IMPORTANT

HERE IS YOUR REGISTRATION CODE TO ACCESS MCGRAW-HILL PREMIUM CONTENT AND MCGRAW-HILL ONLINE RESOURCES

To obtain 30-day trial access to premium online resources for both students and instructors, you need THIS CODE. Once the code is entered, you will be able to use the web resources.

Access is provided for examination purposes only to assist faculty in making textbook adoption decisions.

If the registration code is missing from this examination copy, please contact your local McGraw-Hill representative for access information. If you have adopted this textbook for your course, contact your local representative for permanent access.

To gain access to these online resources

1. **USE** your web browser to go to: www.mhhe.com/writingtoday
2. **CLICK** on "First Time User"
3. **ENTER** the Registration Code printed on the tear-off bookmark on the right
4. After you have entered your registration code, click on "Register"
5. **FOLLOW** the instructions to setup your personal UserID and Password
6. **WRITE** your UserID and Password down for future reference. Keep it in a safe place.

If your course uses WebCT or Blackboard, you'll be able to use this code to access the McGraw-Hill content within your online course. Contact your system administrator for details.

The McGraw-Hill Companies

Higher Education

Thank you, and welcome to your McGraw-Hill Online Resources.

ISBN 0-07-320202-9 PHARR: AIE WRITING TODAY, 1/E

HB6B-KFIC-54DJ-6TZQ-3MYF

REGISTRATION CODE

REGISTRATION CODE

The McGraw-Hill Companies

Mc Graw Hill Higher Education

writing today

DONALD PHARR
Saint Leo University

SANTI V. BUSCEMI
Middlesex County College

CONTEXTS and OPTIONS for the REAL WORLD

Boston Burr Ridge, IL Dubuque, IA Madison, WI New York
San Francisco St. Louis Bangkok Bogotá Caracas Kuala Lumpur
Lisbon London Madrid Mexico City Milan Montreal New Delhi
Santiago Seoul Singapore Sydney Taipei Toronto

Writing Today
Contexts and Options for the Real World

Published by McGraw-Hill, an imprint of The McGraw-Hill Companies, Inc., 1221 Avenue of the Americas, New York, NY 10020.

This book is printed on acid-free paper.

1 2 3 4 5 6 7 8 9 0 DOC DOC 0 9 8 7 6 5

ISBN 0-07-232602-6 (Student's Edition)
ISBN 0-07-297174-6 (Annotated Instructor's Edition)

Vice president and Editor-in-chief: *Emily G. Barrosse*
Publisher: *Lisa Moore*
Sponsoring editor: *Christopher Bennem*
Director of development: *Carla Kay Samodulski*
Marketing manager: *Lori DeShazo*
Senior development editor, media: *Paul Banks*
Senior media producer: *Todd Vaccaro*
Lead production editor: *David M. Staloch*
Lead production supervisor: *Randy Hurst*
Art director: *Jeanne M. Schreiber*
Design manager: *Kim Menning*
Interior designer: *Maureen McCutcheon*
Cover designer: *Laurie Anderson*
Photo research coordinator: *Natalia Peschiera*
Compositor: *Thompson Type*
Typeface: *9.5/12 Stone Serif*
Printer and binder: *RR Donnelley, Crawfordsville*

Library of Congress Cataloging-in-Publication Data
Pharr, Donald.
Writing today : contexts and options for the real world / Donald Pharr, Santi Buscemi.—
Instructor's ed., Full ed.
p. cm.
Includes index.
ISBN 0-07-232602-6 (sc)
1. English language—Rhetoric. 2. Report writing. 3. English language—Grammar—Problems, exercises, etc. I. Buscemi, Santi V. II. Title.
PE1408.P46 2004
808'.042—dc22

2004048287

www.mhhe.com

This book is dedicated to

Mary F. Pharr and

Elaine Buscemi

for their support, love,

and—above all—patience.

ABOUT THE AUTHORS

DONALD PHARR

Donald Pharr received his bachelor's degree from Indiana State University and his master's and doctorate from the University of Georgia. He is the co-author (with Gerald J. Schiffhorst) of *The Short Handbook for Writers,* second edition. He taught for many years in the Florida community college system, where he specialized in applied composition: business, technical, and science writing. As well, he has spent almost two decades consulting as a technical writer and editor. Dr. Pharr currently teaches at Saint Leo University. He lives in Lakeland, Florida, with his wife, Mary.

SANTI V. BUSCEMI

Santi V. Buscemi teaches reading, composition, and literature at Middlesex County College in Edison, New Jersey, where he was chair of the Department of English for twenty-eight years. He is the author of *A Reader for College Writers,* sixth edition, *75 Readings,* ninth edition, *75 Readings Plus,* seventh edition, *The Basics,* fourth edition, and the writing software *AllWrite!* He has lectured on freshman composition and developmental education at regional and national conferences in the United States and South Africa. He also served as a business and technical writing consultant/trainer for the Altria Group, Horizon Blue Cross/Blue Shield, the Port Authority of New York and New Jersey, and Bristol-Myers Squibb. He has also translated *C'era Una Volta,* the fairy tales of Luigi Capuana, from the Italian. Professor Buscemi is past president of the New Jersey College English Association and the New Jersey Association for Developmental Education, and he served on the NADE Adjunct Task Force.

CONTENTS

CHAPTER 3

CHAPTER 4

CHAPTER 5

REFINING YOUR ESSAY: EDITING AND PROOFREADING 99

CHAPTER 6

DESCRIPTION 134

CHAPTER 7

CHAPTER 8

CHAPTER 9

APPLICATIONS
3
PART

CHAPTER 20

THE RESEARCH PROCESS 556

CHAPTER 21

THE RESEARCH PAPER 583

CHAPTER 22

PARTS OF SPEECH 625

PREFACE

The careers that today's students aspire to, and the preparation that they need for those careers, are different from what they were only ten years ago. Much of this change, of course, can be attributed to the electronic revolution in communications, which presents students with increasingly sophisticated tools for researching, writing, revising, and communicating with others. Consequently, in recent years, the English composition course, already essential in a complete and well-planned college curriculum, has also been changing in new and challenging ways.

As composition instructors with sixty years of experience between us, we have learned that today's college students need and want a curriculum that challenges them in the classroom, provides them with skills they can use in other college courses, and, most important, prepares them to communicate effectively in the professional and business worlds. Our goal in *Writing Today* is to give students realistic, practical reasons to master college reading and writing because success in writing is a prerequisite to achieving continued success in college and in their careers. Therefore, we decided to write a text that would focus on both academic and professional contexts for writing. Throughout *Writing Today,* we deliberately address the skepticism of students who see English composition classes as just another hurdle on their way to a degree. *Writing Today* helps them use reading and writing as tools for continued intellectual growth that they can employ in any writing context they confront, long after having completed even their most advanced degrees.

OPTIONS WITHIN DIFFERENT WRITING CONTEXTS

In today's high-tech-dominated world, students are confronted with an exciting, and often bewildering, array of choices in how to write, when to write, and what to write about. A writer's decisions don't happen in a vacuum, of course. As much as possible, we offer scenarios related to the world of writing both inside and outside college. In fact, the chapters in Part 2, "Structures," begin with brief vignettes in which writing and challenges associated with writing play a part in solving problems found in typical business and professional environments. These scenarios help students connect their own daily concerns and their academic and future goals with what the text offers.

In addition, each chapter in Part 2 offers a job-related writing prompt at the end of the chapter along with two prompts that ask students to respond to, analyze, or otherwise discuss a photograph that carries an intriguing message about our history and culture. Other prompts ask them to address questions about popular and/or classic films and encourage them to explore questions by researching Internet sources. In all cases, the text encourages students to focus on specific questions that allow them to apply the techniques and strategies discussed and illustrated in the chapter. Several chapters in Part 3 also emphasize the notion that effective writing makes use of well-defined contexts. For example, the chapter on business formats suggests a variety of scenarios to which students can respond by writing e-mails, letters, and memoranda, including the all-important context of a job search.

PRACTICAL OPTIONS THAT MAKE STUDENTS EFFECTIVE WRITERS

In addition to the many years we have spent teaching English composition, we have both worked closely with corporate executives and government officials who need to communicate better with employees, customers, and the public; we have both designed and delivered corporate training programs; we have written and edited reports, letters, and even speeches for major corporations; and we have taught both business and technical communication in college. Our experience as professional writers in both academia and in the business world has taught us that learning rules and principles, while important, will supply only about a third of what it takes to become an effective writer. The rest depends on the writer's own good judgment and hard work. In any context, writers must constantly make choices among the variety of options that are available to them, from which technique to use to explore their ideas, through which pattern or patterns to use to support their main point, to which suggestions from fellow students or co-workers to follow in revising a draft. That is why we decided to focus on the importance of the writer's responsibility for choosing and to provide as much guidance as possible regarding the process by which writers exercise judgment.

Indeed, the theme of identifying, choosing among, and exercising options runs throughout the text, with "Consider Your Options" notes in the margin that stress the need to make choices. In addition, student writing through much of the first three parts of the text demonstrates how students can employ a spectrum of rhetorical techniques and choices, and annotated first drafts of student essays at the end of each chapter in Part 2 show students in the process of exercising specific rhetorical and linguistic options as they revise their writing. Our experience in field testing the ideas in this text clearly points to the benefits of allowing students to make informed choices as they work their way through the writing process. Doing so simply makes them more responsible and, therefore, more effective writers.

OPTIONS FOR USING TECHNOLOGY

Today, a writer's contexts almost always include some form of technology. In keeping with this reality, we have thoroughly integrated *Writing Today* with *Catalyst*, the most complete electronic resource for research and writing available. "More Options Online" notes in the margin tell students when they can go online to find additional advice, online writing tutors, help with research, diagnostic tests, over 3,000 practice exercises, and more. In addition, the text includes explanations of the use of word processors, the Internet, databases, and other tools generated by the electronic revolution, along with helpful hints for using electronic resources for researching, drafting, and editing.

A FOUR-IN-ONE TEXT OPTION

As a guide to the writing process—with a reader and visual texts integrated into this guide—a guide to research, and a handbook for editing student work, *Writing Today* offers a complete text for the first-year writing course. *Writing Today* is also available in a brief version that omits the handbook.

A Guide to the Writing Process

A Practical Introduction to the Process. The five chapters in Part 1, "Approaches," are a thorough and well-illustrated discussion of the writing process. Chapter 1 provides a definition of the essay and explains its importance as an academic tool and as a way to learn skills that can be applied in the types of writing more often seen in business and professional settings. Through the numerous student and professional examples in the next four chapters, readers easily trace various steps and strategies from which to choose when writing an essay. Again, we emphasize the notion of options for writers and the importance of exercising one's judgment in a particular context.

Patterns Presented as Options. Part 2, "Structures," includes nine chapters that are devoted to discussions of the rhetorical options, or patterns, from description to argument. The tenth chapter, Chapter 15, covers essays that use more than one pattern and explains how to draw on a variety of strategies to address complex questions. Each chapter in Part 2 contains four professional essays, complete with introductory materials and questions for writing and discussion. At the end of each chapter, the final and first drafts of a student essay written using the option covered in that chapter show the process of revision in action.

An Emphasis on Making Choices in Revision. The guidelines for writing an essay in each chapter end by suggesting the kinds of questions a writer must ask and answer as he or she reviews an essay during the revision stage.

Plenty of Options for Writing Topics. Each chapter in Part 2 concludes with a series of suggested assignments, including assignments based on recent and classic films, assignments based on compelling photographs, and one workplace-based assignment.

Readings, Cartoons, and Photographs. The reading selections in *Writing Today* offer students examples of writers facing different contexts and choosing among options, and the visuals help introduce the rhetorical options and give students ideas for their own writing.

Selections from a Variety of Fine Authors. Integrated into each chapter in Part 2, the diverse selection of professional readings includes essays by Bharati Mukherjee, Barbara Ehrenreich, Sandra Cisneros, Thomas McGuane, Maxine Hong Kingston, Fran Lebowitz, Deborah Tannen, Brent Staples, David Sedaris, Lynda Barry, and Sherman Alexie, as well as time-tested classics such as "A Hanging" by George Orwell and "Why I Want a Wife" by Judy Brady. The essays, on engaging topics such as shopping, student employment, and rock lyrics as well as such provocative issues as whether humans are programmed to fight wars and whether torture is ever justified, are enjoyable to read, provide plenty of opportunity for discussion, and serve as strong models.

A Strong Connection Between Reading and Writing. Two complementary sections in each of the chapters in Part 2 are designed to help students make the most of the connection between reading and writing: "Reading with a Writer's Eye" and "Writing with a Reader's Eye." The first section encourages students to engage the text so that they understand the choices professional writers make, the techniques and strategies they employ, and the purposes and contexts they address. Again, our purpose here is to stress the importance of using one's judgment and exercising appropriate options when creating any piece of writing.

The next part of each chapter offers suggestions for every step in the writing process and a part-by-part analysis of a student's essay in the drafting stage. Called "Writing with a Reader's Eye," this section stresses that students need to see themselves as their intended readers and to consider how such an audience might envision, interpret, and react to what they have written.

Visuals That Help Make the Rhetorical Options Real for Students. Engaging cartoons, many of them work-related, open the chapters on rhetorical options in Part 2. At the end of each chapter, a classic photograph and a writing prompt encourage students to use the option presented in that chapter to explore a historical topic that has relevance in today's world.

A Guide to Research and More

Writing in College and Professional Contexts. Part 3, "Applications," covers a number of specialized projects and skills common to college and professional writing. Chapter 16 provides excellent advice on taking various types of examinations, especially the essay exam. Chapter 17 discusses business formats, including appropriate practices for e-mailing in business contexts as well as writing more traditional correspondence. The coverage of writing résumés and letters of application will be especially useful to students seeking employment. Chapter 19, on writing about literature, contains two student essays that analyze works of fiction and poetry included in the text.

Unique Coverage of Using Quotations. Chapter 18, unique to this text, explains how to use quoted material in a paper according to the Modern Language Association (MLA) and the American Psychological Association (APA) formats. As such, this chapter prepares students for the types of writing covered in Chapter 19 ("Writing About Literature"), Chapter 20 ("The Research Process"), and Chapter 21 ("The Research Paper").

Thorough Coverage of Writing and Documenting Research Papers. Chapter 20 provides suggestions on finding and using library and electronic resources. Chapter 21 introduces both the MLA and the APA styles of documentation and contains a complete student research paper in MLA format. Throughout these two chapters, we stress the fact that exercising choice and applying one's judgment are as important when writing a research paper as they are in any other kind of writing. In this regard, we discuss the notion that students are responsible for choosing viable, relevant, and up-to-date sources and that they need to be aware of the many ways in which to incorporate researched material into their work. We discuss the uses of direct quotations, and we explain how and when to paraphrase and to summarize. A complete subsection is devoted to the dangers, as well as the benefits, involved in using the Internet—an unregulated collection of information—as a tool for academic research. Finally, we explain how and why to avoid plagiarism, both intentional and unintentional.

A Handbook

Part 4, "Grammar and Mechanics," is a comprehensive and thorough college handbook that is easy to read and can be used both in class and as an out-of-class reference. We emphasize practical solutions to the most common problems that students face, provide explanations in familiar, easily understood language, and illustrate principles with numerous appropriate examples. Editing exercises throughout and at the end of each chapter give students plenty of opportunities for practice.

KEY FEATURES OF *WRITING TODAY*

We designed this text to help students see reading and writing as practical tools both in college and in the world of work. To meet this goal, *Writing Today* includes the following features:

- **A realistic yet humorous approach to writing.** We understand students' concerns and questions about studying English, so we write directly to our readers, helping them understand how and why writing is valuable to them not only in their composition courses but in all of their other classes and throughout their working lives. To help make a subject many of them find forbidding far more inviting, we offer cartoons at the beginning of chapters in Part Two and practical, often humorous, examples of writing situations and writing pitfalls.
- **Online resources that support writing instruction.** To prepare students for the many electronic options now available in academic life and the work world, *Writing Today* is accompanied by *Catalyst,* the most complete electronic resource for research and writing available. Accessible either on CD or as part of the text's Web site, this electronic resource gives students and instructors a wealth of additional options, including a bank of more than 3,000 grammar exercises, a diagnostic test, writing tutorials, a tutorial on avoiding plagiarism, Bibliomaker software that automatically formats source information in different documentation styles, and an online handbook. Marginal references to the Web site, entitled "More Options Online," appear throughout the text to let students know when additional help is available on *Catalyst.*
- **Plenty of advice on using computers and the Internet.** In keeping with the emphasis on the uses of technology in *Writing Today,* the text offers advice throughout on using the various electronic tools and resources that are available in today's digital writing environment. To make this important advice easy for students to spot, it is identified with an icon.
- **Chapter-opening vignettes from the world of work.** Every chapter in Part 2, "Structures," begins with an often humorous account of an employee using writing to interact with the dreaded Bob, a demanding and sometimes inscrutable supervisor. These scenarios help to make writing real for students by demonstrating how the type of writing they will learn in that chapter has practical applications in the working world. Even more important, they help emphasize the importance of a writer's assessing his or her purpose and audience and of choosing an appropriate strategy for a given writing context.
- **Student writers making choices.** Because student models are so useful to student writers, we offer more than twenty sample student essays. In Part 1, the text follows a student through the process of developing an essay from preliminary activities to final draft. Each chapter in Part 2 includes at least two sample student essays, one in both draft and final form, with comments from the student writer that show how that writer made decisions in moving from the first to the final draft.

- **An extended explanation of and a repeated emphasis on the natural connection between reading and writing.** Through repeated illustration and explanation, we stress that reading and writing are opposite sides of the same coin. As we have noted, each of the ten chapters in Part 2, "Structures," includes two complementary sections to help students make the most of this connection: "Reading with a Writer's Eye" and "Writing with a Reader's Eye." At the same time, these sections impress students with the importance of evaluating and considering the needs of their audiences and contexts. Finally, the text offers a full range of accessible writing prompts that enable students to draw inspiration from the professional and student essays they have read.
- **Consider Your Options notes.** Throughout the text, these marginal notes prompt students to think about what they already do when they write and what their choices are in a given writing situation. As such, they get students to consider numerous and varied questions about intended audiences, purposes, selection of detail, rhetorical approaches, patterns of organization, word choice, and even sentence structure.
- **An emphasis on choices made in revision.** The process of revising an essay for global concerns as well as for errors in grammar, punctuation, and mechanics is covered in Part 1. The need for revision is then reinforced throughout Part 2. Each chapter includes a list of revision questions that students can use to analyze their own and other students' drafts, along with a revision exercise that provides faulty student essays for students to comment on and revise, giving them meaningful practice in critically reviewing and revising essays.

- **Support for students whose first language is not English.** An icon identifies sections throughout the text that are especially relevant to and useful for students whose first language is not English. The notion of options comes into play here as well. Second-language students often agonize over choosing the correct idiom or finding a word with the appropriate connotation. We keep this in mind whenever we discuss ESL-related concerns, and we provide information that makes the process of choosing easier.

- **A variety of collaborative activities.** Today's student will be called on to collaborate not only with other students throughout college but also with colleagues at work. *Writing Today* offers numerous collaborative activities throughout. These activities are identified with an icon that stresses the importance of each individual's contribution to the whole.
- **A complete introduction to the research process.** Chapters 20 and 21 provide commonsense advice for every stage of the research process, along with guidelines for finding print and online sources, models for documenting print and online sources using both the MLA and APA styles, and a sample student research paper.
- **A complete grammar handbook.** In our sixty years in the classroom, we have had plenty of opportunities to observe and analyze the kinds of errors students make; each of us is also the author of a grammar handbook. We apply our combined experience in Part 4, "Grammar and Mechanics," a complete, easily referenced guide to sentence errors, punctuation, and mechanics. It also includes grammar exercises as well as a glossary of usage.

- **A chapter on writing for business.** In keeping with the book's emphasis on writing for the world of work, Chapter 17 offers advice for writing the most common types of business documents students will encounter, including memos, e-mail, letters of application, résumés, and business letters.
- **Chapters on essay examinations and writing about literature.** Chapter 16 offers down-to-earth, practical advice on how students can successfully approach one of the most stressful events in higher education: the essay examination. Chapter 19 offers advice for writing about fiction and poetry, along with two sample student essays and definitions of literary terms.

HELPFUL SUPPLEMENTS FOR STUDENTS AND INSTRUCTORS

For Students

As noted above, *Writing Today* offers students access to the many resources available on *Catalyst*, including diagnostic tests, over 3,000 grammar exercises, an online handbook, writing tutors for each of the rhetorical options covered in Part 2 of the text, a tutorial on avoiding plagiarism, Bibliomaker software, which automatically formats source information in five different documentation styles, and plenty of support for research. McGraw-Hill also offers the following dictionary and vocabulary resources:

- **Random House Webster's College Dictionary (ISBN 0-07-240011-0).** This authoritative dictionary includes over 160,000 entries and 175,000 definitions. The most commonly used definitions are always listed first, so students can find what they need quickly.
- **The Merriam-Webster Dictionary (ISBN 0-07-310057-9).** Based on the best-selling *Merriam-Webster's Collegiate Dictionary,* this paperback dictionary contains over 70,000 definitions.
- **The Merriam-Webster Thesaurus (ISBN 0-07-310067-6).** This handy paperback thesaurus contains over 157,000 synonyms, antonyms, related and contrasted words, and idioms.
- **Merriam-Webster's Vocabulary Builder (ISBN 0-07-310069-2).** This handy paperback introduces 3,000 words and includes quizzes to test progress.
- **Merriam-Webster's Notebook Dictionary (ISBN 0-07-299091-0).** An extremely concise reference to the words that form the core of English vocabulary, this popular dictionary, conveniently designed for 3-ring binders, provides words and information at students' fingertips.
- **Merriam-Webster's Notebook Thesaurus (ISBN 0-07-310068-4).** Conveniently designed for 3-ring binders, this thesaurus helps students search for words they might need in a given context. It provides concise, clear guidance for over 157,000 word choices.
- **Merriam-Webster's Collegiate Dictionary and Thesaurus, Electronic Edition (ISBN 0-07-310070-6).** Available on CD-ROM, this online dictionary contains thousands of new words and meanings from all areas of human endeavor, including electronic technology, the sciences, and popular culture.

For Instructors

- ***Annotated Instructor's Edition.*** The *Annotated Instructor's Edition* provides abundant support for instructors teaching with *Writing Today*, including classroom hints, suggested activities, and answers to exercises. The *AIE* is especially helpful for new teachers of writing as well as instructors who are assigned classes with little advance notice.
- **Advice on the Web site (www.mhhe.com/writingtoday).** The Instructor's portion of the Web site includes advice for new instructors on a variety of subjects, such as teaching the writing process, assigning and teaching the research paper, responding to student writing, and assigning in-class writing, along with sample syllabi.
- **Teaching Composition Faculty Listserv at (www.mhhe.com/tcomp).** Moderated by Chris Anson at North Carolina State University and offered by McGraw-Hill as a service to the composition community, this listserv brings together senior members of the college composition community with newer members—junior faculty, adjuncts, and teaching assistants—through an online newsletter and accompanying discussion group to address issues of pedagogy, both in theory and in practice.
- **PageOut.** McGraw-Hill's own PageOut service is available to help you get your course up and running online in a matter of hours—at no cost. Additional information about the service is available online at **http://www.pageout.net.**

ACKNOWLEDGMENTS

No text is the product of its authors alone. Therefore, we wish to express our sincere appreciation for the work of Carla Samodulski, our developmental editor, who has spent endless hours reviewing, critiquing, guiding, and revising our work. Together we have examined an enormous number of reviews from professional colleagues, culling from them ideas and suggestions to make *Writing Today* the most complete, accessible, and effective introduction to college writing available. Throughout the process, Carla provided the guidance and help so necessary to a project of this magnitude, and she gave us the impetus to keep working even when we became quite tired. Thanks also go to Lisa Moore, publisher for the English group, who oversaw the project in its early stages and who, with Carla Samodulski, helped us through the process of using what we learned from our reviewers to make the text more comprehensive and more useful, as well as to Christopher Bennem, sponsoring editor, and Lori DeShazo, marketing manager. Finally, we want to thank our former editor, Tim Julet, who brought us together several years ago to work on this very rewarding project.

We also wish to thank Laura Barthule, who has helped us with reviewing and review summaries; Bronwyn Becker, Randee Falk, and Judy Voss, all of whom edited various parts of the book; Ben Morrison, who developed the online writing tutor; David Staloch, the project manager; and Kim Menning, the art director. We also need to thank Liana Sutton for her invaluable help with the preparation of the manuscript. In addition, we want to express our gratitude to the students who have allowed us to use their work in order to show how careful essayists approach the writing process: Kevin Hunkovic, Jennifer Janisz, Noelani Jones, Sam Leininger, Manny Meregildo, Curtis Ray Mosley, Claire Reid, and Valerie Richfield. Our thanks also to Christine Francisco, City College of San Francisco, who reviewed the ESL sections in Part 4, and Debora Person,

University of Wyoming Law Library, who reviewed the sections on library and Internet research in Chapter 20. Finally, we want to thank our many colleagues from across the country who reviewed the manuscript in various stages of its development and provided so much insight, direction, inspiration, and encouragement:

Nancy Barrineau, *University of North Carolina at Pembroke*
Mark K. Branson, *Davidson County Community College*
Joyce L. Cherry, *Albany State University*
Laurie Cohen, *Seattle Central Community College*
Avon Crismore, *Indiana University–Purdue University*
Linda A. Dethloff, *Prairie State College*
Betty Dillard, *Forsyth Technical Community College*
Patrick M. Ellingham, *Broward Community College*
Jo N. Farrar, *San Jacinto College Central*
Frederic Giacobazzi, *Kirtland Community College*
Richard A. Greene, *Florida Community College at Jacksonville*
Ashan Hampton, *Morehouse College*
Sarah H. Harrison, *Tyler Junior College*
James E. Hodges, *Thomas University*
Michael Hogan, *Southeast Missouri State University*
Lita Hooper-Simanga, *Georgia Perimeter College*
Clay Holliday, *Valencia Community College*
Michael Hricik, *Westmoreland County Community College*
Richard J. Johnson, *Kirkwood Community College*
Virginia Katzeff, *Lake Land College*
Sandra K. Keneda, *Rose State College*
Sandra G. Lakey, *Pennsylvania College of Technology*
Stephen J. Leone, *Westchester Community College*
Colleen A. Lloyd, *Cuyahoga Community College*
T. Michael Mackey, *Community College of Denver*
Nancy Matte, *Phoenix College*
Yeno Matuka, *Ball State University*
Vernice McCullough, *Glendale Community College*
Leslie Mohr, *Casper College*
John David Moore, *Eastern Illinois University*
Patrice A. Quarg, *Community College of Baltimore County at Catonsville*
Mark Ristroph, *Augusta Technical Institute*
Rachel Ritter, *Miami-Dade Community College*
Sara E. Selby, *Waycross College*
Annabel Servat, *Southeastern Louisiana University*
Phillip Sipiora, *University of South Florida*
Beverly Stamm, *Columbus State Community College*
James Thomas, *Valencia Community College*
William Wade, *Paducah Community College*
Stephen Wilhoit, *University of Dayton*
Fred Wolven, *Miami-Dade Community College*

Donald Pharr
Santi Buscemi

Guided Tour

The following pages illustrate how ***Writing Today*** will help you succeed as a writer, whether in your coursework, at your job, or in another writing context. To get the most out of this text, spend a few minutes getting to know the organization and features of ***Writing Today.***

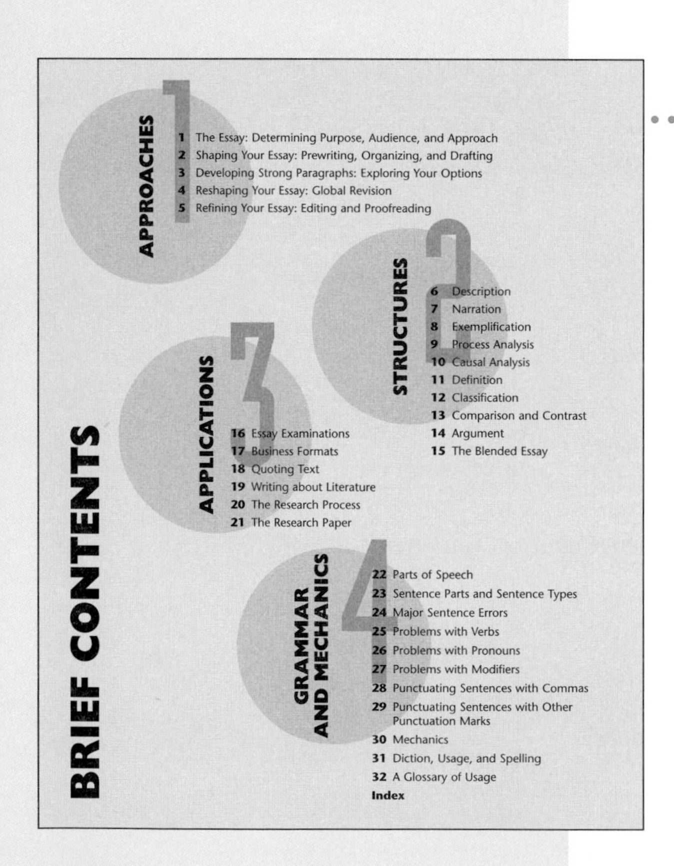

BRIEF CONTENTS

1 APPROACHES

2 STRUCTURES

3 APPLICATIONS

4 GRAMMAR AND MECHANICS

Part I of ***Writing Today*** shows you how learning to write college essays will help you succeed not only in your college work but also in your career. It also introduces you to the stages of the writing process. Part 2 includes chapters on the options you have for developing your writing, and Part 3 explains how to apply those options in different writing contexts, including essay exams, business writing, research papers, and literary analyses. Part 4 will help you edit and proofread your writing.

***Writing Today* means writing with technology.**

Because today's technology gives you more options than ever before as you write, ***Writing Today*** also offers access to *Catalyst*, the most complete electronic resource for research and writing available. Notes in the text margins tell you when you can go online to find additional advice, writing tutors, help with research, diagnostic tests, over 3,000 practice exercises, and more.

404 PART 2 Structures

Suggestions for Writing

1. Are there any advantages to having a "private self" that is very different from the "public self"? Write a 500- to 750-word essay contrasting the private you and the public you.
2. Write a 500- to 750-word essay that recounts a situation in which your cultural upbringing left you uncertain of how to handle the demands of a different culture or context. Possible areas include city versus country, native country versus foreign country, pool hall versus country club.

MORE OPTIONS ONLINE
If you would like to read additional comparison/contrast essays, go to www.mhhe.com/writingtoday.

WRITING THE COMPARISON/CONTRAST ESSAY WITH A READER'S EYE

Students sometimes approach the comparison/contrast assignment as if it were merely an exercise instead of a great opportunity to communicate. All too often, this approach yields mechanical, boring essays that fulfill the assignment's requirements but do little else. Some of these essays seem to have been

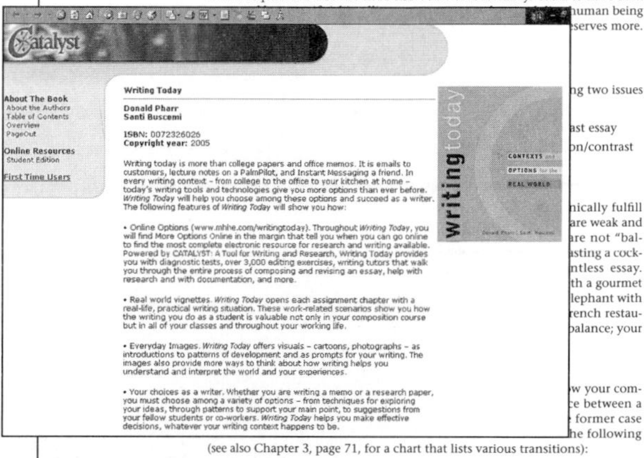

Catalyst

About The Book
About the Authors
Table of Contents
Overview
PageOut
Online Resources
Student Edition
First Time Users

Writing Today

Donald Pharr
Santi Buscemi

ISBN: 0072326026
Copyright year: 2005

Writing today is more than college papers and office memos. It is emails to customers, lecture notes on a PalmPilot, and Instant Messaging a friend. In every writing context – from college to the office to your kitchen at home – today's writing tools and technologies give you more options than ever before. *Writing Today* will help you choose among these options and succeed as a writer. The following features of *Writing Today* will show you how:

• Online Options (www.mhhe.com/writingtoday). Throughout *Writing Today*, you will find More Options Online in the margin that tell you when you can go online to find the most complete electronic resource for research and writing available. Powered by CATALYST: A Tool for Writing and Research, Writing Today provides you with diagnostic tests, over 3,000 editing exercises, writing tutors that walk you through the entire process of composing and revising an essay, help with research and with documentation, and more.

• Real world vignettes. *Writing Today* opens each assignment chapter with a real-life, practical writing situation. These work-related scenarios show you how the writing you do as a student is valuable not only in your composition course but in all of your classes and throughout your working life.

• Everyday Images. *Writing Today* offers visuals – cartoons, photographs – as introductions to patterns of development and as prompts for your writing. The images also provide more ways to think about how writing helps you understand and interpret the world and your experiences.

• Your choices as a writer. Whether you are writing a memo or a research paper, you must choose among a variety of options – from techniques for exploring your ideas, through patterns to support your main point, to suggestions from your fellow students or co-workers. *Writing Today* helps you make effective decisions, whatever your writing context happens to be.

(see also Chapter 3, page 71, for a chart that lists various transitions):

***Writing Today* . . . and tomorrow.**

Each assignment chapter opens with a real-life, practical writing situation. These work-related scenarios show you how the writing you do as a student is valuable not only in your composition course but throughout your working life.

CHAPTER 13

COMPARISON AND CONTRAST

Writing in Context

Bob appears at your cubicle yet again.

"What do you know about optical scanners?" he asks.

"I know what they do. And I know that some of them are geared more toward text processing and some of them are graphics oriented."

"Good," Bob replied. "Here, take this." He hands you two folders. "We need to decide which one of these to buy. Talk to Stephanie if you want the background. I'll need an analysis by Friday."

You start looking through the folders Bob has left with you. They contain mainly sales brochures and listings of technical specifications. You know you'll need to grill Stephanie, and probably other people, before you feel confident about starting the report.

Then it will be a matter of writing an evaluation, a side-by-side examination of the distinctions between the two scanners. Even at this point you can see the "shape" of your report.

You can see its shape because this task so clearly calls for an option known as comparison and contrast, in which two things are compared, often with the aim of producing an evaluation, perhaps an evaluation that will enable readers to arrive at some decision.

NARRATION

CHAPTER 7

Writing in Context

You have been "called back" for a second interview at Osprey. On Wednesday afternoon you show up determined to nail down this job.

First, you have another interview with Bob, the man who would be your boss. Bob is all teeth, smiles, and suit, but you notice that he is smart enough to protect himself by carefully avoiding a commitment at this point.

Next, you are sent back to Human Resources. There is yet another psychological profile test for you to complete, administered by one of the quiet, synthetically pleasant people who hover around the area. (At this point you wouldn't be surprised if one of them produced a rubber mallet and asked to check your reflexes.) After the profile, one of the HR people sits down with you, hands over a clipboard and some writing paper, and asks this question: "Can you tell us about the single most important event in your college years, the one that led you here today?"

And how shall you begin?

Indeed, we all know how to tell stories, but finding the most effective one and telling it to maximum benefit is a complex process.

***Writing Today* involves images as well as words.** Images–cartoons, photographs–serve as introductions to patterns of development and as prompts for your writing. The images also provide more ways to think about how writing helps you understand and interpret the world and your experiences.

388 PART 2 Structures

the next, you give your readers clear accounts of both events. On the other hand, if you were to use a point-by-point approach here, you'd wind up fragmenting those accounts, in a sense reducing the dynamics of the experiences to mere categories of information (hotels stayed at, meals eaten, places seen, and so on). Your reader deserves better treatment. After all, you are trying to fulfill your purpose of providing a clear picture of the two subjects.

In most comparison/contrast essays, the emphasis will be on contrast. Obviously, if your purpose is evaluative, you want to find and focus on differences. Even if your purpose isn't evaluative, it is usually more instructive and interesting to readers to show how two entities are different than to show how they are similar (however, see page 408 for examples of situations in which comparison is the best option). For example, consider this idea: for decades, American automakers tended to produce a car model and then package it under different "nameplates." A midsize Chevy was virtually identical to a midsize Pontiac, and the same was true of Ford and Mercury and Plymouth and Dodge. Presumably, a buyer might buy a Mercury that was virtually the same as the (normally) lower-priced Ford because the Mercury line had more prestige. Would you want to write an essay comparing these two very similar cars? It's hard to see how you could write a fully developed, interesting paper when trying to compare two items that are so similar. However, keep in mind that comparison/contrast essays that emphasize contrast may also use comparison, just as those that emphasize comparison will surely include some contrasts.

Technically, the comparison/contrast option is not limited to two subjects. A writer could compare three subjects (or four, or ten, or twenty, for that matter). But a three-way comparison asks a great deal of your reader, and any number beyond three would probably be too hard for your reader to comprehend in an essay. The three-way approach tends to appear only in technical/business contexts that use a point-by-point approach. In the opening vignette, for example, Bob could have requested an analysis of three scanners rather than of two. However, for general purposes, most essays concentrate on two subjects only. If a situation seems to call for a three-way analysis, you may find that using a classification or definition approach is a better option.

Note also that you can use comparison/contrast to help you develop essays that concentrate on other rhetorical options. For a good example, see Umberto Eco's "How Not to Use the Fax Machine and the Cellular Phone" in Chapter 9 ("Process Analysis"). While showing how consumer technology can come to dominate the consumer, Eco makes a firm distinction between people who need cell phones and those who do not.

The comparison/contrast essay can be difficult to write yet a joy to read, as the following essays indicate.

Consider Your Options

- How might you use comparison/contrast strategies at work?
- How could this approach help you evaluate situations as they arise?

READING THE COMPARISON/CONTRAST ESSAY WITH A WRITER'S EYE

In the works that follow, Ellen Currie contrasts murder in the past with a more contemporary form of murder, namely, serial murder; Bharati Mukherjee examines two very different ways for immigrants to approach life in a new

Writing Today* is about making choices.** Whether you are writing a memo or a research paper, you must choose among a variety of options–from techniques for exploring your ideas, through patterns to support your main point, to suggestions from your fellow students or co-workers. ***Writing Today helps you make better decisions about all your writing: on the job, at home, and in school.

Revision is crucial to *Writing Today. Writing Today* approaches revision in three ways. Part 1 shows you how to revise. Part 2 reinforces this instruction with revision questions for each writing option. Finally, revision exercises with realistic first drafts offer you an opportunity to practice your revision skills.

MORE OPTIONS ONLINE
For more help with the step-by-step development of the comparison/contrast essay, go to www.mhhe.com/writingtoday.

ESSAY B: Point-by-Point Approach

It's obviously true that you can't go home again, and I'm glad I spent another summer in Bristol Park to confirm this idea. At least now I won't be tempted to go back and buy my parents' old house in this now unfriendly, dangerous, and declining neighborhood.

EXERCISE 13.1

Write an outline of either "Let the Unimportant Things Change" or "Neighborhoods and Memories." (For help with outlines, see Chapter 2, pages 41–42.) How effective is the approach the writer has chosen (subject-by-subject or point-by-point)? Would the other approach have been a better choice? If so, why?

Revising Your Draft

After you have completed a draft of your comparison/contrast essay, your next step is to revise it, using your own analysis and comments from classmates and friends. Use the peer review stage to make sure that your essay's structure and

Questions for Reviewing a Comparison/Contrast Essay

1. Does the introduction give the reader enough context? Does it capture the reader's interest? How could the introduction be strengthened?
2. What is the thesis statement? Has the writer placed it in the best position within the essay? How could it be improved?
3. Does the essay have a clear and interesting general point? Is the writer doing more than mechanically comparing and contrasting two subjects?
4. Is the approach that the writer chose—point-by-point or subject-by-subject—appropriate for the topic and for the intended purpose?
5. If the essay uses the point-by-point approach, has the writer established coherence by using the appropriate transitions? Where are transitions needed?
6. If the essay uses the subject-by-subject approach, has the writer referred the reader to the contrasts and/or similarities between the two subjects? In other words, has the writer connected the second subject to the first, or do the two subjects seem separate and unrelated?
7. Regardless of the method used, is the analysis thorough and complete? Has the writer left out any obvious points or areas of discussion? If the essay is intended to paint two pictures, are the pictures vivid? If the essay has an evaluative purpose, is the coverage of the two subjects balanced?
8. Does the essay have an effective conclusion? How could it be improved?

Professionals and students alike are *Writing Today*. When you approach a particular kind of writing, you probably find it most helpful to see real examples from writers facing similar challenges and choosing similar options. Throughout ***Writing Today,*** we stress the importance of reading to developing your skills as a writer. ***Writing Today*** provides more than 20 sample student essays, many in draft as well as final form.

pendent film that makes it to the Gigaplex 9000, and some independent fans are frequenting the latest Hollywood release during the slow time of the year. With any luck, this crossover will be a positive movement: the blockbuster audience may learn to respond to a film in more nuanced ways, and a few of them will even be exposed to higher-quality films. But, more likely, the independent fans may just give in to the ruder ways of the typical moviegoer, and the only place to watch any type of movie in relative peace will be at home—now if I could just get that big screen and film projector installed in the living room.

Sam's First Draft

The Two Sides of the Aisle

Movie studios are concerned with target markets and audiences: they tailer certain movies for certain types of people. The advertising for the latest adventure flick will appeal to different folks than the advertising for the new British art film. And it works. When I go to the movies, I get myself ready in different ways. Most towns have an art-house theater and a few dozen multi-plex theaters that play the big blockbusters, but with independant films gaining a margin of profitability, some of them are showing up at the local multi-plex. Crowds attending independent films have a few distinct characteristics that separate them from the average viewer.

This essay needed more detail—more of a sense of "reality" instead of just commentary.

Independant filmgoers tend to arrive early. The movie is more important to them, whereas it doesn't really matter if you miss the first five minutes of a natural disaster movie. The trip to the concession stand is also a giveaway. The blockbuster crowd loads up on anything they can carry, drag, or stuff in their or their girlfriends' purses. The independant film fan realizes that the concession money supports the movie theater and, not wanting to encourage them, will pass the counter frequently.

I worked on the second and third paragraphs of the rough draft, turning them into three paragraphs.

Once in the theater, audiences are relatively similar—both have the propensity to be just as rude. The talking is directed differently in the two

Writing Today **offers a wide and diverse range of contemporary authors.** The selections include readings by Bharati Mukherjee, Barbara Ehrenreich, Sandra Cisneros, Thomas McGuane, Maxine Hong Kingston, Fran Lebowitz, Deborah Tannen, Brent Staples, David Sedaris, Lynda Barry, and Sherman Alexie.

392 PART 2 Structures

2. Currie treats Ted Bundy as a modern phenomenon. Actually, serial killers are known to have existed in the nineteenth century and before. It is the sheer *number* of these sociopaths in the past few decades that is remarkable. (At the time of this writing, according to FBI estimates, there are several dozen serial killers on the loose in the United States.) In your opinion, what are some of the possible causes of this increase?
3. Why are we so fascinated by serial killers that we name burgers and cocktails after them? What does this say about contemporary society?

Suggestions for Writing

Write a 500- to 750-word essay in which you contrast two motivations for breaking the rules:

1. Shoplifting because of need versus shoplifting for fun
2. Cheating on school assignments out of desperation versus cheating because of laziness
3. Vandalism motivated by anger over political or economic injustice versus vandalism for fun

Two Ways to Belong in America

BHARATI MUKHERJEE

Bharati Mukherjee was born in India, where she received a bachelor's degree and master's degree before immigrating to the United States in 1961. She attended the University of Iowa, where she earned a master's in fine arts and a doctorate in English and comparative literature. A renowned writer of fiction, Mukherjee has published the novels *The Tiger's Daughter* (1972), *Wife* (1975), *Jasmine* (1989), *The Holder of the World* (1993), *Leave It to Me* (1997), and *Desirable Daughters* (2002). Her short-story collection *The Middleman and Other Stories* (1988) won the National Book Critics Circle Award.

Immigration and identity are frequent themes in Mukherjee's works. The following essay was written for the *New York Times* in 1996 to comment upon controversial proposals and legislation regarding the rights of immigrants.

1 This is a tale of two sisters from Calcutta, Mira and Bharati, who have lived in the United States for some 35 years, but who find themselves on different sides in the current debate over the status of immigrants. I am an American citizen and she is not. I am moved that thousands of long-term residents are finally taking the oath of citizenship. She is not.

2 Mira arrived in Detroit in 1960 to study child psychology and pre-school education. I followed her a year later to study creative writing at the University of Iowa. When we left India, we were almost identical in appearance and attitude. We dressed alike, in saris; we expressed identical views on politics, social issues, love, and marriage in the same Calcutta convent-school accent. We would endure our two years in America, secure our degrees, then return to India to marry the grooms of our father's choosing.

3 Instead, Mira married an Indian student in 1962 who was getting his business administration degree at Wayne State University. They soon acquired the labor certifications necessary for the green card of hassle-free residence and employment.

4 Mira still lives in Detroit, works in the Southfield, Mich., school system, and has become nationally recognized for her contributions in the fields of pre-school

Writing Today **is a handbook for writing today.** To help you edit your writing, Part 4 of ***Writing Today*** offers a complete, accessible handbook covering sentence errors, punctuation, and mechanics. It also includes grammar exercises as well as a glossary of usage. ***Writing Today*** is also available in a brief version that does not include the handbook.

660 PART 4 Grammar and Mechanics

SENTENCE FRAGMENTS

As its name suggests, a **sentence fragment** is an incomplete sentence; it "acts" as a sentence, but it is missing a subject, a verb, or a complete thought.

24a PHRASES AS FRAGMENTS

frag 24a

A phrase, by definition, cannot be a complete sentence. Here are some typical phrasal fragments:

Incomplete Verb Form

FRAGMENT The doctor **thinking** that the patient looked better.

REVISED The doctor **was thinking** that the patient looked better.

Prepositional Phrase Used as Sentence

FRAGMENT You'll find the hammer out back. **Beside the rotary saw.**

REVISED You'll find the hammer out back, beside the rotary saw.

MORE OPTIONS ONLINE If you would like to test your knowledge of major sentence errors before reading this chapter, go to www.mhhe.com/writingtoday.

Infinitive Phrase Used as Sentence

FRAGMENT We drove to town. **To buy a new hammer.**

REVISED We drove to town to buy a new hammer.

"Illustration" Phrase Used as Sentence

FRAGMENT Alcoholics can develop many health problems. **For example, cirrhosis of the liver.**

REVISED Alcoholics can develop many health problems—for example, cirrhosis of the liver.

FRAGMENT They were troubled by the motel's location. **Also, the condition of the room they were shown.**

REVISED They were troubled by the motel's location and also by the condition of the room they were shown.

As you can see, many fragments are phrases that clearly belong with an adjacent sentence but that are acting as stand-alone sentences:

FRAGMENT **Wishing that finals week were over.** Jan reluctantly turned back to her studies.

FRAGMENT **To meet our June 1 deadline.** We've got to work hard during the next two weeks.

FRAGMENT **Near the end of its useful life.** The old bridge seemed to sag as heavy trucks strained its rotted timbers.

FRAGMENT Rosa ran to hug her child. **Her eyes filling with tears.**

Of course, you can always correct such fragments by making complete sentences out of them:

PART 1 APPROACHES

The first part of this text discusses the strategies that you will use to complete the assignments given to you in your English composition courses. The finished essay is the goal, but the various parts—large and small—that go into an essay are essential to making the longer form work effectively.

Chapter 1, "The Essay: Determining Purpose, Audience, and Approach," is an introduction to the type of writing that you will use throughout college. Students sometimes object to the importance given to essay writing, failing to see the practical relevance of this form. So let's make an admission: after you finish college, you might spend the rest of your days without ever writing another essay. However (a big *however*), during the remainder of your college years you will face instructors who expect you to know how to write essays and research papers, often with very little specific guidance on approach and format. Furthermore, after you finish school, you might not write essays, but you will be asked to write in a number of contexts using a variety of skills and techniques that you learned in college. Also, the day of the helpful secretary born with the mysterious literacy gene is gone. The computer will sit on your desk, not banished to some support person. And the higher up you go, the better your writing skills will need to be. Most CEOs and leading scientists are also very good writers. Communication in the world of work is not a secondary skill; it is essential.

CLASSROOM HINT Be sure to emphasize the applicability of college essay writing to all other types of writing, especially to practical assignments in the world of work. Doing so is especially important for students who see the composition class simply as another hurdle on the way to getting a diploma.

Chapter 1 shows how the essay is related to its various cousins used in other writing situations. Indeed, if you can write a standard essay, you can write a research paper—or a memo, a feasibility study, a grant proposal, a sales letter, or a narrative cost analysis. The skills you learn in this course will travel with you as long as you need them.

In Chapter 2 ("Shaping Your Essay: Prewriting, Focusing, Organizing, and Drafting"), we look at what happens when your instructor gives you an assignment. What is the specific audience for your task—the reader(s) who will gauge your work's effectiveness? What is your exact purpose for taking the approach that you choose? What are some ways to get started, to generate ideas and words related to your tasks? What will your focus be—in other words, what is the controlling idea, or thesis, of your document? How will you gather and organize evidence to back up your thesis? And what is the best way to write an initial draft of your text?

The primary components of the essay are its paragraphs, and Chapter 3, "Developing Strong Paragraphs: Exploring Your Options," discusses the many different kinds of paragraphs that you will need to develop a variety of essays. You may well be surprised by the great range of options that you have when planning and developing these essential "building blocks."

Chapter 4 ("Reshaping Your Essay: Global Revision") explains how to revise larger units: paragraphs and essays. Paragraphs frequently wander off course as the writer works through new thoughts on paper and forgets his or her original purpose. Essays sometimes promise too much in their introductions and then fail to deliver. Sometimes, an essay starts in one direction and ends with a conclusion quite different from the one the writer planned. Or an essay may be unified and structurally sound but still not be adequate to the demands of the assignment because the writer has neglected to determine the purpose and audience for this effort.

Chapter 5 ("Refining Your Essay: Editing and Proofreading") emphasizes the importance of careful sentence construction and word choice. If paragraphs are the basic components of the essay, then sentences are the elements of paragraphs, and, of course, words make up sentences. Clear communication starts at this level. The chapter includes exercises that ask you to correct the errors in someone else's writing. Once you are comfortable with the concepts explained in Chapter 5, revising your own text, which is never as easy as working on a stranger's text, will become easier and more natural.

One final note: writing is not an art form; it is a skill. If you want to become a better writer and you are willing to work at it, your writing will improve. Writing is not a mysterious practice, nor should it be one that you dread. It is a step-by-step process, and the more you put into this process, the better your results will be. Sometimes this process can even be enjoyable. ●

CLASSROOM HINT Stress the notion that, as with any skill, attaining competence as a writer demands a commitment to exhaustive practice.

CHAPTER 1

THE ESSAY: DETERMINING PURPOSE, AUDIENCE, AND APPROACH

People try to get out of themselves and to escape from the man. This is folly; instead of transforming themselves into angels, they turn themselves into beasts; instead of lifting, they degrade themselves. These transcendental humors frighten me, like lofty and inaccessible heights.

—Michel de Montaigne

Consider Your Options

Very often, sophomores, juniors, and seniors will sigh and then remark, "I wish I had paid more attention in Comp 1." Indeed. Although what you will experience in this course will frequently be rigorous, remember that the more you choose to learn in this course, the better off you'll be in the semesters to come.

The passage on the preceding page was written four hundred years ago by Michel de Montaigne (mon TANE). Montaigne retired early from his law practice and devoted the rest of his life to observing the world and writing about it: the strangeness of human nature, the behavior of animals, the prospect of eternity. Four centuries later, Montaigne's "second career" still makes remarkably good reading, for he was a brilliant thinker and writer who also happened to invent one of the major literary forms: the essay. Montaigne's *Essais* is a collection of his writings, most of them brief and most on a single subject. The French word *essai* means, literally, "attempt"; figuratively, it means "excursion" or "exploration." An important word in the title of this text, *options,* reflects Montaigne's sense of the essay's possibilities. Each document that you produce during your college years—and beyond—will offer you options, choices to be explored as you work through the steps of the writing process.

The essay is only one form of writing practiced in the academic and business worlds. But writing essays will teach you skills necessary for the increasingly complex writing assignments that you will face later in college and for applications in the world of work.

Nevertheless, many students dread the thought of having to write an essay. They see such an assignment as a needlessly formal, artificially narrow means of judging their writing. However, there are three very good reasons that your instructors hold the ability to write essays in such high regard:

CLASSROOM HINT Discuss the fact that the writing you will assign should be seen as a versatile tool for future college work. It prepares students for writing encountered in a variety of disciplines and is excellent preparation for essay examinations.

1. Someone who can write solid essays proves that he or she can communicate effectively with educated, adult readers.
2. Essays provide an unparalleled opportunity for readers to judge someone's critical-thinking, organizational, and language skills.
3. The writer of a successful essay has thought through a topic, taken "ownership" of the developed topic, and worked through the stages of the writing process—thereby creating an essay that can be a source of pride.

SUGGESTED ACTIVITY To familiarize students with the meaning of terms such as *received American usage* and *standard written English,* duplicate and distribute short samples of articles from national newspapers or other periodicals—the *Wall Street Journal,* the *Washington Post,* or the *Atlantic* will do nicely.

Essays may be written on all manner of subjects, and they can be long, sometimes approaching 25,000 words. However, the essays that you will write during your college years will be much shorter. You will be asked to choose a topic of an appropriate size, consider the topic, plan your essay, organize it, and develop it by providing examples, experiences, and other information. At the same time, you will be expected to follow the rules of what is sometimes called "received American usage" or "standard written English"—that is, acceptable grammar and mechanics. If all this sounds like a lot of work to you, you're right. Worthwhile things don't come easy, but the rewards are substantial.

The good news is that there is no single "perfect" way to write an essay. Consider the following situation: a writing instructor has asked her class of twenty-five students to write an in-class essay on one highly specific topic. When the essays are graded, five students receive an *A* for their efforts. The instructor lets you read those five essays. It is very likely that you will be struck by the fact that the five compositions are so *dissimilar:* the five students found their way to a superior result by taking very different approaches.

Writing an essay is not like solving an algebraic equation. Within the limits of traditional mathematics, there is only one answer to $2x + 4 = 8$, and there are only a few approaches that will lead you to the right answer: $x = 2$. However, the five students whose essays you read found very different ways to "solve the problem" of the writing assignment. Looking closer, you see that there are other differences as well. The first essay has beautifully formed phrasing and, interestingly, doesn't show many corrections. Another essay's style is more direct and less elegant, but this essay's strength is its organization. A third essay offers a brilliant analysis of the topic, but a glance at an earlier draft reveals the writer's struggle to communicate: every other word is revised, with arrows and asterisks telling the reader where to look next in a forest of corrections.

The first writer may seem to be "naturally gifted," someone who creates magic as soon as the pen hits the paper, but such a writer is a rare creature. The other two are much more typical. Most *A* writers have *learned* to be *A* writers. Writing isn't an art reserved for the gifted few; it's a *skill,* much like dancing or playing golf or balancing your weekly budget. The purpose of this text is to outline your options, to show you the various strategies, large and small, that will help you learn to be a better writer.

CLASSROOM HINT
Again, remind students that, as a skill, writing demands a great deal of practice.

CHARACTERISTICS OF THE ESSAY

Essays appear in many different forms, but every essay has two features, rhetorical context and rhetorical structure. **Rhetorical context** is the reason that the essay exists: a writer has a purpose and an audience for an essay. **Rhetorical structure** is the way the writer chooses to shape the essay so it best fulfills that purpose and reaches that audience. Note that these two major elements of the essay are also key to *any* document that you might write or read: a business letter, an e-mail, a résumé, or a menu.

SUGGESTED ACTIVITY
Distributing copies of an effective business letter, a newspaper editorial or opinion column, a short technical proposal, or a set of instructions will help demonstrate the importance of communicating a clear purpose.

Rhetorical Context

As you plan an essay, here are two essential issues for you to consider. The first is the **purpose** of your essay—that is, what this essay will be and what you hope to accomplish with it. The second is your **audience.** To whom are you writing? What does this person or persons know or need to know? What will it take to impress this audience?

Defining Your Purpose

"What's gonna be your angle on that kidnapping story, Joe?" said the editor.
"I'll focus on the grieving family—that's the angle as far as I see it right now."

Angle is a word that describes the journalist's purpose for writing. When an instructor gives you an essay assignment, you must first determine *your* purpose, *your* goal. Two of your goals are fairly basic and obvious. One is to get the assignment done, and done on time. The second is to receive a high grade. But you must get past this level. Try not to treat the assignment as an obstacle, a task not unlike having to clean up a mess. Too often, students spend a little time planning and organizing, write a first draft as quickly as possible, and then breathe a sigh of relief as the paper disappears into the instructor's growing stack. There may have been a time in your education when you could take this approach and be rewarded, but in the immortal words of Austin Powers, "That train has sailed." Your instructor of college-level composition will look for evidence that you have used the process of writing—that you have thought, planned, and found your angle. And trying to get a good grade on an essay written with no specific purpose other than to do well is like trying to walk in total darkness.

Traditionally, four categorical purposes for writing are (1) to express, (2) to inform, (3) to entertain, and (4) to persuade. Thinking about these four very general purposes can help you shape your conceptual process and the document that you produce. However, these four are just a starting point; they lead you into a world of options that will enable you to decide on a much more specific purpose for the document that you intend to write.

So how can thinking about a specific purpose help shape your essay? Consider the following scenarios:

1. In response to an assignment that asks you to comment on the fact that young adult citizens of the United States rarely bother to vote in state and federal elections, you plan to argue that young adults are allowing older adults to choose who will be elected, for older people vote at a much higher rate than younger people do. In this case, your purpose is to persuade your audience to agree with you. Will this purpose help guide your choice of language? Will you use bold words and forceful claims, or will your language be descriptive and gentle? Probably the former.
2. You plan to enter an essay in a local writing contest. Your essay will describe your grandmother's small house located in Colorado's Rocky Mountains. This is a magical memory for you; part of your childhood was spent with your grandmother, and those were the best of your growing-up years. Your purpose is to engage your audience and share vivid memories. Will your words be definitive and bold or descriptive and gentle? Probably the latter.

The choices indicated in the preceding examples reflect the necessary relationship between a writer's purpose and the language and evidence that the writer employs. These examples stem from essay topics; however, note the way that a writer's purpose also affects her approach in the following real-life situation.

Jennifer and Diego work in a large department store. Their area is haphazardly maintained because their immediate manager can't be bothered with the need to establish a safe and orderly work environment. Last Tuesday, July 9, a stack of boxed outdoor grills toppled from the summit of a large display rack, bruising Jennifer's elbow but breaking Diego's wrist. This was not the first such incident. Here is Jennifer's e-mail to a friend recounting the incident:

> Yesterday I almost got crushed to death. It was crazy!!!! I wasnt hurt much and I felt rediculus sitting there in a pile of gas cookers and other crap that got carryed down with it. But then I saw Diego, he was white as a ghoste, holding his arm like it was falling off. I ran to get Mr. Wilkins but the creep

was gone. The store manager took care of it. You know, this isnt the first time some one got hurt in our area, last month their was that old man who had the lawnchair fall on his sholder.

Here, Jennifer's purpose is to achieve maximum impact, to tell her friend a good story and show how ludicrous her working life is. Twenty-four hours later, however, Jennifer must write about the same event in a very different context; the store manager, following company policy, has asked her to fill out an incident report. An incident report has a very narrow purpose: to tell what happened as objectively as possible. To fulfill her new purpose, Jennifer will have to refrain from referring to previous accidents or to her contempt for her immediate supervisor.

SUGGESTED ACTIVITY
Discuss the tone, detail, and focus of each of these accident reports. This discussion will help students understand what is required to communicate purpose effectively.

On Tuesday, July 9, I was working with Diego Arteche in the outdoor and patio section. We were creating a display underneath the merchandise rack that contains outdoor grills and related products.

At about 2:20 p.m., we heard a noise. I looked up and saw the stacked boxes of gas grills falling toward us. We both tried to scramble out of the way. A box hit me a glancing blow on my left elbow, but several boxes fell on Diego. He was in severe pain with swelling at his wrist and lower forearm.

I ran to get help. I could not find the area manager, Robert Wilkins, but I was able to summon Marie O'Connor, store manager, who called an ambulance. The EMTs arrived at 2:35 and examined me and Diego Arteche. I had only a bruise on my elbow and arm, but Diego's condition was more serious, so he was taken to the emergency room.

At this point Ms. O'Connor pulled extra personnel into Outdoor and Patio to clean up the mess and put everything back in order. I do not know what caused the boxes to fall.

Jennifer Warne

Two weeks later, however, both Jennifer and Diego have left their place of employment, probably figuring that it's better to take their chances on the open job market than face death by gas grill. Diego, in fact, is in the process of filing a lawsuit for workplace negligence. His attorney asks Jennifer to write her preliminary account of what happened at the store in order to help her prepare Diego's case against the company:

On Tuesday, July 9, I was working with Diego Arteche in the outdoor and patio section of the MegalithMart located at 2304 Sanderson Street. We were creating a display underneath the merchandise rack that contains outdoor grills and related products. All the time I have worked at this store, this rack has been consistently overloaded and the boxes stacked unevenly. Both Diego and I had complained about the situation several times to our area manager, Mr. Robert Wilkins, but his response was always to tell us to take care of it when we had time, then assign us another task and tell us to hurry.

At about 2:20 p.m., we heard a noise. I looked up and saw the stacked boxes of gas grills falling toward us. We both tried to scramble out of the way. A box hit me a glancing blow on my left elbow, but several boxes fell on Diego. He was in severe pain with swelling at his wrist and lower forearm.

I ran to get help. I could not find Robert Wilkins, which did not surprise me, since he is frequently unavailable to his subordinates, but I was able to summon Marie O'Connor, store manager, who called an ambulance. The EMTs arrived at 2:35 and examined me and Diego Arteche. I had only a bruise on my elbow and arm, but Diego's condition was more serious, so he was taken to the emergency room.

Diego and I have been working in an unsafe environment for quite a while. In my encounters with our supervisor, Wilkins, it was clear that he simply did not care about such matters as dangerously overloaded shelves and the possibility of employee and/or customer injury. In fact, just a month prior to our incident, an elderly man was injured when a lawn chair fell—from the same rack—onto his shoulders and neck. For some reason, Mr. Wilkins seemed to find this event quite humorous.

Consider Your Options

Have you ever had to write more than one document about the same event or subject? How did the documents differ?

In this document, Jennifer's purpose is to support Diego's efforts by telling the *whole* story, including her opinion of the negligence shown by Robert Wilkins. The attorney will find such a document useful when preparing a civil action.

Jennifer has experienced one event—the workplace accident—but has written three very different documents. Each document serves a different purpose, and Jennifer has let the purpose guide each writing task. Note that Jennifer's purpose affects the following aspects of each of the documents above:

- The type of information given
- The amount of information given
- The tone used to give information
- The level of formality
- The amount of proofreading and revision done

Finding your purpose is a good way to make any writing assignment your own. Let's start with a worst-case scenario. Your instructor has assigned you and your class a single topic, a fairly narrow one, and you can't believe your eyes: the topic seems absolutely dreadful. Your first instinct is to ignore the assignment, but you realize that this would be a very dangerous course of action to follow. What should you do? You could, of course, work as little as possible, completing the assignment in record time with minimal personal involvement. You could also find a way to let your instructor know how much you dislike this task. However, let's be frank: *in adult life, successful people are very good at pretending to care.* Not every situation will attract and hold your interest. In fact, you might someday even have to write in support of an opinion with which you disagree. Whatever the case, you will have to attack this assignment and find a way to make it yours. Later, when you are "surrounded" by the details of your writing process, you may realize that the topic isn't so horrible after all. Also remember that we are describing a worst-case scenario.

Defining Your Audience

Just as your purpose defines every document that you write, so will your audience. Before you begin an essay, consider these questions:

- Who will read the document that you write?
- Does the audience for your work have specific needs and expectations of which you should be aware?
- Would you characterize your reader(s) as highly skilled text processors or limited in some way?

SUGGESTED ACTIVITY
A good way to introduce the concept of audience is to ask students to write a letter about what they are learning in a particular course to three different readers: a peer, an older relative, and a prospective employer. Have students compare the three versions for diction, amount and type of detail used, and purpose.

These questions are part of an activity known as *audience analysis.* You won't want to "consider" your audience by writing as simply as possible—unless your audience is at the lowest reading level. Instead, you will want to engage your readers at a level that will heighten their experience, allow you to show your level of skill, and help you achieve your purpose.

In the preceding section, we showed how Jennifer Warne had to determine her purpose for each of the three documents that she produced. She also had to recognize her audience: her friend, then the MegalithMart corporate offices, and finally Diego's attorney. Notice that the list of aspects affected by Jennifer's audience analysis is the same as the list of aspects affected by her choice of purpose:

- The type of information given
- The amount of information given
- The tone used to give information
- The level of formality
- The amount of proofreading and revision done

On a practical level, knowing your audience can have crucial benefits in any writing situation, but the opposite is also true. For example, technical writers often create user's manuals for various products. Consider what the following "step" in a user's manual tells the reader:

> Plug the electrical cord into the ampulator, plug the other end into the wall, and your ampulator is ready for use.

Now imagine the pool of consumers who seem to function on Homer Simpson's level. As you know, if Homer bothered to read these directions at all, he would find a way to electrocute himself, "ampulate" his toes, or wreak other havoc. A writer more alert to the needs of the *entire* audience might produce a manual with steps like these:

1. Insert end A of the electrical cord into the opening marked "Power In." You should hear a click. (See diagram 4A.)
2. Insert end B of the electrical cord into a 220-volt grounded wall outlet.
3. Place the ampulator on a smooth, flat, dry surface.

   DANGER: Do not position the ampulator where it can come into contact with water. A severe shock could result!

This writer understands that a great proportion of the retail audience doesn't know much about electrical equipment, and the writer has kept this realization in mind while drafting the instructions. The first writer thinks, "This process is simple," but the second writer thinks, "Nothing is simple, and I need to protect the consumer from harm and my company from liability."

Consider a more complex example. You are a civil engineer, and you have been made manager of a wastewater project for the commissioners of Deadzone County, a rural area in the southern part of your state (few people live there; even fewer visit). Part of your responsibilities will involve preparing a feasibility study, a document that will analyze the practicality of the project. This document will be read by the following parties:

1. Your professional community—the engineers with whom you will work, the Deadzone County engineer, the engineers from the state Environmental Protection Agency (EPA) and federal EPA.
2. Your boss, a highly skilled engineer who will also be the one to decide whether you get a raise next March.
3. Your boss's immediate supervisor, one of the company's vice presidents. This person's expertise is cost accounting, not engineering.
4. The commissioners of Deadzone County, people about whom you know nothing, although you suspect that they were elected because they own businesses or a lot of land. You decide that your best approach to this important group of readers is to assume that they are intelligent but understand little about civil engineering.

Think of the complexity that your task demands. If you needed to address only your professional peers, your document would be relatively straightforward. However, the presence of the second, the third, and—especially—the fourth group forces you to write a feasibility study that can be read by a very diverse audience. How well you are able to understand the needs of this diverse group will play a large role in the success of your report. Indeed, such a diverse audience will force you to use an entirely different vocabulary—even to provide definitions or add a glossary—than you would if you were writing only to your peers.

That's all very well and good, you might say, but at present I'm not a technical writer or an engineer; I'm taking Comp 1. Isn't my audience just one person, my instructor? Perhaps. But who is that instructor? Try another scenario. Your instructor asks you to write a "how-to" paper, an assignment you see as a virtual gift. You love working with cars, and you decide to write an essay explaining how to tune a carburetor. You approach your fortyish female instructor and announce your intentions. She pushes up her glasses and says, "That's a great idea. I've got a four-barrel Carter in my '71 Mustang, and I've had to tune it up twice in the last eighteen months. What a job!" Did your audience just suddenly change for you?

Think further about the idea of audience. For example, your instructor returns your third essay of the semester. Along with a grade, he has included these comments: "Your essays so far show careful analysis and strong organization. However, you're still making careless and harmful grammatical errors, specifically comma splices and subject-verb agreement errors. Next time, concentrate on polishing your final draft—proofread one more time for these grammatical errors before you turn in your essay." In this case, your audience—your instructor—has alerted you that his expectations for your next essay have become more specific. The reverse could also happen; you might get these comments: "Your essays are very 'clean'; you have a firm grasp of grammar and make a point of avoiding errors. However, I don't think you're giving yourself the freedom to develop your ideas. Loosen up a bit next time and explore the topic in greater detail." Once again, your instructor has let you know that the expectations of your audience have changed.

Consider Your Options

Students sometimes say, "I really love to write and would like to make it a career, but how?" If this statement describes you, consider the growing field of technical writing. What do technical writers do? As an example, think of the user's guide that you receive with virtually every product that you purchase. Someone was paid to write, design, and edit that guide.

In addition to demonstrating how instructors' expectations can vary, these examples also indicate the degree to which purpose and audience are connected. In many ways, your audience controls your purpose. An instructor who tells you that his or her expectations for your next essay have changed is also telling you to adjust your purpose. More generally, your purpose is sometimes modified by your sense of a need to do something more for your audience.

Learning to write is not like learning to ride a bicycle. In the latter pursuit, people tend to learn to ride competently and safely, and then they stop learning. They reach a plateau. Rarely would you hear someone say "I want to become a better bike rider." However, there is no plateau in learning to write. Perfection can't be reached, for it doesn't exist. If you keep trying to become a better writer, though, you can only improve. One of your purposes for each writing task will be to build upon the skills that you have already mastered.

Rhetorical Structures

Unfortunately, the word *essay* has developed negative associations for many students; they see this form of writing as divorced from other forms of real-world writing. The truth is quite different. Almost all writing follows what is sometimes called the "classical pattern." Although it has variations, this pattern always includes an introduction, a body, and a conclusion. Your sense of this rhetorical structure will help you to determine the best way to approach any writing situation—in other words, any rhetorical context.

The Classical Pattern of Organization

In the classical pattern, the **introduction** welcomes the reader into the chosen topic, then indicates the specific direction that the essay will take while developing the topic. The **body** paragraphs develop the focus, which is the essay's central idea as expressed formally in a thesis statement. The thesis often appears in the essay's introduction. The **conclusion** comments on the implications raised by the body paragraphs and then brings the essay to an appropriate end.

So how does all this relate to writing tasks outside the academic environment? Consider the following memo:

MEMORANDUM

Bindleburg Software

"Where Tomorrow Is But a Day Away"

TO: All employees
FROM: Erin McGrath, Human Services Director EM
DATE: February 10, 2005
SUBJECT: Absence procedure

This memo indicates a change in the procedure for filing certificates of absence, effective immediately. If you are absent from work for one or more days, bring your completed certificate of absence to Human Services on the day that you return to work. This office will then process your form and return it to your supervisor. Please call me (ext. 239) if you have any questions.

This document is so brief that you might wonder how a single paragraph could be said to follow any kind of "classical pattern." Well, the first sentence is the introduction; it might seem a bit abrupt, but business documents come to the point quickly. The next two sentences function as the body of the document. They are the reason that the memo needed to be written: to announce a procedural change. The final sentence is the conclusion. Good memos almost always employ the device that you see here, asking the reader to call for clarification if necessary. This way, no one can use the otherwise inevitable "I didn't understand" response if caught violating or ignoring the new procedure.

Or consider this personal letter, which also uses the same classical structure:

April 10, 2005

Dear Cousin Walter,

Thank you so much for clearing up my question about my grandfather's second wife's maiden name. Your letter helped me a great deal. I wonder, however, if I could request one more bit of information from you.

In your letter, you mention that her maiden name was Harris and that her father was David Tom Harris, originally from Watkinsville. I checked the county records and found that, in the early 1930s, a Tom Harriss (note the spelling) owned property near Watkinsville on the north side of the Owl River. Could this be the right man?

Thank you so much for your help, and please don't feel the need to hurry with your reply. It's not an urgent matter.

Yours,

Anne Howells

Anne Howells

In the first paragraph, Anne Howells directs the reader to the point of her letter. Then, in the middle section, she once again states the reason she needed to write this letter. The final paragraph graciously concludes her communication.

Anticipating Rhetorical Options

Part 2 of this text discusses **rhetorical options.** These are the basic patterns that writers use to structure essays. The chapters in Part 2 contain student-written essays that illustrate these options. The Part 2 chapters also contain essays written by professional writers, and these writers sometimes "break form." Frequently, their essays aren't so much models as they are examples of how far a pattern of development can be taken.

Part 2 will discuss nine rhetorical options and then illustrate ways that these options can be blended. The ten chapters of Part 2 will examine the following patterns of development:

- Chapter 6: Description (essays that describe a significant person, animal, place, or thing)
- Chapter 7: Narration (essays that tell a story)
- Chapter 8: Exemplification (essays that use examples to prove a point or illustrate an idea)
- Chapter 9: Process analysis (essays that explain how a process unfolds or that tell the reader how to work through a process)
- Chapter 10: Causal analysis (essays that explain why an event happens or explain the effects of an event)
- Chapter 11: Definition (essays that define, explain, and/or illustrate a key idea or term)
- Chapter 12: Classification (essays that analyze a large group of entities by placing them in distinct categories)
- Chapter 13: Comparison and contrast (essays that examine two ideas, people, events, places, or things to show their differences and possible similarities)
- Chapter 14: Argument (essays that support a position on a disputed issue)

- Chapter 15: Blended options (essays that do not depend on a single rhetorical option in their internal development but, instead, use multiple options)

These are the basic patterns of development because they are the way that mature thinkers make sense of the world around them. As well, a writer uses these rhetorical options when they match his or her purpose and the needs of the audience. For example, if asked to tell how a machine works, a writer would not proceed to **describe** the machine but would instead explain the **process** of its operation. If asked to describe a mountain valley, a writer would tell how it looks, sounds, and smells, not **narrate** the history of events that have taken place there. The standard rhetorical options help writers not only to make sense of the world but also to transmit this understanding to their audience.

READING WITH A WRITER'S EYE

CLASSROOM HINT Emphasizing the integral connection between reading and writing is an important step toward helping students achieve collegiate literacy. "Reading with a Writer's Eye" is only one way in which *Writing Today* emphasizes this connection. Throughout the book, students are also encouraged to write their essays with a reader's eye.

You make many choices as you plan and write an essay. You can also make choices as you read the essays in this text or any other reading assignments.

Consider the Writer's Rhetorical Context and Rhetorical Structures

The most basic way to read is merely for information. A more profitable method is sometimes called *critical reading*. However, we prefer the term *active, analytical reading*. In this approach, the reader is aware of not only *what* the writer is trying to say but also *how* the writer is communicating: the rhetorical structure, the use of transitions, the language level, the freshness of expression. Quite simply, readers who read analytically become better writers because they are conscious of the entire writer-reader connection.

Analytical reading can also help you in some very specific ways. Reading the work of professional writers exposes you to skillfully written and edited English. Good writing is judged by standards developed both by academics and by publishing professionals. Reading *Harper's* or the *New Yorker*, for example, or books published by quality presses will show you *how* language works as well as introduce you to a fascinating world of thought.

SUGGESTED ACTIVITY Distributing passages from articles in the *New Yorker*, the *Atlantic*, or another quality periodical will help students understand the kind and level of language they will have to master both as readers and as writers. As an alternative, you might jump ahead in *Writing Today* and discuss sample paragraphs from a few of the professional essays that have been included in Part 2.

Consider Your Purposes as a Reader

Skilled readers have reasons—purposes—that guide their approach to an essay. For example, they may be reading for entertainment, or they may be studying or doing research. To get the most value from this activity, active, analytical readers use the following strategies as they process an essay:

- Interpret the title. Is it straightforward or perhaps ironic?
- Look for any prefatory information. Is there a headnote, an editor's introduction, or a biographical section?
- Look for any stylistic clues—subheadings, for example—that highlight the essay's organization.

- Annotate the text. Write your responses in the margins or between lines. If a passage is confusing, mark it with an asterisk or question mark. If you don't know a word or phrase, circle it. Come back to these areas later.
- Take notes on a separate piece of paper.
- Reread the passages that caused you trouble. Use a college-level dictionary to look up words that you didn't know.
- Summarize the essay in one paragraph.

As this list illustrates, reading is not a passive process. You, the reader, *interact* with the text—questioning, agreeing, disagreeing, wondering. And at some point, you will find yourself *evaluating* the writer's output:

CLASSROOM HINT Emphasize the fact that reading should be as active and conscious an intellectual activity as writing.

- Are the examples sufficient?
- Is the analysis logical?
- Has any information been left out—deliberately or inadvertently—that would have changed the writer's approach had the information been present?
- Is the writer's conclusion warranted?
- Do you *like* what you have read? Does it make you want to learn more about this or other, related subjects?

Read the essay that follows by the professional writer Suzanne Britt, think about it, and then join the discussion that follows.

Neat People vs. Sloppy People

SUZANNE BRITT

1 I've finally figured out the difference between neat people and sloppy people. The distinction is, as always, moral. Neat people are lazier and meaner than sloppy people.

2 Sloppy people, you see, are not really sloppy. Their sloppiness is merely the unfortunate consequence of their extreme moral rectitude. Sloppy people carry in their mind's eye a heavenly vision, a precise plan, that is so stupendous, so perfect, it can't be achieved in this world or the next.

3 Sloppy people live in Never-Never Land. Someday is their métier. Someday they are planning to alphabetize all their books and set up home catalogs. Someday they will go through their wardrobes and mark certain items for tentative mending and certain items for passing on to relatives of similar shape and size. Someday sloppy people will make family scrapbooks into which they will put newspaper clippings, postcards, locks of hair, and the dried corsage from their senior prom. Someday they will file everything on the surface of their desks, including the cash receipts from coffee purchases at the snack shop. Someday they will sit down and read all the back issues of *The New Yorker.*

4 For all these noble reasons and more, sloppy people never get neat. They aim too high and wide. They save everything, planning someday to file, order, and straighten out the world. But while these ambitious plans take clearer and clearer

shape in their heads, the books spill from the shelves onto the floor, the clothes pile up in the hamper and closet, the family mementos accumulate in every drawer, the surface of the desk is buried under mounds of paper and the unread magazines threaten to reach the ceiling.

5 Sloppy people can't bear to part with anything. They give loving attention to every detail. When sloppy people say they're going to tackle the surface of a desk, they really mean it. Not a paper will go unturned; not a rubber band will go unboxed. Four hours or two weeks into the excavation, the desk looks exactly the same, primarily because the sloppy person is meticulously creating new piles of papers with new headings and scrupulously stopping to read all the old book catalogs before he throws them away. A neat person would just bulldoze the desk.

6 Neat people are bums and clods at heart. They have cavalier attitudes toward possessions, including family heirlooms. Everything is just another dust-catcher to them. If anything collects dust, it's got to go and that's that. Neat people will toy with the idea of throwing the children out of the house just to cut down on the clutter.

7 Neat people don't care about process. They like results. What they want to do is get the whole thing over with so they can sit down and watch the rasslin' on TV. Neat people operate on two unvarying principles: Never handle any item twice, and throw everything away.

8 The only thing messy in a neat person's house is the trash can. The minute something comes to a neat person's hand, he will look at it, try to decide if it has immediate use and, finding none, throw it in the trash.

9 Neat people are especially vicious with mail. They never go through their mail unless they are standing directly over a trash can. If the trash can is beside the mailbox, even better. All ads, catalogs, pleas for charitable contributions, church bulletins and money-saving coupons go straight into the trash can without being opened. All letters from home, postcards from Europe, bills and paychecks are opened, immediately responded to, then dropped in the trash can. Neat people keep their receipts only for tax purposes. That's it. No sentimental salvaging of birthday cards or the last letter a dying relative ever wrote. Into the trash it goes.

10 Neat people place neatness above everything, even economics. They are incredibly wasteful. Neat people throw away several toys every time they walk through the den. I knew a neat person once who threw away a perfectly good dish drainer because it had mold on it. The drainer was too much trouble to wash. And neat people sell their furniture when they move. They will sell a La-Z-Boy recliner while you are reclining in it.

11 Neat people are no good to borrow from. Neat people buy everything in expensive little single portions. They get their flour and sugar in two-pound bags. They wouldn't consider clipping a coupon, saving a leftover, reusing plastic nondairy whipped cream containers or rinsing off tin foil and draping it over the unmoldy dish drainer. You can never borrow a neat person's newspaper to see what's playing at the movies. Neat people have the paper all wadded up and in the trash by 7:05 a.m.

12 Neat people cut a clean swath through the organic as well as the inorganic world. People, animals, and things are all one to them. They are so insensitive. After they've finished with the pantry, the medicine cabinet, and the attic, they will throw out the red geranium (too many leaves), sell the dog (too many fleas),

and send the children off to boarding school (too many scuff-marks on the hardwood floors).

Essay Analysis

As we mentioned, there are two ways to read an essay actively and analytically. One way is to look at the rhetorical context—the writer's purpose, audience, and rhetorical pattern. The second way is to look at the essay's effectiveness—its logic, its evidence, and the impact that it makes upon the reader (you). Let's go through Britt's essay with these ideas in mind.

The Essay's Rhetorical Context

"Neat People vs. Sloppy People" is a funny essay; clearly, at least part of Britt's **purpose** was to make us laugh. But good humor is always more than merely funny. Note the opening paragraph:

> I've finally figured out the difference between neat people and sloppy people. The distinction is, as always, moral. Neat people are lazier and meaner than sloppy people.

CLASSROOM HINT
Britt's introduction captures the reader's attention because it contains startling remarks. As such, it is a model of a technique students might use in their own introductions. (Students can find help with their introductions in Chapter 3.)

Here, Britt states a more serious intent of her essay: to draw a "moral" distinction between neat people and sloppy people. For, as she claims, sloppy people act for "noble reasons" (paragraph 4) whereas neat people "are bums and clods at heart" (paragraph 6). Notice Britt's **thesis statement**—the controlling idea—"Neat people are lazier and meaner than sloppy people." This is the idea she will develop throughout her essay.

Britt strives to turn a common set of assumptions upside down. In our culture, we view neatness as part of a package of virtues: hard work, dedication, punctuality, etc. On the other hand, many people consider sloppiness to be a sign of "sorry behavior": laziness, shiftlessness, and so on. Britt attacks these assumptions. She argues that neat people are callous, wasteful, and selfish. On the other hand, she believes that sloppy people properly value objects and correspondence, are careful, and take the long view.

CLASSROOM HINT
Some students might take issue with this interpretation. Invite them to explain their objections; doing so will help ignite a productive class discussion about purpose.

Britt has at least three intentions, or purposes: to make us laugh, to get us to see the world in a different way, and to draw a "moral" distinction between two types of people. To illustrate, consider that the incredibly disorganized home office in your uncle's house is perhaps not managed by a slob, but by a closet humanitarian. And perhaps the immaculate household of your friend's mother, reminiscent of the days of June Cleaver (the Beaver's mother), is actually the work of a flinty-eyed monster who cares about nothing more than tracking you through the house to see where you plan to put down your can of soda.

How about Britt's audience? Part of the appeal of this essay is that it can be read profitably by everyone from intelligent fourth-graders to adults with advanced college degrees. The subject matter is relevant to us all, from the time we are allotted part of a domicile and told "This will be your room." Britt's language, examples, and tone allow this essay to reach such an extended readership.

SUGGESTED ACTIVITY
To drive this point home, analyze the vocabulary in a few paragraphs from the essay.

The Essay's Rhetorical Structure

Britt compares two classes of people, the neat and the unneat, so her rhetorical option is a logical one: comparison/contrast. As we'll see in Chapter 13, when using this approach, most writers tend to concentrate on contrast, not comparison. Think about how few areas of comparison exist between neat people and sloppy people: both are human beings, and both own stuff. Thus, Britt is correct to concentrate on *differences,* not *similarities.*

CLASSROOM HINT Take a few minutes to explain how the point-by-point method—often found in sustained pieces of writing—can be used.

Britt uses one of two possible comparison/contrast strategies. In the subject-by-subject method you see here, the writer discusses the first subject at length, then moves on to the second subject. Thus, Britt discusses the virtues of sloppy people for four paragraphs, then spends seven paragraphs exposing the previously unknown limitations of neat people. Notice the imbalance? Britt's intent is not so much to praise the sloppy as it is to attack the neat; hence, she devotes more "text space" to the latter subject.

As mentioned before, in order to evaluate an essay, a reader needs to analyze its effectiveness—its quality, if you will. To evaluate this essay, we can profit by looking at some of the more specific parts of its rhetorical structure.

Written by a professional writer for publication, "Neat People vs. Sloppy People" breaks some of the guidelines for the standard essay. As you go through the chapters in this text, you will notice the various ways that accomplished writers deviate from the advice offered in this and other writing texts. Sophisticated writers frequently do this, but they always have their reasons, which are inextricably tied to their purpose and audience. Let's evaluate Britt's essay with these thoughts in mind:

CLASSROOM HINT Before discussing these five points, explain the fact that all writers make choices and that the way they exercise their "options" relates to their purpose, audience, and message.

1. The introductory paragraph is very brief. In the essays that you write this term, your instructor will want you to use fully developed introductions, perhaps involving more than one paragraph. In Britt's defense, however, we can point out that she has little reason to spend her first paragraph defining "sloppy person" and "neat person"—the reader probably has a good grasp of those two concepts. (See pages 52–55 in Chapter 3 for more information on developing introductory paragraphs.)
2. Britt tends to write in generalizations. She writes about "people"—never her uncle Bob or friend Susan. She is most specific when writing about physical possessions—desks, letters, and so on. This feature of "Neat People vs. Sloppy People" is perhaps its weakest element. In your writing, you will need to go beyond this level and be more specific, "naming names," as it were. (See pages 55–60 and 74–76 in Chapter 3 for more information on using specific evidence.)
3. Between the "sloppy people" section and the "neat people" section there is an abrupt shift. As mentioned, Britt spends four paragraphs discussing the untidy. She concludes the fourth paragraph with "a neat person would just bulldoze the desk." Her next seven paragraphs discuss neat people and their hidden motivations. This **transition** is abrupt. It works in this essay, but sudden transitions are generally a risky tactic. Your essays will normally include explicit transitions, as we will discuss in Chapter 3 (pages 71–72).

4. The essay has no concluding paragraph. This is another risky choice by Britt, who must have felt that her essay didn't need a final comment. However, your instructor will expect each of your essays to have an effective conclusion that sums up the development of the essay and provides a graceful ending. At times, students skimp on either the conclusion or the introduction, but they do so at their own peril. (See pages 60–63 in Chapter 3 for more information on developing concluding paragraphs.)

5. Britt employs a bold **tone** in this essay and, as we discussed above, accompanies this tone with some fairly risky tactics. All told, does she succeed in impressing the reader? We think so. However, for a different angle on this interpretation, try the exercise below.

EXERCISE 1.1

Using Britt's rhetorical structure (comparison/contrast, subject by subject), write a new version of "Neat People vs. Sloppy People." However, where Britt uses bold declarations and sweeping generalizations, try another approach: write about a person you know who fits Britt's definition of "neat people" and a person who fits the "sloppy people" definition. Concentrate on using specific details and examples to contrast the two people. See if you can make the same "moral" distinction that Britt does.

SUGGESTED ACTIVITY Consider turning this exercise into a brainstorming exercise to be completed in small writing groups or by the class as a whole with you or a student serving as recorder.

EXERCISE 1.1 Answers will vary.

WRITING WITH A READER'S EYE

Being aware of your purpose and audience doesn't mean considering these two issues at the start of the writing process and then forgetting them once you begin to draft. Each sentence that you write and then revise must be a conscious, deliberate gesture toward your audience, reflecting your general purpose and the specific purpose of this particular part of your essay. Your reader depends upon his or her reading skills to interpret your meaning but also upon *you* to provide the clearest possible communication.

CLASSROOM HINT Again, stress the integral connection between reading and writing.

The following essay is the final draft that a student named Verlinda wrote in response to a classroom assignment:

> In 550–750 words, describe a person who is more than what first meets the eye.

Verlinda's earlier drafts were unfocused and somewhat "self-absorbed." Read this essay; then answer the questions that follow. Note that the remaining chapters of Part 1 will show this essay in its earlier forms; you will be able to follow its development through the various stages of the writing process.

A Very Secret Santa

1 All my year growing up, Betty Wallace was my best friend. I spent a lot of time at her house, and she did the same at mine. Our parents were good

friends, and each couple trusted the other implicitly. I grew to see Walter and Leona Wallace as my uncle and aunt.

2 Walter was the more interesting of the two, but not at first glance. An accountant, he seemed to want to fit in. Walter dressed conservatively, which matched his features and size: a black man of middle height, very slightly overweight, with rimless glasses. His only "daring" feature was a neatly trimmed mustache. His personality, at first, also seemed unremarkable. He was quiet, a bit shy, and not really sociable or pleasant. Given his choice, he would sit alone in his big lounge chair and smoke a pipe (an ever-present odor) while watching television. Yet inside Walter Wallace was, if not a heart of gold, then the next best thing: he was the most charitable man I've ever met.

3 I remember the first time I saw an example of Walter's secret side. It was before Christmas, long ago. Betty and I were ten years old and going shopping with Mr. and Mrs. Wallace at the mall. After Walter, swearing under his breath, finally found a parking space, we noticed a commotion a few cars over. A young woman and her seven-year-old were trying to quiet down the three-year-old, who, it seems, had been pulled from the last store they visited without getting what he wanted. The mother looked entirely flustered and was obviously quite poor (the car was dented and covered with rust). The little boy was screaming as if he had been scalded. We walked toward the mall, listening to this drama unfold behind us, and then Walter suddenly disappeared. Mrs. Wallace told us to keep walking, that Walter would catch up. When he did, he said nothing. Confused, I waited until Betty and I were alone to ask for an explanation. "He went back to give that woman some money," Betty explained. "He's done this a thousand times."

4 At the Wallaces' home there were always six to ten dogs and cats. By some radar, strays knew where to go. Over the objections of Leona, Walter would take them in; carry them to the vet; pay for shots, neutering, and medicine; and keep them if he couldn't convince someone else to take them off his hands. As a child, I remember loving the fact that the Wallace home was full of animals, but I don't think Leona Wallace shared my enjoyment.

She didn't like dogs and would freeze in midsentence if a cat jumped in her lap, then launch the cat back towards the floor.

5 Christmastime is wonderful for kids, and Christmases are among my fondest memories. My family and the Wallaces attended Trinity United Methodist, a mostly white church with a middle-class population. However, the arrival of this church's Santa Claus was a great event each year. Walter Wallace as Santa was a complete transformation from Walter Wallace as bespectacled, quiet tax advisor. His voice and laughter boomed through the church as he talked to his small "clients." Walter also took his act on the road; he was a regular fixture at the area hospitals and the children's hospice.

6 Did Walter Wallace have the proverbial heart of gold? Or was he motivated by guilt—a successful man who can't help looking back to a time when he was poor? I don't think either is true. Walter helped young and old, black and white, human and nonhuman only because he couldn't keep himself from doing so. Over the years, Betty told me that her father was miserable if he perceived that he had not done enough in some situation. Betty also told me that Walter's activities caused significant friction in his marriage. But he would not be stopped.

7 In general, I feel that when someone does something "nice" for another, his or her motives are not altogether altruistic—being nice makes the giver feel good about himself or herself. In the case of Walter Wallace, however, his behavior may well have been involuntary. Does this make Walter any less admirable? I don't think so; I wish the world were full of men like him.

EXERCISE 1.2

Answer the following questions to evaluate the final draft of "A Very Secret Santa."

1. What do you think Verlinda's audience and purpose are? Has she successfully addressed the audience and fulfilled her purpose? Explain.
2. The **thesis** of this essay is stated in the last sentence of the second paragraph: "he was the most charitable man I've ever met." Remember that the thesis is a device used to alert the reader to the essay's purpose. Is this thesis significant enough and specific enough to build an essay around?
3. In paragraph 6, Verlinda considers the mystery of Walter Wallace's motives. Should she have mentioned this mystery in her introduction and thesis?

EXERCISE 1.2 Answers will vary. Possible responses:
1. Verlinda's audience comprises members of a typical first-year college writing class. As such, it may be termed "general academic." Her purpose is twofold: to describe an individual and to comment on the motives behind altruism. Whether she has succeeded is a subject for class discussion, but most will see this as an effective essay.
2. The thesis statement works because it focuses on only one aspect of the subject's personality, an aspect that can be developed easily with a few concrete examples.

3. Exploring Walter's motives is helpful, but doing so earlier in the essay would have been distracting. The writer is wise to address her thesis before exploring why Walter acts as he does.
4. She provides all of the consideration needed. After all, the essay is about Walter's charity, not Leona's frustrations over it. Giving more space to Leona's reactions would have weakened the essay's focus.
5. Students may come down on both sides of the question, making it a good point from which to launch class discussion. In our view, however, the evidence is sufficient.
6. Again, this is subject to debate, but we believe the inductive method produces a more believable and intimate portrait.

4. Does Verlinda give enough consideration to the problems that Walter's habits caused for Leona?

5. The writer concludes that Walter acted in the way that he did "because he couldn't keep himself from doing so." Is the evidence that she presents sufficient for her to come to this conclusion?

6. This essay follows an **inductive** method. In other words, the writer presents evidence, then uses that evidence to come to a conclusion. However, she could have made a general claim in her thesis—some people are altruistic because they can't keep themselves from being this way—and then proceeded to use the story of Walter as "evidence" for this claim. If the writer had taken this second approach, would her essay be better? Would it gain or lose any charm for the reader?

The Writing Process

The writer of "A Very Secret Santa," as we have mentioned, did not produce this essay in one step. She employed a series of steps, collectively known as the **writing process.** Here is a brief summary of what this process entails:

- *Planning.* In this stage, you consider the assignment and its requirements. You consider your purpose and your audience, then start to generate ideas.
- *Prewriting.* Some students rush in where angels fear to tread; after the planning stage, they proceed to the drafting stage, producing essays with weak, unfocused structures and poorly developed ideas. However, prewriting allows you to visualize your essay before you begin it. As you cluster, outline, or freewrite (or use some other method of prewriting, as discussed in Chapter 2), you generate more ideas and start to see the logical "shape" of your essay.
- *Drafting.* Your first draft may be very rough, but a very rough draft gives you an opportunity to develop your ideas, as we discuss in chapters 2 and 4. If your planning and prewriting have pointed you in the right direction, then careful revising will lead you to a polished final essay. In any case, be prepared to write multiple drafts if you want to do your best work.
- *Revising for content.* After your first draft, you should put the essay aside for a day, if at all possible. Then go back and read it for its content and its message. Have you written all that you intended, and is what you have written sufficient to meet the assignment's expectations? This revising stage frequently involves **collaboration**, meaning that one or more of your classmates, or readers you recruit on your own, act as your temporary audience. Chapter 4 discusses these issues.
- *Revising for structure.* Is what you have written an essay? Does it produce what its introduction promises? Are all of your paragraphs fully developed around clearly stated topics? See chapters 3 and 4.
- *Revising for grammar and mechanics.* Many students tend to produce as their final draft an essay that sounds very good when read aloud.

However, your reading audience will more likely be looking at paper, not listening to a transcript. This revising stage, sometimes simply referred to as *editing* and *proofreading,* allows you to catch serious errors that can undercut your credibility and also to polish your essay by making final word choices and by fine-tuning your sentences. Chapter 5 concentrates on editing and proofreading.

Chapters 2–5 will take you through these steps of the writing process. Throughout these chapters, we will concentrate on the various **options** that each stage of the writing process will offer you. The personal essay is not a boilerplate document; the writer makes choices at every step along the way.

MORE OPTIONS ONLINE
You can access all of the Web sites listed in "Using the Internet" by going to **www.mhhe.com/writingtoday**.

Using the Internet

Go to these Web sites to find more tips, techniques, and insights on approaches to the essay:

The Purdue University Writing Lab

Students can access useful handouts from this online writing lab (OWL). Included are materials on planning a writing project and writing various types of papers (genres): **http://owl.english.purdue.edu**.

The UVic Writer's Guide

This Web site, sponsored by the University of Victoria's English Department, provides ample support for writing several types of essays as well as successful student models. The site also provides good advice on outlining, organizing, and writing introductions and conclusions: **http://web.uvic.ca/wguide**.

The University of Richmond Writing Center's Writer's Web

This site offers useful suggestions for getting started on a paper and writing thesis statements: **http://writing.richmond.edu/writing/wweb.html**.

CHAPTER 2

SHAPING YOUR ESSAY: PREWRITING, FOCUSING, ORGANIZING, AND DRAFTING

Before musicians give a concert, they practice and plan. Their audience will not welcome slip-ups. Moreover, the audience has expectations about what music will be performed. If it wants to succeed, a musical group will try to determine those expectations and both meet and surpass them. Similarly, when you write an essay, you want to be proud of it.

This essay will also earn a grade that will become part of your final course grade and eventually part of your GPA. Why would you do any less than what entertainers do?

Prewriting, **focusing**, and **organizing** are the preliminary steps that you take before you write your first **draft.** Your instructor will likely require you to show evidence of these preliminary activities. Some instructors ask that you turn in all "pieces" of your assignment response: prewriting output, outline, first draft (and any intermediate drafts), and the finished essay. These instructors will check to see that you did indeed use a process approach to essay writing. Other instructors may choose to grade your preliminary activities. But even if your instructor requires that you turn in nothing more than your finished essay, you will be missing a valuable opportunity if you do not plan your approach before you start to write.

Careful planning will enable you to write a draft that you can revise without having to scrap whole sections and start over. Yes, professional writers sometimes do have to go back to square one, but this problem can usually be avoided by starting out with a plan.

Sometimes, students respond to a discussion of planning by saying, "I just don't have *time* to do all this and write my whole essay." Our response is "You don't have time *not* to plan." Consider this scenario. Next Tuesday at the start of class, your instructor gives you a writing assignment. You have seventy-five minutes, no more, to write an essay. The topic is not given to you until the start of class. This is the type of assignment that most students dread, and with good reason; it's no trip to Maui. The problems here are very much like those faced by runners in a very short sprint: if they start slowly or stumble along the way, there's not enough time to catch up. On the other hand, students who start by immediately writing their introductory paragraph often find themselves in trouble midway through the essay. They realize that their thesis and focus, which seemed fine early on, are now inappropriate or that the initial approach has yielded one or two acceptable paragraphs but little else. As a result, they struggle to finish—to provide evidence that somehow supports the marginal topic sentences and ideas of those last few paragraphs.

There's a way around this quandary. If you spend the first ten minutes putting together an informal "road map," writing a first draft will be dramatically easier. Rather than coming to the end of each body paragraph with the anxious sense that you must now think up something new to say, you can simply refer to your preliminary notes. You will be able to write your entire first draft with confidence because you know where you're going, you know that your ideas are sound, and you have perceived the overall structure of your essay before writing the first word. With a quarter hour left in the period, while others may still be struggling to finish their first drafts, you are on your second pass, revising, and then proofreading. Those ten early minutes have gone a long way toward improving your essay's final quality.

In general, planning also allows you to "test" your topic. Part of the planning process is designed to generate ideas, and during this part of the process, writers often come up with a topic that is superior to their original idea. Such is the nature of writing.

Consider Your Options

What is your current writing process? Does it work for you? What parts of it would you change?

CLASSROOM HINT State your preferences on these questions early in the term and in writing.

CLASSROOM HINT To convince students of the importance of planning, draw analogies between writing and skills or activities with which they may be familiar. For example, discuss the need to stretch before jogging or the importance of choosing just the right foods in order to prepare a holiday dinner.

CHOOSING YOUR TOPIC

Your instructor may assign you a very specific topic, on which you must write within a fairly narrow focus. Or your instructor may give you much more freedom to choose your own topic and approach. Most of the time, instructors' assignments fall between these two ranges, perhaps with a focused topic that leaves the rest of the choices up to you.

One Writer's Decisions

Chapter 1 contains the finished draft of "A Very Secret Santa," an essay we are using to illustrate the steps of the writing process. This essay was written in response to the following topic:

> In 550–750 words, describe a person who is more than what first meets the eye.

Note that the instructor limits the range of the topic but allows the student writer—Verlinda, in this case—to make the rest of the choices. When approaching this assignment, Verlinda immediately realized that the topic could apply to several people she knew, people whose appearance and general aspect belied their reality. However, some of these people did not seem to offer enough "substance" around which to develop an entire essay:

1. Amir Goldman, who teaches Verlinda's survey of art class, had one day mentioned that many years before, he had been a fighter pilot in the Israeli Air Force. This revelation contrasted greatly with Verlinda's early impressions of Dr. Goldman. However, it seemed "anecdotal" and would not provide enough material for an essay.
2. Angie, a fellow student from high school, had been extremely shy when Verlinda knew her. Everything about "school Angie" was seemingly designed to keep people's attention away from her. However, "after-school Angie" was a lead ballet dancer of considerable renown, and she expressed her otherwise apparently repressed emotions through dance. Verlinda thought about Angie as a topic but then realized that she just didn't know her well enough (she couldn't even remember Angie's last name); the essay would be too "external."
3. Eduardo Sanchez-Mejiers, whom Verlinda knows through a friend, will transfer to a Bible college at the end of this term; he wants to become a Baptist minister. Eduardo, a solid citizen, wears hip clothing and drives a Honda coupe with tinted windows and a miniature Puerto Rican flag on the rearview mirror. He is frequently pulled over by the police for vague or trivial reasons—as Eduardo calls it, the crime of "driving while brown." The contrast between what Eduardo is really like and how the police perceive him is extreme, but Verlinda rejects this topic as well, for it is *Eduardo's* topic: personal, complicated, and ongoing.

CLASSROOM HINT The important lesson here is, of course, that even when they are presented with fairly well-defined topics, writers must exercise their "options." Remind students that Verlinda put a great deal of thought into choosing the subject of her essay. In most cases, we advise our students to complete preliminary freewriting about a subject solely for the purpose of determining how much they know or care about it.

Finally, Verlinda realized that Walter Wallace, a man she had known for a decade, presented the best possibilities for her assignment.

As you can see, Verlinda explored many options at this early stage before settling on the one with the most promise. You will have similar choices to make. Time spent wisely at this stage can have substantial benefits. A student who picks the first reasonable-sounding topic, perhaps impatient to get started, may realize—deep into the writing process—that he or she is spending time trying to nurse an inferior topic along. (If you walk onto a car lot and pick the first car that seems desirable, you increase your chances of buying a lemon.) Thinking and choosing carefully at this stage may well help you avoid needless problems later in the day.

Establishing Your Rhetorical Context

Planning also helps you determine two essential features of your approach:

1. Who is my audience?
2. What is my purpose?

As we pointed out in Chapter 1, audience and purpose are inextricably linked. If your instructor asked you to write a process document showing the reader how to perform a specific computer function, your logical next question would be "For whom?" What if your instructor asked you to write these directions for a group of sixth-graders? What could you assume about the computer skills of this group? What language level would you need to employ? On the other hand, what if your instructor asked you to write this document for a group of retirees? What in your purpose would have to change to meet the needs of this older audience?

Even if your audience is one person—your instructor—you will learn more and more about this person as an audience throughout the semester. Each graded assignment that your instructor returns will contain both explicit and implicit clues about what he or she expects of you on your next attempt. Similarly, the topics and ideas that your instructor brings up in class are a way for him or her to establish an audience for your next essay. If your instructor has been leading up to a classification essay assignment, for example, he or she might mention or hint at certain expectations:

> We've looked at various classification essays and seen how they've worked. We've broken down two of them very carefully to see how they were constructed. By now, you should have a pretty good idea of how to write using this approach. And, while I'm at it, I want, in general, to see more evidence of planning when you turn in your essay.

CLASSROOM HINT Explain the expectations of an assignment clearly and in writing. Doing so improves the quality of the essays students produce. It also helps students learn to assess the expectations of assignments made by other instructors.

In this way, your instructor has established the expectations for the new assignment. In effect, your audience has been defined for you.

How about purpose? Your purpose for this new assignment is to try to satisfy the needs of your audience. That sounds simple enough. But look back at the comments and end notes your instructor has written on earlier essays. Shouldn't these, logically, sharpen your sense of purpose?

CLASSROOM HINT Depending upon your students' level of preparation, you might explain each assignment's purpose both in writing and via class discussion.

Of course, you could choose to take the low road. After examining the assignment, you realize that there is an easy way to complete it with a minimum amount of effort. This unmotivated approach implies a very *modest* purpose, one not designed for a productive outcome.

Why not consider a more worthy purpose? After examining the assignment, you see that here you have a chance to really think through a topic and aim for a more ambitious result. (When this happens, you're not just writing for a grade; you're writing for *yourself*.) Your general purpose, then, will be to write an essay that represents more than the average effort and that affects your reader in the way you want it to, consistent with the goals of the assignment. You may want to explain something so that your reader understands it, or make the reader laugh, or convince the reader to change a view or a behavior. But as you expend more effort than usual while dealing with a more ambitious, complicated topic, you'll find that things can go wrong. Don't let this added difficulty discourage you. Instead, make a mental note to allow more time for revising—checking the structure of your essay, its organization, its logic, its voice. Also, set aside more time for proofreading so that the effect your essay has on your reader won't be compromised by easily avoided mistakes.

With these ideas in mind, you have a clear purpose for this essay. If the result doesn't quite live up to your hopes, rest assured that your instructor will notice the ambition inherent in your finished essay. Moreover, if you plan carefully and take the steps that you need—in other words, use the writing process to fulfill your purpose—your final draft should be successful, representing not just a response to an assignment but a document of which you should rightly be proud.

Establishing purpose and audience in the early stages is extremely important. Notice what happens in the following essay, in which the writer never figured out what he wanted to do and how he wanted to say it.

A Modern Marvel

The greatest invention of the 20th Century must be computers. The earliest computers were huge, filling up a big room. My friend, Darren, says that "he can't imagine life before computers." I agree.

You see computers everywhere, stores, doctors offices, etc. They're great for word processing. You can write essays, letters and term papers on them and then revise as you need. Printers are great, too. You can choose any font you want and make the type bigger so that it fills up the page.

My dad had a real bad problem with his computer last month. It crashed right when he was in the middle of something, and he couldn't re-boot. He took it to a repair store and they had to send it to the factory. It took three weeks for it to come back, but it's fine now. Other ways computers are used are with accounting and similar stuff.

As you can see, our lives have been much improved by the computer. Everyone should have one. In fact, why doesn't the Federal Government start a program to give computers to the poor people? Soon we'll be able to watch real television on our computers as well, that is a day I look forward to.

Besides a great number of stylistic lapses and errors, this essay has no purpose and no structure. It wanders; it contradicts itself. The writer, who has apparently never been told about the Internet, among other developments, barely scratches the surface, piling one random thought upon the next.

Frankly, the real problem here is that this essay can't be revised; it must be rewritten. The writer will need to start over. The situation is like taking a car in for major repairs; if the estimate reaches a certain level, the owner knows that the best thing to do is simply buy another car.

CLASSROOM HINT The distinction between revising and rewriting bears repeating in class. It brings home the need for adequate preparation.

With careful prewriting and drafting, on the other hand, you will be able to produce a *serviceable* first draft, one you can deal with and improve upon. This chapter works through the steps of the process, starting from the beginning.

PREWRITING STRATEGIES

Prewriting can help you find a topic and "test" it by seeing how well it holds up under development. It also helps you generate ideas and allows you to see the connections among those ideas. Your choice of prewriting options should be guided by two factors: (1) your rhetorical context (purpose and audience) and (2) your learning style.

Considering Your Purpose and Audience

On one end of the spectrum is a situation faced daily by people writing at work: they need to write a document on a subject that they know intimately, addressed to an audience familiar with the context of the subject matter. This situation requires only a minimal amount of prewriting. On the other end of the spectrum is a complicated document on a subject that the writer is struggling to handle for an audience hostile to the writer's view and needing to be convinced. This situation requires a great deal of prewriting, with careful choices made at this stage as well as at the focusing, organizing, and drafting stages. Your sense of your audience and purpose will help you decide both your most promising prewriting options and the extent to which you develop these options.

Considering Your Learning Style

How do you process language and information? Do you tend to hear it (aural learning) or see it (verbal learning)? Or do you tend to "see" information in a different way—in graphic form (visual learning)? Your answers to these questions reflect your preferred *learning style*. Most of us prefer one of the three basic approaches to learning: aural, verbal, or visual. Your preferred learning style will influence your choice of prewriting option(s), although you should always try several prewriting techniques. Even those that aren't really compatible with your learning style can yield results. Here are the various options according to their type:

1. Aural learners:
   - Brainstorming with peers
   - Brainstorming with a recorder
2. Verbal learners:
   - Brainstorming on paper
   - Freewriting
   - Invisible writing
   - Looping
3. Visual learners
   - Clustering
   - Chart making

Aural Learners: Brainstorming with Peers

What kind of thoughts are discussed or recorded during a brainstorming session? The answer is simple: anything that relates to the assignment. The key value of brainstorming is that, inevitably, one thought leads to another. In a very short time, a writer can work through his or her cognitive process and have the results on paper.

If you can talk about a topic with your classmates, you may get some valuable insights and feedback just by running your ideas past other people and hearing their responses. (Don't forget to take notes.) You can also do the same for them. One of the interesting features of the writing process is that even if you sit, listen, and don't say a word, you will still learn a great deal about the general topic and your peers' approach to it. In other words, the "shape" of the assignment will become clearer to you. However, it is more likely that you will talk to your classmates, receive their feedback, and vice versa. Note that you don't have to be restricted to your classmates; you can brainstorm with a friend or anyone else who is willing to listen and respond.

One Writer's Decisions

When Verlinda was brainstorming to generate ideas for her essay, she found that some of her friends were taking an "oddity" approach to the assignment "Describe a person who is more than what first meets the eye." Stories of janitors who were trained violinists, baseball players who could yodel, and so on kept popping up as her friends considered possible topics.

However, Verlinda really didn't want to write about people with unexpected talents. She wanted to write about a person whose hidden qualities held a moral significance. After thinking through various possibilities, Verlinda knew that she had a good example in mind, but she also knew that she needed to approach this project carefully.

Since grade school, Verlinda had had a very close friend named Betty. Verlinda and Betty spent time at each other's houses, and each regarded the other's parents as uncles and aunts, not just friendly adults. Betty's father, Walter, was an accountant. A short, pudgy man with a clipped mustache, Walter was quiet, was not particularly friendly, and was sometimes at the mercy of his temper. Many people were put off by his apparently gruff exterior. Yet in her time with Betty's family, Verlinda had seen Walter give away hundreds of dollars to the poor, pay hundreds more for veterinary care for stray animals, and transform himself annually into an outgoing, exuberant Santa Claus.

However, Verlinda could see a potential problem with her essay because her audience, the class's instructor, Dr. Marshall, had made it clear through his classroom comments that his view of human nature was not rosy. Verlinda brought up her concern to her writing group. Dr. Marshall questioned people's motives constantly, especially those that seemed self-serving. As someone in the group mentioned, he seemed to be a bit cynical. So Verlinda and her fellow group members knew that a "heartwarming" approach might face problems.

But Walter's situation was not a simple story of charity; Betty had told her of the conflict between her parents because of Walter's charitable acts. Also, Walter was racked with guilt when he perceived that he had not done enough. Was there a sort of compulsion here? One member of Verlinda's group said that the explanation could be that Walter felt an obligation to share his success with other, less fortunate people, but Verlinda told him that made no sense. Walter gave to anyone—or any animal—who needed help. It seemed that Walter helped others because he had a great need to do so. This wasn't an issue of simple goodness on his part; he fulfilled others' needs while simultaneously fulfilling his own. "Surely," Verlinda said, "this is an approach that Dr. Marshall will find interesting." Most of the members of her group agreed.

Aural Learners: Brainstorming with a Recorder

A cassette recorder or a computer with voice-recognition software allows you to brainstorm aloud, then play back or read your spoken thoughts. This method is convenient, but it has drawbacks as well as advantages. A cassette recorder can be used in a variety of situations, but eventually you will need to transcribe your thoughts. Voice-recognition software will create a text file that you can save, but this type of software is still evolving, and today's best programs require a great deal of setup before they will work optimally. Moreover, this type of brainstorming is solitary; you won't get the benefit of a peer's feedback. However, some writers prefer such an approach.

Verbal Learners: Brainstorming on Paper

During brainstorming, no idea is too large or too small. You can use the six questions favored by journalists—*who, what, when, where, how,* and *why*—to generate ideas and details, or you can just jot down thoughts as they occur to you. Remember that you will eventually need specific details in your writing.

Brainstorming is also a time when you should *not* worry about the mechanics of writing. You are compiling a list of ideas, facts, and details. Work quickly; this is no time to let your "internal editor" take over.

One Writer's Decisions

After she met with her group, Verlinda did the following brainstorming on paper:

for significance (moral), only Walter Wallace

harmless looking man, pass him by in a crowd: short, pudgy, clipped mustache, no-rim glasses

accountant, so he wants to fit in

not sociable or talkative—not really pleasant

heart o'gold—but not like some Readers Digest sketch

does he have a heart of gold, or can he just not help helping?

giving money to poor white woman at mall—nonreaction of Mrs. W.

Betty: "happens all the time"

animal adoption business—semipermanent cast of pets, strays taken in constantly, fed, vet bills paid, acquaintances strongarmed to adopt overflow

Mrs. W. doesn't like animals.

Sometimes Mrs. W. doesn't like Mr. W. because of his tendencies.

Santa Claus—if there were an Olympic Saint Nick competition, Walter would win.

Complete transformation

his appeal and help work across gender and color lines—even species

May be compulsive, but the world is a better place with him in it

Verbal Learners: Freewriting

Freewriting is another version of brainstorming, but instead of writing a list of ideas and details, you concentrate on writing out your thoughts as they occur to you. There is no reason to worry about paragraph unity or coherence; just let go and write. Each sentence doesn't necessarily need to "follow" its predecessor.

If you wanted to build a building, you'd need materials—bricks, for instance. Freewriting will help provide you with some of the "bricks" that you'll need to write your essay. Turn off the internal editor and let yourself go.

One Writer's Decisions

Verlinda also used freewriting to come up with ideas about Walter. Here is her response:

No saints here, please, no selfless martyrs—I think Dr. Marshall has a special red pen to grade those with. Also, no janitors who are closet violinists, or gardenors who used to be Asian royalty. I don't know those people, and who cares, anyway?

Walter Wallace, Clark Kent accountant by day, the Charitable Shadow at night. Giving away money, on the quite, like asking a stranger for a cigarette when your suposed to have stopped. $20 here, $10 there. I wish I was close enough to one of those encounters to see the recipients face—shock, awkwardness at this stern looking black man insisting you take money—for your kids, lady, come on.

And that wierd bunch of pets, like discarded pieces of clothing. Cats and dogs lucky as hell, and others fixed, mended, and enoculated and given to protesting friends and family.

Mrs. W, hating animals and fearful of Mr. W's habit—not so much the money but the wierdness. Can't the man help himself? Must be a strain, they've been married over twenty years.

Christmas at church, and a black Santa—kids suprised at first, but swept up by the new Walter, like he'd found a phone booth and changed his personality as well as into the Santa suit. The greatest Santa I've ever seen, a roadshow as well—everyone who needs a free Santa can find one at Walter's house.

Is it charity? Compulsion? One the same as the other? Who knows? A "cure" would make Walter less than what he is, that's for sure. A fascinating man: sitting in that Barcalounger smoking his pipe, watching Monday Night Football, stroking that ancient grey cat.

Verbal Learners: Invisible Writing

Invisible writing sounds very mysterious, but it's actually an enormously successful prewriting technique for writers afflicted with "internal editor syndrome." These people have trouble with brainstorming on paper or freewriting because they have a compulsion to go back and fix errors; they need things to

Consider Your Options

- What is your learning style—aural, verbal, or visual? How can you use this knowledge to help you in the writing process?

be right before they move on. If you are one of these perfectionists, try this technique: open a computer file, but before you start to freewrite, turn down the monitor until it is dark or turn off the monitor altogether. Then you can work without worrying about errors.

Verbal Learners: Looping

Looping is an approach that builds upon any of the five techniques described above. Once you have generated your first set of ideas, go back and list the most important facts/concepts/opinions that you have produced. Then start with this list and *use your original prewriting technique again.* Looping will help you sharpen your focus. Obviously, you can "loop" more than once as you generate more ideas from your narrowing focus. Note that looping is a very valuable technique to use with particularly difficult assignments and/or with writing situations that are complicated by tricky purpose and audience issues.

Visual Learners: Clustering and Chart Making

The preliminary prewriting methods that we've looked at so far have been aural or verbal in nature. However, there is another, more graphically oriented set of methods: clustering and chart making. Students who use these methods prefer to "see" the developing essay. In clustering, you write the topic in the center of a piece of paper, then write ideas suggested by the topic around it, connecting these to the topics with lines. Follow the same procedure with your subtopics.

One Writer's Decisions

Verlinda used a traditional clustering approach when she was trying out various prewriting options:

Here is what Verlinda's clustering output would look like if she had used a chart approach:

quiet, inconspicuous, not very friendly — maybe self-conscious about needing to fit in as accountant	"daring" mustache may be important, because he transforms into a magnificent Santa Clause — big hit at church, hospitals, everywhere
seems very self-contained, cool	but will approach total strangers and give them money when they need it — Why?
quite content in suburban home	but home has a farmload of cats and dogs — he always takes in a stray, fixes what's wrong with it, keeps it or finds a home for it — wife is not impressed. In fact, real friction here: she doesn't like animals.
compulsive?	saint?

a little of both?

SUGGESTED ACTIVITY
Ask students to gather information on an assigned topic by choosing one of the eight prewriting strategies listed under "Verbal" and "Visual" learners on page 30. Make sure that each of the eight strategies is chosen by at least one student. Then distribute copies of their work for discussion. In some cases, what they produce can be used as the prewriting for a formal essay.

Note that this approach allows the writer to arrange information uniformly, left to right, centered on a common theme. It works particularly well for the comparison/contrast option, which makes sense when you realize that Verlinda is implicitly contrasting Walter Wallace's appearance with his reality.

As we mentioned earlier, very few students would want to use all of these prewriting approaches for one essay. Rather, you should pick the approaches that work best for you. This way, you will be ready for the next two steps: focusing your topic and developing your essay's organization.

FOCUSING STRATEGIES

Prewriting helps you think about your ideas and put a range of information and details on paper for future use. By this point, you should have a solid idea of how you will approach your topic. Therefore, now is a good time to determine your **thesis statement**, the guiding idea of your essay.

Establishing Your Working Thesis

A **thesis** is a sentence or group of sentences that states your controlling idea. A good thesis statement both informs the reader about what will follow and interests the reader in the possibilities that lie ahead. A **working thesis** can be defined as "my thesis right now." It may well change, but it's your starting point. Your working thesis gives you a "road map" for your essay. Later, in the drafting stages, you will want to review your thesis to make sure that it still reflects your developing essay.

To come up with a working thesis, look back to your prewriting. If you've done enough preparation, a thesis statement should already be forming in your mind. If not, do additional prewriting or try out another prewriting technique. (See pages 30–35.)

Chapter 1 explains that the thesis statement appears in the introduction of your essay, normally toward the introduction's end. In business documents, the thesis is the point at which readers decide whether to keep reading. Busy—and besieged by all manner of communication—businesspeople need to decide if the latest memo in the day's pile, or the latest arrival in the day's list of e-mail messages, is important ("Wait a minute—read on") or garbage ("Is this how they spend their day up there?").

Similarly, the thesis statement of your essay will either engage or discourage your reader. Unlike most readers, however, your instructor will keep on reading your essay even if your thesis is flat and boring. Obviously, you want to avoid this contingency. Your aim is to make your reader *want* to read your essay. A carefully written thesis statement can confirm and intensify this desire. Note the following thesis:

> If uncontrolled, mosquitoes in swampy areas can produce two negative effects: discomfort and disease.

This thesis does no more than impart information, information that seems obvious when stated in this way. However, notice how the following revision engages the reader:

> Hordes of biting, encephalitis-laden mosquitoes will be swarming all over town unless the swamps are treated this spring.

This version tries to make us actually perceive the insects with our senses. We can visualize the clouds of pests, hear their buzz, feel their bites, and cringe at the possibility of catching a deadly disease.

A thesis statement generally should *not* be a complicated, self-conscious outlining device, such as the following thesis for an essay on tax policy that is intended for general readers:

> In this essay I will prove that the tax increase being considered will have negative consequences: reduced growth, an overburdened citizenry, and unspecified use of revenues.

Writers want to interest and intrigue readers, not bore them to death. Although taxation is not inherently the most fascinating subject, it tends to engage people because most adults pay taxes. A lively approach is more suitable to the writer's audience and purpose. Note this revision:

> Granting the proposed tax increase will allow the county commissioners to pry from overtaxed residents more dollars that they would have otherwise spent in the private sector, where spending belongs.

The revised thesis avoids the dreadful self-consciousness of the original. In your thesis, as elsewhere, don't refer to your essay as if it were some science fair project. Avoid starting out with "In this essay I will discuss . . ." or "In my paper I will show. . . ." Address your reader in natural, mature, clear language, avoiding a didactic and self-referential tone.

Let's look at some more examples of weak and effective thesis statements:

ORIGINAL **A 15 percent across-the-board increase in yearly costs will anger returning students.**

REVISED **Returning students forced to shell out 115 percent of last year's costs for everything from bookstore candy to tuition will probably feel like marching on the president's office.**

ORIGINAL **My aunt Kaye has had a sad life.**

REVISED **Losing her husband to a robber, her life savings to a con man, and her eyesight to diabetes, my aunt Kaye has been cheated of a normal, happy life.**

ORIGINAL **I learned a very good lesson that autumn day.**

REVISED **On that beautiful autumn day I learned that appearances frequently belie reality, that a soft-spoken, well-dressed man could be the monster that my parents always feared.**

CLASSROOM HINT Extend the discussion of the nature of the thesis by considering each of these three examples in class. In each case, the revision is more specific and concrete than the original and, as such, better prepares the reader for what is to come.

MORE OPTIONS ONLINE For more help with thesis statements, go to **www.mhhe.com/writingtoday**.

EXERCISE 2.1

The following thesis statements are too wordy, self-conscious, flat, and/or boring. Working alone, rewrite them. Be creative, and add details as necessary.

1. The food in my dormitory cafeteria is awful.
2. In this essay I hope to prove that stress, although one of the college student's worst enemies, can be successfully combated.
3. At this point in the semester, my dorm's social life has slowed to a crawl.
4. It is impossible to imagine the effects of open admissions across the state university system.
5. Richter Highway, the city's main thoroughfare, needs to be widened.

EXERCISE 2.1 Responses will vary. Some possibilities follow:
1. The food in my dorm cafeteria is always overcooked, over-seasoned, and greasier than the slop offered at most truck stops.
2. Stress might be the college student's worst enemy, but there are several ways to combat it.
3. By the middle of October, students in my dormitory spend their time studying, not attending fraternity parties, homecoming events, or mixers, as they did earlier in the semester.
4. Instituting an open-admissions policy across the state university system might increase educational opportunities for some students, but it might also result in expanded remedial programs, overcrowded classrooms, and a weakening of academic standards.
5. The increase in traffic on Richter Highway, the city's main thoroughfare, necessitates widening it.

Focusing Your Thesis

To be successful, a thesis needs to be neither too narrow nor too broad. A thesis that is too narrow will leave you no freedom, and your essay will likely be of little interest to most audiences.

TOO NARROW **Since my bout with mononucleosis, I've been extremely tired.**

Would you really want to write an essay that is restricted to telling the reader how tired you are? However, note this version:

REVISED **My recent bout with mononucleosis has acquainted me with the pernicious aftereffects of this common yet underestimated disease: extreme fatigue, dizziness, and lack of energy.**

The topic is still not the most exciting one possible, but you could write a much better essay from the revised thesis than from the original because you have broadened the topic a bit. It could be interesting to people who are at risk of catching mononucleosis, whether or not they know you.

The opposite problem occurs when the thesis is too broad—for example, "The treatment of the homeless in this country is shameful." This is the thesis for a long sociological study of the issue—seven or eight hundred pages might cover the varying approaches and policies used by the many cities, counties, and states to deal with the question of how to help the homeless. But with an assignment to write 600 *words,* you would be reduced to writing a series of generalizations if you used this thesis. Even if you did provide a concrete example of the treatment afforded a single homeless person, your example wouldn't prove anything. One homeless person is (unfortunately) just one example, and his or her situation does not necessarily reflect the lives of all the homeless people in this country.

Note how the revised thesis statement allows the writer enough "room" yet restricts the discussion to a manageable range:

REVISED **Our city's new vagrancy law has one purpose, to drive the homeless to the next city: out of sight, out of mind.**

This thesis provides the basis for a lively argument that can be handled in 600 words or less.

Key Elements of an Effective Thesis

An effective thesis (1) indicates your purpose and your controlling idea, (2) provides a general "road map" for your essay, and (3) engages your reader. Here are some ways to ensure that your thesis works:

1. Phrase your thesis as a complete sentence and not as a title or topic.

   NOT **Prohibiting talking on cellular telephones while driving.**

   OR **The dangers of talking on a cellular telephone while driving and the law.**

   BUT **Talking on a cellular telephone while driving is so dangerous that it should be made illegal.**

2. State your point outright; do not announce it.

   NOT **I am going to argue that talking on a cellular telephone while driving is so dangerous that it should be made illegal.**

   OR **This paper will argue that talking on a cellular telephone while driving is so dangerous that it should be made illegal.**

   BUT **Talking on a cellular telephone while driving is so dangerous that it should be made illegal.**

3. Don't bother explaining that your thesis is your opinion or what you believe; readers can be expected to assume that the idea or opinion you are supporting is your own.

   NOT **It is my opinion that talking on a cellular telephone while driving is so dangerous that it should be made illegal.**

OR I believe that talking on a cellular telephone while driving is so dangerous that it should be made illegal.

BUT Talking on a cellular telephone while driving is so dangerous that it should be made illegal.

4. Make your thesis as specific and pointed as you can.

NOT Talking on a cellular telephone while driving is dangerous.

OR Talking on a cellular telephone while driving increases the chances of having an accident.

BUT Talking on a cellular telephone while driving is so dangerous that it should be made illegal.

EXERCISE 2.2

Working alone, read the following scenarios. Decide if each thesis is sufficient, too narrow, or too broad for an essay of 500–700 words. Explain your reasoning.

1. Your college has built a new student union. You were familiar with the old one, and you have had just enough time to acquaint yourself with the new one.

   Topic: How does the new student union differ from its predecessor?

   Audience: Your instructor/fellow students

   Rhetorical option: Comparison/contrast

   Thesis statement: The new student union is a vast improvement over its predecessor.

2. You work as a math tutor in a computer lab. Your job is to help students by using the tutorial software. On Wednesday, your supervisor announces that the long-awaited replacement for the aging software has arrived and will be loaded on Friday. She hands you the user's manual and the technical support documentation, then asks you to write a simplified document to hand out to the students who use the lab.

   Topic: How to use the new math tutorial software

   Audience: Math students in need of academic support

   Rhetorical option: Process analysis

   Thesis statement: The new tutorial software has many features and requirements that differ from those of the old software, but following three basic steps will help you find your way through this program.

3. Your instructor has lectured and led discussions on controversial issues for the past two weeks.

   Topic: Argue one side of an issue about which many Americans have strong feelings.

   Audience: Your instructor

   Rhetorical option: Argument

   Thesis statement: Poverty can be eliminated if we all work together to improve education in our nation.

EXERCISE 2.2 Responses will vary. Some possibilities follow:

1. The thesis might be revised to be more specific: "A larger, better furnished dining hall, a new computer lab, and a large, comfortable commons area make our new student union a vast improvement over its predecessor.
2. Some students might think this thesis is too narrow and might result in a document that lacks interest and development.
3. The thesis is far too broad; the point expressed is impossible to defend in an essay. A far more workable thesis would argue that implementing educational reforms in a particular inner-city school curriculum has produced results.
4. The thesis is acceptable.
5. The thesis seems too narrow for an extended discussion. Even if the writer could provide enough detail to complete a 500- to 700-word essay, its point and purpose would lack significance.

4. You drive a great deal: to work, at work, to school. Your city is becoming increasingly congested, with more cars each year. Your local newspaper asks readers to write in with their opinions.

   Topic: What is a cause or set of causes for local traffic congestion?

   Audience: The newspaper's readership

   Rhetorical option: Causal analysis

   Thesis statement: The real reason for local traffic problems is not congestion but the lack of proper lane-changing procedures by area drivers, leading to unnecessary accidents.

5. You are an outgoing, gregarious person with many, many friends.

   Topic: What types of friends do you have or know about?

   Audience: Your instructor

   Rhetorical option: Classification

   Thesis statement: Friends come in three types: acquaintances, close friends, and lovers.

ORGANIZATIONAL STRATEGIES

CLASSROOM ACTIVITY
You might ask students to prepare—at least once—all three types of outlines for a particular essay just to help them discover which of the three they find most helpful.

At this point, you have moved further in the writing process than you might have guessed. After choosing a topic, establishing audience and purpose, generating ideas, and developing a working thesis, you are now ready for the last step prior to drafting: *structuring* your prewriting so that it can guide you through the rest of the writing process.

Structuring Your Prewriting

The prewriting methods discussed thus far are designed to get you started: to generate ideas, to recall facts and anecdotes, to realize patterns. However, these activities are preliminary; before you begin to write a draft, you need to establish a structure for your essay. Constructing an **outline** of what you intend to do will help you "see" your essay before you begin. An outline can also reveal gaps—places where you need to do more thinking and prewriting. Three basic types of outlines are informal outlines, sentence outlines, and formal outlines.

Informal Outlines

Informal outlines function as guides, giving writers a path to follow and something to fall back upon if the essay takes a wrong turn. Informal outlines have the same general structure as formal outlines (discussed on page 42), but they don't need to follow a rigid hierarchy; they are for your use in planning.

The following outline comes from an essay contrasting the "haves" of the United States with the "have-nots."

Thesis: The divide between rich and poor in the United States is insurmountable.

Intro: Richest country on earth, with poor shut out—literally and figuratively—from this wealth.

Credit

- *U.S. wealthy exploit debt rather than vice versa; poor are either denied access or brutalized by terms.*

Retirement

- *The rich invest and can literally plan out the rest of their lives; the poor survive day to day, investing in the Lotto if anything.*

Residence

- *The rich live where they want; the poor live where no one else would dare to.*

Conclusion

- *Intense separation, which is increasing.*
- *Rich get richer; poor get much poorer.*

This type of outline is very helpful when your time is limited. It is a quick way to structure your thoughts and information while still allowing you to establish a firm plan for your essay.

Sentence Outlines

The sentence outline is a refinement of the informal outline. In a **sentence outline**, you can include not only the subject of each paragraph but also the topic sentence and any major internal supports that you have planned to use. Here is a sentence outline of the essay about the gap between rich people and poor people:

Thesis: The divide between rich and poor in the United States is insurmountable.

I. Credit

- **A.** For the wealthy in the U.S., debt is not a liability; it is an opportunity.
- **B.** The poor, on the other hand, frequently have poor credit or no credit.

II. Retirement

- **A.** Having surplus cash, the rich can invest in their future and for retirement.
- **B.** The poor, however, have no money to "invest"; all their money is used to survive day to day.

III. Place of Residence

- **A.** The rich live where they choose to live.

B. The poor, if they have a home at all, live where no one else wants to live.

IV. Conclusion

A. There is a separation here that seems to be growing more fixed as time goes by.

B. The rich will get richer, and the poor will slide further into their misery.

Formal Outlines

Your instructor may require you to submit a **formal outline** with your essay. However, formal outlines are not often used in the planning stage; they tend to be constructed *after* a preliminary or final draft has been completed. We discuss the formal outline here because of its obvious relation to the other two outline forms we have included.

Every entry in the formal outline is a complete sentence. Note the standard hierarchy of the formal outline:

I. (capitalized roman numeral)

A. (capitalized letter)

1. (Arabic numeral)

This structure will suffice for most short essays; for longer essays, however, you may need to add a fourth level to the hierarchy, using lowercase letters:

I. Main idea

A. Second-level idea

1. Third-level idea

a. Detail supporting third-level idea

MORE OPTIONS ONLINE For more help with outlines, go to **www.mhhe.com/writingtoday**.

Because it reveals an essay's structure, the formal outline can be employed as a revision tool. After finishing a draft, a writer may create a formal outline to check the "skeleton" of his or her essay for discrepancies, errors, or gaps that are not apparent in the full essay.

One Writer's Decisions

Verlinda wrote her formal outline after completing her first draft, partly as a way of locating problems with her draft. (The first draft of Verlinda's essay appears on pages 47–49 at the end of this chapter. The final draft appears in Chapter 1, pages 19–21.)

Thesis: Walter Wallace was the most charitable man I've ever met.

I. Walter practiced "guerilla charity." For example, his convincing the impoverished mother at the mall to take Christmas money for her children was typical of his activities.

II. Walter believed in helping stray animals.

A. No stray was ever turned away.

B. His habits caused strain in his marriage.
   1. Leona did not like animals.
   2. Walter paid out large amounts to veterinarians.

III. Walter transformed into an amazing Santa Claus during the holidays. Specifically, he appeared at the family's church, area hospitals, and the children's hospice.

IV. What are the causes of Walter's "secret side"?
   A. He didn't seem to be the victim of guilt.
   B. He seemed compelled to help anyone who needed it.

V. Whatever the cause, the world is a better place because of Walter Wallace.

DRAFTING STRATEGIES

At this point, you have organized your ideas and are ready to begin a first draft—but don't expect it to be your final draft. No one is able to write a perfect first draft; even people who tend to write very strong first-draft essays realize the need for revision and redrafting. An essay gets stronger as the drafting process continues. As the essay evolves and develops, the writer also gets more and more invested in the process and its outcome.

Essays tend to be written in two distinct circumstances: in supervised classrooms with relatively stringent time requirements or at the writer's discretion, with a time limit (a due date) but no restrictions on when or where the essay will be written. So we have broken this discussion into two sections, one for each situation: (1) supervised writing and (2) writing outside of class.

Drafting In-Class Essays

Writing an essay in class under time constraints is a situation that many students fear. You might not have enough time to do a great deal of planning and prewriting, but as we pointed out earlier, skipping the prewriting stage and moving directly into a draft is a grave mistake. (For more advice on taking essay exams, see Chapter 16.)

After doing as much planning as time will allow—perhaps a quick brainstorming or clustering followed by a rough outline—try to produce the best first draft you can without becoming overly concerned about making it the absolutely best draft you can write. In other words, construct a draft that you can revise. During this process, you may encounter one of the following problems:

1. **The internal editor.** Some writers can't seem to let a mistake go by, even when they're under time pressure. Rather than stopping, going back, and rewriting or fixing the problem area, simply place an asterisk (*) above it so that the error stands out when you begin to revise. Don't obsess over details in the first draft of an essay; instead, concentrate on completing a serviceable, well-structured text, and revise later.
2. **Writer's block.** All writers face this problem from time to time. The words won't come, or they come much more slowly than you want them to. What

to do? First, keep in mind that there is considerable evidence that people who don't prewrite have a lot more trouble with writer's block than people who have planned and prepared. When you prewrite, thoughts arise and percolate in your brain, generating more mental activity. Second, remember that your prewriting exists, waiting on paper. If you get stuck, refer to your prewriting. Scan through it quickly to get your thought patterns moving again.

Have you ever heard of "revisor's block"? Neither have we. Once the first draft has been written, the rest, psychologically speaking, is easier. Our emphasis on prewriting reflects this distinction.

Another issue to consider with writer's block is that your will (in other words, what you want and intend) is not the same as the part of your brain that generates language. Some days, for reasons you may not understand, your will and your language center may not be "in sync"—the words that you write may not match your ideas. This situation is frustrating, and it contributes to writer's block. On difficult days, consider this phenomenon, relax a little, and use the basic steps of the writing process to get yourself going. Sometimes, when writers get past a few minutes of feeling blocked, they find a way into a difficult paragraph or passage and then remember only later that they had been blocked at all.

3. **Panic.** The panic response is part of our genetic heritage. Thousands of years ago, it was quite useful. Walking around a bend in the trail and coming upon a lion, an early human panicked, leading to flight or a defensive response.

   Unfortunately, neither of these urges will help you much in a college classroom. It is trite to tell people experiencing panic to relax, not to worry so much. A more practical piece of advice is this: concentrate on the steps, not the outcome. To write an essay properly, you will need to achieve a series of objectives. Work on each step; the outcome should take care of itself.
4. **Stalled introduction.** If you simply can't put your introduction into words, write the balance of your essay first; then come back and write the introduction. Many writers follow this pattern: prewrite, write the body, write the introduction, write the conclusion. Such an approach may seem odd, but it is one effective way to (a) get your first draft done and (b) establish rhetorical unity.
5. **Bad writing environment.** Classrooms, paradoxically, are sometimes not the best places to work. Try to make yourself as comfortable as possible, and try to ignore distractions—squeaky chairs, talkers, people passing by the door, events outside the window. A distracting environment affects some students more than others; many students are quite comfortable working in an overcrowded room, whereas others get claustrophobic and feel the need for privacy and space.

In the future, students may routinely do in-class writing on computer rather than in longhand. Such a situation will be to the student's advantage. See pages 45–46 of this chapter and pages 85–86 and 97–98 of Chapter 4 for guidelines on using a word processor in the revising stage.

Drafting Out-of-Class Essays

One of the virtues of out-of-class assignments is the extra time that you have to complete them; another benefit is that you can choose your writing environment. Where a writer chooses to work is a highly personal decision. Some writers try to avoid any external stimulation or distraction; others can work while riding on a city bus or while in a room full of people watching the Super Bowl. One of the authors of this book prefers quiet; the other prefers Bruce Springsteen or Lyle Lovett for a low-volume background.

Work where you are comfortable, but if you find yourself becoming distracted, think about moving to a quieter spot. Libraries are great environments for writing; if you've never written an essay in a library, give it a try.

Having five days or two weeks to produce an essay causes many students to fall into the procrastination trap: "The essay's not due until Tuesday; I'll spend all day Sunday on it." We see two problems here. First, if at all possible, you should try to avoid using a single day to go through all the writing-process steps discussed in this chapter. Your work will be improved if you can split the total amount of time spent into two or more days, returning to your writing with a fresh eye (and brain) on each new day. Second, when Sunday rolls around, one of these situations (or one very much like them) has an extremely high probability of happening:

1. You get called in to work.
2. You get invited to a wonderful party.
3. You become ill.

Putting work off only invites problems, as generations of college students have learned the hard way.

Drafting with a Computer

Out-of-class essays normally give you the option to compose your essay using a computer's word-processing program; in fact, many assignments require this approach. If you will be using a computer to write your essay, remember that the faster you get your draft into the computer's memory or onto a backup disk, the better your chances of exploiting the capacities of word-processing software.

Many people prefer to compose in longhand. This approach may help writers work through the stages of developing an essay, but if the final draft must be typed, then another, possibly avoidable, step must be completed. Over the years, we have seen many students develop, revise, and polish handwritten essays only to have their efforts complicated when they had to key their drafts into the computer. Even if these students persisted in wanting to write in longhand, they could have avoided a difficult final step by following this strategy: transferring their first draft to a computer file as soon as they had written it. This step allows them to make all revisions in the computer file and eliminates the possibility of introducing errors when a fine, handwritten essay is hastily typed at the last minute.

Here are some specific guidelines for using a computer in the drafting process:

Consider Your Options

What role do computers play in your writing process? If your computer skills are limited, or if you have "computer phobia," consider taking an introductory computer class. Such courses are designed to sharpen your existing computer skills and to show you new tactics and strategies.

1. **Take advantage of the computer's ability to duplicate your draft.** Here is one student's approach to an assignment requiring a typed essay:

   The essay is the third one of the semester, so all file names start with the label E3. The student has two pieces of prewriting: a freewriting passage and a sentence outline. These two elements are saved in a file called E3P. The student keys in a first draft, named E3A, then copies the file twice under new names: E3B and E3C. Now four files have been saved on the hard drive and on a backup disk. E3B and E3C will be used during revision (see page 85 in Chapter 4), and E3A will be kept as insurance in case the instructor asks to see the first draft or the student is dissatisfied with the revision.

   Disaster stories of hard drives crashing or of lost disks that contain the only version of an essay are commonplace. These calamities can be easily avoided in most situations. Save your work frequently, and keep it in two different storage locations; this way, you'll have a backup if something goes wrong.
2. **Save everything—forever.** Most of us try to avoid being pack rats; we want to clean up, to throw away, to live neatly. Although this mentality may help produce an orderly home, it is dangerous when applied to computer use. *Save all versions of everything you write, save these materials in more than one location, and keep them forever.* "But won't I fill up my computer?" you might ask. No—text takes up very little memory on a modern PC. Graphics—and the programs that handle them—are the items that eat up a computer's memory. If you bought a new computer today and used it only as a word processor, you could save all of your work for fifty years and not exhaust its memory. And diskettes, if you use them, cost about a quarter a piece these days.
3. **Use the printer to your advantage.** By printing out your work at important moments, such as when you are finished working for the day, you will achieve two valuable goals: you will have some more insurance against misadventure, and you will have your writing on paper, which many writers find easier to work with than a monitor's display. Words on paper are not really two-dimensional, as some people believe; there is a "depth" to this form that is absent from characters on a screen.
4. **Listen to your text.** If your computer is equipped with Simpletext or a similar program and has speakers, you can actually "hear" your essay. Talking programs are very useful, especially for writers who are auditory learners rather than visual learners.

Establishing Your Voice

Whether you are writing in class, at home, in longhand, or on a computer, you must determine the voice you will use throughout your essay. Are you planning to write an objective essay, without any references to your feelings and personal impressions? Or are you planning to write about an experience or a person close to you? The answers to these questions will help determine the "voice," or persona, that you create in your essay and will help you resolve a sometimes sticky issue: which pronouns are acceptable in a college-level essay. The following are some frequently asked questions about pronoun use:

SUGGESTED ACTIVITY
Spend class time on the three points listed here. Even some of our strongest writers have needed advice about establishing a voice. You might also distribute copies of two articles that discuss the same subject in very different voices. For example, search the Internet for a journalistic (objective) account of a catastrophic event; then find another account of the same event from a victim's point of view.

1. **Can I use the pronoun *I* to refer to myself in my essay?** The answer is ultimately up to your instructor. For decades, college students were told never to use *I,* but that prohibition rarely stands today. Frequently, your context will determine what you should do. For example, in a technical or legal document, which usually calls for objective writing, *I* is out of place. However, in most of the writing for your composition class, *I* may well be acceptable, especially in essays where you use your own experience as evidence. Once again, check with your instructor.
2. **Can I use the pronoun *you* in my essay?** Be very careful with this issue. *You* is acceptable under only one condition: if the writer is speaking directly to the reader, such as in a letter, a process analysis, or a textbook.
3. **Should I use *one* or *he* or *he or she*?** *One* can sometimes sound absurdly formal ("One can't always tell, can one?"). *He* causes problems unless you're writing about an all-male population and need to refer to an indefinite example from that population. *He or she* (or *she or he*) is certainly standard today but can cause rhythm problems or general awkwardness. We have found that, nine times out of ten, when writers need an indefinite pronoun to refer to a person of either sex, they can rephrase the sentence so that it has a plural context:

   AWKWARD **Every student took his or her seat.**

   IMPROVED **All the students took their seats.**

   However, sometimes the plural won't work, as in the following:

   > The scholarship winner must complete his or her high school education at least four months prior to matriculating at Parker College.

   In this situation, there will be only one winner. (For more information on this subject, consult a grammar handbook.)

One Writer's Decisions

Verlinda wrote her first draft after she had generated ideas by prewriting; then she outlined her draft to get a sense of its structure. Her draft includes errors in grammar, spelling, punctuation, and mechanics. (Verlinda's prewriting is on pages 30, 32, 33, and 34. Her formal outline appears on page 42, and her final draft is in Chapter 1, pages 19–21.)

Verlinda's First Draft

A Very Secret Santa

All my years growing up; Betty Wallace was my very best friend. I spent a lot of time at her house, she spent a lot of time at my house. Our parents were good friends. Each couple trusted the other implecitly. I grew to see Walter and Leona Wallace as uncle and aunt figures.

Walter was more interesting, but not at first glance. An accountent, he seem to want to fit in. Walter dressed conservatively, which matched his features and size: a black man of middle height, a little over weight, rimless glasses and the only "daring" feature a very neatly trimmed mustache. His personality seemed boring. He was quite, a bit shy, and not really sociable or pleasant. Given his choice, he would sit alone in his big lounge chair and smoke a pipe while watching T.V. Yet Walter Wallace, he was the most charitable man I've ever met.

I remember an example of Walter's secret side. It was before Christmas, years ago, Betty and I were ten years old and going shopping with Mr. and Mrs Wallace at the mall. After Walter finaly found a parking space we noticed a comotion a few cars over. A young woman and her seven-year-old were trying to quiet down the three-year-old. He had been pulled from the last store visited without getting what he wanted. The mother looked entirely flustered and she was obviously quite poor, the little boy was screaming like he had been scalded. We walked toward the mall, listening to this squabble unfold behind us, suddenly Walter disappeared. Mrs. Wallace told us to keep walking, that Walter would catch up. When he did he said nothing.

I waited until Betty and I were alone to ask for an explanation. "He went back to give that woman some money", Betty explained, "He's done this a thousand times".

At the Wallaces' home there was always six to ten dogs and cats. Strays knew where to go. Over the objections of Leona, Walter would take them in, carry them to the vet, pay for shots, nutering, and medicine, and keep them if he couldn't convince some one else to take them off his hands. As a child I remember loving the fact that the Wallace home was full of animals, but I don't think Leona Wallace shared my enjoyment. She didn't like dogs, and would freeze in midsentence if a cat jumped in her lap. Then launching the cat back towards the floor.

Christmastime is wonderful for kids, and it is one of my fondest memories'. My family and the Wallaces attended Trinity United Methodist, a mostly white church with a middle class population. The arrival of Santa Claus was a great event. Walter Wallace as Santa was a complete transformation from Walter Wallace as bespectacled, quiet taxadvisor. His voice and laughter booms through the church as he talks to his small "clients". Walter took his act on the road, at the area hospitals and the children's hospise.

Did Walter Wallace have the proverbeal heart of gold? Or was he motivated by guilt--a successful man who can't help looking back to a time when he was poor? Neither one. Walter helped young and old, black and white, human and nonhuman; only because he couldn't keep himself from doing so. Betty told me that her father was miserable, if he percieved that he had not done enough. She told me that Walter's activities caused signifigant friction in his marriage. But he would not be stopped.

I feel that when people do something "nice" for another that their motives are not altogether altruistic—being nice makes the giver feel good about him or herself. In the case of Walter Wallace however the motive seems to have been more involuntary. Does this make Walter less admirable? I don't think so, I wish the world was full of men like him.

EXERCISE 2.3

Choose one of the general topics below. Then develop the topic by using the following steps:

1. Identify your purpose and audience.
2. Use a preliminary prewriting method to narrow your topic and generate ideas: either brainstorming/freewriting or clustering/chart making.
3. Decide upon a working thesis.
4. Structure your essay by using an informal outline or a sentence outline.
5. Compose your first draft.

EXERCISE 2.3 Responses will vary.

SUGGESTED ACTIVITY
Consider assigning each of the topics listed here to a different writing group or discussing each topic and the appropriate approach with the class as a whole.

Topics:

1. In what ways is your life easier than your parents' or grandparents' lives were when they were about your age? In what ways is it more difficult? Try interviewing a parent, grandparent, or older relative to gather information for this assignment.

2. "First impressions are essential." Agree or disagree.
3. One local, state, or federal law that should be immediately repealed.
4. The strangest person in your extended family.
5. The reasons that students are tempted to cheat on exams or plagiarize papers.
6. Three very different types of physical exercise.
7. An incident in which you were lucky to escape with your life.
8. An anonymous benefactor has given you a restaurant, with the condition that you do not change the nature of the restaurant or sell it to someone else. You must make the restaurant profitable. Unfortunately, the restaurant's name is "Ed's House of Thin Gruel." How will you achieve success?

MORE OPTIONS ONLINE
You can access the Web sites listed in "Using the Internet" by going to **www.mhhe.com/writingtoday**.

Using the Internet

Go to these Web sites to find more tips, techniques, and insights on prewriting and drafting:

The University of Richmond Writing Center's Writer's Web

This site offers excellent advice on writing first drafts in various academic disciplines. The section on "focusing and connecting ideas" is also helpful. A topic index and search engine make finding useful material easy, especially in regard to addressing your audience, determining your voice, and deciding on your purpose in various contexts. This Web site also discusses freewriting, brainstorming, clustering, and other prewriting techniques: **http://writing.richmond.edu/writing/wweb.html**.

University of Buffalo Composition Web Site

This multilayered site contains numerous pages on the writing process and describes valuable strategies for planning and drafting an academic paper. It also contains a link to a Dartmouth University site that explains the differences between academic writing and other types of writing: **http://icarus.ubetc.buffalo.edu/engcomp/writing_strategies.htm**.

Garbl's Writing Process Links

This site provides an annotated list of several other valuable Web sites (with links) that provide information on the writing process—from overcoming writer's block to planning and drafting to proofreading: **http://home.comcast.net/~garbl/writing/process.htm**.

CHAPTER 3

DEVELOPING STRONG PARAGRAPHS: EXPLORING YOUR OPTIONS

As we saw in Chapter 1, paragraphs are the building blocks of essays. An essay begins with an introductory paragraph or paragraphs, and this section sets up the rest of the text by leading to the **thesis statement**—the controlling idea of the essay. After the introduction, the body of the essay includes paragraphs that develop and support the thesis statement.

The concluding paragraph or paragraphs reflect on the essay and offer final thoughts on the issue being discussed.

Using this structure, a writer might develop an essay as short as three paragraphs (introduction, body, conclusion) or as long as fifty or more paragraphs, with several in the introduction and the conclusion and a great number forming the body. Whatever the length of the essay, however, paragraphs are its building blocks. In essays of the length you will likely be asked to write in this course, a poorly conceived and constructed paragraph will lodge in the reader's memory and override his or her perception of other, better-written parts of your essay. Carefully developed paragraphs are the essential components of effective short essays.

PARAGRAPHS IN CONTEXT

In this section, we'll concentrate on how to develop the paragraphs that make up the three sections of a classically structured essay.

Introductory Paragraphs

An essay's introduction might consist of only one paragraph or of more than one. In either case, the introduction serves two functions: to provide the background or context of the essay and to indicate the **thesis statement**, the essay's controlling idea.

Positioning the Thesis

The thesis statement *often* appears at or toward the end of the introduction, as in the following example (the thesis is highlighted):

> I've been dating Scott for about six weeks. During that time we've had "normal" dates—coffee, lunch, movies at the multiplex, movies on his DVD player—but last Wednesday he asked if I would consent to go with him to the last day of a professional golf tournament. I like Scott, I want to see our relationship progress, and I'm a decent actor. Swallowing my horror, I said, "Sure, sounds like fun." What it actually sounded like was unadulterated boredom. **This past Sunday, however, proved that my expectations were completely off base.**

The writer provides us with the necessary background by telling of her relationship with Scott and of her desire to further that relationship. The conflict is brought about by his unexpected invitation to the golf tournament, which leads her to have a set of expectations about the experience. The thesis statement then lets us know that the writer's fears of boredom turned out to be unfounded.

Of course, the thesis statement might also appear in the essay's first sentence. The following revision of the previous example illustrates this approach:

> **This past Sunday I had an experience that showed me how far apart expectations and reality can be.** I've been dating Scott for about six weeks. During that time we've had "normal" dates—coffee, lunch, movies at the multiplex, movies on his DVD player—but last Wednesday he asked if I would consent to go with him to the last day of a professional golf tournament. I like Scott, I want to see our relationship progress, and I'm a decent actor. Swallowing my horror, I said, "Sure, sounds like fun." What it actually sounded like was unadulterated boredom.

Which approach works better? Probably the original version is preferable in this case. For one thing, starting an essay with a generalization ("This past Sunday I had an experience that showed me how far apart expectations and reality can be") does not interest the reader as much as the lead sentence of the original paragraph ("I've been dating Scott for about six weeks"). Who's Scott? We're curious to learn more. Second, the original version ends the introduction with a clear message that the essay will support the idea that negative expectations can be confounded. In the revised version, the introduction is "leaning" in the wrong direction (toward "unadulterated boredom") as it concludes.

CLASSROOM HINT You can underscore the importance of placing the thesis effectively by referring to one or two of the essays in the chapter on illustration, comparison/contrast, or argumentation.

As we mentioned, an essay's introduction does not have to be confined to one paragraph. Note how this writer uses a personal experience in her first paragraph to set up the theme of her essay and its eventual thesis:

> Last week in my American history class, Dr. Rodriguez posed an interesting question: "A hundred years ago, what would have been the ways that you could have listened to music?" The answer, of course, is only if someone decided to play or sing live music while you were in hearing range. The idea eventually led me to think of a much quieter, less obtrusive United States in which radio, TV, intercoms, telephones, and all manner of uninvited advertising were not in a person's face during every waking hour.
>
> I also started thinking about another, very prevalent problem today: boredom. I see it all around me. I plan to be a math major, and in my introductory classes I notice students who seem almost stunned by boredom. And why not? **We live in a culture where competing forms of entertainment always try to top previous efforts. We also are so saturated with invasive advertising and entertainment that we are stupefied by any "performer" who doesn't dance and sing.**

Notice that the thesis statement for this essay spans two sentences. The thesis should be as clear and concise as possible. A one-sentence thesis is often preferable, but trying to fit a complicated thesis into one sentence can produce an awkward and/or overly long statement. In some cases you may need two or more sentences to express your thesis.

CLASSROOM HINT Advise students who are struggling with their introductions to keep to a simple, straightforward thesis expressed in one sentence.

Getting Your Reader's Attention

How can you get your reader's attention? Writers use many different techniques. Notice the devices used by the writers of the following introductory paragraphs.

Using an Engaging Anecdote

> Two hurricanes have visited me recently, and except for a few rather hasty observations of my own (which somehow seem presumptuous), all I know about these storms is what I've heard on the radio. I live on the Maine coast, to the east of Penobscot Bay. Formerly, this coast was not in the path of hurricanes, or if it was we didn't seem to know it, but times change and we must change with them. My house is equipped with three small, old-fashioned radios, two of them battery sets, one a tiny plug-in bedside model on which my wife sometimes manages to get the Giants after I have turned in. We do not have TV, and because of this curious omission we are looked upon as eccentrics, possibly radicals.
>
> —from E. B. White, "The Eye of Edna"

Here, White opens with an anecdote that is alarming in its understatement ("Two hurricanes have visited me lately . . ."), as if mild-mannered acquaintances had dropped in for social visits. The reader is instantly engaged. Furthermore, living through one hurricane would be bad enough, but two?

Using a Provocative Statement

> If you're a novice in Cyberspace, you may think that buying a computer is a scary and confusing process. But the truth is that if you take a little time to learn a few basic principles and some of the technical lingo, buying the right computer and getting it to work properly is no more complicated than building a nuclear reactor from wristwatch parts in a darkened room using only your teeth. So let's get started!
>
> —from Dave Barry, "How to Buy and Set Up a Computer"

Barry opens Chapter 3 of *Dave Barry in Cyberspace* with an intentionally provocative statement to which the reader instantly reacts. ("A new computer can't be *that* difficult.") Then Barry continues with an extremely funny account of the various pitfalls that one can encounter with retail salespeople, "customer support," and incompatible software.

Questioning an Assumption In the next example, Bill Cosby opens an essay by questioning, both implicitly and explicitly, one of our most cherished assumptions—that children are necessary for personal fulfillment:

> So you've decided to have a child. You've decided to give up quiet evenings with good books and lazy weekends with good music, intimate meals during which you finish whole sentences, sweet private times when you've savored the thought that just the two of you and your love are all you will ever need. You've decided to turn your sofas into trampolines and to abandon the joys of leisurely contemplating reproductions of great art for the joys of frantically coping with reproductions of yourselves. Why?
>
> —from Bill Cosby, "The Baffling Question"

Cosby's essay then goes on to illustrate some of the "joys" of parenthood.

Using a Quotation In *Trials of an Expert Witness,* Dr. Harold L. Klawans recalls his experiences as a witness in medical malpractice cases. His thesis is that in a court of law, winning is everything, whether we like this idea or not. Klawans sees sports as a metaphor for courtroom struggles, and he opens his first chapter with a quotation from the prominent scholar Jacques Barzun to illustrate his point:

> Jacques Barzun is credited with having proclaimed that "whoever would know the heart and mind of America had better learn baseball." While I will never dispute that axiom, the single action that has come to epitomize much of the American character to me belonged to a figure from an entirely different and much more international sport, namely, basketball. "Red" Auerbach was for many years the coach of the most successful basketball team in the world, the Boston Celtics, who won ten championships in a single eleven-year stretch under his leadership. He was an intense competitor who fought tooth and nail, but as soon as he knew that the game was won, Red relaxed, sat back, and lit a cigar, barely watching either his team or their opponents play out the rest of the game. That act was not one of disdain or arrogance. He had won. He had no more worries. He could relax and enjoy himself. He could sit back and feel the thrill of victory. If his actions increased the agony of defeat, so be it.
>
> —from Harold L. Klawans, *Trials of an Expert Witness*

Note that the quotation is integrated into the text, not just there to be admired, as in the following example:

> "When it rains, it pours." Whoever first said that was right on track.

Opening your essay with a quotation can be effective as long as you integrate the quoted text; don't let it "float."

Here are two other methods to capture the reader's attention:

1. Ask a question. For example: *Why is the cafeteria food at this college so uniformly inedible?*
2. Relate compelling statistics. For example: *A recent study by the state human services commission reveals that 15 percent of our children are abused by their twelfth birthday.*

SUGGESTED ACTIVITY
As an excellent in-class exercise, ask students to write an opening paragraph using one of these techniques. If you use writing groups, assign a different technique to each group.

Remember that you are trying to engage your reader's attention, to make that person *want* to continue reading your essay. For this reason, you should *never* use the self-conscious, reflexive approach seen in the work of so many inexperienced writers ("This essay will attempt to prove . . ."). The guideline is simple: don't refer to your essay as an essay while writing it.

MORE OPTIONS ONLINE
For more help with thesis statements and introductory paragraphs, go to **www.mhhe.com/writingtoday**.

Body Paragraphs

Your choice of body paragraphs will largely be determined by which rhetorical option (description, narration, and so on) you are using to develop your essay. However, since you will often use more than one rhetorical option within an essay, you may need to use several of the following types of paragraphs in one piece of writing.

Description

In description, the emphasis is on sensory detail—engaging the reader's ability to see, hear, feel, smell, and so on. (For more on sensory detail, see Chapter 6.) Note how the following paragraph from "A Very Secret Santa" focuses on these elements:

SUGGESTED ACTIVITY Have students meet in pairs and describe each other's clothing, facial features, and other physical characteristics. This in-class exercise never fails to demonstrate how difficult and how useful effective description can be.

CLASSROOM HINT Remind students of the versatility of description: it appears frequently in science, journalism, literature, history, and jurisprudence.

> Walter was the more interesting of the two, but not at first glance. An accountant, he seemed to want to fit in. Walter dressed conservatively, which matched his features and size: a black man of middle height, very slightly overweight, with rimless glasses. His only "daring" feature was a neatly trimmed mustache. His personality, at first, also seemed unremarkable. He was quiet, a bit shy, and not really sociable or pleasant. Given his choice, he would sit alone in his big lounge chair and smoke a pipe (an ever-present odor) while watching television. Yet inside Walter Wallace was, if not a heart of gold, then the next best thing: he was the most charitable man I've ever met.

Narration

The narrative essay, or the narrative paragraph within an essay, tells a story in order to entertain the reader or point out a significant effect caused by the story's events. (For more on narration, see Chapter 7.) Narrative paragraphs use time order, with the writer employing transitions to ensure that the reader can follow the events without losing the "thread" of the story (for a list of transitions, see page 71):

> The game was close, start to finish. With ten seconds left to go, Demetrius fouled out by stopping the Garfield point guard from driving to the basket. The guard made one of the two resulting foul shots, and our enemy had a one-point lead. After a timeout, we had the ball in our forecourt, and guess who was trying to get position on Garfield's very athletic center? Me. It was like a housecat trying to get position on a cougar. We ran a set play, in which our best shooter shot from an angle after our small forward set a pick to block out the defender. Our guard arced the ball toward the basket, and next there was one of those frozen moments while everyone judged the apparent accuracy of the attempt. Then the ball clanged down on the back of the rim and bounced straight up. Robert McAlester leaped up after it, and I followed with my normal tape-delay reaction time.

The writer is trying to accomplish two tasks here. The first task is to recount the events of the basketball game without using too much jargon. After all, even though basketball is a popular sport, not everyone has an intimate knowledge of its structure and language. The writer's second task is to tell the story of the climactic, exciting final moments. He uses transitions (*next, then*) to good effect here, moving the reader right along with the narrative.

CLASSROOM HINT Explain that examples are concrete and specific applications of a concept, which is general by its very nature.

Exemplification

When writers use the exemplification option, they are trying to prove a general assertion by providing specific evidence to back the assertion up. (For more on exemplification, see Chapter 8.) Notice how the following paragraph depends on its example:

> We have been preached at for years by the National Safety Council, among others, to obey the posted speed limits. "Speed kills," they tell us. Actually, however, speeding doesn't cause accidents; failure to yield the right-of-way and inability to control a vehicle account for almost all accidents. But excessive speeding can lead to both of these errors. Driving ten miles an hour over the speed limit is the norm for most Americans (including me), but I always shudder when I see someone driving, say, 70 in a 45-mile-per-hour zone. This driver is going so much faster than the surrounding cars that he or she can get in trouble merely due to the other drivers' expectations. Unless a "normal" driver in the traffic is explicitly aware of the high speed of the fastest car, he or she may well make a lane change without realizing that the fast car is now trapped with nowhere to go and not enough time to stop. Did the slower car "cause" the accident? Maybe in one sense, yes, but rear-end a car when you're doing 70 in a 45-mile-per-hour zone and see how fast you need a lawyer.

SUGGESTED ACTIVITY Ask students to add their own examples to this paragraph. Doing so will help them grasp the value of exemplification in achieving clarity and persuasiveness.

Process Analysis

The process analysis strategy has two possible purposes. One is to explain to the reader how to do something: perform a task, repair machinery, and so on. The second purpose is to explain how an activity happened in the past or happens routinely. (For more on process analysis, see Chapter 9.)

The first of the following two examples uses the "how to" approach to lead the reader through the "process" of falling asleep:

CLASSROOM HINT Remind students that process analysis is useful in many disciplines: the physical sciences, the social sciences, technology, journalism, and business.

> The first step takes place in the two or three hours before bedtime. This period is not a good time to eat the evening meal, unless you want to run the risk of being awakened by indigestion. Similarly, anything containing alcohol or caffeine can disrupt your ability to fall asleep. Old novels tell of characters drinking a glass of heated milk before bed. It sounds awful, but it works for many people. A warm bath just before bed may also help. The main objectives are to avoid anything that will disrupt sleep and to take measures conducive to sleep.

SUGGESTED ACTIVITY To help students appreciate how much effort is involved in producing effective process analysis, ask them to explain in writing how to tie a shoe, hammer a nail, open a soft drink can, or complete another simple task. Then ask them to read their work to a listener who, pretending to know nothing about the subject, tries to follow the instructions. The questions the listener asks will surely prompt the writer to add detail.

The next example shows how otherwise promising sales presentations can fail:

> The other extreme has its own problems. In my division we call these presentations "two young guys in red flannel shirts." When the techies show up, they are prepared to wow you. And they do. Their fingers fly across their ergonomic keyboards; technical wizardry rises up like a powerful genie in the room. However, the real problem with this type of presentation happens, oddly enough, at the same juncture as in the previous type. Ask one of these phenoms an application question, and watch what happens. Some of them can't communicate at all; some can't even look you in the eye. All in all, the solitude that draws many very smart but very shy people into computer/software design does not lend itself to interaction with the lay public.

The process that the writer is analyzing has happened in the past; presumably, it will happen in the future as well. Note that this paragraph comes from a definition essay that uses process analysis as an internal strategy.

Causal Analysis

CLASSROOM HINT A good way to introduce causal analysis is to compare and contrast it to process analysis. In a nutshell, process focuses on "how"; causal focuses on "why."

Paragraphs developed using causal analysis normally concentrate on either cause or effect. (For more on causal analysis, see Chapter 10.) In this first example, Naomi Wolf considers possible causes for a perceived change in attitude:

> Thus, feminism stopped being seen as guaranteeing every woman's choice—whatever that may be—and fell captive to social attitudes held only by a minority that often could not even reach agreement among its own members. To be sure, this development might have been inescapable, a result of the abortion wars that demanded an us-and-them worldview. But, the ideological overloading closed the word "feminism" off to enormous numbers of people: women who are not sure about, or who actively oppose, abortion; women who are terrified of being tarred with the brush of homophobia; women who strongly resist identifying themselves as victims; women who are uneasy with what they see as man bashing and blaming; conservative women; and men themselves.
>
> —from Naomi Wolf, *Fire with Fire*

The second example concentrates on effects:

> To the British, the Eskimos were like children—untutored savages who could only benefit from the white man's ways. This paternalism was quite unjustified. In the decades that followed, the real children in the Arctic would be the white explorers. Without the Eskimos to care for them, hunt for them, and guide them through that chill, inhospitable realm, scores more would have died of starvation, scurvy, exhaustion, or exposure. Without the Eskimos, the journeys to seek out the Pole and the Passage would not have been possible. Yet their contribution has been noted only obliquely. It was the British Navy's loss that it learned so little from the natives. Had it paid attention, the tragedies that followed might have been averted.
>
> —from Pierre Berton, *The Arctic Grail*

If, Berton argues, the British naval explorers had tried to learn from the Inuit rather than seeing them as hopeless savages, the exploration of the Arctic would have been easier and not quite so deadly.

Definition

CLASSROOM HINT Beginning writers tend to create brief, stilted, and unconvincing definitions. Remind them that definition is really the heart of exposition and that unlike a dictionary definition, a definition within an essay demands both specificity and creativity. In addition, effective definitions need to have a clear purpose.

Writers use definition to clear up possible confusion about a troublesome term or to bring new meaning to a commonplace word or idea. (For more on definition, see Chapter 11.) Note how the following paragraph defines the idea of "living on the economy budget":

> Members of families existing on the economy budget never go out to eat, for it is not included in the food budget; they never go out to a movie, concert, or ball game or indeed to any public or private establishment that charges

admission, for there is no entertainment budget; they have no cable television, for the same reason; they never purchase alcohol or cigarettes; never take a vacation or holiday that involves any motel or hotel or, again, any meals out; never hire a baby-sitter or have any other paid child care; never give an allowance or other spending money to the children; never purchase any lessons or home-learning tools for the children; never buy books or records for the adults or children, or any toys, except in the small amounts available for birthday or Christmas presents ($50 per person over the year); never pay for a haircut; never buy a magazine; have no money for the feeding or veterinary care of any pets; and, never spend any money for preschool for the children, or educational trips for them away from home, or any summer camp or other activity with a fee.

—from John E. Schwarz and Thomas J. Volgy, *The Forgotten Americans*

Notice the internal strategy that Schwarz and Volgy use. They define the economy budget by using exemplification; we learn the misery faced by people trapped in this economic bracket by example after example of what the poor can't afford to do. Almost involuntarily, the reader compares these examples to his or her situation.

Classification

Writers classify when they take large subjects and divide them into smaller subjects. (For more on classification, see Chapter 12.) Classification is a way of making a subject clear by discussing its parts or categories, as in the following example:

In this country, we waste an enormous amount of time and energy disapproving of one another in three categories where only personal taste matters: hair, sports, and music. We need not review the family trauma, high dudgeon, tsk-tsking, and lawsuits caused over the years by hair and how people wear it. Consider the equally futile expenditure of energy in condemning other people's sports. And in music, good Lord, the zeal put into denouncing rock, sneering at opera, finding classical a bore, jazz passé, bluegrass fit only for snuff-dippers—why, it's stupefying. It's incomprehensible.

—from Molly Ivins, "Honky Tonking"

Comparison/Contrast

When you compare and contrast two subjects, you have two options for structuring your paragraph or essay. If you use the subject-by-subject approach, you discuss one of the subjects first, then the other. In an essay, you can use various paragraph strategies, including most of the ones in this section. If you use the point-by-point approach, however, you compare and contrast the two subjects in relation to one point of comparison per sentence or group of sentences. (For more on comparison/contrast, see Chapter 13.) The point-by-point approach requires a careful use of transitions, as in the following example:

CLASSROOM HINT
Begin your discussion of comparison/contrast by explaining that, strictly speaking, comparison identifies similarities while contrast points out differences.

In terms of gas mileage, my current vehicle is vastly superior to its predecessor. My old car averaged 22 miles per gallon. In contrast, my new vehicle

> averages 36 m.p.g. The clunker that I suffered with for so long needed a tune-up every year; however, my new car is guaranteed not to need a tune-up for at least 100,000 miles. Finally, I'm saving a dime each time I buy a gallon of gas, for my old car needed mid-grade gas whereas my new one burns regular.

Argument

You could use any type of paragraph when developing an argument, but most paragraphs used in an argument make and support assertions. (For more on argument, see Chapter 14.) In the following example, the writer is arguing against a proposal to offer free tuition to community college students in her state:

> I would feel sorry for college instructors who suddenly had to teach this newly defined group of students. A college professor must be seen as an expert, and suddenly he or she must teach students with no incentive to learn whatsoever. Surely this situation would be demoralizing. Community college faculty would become like those notorious American high school teachers I've heard about so much: tired, depressed functionaries with no control and no hope.

In an argument essay, you are, obviously, trying to prove your point. However, any subject worth arguing has very good arguments on each side. The **yield** is a type of paragraph that acknowledges the other side's assertions. Yield paragraphs do not appear in all argument essays, but they are useful devices. The following yield is the second paragraph of the same argument about tuition:

> To one style of thinking, it is hard to oppose this idea. There are a great many people who find one difficulty standing between them and a college degree: money. These folks will become the very smart mechanic, the brilliant secretary, the underused office manager. Telling these people "no" just seems wrong.

MORE OPTIONS ONLINE For more help with body paragraphs, go to **www.mhhe.com/writingtoday**.

In this paragraph, the writer acknowledges that her position may seem harsh and that those who oppose her may well have sound reasons for doing so. The writer is—temporarily—yielding to the other side before resuming her argument.

EXERCISE 3.1

EXERCISE 3.1 Responses will vary.

CLASSROOM HINT Discussing one or two photographs in class and suggesting possible approaches will help students get started.

Each chapter in Part 2 (chapters 6–15) ends with a photograph chosen to illustrate the rhetorical option that the chapter discusses. For example, the narration chapter (Chapter 7) has a photograph reflecting a story, the comparison/contrast chapter (Chapter 13) has a photograph showing a sharp contrast between two images, and so on. Turn to Part 2, and select a photograph that interests you. Note the title of the chapter, and write a paragraph in response to the photograph, using the rhetorical option covered in the chapter to develop your idea.

Concluding Paragraphs

A short essay normally ends with only one concluding paragraph. Along with the introduction, the conclusion of an essay often gives students trouble.

Many students make the error of bringing up new topics in the conclusion, frequently topics that beg to be explored, but not at the end of an essay. If you find yourself in this situation, reexamine the structure of your introduction and your body paragraphs. Should the new topic or topics be developed within your essay, or should they not be mentioned at all?

The worst approach to take in a conclusion is to contradict the ideas and positions already developed in the body paragraphs. You might shake your head and wonder who would do such a thing, but we see this problem often enough in students' essays to mention that it is a common pitfall.

The conclusion is the last part of your essay; it should logically derive from the paragraphs that precede it. Therefore, avoid using "In conclusion" or similar phrasing. Your reader can see that this is the end of your essay, so there is no need to announce it. Also avoid stilted sentences such as "As this essay has shown. . . ." Such language can lower the reader's evaluation of an otherwise effective essay.

Short essays rarely need a summary in their conclusion. Readers are frequently put off by encountering a recap of what they have just read and can still easily remember. Instead, you should use your conclusion to comment about your essay and its implications. Here are some proven approaches to writing effective conclusions.

Consider Your Options

Exercise 3.1 asks you to examine a visual representation (a photograph), consider an abstraction (a rhetorical option), and then respond in words (by writing a paragraph). The rhetorical options discussed in this section and in Part 2 are not merely essay patterns; they are ways of thinking. Try this: listen to your favorite music for a day, and list the rhetorical options that you hear used by your favorite artists.

Reinforcing Your Thesis

Don't *repeat* your thesis; *reinforce* it. In "A Very Secret Santa," Verlinda includes her thesis statement within this sentence:

> Yet inside Walter Wallace was, if not a heart of gold, then the next best thing: he was the most charitable man I've ever met.

If in her conclusion Verlinda had repeated her thesis—"he [Walter] was the most charitable man I've ever met"—she would have missed an opportunity to make a strong final impression. However, note her very effective conclusion, especially its last sentence, which *reinforces* her thesis:

> In general, I feel that when someone does something "nice" for another, his or her motives are not altogether altruistic—being nice makes the giver feel good about himself or herself. In the case of Walter Wallace, however, the motive seems to have been more involuntary. Does this make Walter any less admirable? I don't think so; I wish the world were full of men like him.

Commenting on Your Essay's Implications

If in your essay you have analyzed a situation, for example, now is the time to comment on the implications of your analysis. The following paragraph concludes an essay that examines the problem of boredom in modern life (see page 53 for the first two paragraphs of this essay). The writer believes that the modern world's noisy and intrusive entertainment and advertising culture is one of the main causes of boredom.

> In the future, two things are likely to happen. One is that the entertainment/advertising phalanx will turn to even more violence, noise, and intrusion. These

techniques have worked for a long time, and they are not likely to disappear. Correspondingly, the ability to appreciate anything that requires a "quiet faculty"—such as a garden, an art museum, or an algebra textbook—will certainly dwindle even more. Our culture is about to become the slave of its own entertainment industry.

Using a Call to Action

An essay that analyzes a problem can make a recommendation on how to solve the problem or at least improve the situation. The following paragraph concludes an essay defining the ideal sales presentation (excerpted on page 57). The essay points out what is wrong with most corporate sales presentations, and the concluding paragraph offers a remedy for this ongoing problem:

> I have a feeling that most vendors would prosper if they were able to sit in on presentations that actually convinced my company to pull the trigger. The androids-in-suits crowd would be horrified by how "unprofessional" a successful presentation is; the red-flannel boys would be alarmed at the apparent lack of nuclear widgets. However, in the middle is not mediocrity, but success.

Showing the Aftermath

Many essays are either straight narratives or use a narrative framework to accomplish another purpose. In such essays, the conclusion can explain what happens *after* the narrative. The following example concludes a narrative of unexpected heroism in a basketball game (excerpted on page 56). The story itself ends in the last body paragraph, and the conclusion provides the aftermath, allowing the writer to comment on his life since basketball:

> My height is useful in different ways now. While going to college, I work part time as a stocker for Target, and I can reach shelves unattainable by my colleagues. The rest of the time, I study. I don't even own a basketball, but my brief moment of glory will never fade.

Referring to an Earlier Anecdote or Example

Page 57 of this chapter contains a paragraph from an exemplification essay in which the writer discusses dangerous driving. In that paragraph, the writer introduces the example of a car moving at 70 mph in a 45-mph speed zone. The writer uses this hypothetical example in each of his body paragraphs, then returns to it in his conclusion:

> The driver cruising at 70 mph in a 45-mph zone is one of the worst of all traffic problems. Mr. Careless is driving too fast to react to slower traffic. The drivers of the slower cars, in turn, may not realize that a maniac is in their midst. And, if the distractions of cell phones, CD players, radios, and refreshments are present—for any or all of the drivers—then a dynamic recipe for trouble emerges.

Using an Authoritative Quotation

Taking advantage of someone else's words can produce a powerful conclusion. The following is the concluding paragraph of an essay warning of the dangers of credit-card debt for college students:

> All students want to have fun while going to school; it's part of the tradition. But do they want to be paying for that fun many years from now? When I talked to Teresa Espinoza, a Student Life counselor, she provided a grisly anecdote: "The worst case this office has seen was a student who—beyond the normal package of student loans—owed $27,000 in credit debt at the end of her junior year. When this student is in her forties or fifties, she may still be paying off this debt."

MORE OPTIONS ONLINE
For more help with concluding paragraphs, go to **www.mhhe.com/writingtoday.**

WRITING EFFECTIVE TOPIC SENTENCES

Just as the thesis statement represents the controlling idea of an essay, the **topic sentence** indicates the specific subject of a paragraph. Readers of English-language essays expect a clear topic sentence and a unified paragraph that deals with one idea. Moving from one main idea to another within a paragraph, or digressing from the main idea and then returning to it, will result in a lack of unity.

The topic sentence may be handled in a variety of ways, normally depending on its placement in the paragraph. The topic sentence may also be implied—in other words, not stated but evident from the development of the paragraph—or it may be carried over from the preceding paragraph.

The following sections discuss your options when writing topic sentences and creating paragraphs. As you draft the paragraphs in an essay, you may want to create a **Save** directory or folder in your word-processing program. Here you can keep drafts of paragraphs that did not quite work out. Then, if your purpose changes later in the writing process, you can come back to these old versions to see if they are suddenly more useful to you.

Topic Sentence at the Paragraph's Beginning

Starting a paragraph with a topic sentence is the most common approach, as in the following example (the topic sentence is highlighted):

> **It was a world of difference marked by possessions.** Between Saturday night movies and winter vacations; weekly pay envelopes and checking accounts; Easter outfits bought on the layaway plan and designer clothes ordered a season ahead; social security checks and stock dividends; kids who slept on sofa beds and children with nannies; in short, between an envious life and an enviable one. Because these symbols of class changed visibly from top to bottom, they seemed unnatural, perhaps unjust, and we resented them. Because male-female roles changed very little from their elegant dinner parties to our kitchen tables, they seemed natural, and very just indeed.
>
> —from Gloria Steinem, *Moving Beyond Words*

Steinem, who is writing about a "traditional" era before modern feminism, illustrates the general statement in her topic sentence with specific evidence. Her concluding sentences comment on the situation that she describes.

Steinem's paragraph is part of an analytical discussion of a complex subject, and her topic sentence is appropriate for her subject matter. In more informal writing, however, a topic sentence might try to engage, interest, or even humor the reader. The following paragraph presents a great deal of information and develops it quite well, but the topic sentence is as flat as roadkill:

> **There are many problems with local road construction.** The expansion of the Midtown Expressway toll plaza seems to take place only between the hours of 7 and 9 a.m. and 4 and 6 p.m. It's as if the Department of Transportation is trying to show us their sincerity. An obvious solution would be to move this work to nighttime hours, when traffic on the Midtown is about one-tenth of rush-hour volume. Another example is the widening of the emergency lanes on the six miles of the interstate east of downtown. This project has already consumed two years and doesn't seem close to being finished. One wonders how much work is actually being done.

Notice how much better a livelier topic sentence would work with the same paragraph:

> Is anyone in our area actually "in charge" of road construction?

In this case, asking a pointed question is a much more effective lead-in than the boring "There are many . . ." approach. Writing topic sentences intended to "hook" the reader is largely a matter of judgment and degree; starting every paragraph with a question would seem labored and artificial. However, keep in mind that the purpose of an essay is not just to pass along information; a well-written essay engages the reader.

Ending with the Topic Sentence

The standard development pattern—with the topic sentence first, followed by supporting details—can be reversed. Some paragraphs begin with evidence and details, then conclude with the topic sentence, which gathers the preceding sentences into a general idea. The following paragraph uses this technique effectively:

> But then there was Spanish. *Español:* my family's language. *Español:* the language that seemed to me a private language. I'd hear strangers on the radio and in the Mexican Catholic church across town speaking in Spanish, but I couldn't really believe that Spanish was a public language, like English. Spanish speakers, rather, seemed related to me, for I sensed that we shared—through our language—the experience of feeling apart from *los gringos.* It was thus a ghetto Spanish that I heard and I spoke. Like those whose lives are bound by a barrio, I was reminded by Spanish of my separateness from *los otros, los gringos* in power. **But more intensely than for most barrio children—because I did not live in a barrio—Spanish seemed to me**

the language of home. (Most days it was only at home that I'd hear it.) It became the language of joyful return.

—from Richard Rodriguez, "Los Otros, Mis Hermanos"

In his essay, Rodriguez uses the comparison/contrast option as his overall strategy, but he uses narrative as this paragraph's internal strategy. This approach works well in paragraphs that recount events and then build up to a defining conclusion. Note that Rodriguez's topic sentence is actually three sentences, the last three of the paragraph.

Placing the topic sentence at the end of a paragraph is a strategy that works only in certain situations. Writers who use this device too often have probably planned poorly. In other words, they wrote the paragraph, figured out what they meant, and then added a topic sentence at the end. Note the following example:

The presenters have spent a great deal of time—and money—in ensuring that they look just right. The women dress like Miranda in *Sex and the City;* the men all watch *The Practice.* Somewhere in the histories of these people are rich orthodontists, as their teeth could blind you in direct sunlight. Their delivery is practiced and polished. These people are, to be frank, very easy to look at. So what's the problem? It's obvious: most of these people could push Chryslers or furniture as well as they can move whatever technical stuff they're trying to sell my company. Over the past fifteen years, computer/software/support items have been the focus of many of these presentations, and lately that focus has narrowed, with the Internet and its possibilities taking over. But ask one of these well-tailored androids a question that's not in the "script," and the façade weakens. Then a noticeable anger rises from me and my colleagues. **Most high-powered presentations favor style over substance.**

The logical position for the topic sentence in this paragraph is at the beginning, not the end, where it seems like an afterthought. Consider how much better the paragraph would read, and how much easier it would be to understand, if its topic sentence appeared at the beginning.

Topic Sentence Within the Paragraph

The strategy of placing the topic sentence within the paragraph can be very useful, especially when you need to give your reader background information. A few (or several) sentences introduce the main idea, which is then presented; the rest of the paragraph develops and supports the main idea, as in the following example:

There've been a lot of famous corpses in Chicago over the years, but John Wilkes Booth probably wasn't one of them. You do bring up an interesting topic, though. **The circumstances surrounding the death of John Wilkes Booth are hazy—hazy enough, in fact, to have kept a rumor in circulation for some years after his death (or "death," if you prefer) that J. W.**

> **was alive and kicking.** According to the history books, Booth died on the night of April 26, 1865. Heading south from Washington after the assassination, he reached the rolling Rappahannock River in Virginia on the twelfth night of his flight, and took refuge, along with one of his co-conspirators, in a tobacco barn belonging to the farm of one Richard Garrett. Federal troops in the area were tipped off, and the barn was surrounded and set on fire at about three in the morning. The troops had been instructed to take Booth alive, but he was found inside the burning building with a fatal bullet wound, an apparent suicide. A sergeant named Boston Corbett later took credit for the shooting, claiming that "Providence directed me" to disobey the order, but the point was never settled. Booth lived for some hours after the shooting, muttering the words "useless, useless," according to a popular account. The badly burned body was taken to Washington, where it was identified by some of Booth's friends, but the corpse had been damaged severely enough to make a positive identification impossible. The body, whoever it was, was secretly buried in the floor of a Washington warehouse to keep it safe from molestation. Four years later, the corpse was exhumed and taken to the Booth family plot in Baltimore, where as far as anybody knows or cares, it has remained ever since.
>
> —from Cecil Adams, *The Straight Dope*

SUGGESTED ACTIVITY For an effective in-class exercise, ask students to write paragraphs with topic sentences in different places. Suggest topics students are familiar with and can write about easily. This exercise can be used with writing groups.

The purpose of Adams's very popular newspaper column is to entertain as well as inform; thus, he prefaces his serious topic sentence ("The circumstances surrounding the death . . .") with sentences that establish his context and provide an effective lead-in. A more straightforward approach would have been informative but much less conversational in tone and, hence, less entertaining.

Topic Sentence Used for Two Paragraphs

CLASSROOM HINT Remind beginning writers that while using one topic sentence for two paragraphs or relying on an implied central idea can be effective, such approaches can result in paragraphs that lack unity.

Occasionally, a writer will begin a paragraph with a topic sentence and then develop the idea over two paragraphs (and sometimes more). Remember, a paragraph must develop a single idea, but this guideline does not mean that every idea must be developed in only one paragraph. For the sake of the reader, careful writers will break up long paragraphs into shorter paragraphs that are more easily digested. The following example includes one medium-length paragraph followed by a quite long one on the same topic. If the two paragraphs had been combined, the result would have been difficult for readers to manage:

> **Once the stormy years of his early struggles were over, Dr. Juvenal Urbino had followed a set routine and achieved a respectability and prestige that had no equal in the province.** He arose at the crack of dawn, when he began to take his secret medicines: potassium bromide to raise his spirits, salicylates for the ache in his bones when it rained, ergosterol drops for vertigo, belladonna for sound sleep. He took something every hour, always in secret, because in his long life as a doctor and teacher he had always opposed prescribing palliatives for old age: it was easier for him to bear other people's pains than his own. In his pocket he always carried a

little pad of camphor that he inhaled deeply when no one was watching to calm his fear of so many medicines mixed together.

He would spend an hour in his study preparing for the class in general clinical medicine that he taught at the Medical School every morning, Monday through Saturday, at eight o'clock, until the day before his death. He was also an avid reader of the latest books that his bookseller in Paris mailed to him, or the ones from Barcelona that his local bookseller ordered for him, although he did not follow Spanish literature as closely as French. In any case, he never read them in the morning, but only for an hour after his siesta and at night before he went to sleep. When he was finished in the study he did fifteen minutes of respiratory exercises in front of the open window in the bathroom, always breathing toward the side where the roosters were crowing, which was where the air was new. Then he bathed, arranged his beard and waxed his mustache in an atmosphere saturated with genuine cologne from Farina Gegenüber, and dressed in white linen, with a vest and a soft hat and cordovan boots. At eighty-one years of age he preserved the same easygoing manner and festive spirit that he had on his return from Paris soon after the great cholera epidemic, and except for the metallic color, his carefully combed hair with the center part was the same as it had been in his youth. He breakfasted *en famille* but followed his own personal regimen of an infusion of wormwood blossoms for his stomach and a head of garlic that he peeled and ate a clove at a time, chewing each one carefully with bread, to prevent heart failure. After class it was rare for him not to have an appointment related to his civic initiatives, or his Catholic service, or his artistic and social innovations.

—from Gabriel García Márquez, *Love in the Time of Cholera*

Notice that García Márquez uses a wealth of detail over two paragraphs to develop a topic sentence that appears at the beginning of the first one.

The Implied Topic Sentence

When a writer implies the main idea rather than stating it, he or she is gambling that the development and support within the paragraph will make the main idea obvious, as in the following example:

I am over 21 years of age. I am a citizen of the United States. I have not been convicted of a felony. And I have not been treated or confined for drug addiction, drunkenness, or mental illness. According to the National Firearms Act of 1934, I thus qualify to purchase a fully automatic machine gun capable of firing hundreds of bullets with a single squeeze of the trigger. A few months ago, I decided to try.

—from Mathew Maranz, "Guns 'R' Us"

What is the topic of this paragraph? It could be stated this way: "Guns are too readily available in the United States." Would the paragraph be better if it had included this sentence? No—Maranz's point is self-evident, and reinforcing this point so obviously would detract from the paragraph's effectiveness.

However, think about the danger that lurks in the word *implied*. As a writer, you can attempt to imply your point, but your attempt will be fruitless if your

MORE OPTIONS ONLINE
For more help with topic sentences, go to **www.mhhe.com/writingtoday.**

reader does not grasp your implication. In other words, you are assuming that your reader will *infer* your meaning, a risky proposition. Be careful.

EXERCISE 3.2

EXERCISE 3.2 Responses will vary. This exercise promotes active classroom discussion.

Each of the following paragraphs is missing its topic sentence. Read the paragraph carefully; then add the topic sentence where it will be most effective.

1. I wake up too late, and have to rush to get ready. Because I've been rushing, I forget a key piece of my schoolwork. And the later I start in the morning, the worse the traffic is during rush hour. I get to school late and enter my first class ten minutes after it has begun, receiving a puzzled glare from the instructor, who probably believes that I'll be late for my own funeral. And finally, to make my day complete, I learn much later in the afternoon that he increased our reading assignment and announced a quiz for the next class—information I would have received earlier if my day wasn't so off-kilter.
2. According to a story in yesterday's student newspaper, this school has spent $11 million on its football program over the last four years. During this time, the team's record has been a combined 12 wins, 32 losses. Seven football players have been arrested for violent crimes, and fifteen more have been arrested for theft, drug possession, or alcohol-related offenses. The university also plans to spend $15 million to renovate its football stadium.

ACHIEVING UNITY

A paragraph needs to develop one idea. When a paragraph has done this successfully, it is said to be unified. Lack of **unity** is a problem that hinders many student writers, but paragraphs with unity problems are frequently the result of poor planning and no sense of purpose.

Chapter 2 discusses the need for planning and offers prewriting techniques that writers can use to help them determine where they are going before they begin the first draft of a paragraph or an essay. Trying to write the first draft of any text with no more preparation than the thoughts you have in your mind is risky. You are exploring, thinking your way through the text's development as you write it. When you take this approach, you are almost always forced to rely too much on the revision process, and sometimes, as we saw in Chapter 2, a first draft completed in this way is useless: it really can't be revised and must instead be discarded.

Part of the preparation/prewriting step is determining your purpose for writing. Knowing the effect that you intend to produce with a paragraph or an essay is essential if you want to produce a unified result.

The following paragraph is a good example of what happens when someone starts writing on a subject without prewriting and without determining a specific purpose:

> America is a melting pot, and Florida is a state, like New York or Massachusetts, that has an incredibly diverse population. Immigrants have come to

Florida for more than four centuries. Florida became a state in 1837. The first immigrants in Florida were the Spanish in the 1500s. Then came French and British settlers. Today, many immigrants from Cuba, Puerto Rico, and the non-Hispanic parts of the Caribbean live in Florida. These people are largely from Jamaica, Haiti, and the Bahamas. Early in the century, many Greeks settled on the Gulf Coast north of Clearwater in the Tarpon Springs area. Tarpon Springs is neat. They have a Sponge Museum and other sponge-related attractions. Many black people were brought to Florida as slaves, and many more came to Florida after the Civil War. Also, the Minorcans helped settle Florida in the St. Augustine–New Smyrna area in the 1800s. Only the Native Americans of South Florida are nonimmigrants.

This paragraph wanders like a toy boat in a gale. What is the writer's purpose? If it is to point out that different areas of Florida retain an ethnic flavor due to immigration patterns, it fails. If it is to list the major waves of immigration to Florida over time, it fails as well. There is no sense of chronology here.

Let's assume that the purpose of this paragraph is the second one: to list—generally—the historical immigration patterns in Florida. Using a narrative (chronological) strategy for development, the writer can revise the paragraph so that it is unified:

The United States has often been described as a melting pot, and one of its largest states, Florida, is a very good example of the immigrant tradition. Florida has received immigrants for over four centuries. The first were the Spanish, who arrived on the Atlantic coast in the 1500s, followed in later centuries by the French and the British. An interesting (and ultimately tragic) contingent was the Minorcans, who were brought to the St. Augustine–New Smyrna area as laborers. Black slaves became involuntary Florida residents up to the end of the Civil War. In the twentieth century, various groups have settled in specific areas of the state: Greeks who were attracted by the sponges off the Tarpon Springs coastline, Cubans and Puerto Ricans who settled in Miami and other population centers. The most recent wave of immigrants has come from Jamaica, Haiti, and the Bahamas. The only Floridians who aren't immigrants are the Native Americans of South Florida, and relatively few of this band remain, concentrated in the area around the Everglades.

Another problem with unity occurs when a writer has a clear purpose for a paragraph but includes irrelevant statements within it, leading the reader off the track of the paragraph's central idea. Called *digressions,* these wanderings distract and confuse a reader who is expecting the paragraph to illustrate the development of a single idea, as in the following example (the irrelevant sentences are highlighted):

If current trends continue, stores will soon start offering Christmas merchandise on June 1. For years, the Christmas shopping season commenced on the day after Thanksgiving. Everyone remembers that frantic Friday. (Once, I saw a four-way fistfight over a mall parking spot.) However, retailers have now succeeded in pushing this date forward to mid-October. There is no law against this practice. The general freedom given to business in this country

MORE OPTIONS ONLINE
For more help with paragraph unity, go to **www.mhhe.com/writingtoday.**

allows Wal-Mart, say, to sell Christmas decorations in March if company officials feel like it. **This kind of freedom is what has allowed the United States to become so wealthy. The marketing genius of American retailers is the envy of the rest of the world.** But starting the Christmas shopping season earlier every year is becoming increasingly bizarre. Also, this practice is turning an occasion that is already a problem for many people into a true ordeal.

EXERCISE 3.3

EXERCISE 3.3 Revised paragraphs will vary.
1. The fourth, fifth, sixth, and eighth sentences do not relate to the topic sentence.
2. The fifth, sixth, ninth, and tenth sentences do not relate to the topic sentence.

The following paragraphs lack unity. Read each and underline the sentences that lead the text in the wrong direction. Then revise the paragraph to correct the problem.

1. The dog is the most useful creature humanity has ever known. Farmers and ranchers, in particular, have made great use of dogs. Dogs can be used to herd sheep and to help in the herding of horses. Horses themselves are quite useful agrarian animals. So is the mule, which is the offspring of a male donkey and a female horse, and the hinny, which is the offspring of a male horse and a female donkey. Oxen have also been used on farms and ranches. Dogs in rural areas can be used to guard property against trespassers and to help control vermin. Cats can also be used to control vermin, but not to repel intruders.
2. My roommate had his semester fall apart on him this weekend, and while I feel sorry for him, he has only himself to blame. Mike is taking three classes and working thirty hours a week. On Friday afternoon, he got his latest calculus test back and found that he made a 51. Now he probably can't pass the course. Calculus is one of the hardest courses for many students at this school. Of course, it's not as boring as statistics, but that's its only saving grace. I tried to commiserate with Mike; however, he was down and stayed there. He went out to a local club that night and didn't get back until 4:00 a.m. A good band was playing at the Emerald, which is one of my favorite night spots. They have great specials and attract the best crowds in town. Mike stayed much too long and then came home and slept until 2:30 p.m. When he awoke, he found a message on the answering machine from his boss, letting Mike know that he had been fired for missing work. On both Saturday night and Sunday night, Mike also hit the club scene. On Monday, he managed to sleep both through his biology exam and past the deadline for his research paper in Comp 2. I'm going to have a talk with him about getting some help over at the counseling center.

ACHIEVING COHERENCE

When someone is trying to talk and is babbling or cannot form words, the person is said to be incoherent. In terms of paragraph development, however, **coherence** has a more technical meaning. A paragraph is coherent when the writer has succeeded in guiding the reader through the text. Three common techniques that will help you achieve coherence in your paragraphs are

(1) using effective transitions, (2) choosing nouns and pronouns carefully, and (3) writing with parallel structures.

Using Effective Transitions to Improve Coherence

Transitions are text markers—words and phrases that guide the reader through the text. When a paragraph does not include transitions, the reader faces a string of unconnected sentences and is forced to impose order on and make connections among the various thoughts without the writer's help.

Your reader shouldn't have to go back and reread your sentences—in other words, your writing should contain clearly marked transitions that allow the reader to make the right connections the first time that he or she approaches your text. Transitions make these connections for readers.

TRANSITIONAL EXPRESSIONS

Relationship	Expression
Addition	also, in addition, too, moreover, and, besides, furthermore, equally important, then, finally
Example	for example, for instance, thus, as an illustration, namely, specifically
Contrast	but, yet, however, on the other hand, while, nevertheless, nonetheless, conversely, in contrast, still, at the same time
Comparison	similarly, likewise, in the same way
Concession	of course, to be sure, certainly, granted
Time	first, second, third, next, then, finally, afterwards, before, soon, later, meanwhile, subsequently, immediately, eventually, currently
Location	in the front, in the foreground, in the back, in the background, at the side, adjacent, nearby, next to, in the distance, here, there, to the left, to the right, inside, outside
Result	therefore, thus, as a result, so, accordingly
Summary	hence, in short, in brief, in summary, in conclusion, finally

SUGGESTED ACTIVITY
Ask each student to use one transition between a pair of sentences he or she creates. Then ask a few students to read their work aloud or write it on the blackboard.

Effective transitions are one of the true marks of good writing—and this technique is one of the most painless to learn. Note the following paragraph, which uses no transitions at all:

> On our date last Saturday, my boyfriend ran over a nail. His left front tire went flat. The car jack had never been used before. It was stiff. Eduardo tried to loosen the tire lugs. They were almost frozen. He found a piece of pipe. He used it to gain leverage on the tire iron. The car was parked in some mud. Eduardo got the flat tire off and slipped and fell into the mud. He was filthy. Eduardo got the spare tire in place. We continued on our "date."

This paragraph is written in a telegraphic style: Sentence. Stop. Sentence. Stop. Now see how adding transitional words and phrases improves the paragraph's coherence:

On our date last Saturday, my boyfriend ran over a nail, **so** his left front tire went flat. The car jack had never been used before; **as a result,** it was stiff. **First,** Eduardo tried to loosen the tire lugs, **but** they were almost frozen. **Then** he found a piece of pipe, **and** he used it to gain leverage on the tire iron. **However,** the car was parked in some mud. **Once** Eduardo got the flat tire off, he slipped and fell into the mud. **Thus,** he was filthy **by the time** he got the spare tire in place **and** we could continue on our "date."

Most of the transitions used in this paragraph show the passage of time (*first, then, once*) and cause/effect (*so, as a result, thus*). The transitions in the following paragraph help the writer build a sense of opposition, or contrast:

The key to the industrial revolution was discovering that non-human forms of energy substituted for human forms could increase the wealth of a nation beyond anyone's wildest dreams. **But** there was a catch. To realize this great wealth, non-human energy needed huge complexes called factories with hundreds, even thousands of workers collected into one factory. **Moreover,** several factories in one central place made the generation of energy more efficient. **Almost overnight,** the Western world was transformed from a rural and agricultural country to an urban and industrial state. Our technological advance seems to no longer fit our social structure: In a sense, the Japanese can better cope with modern industrialism. **While** Americans still busily protect our rather extreme form of individualism, the Japanese hold their individualism in check and emphasize cooperation.
—from William Ouchi, "Japanese and American Workers: Two Casts of Mind"

MORE OPTIONS ONLINE
For more help with paragraph coherence, go to **www.mhhe.com/writingtoday**.

This paragraph is part of Ouchi's argument that Japanese workers and American workers approach their jobs very differently. Hence, Ouchi uses transitions of opposition, such as *but* and *while,* as well as other transitions, such as *moreover,* which help him introduce additional details.

EXERCISE 3.4

EXERCISE 3.4 Responses will vary. Here are some possibilities:
1. As a result, these brave souls . . . beaches or hills. Today, however, soldiers are frequently . . . up close. Therefore, they are able. . . .
2. Before long, SA hired . . . Of course, he needed someone. . . . Therefore, he hired a secretary. However, the coordinator found. . . . Therefore, she hired two student assistants. . . .

The following paragraphs have very few transitions and, as a result, very little coherence. Revise each paragraph, adding transitional words and phrases to improve the paragraph's coherence.

1. Today, war is fought differently than it was in the past. Traditional combat depended on information gained from scouts and spies. These brave souls placed their lives in danger by infiltrating enemy lines or attacking exposed areas such as beaches or hills. Modern combat uses satellites and computers to get the job done. In the past, soldiers fought hand to hand and face to face. Soldiers today are frequently miles apart and never see their opponents up close. They are able to kill much more efficiently due to the technology at their command.

2. Colleges sometimes spend money like water, as one need leads to another. I work as a student assistant for the Student Activities (SA) office, which recently launched a new and revamped intramural program. SA hired a new coordinator. He needed someone to answer the phone and handle written communication. He hired a secretary. The coordinator found that he could not trust the secretary to make decisions while he was away. He then hired a woman to be his assistant. She is an organizational type who likes delegating authority. She hired two student assistants. First we had one person hired to perform a function. Now we have five, all in the space of a month.

Achieving Coherence Through Careful Choice of Nouns and Pronouns

Pronouns enable us to avoid the needless repetition of nouns, thereby making reading easier and faster. At the same time, the words that pronouns are replacing—their **antecedents**—must be clear, or the reader will wonder what the writer is referring to. Developing a sense of how to use pronouns and when *not* to use a pronoun—instead, repeating the noun for clarity and emphasis—will help you make your paragraphs and essays more coherent.

Note the skillful use of pronouns in the following two paragraphs by Axel Madsen:

> Gabrielle was twenty-seven when **she** fell in love with Arthur Capel. To **her,** Boy Capel was someone solid, someone who assumed **she** had a mind and asked what **she** thought. To **him, she** was a singular beauty. Slim, straight, and with an aristocratic head on a long, graceful neck, **she** looked like a Gainsborough duchess in profile. Yet full face, with **her** mocking raven eyes, generous mouth, charming dimple and knowing presence, **she** was an alluring street urchin.
>
> During the week in the Pyrenees **he** had come to appreciate **her** acid charm, **her** spontaneity and sharp tongue. **She** was energetic, frank, and witty, yet just beneath **her** deceptively accessible and limpid demeanor there was something severe. **She** loved what was beautiful and detested what was merely pretty. **Her** taste was nervy and **she** divined the phony, the contrived, the spurious in people. That **she** was Etienne's mistress somehow added to **her** stature in Boy's eyes. Etienne's persistent reminders that **he** would be going to Argentina for an extended visit practically invited Boy to attempt **her** conquest.
>
> —from Axel Madsen, *Chanel: A Woman of Her Own*

Here the pronouns *she, her, he,* and *him* are used twenty-one times, but there is never a question about which person each pronoun refers to. Notice in the last two sentences that Madsen is able to continue to use *she* and *her* (referring to Gabrielle) while using mostly nouns to refer to the two men, Arthur ("Boy") and Etienne.

In the preceding example, the careful use of pronouns contributes to clarity and ease of reading. Sometimes, however, to achieve greater emphasis, writers deliberately repeat nouns or use synonyms for greater emphasis, as in the following example:

Social **change** may be slow to occur, but as we have seen, the **democratic process** is the best way to effect equitable **progress.** The **democratic process** lets people have their say. The **democratic process** then lets elected leaders judge the desires of the populace and make informed decisions. Finally, the **democratic process** allows judicial, principled review of new laws to ensure that our nation's basic ideas are not violated.

Using Parallelism to Improve Coherence

Parallelism is the use of the same constructions for similar ideas. The following sentence has a problem with parallelism:

John enjoyed reading, dancing, and to swim.

The writer's pattern is gerund ("reading"), gerund ("dancing"), and then, illogically, infinitive ("to swim"). Obviously, the writer should have continued the pattern established by the two gerunds:

John enjoyed reading, dancing, and swimming.

Problems with parallelism can also occur within paragraphs. Note in the following paragraph how careless wording causes a lack of parallelism and a corresponding lack of coherence:

To change a practice that has long been followed can be difficult. **Modifying** the practice may be seen as the first step. Smokers find that **to vary** the intervals between cigarettes may help disturb the pattern of counting on a smoke at certain times. **To modify** one element of a habit can be the first step in **losing** the habit altogether.

The boldface terms should be made parallel for greater coherence, as in the revision below:

Changing a practice that has long been followed can be difficult. **Modifying** the practice may be seen as the first step. Smokers find that **varying** the intervals between cigarettes may help disturb the pattern of counting on a smoke at certain times. **Modifying** one element of a habit can be the first step in **losing** the habit altogether.

See Chapter 5 for more on the subject of parallelism.

ACHIEVING SPECIFICITY THROUGH THE USE OF CONCRETE DETAILS

Effective paragraph development is always a matter of degree and a matter of context. Some paragraphs deal with abstract or general subjects and do not—and should not—depend on specific, concrete details, as in the following example:

> The American premise is an existential one, and our moral code is political, its object being to allow for the widest horizons of sight and the broadest range of expression. We protect the other person's liberty in the interest of protecting our own, and our virtues conform to the terms and conditions of an arduous and speculative journey. If we look into even so coarse a mirror as the one held up to us by the situation comedies on prime-time television, we see that we value the companionable virtues—helpfulness, forgiveness, kindliness, and, above all, tolerance.
>
> —from Lewis H. Lapham, "Who and What Is American?"

The closest that Lapham gets to using concrete details is his reference to television. Yet there's nothing wrong with this paragraph (and a great deal that is right). Many paragraphs in academic writing take this approach.

However, in essays that deal with more specific and more practical issues, using concrete details will help develop your paragraphs and inform your reader. We frequently groan (sometimes inwardly, sometimes not) when we read paragraphs like this one:

> Breakfast is the most important meal of the day. Getting nutritious food into your system in the morning starts your metabolism working and provides you with energy. People who don't eat breakfast sometimes encounter ill effects later in the morning.

We don't learn much from this paragraph. How about some specific breakfast-food choices? Are some better than others? Should we ingest all the sugar-laden products that we can find? What if we want to eat a couple of barbecue sandwiches? And what, exactly, happens to people who don't eat breakfast? Do they feel a sudden lack of energy, experience a mild headache, or start lurching about like the zombies in *Night of the Living Dead*? This paragraph cries out for specific examples. Note the following revision:

> Breakfast is the most important meal of the day. When people wake up, they need energy for the morning, and energy comes from food. What kind of food, though? The remains of last night's pizza or barbecue? Sugar-loaded Breakfast Bombs? Technically, these are sources of energy, but not very good ones. Better choices are bran cereal, fruit, or even green vegetables. The last suggestion may sound strange, but a simple salad is a very nutritious breakfast, and a good breakfast can help avoid problems later in the morning. People who don't eat breakfast—or who eat very little at breakfast—can suffer a variety of late-morning problems, such as lack of energy, headaches, and fluctuating glucose levels. Taking the time to eat a good breakfast is a simple way to make the morning better and the day easier.

Consider Your Options

Think about the last paragraph that you have written—for this or another class, at work, or in a message to a friend. Could it have been improved by adding more concrete and specific details? What details could you have chosen to add?

EXERCISE 3.5

Read the following paragraphs. Determine if each one is sufficiently specific in terms of its subject matter and purpose. If it is not, add specific details of your choosing.

EXERCISE 3.5 Answers will vary. Some possibilities follow:
1. The writer might get specific about how exercise makes one feel better (e.g., raises energy levels, fights depression) and look better (e.g., tones muscles, improves complexion). "Significant health problems" might be replaced with "obesity, diabetes, and coronary disease."
2. The writer might include specific examples to show that major computer, financial, and retail corporations put recent college graduates through focused training programs before they integrate them into their work forces. The writer might also include examples of "tradition and bureaucracy" as seen in his or her college.
3. Naming and describing a particular building—broken windows, dirty staircases, peeling paint, crumbling façades—would help make this paragraph more convincing. So would a description of the "decaying commercial strip." For example, how many stores have gone out of business? What does the "strip" look like? Are storefronts boarded up? Are the streets full of litter? Are homeless people sleeping in doorways?

1. Most people don't exercise enough. Exercise gets the heart and lungs working. It also helps burn calories and leads to weight loss. People who exercise feel better and look better. A lack of exercise can lead to significant health problems in later life.
2. Many observers note that college does a poor job of training students for the world of work. Although such training is only a part of what colleges do, these complaints are valid. However, such a discrepancy is inevitable. For one thing, the business world changes faster than the academic world can adapt. Business is based on the need for profit, and decisions on changing policies can be made in an afternoon. Colleges, on the other hand, are based on tradition and bureaucracy. Change occurs more slowly here. Another problem is that "training" in college comes from professors, and many professors do not alter their methods over time. In other words, if they see that their approaches are reasonably successful, most instructors won't alter them just to "keep up" with the needs of the private-sector workplace.
3. This university has a very good reputation, but it may have the ugliest campus in North America. The buildings are very old, for one thing—not distinguished old but crumbling old. They are dirty and poorly maintained as well. The campus is very bare, with almost no greenery. A busy commercial section of town is literally next door, and this strip is decaying, not improving. All in all, our campus is not much of an advertisement for this university.

EXERCISE 3.6

Write a fully developed paragraph on one of the following topics. Remember to use specific, concrete examples and details.

1. **Description.** Choose an object that you are planning to buy or want to buy in the future.
2. **Narration.** What was the most amazing thing you heard someone say this week? Go beyond one or two sentences. For example, explain the circumstances or context in which it was said. Narrate the events that led up to and came after this comment. Identify the speaker and the listeners.
3. **Exemplification.** State a general "rule of thumb"; then give an example of what happens if someone violates this rule.
4. **Process analysis.** Show the reader how to get up and get ready in the morning without wasting time. Or write about another task that you complete regularly.
5. **Causal analysis.** What is one cause of student failure? What is one effect experienced by spending too much time surfing the Internet? Choose one of these questions.
6. **Definition.** What is the ideal roommate? What is the ideal neighbor? What is the ideal boss? Choose one of these questions. Rely on definition, but also use examples as necessary.

EXERCISE 3.6 Responses will vary.

CLASSROOM HINT Discussing each of these topics and helping students complete prewriting in class will improve their chances of writing successful papers.

7. **Comparison and contrast.** Contrast your two closest friends in terms of one personality trait.
8. **Argument.** Argue against one policy of your college or university.

Using the Internet

Go to these Web sites to find more tips, techniques, and insights on developing paragraphs:

MORE OPTIONS ONLINE
You can access the Web sites listed in "Using the Internet" by going to **www.mhhe.com/writingtoday**.

Guide to Grammar and Writing

This Web site, maintained by Capital Community College, provides a discussion of several topics relating to paragraph unity, coherence, development, and variety: **http://webster.commnet.edu/grammar/index.htm**.

The UVic Writer's Guide

The University of Victoria's English Department Web site includes helpful information on the rhetorical functions of paragraphs, the topic sentence, unity and coherence, paragraph development, and paragraph patterns: **http://web.uvic.ca/wguide**.

CHAPTER 4

RESHAPING YOUR ESSAY: GLOBAL REVISION

The Renaissance dramatist Ben Jonson once wrote about his contemporary, William Shakespeare, that he was believed to have "never blotted out a line." The implication is that Shakespeare produced flawless first drafts, never needing to revise or make corrections. This statement is surely a

product of Elizabethan hype; no one believes that Shakespeare wrote his prodigious body of work as a series of uncorrected first drafts.

All writers revise. **Revision** is the process of modifying what you have written so that it is more effective and economical. You can forgo revising only when time pressures keep you from it, such as when you are taking an essay examination that asks for more than you can deliver in the allotted time. In that situation, you must simply crank up your output and hope for the best. The rest of your writing experiences will require that you spend time carefully revising your work.

In this chapter, we concentrate on comprehensive issues that are sometimes called, collectively, "global" revision. (The following chapter focuses on editing sentences and words.) Global issues include unity, coherence, language level, tone, and the effectiveness of an essay's introduction, body, and conclusion. Being able to write dynamic sentences is a valuable ability; unfortunately, it is possible to write a paragraph or essay full of strong sentences that don't relate to one another and don't work together to develop the paragraph's or essay's controlling idea. Consider this example:

> Parker County's attempts to improve the quality of education are a failure. The county's history is full of such inept and misguided reform attempts. A fairly recent example was the attempt to change the county jail from a dilapidated, sadistic hellhole into a modern facility providing uniform, humane treatment for inmates. The result? We got a new jail, of course, but one that took sixteen months and $21 million more to build than had been projected, along with $5 million more in "repair" costs in its first year of existence. The same crew of undereducated guards is staffing this new facility, and the stories of inmate abuse have not abated. The education reform efforts have met a similar fate. Throwing money at the schools in poorer areas of the county has only helped principals fulfill their wish lists. As a result, Parkersville High School, arguably the worst in the county, now has a new scoreboard for its baseball field while students use ragged editions of textbooks and see a computer only by glimpsing one through a staff member's office door.

This paragraph does a fairly good job sentence by sentence, but what is its topic? Its first sentence indicates that the paragraph is about a county's failure to "improve" education. But then the writer shifts into a general rant against the county's incompetent managers, followed by a specific complaint about jail reform. Jails aren't usually the concern of a county school board. Then the writer comes back to education reform but is really on a different topic than the one suggested by the paragraph's first sentence. Attempts to equalize funding aren't the same as attempts to improve education. Finally, the example with which the writer concludes is effective in terms of the revised topic, but a closing comment would help put this example in context.

This paragraph needs global revision, yet the direction that the revision will take depends upon the writer's true purpose, and we can't be sure of that

Consider Your Options

When you write, how much revising do you normally do? (Be honest.) Has anyone ever pointed out that your writing process seems incomplete? In our experience, lack of revision is the main cause of weak writing at the college level.

purpose from reading this paragraph. Does the writer want to convince readers that the county's attempts at improving education have failed? Then the jail example has no place here, and the Parkersville High School section needs to be clarified and expanded. Is the writer's purpose to show that the county is run by incompetents? Then the topic sentence should be stated more generally to reflect that purpose.

When a student is writing an essay, he or she needs to think on many levels. Here are some of the more general cognitive concerns that a writer usually has:

1. Is my essay unified in terms of its thesis and development?
2. Is this paragraph (a) supporting the thesis and (b) unified and coherent in and of itself?
3. Does this sentence make sense?
4. This word clearly isn't right. Where are my dictionary and thesaurus?

It's difficult to keep all of these considerations balanced while writing and at the same time dealing with more fleeting concerns, such as the following:

"I really have only a couple of hours more that I can give to this."

"Jeez, this room is cold."

"What a time to start sneezing."

"Do I have to work tonight or not?"

"When are they going to call?"

Just as most writers need to pay attention to several different levels as they write, they need to review their drafts for different levels of problems as well. Therefore, to be effective, revision should take place in stages. In this chapter, we will offer practical approaches to the process of turning a workable first draft into a polished final draft, providing advice on soliciting and using peer comments, using word-processing software to revise, and addressing global concerns.

PEER RESPONSE AND REVIEW

A good way to approach revision is to ask for the opinions of your peers. Consulting another person or persons allows you to get past the "blinders" that all writers have, to one degree or another, regarding their own work. "Everyone needs an editor" is a statement that sounds like a simpleminded aphorism, but it is not. It is true. Why? One reason has to do with human nature and the need for self-esteem (It's mine! I wrote what I meant! Leave it alone!), but the full picture is not as obvious. Even professionals who are deeply involved with the mysteries of language—rewrite specialists and copy editors—report that they have trouble editing their own work.

Therefore, the reactions of your student colleagues can be an essential part of your revising process. As in any other potentially worthwhile activity, however, pitfalls lurk. The following are some guidelines to help you avoid wasting your peer response time or, even worse, incorporating changes into your writing that will actually damage it:

1. **Treat peer review seriously.** Meeting with your peers is not a time for getting together with friends, or finding someone to date, or discussing the new film opening this weekend. If your peer review time degenerates into socializing, you will have lost a valuable opportunity and gained the ire of both your instructor and the more serious members of your group.
2. **Take part.** Some students are shy, and some come from cultures in which group interaction is much more formal than the atmosphere typically found in a peer review session. If you are uncomfortable with the peer review process, remember that its rewards will outweigh its problems. Try to exploit this process, not shrink from it.
3. **Understand how groups operate.** Some people like to take charge (in current pop terminology, they are "alphas"); others ("betas") prefer to cooperate and get along. However, the desire to be in charge doesn't correspond to the ability to revise English prose. An alpha member may have the worst skills or judgment of the group; he or she may also be the one who wants to talk, not work.
4. **Be receptive to suggestions.** For the same reason that it is hard for writers to read their own work with a cold eye, most of us resist the help of others. Group review was not invented for the purpose of challenging your ego; therefore, listen to what your classmates tell you without reacting defensively. If, for example, you are working with a partner who marks twenty-four places that need improvement, do not take offense. Perhaps only twelve of the responses are actually valid; if so, your partner has done you a huge favor. And, as careful and particular as your partner might be, your instructor will be a much more stringent judge of your work.
5. **Use a checklist.** To make sure that you have covered all the important revision issues, use a checklist of standard questions (see page 82).
6. **Refer matters of grammar and punctuation to the authorities.** Suppose that you are a beta type, and your essay is being reviewed by the group's alpha person. "Aha!" he says. "I think this is a comma splice. In fact, I'm *sure* it is." Two other group members then read the sentence, and their responses are not helpful: "I'm not sure." "Beats me." Here is the sentence:

   Some scientists believe that viruses are immortal, whereas other researchers are finding ways to combat these destructive organisms.

   If you follow the alpha person's guidelines, here is the result:

   Some scientists believe that viruses are immortal; whereas, other researchers are finding ways to combat these destructive organisms.

   You've just changed a perfectly good complex sentence into a sentence with an error—a semicolon should not be used to join an independent and a dependent clause. And your "helpful reviewer" will not share in the harm

CLASSROOM HINT Reviewing these six cautionary statements in class is always worthwhile. You can also stress the fact that peer review gives the reader an audience other than the instructor. In most cases the chief task of such an audience is to evaluate and offer suggestions about development, logic, and clarity. Less reliable are peer comments about sentence structure, punctuation, and other editing concerns.

Consider Your Options

A sign of true maturity is the ability to listen to constructive criticism, not get upset, and then profit from the advice. Can you recall a situation in your life when you used constructive criticism as it was intended?

Peer Review Checklist

CLASSROOM HINT
Spending class time discussing each of these points is often a necessity.

Answer the following questions as you review your partner's draft:

1. Does the introduction provide sufficient and appropriate background and context?
2. Does the introduction include a clear thesis statement?
3. After you read the rest of the essay, reread the thesis statement. Is it supported by the rest of the essay? If not, should it be revised, or should one or more body paragraphs be revised?
4. Is the topic sentence of each body paragraph effective? If not, should it be revised, or should the rest of the paragraph be revised?
5. Are the topic sentences in the body paragraphs supported by specific and concrete evidence?
6. Is the conclusion an effective commentary on the essay, or does it merely repeat the thesis and summarize the essay or have other problems?
7. Overall, does the essay suffer from problems in any of the following areas?
   - Unity (in terms of the essay as a whole and each paragraph)
   - Coherence (in terms of the essay as a whole and each paragraph)
   - Language level (see Chapter 5)
   - Tone (see Chapter 5)

he caused. On questions about grammar, punctuation, and mechanics, consult your instructor or a grammar handbook.

One additional note: peer review sessions are not intended to be error-hunting sessions. Larger issues, such as organization and level of detail, should be dealt with here; finding specific grammatical or mechanical errors is a matter of editing and proofreading—*your* editing and proofreading.

Responding to Suggestions for Revision

When another person—a peer, a tutor, your instructor—has reviewed your draft and suggested changes, you are faced with a series of choices and decisions. Your relationship with your reviewer is not the same as that between a typesetter and a proofreader. In that relationship, the proofreader brings pages with specific corrections marked, and the typesetter is simply expected to follow the directions. If someone has gone over a draft for you, you will see specific corrections that you will want to make without delay, but you will also note suggestions, queries, and overview comments, all of which you will need to consider carefully before choosing which revisions to make.

MORE OPTIONS ONLINE
For more help with peer review, go to **www.mhhe.com/writingtoday**.

One Writer's Decisions

After Verlinda wrote the first draft of "A Very Secret Santa," she exchanged drafts with her partner, Daniel, and each reviewed the other's work. Here is Daniel's response to Verlinda's draft, followed by Verlinda's handwritten revision plan. Can you suggest any further changes?

CLASSROOM HINT Students can gain a great deal by reviewing Verlinda's revision on their own. On the other hand, her peer-reviewed draft is an excellent vehicle for class discussion.

Peer-Reviewed Draft

A Very Secret Santa

All my years growing up; Betty Wallace was my very best friend. I spent a lot of time at her house, she spent a lot of time at my house. Our parents were good friends. Each couple trusted the other implecitly. I grew to see Walter and Leona Wallace as uncle and aunt figures. [seems wordy]

Walter was more interesting [than what?], but not at first glance. An accountent, he seem to want to fit in. Walter dressed conservatively, which matched his features and size: a black man of middle height, a little over weight, rimless glasses and the only "daring" feature a very neatly trimmed mustache. His personality also seemed boring. He was quite, [wrong word] a bit shy, and not really sociable or pleasant. Given his choice, he would sit alone in his big lounge chair and smoke a pipe while watching T.V. Yet Walter Wallace, he [?] was the most charitable man I've ever met. [strengthen thesis]

I remember an example of Walter's secret side. It was before Christmas, years ago, Betty and I were ten years old and going shopping with Mr. and [wordy] Mrs Wallace at the mall. After Walter finaly found a parking space we noticed a comotion a few cars over. A young woman and her seven-year-old were trying to quiet down the three-year-old. He had been pulled from the last store visited without getting what he wanted. The mother looked entirely flustered and she was obviously quite poor, the little boy was screaming [Make two sentences] like he had been scalded. We walked toward the mall, listening to this squabble unfold behind us, suddenly Walter disappeared. Mrs. Wallace told us to keep walking, that Walter would catch up. When he did he said nothing.

I waited until Betty and I were alone to ask for an explanation. "He went back to give that woman some money", Betty explained, "He's done this a thousand times". [fix dialogue] (why tiny paragraph?)

At the Wallaces' home there was always six to ten dogs and cats. Strays knew where to go. Over the objections of Leona, Walter would take them in, carry them to the vet, pay for shots, nutering, and medicine, and keep them if he couldn't convince some one else to take them off his hands. As a child I remember loving the fact that the Wallace home was full of animals, but I don't think Leona Wallace shared my enjoyment. She didn't like dogs, and would freeze in midsentence if a cat jumped in her lap. Then launching the cat back towards the floor. abrupt

Christmastime is wonderful for kids, and it is one of my fondest memories'. My family and the Wallaces attended Trinity United Methodist, a mostly white church with a middle class population. The arrival of Santa Claus was a great event. Walter Wallace as Santa was a complete transformation from Walter Wallace as bespectacled, quiet taxadvisor. His voice and laughter booms through the church as he talks to his small "clients". Walter took his act on the road, at the area hospitals and the children's hospise. shift?

Did Walter Wallace have the proverbeal heart of gold? Or was he motivated by guilt—a successful man who is a success story and can't help looking back to a time when he was poor? Neither one. Walter helped young and old, black and white, human and nonhuman; only because he couldn't keep himself from doing so. Betty told me that her father was miserable, if he percieved that he had not done enough. She told me that Walter's activities caused signifigant friction in his marriage. But he would not be stopped. confusing

I feel that when people do something "nice" for another that their motives are not altogether altruistic - being nice makes the giver feel good about him or herself. In the case of Walter Wallace however the motive seems to have been more involuntary. Does this make Walter less admirable? I don't think so, I wish the world was full of men like him.

V: This is a good start. Walter sounds like a really good guy. Here are some problem areas you might went to look at, though:

1. *It's like you're writing to yourself. Why would your reader be interested in Walter?*
2. *I'm not sure what you're trying to accomplish here. Think about your thesis.*

3. In places, this doesn't hang together—more transitions?
4. I noticed a lot of specific stuff that we're not really supposed to mark.

You might want to drop by the Writing Center. Good Luck!

1. *Daniel's right—it's like I'm talking to myself. This doesn't flow.*
2. *Transitions will help my paragraphs. It's like they start at one point and then jump from sentence to sentence without much connection.*
3. *Read this aloud when revising.*
4. *Proofread—yes, the Writing Center could help.*

Using a Word Processor to Revise

If your assignment requires a typed essay and you prefer to work with a pen, eventually you will have to transfer your handwritten work to a computer file. If, however, you start your assignment on the computer—including your preliminary thoughts and your prewriting strategies—you will be able to exploit your computer's memory by building upon each previous step. Even if you realize that your first draft will need substantial revision, it's there for you to revise; you won't have to reinvent the wheel at each stage.

The following guidelines will help you as you revise your essay on a computer:

CLASSROOM HINT You need not discuss "Using a Word Processor to Revise" in class, especially if your time is limited. Just remind students to read this section carefully.

1. **Take advantage of the computer's ability to duplicate your draft.** In Chapter 2 we saw how a student sets up files for prewriting and drafting the third essay of the semester. All draft file names start with "E3." The student keys in a first draft, named E3A, then copies the file twice under new names: E3B and E3C. Now four files have been saved on the hard drive and on a backup disk. E3B is the file that the student will revise. As she revises E3B, the student marks any text that seems questionable, adds parenthetical comments, and suggests new wording, all by using boldface type. Why boldface? It is easy to see on the computer screen, and words and sentences in bold type can be easily changed or deleted in the final draft. After revising file E3B, the student has two choices: (1) merge E3B into E3C or (2) if the software permits, view E3C and E3B simultaneously. Recall that E3C is a duplicate of E3A. The student can now revise the first draft by using the revision notations in E3B. If anything goes wrong, the student still has a copy of the original first draft.

   This cautious approach costs very little time and no more money than the reckless method of continually revising the same file. Two major problems can occur when you work with only one file: (1) if you decide to go back to text used in a previous version, that text no longer exists and must be reconstructed, and (2) you may lose the single file due to some unthinkable misadventure. Caution is a virtue, especially when it is so little trouble and the downside is so great.

   Note: Many word processors allow you to make revisions in a different color font so that you can easily compare one draft with another.

2. **Use your printer frequently.** Print out your work at important moments, such as when you are finished working for the day or have completed a revision stage. It is easier to work on paper than on a computer screen, and you give yourself more insurance against misadventure by keeping paper copies.
3. **Learn the cut-and-paste (block) functions.** The great advantage of using word-processing software is that it gives you the ability to duplicate, move, and save text. You can change the order of your body paragraphs with a few mouse clicks, or you can go into the file containing your first draft or prewriting and "salvage" text that you have left behind.
4. **Listen to your text.** If your computer is equipped with Simpletext or a similar program and has speakers, you can "hear" your essay. Talking programs are very useful, especially for writers who are auditory learners.

REVISING ESSAYS

Essays can go wrong in a number of ways. For example, an essay can have a faulty structure, sound a false note, confuse the reader, or have an impact that you really never intended. Quite often, students are surprised by comments made by their instructors in the margins of their graded essays. "But I didn't mean it that way" is a frequent student response.

Remember that your instructor can't read your mind. Your intentions are, essentially, private. Your instructor's judgment of your work is based on the pieces of paper that you submit. We all know about good intentions and where they can lead.

As we have already pointed out, what happens between the time that you start planning an essay and the time that your instructor finishes reading it is a complicated process with many sometimes mysterious variables. For example, you can't control your instructor's reaction, nor is there any single "correct" response to a writing assignment. However, most of these variables *can* be controlled, and the revision process is the point at which you are in the best position to do so.

We'll begin by looking at general areas of concern, then tackle more specific problems. Remember that your ability to address these issues successfully can make the difference between an *A* essay and a *C* essay.

Checking for Unity

Does your essay address the ideas you have asserted in your thesis statement, or does it wander from idea to idea, like a moth flying near stadium lights? Remember that **unity** is closely connected to purpose. (See Chapter 3, page 68.) If you clearly understand your purpose for writing an essay, then unity is easier to achieve. For example, if your purpose is to convince the reader that real-estate developers are corrupting your local zoning commission, then a paragraph about the history of "old downtown" will probably be out of place.

Sometimes, however, students have an overly narrow view of unity. They are afraid to let *anything* appear in their essays that is not strictly related to the thesis. These students sometimes produce "tunnel vision" essays that read like product manuals or other rigidly focused forms of writing. However, skillful essay writers know that they have the option of introducing brief comparisons to related ideas, adding the occasional funny or ironic comment, and conveying a sense, generally, of the world around them. Their writing has a thematic texture that goes beyond their thesis. Effective writing is always a balancing act, with the writer constantly thinking thoughts such as the following:

> I love this paragraph, but have I gone too far this time? The rest of my essay is rather sober, but this part of the subject is always something that I've found ludicrous. Still. . . .

For an example of a student writer's work that reflects this kind of balance, see Sam Leininger's essay contrasting two types of moviegoers (Chapter 13, pages 415–417).

Achieving unity requires a series of judgment calls about what to keep and what to drop, decisions that you will have to make during the revision process. If any directive works uniformly, it's probably this one: if you err, err on the side of conservativism. In other words, is the potential reward worth risk that you're considering?

Improving Coherence

As you will recall from Chapter 3, a document that is **coherent** will (1) follow the direction implied by its thesis statement and (2) use effective transitions to help make connections between paragraphs. When you revise, you need to ask yourself if you have made all the relationships clear for your readers. Will they be able to read your essay straight through without having to reread some of the sections?

Coherence is closely related to the issue of audience. As a writer, you should be trying to write an essay that accommodates the needs of an adult reader. This is not a matter of keeping your text simple (using common words, simple sentences, and easy transitions). It is more an issue of being able to perceive a possible interpretation problem and taking steps to avoid confusion.

Chapter 3 provides strategies for achieving coherence at the paragraph level, including the use of transitional expressions, pronouns, repeated nouns and synonyms, and parallel structures. (See pages 71–74.) All four of these strategies are useful at the essay level as well. In addition, transitional sentences such as the following can help you clearly link a paragraph to the one that precedes or follows it:

> Although Buffalo's location on Lake Erie has been a blessing, the heavy industry that was attracted by its access to the cities on the Great Lakes and the abundant energy provided by Niagara Falls has also brought a curse: pollution.

The sentence refers back to the preceding paragraph about the advantages of Buffalo's location and, at the same time, prepares readers for the topic of the next paragraph.

Using the Appropriate Language Level

There are many ways to categorize language levels, but for our purposes let us concentrate on three types: informal, standard, and formal.

Informal English is conversational. In many ways, it reflects the diction of spoken English, of good friends talking to one another without worrying about being overheard. Because informal English is casual in tone and tends to include slang, it is usually not appropriate for college-level writing, although it may be suitable for a personal narrative. Developing and using a personal voice is important, but at the same time you must consider your audience; in the case of slang, which changes very quickly, your audience may not even know what your words mean.

Here is an example of a paragraph written in informal English:

> The downtown club scene must be real trouble for newcomers. There're more than twenty clubs and seventy bands coming and going, so who knows where to look for the good stuff. One thing is key: the choice bands don't hook up with the "nice" clubs. A rule of thumb: the cleaner the club and the higher the cover, the worse the act and the general scene. The "nice" places will be filled with burb types, along with the crews moving in and out. Downtown is like what Austin and Athens used to be: if you want the hot sound, find the grungy-looking crib.

Consider Your Options

- Which language level do you use most frequently? Can you recall an instance in which using an inappropriate language level caused you trouble?

Standard English avoids the casual tone and slang of informal English but also avoids the complex vocabulary and syntax of formal English. This paragraph is a good example of standard English:

> A few yards up the hill, I found a protected platform beneath a thick barrier of trees. The forest canopy deflected the wind, filtered the sunlight, and dispersed the rain into a fine mist. The green mosses and yellow-green lichens on the forest floor were spongy and comfortable. A roar in the canopy overhead reminded me that the storm still raged, but that was another world, far removed from my burrow within the rain forest. I sat in the mist with my back against a rock, watched the water drip off my parka, and relaxed. Then I pitched my tent and crowded inside to brew a hot cup of tea.
>
> —from Jon Turk, *Cold Oceans*

Formal English is the language of scholarly writing and applied technology. It avoids the personal voice and uses complex sentence structure and diction to achieve a tone of thoroughly objective discussion. Here is an example:

> The habitual reference to the emotions and processes of the poet's mind for the source of poetry altered drastically the established solutions to that basic problem of aesthetics, the discrepancy between the subject matter in poetry and the objects found in experience. According to the central tradition hitherto, poetry departs from fact principally because it reflects a nature which has been reassembled to make a composite beauty, or filtered to reveal a central form or the common denominator of a type, or in some fashion culled and ornamented for the greater delight of the reader. To the

romantic critic, on the other hand, though poetry may be ideal, what marks it off from fact is, primarily, that it incorporates objects of a sense which have already been acted on and transformed by the feelings of the poet.
—from M. H. Abrams, *The Mirror and the Lamp: Romantic Theory and the Critical Tradition*

You probably won't be expected to write at precisely the same language level in all of your essays. What is appropriate for one purpose may well be unsuitable for another. For example, as noted above, the personal narrative tends to employ informal language, whereas the analytical options—process, cause and effect, and classification—tend to require a language level closer to standard English or even formal English. For most of your college-level writing, your safest choice is standard English. For some writing assignments, however, you may need to move toward formal English.

Consider your purpose as you start revising a first draft. Is your language level appropriate for this purpose? If the language level seems generally adequate, then think about this possible problem: Are there some places where you've used language that clashes with the rest of your text? In other words, have you used a slang expression in, say, the fourth paragraph? If so, then this gaffe may lodge in the reader's memory. For example, we occasionally read otherwise sound essays and then come across a minor or mid-level obscenity, perhaps thrown in for effect. Such a usage is almost always inappropriate in academic writing, and this misjudgment truly stands out.

EXERCISE 4.1

The following passage is written in informal English. Working alone, revise the paragraphs so that they are more suitable for college-level work.

My favorite computer/music/video store gives me a load of problems at the same time. It's in the low-rent part of town, but that's the least of my worries. Great merchandise, scuzzy store, weird salesguys are the normal bill of fare.

I went there last Saturday to look at some new speakers. Walking past a pack of Netheads arguing about the latest monitor, I tripped over a gizmo that even I, good with computers, couldn't put a name to. In the stereo section I ran into the guy who would help my quest. He had obviously been hiding when the Dork Patrol made its latest sweep. But he knew a lot about sound systems. He found me the speakers I wanted. He dug up a rebate coupon from somewhere. He gave me enough info so that I wouldn't fry myself when I got home. And the price was right. So, what's to moan about?

EXERCISE 4.2

The following passage uses elevated language and syntax to describe a subject that would be better handled with standard English. Working with a partner or in a small group, revise it. Use a dictionary if needed.

Television serial comedies have reached their nadir. This reference is, of course, to the programs that display young people using the workplace for

EXERCISE 4.1 Responses will vary. Here is one possibility.

My favorite computer/music/video store gives me many problems at the same time. It is located in a poor neighborhood, but that is the least of its drawbacks. While the store offers quality merchandise, it is dirty and disorganized, and the sales representatives seem odd.

I went there last Saturday to look at new speakers. Walking past a few customers arguing about the latest modem, I tripped over an apparatus that even I, though I am familiar with computers, couldn't put a name to. In the stereo section, I met a man who could help me. He lacked personality, but he knew a lot about sound systems. He found me the speakers I wanted. He also found a rebate coupon from somewhere. He gave me enough information to set up my speakers correctly when I got home. Moreover, the price was right. I had nothing to complain about.

EXERCISE 4.2 Responses will vary. Here is one possibility.

Television serial comedies have reached their low point. The worst are the programs that display young people using the workplace for both legitimate work and romance. The result is an unfortunate mixture of unproductive work hours and chaotic personal lives.

Until now, workplace relationships, a natural issue, were less common on network broadcasts. The work environment was seen as the setting for comedy, not for romance. Today, young people on these shows seem to go to work only to wear the latest fashions and spend their time trying to attract members of the opposite sex, who are there for the same reasons.

both gainful employment and riotous romance. The result is an unfortunate admixture of unproductive work hours and chaotic personal lives.

Hitherto, workplace propinquity, an issue of some inevitability, was less of a staple on network broadcasts. To be sure, the work environment was seen as a source of humor, but not as a breeding ground. In current offerings, young people seem to attend work only to wear the latest accoutrements and spend their tenure trying to gain the amorous attention of other similarly attired and like-intentioned foragers. The results are ludicrous, pathetic, and forced.

Making Your Language More Concrete and Specific

Concrete language usually communicates your ideas and details more effectively than abstract language. Concrete language appeals to the senses: sight, hearing, taste, smell, and touch. Notice the strength of impact, interest, and precision that the sentences on the right have when compared to those on the left:

Abstract	Concrete
He often became envious of the success of others.	He often sneered at and cursed others who were successful.
My grandmother was affectionate.	My grandmother often kissed and hugged us.
The two candidates hated each other.	The two candidates scowled at each other.
We were uncomfortable in the overcrowded waiting room.	Our faces and hands became sweaty, and we had trouble breathing in the overcrowded waiting room.
The old man's fingers were arthritic.	The fingers of the old man's right hand were swollen, and they curled into a useless claw.

Remember, concrete language gives your readers a verbal portrait of what you are communicating and allows them to experience it in their imaginations. Abstract language simply tells readers something. In some contexts, however, abstract language is appropriate, as in the following example, excerpted from Lewis H. Lapham's "Who and What Is American?"

> We [Americans] protect the other person's liberty in the interest of protecting our own, and our virtues conform to the terms and conditions of an arduous and speculative journey.

Nevertheless, when you want to transmit your experience of a person, object, place, or problem, abstract language often leaves your readers with only a vague sense of what you mean. Even when student writing is unified, coherent, and pointed, it can be weakened by discussions that take place in the realm of the abstract—no concrete details support the student's assertions.

The following paragraph is a good example of writing that lacks specificity:

> During fall and spring registration, a place that students avoid and dread is the preliminary table. If their advising forms are complete, students can avoid this step. However, students who are forced to deal with the preliminary table will face general rudeness, incompetence, and delay.

This paragraph is not badly written, but it could be so much stronger if specific, concrete detail were included, as in the following revision:

> A careful student never goes to registration at Parker College without having his or her documents in order. Much like a hero trying to cross a European border in a World War II movie, it is worth one's health and future to have these documents in order. "Your papers, please?" is what I remember the monocled inspector demanding in those old films. At Parker's registration, students breathe a sigh of relief if they pass this stage. If not, they are directed to the dreaded preliminary table. Here members of the Records Department shuffle paper, lose forms, and stamp the wrong documents. My friend Heather once waited five minutes for the "registration specialist" to find her name in an alphabetized printout. "It was pathetic," Heather reported. "I can read upside-down, like most people, and I saw the man go past my name at least six times. But you don't want to anger these people." Another acquaintance, Jeff, waited for over a half hour. The person who was "helping" him got up and took his documents to a supervisor's office. Along the way, this nimrod got distracted and laid the documents down. Most of the delay, Jeff figured, was spent in finding the missing forms. The conclusion to be drawn? Avoid the preliminary desk if at all possible, for there be monsters.

As you revise your essay, look for places where specific, concrete details would make your ideas clearer for your audience.

Achieving Specificity

Notice that the items on the right are much more effective and clear than those on the left.

General	More Specific	Very Specific
book	novel	*The Scarlet Letter*
artwork	oil painting	Rembrandt's self-portrait
residence	house	three-bedroom ranch
exercise	aerobic exercise	jogging
motor vehicle	sports utility vehicle	Ford Explorer
restaurant	fast-food restaurant	McDonald's
evergreen	pine	Norwegian spruce
municipality	city	Los Angeles
boat	sailboat	schooner

EXERCISE 4.3 Responses vary. Some possibilities for Paragraph 1 follow:
1. Name specific stores, malls, and home-decorating warehouses.
2. Name specific products.
3. Describe a product that "has felt many hands."
4. Rethink and rewrite sentence 2.

Paragraph 2:
1. Name breeds of large dogs, mid-size dogs, and small dogs.
2. Describe the kind of exercise large and mid-size breeds need.
3. Relying on personal experience or observation, describe the behavior of a small dog with an "irritating disposition" and provide an example of a small dog's "irritating habits."

EXERCISE 4.3

Working alone, read the following paragraphs. Each lacks concrete, specific details that would make the writer's meaning clearer. Prepare a list of suggestions for each paragraph's writer to indicate where specific examples and support will help.

1. Shopping for home-decorating products is a lot of fun, but there are also pitfalls. The same products can vary in price by 100%. The worst offenders are, of course, mall stores. An item costing $40 at the mall may well be available for $20–$25 at the discount department stores or the "warehouse" home-decorating outfits. Deep sales at the mall don't really equalize matters either. A 40%-off sale sounds great, but the $40 item now costs $24, and the off-price outlet only needs a 10% sale to stay lower. A final problem is that many people seem to use the mall as a place to handle things, touching them almost compulsively. By the time the 40%-off sale takes place, the desired item has felt many hands, and this is not a picture that I find appealing.
2. Getting the right dog is a matter of getting the right sized dog. Large dogs need to live in the country or near a park. They may also eat upwards of a pound of food per day. Mid-size dogs can live inside a house, but most of them prefer the outdoors. Like large dogs, they need plenty of exercise. Small dogs are better off inside houses or apartments, but many small dogs have irritating dispositions and habits. Whatever the case, let the size of your home be the first factor in deciding what type of dog to acquire.

Finding the Right Tone

Your **tone** is your essay's attitude toward your subject. Should your essay's tone be angry, calm, impassioned, or joyful? Usually, your rhetorical option, your purpose, and your subject matter will help determine the appropriate tone of a final draft. A humorous tone may well be appropriate for a narrative essay about misinterpreted directions, but it is hard to see how a similarly humorous tone would work in an essay about the lives of terminally ill children.

Another issue is consistency of tone. Does your essay start off with an edge of anger but then end with a completely different tone? If so, why? Examine your purpose again; then try to tell where and why the tone of your essay changed.

Checking Your Introductory Paragraphs and Thesis

Remember that your introduction should (1) establish a context for your essay and (2) include a thesis statement that both informs your reader of the essay's direction and expresses the essay's controlling idea. Read your draft's introduction to make sure that it provides the proper context. Students frequently err by doing too little or too much here, either writing a huge explanation for their essay that threatens to dwarf the essay itself or a tiny introduction: "Last summer I moved to a new apartment with no help. I'll never forget that day." (Chapter 3, pages 52–55, provides a list of ways to introduce an essay.)

Next, check your thesis statement against the body of your draft. Read your thesis, then each topic sentence. Does your thesis accurately reflect your essay's content, or did your essay take a new direction during the writing process? If the latter is true, do you need to revise your thesis statement so that it reflects this change in approach? Or, as we discuss in the next section, do you need to revise body paragraphs to bring them back into line with your controlling idea and the purpose implied in your thesis?

Checking Your Topic Sentences and Body Paragraphs

Your thesis statement promises the reader that your essay will follow a specific approach. When you read your first draft, do the essay's body paragraphs deliver on this promise? Or do they begin to deliver and then change course or seem to weaken?

If there is a conflict or weakness, many students are tempted to go back to the introduction and modify the thesis. After all, it's easier to rewrite the thesis than to rewrite a whole paragraph or two. However, revising the thesis isn't always the best approach. If the body of your essay has lost its direction or doesn't seem to fulfill the promise of your thesis, then patching the thesis statement won't fix the problem. You will need to revise the body so that it corresponds to your purpose.

Revising for Effective Topic Sentences

Pay close attention to the topic sentences of your body paragraphs if you find a unity problem in the body of your essay. Frequently, a key to your problem can be found here. Does each topic sentence support your thesis, or does one or more of them wander off in a different direction? If so, ask yourself if you can revise them to fix the problem or if you need to delete and replace the paragraph.

Even if the topic sentences support the thesis, you also need to make sure that they are strong topic sentences that work with the rest of the paragraph. Just as a thesis statement controls an essay, a topic sentence controls a paragraph. Sometimes, a topic sentence is too general, providing a weak focus. Other times, a topic sentence can be misleading, promising one type of development while the paragraph actually develops in new, unexplained directions. And when the topic sentence appears at the end of the paragraph as a summary of the paragraph's ideas, the summary may not adequately reflect the paragraph that it is concluding.

EXERCISE 4.4

Each of the following paragraphs has a faulty topic sentence. Working alone, read the paragraph and then replace the topic sentence with a more effective one.

1. TV weather forecasters make inaccurate judgments about the weather. These "specialists" are upbeat in any situation except for the truly catastrophic. A

EXERCISE 4.4 Responses will vary. Some possibilities follow:
1. Unfortunately, TV weather forecasters pander to their audiences' desires rather than provide clear and important insights about the weather.
2. Shoplifting is becoming child's play.

case in point: last July, our area went the entire month without rain. Both the days and nights were extremely hot. But each morning and evening, the local forecasters would chirp on about the beautiful day we were about to have, when a more mature judgment would have been to concentrate on the need for rain. However, Mr. or Ms. Tallhair is just giving us what surveys tell TV consultants that we really want: happy weather. Commercial television is a business, and I suppose that in one sense we shouldn't blame these "forecasters" for fulfilling our stated needs.

2. A sixteen-year-old boy wanders through Landon Department Store. He finally comes to the music department and spends almost an hour looking through the compact discs. Eventually, he goes to a cash register and pays $12 for a CD, takes his purchase, and leaves the store. But although he has paid for one CD, he has shoplifted three more, hidden in his backpack. Shoplifting is a problem that must be stopped.

Revising for Stronger Body Paragraphs

Just as you need to check your essay as a whole for unity and coherence, you should check each of your body paragraphs to make sure that your ideas all relate to the topic sentence and that a reader can follow your ideas without having to double back. Delete any sentences that do not support your topic sentence. Add transitional expressions and use parallelism to help readers follow your ideas. (For help with improving a paragraph's coherence, including a list of transitional expressions, see pages 70–74.) Finally, as you read each paragraph, look for opportunities to add the specific, concrete details that will make your essay clearer and more forceful.

EXERCISE 4.5

EXERCISE 4.5
1. The second, third, sixth, seventh, and eighth sentences have strayed from the point.
2. The third, eleventh, and twelfth sentences have strayed from the point.

Working alone, read the following paragraphs. Underline sentences that have strayed from the point.

1. Students who disrupt college classes should be removed from those classes. My major will be economics, and I'm taking the intro economics courses as well as finishing up my general-ed courses. Three of these courses are in Ryan Hall. In every one of my classes this semester there is at least one clown who detracts from the lecture or discussion by calling attention to himself. In fact, the same clown is in two of my classes—Renaissance humanities and macroeconomics. These two aren't the best anyway. The humanities instructor is a complete bore who reads from the textbook. The economics professor mumbles while he is facing the board and trying to clarify his shaky graphs. The clown sits and talks to his friends and laughs at anything unexpected coming from either instructor. He seems to have learned how to approach a college lecture by watching too many episodes of *Mystery Science Theater 3000.* I dream that someday a large campus security officer will loom up behind him and take him away. He'll never be seen again, of course, and this fact will help dissuade future clowns from making the same mistake.

2. My uncle Roy is an example of someone who has turned his life around. Up until the time that he was about twenty-five years old, Uncle Roy

was hell on wheels. He was also a champion bowler, once winning five tournaments in six weeks. Two things happened to Roy in his twenty-sixth year. One was that he nearly died while riding in a car driven by a drunk driver. The car hit a bridge abutment, and Uncle Roy, who was also drunk, was the only survivor. The second event was Roy's meeting my aunt Linda, a divorcée with a child. Linda told Roy that his wild days were over, that she'd already run off one husband for drinking and didn't intend to do so again. Roy married Aunt Linda and became a family man. He is devoted to his adopted daughter, Laura. Laura was born virtually deaf and hears only with very strong hearing aids and lipreading. She attends a regular school, though, and is very well adjusted. At the urging of Aunt Linda, Roy went to college part time for several years. Today he is a cost accountant, a change that must come as a shock to his old rounder buddies—those who still survive.

EXERCISE 4.6

Working with a partner or in a small group, read the following paragraphs, and make any changes that will improve coherence. (For suggestions on how to improve a paragraph's coherence, see pages 70–74 in Chapter 3.)

1. Many people these days seem desperate to produce children. These people can spend a fortune on "pre-pregnancy" treatments: fertility testing, genetic testing, artificial fertilization. If successful, these people then produce a child. The costs of raising and to educate a child are immense. The costs can average a half million dollars per child. The costs are prohibitive. Personal pressure, family pressure, and pressure from society all work together to ensure that people continue to want babies.
2. Our entertainment options today are vastly different from the opportunities for entertainment before World War II. In the 1930s, the standard picture was of families sitting in the living room listening to the huge radios or record players of the time. Or perhaps the family would go to a live concert, or perhaps a play was being performed. Modern families have radio, television is available, computer games and the Internet are popular. Modern families don't have to go to a performance to be entertained. Modern families can have the entertainment come to them. Pay-per-view movies can be ordered, and premium sporting events can be ordered. Modern families have a wealth of entertainment options.

EXERCISE 4.6 Responses will vary. Possible revisions follow:

A. Many people these days . . . children. They can spend a fortune. . . . If successful, they then produce a child. However, the costs of raising and educating a child are immense. They can average . . . per child. As such they are often prohibitive. Nonetheless, personal pressure. . . .

B. Our entertainment options today . . . before World War II. In the 1930s, families often sat in the living room during the evening listening. . . . perhaps the family would go to a live concert or to a play. Modern families have radio, television, computer games, and the Internet. They don't have to go . . . to be entertained. In fact, the entertainment comes to them. They can order pay-per-view movies or premium sporting events. In short, modern families. . . .

Checking Your Conclusion

Finally, ask these questions about your conclusion:

1. Does this paragraph appear very brief when compared to the other paragraphs in my essay?
2. Is the conclusion a simple summary of my essay?
3. Have I brought up any new topics here that will divert my reader from the main idea of the essay that he or she has just read?

4. Have I included a self-conscious reference to my essay ("In this essay I have shown . . .")?

If your answer to any of these questions is yes, then you need to revise your conclusion. (For ways to conclude an essay, see Chapter 3, pages 60–63.) Students sometimes forget a very basic fact: normally, the conclusion is the last part of the essay that an instructor reads before determining a grade. An otherwise strong essay with a weak or confusing conclusion has made its mistake in the wrong place. It's as if you met a new person, made a satisfactory first impression, had a positive conversation, and then muttered an obscure thought while parting.

EXERCISE 4.7

EXERCISE 4.7 Responses will vary.

At the end of Chapter 2, you were asked to prepare, prewrite, and draft a response to one of the topics on page 49. (If you haven't completed this assignment yet, do so now.) Find and revise this draft, using the techniques discussed in this section. Then exchange drafts with a partner and review (1) the first draft and (2) your partner's suggested changes to his or her essay. Use the checklist questions on page 82 to guide your review. What else can you suggest that will improve your partner's revision?

MORE OPTIONS ONLINE For more information about revision checklists, go to **www.mhhe.com/writingtoday**.

Writing an Effective Title

At this point, the structure of your essay is in place, so it's time to give your essay a title. The following guidelines explain your options:

1. Avoid using a vague or an overly general title:

   My Adventure   Aunt Rita's Greenhouse

   Such titles sound juvenile and tell your reader very little.

2. Avoid a strained and overly specific title:

   The Problem Caused by Feral Cats and What the Current Proposal (AR-1789) Before the Sparks County Commission Can Do to Solve It

3. Use a title suitable to your purpose. Narratives and descriptions frequently have fairly short titles primarily designed to entice the reader:

   The Mystery of Spring Water   Jason's Revenge

   Remember the title of Verlinda's essay: "A Very Secret Santa." It is both accurate, meaning that it reflects the essay as a whole, and interesting.

   In the case of more analytical essays, however, titles need to be more informative. Consider using a colon to separate the main part of a title from its descriptive second part. "How to Wax a Car" is a factual (and probably accurate) but boring title. How about "Waxing a Car: Three Easy Steps"? "The Modern Root Canal" is off-putting, to say the least. How about "The Modern Root Canal: Less Pain, Less Time"? This title would interest readers, not repel them.

Completing Your Essay on a Computer

If you are using a computer to write your essay, at this point you should have your latest draft on a backup disk and also on the hard drive, if possible. You should also have a paper copy of the draft with handwritten revision comments on it. Now you are ready to finish your essay by revising your existing file. The following guidelines will help:

1. Check your existing electronic draft for any areas that are highlighted or marked in boldface. Also check for any annotations or comments that you may have inserted.
2. Make your revisions from paper to screen. Once you are satisfied that you have finished this step, save and print out the corrected version. Now check this printout against the paper source; it's easy to miss corrections when revising on computer.
3. After you have made your last correction, print out a paper copy and read it again. This is the proofreading stage, in which you try to find the last few errors. (For help with proofreading, see Chapter 5.)
4. Run the spell-checker. If your computer has a grammar-checking program, you might use this as well. You should not *rely* on either one, however. Such software programs aren't perfect. For example, a spell-checker can't distinguish among *their, there,* and *they're*. A grammar checker might highlight sentences that have no errors but seem too long, according to the software's programming. Remember that the quality of the essay is your responsibility.
5. Read your essay aloud. (If your computer has the appropriate software, let your computer read your essay back to you.) *Listen* for problems that you might not *see* when reading silently. At this stage, you can catch awkward phrasings and unintentional rhymes.
6. When preparing your essay for its final printing, check your assignment one last time. Is there any requirement that you missed or forgot? Does the instructor include information about how he or she wants your typed essay to be formatted? Now is the time to confirm that your response meets the physical demands of the assignment.
7. Use a standard typeface of easily readable size, and double-space your printout. One of the great advantages of the computer is that it allows you to determine font, point size, and line spacing, so is it any wonder that composition instructors get angry when they receive a paper in ten-point type, single-spaced? Use a nondisplay font—the older, conservative fonts such as Times Roman, Courier, Garamond, Goudy, and Palatino will work well. Use 12-point type unless your instructor specifies differently. Don't use a cursive font, all-capital letters, or any other formatting that will distract your reader. Use one-inch margins, and don't crowd your page.
8. After you have printed out the final draft of your essay, save your work once again to two different places, in case disaster strikes. Also, consider keeping an "electronic portfolio": your entire semester's work on a backup disk. You never know when you might need a file from the disk, and it is often useful to be able to look back over your semester's work and see how far you've progressed.

4. Do not add extra formatting to your title (extra quotation marks, bold type, italic type, underlining, or all-capital letters). Center it, and capitalize its important words. (For more on capitalization, consult a grammar handbook.)

To the Losers Go the Rest

Using the Internet

MORE OPTIONS ONLINE
You can access the Web sites listed in "Using the Internet" by going to **www.mhhe.com/writingtoday**.

Go to these Web sites to find more tips, techniques, and insights on revising essays:

The UVic Writer's Guide

The section titled "Writing Your Essay: Getting It Down" offers suggestions on writing and revising first drafts and creating effective introductions and conclusions. Other advice covers writing well-developed, coherent body paragraphs that relate to the essay's thesis: **http://www.web.uvic.ca/wguide**.

The Write Place Catalogue

Maintained by St. Cloud University, this site provides advice on organization and coherence in paragraphs and essays. Transitions and thesis statements receive special coverage. You can also find information on writing essay introductions and conclusions: **http://leo.stcloudstate.edu/catalogue.html**.

CHAPTER 5

REFINING YOUR ESSAY: EDITING AND PROOFREADING

All experienced writers edit and proofread their work, and learning to do so will only improve your college-level writing. Your writing instructor, along with your other instructors, is an expert reader. Such readers are impatient with sloppy, wasteful writing: twelve words used when six would suffice; "weasel words," which are terms used in an attempt to avoid speaking plainly;

and euphemisms, terms constructed to avoid the painful facts of human existence and/or the responsibilities of the person controlling the situation.

In addition, an expert reader—and any other reader, for that matter—hates being made to squint. "Squinting" is an expression normally used to describe poorly placed modifiers, but the idea can be applied more generally. You make your reader squint when he or she has to read a sentence or larger passage more than once. Yes, it is possible that your reader has simply misread your passage (it happens to the best of us), and it is possible that your reader has decided to go back and reread your text because it is wonderful. In general, however, writing that needs to be read more than once is simply unclear, ambiguous, or without a controlling focus. Effective writers make sure that their readers can comprehend their meaning in one attempt.

Finally, learning to edit and proofread will help you in the competitive environment of higher education. You are a smart person pitted against other smart people. Your instructors will inevitably compare your work with that of your classmates. Be assured that the best writers in all of your classes will be taking the time to refine their work by editing and proofreading.

This chapter concentrates on revising sentences and words. We discuss here the problems that afflict most English prose, along with ways to fix these problems. If you need additional help with the topics covered in this chapter, consult a grammar handbook. Most handbooks contain extensive treatment of these grammatical issues.

MORE OPTIONS ONLINE
For more help with the topics in this chapter, go to **www.mhhe.com/writingtoday**.

COMBINING SENTENCES

The Internet is a new world. It is an exciting world. This world contains many possibilities. One possibility is research. Another possibility is shopping. Another possibility is investing. Students can research topics from home. They don't have to go to a library. Shoppers can buy products. They don't have to go to a store. Investors can buy mutual funds directly. They don't have to call a broker. The Internet is a major convenience.

CLASSROOM HINT
Reading this paragraph aloud or asking a student to do so usually brings the point home.

As the passage suggests, you can write English prose in single-clause sentences, with each sentence containing a subject and verb and expressing a single idea. These are called **simple sentences**, the most basic type. However, this approach has two major limitations:

1. The resulting text sounds immature, as if written by a child.
2. The text is inefficient—too many words and too much space are wasted when you use a sentence for each thought.

Sentence combining allows writers to create mature, economical text by merging connected ideas and showing their relationships to one another. In this section, we'll look at two methods of combining sentences:

1. Merging and submerging
2. Coordinating and subordinating

Merging and Submerging Related Ideas

Merging

The most basic way to combine sentences is to merge parallel ideas:

ORIGINAL **The Internet is a new world. It is an exciting world.**

REVISED **The Internet is a new, exciting world.**

Note that the unnecessary words in the second original sentence have been deleted in the revised version.

ORIGINAL **The Civic Center is old. It is run-down. It is hazardous.**

REVISED **The Civic Center is old, run-down, and hazardous.**

Merging the ideas of one or more sentences with the ideas of another sentence is a powerful revision method. Note how this choppy passage can be revised to read more smoothly:

ORIGINAL **The Parker Hotel was built in 1911. It was once a resort hotel. Time passed by. The hotel is now a collection of apartments. These apartments are used by senior citizens.**

REVISED **The Parker Hotel, built in 1911 and once regarded as a resort, now provides apartments for senior citizens.**

Submerging

There are five basic ways to join sentences by submerging:

CLASSROOM HINT Remind students that when they submerge ideas, they subordinate one idea to another. In other words, they make one idea less important than another. If necessary, supplement these examples with a few taken from your own student papers or from McGraw-Hill's *Catalyst*.

1. **Turn one of the sentences into a relative clause.** A **relative clause** has a subject and verb and starts with *who, whom, whose, that,* or *which.* Relative clauses modify nouns. Note the following examples:

   ORIGINAL **There is the car. I saw it near the elementary school yesterday.**

   REVISED **There is the car that I saw near the elementary school yesterday.**

   ORIGINAL **Atlanta is the capital of Georgia. It is located in the northern half of the state.**

   REVISED **Atlanta, which is the capital of Georgia, is located in the northern half of the state.**

   Notice the distinction between *that* and *which. That* is used to begin **essential clauses,** which are clauses that define. ("There's the car." "Which car?" "The car that I saw near the elementary school yesterday.") Do not use commas to set off essential clauses. On the other hand, **nonessential clauses** offer extra, explanatory information, not defining information. Atlanta is a well-known city and doesn't need to be defined; that it is the capital of Georgia is extra information. Use *which,* along with a comma or commas, for nonessential clauses.

   Here is an easy way to remember the essential/nonessential distinction. Note the following phrases:

   my sister Mary
   my sister, Mary

The writer of the first phrase has more than one sister. The name *Mary* answers the question "Which sister?" The writer of the second phrase has only one sister. The comma precedes the name, which is extra, explanatory information.

You will sometimes see *which* used in place of *that* at the beginning of an essential clause:

ACCEPTABLE **There is the car which I saw near the elementary school yesterday.**

However, the reverse won't work. In a nonessential relative clause, a comma + *that* can't be substituted for a comma + *which:*

INCORRECT **Atlanta, that is the capital of Georgia, is located in the northern half of the state.**

That and *which* are used to refer to everything except people and named animals. *Who* is used for these two groups. When you are forming an essential relative clause beginning with *who,* do not use a comma or commas; for a nonessential clause, use a comma or commas:

NONESSENTIAL MODIFIER **I'm going back home to help my father, who is moving to an apartment.**

Each human can have only one father.

ESSENTIAL MODIFIER **Ed is my cousin who once served in the legislature.**

Each person can have many cousins. The relative clause *who once served in the legislature* answers the question "Which cousin?"

CLASSROOM HINT
Essential clauses are also called restrictive clauses. You can find more on essential and nonessential modifiers in *Catalyst*.

2. **Change one sentence into an appositive.** An **appositive** is a word or phrase used to modify an adjacent noun. As with relative clauses, you must use a comma or commas to set off an appositive if it provides extra information:

Atlanta, the capital of Georgia, is located in the northern half of the state.

CLASSROOM HINT
You can supplement these examples with samples from your own students' writing or with those taken from *Catalyst*.

In this sentence, the appositive functions in much the same way as does the relative clause in the example on page 101, but *which is* has been deleted, turning the clause into a phrase.

Appositives can also function as essential modifiers:

My sister Mary is here for the weekend.

No commas are used here because the writer has more than one sister; *Mary* answers the question "Which sister?"

3. **Change one sentence into a participial phrase. Participles** are adjectives formed from verbs; they end in *-ed, -d, -t, -en,* or *-ing.* Note the following sentences:

Butter is derived from milk. Butter is high in fat content.

We can combine these two short sentences by changing the first sentence into a phrase beginning with the participle *derived:*

Butter, derived from milk, is high in fat content.

4. **Turn one sentence into a prepositional phrase.** A **prepositional phrase** begins with a preposition such as *for, at, to, in, by,* or *on.*

ORIGINAL **The hitter wished for good luck. He tapped the plate three times with the end of the bat.**

REVISED **For good luck, the hitter tapped the plate three times with the end of the bat.**

For good luck is a prepositional phrase beginning with the preposition *for.*

5. **Change one sentence into an absolute phrase.** An **absolute phrase** modifies the entire sentence.

ORIGINAL **The car's front tires were flat. The car limped along the shoulder of the road.**

REVISED **Its front tires flat, the car limped along the shoulder of the road.**

EXERCISE 5.1 Responses will vary. The following are suggestions:
1. The search engine, which was slow today, completed the Web search in seven minutes.
2. That's Angela, my cousin's wife.
3. Tomatoes, once thought to be poisonous, are now enjoyed by millions of people.
4. *Manhunter,* which is based on Thomas Harris's *Red Dragon,* is the "prequel" to *Silence of the Lambs.*
5. Sunshine came through the open window, keeping me awake.
6. There's the skeleton of the snake that was run over last month.
7. The death of Ralph Miley, who was mayor for twelve years, came as a shock.
8. Not having financial support, Jason's new company was doomed.

EXERCISE 5.2 Responses will vary. The following are suggestions:
1. Hepatitis C, a very serious disease, affects the liver. Many people who suffer from the disease may not know they have it. Without medical treatment, they can become very ill and even die. So far, scientists have been unsuccessful in finding a cure.

EXERCISE 5.1

Working alone, combine the following sentence pairs by using any of the methods discussed in this section.

1. The search engine was slow today. The Web search took seven minutes.
2. That's Angela. She is my cousin's wife.
3. Tomatoes were once thought to be poisonous. They are now enjoyed by millions of people.
4. The movie *Manhunter* is based on Thomas Harris's novel *Red Dragon.* The movie is the "prequel" to *Silence of the Lambs.*
5. Sunshine came through the open window. The sunshine kept me awake.
6. There's the skeleton of the snake. The snake was run over last month.
7. The death of Ralph Miley came as a shock. He was mayor for twelve years.
8. Jason's new company didn't have outside financial support. The new company was doomed.

EXERCISE 5.2

Working with a partner or in a small group, revise the following paragraphs, which are strings of related sentences. Combine the sentences by merging or submerging related ideas.

1. Hepatitis C is a very serious disease. It affects the liver. Many people have it. However, they may not know that they have it. Some victims may not get medical treatment. If so, these people could become very ill and die. Scientists are working on a cure. So far, they have been unsuccessful.

2. The storm caused a great deal of damage, mainly in the eastern part of the city. Trees and power lines were knocked down. The torrential rain lasted for three hours. However, the wind, which approached tornado strength, did most of the damage. Luckily, the storm hit at 3:00 a.m., when most people were not out in the open or driving their cars.

2. The storm caused a great deal of damage. The damage was mainly in the eastern part of the city. Trees were knocked down. Power lines were also knocked down. The rain lasted for three hours. It was torrential. However, the wind did most of the damage. It approached tornado strength. Luckily, the storm hit at 3:00 a.m. Very few people were out in the open or driving in their cars.

Coordinating and Subordinating Related Ideas

The preceding section illustrates techniques that you can use to combine sentences and make your writing more efficient, deleting unnecessary words and making your point as succinctly as possible. **Coordination** and **subordination** are additional sentence-combining techniques designed to connect sentences of roughly equal weight. You do not use these techniques for economy but, instead, to show the connection between two related sentences. When you combine sentences by using coordination and subordination, you can indicate both obvious and subtle connections, control your level of formality, and produce sentences appropriate for your purpose.

Conjunctions, words used to join words, phrases, and sentences, come in four varieties. Of the four types, two are related: **coordinating conjunctions** and **conjunctive adverbs/transitional expressions.** (See the chart on pages 105 and 106.) These two types are used to join **independent clauses**, word groups that can stand alone as sentences, in order to form **compound sentences**, sentences made up of more than one independent clause. For example,

ORIGINAL **Alice enjoyed spending time in online chat rooms. Lisa had never even been on the Internet.**

REVISED **Alice enjoyed spending time in online chat rooms, but** Lisa had **never even been on the Internet.**

Here the two sentences are joined with the coordinating conjunction *but,* preceded by a comma, to form a compound sentence. Notice how a similar effect can be achieved by using a conjunctive adverb:

> Alice enjoyed spending time in online chat rooms; **however,** Lisa had never even been on the Internet.

When you use *however* or any other conjunctive adverb/transitional expression to join two sentences, place a semicolon before it and a comma after it. Note that this sentence has a more formal tone than the compound sentence formed by using *but.*

Notice how another type of sentence connector, the **subordinating conjunction**, can be used to join two sentences:

ORIGINAL **Lisa had an unreasonable fear of the Internet. She had read stories about cybercrime.**

REVISED **Lisa had an unreasonable fear of the Internet because she had read stories about cybercrime.**

OR **Because** Lisa had read stories about cybercrime, she had an unreasonable fear of the Internet.

The revised sentence is not a compound sentence; it is called a **complex sentence** because it has one independent clause and one dependent clause. What happened to the other independent clause? The addition of the subordinating conjunction *because* made it dependent. As the name suggests, this type of word is used to *subordinate* an independent clause—to make it lower in rank, so to speak. It has become a **dependent clause**, one that cannot stand alone as a sentence.

The following chart lists coordinating conjunctions, conjunctive adverbs/transitional expressions, and subordinating conjunctions.

CLASSROOM HINT
Bringing these lists to students' attention in class is worthwhile.

SENTENCE CONNECTORS

Coordinating Conjunctions	Conjunctive Adverbs/ Transitional Expressions	Subordinating Conjunctions
and	accordingly	after
but	additionally	although
for	also	as
nor	as an illustration	because
or	at the same time	before
so	besides	even if
yet	certainly	even though
	consequently	if
	conversely	in order that
	finally	once
	for example	provided that
	for instance	rather than
	furthermore	since
	hence	so that
	however	so (that)
	in addition	than
	in brief	that
	in conclusion	though
	in contrast	unless
	in short	until
	in summary	when
	in the same way	whenever
	indeed	where
	instead	whereas
	likewise	wherever
	meanwhile	whether
	moreover	while
	namely	
	nevertheless	

SENTENCE CONNECTORS (*continued*)		
Coordinating Conjunctions	**Conjunctive Adverbs/ Transitional Expressions**	**Subordinating Conjunctions**
	next	
	nonetheless	
	of course	
	on the other hand	
	otherwise	
	similarly	
	specifically	
	still	
	subsequently	
	then	
	therefore	
	thus	
	to be sure	
	(Note that other adverbs can also function as conjunctives: *clearly, slowly, eagerly,* and so on.)	

The fourth type, correlative conjunctions, is discussed on page 111.

Using Coordinating Conjunctions

The words in the first column on page 105 are the seven coordinating conjunctions. Small words of either two or three letters, they are very old members of the English language. When you use them as sentence connectors, be aware of these key issues:

1. Don't place a comma in front of every *and* or *but* that you write. Besides being used with a comma to form compound sentences, these seven words can also be used as simple conjunctions, joining two nouns, verbs, or phrases. In both of the following sentences, the conjunction is not used as a sentence connector but as a simple conjunction—hence, no preceding comma is needed:

   Miguel **and** Angelica are here.

   We traveled to Tampa **but** not to Clearwater.

   For a complete discussion of comma usage, consult a grammar handbook.

CLASSROOM HINT See *Catalyst*, for more about comma splices and fused sentences.

2. By using a coordinating conjunction with a comma to form a compound sentence, you can avoid the major errors known as the **comma splice** and the **fused sentence.** The following sentence is an example of a comma splice:

   COMMA SPLICE **Julia reminded Eddie to set his alarm clock, he still overslept.**

   In a compound sentence, a comma can separate the two independent clauses only if a coordinating conjunction follows the comma:

CORRECT **Julia reminded Eddie to set his alarm clock, yet he still overslept.**

The fused sentence is the comma splice made worse. Here, even the comma is missing:

FUSED SENTENCE **Julia reminded Eddie to set his alarm clock he still overslept.**

CORRECT **Julia reminded Eddie to set his alarm clock, yet he still overslept.**

3. The coordinating conjunctions are useful little words, but as a category they have some limitations. Although there are seven coordinating conjunctions, two of them—*but* and *yet*—are synonyms and are virtually interchangeable. Also, two more of the coordinating conjunctions—*or* and *for*—are not used very often to connect independent clauses. Note this sentence:

   We will drive to St. Louis, **or** we will fly to Kansas City.

   This construction, although a clear example of a compound pattern, is probably not the way that most writers would express this idea. Normally, a reader would expect a more concise pattern:

   We will either drive to St. Louis or fly to Kansas City.

   If you were to use only coordinating conjunctions to connect sentences, you would show that you have mastered a punctuation strategy, avoid comma splices and fused sentences, and communicate in a common, centuries-old sentence pattern. However, you would also severely restrict your ability to communicate precisely. Look at the much longer list of words and phrases in the second column of the sentence connector chart on pages 105 and 106. These connectors, discussed in the following section, cover a far wider range of meanings than do the seven coordinating conjunctions.

Using Conjunctive Adverbs/Transitional Expressions

The conjunctive adverbs and the words and phrases collectively known as **transitional expressions** are the other group of sentence connectors that you can use to form compound sentences.

These words and phrases are extremely useful, provided that you choose carefully and keep the following issues in mind:

1. The semicolon-before, comma-after pattern holds for all these connectors except one, the last in the following group of sentences:

   Trouble awaits applicants who put off filing; **however,** the deadline is still two weeks away. Anyone who needs help with the paperwork can call on a number of resources; **for instance,** there is a company office not two blocks from here. Most people call this office first; **then** they can get all the assistance they need.

   Note that in these examples, *then* is the only connector not followed by a comma. All the other words and phrases in the second column of the chart on pages 105 and 106 follow the semicolon-connector-comma pattern.

2. Unlike coordinating conjunctions, conjunctive adverbs/transitional expressions can appear in different positions within a clause:

   Maria was ready; **however,** Eduardo was not.

   Maria was ready; Eduardo, **however,** was not.

   Maria was ready; Eduardo was not, **however.**

   The semicolon is the boundary point between the two independent clauses, but the conjunctive adverb *however* can be placed at the beginning, in the middle, or at the end of the second independent clause.

   Is there a preferred position? You should normally place the connector at the beginning, for two reasons. In the first sentence, *however* doesn't break up the logical relation between the subject (*Eduardo*) and the verb (*was*). Writers sometimes have a habit of placing the conjunctive adverb between the subject and the verb on the erroneous assumption that this placement makes their sentence sound more formal. In the following sentence, notice how the conjunctive adverb gets in the way of the reader's progress from subject to verb:

   Eduardo, **however,** was not.

   As well, when the connector appears in the beginning position, the reader sees how the two independent clauses are related before reading the second clause. In the third example, the reader doesn't get to the negative transition until the very end: "Eduardo was not, however." The word *however* doesn't appear when the reader really needs it (at the beginning).

3. The semicolon can stand alone without a connector. Think of the semicolon as an internal period: it brings the sentence to a stop but, unlike the period, allows the writer to continue with the sentence instead of starting a new one. Strictly speaking, you don't need a conjunctive adverb or a transitional expression to connect the two clauses, as in the following example:

   Maria was ready; Eduardo was not.

   This sentence communicates well enough. It seems a bit abrupt, yet not drastically so. But notice how much the sentence improves with the addition of a conjunctive adverb:

   Maria was ready; **however,** Eduardo was not.

   Here the writer has given his or her audience more direction.

4. Many conjunctive adverbs can also function as regular adverbs. An **adverb** is a word that modifies a verb, an adjective, or another adverb.

   We are asked to vote for every referendum the mayor proposes, **however** misguided it might be.

   In this sentence, *however* is a simple adverb modifying the adjective *misguided*. It is not a conjunction and should not be preceded by a semicolon.

5. If you are careless when punctuating compound sentences that use conjunctive adverbs or transitional expressions, you can end up with comma splices or fused sentences (see pages 106–107):

CLASSROOM HINT See *Catalyst* for more about semicolons.

COMMA SPLICE	**D. W. Griffith was one of the first great film pioneers, in addition, he was one of the founders of United Artists.**
CORRECT	**D. W. Griffith was one of the first great film pioneers; in addition, he was one of the founders of United Artists.**
FUSED SENTENCE	**Most people remember Mary Pickford as a silent-film star nevertheless she was also a founder of United Artists.**
CORRECT	**Most people remember Mary Pickford as a silent-film star; nevertheless, she was also a founder of United Artists.**

Using Subordinating Conjunctions

Subordinating conjunctions connect sentences in a fundamentally different way than do coordinating conjunctions or conjunctive adverbs/transitional expressions. When you join two sentences by adding a subordinating conjunction, one of the two sentences loses its status as an independent clause. For example, note the following two sentences:

I wasn't sure that I knew how to use the new software. I gave it a try.

We can use the word *although* to subordinate the first clause:

Although I wasn't sure that I knew how to use the new software, I gave it a try.

We can also subordinate the second clause:

I wasn't sure that I knew how to use the new software, **although** I gave it a try.

When the second clause starts with a subordinating conjunction, it usually doesn't need to be preceded by a comma unless it represents a contrasting thought, as in the example above. However, the use of the comma is optional, even when a contrasting thought is expressed.

As with coordinating conjunctions and conjunctive adverbs/transitional expressions, subordinating conjunctions have special features that you should keep in mind:

1. Most of the time, a writer will use a complex sentence (independent clause followed by dependent clause, or the reverse order) to show that the independent clause contains information that is more important than the information contained in the dependent clause, as in this construction:

Although she stumbled at the start, Angela won the race easily.

The outcome of the race is more important than an event that happened during the race, so the incident (stumbled) is subordinated to the outcome (winning).

However, writers sometimes use complex sentences simply to provide variety. The two sentences are equal in weight, and the writer subordinates one to the other only to vary the sentence pattern for his or her reader, who might otherwise become tired of sentences joined by *and, but,* and *however.*

The Wallace family loved Christmas, whereas the Jacksons saw it as merely a grim duty.

Which fact is more important, that the Wallaces are Christmas lovers or the Jacksons are Christmas haters? Neither is. The writer is using the subordinating conjunction *whereas* to provide stylistic variety.

CLASSROOM HINT See *Catalyst* for more about fragments.

2. A dependent clause standing alone is not a complete sentence; it is a **sentence fragment**, a group of words that is treated like a sentence but is missing a subject and/or a verb or that does not represent a complete thought. A fragment is as severe an error as a comma splice or a fused sentence.

   In the following example, the first sentence is correct; the second is a fragment:

   FRAGMENT **I couldn't get to work on time. Because my car wouldn't start.**

   Revision is easy in this case; simply form a complex construction by combining the sentence and the fragment:

   CORRECT **I couldn't get to work on time because my car wouldn't start.**

   The next example is more troubling:

   FRAGMENT **Although, I could have asked my neighbor for a ride.**

   In this case, the writer obviously believes that *although* is a conjunctive adverb, not a subordinating conjunction. Fixing this fragment is easy; simply replace *although* with the appropriate conjunctive adverb:

   CORRECT **Nevertheless, I could have asked my neighbor for a ride.**

   For more help with recognizing and correcting sentence fragments, consult a grammar handbook.

3. Two of the subordinating conjunctions—*since* and *while*—are troublesome because each has two different meanings. *Since* can mean either "during the time after" or "because":

   AMBIGUOUS **Since my refund check arrived, I have felt better.**

   Has the writer felt better in the days after the check arrived, or because the check arrived? Does it make any difference? Of course it does, especially if the reader has to sit and think about the meaning.

   While can mean "during the time that" or "whereas":

   AMBIGUOUS **Jane enjoyed swimming while Kathryn played the piano.**

   The writer probably intended *while* to mean "whereas" in this case. Otherwise, the scene it brings to mind is a bit bizarre, though possible. If the writer did mean "whereas," why not just use that word and avoid the possible confusion?

Using Correlative Conjunctions

Correlative conjunctions, a fourth type of conjunction, are not used to join sentences, so they do not appear in the sentence connectors chart. These are paired conjunctions that emphasize relationships *within* sentences:

> **Both** walnuts **and** cashews are delicious.
>
> **Either** Juan **or** Elena will be here soon.
>
> **Neither** Bill **nor** Edna voted in the last election.
>
> You should **not only** study for your physics test **but also** attend the group study session.

Remember to use a "whole" pair of correlative conjunctions. For example, *not only* must be followed by *but also,* not *but* alone.

EXERCISE 5.3 Responses will vary. The following are suggestions:
1. Last summer, while driving through New England with three of my friends, I fell in love with New Hampshire. Not many people live in this state, and the winters there are very cold. However, it contains lovely natural features and interesting small towns. We didn't have enough time to drive to the northern part of the state, so we concentrated on thoroughly exploring New Hampshire's middle and southern sections.

2. Someone needs to establish a janitorial service for the Internet—not to clean up the raunchy parts but to get rid of the abandoned, ancient Web sites. The Internet has been in popular use for a relatively short amount of time, but it contains an alarming number of outmoded, useless sites. New Web sites tend to have all the bells and whistles and to rely on graphics. Old Web sites reek of early technology, are dependent on text, and contain information that was once current but is no longer needed. Perhaps someday an agency will be allowed to do a search-and-destroy mission on these ancient outposts.

EXERCISE 5.3

Each sentence in the following paragraphs consists of a single independent clause. Working with a partner or in a small group, use coordination and subordination to combine sentences and make the paragraph read more smoothly. If necessary, add the appropriate sentence connector to show logical relations between ideas. Make sure that you punctuate your newly combined sentences correctly.

1. Last summer, three of my friends and I were driving through New England. In particular, I loved New Hampshire. It contained lovely natural features and interesting small towns. Not many people live there. The winters are very cold. We didn't have enough time to drive to the northern part of the state. We concentrated on thoroughly exploring New Hampshire's middle and southern sections.
2. Someone needs to establish a janitorial service for the Internet—not to clean up the raunchy parts but to get rid of the abandoned, ancient Web sites. The Internet has been in popular use for a relatively short amount of time. However, there are an alarming number of outmoded, useless sites. New Web sites tend to have all the bells and whistles. Old Web sites have a reek of early technology. New Web sites tend to rely on graphics. Old Web sites are dependent on text. Old Web sites also tend to contain information current in the year they were last updated—say, 1996. This information is no longer needed. Perhaps someday an agency will be allowed to do a search-and-destroy mission on these ancient outposts.

EXERCISE 5.4

Many of the following sentences are incorrectly punctuated, causing comma splices and fused sentences. Working alone, correct any faulty punctuation.

1. I frequently hear people complain about the high salaries paid to professional athletes. They make too much money, no one should get that much for

EXERCISE 5.4 Responses will vary. The following are suggestions:
1. . . . They make too much money; no one . . . game. . . . People complain all the time about athletes; however, you rarely hear them complain about movie actors. . . . One is that most of us have played sports at some time in our lives; therefore, we have . . . doing. The second is the opposite. Most of us . . . deserve.
2. . . . I like the looks of jays . . . in particular; nevertheless, we're locked in battle. . . . This is not to say . . . instinct. I just wonder why jays are the only ones that act this way. When you walk past a nesting robin, nothing happens. . . .

playing a game. This is the way that the argument normally goes. People complain all the time about athletes, however you rarely hear them complain about movie actors. I believe the reason is twofold. One is that most of us have played sports at some time in our lives therefore we have a familiarity with what athletes are doing. The second is the opposite, most of us have never tried to act, so we give actors more credit than they might deserve.

2. I'm at war with a bluejay that lives in a tree near my apartment's parking lot. I like the looks of jays in general and this one's looks in particular, nevertheless, we're locked in battle. The jay is guarding a nest, so anyone who walks by is a threat. The bird will fly fifty feet to swoop down at me. This is not to say I disapprove of the bird's protective instinct, I just wonder why jays are the only ones that act this way. You walk past a nesting robin nothing happens. Jays, however, treat humans as enemies.

EXERCISE 5.5

The following paragraph contains fragments caused by treating dependent clauses as sentences. Working alone, find the fragments and fix them in one of two ways: (1) by revising the fragment so that it becomes part of an adjacent sentence or (2) by changing the subordinating conjunction into a conjunctive adverb. Make sure that you punctuate your revised sentences correctly.

The era of the box-office idol seems a thing of the past. People used to go to movies based on who was starring. Because these stars had drawing power that in some cases lasted for decades. Today, no star seems to be able to carry a film singlehandedly. Tom Cruise, Julia Roberts, Brad Pitt, and Tom Hanks are all contemporary superstars. Although, each of these actors has seen failure at the box office. Perhaps the director is today's new superstar. People will turn out in droves to see anything directed by Steven Spielberg or James Cameron. Maybe because these directors always aim for blockbuster success.

EXERCISE 5.5 Responses will vary. The following are suggestions:
. . . People used to go to movies based on who was starring; in fact, these stars had drawing power that in some cases lasted for decades. . . . Tom Cruise, Julia Roberts, Brad Pitt, and Tom Hanks are all contemporary superstars, but each of these actors has seen failure at the box office. . . . People will turn out in droves to see anything directed by Steven Spielberg or James Cameron because these directors always aim for blockbuster success.

MORE OPTIONS ONLINE
For more help with sentence combining, go to **www.mhhe.com/writingtoday**.

Using Hybrid Sentence Patterns

Sentences joined by coordination and subordination form recognizable patterns with formal names, some of which we have already encountered:

COMPOUND SENTENCES

My computer is three years old, but it still suits my needs.

My computer is three years old; however, it still suits my needs.

COMPLEX SENTENCES

Although my computer is three years old, it still suits my needs.

My computer still suits my needs although it is three years old.

When a sentence contains both compound and complex elements, it is called a **compound-complex sentence:**

COMPOUND-COMPLEX SENTENCES

Although my computer is three years old, it still suits my needs, so I probably won't buy a new one for a few more years.

Although my computer is three years old, it still suits my needs; therefore, I probably won't buy a new one for a few more years.

My computer still suits my needs although it is three years old, so I probably won't buy a new one for a few more years.

My computer still suits my needs although it is three years old; therefore, I probably won't buy a new one for a few more years.

I probably won't buy a new computer for a few more years; my current computer still suits my needs although it is three years old.

I probably won't buy a new computer for a few more years; although my current computer is three years old, it still suits my needs.

You can generate a limitless number of new sentences by changing the subject, changing the verb, changing the connector, and so on. You can also generate sentences that contain many clauses—collections of independent clauses and dependent clauses that represent increasingly complex thoughts. However, be careful: long sentences are not necessarily wrong, but think of your reader. Do you want to subject your audience to eighty-five-word sentences? Of course not. The patterns that we have explored will allow you to generate sentences of any length, long or short. It is up to you to use these options wisely.

Using Periodic and Climactic Sentence Structure to Create Emphasis

Creating emphasis may require you to structure sentences so that your most important words and phrases are highlighted. Two methods of highlighting are the periodic sentence and the climactic sentence.

The majority of declarative sentences are **cumulative;** they begin with the main idea and then add any modifiers or details needed. For emphasis (and variety), try using a **periodic** sentence from time to time; in such a sentence, the main idea comes *last,* preceded by its modifiers. Note the difference in emphasis between the following two sentences:

CUMULATIVE **The governor is in sad shape, beset by a hostile press, charges of corruption, and dissension within her own party.**

PERIODIC **Beset by a hostile press, charges of corruption, and dissension within her own party, the governor is in sad shape.**

A **climactic** sentence arranges its ideas in order of importance, ending with the most important idea:

CLIMACTIC **During that week, Jason sold his car, found someone to date, and graduated from college after six years of trying.**

EXERCISE 5.6 Responses will vary. The following are suggestions:
1. In 1997, my friend Jason graduated, got engaged, and moved to Oregon.
2. Dark clouds, high winds, and heavy rains ruined the picnic.
3. Despite bad relief pitching, slow base running, and strange managerial decisions, we won 11–3.
4. It was a strange day at work: I got a flat tire and my hard drive crashed, but I won a monthly sales award and got a nice bonus.
5. His torn ear, blind eye, and arthritic hip make Ralph a horrible excuse for a dog.

CLASSROOM HINT Reviewing this section in class is always worthwhile.

EXERCISE 5.6

Examine each set of word groups below, and construct a sentence displaying the best possible emphasis.

1. My friend Jason. 1997. Graduated. Got engaged. Moved to Oregon.
2. Dark clouds. High winds. Heavy rains. Ruined picnic.
3. Bad relief pitching. Slow base runners. Strange managerial decisions. Won 11–3.
4. Flat tire. Crashed hard drive. Monthly sales award. Nice bonus. Strange day at the office.
5. Torn ear. Blind eye. Arthritic hip. Horrible excuse for a dog.

CHOOSING WORDS CAREFULLY

When revising, you may find that your first draft contains phrases and sentences that are overly complicated. You may also find phrases or sentences that do not say what you intended them to; when thinking your way through a first draft, you may not always choose the best words and phrasings. You may also find passages that are not emphatic; weak phrasing has caused your writing to lose its punch. And you may also discover passages that are simply awkward, for any number of reasons. This section discusses these problems and ways to correct them.

Striving for Parallelism

When you give equal emphasis to two or more ideas, actions, things, or feelings, try to use **parallel** structures. In other words, group nouns with nouns, verbs with verbs, prepositional phrases with prepositional phrases, and so on:

NOT PARALLEL — **In Japan, heavy rains are frequent, and the country also experiences volcanic eruptions as well as typhoons.**

MADE PARALLEL BY USING NOUNS — **In Japan, heavy rains, typhoons, and volcanic eruptions are frequent.**

NOT PARALLEL — **Mia has two ambitions: graduating from college and to get a job.**

MADE PARALLEL BY USING INFINITIVES — **Mia has two ambitions: to graduate from college and to get a job.**

Parallelism can also help make comparisons and contrasts clear and emphatic:

UNCLEAR — **The candidate was greeted with cheers, and he did not hear the hisses and boos he had expected.**

MADE PARALLEL BY USING PREPOSITIONS — **The candidate was greeted with cheers, not with the hisses and boos he had expected.**

Some pairs of words help make a sentence parallel if used correctly. These are the correlative conjunctions: *both/and, either/or, neither/nor,* and *not only/but also* (see also page 111 in this chapter). When you use these correlatives, make sure the elements they are joining are parallel:

NOT PARALLEL **In January, the weather is either cool and rainy or we get frigid temperatures and lots of snow.**

PARALLEL **In January, the weather is either cool and rainy or cold and snowy.**

Note that not everything in English can be made parallel. As the examples below illustrate, sometimes you might have to restructure the sentence:

INCORRECT **Raul is poised, witty, and gives great presentations.**

CORRECT **Raul is poised and witty; therefore, he gives great presentations.**

Including All Necessary Words

Faulty parallelism and poor communication are frequently caused by the omission of key words. Note how such omissions cause problems with parallelism in the following sentences:

WORD OMITTED **The striking workers were angry and grumbling in low tones.**

REVISED **The striking workers were angry and were grumbling in low tones.**

WORD OMITTED **The professor gave high grades to Laura, Bill, and to Anne.**

REVISED **The professor gave high grades to Laura, to Bill, and to Anne.**

Although words can often be omitted from a pair or series without sacrificing clarity, make sure that the word you are leaving out is expendable. If not, you may create an error like the one below:

WORD OMITTED **Is it similar or different from our old model?**

REVISED **Is it similar to or different from our old model?**

In this situation, each verb requires its own preposition: *to* and *from,* respectively. Preposition usage is highly idiomatic; refer to a grammar handbook or a dictionary if you are unsure about which preposition to use in a given context.

A similar problem is sometimes caused by the omission of the subordinator *that.* Most of the time, writers can leave out this word:

Shannon believed [that] she would win the race.

In this instance, omitting *that* causes no problem for the reader. But how about this example?

AWKWARD **Mark felt the car was overpriced.**

The reader understands what is meant, but *Mark felt the car* can be misread. Don't omit *that* if doing so causes your reader to pause or to stumble.

CLEAR **Mark felt that the car was overpriced.**

You should also avoid constructions such as this one:

FAULTY **Keith understood the process would be lengthy and that he was looking at three months of hard work.**

Here, the writer has used *that* to *explicitly* subordinate the second idea but, by omitting *that,* has only *implicitly* subordinated the first idea. It is clearer and more logical to treat both ideas in the same way by subordinating them explicitly.

CLEAR **Keith understood that the process would be lengthy and that he was looking at three months of hard work.**

The following sentence omits a needed word in a comparison:

INCORRECT **Ms. Tompkins sings better than any member of her church choir.**

Ms. Tompkins is a member of the choir, so the comparison indicates that she sings better than herself. Note the revision:

CORRECT **Ms. Tompkins sings better than any other member of her church choir.**

Because of missing words, some comparisons are ambiguous:

AMBIGUOUS **Anna likes Pablo more than Esteban.**

The meaning is unclear. Here are two revisions:

CLEAR **Anna likes Pablo more than she likes Esteban.**

CLEAR **Anna likes Pablo more than Esteban does.**

Avoiding Awkward Repetition

Key words and concepts can be repeated for emphasis:

Mr. Desmond is a **fine** employee and a **fine** human being.

Oral presentations enable an instructor **to gauge a student's** thinking, **to gauge a student's** preparation, and **to gauge a student's** confidence.

However, needless repetition should be avoided. Here, using the words *teacher, teaches,* and *teaching* in the same sentence is repetitious:

AWKWARD **A teacher who teaches middle school students usually learns a great deal about teaching.**

REVISED **A middle school teacher usually learns a great deal about teaching.**

Avoiding Faulty Comparisons

When you compare things, they have to be logically comparable. Note the problem in the following sentence:

INCORRECT **More Euromongo Supremes are on the highways than any other car company.**

In effect, this sentence tries to compare a car to a car company. Note the revision:

CORRECT **More Euromongo Supremes are on the highways than any other car.**

EXERCISE 5.7

Check for faulty parallelism, omitted words, awkward repetition, or faulty comparisons in the following sentences, and revise them.

1. Do you want to walk or go swimming?
2. The fighter fought four fighters in the next weight class up.
3. Lisa can spell better than any six-year-old I've ever known.
4. The painting was more complicated than any other modern artist.
5. Mario likes to swim, to dance, and he likes playing soccer.

EXERCISE 5.7 Responses will vary. The following are suggestions:
1. Do you want to walk or to swim?
2. The fighter faced four opponents in the next weight class.
3. Lisa can spell better than any other six-year-old I've ever known.
4. The painting was more complicated than the works of other modern artists.
5. Mario likes to swim, to dance, and to play soccer.

Using Only Words That Matter

You do not necessarily need to write each thought in as few words as possible. Writing in this manner produces text that is flat and over-controlled; it sounds as if it has been produced by a machine. Our advice is simply this: don't waste words. Don't use six words when two will suffice. If your reader has to spend too much time processing six words when two words would have provided the same meaning, he or she will become impatient with your text, much as a listener grows edgy when a speaker takes five minutes to tell a thirty-second story.

AVOID WORDINESS

Wordy Phrase	Simpler Equivalent
during the time that	while
due to the fact that	because
in excess of	more than
in all probability	probably
in many instances	often
in a similar manner	similarly
in the event that	if
whether or not	whether
on the part of	by
a large number of	many
a large amount of	much
a small number of	few
a small amount of	little
it is clear that	clearly
it is obvious that	obviously
speaking with the truth	speaking truthfully
walking with care	walking carefully
shouting with excitement	shouting excitedly
not a few	many

Don't think that you must always avoid using a phrase from the left-hand column; at times, one of these phrases may be useful and appropriate. However, if you *consistently* use these terms in place of their simpler equivalents, your writing will seem bloated.

You should also avoid using **fillers**, well-known but essentially empty expressions used when a more basic expression—or none at all—would suffice:

all in all

needless to say

first and foremost

Note the following paragraph and its revision:

WORDY **It can be clearly seen that our division's profits may or may not increase next year, with this issue based on the question of whether or not a large number of our current clients adopt the offer on the part of our main competition to sign package deals. Needless to say, in the event that our competitor succeeds, our business's profits, in all probability, will falter.**

REVISED **Clearly, our division's profits next year depend on whether many of our current clients adopt our rival's package-deal offer. If our competitor succeeds, our business's profits will falter.**

The most practical difference between the two versions is that the reader is forced to process sixty-six words in the original version to get the same meaning contained in the twenty-eight words of the revised version. Unrevised first drafts are frequently as wordy as the original paragraph above. One of the purposes of revision is to clear away some of the deadwood from the original forest of prose.

EXERCISE 5.8 Responses will vary. The following are suggestions:
1. The art gallery's new show is a hit.
2. When the new stadium is completed, I doubt it will meet the planning committee's financial estimates.
3. The art gallery management's attempt to restrict audience numbers to seventy-five will be futile.
4. The planning committee's estimates will probably be exceeded by 50 percent or more.
5. Shouting happily, Robert approached Anne, who shivered nervously.
6. Many art gallery patrons complained about the number of restrictions; however, the majority who got in enjoyed the experience.
7. The company's profit margin is my main concern.
8. A few of the new stadium's supporters are speaking carefully about the rash optimism of the initial budget planning process.

EXERCISE 5.8

Working alone, revise the following sentences so that they are more concise.

1. When all is said and done, I believe that the art gallery's new show is a hit.
2. If and when the new stadium is completed, I doubt that it will meet the financial estimates of the planning committee.
3. The attempt on the part of the art gallery's management to restrict audience numbers in excess of seventy-five will be seen to be futile.
4. In all probability, the planning committee's estimates will be exceeded by 50 percent or more.
5. Shouting with happiness, Robert approached Anne, who shivered with nervousness.
6. Not a few of the art gallery patrons complained about the number of restrictions; however, the vast majority of those who got in were made happy by the experience.
7. Needless to say, the company's profit margin is my main concern.

8. A small number of the new stadium's supporters are speaking with care about the rash optimism that prevailed during the time that the initial budget planning took place.

EXERCISE 5.9

Working with a partner or in a small group, revise the following paragraphs to eliminate wordiness.

1. The deep rivers of the Midwest and Great Plains have always fascinated not a small number of visitors. During the time that Mark Twain wrote about attempts on the part of steamship companies to master the Mississippi, it is obvious that the romance of the great rivers existed in a prior time and that Twain was building on a myth that was not new. Due to the fact that obstacles placed in the river by nature and obstacles placed in the river by accident forced riverboat pilots to navigate in a cautious manner, an inevitable theme rose up of the fact of humanity at war with its natural environment.
2. "Dahlia, if you'll join me in matrimony, I think you'll find in all probability that in many measures I will surprise you as a husband. I am not ungifted in the arts of love, despite any preconceptions on that issue you might have formed, and in a similar way you will grow to love my home bequeathed to me by my ancestors. Ignore those attempts on the part of your friends to persuade you; it is obvious that they do not know the interests that are best for you."

EXERCISE 5.9 Responses will vary. The following are suggestions:
1. The deep rivers of the Midwest and Great Plains have always fascinated visitors. By the time Mark Twain wrote about steamship companies' attempts to master the Mississippi, the romance of the great rivers had passed, and Twain was building on an old myth. Obstacles placed in the river by nature and by accident forced riverboat pilots to navigate cautiously, thereby generating the inevitable theme of humanity at war with nature.
2. "Dahlia, if you'll marry me, I will surprise you as a husband. Despite what you think, I am a gifted lover, and I am sure you will like my ancestral home. Ignore your friends' advice; they do not know what is best for you."

Avoiding Redundancy

Redundancy—the use of two or more words together that mean the same thing—is another common word-choice problem. The following are common redundancies:

Redundant Phrase	Simpler Equivalent
small in size	small
brown in color	brown
and therefore	therefore
so therefore	so *or* therefore
and so	so
and yet	yet
but yet	but *or* yet
outside of	outside
future plans	plans
advance reservations	reservations
prior planning	planning
visible to the naked eye	visible

Redundant Phrase	Simpler Equivalent
square in shape	square
quite precise	precise
vanish from view	vanish
recur again	recur
advance ahead	advance
can possibly	can
very unique	unique
plan ahead	plan
retreat backward	retreat
completely clear	clear
totally obvious	obvious
in this day and age	now
over and over	continually *or* regularly
each and every	each *or* every
deliberately plan	plan
review again	review
past experience	experience
prior experience	experience
personal friend	friend
review again	review
final result	result
end result	result
final total	total
my own personal	my
my own	my

EXERCISE 5.10 Responses will vary. The following are suggestions:

1. Experience tells us that this initiative will fail.
2. Jared planned to ruin my party.
3. Your motives are obvious, Laura.
4. After failing to break the enemy lines, the patrol returned to headquarters.
5. The mall was closed, so we had to postpone our Christmas shopping.
6. Eddie left the car, but he forgot to give me his key.
7. The mysterious guest vanished when approached by Dr. Herzel.
8. This small, gray, oval device is unique.
9. Modern physics has become too specialized for anyone except people with doctorates in the subject.
10. Unless you have the surgery, Mr. Walker, these symptoms will recur.

A writer who uses any of the terms from the left-hand column in a final draft is not paying enough attention to what he or she is actually communicating.

EXERCISE 5.10

Working alone, revise the following sentences to eliminate redundant constructions.

1. Prior experience tells us that the end result of this initiative will be failure.
2. I think that Jared deliberately planned to ruin my party.
3. Your motives are totally obvious, Laura.
4. After failing to break the enemy lines, the patrol returned back to headquarters.
5. The mall was closed, and so we had to postpone our Christmas shopping.
6. Eddie left the car, but yet he forgot to give me his key.

7. The mysterious guest vanished from view when approached by Dr. Herzel.
8. It's a small device, gray in color and oval in shape—it's absolutely unique.
9. My own personal opinion is that modern physics has become too specialized for anyone except people with doctorates in the subject.
10. Unless you have the surgery, Mr. Walker, these symptoms will recur again.

Avoiding Euphemisms

Another problem that you need to watch for as you edit is the use of **euphemisms:** words and phrases used to mask the painful realities of life. We sometimes use euphemisms to avoid making a troubling situation worse ("Uncle Mike passed on last night") or to avoid saying what we actually mean ("Jenkins, we're going to have to let you go"). In some situations, a euphemism can be appropriate—for example, "going to the bathroom." However, if you want to write directly and clearly, using euphemisms is a bad habit.

EXERCISE 5.11

Working alone, read the following sentences, each of which contains a highlighted term. Decide if that term is a euphemism. If so, replace it with a more direct or appropriate expression. Not all sentences contain euphemisms.

1. Wanda's in trouble with the boss; it looks like she **fudged** on her travel account.
2. Our former accountant **expired** this morning.
3. During our journey, we frequently had to stop so that my young son could go **tinkle.**
4. The police arrested seventeen people after last night's **civil unrest** in which cars were smashed and businesses were looted.
5. The new tolls on the Midtown Expressway will **enhance revenues** for the city.
6. Henry never gives to any charities; he's very **parsimonious.**
7. Seventy-four employees were **downsized** in the company's latest cost-cutting efforts.
8. Aunt Linda's **frugality** kept her family going after the death of Uncle Carter.

EXERCISE 5.11
Responses will vary. The following are suggestions:
1. . . . it looks like she *lied* on her travel account.
2. Our former accountant *died* this morning.
3. . . . my young son could *use the restroom.*
4. . . . after last night's *riot* . . .
5. . . . will *increase* revenues for the city.
6. . . . *stingy.*
7. Seventy-four employees were *laid off* in the company's latest cost-cutting efforts.
8. Correct.

Using Figurative Language Appropriately

Figurative language does not represent a subject directly or literally; instead, it compares the subject in some way to something else. The result creates a relationship that helps explain, define, or add information about the subject.

> Harrison's wrongful-termination lawsuit is **the wheel upon which our company may be broken.**

The lawsuit is not literally a wheel; it's a legal filing. But claiming that the lawsuit is "the wheel upon which our company may be broken" evokes images of a torturer's wheel, a medieval device used to strain and kill its victim.

Note how the author of the following passage uses figurative language to help him make his point:

> The whiskey-jack showed up again around here a couple of years ago. I encountered one down in the cedar swamp in the pasture, where I had gone to look for a fox's den. The bird, instead of showing alarm at my intrusion, followed me about, jumping silently from branch to branch in the thick woods, seemingly eager to learn what I was up to. I found it spooky yet agreeable to be tailed by a bird, and a disreputable one at that. **The Canada jay looks as though he had slept in his clothes.**
>
> —from E. B. White, "Home-Coming"

In this passage, White uses a **simile.** This figure of speech is a direct comparison, claiming that something is *like* something else ("looks *as though*"). White's use of the simile gives the paragraph a vivid conclusion.

Here is another approach:

> Prices continued to move firmly upward on the Wall Street stock exchanges, and Alan Greenspan, that great and good chairman of the Federal Reserve Bank named *de facto* captain of the American ship of state since President Clinton had fallen overboard with Monica Lewinsky, saw nothing on the calm horizon but blue sky and white sailboats.
>
> —from Lewis H. Lapham, "Sucking at Straws"

Lapham is using a **metaphor.** Like a simile, a metaphor tries to amplify meaning by linking one idea to another, but a metaphor does so directly, without using *like* or similar words that signal comparison. With a metaphor, the writer says that the item being described *is* (figuratively) the other. Lapham takes the old idea of the U.S. government as a "ship" crossing rough and uncharted waters, then extends the idea by suggesting that Alan Greenspan has become "captain" in place of the embattled President Clinton.

Note the following two examples:

SIMILE **After Mike's grueling day at the office, Laura's welcoming smile was like a rainbow of sanctuary.**

METAPHOR **After Mike's grueling day at the office, Laura's welcoming smile was a rainbow of sanctuary.**

As you can see in the two examples above, the metaphor is more forceful than the simile. However, the metaphor is also somewhat harder to use properly. Note that in the passages by White and Lapham, each writer uses just one comparison—in White's case, the bird that looks disreputable, and in Lapham's case, the metaphor of the U.S. "ship" of state.

A problem area in figurative language involves **mixed metaphors**, which occur when multiple comparisons are used in a single text passage:

> The bottom line is that Geena would be in the lap of luxury if she had nipped that drinking problem in the bud. When push came to shove, the

world was her oyster last year; now, she'll be lucky if her company doesn't kick the bucket before the cows come home.

This isn't direct communication; it's a form of code. Seven different themes are used here, and the reader is being bounced from figurative phrase to figurative phrase—to no purpose. Moreover, each figurative phrase is a cliché, discussed in the next section of this chapter.

A third type of figurative language is **personification**, in which human characteristics are given to nonhuman entities:

The moon smiled at us.

The night's wind whispered a mystery story.

Obviously, as the second sentence indicates, writers who use personification must keep control of their imagination. A sentence that personifies the night wind is striking, but if the wind whispers through an entire paragraph, readers will soon tire of the idea.

Avoiding Clichés

Using vivid figures of speech will improve your writing; using **clichés** will hurt it. How can you tell the difference? If an expression is very common, a phrase that you've known most of your life, an "old standard," it's probably a cliché. Note the cliché in the following sentence:

My sister is blind as a bat without her glasses.

Besides the needless cruelty of *blind as a bat,* this worn-out phrase is not going to make your reader admire your language skills. The expression is not only a cliché; it is an *ancient* cliché. However, note how the writer of the following passage makes good use of a cliché:

Peter McMichaels was hired at the same time as four other people. His work has been no better or worse than theirs. He has no outstanding characteristics other than his willingness to complain when he doesn't get his way. Yet Peter got a raise this month whereas the other four people didn't. It's clearly an instance of the "squeaky wheel" syndrome.

The writer has taken a very old cliché ("The squeaky wheel gets the grease") and used it to good effect. The reader can be expected to know the cliché and not to need to see it spelled out, which would belabor the obvious. However, remember that only rarely can you put a cliché to good use; you should avoid clichés as much as possible.

EXERCISE 5.12

Working alone, read the following sentences. If a sentence can be made more lively, revise it. Be creative. If a sentence contains a cliché or a mixed metaphor, revise the sentence to eliminate the problem. Some sentences are acceptable.

EXERCISE 5.12 Responses will vary. The following are suggestions:
1. Mrs. Parker was correct when she suggested that we call everyone in the neighborhood.
2. Acceptable.
3. Do everything you can to find him!
4. Myra's career advanced rapidly until her company was taken over.
5. The recent campaign to "beautify" Parkersville is futile. (The figurative language in the original sentence is too intense, though some students might disagree.)
6. The salmon swam against the current like a fish possessed.
7. After her oral presentation failed, Laurel considered dropping her business communications class.
8. This cake batter is very light.
9. Luis's petition gathered strength when the committee rejected the only objection.
10. Here's the truth.

1. Mrs. Parker hit the nail on the head when she suggested that we pull out all the stops and call everyone in the neighborhood.
2. My brother-in-law isn't the swiftest arrow in the quiver, but he's a good family man.
3. Find him—leave no stone unturned!
4. Myra went up the corporate ladder quickly until her career ran aground after her company was taken over.
5. The recent campaign to "beautify" Parkersville is like putting makeup on a hog.
6. The salmon swam very hard against the current.
7. After her oral presentation bit the dust, Laurel considered dropping her business communications class.
8. This cake batter is as light as a feather.
9. Luis's petition got a shot in the arm when the committee steamrolled the only objection.
10. In a nutshell, here's the straight dope.

Learning to Use Denotation and Connotation

Denotation refers to the actual meaning or meanings of a word. Students sometimes misunderstand the denotative meaning of a word and misuse it. When this happens, the reader may understand what the writer intends but will still note the error. In the worst cases, however, the reader has no idea what the writer is attempting to communicate. A college-level dictionary is your best guide when you want to be sure that you are using a word with the correct denotation. As well, a usage glossary such as the ones found in grammar handbooks will help you make accurate decisions.

EXERCISE 5.13

Working with a partner or in a small group, read the following sentences. Do the highlighted terms mean what the writer seems to intend? If not, replace the term with a correct one or revise the sentence so that the term is correct. Use a college-level dictionary and/or a handbook's usage glossary for help.

1. The disabled singer received **fulsome** praise from her proud fans.
2. The judge was clearly **biased** in his opinion.
3. A crime was **omitted** last night in Parkersville.
4. I had to have my car's **breaks** replaced again; this kind of **maintenance** drives me crazy.
5. My government teacher has given me five *A*'s in a row—I can't stand all this **opprobrium**.
6. Go to the **Personal** Department if you want to get your health insurance forms.

7. When you spoke harshly to me, were you **inferring** that I was to blame for our financial situation?
8. Michael's father was a **conscious** objector during the Vietnam War era.

Whereas **denotation** is what words *mean* (their dictionary definition), **connotation** is what words *suggest.* Note the difference between these two sentences:

Mr. Newsome owned and managed old apartment complexes in the central city.

Mr. Newsome was a slum lord.

The first sentence is an objective statement; it does not imply anything about Newsome and his buildings. However, the second sentence is highly *suggestive.* What comes to mind when you hear the term *slum lord*? Probably you have a raft of associations for this phrase, none of them positive. These associations are called the connotation of a term.

EXERCISE 5.13 Responses will vary. The following are suggestions:
1. The disabled singer received *adoring* praise . . .
2. Correct.
3. A crime was *committed* . . .
4. I had to have my car's *brakes* replaced . . . *repairs* drive me crazy.
5. . . . I can't stand all this *approval.*
6. Go to the *Personnel* Department . . .
7. . . . were you *implying* . . . ?
8. Michael's father was a *conscientious* objector . . .

Two Connotation Pitfalls

1. Sometimes, writers who fail to recognize the connotations of words can create sentences with unintended and inappropriate humor:

   The directions for this laxative are very irregular.

   The writer has made an inadvertent pun—wouldn't *unusual* work better than *irregular*? Humor is frequently a plus, but missteps such as this one will cause people to laugh *at* you, not *with* you.
2. Frequently, inadvertent **sexism** is another result of problems with connotation. If a friend mentions that she plans to run for the Student Assembly, the following response may not have the desired effect:

   Brenda, I'm so happy that you're going to try to become an assemblyman.

For Brenda to do so will involve both (a) winning the election and (b) having a sex-change operation. We doubt that she is considering the second option. Many traditional terms and titles of standard English were formed when, largely, men ran things and women kept house. This situation hasn't been true for a very long time.

Concern about sexism in language is frequently described as "political correctness," as if avoiding sexism (and racism and ageism, for that matter) were something that people *had* to do under the watchful eye of some shadowy monitoring group. No—careful writers avoid sexist language because they don't want to cause unnecessary pain or embarrassment to others or to alienate their readers.

Therefore, Brenda probably doesn't want to become an "assemblyman." But she likely wants to be a *member* of the Student Assembly or, perhaps, a *representative.* If a writer shows no sensitivity about this issue, the reader will think that the writer doesn't know any better or, worse, doesn't care. Remember, you should always write for your audience, not for yourself.

The built-in sexism of American English can be countered, but we'd like to add one more guideline: don't make flamboyant, highly noticeable attempts to avoid sexist language. That is, you don't have to sacrifice your style to meet this need. For example, you can't change every word ending in *-man* to a word ending in *-person* without producing awkwardness. Use common sense. For instance, "guard" seems more logical than "watch person," and "postal carrier" seems more natural than "mail person."

EXERCISE 5.14

Working with a partner or in a small group, read the following sentences and choose the *best* word or phrase from the choices in parentheses.

1. Her job as a (waiter, waitress, waitperson, server) kept Gwen afloat during her senior year.
2. The accused man looked (nervous, shifty) as the bailiff ordered all to rise.
3. Irena del Valles is the (congressman, congresswoman, representative) for our district.
4. I felt (strange, funny) as I waited for the comedian to start his act.
5. If they don't fix that pothole in front of my house, I'm going to call the city (ombudsman, ombudsperson, mediator).
6. Moria went to school to learn how to become a computer (repairman, repairwoman, technician).
7. We elected Lydia Kelly as (chairman, chairwoman, chair) of the Goals 2010 committee.
8. Your grandfather seems rather (crotchety, irritable) today.
9. Her hands visibly (shaking, fluttering), Ms. Walters asked the (policeman, police officer) to come inside.
10. That pile of dead spiders is (creepy, disturbing).

EXERCISE 5.14
1. server
2. nervous
3. representative
4. strange
5. mediator
6. technician
7. chair
8. irritable
9. shaking, police officer
10. disturbing

Using Idiomatic English

Like all languages, English has its own **idioms**—customarily accepted phrasings and ways of ordering words. To an international student who is learning English, a sentence such as "The butler called me a cab" must seem very strange indeed. (A native speaker of English would find similar oddities in the international student's first language.)

However, even experienced writers of English sometimes run into trouble with idioms. (Should you use *different from* or *different than*? The former, usually.) People who read a great deal have an advantage in this area because they see edited language that, by virtue of sheer repetition, helps them learn the correct forms. But for everyone else, the problem remains, and some phrasings can't be constructed logically: you must either know the correct form or look it up. You can get help choosing the correct word or phrase by using a good ESL dictionary, such as *The Newbury House Dictionary of American English,* or the usage notes in a college-level dictionary.

EXERCISE 5.15

In the following passage, the highlighted words and phrases are unidiomatic. Working with a partner or in a small group, revise this passage to eliminate the errors. Use a college-level dictionary or an ESL dictionary for assistance.

I went to get my mail **at my mailbox** last Sunday, and **from the mail** I got a shock. It seems that my health insurance claims were not approved **through school's insurance policy.** I had to make a special trip to school, **during that** I planned my argument.

The health insurance office is **found at** the Student Services Building, **besides** the financial aid office. I **asked** with the representative for almost an hour, and she apologized about the problem. She **told me also** what she planned on doing to correct the error. I concurred **about** her idea; it seemed to be a good way **of to take care with** the problem.

A friend of **my** later told **to me** to **be accustomed with** this mixup; it happens **all the while.** She also told me that the university **health blanketing** is **much preferable than providers on the outside** because of its **lowered** cost. So I **took a word with the wise** and will be prepared **for scrutinizing** all **documents of university health insurance sent at me.**

EXERCISE 5.15 Responses will vary. The following is a suggested revision:

When I got my mail last Sunday, I received a shock. It seems that my health insurance claims were not approved by the school's insurance policy. I had to make a special trip to school, during which I planned my argument.

The health insurance office is located in the Student Services Building, beside the financial aid office. I spoke with the representative for almost an hour, and she apologized about the problem. She also told me what she planned on doing to correct the error. I concurred with her idea; it seemed to be a good way to take care of the problem.

A friend of mine later told me to get accustomed to this mixup; it happens all the time. She also told me that the university health coverage is preferable to that of outside providers because of its low cost. So I took a word to the wise and will be prepared to scrutinize all documents sent to me by the university health insurance.

Using Active, Specific Language

Students in college-level writing classes sometimes make the process of composing more complicated than it is. In their attempt to sound "formal," they forget one of the first guidelines for communicating clearly: *good writing is good speaking correctly transcribed to paper.* Students sometimes write sentences that they would not dream of saying, such as "Formulated in the early morning hours, the proposal was designed to facilitate interaction among the two sides in the labor dispute." First off, is it necessary to "formulate" a proposal? Second, who did this deed? Third, what in the world does *facilitate* really mean, anyway? Here is a plainer version of this sentence: "Early in the morning, the committee finished the proposal that would bring both sides to the bargaining table." In other words, write what you mean. Don't cloak your meaning in ornate language.

In this section, we look at three related problems that can make your writing seem static instead of active: relying on complicated noun structures when direct verbs would be better, relying too much on the passive voice, and relying on abstract words when concrete words would be more emphatic.

1. **Prefer verbs over nouns.** Examine the following sentence:

   There was an immediate burst of applause from the crowd when the popular governor started her speech.

   It communicates well enough, but it lacks a certain punch. Note the revision:

   The crowd applauded immediately when the popular governor started speaking.

The revised sentence depends on verbs (*applauded, started speaking*), not nouns, to show what happened, and it gets directly to the point. In the next two examples, the original sentences have a similar problem:

ORIGINAL **The baking of cakes is a source of much pleasure for my retired uncle.**

REVISED **My retired uncle really enjoys baking cakes.**

ORIGINAL **It was in the supervision of trainees that Manuel Gomez found his niche.**

REVISED **Manuel Gomez excelled at supervising trainees.**

As we mentioned earlier, the goal is not to write each sentence with the fewest possible words, but to remember that each sentence tells the story of an actor and an action. Concentrate on showing this relationship with active verbs and clear, direct expression.

2. **Prefer the active voice.** In sentences in the active voice, subjects act; in sentences in the passive voice, subjects are acted upon. Overusing the passive voice causes weak, flabby writing. Examine these two sentences:

PASSIVE **The bonus money was given to us by Ms. Thompson.**

ACTIVE **Ms. Thompson gave us the bonus money.**

The sentence using the passive voice fades away like the dying note of a song, whereas the sentence in the active voice gives the reader the information directly. Keep in mind these simple guidelines: use the passive voice only (1) when you can't—or really don't want to—reveal who did the action or (2) when you want to emphasize the receiver of the action.

Consider the following situation. Police officers checking the back door of a restaurant find a male corpse. It has four visible bullet wounds. No other human beings are in the area. How will the local newspaper "lead" with this story? Probably this way:

A man was murdered last night. . . .

The active voice won't work here, because the writer doesn't know the identity of the actor.

Also, you may want to choose the passive voice when you know the responsible party but don't want to mention the name—perhaps the guilty party is your boss, for example.

TACTFUL **Mistakes were found in the billing of the Andrews project.**

The alternative might be dangerous:

BLUNT **Mr. Waddell committed errors when billing the Andrews project.**

Finally, sometimes you will want to emphasize the receiver, not the actor:

The murder weapon was found behind a shed.

The person who found the weapon is not important; the actual discovery is.

3. **Use concrete terms.** Don't overuse abstract words when specific, concrete words would work much better. (See Chapter 4, pages 90–91.) Most readers find that "weasel words" such as *facilitate, facilitation, enable, enabler, utilize,* and *utilization* make their skin crawl. Again, college-level writing does not require the construction of such jewels as "I perceived the letter carrier at the door." You wouldn't say such a thing, so why put it on paper?

   In "Politics and the English Language," the British novelist and essayist George Orwell claims that sloppy, inefficient writing is the result of sloppy, inefficient thinking. Moreover, Orwell points out that one breeds the other in a vicious cycle. However, the opposite is also true. Think clearly, and write your thoughts clearly; then you are ready for an even better attempt the next time out.

MORE OPTIONS ONLINE
For more help with word choice, go to **www.mhhe.com/writingtoday**.

EXERCISE 5.16

Working alone, look for problem areas in the following sentences and revise as needed. Use a college-level dictionary for reference.

1. Hi, I'm here to facilitate this meeting.
2. According to our statistics, utilization of coffee by our secretaries has undergone an increase of 20 percent.
3. The bad news was communicated by Inspector Laurence.
4. Don't bug me, Eddie; I'm cogitating!
5. The termination process of an employee found to be ineffective has been estimated by our personnel department to cost over $5,000.
6. I'm trying to conceptualize the scene that you're describing.
7. The ball was hit by the bat and began the process of arcing through the air in the general proximity of the shortstop.
8. My apprehension of your meaning is faulty.

EXERCISE 5.16
Responses will vary. The following are suggestions:
1. Hi, I'm here to lead this meeting.
2. According to our statistics, our secretaries are drinking 20 percent more coffee than they were before.
3. Inspector Laurence told us the bad news.
4. Don't bother me, Eddie; I'm thinking!
5. Our personnel department estimates that firing an ineffective employee costs over $5,000.
6. I'm trying to imagine the scene that you're describing.
7. The bat hit the ball which began arcing toward the shortstop.
8. I don't understand you.

EXERCISE 5.17: SUMMARY

The following paragraphs contain all the problems that we have discussed in the second half of this chapter. Working with a partner or a small group, revise these paragraphs so that they are clear, concise, and active. Use a college-level dictionary for reference.

1. The endless parade of children in their trick-or-treat regalia I find fascinating, but yet I feel a sensation of pleasure when I perceive that the last child is here no more. The last piece of firm confectionary made largely of sucrose has been given out, and the final, last gamine has been dispatched. I sink back and down into my soft recliner, and I cogitate back to my days of youthfulness. During the time that my days of trick-or-treating were active, a hard doughnut or roll was our most frequent gift. Costumes were hand sewn by our mothers using needle and thread, and no child ever faced the eventuality of a cookie infiltrated with medicine, or some other unspeakable, monstrous

EXERCISE 5.17 Responses will vary. The following are suggestions:

1. I find the endless parade of children in their trick-or-treat costumes fascinating, but I am pleased when the trick-or-treating is over. When I have given out the last piece of hard candy and the last child has been sent home, I sink into my soft recliner, and I think back to my youth. During my trick-or-treating days, a hard doughnut or roll was our most frequent gift. Our mothers sewed our costumes by hand, and no child ever received a drug-filled cookie or some other nasty surprise. Times change, but never for the better.
2. Ms. Lawrence, as safety crew leader, your conduct has been above average. We wish we could give you a cash reward, but our shaky finances prevent that. So we ask you to continue working hard, for someday you will be rewarded.

3. Thank you for your generous offer, Jeffrey, but I am confused. I have considered your suggestion carefully, and I believe it has promise. Perhaps I will be able to give you my answer soon.
4. I plan to attend Camptown Races' unprecedented evening performance. My biggest bet will be on the horse with the short tail, and my odds will improve if someone makes the same bet on the bay-colored horse. One of us will win, for these horses have been bred to run at night as well as during the day.

act. Ah, each and every time I think of it, times change, but never for the better.

2. Ms. Lawrence, in your role as foreman of the safety crew, your conduct has been found to be above average. We wish that there were some financial perquisite that you could receive, but our shaky contingencies forbid that eventuality. So, therefore, we ask you to toe the line and act like a trouper, for your day in the sun will come.
3. Don't think that I'm not receptive to your generous and charitable offer, Jeffrey. My mind has entered a state of chaos, much like a horde of flies fighting over an abandoned pudding. I have perused your suggestion with care, Jeffrey, and its potentialities and possibilities are not unpleasant to my style of thought. Perhaps at some time of a future date I will be able to give you my final and ultimate response.
4. Camptown Races will have an unprecedented evening performance, and I plan to be in attendance. My central wager will be on the horse with a shortened tail, and my relative odds will be improved if someone makes an equal and commensurate wager on the horse of a distinctive bay color. Success will surely accrue to one or the other of us, for these horses look to have been bred by a management team that desired steeds which could run in the nocturnal hours as well as the diurnal hours.

EXERCISE 5.18: SUMMARY

The following paragraph is from the first draft of "A Very Secret Santa." Working with a partner or in a small group, fix any error that you find. Then compare your corrected version of the paragraph with the final version on page 20.

I remember the first time I saw an example of Walter's secret side. It was before Christmas, years ago, Betty and I were ten years old and going shopping with Mr. and Mrs Wallace at the mall. After Walter finaly found a parking space we noticed a comotion a few cars over. A young woman and her seven-year-old were trying to quiet down the three-year-old. He had been pulled from the last store visited without getting what he wanted. The mother looked entirely flustered and she was obviously quite poor, the little boy was screaming like he had been scalded. We walked toward the mall, listening to this squabble unfold behind us, suddenly Walter disappeared. Mrs. Wallace told us to keep walking, that Walter would catch up. When he did he said nothing.

Using the Internet

Go to these Web sites to find more tips on, techniques for, and insights on revising words and sentences:

The American Heritage Book of English Usage

This commercial online reference tool contains sections on style, word choice, and matters regarding gender in writing: **http://www.bartleby.com/64.**

MORE OPTIONS ONLINE You can access all of the Web sites listed in "Using the Internet" by going to **www.mhhe.com/writingtoday**.

The Elements of Style

This is an online edition of the classic work of American usage, written by William Strunk, Jr., for his students at Cornell University. It was later revised by E. B. White, who had been one of those students: **http://www.bartleby.com/141.**

Guide to Grammar and Style

Created by Professor Jack Lynch of Rutgers University, this Web site contains a search engine that allows you to access information on English usage. The list of additional readings on grammar and usage is also useful: **http://andromeda.rutgers.edu/~jlynch/Writing.**

Guide to Grammar and Writing

Among the most useful pages on this site are "Notorious Confusables," which lists words "we get mixed up," and "Plague Words and Phrases," which "we should avoid": **http://webster.comnet.edu/grammar/index.htm.**

The Write Place Catalogue

Maintained by St. Cloud University, this site contains abundant resources on sentence structure and style, including advice on how to combine sentences for variety and clarity, techniques to avoid and correct wordiness, and coverage of matters pertaining to word choice: **http://leo.stcloudstate.edu/catalogue.html.**

The Writer's Web

The Web site of the University of Richmond's Writing Center, the Writer's Web contains advice on editing for clarity and style, with emphasis on avoiding sexist language, distinguishing between commonly confused words, and avoiding clichés: **http://writing2.richmond.edu/writing/wweb.html.**

Your college and the working world **that looms before you contain a number of discourse communities. Each field of study or employment has its own preferred approaches to communication, its own specialized language and shorthand. These you will learn as you choose your major and immerse yourself in a field of study and application.**

However, you need some general tools and skills before you begin to specialize in a chosen field. The chapters in Part 2 discuss strategies that underlie the writing you will be expected to produce. Each chapter concentrates on one strategy. We call these strategies rhetorical options. They are ways to approach a writing situation.

Students sometimes find the process of learning one new approach after another to be stressful. Having become comfortable with one strategy, they don't see the point of learning a new one. They believe that in the working world, they won't need all of these specific approaches. It's true that your boss will never assign you a project report and say "Write a process analysis." By the same token, your boss will know what he or she wants—a process analysis—and will expect you to be able to write the appropriate document without having to tell you how to proceed. Similarly, if your boss sends you a set of data and asks you to analyze it, he or she is probably not going to tell you which algebraic technique to employ—sampling, graphing, guessing, or consulting a psychic. But your algebra instructor made you process similar data in a specific way—the most reliable and economical way—so that you could avoid guesswork. In short, the techniques that you learn in college "skill classes" will extrapolate to the world of work.

We do not see composition as a captive part of the humanities. Instead, we see writing as a responsibility that every adult has—both on the job and off. To that end, we offer the following ten chapters with the "real" world in mind. Each chapter begins with a vignette from the business world. A new employee is faced with a boss (Bob) who is sometimes lazy and sometimes sadistic—and who always seems to need a new report written. The new hire is forced to scramble, to conceive, to come up with the best way to respond to Bob's need for documents. As a manager, Bob is not atypical of a supervisor in the corporate world, and his requests (demands) will show you how the skills discussed in each chapter can be extrapo-

lated into "real" situations (as if the sweat and hope and worry that you'll put into English composition aren't "real").

Nine of the ten chapters in Part 2 are each devoted to a specific rhetorical option. The final chapter in this part, "The Blended Essay," takes a combined approach, covering situations that do not fit well under the umbrella of one particular strategy or another. In these situations, the writer needs to employ multiple strategies, and we discuss how to choose the best strategies for such an essay and produce a well-organized, successful piece of writing.

When working through these chapters, remember that *options* is an important word in the title of this text. Our aim is always to avoid a formulaic, cookie-cutter approach to writing an essay. When we include a model essay, it is just that—a model—not a blueprint. As we mention elsewhere, if five students earn an *A* on the same writing assignment and you had the opportunity to read all five essays, you would be surprised at how *different* the essays are. If you had access to each student's writing process—prewriting, first draft, revisions, and final draft—you would also see that each student took a very different road to get to the same good outcome. Learn the strategies in the following ten chapters, and make them your own.

PART 2 STRUCTURES

DILBERT reprinted by permission of United Feature Syndicate, Inc.

DESCRIPTION

CHAPTER 6

Writing in Context

You've had a busy afternoon. After applying to Osprey Online Technologies last month, you had your interviews today.

You had a good experience. The preliminary interviews went well, and the next meeting—with Bob, the man who would be your supervisor—went quite well indeed.

Returning home, you make a phone call, as promised, to a friend who wants a report on your big day. When you start telling her about what happened, she interrupts: "No, tell me what the company is *like*. The *place*. The *people*."

Note that the friend doesn't want to hear a story but wants, instead, a "picture" of the experience.

SUGGESTED ACTIVITY Point out that Dilbert's colleagues are using figurative language, a common technique in descriptive writing. Choose some object in the room, and ask students to use figurative language to describe it (for a discussion of figurative language, see Chapter 5).

HOW DOES DESCRIPTION WORK?

As a general strategy, **describing** is used in many forms of writing. Readers employ their imagination as they are reading, and descriptive details help make the subject matter become real for them. Visual forms of expression—photography, painting, and film, to name a few—have the advantage of fully engaging one of our senses—sight—but they are still limited. For example, film can appeal to both our eyes and our ears, but three more senses remain: touch, taste, and smell. Good descriptive writing can stimulate the reader's imagination to form sensory responses from all five senses. Frequently, the reader has no choice: many people cannot read an article about the taste of citrus fruits, for example, without having a physical response to the imagined taste. And a passage about a specific food left out of the refrigerator too long will produce a shudder from readers as they imagine the resulting smell.

Description is a powerful strategy, one that allows the writer to exercise a great deal of control over the reader's perceptions. Compare these two sentences:

> The boy stood outside the shack.
>
> The small, ragged boy, who looked like he hadn't bathed for a few days, stood outside the lopsided, unpainted shack.

The first sentence provides a dim picture, a stick-figure outline of the scene. The second sentence indicates dysfunction and despair. Poverty is the obvious problem, but the alert reader will infer that the boy has another, more sinister problem as well: in our culture, poor hygiene is seen as a symptom of abuse, neglect, and/or depression.

Description is also a strategy we use in our daily interactions. No doubt, you frequently describe different kinds of subjects to your friends and family. One category consists of objects and items:

CLASSROOM HINT Consider using these topics for short, in-class writing.

- The outfit you spotted at the mall and are now thinking of buying
- The new sports car from Mongo Euromotors that fills you with consumer lust
- The weird bone that the dog brought into the yard
- The Picasso on loan to the local art museum
- The meal of a lifetime—a five-course extravaganza at your city's finest restaurant

You can also describe places—either natural or constructed:

- The amazing tide swing in the Bay of Fundy
- A large, ornate house that sits in the middle of a group of smaller houses with much more modest designs
- The new sports stadium
- A quiet street lined with camphor trees
- A desert scene at night
- Your dorm during finals week

Taking a slightly different tack, you can describe people: the very old, the very young, those who are striking, those who are extremely unattractive, those who are in any way distinctive.

Obviously, you can use description as a specific strategy within an essay written with a different overall strategy. An essay contrasting the performance styles of two popular singers might describe each singer's physical appearance to help the reader get a fuller picture. An essay narrating a senseless crime in a quiet neighborhood would probably describe the neighborhood prior to telling the shocking story. Used as a strategy—as an option—description brings texture to any type of writing.

CLASSROOM HINT
Distribute and read news and feature stories from local newspapers or selections from college textbooks to emphasize the versatility of description as an option.

However, in some essays your main strategy will be to describe something, perhaps simply to entertain your audience or to make a serious point about your subject. Here, you attempt to convey the *essence* of the subject by using sensory details to appeal to your reader's imagination. As much as possible, you should try to evoke all five senses:

- Sight: "The mountain rose, green and verdant, above the white, sandy beach below."
- Hearing: "The quail burst out of the thicket with an explosion of pounding wings."
- Touch: "Weathered by almost a century, the old man's arm felt as if it were covered with elephant skin."
- Taste: "My slice of apple pie tasted the way I expected it to until I noticed a hint of raspberries."
- Smell: "The part of the cave where the bear had nested had a sharp, earthy, almost rank scent."

Not every context will allow you to provide details that appeal to all five senses. However, remember that your purpose is to capture for your audience the essence of the subject you are describing, using as much detail as your writing context allows you.

The descriptive essay comes in two basic forms: objective and subjective. **Objective description** is used in the sciences, in business, and in technology; writers using this approach attempt to describe their subject without including their personal responses. A medical examiner's report on what caused the death of a person found in an alley is an example of objective description. So is the report of a business planner who has been sent to look at a tract of land and determine its suitability for development as a shopping center. When a certain type of machinery is needed for production, a company's engineers will describe the machine *before* it is built, laying out the required physical and dynamic specifications. Note that personal bias is out of place in this context. Instead, the emphasis is on impartiality—on providing a disinterested description.

CLASSROOM HINT
Paragraphs from a biology or chemistry textbook can help illustrate objective description. Passages from an art history or humanities text or from a short story are more likely to illustrate subjective description.

Subjective description, on the other hand, allows the writer to show a personal connection to his or her subject. For example, if you wrote an essay describing your aunt's dog, Rusty—a lovable rogue with a talent for madcap adventures and digging up disgusting objects—you would be writing from your limited experience of this dog. If your aunt had taken on this assignment, however, her response would probably be much different. She's the one who has to deal with this creature day in and day out, and what seems "lovable" to an occasional visitor may well require teeth-gritting forbearance from the caretaker.

Such a difference in response to a subject is normal and to be expected. After all, a subjective description requires a *personal* bias. A subjective description is also different from an objective description in this way: the writer is usually exploring his or her emotions. In this context, "feelings" aren't really physical responses. However, our emotional reaction to a subject will help determine the physical details we will choose to describe it. Think of the example of the small boy standing outside the shack (page 136). The first, unadorned description is neutral. The second description implies that the writer feels pity for the young boy and his obviously troubled life. In general, we describe positively those things or people that we personally like; we describe sympathetically those things or people that we pity. The opposite is also true.

Some contexts will require both subjective and objective description. In the first reading selection of this chapter, Thomas McGuane's "Roanie" (pages 139–143), the author describes a horse that is both a working animal (requiring objective description) and a personal pet (requiring subjective description). McGuane's context dictated his approach.

Whether you are using an objective or a subjective approach (or a combination of both), you need to work from a **dominant impression**, a focus that controls the structure and details of your descriptive essay. In an objective description, your intellectual evaluation of the qualities of your subject matter will shape your dominant impression; in a subjective description, your feelings toward the person or thing you are describing will govern your approach.

Consider Your Options

List various environmental stimuli with which you come into contact every day. Then, referring to one or more of the five senses, describe the way each stimulus in the list affects you.

READING THE DESCRIPTIVE ESSAY WITH A WRITER'S EYE

The following four essays are largely subjective descriptions. In the first one, Thomas McGuane describes the best horse that he ever owned, an animal of quirky genius. In the second, Maxine Hong Kingston gives us her impressions of an old photograph of her mother and father. Next, the actress Hildegard Knef describes her father and what his death did to her as a young girl. Finally, Sherman Alexie describes his chaotic childhood on the Spokane Reservation. As you read each essay, try to judge the writer's connection with his or her audience. For what audience is each essay written?

Following the essays, the second half of this chapter features strategies for writing the descriptive essay with a reader's eye (pages 155–165). If you decide to write on one of the topics that follow the four essays below, make sure that you have read the strategies section before you begin. Also note that additional writing topics are listed at the end of the chapter (pages 169–170).

Roanie

THOMAS MCGUANE

Thomas McGuane is the author of ten novels, including *Ninety-Two in the Shade*, which was nominated for the 1973 National Book Award; *Panama* (1978); *Nothing But Blue Skies* (1999); and *The Cadence of Grass* (2002). He has also written screenplays, including those for *Missouri Breaks* (1976) and *Tom Horn* (1980). Increasingly, however, McGuane is becoming well-known for his skills as an essayist, especially after the publication of his 2000 collection *The Longest Silence: A Life in Fishing*, which showcased his sharp wit and elegant style. McGuane lives in Sweet Grass County, Montana.

In this essay, from McGuane's collection *Some Horses* (1999), the author describes a rather remarkable horse, one that seems to transcend his species. "Cutting horses" have traditionally been used to separate a chosen cow from a herd. Typically, the cow does not want to leave the herd's safety and will do everything in its power to elude the horse. The cutting horse must be smarter, faster, and more agile than the cow. In the twentieth century, cutting evolved into a sport, with regular competitions and even a hall of fame. "Roanie" describes this world.

There is a notion that you get only one great horse in a lifetime, a persistent notion that I hope isn't true; because, if that is the case, I've already had mine, in fact still have him though he is an arthritic old man twenty-six years old. His name is Lucky Bottom 79 and he was already a terrific horse when I acquired him over twenty years ago, though for some reason, he wasn't doing much and had a reputation for being a bronc that had probably kept someone else from buying him. He is called Roanie for his red roan coat, a coat that turns almost purple in the summer, and he is not a very pretty horse. In fact, he won an informal contest one year in Hamilton for being the ugliest horse in Montana. He has a slight Roman nose, actually called the "Burt bump" for a trait inherited from his grandsire Burt. As to the length of his head, it's been remarked that he can drink from a fifty-gallon drum and still keep an eye on you. His sire was a good horse called Lucky Star Mac, an Oklahoma Star–bred horse; and his mother was a racehorse named Miss Glimpse. Roanie is one of those hotheaded horses about which people say, "The only safe place is on his back." He can kick in any direction, has actually stripped the buttons off the front of a man's shirt, and the extreme suspicion that is continuously in his eye doesn't come from nowhere. Roanie was not the sort of horse Buster prefers but he once said to me, "Boy, when he was on, that roan horse was unbelievable!" 1

Lucky Bottom 79 was trained by a part-Cherokee cowboy named Ed Bottom, who is, any way you look at it, an outstanding horseman who had made an everlasting mark training calf-roping and cutting horses for nearly half a century. Like Buster Welch, Ed is a member of the Cutting Horse Hall of Fame. Yesterday, I tried to catch swaybacked old Roanie in a twenty-foot loafing shed. He went by me like mercury, low, quick, and throwing me such an elegant head fake I'm lucky I didn't fall down. 2

Ed Bottom lives in Asher, Oklahoma, next door to the Barrow farm, former home of Clyde Barrow. One of Ed's childhood heroes was a family friend, Pretty Boy Floyd, and Ed remembers Pretty Boy coming home from robberies, hiding his shot-up Hudson in a sheep shed, giving all the kids silver dollars, and pitching horseshoes with the grown-ups. 3

I traveled to Oklahoma to try Roanie and I remember two things distinctly. When I went out to the corral to saddle and work a cow on him, Mrs. Bottom said, "Don't fall off." 4

Responding to this nicety, I said, "I won't." 5

Mrs. Bottom said, "You won't?" 6

I had some time to think about this as we got Roanie ready. Roanie hadn't seen me before and I have never been around a horse that exuded such all-consuming distrust of strangers. However, once I was on his back and loping in a circle all was well, with the exception of one small thing: the horse kept his head turned so that he could look back and watch me the whole while. 7

I cut the first cow on him. The cow stopped, looked, prepared for sudden motion, and Roanie began to sink. I guess you would call it a crouch. But it was level all around and I simply sensed the ground coming up: this horse had a working altitude of about a man's waist and I soon found that he had real speed and the ability to turn right through himself like a dishrag. And he understood cattle. He could mesmerize them or stop them with sheer speed, all at hot-rod roadster height. And as I would learn over the years, either his sense of play or his sense of rightness in the world made him purely at home only when he was working cattle. At such a time, you couldn't spur him or misride him to the wrong spot with the strength of Superman. He knew with certainty where he wanted to be and the door to the suggestion box was nailed shut. Over the years, several outstanding cutting-horse riders have competed on him without success. Evidently, he disliked all their opinions and convictions. I was too ignorant and perhaps intimidated by him to let him do anything but what he wanted to do. That proved to be the right approach. For a few years, I made more money on his back than I did at my actual job. It was a great feeling to know you were probably going to win a cutting before you even unloaded the horse from the trailer. 8

I bought Roanie on the condition he pass a veterinary exam. We took him to the local vet and after Roanie kicked the X-ray plates all over the building and took a couple of shots at the X-ray machine itself, we decided to forgo the exam and accept instead Ed's statement, "You can't hurt him with an axe handle." The demoralized veterinarian was reduced to inquiring rhetorically, "Why do you people always want to X-ray everything?" Ed gave me two bits made by another Cherokee, John Israel, identical except for the length of the shanks and beautifully fashioned from salvaged old hay rakes. "Tune him in the long shanks and show him in the short ones." That was the end of the operating instructions. We headed home. 9

It was early spring on the ranch, snowy and muddy. A friend of mine stopped by to see Roanie and the muck sucked his overshoe off in the corral. He looked at the slush filling the boot as he stood in his stocking foot. "There it is," he said, "ag world." I led Roanie around, then put him in a box stall to protect him from the change of Montana weather and settled in to start building a relationship with him. 10

Roanie had not always done well in box stalls. At the national futurity for three-year-olds, he had a record-setting run that brought the audience to its feet. Afterward, Ed put him in one of the assigned box stalls. Someone had placed a blanket in the stall that Roanie had never seen before. By the time Roanie spotted it, his friend Ed was back in the bleachers and Roanie felt he had little choice but to kick the door, its latch and hinges, off the box stall and race out in equine hysteria to scatter spectators. Ed was summoned on the loudspeaker and things were soon put right. If there was a big problem, it was lost on Ed, who is the last word in coolheaded. His comment on Roanie's escapade: "I guess he didn't want to be in there." 11

I didn't know that story at the time I got Roanie home. All I know is that when I went into the box stall with him, he flattened himself against the wall in terror and when I moved, he began to whirl. . . . Sharing a tiny room with an eleven-hundred-and-fifty pound whirling panicked animal is a situation that impresses one with its gravity. I had to do something. The check hadn't cleared yet and I could hardly confine our relationship to watching him through the window. This was not a public aquarium. 12

The next day, I moved a small school desk into Roanie's stall. Then I went in and sat down and did my work. For the first hour, Roanie seemed to be trying to smear himself into the plank walls. He trembled from head to toe. At the end of the hour, I was still writing and he was getting tired of his exertions. He was standing with his weight equally distributed on all four feet. When I got up to pet him, he flattened himself once more. I found myself, pen in hand, seated at my desk, hunched over a legal pad, making such plaintive cries as, "Roanie, I gotta take a leak!" In three days, he was tired of my writing life, trying to figure out how to get around the desk to the hay. We'd made a start. 13

We began riding out on the ranch. This he adored: new country. It was always a special pleasure to simply use him as a saddle horse because he was the sort of horse that always seemed to pull you through the country, head stretched forward, ears pricked, drinking up the new space. There is nothing quite like looking over wild land from horseback. 14

I don't know how Roanie would have done in battle though I think once he'd gotten the idea of what the job was, he would have excelled. His panic attacks, however, would have been dangerous to friend and foe alike. Early in my ownership of him, his feet, accustomed to red Oklahoma dirt, got sore on the rocks where I live. Finally, he went quite lame. It turned out to be merely a stone bruise but a shadow on his X-rays suggested a fractured coffin bone. I sent him immediately to Colorado State University's outstanding equine veterinary center in Fort Collins and called the excellent lameness specialist there. I explained to this specialist that Roanie could be quite unpredictable; to avoid having people getting hurt, I urged caution. 15

"Mr. McGuane, we are well accustomed to handling horses of all kinds. Owners often give us these sorts of warnings and, while we think it is considerate, we don't worry about it too much." The doctor, a cultivated Australian, took me for a nervous sort. 16

Within a few days, he called me. His voice was elevated in both pitch and intensity. "Your horse is going to get this university sued back to the stone age! I have had to rescue several of my graduate students from him and I have hung a skull and crossbones on his stall!" They had tranquilized my horse from the sort of range usually considered appropriate for the rhinoceros and managed to examine him enough to conclude that his hoof injury wasn't serious. When his health papers came back with him, a notation read, "Lucky Bottom 79's rectal temperature not taken as he continually endangered human life." 17

"I'd like a photograph of someone riding this horse," were the doctor's last words to me. 18

"The only safe place is on his back," I said but I think it fell on deaf ears. 19

In any case, he was soon sound once again and in glistening physical condition. We worked cattle at home and he was quick and smooth. I decided to take 20 him to a cutting-horse contest in Blackfoot, Idaho, on the weekend. I knew I had a special horse.

21 The cutting was held in a city park right in the middle of town. It seemed kind of odd not to have a lot of open country around us but the cattle had been, in the words of Chuck Tyson, a great old cow man, "surrounded by cleverness" and things were rather orderly. Roanie had not been to a cutting in a good while and, as I was to learn, he knew the difference between a cow in a contest and a cow anywhere else. As soon as I unloaded him and he heard the bawling cattle and saw the spectators, his blood began to boil. I tried to gallop him down but he just got crazier. I decided to walk him and keep him calm. He gaped around at everything, froze, and shied from paper cups, cigarette wrappers, the light off windshields; children who'd never seen a horse flare its nostrils, snort, and run backward from a gum wrapper gathered around and made my composure worse with their astonished questions. "Hey mister, what's the matter with your horse?" Or, "He's loco, ain't he?" I consoled myself by knowing that as soon as I rode him into the herd, everything would settle down and the eternal cowhorse logic would take over. Boldly, I entered both the open and the non-professional classes.

22 I had an excellent draw in the open. I hired my herd holders and turn-back man and rode confidently toward the herd. I thought Roanie's walk was uncustomarily jerky but gave it little thought as we turned through the cattle and began to drive out. A pretty baldface heifer slipped up onto the point of the herd and I eased forward, cut her, and put my rein hand down on Roanie's neck. Roanie stood bolt upright, the perfect position, I thought, for him to jump out of his skin. He looked bug-eyed at the cow until she moved and then he reared up on his hind legs, pawing the air like Roy Rogers' Trigger on LSD, and with several huge kangaroo leaps shot past the turn-back horses, blowing snot in two directions, and bolted into the Blackfoot city park, scattering strollers and people of all ages. When I got him stopped, I turned to look back at the cutting-horse contest. All I could see was a wall of blank faces. The judge gave me a zero because he was unaware of a lower number.

23 I decided that the only way around this was through it and so I did not scratch from the next class; and I was only mildly unnerved by the voices I heard as I rode toward the cattle: "He's not going in there *again,* is he?" In the crowd were some unmitigated gawkers of the kind that swarm to accident scenes. I cut two cows in the course of my run and Roanie laid down a performance that was absolutely faultless. We won the cutting by a serious margin. It seemed to be that we had gotten through something together because I became abruptly more sensitive to the world as he saw it. I used to think that when I led him out of his box stall at a cutting I could tell by the look in his eye if he was going to win it that day. If he seemed to gaze upon the world with easy vigilance, I knew that we would be deep in the money. If the look of incomplete understanding was there, if he fixated on a bucket or a snakelike curve of garden hose, I knew we would have to find some way to cool out before we began, often by a ride around the neighborhood or, if we were at a local Montana cutting, a visit to one of his horse friends at another trailer. In any case, from then on the pressure was on me to cut my cows correctly and to ride him well; in doing such a tremendous job of holding up his end, he gave me much room for error. I tried not to abuse it.

24 I felt so competitive when I was riding this horse that I went to every last little cutting in the region and got a wonderful education in the geography of the North-

ern Rockies, so many little towns in which the fairgrounds were the only public gathering place. It's been more than a decade since I rode him in a contest but people still inquire about him everywhere I go. "How's the old roan horse?" they ask, shaking their heads in awe. It's so nice to tell them he's fine, and free, in a big grassy place. Not that I don't sometimes wish it were long ago and I were throwing a saddle up on his powerful withers with the feeling that I could hardly wait for my draw.

Vocabulary

The following terms are identified by paragraph number. Make sure that you understand each term's meaning in its context. If you're not sure that you understand a term, look it up in a college-level dictionary.

notion (1)	mesmerize (8)	gravity (12)
bronc (1)	rhetorically (9)	plaintive (13)
swaybacked (2)	equine (11)	unmitigated (23)
exuded (7)	escapade (11)	vigilance (23)

Style and Strategy

1. Which of the five senses does McGuane evoke in this essay?
2. What is your dominant impression of McGuane's horse?
3. Find examples of McGuane's use of the following strategies: narration (see Chapter 7), process analysis (Chapter 9), causal analysis (Chapter 10), definition (Chapter 11), and comparison/contrast (Chapter 13). What does each strategy contribute to the essay as a whole?

STYLE AND STRATEGY
1. Sight is appealed to throughout; sound in paragraphs 10, 17, 21; touch in paragraphs 13, 15, 22.
2. Most students recognize the spirited nature of the horse; others mention his nobility.
3. Narration appears in paragraphs 2–11 and 14–19; causal analysis in paragraphs 11 and 21–23; definition in paragraph 1; comparison/contrast in paragraphs 9, 12, and 22.

Questions for Critical Thinking and Discussion

1. Many people who work in farming and ranching do so because they grew up on a farm or a ranch. However, Thomas McGuane *chose* to become a rancher. Thus, what is the significance of the comment of McGuane's friend whose boot is sucked away by the mud: "There it is . . . ag world" (paragraph 10)?
2. Some observers believe that using animals such as horses and dogs on ranches and farms is acceptable but that using animals in sports such as racing or rodeos is not. What is the difference between the two types of activities? In your opinion, is the competition that McGuane describes a "fair use" of a horse like Roanie? Why or why not?
3. Someone who answers "yes" to the preceding question might point out that without competitions such as racing and shows, a horse such as Roanie would never have been bred at all—in other words, Roanie owes his very existence to cutting competitions. Is this a valid argument? Why or why not?

QUESTIONS FOR CRITICAL THINKING AND DISCUSSION All three questions make for good classroom discussion, but they can be turned into prompts for short writing, too.

Suggestions for Writing

1. Write a 500-word description of the strangest animal that you've ever known.

SUGGESTIONS FOR WRITING For item 1, consider allowing students to write about animals that they have read about in fantasy or science fiction or that they can conjure up in their own imaginations. Item 2 is the more difficult assignment. Remind students that personality can be revealed through behavior.

2. In 500 to 750 words, describe someone you know who, like Roanie, is brilliant at a particular skill or activity but seems to require "special handling" in other areas of life.

Photographs of My Parents

MAXINE HONG KINGSTON

Born in Stockton, California, Maxine Hong Kingston grew up in the United States listening to her immigrant parents and relatives talk of their homeland in China. Two of Kingston's books, *The Woman Warrior: Memoirs of a Girlhood Among Ghosts* (1975) and *China Men* (1980), reflect both her own and her parents' and ancestors' diverse experiences.

"Photographs of My Parents" shows the world of meaning that a picture can convey—especially if the photo is from another time and place.

1 Once in a long while, four times so far for me, my mother brings out the metal tube that holds her medical diploma. On the tube are gold circles crossed with seven red lines each—"joy" ideographs in abstract. There are also little flowers that look like gears for a gold machine. According to the scraps of labels with Chinese and American addresses, stamps, and postmarks, the family airmailed the can from Hong Kong in 1950. It got crushed in the middle, and whoever tried to peel the labels off stopped because the red and gold paint came off too, leaving silver scratches that rust. Somebody tried to pry the end off before discovering that the tube pulls apart. When I open it, the smell of China flies out, a thousand-year-old bat flying heavy-headed out of the Chinese caverns where bats are as white as dust, a smell that comes from long ago, far back in the brain. Crates from Canton, Hong Kong, Singapore, and Taiwan have that smell too, only stronger because they are more recently come from the Chinese.

2 Inside the can are three scrolls, one inside another. The largest says that in the twenty-third year of the National Republic, the To Keung School of Midwifery, where she has had two years of instruction and Hospital Practice, awards its Diploma to my mother, who has shown through oral and written examination her Proficiency in Midwifery, Pediatrics, Gynecology, "Medecine," "Surgary," Therapeutics, Ophthalmology, Bacteriology, Dermatology, Nursing and Bandage. This document has eight stamps on it: one, the school's English and Chinese names embossed together in a circle; one, as the Chinese enumerate, a stork and a big baby in lavender ink; one, the school's Chinese seal; one, an orangish paper stamp pasted in the border design; one, the red seal of Dr. Wu Pak-liang, M.D., Lyon, Berlin, president and "Ex-assistant étranger à la clinique chirugicale et d'accouchement de l'université de Lyon"; one, the red seal of Dean Woo Yin-kam, M.D.; one, my mother's seal, her chop mark larger than the president's and the dean's; and one, the number 1279 on the back. Dean Woo's signature is followed by "(Hackett)." I read in a history book that Hackett Medical College for Women at Canton was founded in the nineteenth century by European women doctors.

3 The school seal has been pressed over a photograph of my mother at the age of thirty-seven. The diploma gives her age as twenty-seven. She looks younger than I do, her eyebrows are thicker, her lips fuller. Her naturally curly hair is parted on the left, one wavy wisp tendrilling off to the right. She wears a scholar's white

gown, and she is not thinking about her appearance. She stares straight ahead as if she could see me and past me to her grandchildren and grandchildren's grandchildren. She has spacy eyes, as all people recently from Asia have. Her eyes do not focus on the camera. My mother is not smiling; Chinese do not smile for photographs. Their faces command relatives in foreign lands—"Send money"—and posterity forever—"Put food in front of this picture." My mother does not understand Chinese-American snapshots. "What are you laughing at?" she asks.

4 The second scroll is a long narrow photograph of the graduating class with the school officials seated in front. I picked out my mother immediately. Her face is exactly her own, though forty years younger. She is so familiar, I can only tell whether or not she is pretty or happy or smart by comparing her to the other women. For this formal group picture she straightened her hair with oil to make a chinlength bob like the others'. On the other women, strangers, I can recognize a curled lip, a sidelong glance, pinched shoulders. My mother is not soft; the girl with the small nose and dimpled underlip is soft. My mother is not humorous, not like the girl at the end who lifts her mocking chin to pose like Girl Graduate. My mother does not have smiling eyes; the old woman teacher (Dean Woo?) in front crinkles happily, and the one faculty member in the western suit smiles westernly. Most of the graduates are girls whose faces have not yet formed; my mother's face will not change anymore, except to age. She is intelligent, alert, pretty. I can't tell if she's happy.

5 The graduates seem to have been looking elsewhere when they pinned the rose, zinnia, or chrysanthemum on their precise black dresses. One thin girl wears hers in the middle of her chest. A few have a flower over a left or right nipple. My mother put hers, a chrysanthemum, below her left breast. Chinese dresses at that time were dartless, cut as if women did not have breasts; these young doctors, unaccustomed to decorations, may have seen their chests as black expanses with no reference points for flowers. Perhaps they couldn't shorten that far gaze that lasts only a few years after a Chinese emigrates. In this picture too my mother's eyes are big with what they held—reaches of oceans beyond China, land beyond oceans. Most emigrants learn the barbarians' directness—how to gather themselves and stare rudely into talking faces as if trying to catch lies. In America my mother has eyes as strong as boulders, never once skittering off a face, but she has not learned to place decorations and phonograph needles, nor has she stopped seeing land on the other side of the oceans. Now her eyes include the relatives in China, as they once included my father smiling and smiling in his many western outfits, a different one for each photograph that he sent from America.

6 He and his friends took pictures of one another in bathing suits at Coney Island beach, the salt wind from the Atlantic blowing their hair. He's the one in the middle with his arms about the necks of his buddies. They pose in the cockpit of a biplane, on a motorcycle, and on a lawn beside the "Keep Off the Grass" sign. They are always laughing. My father, white shirt sleeves rolled up, smiles in front of a wall of clean laundry. In the spring he wears a new straw hat, cocked at a Fred Astaire angle. He steps out, dancing down the stairs, one foot forward, one back, a hand in his pocket. He wrote to her about the American custom of stomping on straw hats come fall. "If you want to save your hat for next year," he said, "you have to put it away early, or else when you're riding the subway or walking along Fifth Avenue, any stranger can snatch it off your head and put his foot through it. That's the way they celebrate the change of seasons here." In the winter he wears

a gray felt hat with his gray overcoat. He is sitting on a rock in Central Park. In one snapshot he is not smiling; someone took it when he was studying, blurred in the glare of the desk lamp.

7 There are no snapshots of my mother. In two small portraits, however, there is a black thumbprint on her forehead, as if someone had inked in bangs, as if someone had marked her.

8 "Mother, did bangs come into fashion after you had the picture taken?" One time she said yes. Another time when I asked, "Why do you have fingerprints on your forehead?" she said, "Your First Uncle did that." I disliked the unsureness in her voice.

9 The last scroll has columns of Chinese words. The only English is "Department of Health, Canton," imprinted on my mother's face, the same photograph as on the diploma. I keep looking to see whether she was afraid. Year after year my father did not come home or send for her. Their two children had been dead for ten years. If he did not return soon, there would be no more children. ("They were three and two years old, a boy and a girl. They could talk already.") My father did send money regularly, though, and she had nobody to spend it on but herself. She bought good clothes and shoes. Then she decided to use the money for becoming a doctor. She did not leave for Canton immediately after the children died. In China there was time to complete feelings. As my father had done, my mother left the village by ship. There was a sea bird painted on the ship to protect it against shipwreck and winds. She was in luck. The following ship was boarded by river pirates, who kidnapped every passenger, even old ladies. "Sixty dollars for an old lady" was what the bandits used to say. "I sailed alone," she says, "to the capital of the entire province." She took a brown leather suitcase and a seabag stuffed with two quilts.

Vocabulary

The following terms are identified by paragraph number. Make sure that you understand each term's meaning in its context. If you're not sure that you understand a term, look it up in a college-level dictionary.

ideographs (1)	posterity (3)	emigrants (5)
abstract (1)	expanses (5)	province (9)
enumerate (2)	emigrates (5)	

Style and Strategy

1. Kingston first describes the photographs of her mother, then the ones of her father. In your opinion, why did she choose this order?

2. Reread Kingston's description of her mother's photographs. How much of her discussion is based on pure observation, and how much is her interpretation of what she observes?

3. The last paragraph tells of the death of the couple's first two children. Were you surprised by this development? Why do you think Kingston saved this information for the end of her essay?

STYLE AND STRATEGY

1. The centerpiece of this essay is the author's mother and the world that was left behind when her father emigrated. Interestingly, her parents' long separation enabled Hong Kingston's mother to become educated.
2. Most of paragraphs 3–5 is subjective.
3. Saving this information for the end of the essay forces the reader to rethink what has come before and apply a new perspective when considering both parts of the question.

Questions for Critical Thinking and Discussion

1. In our digital era, photographs can be scanned, altered, and output again. In addition, many good-looking people don't photograph well, whereas many ordinary-looking people are quite photogenic. In terms of "capturing a moment," how reliable is photography?
2. Many people in the United States use up dozens of rolls of film each year to chronicle their family or to document their travels. Why is photography so popular?

QUESTIONS FOR CRITICAL THINKING AND DISCUSSION Both questions can be used as in-class writing prompts.

Suggestions for Writing

1. Obtain a photograph of one of your deceased relatives, preferably one you never met. In a 500- to 750-word essay, describe this person. How is he or she similar to or different from the way you perceive yourself?
2. Obtain a photograph of yourself from your childhood. In a 500-word essay, describe this person.

SUGGESTIONS FOR WRITING Encourage students to interview other relatives to gather information for item 1.

From *The Gift Horse*

HILDEGARD KNEF

Translated by David Anthony Palastanga

Born in Germany, Hildegard Knef (1925–2002) survived her father's early death, the Nazi regime, and cancer to become an international film star. Late in her career she published two highly regarded memoirs, *The Gift Horse* (1970) and *The Verdict* (1975). These fascinating accounts of Knef's life clearly transcend the typical movie star "autobiography."

In this selection (Chapter 4 of *The Gift Horse*), Knef paints a portrait of herself as a very conflicted and thoroughly unpromising young girl.

1 I, Hildegard Frieda Albertina, had given my mother, Frieda Auguste, very little joy. There were the constant, endless, countless, family-disrupting illnesses, streams of drops and medicines. "Hilde is always ill," they said. There was my fear when she was out, my fear when she was there, fear that she might go out again. There was the waiting around hallway doors, fear of darkness, fear of being alone, of forgetfulness. There were swollen eyes and sties, wobbly polio legs, a broken collarbone that wouldn't mend, rheumatism that kept me and her awake all night. One nose, broken; one jaw, operated on; one foot, cut open with a razor blade because Mother was at the movies and still not home at eleven. There was anemia and there were blood tests, ghostly pale face, shadows under the eyes, and there was jolly sympathy from the neighbors. And if the flood of horror was once stemmed for a short while and I was allowed to visit her, perhaps, one afternoon at Siemens in the big room where she typed, where forty typewriters all chattered simultaneously, where she typed until the chain of chocolate, tobacco, shoemaker shops began—then I promptly fell down. Fell on the stairs, got bumps on my forehead and other places, brought disgrace, snot, and pain where proud presentation had been wished for, expected.

2 "It really is a trial with that child," she would sometimes say, when all hope forsook her. And the grand ball, the only one—I spoiled that for her too. Ruined it. It was at the Imperial Ballroom in Lichterfelde. Mother and Stepfather's first ball

together—Mother in long gown, Stepfather in navy blue, scrubbed and eager, already in the taxi. And the torchlight procession for the children. Chinese lanterns in the twilight, orchestra plays something by Lincke, parents clap, beam, are proud, puffed up. I stand there, look at torches, the procession does a sudden turn, I lose sight of Mother—panic. A man comes, lifts me onto the stage, light, fanfare.

"We have found a stray child. Now what's your name?" Chuckles and sniggers from below. "What's your name?" Louder, sharper. Don't know. Panic. "Now, now," he says beside me, above me, "it's not as bad as all that." 3

Mother pulls me down. "Dear God," she says, "dear God, can't you take care of yourself for two minutes?" 4

The children poke each other in the ribs, laugh. The adults exchange glances, smile. Stepfather drinks a quick beer, too quick, starts coughing, goes his asthma color, lilac at its most lilac. We go. No one says a word. Go home on the train, in long festive black. 5

And I wasn't pretty either, God knows, nobody but Grandfather thought I was pretty. The saleswoman in the bookshop next door once said: "You get more like your Aunt Hulda every day," and although I loved Aunt Hulda dearly, I didn't want to look like her. And Mother said to Stepfather, one night as it was getting dark: "A pity Hilde isn't prettier." And Stepfather, cranky, wanting to sleep, murmured: "Yes, but she looks quite interesting." 6

That was a blow. A worse one fell the day Lieselotte wanted to go to the movies with her friend. She took me along because her mother had said, "You're not to go alone." Her friend brought his friend, pimply, damp hands, rubbing his cheeks and rolling his eyes, sighing: "This shaving drives me crazy." When the film was over, the three of them said: "Auf Wiederseh'n." Left me standing at the cinema in the black-out, said Wiederseh'n and went. 7

And Mother was beautiful, very beautiful. She had the longest, loveliest legs in Schöneberg, the greenest eyes, was healthy, slender, tough, powerful, fearless. A little disappointed perhaps, disappointed because she had such a lovely clear high voice, but had not, after all, become a singer. There wasn't enough money for the training, and to go around begging for a scholarship—no, one was too proud for that, if it came to that, one would rather not fulfill one's most cherished dreams. She had been brought up on Prussian discipline and when she was twenty-three my grandmother asked her whether she still had a right to wear that white summer dress. She didn't. She had met my father. It was love at first sight and I believe my mother still loved him when she died thirty-five years after him. 8

His name was Hans Theodor, he was big, wild, restless, red-haired, he charged through life and professions like an express train through stations, won races swimming against the current in the Rhine, football trophies, amateur boxing contests. 9

He was desperate. 10

I would like to have known him. 11

At seventeen he was awarded the Iron Cross second class, at seventeen and a half the Iron Cross first class. He had volunteered, was at the Somme, at Verdun, and was once in a brothel. And when the war was over, the revolutionaries tore off his ribbons and epaulettes at the railway station in Berlin. What remained was the illness. "Cured," the doctor said a year later, "got away with it this time." 12

He had trouble adjusting himself to a Germany reeking of cabbages and turnips, sought war, sought a fight—until he found his Frieda Auguste. They got 13 married. Packed, unpacked, moved, moved again; it was a marriage on the move. He had success and a chauffeur-driven car, lost both, landed in Ulm. Then came the biggest, once-in-a-lifetime, puts-everything-else-in-the-shade chance: Turkey, own factory, independence. I put an end to that. I made my entrance in December. My father ran through the apartment shouting: "Is her blood all right, Doctor, is her blood in order too?" It was.

14 A month later Mother found the syringe. In the hall was a high cupboard, in the high cupboard a carton, in the carton the syringe. What's the syringe for? she asked.

15 The illness I had once has come back. I'm having treatment, giving myself the injections, they say it will go away again.

16 It didn't. He got fever, he got angina. Whether the one had anything to do with the other the doctors didn't know. He was taken to the hospital. Mother too—she had appendicitis. He lay on the second floor, she on the first. Ten days later he screamed for his Auguste, the priest came. Taking him gently by the hand, he spoke: My son, he said, we all have to die one day, it is God's will. We have to find the way to *Him, He* is good, *He* is great. *He,* in his mercy, will take care of you, let us pray.

17 Hans Theodor stood up, took the comforting priest by the throat and throttled him until he turned purple, screamed and screamed: I am twenty-eight I have a wife and a child of six months it's not true it isn't *His* will can't be *His* will you're lying. . . . Then he fell over the unconscious priest and died.

18 My mother was informed four hours later; they had simply forgotten about her.

19 She took the urn and a hammock, strung me up between two luggage racks, and traveled back to Berlin and her parents. There was no money left, she had to work in offices again, as she had done before she was married. Grandmother and I went regularly to the Schöneberg cemetery and she said, "If we water the grave well enough, perhaps Father will grow again, we must be patient and wait until spring," but in spring the cemetery and the grave looked the same as ever, Father had not grown again and I was disappointed and cried all the way home.

20 When in thirty-three the Nazis took over Berlin with parades and uproar and children waving little flags and squealing Heil Hitler, my mother said: "A blessing that he's not alive, a blessing that he's not alive." He had been a Social Democrat, and despite his many professions, had even spoken in the Reichstag* once; but she wasn't thinking of this so much as his inability to avoid a row, to take anything lying down; stupidity and fanaticism threw him into a rage, besides which he'd never been averse to a good fight.

21 My stepfather went about things in a more prudent manner. He had a shop together with a Herr Gold, and when the Nazis advised him to join the party and get rid of Herr Gold, he asked simply and quietly how much it might cost not to become a party member as he had asthma and would not be able to take part in the sporting activities of the community. They said uncertainly that they would leave this up to him, so he pulled out his wallet and cordially placed a one-mark piece on the table. He was looking for a new shop the next day.

22 He didn't like hanging out the flag either and was currently being warned by the Blockleiter. Finally he bought one, about the size of a child's handkerchief, and

***Reichstag:** German legislature.

was warned again. The Blockleiter said severely that the flag must be relative in size to the shop window. So Stepfather bought one relative in size to the shop window, but it hung down onto the pavement and people got tangled up in it; with a really good gust of wind it would envelope whole families. The Blockleiter came again and demanded something shorter, so Stepfather rolled it up around the pole so that the black swastika in the white circle disappeared and we now had a flag of exactly the requisite dimensions, but red—which at that time was not at all fashionable. Several inquisitive people, who probably thought that they'd misunderstood the latest news bulletins, gathered in front of the shop and asked excitedly what the new flag meant. The purple-faced Blockleiter steamed up and put an end to the disorder with a threatening: "If one more incident comes to my notice . . ." and then left Stepfather's haven of quiet mirth without reporting him.

23 I always carried with me a small photo of my father; he looked sad and angry with his deep-set, somewhat slanting eyes, his square chin and soft mouth. I always looked at him when I had troubles, or when I was especially happy about something. My stepfather was jealous of my quiet photo love affair, Mother pacified him with: "But she's only a child." As I got bigger, she often looked at me in astonishment and said: "You laugh just like your father—he always bellowed like that too and laughed till the tears rolled down his face." I tried to tame my wild laughter, but sometimes I forgot and then Mother looked startled, grew pale, went out.

Vocabulary

The following terms are identified by paragraph number. Make sure that you understand each term's meaning in its context. If you're not sure that you understand a term, look it up in a college-level dictionary.

polio (1)	reeking (13)	cordially (21)
rheumatism (1)	syringe (14)	envelope (22)
anemia (1)	throttle (17)	requisite (22)
forsake (2)	urn (19)	inquisitive (22)
procession (2)	fanaticism (20)	mirth (22)
fanfare (2)	averse (20)	bellow (23)
epaulettes (12)	prudent (21)	

Style and Strategy

STYLE AND STRATEGY
1. Touch, sound, and sight are evoked.
2. There are many to choose from. Such sentences create interest and empathy in readers.
3. The clearest example is the contrast between her father and her stepfather.
4. There seems to be a hint of sadness over the fact that she never realized the joy and comfort naturally associated with childhood.

1. Descriptive essays need to evoke the senses. How well does Knef accomplish this? To which senses does she appeal the most? Does she neglect to evoke any of the five senses?
2. Find the two most *emphatic* sentences in this essay. How does Knef use these as part of her description?
3. Knef uses the internal strategy of comparison/contrast (see Chapter 13) several times during this essay. Find these instances, and analyze why Knef uses this strategy.
4. What is the tone of this essay? How does Knef achieve this tone, and how does she use it to make her point?

Questions for Critical Thinking and Discussion

1. In your childhood, did you have to adjust to the presence of a new stepparent? If so, how were you affected?
2. As a person ages, does the loss of a close relative ever get any easier to bear?
3. Are you the same person you were as a child? If not, how have you changed, and what caused you to change?

QUESTIONS FOR CRITICAL THINKING AND DISCUSSION Items 1 and 2 can be turned into prompts for short writing.

Suggestions for Writing

1. Write a 500- to 750-word essay in which you describe yourself at a time in your life when you felt supremely awkward and out of place.
2. In a 500- to 750-word essay, describe your most notable or interesting relative.

SUGGESTIONS FOR WRITING Encourage students to use anecdotes to develop these assignments. (See page 157 and Chapter 7 for more on anecdotes.)

Family Portrait

SHERMAN ALEXIE

Sherman Alexie is a Native American of Spokane/Coeur d'Alene background. After growing up on the Spokane Reservation in Washington State, Alexie has gone on to establish a reputation as one of the most promising writers in the United States. His books include *The Business of Fancydancing* (1992), *First Indian on the Moon* (1993), *Reservation Blues* (1996), *Indian Killer* (1996), and *One Stick Song* (2000).

"Family Portrait," from *The Lone Ranger and Tonto Fistfight in Heaven* (1993), will probably puzzle you, and you may find that you need to read this essay more than once. Alexie's descriptions are highly impressionistic and sometimes almost hallucinatory. However, the result will be worth your trouble.

1 The television was always loud, too loud, until every conversation was distorted, fragmented.

2 "Dinner" sounded like "Leave me alone."

3 "I love you" sounded like "Inertia."

4 "Please" sounded like "Sacrifice."

5 Believe me, the television was always too loud. At three in the morning I woke from ordinary nightmares to hear the television pounding the ceiling above my bed. Sometimes it was just white noise, the end of another broadcasting day. Other times it was a bad movie made worse by the late hour and interrupted sleep.

6 "Drop your weapons and come out with your hands above your head" sounded too much like "Trust me, the world is yours."

7 "The aliens are coming! The aliens are coming!" sounded too much like "Just one more beer, sweetheart, and then we'll go home."

8 "Junior, I lost the money" sounded too much like "You'll never have a dream come true."

9 I don't know where all the years went. I remember only the television in detail. All the other moments worth remembering became stories that changed with each telling, until nothing was aboriginal or recognizable.

10 For instance, in the summer or 1972 or 1973 or only in our minds, the reservation disappeared. I remember standing on the front porch of our HUD house, practicing on my plastic saxophone, when the reservation disappeared.

Finally, I remember thinking, but I was six years old, or seven. I don't know for sure how old; I was Indian. 11

Just like that, there was nothing there beyond the bottom step. My older brother told me he'd give me a quarter if I jumped into the unknown. My twin sisters cried equal tears; their bicycles had been parked out by the pine trees, all of it vanished. 12

My mother came out to investigate the noise. She stared out past the bottom step for a long time, but there was no expression on her face when she went back to wash the potatoes. 13

My father was happily drunk and he stumbled off the bottom step before any of us could stop him. He came back years later with diabetes and a pocketful of quarters. The seeds in the cuffs of his pants dropped to the floor of our house and grew into orange trees. 14

"Nothing is possible without Vitamin C," my mother told us, but I knew she meant to say, "Don't want everything so much." 15

Often the stories contain people who never existed before our collective imaginations created them. 16

My brother and I remember our sisters scraped all the food that dropped off our plates during dinner into a pile in the center of the table. Then they placed their teeth against the edge of the table and scraped all the food into their open mouths. 17

Our parents don't remember that happening, and our sisters cry out, "No, no, we were never that hungry!" 18

Still, my brother and I cannot deny the truth of our story. We were there. Maybe hunger informs our lives. 19

My family tells me stories of myself, small events and catastrophic diseases I don't remember but accept as the beginning of my story. 20

After surgery to relieve fluid pressure on my brain, I started to dance. 21

"No," my mother tells me. "You had epileptic seizures." 22

"No," my father tells her. "He was dancing." 23

During "The Tonight Show" I pretended to sleep on the couch while my father sat in his chair and watched the television. 24

"It was Doc's trumpet that made you dance," my father told me. 25

"No, it was grand mal seizures punctuated by moments of extreme perception," my mother told him. 26

She wanted to believe I could see the future. She secretly knew the doctors had inserted another organ into my skull, transplanted a twentieth-century vision. 27

One winter she threw me outside in my underwear and refused to let me back into the house until I answered her questions. 28

"Will my children love me when I'm old?" she asked, but I knew she wanted to ask me, "Will I regret my life?" 29

Then there was music, scratched 45's and eight-track tapes. We turned the volume too high for the speakers, until the music was tinny and distorted. But we danced, until my oldest sister tore her only pair of nylons and wept violently. But we danced, until we shook dust down from the ceiling and chased bats out of the attic into the daylight. But we danced, in our mismatched clothes and broken shoes. I wrote my name in Magic Marker on my shoes, my first name on the left toe and my last name on the right toe, with my true name somewhere in between. 30

But we danced, with empty stomachs and nothing for dinner except sleep. All night we lay awake with sweat on our backs and blisters on our soles. All night we fought waking nightmares until sleep came with nightmares of its own. I remember the nightmare about the thin man in a big hat who took the Indian children away from their parents. He came with scissors to cut hair and a locked box to hide all the amputated braids. But we danced, under wigs and between unfinished walls, through broken promises and around empty cupboards.

31 It was a dance.

32 Still, we can be surprised.

33 My sister told me she could recognize me by the smell of my clothes. She said she could close her eyes and pick me out of a crowd by just the smell of my shirt.

34 I knew she meant to say *I love you.*

35 With all the systems of measurements we had available, I remember the degree of sunlight most. It was there continuously, winter or summer. The cold came by accident, the sun by design.

36 Then there was the summer sniffing gas. My sisters bent their heads at impossible angles to reach the gas tanks of BIA vehicles. Everything so bright and precise, it hurt the brain. Eardrums pounded by the slightest noise; a dog barking could change the shape of the earth.

37 I remember my brother stretched out over the lawnmower, his mouth pressed tightly to the mouth of the gas tank. It was a strange kiss, his first kiss, his lips burnt and clothes flammable. He tried to dance away, he named every blade of grass he crushed when he fell on his ass. Everything under water, like walking across the bottom of Benjamin Lake, past dead horses and abandoned tires. Legs tangled in seaweed, dance, dance again, kick the feet until you break free. Stare up at the surface, sunlight filtered through water like fingers, like a hand filled with the promise of love and oxygen.

38 WARNING: *Intentional misuse by deliberately concentrating and inhaling the contents can be harmful or fatal.*

39 How much do we remember of what hurts us most? I've been thinking about pain, how each of us constructs our past to justify what we feel now. How each successive pain distorts the preceding. Let's say I remember sunlight as a measurement of this story, how it changed the shape of the family portrait. My father shields his eyes and makes his face a shadow. He could be anyone then, but my eyes are closed in the photo. I cannot remember what I was thinking. Maybe I wanted to stand, stretch my legs, raise my arms above my head, open my mouth wide, and fill my lungs. *Breathe, breathe.* Maybe my hair is so black it collects all the available light.

40 Suddenly it is winter and I'm trying to start the car.

41 "Give it more gas," my father shouts from the house.

42 I put my foot to the fire wall, feel the engine shudder in response. My hands grip the steering wheel tightly. They are not mine this morning. These hands are too strong, too necessary for even the smallest gestures. I can make fists and throw my anger into walls and plasterboard. I can pick up a toothbrush or a pistol, touch the face of a woman I love. Years ago, these hands might have held the spear that held the salmon that held the dream of the tribe. Years ago, these hands might have touched the hands of the dark-skinned men who touched medicine and the magic of ordinary gods. Now, I put my hand to the gearshift, my heart to the cold wind.

"Give it more gas," my father yells. 43

I put the car into Drive and then I am gone, down the road, carefully, touching the brake like I touch my dreams. Once, my father and I drove this same road and he told the story of the first television he ever saw. 44

"The television was in the window of a store in Coeur d'Alene. Me and all the guys would talk down there and watch it. Just one channel and all it showed was a woman sitting on top of a television that showed the same woman sitting on top of the same television. Over and over until it hurt your eyes and head. That's the way I remember it. And she was always singing some song. I think it was 'A Girl on Top of the World.'" 45

This is how we find our history, how we sketch our family portrait, how we snap the photograph at the precise moment when someone's mouth is open and ready to ask a question. *How?* 46

There is a girl on top of the world. She is owldancing with my father. That is the story by which we measure all our stories, until we understand that one story can never be all. 47

There is a girl on top of the world. She is singing the blues. That is the story by which we measure heartbreak. Maybe she is my sister or my other sister or my oldest sister dead in the house fire. Maybe she is my mother with her hands in the fry bread. Maybe she is my brother. 48

There is a girl on top of the world. She is telling us her story. That is the story by which we measure the beginning of all of our lives. *Listen, listen, what can be calling?* She is why we hold each other tight; she is why our fear refuses naming. She is the fancydancer; she is forgiveness. 49

The television was always loud, too loud, until every emotion was measured by the half hour. We hid our faces behind masks that suggested other histories; we touched hands accidentally and our skin sparked like a personal revolution. We stared across the room at each other, waited for the conversation and the conversion, watched wasps and flies battering against the windows. We were children; we were open mouths. Open in hunger, in anger, in laughter, in prayer. 50

Jesus, we all want to survive. 51

STYLE AND STRATEGY
1. Alexie's childhood was difficult. The family was poor and dysfunctional. Alexie creates this impression by the disjointed scenes and sensations that he chooses to describe and by themes that run throughout the piece such as the noise from the television and dancing.
2. Literally speaking, the reservation may have been disbanded, but students may in fact find other interpretations.
3. This is the kind of desperate statement that captures the suffering experienced by the author and his family, as well as their ability to endure.

Vocabulary

The following terms are identified by paragraph number. Make sure that you understand each term's meaning in its context. If you're not sure that you understand a term, look it up in a college-level dictionary.

aboriginal (9)	collective imagination (16)	fire wall (42)
HUD (10)	grand mal (26)	

Style and Strategy

1. What is the dominant impression you have of Alexie's childhood, based on this account? How does Alexie create this impression?
2. In paragraph 10, Alexie mentions that "the reservation disappeared." Although what the writer intends is not clear, what do you think he means? What purpose does this kind of ambiguity serve in this essay?

3. Alexie concludes with a one-sentence paragraph: "Jesus, we all want to survive." Is this sentence the thesis of "Family Portrait"? Why or why not?

Questions for Critical Thinking and Discussion

1. "The most important social obligation of any culture is to its children." Do you agree? Explain.
2. In paragraph 11, Alexie writes that "I was six years old, or seven. I don't know for sure how old; I was Indian." What does he mean by this statement?
3. In paragraphs 16–31, Alexie writes about how different members of his family had different memories of events from the time period covered in this essay. What point is Alexie trying to make here?
4. Can a person ever escape his or her childhood, whether it was good or bad?

QUESTIONS FOR CRITICAL THINKING AND DISCUSSION Items 2 and 3 point to a theme that needs discussing: in such a social environment, time and history become blurred, and recognizing reality sometimes becomes difficult. For item 3, you might point out that the memories different family members have of the same events often differ and encourage students to consider how Alexie uses this phenomenon in his essay.

Suggestions for Writing

1. Was your childhood chaotic, orderly, or somewhere in between? Write a 500- to 750-word essay describing a childhood situation that best exemplifies the conditions under which you grew up.
2. From the nineteenth century until the present, many Native Americans have been under the "custodial care" of the federal government and have lived on reservations. Have the lives of the first Americans been improved or degraded by reservation life? Research this issue by choosing one tribe or reservation and describing the condition of its people. (For help with research, see chapters 20 and 21.)

SUGGESTIONS FOR WRITING Item 1 can be completed without research, but students should be encouraged to interview family members to gather additional information and other perspectives.

WRITING THE DESCRIPTIVE ESSAY WITH A READER'S EYE

MORE OPTIONS ONLINE If you would like to read additional descriptive essays, go to **www.mhhe.com/writingtoday**.

When you write, you are striving to produce a document that successfully meets your goals (your purpose) while satisfying your reader's needs. Think like a reader as you write. For example, if a passage seems unclear to you or lacks sufficient details, your reader will undoubtedly also sense this flaw. Externalize your effort by trying to foresee how what you write will be perceived by your audience. The following advice will help you think like your reader as you consider your assignment and then prewrite, draft, revise, and edit your descriptive essay.

Issues to Keep in Mind

Some students find that a descriptive essay is relatively easy to write; others struggle with this type of essay. Here are four issues for you to consider as you work on your essay:

1. Audience and language level
2. The tendency to write a narrative essay instead of a description

3. The question of objective approach versus subjective approach
4. Choosing an effective structure for description

Audience and Language Level

Depending on the topic that you choose and the focus of your assignment, you will need to think hard about your essay's effect on the person or persons who will read it. For example, if you are writing a straightforward, objective description of an orange for your writing class (it sounds like an easy task, but it's not—try it), considering your audience should be fairly easy. You are trying to find clear, specific language to draw a "word picture" of this common fruit. You can probably think of words that both you and your reader will understand; the challenge will be to find a way to engage your reader's imagination.

But suppose that you have been assigned to write about your most treasured possession. In your case, it would be your retooled 1971 Plymouth Roadrunner with hemispheric carburetion and all the "improvements" that you have been able to add to it. The danger here is that you might lapse into technological shorthand and **jargon**—the specialized language that is acceptable if your audience is composed of fellow Roadrunner fans but that is strange and even unintelligible to people who don't share that interest. Failure to define or clarify terms that readers are not likely to know—in general, failure to consider your reader—may well result in a negative reception for your essay. Unfortunately, some writers see writing in the language of a specialized field as a form of showing off. However, most readers hate a show-off.

For a general audience, then, you should avoid jargon. But even when you are writing for a general audience, you may find it necessary to use technical language; just make sure that you define an unfamiliar term the first time you use it, as in the following example:

> The ancient skeleton had ossified (hardened until brittle).

Thereafter, you are free to use *ossified* whenever it is appropriate.

Often, descriptions are too bland rather than too technical. When describing a common object or scene, a writer may fail to realize that his or her description adds little to the reader's understanding, as in this example:

> The beach had white sand leading down to the water.

The reader's response to such a sentence is likely to be something like "Noted." This description is what most readers will picture when they see the word *beach*. However, you can find ways around this problem. Note the following revision:

> The beach was like a postcard, with gleaming white sand leading to azure water that broke in a gentle surf.

Descriptive writing is a natural context for **figurative language**, especially **similes** such as the one in the sentence above (see pages 121–123 in Chapter 5 for more on figurative language). Frequently, writers will describe something by comparing it to another, more familiar object:

> This variety of orange has a brownish tint, the same color as a regulation basketball.
>
> The tiny house on the slope of the mountain looked like a person hanging on to the edge of a cliff.
>
> The indigo snake's skin feels like an expensive glove.
>
> The old firefighter had a voice like a foghorn: loud, insistent, and monotonous.

However, remember to avoid **clichés,** which are overused figures of speech (for example, "old as the hills"). As noted in Chapter 5, if you use an expression fairly frequently, it's probably not going to be fresh for your readers.

CLASSROOM HINT Remind students of the need to avoid clichés. Write a few on the board or turn back to Chapter 5.

Description and Narration

Many descriptive essays concentrate on sensory details and emotional responses. Maxine Hong Kingston's "Photographs of My Parents" (pages 144–146) is a good example of this type. However, in many descriptive essays, description is embedded in a narrative structure. **Narrative** (see Chapter 7) is a powerful tool for communicating our ideas about people and places: our first impulse is always to tell a story—to recount events—when we are asked to explain ourselves or something outside ourselves. And many descriptive essays use brief narratives, or *anecdotes,* to good effect. In this chapter, Thomas McGuane's "Roanie" (pages 139–143) includes a good deal of narration. However, note that the anecdotes McGuane loosely groups together are not the dominant feature in the essay; instead, he concentrates on sensory descriptions that help readers see what makes his horse unique, and these sensory details are what readers will most likely remember.

When you are writing a descriptive essay, you can use anecdotes to help make your subject come to life for your readers, and you can even use a narrative structure to arrange your details. However, make sure that if the assignment calls for a description, you are not just writing a narrative with some description added here and there.

Objective Description Versus Subjective Description

Although we have discussed *objective* and *subjective* description as two separate concepts, rarely, if ever, can an essay be described as purely objective or purely subjective. Instead, essays tend to lean in one direction or the other, being *primarily* objective or *primarily* subjective.

SUGGESTED ACTIVITY Take this opportunity to assign a short project in which students describe something both objectively and subjectively. A magazine photograph or advertisement can be a good stimulus.

You should determine whether your essay will be primarily objective or subjective either before or during the prewriting stage. Often, this decision is made for you—your instructor might specifically request an objective approach or a subjective approach as part of the assignment. In general, though, the subject matter and your purpose for writing will help determine your response. If you are asked to describe your favorite vacation location in order to entertain your readers, then a subjective response is obviously appropriate. On the other hand, if you are asked to describe a car, a basketball, or a hand tool in order to inform your readers, then an objective response is clearly indicated.

However, problems can occur when the writer suddenly shifts gears. A writer should not suddenly switch from impartial, unbiased description to an overtly personal or subjective approach; similarly, a subjective description that suddenly becomes dry and objective will seem strange. In either case, the essay will have lost its **unity.**

Structuring Your Description

How you present your description to your reader will affect its impact. If your description jumps from detail to detail without a logical or coherent plan, the essay will be disjointed and the reader will be confused and unsure of the dominant impression you are trying to convey. Note how the following paragraph proceeds without plan or logic:

> The old woman sat across the table from me. Her eyes were dark and very small, almost beady, and they nervously flitted from left to right. Her clothing was old, a faded windbreaker worn over a man's shirt. Her hair was almost white and flew out of control away from her head. The skin on the woman's hands was very thin, with freckles and liver spots covering her knuckles. The wrinkles in her brow and cheeks showed the effects of too much worry, a life spent in anxiety over what would happen next.

This passage is in many ways competent, with a number of well-chosen, specific details, but it suffers because of its poor structure. The writer moves haphazardly through the woman's eyes, clothes, hair, hands, and face without establishing a logical pattern. Unless there is a good—and apparent—reason for taking such a scattered approach, the writer is asking the reader to make connections that would not have been necessary if the writer had done a better job of organizing and planning. The revised paragraph paints a clearer picture because it is logically structured. The writer first describes the woman's clothes and hands, then focuses on her face:

> The old woman sat across the table from me. Her clothing was old, a faded windbreaker worn over a man's shirt. The skin on the woman's hands was very thin, with freckles and liver spots covering her knuckles. Her hair was almost white and flew out of control away from her head. Her eyes were dark and very small, almost beady, and they nervously flitted from left to right. The wrinkles in her brow and cheeks showed the effects of too much worry, a life spent in anxiety over what would happen next.

The following two patterns are commonly used options for descriptive essays. Both patterns are *logical* and *natural* ways of arranging descriptive details:

1. **Outside (fringes) to inside (nucleus).** This approach works well if the most important feature that you are describing is at the center of an area:

   > The large room was mainly empty, with only a few papers next to several computer terminals and artists' tables. As I moved closer to the center of

the room, however, evidence of hard work began to appear: stacks of yellowing pages, drawings, artists' tools. Then I came upon a blizzard of activity: two graphic artists, one at a computer and the other at her inclined table, talked feverishly as cigarette smoke swirled around them and coffee fumes filled the air. The hubbub was intense; these two nervous people faced a ten o'clock deadline, and time was running out.

Note that you can reverse this pattern for ironic effect:

The two nervous graphic artists faced a ten o'clock deadline, and time was running out. One sat at a computer, the other at her inclined table. Both were talking feverishly as cigarette smoke and coffee fumes filled the air. But the two occupied only the center of a large room, and as I walked away, I noticed the vestiges of past projects at several computer terminals and artists' tables. The rest of the room was empty.

2. **Left to right, right to left, top to bottom, bottom to top.** In this approach, the writer cues the reader to the pattern by using **transitions of location** (see also page 71 in Chapter 3). These words and terms "show" your reader where one item is located relative to another, as in the following example:

SUGGESTED ACTIVITY
Ask students to write a short description of a classroom building, their home, or a dorm room using one of these two patterns.

The used-car lot had ten rows of about fifteen cars apiece. The row **nearest** to the highway had bright, shiny models with high prices. Obviously, these were the most desirable cars with the highest potential for profit. In the **next row back,** the cars were a bit less desirable. But when you walked four or five rows **deeper** into the lot, the segregation became even more pronounced: cars with weird, rough paint jobs, dents, and hopeful window signs (Air works great!). The **farthest** row from the highway held the dregs, cars whose bright and shiny days were long past. These cars were **distanced** from most customers and would attract only those driving similar eyesores.

Remember to build your description with your audience in mind. You are trying to *help* your reader, who should be able to perceive the organization you are using and comfortably follow your progress through the arrangement of your details and your use of transitions.

MORE OPTIONS ONLINE
For more help with problem areas in the descriptive essay, go to **www.mhhe.com/writingtoday**.

Choosing a Topic

Your instructor may assign you a specific topic for your description: an item or object, a place or building on campus, a person you know well, and so on. Alternatively, your instructor may allow you to choose a specific topic from some general categories or from the suggestions for writing that follow the readings in this chapter. If you are allowed to choose your own topic, you have two factors to consider: the "size" of your topic and its level of difficulty.

1. If you choose a topic that is too broad, you will find yourself trying to describe something too large to fit into a standard essay. If you tried to describe your college's campus in 600 to 700 words, for example, your essay would need to be very general in order to cover all of the campus's features. Remember that good description captures *specific* sensory details. You might be able to provide specific details for one of the campus's buildings in an essay of this size, but then you would have even less room to describe the rest of the campus.

   On the other hand, if you choose a very limited topic, you may not have enough subject matter to work with. Suppose you decide to describe an ornate hairbrush that has been handed down through your family for two centuries. You may find yourself working very hard to "fill" your essay. This topic is also so personal that it may not result in an essay that interests your audience. Although highly personal topics can be the source of excellent essays, when you describe something that is both very limited and extremely personal, you run the risk of developing a "private" essay that does not engage its intended audience. Lacking a personal connection to the hairbrush, the reader might very well think, "So what?"
2. You also need to consider your topic's degree of difficulty. Although you don't necessarily need to choose the most difficult topic from a list of possibilities—this is not mountain climbing, after all—you should keep in mind the need for a certain "perceived level of difficulty" in your writing. Have you ever watched high divers in competition, perhaps in the Olympics? Each dive is first judged by its level of difficulty. Potentially, a diver can earn a higher score by attempting a more difficult combination. Instructors often use similar—though usually unstated—criteria when judging essays. If you choose the easiest possible subject to describe—a treasured object with which you are completely familiar—it is likely that your essay will be somewhat limited. Push yourself a bit—try to go beyond the easy or the expected. Your instructor will notice your effort, and you will grow as a writer by taking on more difficult tasks.

Prewriting

Chapter 2 presents a variety of prewriting strategies to choose from. Many writers find that the less formal strategies work best when they are generating ideas for a descriptive essay. For example, clustering and brainstorming are very useful for generating sensory details. (See pages 30–35 for help with these two strategies.) Remember, when you are prewriting, more is better. Having more details than you can possibly use is preferable to straining for details as you write your initial draft. Write down everything you can think of about your subject.

As you prewrite, you can also start to make some important decisions about your essay. First, if you are not sure whether a subjective approach or an objective approach is appropriate, the details you generate while you are

farce. Second, her clothes indicate her class. Although she is clearly in a recreational setting, her sundress has almost a cowl effect as it rises over her bathing suit. Third, although the setting is apparently a beach, the mother and son seem to be alone. If the woman is at the beach, then she is probably using the umbrella/parasol to avoid the direct sunlight, which could harm her skin tone. Also, a beach setting would explain the woman's apparent lack of makeup, which makes her look older than she would probably like. She is about 40 but looks a bit older here: a regal woman holding her prize, her son.

The boy's face lacks the extreme definition that characterizes his mother's face, but he is still clearly an aristocrat in the making. The button nose sets off a handsome profile, much more formal than you would normally see in a boy who is only two to three years old. Even at that young age, he does not turn to Mother but looks with her: to sea, to his limitless future. The world should be his, if this photograph tells us anything at all.

Carefully constructed topic sentences such as the ones in these paragraphs give both you and your reader a focus for each body paragraph and keep the essay on track.

The Conclusion

Students frequently dread writing the conclusion even more than the introduction. For one thing, they are often tired at this point, having expended a great deal of mental energy on developing the draft. Second, many students don't see the necessity for a conclusion and resist putting too much effort into it. However, keep in mind that your conclusion allows you to bring the points you have made throughout your essay together and emphasize them. It's your chance to leave your reader with a strong final impression. The conclusion is *not* a place to (a) summarize your essay or (b) bring up new ideas that lead off in startling directions. However, note that the conclusion may include *evaluative* statements, as the sample descriptive essay does:

Lisa Fonssagrives-Penn and her son present an image of pride, almost arrogance. The future (as well as the present) belongs to people such as these two, but seeing these shining specimens also reminds viewers of the aging process and the inevitability of decay. The woman will grow old and die, and her son will go through the same heartbreaks and tragedies that happen to all of us. Yet for one frozen moment, these bluebloods dominate the camera's eye.

Consider Your Options

Consider description as a way to conclude any type of writing. For example, describing the mangled wreck of a car might be an effective way to end an essay arguing for stiffer penalties for drunk driving.

EXERCISE 6.1

Write a sentence outline of "Frozen Moment." (For help with sentence outlines, see Chapter 2, pages 41–42.) What does the outline reveal about the essay's organization? Would a different organization work better? Why?

Revising Your Draft

After you have completed a draft of your descriptive essay, your next step is to revise it, using your own analysis and comments from classmates or friends. During peer review, answer the questions below about the draft you are reviewing, whether it is yours or another student's.

After reviewing for content, you need to go over your peer reviewers' responses to your essay and then revise for unity, coherence, language level, and tone (see Chapter 4). When you have revised your draft and are basically satisfied with it, read your draft for grammatical and mechanical errors. Concentrate on finding and correcting major sentence errors (fragment, comma splice, fused sentence), errors in pronoun agreement and subject-verb agreement, and spelling.

Once you have made your corrections, *read your essay one more time* to catch any errors made during revision and find errors missed during your earlier reviews.

MORE OPTIONS ONLINE For more help with the step-by-step development of the descriptive essay, go to **www.mhhe.com/writingtoday**.

MORE OPTIONS ONLINE For more help with revision, go to **www.mhhe.com/writingtoday**.

Questions for Reviewing a Descriptive Essay

CLASSROOM HINT Discuss these questions and emphasize their importance in class.

1. Does this essay have an introduction that engages the reader and sufficiently explains the situation? How could it be improved?
2. What is the thesis statement? In what ways, if any, could it be strengthened?
3. Does the description create a complete picture of the subject? Has the writer fulfilled his or her purpose for writing the essay?
4. Is the pattern of organization effective? Would another pattern work better?
5. Are the topic sentences clear and properly located? Where is a more effective topic sentence needed?
6. Are the body paragraphs fully developed? Where are additional details, or more specific details, needed?
7. Does the writer use transitions to guide the reader? Where are transitional words or sentences needed?
8. Does the essay have an effective conclusion? How could it be improved?

Student Essay

The following essay is Jennifer Janisz's response to an assignment that asked for a descriptive essay. The final draft is presented first. Then Jennifer's first draft is presented, with her comments about this draft and what she needed to do in the revision stage.

In the essay, Jennifer describes her sensations during what must be a major life event for anyone who has experienced it: the removal of her wisdom teeth.

EXERCISE 6.1 (page 164) Answers will vary. The following sentence outline is suggested. Thesis: Lisa Fonssagrives-Penn and her son are born to dominate.
I. The woman is clearly from the upper class.
  A. She has a hyphenated name.
  B. Her clothes indicate her class.
  C. Mother and son are alone at the beach.
II. The son is clearly an aristocrat in the making.
  A. He has a handsome profile.
  B. He looks to the sea and his limitless future.
III. Mother and son present an image of pride but, like all of us, are subject to decay.

Jennifer's Final Draft

Help! Anyone!

1 The moment I walk through the mirrored door and into the peach reception room, a sense of trepidation washes over me as a mixture of plastic and mint invades my nostrils. Slowly, I approach the Hispanic woman at the circular, cream desk. "Can I help you?" she asks with a smile, flashing her perfect white teeth. I give her my name and drag myself over to one of the chairs covered in scratchy cloth, which makes it impossible to get comfortable and perhaps pretend, for just a moment, that I am anywhere else but here. Gazing around the room, desperate for anything to get my mind off of the pain I know I'm about to endure, I find only children's books and little toy blocks. My eyes fixate on the pyramid design on the wallpaper.

2 Before I can count to 200 blocks of pyramid, my name is called. The tingling in my legs becomes more paralyzing with every step I take closer to the back room. Passing through the heavy apricot-colored door, I swear I hear shrieks from the poor victims of the dental hygienist. Other dental hygienists are crowded around a sink putting on fresh latex gloves. My jaw starts throbbing at the very sight of the torture devices neatly lined up on the table next to them. The receptionist ushers me past tearful children, strapped down to chairs and enduring the same fate I will soon have the pleasure of enduring. She leads me into a brightly lit, private room. I have no choice but to sit down in the cold, gray, vinyl chair.

3 Silently, I wait in agony for the torment to begin. My premonitions get stronger, and my heart starts racing faster and faster, yet nothing happens. I sit in complete silence, except for the second hand on the

black-and-white wall clock that my eyes are fixated on. I desperately want this experience to just be over so I can go home and block it all out of my memory. Maybe I should make a run for it while I still can. Too late, the door opens, and in walks the dentist in his blue paper face mask and cap. He slips on his funny-looking glasses and sits down with a sigh.

4 Much against my will, the dentist is now in control of my mouth. My thoughts are screaming at me to clamp my mouth shut and do as much damage to his hand with my teeth as I possibly can. My mouth doesn't listen to the screams and continues to do whatever the dentist requests. I can feel my blood pounding through my entire body as I open my eyes just in time to see the dentist reach for a pair of blindingly shiny, silver clamps. "All right, now keep your head steady and your mouth open wide. You shouldn't feel that much pain." I would love to believe him. Still, even though I taste the piña-colada-flavored numbing gel and my lip feels like it's touching the ground, I know better. In complete agony I lie in the chair, unable to shut my eyes, move, or even utter a sound. Yet I'm very able to feel and hear him searing through my gums and into my jaw. The clamps enclose my tooth, and I can literally hear each crack as he tries as gingerly as possible to extract it from my jaw. Blood gushes from my mouth as tears cascade down my cheeks. I have no idea how much longer I will be able to survive this suffering as I feel my tooth dangling from just one side of my jaw. I hear one final snap, and relief washes over me as the pain slowly subsides.

5 "Great job! Only three more left to go!" exclaims the dentist. I shudder at the thought of even one more second in this chair. I take a deep breath and just thank God that I only have one set of wisdom teeth.

Jennifer's First Draft

My goal was to make the reader feel what it was like to be in the dentist chair and understand why I hate that place so much.

Help! Anyone!

The moment I walk through the mirrored door and into the peach receptionist room, a sense of trepidation washes over me, plastic and mint invade my nostrils. Slowly, I approach the Spanish looking receptionist.

"Can I help you?" she asks with a smile, flashing her perfect white teeth. I give her my name and sit down in one of the chairs in the room covered in scratchy cloth, which makes it impossible for me to get comfortable and perhaps, just for a moment, that I'm anywhere else. Gazing around the room, desperate for something to get my mind off of the pain I know I'm about to endure, I find only children's books and toys. My eyes fixate on the pyramid design on the wallpaper. Before I could reach 200 blocks of pyramids my name is called. The tingling in my legs gets stronger with every step I take towards the back room. Passing through the heavy apricot colored door, I swear I hear the screams of dental hygienist victims. A group of dental hygienists are crowded around a sink putting on fresh latex gloves. My jaw starts throbbing at the very sight of the torture devices neatly lined up on the table next to them. The receptionist ushers me into a private room and into a gray colored vinyl chair. Silently I wait for the torture to begin. Although my premonitions get stronger and my heart races faster and faster, nothing happens. The only thing moving is the second hand on the black and white wall clock that my eyes are fixated on. I just want to go hone and forget about it. Maybe I should make a run for it while I still can. Too late, the door slides open and in walks the dentist with his blue paper face mask and cap and funny looking glasses. Very unwillingly, the dentist is in control of my mouth. My brain's telling me to clamp shut, but my mouth does exactly what the dentist requests. I can feel my blood pounding through my entire body as I open my eyes just in time to see the dentist reach for a pair of blindingly shiny, silver clamps. "Alright, now keep your head steady and your mouth open wide. You shouldn't feel much pain." I would love to believe him. And even though I taste the pina colada flavored numbing gel and my lip feels about ten times too big, I know better. In complete agony I lay in the chair, unable to shut my eyes, move or even scream. Yet very able to feel and hear him searing through my gums and into my jaw. The clamps enclose on the tooth and I can literally hear each cracking of my tooth as he tries as gingerly as possible to extract the tooth from my jaw. Blood

I added more description of the walk to the examining room and the room itself so that the reader could actually picture the events.

I also tried to make my essay a little bit longer, but I chose the details I added carefully so that the reader would think about my overall impression.

I wrote my first draft in one fast block. When I revised, I had to go back and establish my paragraphs. Since I was using a narrative structure, I started a new paragraph each time something happened.

gushes from my mouth as tears cascade down my cheeks. "Great job! Only three more to go!" the dentist exclaims. I shudder at the thought of even one more second in this chair. I just thank God that you only get wisdom teeth once.

EXERCISE 6.2: REVISING

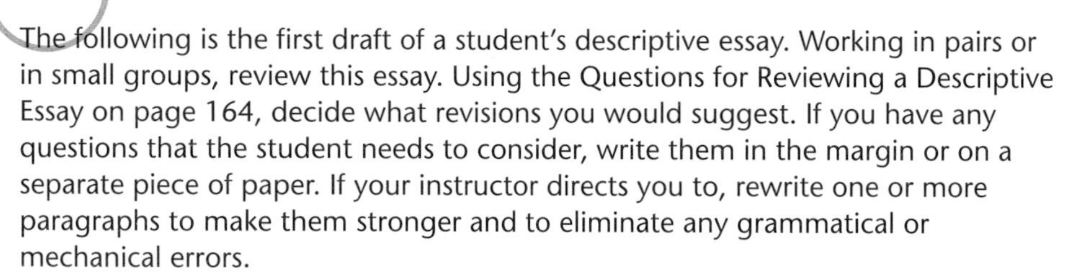

The following is the first draft of a student's descriptive essay. Working in pairs or in small groups, review this essay. Using the Questions for Reviewing a Descriptive Essay on page 164, decide what revisions you would suggest. If you have any questions that the student needs to consider, write them in the margin or on a separate piece of paper. If your instructor directs you to, rewrite one or more paragraphs to make them stronger and to eliminate any grammatical or mechanical errors.

EXERCISE 6.2 Answers will vary. Students should point out the need for a stronger introduction, the informal language and use of slang, and the need for more specific details in paragraphs 2, 3, and 4.

SUGGESTED ACTIVITY Consider asking students to meet in writing groups, each of which is charged with producing a more developed and effective version of this essay. Encourage students to use their imaginations when adding appropriate details.

"Dorm Room From Hell"

1 I live in a dorm room with too other dudes, they are also students here. The place is always a mess, pizza boxes and beer cans everwhere. Tim is the worst offender but James at least trys to keep things neet. I'm sort of in the middle.

2 The livingroom has a couple of chairs, a couch and a T.V. The rug hasn't been cleaned in awhile and it needs it. Weve spilled stuff everywhere. One Saturday we were all going to pitch in to cleanup, but James got called into work and Tim was sleeping off one. Somehow nothing got done.

3 We each have a bedroom, Tim's is the worse as you might imagine. There's stuff everywhere, including old food. He hasn't made his bed in months and he rarely change the sheets. His girl friend says, it looks like hes a tornado victim.

4 James' room is the neatest, he at least trys to keep it neat. But, he works so much that he doesn't have a lot of time. My room is sometimes neat only do to the fact that I try to keep my possesions at a minemum. Otherwise I'm almost as bad of a slob as Tim.

5 Whenever we move out of this apartment well have a lot of cleaning to do. Unless, of course, the land lord wants to donate it as a museum of male messiness.

Additional Writing Topics

1. Some people look different because of birth, disease, or accident, but many people have a distinctive appearance because of personal choice. Choose a person you know who has a very personal style, and describe him or her.
2. What is the most distinctive public building or private house that you have seen lately? Describe the exterior of this structure.
3. Have you been in a very interesting room in a public building or in someone's house? Describe it.
4. Where do you go to get comfortable and be alone? Describe this place.
5. **Writing on the job.** Think of the place where you work or where you used to work. Choose a distinctive physical feature of this workplace, and write an essay describing it for a potential employee.

Responding to a Photograph

During the Great Depression, Walker Evans worked for the Farm Security Administration, a branch of the federal government that tried to aid the nation's farmers. Evans traveled widely, photographing the inhabitants of rural areas. While roaming through Alabama in 1936, Evans did an extensive study of the Floyd Burroughs family. One of his photographs is reproduced below.

CLASSROOM HINT You might discuss this photograph in class before asking students to write about it.

Walker Evans, *Squeakie Burroughs and Friend, Hale County, Alabama, Summer 1936.* The Library of Congress [LC-USF33-31297-M2].

1. Write an informal response to the photograph. What do you notice? How does the image make you feel? How does the photograph make use of the description option?

2. In 1936 many of the safeguards that we now take for granted—Social Security, Medicare, and Medicaid, for instance—did not exist. The Great Depression was also marked by an extensive drought, so U.S. farmers struggled with poor agricultural conditions as well as a poor economy. Some farm families lost their land; others actually starved. Using a combination of library and online research, explore the life of the small farmer or sharecropper of the 1930s. Write a documented essay describing what daily life was like for a representative family. (For more information on documented essays, see Chapter 21.)

Writing About Film

Princess Mononoke (1999, PG-13) is a Japanese animated film about nature and humanity's complex relationship to it. Choose a key scene—preferably one depicting a "nature spirit"—and write an essay describing what you see.

Howards End (1990, PG-13) is about an English estate of the same name and the differing attitudes toward that place. The property has great nostalgic value for its owner and becomes the object of a power struggle within her family. Write an essay describing the estate called Howards End.

Using the Internet

Search the Internet for insights and information to use in descriptive papers.

1. Visit at least two Web sites containing information on a city, state, country, or region of the world that you have always wanted to see. Take notes on points of interest. Gather information about one or more of the following: historical attractions, important buildings, museums and galleries, folk festivals, native food and dress, and social and religious observances. However, don't forget to gather information about the natural environment of the place as well. Turn these notes into a full-length descriptive essay designed to entice outsiders to visit this locale.

2. Search for information on the places in which your parents or grandparents were born, grew up, or lived most of their lives. Draw this material from at least two different Web sites. Then write a descriptive essay that explains the kind of place where your parents or grandparents once lived. Be as specific as you can about special aspects of the natural and social environment of this town or city. Also describe the kind of people who inhabit it, if possible. If you have visited this place, draw on your own experience as well as the information you gather from the Web.

3. In her essay about the extraction of her wisdom teeth, Jennifer Janisz does more than describe a place or explain a dental procedure. She also describes her state of mind, and she even verges on technical description when she talks about those "shiny silver clamps." Using her essay as inspiration, search the Internet to learn about a new instrument or

machine that represents a significant advance in medicine, dentistry, or another health-related field. You might want to search for information about a device used to treat an illness that you or someone you know is suffering from. Describe what this instrument looks like, and explain what it can do.

HELLO?
HI, DAD! IT'S ME, CALVIN. WILL YOU TELL ME A STORY?

CALVIN, I'M AT WORK! I DON'T HAVE TIME TO TELL YOU A STORY NOW! I'M VERY BUSY! GET OFF THE PHONE. I'M EXPECTING IMPORTANT CALLS.

OK, DAD. I'LL JUST STAY HERE QUIETLY GROWING UP AT AN UNBELIEVABLE RATE, NEVER SPENDING MUCH SPECIAL TIME WITH MY OWN DAD, WHO'S ALWAYS WORKING.

CHAPTER 7

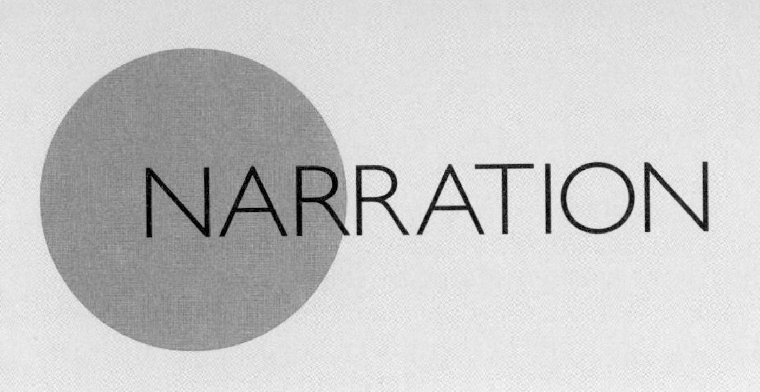

NARRATION

Writing in Context

You have been "called back" for a second interview at Osprey. On Wednesday afternoon you show up determined to nail down this job.

First, you have another interview with Bob, the man who would be your boss. Bob is all teeth, smiles, and suit, but you notice that he is smart enough to protect himself by carefully avoiding a commitment at this point.

Next, you are sent back to Human Resources. There is yet another psychological profile test for you to complete, administered by one of the quiet, synthetically pleasant people who hover around the area. (At this point you wouldn't be surprised if one of them produced a rubber mallet and asked to check your reflexes.) After the profile, one of the HR people sits down with you, hands over a clipboard and some writing paper, and asks this question: "Can you tell us about the single most important event in your college years, the one that led you here today?"

And how shall you begin?

Indeed, we all know how to tell stories, but finding the most effective one and telling it to maximum benefit is a complex process.

SUGGESTED ACTIVITY
Ask students to take five to ten minutes to write a brief story their parents told them as children or a story that they like to tell their children. As a class, examine one or two of these stories for elements of narration such as strategies for expanding or compressing time, dialogue, and the point that the storyteller is making.

HOW DOES NARRATION WORK?

The **narrative** is the oldest structured form of human communication. The ability to process the standard elements of a narrative seems to be genetically hardwired into the human system. Parents teach language to very young children by telling them stories. Moreover, people spend the rest of their lives telling stories: informing the traffic officer about what happened in the accident, explaining to the boss what happened in the client conference, letting the spouse know about the huge argument at work, explaining to children the events that happened when they were too young to remember. When you are old, you will probably tell young people about how strange the decades before and after the turn of the century were.

Except when people are asleep and slaves to their subconscious, the events of their world unfold in a continuous narrative. In some sense, every life is a narrative, a chronology of events both small and large.

Most of life's events are, indeed, small. Think what your typical morning would look like if captured on film. You wake up, shower, prepare, dress. You leave for school. Your first class is algebra, where you are either attentive or bored, depending on your general level of interest, the specific subject matter, and the lecturer's skill. Your next class is economics, where you go through the same scenario. At 10:00 you have an hour break, during which you grab some food and study for a while. At 11:00 you have English. At noon your morning is over.

The resulting "film" of your average morning is unlikely to win any best-documentary awards. More likely, it would bore viewers to tears. This narrative is *unstructured,* like most of our experiences in real life. In fact, there is a significant subcategory of narrative writing that is deliberately unstructured. Read a police officer's incident report or the court transcript of eyewitness testimony, and you'll find narratives in which the "story" is lost in a mass of seemingly extraneous details and impressions. However, the person relating the narrative is just following directions. The *whole* story is needed; others will figure out what is important. The minutes of meetings produce a similar effect: all motions and discussions are listed in order, the important along with the trivial, and the reader is left to interpret the results. However, most written narratives are *structured*—that is, they convey a sense of their significance and a point or "moral." Moviemakers edit out the dull parts; similarly, writers of short stories, novels, and plays concentrate on the significant events of the plot and minimize others.

The success of a personal narrative essay depends on this search for significance. The narrative essay tells a story, to be sure, but the true value of the narrative comes from what the writer and reader learn from it. Thus, what may well be suitable in a short story—for example, an amusing series of events—may not work so well as the subject of a personal narrative essay. Read the following short essay, and then consider its "point":

> In 1958 I was three years old. My father had just been transferred seven hundred miles from our home to a power-plant construction project in a very remote part of the lower Midwest. The place and the area must have been

hellish for my parents—especially my mother—but I didn't care. At three years of age, I found the world an endlessly fascinating place no matter where I was.

During the day I played outside in the yard, or watched life through the window. One afternoon in the late summer of 1958, I saw a strange episode unfold. Our next-door neighbor, Joe Marshall, was Dad's age, and the next neighbor down was a retired coal miner, Albert McGinnis. For some reason, Mr. Marshall was home from work that day, working in his yard, and for a probably more complicated reason, Mr. McGinnis snapped and took out after Mr. Marshall with a shovel.

The old man chased Joe Marshall down the middle of the street, and suddenly Joe stopped and started to chase Mr. McGinnis. After this went on for a few hundred feet, the old man apparently realized that he was the one with the deadly weapon, and the race suddenly reversed itself again.

Finally, Joe Marshall took the shovel away from Albert McGinnis, and eventually the sheriff came. Mr. McGinnis was taken away, and Mr. Marshall recovered his equilibrium.

That night at supper, my parents discussed the incident. My mother asked me if I'd seen this bizarre event. When I answered yes, she was amazed: "Why didn't you *say* anything?"

"Because it was like a cartoon," I answered. I didn't have to say anything else. My parents looked at each other, and the conversation ended.

Even at the age of three, I was sure that no one was going to be hurt during the Marshall-McGinnis debacle. For it *was* just like a cartoon, and I'm sure that I, somehow, some way, would have known otherwise if actual violence had been about to occur.

SUGGESTED ACTIVITY
Ask students to add detail to or reconstruct this essay in order to make a point.

Do you see the problem with this essay? The writer recounts an odd event, one that could be very funny in a movie or a novel, but what is the point? Cartoons are bad? Encounters that initially seem violent can end up being comical? No, there isn't really a resulting message issuing from this essay. The raw materials are certainly present, but they really don't lead anywhere.

However, the structured personal essay—the formal type that you'll be writing in response to classroom assignments—*does* need to make a point. The writer has experienced something in his or her past that proved significant; perhaps it changed the way that he or she understands the world. The preceding essay about the young boy, though interesting, has no real point, but a less interesting narrative—say, one about the day you learned the result of touching a hot stove top—would be about an event that changed the way you experience the world: a narrative whose significance is lasting. Note that we're not advising dreary, moralistic approaches to the essay. "How I Learned Not to Drive Drunk" and "My Horrible Experience with Credit-Card Debt" may well be the titles of interesting essays, but you don't need to take this approach. People learn from good experiences as well as from bad ones.

Another way you will employ structured narrative is to develop paragraphs for essays based on other rhetorical options. For example, a process analysis essay (see Chapter 9) is frequently ordered chronologically, as the writer explains to the reader how to complete a series of steps. As well, you will find

Consider Your Options

When was the last time you chose to *use* a narrative? What was your purpose? How did this purpose help you shape your account?

yourself using smaller narratives (brief recountings of events known as **anecdotes**) to help develop paragraphs in almost every type of essay that you write. Narrative pervades our world.

The effective personal narrative has a story to tell and a point to make; it also uses an economical structure and has a clear sense of its audience. Later in this chapter we talk about how to handle time in an essay and how to use transitions to guide the reader. Note how the writers of the following professional essays make their points, structure their stories, and engage their readers.

READING THE NARRATIVE ESSAY WITH A WRITER'S EYE

In the four works that follow, Lynda Barry writes about a childhood spent in such dysfunctional circumstances that school became a haven for her, Sandra Cisneros shows how going against her father's very traditional expectations paid off for her, Annie Dillard recounts an experience from her youth in Pittsburgh, and George Orwell presents the stark reality of capital punishment. As you read each essay, concentrate on the writer's **thesis**—the point that the writer is trying to make and the focus that drives each of these narratives.

The second half of this chapter features strategies for writing the personal narrative with a reader's eye (pages 190–200). If you decide to write on one of the topics that follow the four essays, make sure that you have read the strategies section before you begin. Additional writing topics are listed at the end of the chapter (pages 205–207).

The Sanctuary of School

LYNDA BARRY

Lynda Barry is best known for her syndicated cartoons, but she has also written an important novel about adolescence, *The Good Times Are Killing Me* (1988). She has a profound understanding of the issues facing children and teenagers.

"The Sanctuary of School" first appeared in the *New York Times* in 1992. In it, Barry portrays her childhood response to her family situation, made dysfunctional by strife and alcohol.

1 I was 7 years old the first time I snuck out of the house in the dark. It was winter and my parents had been fighting all night. They were short on money and long on relatives who kept "temporarily" moving into our house because they had nowhere else to go.

2 My brother and I were used to giving up our bedroom. We slept on the couch, something we actually liked because it put us that much closer to the light of our lives, our television.

3 At night when everyone was asleep, we lay on our pillows watching it with the sound off. We watched Steve Allen's mouth moving. We watched Johnny Carson's mouth moving. We watched movies filled with gangsters shooting machine guns into packed rooms, dying soldiers hurling a last grenade and beautiful women crying at windows. Then the sign-off finally came and we tried to sleep.

The morning I snuck out, I woke up filled with a panic about needing to get to school. The sun wasn't quite up yet but my anxiety was so fierce that I just got dressed, walked quietly across the kitchen and let myself out the back door. 4

It was quiet outside. Stars were still out. Nothing moved and no one was in the street. It was as if someone had turned the sound off on the world. 5

I walked the alley, breaking thin ice over the puddles with my shoes. I didn't know why I was walking to school in the dark. I didn't think about it. All I knew was a feeling of panic, like the panic that strikes kids when they realize they are lost. 6

That feeling eased the moment I turned the corner and saw the dark outline of my school at the top of the hill. My school was made up of about 15 nondescript portable classrooms set down on a fenced concrete lot in a rundown Seattle neighborhood, but it had the most beautiful view of the Cascade Mountains. You could see them from anywhere on the playfield and you could see them from the windows of my classroom—Room 2. 7

I walked over to the monkey bars and hooked my arms around the cold metal. I stood for a long time just looking across Rainier Valley. The sky was beginning to whiten and I could hear a few birds. 8

In a perfect world my absence at home would not have gone unnoticed. I would have had two parents in a panic to locate me, instead of two parents in a panic to locate an answer to the hard question of survival during a deep financial and emotional crisis. 9

But in an overcrowded and unhappy home, it's incredibly easy for any child to slip away. The high levels of frustration, depression and anger in my house made my brother and me invisible. We were children with the sound turned off. And for us, as for the steadily increasing number of neglected children in this country, the only place where we could count on being noticed was at school. 10

"Hey there, young lady. Did you forget to go home last night?" It was Mr. Gunderson, our janitor, whom we all loved. He was nice and he was funny and he was old with white hair, thick glasses and an unbelievable number of keys. I could hear them jingling as he walked across the playfield. I felt incredibly happy to see him. 11

He let me push his wheeled garbage can between the different portables as he unlocked each room. He let me turn on the lights and raise the window shades and I saw my school slowly come to life. I saw Mrs. Holman, our school secretary, walk into the office without her orange lipstick on yet. She waved. 12

I saw the fifth-grade teacher, Mr. Cunningham, walking under the breezeway eating a hard roll. He waved. 13

And I saw my teacher, Mrs. Claire LeSane, walking toward us in a red coat and calling my name in a very happy and surprised way, and suddenly my throat got tight and my eyes stung and I ran toward her crying. It was something that surprised us both. 14

It's only thinking about it now, 28 years later, that I realize I was crying from relief. I was with my teacher, and in a while I was going to sit at my desk, with my crayons and pencils and books and classmates all around me, and for the next six hours I was going to enjoy a thoroughly secure, warm and stable world. It was a world I absolutely relied on. Without it, I don't know where I would have gone that morning. 15

Mrs. LeSane asked me what was wrong and when I said "Nothing," she seemingly left it at that. But she asked me if I would carry her purse for her, an honor above all honors, and she asked if I wanted to come into Room 2 early and paint. 16

She believed in the natural healing power of painting and drawing for troubled children. In the back of her room there was always a drawing table and an easel with plenty of supplies, and sometimes during the day she would come up to you for what seemed like no good reason and quietly ask if you wanted to go to the back table and "make some pictures for Mrs. LeSane." We all had a chance at it—to sit apart from the class for a while to paint, draw, and silently work out impossible problems on 11 × 17 sheets of newsprint. 17

Drawing came to mean everything to me. At the back table in Room 2, I learned to build myself a life preserver that I could carry into my home. 18

We all know that a good education system saves lives, but the people of this country are still told that cutting the budget for public schools is necessary, that poor salaries for teachers are all we can manage and that art, music and all creative activities must be the first to go when times are lean. 19

Before- and after-school programs are cut and we are told that public schools are not made for baby-sitting children. If parents are neglectful temporarily or permanently, for whatever reason, it's certainly sad, but their unlucky children must fend for themselves. Or slip through the cracks. Or wander in a dark night alone. 20

We are told in a thousand ways that not only are public schools not important, but that the children who attend them, the children who need them most, are not important either. We leave them to learn from the blind eye of a television, or to the mercy of "a thousand points of light" that can be as far away as stars. 21

I was lucky. I had Mrs. LeSane. I had Mr. Gunderson. I had an abundance of art supplies. And I had a particular brand of neglect in my home that allowed me to slip away and get to them. But what about the rest of the kids who weren't as lucky? What happened to them? 22

By the time the bell rang that morning I had finished my drawing and Mrs. LeSane pinned it up on the special bulletin board she reserved for drawings from the back table. It was the same picture I always drew—a sun in the corner of a blue sky over a nice house with flowers all around it. 23

Mrs. LeSane asked us to please stand, face the flag, place our right hands over our hearts and say the Pledge of Allegiance. Children across the country do it faithfully. I wonder now when the country will face its children and say a pledge right back. 24

Vocabulary

The following terms are identified by paragraph number. Make sure that you understand each term's meaning in its context. If you're not sure that you understand a term, look it up in a college-level dictionary.

sign-off (3)	easel (17)
nondescript (7)	abundance (22)

Style and Strategy

1. What was the only part of Barry's home that she enjoyed? How does she illustrate this aspect of her home life?

2. Where does the narrative end? What follows the end of the narrative?

STYLE AND STRATEGY

1. Watching television with the sound off provided the narrator with the peace and comfort that can be compared with what she experienced at school. Paragraphs 11–18 are worth discussing.
2. The narrative concludes with paragraph 18. What follows is an argument for increased funding of public education.
3. The name reflects the "clarity" and "sanity" of the narrator's school environment.
4. Such questions draw readers into the discourse by having them consider consequences that are important to Barry's argument.

3. Barry tells us that her second-grade teacher was named Claire LeSane, an obviously fictional name. Why did Barry choose this pseudonym for her teacher?
4. In paragraph 22, note the two questions that Barry asks. These are called *rhetorical* questions because Barry does not intend to answer them. Why, then, does she ask them? What do they contribute to her narrative?

Questions for Critical Thinking and Discussion

1. Do you know a family whose situation is similar to the situation that Barry describes? If so, how do the children cope? What options do they have?
2. Comment on this statement: "You have to buy a license to catch fish, but you can produce all the children that you want while the government turns a blind eye." Given the high value most people in the United States attach to individual liberty and freedom of choice, what, if anything, can the government do about situations such as the one Barry faced as a child?

QUESTIONS FOR CRITICAL THINKING AND DISCUSSION Both items produce interesting discussion. The first can be turned into a writing prompt that students might research on the Internet.

Suggestions for Writing

1. When you were a child, where did you go to "hide"? Write a 500-word essay about a time when you felt the need to escape to that place.
2. In 500 to 750 words, write about a family crisis and how you reacted to it.

SUGGESTIONS FOR WRITING Remind students who choose the first prompt to cast their writing in the form of a narrative that explains why they needed to escape and why they chose a particular place.

Only Daughter

SANDRA CISNEROS

Sandra Cisneros was born in Chicago to a Mexican father and a Mexican American mother. She attended the prestigious Master of Fine Arts program at the University of Iowa before producing her well-regarded collections of short stories and poetry—*The House on Mango Street* (short fiction, 1983), *My Wicked Wicked Ways* (poetry, 1987), *Woman Hollering Creek* (short fiction, 1991), and *Loose Women* (poetry, 1994). She has also written a children's book, *Hairs-Pelitos* (1994). In 1995, Cisneros was awarded a MacArthur fellowship.

In "Only Daughter," first published in 1990 in *Glamour,* Cisneros writes about the push/pull of traditional culture (her father's) and modern culture (North America's).

1 Once, several years ago, when I was just starting out my writing career, I was asked to write my own contributor's note for an anthology I was part of. I wrote: "I am the only daughter in a family of six sons. *That* explains everything."

2 Well, I've thought about that ever since, and yes, it explains a lot to me, but for the reader's sake I should have written: "I am the only daughter in a *Mexican* family of six sons." Or even: "I am the only daughter of a Mexican father and a Mexican-American mother." Or: "I am the only daughter of a working-class family of nine." All of these had everything to do with who I am today.

3 I was/am the only daughter and *only* a daughter. Being an only daughter in a family of six sons forced me by circumstance to spend a lot of time by myself because my brothers felt it beneath them to play with a *girl* in public. But that aloneness, that

loneliness, was good for a would-be writer—it allowed me time to think and think, to imagine, to read and prepare myself.

4 Being only a daughter for my father meant my destiny would lead me to become someone's wife. That's what he believed. But when I was in the fifth grade and shared my plans for college with him, I was sure he understood. I remember my father saying, "*Que bueno, ni'ja,* that's good." That meant a lot to me, especially since my brothers thought the idea hilarious. What I didn't realize was that my father thought college was good for girls—good for finding a husband. After four years in college and two more in graduate school, and still no husband, my father shakes his head even now and says I wasted all that education.

5 In retrospect, I'm lucky my father believed daughters were meant for husbands. It meant it didn't matter if I majored in something silly like English. After all, I'd find a nice professional eventually, right? This allowed me the liberty to putter about embroidering my little poems and stories without my father interrupting with so much as a "What's that you're writing?"

6 But the truth is, I wanted him to interrupt. I wanted my father to understand what it was I was scribbling, to introduce me as "My only daughter, the writer." Not as "This is my only daughter. She teaches." *Es maestra*—teacher. Not even *profesora.*

7 In a sense, everything I have ever written has been for him, to win his approval even though I know my father can't read English words, even though my father's only reading includes the brown-ink *Esto* sports magazines from Mexico City and the bloody *¡Alarma!* magazines that feature yet another sighting of *La Virgen de Guadalupe* on a tortilla or a wife's revenge on her philandering husband by bashing his skull in with a *molcajete* (a kitchen mortar made of volcanic rock). Or the *fotonovelas,* the little picture paperbacks with tragedy and trauma erupting from the characters' mouths in bubbles.

8 My father represents, then, the public majority. A public who is uninterested in reading, and yet one whom I am writing about and for, and privately trying to woo.

9 When we were growing up in Chicago, we moved a lot because of my father. He suffered bouts of nostalgia. Then we'd have to let go of our flat, store the furniture with mother's relatives, load the station wagon with baggage and bologna sandwiches, and head south. To Mexico City.

10 We came back, of course. To yet another Chicago flat, another Chicago neighborhood, another Catholic school. Each time, my father would seek out the parish priest in order to get a tuition break, and complain or boast: "I have seven sons."

11 He meant *siete hijos,* seven children, but he translated it as "sons." I have seven sons. To anyone who would listen. The Sears Roebuck employee who sold us the washing machine. The short-order cook where my father ate his ham-and-eggs breakfasts. "I have seven sons." As if he deserved a medal from the state.

12 My papa. He didn't mean anything by that mistranslation, I'm sure. But somehow I could feel myself being erased. I'd tug my father's sleeve and whisper: "Not seven sons. Six! And *one daughter.*"

13 When my oldest brother graduated from medical school, he fulfilled my father's dream that we study hard and use this—our heads, instead of this—our hands. Even now my father's hands are thick and yellow, stubbed by a history of

hammer and nails and twine and coils and springs. "Use this," my father said, tapping his head, "and not this," showing us those hands. He always looked tired when he said it.

14 Wasn't college an investment? And hadn't I spent all those years in college? And if I didn't marry, what was it all for? Why would anyone go to college and then choose to be poor? Especially someone who had always been poor.

15 Last year, after ten years of writing professionally, the financial rewards started to trickle in. My second National Endowment for the Arts Fellowship. A guest professorship at the University of California, Berkeley. My book, which sold to a major New York publishing house.

16 At Christmas, I flew home to Chicago. The house was throbbing, same as always; hot *tamales* and sweet *tamales* hissing in my mother's pressure cooker, and everybody—my mother, six brothers, wives, babies, aunts, cousins—talking too loud and at the same time, like in a Fellini film, because that's just how we are.

17 I went upstairs to my father's room. One of my stories had just been translated into Spanish and published in an anthology of Chicano writing, and I wanted to show it to him. Ever since he recovered from a stroke two years ago, my father likes to spend his leisure hours horizontally. And that's how I found him, watching a Pedro Infante* movie on Galavisión* and eating rice pudding.

18 There was a glass filmed with milk on the bedside table. There were several vials of pills and balled Kleenex. And on the floor, one black sock and a plastic urinal that I didn't want to look at but looked at anyway. Pedro Infante was about to burst into song, and my father was laughing.

19 I'm not sure if it was because my story was translated into Spanish, or because it was published in Mexico, or perhaps because the story dealt with Tepeyac, the *colonia* my father was raised in and the house he grew up in, but at any rate, my father punched the mute button on his remote control and read my story.

20 I sat on the bed next to my father and waited. He read it very slowly. As if he were reading each line over and over. He laughed at all the right places and read lines he liked out loud. He pointed and asked questions: "Is this So-and-so?" "Yes," I said. He kept reading.

21 When he was finally finished, after what seemed like hours, my father looked up and asked: "Where can we get more copies of this for the relatives?"

22 Of all the wonderful things that happened to me last year, that was the most wonderful.

Vocabulary

The following terms are identified by paragraph number. Make sure that you understand each term's meaning in its context. If you're not sure that you understand a term, look it up in a college-level dictionary.

retrospect (5)	philandering (7)	Chicano (17)
embroidering (5)	nostalgia (9)	

***Pedro Infante (1917–1957):** a Mexican film star and singer.

***Galavisión:** a major Hispanic cable television network in the United States.

STYLE AND STRATEGY
1. People, like words, are often defined in contexts. Paragraphs 3, 4, 7, and 8 are helpful when responding to this question.

2. The best statement of a thesis comes at the beginning of paragraph 7. But Cisneros's thesis really goes beyond this statement. Her purpose is to illustrate the anguish of seeking parental approval, but through it all shines the author's unmitigated joy over her father's affirmation.
3. In paragraph 12, the narrator realizes that attempts to win her father's approval will not be rebuffed.

QUESTIONS FOR CRITICAL THINKING AND DISCUSSION The first item can be turned into a short writing prompt quite easily. However, advise students to use an anecdote from the subject's life to develop this assignment. One of the purposes of this assignment is to demonstrate the versatility of narration. The second item prompts discussion of Cisneros's purpose and, again, of the versatility of narration.

SUGGESTIONS FOR WRITING The information students use to respond to the items under Questions for Critical Thinking and Discussion can help them get started on the essay called for in item 1.

Style and Strategy

1. Cisneros spends the first four paragraphs of her essay commenting on the significance of her being the only sister of six brothers. Why does she open the essay in this way? How successful is this strategy?
2. What is this essay's thesis? Is it stated overtly, or is it implied?
3. "The turning point of this narrative is paragraph 12." Do you agree with this statement? Why or why not?

Questions for Critical Thinking and Discussion

1. The idea that young women should be given the same opportunities as young men is widely accepted in modern North American culture. However, Cisneros's father believed that young women should be both protected and provided for. Do you know someone who holds a similar opinion? What might be some of the consequences of this idea?
2. What do your parents expect of you over the next ten years? Are you willing to try to satisfy those expectations? What are your own expectations? If any of your expectations differ from those of your parents, how have you handled this conflict?

Suggestions for Writing

1. Write a 500- to 750-word essay about an occasion when you succeeded at a task despite the negative expectations of an authority figure—for example, a parent, a teacher, or an employer.
2. Write a 500- to 750-word essay about an occasion in which you had every reason to succeed at a task but somehow failed.

The Chase

ANNIE DILLARD

Annie Dillard, best known for her Pulitzer Prize-winning *Pilgrim at Tinker Creek* (1975), is the author of eight other books, including a novel, *The Living* (1992); a collection of essays, *Teaching a Stone to Talk: Expeditions and Encounters* (1982); and her memories of growing up, *An American Childhood* (1987).

In "The Chase," excerpted from *An American Childhood*, Dillard looks back at her early days in Pittsburgh and recounts a moment in which she gained a better understanding of the nature of adults. Have you ever had a similar experience?

1 Some boys taught me to play football. This was fine sport. You thought up a new strategy for every play and whispered it to the others. You went out for a pass, fooling everyone. Best, you got to throw yourself mightily at someone's running legs. Either you brought him down or you hit the ground flat out on your chin, with your arms empty before you. It was all or nothing. If you hesitated in fear, you would miss and get hurt; you would take a hard fall while the kid got away, or you would get kicked in the face while the kid got away. But if you flung yourself wholeheartedly at the back of his knees—if you gathered and joined body and soul and pointed them diving fearlessly—then you likely wouldn't get hurt, and you'd stop

the ball. Your fate, and your team's score, depended on your concentration and courage. Nothing girls did could compare with it.

2 Boys welcomed me at baseball, too, for I had, through enthusiastic practice, what was weirdly known as a boy's arm. In winter, in the snow, there was neither baseball or football, so the boys and I threw snowballs at passing cars. I got in trouble throwing snowballs, and have seldom been happier since.

3 On one weekday morning after Christmas, six inches of new snow had just fallen. We were standing up to our boot tops in snow on a front yard on trafficked Reynolds Street, waiting for cars. The cars traveled Reynolds Street slowly and evenly; they were targets all but wrapped in red ribbons, cream puffs. We couldn't miss.

4 I was seven; the boys were eight, nine, and ten. The oldest two Fahey boys were there—Mikey and Peter—polite blond boys who lived near me on Lloyd Street, and who already had four brothers and sisters. My parents approved Mikey and Peter Fahey. Chickie McBride was there, a tough kid, and Billy Paul and Mackie Kean too, from across Reynolds, where the boys grew up dark and furious, grew up skinny, knowing, and skilled. We had all drifted from our houses that morning looking for action, and had found it here on Reynolds Street.

5 It was cloudy but cold. The cars' tires laid behind them on the snowy street a complex trail of beige chunks like crenellated castle walls. I had stepped on some early; they squeaked. We could have wished for more traffic. When a car came, we all popped it one. In the intervals between cars we reverted to the natural solitude of children.

6 I started making an iceball—a perfect iceball, from perfectly white snow, perfectly spherical, and squeezed perfectly translucent so no snow remained all the way through. (The Fahey boys and I considered it unfair actually to throw an iceball at somebody, but it had been known to happen.)

7 I had just embarked on the iceball project when we heard tire chains come clanking from afar. A black Buick was moving toward us down the street. We all spread out, banged together some regular snowballs, took aim, and, when the Buick drew nigh, fired.

8 A soft snowball hit the driver's windshield right before the driver's face. It made a smashed star with a hump in the middle.

9 Often, of course, we hit our target, but this time, the only time in all of life, the car pulled over and stopped. Its wide black door opened; a man got out of it, running. He didn't even close the car door.

10 He ran after us, and we ran away from him, up the snowy Reynolds sidewalk. At the corner, I looked back; incredibly, he was still after us. He was in city clothes: a suit and tie, street shoes. Any normal adult would have quit, having sprung us into flight and made his point. This man was gaining on us. He was a thin man, all action. All of a sudden, we were running for our lives.

11 Wordless, we split up. We were on our turf; we could lose ourselves in the neighborhood backyards, everyone for himself. I paused and considered. Everyone had vanished except Mikey Fahey, who was just rounding the corner of a yellow brick house. Poor Mikey, I trailed him. The driver of the Buick sensibly picked the two of us to follow. The man apparently had all day.

12 He chased Mikey and me around the yellow house and up a backyard path we knew by heart: under a low tree, up a bank, through a hedge, down some snowy steps, and across the grocery store's delivery driveway. We smashed through a gap

in another hedge, entered a scruffy backyard and ran around its back porch and tight between houses to Edgerton Avenue; we ran across Edgerton to an alley and up our own sliding woodpile to the Halls' front yard; he kept coming. We ran up Lloyd Street and wound through mazy backyards toward the steep hilltop at Willard and Lang.

13 He chased us silently, block after block. He chased us silently over picket fences, through thorny hedges, between houses, around garbage cans, and across streets. Every time I glanced back, choking for breath, I expected he would have quit. He must have been as breathless as we were. His jacket strained over his body. It was an immense discovery, pounding into my hot head with every sliding, joyous step, that this ordinary adult evidently knew what I thought only children who trained at football knew: that you have to fling yourself at what you're doing, you have to point yourself, forget yourself, aim, dive.

14 Mikey and I had nowhere to go, in our own neighborhood or out of it, but away from this man who was chasing us. He impelled us forward; we compelled him to follow our route. The air was cold; every breath tore my throat. We kept running, block after block; we kept improvising, backyard after backyard, running a frantic course and choosing it simultaneously, failing always to find small places or hard places to slow him down, and discovering always, exhilarated, dismayed, that only bare speed could save us—for he would never give up, this man—and we were losing speed.

15 He chased us through the backyard labyrinths of ten blocks before he caught us by our jackets. He caught us and we all stopped.

16 We three stood staggering, half blinded, coughing, in an obscure hilltop backyard: a man in his twenties, a boy, a girl. He had released our jackets, our pursuer, our captor, our hero: he knew we weren't going anywhere. We all played by the rules. Mikey and I unzipped our jackets. I pulled off my sopping mittens. Our tracks multiplied in the backyard's new snow. We had been breaking new snow all morning. We didn't look at each other. I was cherishing my excitement. The man's lower pants legs were wet; his cuffs were full of snow, and there was a prow of snow beneath them on his shoes and socks. Some trees bordered the little flat backyard, some messy winter trees. There was no one around: a clearing in a grove, and we the only players.

17 It was a long time before he could speak. I had some difficulty at first, recalling why we were there. My lips felt swollen; I couldn't see out of the sides of my eyes; I kept coughing.

18 "You stupid kids," he began perfunctorily.

19 We listened perfunctorily indeed, if we listened at all, for the chewing out was redundant, a mere formality, and beside the point. The point was that he had chased us passionately without giving up, and so he had caught us. Now he came down to earth. I wanted the glory to last forever.

20 But how could the glory have lasted forever? We could have run through every backyard in North America until we got to Panama. But when he trapped us at the lip of the Panama Canal, what precisely could he have done to prolong the drama of the chase and cap its glory? I brooded about this for the next few years. He could only have fried Mikey Fahey and me in boiling oil, say, or dismembered us piecemeal, or staked us to anthills. None of which I really wanted, and none of which any adult was likely to do, even in the spirit of fun. He could only chew us out there

in the Panamanian jungle, after months or years of exalting pursuit. He could only begin, "You stupid kids," and continue in his ordinary Pittsburgh accent with his normal righteous anger and the usual common sense.

If in that snowy backyard the driver of the black Buick had cut off our heads, Mikey's and mine, I would have died happy, for nothing has required so much of me since as being chased all over Pittsburgh in the middle of winter—running terrified, exhausted—by this sainted, skinny, furious redheaded man who wished to have a word with us. I don't know how he found his way back to his car. 21

Vocabulary

The following terms are identified by paragraph number. Make sure that you understand each term's meaning in its context. If you're not sure that you understand a term, look it up in a college-level dictionary.

trafficked (3)	scruffy (12)	perfunctorily (18)
cream puff (3)	mazy (12)	redundant (19)
crenellated (5)	improvising (14)	dismembered (20)
translucent (6)	exhilarated (14)	piecemeal (20)
turf (11)	labyrinth (15)	exalting (20)

Style and Strategy

1. Dillard uses a brief thesis statement (see paragraph 2). Could she have expanded it, or is it more effective the way it is? Explain.
2. Why does Dillard open her essay with some comments about playing football? How is this section relevant to the rest of her essay? How does Dillard establish this relevance for readers?
3. How does Dillard use description (see Chapter 6) in this essay?
4. In paragraph 13, Dillard comes to an important realization about adults. Restate this realization in your own words.

STYLE AND STRATEGY
1. The thesis is appropriate. Anything more would have been superfluous.
2. The danger that she depicts in paragraph 1 prepares us for the excitement we experience in the rest of the essay.
3. Paragraphs 5–10, 12–13, and 16 are worth discussing in this regard.
4. Few students have trouble understanding Dillard's comments about the importance of being focused and resolute.

Questions for Critical Thinking and Discussion

1. In what way or ways can the unidentified "furious redheaded man" be said to function as a role model for Dillard and her friends?
2. Although this narrative about Dillard and her childhood friends has a satisfactory outcome, consider this question: What could have gone very wrong during such an encounter?

QUESTIONS FOR CRITICAL THINKING AND DISCUSSION
1. Try using this question as a prompt for short writing. Students can trace the same dedication and focus in the children's actions that they see in those of the "redheaded man."

2. This item can be used as a prompt for a full-length essay.

Suggestions for Writing

1. When you were a child, did you ever have an initially negative encounter with an adult that ended up having a positive outcome? Write a 500- to 750-word essay about such an encounter.
2. Sober, industrious adults will sometimes display an otherwise hidden joy for life. In 500 to 750 words, write a narrative about an event in which an adult of your acquaintance showed such an unexpected side.

SUGGESTIONS FOR WRITING
1.–2. Students who write in response to either of these prompts should be encouraged to use concrete, vivid language like the kind we see in Dillard's essay.

A Hanging

GEORGE ORWELL

Eric Arthur Blair, who took the pseudonym George Orwell, was born in 1903 to English parents stationed in India. As a young man, he joined the British Imperial Police in Burma (now Myanmar). Later, he returned to Europe and became a writer. *Homage to Catalonia* (1938), the account of his volunteer soldiering in the Spanish Republican army, reflects his sympathies with left-wing political movements. Later, Orwell shed his left-wing politics and concentrated on the evils of totalitarian government. His two best-known books, *Animal Farm* (1945) and *1984* (1949), reflect this growing concern. Orwell died in 1950.

In "A Hanging," first published in 1931, Orwell recounts in a spare, unemotional style the execution of a Burmese convict. This essay is not a statement for or against capital punishment but instead a look at a process that most of us are happy to leave to the responsibility of others.

It was in Burma, a sodden morning of the rains. A sickly light, like yellow tinfoil, was slanting over the high walls into the jail yard. We were waiting outside the condemned cells, a row of sheds fronted with double bars, like small animal cages. Each cell measured about ten feet by ten and was quite bare within except for a plank bed and a pot for drinking water. In some of them brown silent men were squatting at the inner bars, with their blankets draped round them. These were the condemned men, due to be hanged within the next week or two. 1

One prisoner had been brought out of his cell. He was a Hindu, a puny wisp of a man, with a shaven head and vague liquid eyes. He had a thick, sprouting moustache, absurdly too big for his body, rather like the moustache of a comic man on the films. Six tall Indian warders were guarding him and getting him ready for the gallows. Two of them stood by with rifles and fixed bayonets, while the others handcuffed him, passed a chain through his handcuffs and fixed it to their belts, and lashed his arms tight to his sides. They crowded very close about him, with their hands always on him in a careful, caressing grip, as though all the while feeling him to make sure he was there. It was like men handling a fish which is still alive and may jump back into the water. But he stood quite unresisting, yielding his arms limply to the ropes, as though he hardly noticed what was happening. 2

Eight o'clock struck and a bugle call, desolately thin in the wet air, floated from the distant barracks. The superintendent of the jail, who was standing apart from the rest of us, moodily prodding the gravel with his stick, raised his head at the sound. He was an army doctor, with a grey toothbrush moustache and a gruff voice. "For God's sake hurry up, Francis," he said irritably. "The man ought to have been dead by this time. Aren't you ready yet?" 3

Francis, the head jailer, a fat Dravidian in a white drill suit and gold spectacles, waved his black hand. "Yes sir, yes sir," he bubbled. "All iss satisfactorily prepared. The hangman iss waiting. We shall proceed." 4

"Well, quick march, then. The prisoners can't get their breakfast till this job's over." 5

We set out for the gallows. Two warders marched on either side of the prisoner, with their rifles at the slope; two others marched close against him, gripping him by arm and shoulder, as though at once pushing and supporting him. The rest of us, magistrates and the like, followed behind. Suddenly, when we had gone ten yards, the procession stopped short without any order or warning. A dreadful thing 6 had happened—a dog, come goodness knows whence, had appeared in the yard. It came bounding among us with a loud volley of barks, and leapt round us wagging its whole body, wild with glee at finding so many human beings together. It was a large woolly dog, half Airedale, half pariah. For a moment it pranced round us, and then, before anyone could stop it, it had made a dash for the prisoner and, jumping up, tried to lick his face. Everyone stood aghast, too taken aback even to grab at the dog.

"Who let that bloody brute in here?" said the superintendent angrily. "Catch it, someone!" 7

A warder, detached from the escort, charged clumsily after the dog, but it danced and gambolled just out of his reach, taking everything as part of the game. A young Eurasian jailer picked up a handful of gravel and tried to stone the dog away, but it dodged the stones and came after us again. Its yaps echoed from the jail walls. The prisoner, in the grasp of the two warders, looked on incuriously, as though this was another formality of the hanging. It was several minutes before someone managed to catch the dog. Then we put my handkerchief through its collar and moved off once more, with the dog still straining and whimpering. 8

It was about forty yards to the gallows. I watched the bare brown back of the prisoner marching in front of me. He walked clumsily with his bound arms, but quite steadily, with that bobbing gait of the Indian who never straightens his knees. At each step his muscles slid neatly into place, the lock of hair on his scalp danced up and down, his feet printed themselves on the wet gravel. And once, in spite of the men who gripped him by each shoulder, he stepped slightly aside to avoid a puddle in the path. 9

It is curious, but till that moment I had never realized what it means to destroy a healthy, conscious man. When I saw the prisoner step aside to avoid the puddle I saw the mystery, the unspeakable wrongness, of cutting a life short when it is in full tide. This man was not dying, he was alive just as we were alive. All the organs of his body were working—bowels digesting food, skin renewing itself, nails growing, tissues forming—all toiling away in solemn foolery. His nails would still be growing when he stood on the drop, when he was falling through the air with a tenth-of-a-second to live. His eyes saw the yellow gravel and the grey walls, and his brain still remembered, foresaw, reasoned—reasoned even about puddles. He and we were a party of men walking together, seeing, hearing, feeling, understanding the same world; and in two minutes, with a sudden snap, one of us would be gone—one mind less, one world less. 10

The gallows stood in a small yard, separate from the main grounds of the prison, and overgrown with tall prickly weeds. It was a brick erection like three sides of a shed, with planking on top, and above that two beams and a crossbar with the rope dangling. The hangman, a grey-haired convict in the white uniform of the prison, was waiting beside his machine. He greeted us with a servile crouch as we entered. At a word from Francis the two warders, gripping the prisoner more closely than ever, half led half pushed him to the gallows and helped him clumsily up the ladder. Then the hangman climbed up and fixed the rope round the prisoner's neck. 11

We stood waiting, five yards away. The warders had formed in a rough circle round the gallows. And then, when the noose was fixed, the prisoner began crying out to his god. It was a high, reiterated cry of "Ram! Ram! Ram! Ram!" not urgent 12 and fearful like a prayer or cry for help, but steady, rhythmical, almost like the tolling of a bell. The dog answered the sound with a whine. The hangman, still standing on the gallows, produced a small cotton bag like a flour bag and drew it down over the prisoner's face. But the sound, muffled by the cloth, still persisted, over and over again: "Ram! Ram! Ram! Ram! Ram!"

13 The hangman climbed down and stood ready, holding the lever. Minutes seemed to pass. The steady, muffled crying from the prisoner went on and on, "Ram! Ram! Ram!" never faltering for an instant. The superintendent, his head on his chest, was slowly poking the ground with his stick; perhaps he was counting the cries, allowing the prisoner a fixed number—fifty, perhaps, or a hundred. Everyone had changed color. The Indians had gone grey like bad coffee, and one or two of the bayonets were wavering. We looked at the lashed, hooded man on the drop, and listened to his cries—each cry another second of life; the same thought was in all our minds: oh, kill him quickly, get it over, stop that abominable noise!

14 Suddenly the superintendent made up his mind. Throwing up his head he made a swift motion with his stick. "Chalo!" he shouted almost fiercely.

15 There was a clanking noise, and then dead silence. The prisoner had vanished, and the rope was twisting on itself. I let go of the dog, and it galloped immediately to the back of the gallows; but when it got there it stopped short, barked, and then retreated into a corner of the yard, where it stood among the weeds, looking timorously out at us. We went round the gallows to inspect the prisoner's body. He was dangling with his toes pointed straight downwards, very slowly revolving, as dead as a stone.

16 The superintendent reached out with his stick and poked the bare brown body; it oscillated slightly. "*He's* all right," said the superintendent. He backed out from under the gallows, and blew out a deep breath. The moody look had gone out of his face quite suddenly. He glanced at his wrist-watch. "Eight minutes past eight. Well, that's all for this morning, thank God."

17 The warders unfixed bayonets and marched away. The dog, sobered and conscious of having misbehaved itself, slipped after them. We walked out of the gallows yard, past the condemned cells with their waiting prisoners, into the big central yard of the prison. The convicts, under the command of warders armed with lathis, were already receiving their breakfast. They squatted in long rows, each man holding a tin panikin, while two warders with buckets marched round ladling out rice; it seemed quite a homely, jolly scene, after the hanging. An enormous relief had come upon us now that the job was done. One felt an impulse to sing, to break into a run, to snigger. All at once everyone began chattering gaily.

18 The Eurasian boy walking beside me nodded towards the way we had come, with a knowing smile: "Do you know, sir, our friend [he meant the dead man] when he heard his appeal had been dismissed, he pissed on the floor of his cell. From fright. Kindly take one of my cigarettes, sir. Do you not admire my new silver case, sir? From the boxwalah, two rupees eight annas. Classy European style."

19 Several people laughed—at what, nobody seemed certain.

20 Francis was walking by the superintendent, talking garrulously: "Well, sir, all hass passed off with the utmost satisfactoriness. It was all finished—flick! like that. It iss not always so—oah, no! I have known cases where the doctor wass obliged to go beneath the gallows and pull the prisoner's legs to ensure decease. Most disagreeable!"

"Wriggling about, eh? That's bad," said the superintendent. 21

"Ach, sir, it iss worse when they become refractory! One man, I recall, clung to the bars of hiss cage when we went to take him out. You will scarcely credit, sir, that it took six warders to dislodge him, three pulling at each leg. We reasoned with him. 'My dear fellow,' we said, 'think of all the pain and trouble you are causing to us!' But no, he would not listen! Ach, he wass very troublesome!" 22

I found that I was laughing quite loudly. Everyone was laughing. Even the superintendent grinned in a tolerant way. "You'd better all come out and have a drink," he said quite genially. "I've got a bottle of whisky in the car. We could do with it." 23

We went through the big double gates of the prison into the road. "Pulling at his legs!" exclaimed a Burmese magistrate suddenly, and burst into a loud chuckling. We all began laughing again. At that moment Francis' anecdote seemed extraordinarily funny. We all had a drink together, native and European alike, quite amicably. The dead man was a hundred yards away. 24

Vocabulary

The following terms are identified by paragraph number. Make sure that you understand each term's meaning in its context. If you're not sure that you understand a term, look it up in a college-level dictionary.

sodden (1)	gait (9)	oscillated (16)
sickly (1)	servile (11)	refractory (22)
condemned (1)	reiterated (12)	magistrate (24)
whence (6)	abominable (13)	amicably (24)
gambolled (8)	timorously (15)	

Style and Strategy

1. What is the tone of this narrative? How does Orwell's tone affect you as a reader?
2. What does the description of the dog's behavior add to the story? Do you think Orwell added this detail for comic relief, or does it have another purpose?
3. What effect does the recounting of the post-hanging "celebration" have?
4. Most of this narrative is straightforward, but at one point Orwell stops to comment on its significance. Where does this break occur, and what effect does it have on your sense of the tale?
5. In the last few paragraphs, the executioners are nervously celebrating the event. How does Orwell use the abrupt last sentence of the essay ("The dead man was a hundred yards away") to comment on this celebration?

STYLE AND STRATEGY
1. The tone is obviously bleak. One need only reread paragraph 1 to make the point.
2. Orwell uses the dog as a symbol of nature's opposition to what is occurring.
3. This is not an attempt at comic relief. The forced and awkward humor of the last few paragraphs proves how uncomfortable the participants have become. They need to turn away from the reality of what they have done.
4. Paragraph 10 communicates Orwell's point of view. It is at this point that we are sure of the essay's purpose.
5. The juxtaposition of life and death is clear in this image.

Questions for Critical Thinking and Discussion

1. There are many jobs that most of us don't want and prefer not to think about: executioner, slaughterhouse worker, solid-waste technician, health care worker specializing in caring for terminally ill children or adults.

QUESTIONS FOR CRITICAL THINKING AND DISCUSSION Both questions elicit lively classroom discussion. Ask students to refer to specific places in the text to support their comments.

How do you think people who have such jobs get used to dealing with them psychologically? In other words, how would such a job become just a "job," with all the routine and boredom we associate with a steady position?

2. Consider this statement and the questions that follow it: "There are many hundreds of people—almost all male—on Death Row in the United States. Yet there are only a few dozen executions each year. I believe that these token executions are just that—symbols that make us feel better. Some justice has been done; someone *finally* got what he deserved." If we "cleaned out" Death Row, as some advocate, with a couple of executions every day for two or three years, how do you think the American public would react? Do the people who support capital punishment really want it carried out regularly, or do they want the idea of it, an occasional symbolic instance of putting a murderer to death? What is your view on the issue of capital punishment?

SUGGESTIONS FOR WRITING Discuss the kinds of thesis statements readers should expect to find in essays like those called for by these assignments.

Suggestions for Writing

1. Write a 500- to 750-word narrative about an incident that you witnessed or know about involving substantial harm done to someone but with no punishment for the offender. The offender, after all, could be a police officer merely doing his or her job or a parent making an earnest attempt to deal with a misbehaving child.
2. Write a 500- to 750-word narrative about an occasion in which you unintentionally harmed someone. What were the consequences? How did you feel?

MORE OPTIONS ONLINE If you would like to read additional narrative essays, go to www.mhhe.com/writingtoday.

WRITING THE PERSONAL NARRATIVE WITH A READER'S EYE

The audience for a personal narrative wants to read an interesting, well-structured story that has a point to make. The advice that follows will help you think like your reader as you consider your assignment and then prewrite, draft, revise, and edit your narrative essay.

Issues to Keep in Mind

The personal narrative deals with events that transpire over a period of time; time itself, along with how it is presented, is the most central issue in structuring this type of writing. Here are four aspects of presenting time for you to consider as you plan, write, and revise your personal narrative:

1. Strategies that expand, compress, and manipulate time
2. Transitions
3. Paragraphing and topic sentences
4. Dialogue

Using Time Economically

The writer of a personal narrative needs to make choices similar to those made by a film editor. Think about how movies work. The events of two days, or two weeks, or two years are condensed into a product that takes about two hours to view. The boring parts are left out. So it is with the personal narrative essay. Events taking hours or days can be covered in a relatively small number of paragraphs if the writer carefully selects what is central to the narrative and ignores what is not.

Similarly, the film editor can *expand* time. Say that the hero, played by Ben Affleck, is fighting his penultimate battle against the villain, played by Gary Oldman. They are on a balcony three stories above the street. By a singularly underhanded maneuver, Oldman is able to tumble Affleck off the balcony. In real life, the ensuing fall would take about five seconds. However, the smart film editor will make it last twenty seconds to exploit the audience's horror over the possibility of Ben's going splat. Slow motion, various camera angles, long shots, and close-ups will be used to show the falling Ben, and "reaction shots"—the smirk of the evil villain, the terror of Ben's sweetheart, the upturned faces of the pedestrians below—will prolong and accentuate the moment.

When you write a personal narrative, the duration of the event about which you're writing becomes a raw resource; you can use it, alter it, and control it. Of course, you could write a "straight" narrative that sticks closely to **chronological** time, but very few narrative topics work well this way. Think about it: you can read the body paragraphs of a 700-word essay in under five minutes. Do you want to write your essay about a five-minute life experience? Perhaps, but searching for such a topic would truly restrict your opportunities.

More likely, you will want to depend on the use of **psychological** time—time as we remember it, time as it is important in a narrative structure. This approach can sometimes result in the expansion of time, as you describe your reaction to a small but extremely important event. Normally, however, you will need to condense a longer event into a narrative that is more compact and therefore more compelling. Notice how the writer of the following narrative passage, not wanting to leave anything out, tells us a bit more than we need to know:

> Highway 35 is a big bunch of curves, and Jason seemed to take this as a challenge. On we rode, going much too fast in his car with its brakes that Jason knew to be bad. After about two miles the idiot finally learned the reality of his situation when the car ran straight through a curve and landed us in a shallow ditch. No one was hurt, thank God, but we were certainly stuck.
>
> Laura used her cell phone to call a wrecker, and we waited. I had been having a nagging problem with the little toe on my right foot, so I took my shoe off and rubbed the toe, but it still hurt. Then I remembered that I had a test on the following Friday in U.S. government, and I made a mental note

> to set aside some time on Thursday evening to study, which meant going home right after work and not going out with Laura.
>
> When help arrived, it wasn't a wrecker; it was a county deputy. She asked what had happened, and Jason, the idiot, said, "My brakes failed." (Not "I swerved to avoid a cat" or "I overcorrected coming into the curve.") The cop wrote Jason a ticket for going too fast for conditions and also one for not maintaining a safe vehicle. If he had had a brain, he probably could have avoided both tickets and the inevitable lecture.

Do you see the problem with this passage? The first paragraph is fine, as is the third. But the second paragraph has only one useful sentence: "Laura used her cell phone. . . ." Whatever narrative tension has been built up by the first paragraph is dissipated in the rest of the second paragraph, as the reader lets us know about the problems with her foot (thanks!) and her need to study (yawn). Then the third paragraph picks us up again, but the damage has already been done.

What would have worked better here is a **flashforward,** going from one significant narrative event to the next while omitting the waiting period. (Waiting is almost always boring, unless a quarrel breaks out.) Note how the writer could have used this device to unify her narrative:

> Highway 35 is a big bunch of curves, and Jason seemed to take this as a challenge. On we rode, going much too fast in his car with its brakes that Jason knew to be bad. After about two miles the idiot finally learned the reality of his situation when the car ran straight through a curve and landed us in a shallow ditch. No one was hurt, thank God, but we were certainly stuck.
>
> Laura used her cell phone to call a wrecker, and we waited. **And waited. And waited. Surely, I thought, we're not that far from town. But it took forever.**
>
> **Finally,** when help arrived, it wasn't a wrecker; it was a county deputy. . . .

The highlighted words act as a "bridge" between the two important events.

A similar technique is a **flashback,** which takes the reader to a significant moment in a time preceding the immediate event:

> It was three minutes until ten, and Randall still hadn't arrived. I was cursing myself for allowing the least active group member to "finally do something" at the end, and he was carrying the folder that contained our

project. A glance at Luis and Brenda indicated that they were also beating themselves up.

Years ago, when I was in middle school, a similar disaster occurred. I remember my mother's verdict: "Don't trust important stuff to trivial people. They'll screw you up every time, and then they'll ask 'What's the big deal?'"

Today I thought about my mother, who had spent her working life managing teenagers at a restaurant, and I realized how right she was. I—and my team—faced an *F* on a crucial assignment because of our heedless trust in Randall.

You'll probably use the flashforward technique more often than the flashback; the latter strategy is more specialized and stylistic whereas the former strategy fulfills a routine, practical need in narratives.

Transitions

Too often, students' narratives suffer from the "and then" syndrome, as in the following paragraph:

Then Bobby decided to end the foolishness, and he grabbed the dead raccoon by the tail and heaved it off the roof. Then Bobby and Jane climbed down and got ready to leave. Mr. Johnson, Jane's dad, was there and he was mad. The raccoon corpse had narrowly missed him on the way down, and he was standing beside it. Then Bobby took off running, and Mr. Johnson took off after him.

And so on. Then so on some more. Narratives that depend on *and then* have the rushed quality of stories reported by children: a sort of needlessly breathless effect. Remember from Chapter 3 that there are many transitions you can use to indicate shifts in chronological time:

first, second, third, next, then, finally, afterwards, before, soon, later, meanwhile, subsequently, immediately, eventually, currently

Such time transitions help you create a *smooth* narrative; they also help you control the way that your reader processes your text. Note how even a straightforward use of transitions (shown highlighted) shapes the following paragraph:

Our **first** problem occurred because Amy and I were physically separated and couldn't communicate. I was in Chicago, and she was in Milwaukee. I assumed that buying the Christmas tree was my responsibility, and I **immediately** started scouring the church, school, and commercial lots. **Meanwhile,** Amy's search exemplified our **second** confusion: she thought we needed an artificial tree for our Christmas celebrations. **Subsequently,** she arrived at our apartment with a six-foot spruce in a box, thinking she had done her part. Imagine her surprise when I **finally** arrived, dragging a seven-foot fir up the steps.

Time transitions can also allow you to delay climactic moments or to surprise your reader when he or she least expects it.

Paragraphing and Topic Sentences

A problem related to the "and then" syndrome is the formless narrative. In this kind of faulty narrative, the body paragraphs tell a continuous story, but in one big sweep. The paragraphs begin and end for no discernible reason, as if the writer had decided "that one's long enough" and then embarked on a new one.

Remember that paragraphs are controlled by ideas, not word count. A narrative can be organized into a logical structure in the same way that any piece of writing can be organized. When prewriting, look for logical breaks in the action, such as these:

1. Sudden complications—in other words, the direction of the narrative is quickly changed by a new and surprising event.
2. Cause and effect—one event logically leads to another.
3. Dead time—as mentioned, the waiting time between key events is frequently a good point to flashforward to the next event.

Don't let your narrative just unfold; instead, plan your series of paragraphs carefully. Then make sure that the topic sentences of your body paragraphs clearly indicate the narrative's structure. Readers don't need topic sentences that read like directions from the owner's manual for a hair dryer; however, readers do look for structure in a narrative, and it is your job as the writer to provide it. Using time transitions will help you in this effort.

Dialogue

Effective narratives often include conversations between people in the story by placing these exchanges in quotation marks ("/"). This is called **dialogue.** If you summarize or report what was said in a conversation, the reader processes this information quickly. However, using dialogue slows down the pace of a narrative—sometimes a good idea—and is also more specific and "real." Dialogue can also be used to communicate a person's conversations with himself or herself. In other words, it can be a good way to reveal what an individual is thinking.

Dialogue can serve many purposes in a narrative. It can be used to introduce important information that the reader needs to learn to understand the significance of the events being related. In some cases, a character's words will recall events that occurred well before the story began. In others, a character's words will help advance the plot by telling the reader what is happening. In still others, they will convey information about the time and place in which the story is set. However, the most important functions of dialogue are to reveal important information about the people who inhabit the story—their motives, values, and personalities—and to develop the narrative's theme or implied thesis.

Look back to "Only Daughter," by Sandra Cisneros. Here, the author uses her father's words to explain his hopes and fears for her future, to describe their relationship, and, most important, to convey the strength and nobility of the man's character. Orwell's "A Hanging" also makes good use of dialogue. In this essay, however, the author puts telling language into the mouths of his characters in order to dramatize the fact that the death penalty is such an extreme measure.

You can use the essays in this chapter as sources from which to learn techniques for the inclusion of dialogue. Note that the authors take pains to make sure that speakers are always identified and that each question is directly attributable to someone. For example, when a dog runs on to the field and interrupts the execution in "A Hanging," Orwell writes: *"Who let that bloody brute in here?"* ***said the superintendent*** *angrily. "Catch it, someone!"* In another instance, he embeds the attribution in the narrative: *And then when the noose was fixed, the prisoner began crying out to his god. It was a high, reiterated cry of "Ram! Ram! Ram!"* In both cases, the speaker is clearly identified. As well, remember that when you use dialogue from two or more speakers, each speaker gets a new paragraph, as in this example.

> "Are you going to the party?" Andrea asked.
> "Nope. Got too much to do," I mumbled.

(For more on the mechanics of including dialogue, see Chapter 18.)

MORE OPTIONS ONLINE
For more help with problem areas in the narrative essay, go to **www.mhhe.com/writingtoday**.

Choosing a Topic

Many of the problems students have with narrative essays are caused by the topics they choose. The following guidelines will help you choose a subject that can be handled in an academic assignment:

CLASSROOM HINT
If you have time, discuss these six items in detail during class.

1. Write about one event or sequence of events, not your life's story. If the assignment asks for 700 words, you will have trouble recounting your sophomore year in high school, or the summer that followed, or perhaps even a week during that summer. Choose a *limited* subject, one that you can exploit within the limits of the assignment.
2. Avoid personally painful issues. No one gets through life unscathed, and many people suffer horrible, unspeakable wrongs along the way. If you have been the victim of a dreadful circumstance, this experience might not be a good subject for your narrative. Writing an essay about a personal tragedy may require you to deal with your emotions as much as the demands of the assignment. Remember that your goals are to write an accomplished essay, improve your composition skills, and receive a desirable grade. Choose

a topic that will allow you to concentrate on the writing process, not on your emotions.

3. Consider your audience. Sometimes, a personal experience may seem so intense and special to a writer that he or she may forget that it is old news to an adult audience. For example, instructors really don't like to read a personal narrative about the loss of the writer's virginity—not necessarily for prudish reasons, but because this life event happens to most people in much the same way. In other words, an event that seems unique to the writer is simply part of the general human experience.
4. Be sure that you can make a thematic point. As we illustrated in the passage on pages 174–175, some narratives recount interesting but essentially pointless events: random violence, sudden bad luck, and so on. Instead, look for events that taught you something, or changed your career goals, or put you in a new city or in a new school when you were quite happy with the old city or school.
5. Consider choosing a humorous topic. Humor has an honorable place in the long history of the personal narrative. There's no reason that you should look for a serious, sober topic if you tend to see the funny side of most situations. Besides, if you are able to bring a smile to your instructor's face during the sometimes grim process of grading a stack of papers, you may well have accomplished something.
6. Consider writing about someone close to you. The personal essay doesn't always have to be about the narrator. Many students would rather write about someone other than themselves, and the experiences of a family member or close friend may prove to be a promising topic. You were there; you saw what your sister or your boyfriend went through; you commiserated or joined in the celebration; you learned something about life because of your connection to the story's central figure. Some excellent essays have been written using this approach; however, check with your instructor before you proceed.

Prewriting

CLASSROOM HINT If necessary, review what students read in Chapter 2 about prewriting, outlining, and organizing.

Use one of the "data-gathering" strategies—freewriting, listing, or clustering—outlined in Chapter 2 to generate the raw material of your composition. After having done so, determine the most important events of the story. Concentrate on these, and decide how you will deal with the less important events. Also, review your prewriting to see if your resulting essay will make a point. If so, you should be able to come up with your working thesis at this time.

Organizing

Use one of the outlining methods discussed in Chapter 2 to help you find a coherent structure for your story. Remember, you want to avoid writing a formless narrative with indeterminate paragraphs. You might consider writing the topic sentences for body paragraphs before you begin drafting. You may end up revising these sentences, but they will help you to establish an initial structure for your narrative.

Drafting

To illustrate one writer's approach to writing the narrative essay, we have included the essay "Chaos at the Veterinary Clinic."

The Introduction

Too often, students dive into their narrative without establishing its context. Remember that your reader knows very little about you. If, for example, you are writing about being uprooted from your home in Portland, Oregon, and moving to a new home in Portland, Maine, because of your mother's job transfer, you first need to tell readers something about your life prior to the move. What was Oregon like? Were you happy? How many siblings did you have, if any? Was the move a complete surprise, or was it an issue that your family had discussed at length? Notice how the writer of the following essay uses two introductory paragraphs to establish her story:

Consider Your Options

Avoid starting your narrative in your introduction. Use the introduction for context and background. The reader needs this information to make sense of the story that follows. (See Chapter 3 for more on introductions.)

Chaos at the Veterinary Clinic

My five-year-old cat, Raymond, is a magnificent creature. He is coal-black and very large, weighing eighteen pounds with no apparent fat. But it's his personality that makes Raymond special. He has very little fear, rather a bold curiosity with which he meets the world. He's a very loving cat as well and a good judge of my moods. His only drawback is his habit of jumping on my lap when I'm preoccupied, landing with a force strong enough to almost knock the wind out of me.

Raymond's health needs are dealt with at the Oakland Veterinary Clinic, owned and run by the very skillful (and very cute) Dr. Scott McNabb. Dr. McNabb has treated Raymond since he was a kitten, and I've made many trips there, carrying increasingly large cat carriers. However, last Tuesday the cat carrier was under a bunch of boxes in the utility room, so, on a whim, I carried Raymond to the car and let him ride in the passenger seat. As I expected, he was fine during the six-block ride to the clinic, standing up and watching the world go by outside the window. **However, the fun really began at the clinic.**

Note that the last sentence of the introduction is the writer's thesis statement. Should she have been more explicit about the events that were about to unfold? No—to do so would have spoiled the story for her readers.

The Body

The main section of the narrative is where the actual event or sequence of events is recounted. Note how the writer maintains control of the reader's perception of time while adding sensory detail to help amplify her story's effect:

> The waiting room looked peaceful enough. Three people were there with dogs in carriers, and two people had cats. Besides Raymond, the only "loose" animal was a small kitten playing on the lap of its owner. After surveying the room and sniffing the weird, ever-present medicinal smell, Raymond settled down on my lap and seemed perfectly happy.
>
> Suddenly, the door to the kennel burst open and a stream of dogs rushed into the waiting area. The dogs in their carriers immediately started barking, as did the intruders, who rushed up to their caged colleagues and checked them out. From the cat carriers came a frenzied clicking sound, as if someone had poured ice water on a nest of rattlesnakes. The kitten disappeared. Raymond stood up on my lap, digging in with his back claws (thank heaven his front ones had been removed), swelling up like a cobra. To say he resembled a black cat in a Halloween decoration would be both a cliché and an understatement; those cats aren't nearly as big as Raymond was at that point.
>
> Next, a loud rumbling bark reverberated from the kennel; a huge Rottweiler appeared, followed by Dr. McNabb. I've never really cared for Rottweilers, especially this one, which headed straight for me and Raymond. My great tom had met his match. He became very small (as small as an eighteen-pound cat can become), sinking down in my lap as if he were in a World War I bunker, staring at the approaching foe.
>
> During the crisis, Dr. McNabb retained his cool, acting as if this were business as usual. He grabbed the Rottweiler by the collar and had the presence of mind to reach over and scratch Raymond's ears. Behind Dr. McNabb,

EXERCISE 7.1 Answers will vary. The following sentence outline is suggested.
Thesis: The fun really began at the clinic.

I. Background: Raymond is a magnificent cat.
   A. He is large.
   B. He has little fear and is loving.
   C. His only drawback is his need to jump on his owner's lap.
II. The owner took Raymond to the veterinary clinic without his carrier.
III. The waiting room looked peaceful.
   A. Three people had dogs; two had cats.
   B. Raymond settled on his owner's lap.
IV. Suddenly, the kennel door burst open, and a stream of dogs rushed in.
   A. Animals in the waiting room reacted.
   B. Raymond stood and dug in his claws.

his assistants rounded up the remaining dogs, which seemed to take an hour but actually took about five minutes.

Finally, all the dogs were led, dragged, or carried back to the kennel. The waiting room was eerily silent. The dogs had stopped barking, but the cats still apparently believed that Armageddon was in process. Raymond didn't move; his only reaction was to let down his hackles.

V. A Rottweiler appeared, followed by Dr. McNabb.
  A. The Rottweiler headed for the narrator.
  B. Raymond became small.
VI. Dr. McNabb stayed cool and grabbed the Rottweiler.
  A. Assistants rounded up the rest of the dogs.
  B. Raymond let down his hackles.
VII. Dr. McNabb explained the incident.
VIII. Raymond will travel to the vet in a carrier from now on.

The Conclusion

The concluding section of your essay recounts the aftermath, the wrapping up of loose ends. What were the immediate effects of your experience? What did you learn? Note how the writer of our model essay used two paragraphs to wrap up the story of her chaotic experience at the clinic:

When it was finally time for Raymond's shots, he submitted meekly. I waited until Dr. McNabb had finished before I asked the obvious question: "What happened?" He answered sheepishly, "My son's day care is closed today because of renovations. I brought him in to work with me, and he decided it would be fun to set the kennel dogs free."

Raymond has another appointment with Dr. McNabb in six weeks. I can only expect that we won't see a repeat of last Tuesday's events, but if we do, Raymond will be watching from inside his carrier. His days as a free-range clinic cat are over.

Consider Your Options

You need not conclude a narrative with a narrative paragraph. An appropriate ending for such an essay might describe, offer advice, or look to the future. (See Chapter 3.)

EXERCISE 7.1

Write a sentence outline of "Chaos at the Veterinary Clinic." (For help with sentence outlines, see Chapter 2, pages 40–42.) What does the outline reveal about the essay's organization?

MORE OPTIONS ONLINE
For more help with the step-by-step development of the narrative essay, go to **www.mhhe.com/writingtoday**.

Revising Your Draft

After you have completed a draft of your narrative essay, your next step is to revise it, using your own analysis and comments from classmates or friends. During peer review, answer the Questions for Reviewing a Narrative Essay (page 200) in regard to the draft you are reviewing, whether it is yours or another student's.

After reviewing for content, you need to go over your peer reviewers' responses to your essay and then revise for unity, coherence, language level, and tone (see Chapter 4). When you have revised your draft and are basically satisfied with it, read your draft for mechanical and grammatical errors. Concentrate on finding and correcting major sentence errors (fragment, comma splice,

MORE OPTIONS ONLINE
For more help with revision, go to **www.mhhe.com/writingtoday**.

Questions for Reviewing a Narrative Essay

CLASSROOM HINT Review these questions in class if time permits.

1. Does the introduction give the reader enough context? Does it capture the reader's interest? How could the introduction be strengthened?
2. What is the thesis statement? Has the writer placed it in the best position within the essay? How could it be improved? If there is no thesis statement, is the main point of the narrative clear from the way the writer presents the key events?
3. Does the narrative relate a significant event or series of events? How has the writer fulfilled his or her purpose for writing the essay?
4. Is the organization effective? Where would a flashforward help the writer get from one key event to the next? Where would a flashback be useful?
5. Do the topic sentences indicate the structure of the narrative?
6. Are the body paragraphs fully developed? Where are additional sensory details needed? Where could dialogue be added to make the narrative more lively and immediate?
7. Does the writer use time transitions to guide the reader? Where are transitional words or sentences needed?
8. Does the essay have an effective conclusion? How could it be improved?

---

fused sentence), errors in pronoun agreement and subject-verb agreement, inappropriate shifts in verb tense, and spelling.

Now that you have made your corrections, *read your essay one more time* to catch any errors made during revision and find errors missed during your earlier reviews.

Student Essay

The following essay is Claire Reid's response to a narrative assignment. Claire's mother had gone to considerable trouble so that her daughter could "come out in society." However, Claire had other ideas. This essay won first place in the personal essay contest held at her college. The final draft is presented first, followed by Claire's first draft, with her comments about this draft and what she needed to do in the revision stage.

Claire's Final Draft

After the Fray

1 From the earliest time I can remember, my mother was always instructing me on how to be a lady. She would dress me every morning in a freshly

pressed dress, pin my hair back perfectly with tiny bows, and polish my patent leather shoes until they gleamed. "Sugar, spice, and everything nice, that's what little girls are made of," she'd say as she handed me my Barbie lunchbox and kissed me goodbye. I would come home at the end of the day, pink taffeta dress saturated in mud, hair matted into little knots around my bows, and pantyhose run clear to my thigh. "Claire," my mother would exclaim as she stripped me down and ripped through my hair, "someday I'm gonna make a lady out of you, even if it kills me!" I never doubted her when she took that tone of voice, and something told me, even then, that it was going to take a fight.

My time finally came when I was thirteen years old. One morning I woke up to find an invitation to the Winter Park Women's Club Ball placed neatly on my breakfast plate. I ate that meal like it was my last supper. As my mother busied herself with invitations, reservations, and other plans to carry out my doom, I followed behind her, making it quite clear that I would rather die a miserable death than submit to this form of torture. I was convinced that she hated me and relished my suffering. 2

The following week was a whirlwind of dancing and etiquette classes, fitting sessions, and rehearsals for the gala event. Out of pure spite toward my mother, I fought the whole way. I made every retailer on Park Avenue suffer as I flung dresses out of the stalls, raked the nerves of even the most composed etiquette teachers, and dragged my mother, exasperated and humiliated, through it all. After a week of all-out temper tantrums (on both of our parts), the day had finally come to take my place among society's finest bunch of clueless individuals. I spent the morning raging through the house, performing the grand finale I had worked up all week. She spent the morning locked in her room crying to my father, thinking I was disconnected and extreme, and blaming herself for all of my shortcomings. Finally, my father, put out by this whole chain of events, demanded I put on my dress and comply with my mother's wishes for the rest of the evening. He then rounded up the family and herded us to the car. 3

The event went by in a whirlwind, and I hardly even noticed the elders who stopped to compliment me on my hair or tell me what an absolute princess I had become. I soon felt the room closing in on me and sought refuge behind the clubhouse on the fairway. As I stepped outside, I thought I could hear the faint sniffles of someone crying. Turning to my right and walking down the green, I stumbled upon my mother, sitting on the grass in her rumpled peach dress, crying like a baby. In her left hand was a wad of tissues, and in her right, much to my dismay, was a cigarette. "You know I don't usually smoke," she blurted out. 4

"I know," I replied, and plopped down next to her on the soft, fragrant grass. I'm not so sure how it happened, but in those few minutes behind that clubhouse full of little debutantes and their estranged parents, I caught the first glimpse of my mother. I saw her not as the one who cleans your cuts and tucks you in at night, but as a real person . . . and right then and there began our everlasting quest to understand each other. 5

Even now, my mother still swears she'll make a lady out of me or die trying. But after that day, she became a little less pushy and a little more trusting. She tells me she's gonna let the cards fall where they may, but she hopes the wind will push them in the right direction. And I, well, I'm learning that having an overbearing mother isn't so bad after all, and sometimes, just sometimes, it helps to take your mother's advice. The older I get, the more frequently I tell her, half joking but more seriously than she knows, that someday she just may make a lady out of me. "I've never doubted you when you use that tone of voice," she replies, "but I have a feeling it's gonna be a fight." 6

Claire's First Draft

After the Fray

I added details about how my mother would dress me to give the reader a better sense of our conflict.

From the time I can Remember, my mother was always instructing me on how to be a lady. "Sugar, spice, and everything nice, that's what little girls are made of", she'd say as she hand me my Barbie lunchbox and kissed 1 me goodbye. I would come home at the end of the day, pink taffetta dress saturated in mud, hair matted into little knots around my bows, and panty-hose run clear to my thigh. "Claire", my mother would exclaim as she stripped me down and ripped through my hair, "someday I'm gonna make a lady out of you, even if it kills me"! I never doubted her when she took that tone of voice, and something told me, even then, that it was going to take a fight.

2

My time finally came when I was thirteen years old. One morning I woke up to find an invitation to the Winter Park woman's club Ball placed neatly on my breakfast plate. I ate that meal like it was my last supper. I was convined that she hated me and relished in my suffering.

I added some details here to show our conflict more clearly.

3

The following week was a whirlwind of dancing and etiquette classes, fitting sessions, and rehersals for the gala event.Out of pure spite toward my mother, I fought the whole way. I made every retailer on Park avenue suffer as I flung dresses out of the stalls, raked the nerves of even the most composed etiquitte teachers, and dragged my mother, exasperated and humiliated, through it all. after a week of all out temper tantrums (on both of our parts), the day had finally come to take my place among society's finest bunch of clueless individuals. I spent the morning raging through the house, performing the grand finale I had worked up all week. She spend the morning locked in her room crying to my father, thinking I was disconnected and extreme, and blaming herself for all of my shortcomings. Finally my father, put out by this whole chain of events, demanded I don on my dress and comply for the rest of the evening. He then rounded up the family, and herded us to the car.

I'm not the best speller in the world, or the best typist. I made five proof-reading passes through this to get rid of all the errors, but I didn't do the proof-reading all at the same sitting.

4

The event went by in a whirlwind, and I hardly even noticed the elders who stopped to complement me on my hair, or ell me what an absolute princess I had become. I soon felt the room closing in on me and sought refuge behind the clubhouse on the fairway. As I stepped outside, I thought I could hear the faint sniffles of someone crying. Turning to my right and walking down the green, I stumbled upon my mother, sitting on the grass in her rumpled peach dress, crying like a baby. In her

I added some dialogue here to make the scene stronger.

left hand was a wad of tissues, and in her right, much to my dismay, was a cigarette. I'm not so sure how it happened, but in those few minutes behind that clubhouse full of little debutantes and their estranged parents, I caught the first glimpse of my mother. I saw her as not the one who cleans you cuts and tucks you in at night, but the real person . . . and right then and there began the everlasting quest to understand eachothter.

My classmate thought I needed more here so I added a final quote.

Even to this day, my mother still swears she'll make a lady out of me, or die trying. but after that day, she became a little less pushy and a little more trusting. She tells me she's gonna let the cards fall where they may, but she hopes the wind will push them in the right direction. And I, well, I'm learning that having an overbearing mother isn't so bad after all, and sometimes, just sometimes, it helps to take your mothers advice. 5

EXERCISE 7.2: REVISING

EXERCISE 7.2 Answers will vary. Students should point out the need for a stronger introduction and conclusion, more details, and more of an indication of the significance of the event.

SUGGESTED ACTIVITY
Consider asking students to meet in writing groups, each of which is charged with producing a more developed and effective version of this essay. Encourage students to add appropriate details from their own childhood experiences with siblings.

The following is the first draft of a student's narrative essay. Working in pairs or in small groups, review this essay. Using the Questions for Reviewing a Narrative Essay on page 200, decide what revisions you would suggest. If you have any questions the student needs to consider, write them in the margin or on a separate sheet of paper. If your instructor directs you to, rewrite one or more paragraphs to make them stronger and to eliminate any grammatical or mechanical errors.

"stupid is it's own reward"

When I was seven I did the dumbest thing imaginable, I got my tongue stuck to a pumphandle. 1

I new not to do this. Like every one. But my brother Mike talk me in to it. 2

It was very cold that day, it was atleast 20 degrees. We got up and got dress in a hury, it was so cold. Mike and me went out side and we noticed what snow had left was frozen into ice. 3

Then we saw the old pump the one not hookedup any more. Then Mike dared me to put my tongue on the handle. I told him he was loony if he thought Id do that. Then he 'called me chicken'. And I couldnt let that go. 4

I was 8 years old, Mike was ten. He was my big brother - still is, but I 5 new he was likely to play crule tricks on me. 'Just touch it with your tongue', he said, 'be quick and you wont get hurt'.

I did as he said my tongue froze instantly to the handle. Mike ran away laughing and I was trapped with terror and pain. 6

I forgiven Mike after awhile. Although, I still dont trust him. 7

Additional Writing Topics

1. What is the most significant event that happened to you before you were five years old?
2. We all end up spending a great deal of our time in school. Write about an event that occurred in your K–12 years.
3. During high school, what was your single most "formative" experience? That is, was there an event that led you here today?
4. **Writing on the job.** What's the most interesting experience that you have had while working? Did it change your view of the job market? Write a narrative for someone who is about to enter the work force.

Responding to a Photograph

After World War II, the United States settled in to an economic boom that lasted through the 1960s. In 1951 Alex Henderson took this photograph of an American family posed in the middle of a grocery store.

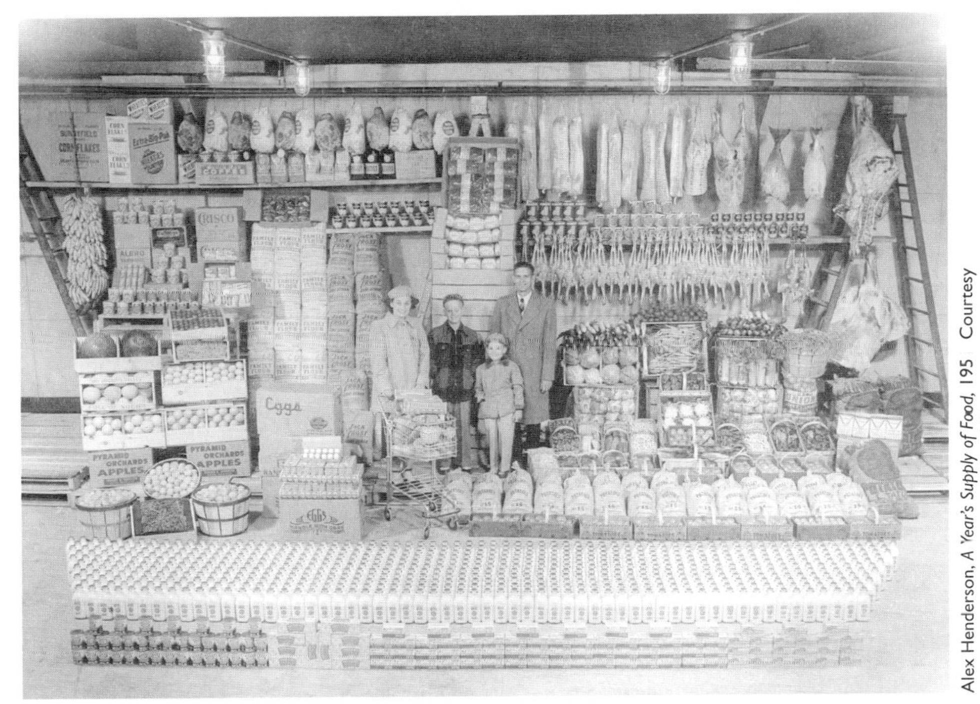

Alex Henderson, *A Year's Supply of Food*, 195 Courtesy Hagley Museum and Library [72-341].

CLASSROOM HINT Discuss this photograph before assigning item 1. Students should be comfortable with the process of including and citing researched materials before you assign item 2.

1. Write an informal response to the photograph. What do you notice? How does the image make you feel? How does the photograph exploit the narration option—in other words, what could be the story of this family?
2. Today, many people view the 1950s as a "golden age": peace, prosperity, and unlimited prospects. Others view the same era as a remarkably narrow time of middle-class insularity. Using a combination of library and online research, explore a day in the life of a "typical" U.S. family of the 1950s. Write a documented essay about this hypothetical day. (For more information on documented essays, see Chapter 21.)

Writing About Film

Big Night (1995, R) tells the story of two brothers who come to America to establish an authentic Italian restaurant. However, their great gamble ultimately fails, and the film's ending is ambiguous. Write an essay that tells the story of the sequel. What do you think that Primo and Secondo (the two brothers) would do next?

Memento (2001, R) depicts a man who is trying to find the murderer of his wife. Unfortunately, the man has severe short-term amnesia. Moreover, the film's director chose to show each scene in reverse chronological order. Write an essay in which you unravel this film and show the actual linear narrative of *Memento.*

Using the Internet

Search the Internet for insights and information to use in narrative essays.

1. "A Hanging" is George Orwell's indictment of capital punishment. Search the Internet to find information about the use or prohibition of the death penalty in your state, in a neighboring state, or in another country. Use this information to write a short history of capital punishment in your state. Focus on a few questions:
   - When was capital punishment first used?
   - How often has it been used and for what crimes?
   - Is capital punishment still used? Has it ever been banned by law?
   - What method(s) of execution have been used?
   - Have any death row inmates been exonerated?

   Rely on more than one Internet source to find information.
2. Go online to find sites that contain and/or discuss myths, tales, or legends used by any culture of your choice to teach people about death, illness, poverty, suffering, infidelity, sin, or some other aspect of the darker side of human existence. Write about this topic by first summarizing a tale or

myth. Then explain how this story might help you explain the existence of a particular evil or harsh reality to a child. As an alternate assignment, summarize two different myths or tales on the same subject; then compare and/or contrast their messages (see Chapter 13) and how the stories present them.

DILBERT reprinted by permission of United Feature Syndicate, Inc.

EXEMPLIFICATION

CHAPTER 8

Writing in Context

Bob has called a meeting to discuss subcontracting part of a new software project. Osprey Online Technologies has used various vendors for this kind of help in the past, with varying results. The boss wants to talk about which company is best suited for the current project.

The meeting is attended by Bob, Stephanie (his assistant), two software developers, and Jason, who, along with you, will supervise the subcontractors.

Shortly after the meeting begins, Jason raises his hand. "I just want to say that whichever outfit we choose, I hope it's not IBDmc. We've had a lot of trouble with them in the past two years. They're sloppy. I figure ——"

Bob interrupts. "Give me some specifics."

"What?" Jason seems surprised, as if Bob had happened to question whether the sun will rise and set.

"Refresh my memory. Give me some *examples* of problems that we've had. In writing, please."

Bob is making a reasonable request here: ground the complaint in actual fact. Jason's distrust of the vendor may be justified, but where's the evidence?

SUGGESTED ACTIVITY Dilbert supports his thesis—that he is the perfect employee—with a number of intentionally overblown examples of his excellence. Ask students to take five to ten minutes to come up with examples to support a thesis about themselves (that they are the perfect student, the perfect employee, the perfect parent, and so on).

HOW DOES EXEMPLIFICATION WORK?

When writers back up their assertions with a specific example or examples, they are using **exemplification.** Exemplification has two distinct uses. One is as an internal strategy, a way of providing concrete details to back up assertions and claims of every type. Most essays that you write will use these concrete details. You will find that you need to provide examples to develop paragraphs and essays written for many different purposes. Readers appreciate a well-written passage that presents an interesting or provocative general statement ("Rubbernecking is as dangerous as drunk driving"), but they will like that passage much more if it backs up the general statement with concrete evidence and details. Notice the difference between the following two paragraphs:

> Sometimes a false picture emerges of the U.S. generals in World War II. The exploits of a few romantic individuals, each of whom saw himself as the leader of a historical crusade, tend to overshadow the reality of how the American end of the war was run. Our command was actually in the hands of generals who were effectively bureaucrats—competent managers who didn't let their personalities get in the way of the larger effort.

CLASSROOM HINT Asking students to pick out specific differences between these two paragraphs helps them understand the value of examples.

> Sometimes a false picture emerges of the U.S. generals in World War II. A few generals had a somewhat romantic view of their roles. George S. Patton in the European theater and Douglas MacArthur in the Pacific each saw himself as the leader of a historical crusade. But such individuals overshadow the reality of how the American end of the war was run. Our command was actually in the hands of generals who were effectively bureaucrats—competent managers such as Dwight Eisenhower, Omar Bradley, and Mark Clark. These men didn't let their personalities get in the way of the larger effort. They in turn reported to the ultimate manager, George Marshall, who "ran the war" just as a company president "runs the firm."

The first paragraph seems acceptable until you read the second one. Your writing instructor knows the value of specific examples and will likely prompt you to include them if you have neglected to do so. No other strategy connects abstract thought to human reality as effectively as a well-chosen example.

The second use of exemplification is as an overall pattern for an essay. A writer of an exemplification essay wants to illustrate a situation or make a point; the writer explains and supports the thesis with examples drawn from his or her experience or research into a topic. Some essays will analyze one extended example for this purpose. But how does exemplification differ from the other rhetorical options that are used to explain something to readers?

In Chapter 9 and Chapter 10 you will be introduced to two forms of **analysis:** process analysis in Chapter 9 and causal analysis in Chapter 10. Process analysis shows *how* something happens or has happened. Causal analysis shows *why* something happened or what might happen as the result of some action. The exemplification essay has a similar but more general goal—to explain a situation or problem. Exemplification is actually a form of analysis, a way of looking into a problem or situation and explaining it.

Consider the following scenario: your campus has been ravaged by tornadoes, but so far the administration has managed to avoid canceling a large number of classes. Here is how the three types of analysis could be used to address this situation:

- **Causal analysis.** You could write an essay that answers this question: What were the *effects* of the tornadoes? In your essay, you would probably discuss the destruction of all or parts of buildings on campus, the classes that had to be moved from their normally scheduled rooms to temporary areas, and whatever class cancellations were inevitable.
- **Process analysis.** You could write an essay that considers *how* the administration is coping with the problems caused by the storms. In your essay, you would probably focus on the steps that the administration has taken: ordering emergency repair estimates, moving classes, rescheduling labs, and so on.
- **Exemplification.** For this kind of essay, you would probably answer this question: *What is* the current situation on campus after the recent tornadoes? In your essay, you would concentrate on *illustrating* the problems faced by students, staff, and faculty by providing specific examples of each one. For instance, you might mention the decrease in the number of student parking spots resulting from the fact that a large oak fell onto the main student lot.

You will use exemplification in many writing situations throughout your college career. For example, Chapter 16 of this text covers the essay examination, a form of testing that you can expect to face in many of your courses. In an American history class, for instance, you might see this item on an essay test: "Discuss the situation faced by the Confederate army after its defeat at Gettysburg." This question is designed to let you display your knowledge in an essay format. Let's say that you decide to concentrate on these three areas in your essay: momentum, morale, and manpower. Besides the nifty alliteration produced by those *m*'s, you believe that these were the three most important issues for the Confederates after Gettysburg. However, your history instructor doesn't want to read an essay filled with generalizations. ("Both sides fought hard." "Many lives were lost." "It was a great victory for the North.") Instead, he or she wants to see general statements backed up by **evidence:** examples that consist of facts, quotations, and statistics. When you support your general statements with this kind of evidence, you demonstrate that you have studied and assimilated the material; your resulting essay shows that you are able to understand the evidence in context.

CLASSROOM HINT Ask students to recall essay exam questions from other college or high school courses that required the use of exemplification.

The exemplification option is useful not only in response to essay examination questions but in many other writing situations as well. For example, suppose that a student journalist were given this assignment: "Describe the current controversy over the misuse of Student Government funds." Despite the presence of the word *describe,* the prompt is really asking the writer to explain, to *elucidate,* using examples.

Exemplification is enormously versatile. Writers often use it to explain their world, as we see in the readings that follow.

Consider Your Options

How might you use exemplification strategies on the job? What circumstances would call for you to explain a workplace situation by using specific examples?

READING THE EXEMPLIFICATION ESSAY WITH A WRITER'S EYE

In the four works that follow, Phyllis Rose examines the world of modern shopping, Brent Staples writes about dealing with the general public's fear of unknown black men, Lars Eighner writes about what it is like to dine from a Dumpster, and Harry F. Waters illustrates the false picture of American society that television provides. As you read these essays, concentrate on the authors' *purpose*. What are they trying to prove? Writers of exemplification essays are usually presenting their generalizations and examples for a reason; readers always appreciate concrete examples, which makes this option ideal for getting a writer's message across.

Following the essays, the second half of this chapter features strategies for writing the exemplification essay with a reader's eye (pages 230–236). If you decide to write on one of the topics that follow the four essays below, make sure that you have read the strategies section before you begin. Also note that additional writing topics are listed at the end of the chapter (pages 240–243).

Shopping and Other Spiritual Adventures in America Today

PHYLLIS ROSE

Phyllis Rose is professor of English at Wesleyan University. She has published several books, including *Woman of Letters: A Life of Virginia Woolf* (1978), *Parallel Lives: Five Victorian Marriages* (1983), *Jazz Cleopatra: Josephine Baker in Her Time* (1989), and *The Year of Reading Proust* (1997). "Shopping and Other Spiritual Adventures in America Today" is an essay from Rose's 1990 collection *Never Say Goodbye*.

Shopping is a necessity, but it can become a frivolous waste of time if taken to extremes. However, Phyllis Rose sees a higher purpose in this common activity. The following essay shows how exemplification can be used as a springboard to analysis and evaluation.

Last year a new Waldbaum's Food Mart opened in the shopping mall on Route 66. It belongs to the new generation of superduper-markets open twenty-four hours that have computerized checkout. I went to see the place as soon as it opened and I was impressed. There was trail mix in Lucite bins. There was freshly made pasta. There were coffee beans, four kinds of tahini, ten kinds of herb teas, raw shrimp in shells and cooked shelled shrimp, fresh-squeezed orange juice. Every sophistication known to the big city, even goat's cheese covered with ash, was now available in Middletown, Conn. People raced from the warehouse aisle to the bagel bin to the coffee beans to the fresh fish market, exclaiming at all the new things. Many of us felt elevated, graced, complimented by the presence of this food palace in our town. 1

This is the wonderful egalitarianism of American business. Was it Andy Warhol who said that the nice thing about Coke is, no can is any better or worse than any other? Some people may find it dull to cross the country and find the same chain stores with the same merchandise from coast to coast, but it means that my town is as good as yours, my shopping mall as important as yours, equally filled with wonders. 2

Imagine what people ate during the winter as little as seventy-five years ago. They ate food that was local, long-lasting, and dull, like acorn squash, turnips, and cabbage. Walk into an American supermarket in February and the world lies before you: grapes, melons, artichokes, fennel, lettuce, peppers, pistachios, dates, even strawberries, to say nothing of ice cream. Have you ever considered what a triumph of civilization it is to be able to buy a pound of chicken livers? If you lived on a farm and had to kill a chicken when you wanted to eat one, you wouldn't ever accumulate a pound of chicken livers. 3

Another wonder of Middletown is Caldor, the discount department store. Here is man's plenty: tennis racquets, panty hose, luggage, glassware, records, toothpaste, Timex watches, Cadbury's chocolate, corn poppers, hair dryers, warm-up suits, car wax, light bulbs, television sets. All good quality at low prices with exchanges cheerfully made on defective goods. There are worse rules to live by. I feel good about America whenever I walk into this store, which is almost every mid-winter Sunday afternoon, when life elsewhere has closed down. I go to Caldor the way English people go to pubs: out of sociability. To get away from my house. To widen my horizons. For culture's sake, Caldor provides me, too, with a welcome sense of seasonal change. When the first outdoor grills and lawn furniture appear there, it's as exciting a sign of spring as the first crocus or robin. 4

Someone told me about a Soviet emigré who practices English by declaiming, at random, sentences that catch his fancy. One of his favorites is, "Fifty percent off all items today only." Refugees from Communist countries appreciate our supermarkets and discount department stores for the wonders they are. An Eastern European scientist visiting Middletown wept when she first saw the meat counter at Waldbaum's. On the other hand, before her year in America was up, her pleasure turned sour. She wanted everything she saw. Her approach to consumer goods was insufficiently abstract, too materialistic. We Americans are beyond a simple, possessive materialism. We're used to abundance and the possibility of possessing things. The things, and the possibility of possessing them, will still be there next week, next year. So today we can walk the aisles calmly. 5

It is a misunderstanding of the American retail store to think we go there necessarily to buy. Some of us shop. There's a difference. Shopping has many purposes, the least interesting of which is to acquire new articles. We shop to cheer ourselves up. We shop to practice decision-making. We shop to be useful and productive members of our class and society. We shop to remind ourselves how much is available to us. We shop to remind ourselves how much is to be striven for. We shop to assert our superiority to the material objects that spread themselves before us. 6

Shopping's function as a form of therapy is widely appreciated. You don't really need, let's say, another sweater. You need the feeling of power that comes with buying or not buying it. You need the feeling that someone wants something you have—even if it's just your money. To get the benefit of shopping, you needn't actually purchase the sweater, any more than you have to marry every man you flirt with. In fact, window-shopping, like flirting, can be more rewarding, the same high without the distressing commitment, the material encumbrance. The purest form of shopping is provided by garage sales. A connoisseur goes out with no goal in mind open to whatever may come his or her way, secure that it will cost very little. Minimum expense, maximum experience. Perfect shopping. 7

I try to think of the opposite, a kind of shopping in which the object is all-important, the pleasure of shopping at a minimum. For example, the purchase of blue jeans. I buy new blue jeans as seldom as possible because the experience is so humiliating. For every pair that looks good on me, fifteen look grotesque. But even shopping for blue jeans at Bob's Surplus on Main Street—no frills, bare-bones shopping—is an event in the life of the spirit. Once again I have to come to terms with the fact that I will never look good in Levi's. Much as I want to be mainstream, I never will be. 8

In fact, I'm doubly an oddball, neither Misses nor Junior, but Misses Petite. I look in the mirror, I acknowledge the disparity between myself and the ideal. I resign myself to making the best of it: I will buy the Lee's Misses Petite. Shopping is a time of reflection, assessment, spiritual self-discipline. 9

It is appropriate, I think, that Bob's Surplus has a communal dressing room. I used to shop only in places where I could count on a private dressing room with a mirror inside. My impulse then was to hide my weaknesses. Now I believe in sharing them. There are other women in the dressing room at Bob's Surplus trying on blue jeans who look as bad as I do. We take comfort from one another. Sometimes a woman will ask me which of two items looks better. I always give a definite answer. It's the least I can do. I figure we are all in this together, and I emerge from the dressing room not only with a new pair of jeans but with a renewed sense of belonging to a human community. 10

When a Solzhenitsyn rants about American materialism, I have to look at my digital Timex and check what year this is. Materialism? Like conformism, a hot moral issue of the fifties, but not now. How to spread the goods, maybe. Whether the goods are the Good, no. Solzhenitsyn, like the visiting scientist who wept at the beauty of Waldbaum's meat counter but came to covet everything she saw, takes American materialism too materialistically. He doesn't see its spiritual side. Caldor, Walbaum's, Bob's Surplus—these, perhaps, are our cathedrals. 11

STYLE AND STRATEGY
1. Good examples, which make her writing credible and relevant, appear in paragraphs 1, 3, 4, 6, 8, 9, and 10.
2. Shopping is a spiritual adventure because
   - Contemporary American business has created a new type of egalitarianism.
   - American materialism goes beyond the simple desire to acquire goods.
   - Shopping has a spiritual side.
   - American materialism has a "spiritual side."
3. Rose's tone is positive and appropriate to purpose; at the same time, students should see that she is poking fun at herself and her fellow shoppers when she writes sentences such as "here is man's plenty" (paragraph 4).

Vocabulary

The following terms are identified by paragraph number. Make sure that you understand each term's meaning in its context. If you're not sure that you understand a term, look it up in a college-level dictionary.

exclaiming (1)	declaiming (5)	encumbrance (7)
egalitarianism (2)	materialism (5)	connoisseur (7)
sociability (4)	abstract (5)	conformism (11)

Style and Strategy

1. What are the major examples that Rose uses? How do they help her develop her thesis?

2. List Rose's main points. Do they add up to a unified idea? Do the examples she has chosen support this idea? Explain.

3. This essay is a serious analysis of important issues: human behavior, leisure-time activities, cultural similarities and differences. What is Rose's prevailing tone? Does her tone reinforce, or detract from, the point she is making about shopping?

Questions for Critical Thinking and Discussion

1. Do you think shopping is a harmless activity? Why or why not?
2. Why does Rose refer to shopping as a "spiritual" adventure?
3. How does shopping on the Internet differ from shopping in a store or in a mall? Does shopping on the Internet have a "spiritual side"? Why or why not?
4. Many commentators have pointed out the increasing isolation and lack of community among Americans today. Is shopping a response to this phenomenon? Explain.

QUESTIONS FOR CRITICAL THINKING AND DISCUSSION As you discuss these in class, ask students to refer to Rose's essay. Item 3 can be turned into a comparison/contrast assignment.

Suggestions for Writing

1. Write a 500-word essay about one of your hobbies that some people find trivial or unimportant but that you find loaded with significance. Use examples to back up your assertions.
2. In a 500- to 750-word essay, give examples of the behaviors that you encounter at the places where you shop.

SUGGESTIONS FOR WRITING Both items require students to engage in careful observation and note taking.

Just Walk on By

BRENT STAPLES

Brent Staples received a doctorate in psychology from the University of Chicago and taught psychology before becoming a writer and an editor. He worked for the *Chicago Sun-Times* and then the *New York Times*, where he serves on the editorial board and is an editorial writer. His 1994 memoir, *Parallel Time: Growing Up in Black and White*, won the Anisfield Wolff Book Award.

"Just Walk on By" originally appeared in *Ms.* in 1986 and then in a revised version, "Black Men and Public Space," in *Harper's* (1987). In this widely anthologized essay, Staples gives readers vivid examples of one middle-class black man's experience in a country dominated by whites.

My first victim was a woman—white, well dressed, probably in her early twenties. I came upon her late one evening on a deserted street in Hyde Park, a relatively affluent neighborhood in an otherwise mean, impoverished section of Chicago. As I swung onto the avenue behind her, there seemed to be a discreet, uninflammatory distance between us. Not so. She cast back a worried glance. To her, the youngish black man—a broad six feet two inches with a beard and billowing hair, both hands shoved into the pockets of a bulky military jacket—seemed menacingly close. After a few more quick glimpses, she picked up her pace and was soon running in earnest. Within seconds she disappeared into a cross street. 1

That was more than a decade ago. I was 22 years old, a graduate student newly arrived at the University of Chicago. It was in the echo of that terrified woman's footfalls that I first began to know the unwieldy inheritance I'd come into—the ability to alter public space in ugly ways. It was clear that she thought herself the quarry of a mugger, a rapist, or worse. Suffering a bout of insomnia, however, I was stalking sleep, not defenseless wayfarers. As a softy who is scarcely able to take a knife to a raw chicken—let alone hold it to a person's throat—I was surprised, embarrassed, and dismayed all at once. Her flight made me feel like an accomplice in tyranny. It also made it clear that I was indistinguishable from the muggers who 2 occasionally seeped into the area from the surrounding ghetto. That first encounter, and those that followed, signified that a vast, unnerving gulf lay between nighttime pedestrians—particularly women—and me. And I soon gathered that being perceived as dangerous is a hazard in itself. I only needed to turn a corner into a dicey situation, or crowd some frightened, armed person in a foyer somewhere, or make an errant move after being pulled over by a policeman. Where fear and weapons meet—and they often do in urban America—there is always the possibility of death.

3 In that first year, my first away from my hometown, I was to become thoroughly familiar with the language of fear. At dark, shadowy intersections in Chicago, I could cross in front of a car stopped at a traffic light and elicit the *thunk, thunk, thunk, thunk* of the driver—black, white, male, or female—hammering down the door locks. On less traveled streets after dark, I grew accustomed to but never comfortable with people who crossed to the other side of the street rather than pass me. Then there were the standard unpleasantries with police, doormen, bouncers, cab drivers, and others whose business it is to screen out troublesome individuals *before* there is any nastiness.

4 I moved to New York nearly two years ago and I have remained an avid night walker. In central Manhattan, the near-constant crowd cover minimizes tense one-on-one street encounters. Elsewhere—visiting friends in SoHo, where sidewalks are narrow and tightly spaced buildings shut out the sky—things can get very taut indeed.

5 Black men have a firm place in New York mugging literature. Norman Podhoretz in his famed (or infamous) 1963 essay, "My Negro Problem—And Ours," recalls growing up in terror of black males; they "were tougher than we were, more ruthless," he writes—and as an adult on the Upper West Side of Manhattan, he continues, he cannot constrain his nervousness when he meets black men on certain streets. Similarly, a decade later, the essayist and novelist Edward Hoagland extols a New York where once "Negro bitterness bore down mainly on other Negroes." Where some see mere panhandlers, Hoagland sees "a mugger who is clearly screwing up his nerve to do more than just *ask* for money." But Hoagland has "the New Yorker's quickhunch posture for broken-field maneuvering," and the bad guy swerves away.

6 I often witness that "hunch posture," from women after dark on the warrenlike streets of Brooklyn where I live. They seem to set their faces on neutral and, with their purse straps strung across their chests bandolier style, they forge ahead as though bracing themselves against being tackled. I understand, of course, that the danger they perceive is not a hallucination. Women are particularly vulnerable to street violence, and young black males are drastically overrepresented among the perpetrators of that violence. Yet these truths are no solace against the kind of alienation that comes of being ever suspect, against being set apart, a fearsome entity with whom pedestrians avoid making eye contact.

7 It is not altogether clear to me how I reached the ripe old age of 22 without being conscious of the lethality nighttime pedestrians attributed to me. Perhaps it was because in Chester, Pennsylvania, the small, angry industrial town where I came of age in the 1960s, I was scarcely noticeable against a backdrop of gang warfare, street knifings, and murders. I grew up one of the good boys, had perhaps a half-dozen fist fights. In retrospect, my shyness of combat has clear sources.

8 Many things go into the making of a young thug. One of those things is the consummation of the male romance with the power to intimidate. An infant dis-

covers that random flailings send the baby bottle flying out of the crib and crashing to the floor. Delighted, the joyful babe repeats those motions again and again, seeking to duplicate the feat. Just so, I recall the points at which some of my boyhood friends were finally seduced by the perception of themselves as tough guys. When a mark cowered and surrendered his money without resistance, myth and reality merged—and paid off. It is, after all, only manly to embrace the power to frighten and intimidate. We, as men, are not supposed to give an inch of our lane on the highway; we are to seize the fighter's edge in work and in play and even in love; we are to be valiant in the face of hostile forces.

9 Unfortunately, poor and powerless young men seem to take all this nonsense literally. As a boy, I saw countless tough guys locked away; I have since buried several, too. They were babies, really—a teenage cousin, a brother of 22, a childhood friend in his mid-twenties—all gone down in episodes of bravado played out in the streets. I came to doubt the virtues of intimidation early on. I chose, perhaps even unconsciously, to remain a shadow—timid, but a survivor.

10 The fearsomeness mistakenly attributed to me in public places often has a perilous flavor. The most frightening of these confusions occurred in the late 1970s and early 1980s when I worked as a journalist in Chicago. One day, rushing into the office of a magazine I was writing for with a deadline story in hand, I was mistaken for a burglar. The office manager called security and, with an ad hoc posse, pursued me through the labyrinthine halls, nearly to my editor's door. I had no way of proving who I was. I could only move briskly toward the company of someone who knew me.

11 Another time I was on assignment for a local paper and killing time before an interview. I entered a jewelry store on the city's affluent Near North Side. The proprietor excused herself and returned with an enormous red Doberman pinscher straining at the end of a leash. She stood, the dog extended toward me, silent to my questions, her eyes bulging nearly out of her head. I took a cursory look around, nodded, and bade her good night. Relatively speaking, however, I never fared as badly as another black male journalist. He went to nearby Waukegan, Illinois, a couple of summers ago to work on a story about a murderer who was born there. Mistaking the reporter for the killer, police hauled him from his car at gunpoint and but for his press credentials would probably have tried to book him. Such episodes are not uncommon. Black men trade tales like this all the time.

12 In "My Negro Problem—And Ours," Podhoretz writes that the hatred he feels for blacks makes itself known to him through a variety of avenues—one being his discomfort with that "special brand of paranoid touchiness" to which he says blacks are prone. No doubt he is speaking here of black men. In time, I learned to smother the rage I felt at so often being taken for a criminal. Not to do so would surely have led to madness—via that special "paranoid touchiness" that so annoyed Podhoretz at the time he wrote the essay.

13 I began to take precautions to make myself less threatening. I move about with care, particularly late in the evening. I give a wide berth to nervous people on subway platforms during the wee hours, particularly when I have exchanged business clothes for jeans. If I happen to be entering a building behind some people who appear skittish, I may walk by, letting them clear the lobby before I return, so as not to seem to be following them. I have been calm and extremely congenial on those rare occasions when I've been pulled over by the police.

14 And on late-evening constitutionals along streets less traveled by, I employ what has proved to be an excellent tension-reducing measure: I whistle melodies from Beethoven and Vivaldi and the more popular classical composers. Even steely New Yorkers hunching toward nighttime destinations seem to relax, and occasionally they even join in the tune. Virtually everybody seems to sense that a mugger wouldn't be warbling bright, sunny selections from Vivaldi's *Four Seasons*. It is my equivalent of the cowbell that hikers wear when they know they are in bear country.

Vocabulary

The following terms are identified by paragraph number. Make sure that you understand each term's meaning in its context. If you're not sure that you understand a term, look it up in a college-level dictionary.

affluent (1)	errant (2)	consummation (8)
discreet (1)	elicit (3)	bravado (9)
billowing (1)	extol (5)	labyrinthine (10)
unwieldy (2)	bandolier (6)	affluent (11)
quarry (2)	perpetrator (6)	proprietor (11)
insomnia (2)	solace (6)	cursory (11)
wayfarer (2)	alienation (6)	bade (11)
tyranny (2)	entity (6)	berth (13)
dicey (2)	lethality (7)	skittish (13)
foyer (2)	retrospect (7)	congenial (13)

STYLE AND STRATEGY
1. This startling opening is intentionally ironic.
2. The contrast is stated explicitly in paragraphs 2, 5, 7, 10, and 11.
3. In paragraph 9, he mentions childhood friends who wound up in prison. However, the most telling example involves a fellow black journalist in paragraph 11.
4. No, his tone is quite controlled. Paragraphs 12–14 are worth discussing in this regard.

Style and Strategy

1. In the opening sentence, why does Staples refer to his "first victim"? How does Staples's opening paragraph capture readers' attention?
2. What is the contrast between the "real" Staples and how he is perceived by others? How does Staples make that contrast clear?
3. Most of Staples's examples are from his own experience. What other examples does he provide? What do they add to the essay?
4. Staples has every right to be angry about what he has gone through. Is the tone of this essay angry? Explain.

QUESTIONS FOR CRITICAL THINKING AND DISCUSSION Each of these questions can be used as a prompt for a short writing assignment, which students can address when they prepare for classroom discussion of the essay.

Questions for Critical Thinking and Discussion

1. This essay is about the harmful effects of stereotyping—white Americans frequently fear young black men, so Staples is feared. How often, and in what contexts, do you see negative stereotyping in your daily life?
2. Consider the following situation. You walk into a busy office where four young workers are frantically running around and getting into loud arguments with one another. In the midst of these four is an older woman working calmly and serenely, never showing the tension and apprehensiveness that afflict her colleagues. Who are you going to go to for assistance? If you said "the older woman," is this an example of positive stereotyping? How?

3. We all depend a great deal on first impressions—how a person looks and behaves, and how those features fit in with our past experiences. How often are your first impressions wrong? In other words, explain a situation in which you got to know a person and found him or her to be quite unlike your presumption.

Suggestions for Writing

1. Are you sometimes or regularly misperceived by those around you? Write a 500- to 750-word essay in which you give several examples of situations in which your self-perception is at odds with how others seem to regard you.
2. Write a 500- to 750-word essay about an experience in which the members of a group you belonged to were all victims of the same incorrect assumption. Give examples of group members' reactions.

SUGGESTIONS FOR WRITING Encourage students to gather as much information as possible before they begin to write. Brainstorming might be appropriate for item 2.

On Dumpster Diving

LARS EIGHNER

When Lars Eighner wrote "On Dumpster Diving," he was homeless after having been fired from his job in Austin, Texas. With Lizbeth, his Labrador retriever, Eighner spent three years on the streets.

"On Dumpster Diving" is a revised version of an essay originally published in 1991 in *Threepenny Review* and included in the book *Travels with Lizbeth: Three Years on the Road and on the Streets* (1993). In it, Eighner uses a series of examples to comment on how what we throw away defines the way we live.

1 Long before I began Dumpster diving I was impressed with Dumpsters, enough so that I wrote the Merriam-Webster research service to discover what I could about the word *Dumpster.* I learned from them that it is a proprietary word belonging to the Dempster Dumpster company. Since then I have dutifully capitalized the word, although it was lowercased in almost all the citations Merriam-Webster photocopied for me. Dempster's word is too apt. I have never heard these things called anything but Dumpsters. I do not know anyone who knows the generic name for these objects. From time to time I have heard a wino or hobo give some corrupted credit to the original and call them Dipsy Dumpsters.

2 I began Dumpster diving about a year before I became homeless.

3 I prefer the word *scavenging* and use the word *scrounging* when I mean to be obscure. I have heard people, evidently meaning to be polite, use the word *foraging,* but I prefer to reserve that word for gathering nuts and berries and such, which I do also according to the season and the opportunity. *Dumpster diving* seems to me to be a little too cute and, in my case, inaccurate because I lack the athletic ability to lower myself into the Dumpsters as the true divers do, much to their increased profit.

4 I like the frankness of the word *scavenging,* which I can hardly think of without picturing a big black snail on an aquarium wall. I live from the refuse of others. I am a scavenger. I think it a sound and honorable niche, although if I could I would naturally prefer to live the comfortable consumer life, perhaps—and only perhaps—as a slightly less wasteful consumer, owing to what I have learned as a scavenger.

5 While Lizbeth and I were still living in the shack on Avenue B as my savings ran out, I put almost all my sporadic income into rent. The necessities of daily life I began

to extract from Dumpsters. Yes, we ate from them. Except for jeans, all my clothes came from Dumpsters. Boom boxes, candles, bedding, toilet paper, a virgin male love doll, medicine, books, a typewriter, dishes, furnishings, and change, sometimes amounting to many dollars—I acquired many things from the Dumpsters.

6 I have learned much as a scavenger. I mean to put some of what I have learned down here, beginning with the practical art of Dumpster diving and proceeding to the abstract.

7 What is safe to eat?

8 After all, the finding of objects is becoming something of an urban art. Even respectable employed people will sometimes find something tempting sticking out of a Dumpster or standing beside one. Quite a number of people, not all of them of the bohemian type, are willing to brag that they found this or that piece in the trash. But eating from Dumpsters is what separates the dilettanti from the professionals. Eating safely from the Dumpsters involves three principles: using the senses and common sense to evaluate the condition of the found materials, knowing the Dumpsters of a given area and checking them regularly, and seeking always to answer the question "Why was this discarded?"

9 Perhaps everyone who has kitchen and a regular supply of groceries has, at one time or another, made a sandwich and eaten half of it before discovering mold on the bread or got a mouthful of milk before realizing the milk had turned. Nothing of the sort is likely to happen to a Dumpster diver because he is constantly reminded that most food is discarded for a reason. Yet a lot of perfectly good food can be found in Dumpsters.

10 Canned goods, for example, turn up fairly often in the Dumpsters I frequent. All except the most phobic people would be willing to eat from a can, even if it came from a Dumpster. Canned goods are among the safest of foods to be found in Dumpsters but are not utterly foolproof.

11 Although very rare with modern canning methods, botulism is a possibility. Most other forms of food poisoning seldom do lasting harm to a healthy person, but botulism is almost certainly fatal and often the first symptom is death. Except for carbonated beverages, all canned goods should contain a slight vacuum and suck air when first punctured. Bulging, rusty, and dented cans and cans that spew when punctured should be avoided, especially when the contents are not very acidic or syrupy.

12 Heat can break down the botulin, but this requires much more cooking than most people do to canned goods. To the extent that botulism occurs at all, of course, it can occur in cans on pantry shelves as well as in cans from Dumpsters. Need I say that home-canned goods are simply too risky to be recommended.

13 From time to time one of my companions, aware of the source of my provisions, will ask, "Do you think these crackers are really safe to eat?" For some reason it is most often the crackers they ask about.

14 This question has always made me angry. Of course I would not offer my companion anything I had doubts about. But more than that, I wonder why he cannot evaluate the condition of the crackers for himself. I have no special knowledge and I have been wrong before. Since he knows where the food comes from, it seems to me he ought to assume some of the responsibility for deciding what he will put in his mouth. For myself I have few qualms about dry foods such as crackers, cookies, cereal, chips, and pasta if they are free of visible contaminates and still dry and

crisp. Most often such things are found in the original packaging, which is not so much a positive sign as it is the absence of a negative one.

15 Raw fruits and vegetables with intact skins seem perfectly safe to me, excluding of course the obviously rotten. Many are discarded for minor imperfections that can be pared away. Leafy vegetables, grapes, cauliflower, broccoli, and similar things may be contaminated by liquids and may be impractical to wash.

16 Candy, especially hard candy, is usually safe if it has not drawn ants. Chocolate is often discarded only because it has become discolored as the cocoa butter de-emulsified. Candying, after all, is one method of food preservation because pathogens do not like very sugary substances.

17 All of these foods might be found in any Dumpster and can be evaluated with some confidence largely on the basis of appearance. Beyond these are foods that cannot be correctly evaluated without additional information.

18 I began scavenging by pulling pizzas out of the Dumpster behind a pizza delivery shop. In general, prepared food requires caution, but in this case I knew when the shop closed and went to the Dumpster as soon as the last of the help left.

19 Such shops often get prank orders; both the orders and the products made to fill them are called *bogus*. Because help seldom stays long at these places, pizzas are often made with the wrong topping, refused on delivery for being cold, or baked incorrectly. The products to be discarded are boxed up because inventory is kept by counting boxes: A boxed pizza can be written off; an unboxed pizza does not exist.

20 I never placed a bogus order to increase the supply of pizzas and I believe no one else was scavenging in this Dumpster. But the people in the shop became suspicious and began to retain their garbage in the shop overnight. While it lasted I had a steady supply of fresh, sometimes warm pizza. Because I knew the Dumpster I knew the source of the pizza, and because I visited the Dumpster regularly I knew what was fresh and what was yesterday's.

21 The area I frequent is inhabited by many affluent college students. I am not here by chance; the Dumpsters in this area are very rich. Students throw out many good things, including food. In particular they tend to throw everything out when they move at the end of a semester, before and after breaks, and around midterm, when many of them despair of college. So I find it advantageous to keep an eye on the academic calendar.

22 Students throw food away around breaks because they do not know whether it has spoiled or will spoil before they return. A typical discard is a half jar of peanut butter. In fact, nonorganic peanut butter does not require refrigeration and is unlikely to spoil in any reasonable time. The student does not know that, and since it is Daddy's money, the student decides not to take a chance. Opened containers require caution and some attention to the question. "Why was this discarded?" But in the case of discards from student apartments, the answer may be that the item was thrown out through carelessness, ignorance, or wastefulness. This can sometimes be deduced when the item is found with many others, including some that are obviously perfectly good.

23 Some students, and others, approach defrosting a freezer by chucking out the whole lot. Not only do the circumstances of such a find tell the story, but also the mass of frozen goods stays cold for a long time and items may be found still frozen or freshly thawed.

Yogurt, cheese, and sour cream are items that are often thrown out while they are still good. Occasionally I find a cheese with a spot of mold, which of course I just pare off, and because it is obvious why such a cheese was discarded, I treat it with less suspicion than an apparently perfect cheese found in similar circumstances. Yogurt is often discarded, still sealed, only because the expiration date on the carton had passed. This is one of my favorite finds because yogurt will keep for several days, even in warm weather. 24

Students throw out canned goods and staples at the end of semesters and when they give up college at midterm. Drugs, pornography, spirits, and the like are often discarded when parents are expected—Dad's Day, for example. And spirits also turn up after big party weekends, presumably discarded by the newly reformed. Wine and spirits, of course, keep perfectly well even once opened, but the same cannot be said of beer. 25

My test for carbonated soft drinks is whether they still fizz vigorously. Many juices or other beverages are too acidic or too syrupy to cause much concern, provided they are not visibly contaminated. I have discovered nasty molds in vegetable juices, even when the product was found under its original seal; I recommend that such products be decanted slowly into a clear glass. Liquids always require some care. One hot day I found a large jug of Pat O'Brien's Hurricane mix. The jug had been opened but was still ice cold. I drank three large glasses before it became apparent to me that someone had added rum to the mix, and not a little rum. I never tasted the rum, and by the time I began to feel the effects I had already ingested a very large quantity of the beverage. Some divers would have considered this a boon, but being suddenly intoxicated in a public place in the early afternoon is not my idea of a good time. 26

I have heard of people maliciously contaminating discarded food and even handouts, but mostly I have heard of this from people with vivid imaginations who have had no experience with the Dumpsters themselves. Just before the pizza shop stopped discarding its garbage at night, jalapeños began showing up on most of the thrown-out pizzas. If indeed this was meant to discourage me, it was a wasted effort because I am a native Texan. 27

For myself, I avoid game, poultry, pork, and egg-based foods, whether I find them raw or cooked. I seldom have the means to cook what I find, but when I do I avail myself of plentiful supplies of beef, which is often in very good condition. I suppose fish becomes disagreeable before it becomes dangerous. Lizbeth is happy to have any such thing that is past its prime and, in fact, does not recognize fish as food until it is quite strong. 28

Home leftovers, as opposed to surpluses from restaurants, are very often bad. Evidently, especially among students, there is a common type of personality that carefully wraps up even the smallest leftover and shoves it into the back of the refrigerator for six months or so before discarding it. Characteristic of this type are the reused jars and margarine tubs to which the remains are committed. I avoid ethnic foods I am unfamiliar with. If I do not know what it is supposed to look like when it is good, I cannot be certain I will be able to tell if it is bad. 29

No matter how careful I am I still get dysentery at least once a month, oftener in warm weather. I do not want to paint too romantic a picture. Dumpster diving has serious drawbacks as a way of life. 30

Vocabulary

The following terms are identified by paragraph number. Make sure that you understand each term's meaning in its context. If you're not sure that you understand a term, look it up in a college-level dictionary.

proprietary (1)	refuse (4)	pathogens (16)
dutifully (1)	niche (4)	advantageous (21)
citations (1)	sporadic (5)	deduced (22)
apt (1)	bohemian (8)	expiration (24)
generic (1)	dilettanti (8)	staples (25)
corrupted (1)	phobic (10)	spirits (25)
frankness (4)	qualms (14)	dysentery (30)

Style and Strategy

1. Many Americans see homelessness as a vast national tragedy. (In such a prosperous country, how could so many people be adrift?) Does Eighner's tone reflect this attitude, or does it indicate that he is taking a different approach? Explain.
2. At times, this essay almost seems as if it were written by a sociologist studying Americans' discards in order to analyze consumer habits. (Such studies have been conducted.) But who is Eighner's audience? How will this audience react to Eighner's examples?
3. Explain how Eighner incorporates the following three strategies as part of his exemplification essay: process analysis (see Chapter 9), causal analysis (Chapter 10), and comparison and contrast (Chapter 13).

STYLE AND STRATEGY
1. The opening paragraphs reveal Eighner's tone. He is usually light and direct, but sometimes he engages in whimsy.
2. The intended audience is well educated and sophisticated. They are familiar with large urban settings. In the hands of another writer, Eighner's examples might seem shocking, but with his practical approach Eighner uses these examples to inform and to entertain.
3. Process analysis is seen in paragraphs 10–12, 14–17, and 26; causal analysis in paragraphs 5, and 19–25; comparison/contrast in paragraphs 8 and 28–29.

Questions for Critical Thinking and Discussion

1. Are there people in your city or town who are *involuntarily* homeless? Do you know what caused them to lose their homes?
2. Why would someone *choose* to be homeless?
3. Are you an efficient consumer, or would a "scavenger" welcome the chance to sort through your garbage? Explain.
4. Would you take something from a garbage can or a Dumpster if the item appealed to you? Explain.

QUESTIONS FOR CRITICAL THINKING AND DISCUSSION All four items can lead to interesting class discussions. The third can be turned into a prompt for short writing, in which students attempt self-analysis.

Suggestions for Writing

1. Write a 500-word essay about an activity that most people dislike and avoid (for example, cleaning an apartment or doing laundry) but that you perversely enjoy. Give examples that show why you enjoy this activity.
2. Write a 500-word essay about an activity that most people enjoy but that you dread. Give examples that show why you dislike this normally "positive" experience.

SUGGESTIONS FOR WRITING Encourage students to brainstorm in small study groups in order to gather information for essays on these topics.

Life According to TV

HARRY F. WATERS

Television plays a major role in the United States, even for people who don't watch it very often. Television's influence is vast and incalculable. However, is television an accurate reflection of life in the United States? Harry F. Waters, a staff writer for *Newsweek* (where this essay appeared on December 6, 1982), doesn't think so. Drawing on the work of media scholar George Gerbner, Waters's essay shows, by example after example, that television is a faulty mirror of American society.

1 The late Paddy Chayefsky, who created Howard Beale,* would have loved George Gerbner. In *Network,* Chayefsky marshaled a scathing fictional assault on the values and methods of the people who control the world's most potent communications instrument. In real life, Gerbner, perhaps the nation's foremost authority on the social impact of television, is quietly using the disciplines of behavioral research to construct an equally devastating indictment of the medium's images and messages. More than any spokesman for a pressure group, Gerbner has become the man that television watches. From his cramped, book-lined office at the University of Pennsylvania springs a steady flow of studies that are raising executive blood pressures at the networks' sleek Manhattan command posts.

2 George Gerbner's work is uniquely important because it transports the scientific examination of television far beyond familiar children-and-violence arguments. Rather than simply studying the link between violence on the tube and crime in the streets, Gerbner is exploring wider and deeper terrain. He has turned his lens on TV's hidden victims—women, the elderly, blacks, blue-collar workers and other groups—to document the ways in which video-entertainment portrayals subliminally condition how we perceive ourselves and how we view those around us. Gerbner's subjects are not merely the impressionable young; they include all the rest of us. And it is his ominous conclusion that heavy watchers of the prime-time mirror are receiving a grossly distorted picture of the real world that they tend to accept more readily than reality itself.

3 The 63-year-old Gerbner, who is dean of Penn's Annenberg School of Communications, employs a methodology that meshes scholarly observation with mundane legwork. Over the past 15 years, he and a tireless trio of assistants (Larry Gross, Nancy Signorelli and Michael Morgan) videotaped and exhaustively analyzed 1,600 prime-time programs involving more than 15,000 characters. They then drew up multiple-choice questionnaires that offered correct answers about the world at large along with answers that reflected what Gerbner perceived to be the misrepresentations and biases of the world according to TV. Finally, these questions were posed to large samples of citizens from all socioeconomic strata. In every survey, the Annenberg team discovered that heavy viewers of television (those watching more than four hours a day), who account for more than 30 percent of the population, almost invariably chose the TV-influenced answers, while light viewers (less than two hours a day), selected the answers corresponding more closely to actual life. Some of the dimensions of television's reality warp:

***Howard Beale:** a character in the film *Network,* a satire of the television industry's pursuit of ratings. Played by Peter Finch, Beale is remembered for screaming "I'm mad as hell, and I'm not going to take this anymore!"

Sex

Male prime-time characters outnumber females by 3 to 1 and, with a few star-turn exceptions, women are portrayed as weak, passive satellites to powerful, effective men. TV's male population also plays a vast variety of roles, while females generally get typecast as either lovers or mothers. Less than 20 percent of TV's married women with children work outside the home—as compared with more than 50 percent in real life. The tube's distorted depictions of women, concludes Gerbner, reinforce stereotypical attitudes and increase sexism. In one Annenberg survey, heavy viewers were far more likely than light ones to agree with the proposition: "Women should take care of running their homes and leave running the country to men." 4

Age

People over 65, too, are grossly underrepresented on television. Correspondingly, heavy-viewing Annenberg respondents believe that the elderly are a vanishing breed, that they make up a smaller proportion of the population today than they did 20 years ago. In fact, they form the nation's most rapidly expanding age group. Heavy viewers also believe that old people are less healthy today than they were two decades ago, when quite the opposite is true. As with women, the portrayals of old people transmit negative impressions. In general, they are cast as silly, stubborn, sexually inactive and eccentric. "They're often shown as feeble grandparents bearing cookies," says Gerbner. "You never see the power that real old people often have. The best and possibly only time to learn about growing old with decency and grace is in youth. And young people are the most susceptible to TV's messages." 5

Race

The problem with the medium's treatment of blacks is more one of image than of visibility. Though a tiny percentage of black characters come across as "unrealistically romanticized," reports Gerbner, the overwhelming majority of them are employed in subservient, supporting roles—such as the white hero's comic sidekick. "When a black child looks at prime time," he says, "most of the people he sees doing interesting and important things are white." That imbalance, he goes on, tends to teach young blacks to accept minority status as naturally inevitable and even deserved. To access the impact of such portrayals on the general audience, the Annenberg survey forms included questions like "Should white people have the right to keep blacks out of their neighborhoods?" and "Should there be laws against marriages between blacks and whites?" The more that viewers watched, the more they answered "yes" to each question. 6

Work

Heavy viewers greatly overestimated the proportion of Americans employed as physicians, lawyers, athletes and entertainers, all of whom inhabit prime-time in hordes. A mere 6 to 10 percent of television characters hold blue-collar or service jobs vs. about 60 percent in the real work force. Gerbner sees two dangers in TV's skewed division of labor. On the one hand, the tube so overrepresents and glamorizes the elite occupations that it sets up unrealistic expectations among those who must deal with them in actuality. At the same time, TV largely neglects portraying the occupations that most youngsters will have to enter. "You almost never see the farmer, the factory worker or the small businessman," he notes. "Thus not only do 7 lawyers and other professionals find they cannot measure up to the image TV projects of them, but children's occupational aspirations are channeled in unrealistic directions." The Gerbner team feels this emphasis on high-powered jobs poses problems for adolescent girls, who are also presented with views of women as homebodies. The conflicting views, Gerbner says, add to the frustration over choices they have to make as adults.

Health

8 Although video characters exist almost entirely on junk food and quaff alcohol 15 times more often than water, they manage to remain slim, healthy and beautiful. Frequent TV watchers, the Annenberg investigators found, eat more, drink more, exercise less and possess an almost mystical faith in the curative powers of medical science. Concludes Gerbner: "Television may well be the single most pervasive source of health information. And its over-idealized images of medical people, coupled with its complacency about unhealthy life-styles, leaves both patients and doctors vulnerable to disappointment, frustration and even litigation."

Crime

9 On the small screen, crime rages about 10 times more often than in real life. But while other researchers concentrate on the propensity of TV mayhem to incite aggression, the Annenberg team has studied the hidden side of its imprint: fear of victimization. On television, 55 percent of prime-time characters are involved in violent confrontations once a week; in reality, the figure is less than 1 percent. In all demographic groups in every class of neighborhood, heavy viewers overestimated the statistical chance of violence in their own lives and harbored an exaggerated mistrust of strangers—creating what Gerbner calls "mean-world syndrome." Forty-six percent of heavy viewers who live in cities rated their fear of crime "very serious" as opposed to 26 percent of light viewers. Such paranoia is especially acute among TV entertainment's most common victims: women, the elderly, nonwhites, foreigners and lower-class citizens.

10 Video violence, proposes Gerbner, is primarily responsible for imparting lessons in social power: it demonstrates who can do what to whom and get away with it. "Television is saying that those at the bottom of the power scale cannot get away with the same things that a white, middle-class American male can," he says. "It potentially conditions people to think of themselves as victims."

11 At a quick glance, Gerbner's findings seem to contain a cause-and-effect, chicken-or-the-egg question. Does television make heavy viewers view the world the way they do or do heavy viewers come from the poorer, less experienced segment of the populace that regards the world that way to begin with? In other words, does the tube create or simply confirm the unenlightened attitudes of its most loyal audiences? Gerbner, however, was savvy enough to construct a methodology largely immune to such criticism. His samples of heavy viewers cut across all ages, incomes, education levels and ethnic backgrounds—and every category displayed the same tube-induced misconceptions of the world outside.

12 Needless to say, the networks accept all this as enthusiastically as they would a list of news-coverage complaints from the Ayatollah Khomeini.* Even so, their responses tend to be tinged with a singular respect for Gerbner's personal and pro-

---

***Ayatollah Khomeni:** a religious leader who came to power after the 1979 Iranian revolution.

fessional credentials. The man is no ivory-tower recluse. During World War II, the Budapest-born Gerbner parachuted into the mountains of Yugoslavia to join the partisans fighting the Germans. After the war, he hunted down and personally arrested scores of high Nazi officials. Nor is Gerbner some videophobic vigilante. A Ph.D. in communications, he readily acknowledges TV's beneficial effects, noting that it has abolished parochialism, reduced isolation and loneliness and provided the poorest members of society with cheap, plug-in exposure to experiences they otherwise would not have. Funding for his research is supported by such prestigious bodies as the National Institute of Mental Health, the Surgeon General's office, and the American Medical Association, and he is called to testify before congressional committees nearly as often as David Stockman.*

Mass Entertainment

13 When challenging Gerbner, network officials focus less on his findings and methods than on what they regard as his own misconceptions of their industry's function. "He's looking at television from the perspective of a social scientist rather than considering what is mass entertainment," says Alfred Schneider, vice president of standards and practices at ABC. "We strive to balance TV's social effects with what will capture an audience's interests. If you showed strong men being victimized as much as women or the elderly, what would comprise the dramatic conflict? If you did a show truly representative of society's total reality, and nobody watched because it wasn't interesting, what have you achieved?"

14 CBS senior vice president Gene Mater also believes that Gerbner is implicitly asking for the theoretically impossible. "TV is unique in its problems," says Mater. "Everyone wants a piece of the action. Everyone feels that their racial or ethnic group is underrepresented or should be portrayed as they would like the world to perceive them. No popular entertainment form, including this one, can or should be an accurate reflection of society."

15 On that point, at least, Gerbner is first to agree; he hardly expects television entertainment to serve as a mirror image of absolute truth. But what fascinates him about this communications medium is its marked difference from all others. In other media, customers carefully choose what they want to hear or read: a movie, a magazine, a best seller. In television, notes Gerbner, viewers rarely tune in for a particular program. Instead, most just habitually turn on the set—and watch by the clock rather than for a specific show. "Television viewing fulfills the criteria of a ritual," he says. "It is the only medium that can bring to people things they otherwise would not select." With such unique power, believes Gerbner, comes unique responsibility: "No other medium reaches into every home or has a comparable, cradle-to-grave influence over what a society learns about itself."

Match

16 In Gerbner's view, virtually all of TV's distortions of reality can be attributed to its obsession with demographics. The viewers that prime-time sponsors most want to reach are white, middle-class, female and between 18 and 49—in short, the audience that purchases most of the consumer products advertised on the tube. Accordingly, notes Gerbner, the demographic portrait of TV's fictional characters

*__David Stockman:__ a prominent and controversial official during Ronald Reagan's presidency.

largely matches that of its prime commercial targets and largely ignores everyone else. "Television," he concludes, "reproduces a world for its own best customers."

17 Among TV's more candid executives, that theory draws considerable support. Yet by pointing a finger at the power of demographics, Gerbner appears to contradict one of his major findings. If female viewers are so dear to the hearts of sponsors, why are female characters cast in such unflattering light? "In a basically male-oriented power structure," replies Gerbner, "you can't alienate the male viewer. But you can get away with offending women because most women are pretty well brainwashed to accept it." The Annenberg dean has an equally tidy explanation for another curious fact. Since the corporate world provides network television with all of its financial support, one would expect businessmen on TV to be portrayed primarily as good guys. Quite the contrary. As any fan of "Dallas," "Dynasty," or "Falcon Crest" well knows, the image of the company man is usually that of a mendacious, dirty-dealing rapscallion. Why would TV snap at the hand that feeds it? "Credibility is the way to ratings," proposes Gerbner. "This country has a populist tradition of bias against anything big, including big business. So to retain credibility, TV entertainment shows businessmen in relatively derogatory ways."

18 In the medium's Hollywood-based creative community, the gospel of Gerbner finds some passionate adherents. Rarely have TV's best and brightest talents viewed their industry with so much frustration and anger. The most sweeping indictment emanates from David Rintels, a two-time Emmy-winning writer and former president of the Writers Guild of America, West. "Gerbner is absolutely correct and it is the people who run the networks who are to blame," says Rintels. "The networks get bombarded with thoughtful, reality-oriented scripts. They simply won't do them. They slam the door on them. They believe that the only way to get ratings is to feed viewers what conforms to their biases or what has limited resemblance to reality. From 8 to 11 o'clock each night, television is one long lie."

19 Innovative thinkers such as Norman Lear, whose work has been practically driven off the tube, don't fault the networks so much as the climate in which they operate. Says Lear: "All of this country's institutions have become totally fixated on short-term bottom-line thinking. Everyone grabs for what might succeed today and the hell with tomorrow. Television just catches more of the heat because it's more visible." Perhaps the most perceptive assessment of Gerbner's conclusions is offered by one who has worked both sides of the industry street. Deanne Barkley, a former NBC vice president who now helps run an independent production house, reports that the negative depictions of women on TV have made it "nerve-racking" to function as a woman within TV. "No one takes responsibility for the social impact of their shows," says Barkley. "But then how do you decide where it all begins? Do the networks give viewers what they want? Or are the networks conditioning them to think that way?"

20 Gerbner himself has no simple answer to that conundrum. Neither a McLuhanesque* shaman nor a Naderesque crusader, he hesitates to suggest solutions until pressed. Then out pops a pair of provocative notions. Commercial television will never democratize its treatments of daily life, he believes, until it finds a way to broaden its financial base. Coincidentally, Federal Communications Commission chairman Mark Fowler seems to have arrived at much the same conclusion. In exchange

*__McLuhanesque:__ derived from the name Marshall McLuhan (1911–1980), a pioneer in media studies and the source of the observation, "The medium is the message."

for lifting such government restrictions on TV as the fairness doctrine and the equal-time rule, Fowler would impose a modest levy on station owners called a spectrum-use fee. Funds from the fees would be set aside to finance programs aimed at specialized tastes rather than the mass appetite. Gerbner enthusiastically endorses that proposal: "Let the ratings system dominate most of prime time but not every hour of every day. Let some programs carry advisories that warn: 'This is not for all of you. This is for nonwhites, or for religious people or for the aged and the handicapped. Turn it off unless you'd like to eavesdrop.' That would be a very refreshing thing."

Role

21 In addition, Gerbner would like to see viewers given an active role in steering the overall direction of television instead of being obliged to passively accept whatever the networks offer. In Britain, he points out, political candidates debate the problems of TV as routinely as the issue of crime. In this country, proposes Gerbner, "every political campaign should put television on the public agenda. Candidates talk about schools, they talk about jobs, they talk about social welfare. They're going to have to start discussing this all-pervasive force."

22 There are no outright villains in this docudrama. Even Gerbner recognizes that network potentates don't set out to proselytize a point of view; they are simply businessmen selling a mass-market product. At the same time, their 90 million nightly customers deserve to know the side effects of the ingredients. By the time the typical American child reaches the age of reason, calculates Gerbner, he or she will have absorbed more than 30,000 electronic "stories." These stories, he suggests, have replaced the socializing role of the preindustrial church: they create a "cultural mythology" that establishes the norms of approved behavior and belief. And all Gerbner's research indicates that this new mythological world, with its warped picture of a sizable portion of society, may soon become the one most of us think we live in.

23 Who else is telling us that? Howard Beale and his eloquent alarms have faded into off network reruns. At the very least, it is comforting to know that a real-life Beale is very much with us . . . and *really* watching.

Vocabulary

The following terms are identified by paragraph number. Make sure that you understand each term's meaning in its context. If you're not sure that you understand a term, look it up in a college-level dictionary.

late (1)	curative (8)	derogatory (17)
scathing (1)	acute (9)	adherents (18)
cramped (1)	savvy (11)	conundrum (20)
subliminally (2)	recluse (12)	shaman (20)
strata (3)	parochialism (12)	levy (20)
satellites (4)	mendacious (17)	proselytize (22)
quaff (8)	rapscallion (17)	

Style and Strategy

1. What is the thesis of this essay? Where is it?
2. Waters's *primary* purpose is to provide examples of ways that television,

STYLE AND STRATEGY

1. The thesis is plainly stated in the last sentence of paragraph 2.
2. The author's secondary purpose becomes clear as he discusses each of the "dimensions of television's reality warp" (paragraph 3). He argues that TV executives intentionally create programming featuring lifestyles, behaviors, and ideals to which viewers cannot and, in most cases, should not aspire. Therefore, TV's distortion of reality has a sinister effect on the evolution of our society.
3. Causal analysis appears in several paragraphs, most notably 7, 8, 10, 16, 17, and 19. Classification is evident in the very way the essay is organized.
4. The conclusion to such an essay cannot be definitive, but discussing the last three paragraphs provides insight into the art of ending an essay.

overall, presents a distorted picture of life in the United States. What is his *secondary* purpose? (Hint: look for his references to causes and effects.)

3. Find and list examples of Waters's use of (1) causal analysis (see Chapter 10) and (2) classification (Chapter 12) as internal strategies.
4. Does Waters come to a definitive conclusion? Summarize the last three paragraphs of this essay.

QUESTIONS FOR CRITICAL THINKING AND DISCUSSION Students have little trouble discussing these items in class. The first question can be turned into a prompt for a comparison/contrast essay that requires close textual analysis of Waters's essay. It also requires some careful TV watching.

SUGGESTIONS FOR WRITING Suggest that students do some research before attempting these assignments. The Internet is a good place to start.

Questions for Critical Thinking and Discussion

1. This essay is more than twenty years old. How has television changed since this essay was published in 1982? Is television now a more accurate reflection of society, or has it become even less accurate?
2. In paragraphs 13 and 14, Waters includes rebuttals from two network executives, who point out that (a) people don't want to see social realism on television and (b) television cannot please everyone. Discuss these ideas. Would you watch a prime-time drama about families living on the social and economic margin?

Suggestions for Writing

1. Today, companies and institutions seem devoted to "mission statements" and "values statements." Write a 500- to 750-word essay about a company or institution whose "projected" image is at odds with the reality of the company or institution itself. Use specific examples.
2. Select a local company or institution whose services are undervalued or unappreciated—a food bank, for instance. Write a 500- to 750-word essay explaining the value that this company or institution provides.

MORE OPTIONS ONLINE If you would like to read additional exemplification essays, go to **www.mhhe.com/writingtoday**.

WRITING THE EXEMPLIFICATION ESSAY WITH A READER'S EYE

Essays that depend on abstractions and generalities usually fail to connect with the audience and fulfill their purpose. Use effective, believable examples to support your general statements and reach out to your readers. The advice that follows will help you think like your reader as you consider your assignment and then prewrite, draft, revise, and edit your exemplification essay.

Issues to Keep in Mind

The usual purpose of an exemplification essay is to inform your reader about a topic or persuade your reader by providing clear, concrete examples. Consequently, as you begin to think about your essay, you'll need to decide on the kinds of examples you'll need and where to find them. Thinking about the following issues will help you to choose the best examples for your purpose:

1. Using examples from personal experience and from sources
2. Finding relevant and representative examples

Sources of Examples

For a great many essays, you can find plenty of examples from your personal experience, often more than you can use. However, if you have been assigned a topic that does not ask you to depend on your personal experience, you may need to spend some time at the library or online to find supporting information for your thesis. In fact, some assignments will stipulate that you do some basic research. Such assignments aren't necessarily asking you to produce a full-fledged research paper, just to go beyond your own experience. Whether you are required to use sources or not, if you use researched information in an essay, remember that you will be expected to cite the source. Moreover, there is a substantial difference between widely available information, known as **common knowledge**, that you encountered for the first time during your research and highly specific, specialized information that needs to be documented, including facts that are not readily available, opinions, and someone else's words. For example, if your instructor read the following sentence in one of your essays, he or she would probably not even slow down:

> Wyoming is one of the western states that regularly experiences heavy snowfalls.

All the people who live in Wyoming, and many people who live elsewhere, know that it snows a great deal in that state. However, the following sentence would probably draw a comment:

> Wyoming's population was only 340,000 in 1970, and the state remains sparsely settled today.

"What's your source?" "Where did you find this?" "You must give credit to the source that provided this information." These are the types of comments you could expect to find in the margin next to a sentence like this one. Your instructor would be trying to alert you to the dangers of playing fast and loose with researched material.

In the academic world, you are allowed to borrow from someone else's work, whether it be published or unpublished, but only if you acknowledge having done so. Not citing the sources of any facts (other than common knowledge), opinions, or quotations that you use is **plagiarism**, a term that you should hope to encounter only in the abstract. You don't want to be accused of lifting someone else's work. When in doubt, as always, ask your instructor. (Chapter 21 gives more details about the various transgressions that can be interpreted as plagiarism and provides guidelines for documenting your sources.)

When writing an essay that draws on their personal experience, some students are tempted to "construct" examples. Whatever your opinion on the morality of such a practice, we advise against it. Our opinion is rooted in practicality: a constructed example tends to stick out a bit, like a third eye in the center of someone's forehead. Most of us aren't very good writers of fiction, and most of us aren't very convincing liars; constructing examples requires talent in both areas. A paragraph like this one reeks of artificiality:

> The endless period of rain we have lived through is interesting, but everyone wishes it was gone. For example, my friend Emily has had a cold for two weeks. The walkways are slippery as well. For example, my friend Jennifer slipped on the sidewalk and sprained her ankle.

The paragraph is generally routine and lifeless; moreover, its two examples seem more like chalk outlines than real human beings. Working hard to come up with genuine examples will always help your essay; constructing examples will almost always introduce a false note.

Relevant and Representative Examples

CLASSROOM HINT
Devote some classroom time to a discussion of this section.

For each example that you find, you need to ask yourself the following questions: Does the example actually help illustrate my point, or is it irrelevant? Even worse, does it *contradict* my point? Once again, careful planning and prewriting will allow you to weed out defective examples, perhaps preventing you from writing a paragraph like this one on the topic of laws against drunk driving:

> Our state's new .08 blood alcohol content limit for drunk driving is a problem. For example, my roommate, Eddie, blew a .10 and was convicted of driving while intoxicated (DWI). He lost his license for six months, he has to complete 100 hours of community service, he had to pay his lawyer $1500.00, and he will be facing sky-high insurance rates when he gets his license back.

Although admirable in its use of specific details, this paragraph does not illustrate the writer's idea that the new law is a problem; instead, it proves that Eddie behaved foolishly. A DWI law is not passed in secrecy. The issue of drunk driving always generates publicity and controversy, and Eddie either didn't pay attention or decided to ignore the new reality. Moreover, the writer has let his sympathy for his roommate override his common sense.

Here is another question to ask yourself about each example that you consider: Is it truly representative? For example, a student who is developing an essay claiming that "volunteerism" has become a major part of student life at her college may want to use as an example a truly committed volunteer, a young man who has been profiled in the student newspaper for his involvement in six different charity drives and fund-raisers. But this person is not *representative* of the student body; instead, he is the *model* of the student volunteer. To find more effective examples, the student would need to do research on the total number of fund-raisers and charity drives on campus and the level of student involvement with these activities. With more broad-based examples, the writer can more convincingly support her assertion that volunteering has indeed become a fact of student life.

MORE OPTIONS ONLINE
For more help with problem areas in the exemplification essay, go to **www.mhhe.com/writingtoday**.

Choosing a Topic

To write an effective exemplification essay, you need to find a general statement about your topic that you can illustrate with clear, relevant, and representative examples. The following guidelines will help you choose a promising topic for your essay:

1. Choose a topic that you're comfortable with. Why choose a topic such as "the great value of books" if you don't like to read but prefer to watch seven hours of television every day? Wouldn't you be better off with "television: an underrated resource"?
2. Look for a topic that you can successfully illustrate. Exemplification works best when connected to the particulars of everyday life. Think of the subject matter of the four readings in the previous section: shopping, walking the streets at night, sorting through garbage, watching television. The four authors drew upon observable reality. You would have trouble developing an exemplification essay on a large, abstract, and complicated subject such as the inequities in U.S. immigration laws because such a topic requires a great deal of abstract discussion.
3. Consider your audience and the interaction that readers will bring to your text. Many essay assignments will include a specific audience and purpose, and you can use this context to guide you as you work. The more that you consider your audience, the better your chances of success. As you select your topic, though, don't try to "score points" with your audience by attempting to determine the culturally appropriate response—the response you think they expect. If given a choice between reading a well-written essay on the value of books or a well-written essay on the undervaluation of television, we'd go straight for the latter. It's got more potential; the challenge is greater.

Prewriting

Once you have chosen your topic, use one of the informal prewriting strategies to generate ideas and examples: listing, freewriting, or clustering. (See Chapter 2 for more on these strategies.) Remember that you are always better off generating more examples than you will actually use. If examples from your personal experience will not be enough to support the topic, consider going to the library or on the Internet to look for additional support. If you plan to research your topic, however, check with your instructor first.

At this point, see if you can develop a working or preliminary thesis. If you can do so, and if you begin to visualize the direction that your essay will take, you are now ready to organize your prewriting.

Organizing

Once you have generated a sufficient number of examples and developed your working thesis, the best way for you to organize this raw material is to arrange it into an outline. (Chapter 2 covers informal, sentence, and formal outline structures.) The typical structure of an exemplification essay is straightforward and logical: a thesis supported by topic sentences supported by specific examples. As well, make sure that you consider the most effective order for your body paragraphs and examples. Ending with your most compelling example is frequently a good approach.

Drafting

To illustrate one approach to writing an exemplification essay, we have included the essay "Tattoos: Thinking in the Present Tense."

The Introduction

The introductory paragraphs of an exemplification essay should literally introduce your reader to your main idea and the world that it inhabits. If readers do not have sufficient context, it can hinder their ability to appreciate an exemplification essay. Someone has forgotten to turn on some of the lights, as it were, and the reader is forced to stumble around in the dark, trying to get a fix on what the writer is up to. Note how the following introductory paragraph grounds the reader in the writer's reality:

Consider Your Options

Context and background are essential to your introduction. Too often we read exemplification essays with brief introductions that seem almost a formality. Make sure that you choose an approach that enables you to set up the situation for your reader before you start to explain it in your essay's body paragraphs. (See Chapter 3 for more on introductions.)

Tattoos: Thinking in the Present Tense

Recently, I heard a caller to a conservative talk-radio show complain about the appearance of young people: their weird hair, their body piercings, their tattoos. I told myself that young people always look strange to older people, and the caller sounded old. But of her three points, only one is truly worth exploring. **Tattoos are effectively permanent, and a person who has decided to get a tattoo is saying a lot about his or her view of life, especially in the location and type of tattoo.** Is it visible, or is it hidden? What is its subject matter?

Note the position of the thesis statement, toward the end of the paragraph, but with two questions following it for elaboration.

EXERCISE 8.1 Answers will vary. The following sentence outline is suggested.
Thesis: Tattoos are permanent, and the location and type of tattoo says a lot about a person's view of life.
I. People who have easily visible tattoos are making the strongest statement.
A. Tattoos worn by characters in movies are the first traits a viewer notices.

The Body

Here the writer proceeds to develop the ideas presented in her introduction with topic sentences and examples:

People who have easily visible tattoos are making the strongest statement. A tattoo on the hand/wrist, leg/calf, or face or neck will almost always be there for anyone to examine. The striking shoulder and neck tattoo worn by George Clooney's character in *From Dusk Till Dawn* and Harvey Keitel's facial cat stripes in *The Piano* were the first traits that viewers noticed. However, many young people get "in-your-face" tattoos without realizing that within a short time they may be going on an interview for that big first career job and looking into the eyes of an interviewer who is transfixed by the impossible-to-hide choice made in a somewhat more exuberant moment.

People who have hidden tattoos are playing it safe, in one sense. The tattoo won't prevent them from landing a good job. But the hidden tattoo can play a more devious role. My friend Siobhan uses hers as a flirtation device. When she's at a club and meets a guy she likes, she always lets him know that she has a tattoo. When the stooge asks "Where?" Siobhan always says "I'm not telling." It's obvious where that strategy is designed to lead.

The subject matter of the tattoo is also important. The favorite tattoos of the past—"Mom" and "Born to Lose"—seem to have been replaced by images only—a rose, a floral design, a snake. Images can be taken to extremes, however. I recently saw a man at a convenience store who was shirtless, and around his chest and back was a mural, a cyclorama, of the man's sexual fantasies. It was utterly ghastly. This man should not be allowed go into public without a shirt, or at least an NC-17 rating.

B. Young people who get "in-your-face" tattoos may face unanticipated consequences during job interviews.
II. People who have hidden tattoos are playing it safe.
A. The tattoo won't prevent them from landing a job.
B. The tattoo can have more devious purposes.
III. The subject matter of the tattoo is important.
A. Popular tattoos of the past have been replaced.
B. Images can be extreme, even sexually explicit.
IV. People shouldn't be allowed to get tattoos until they are old enough to consider the consequences.

The Conclusion

Your conclusion needs to reinforce your thesis—the idea that your body paragraphs and examples have developed. You might even go further and offer a judgment based on the evidence you have presented. Note here how the writer comes to two judgments about the decision to get a tattoo, both of which are logically derived from her essay's body paragraphs:

Tattoos seem like a lot of fun, but they are indeed permanent. Attempts to surgically remove tattoos always leave a scar. Perhaps my father, who is from Texas, sums it up best: "Sure, tattoos should be legal. But the minimum age ought to be 65. By then, people'd be mature enough not to screw up their future."

Consider Your Options

In the conclusion of a short essay you don't need to summarize, nor do you need to repeat your thesis. But keep your thesis in mind as you choose your approach. One common approach for this type of essay is to comment on the situation or problem that you have just explained. (See Chapter 3 for more approaches.)

MORE OPTIONS ONLINE
For more help with the step-by-step development of the exemplification essay, go to **www.mhhe.com/writingtoday**.

EXERCISE 8.1

Write a sentence outline of "Tattoos: Thinking in the Present Tense." (For help with sentence outlines, see Chapter 2, pages 40–42.) What does the outline reveal about

Questions for Reviewing an Exemplification Essay

CLASSROOM HINT Review these questions in class if time permits.

1. Does the introduction give the reader enough context? Does it capture the reader's interest? How could the introduction be strengthened?
2. What is the thesis statement? Has the writer placed it in the best position within the essay? How could it be improved?
3. Has the writer offered enough examples to support the thesis? If not, should the writer add more? Has the writer fulfilled his or her purpose for writing the essay?
4. Do the content and the structure work together, or is there a better way of organizing the examples? If so, how should they be organized?
5. Does the draft sound mechanical, as if each paragraph has been "set up" so that an example can illustrate it? Or are the examples integral and natural elements of their respective paragraphs? Where are transitional words or sentences needed?
6. Do any of the examples seem irrelevant, contradictory, artificial, or just strange? If so, point them out.
7. Are the body paragraphs fully developed? Where are additional details, or more specific details, needed?
8. Does the essay have an effective conclusion? How could it be improved?

the essay's organization? Could you suggest a different organization for this essay? Why?

Revising Your Draft

After you have completed a draft of your exemplification essay, your next step is to revise it, using your own analysis and comments from classmates or friends. During peer review, answer the Questions for Reviewing an Exemplification Essay (above) about the draft you are reviewing, whether it is yours or another student's.

After reviewing for content, you need to go over your peer reviewers' responses to your essay and then revise for unity, coherence, language level, and tone (see Chapter 4). When you have revised your draft and are basically satisfied with it, read your draft for mechanical and grammatical errors. Concentrate on finding and correcting major sentence errors (fragment, comma splice, fused sentence), errors in pronoun agreement and subject-verb agreement, and spelling.

MORE OPTIONS ONLINE For more help with revision, go to **www.mhhe.com/writingtoday**.

Now that you have made your corrections, *read your essay one more time* to catch any errors made during revision and find errors missed during your earlier reviews.

Student Essay

The following essay is Jennifer Janisz's response to an exemplification assignment. The final draft is presented first. Then Jennifer's first draft is presented, with her comments about this draft and what she needed to do in the revision stage.

Jennifer's Final Draft

Three Families

1 It's Christmas day, and the entire family is at my house. Eating dinner, I overhear several conversations and start to realize just how different the branches of my family are. I have three sets of aunts and uncles: my mom's sister, Gwen, and her husband, Ben; my dad's brother, John, and his wife, Kelly; and my dad's sister, Nicole, and her husband, Tom. Each set of relatives has at least one child yet very distinct ideas about how to raise and treat him or her. Gwen's family is laid back and cooperative. John's family is under his strict watch and command at all times. Nicole's family is free to do whatever they desire without repercussions. Though all three of these families have personal theories on the process of raising children, it's clear that no single approach is the perfect solution for everyone.

2 Gwen's family is the easygoing type. She and Ben don't worry too much about anything. Basically, they can have this attitude because the family members all trust one another. Gwen and Ben have two children, Billy and Christie. These two are responsible and levelheaded and do not need to be constantly watched by their parents. Billy and Christie are not perfect children. Like every child who is growing up, they make mistakes. Because of the respect these family members have for one another, however, it is easy for them to trust each other. When something does go wrong, the problem is handled rationally. A perfect example of this approach happened when Billy was sixteen. He went to a party that provided alcohol, and he ended up getting drunk. Most kids his age would have kept this secret from their parents. Billy, though, told his parents exactly what happened. Instead of grounding him, Gwen and Ben felt that he had learned his lesson from the experience and trusted him not to do it again.

3 John's family is not that trusting. The respect in this house is built out of fear. John and Kelly have one daughter, Mariah, who is far from meeting their high expectations. When Mariah does something wrong, even something

petty, she can be sure that the punishment will be severe. John and Kelly don't want to take chances in raising their daughter. They want to make sure that she knows what is expected of her and feel that she should respect their wishes, simply because they are her parents. Unfortunately, Mariah craves attention of any kind, so she doesn't strive to be what her parents demand, which only angers them that much more. Neither John nor Kelly smokes, so when Mariah brought home a pack of cigarettes she got from her friend, her parents were furious. John caught her with the pack and made her smoke every last cigarette in front of him. Indeed, John and Kelly can be sure that she won't smoke again for a long time. But even though John and Kelly's rules are effective, the motives behind their rules aren't based on trust.

4 Nicole's family, on the other hand, is entirely different from both of the other two families. Although Gwen's and John's families are dissimilar, both are based on respect. By contrast, Nicole and Tom, who have two sons, Martin and Charlie, get no respect from either one. Martin and Charlie come and go as they please and don't bother to tell their parents where they're going and when they might be home. If Nicole and Tom were to punish one of them, he would simply ignore his parents and continue to enjoy his freedom. Once when Martin was seventeen, he "borrowed" Tom's car. After a week he finally returned but only to ask for money from his parents (which they gave without question). Nicole and Tom are not worried about whether they are raising their children right. They believe that the most important role they play is to make sure that their children are happy. This method doesn't seem to work with many families because people usually don't have an unlimited supply of patience and understanding. However, it works for Nicole and Tom.

5 As I look around the table, it is easy to see just how different these families are. Their actions and reactions all seem unusual to me, but each family has its own vision of how children should be raised and treated, and I can't say if any particular method is the best one. A one-size-fits-all plan clearly wouldn't work in my family.

Jennifer's First Draft

Three Families

1 It's Christmas day, and the whole family is at my house. Listening to three different conversations at the dinner table I start to realize just how diffrent the branches of my family are. I have three sets of aunts and uncles: my mom's sister, Gwen, and her husband Ben, my dad's brother, John, and his wife Kelly, and my dad's sister, Nicole, and her husband Tom. Each set has at least one child, yet very distinct ways of raising them. Gwen's family is laid back and co-operative, John's family is under his strict watch at all times, Nicole's family is free to do whatever they desire. All of these families are different.

The rough draft was the "bones" of what I eventually wanted to write. I wanted to get the basic structure and events on paper.

2 John's family is not very trusting. The respect in that house is built on fear. John and Kelly have one daughter, Mariah. John and Kelly are extremely strict with Mariah; who is far from their high expectations. When Mariah does something wrong, she can be sure that the punishment will be severe. Unfortunately, Mariah craves attention of any kind so she doesn't strive to be who her parents want. True, John and Kelly's rules are effective, but that couldn't be too happy of a living environment.

I changed the order of these two paragraphs because I thought that it would be more effective to move from the less strict family to the more strict one.

3 By contrast, Gwen's family is the easy going type. Her and Ben never worry about too much about anything. Basically, they can do this because there is a trust that bonds their family together. Gwen and Ben have two children, Billy and Christie. They are responsible and level headed and do not need to be constently watched by their parents. Billy and Christie are not perfect children, like every child who is growing up, they make mistakes too, but because of the strong respect these family members have for one another, it is easy for them to trust each other, and when something does go wrong, it is handled rationally.

In the final draft I added detail like the story about Billy and the party. I realized that a reader of the first draft would be seeing just names and my opinions. I needed more.

4 Nicole's family is entirely diffrent from both of the others. Gwen's and John's families, though unalike, were both based on respect. Nicole and Tom, who have two sons, Martin and Charlie, get no respect from either. Martin and Charlie come and go as they please. When Martin was seventeen, he "borrowed" Tom's car. He finally returned only to withdraw

Also, I worked on adding transitions. I almost never have enough transitions in a first draft.

more money from his parents. This method doesn't really appear to get results, but all Nicole and Tom are worried about is their childrens happiness.

As I look around the table, it is easy to see just how diffrent these families are. There actions and reactions are all unusual, but the results each separate family desire is unusual also. So even though no particular method is the best one, the chosen method for each individual family is the best for them. 5

As always, I read the essay—three times—for mechanical errors.

EXERCISE 8.2: REVISING

The following is the first draft of a student's exemplification essay. Working in pairs or in small groups, review this essay. Using the Questions for Reviewing an Exemplification Essay on page 236, decide what revisions you would suggest. If you have any questions the student needs to consider, write them in the margin or on a separate sheet of paper. If your instructor directs you to, rewrite one or more paragraphs to make them stronger and to eliminate any grammatical or mechanical errors.

EXERCISE 8.2 Answers will vary. Students should point out the need for a stronger introduction and stronger topic sentences, as well as more fully developed paragaphs and a stronger conclusion.

"T.V. ads"

T.V. ads tell us a lot about ourselves, as Americans. They tell us we are thrifty, love luxury and want to be sexey. 1

We love luxury, for example, there is the car ads on TV; also, the cruise-line ads. Car dealers advertise cars costing up to $60,000 dollars; the price of a small house. These cars are like living space, in fact, they're nicer than some people's living space. Many people lust at these. 2

We are thrifty, we love to save a buck. TV ads frequently scald the viewer for spending to much for a products. Whereas savers are seen as smart. 3

We wont to be sexey. Back to the car ads again. They don't show ugly people or fat people or deformed people. Rich sleke people drive rich sleke cars. The women are prizes. Buy one and your sex life will improve. 4

Obviously the ideal American is thrifty, luxury loving and sexy. 5

SUGGESTED ACTIVITY
Consider asking students to meet in writing groups, each of which is charged with producing a more developed and effective version of this essay. Encourage students to add appropriate details from their own experience with television advertisements.

Additional Writing Topics

1. Proverbs frequently become clichés, but they always have some truth built into them. Write an essay explaining one of the following proverbs, using examples to illustrate the proverb's core meaning:

a. A rolling stone gathers no moss.
b. Make hay while the sun shines.
c. Clothes make the person.
d. Let a smile be your umbrella.
e. A bird in the hand is worth two in the bush.
f. Don't put all your eggs in one basket.
g. It's always darkest before the dawn.
h. You can't judge a book by its cover.
i. Every cloud has a silver lining.
j. Still waters run deep.
k. Don't look a gift horse in the mouth.
l. You can't make a silk purse out of a sow's ear.
m. If wishes were horses, beggars would ride.
n. It was the straw that broke the camel's back.
o. In for a penny, in for a pound.

2. **Writing on the job.** Think of the place where you work or where you used to work. Choose one workplace policy, procedure, or practice that you believe to be either highly effective or highly ineffective. Write a memo for your boss essay analyzing this policy by using examples to support your assertions. (See Chapter 17 for help with writing a memo.)

Responding to a Photograph

In the first half of the twentieth century, the rise of unions and the reaction to them from business leaders often led to severe violence. An unknown photographer took a picture of a young woman (see page 242) to commemorate her violent death.

CLASSROOM HINT Discuss this photograph in class before assigning item 1. Students should be comfortable with the process of including and citing researched material before you assign item 2.

1. Write an informal response to the photograph. What do you notice? How does the image make you feel? How does the photograph make use of the exemplification option?
2. Using a combination of library and online research, explore one incident of labor-related violence in the early twentieth century. Write a documented essay that explains what happened and gives examples of the results of this conflict. (For more information on documented essays, see Chapter 21.)

Writing About Film

A League of Their Own (1992, PG) tells the story of a women's professional base ball team during World War II. The players come from various cultural and social backgrounds. Write an essay explaining how each player is an example of a "type."

Saving Private Ryan (1998, R) shows the 1944 D-Day assault on the beaches of France and then follows one army company's attempts to locate and save Private Ryan, the last survivor of five brothers who fought in World War II. The men in the company are drawn from all walks of life. Write an essay showing

IN MEMORY OF

IDA BRAYMAN

17 YEARS OLD

who was shot & killed by an Employer Feb. 5th 1913 during the great struggle of the Garment Workers of Rochester.

 60

Copyrigted 1913 by U. G. W. Local 14 Rochester N. Y.

Unknown photographer, *In Memory of Ida Brayman*, 1913. Collection of Gotham Book Mart, New York City.

how each soldier is an example of a "type." (Warning: the first major scene of this film—the assault on the beach—is extremely violent and intense.)

Using the Internet

Search the Internet for insights and information to use when developing essays with examples.

1. Write an exemplification essay on the popularity of online shopping. Locate the Web sites of as many "e-tailers" as you can, and use these examples to demonstrate the variety of goods and services on the Web and the extent to which e-business is expanding. Refer in detail to as many specific Web sites as you can.
2. We often hear that government wastes our tax money. Using the Internet, find outlandish examples of government waste on the local, state (provincial), or national level. Use these examples in an essay that alerts your reader to the extent of the problem.

   As an alternate assignment, search the Web for examples of useful human services that a government—local, state (provincial), or national—provides its citizens. Using these examples, write an essay that you or someone you know might find helpful as a guide to government assistance, information, or funding.

"O.K. now. You got it straight what you're supposed to do?"

CHAPTER 9

PROCESS ANALYSIS

Writing in Context

You are at your desk one afternoon finishing an intermediate report on the Medlock project when you sense the presence of another. It is, of course, Bob, and he is wearing his shifty expression, the one that says he is about to give you work that he should be doing himself but finds too difficult.

"This new software documentation is brutal. Read through this and see if you can make me sort of a summary of steps to follow."

You sigh. Stephanie the Capable, Bob's assistant, is out of the office today, or she would have been stuck with this task. You also want to finish your report on the Medlock project by quitting time. You wonder darkly why you are working for a man who can't read.

When you go through the documentation, however, you agree with Bob about the central problem: this stuff is atrocious. You read the instructions again, and this time you find yourself making notes. These notes become a clear set of steps for you to hand to Bob so that he can begin to use his new software update.

The documentation that has stymied Bob is a poorly written example of process analysis, a rhetorical option that is used throughout the business world and in many other writing situations as well.

SUGGESTED ACTIVITY Have students ask themselves the question posed in the cartoon about some relatively simple process that they are asked to do routinely. Give them five to ten minutes to write out the answer, and then ask one or two students to volunteer to share their responses with the class. Discuss the elements of process analysis that the responses reveal.

HOW DOES PROCESS ANALYSIS WORK?

When people want to learn how to do something, or how something works or is done, most try to find an expert who can break the process down into a clear set of steps (and not make the listener or reader feel stupid in the bargain). In other words, they look for a process analysis. Writing that uses process analysis is seemingly everywhere. For example, most bookstores feature a large number of titles in the self-help section. Here, people can buy books that are designed to improve their sex life, self-esteem, negotiating skills, and hairstyle, just to name a few areas for self-improvement. Other sections of the bookstore contain books and magazines that claim to help the reader improve his or her golf swing, learn to use the latest tax-accounting program, attract a desirable mate, and transform a mundane picnic into a gala affair.

The instructions that come with most of the products that you buy are an even more specific form of process analysis. Product instructions are examples of technical writing, and here the ever-important need for the writer to know his or her audience is especially critical. Everyone has had to deal with defective product instructions. If the product is imported, the confusion may have been caused by a writer who was struggling with English. More often, however, the writer simply forgot to think about the reader's needs. The following instructions for formatting a computer diskette for a different use may or may not have actually accompanied a product, but they illustrate the risks—and possible disturbing consequences—of ignoring the audience:

Step 1. Erase all existing files from the disk.

Step 2. Make sure that you have saved any important files before proceeding with Step 1.

These two types of process analysis—self-help and product directions—have an **instructional** purpose. However, most academic writing that uses process analysis is more likely to be **informative.** In other words, a writer tells you how something happened—for example, how the Confederacy, although it was the underdog, kept the American Civil War going on for so long. Or how the "Miracle Mets," a baseball franchise that had been in existence for only seven years at the time, won the 1969 World Series. Or how Mother Teresa's humble street mission eventually brought its founder international acclaim and the Nobel Peace Prize. Sometimes writers use process analysis to explain why a problem or situation is so hard to change or remedy—for example, why it is so hard to keep stalkers away from their victims; why teenagers continue to take up cigarette smoking, despite the overwhelming evidence of the harmful effects of this habit and the billions of dollars spent on cautionary advertising campaigns each year; why the heroin market remains such a profitable enterprise; why it is becoming more and more difficult for college students to complete a traditional four-year degree in four years.

CLASSROOM HINT Consider discussing additional topics relating to other courses students take, especially those in the sciences and social sciences.

Process writing that attempts to inform or comment has a broader focus than instructional writing. Often, the writer has a larger purpose for presenting information in this way: to argue against an injustice, for example, or to show why a particular government policy that looks good on paper is imbecilic in practice. Usually, the writer will make this aim clear in a thesis statement that makes a point about the process being described. The essays in the following section are examples of process analysis, but in each one the writer has a compelling point to make about the process that he or she is describing.

In addition, think about the value of using process analysis in other types of essays. An analysis of the cause of a problem (see Chapter 10) might also need to explore *how* the problem developed as well as *why* the problem developed. An essay arguing that a policy is ineffective and/or unfair (see Chapter 14) will need to explain *how the policy works*. Process analysis is a "core option," one that appears in a variety of contexts and with a variety of purposes.

Consider Your Options

What is the worst example of instructional process analysis that you have encountered in the past year? Think about the instructions that come with consumer products. What can go wrong with these documents? How could their writers make better choices?

READING THE PROCESS ANALYSIS ESSAY WITH A WRITER'S EYE

In the following essays, Jerry Jesness shows how the high schools in which he has taught have corrupted the academic process. Joan Gould describes her bizarrely careful preparations before a first date in 1950. Malcolm X writes about the time in the 1940s when he was still Malcolm Little, not Malcolm X, and had his hair straightened—a seemingly innocuous process that leads the author to comment on a much more insidious practice. Finally, Umberto Eco explains how the advent of fax machines and cell phones has led to unexpected—and mostly negative—situations. As you read these essays, be aware of the authors' purpose: each author is using the process option as a useful strategy to reveal a higher meaning.

Following the essays, the second half of this chapter features strategies for writing the process analysis essay with a reader's eye (pages 263–270). If you decide to write on one of the topics that follow the four essays, make sure that you have read the strategies section before you begin. Also note that additional writing topics are listed at the end of the chapter (pages 274–277).

Why Johnny Can't Fail

JERRY JESNESS

Jerry Jesness teaches special education in Los Fresnos, Texas. He has published more than forty articles, columns, and commentaries on the subject of education. This essay first appeared in *Reason* magazine in August 1999. (*Reason* is a publication devoted to "free minds and free markets," seeking to make "a principled case for liberty and individual choice in all areas of human activity.") Do you recognize any of the occurrences that Jesness describes?

1 I confess. I am a grade-inflating teacher guilty of "social promotion." I have given passing grades to students who failed all of their tests, to students who refused to read their assignments, to students who were absent as often as not, to students who were not even functionally literate. I have turned a blind eye to cheating and outright plagiarism, and have given As and Bs to students whose performances were at best mediocre. Like others of my ilk, I have sent students to higher grades, to higher education, and to the workplace unprepared for the demands that would be made of them.

I am, in short, a servant of the force that thwarts nearly every effort to reform American education. I am a servant of the floating standard. 2

I was introduced to the floating standard in 1979, while teaching for the Bureau of Indian Affairs on a reservation in western South Dakota. My predecessor, considered a capable if imprudent instructor by his former students and peers, had been forced to resign after failing nearly half of his students. In his absence, the failing grades were changed and his students were promoted to the next grade. 3

Even though I knew my predecessor's fate, I gave some failing grades the first term. After a few warnings, however, I fell into line. There was no point in doing otherwise. The students already knew that failing grades would mysteriously self-correct over the summer. I opted for self-preservation. 4

A few years later I moved to Texas's lower Rio Grande Valley. Since I now was more experienced, I was confident that I would be able to grade fairly. Besides, my future principal spoke movingly at my interview about the need to push our students to their limits. In the first grading period, I boldly flunked a number of students, including the daughter of an administrator of a local elementary school and a star fullback who was also the nephew of a school-board member. 5

Shortly thereafter I was called in to meet with my principal and the aggrieved parents. Such was my naïveté that I actually bothered to bring evidence. I showed the administrator her daughter's plagiarized book report and the book from which it had been copied, and I showed the fullback's father homework bearing his son's name but written in another person's handwriting. The parents offered weak apologies but maintained that I had not treated their children fairly. 6

My principal suddenly discovered a number of problems with my teaching. For the next few weeks he was in my class almost daily. Every spitball, every chattering student, every bit of graffiti, was noted. When there were discipline problems, my superiors sided with the offending students. Teaching became impossible. 7

So again I learned to turn a blind eye to cheating and plagiarism, and to give students, especially athletes, extra credit for everything from reading orally in class to remembering to bring their pencils. Along the way, I gained the cooperation of my students and the respect and support of my superiors. 8

But not until my fifth year of teaching did I finally accept that my only choices were to embrace the floating standard or to abandon public education. That year my assignment was to teach English as a second language and lower-level language arts. My principal was particularly adamant about having all the students pass. 9

In language arts, no test was to be graded below 50, even one that was turned in blank. Daily assignments were to be graded according to the number of questions answered, even if all of the answers were wrong. If eight of ten questions were answered, the grade was to be 80, regardless of the quality of the answers. Those who still were failing at the end of the grading period were to be offered the opportunity to do reports or projects for extra credit. My neighbor, another lower-group teacher who was held up to me as a mentor, boasted that he left the week's spelling words on the blackboard during spelling tests and recommended that I do the same. I pulled in my horns too late to save myself that year. The principal recommended that my contract not be renewed. 10

That job and its $17,000 annual salary were hardly worth fighting for, so I left quietly. After a year as a salesperson and graduate student, however, I began to miss the classroom and decided to give teaching one more try. I returned to the 11 district where I had flunked the star fullback. My superiors correctly assumed that I had learned my lesson and welcomed the return of the prodigal teacher. Just as Orwell's Winston Smith was finally able to achieve victory over himself and love Big Brother, I was ready to embrace the floating standard.

12 In the ensuing seven years, only two of my students failed. My evaluations were "above expectations" twice and "clearly outstanding" five times. By my fifth year I had climbed to the top of the Texas teachers' career ladder and earned an annual bonus of $3,300.

13 The funny thing is that I really did become a better teacher after my reincarnation, if only because my students and superiors were now cooperative. My classes were better behaved once I stopped trying to force students to learn more than they cared to. I no longer met with hostility when I sent students to the principal's office. I tried to be as honest as possible with my charges. All of my students and any parents who bothered to visit my classroom or return my phone calls understood that grades above 80 honestly reflected performance, while those in the 70 range were fluffed up with extra credit. I explained to the parents of my immigrant students that here in America passing grades may be given for attendance and minimal effort and do not necessarily reflect mastery of the course material. Students who needed to be pushed lost out, but that was the price of harmony.

14 It does not matter what changes we make in curricula. The floating standard guarantees the reign of mediocrity. If standards are set high but students lack the skills or motivation to meet them, the standards will inevitably change. If a number of students in a given class take part-time jobs, homework will be reduced. If drugs sweep through a school, lower expectations will compensate for weakened ability. Americans want quality education, but when lower grades and higher failure rates reach their own children's classes, they rebel and schools relent. Americans hate public education because standards are low but love their local schools because their children perform so well there.

15 Schools have their own reasons to play along. Flexible standards mean fewer complaints. When parents are happy, there are fewer lawsuits; when students are happy, there are fewer discipline problems. What's more, schools that fail students assume the expense and unpopular obligation of retaining them.

16 In the short term, floating standards make everybody a winner. Students build self-esteem, parents gain peace of mind, and schools save money. By giving high grades and class credit to anyone willing to occupy space in a classroom, schools create the illusion that their students are learning. Only after leaving school and facing work or college do the students discover that they are ignorant and ill prepared.

17 Imagine that you are required to teach *Hamlet* to a group of students who are either unwilling or unable to read such a work. If you demand that your charges read and understand the play, most will fail and you will be blamed. If you drop *Hamlet* and convert the class into a remedial reading course, you will be out of compliance with the curriculum. If you complain that your students are not up to the mandated task, you will be labeled insensitive and uncaring.

18 Fear not: The floating standard will save you. If the students will not or cannot read the play, read it to them. If they will not sit still long enough to hear the whole play, consider an abridged or comic-book version, or let them watch the movie. If they cannot pass a multiple-choice test, try a true-or-false or a fill-in-the-blank test that mirrors the previous day's study sheet. If they still have not passed, allow them

to do an art project. They could make a model of the Globe Theatre with Popsicle sticks or draw a picture of a Danish prince, or Prince Charles, or even the Artist Formerly Known As Prince. Those not artistically inclined could make copies of Shakespearean sonnets with macaroni letters on construction paper. If all else fails, try group projects. That way you can give passing grades to all the students, even if only one in five produces anything.

19 Keep dropping the standard, and sooner or later everyone will meet it. If anyone asks, you taught *Hamlet* in a nonconventional way, one that took into account your students' individual differences and needs.

20 For three decades, dismayed Americans have watched their children's test scores slip relative to those of children in other industrialized nations. Our leaders have responded with hollow excuses. Too many American children live in poverty, they say. But so do many Koreans. Many American children are raised in single-parent homes. But so are many Swedes. The United States is an ethnically diverse country. But so is Singapore. The biggest lie is that we are the only nation in the world that seeks to educate children of all socioeconomic classes. That has not been true for decades. The reality is simpler than that. Those other nations have fixed standards.

21 American schools offer fixed standards for their best and worst students, but not for the largest group, those in the middle. Advanced Placement tests are the same throughout the country. The International Baccalaureate program offers uniform curricula and standards to top-notch students in the United States and in English-language schools throughout the world. Ever-increasing numbers of states have mandated that their students pass a basic skills test before graduating. In Texas, the Texas Assessment of Academic Skills (TAAS) is the standard. In order to prevent schools from ignoring any class of students, Texas wisely chose to track test scores by racial and economic group. The state has demanded basic skills for all students, and the schools are delivering.

22 For those who seek to learn more than basics, however, the result has been negative. Like other state-mandated minimum skills tests, the TAAS is helping to solve one problem while creating another: basic skills are now so strongly stressed that real academics suffer. It should be obvious that a student who has read and analyzed the works of Charles Dickens or Mark Twain would be better able to determine the sequence of events or identify the main idea of a paragraph than would a student who spent his academic year reading sample test passages, yet teachers who once taught from novels now assign reams of single-page reading passages followed by multiple-choice questions.

23 Perhaps there is another way. Those who take Advanced Placement or International Baccalaureate tests submit to a voluntary outside standard. There is no reason that we cannot extend this option to other students as well. Textbook publishers, educators, and others could produce competing tests, to be given at the end of certain courses. Schools could submit the works of literature read and historical eras studied to private testing companies and receive tests based on that material. These tests would free teachers from the pressure to adjust the content of their courses and would assure students and their parents that the standard for each course is fixed, not floating. If *Hamlet* is tested, then *Hamlet,* not Popsicle-stick or macaroni art, will be taught.

Vocabulary

The following terms are identified by paragraph number. Make sure that you understand each term's meaning in its context. If you're not sure that you understand a term, look it up in a college-level dictionary.

social promotion (1)	adamant (9)	remedial (17)
functionally literate (1)	prodigal (11)	compliance (17)
plagiarism (1)	ensuing (12)	mandated (17)
thwart (2)	reincarnation (13)	sonnets (18)
imprudent (3)	harmony (13)	diverse (20)
aggrieved (6)	curricula (14)	reams (22)
naïveté (6)		

Style and Strategy

1. What is this essay's intended audience?
2. What is the author's thesis, and where is it located? Find the specific examples that Jesness uses to back up his thesis.
3. What is the problem that the author analyzes, and what process must teachers follow in order to deal with the problem?
4. How would you evaluate the author's tone?
5. At the end of the essay, the author proposes a solution. Given the tone of his essay, do you think that he expects the solution to be adopted? Explain.
6. Jesness uses process analysis and exemplification. What other rhetorical options does he use in this essay? Point to specific paragraphs.

STYLE AND STRATEGY
1. Jesness is writing to an upper-middle class, well-educated audience.
2. The thesis appears in paragraph 14: "The floating standard guarantees the reign of mediocrity." Specific examples appear in paragraphs 10, 14, 16, 17, and 18.
3. Paragraphs 14–16 and 21–23 are worth discussing.
4–5. Jesness adopts a serious and, at times, imploring tone coupled, unfortunately, with a touch of despair. In light of this tone, it hard to believe that he has any faith that his solution will be adopted.
6. Narration appears in paragraphs 3–11; cause/effect in 13–19; comparison/contrast in 14, 16, 20, and 22.

Questions for Critical Thinking and Discussion

1. Consider the following statement: "The American system of education in grades K through 12 is a complete fraud—they might as well call it the national day-care initiative." Do you agree or disagree? Explain.
2. Some states have adopted a version of the voucher system, in which parents have the option of placing their children in private schools and receiving some form of tuition reimbursement from tax revenues. What is your opinion of this policy?
3. What is the main problem—or group of problems—that you remember from your K–12 years? Can you suggest a way to solve this problem?

QUESTIONS FOR CRITICAL THINKING AND DISCUSSION Be prepared for a variety of opinions in response to these items. However, the discussion that ensues generates interesting topics and information for student essays.

Suggestions for Writing

1. Have you ever participated in an organization that didn't follow its own rules or practices, leaving you feeling somehow defrauded? Write a 500-word essay about this experience.
2. Write a 500- to 750-word process analysis essay that shows how an activity turned sour—for example, a party, a trip, or a sporting event that started promisingly but went bad.

SUGGESTIONS FOR WRITING Students rarely have difficulty gathering sufficient information for either of these.

Binding Decisions

JOAN GOULD

Joan Gould is a freelance writer who has contributed essays to major U.S. publications. Her work frequently centers on the events of her life: growing up in the middle of the twentieth century and becoming a wife, a mother, and a caregiver. Many of her essays were collected in *Spirals: A Woman's Journey Through Family Life* (1988). The following selection first appeared in *Memories* magazine in 1989.

I'm out of the bathtub. I'm ready to get dressed for my date tonight, which is a blind date, serious business in this year of 1950 for any girl who's over 20 and still single. I'm 22. No matter how much money I may earn in my job, I'll never be allowed to have an apartment of my own; I'll never pay an electric bill or buy a bedspread or spend a night away from home without my parents; in fact, I'll never be a grown-up as long as I remain single. 1

How shall I dress? I want to look sexy enough to attract this unknown man, so that he'll call and ask me for another date next week. (Needless to say, I won't call him, even if my life depends on it.) On the other hand, I don't want to hide the fact that I'm what's known as a Nice Girl, addicted to Peter Pan collars and velvet hats and white gloves, which means that I'm good wife material, and also makes it clear that he'll get nothing more than a goodnight kiss from me tonight. 2

And so I dress carefully. Every single item that I put on not only is complicated in itself but carries an even more complicated message. 3

My girdle comes first. Here's the badge, the bind, the bondage of womanhood. Here's the itch of it. This is the garment that tells me I'm not a little girl anymore, who wears only underpants, but neither am I middle-aged like my mother, who wears a real corset with bones that dig into her diaphragm and leave cruel sores there. I can get away with either a panty girdle or a two-way stretch, both of which are made of Lastex with a panel of stiff satin over the abdomen. The basic difference is that a panty girdle, unlike a two-way stretch, covers the crotch, which was considered a shocking—indeed obscene—idea when first introduced. Victorian women were obliged to wear half a dozen petticoats at a time to be respectable, but never, never would they put on anything that slipped between their thighs, like a pair of pants. 4

But why should I be bothering with this sausage casing when I weighed a grand total of a hundred and two pounds? 5

I bother because being thin has nothing to do with it. A girdle is a symbolic garment, and unless I wanted to be regarded as a child or a slut I have to put it on. When I go out with girlfriends in the daytime I may choose to be more comfortable in only a garter belt, a device with four long, wiggly elastics that dangle down my thighs like hungry snakes lunging at my stockings. When I'm with a boy, however, it would be unthinkable—it would be downright indecent—to let him see my rear end jiggle or let him notice it has two halves. (All males are called "boys," no matter what their age, so long as they're single.) My backside is supposed to be molded in a rigid piece that divides into two legs, like a walking clothespin. 6

Besides, if I don't wear a girdle every day, the older girls warn me, I'm going to "spread." Spreading is somehow related to letting my flesh hang loose, which is in turn related to the idea of the "loose" woman, and none of us wants to be consid- 7 ered loose. A man doesn't buy a cow if he can get milk for free, our mothers tell us in dire tones. We don't point out that we're not cows, and we don't fight against girdles, which apparently do a good job of discouraging wandering hands, since most of the single girls I know are virgins.

8 But which girdle should I wear? If I pick the panty girdle, I'll need 10 minutes' advance notice before going to the toilet. If I wear the two-way stretch, it will ride up and form a sausage around my waist. Either way, my flesh will be marked with welts and stripes when, at that delirious moment in my bedroom, I can strip off my clothes and scratch and scratch.

9 I pick the two-way stretch but, born compromiser that I am, put underpants over it.

10 Next comes the bra. I don't dare look at myself in the mirror as I put it on. This is the era of the pinup girl, the heyday of Lana Turner and Betty Grable,* when breasts bubble and froth over the rims of C-cups and a flat chest is considered about as exciting as flat champagne. Not until Twiggy* appears on the scene in the 1960's will thinness become acceptable in a girl, much less desirable—but how am I supposed to survive until then? The answer is the garment I've just put on, the confession of my disgrace—a padded bra. If I wear a strapless gown, I pin foam-rubber bust pads, which are known as "falsies," in place. Occasionally one of these breaks loose during a particularly ardent conga or mambo and rises above my dress like the rim of the sun peering over a hilltop.

11 At least the bra won't show under my silk slip. Silk is expensive, of course, and no male will see my underwear unless he marries me or I'm carried off to a hospital emergency room—but then, as all the mothers warn us, accidents do happen.

12 Stockings next. During World War II, just as I became old enough to wear them, our wonderful new nylons were snatched away from us in order to make parachutes for what was known as the "war effort." What were we girls supposed to do—go out on a date in socks, like little children? If there weren't any stockings around, we'd have to create them. And so we bought bottles of makeup base and painted stockings on our legs and drew seams up the back with eyebrow pencils, which was undoubtedly the last time my seams were ever straight.

13 My dress, oddly enough, is easy to choose. For a woman of my years, a skirt-and-sweater is out of the question on a date. The dress mustn't be too high-style or expensive, however, or else the young man will think that I'm spoiled, a fatal defect in a girl who might otherwise qualify as good wife material. Never mind that I earned the money to buy my own clothes; I still have to show that it won't cost much to support me once we marry and I quit my job. For the same reason, wherever we go—which is always at his expense, of course—I'll insist that we travel by bus or subway, never by taxi. If he invites me out to dinner (which doesn't happen often, because of cost, and never on a first date), I'll eat a sandwich at home before I leave, to make sure I won't be tempted to order an appetizer or dessert in the restaurant.

14 Shoes. I'd like to wear my fashionable new ones, with their ankle straps crisscrossing in back and fastening above the ankle bone, but they have 3½-inch heels,

---

***Lana Turner and Betty Grable:** U.S. movie stars of the 1940s and 1950s.

***Twiggy:** an extremely thin fashion model and actress, most famous from the 1960s through the early 1970s.

and I have no idea if I'll tower over this unknown man. If I choose low heels, on the other hand, he may think that I'm condescending. I pick the high heels but hide a low-heeled pair in the hall closet, just in case. Blind dates have their special hazards.

I still have to put on my makeup, which includes lots of lipstick, loose face powder and an eyebrow pencil to extend my brow line, but no eye shadow, much less liner. I also have to do my hair, which is set with heavy lotion and rollers in the beauty parlor every week. (At night I sleep in a cotton mesh hairnet that I tie around my head, in order to preserve the set for at least a week.) 15

Speeding up the pace, I rush to equip my pocketbook with a monogrammed handkerchief and some "mad money," including several nickels for phone calls or a bus, obligatory for a blind date. I run to my glove drawer and hunt up a pair in white kid, since he's invited me to a concert. I won't need a hat. He'll wear one, of course. 16

The doorbell rings. I dab Shalimar on a tuft of cotton, which I tuck inside my bra; I check my stocking seams and move toward the door. For an instant, my hand rests on the knob, while I wonder what sort of person is breathing out there, only inches away from me but still unrevealed, unexplored. And then I open the door, and I see his face and hear his voice, because he's already in mid-sentence. As a matter of fact, he's in mid-story, as if it's inconceivable that anyone could be less than fascinated with what he's saying, which happens to be true, or as if he's my husband already and has waited all day, or maybe all his life, to tell me what happened to him that afternoon. 17

A box of Kleenex is tucked under his arm, because he has a cold, and he lays the box down on the hall table with the assurance of the rightful prince stepping into his kingdom at last. This one I'll marry or I'll marry no one, I say to myself an hour later. 18

Three dates—which means three weeks—later, he proposes. "Wait. I have to tell you something first," I declare in distress. He waits. I'm in turmoil. I'm risking everything on candor, and candor isn't a virtue in which I've much practice. I've never said anything like this out loud before. "You have a right to know," I announced. "I wear a padded bra." 19

He says he imagines he can handle that. 20

We were married three months later. I wonder, if he hadn't proposed so promptly, how much longer it would have been before he discovered my secret for himself. 21

STYLE AND STRATEGY

1. Gould uses figurative language and double entendre to create humor. She also slips in rhetorical questions, anticipates a variety of outcomes, and most important, fills the essay with specific and recognizable details. To add even more credibility and interest, she reminds us of exhortations that mothers—perhaps our own—made to their single daughters.
2. The use of the first person and the present tense in this narrative gives the essay an immediacy and relevance that might not have been possible had Gould written a set of instructions using the imperative mood. Indeed, male readers might be put off by such an approach. (Note that the last paragraph is in the past tense).
3. Take the opportunity to remind students that an essay's purpose need not be one-dimensional. Both answers apply here.
4. Time-order transitions appear in paragraphs 3, 4, 10, 12, 15, 16, 17, 19, 21; cause/effect transitions appear in paragraphs 6, 7, 8, and 14; and opposition transitions appear in paragraphs 2, 6, 8, and 13.
5. The conclusion is logical and in keeping with the tone and purpose of what has come before.

Vocabulary

The following terms are identified by paragraph number. Make sure that you understand each term's meaning in its context. If you're not sure that you understand a term, look it up in a college-level dictionary.

diaphragm (4)	compromiser (9)	condescending (14)
dire (7)	conga (10)	obligatory (16)
delirious (8)	mambo (10)	candor (19)

Style and Strategy

1. Gould spends almost a whole essay painstakingly describing how she prepared for a date with someone she had never seen before. What strategies does Gould use to interest her readers?

2. Although "Binding Decisions" is a process essay, its internal strategy is narration (see Chapter 7). What does the narrative option add to this essay's effect? What other option could Gould have used?
3. What is Gould's purpose in describing her preparations for a date? Is she trying to tell the reader how to find someone to marry, or is she commenting on the rigorous process that she went through to find her own husband?
4. How often does Gould use transitions? Read her essay again, and mark the places where she uses transitions to indicate time order, cause and effect, and opposition.
5. How did you react to the conclusion of this essay, when Gould makes her "confession"? Is this conclusion a logical end to Gould's careful analysis of her dating ritual?

Questions for Critical Thinking and Discussion

QUESTIONS FOR CRITICAL THINKING AND DISCUSSION Item 1 invites close analysis of the text. Items 2 and 3 lead to lively discussion, with members of the two sexes generally taking predictable sides. Item 4 can be used to brainstorm information that students might put into an essay.

1. Consider this statement: "Joan Gould does an excellent job of showing us that American social customs can be just as bizarre and complicated as those of some newly discovered tribe located far from nowhere and shielded from the influences of 'civilization.'" Do you agree? Why or why not?
2. Why would a culture make it so difficult for someone to find a spouse? Do you think that the man whom Gould met had to go through a complicated ritual before he arrived at her door?
3. After a series of successful dates and a proposal of marriage, Joan Gould decides that it is time for "candor," or a sincere admission. Do you find the use of this term ironic? (Writers use *irony* when they say the opposite of what they mean to create humor or emphasize a point.) Isn't the very nature of the "game" that Gould must play in the traditional dating culture of 1950 one of deception and hidden truths, as opposed to candor?
4. The "rules" of dating have changed a good deal in the five decades since Gould's courtship, but are they any less complicated?

Suggestions for Writing

SUGGESTIONS FOR WRITING It helps to prepare students for these assignments by discussing them in class.

1. In a 500- to 750-word essay, explain how you prepare for a first date with someone you don't know.
2. In 500 to 700 words, explain a process that you find unnecessarily complex and strange—for example, registering for classes, getting ready to attend a formal event, training for a particular sport, keeping up with the latest fads and fashions in clothes.

My First Conk

MALCOLM X

The civil rights movement of the 1950s and 1960s had two great leaders: Martin Luther King, Jr., and Malcolm X (1925–1965). King believed in civil disobedience—peaceful resistance to unfair and unconstitutional laws (see his essay in Chapter 12, pages 361–363). However, Malcolm X believed that African Americans had been acquiescent for too long; he favored a more militant response. A native of Omaha, Nebraska, Malcolm Little converted to Islam while serving a prison sentence and later became a leading member of the Black Muslim movement. In his middle age, he returned to orthodox Islam and channeled his political energy into his black separatist movement, the Organization for Afro-American Unity. Malcolm X was assassinated in 1965.

"My First Conk," excerpted from *The Autobiography of Malcolm X* (1965), is about two processes, one physical and one social. Notice how easily the author moves from one to the other.

Shorty soon decided that my hair was finally long enough to be conked. He had promised to school me in how to beat the barber shops' three- and four-dollar price by making up congolene, and then conking ourselves. 1

I took the little list of ingredients he had printed out for me, and went to a grocery store, where I got a can of Red Devil lye, two eggs, and two medium-sized white potatoes. Then at a drugstore near the poolroom, I asked for a large jar of vaseline, a large bar of soap, a large-toothed comb and a fine-toothed comb, one of those rubber hoses with a metal spray-head, a rubber apron, and a pair of gloves. 2

"Going to lay on that first conk?" The drugstore man asked me. I proudly told him, grinning, "Right!" 3

Shorty paid six dollars a week for a room in his cousin's shabby apartment. His cousin wasn't at home. "It's like the pad's mine, he spends so much time with his woman," Shorty said. "Now, you watch me—" 4

He peeled the potatoes and thin-sliced them into a quart-sized Mason fruit jar, then started stirring them with a wooden spoon as he gradually poured in a little over half the can of lye. "Never use a metal spoon; the lye will turn it black," he told me. 5

A jelly-like, starchy-looking glop resulted from the lye and potatoes, and Shorty broke in the two eggs, stirring real fast—his own conk and dark face bent down close. The congolene turned pale-yellowish. "Feel the jar," Shorty said. I cupped my hand against the outside, and snatched it away. "Damn right, it's hot, that's the lye," he said. "So you know it's going to burn when I comb it in—it burns bad. But the longer you can stand it, the straighter the hair." 6

He made me sit down, and he tied the string of the new rubber apron tightly around my neck, and combed up my bush of hair. Then, from the big vaseline jar, he took a handful and massaged it hard all through my hair and into the scalp. He also thickly vaselined my neck, ears and forehead. "When I get to washing out your head, be sure to tell me anywhere you feel any little stinging," Shorty warned me, washing his hands, then pulling on the rubber gloves, and tying on his own rubber apron. "You always got to remember that any congolene left in burns a sore into your head." 7

The congolene just felt warm when Shorty started combing it in. But then my head caught fire. 8

I gritted my teeth and tried to pull the sides of the kitchen table together. The comb felt as if it was raking my skin off. 9

My eyes watered, my nose was running. I couldn't stand it any longer; I bolted to the washbasin. I was cursing Shorty with every name I could think of when he got the spray going and started soap lathering my head. 10

He lathered and spray-rinsed, lathered and spray-rinsed, maybe ten or twelve times, each time gradually closing the hot-water faucet, until the rinse was cold, and that helped some. 11

"You feel any stinging spots?" 12

"No," I managed to say. My knees were trembling. 13

"Sit back down, then. I think we got it all out okay." 14

The flame came back as Shorty, with a thick towel, started drying my head, rubbing hard. "*Easy, man, easy!*" I kept shouting. 15

"The first time's always worst. You get used to it better before long. You took it real good, homeboy. You got a good conk." 16

When Shorty let me stand up and see in the mirror, my hair hung down in limp, damp strings. My scalp still flamed, but not as badly; I could bear it. He draped the towel around my shoulders, over my rubber apron, and began again vaselining my hair. 17

I could feel him combing, straight back, first the big comb, then the fine-tooth one. 18

Then, he was using a razor, very delicately, on the back of my neck. Then, finally, shaping the sideburns. 19

My first view in the mirror blotted out the hurting. I'd seen some pretty conks, but when it's the first time, on your *own* head, the transformation, after the lifetime of kinks, is staggering. 20

The mirror reflected Shorty behind me. We both were grinning and sweating. And on top of my head was this thick, smooth sheen of shining red hair—real red—as straight as any white man's. 21

How ridiculous I was! Stupid enough to stand there simply lost in admiration of my hair now looking "white," reflected in the mirror in Shorty's room. I vowed that I'd never again be without a conk, and I never was for many years. 22

This was my first really big step toward self-degradation: when I endured all of that pain, literally burning my flesh to have it look like a white man's hair. I had joined that multitude of Negro men and women in America who are brainwashed into believing that the black people are "inferior"—and white people "superior"—that they will even violate and mutilate their God-created bodies to try to look "pretty" by white standards. 23

Look around today, in every small town and big city, from two-bit catfish and soda-pop joints into the "integrated" lobby of the Waldorf-Astoria, and you'll see conks on black men. And you'll see black women wearing these green and pink and purple and red and platinum-blonde wigs. They're all more ridiculous than a slapstick comedy. It makes you wonder if the Negro has completely lost his sense of identity, lost touch with himself. 24

You'll see the conk worn by many, many so-called "upper class" Negroes, and, as much as I hate to say it about them, on all too many Negro entertainers. One of the reasons that I've especially admired some of them, like Lionel Hampton and Sidney Poitier, among others, is that they have kept their natural hair and fought to the top. I admire any Negro man who has never had himself conked, or who has had the sense to get rid of it—as I finally did. 25

I don't know which kind of self-defacing conk is the greater shame—the one you'll see on the heads of the black so-called "middle class" and "upper class," who ought to know better, or the one you'll see on the heads of the poorest, most downtrodden, ignorant black men. I mean the legal-minimum-wage ghetto-dwelling kind of Negro, as I was when I got my first one. It's generally among these poor fools that you'll see a black kerchief over the man's head, like Aunt Jemima; he's trying to make his conk last longer, between trips to the barbershop. Only for special occasions is this kerchief-protected conk exposed—to show off how "sharp" 26 and "hip" its owner is. The ironic thing is that I have never heard any woman, white or black, express any admiration for a conk. Of course, any white woman with a black man isn't thinking about his hair. But I don't see how on earth a black woman with any race pride could walk down the street with any black man wearing a conk—the emblem of his shame that he is black.

27 To my own shame, when I say all of this, I'm talking first of all about myself—because you can't show me any Negro who ever conked more faithfully than I did. I'm speaking from personal experience when I say of any black man who conks today, or any white-wigged black woman, that if they gave the brains in their heads just half as much attention as they do their hair, they would be a thousand times better off.

STYLE AND STRATEGY
1. The thesis appears in the last sentence of paragraph 23. Malcolm X waits until this point because he must first reveal the suffering and stupidity associated with "conking" if the thesis is to have full effect.
2. Comparison/contrast appears in paragraphs 24 and 25; causal analysis in paragraphs 5–9; argument in paragraphs 22–27; exemplification in paragraphs 24–26; and definition in paragraphs 6 and 26.
3. The first is "conking." The second is the process by which some black people display their "shame" over being black, as they "try to look 'pretty' by white standards" (paragraph 23).

Vocabulary

The following terms are identified by paragraph number. Make sure that you understand each term's meaning in its context. If you're not sure that you understand a term, look it up in a college-level dictionary.

conk (1)	lye (2)	slapstick (24)
congolene (1)	self-degradation (23)	

Style and Strategy

1. In which paragraph does the thesis appear? Why does Malcolm X reveal his purpose at that point of the essay?
2. Locate the following internal strategies: comparison/contrast (see Chapter 13), causal analysis (Chapter 10), argument (Chapter 14), exemplification (Chapter 8), and definition (Chapter 11). What does each rhetorical option contribute to the essay?
3. In this process analysis, Malcolm X is actually analyzing two processes. What are they?

QUESTIONS FOR CRITICAL THINKING AND DISCUSSION Students have little trouble bringing up relevant examples and arguments.

Questions for Critical Thinking and Discussion

1. When Malcolm X got his hair conked, he was clearly bowing to peer pressure—the desire to look like his contemporaries so that they would accept him. How much peer pressure do you experience or notice your friends experiencing?
2. Can peer pressure ever be a positive phenomenon?
3. Malcolm X is writing about a situation that reflects the social structure that was prevalent in the middle of the twentieth century, when African Americans were encouraged to imitate the look and standards of the dominant European American majority. In what ways has this situation changed, and even reversed? In what ways is it the same?

Suggestions for Writing

1. Write a 500-word essay about a time when you underwent a process designed to radically alter your appearance—a tattoo, a piercing, an abrupt change in your hairstyle. What were the results?

2. Write a 500- to 750-word essay about one of these processes: (a) conforming to a trend in order to be perceived as stylish or hip; (b) ignoring current trends in clothing and personal appearance and seeking to create a personal style and image.

SUGGESTIONS FOR WRITING Both items produce good writing. However, some students prefer causal to process analysis when responding to item 1. Remind students to go beyond pure narration for either prompt.

How Not to Use the Fax Machine and the Cellular Phone

UMBERTO ECO

Umberto Eco is professor of semiotics at the University of Bologna, in Italy. (Semiotics is the linguistic study of signs, symbols, and meanings.) Eco is best known for his novels, such as *Foucault's Pendulum* (1989), *The Name of the Rose* (1994), *The Island of the Day Before* (1995), and *Baudolino* (2002). Eco has also written numerous scholarly works and collections of essays.

The following essay, from *How to Travel with a Salmon* (1995), examines two processes: how people use technology and how technology can dominate people's lives.

1 The fax machine is truly a great invention. For anyone still unfamiliar with it, the fax works like this: you insert a letter, you dial the number of the addressee, and in the space of a few minutes the letter has reached its destination. And the machine isn't just for letters: it can send drawings, plans, photographs, pages of complicated figures impossible to dictate over the telephone. If the letter is going to Australia, the cost of transmission is no more than that of an intercontinental call of the same duration. If the letter is being sent from Milan to Saronno, it costs no more than a directly dialed call. And bear in mind that a call from Milan to Paris, in the evening hours, costs about a thousand lire.* In a country like ours, where the postal system, by definition, doesn't work, the fax machine solves all your problems. Another thing many people don't know is that you can buy a fax for your bedroom, or a portable version for travel, at a reasonable price. Somewhere between a million five and two million lire.* A considerable amount for a toy, but a bargain if your work requires you to correspond with many people in many different cities.

2 Unfortunately, there is one inexorable law of technology, and it is this: when revolutionary inventions become widely accessible, they cease to be accessible. Technology is inherently democratic, because it promises the same services to all; but it works only if the rich are alone in using it. When the poor also adopt technology, it stops working. A train used to take two hours to go from A to B; then the motor car arrived, which could cover the same distance in one hour. For this reason cars were very expensive. But as soon as the masses could afford to buy them, the roads became jammed, and the trains started to move faster. Consider how absurd it is for the authorities constantly to urge people to use public transport, in the age of the automobile; but with public transport, by consenting not to belong to the elite, you get where you're going before members of the elite do.

3 In the case of the automobile, before the point of total collapse was reached, many decades went by. The fax machine, more democratic (in fact, it costs much

*Up until 2002, the *lira* was the basic unit of currency in Italy. In 1995, a thousand lire was equivalent to approximately sixty-three cents.

***A million five lire** was approximately $945 in 1995; **two million lire** was approximately $1,260.

less than a car), achieved collapse in less than a year. At this point it is faster to send something through the mail. Actually, the fax encourages such postal communications. In the old days, if you lived in Medicine Hat, and you had a son in Brisbane, you wrote him once a week and you telephoned him once a month. Now, with the fax, you can send him, in no time, the snapshot of his newborn niece. The temptation is irresistible. Furthermore, the world is inhabited by people, in an ever-increasing number, who want to tell you something that is of no interest to you: how to choose a smarter investment, how to purchase a given object, how to make them happy by sending them a check, how to fulfill yourself completely by taking part in a conference that will improve your professional status. All of these people, the moment they discover you have a fax, and unfortunately there are now fax directories, will trample one another underfoot in their haste to send you, at modest expense, unrequested messages.

4 As a result, you will approach your fax machine every morning and find it swamped with messages that have accumulated during the night. Naturally, you throw them away without having read them. But suppose someone close to you wants to inform you that you have inherited ten million dollars from an uncle in America, but on condition that you visit a notary before eight o'clock: if the well-meaning friend finds the line busy, you don't receive the information in time. If someone *has* to get in touch with you, then, he has to do so by mail. The fax is becoming the medium of trivial messages, just as the automobile has become the means of slow travel, for those who have time to waste and want to spend long hours in gridlocked traffic, listening to Mozart and Dire Straits.*

5 Finally, the fax introduces a new element into the dynamics of nuisance. Until today, the bore, if he wanted to irritate you, paid (for the phone call, the postage stamp, the taxi to bring him to your doorbell). But now you contribute to the expense, because you're the one who buys the fax paper.

6 How can you react? I have already had letterhead printed with the warning "Unsolicited faxes are automatically destroyed," but I don't think that's enough. If you want my advice, I'd suggest keeping your fax disconnected. If someone has to send you something, he has to call you first and ask you to connect the machine. Of course, this can overload the telephone line. It would be best for the person who has to send a fax to write you first. Then you can answer, "Send your message via fax Monday at 5.05.27 P.M., Greenwich mean time, when I will connect the machine for precisely four minutes and thirty-six seconds."

7 It is easy to take cheap shots at the owners of cellular phones. But before doing so, you should determine to which of the five following categories they belong.

8 First come the handicapped. Even if their handicap is not visible, they are obliged to keep in constant contact with their doctor or the 24-hour medical service. All praise, then, to the technology that has placed this beneficent instrument at their service. Second come those who, for serious professional reasons, are required to be on call in case of emergency (fire chiefs, general practitioners, organ-transplant specialists always awaiting a fresh corpse, or President Bush,* because if he is ever unavailable, the world falls into the hands of Quayle). For them the

---

***Dire Straits:** a band popular in the mid- to late 1980s.

***President George H. W. Bush:** 41st President of the United States and father of President George W. Bush. Dan Quayle was his vice president.

portable phone is a harsh fact of life, endured, but hardly enjoyed. Third, adulterers. Finally, for the first time in their lives, they are able to receive messages from their secret lover without the risk that family members, secretaries, or malicious colleagues will intercept the call. It suffices that the number be known only to him and her (or to him and him, or to her and her: I can't think of any other possible combinations). All three categories listed above are entitled to our respect. Indeed, for the first two we are willing to be disturbed even while dining in a restaurant, or during a funeral; and adulterers are very discreet, as a rule.

9 Two other categories remain. These, in contrast, spell trouble (for us and for themselves as well). The first comprises those persons who are unable to go anywhere unless they have the possibility of chattering about frivolous matters with the friends and relations they have just left. It is hard to make them understand why they shouldn't do it. And finally, if they cannot resist the compulsion to interact, if they cannot enjoy their moments of solitude and become interested in what they themselves are doing at that moment, if they cannot avoid displaying their vacuity and, indeed, make it their trademark, their emblem, well, the problem must be left to the psychologist. They irk us, but we must understand their terrible inner emptiness, be grateful we are not as they are, and forgive them—without, however, gloating over our own superior natures, and thus yielding to the sins of spiritual pride and lack of charity. Recognize them as your suffering neighbor, and turn the other ear.

10 In the last category (which includes, on the bottom rung of the social ladder, the purchasers of fake portable phones) are those people who wish to show in public that they are greatly in demand, especially for complex business discussions. Their conversations, which we are obliged to overhear in airports, restaurants, or trains, always involve monetary transactions, missing shipments of metal sections, an unpaid bill for a crate of neckties, and other things that, the speaker believes, are very Rockefellerian.*

11 Now, helping to perpetuate the system of class distinctions is an atrocious mechanism ensuring that, thanks to some atavistic proletarian defect, the nouveau riche, even when he earns enormous sums, won't know how to use a fish knife or will hang a plush monkey in the rear window of his Ferrari or put a San Gennaro* on the dashboard of his private jet, or (when speaking his native Italian) use English words like "management." Therefore he will not be invited by the Duchesse de Guermantes (and he will rack his brain trying to figure out why not; after all, he has a yacht so long it could almost serve as a bridge across the English Channel).

12 What these people don't realize is that Rockefeller doesn't need a portable telephone; he has a spacious room full of secretaries so efficient that at the very worst, if his grandfather is dying, the chauffeur comes and whispers something in his ear. The man with power is the man who is not required to answer every call; on the contrary, he is always—as the saying goes—in a meeting. Even at the lowest managerial level, the two symbols of success are a key to the executive washroom and a secretary who asks, "Would you care to leave a message?"

13 So anyone who flaunts a portable phone as a symbol of power is, on the contrary, announcing to all and sundry his desperate, subaltern position, in which he is

*__Rockefellerian:__ an adjective derived from "Rockefeller," the surname of a wealthy American family.

*__San Gennaro:__ a statue of the patron saint of the Italian city of Naples.

obliged to snap to attention, even when making love, if the CEO happens to telephone; he has to pursue creditors day and night to keep his head above water; and he is persecuted by the bank, even at his daughter's First Holy Communion, because of an overdraft. The fact that he uses, ostentatiously, his cellular phone is proof that he doesn't know these things, and it is the confirmation of his social banishment, beyond appeal.

Vocabulary

The following terms are identified by paragraph number. Make sure that you understand each term's meaning in its context. If you're not sure that you understand a term, look it up in a college-level dictionary.

dictate (1)	adulterer (8)	monetary (10)
duration (1)	malicious (8)	perpetuate (11)
lire (1)	suffices (8)	atrocious (11)
inexorable (2)	comprises (9)	atavistic (11)
inherently (2)	frivolous (9)	proletarian (11)
elite (2)	compulsion (9)	nouveau riche (11)
notary (4)	solitude (9)	chauffeur (12)
dynamics (5)	vacuity (9)	flaunts (13)
unsolicited (6)	trademark (9)	sundry (13)
beneficent (8)	irk (9)	subaltern (13)
practitioners (8)	gloating (9)	ostentatiously (13)

STYLE AND STRATEGY

1. The thesis appears at the beginning of paragraph 2. Students will interpret these first few sentences in different ways, but one common message is that both fax machines and cellular phones are becoming so popular that they are losing their effectiveness.
2. The problem with fax machines is articulated in paragraph 4: "The fax is becoming the medium of trivial messages." The problem with cellular phones belongs chiefly to those people described in paragraphs 11–13.
3. The paradox illustrated when Eco discusses the invention of the railroad and the automobile is that the more "accessible" an invention becomes, the more "inaccessible" it becomes.
4. Perhaps this is an exaggeration, but students can easily replace this example with that of e-mails.
5. Categorization prevents the author from generalizing about the users of cellular phones. It also projects a modicum of objectivity—genuine or not.
6. The reader can easily infer a conclusion about the social implications of using fax machines and cellular phones.

Style and Strategy

1. In which paragraph is Eco's thesis? Restate it in your own words.
2. Eco analyzes a process, the development of problems with fax machines and with cellular phones, but they aren't the same problems. In your own words, explain the problems that Eco identifies with each type of technology.
3. In paragraphs 2–3, Eco explains a *paradox* (contradiction) that developed when fax machines went on the market. What is this paradox, and what historical *analogy* (extended comparison) does Eco use to illustrate it?
4. In paragraph 4, Eco explains the effects of the proliferation of fax machines. Is this paragraph meant to be taken literally? Explain.
5. Eco uses classification in paragraphs 7–13. What is his purpose for doing so?
6. This essay does not have a formal conclusion. Would it have been improved by the addition of a final, concluding paragraph? Explain.

Questions for Critical Thinking and Discussion

1. Comment on the following statement: "The recent developments in consumer technology have had the unfortunate result of making U.S. culture noisier and ruder. Cell phones, pagers, boom boxes, and modern sound systems for cars have turned rudeness into an art form."

2. Comment on the following statement: "Cell phones don't play the same role they did in the past. For many people, the vast number of minutes they have to use each month prompts them to use the phone as much as possible. Some people can't seem to walk a hundred yards without making a 'Whassup?' phone call."

QUESTIONS FOR CRITICAL THINKING AND DISCUSSION While these make excellent prompts for class discussion, they can also be used as prompts for short and sustained writing. Students can tap a wellspring of information from their own experiences when addressing these items.

Suggestions for Writing

1. Write a 500- to 750-word essay on the following topic: "how not to use e-mail." Note that this essay could employ either the instructional approach or the informational approach.
2. Has a specific kind of technology—cell phones or personal digital assistants (PDAs), for example—ever taken up more of your life than you expected it to? Write a 500- to 750-word essay that analyzes how this process developed.
3. Write a 500- to 750-word essay on the following topic: how to use a cell phone responsibly.

SUGGESTIONS FOR WRITING All three suggestions can lead to successful essays. You might ask students who have chosen to write on the same prompt to meet in small groups and to begin gathering information via brainstorming.

WRITING THE PROCESS ANALYSIS ESSAY WITH A READER'S EYE

MORE OPTIONS ONLINE If you would like to read additional process analysis essays, go to **www.mhhe.com/writingtoday**.

When you are writing a process essay, your ability to understand your reader's needs is crucial. Look at it this way: you are telling your reader how to do something or how a process occurs. Since you probably know more about the subject than your reader does, you shouldn't assume that your reader will understand the process if you write down the steps just as they occur to you. Beware of writing an essay that seems very effective—to you—but that baffles an intelligent reader who needs a clearer, more detailed explanation of the process you are analyzing. The advice that follows will help you think like your reader as you consider your assignment and then prewrite, draft, revise, and edit your process analysis essay.

Issues to Keep in Mind

When writing a process analysis, you may choose a topic that leads you to write an instructional ("how-to") essay, or you may prefer the informational approach, in which you show how a significant process works. In either case, take some time to think about the following three issues:

1. Audience analysis
2. Language level
3. Voice

Audience Analysis

If you needed to explain how to use a new type of optical scanner, you wouldn't write the same instructions for every possible audience. A novice computer user would need a simple, painstakingly clear set of steps, whereas someone with extensive computer experience could probably understand a less detailed set of instructions. Therefore, before you begin to write any kind of process analysis, you need to consider how much you can expect your audience to know about the process that you are analyzing. The answer to this question will determine both how you plan your essay and how much explanatory information you will need to include.

In addition, once you have completed a draft, you can use peer review to help you discover places where readers will have problems following the process. Choose a reviewer who is part of your target audience, and ask him or her this question at the start: "Does my essay make *sense* to you?"

CLASSROOM HINT If possible, use class time to discuss language appropriate to various audiences of process analysis.

Language Level

As you think about how much your audience is likely to know, you also need to think about the kind of language to use in your essay. If you are writing about a mechanical or technical process, you need to be careful about including **jargon**, specialized language that only members of a particular group are likely to understand. For example, the following sentence appeared in an essay for a general audience on how baseball managers choose relief pitchers: "Craig Biggio went yard with the bases juiced." Perhaps one out of three U.S. readers would understand the meaning of this mysterious line—that Craig Biggio (the batter) hit a grand slam (a home run with runners on all three bases). Unless you know that all of the members of your audience will understand it, it's usually best to avoid using jargon in a process analysis.

Although you can usually avoid jargon, sometimes you will need to explain general technical terms in order to make readers understand the process you are describing. In an essay on working out, for instance, the writer could use a parenthetical definition to clarify a term that some readers might not know: "Performing regular sets of this exercise will strengthen the deltoids (shoulder muscles)." As in this example, you should usually define terms simply and economically; an essay filled with complex definitions will frustrate readers. Moreover, any topic that requires you to define a large number of terms may be too specialized for your purposes.

Voice

CLASSROOM HINT Spend class time discussing the importance of the imperative mood in essays that give instructions.

Students are usually told to avoid using *you* in their essays. Normally, when students write *you,* they mean a generalized, vague "someone." However, in an instructional process analysis, the writer is addressing a specific *you:* the reader. Using *you* is appropriate in this situation. On the other hand, an informational process essay does not tell the reader how to perform a process, so the use of *you* should usually be avoided in such writing.

Choosing a Topic

MORE OPTIONS ONLINE For more help with problem areas in the process analysis essay, go to **www.mhhe.com/writingtoday.**

As always, think of your reader. Most writing instructors have already read a great many weak, boring papers on such topics as "How to Pack a Suitcase" and "How to Change a Flat Tire on an Imported Car." At the very least, you want your essay to be informative *and* entertaining. The following guidelines will help you choose a promising topic for your process analysis:

1. Find a topic that is neither too narrow nor too broad. A narrow, mundane topic will probably lead to a narrow, mundane essay, like the sleep-inducing essays on packing suitcases and changing tires mentioned above. On the other hand, some topics are clearly too broad for the confines of the short essay. "How the Federal Reserve Came to Be More Important Than the Supreme Court" is an interesting subject, but you could spend the rest of your life researching it and writing about it. Find a topic that can be successfully undertaken within the limits of your assignment—for example, the process that the justices of the U.S. Supreme Court use to decide whether to hear a case.
2. Find a topic that interests you. Students sometimes worry that their interests and those of their instructor may be very far apart; hence, they may discard certain topics because they fear the topic will not be "pleasing" to the instructor. Remember that composition teachers tend to be a fairly open-minded group of people. They like good writing, regardless of the subject, and they are continually surprised by students' ability to develop interesting papers on unexpected themes. Consider the following topic: "How Country Music Videos Have Succeeded as Television Programming." One of the authors of this text believes that country music is enjoyable, historically important, and culturally significant; the other hates country music, doesn't listen to it, and wishes that it would go away. Yet we'd both like to read a student's paper on this subject.
3. Consider whether you want to choose a topic that will require research. Although you may know a great deal about a particular subject, research might help broaden your scope. However, before proceeding with a topic that requires research, check with your instructor about whether he or she will allow you to include secondary material in your essay. And if you do include information from other sources, make sure that you document this information properly (see also Chapter 21).

Prewriting

The process essay sets forth a series of steps. To develop these steps, you need to generate plenty of material before you decide how to organize your essay. Freewriting works well for generating the steps or stages in a process, as does clustering or brainstorming (see Chapter 2, pages 31–34). As you choose your topic and start your prewriting, you will be able to determine whether your essay will be instructional or informational, and this decision will help later as you begin to draft your introduction. If your essay will use the instructional approach, you should think about how learning the process will help your reader. If your essay is informational, you should consider the overall point that you are trying to make. Also at this time, you should be able to develop a preliminary thesis statement.

Organizing

Once you have generated a list of the steps or stages in the process and developed your working thesis, the best way for you to organize this raw material is to arrange it into an outline. (Chapter 2 covers informal, sentence, and formal outline structures. See pages 40–42.) A sentence outline works well for process analysis, giving you (and perhaps your peer reviewer) a look at how the essay will present the process for readers. Make sure that you are comfortable with your essay's proposed outline before you begin drafting and that your outline doesn't reveal gaps in the process. Outlines are easy to revise, but essays can be much more of a problem.

Drafting

To illustrate one approach to writing a process analysis essay, we have included the essay "Shaping a Better Beast."

The Introduction

The introduction to a process analysis must establish background and context—what your reader needs to know before working through your process analysis. Many students, concentrating on the process that will form the body of the essay, write very short introductions, forgetting what the reader needs to know:

- In an informational essay, the context and the larger significance of the process being analyzed
- In an instructional essay, the context and the importance of learning how to master the process (and in the case of a highly practical essay, such as how to sand and finish a wooden cabinet, the tools and other materials that will be required)

Remember that you can write your introduction after you write the body of your essay. Many writers find it hard to introduce text that has not yet been written, so consider postponing the introduction until after you have written the draft of your body paragraphs.

The introductory paragraph for our sample essay effectively establishes the importance of the process, setting up the rest of the essay:

Shaping the Better Beast

Today, cats are the most popular pets in American homes. But before cats grow up, they start as kittens, creatures that are very different from mature felines in many ways. Most people love kittens; they are a delight to be around. As the saying goes, though, "The problem with kittens is that they grow up and become CATS." Many adult cats are mean, distant, neurotic, or just plain weird. However, the personality of a mature cat is not "hard-wired" genetically. The development of a cat's temperament is a function of environment and handling. **By working closely with a kitten from the moment you bring it home, you can have a good chance of developing a kind, loving companion.**

Note the thesis statement at the end of this paragraph. In many types of writing that you will be assigned, your instructor may require a specific thesis statement that lists all the issues you plan to cover. Such a thesis can help readers follow the structure of your essay, but in a process essay this "list" approach can make the essay seem more mechanical than it needs to. Moreover, in some cases listing all the steps in the process is unwieldy; your thesis would have to consist of either multiple sentences or one long, crowded sentence that would be hard to make parallel. Therefore, a general thesis statement is usually the best option for a process essay.

Consider Your Options

A process analysis might be written in different ways to fulfill a variety of purposes. Make sure to understand your purpose and to state it clearly in your introduction. (For more on introductions, see Chapter 3.)

The Body

The writer now provides the steps—both specific and general—that the reader should follow:

> First, make sure that you bring your kitten home to a nonthreatening environment. A dwelling filled with noisy roommates, parties, and loud music is not a good place to raise a kitten. Cats are afraid of loud noises and prefer quiet. Similarly, if you own a dog or other cats, these other animals will make it more difficult for your kitten to adjust and develop. You should also be aware that your kitten needs quiet places: things to hide under, such as table coverings and drapes. A kitten is much more likely to feel at home in a place that matches its instinctive needs.
>
> Second, spend as much time as possible playing with your kitten. Human children who are routinely ignored can grow up to be cold, distant adults. The same is true with cats. Kittens are dynamos: they want to play, sometimes at a maniacal level. Indulge this need: play with your kitten as much as you can if you want it to bond with you for life. For better or for worse, your kitten sees you as a surrogate mother, so spend as much time as you can with your "child."
>
> Finally, listen to your kitten and be aware of its signals. Each cat is different. Try to figure out your kitten's personality very early on. For example, if you are playing with your kitten and it suddenly seems angry or aggressive, let it cool off. As you interact with your kitten, you can also let it know that some of its signals are unacceptable. Biting, excessive use of claws, and interminable crying in the presence of a closed door are behaviors that you can adjust at this point. However, although you can mold your kitten's behavior to a degree, keep in mind that cats aren't robots. A friend of mine

thinks she has raised the perfect cat, and her cat is usually docile and pleasant, but if he has access to her bedroom at night, she will invariably wake up at three or four in the morning with a sixteen-pound Bengal Tiger perched on top of her head. She has tried to change his behavior, but it continues. Oddly enough, her cat didn't start this behavior until he was four years old.

Note the writer's use of topic sentences:

- First, make sure that you bring your kitten home to a nonthreatening environment.
- Second, spend as much time as possible playing with your kitten.
- Finally, listen to your kitten and be aware of its signals.

EXERCISE 9.1 (page 269) Answers will vary. The following sentence outline is suggested.
Thesis: By working closely with a kitten, you can develop a kind and loving companion.
I. Bring the kitten home to a nonthreatening environment.
  A. Cats prefer quiet.
  B. Dogs or other cats will make adjustment difficult.
II. Spend time playing with the kitten.
  A. Kittens who are ignored become cold and distant.
  B. Kittens like to play.
III. Listen to the kitten and be aware of its signals.
  A. Figure out your kitten's personality.
  B. Let it know when behavior is unacceptable.
  C. Some behavior will persist or will begin later.
IV. As the example of Amy's cat shows, the process of raising a kitten is important.

These sentences guide the reader effectively through the process. In Chapter 3, "Developing Strong Paragraphs," we point out that writers can sometimes use implied topic sentences or topic sentences that end, rather than begin, a paragraph. However, avoid these approaches in an instructional process essay. Instead, begin each body paragraph with a clear topic sentence.

Second, notice how the writer has used transitions to link ideas. Time-order transitions (for example, *first, next, then, finally*) are frequently useful in process analysis, as this essay proves, but causal transitions such as *therefore* and *consequently* can also work well. See Chapter 3, page 71, for the chart on transitions, and use them liberally in any process analysis essay you write. Especially if your essay tells readers how to do something, it may sound a bit more formulaic and mechanical than other essays you write. If readers find it clear and easy to follow, though, they will be grateful and your essay will be a success.

Third, notice how the writer employs other rhetorical options as she develops her body paragraphs. Description, narration, exemplification, causal analysis, definition, and comparison/contrast all help to make these paragraphs more effective.

The Conclusion

The dreaded "summary" approach to concluding your process essay ("In this essay I have explained three steps for making the shoe-shining process a snap. These are . . .") is rarely a good choice. Although you should avoid bringing up new subjects in your conclusion, you should certainly feel free to comment on the significance of your subject or offer an effective anecdote:

Consider Your Options

Instead of summarizing your essay in the conclusion of a process analysis, ask yourself what needs to be stressed to your reader at this point. (For more on conclusions, see Chapter 3.)

A few weeks ago, my friend Amy asked me to come by and see her cat, a Russian Blue named Nita. I knew that Amy already had a dog and another cat, and I knew as well that Russian Blues are sometimes neurotic, so I was curious to see what this one might be like. During my ninety minutes at Amy's, I got just three brief glimpses of her "pet." Whenever Nita emerged from her hiding place, either the Labrador or the orange tom ran after her

Questions for Reviewing a Process Analysis Essay

CLASSROOM HINT If time permits, discuss these seven questions in class.

1. Does the introduction sufficiently explain the background and context for the process?
2. Does the essay include a thesis statement that informs the reader about the analysis to follow, either stating why it is important to learn or making a point about it? Is the writer's purpose clear?
3. Do the steps and the commentary make sense? Do you feel that you understand the process that is being described? Point out any places where you were confused.
4. Point out any step or comment that doesn't ring true.
5. Are topic sentences both clear and properly located? Where are the steps unclear for readers, and where does a step need more explanation?
6. Does the writer use enough transitions to guide the reader through the process? Where are transitional words and sentences needed?
7. Does the essay have an effective conclusion? How could it be improved?

and chased her away. When I tried to pick Nita up, she raked my arm because of her fear of contact. Amy said, "I haven't been home much since I adopted Nita. I've been letting her get to know the others on her own." Because of Amy's "process" of raising her kitten, she doesn't have a pet; she has a hostage.

The conclusion to the process essay is your opportunity to finish what is sometimes a fairly mechanical essay with your own signature flourish. Take advantage of this opportunity.

MORE OPTIONS ONLINE For more help with the step-by-step development of the process analysis essay, go to **www.mhhe.com/writingtoday**.

EXERCISE 9.1

Write a sentence outline of "Shaping the Better Beast." (For help with sentence outlines, see Chapter 2, pages 40–42.) What does the outline reveal about this essay's organization? How would a different organization work for this essay?

Revising Your Draft

After you have completed a draft of your process analysis essay, your next step is to revise it, using your own analysis and comments from classmates or friends. During peer review, answer the Questions for Reviewing a Process Analysis Essay (above) whether you are reviewing your own draft or the work of another student.

After reviewing for content, you need to go over your peer reviewers' responses to your essay and then revise for unity, coherence, language level, and

MORE OPTIONS ONLINE For more help with revision, go to **www.mhhe.com/writingtoday.**

tone (see Chapter 4). When you have revised your draft and are basically satisfied with it, read your draft for mechanical and grammatical errors. Concentrate on finding and correcting major sentence errors (fragment, comma splice, fused sentence), errors in pronoun agreement and subject-verb agreement, and spelling.

Now that you have made your corrections, *read your essay one more time* to catch any errors made during revision and find errors missed during your earlier reviews.

Student Essay

In the following essay, Manny Meregildo writes about the problem of trying to hold down a job while attending college. The final draft is presented first. Then Manny's first draft is presented, with his comments about this draft and what he needed to do in the revision stage.

Manny's Final Draft

Get the Right Job

1 Unfortunately, most of us do not live in an ideal world where Mom and Dad pay for all of our school and living expenses. If most college students plan to have any type of social life or buy their first car, they will have to find a job. Eventually, serious college students find out that attending college is extremely difficult, and having to get a job to pay for some of the expenses is not a pleasant experience. Even though most employers value a higher education, the business world and the college environment sometimes collide, creating extreme conflicts.

2 Attending college is a job in itself. You are expected to be on time for class and attend every lecture—which in some cases means attending a class three times a week. You are also expected to study several hours a day and complete any assignment that has been given, which can take several hours as well. That leaves very little time for an employer to work with; however, when managers are creating the schedules for the following week, they are not concerned about the number of hours that you need for studying or whether the schedule they are creating conflicts with your current course schedule. Fortunately, there is a way out of this situation: find a job with flexible hours and a work environment that is not tyrannical.

3 Flexibility is an extremely important attribute for both school and work. Usually, college instructors will hand out a syllabus listing what will be done

during that semester, and this schedule is normally followed. However, there are always unexpected circumstances when the class runs late, you need to stay after class to speak with the professor, or the date of an exam is pushed back. These unexpected events can cause problems when you have to work on the same day. Unfortunately, some students have to deal with an employer like mine, who will refuse to give anyone the day off, even if it means failing the class. Is having to deal with this dilemma worth the risk of losing three months of your life?

4 For every class hour, students should spend a minimum of three hours studying—well, at least that is the recommended time given by instructors. Your main goal is to achieve an *A* in the class; therefore, to accomplish this task, you need to study as much as possible. Unfortunately, having a job takes away precious studying time—doing the math shows why. Some employers allow their employees to bring their schoolbooks to work so that they can study while on the job. However, if your boss is strict like mine, and he or she doesn't care if business is slow or not, the boss will not allow any materials that are not work-related on the floor. Nevertheless, what your boss and other bosses do not know won't hurt them. You can usually find a way to study where you work.

5 The best option is to avoid working altogether while attending college, unless you can find a supervisor who believes that education comes first and will fight for you, or who needs the extra studying time too and is willing to overlook some of the company's policies. However, not all of us are fortunate enough to enjoy such pleasures; instead, we battle with time to get everything done.

Manny's First Draft

Getting the Right Job

1 Unfortunately, we all do not live in an ideal world where mom and dad pay for all of our school or living expenses. If we as students plan to have any type of life, we will have to find a job. Eventually, serious college students find out that attending college is extremely difficult, and having to get a job

When I wrote my first draft, I wasn't really sure which way to go with it, so it didn't seem very focused when I read it over. Sometimes it's informational, sometimes instructive. I realized that I was better off giving advice here, even though that complicated the revision.

to pay for some of the expenses is not a pleasant experience. Even though most employers value a higher education, the business world and the college environment sometimes collide, creating a catastrophic event.

2 Attending college is a job in itself. We as college students are expected to attend every lecture - which in some cases are about three times a week. We are also expected to study several hours a day, which can take several hours as well. That leaves very little time for an employer to work with; however, when managers are creating the work schedules for the following week, they are not concerned about whether the schedule they are creating conflicts with our current course schedule, creating a problem for the student. Fortunately, there is an easy way out of this situation: finding the right job, one that is flexible and not tyrannical.

I wasn't sure whether to use "you" or talk about college students—this went along with my problems in focusing the essay.

3 College instructors usually will hand out a listing of what would be done during that semester. Thus, there are those unexpected circumstances where the class runs late, if the students needs to stay after class to speak with the professor, or if the date of an exam is pushed back. This could be a problem, because the student might have to work that day. Unfortunately, some students have to deal with an employer like mine who will refuse to give any one the day off. Is having to deal with this dilemma worth the risk of losing three months of your life?

A classmate pointed out that this paragraph needed a point, so I added a topic sentence.

4 For every class hour there should be a minimum of three hours of studying. A student's main goal is to achieve an A in the class; therefore, to accomplish this task, lots of studying is required. Unfortunately, having a job takes away from our studying time, and if we were to do the math we will see why. Some employers would allow their employees to bring their schoolbooks to work so that they could study while on the job. Thus, if the student has a strict boss like I do who does not care if business is slow or not, the boss will not allow any materials that are not work related on the floor.

My first drafts frequently have verb problems and clunky language; this one is a good example.

5 If possible, avoid working while attending college at all cost, unless you can find a supervisor who will fight for you and believes that education comes first or he or she needs the extra studying time too and is willing to overlook some of the company's policies. However, we are all not that fortu-

nate to enjoy such pleasures; instead, we battle with time to get the job done.

SUGGESTED ACTIVITY
Consider asking students to meet in writing groups, each of which is charged with producing a more developed and effective version of this essay. Encourage students to add appropriate details from their own experience with weight control.

EXERCISE 9.2: REVISING

The following is the first draft of a student's process analysis essay. Working in pairs or in small groups, review this essay. Using the Questions for Reviewing a Process Analysis Essay on page 269, decide what revisions you would suggest. If you have any questions the student needs to consider, write them in the margin or on a separate sheet of paper. If your instructor directs you to, rewrite one or more paragraphs to make them stronger and to eliminate any grammatical or mechanical errors.

"Losing Weight"

1 Everyone seems to be trying to lose weight. A good idea, since most Americains are overweight to some degree or the other. Irregardless of how much weight people want - or need - to loose, there are three simple steps that will help bring the gross weight down and help to acheive a healthy life style; eliminating fat from the diet, regualar intake and an exercise program.

EXERCISE 9.2 Answers will vary. Students should point out that the thesis needs to be clearer (what is "regular intake"?), and the third point and conclusion need further development.

2 A large cheese burger from a fastfood restarant may contain as many as 125 grams of fat. This is enough fat for a week! on the other hand, chicken - with the skin removed - has far less fat. And so does fish. But you cant fry either chicken or fish and hope to loose weight do to the fat in the fring oils. Never the less, avoiding fastfoods is one way to cut down fat. A diet that consists of skinless chicken and fish are the way to go, therefore, think of these as your key to thiness.

3 When I start my tuesdays they are very different than my Mondays which are very different from my wednesdays and so on, etc. My schedual changes everyday. So does my meal times. Eating on a regualar schedual helps one acheive selfdiscipline, and you can then look forward to a self controlled diet. If you cant eat on a regualar schedual than try to plan what you eat before its time to eat it. It might be that it is dificult for you to plan a meal before you eat it, never the less, make the attempt.

4 Exercise has any number of health related benefits and it is the best way to burn extra calories and it is also the way to tone the bodies mussels. Hard exercise is best it strenthens the muscles and improves the heart's activities.

Any one of any age, from infants to geezers will have their life improved by hard exersise.

So, as you can see, in the previous essay I have given three easy steps to improve your health: exercise, avoid fat and eat regualar. Try it, it just might make a differance! 5

Additional Writing Topics

1. *Deflated expectations.* You had great hopes for that first date with a new someone, but after ten minutes you realize that you are in what government types call a "damage control situation." What steps can you take to survive the evening and return to the safety of your home?
2. *The collection agent awaits.* The credit cards have been fun, but the bills are piling up. What can you do to stabilize your financial situation?
3. *Grand Central Station.* You live in a home with three (or four, or whatever) roommates. How can this situation be managed so that chaos is not the normal condition?
4. *Time control.* You love to shop, but time is not as free for you as it used to be. How can you efficiently maximize your enjoyment of shopping in a limited amount of time?
5. *Practical stuff.* Teach your readers how to
   a. Customize a Web browser.
   b. Change the oil in a fifty-year-old car.
   c. Improve their poker-playing skills.
   d. Get rid of a slice (or a hook) in golf.
   e. Accessorize clothing.
   f. Use a zip drive.
   g. Meet new friends.
   h. Break up with a sweetheart.
   i. Improve their public image.
   j. Become a better public speaker.
   k. Set up an aquarium.
   l. Keep a ferret, an iguana, or other exotic animal as a pet.
   m. Make a good first impression.
   n. Make a horrible first impression.
   o. Pass a particularly difficult course.
   p. Fail a particularly easy course.
6. **Writing on the job.** Write an essay in which you explain to the reader either (a) how to succeed in a job interview or (b) how to fail miserably in a job interview.

Responding to a Photograph

In the mid-1980s, the price of gold soared, and gold mines like this one in Brazil became feverishly active. Sebastião Salgado took this photograph in 1986.

Sebastião Salgado, *Serra Pelada Gold Mine*, Pará, Brazil, 1986. © Sebastião Salgado (Amazonas/Contact Press Images).

CLASSROOM HINT To help your students write successful papers in response to these two prompts, discuss them in class or as part of a student-teacher office conference. Students should be comfortable with the process of including and citing researched material before you assign item 2.

1. Write an informal response to the photograph. What do you notice? How does the image make you feel? How is the photograph an example of process analysis?

2. Many of the people working in this mine were desperately poor and were willing to withstand horrible working conditions in order to have a job. Using a combination of library and online research, choose a type of business or industry in a developing country—such as Brazilian mining, the factories of northern Mexico, the garment and footwear manufacturers of Southeast Asia, or telephone help centers in India—and explore the labor process. How do people get jobs? How much are they paid? Are they protected from unfair working conditions and predatory practices? Remember to narrow your topic so that you can adequately address it. Write a documented essay explaining how labor is hired and treated in one of these types of industries. (For more information on documented essays, see Chapter 21.)

Writing About Film

The Princess Diaries (2001, PG) tells the story of a normal young girl who learns that she is actually a princess of a small European country. Under the tutelage of her grandmother, the girl must "become" a princess. How does this transformation occur?

Ocean's Eleven (2001, PG-13) depicts Danny Ocean and his band of highly skilled thieves who plan to rob a Las Vegas casino. The casino's owner knows about the planned heist and exercises his considerable wherewithal to prevent it. However, the robbery takes place right under his nose. How?

Using the Internet

Search the Internet for insights and information to use when explaining a process.

1. Use the Internet to find information on an art, task, or process that is now rare or no longer practiced. Examples include mummifying the body of an ancient Egyptian; making wine without the use of a press; churning butter; building an Egyptian or Mayan pyramid; cremating a Viking chieftain; building a cliff dwelling, long house, or other Native American home; painting a fresco; hunting with falcons; printing a book or newspaper in colonial America; throwing a masquerade ball; hauling freight along the Erie Canal; sailing a merchant schooner; practicing medicine with leeches; and fueling and driving a coal-fired steam locomotive. Use this information to write an essay that instructs the reader in the steps required to perform this art, task, or process.

2. Explain a natural process such as photosynthesis, the circulation of the blood in a human body, the formation of rain clouds, the eruption of a

volcano, the creation of oil or coal deposits, the migration of birds, or the metamorphosis of a butterfly. Once again, use the Internet to find sources of information.

3. Go online to learn how to build a Web page and to put it on the Internet. Explain this process in an essay addressed to a novice Web user.

DILBERT reprinted by permission of United Feature Syndicate, Inc.

CHAPTER 10

CAUSAL ANALYSIS

Writing in Context

One of Osprey's major revenue sources is the sale of networking software; unfortunately, because of the way that the software has been developed over time, some clients have older versions, with updates provided only by high-level client-specific "patches" to the ongoing software program.

Bob has called a meeting to unveil his new marketing plan. Bob's plan is both simple and audacious: offer all current business users an up-to-date version of the program, which would cost the clients a hefty sum, then guarantee future updates at a reduced price. This is a one-time-only offer; clients must decide within thirty days.

The idea sounds good to you, but Bert Alvarez, one of the company's vice presidents, has doubts. "Perhaps a feasability study would be in order," he says.

"Exactly," Bob agrees. He turns in your direction. "How are our current clients likely to react? Will they run to our competitors? Speaking of them, will they try to undercut us? You've got till Friday to give us an answer."

The document that Bob has requested, a *feasibility study,* examines the possible *effects* of a change in policy. A very common type of business writing, it calls for an option that is used widely in the academic and business worlds.

SUGGESTED ACTIVITY
Point out that Dilbert's instructor is attempting to explain the causes of his own eccentric style of dress. Have students take five to ten minutes to write a brief explanation of why they dress the way they do. Examine one or two responses for the elements of causal analysis.

HOW DOES CAUSAL ANALYSIS WORK?

Feasibility studies such as the one Bob has asked for require use of the **causal analysis** option, in which a writer explores the causes and/or effects of an event, a policy, or a situation. Note that this feasibility study will need to be *hypothetical*. The writer is being asked to predict the future by considering the firm's current circumstances and researching the past behavior of its clients.

In other circumstances, the writer might be asked to write a report exploring the effects of a past event. For example, perhaps a policy change was made in the past, and the vice president wants to determine its effects. Did everything go according to plan, or were there any surprises?

This kind of causal analysis can be used for a great many subjects in numerous academic disciplines as well as in business and in daily life, as the following brief list of possible topics for an essay exploring effects makes clear:

- In 1990, Iraq invades Kuwait and goads the United States into the military response that came to be known as Desert Storm. What happened to Iraq after losing this war?
- A year ago, a twenty-two-year-old woman decided to divorce her chronically unemployed husband, return to college, and try to establish a better life for herself and her two very young children. Did she succeed? What were the effects of this momentous choice?
- Ten years ago, a student informed his parents that he was changing his major from finance to humanities and planned to attend graduate school after receiving his bachelor's degree. Ten years later, how have things worked out for him?
- A maple tree has been encroaching on the sight lines of motorists as they approach a stop sign. The county commission has been told repeatedly that the tree must be cut back, but it has never taken action. What are the effects of this nondecision?
- A state decides to limit welfare benefits to two years, after which the recipients must fend for themselves. Five years after the new law has been enacted, the state commissions a study to find out what has happened to the people who were affected by the law. Did they thrive, or did they starve?

When a writer explores the effects of past events, he or she concentrates on factual situations that can be studied and understood. In the case of a state cutting back on welfare availability, though, it is likely that both approaches have been used. Before the law was approved, the state government would have looked into what *would probably* happen as a result of the new welfare law (the feasibility approach); five years later, the state orders a study to examine what *actually* happened.

The third basic version of causal analysis looks at *why* events happened or why a situation has transpired, such as in the following instances:

- Police intervene in an argument between two patrons outside a downtown club. Five minutes later, a riot is in progress.

- A weird odor fills the air near the water treatment plant on the Generic River.
- In the past three years, the student dropout rate has tripled at Area Consolidated Comprehensive High School.
- Your cat insists on sitting directly in front of the television during *Joan of Arcadia*.
- It has become almost impossible to find a parking spot on your college's campus.

A writer investigating these situations needs to concentrate on *causes*. What is the explanation for these curious events? What factors have changed? Are there any causes that are not immediately evident but seem obvious after some thought and investigation?

Writers who use causal analysis tend to concentrate on either causes or effects (whether historical or hypothetical); however, it is impossible to discuss causes without discussing effects, and vice versa. The distinction is more a matter of emphasis, of looking at a situation and finding the best way to analyze it. For example, would you emphasize causes or effects when writing about the following situations?

- Your university has announced that any student who misses more than three classes, or "contact hours," in a semester will be dropped from that class.
- Over the past month, your lover has become listless, moody, and irritable.
- In 1863, Robert E. Lee ignored the advice of his generals and continued on with his plans during the battle of Gettysburg.

In each of these situations, the best strategy seems fairly obvious. The first scenario makes one wonder what the effects of the change in attendance policy will be. Will students have to put in extra semesters to make up for uncompleted classes? Will students need to change their habits? If you were writing about this situation, you would probably look at the hypothetical: What effects could be *expected*? On the other hand, the second scenario would prompt you to look for *causes*. What's going on with your loved one? Why is he or she changing? The third scenario would most likely lead you to investigate what actually happened after Lee made his ill-fated decision: the Confederacy lost its vital momentum, and the Civil War turned in favor of the Union.

Causal analysis essays tend to follow these basic patterns:

CLASSROOM HINT
Consider spending class time discussing the three versions of causal analysis explained above as well as the four patterns listed here.

- **Multiple causes of one effect.** In this pattern, a writer concentrates on the cause of a situation by explaining how an outcome is the product of a combination of causes—for example, a failed birthday party caused by a number of factors that went awry.
- **One major cause with several effects.** Here, one event or factor has various ramifications, and the essay concentrates on effects—for example, a writer might relate how the death of his or her father just after the writer's graduation from high school affected (a) the

emotional well-being of all the surviving family members, (b) the financial/occupational status of the writer's mother, and (c) the college prospects of both the writer and his or her brothers and sisters.

- **Hypothetical effects of a proposed change.** This approach speculates: "What would happen if . . . ?" The writer produces a hypothetical scenario that attempts to logically forecast the results of a policy change or structural change, such as "What would happen if the United States severely restricted immigration quotas?" The essay would explore the positive and negative outcomes that could be expected from such a change in policy.
- **Causal chains.** This term may best be explained as "one thing leads to another." In a basic example, the writer might explain about one recent morning when she overslept, causing her to run late in getting her daughter ready for school, resulting in her daughter's missing the school bus, requiring the writer to call a taxi and accompany her daughter to school and then return home, making her late for her own city bus to college, causing her to miss half of her economics class on final exam day, fail the exam, and have to take economics again.

In the examples above, the purpose for writing determines whether the emphasis is on cause or effect.

Occasionally, an essay will weigh causes and effects equally. How might you respond to the following scenario? Your paternal grandparents have been married for forty-eight years. They suddenly announce that they are splitting up. What is the best way to write about this situation? One approach would be to look at the causes of this surprising decision. Were your grandparents secretly unhappy with each other? Did one of them, at around age seventy, fall in love with someone else? (Don't laugh; it happens.) Has one of them changed so much over the last several years that the marriage is no longer viable?

The other approach would be to examine the potential effects of this decision. Will one (or both) of your grandparents be emotionally devastated? Financially devastated? How about the effects on their children, including, of course, your father? How about the effects on their grandchildren, including you?

Actually, your grandparents' divorce could be discussed from either angle. The situation also presents an opportunity to write an essay in which you concentrate equally on causes and effects, with causes discussed first and effects discussed later. However, most topics lead the writer in one direction or the other.

As these examples demonstrate, causal analysis, along with two other forms of analysis—exemplification (Chapter 8) and process analysis (Chapter 9)—are powerful tools that enable us to look at the world around us and make sense of it. For this reason, these strategies are commonly used by instructors in other courses when they ask you to explain the content you have learned in their classes. And your future writing, on the job or in the laboratory, will doubtless require you to employ these standard options.

In many essays that use a different overall strategy, you will need to consider either causes or effects in order to support your thesis and fulfill your purpose. For example, if you are explaining how to do something on the job (a process analysis essay), you may need to warn readers about the effects of neglecting to follow a particular step. If you are classifying a group of events for a history course, you might decide to categorize them according to their causes or their effects.

In other essays, however, causal analysis will be your main strategy. A note of caution: students occasionally get so fixated on the idea of causal analysis that they never stray from their initial idea, producing essays showing how one event leads to another, which leads to another, and so on, like some kind of demented parlor game. However, the purpose of causal analysis is much broader. Here, as in the other two analytical options—exemplification and process analysis—the writer has the opportunity to discuss the world as he or she sees it. The causal option forms the backbone of such an essay. A writer might explore the causes and/or effects of a situation, event, or policy in order to explain to readers how it came about or how it will affect them. Alternatively, the writer might analyze causes and/or effects in order to persuade the reader to do something about them—for example, to agree to an increase in student fees so that the college can build more parking lots.

Being able to show the linkages that make up our world is a powerful skill, as demonstrated in the essays that follow.

Consider Your Options

How might you use causal analysis on the job? What circumstances would call for you to analyze a situation by using this strategy?

READING THE CAUSAL ANALYSIS ESSAY WITH A WRITER'S EYE

In the works that follow, the social commentator Barbara Ehrenreich examines a modern attitude toward being busy, journalist Natalie Angier looks at scientific theories about the causes of war, Gore Vidal examines the causes and results of the "war on drugs," and Richard Rhodes attacks the idea that entertainment violence leads to real violence. These essays all demonstrate the importance of **prewriting.** As you read them, you will notice that a great deal of thought went into constructing the causal connections that these writers present.

The second half of this chapter features strategies for writing the causal analysis essay (pages 296–307). If you decide to write on one of the topics that follow the four essays below, make sure that you have read the strategies section before you begin. Note that additional writing topics are listed at the end of the chapter (pages 312–315).

The Cult of Busyness

BARBARA EHRENREICH

Barbara Ehrenreich is a keen observer of the world. Writing on a wide variety of social topics, she has published scores of magazine articles and a number of books of social criticism, including the following: *Fear of Falling: The Inner Life of the Middle Class* (1989), *The Worst Years of Our Lives: Irreverent Notes on a Decade of Greed* (1990), *The Snarling Citizen* (1995), *Blood Rites: The Origins and History of the Passions of War* (1997), and *Nickel and Dimed: On (Not) Getting By in America* (2001). In the following essay, she illustrates a problem by approaching it with common sense and a clear eye.

Not too long ago a former friend and soon-to-be acquaintance called me up to tell me how busy she was. A major report, upon which her professional future depended, was due in three days; her secretary was on strike; her housekeeper had fallen into the hands of the Immigration Department; she had two hours to prepare a dinner party for eight; and she was late for her time-management class. Stress was taking its toll, she told me: her children resented the fact that she sometimes got their names mixed up, and she had taken to abusing white wine. 1

All this put me at a distinct disadvantage, since the only thing I was doing at the time was holding the phone with one hand and attempting to touch the opposite toe with the other hand, a pastime that I had perfected during previous telephone monologues. Not that I'm not busy too: as I listened to her, I was on the alert for the moment the dryer would shut itself off and I would have to rush to fold the clothes before they settled into a mass of incorrigible wrinkles. But if I mentioned this little deadline of mine, she might think I wasn't busy enough to need a housekeeper, so I kept on patiently saying "Hmm" until she got to her parting line: "Look, this isn't a good time for me to talk, I've got to go now." 2

I don't know when the cult of conspicuous busyness began, but it has swept up almost all the upwardly mobile, professional women I know. Already, it is getting hard to recall the days when, for example "Let's have lunch" meant something other than "I've got more important things to do than talk to you right now." There was even a time when people used to get together without the excuse of needing something to eat—when, in fact, it was considered rude to talk with your mouth full. In the old days, hardly anybody had an appointment book, and when people wanted to know what the day held in store for them, they consulted a horoscope. 3

It's not only women, of course; for both sexes, busyness has become an important insignia of upper-middle-class status. Nobody, these days, admits to having a hobby, although two or more careers—say, neurosurgery and an art dealership—is not uncommon, and I am sure we will soon be hearing more about the tribulations of the four-paycheck couple. Even those who can manage only one occupation at a time would be embarrassed to be caught doing only one *thing* at a time. Those young men who jog with their headsets on are not, as you might innocently guess, rocking out, but are absorbing the principles of international finance law or a lecture on one-minute management. Even eating, I read recently, is giving way to "grazing"—the conscious ingestion of unidentified foods while drafting a legal brief, cajoling a client on the phone, and, in ambitious cases, doing calf-toning exercises under the desk. 4

But for women, there's more at stake than conforming to another upscale standard. If you want to attract men, for example, it no longer helps to be a bimbo with time on your hands. Upscale young men seem to go for the kind of woman who plays with a full deck of credit cards, who won't cry when she's knocked to the ground while trying to board the six o'clock Eastern shuttle, and whose schedule doesn't allow for a sexual encounter lasting more than twelve minutes. Then there is the economic reality: any woman who doesn't want to wind up a case study in the feminization of poverty has to be successful at something more de- 5 manding than fingernail maintenance or come-hither looks. Hence all the bustle, my busy friends would explain—they want to succeed.

6 But if success is the goal, it seems clear to me that the fast track is headed the wrong way. Think of the people who are genuinely successful—path-breaking scientists, best-selling novelists, and designers of major new software. They are not, on the whole, the kind of people who keep glancing shiftily at their watches or making small lists entitled "To Do." On the contrary, many of these people appear to be in a daze, like the distinguished professor I once had who, in the middle of a lecture on electron spin, became so fascinated by the dispersion properties of chalk dust that he could not go on. These truly successful people are childlike, easily distractable, fey sorts, whose usual demeanor resembles that of a recently fed hobo on a warm summer evening.

7 The secret of the truly successful, I believe, is that they learned very early in life how *not* to be busy. They saw through that adage, repeated to me so often in childhood, that anything worth doing is worth doing well. The truth is, many things are worth doing only in the most slovenly, halfhearted fashion possible, and many other things are not worth doing at all. Balancing a checkbook, for example. For some reason, in our culture, this dreary exercise is regarded as the supreme test of personal maturity, business acumen, and the ability to cope with math anxiety. Yet it is a form of busyness which is exceeded in futility only by going to the additional trouble of computerizing one's checking account—and that, in turn, is only slightly less silly than taking the time to discuss, with anyone, what brand of personal computer one owns, or is thinking of buying, or has heard of others using.

8 If the truly successful manage never to be busy, it is also true that many of the busiest people will never be successful. I known this firsthand from my experience, many years ago, as a waitress. Any executive who thinks the ultimate in busyness consists of having two important phone calls on hold and a major deadline in twenty minutes, should try facing six tablefuls of clients simultaneously demanding that you give them their checks, fresh coffee, a baby seat, and a warm, spontaneous smile. Even when she's not busy, a waitress has to look busy—refilling the salt shakers and polishing all the chrome in sight—but the only reward is the minimum wage and any change that gets left on the tables. Much the same is true of other high-stress jobs, like working as a telephone operator, or doing data entry on one of the new machines that monitors your speed as you work: "success" means surviving the shift.

9 Although busyness does not lead to success, I am willing to believe that success—especially when visited on the unprepared—can cause busyness. Anyone who has invented a better mousetrap, or the contemporary equivalent, can expect to be harassed by strangers demanding that you read their unpublished manuscripts or undergo the humiliation of public speaking, usually on remote Midwestern campuses. But if it is true that success leads to more busyness and less time for worthwhile activities—like talking (and listening) to friends, reading novels, or putting in some volunteer time for a good cause—then who needs it? It would be sad to have come so far—or at least to have run so hard—only to lose each other.

STYLE AND STRATEGY
1. The sarcasm with which Ehrenreich opens is so well done that it draws us into the essay.
2. The thesis appears in paragraph 7. It has greater impact here than at the beginning of the essay because Ehrenreich needs to explain and condemn the "cult of busyness" before she explains that busyness is not a prerequisite for success.
3. Paragraphs 6–8 help explain the paradox.
4. Definition, which appears in paragraphs 4, 5, and 6, is used to explain the creation of certain phenomena caused by the "cult of busyness." The author also uses definition to explain what she means by the "truly successful" person.
5. The last line of the essay usually prompts class discussion about the purpose of this selection: to show that all of this busyness prevents us from appreciating what is most important in life—"each other."

Vocabulary

The following terms are identified by paragraph number. Make sure that you understand each term's meaning in its context. If you're not sure that you understand a term, look it up in a college-level dictionary.

pastime (2)	tribulations (4)	distractable (6)
monologue (2)	ingestion (4)	fey (6)
incorrigible (2)	upscale (5)	demeanor (6)
conspicuous (3)	feminization (5)	adage (7)
upwardly mobile (3)	shiftily (6)	slovenly (7)
insignia (4)	dispersion (6)	acumen (7)
neurosurgery (4)		

Style and Strategy

1. Describe the way Ehrenreich opens her essay. Is her introduction effective? Why or why not?
2. What is the author's thesis? Where has she placed it?
3. Ehrenreich presents the contemporary "cult of busyness" as a *paradox,* a statement that seems contradictory but that is nevertheless true. Explain this paradox.
4. Find two instances where the author uses definition (see Chapter 11). How does her use of definition support her causal analysis?
5. Do you accept Ehrenreich's conclusion? Why or why not?

QUESTIONS FOR CRITICAL THINKING AND DISCUSSION Both prompts encourage close analysis of the text, and both can be turned into writing prompts.

Questions for Critical Thinking and Discussion

1. "Success in United States culture is becoming more and more dependent on personal image. It doesn't matter whether you're any good at what you do as long as you *say* you're good at what you do and look and dress the part." Do you agree or disagree with this statement?
2. Over the past twenty years, the media have devoted considerable attention to Americans who are too busy to pause for breath. Yet it is likely that these career-fixated, time-obsessed people are still a distinct minority. The majority still follow the example of Homer Simpson: come home at 5:30, eat supper, and watch television. What have you observed about people and their attitudes toward work? Have you noticed any differences between the way women approach this issue of work versus leisure time and the way men do?

SUGGESTIONS FOR WRITING Item 2 is easier to approach because students can readily focus on a concrete subject for discussion.

Suggestions for Writing

1. Write a 500- to 750-word essay in which you analyze a well-intentioned approach to solving a problem or completing a project that got bogged down. Consider what caused the problem. Were there defects in the planning stage and/or misplaced priorities?

2. Write a 500- to 750-word essay about a person who has a positive reputation that is unearned. How did this person come to be seen as smart, able, kind, or "cool"?

Is War Our Biological Destiny?

NATALIE ANGIER

Natalie Angier worked as a staff writer for *Time* and *Discover* before joining the *New York Times* in 1990 as a writer specializing in science. She was awarded the Pulitzer prize in 1991. Among her books are *The Beauty of the Beastly: New Views on the Nature of Life* (1995) and *Women: An Intimate Geography* (1999).

In the following essay, first published in the *New York Times* on November 11, 2003, Angier explores the causes of war. Is war somehow caused by human genetics, or is it a learned behavior?

In these days of hidebound militarism and round-robin carnage, when even that beloved ambassador of peace, the Dalai Lama, says it may be necessary to counter terrorism with violence, it's fair to ask: Is humanity doomed? Are we born for the battlefield—congenitally, hormonally incapable of putting war behind us? Is there no alternative to the bullet-riddled trapdoor, short of mass sedation or a Marshall Plan* for our DNA? 1

Was Plato right that "Only the dead have seen the end of war"? 2

In the heartening if admittedly provisional opinion of a number of researchers who study warfare, aggression, and the evolutionary roots of conflict, the great philosopher was, for once, whistling in a cave. As they see it, blood lust and the desire to wage war are by no means innate. To the contrary, recent studies in the field of game theory show just how readily human beings establish cooperative networks with one another, and how quickly a cooperative strategy reaches a point of so-called fixation. Researchers argue that one need not be a Pollyanna, or even an aging hippie, to imagine a human future in which war is rare and universally condemned. 3

They point out that slavery was long an accepted fact of life; if your side lost the battle, tough break, the wife and kids were shipped off as slaves to the victors. Now, when cases of slavery arise in the news, they are considered perverse and unseemly. 4

The incentive to make war similarly anachronistic is enormous, say the researchers, though they worry that it may take the dropping of another nuclear bomb in the middle of a battlefield before everybody gets the message. "I know not with what weapons World War III will be fought," Albert Einstein said, "but World War IV will be fought with sticks and stones." 5

Admittedly, war making will be a hard habit to shake. "There have been very few times in the history of civilization when there hasn't been a war going on somewhere," said Victor Davis Hanson, a military historian and classicist at California State University in Fresno. He cites a brief period between A.D. 100 and A.D. 200 as perhaps the only time of world peace, the result of the Roman Empire's having everyone, fleetingly, in its thrall. 6

Archaeologists and anthropologists have found evidence of militarism in perhaps 95 percent of the cultures they have examined or unearthed. Time and again 7

***Marshall Plan:** a program of economic aid and loans from the United States that helped the countries of western Europe recover from World War II.

groups initially lauded as gentle and peace-loving—the Mayas, the !Kung of the Kalahari, Margaret Mead's Samoans—eventually were outed as being no less bestial than the rest of us. A few isolated cultures have managed to avoid war for long stretches. The ancient Minoans, for example, who populated Crete and the surrounding Aegean Islands, went 1,500 years battle-free; it didn't hurt that they had a strong navy to deter would-be conquerors.

8 Warriors have often been the most esteemed of their group, the most coveted mates. And if they weren't loved for themselves, their spears were good courtship accessories. This year, geneticists found evidence that Genghis Khan, the 13th century Mongol emperor, fathered so many offspring as he slashed through Asia that 16 million men, or half a percent of the world's male population, could be his descendants.

9 Wars are romanticized, subjects of an endless, cross-temporal, transcultural spool of poems, songs, plays, paintings, novels, films. The battlefield is mythologized as the furnace in which character and nobility are forged; and, oh, what a thrill it can be. "The rush of battle is a potent and often lethal addiction," writes Chris Hedges, a reporter for The New York Times who has covered wars, in "War Is a Force That Gives Us Meaning." Even with its destruction and carnage, he adds, war "can give us what we long for in life."

10 "It can give us purpose, meaning, a reason for living," he continues.

11 Nor are humans the only great apes to indulge in the elixir. Common chimpanzees, which share about 98 percent of their genes with humans, also wage war: gangs of neighboring males meet at the borderline of their territories with the express purpose of exterminating their opponents. So many males are lost to battle that the sex ratio among adult chimpanzees is two females for every male.

12 And yet there are other drugs on the market, other behaviors to sate the savage beast. Dr. Frans de Waal, a primatologist and professor of psychology at Emory University, points out that a different species of chimpanzee, the bonobo, chooses love over war, using a tantric array of sexual acts to resolve any social problems that arise. Serious bonobo combat is rare, and the male-to-female ratio is, accordingly, 1:1. Bonobos are as closely related to humans as are common chimpanzees, so take your pick of which might offer deeper insight into the primal "roots" of human behavior.

13 Or how about hamadryas baboons? They're surly, but not silly. If you throw a peanut in front of a male, Dr. de Waal said, it will pick it up happily and eat it. Throw the same peanut in front of two male baboons, and they'll ignore it. "They'll act as if it doesn't exist," he said. "It's not worth a fight between two fully grown males."

14 Even the ubiquitousness of warfare in human history doesn't impress researchers. "When you consider it was only about 13,000 years ago that we discovered agriculture, and that most of what we're calling human history occurred since then," said Dr. David Sloan Wilson, a biology and anthropology professor at Binghamton University in New York, "you see what a short amount of time we've had to work toward global peace."

15 In that brief time span, the size of cooperative groups has grown steadily, and by many measures more pacific. Maybe 100 million people died in the world wars of the 20th century. Yet Dr. Lawrence H. Keeley, a professor of anthropology at the University of Illinois at Chicago, has estimated that if the proportion of casualties in the modern era were to equal that seen in many conflicts among preindustrial groups, then perhaps two billion people would have died.

16 Indeed, national temperaments seem capable of rapid, radical change. The Vikings slaughtered and plundered; their descendants in Sweden haven't fought a war in nearly 200 years, while the Danes reserve their fighting spirit for negotiating better vacation packages. The tribes of highland New Guinea were famous for small-scale warfare, said Dr. Peter J. Richerson, an expert in cultural evolution at the University of California at Davis. "But when, after World War II, the Australian police patrols went around and told people they couldn't fight anymore, the New Guineans thought that was wonderful," Dr. Richerson said. "They were glad to have an excuse."

17 Dr. Wilson cites the results of game theory experiments: participants can adopt a cheating strategy to try to earn more for themselves, but at the risk of everybody's losing, or a cooperative strategy with all earning a smaller but more reliable reward. In laboratories around the world, researchers have found that participants implement the mutually beneficial strategy, in which cooperators are rewarded and non-cooperators are punished. "It shows in a very simple and powerful way that it's easy to get cooperation to evolve to fixation, for it to be the successful strategy," he said. There is no such quantifiable evidence or theoretical underpinning in favor of Man the Warrior, he added.

18 As Dr. de Waal and many others see it, the way to foment peace is to encourage interdependency among nations, as in the European Union. "Imagine if France were to invade Germany now," he said. "That would upset every aspect of their economic world," not the least one being France's reliance on the influx of German tourists. "It's not as if Europeans all love each other," Dr. de Waal said. "But you're not promoting love, you're promoting economic calculations."

19 It's not just the money. Who can put a price tag on the pleasures to be had from that wholesome, venerable sport—making fun of the tourists?

Vocabulary

The following terms are identified by paragraph number. Make sure that you understand each term's meaning in its context. If you're not sure that you understand a term, look it up in a college-level dictionary.

hidebound (1)	classicist (6)	sate (12)
militarism (1)	fleetingly (6)	tantric (12)
carnage (1)	thrall (6)	ubiquitousness (14)
congeniality (1)	lauded (7)	subterranean (12)
sedation (1)	outed (7)	pacific (15)
provisional (3)	bestial (7)	foment (18)
fixation (3)	cross-temporal (9)	influx (18)
anachronistic (5)	elixir (11)	venerable (19)

Style and Strategy

1. What is the tone of this essay? Is the tone suitable to the subject and the thesis?
2. Is this essay's thesis directly stated or implicitly stated? In your own words, restate Angier's thesis in one sentence.

STYLE AND STRATEGY

1. The essay's tone is sophisticated but not formal. Angier's approach is serious but also energetic, forthright, and colorful. While somewhat unorthodox for an essay that discusses the possibility of avoiding world annihilation, her tone is appropriate to the audience, and it works well. After all, most readers of the *New York Times* are generalists, people who might not want to plod through the kind of prose some times heavy and specialized—found in foreign-relations journals.
2. The thesis appears in paragraph 3.
3. Information in paragraph 8, as well as that in paragraphs 9, 10, and 11, helps present the opposing argument, which Angier must discuss first if she is to convince the reader that she has thought about this issue seriously and systematically. In short, these paragraphs

establish her authority and credibility.
4. Each of these arguments is persuasive. You can launch an excellent classrooom discussion by asking students to explain and argue for their favorite. This question can also be used as a prompt for a short writing or for a journal

entry, from which class discussion can then be launched.
5. Paragraphs 15 and 16 use comparison/contrast; paragraph 17 uses process analysis.

QUESTIONS FOR CRITICAL THINKING AND DISCUSSION
1. This item can be used as a prompt for narrative writing and will allow students to practice interviewing skills.
2–4. These items make excellent prompts for classroom discussion. However, they can also be used as prompts for short argumentative essays in which students state a position and then support it with historical facts, illustrations, and anecdotes. All three produce effective essays, but you might want to discuss each prompt ahead of time in class or during an office conference.

SUGGESTIONS FOR WRITING These prompts encourage students to think carefully. It helps to discuss in class the kind of response you expect as a way to introduce them. Try assembling students into groups, each of which brainstorms information about one of the four prompts. Whether students answer the question positively or negatively, they should be urged to provide concrete details and logical arguments to support their responses. When the class reassembles, ask each group to report. Before you dismiss the class,

3. In paragraph 8, Angier cites the example of the estimated number of the descendants of Genghis Khan. What purpose does this example serve?
4. Starting in paragraph 14, Angier cites four authorities who support the idea that the habit of war can be "unlearned." Which of these opinions best supports Angier's analysis? Why?
5. Explain how Angier uses (a) process analysis (see Chapter 9) and (b) comparison/contrast (see Chapter 13) to help develop her thesis.

Questions for Critical Thinking and Discussion

1. Have you, a relative, or a friend ever been directly affected by a war or a military action? If so, how did the event occur? What were its effects?
2. Consider some ways in which war can be seen as a positive process. What are some acceptable reasons for waging war, and what are some possible benefits of war?
3. Do you believe that the future will contain fewer wars, as Angier suggests is possible? Explain your answer.
4. Respond to this statement: "Once the speeches and the flag waving are out of the way, nations always fight wars for the same reason: economic gain." Do you agree? Why or why not?

Suggestions for Writing

Angier wrote her essay while realizing that many people view war as an unfortunate inevitability of human experience. However, she points out that war is a "learned" experience for humans, not a biological necessity. Choose one of the following topics, and write a similar essay of 500–750 words:

1. Proportionately, teenagers are involved in more traffic accidents than any other age group. Is this situation inevitable?
2. Every year, a substantial proportion of first-year college students will drop out of school. Is this situation inevitable?
3. Statistically, people living in poverty are arrested more often than people at other socioeconomic levels. Is this situation inevitable?
4. At all socioeconomic levels, men are arrested more often for violent crime than women are. Is this situation inevitable?

Drugs

GORE VIDAL

Novelist, playwright, screenwriter, actor, and political commentator, Gore Vidal has alternately edified and infuriated his audience for more than fifty years. As an unabashed political independent, Vidal has found himself arguing unorthodox and/or unpopular positions for decades. He published his first novel, *Williwaw* (1946), at the age of nineteen, and has written more than thirty books, including *Burr* (1973), *1876* (1976), *Duluth* (1983), *Lincoln* (1984), *Empire* (1987), and *The Golden Age* (2000).

"Drugs," first published in 1970 in the *New York Times*, examines both the causes and the effects of the ongoing American war on illegal narcotics.

It is possible to stop most drug addiction in the United States within a very short time. Simply make all drugs available and sell them at cost. Label each drug with a precise description of what effect—good and bad—the drug will have on the taker. This will require heroic honesty. Don't say that marijuana is addictive or dangerous when it is neither, as millions of people know—unlike "speed," which kills most unpleasantly, or heroin, which is addictive and difficult to kick.

remind students that this assignment lends itself to the inclusion of library and Internet research.

For the record, I have tried—once—almost every drug and liked none, disproving the popular Fu Manchu theory that a single whiff of opium will enslave the mind. Nevertheless many drugs are bad for certain people to take and they should be told why in a sensible way.

Along with exhortation and warning, it might be good for our citizens to recall (or learn for the first time) that the United States was the creation of men who believed that each man has the right to do what he wants with his own life as long as he does not interfere with his neighbor's pursuit of happiness (that his neighbor's idea of happiness is persecuting others does confuse matters a bit).

This is a startling notion to the current generation of Americans. They reflect a system of public education which has made the Bill of Rights, literally, unacceptable to a majority of high school graduates (see the annual Purdue reports) who now form the "silent majority"—a phrase which that underestimated wit Richard Nixon took from Homer who used it to describe the dead.

Now one can hear the warning rumble begin: if everyone is allowed to take drugs everyone will and the GNP will decrease, the Commies will stop us from making everyone free, and we shall end up a race of Zombies, passively murmuring "groovie" to one another. Alarming thought. Yet it seems most unlikely that any reasonably sane person will become a drug addict if he knows in advance what addiction is going to be like.

Is everyone reasonably sane? No. Some people will always become drug addicts just as some people will always become alcoholics, and it is just too bad. Every man, however, has the power (and should have the legal right) to kill himself if he chooses. But since most men don't, they won't be mainliners either. Nevertheless, forbidding people things they like or think they might enjoy only makes them want those things all the more. This psychological insight is, for some mysterious reason, perennially denied our governors.

It is a lucky thing for the American moralist that our country has always existed in a kind of time-vacuum: we have no public memory of anything that happened before last Tuesday. No one in Washington today recalls what happened during the years alcohol was forbidden to the people by a Congress that thought it had a divine mission to stamp out Demon Rum—launching, in the process, the greatest crime wave in the country's history, causing thousands of deaths from bad alcohol, and creating a general (and persisting) contempt among the citizenry for the laws of the United States.

The same thing is happening today. But the government has learned nothing from past attempts at prohibition, not to mention repression.

Last year when the supply of Mexican marijuana was slightly curtailed by the Feds, the pushers got the kids hooked on heroin and deaths increased dramatically, particularly in New York. Whose fault? Evil men like the Mafiosi? Permissive Dr. Spock? Wild-eyed Dr. Leary? No.

The Government of the United States was responsible for those deaths. The bureaucratic machine has a vested interest in playing cops and robbers. Both the

Bureau of Narcotics and the Mafia want strong laws against the sale and use of drugs because if drugs are sold at cost there would be no money in it for anyone.

11 If there was no money in it for the Mafia, there would be no friendly playground pushers, and addicts would not commit crimes to pay for the next fix. Finally, if there was no money in it, the Bureau of Narcotics would wither away, something they are not about to do without a struggle.

12 Will anything sensible be done? Of course not. The American people are as devoted to the idea of sin and its punishment as they are to making money—and fighting drugs is nearly as big a business as pushing them. Since the combination of sin and money is irresistible (particularly to the professional politician), the situation will only grow worse.

Vocabulary

The following terms are identified by paragraph number. Make sure that you understand each term's meaning in its context. If you're not sure that you understand a term, look it up in a college-level dictionary.

exhortation (3)	prohibition (8)	vested interest (10)
mainliners (6)	curtailed (9)	wither (11)
perennially (6)	bureaucratic machine (10)	

STYLE AND STRATEGY
1. Vidal's proposal appears in paragraph 1, where it draws us into the essay.
2. Causes can be found in paragraphs 3, 4, 6, 7, 11, and 12.
3. Effects can be found in paragraphs 6, 8, 9, and 12.
4. Students have little trouble identifying sarcasm in this piece.
5. Paragraphs 6 and 12 use rhetorical questions as a way to allow the author to create a dramatic introduction to his opinions and to maintain reader interest.

Style and Strategy

1. What is Vidal's proposal? Does he qualify or weaken it in any way? Where does he present it, and what is the effect of its placement in the essay?
2. List the causes that Vidal cites for the ongoing American war on illegal substances.
3. List the effects of the war on illegal substances, as Vidal sees them.
4. How would you describe Vidal's tone?
5. A *rhetorical question* is one asked by a writer who really doesn't want an answer but wants to raise the issue mentioned in the question. Where in this essay does Vidal use rhetorical questions? In what way does he use them? What is their effect?

QUESTIONS FOR CRITICAL THINKING AND DISCUSSION These items are intended to encourage rereading of the essay and close analysis.

Questions for Critical Thinking and Discussion

1. What would the United States be like if all currently illegal drugs could be sold legitimately? Would our society find a way to accommodate the open use of these drugs, or would chaos reign?
2. Do you think that people who do not take illegal drugs would try them if they were legal?
3. Most adult Americans believe that marijuana is less harmful than alcohol, but alcohol is legal (and culturally accepted) whereas possession of marijuana will lead straight to arrest. Moreover, some commentators believe that this apparent paradox reflects the power struggle among the American social classes—in other words, the rich make the rules and the

rich prefer alcohol, so drinking is encouraged whereas smoking pot is a criminal offense. Do you agree or disagree?

4. "If all drugs were legalized, the inner-city ghetto and barrio would disappear." What is the reasoning behind this comment?
5. Reread paragraph 12. What assumptions does Vidal make here about the American public and its government? Do you agree? Why or why not?

Suggestions for Writing

SUGGESTIONS FOR WRITING All three items can be used as prompts for a fully documented research paper.

1. Write a 500- to 750-word essay about a social program or policy that doesn't seem worth the trouble—in other words, the effects of this program fail to justify the program's costs.
2. When Vidal writes about the rise of organized crime during the 1920s, he is referring to the Law of Unintended Consequences. In other words, the federal government made the sale of alcoholic beverages illegal; then, to everyone's horror, organized, vicious criminals appeared to satisfy the national demand for alcohol. Write a 500- to 750-word essay about a situation in which a change in a policy or procedure brought about an unintended consequence—whether positive or negative.
3. Write a 500- to 750-word essay in which you argue for a change in or the reversal of a college policy that you believe is counterproductive or unfair. Try to predict the effects of this change or reversal, using as much detail as possible in order to support your thesis and convince your readers.

Hollow Claims About Fantasy Violence

RICHARD RHODES

Richard Rhodes is best known for his *The Making of the Atomic Bomb* (1987), which was awarded the Pulitzer Prize for Nonfiction, the National Book Award, and a National Book Critics Circle Award. He is also the author of eighteen other books, including *Nuclear Renewal: Common Sense About Energy* (1993), *Dark Sun: The Making of the Hydrogen Bomb* (1995), *Why They Kill: The Discoveries of a Maverick Criminologist* (1999), and *Masters of Death: The SS-Einsatzgruppen and the Invention of the Holocaust* (2002).

"Hollow Claims About Fantasy Violence," which first appeared in the *New York Times* on September 17, 2000, challenges beliefs held by many laypersons as well as many social scientists. Does violent entertainment cause violent behavior? Rhodes doesn't think so.

1 The moral entrepreneurs are at it again, pounding the entertainment industry for advertising its Grand Guignolesque* confections to children. If exposure to this mock violence contributes to the development of violent behavior, then our political leadership is justified in its indignation at what the Federal Trade Commission has reported about the marketing of violent fare to children. Senators John McCain and Joseph Lieberman have been especially quick to fasten on the FTC report as they make an issue of violent offerings to children.

2 But is there really a link between entertainment and violent behavior?

3 The American Medical Association, the American Psychological Association, the American Academy of Pediatrics, and the National Institute of Mental Health all

*__Grand Guignolesque:__ referring to a Parisian theater that specialized in productions that were designed to shock and horrify audiences.

say yes. They base their claims on social science research that has been sharply criticized and disputed within the social science profession, especially outside the United States. In fact, no direct, causal link between exposure to mock violence in the media and subsequent violent behavior has ever been demonstrated, and the few claims of modest correlation have been contradicted by other findings, sometimes in the same studies.

4 History alone should call such a link into question. Private violence has been declining in the West since the media-barren late Middle Ages, when homicide rates are estimated to have been 10 times what they are in Western nations today. Historians attribute the decline to improving social controls over violence—police forces and common access to courts of law—and to a shift away from brutal physical punishment in child-rearing (a practice that still appears as a common factor in the background of violent criminals today).

5 The American Medical Association has based its endorsement of the media violence theory in major part on the studies of Brandon Centerwall, a psychiatrist in Seattle. Dr. Centerwall compared the murder rates for whites in three countries from 1945 to 1974 with numbers for television set ownership. Until 1975, television broadcasting was banned in South Africa, and "white homicide rates remained stable" there, Dr. Centerwall found, while corresponding rates in Canada and the United States doubled after television was introduced.

6 A spectacular finding, but it is meaningless. As Franklin E. Zimring and Gordon Hawkins of the University of California at Berkeley subsequently pointed out, homicide rates in France, Germany, Italy, and Japan either failed to change with increasing television ownership in the same period or actually declined, and American homicide rates have more recently been sharply declining despite a proliferation of popular media outlets—not only movies and television but also video games and the Internet.

7 Other social science that supposedly undergirds the theory, too, is marginal and problematic. Laboratory studies that expose children to selected incidents of televised mock violence and then assess changes in the children's behavior have sometimes found more "aggressive" behavior after the exposure—usually verbal, occasionally physical.

8 But sometimes the control group, shown incidents judged not to be violent, behaves more aggressively afterward than the test group; sometimes comedy produces the more aggressive behavior; and sometimes there's no change. The only obvious conclusion is that sitting and watching television stimulates subsequent physical activity. Any kid could tell you that.

9 As for those who claim that entertainment promotes violent behavior by desensitizing people to violence, the British scholar Martin Barker offers this critique: "Their claim is that the materials they judge to be harmful can only influence us by trying to make us be the same as them. So horrible things will make us horrible—not horrified. Terrifying things will make us terrifying—not terrified. To see something aggressive makes us feel aggressive—not aggressed against. This idea is so odd, it is hard to know where to begin in challenging it."

10 Even more influential on national policy has been a 22-year study by two University of Michigan psychologists, Leonard D. Eron and L. Rowell Huesmann, of boys exposed to so-called violent media. The Telecommunications Act of 1996, which mandated the television V-chip, allowing parents to screen out unwanted program-

ming, invoked these findings, asserting, "Studies have shown that children exposed to violent video programming at a young age have a higher tendency for violent and aggressive behavior later in life than children not so exposed."

11 Well, not exactly. Following 875 children in upstate New York from third grade through high school, the psychologists found a correlation between a preference for violent television at age 8 and aggressiveness at age 18. The correlation—0.31—would mean television accounted for about 10 percent of the influences that led to this behavior. But the correlation only turned up in one of three measures of aggression: the assessment of students by their peers. It didn't show up in students' reports about themselves or in psychological testing. And for girls, there was no correlation at all.

12 Despite the lack of evidence, politicians can't resist blaming the media for violence. They can stake out the moral high ground confident that the First Amendment will protect them from having to actually write legislation that would be likely to alienate the entertainment industry. Some use the issue as a smokescreen to avoid having to confront gun control.

13 But violence isn't learned from mock violence. There is good evidence—causal evidence, not correlational—that it's learned in personal violent encounters, beginning with the brutalization of children by their parents or their peers.

14 The money spent on all the social science research I've described was diverted from the National Institute of Mental Health budget by reducing support for the construction of community mental health centers. To this day there is no standardized reporting system for emergency-room findings of physical child abuse. Violence is on the decline in America, but if we want to reduce it even further, protecting children from real violence in their real lives—not the pale shadow of mock violence—is the place to begin.

Vocabulary

The following terms are identified by paragraph number. Make sure that you understand each term's meaning in its context. If you're not sure that you understand a term, look it up in a college-level dictionary.

entrepreneur (1)	barren (4)	desensitizing (9)
Grand Guignol (1)	attribute (4)	critique (9)
confections (1)	endorsement (5)	mandated (10)
mock (1)	proliferation (6)	invoked (10)
indignation (1)	undergird (7)	smokescreen (12)
fare (1)	marginal (7)	diverted (14)

Style and Strategy

1. In paragraph 1, Rhodes refers to the "moral entrepreneurs." What does he mean by this term?
2. Rhodes uses an implicit thesis statement. State his thesis in your own words.
3. What does Rhodes see as the real cause of juvenile violence?
4. In analyzing a very complicated and controversial subject, Rhodes refers

STYLE AND STRATEGY
1. Rhodes implies strongly that those accusing the media of promoting violence have something to gain by taking this stand.
2. Answering the question in paragraph 2 will lead students to the author's thesis.
3. Paragraphs 4 and 13 should be discussed in response to this question.
4. Responses vary, but this is an essay that uses and responds to researched information in a manner that can serve as a model for students.

QUESTIONS FOR CRITICAL THINKING AND DISCUSSION
1. This item can be used both as a prompt for

class discussion and as a writing assignment.
2. In discussing censorship, you might ask students to focus on a particular subtopic such as censoring the Internet or censoring the music industry.

SUGGESTIONS FOR WRITING All four prompts call for the inclusion of researched materials. You might advise students to begin with a short discussion of the commonly accepted cause that includes an explanation about why so many people accept it. They might spend the rest of the essay arguing for the real cause.

to a number of studies and authorities, sometimes specifically and sometimes more generally. In your opinion, does he present a convincing analysis? Explain.

Questions for Critical Thinking and Discussion

1. "Rhodes may be right about violent entertainment not causing violent behavior. However, the barrage of media violence faced by Americans of all ages is coarsening us as a people. We *are* becoming desensitized to violence, if to the extent only that reports of it on the news don't affect us the way they might have in the past." Do you agree?
2. Do you believe in censorship? If not, do you believe that under certain circumstances you could change your mind? Explain.

Suggestions for Writing

Rhodes's essay is about *false* (or *spurious*) *causality*—the tendency of people to believe they understand the cause of a phenomenon even without sufficient proof. Write a 500- to 750-word essay in which you examine one of the following phenomena and explain why its commonly accepted cause is not its real cause:

1. Why the U.S. high school dropout rate is very high
2. Why many U.S. teenage girls become pregnant before marriage
3. Why many U.S. college students gain weight during their freshman year
4. Why the voting rate among U.S. college students is very low

MORE OPTIONS ONLINE If you would like to read additional causal analysis essays, go to **www.mhhe.com/writingtoday**.

WRITING THE CAUSAL ANALYSIS ESSAY WITH A READER'S EYE

Causal analysis essays must have a logical, believable development; otherwise, they will not connect with their audience and will fail to accomplish their purpose. The advice that follows will help you think like your reader as you consider your assignment and then prewrite, draft, revise, and edit your causal analysis essay.

Issues to Keep in Mind

The usual purpose of a causal analysis essay is to explain a situation to the reader. Consequently, as you begin to plan your essay, you will need to consider the best way to present causes and/or effects. Thinking about the following two issues will help you as you prepare:

1. Considering the nature and importance of each cause or effect
2. Choosing internal development strategies

Weighing Causes or Effects

Three critical issues in developing a causal analysis essay are the following:

1. **Determining major causes and/or effects and then concentrating on them.** Many events, policies, or situations have more than one cause and result in more than one effect. Because of this complexity, writers often have to sort out primary causes or effects from minor ones or even from false ones. One pitfall that you need to watch out for in particular is building an essay on a bad foundation—a cause or effect that turns out to be minor—while the essay ignores the much more important—and obvious—primary cause or effect.

   To avoid this potential problem, you need to spend the time necessary to consider—and weigh—all of the causes or effects. As you prewrite, don't just seize the first causes or effects that come to mind. Evaluate the results of your prewriting to determine the *most* important causes or effects; then concentrate on these as you develop your essay. For example, suppose you write about the *nearest* cause—the one that happened closest in time to the situation you are considering—as if it were the sole reason for the situation. But reality is complicated; the *nearest* cause may not be the *primary* cause. Notice how the writer of the following passage avoids this error by moving from an immediate, superficial reason for a new law to a less obvious but more substantial one:

   The city council has stated that the guidelines it recently passed to curtail downtown activity are meant "to bring stability to the central business district in the nighttime hours." Thus, more police officers will now patrol the sidewalks and check for violations of the open-container law, apprehend the inebriated, and enforce the parking regulations, which now extend around the clock.

   Yes, downtown activity will be "controlled" all right—to the point of extinction. And this is the council's true motive. The city council—and, presumably, their most vocal constituents—are made uncomfortable by the strange-looking young people who congregate downtown after hours to hear the latest bands in the most current club. Surely they must be sent away.

   This metropolis was a much smaller city only a few decades ago, and it is still run as if the year were 1959. The city council members are always mourning the death of "family values," and clearly the young people with the brilliant hair, the tattoos, and the pierced noses and lips don't have a place in the family values picture. But here's where the city council has missed the point: without those clubs, downtown is as dead as a post. The kids spend money, they cause very little real trouble, and they make this city a greater draw than it would be otherwise. Perhaps the city council members should actually go downtown and watch. In fact, they could go along with me; I'm a cop, and I've spent the last year patrolling the downtown district. Perhaps the "family values" crowd could then get past their horror over weird hair and look at the vibrant downtown scene for what it is: a cultural and financial bonanza.

   On the other hand, sometimes the primary cause is important but doesn't warrant much discussion. Suppose, for example, that your area has been ravaged by wildfires that have been able to spread because of an ongoing drought. The primary cause of this situation is a shift in the El Niño weather patterns. Although this shift needs to be mentioned in any discussion of the causes of the fires, there is very little that can be done about it—scientists can't, at this point, reprogram El Niño. Hence, even though the drought is a secondary cause, writers will probably concentrate on its nature, predictions about its duration, and ways to counter its effects in order to prevent additional fires.

You will also need to keep the big picture in mind when you write about effects. For instance, suppose that your school has decided to increase fees by fifty dollars per student per year in order to augment its construction fund. An essay in which you complain about the narrow, short-term effect of this increase on students (meaning the writer of the essay, who is speaking personally) would probably appear to be self-indulgent because the writer is not considering the long-term effects of the increase. Wouldn't it be nice to have an extra parking lot or two so that students could park more quickly and get to their classes sooner, thus ending the usual morning madness? Even if the parking lots will not be completed until after the writer graduates, he or she will gain credibility by considering long-term benefits rather than debating the issue solely in terms of how it affects students right now. Composition instructors tend to view causal analysis essays written with a narrow, self-interested focus as products of immaturity; the responsible writer will look instead to the larger picture.

Thus, it is essential to weigh all possible causes or effects when you are preparing to write a causal analysis essay. Peer review can help you do this at every stage. Consider showing a classmate your completed prewriting, in which you've listed all of the causes or effects and indicated the ones you consider most important. Your classmate's comments may alert you to potential problems in your thinking. Also, keep in mind that a causal essay is easy to "repair" early in the process, but if it is not built on a solid base, it is a nightmare to revise.

2. **Mistaking correlation for causation.** Events often occur simultaneously and are even associated with each other in people's minds, but that does not necessarily mean that one event has caused the other, only that they are correlated. For instance, dark, puffy cumulus clouds normally accompany rain, but do they *cause* rain? No. Rain is the product of a much more complicated **causal chain**—defined above as a scenario in which "one thing leads to another"—and cumulus clouds are but one link in that chain. As another example, you may have noticed a bitter, cold wind blowing on each of the last five mornings. At the same time, each morning you have noticed that your neighbor's dog, which lives outdoors, has been steadily barking. Did the wind cause the dog's behavior? Maybe—further investigation is required. Did the dog's barking cause the wind to blow? We hope not (tabloid headline: "Demon Dog Controls Local Climate"). As with the issue of choosing the *most* important causes or effects, you must think critically about how causation occurs: this rhetorical option requires an active brain.

3. **Recognizing the Law of Unintended Consequences.** Sometimes an organization will change one of its policies or rules with a confident sense that the organization will benefit from the effects of this new approach. However, such confidence can fall victim to the "Law of Unintended Consequences." This maxim, loosely related to the general series of laws associated with Mr. Murphy, states that we cannot know what the future will bring—that if we change the dynamics of a situation, then we cannot predict the outcome with certainty. As an example, Gore Vidal points out in "Drugs" (pages 290–292) that the American people and their legislators greatly misjudged the situation in 1919 when the legislation outlawing alcoholic beverages, known as the Volstead Act, was enacted and Prohibition became the law of the land. Americans didn't stop drinking; they just started buying their alcohol from illegal providers. Hence, organized crime was born on a national level and, of course, remains with us today.

   You need to be aware of unintended consequences in two varieties of causal analysis essays. The first is an essay in which you explain how a change in policy caused an important and unanticipated effect—much as Vidal does in "Drugs." The second is an essay in which you are exploring a "what-if" scenario. As you prewrite your essay, you need to be aware that the policy change that you are considering might have unexpected consequences of its own—ones that you might miss but that your reader could see as obvious.

Choosing Internal Strategies

Good causal analysis essays avoid a narrow, formulaic approach to their subjects. You will most likely need to use several internal strategies to develop your essay fully and to fulfill your purpose. For example, consider how the four readings in the first half of the chapter were developed:

CLASSROOM HINT
Consider taking a few minutes of class time to discuss each item, with specific reference to the essay mentioned.

- In "The Cult of Busyness," Barbara Ehrenreich uses narrative (see Chapter 7) and process analysis (Chapter 9) as she asks the question "Why are people suddenly so busy?"
- In "Is War Our Biological Destiny?" Natalie Angier uses comparison/contrast (see Chapter 13) to analyze the causes of war and to conclude that war does not necessarily need to be as much a part of humanity's future as it was of humanity's past.
- In "Drugs," Gore Vidal uses comparison and contrast (comparing the war on drugs to the previous war on alcohol—see Chapter 13) and argument (presenting these campaigns as illogical and impractical—see Chapter 14) to illustrate the unanticipated effects of the anti-drug campaign.
- In "Hollow Claims About Fantasy Violence," Richard Rhodes uses argument (see Chapter 14) to criticize the claims of those who see a link between media violence and real violence.

The internal strategies that you will need to use to develop your causal analysis will depend on your context—your subject, your focus (emphasizing cause or effect), your audience, and your purpose.

MORE OPTIONS ONLINE
For more help with problem areas in the causal analysis essay, go to **www.mhhe.com/writingtoday**.

In the "Drafting" section (pages 301–306), we will show how two student essays were developed, one concentrating on causes and the other on effects. When you read these examples, notice the number and range of internal strategies used.

Choosing a Topic

When you are writing a causal analysis essay, bear in mind that you will need to choose a topic that you can deal with adequately within the scope of the assignment. If you have been assigned a topic, you will still need to narrow it down to a manageable size. You should also decide whether to concentrate on causes or effects or both and consider whether you will need to do some research in order to gain a fuller understanding of your topic.

1. Choose a topic that you can deal with. Would any of the following be good topics for a causal analysis essay?
   - The reasons behind the Civil War
   - Why salmon migrate upstream
   - The fallout from the Great Depression

   Perhaps these topics would work, if you don't mind writing an essay the length of an encyclopedia. If that prospect doesn't appeal to you, could you investigate causes and effects by limiting one of these topics into a more specific, manageable form? Certainly, but note how even a very limited version of each of the above ideas might be hard to handle in a 750-word essay:
   - The South went to war against the North because it followed the hotheads of a relatively unimportant state, South Carolina, rather than the more reasoned attitudes of a key state, Virginia.
   - What is important about the spawning migration of salmon is not that they swim upstream, swim downstream, or perhaps hitchhike; it's that they are genetically programmed to return home to breed.
   - One effect of the Great Depression is our current crop of retirees, the richest group of older people in our nation's history, who still eat at early-bird specials and order water with meals.

   Handling any of these revised topics in under a thousand words would be difficult. The more you limit your topic, the better you can control the resulting essay. One way to test the "size" of your topic is to measure the amount of prewriting that you produce. If your prewriting seems to go on forever, you probably need to scale down the size of your topic—and the reverse is also true. If you find it difficult to generate ideas in the prewriting stage, you need to broaden your topic.
2. Decide whether to concentrate on causes or effects or both. As we discuss in the introduction to this chapter (see pages 280–284), this decision is usually a fairly straightforward one—your subject matter and writing context tend to make the decision for you.
3. Consider the possible need to research the topic and, if so, the kind of research you will need to conduct. Whether your instructor has assigned a specific topic or set of topics from which to choose or you are choosing

your own topic, you will need to decide if the topic is within your "comfort zone" of knowledge or is one that you need to research in the library or on the Internet. For a personal topic, you can usually rely on your own knowledge. For most other topics, however, you may need to conduct research either for specific information or for general background knowledge in order to write authoritatively. Chapters 20 and 21 offer advice on locating and documenting library and Internet sources.

Prewriting

As mentioned, causal analysis essays are easy to fix in the early stages but hard to revise if the fundamental analysis is wrong. The following approach will help you to generate ideas. First, use an informal, idea-gathering strategy such as brainstorming, clustering, or freewriting to develop possible causes or effects (see Chapter 2, pages 31–34). Review your results carefully. At this point, you may want to stop, come back later, and prewrite some more. If you have determined that you need to research your topic, this is the time to do so. As we discuss in "Issues to Keep in Mind" (pages 296–300), your analysis of your prewriting is crucial: your essay must concentrate on major causes or effects, must avoid confusing cause and correlation, and must not miss any obvious (and important) causes or effects that an able reader would expect to see. Make sure that you have done thorough prewriting before you go on to the organizing stage. Consider having a peer reviewer go over your prewriting as well and give you his or her thoughts on your analysis.

Organizing

After your prewriting, you should have a good idea of how to "shape" your essay. You may be writing about multiple effects stemming from a single cause or about a major effect caused by multiple factors. If your prewriting indicates a causal chain (one factor causing another, which causes another, and so on), keep in mind that your essay will most likely employ a narrative framework. Now is the time to build a thorough sentence outline. (For help with sentence outlines, see Chapter 2, pages 40–42.) When you review your completed outline, you will have a good sense of where your essay will go, and you may also find some weaknesses, which are much easier to correct at this stage than later in the writing process. As in the prewriting stage, consider having a peer reviewer go over your outline at this point; a second pair of eyes—and accompanying brain—are always helpful.

Drafting

Because causal analysis includes two differing strategies, we have included two causal analysis essays: "Listening Intently," which explores the causes of an ironic world view, and "Never a Dull Moment," which looks at the unintended effects of a change in educational policy.

Consider Your Options

As is true of other types of writing, introductions to causal analysis essays can take a variety of forms. Consider description or definition as strategies to build an effective introduction. Other strategies are to contradict a popular opinion or belief, to define a controversial issue, to state a problem, or to ask a question that the rest of the essay will answer.

The Introduction

In the introduction to your causal analysis essay, you need to provide your reader sufficient context: your reader needs the background of your subject. Sometimes, this situation requires two or more introductory paragraphs, but in most essays of under 1,000 words, a single, well-developed paragraph will suffice.

Both of the introductory paragraphs that follow were written after the writer had completed the body of the essay. Since causal analysis can be a fairly complex option, developing the essay first and then creating its introduction is frequently a good idea. With this approach, you avoid the danger that your body paragraphs will drift away from what your introduction has promised.

Essay A: Cause Focus

Listening Intently

During the late 1990s, the media were obsessed with "Generation X": the slackers, the irony-transfixed whiners who seemed to have no productive place in society. In a time when wealth was readily available to those who were bright and ambitious, the Gen X crowd seemed to prefer black clothes, black coffee, and black humor. Why? Centrally, irony (and its related negativisms, cynicism and nihilism) is learned, not innate. **Three American institutions have a lot to answer for in fostering this negativity: our politicians, our schools, and our parents.**

The writer sets up his analysis by contrasting the go-go acquisitiveness of the late twentieth century with the values of the quizzical, passive generation that was just coming into adulthood at that time. The thesis statement, which appears at the end of the paragraph, is specific, pointing to three causes of the phenomenon.

Essay B: Effects Focus

Never a Dull Moment

Because of the recent budget surplus in our state, the legislature has decided to use some of the extra money to establish merit scholarships. Basically, any student who maintains a 3.0+ GPA through high school and then keeps above this threshold in college gets a sizable scholarship. This program has made the difference for a lot of students who either couldn't have afforded to attend a state university or any other kind of college or would have gone heavily into debt. However, a perhaps unexpected problem has resulted. To maintain the scholarship, students must earn a 3.0 or better cumulative GPA. As an outcome, our student body is grade conscious to an extent that is terrifying. Learning seems to be way back on this bus; the magical GPA now rules everything.

In this introduction, the writer refers to the Law of Unintended Consequences as she sets up the rest of her essay. Note that, unlike the previous introduction, the thesis statement does not offer a preview of what will follow; however, the reader's interest is sufficiently aroused.

The Body

Each writer has set up a context in which he or she can explore causes or effects, thus avoiding the "cookie-cutter" phenomenon, wherein causes and effects are discussed as if they followed a formula. Note how the two sets of body paragraphs develop in very different ways:

ESSAY A: Cause Focus

Americans' contempt for politicians and the political process is nothing new, but our negative attitudes have sharpened ever since the Watergate scandal in the 1970s. Part of the cause lies with the media themselves. In the past, the media's attitude toward public figures was more respectful. For example, White House correspondents knew that President Kennedy had extramarital affairs, but there was never any question of publishing this information. Today, of course, the media see the private lives of politicians as a gold mine of opportunity. Furthermore, the media breed cynicism by openly questioning politicians' motives. The way elected figures now tend to exploit the media also exacerbates this problem. Many thought the media had hit a new low when then governor Bill Clinton played his saxophone on *Arsenio Hall;* however, that performance was topped several years later by former senator Bob Dole's shilling for Viagra. (At this point the concept of "new low" becomes frightening.) Growing up during this era, I—and the vast majority of my contemporaries—did not see politicians as public servants; we saw them as money-grubbing hypocrites. Can you imagine one of us hanging a printed portrait of the president on our living room wall?

The cynicism bred by politics is more than matched, however, by the pessimism four years in high school can cause. When I watch *The Simpsons,* I view this program as sociology as much as entertainment, especially in its depiction of the school Bart and Lisa attend. After talking to my peers, I find that my experiences in public education were typical, which is a frightening thought. My high school classes were presided over by two types of teachers: those who passed the time and those who used their cleverness to pass the time. For the first group, a successful day at the job site meant that no student became mutilated, pregnant, unconscious, or dead while in their charge. This is the Daycare Model. The second group was actually worse. These teachers depended on clever, gimmick assignments to "stimulate" students, to somehow prod them into a "passion for learning." Thus, in the space of one week during my sophomore year I was asked to write my own obituary (Journalism), to write a letter to my long-dead great-grandparents to let them know what 1995 was like (English), and to "design my ideal mammal" (Biology). When I got to college, I learned that my language classes would have done me a favor if they had taught me how to analyze text, and that if I had learned something about the human musculoskeletal system I would be better prepared for university-level biology. But such activities wouldn't have been "stimulating," just a lot of hard work, and they wouldn't have been "fun" either—for the teachers as well as for their intellectually dispossessed students.

Our parents are another source of cynicism. In the past, parents were portrayed as remote, prepossessing figures who sacrificed a good deal for the welfare of their brood. I don't see these traits in my parents or in most of the parents I know. They seem to be merely older versions of adolescents. They still have a mania to get and spend (does this never end?), and they work hard in order to buy more toys and satisfy the credit card companies. If this is maturity, I don't see much to look forward to.

See if you can find the following internal strategies used in the body paragraphs above: classification (see Chapter 12), exemplification (Chapter 8), and process analysis (Chapter 9).

Essay B: Effects Focus

EXERCISE 10.1 (page 306) Answers will vary. The following sentence outlines are suggested.

The first visible result of the pressures to maintain grade point average is rampant cheating. Before, most students who cheated probably did so out of a desire for convenience: too lazy to study, they got the answers the easy way. Now, however, students have a very real need to practice this dishonesty: they need to stay in school. According to a recent article in the *Signal,* the number of cases of academic dishonesty referred to the Review Council has tripled from the same time period over two years ago. A girl down my hall was caught with her boyfriend breaking into a chemistry instructor's office. Not only did they get expelled from school, but they are facing criminal charges as well.

Professors with a reputation for difficult classes are being avoided at all costs. Softer touches, formerly just popular, are now being mobbed. An interesting incident happened during the drop/add period for this term. A certain tenured humanities professor reacted to a dispute with his department head by giving all A's to all four sections that he taught in the fall semester. Once news of his generosity got around, students were lined up around the block trying to get into this man's spring classes, on the hope that his campaign would continue.

Faculty members who teach classes where the grading is perceived by students as "subjective" must really hate the new scholarship program. At the end of each semester since the program's inception, they have been pestered by students trying to wheedle a better grade. Some real sob stories are offered. I sat outside my speech instructor's office one afternoon in December as someone from my dorm went through a real psychodrama. At first I thought she really might have been responding to some bizarre academic assignment, but then I realized she was merely having a fit. When she emerged her face was flushed, she had tears streaming down her cheeks, and she muttered imprecations as she sped down through the hall. I asked Mr. Gonzalez if I should come back later, but he said that I should stick around, unless I had something similar in mind.

See if you can find the following internal strategies used in the body paragraphs above: exemplification (see Chapter 8), comparison/contrast (Chapter 13), narration (Chapter 7), and description (Chapter 6).

Essay A
Thesis: Three institutions fostered the negativity of "Generation X."

I. Negative attitudes about politicians have sharpened since the Watergate scandal.
   A. Part of the cause lies with the media, which cover politicians' private lives.
   B. The media also breed cynicism by questioning politicians' motives.
II. Cynicism about politicians is matched by pessimism caused by high school.
   A. The portrayal of high school on *The Simpsons* is close to reality.
   B. Two types of teachers presided over the writer's high school classes: the Daycare Model and the excessively creative.
III. Parents are a third source of cynicism—they are merely older adolescents.
IV. Generation X has learned that truth is rare and that greed, mendacity, and ineptitude control the world.

Essay B
Thesis: The new merit scholarships in our state have had an unintended effect: because students need to maintain a 3.0 GPA, they have become too grade conscious.

I. The first result of the pressure to maintain grade point average is rampant cheating.
   A. In the past, students cheated out of a desire for convenience.
   B. Now students have a real need to practice dishonesty: they need to stay in school.
II. Professors with a reputation for difficult classes are being avoided.
III. Faculty members who teach classes where grading is "subjective" are pestered by students hoping to improve their grades.
IV. The unintended effect of the scholarship program is to cheapen education and alter the process.

The Conclusion

As in most essays, you should avoid a summary conclusion, which is often dull and adds little to the essay. Instead, try to come to an *evaluative* conclusion,

Consider Your Options

Good ways to end a causal analysis are to offer your reader advice, look to the future, or explain the applicability of the analysis to your reader's life. (For more on conclusions, see Chapter 3.)

which comments on the implications of the essay's analysis. The evaluative conclusion is a more effective and informative approach. Note the angles the two writers use to end their essays on Generation X and the problematic education policy.

Essay A: Cause Focus

Children learn by imitation. What the members of so-called Generation X have learned is that truth is rare and that greed, mendacity, and ineptitude are the controlling features of their world. So why should they be enthusiastic, and why isn't irony an appropriate lens through which to view this mess?

Essay B: Effects Focus

The legislators undoubtedly had good intentions when they passed the scholarship bill, but they have opened a particularly active can of worms with the new merit scholarship initiative. Letting deserving students go to college is a good idea, but not if a secondary effect is to cheapen education and alter the whole process.

MORE OPTIONS ONLINE
For more help with the step-by-step development of the causal analysis essay, go to **www.mhhe.com/writingtoday**.

EXERCISE 10.1

Write a sentence outline of "Listening Intently" or "Never a Dull Moment." (For help with sentence outlines, see Chapter 2, pages 40–42.) What does the outline reveal about each essay's organization? How would a different organization work?

Revising Your Draft

After you have completed a draft of your causal analysis essay, your next step is to revise it, using your own analysis and comments from classmates or friends. Use the peer review stage to make sure that your essay's structure and content are sound. During peer review, answer the questions on page 307 about the draft you are reviewing, whether it is yours or another student's.

After reviewing for content, you need to go over your peer reviewers' responses to your essay and then revise for unity, coherence, language level, and tone (see Chapter 4). When you have revised your draft and are basically satisfied with it, read your draft for mechanical and grammatical errors. Concentrate on finding and correcting major sentence errors (fragment, comma splice, fused sentence), errors in pronoun agreement and subject-verb agreement, and spelling.

MORE OPTIONS ONLINE
For more help with revision, go to **www.mhhe.com/writingtoday**.

Now that you have made your corrections, *read your essay one more time* to catch any errors made during revision and find errors missed during your earlier reviews.

Questions for Reviewing a Causal Analysis Essay

1. Is the writer's purpose for the essay clear? Does the essay include an introduction that gives readers important background information?
2. Is there a clear thesis statement that indicates whether the writer is concentrating on causes, effects, or both? If not, how could the thesis be improved?
3. Point out any explanation of a cause or an effect that doesn't ring true. Point out any place where the writer has mistaken correlation for causation.
4. Has the writer used an effective organization for the causes and/or effects? What other organization would be more effective?
5. Has the writer used the right strategy to explain each cause or effect? Where does a cause or an effect need additional clarification or development?
6. Are topic sentences both clear and properly located?
7. Does the writer use transitions to guide the reader? Where are transitions needed?
8. Does the essay have an effective conclusion? How could it be improved?

CLASSROOM HINT
These questions are worth discussing in class.

Student Essay

The following essay is Noelani Jones's response to a causal analysis assignment. Noelani, a native of Hawaii, writes about the effects caused by that state's isolation from the U.S. mainland. The final draft is presented first. Then Noelani's first draft is presented, with her comments about this draft and what she needed to do in the revision stage.

Noelani's Final Draft

Worlds Apart

1 When people make general statements about the United States as a whole country, I notice that their comments often exclude Hawaii and Alaska. This often bothered me, growing up in Hawaii, but now that I also live in the continental United States I can understand how easy it is to exclude Alaska and Hawaii when thinking of the "United" States. Hawaii's detachment from the rest of the states truly makes it special and gives Hawaii its unique identity, but this isolation comes with several pitfalls for the people of Hawaii as well.

2 The remoteness and unique tropical beauty of this small chain of islands are what make it so attractive to the world. Hawaii benefits greatly from

tourism, its leading industry. Hundreds of thousands of beach-loving tourists make their way to the shores of Hawaii each year. You can always find a game show or sweepstakes offering a free vacation to Hawaii as a prize because a trip to Hawaii is something that just about anyone in the general population would want to have. The film industry in Hawaii is also booming. Hundreds of television shows and movies have been and are now still being filmed in Hawaii because viewers love to see its rare beauty. Hawaii's reputation as a remote tropical paradise is the bread and butter of its people because most of the jobs in Hawaii depend upon the tourism industry.

3

Hawaii's seclusion from the rest of the United States leads to a much higher cost of living, however. Just about everything under the sun, other than the local agricultural produce, must be shipped to the islands by barge or by plane over the wide, blue ocean, which makes practically everything more expensive. A good example of this is oil. Because oil needs to be shipped in by boat, the average price for gas these days is one and a half times as much as it is in Florida. In addition to that, prices are also hiked because the major consumers are the wealthy tourists who can afford to pay a little more while they're on vacation. All the same, limited space, the high demand for real estate, and the additional difficulty of importing building materials lead to a much higher cost of housing than in most other states.

4

The Hawaiian people are just as unique as the character of their land. Hawaii is often called the "melting pot of the Pacific." Hawaii is just as close to, or even closer to, Asia than it is to America, and just as the continental United States has received many immigrants from European and Latin American countries, Hawaii over the years has seen a great influx of Asians and Polynesians. The Asian influence on Hawaii today is strong and predominant in all aspects of our culture. I myself am not native Hawaiian by race; I am a mixture of Chinese, Japanese, Irish, and Welsh blood. The Asian influence is very evident in the personality of our people, our gift-giving customs, the style of food we eat, even the language we use. "Pidgin English," our colloquial language, is a random mixture of broken English, Hawaiian, Japanese,

Filipino, and Chinese, and it is one of the many differences that separate us from the "haoles" (Caucasians) on the mainland. "We no can understand what da haoles say, 'cuz dey talk da kine proper English," I might say.

5 Isolation from the rest of the United States has created a strong subculture that quite surpasses the small variations between the different regions of the continental United States. This great difference between cultures makes it fairly difficult for people who grow up in Hawaii to move to other states. Most often, students who stay in Hawaii for college end up staying in Hawaii their whole lives. But Hawaii is losing its highest-quality students to the renowned universities on the mainland, which in turn means that the islands also lose the best of their work force. The students with the most potential are most often the ones who do leave Hawaii for college. They often remain on the mainland, adapting to the mainland's culture, its low cost of living, and its large job market, none of which can be found in Hawaii. The saddest aspect of the situation is that the students have to travel so far from home to access such opportunities.

6 Whenever I call home to Hawaii, my brother and sister always remark in a remorseful way how I've lost my Hawaiian accent. They tease me that I've become like the haoles. The stark contrast between the two cultures and its effect on me is evident even over the phone. I am one of these students who have left Hawaii for the vast opportunities of the mainland. Hawaii will always be my homeland, but it's not likely that I will ever choose to go back to live there. To me, Hawaii would just be a great place to visit for a vacation.

Noelani's First Draft

Worlds Apart

1 When people make general statements about the United States as a whole country, I notice they often leave out Hawaii, and Alaska. This often bothered me growing up in Hawaii, but now that I also live on the continental United States I can understand how easy it is to forget that the union extends past the boarders of California, Oregon and Washington. Hawaii's isolation

from the rest of the "united" states makes it special and gives Hawaii its unique identity but isolation has it's pitfalls for the islanders of Hawaii as well.

2 The remoteness and unique tropical beauty of this small, chain of islands is what makes it so attractive to the world. Tourism is by far Hawaii's leading industry. Hundreds of thousands of beach-loving tourist make their way to the shores of Hawaii a year. A free trip to Hawaii is always a popular game show prize, because it's everyone's dream to vacation there. The film industry in Hawaii is booming. Thousands of television shows, and movies have shown the world the beauty of Hawaii. And new upcoming shows have recently been contracted to be filmed there, because viewers love to see the rare beauty of Hawaii. Many wealthy people own beautiful houses in Hawaii because it's a great place to "get away from it all" if you can afford it. Hawaii is known worldwide as a remote tropical paradise, and the people profit from this reputation with an economy supported heavily by tourism.

I shortened and refined the end of the second paragraph because it did not support the topic sentence, and it included altogether too much information.

3 But isolation and remoteness from the rest of the United States leads to a higher cost of living. Just about everything, except for the local agricultural produce, must be shipped in by barge or by plain, which makes practically everything, we buy more expensive. A good example of this is oil. Because oil needs to be shipped in by boat, the average price for gas these days is one and a half times as much as it is in Florida. In addition to that, prices are also hiked because the major consumers are the wealthy tourists who can afford to pay a little more while they're on their two week vacation. Limited space, and the high demand for real estate in Hawaii leads to an extremely higher cost of housing in Hawaii, than in most other states of America.

I took out most of the "we's" and "our's" in the essay because I didn't use them throughout the paper consistently, and it seemed misleading for me to write as if I were still a part of Hawaii, when the main focus was to show that I am now separate from Hawaii.

4 Being isolated from the rest of the United States makes it difficult for people from the state of Hawaii to know, understand, or distinguish the different cultural regions that make up the conitental U.S. A man from New York could most likely distinguish a Texan from a Californian by their dress, and accent, because he's had friends that came from those parts, he's had business dealings with companies in those states, and he often visits his cousins who live in LA, and his sister who is studying in Austin, TX . But Americans

I repeated the words "isolation" and "isolated" too many times, so I replaced them with other similar words.

who grow up in Hawaii often refer to people from all other states simply as "Mainlanders" or "haole's", which means "white foreigners". They have a hard time, because they are not exposed as much to the different types of cultures in the U.S. The distance limits our interaction with the rest of the US, thus making it harder for us to learn about different types of mainlanders or be able to distinguish them apart

I totally deleted the fourth paragraph because it was too trivial and discussed a very small idea in a roundabout, wordy way. The main idea I wanted to emphasize was also a part of the fifth paragraph, so I just eliminated the whole fourth paragraph.

5

Hawaii's people are unique. Hawaii is often called the "melting pot of the Pacific." Hawaii is just as close, or even closer to Asia than it is to America, and just as (while) the continental US received many immigrants from European and Latin American countries, Hawaii, over the years has seen a great influx of Asians, and Polynesians. The Asian influence on Hawaii today is strong and predominant in all aspects of our culture and greatly contrasts the similar regional cultures of the continental US. It is evident in the personality of our people, our gift giving customs, the style of food we eat, even the language we use. "Pidgin English", our colloquial language, is a random mixture of broken English, Hawaiian, Japanese, Filipino, and Chinese, and is one of the many differences that separate us from the "haole's" (Caucasians) on the mainland. "We no can understand what da haole's say, 'cuz dey talk da kine proper English," I might say. Isolation from the rest of the United States has created a strong and quite (far away) subculture that quite surpasses the small variations between the different regions of the continental US. This great difference between cultures makes it fairly difficult for people who grow up in Hawaii to move to other states. Most often, students who stay in Hawaii for college end up staying in Hawaii their whole lives. But Hawaii is loosing its highest quality students to the renowned universities on the mainland, which in turn means that it also loses the best of our potential work force. The students that do leave often end up staying on the mainland, because they've adapted to the mainland culture, the low cost of living, and the large job market that they can not find in Hawaii.

I changed the first sentence of the fifth paragraph because it was choppy/messy. I added the fifth sentence to the fifth paragraph to back up the sentence before it and to give interesting insight into my life and viewpoint, that of an average person from Hawaii. I also broke up this paragraph because it seemed too long.

6

I am one of these students who have left Hawaii for college, and I may never return to live there again. Whenever I call home, my brother and sister

In the last paragraph I gave more personal information to show the effects on my personal life. And I reorganized the sentences to keep the related ideas together and make them stronger.

always remark in a remorseful way that I've lost my pidgin accent. They tease me and tell me I've become a haole. Hawaii will always be my homeland, but now it seems like just a great place to visit and take vacations in. I don't think I could every call it home again.

EXERCISE 10.2: REVISING

The following is the first draft of a student's causal analysis essay. Working in pairs or in small groups, review this essay. Using the Questions for Reviewing a Causal Analysis Essay on page 307, decide what revisions you would suggest. If you have any questions that the student needs to consider, write these in the margin or on a separate sheet of paper. If your instructor directs you to, rewrite one or more paragraphs to make them stronger and to eliminate any grammatical or mechanical errors.

SUGGESTED ACTIVITY Consider asking students to meet in writing groups, each of which is charged with producing a more developed and effective version of this essay. Encourage students to use their imaginations, or details from their own experience.

EXERCISE 10.2 Answers will vary. Students should point out the weak thesis statement, the lack of evidence for the writer's main points, underdeveloped paragraphs, and the weak conclusion. .

"A Bad Move Gentleman"

1 Our college has a new policy, it's a horrible policy: any student that misses more than 3 'contact hours' will be dropped from their class. The effects are going to hurt badly individual students: they will be punished unfairly.

2 First in a three-day a week class over 16 weeks has 45 class meetings, therefore, at least 42 classes must be attended orelse the student is dropped. Thats too much. What if you get sick. What if your car wont start. And besides everyone gets a day off every once in a while, dont they?

3 Students with too absenses could find themselves living in fear because they know their on the edge.

4 Moreover students, we, pay the tuition that runs this school, who is the school to cancel us after we've paid are money? The whole thing sucks if you ask me. We putup with alot with this school anyway; bad parking, old classrooms. What are they thinking?

5 In conclusion, as I have clearly pointed out, the new rules is too hard on students and unfair toboot. Think it over, gentleman.

Additional Writing Topics

1. Are you a different person than you were four years ago? If so, why?
2. Describe a problem that exists at your college, and discuss (a) its cause, (b) its effects, or (c) both.

3. Most college students are eighteen or older, so they are normally eligible to vote. However, college students are notoriously underrepresented among voters in local, state, and federal elections. Why?
4. Over the past fifteen years, most states have raised their drinking ages to twenty-one (in other states, twenty-one was already the legal drinking age). In your experience, what have been the effects of this change?
5. How would your life change, in all probability, if you found yourself in one of the following situations?
   - A close relative dies, leaving you with custody of her two-year-old son.
   - Your physician tells you that you must avoid all caffeine.
   - Because of a change in your financial situation, you find that you must work twenty more hours per week at your current job or at a new one.
   - You find, to your amazement, that you have the winning ticket in the state Lotto drawing. You will receive, after taxes, $247,395 for each of the next twenty years.
6. **Writing on the job.** In any line of work, workers can count on foul-ups with at least one procedure. At your current job or at a former job, what was the major procedural difficulty? Write a memo for your supervisor that analyzes this problem and discusses its causes and possible solutions to it. (For help with writing memos, see Chapter 17.)

Responding to a Photograph

In 1955, in Montgomery, Alabama, Rosa Parks, an African American, refused to surrender her bus seat to a white passenger. Parks was arrested, and in response to the incident, black citizens of Montgomery boycotted the city bus system. Dan Weiner took this photograph soon after the boycott began.

CLASSROOM HINT
Review these assignments in class as a way to gather information and insights students can use in their essays.

Dan Weiner, *Boycotted Bus, Montgomery, 1956* Courtesy of Sandra Weiner.

1. Write an informal response to the photograph. What do you notice? How does the image make you feel? How does the photograph make use of the causal analysis option?

2. The 1950s and 1960s were the heyday of the U.S. civil rights movement. In response to racial discrimination, leaders such as Martin Luther King, Jr., planned nonviolent actions to show the resolve of the African American citizenry. Using a combination of library and online research, explore an event that prompted a coordinated, nonviolent response from King or from another black leader. Write a documented essay exploring the causes and the effects of the event. (For more information on documented essays, see Chapter 21.)

Writing About Film

In the Bedroom (2001, R) takes place in a small seaside town in Maine. The son of a local doctor and high school teacher is having an affair with a married woman who is estranged from her abusive husband. The woman's husband confronts and then murders the young man. What are the complex effects of this violent act?

In *Run Lola Run* (German with subtitles, 1998, R), Lola is in love with Manni, a small-time criminal who will be murdered if he does not replace the 100,000 marks he has lost due to his bungling. Lola has twenty minutes to get the cash. She tries once and fails, but realizes (in a type of magic realism) that she is able to start over and try again. Lola "runs" a total of three times in her attempt to save Manni. What effects do her attempts have on the people with whom she comes in contact?

Using the Internet

Search the Internet for insights and information to use when explaining causes and effects.

1. Find several Web sites that use a layperson's language to explain the causes, symptoms, and probable outcomes of physical or mental illnesses. After some preliminary "surfing," focus on a particular disease and gather information about your subject from at least three different Web sites. Use this information in an essay that explains the causes, symptoms, and probable outcomes of this illness. If the disease can be treated, explain how this treatment works and discuss the extent to which it is effective in arresting the disease's progress, alleviating its symptoms, or curing the patient entirely.

2. Natalie Angier discusses war as an activity that, paradoxically, has served human needs, no matter how horrible war can be. What are some other paradoxical and complicated human "needs"? For example, some people use tobacco, despite an extensive medical literature telling them not

to do so; others are addicted to alcohol or drugs; and still others are pathological shoppers. Focus on a physiological or psychological craving or dependency. Go online to learn more about its causes and effects, and put this information into a well-developed causal analysis paper.

"I'm sorry, but the director of the film has asked specifically that people like you not be allowed to see it."

CHAPTER 11

DEFINITION

Writing in Context

You've been at Osprey Online for over a month now. At lunch, you are talking to a colleague, Jason, about Bob and his shortcomings as a manager. Jason has worked for Bob for two years, and he has a long list of complaints.

"Bob's manipulative, lazy, and—frankly—rude. Sometimes he's talking to a client and forgets that he's not dealing with one of us. Then you see something click in his face, and suddenly he becomes nice again. He doesn't have an ounce of sincerity. He's successful because of the hard work of people like you and me, not that this fact has ever occurred to him, and not that he'd ever admit it."

Jason's description matches some of the traits you've noticed during your brief working relationship with Bob; however, you decide to play devil's advocate.

"Jason, all bosses cause problems for the people who work for them, even the best ones. What's your definition of the ideal manager, anyway?"

Jason might find that the answer to this question requires some serious thought.

SUGGESTED ACTIVITY
Moviemakers target certain groups in their marketing campaigns. Discuss why the couple in the cartoon might be considered the wrong "demographic" for a film such as an action picture or a slasher movie. Have students take five minutes to write a definition of their own demographic, and discuss a few sample definitions as a class.

HOW DOES DEFINITION WORK?

A writer trying to explain the qualities of an ideal manager might be in for a few surprises. The ideal manager wouldn't let his or her workers goof off all day, call in "sick" whenever they felt like it, or come and go as they pleased. With such lax supervision, the enterprise would soon go bankrupt, and all concerned would lose their jobs. No, the writer would likely discover—and reveal to the reader—that the ideal boss would insist on professional behavior and productivity.

When you use **definition**, you explain the meaning of a term or concept in order to shed new light on it. Your purpose is to show your readers a new way of looking at a concept, perhaps with the goal of changing their attitudes. You can use definition as an internal strategy, in which you define a term or concept in order to clarify some larger issue or discussion. You can also use definition as the basis of an entire essay.

CLASSROOM HINT
Make sure students understand this distinction.

Often, students will use a dictionary definition in the course of an essay, sometimes making the definition part of their introduction. However, most of the time a formal definition does not tell the reader anything new and sometimes even insults the reader's intelligence. Quoting the formal definition of a word from a standard college dictionary won't help your essay unless you are able to use the word's meaning in a fresh, surprising way. For example, in the following paragraph from an essay about the stock market boom of the 1990s, a secondary meaning of the word *rush* proves to be illuminating:

> According to my dictionary, one of the definitions of *rush* is "the movement of people to a new site in search of financial reward," as in a gold rush. Just as the hopeful thronged to California in the middle of the nineteenth century and to Alaska at the end of the century, during the 1990s investors "rushed" to the brave new digital world of Internet stocks. The movement wasn't so much a boom as it was an exploratory adventure. Like the gold-obsessed pilgrims of the nineteenth century, many of the investors had no idea where to look for treasure and what to do when they found promising options. Thus, fortunes were made and lost in weeks or days, as some new companies paid off dramatically and others turned out to be empty mines.

In order to shed light on a subject, a writer can also examine the historical roots of the word being defined, as Nancy Gibbs does in the following excerpt from "When Is It Rape?"

CLASSROOM HINT
Students profit from class discussion of the three types of definition listed here.

> The present debate over degrees of rape is nothing new: All through history, rapes have been divided between those that mattered and those that did not. For the first few thousand years, the only rape that was punished was the defiling of a virgin, and that was viewed as a property crime. A girl's virtue was a marketable asset, and so a rapist was often ordered to pay the victim's father the equivalent of her price on the marriage market. In early Babylonian and Hebrew societies, a married woman who was raped suffered the same fate as an adulteress—death by stoning or drowning. Under William the Conqueror, the penalty for raping a virgin was castration and

> loss of both eyes—unless the violated woman agreed to marry her attacker, as she was often pressured to do. "Stealing an heiress" became a perfectly conventional means of taking—literally—a wife.

Here Gibbs uses the history of the concept of *rape* to help explain current attitudes toward sexual violence.

Sometimes, a writer may need to use a highly personal definition of a word, called a **stipulated definition.** In other words, the writer asks the reader to agree to his or her "spin" on a term's meaning, as in the following example:

> When I think of "welfare," I don't think about small sums of money going to mothers trying to raise children on their own. Instead, I think about state legislatures and the U.S. Congress finding new ways to give businesses money to keep them afloat. I think of the artificial price structures that are maintained for tobacco and sugar so that American businesses can compete in the global marketplace. I think about companies that never actually pay fines for their illegalities; they simply pass the costs on to their customers, who foot the bill. That's what "welfare" means to me.

In an **extended definition,** the writer devotes an entire essay to exploring the meaning of a term or concept—once again, to show the reader a new way of looking at the topic or to change the reader's opinion. Writers can choose from a limitless number of possible topics and employ a wide variety of internal strategies. For example, over the course of an essay you could define selfishness, honesty, the optimum fitness plan, the perfect dinner date, or the typical fraternity member. To explain the **defining features** of your term or concept, the aspects of it that set it apart, you could use one or more of the rhetorical options that are discussed in Part 2 of this book.

Definition essays normally have an **objective** focus or a **subjective** focus. An objective definition seeks to inform the reader and usually does not contain the preferences or opinions of the writer. A subjective definition represents the writer's personal definition of a term or concept. However, note that rarely is a definition completely objective or completely subjective; the focus is more on one than the other.

Consider Your Options

Make a list of topics relating to your role as a student that might be discussed by using an extended definition.

READING THE DEFINITION ESSAY WITH A WRITER'S EYE

In the four essays that follow, the writers present extended definitions on a range of topics. Judy Brady offers an exhaustive (and daunting) definition of society's expectations of wives, William Raspberry points out that social definition can be self-perpetuating, Annie Dillard provides a subjective definition of adolescence, and Tony Earley defines vernacular language. As you read these selections, note the effects that the authors are able to achieve from the starting point of definition. As a rhetorical option, definition may seem basic; however, it is anything but that. A good definition can change a reader's most strongly held assumptions.

Following the essays, the second half of this chapter provides strategies for writing the definition essay with a reader's eye (pages 333–342). If you decide to write on one of the topics that follow the four essays below, make sure that you have read the strategies section before you begin. Also note that additional writing topics are listed at the end of the chapter (pages 348–349).

Why I Want a Wife

JUDY BRADY

Written by essayist and political activist Judy Brady, "Why I Want a Wife" is one of the most famous and enduring essays of our times. First published in the Spring 1972 issue of *Ms.*, it has become both a rallying cry for women seeking equality and a penetrating look into the sociology of the American family.

I belong to that classification of people known as wives. I am A Wife. And, not altogether incidentally, I am a mother. 1

Not too long ago a male friend of mine appeared on the scene fresh from a recent divorce. He had one child, who is, of course, with his ex-wife. He is looking for another wife. As I thought about him while I was ironing one evening, it suddenly occurred to me that I, too, would like to have a wife. Why do I want a wife? 2

I would like to go back to school so that I can become economically independent, support myself, and, if need be, support those dependent upon me. I want a wife who will work and send me to school. And while I am going to school I want a wife to take care of my children. I want a wife to keep track of the children's doctor and dentist appointments. And to keep track of mine, too. I want a wife to make sure my children eat properly and are kept clean. I want a wife who will wash the children's clothes and keep them mended. I want a wife who is a good nurturant attendant to my children, who arranges for their schooling, makes sure that they have an adequate social life with their peers, takes them to the park, the zoo, etc. I want a wife who takes care of the children when they are sick, a wife who arranges to be around when the children need special care, because, of course, I cannot miss classes at school. My wife must arrange to lose time at work and not lose the job. It may mean a small cut in my wife's income from time to time, but I guess I can tolerate that. Needless to say, my wife will arrange and pay for the care of the children while my wife is working. 3

I want a wife who will take care of *my* physical needs. I want a wife who will keep my house clean. A wife who will pick up after me. I want a wife who will keep my clothes clean, ironed, mended, replaced when need be, and who will see to it that my personal things are kept in their proper place so that I can find what I need the minute I need it. I want a wife who cooks the meals, a wife who is a *good* cook. I want a wife who will plan the menus, do the necessary grocery shopping, prepare the meals, serve them pleasantly, and then do the cleaning up while I do my studying. I want a wife who will care for me when I am sick and sympathize with my pain and loss of time from school. I want a wife to go along when our family takes a vacation so that someone can continue to care for me and my children when I need a rest and change of scene. 4

I want a wife who will not bother me with rambling complaints about a wife's duties. But I want a wife who will listen to me when I feel the need to explain a rather difficult point I have come across in my course of studies. And I want a wife who will type my papers for me when I have written them. 5

I want a wife who will take care of the details of my social life. When my wife and I are invited out by friends, I want a wife who will take care of the babysitting arrangements. When I meet people at school that I like and want to entertain, I want a wife who will have the house clean, will prepare a special meal, serve it to me and my friends, and not interrupt when I talk about the things that interest me and my friends. I want a wife who will have arranged that the children are fed and ready for bed before my guests arrive so that the children do not bother us. I want a wife who takes care of the needs of my guests so that they feel comfortable, who makes sure that they have an ashtray, that they are passed the hors d'oeuvres, that they are offered a second helping of the food, that their wine glasses are replenished when necessary, that their coffee is served to them as they like it. And I want a wife who knows that sometimes I need a night out by myself. 6

I want a wife who is sensitive to my sexual needs, a wife who makes love passionately and eagerly when I feel like it, a wife who makes sure that I am satisfied. And, of course, I want a wife who will not demand sexual attention when I am not in the mood for it. I want a wife who assumes the complete responsibility for birth control, because I do not want more children. I want a wife who will remain sexually faithful to me so that I do not have to clutter up my intellectual life with jealousies. And I want a wife who understands that *my* sexual needs may entail more than strict adherence to monogamy. I must, after all, be able to relate to people as fully as possible. 7

If, by chance, I find another person more suitable as a wife than the wife I already have, I want the liberty to replace my present wife with another one. Naturally, I will expect a fresh, new life; my wife will take the children and be solely responsible for them so that I am left free. 8

When I am through with school and have a job, I want my wife to quit working and remain at home so that my wife can more fully and completely take care of a wife's duties. 9

My God, who *wouldn't* want a wife? 10

Vocabulary

The following terms are identified by paragraph number. Make sure that you understand each term's meaning in its context. If you're not sure that you understand a term, look it up in a college-level dictionary.

nurturant (3)	hors d'oeuvres (6)	adherence (7)
attendant (3)	replenish (6)	monogamy (7)

Style and Strategy

1. Write down the major defining features of wives that Brady includes, and note their arrangement. How does Brady organize her definition?

STYLE AND STRATEGY
1. This question makes a good prompt for an in-class group writing assignment.
2. Irony appears at the end of paragraph 1 and in paragraphs 9 and 10. Sarcasm appears throughout, most notably at the end of paragraph 3, at the beginning and end of paragraph 4, at the beginning of paragraph 5, and throughout paragraphs 7 and 8.

3. The introduction establishes Brady's authority. The last paragraph invites the reader into the discussion and reinforces Brady's argument.

2. Writers use *irony* when they say the exact opposite of what they mean in order to create humor or emphasize a point. *Sarcasm,* a form of irony, has a biting or critical tone. Locate the places where Brady uses irony and/or sarcasm.
3. Both the first paragraph and the last paragraph are very brief, but they are also very effective. Explain why.

QUESTIONS FOR CRITICAL THINKING AND DISCUSSION
1. Ironing is, of course, thought of as a "wifely duty" by some husbands.
2–3. These items can be used as catalysts for class discussion and as a way to gather information for essay writing.
4. This question can be turned into an essay prompt that requires both close textual analysis and comparison/contrast. Ask students what Gould can tell us about Brady's essay or what Brady can tell us about Gould's essay.

Questions for Critical Thinking and Discussion

1. Why is it appropriate that Brady thought of this subject "while I was ironing one evening" (paragraph 2)?
2. Brady is writing about the typical wife's domestic duties in the early 1970s. Three decades later, how much has changed for the "typical wife"? How much has changed for the "typical husband"?
3. James Thurber, another chronicler of relationships and strife, titled one of his books *The War Between Men and Women.* What, do you think, causes resentment between men and women?
4. Chapter 9 includes an essay by Joan Gould called "Binding Decisions" (pages 252–254). Gould describes her elaborate, painstaking preparations for a first date at a time (1950) when she dearly wanted to get married before she was "too old" (she was twenty-one at the time). Read Gould's essay, and then discuss what Gould's perspective tells us about Brady and how Brady's experience fulfills, or does not fulfill, Gould's expectations about marriage.

SUGGESTIONS FOR WRITING Students rarely have difficulty addressing these assignments.

Suggestions for Writing

1. Complete the following sentence: "I want a _____." Then, in a 500-word essay, define your term by using irony.
2. Write a 500- to 750-word essay that uses definition to explain why "I want/don't want to get married."

The Handicap of Definition

WILLIAM RASPBERRY

A native of Mississippi, William Raspberry is one of the most respected journalists in the United States, with a commanding insight into the problems of American society and politics. In 1991, Raspberry published *Looking Backward at Us,* a collection of his nationally syndicated columns for the *Washington Post,* where the following essay was first published in 1982.

In "The Handicap of Definition," Raspberry explains the problems caused by accepting a narrow definition of oneself and one's culture. He then shows how these limitations can be overcome.

1 I know all about bad schools, mean politicians, economic deprivation and racism. Still, it occurs to me that one of the heaviest burdens black Americans—and black children in particular—have to bear is the handicap of definition: the question of what it means to be black.

Let me explain quickly what I mean. If a basketball fan says that the Boston Celtics' Larry Bird plays "black," the fan intends it—and Bird probably accepts it—as a compliment. Tell pop singer Tom Jones* he moves "black" and he might grin in appreciation. Say to Teena Marie or the Average White Band* that they sound "black" and they'll thank you. 2

But name one pursuit, aside from athletics, entertainment or sexual performance, in which a white practitioner will feel complimented to be told he does it "black." Tell a white broadcaster he talks "black" and he'll sign up for diction lessons. Tell a white reporter he writes "black" and he'll take a writing course. Tell a white lawyer he reasons "black" and he might sue you for slander. 3

What we have here is a tragically limited definition of blackness, and it isn't only white people who buy it. 4

Think of all the ways black children can put one another down with charges of "whiteness." For many of these children, hard study and hard work are "white." Trying to please a teacher might be criticized as acting "white." Speaking correct English is "white." Scrimping today in the interest of tomorrow's goals is "white." Educational toys and games are "white." 5

An incredible array of habits and attitudes that are conducive to success in business, in academia, in the nonentertainment professions are likely to be thought of as somehow "white." Even economic success, unless it involves such "black" undertakings as numbers banking, is defined as "white." 6

And the results are devastating. I wouldn't deny that blacks often are better entertainers and athletes. My point is the harm that comes from too narrow a definition of what is black. 7

One reason black youngsters tend to do better at basketball, for instance, is that they assume they can learn to do it well, and so they practice constantly to prove themselves right. 8

Wouldn't it be wonderful if we could infect black children with the notion that excellence in math is "black" rather than white, or possibly Chinese? Wouldn't it be of enormous value if we could create the myth that morality, strong families, determination, courage and love of learning are traits brought by slaves from Mother Africa and therefore quintessentially black? 9

There is no doubt in my mind that most black youngsters could develop their mathematical reasoning, their elocution and their attitudes the way they develop their jump shots and their dance steps: by the combination of sustained, enthusiastic practice and the unquestioned belief that they can do it. 10

In one sense, what I am talking about is the importance of developing positive ethnic traditions. Maybe Jews have an innate talent for communication; maybe the Chinese are born with a gift for mathematical reasoning; maybe blacks are naturally blessed with athletic grace. I doubt it. What is at work, I suspect, is assumption, inculcated early in their lives, that this a thing our people do well. 11

Unfortunately, many of the things about which blacks make this assumption are things that do not contribute to their career success—except for that handful 12

***Tom Jones:** a pop singer who had a number of hit songs in the late 1960s and early 1970s.

***Teena Marie; the Average White Band:** *Teena Marie* is a singer and songwriter whose most popular hits were released in the eighties; *Average White Band* is a popular soul group from the seventies.

of the truly gifted who can make it as entertainers and athletes. And many of the things we concede to whites are the things that are essential to economic security.

13 So it is with a number of assumptions black youngsters make about what it is to be a "man": physical aggressiveness, sexual prowess, the refusal to submit to authority. The prisons are full of people who, by this perverted definition, are unmistakably men.

14 But the real problem is not so much that the things defined as "black" are negative. The problem is that the definition is much too narrow.

15 Somehow, we have to make our children understand that they are intelligent, competent people, capable of doing whatever they put their minds to and making it in the American mainstream, not just in a black subculture.

16 What we seem to be doing, instead, is raising up yet another generation of young blacks who will be failures—by definition.

Vocabulary

The following terms are identified by paragraph number. Make sure that you understand each term's meaning in its context. If you're not sure that you understand a term, look it up in a college-level dictionary.

deprivation (1)	conducive (6)	innate (11)
diction (3)	numbers banking (6)	inculcated (11
reasons (3)	quintessential (9)	prowess (13)
slander (3)	elocution (10)	subculture (15)
scrimping (5)		

Style and Strategy

STYLE AND STRATEGY
1. The first paragraph might have been developed further with the author explaining why he mentions "mean politicians," etc. In addition, he might have waited until the fourth or fifth paragraph to state his thesis, beginning the essay with the reference to Larry Bird.
2. The flaw is explained in paragraph 4, but you might also discuss paragraphs 7, 8, 11, 12, and 14 in this connection.
3. The contrast Raspberry makes is better executed in two paragraphs.

1. This essay was originally published as a newspaper column. Newspaper columnists have a limited amount of space in which to make their point. Note that Raspberry delivers his thesis early—in the second sentence. How might Raspberry have begun this essay if he had written it for a different audience and purpose?

2. Raspberry first attacks a number of definitions or assumptions about African Americans, then provides a better definition for the future. What does he claim to be the fatal flaw of the existing assumptions?

3. Paragraphs 15 and 16 serve as Raspberry's conclusion. Raspberry is following journalistic convention by using short paragraphs throughout his essay; however, these two paragraphs could be easily be merged into one. Can you think of another reason why using two paragraphs is effective here?

Questions for Critical Thinking and Discussion

1. Chapter 8 contains an essay by Brent Staples titled "Just Walk on By" (pages 215–218). In it, Staples describes a series of typical experiences he had as a young black male walking alone at night. He found that if people saw him approaching on the sidewalk, they would nervously cross the street to avoid him because he fit their definition of "danger." How much of this perhaps unconscious definition do you experience in your life? Do you act on it? Have you ever been the victim of it?

2. Many observers believe that young people can be trapped in their parents' or families' expectations—in other words, the previous generation's "definition" of a young person's future. Is this syndrome a factor in your life?

QUESTIONS FOR CRITICAL THINKING AND DISCUSSION These questions often produce energetic discussion in class. However, you might ask students to record their reactions in writing first.

Suggestions for Writing

1. Write a 500- to 750-word essay about a teacher or supervisor who had an inaccurate perception of you. Explain how you overcame (or were unable to overcome) this definition.
2. Write a 500- to 750-word essay on the following topic: "I may appear to be a(n) _____, but I'm actually a(n) _____."

SUGGESTIONS FOR WRITING Both of these items require students to contrast, so make sure you have introduced comparison/contrast before you assign these prompts.

So This Was Adolescence

ANNIE DILLARD

Annie Dillard, best known for her Pulitzer Prize–winning *Pilgrim at Tinker Creek* (1975), is the author of eight other books, including a novel, *The Living;* a collection of essays, *Teaching a Stone to Talk: Expeditions and Encounters* (1982); and her memories of growing up, *An American Childhood* (1987).

In "So This Was Adolescence," excerpted from *An American Childhood,* Dillard looks back at her adolescence. As you read this selection, think about your own adolescence. Do you recognize any of the situations, problems, and emotions that Dillard recounts?

1 When I was fifteen, I felt it coming; now I was sixteen, and it hit.

2 My feet had imperceptibly been set on a new path, a fast path into a long tunnel like those many turnpike tunnels near Pittsburgh, turnpike tunnels whose entrances bear on brass plaques a roll call of those men who died blasting them. I wandered witlessly forward and found myself going down, and saw the light dimming; I adjusted to the slant and dimness, traveled further down, adjusted to greater dimness, and so on. There wasn't a whole lot I could do about it, or about anything. I was going to hell on a handcart, that was all, and I knew it and everyone around me knew it, and there it was.

3 I was growing and thinning, as if pulled. I was getting angry, as if pushed. I morally disapproved most things in North America, and blamed my innocent parents for them. My feelings deepened and lingered. The swift moods of early childhood—each formed by and suited to its occasion—vanished. Now feelings lasted so long they left stains. They arose from nowhere, like winds or waves, and battered at me or engulfed me.

4 When I was angry, I felt myself coiled and longing to kill someone or bomb something big. Trying to appease myself, during one winter I whipped my bed every afternoon with my uniform belt. I despised the spectacle I made in my own eyes—whipping the bed with a belt, like a creature demented!—and I often began half-heartedly, but I did it daily after school as a desperate discipline, trying to rid myself and the innocent world of my wildness. It was like trying to beat back the ocean.

Sometimes in class I couldn't stop laughing; things were too funny to be borne. It began then, my surprise that no one else saw what was so funny. 5

I read some few books with such reverence I didn't close them at the finish, but only moved the pile of pages back to the start, without breathing, and began again. I read one such book, an enormous novel, six times that way—closing the binding between sessions, but not between readings. 6

On the piano in the basement I played the maniacal "Poet and Peasant Overture" so loudly, for so many hours, night after night, I damaged the piano's keys and strings. When I wasn't playing this crashing overture, I played boogie-woogie, or something else, anything else, in octaves—otherwise, it wasn't loud enough. My fingers were so strong I could do push-ups with them. I played one piece with my fists. I banged on a steel-stringed guitar till I bled, and once on a particularly piercing rock-and-roll downbeat I broke straight through one of Father's snare drums. 7

I loved my boyfriend so tenderly, I thought I must transmogrify into vapor. It would take spectroscopic analysis to locate my molecules in thin air. No possible way of holding him was close enough. Nothing could cure this bad case of gentleness except, perhaps, violence: maybe if he swung me by the legs and split my skull on a tree? Would that ease this insane wish to kiss too much his eyelids' outer corners and his temples, as if I could love up his brain? 8

I envied people in books who swooned. For two years I felt myself continuously swooning and continuously unable to swoon; the blood drained from my face and eyes and flooded my heart; my hands emptied, my knees unstrung, I bit at the air for something worth breathing—but I failed to fall, and I couldn't find the way to black out. I had to live on the lip of a waterfall, exhausted. 9

When I was bored I was first hungry, then nauseated, then furious and weak. "Calm yourself," people had been saying to me all my life. Since early childhood I had tried one thing and then another to calm myself, on those few occasions when I truly wanted to. Eating helped; singing helped. Now sometimes I truly wanted to calm myself. I couldn't lower my shoulders; they seemed to wrap around my ears. I couldn't lower my voice although I could see the people around me flinch. I waved my arm in class till the very teachers wanted to kill me. 10

I was what they called a live wire. I was shooting out sparks that were digging a pit around me, and I was sinking into that pit. Laughing with Ellin at school recess, or driving around after school with Judy in her jeep, exultant, or dancing with my boyfriend to Louis Armstrong across a polished diningroom floor, I got so excited I looked around wildly for aid; I didn't know where I should go or what I should do with myself. People in books split wood. 11

When rage or boredom reappeared, each seemed never to have left. Each so filled me with so many years' intolerable accumulation it jammed the space behind my eyes, so I couldn't see. There was no room left even on my surface to live. My rib cage was so taut I couldn't breathe. Every cubic centimeter of atmosphere above my shoulders and head was heaped with last straws. Black hatred clogged my very blood. I couldn't peep, I couldn't wiggle or blink; my blood was too mad to flow. 12

For as long as I could remember, I had been transparent to myself, unselfconscious, learning, doing, most of every day. Now I was in my own way; I myself was a dark object I could not ignore. I couldn't remember how to forget myself. I didn't want to think about myself, to reckon myself in, to deal with myself every livelong 13 minute on top of everything else—but swerve as I might, I couldn't avoid it. I was a boulder blocking my own path. I was a dog barking between my own ears, a barking dog who wouldn't hush.

14 So this was adolescence. Is this how the people around me had died on their feet—inevitably, helplessly? Perhaps their own selves eclipsed the sun for so many years the world shriveled around them, and when at last their inescapable orbits had passed through these dark egoistic years it was too late, they had adjusted.

15 Must I then lose the world forever, that I had so loved? Was it all, the whole bright and various planet, where I had been so ardent about finding myself alive, only a passion peculiar to children, that I would outgrow even against my will?

Vocabulary

The following terms are identified by paragraph number. Make sure that you understand each term's meaning in its context. If you're not sure that you understand a term, look it up in a college-level dictionary.

roll call (2)	overture (7)	exultant (11)
witlessly (2)	transmogrify (8)	ardent (15)
appease (4)	spectroscopic (8)	peculiar (15)
demented (4)	swoon (9)	
borne (5)	live wire (11)	

Style and Strategy

1. Where is Dillard's thesis statement? Why did she present the thesis in this position?
2. Besides definition, what other rhetorical options does Dillard employ in this essay? Cite specific passages and paragraphs.
3. In the first paragraph, Dillard writes that "When I was fifteen, I felt it coming. . . ." As you read this essay, when did you realize what "it" is?
4. In your opinion, does Dillard expect the questions in the final paragraph to be answered? Explain.

STYLE AND STRATEGY
1. Dillard waits until paragraph 14 to reveal her thesis so that the reader can share a bit of the confusion she herself experienced at this state in her life.
2. Narration appears in paragraphs 4, 9, and 10; contrast in 5 and 13; analogy in 2 and 11; process in 8; and description in 12.
3. Responses vary, but some students see the first clues of the self-absorption and rebelliousness typical of adolescence in paragraph 3.
4. Answers will vary.

Questions for Critical Thinking and Discussion

1. "Anyone who survives to age twenty-one can probably expect to live to be eighty." Comment on this statement. What does it imply about the vicissitudes of adolescence?
2. What advice would you give to teenagers undergoing adolescence?

QUESTIONS FOR CRITICAL THINKING AND DISCUSSION Before discussing item 1, make sure students understand "vicissitudes." Item 2 can be turned into a process paper.

Suggestions for Writing

1. Choose a period in your life, and define it in an essay of 500 to 750 words.
2. Was your adolescence different from the stormy times that Dillard describes? If so, write a 500- to 750-word essay defining adolescence in terms of your experience.

SUGGESTIONS FOR WRITING Remind students that both essays, like Dillard's, require a great deal of specific detail.

The Quare Gene

TONY EARLEY

Tony Earley is a professor of English at Vanderbilt University. He is the author of a collection of short stories, *Here We Are in Paradise* (1994); a novel, *Jim the Boy* (2000); and a collection of essays, *Somehow Form a Family: Stories That Are Mostly True* (2001).

"The Quare Gene" first appeared in *The New Yorker* in 1998. This essay is an extended definition of the concept of vernacular language. Be forewarned that Earley uses a number of words that may be unfamiliar to you. However, the topic of this essay is quite approachable.

1 I do not like, I have never liked, nor do I expect to like watermelon. For the record, I consider this a private, dietary preference, not a political choice, neither a sign of failing character nor a renunciation of Southern citizenship. I simply do not like watermelon. Nor, for that matter, do I like grits, blackberries, cantaloupe, buttermilk, okra, baked sweet potatoes, rhubarb, or collard greens. Particularly collard greens. I don't even like to look at collard greens. But, because I am a Southerner—a North Carolinian, of Appalachian, Scots-Irish descent, the offspring of farming families on both sides—my family finds my refusal to like the foods they like somehow distressing. When I eat at my grandmother's red-roofed, high-ceilinged Victorian barn of a house, in Polk County, North Carolina, my relatives earnestly strive to persuade me that I am making a big mistake by not sampling this or that, that I should just *try* the greens, have just a little *slice* of watermelon, a small *bite* of cantaloupe. They tell me that I will get used to the seeds in blackberries, the mealiness of grits, the swampy odor of greens boiled too long in a big pot. And when I passionately and steadfastly refuse, as I have done for the last thirty-seven years, they stare at me for a few seconds as if they didn't know me, their mouths set sadly, before looking down at their plates as if preparing to offer up a second grace. Then my grandmother pronounces, "Tony Earley, you're just quare."

2 According to my edition of the Shorter Oxford English Dictionary, "quare" is an Anglo-Irish adjective from the early nineteenth century meaning "queer, strange, eccentric." Most other dictionaries, if they list the word at all, will tell you that it is dialectical, archaic, or obsolete, an anachronism, a muted, aging participant in the clamoring riot of the English language. But when spoken around my grandmother's table, by my parents and aunts and uncles and cousins, "quare" is as current as the breath that produces it, as pointed as a sharpened stick. In my family's lexicon, "quare" packs a specificity of meaning which "queer," "strange," "eccentric," "odd," "unusual," "unconventional," and "suspicious" do not. The only adjective of synonymous texture would be "squirrelly," but we are a close bunch and would find the act of calling one another squirrelly impolite. So, in my grandmother's dining room, when "quare" is the word we need, "quare" is the word we use.

3 Nor is "quare" the only word still hiding out in my grandmother's house which dictionaries assure us lost currency years ago. If I brought a quare person to Sunday dinner at Granny's and he ate something that disagreed with him, we might say that he looked a little peaked. Of course, we might decide that he was peaked not because he had eaten something that disagreed with him but because he had eaten a bait of something he liked. We would say, Why, he was just too trifling to leave the table. He ate almost the whole mess by himself. And now we have this quare, peaked, trifling

person on our hands. How do we get him to leave? Do we job him in the stomach? Do we hit him with a stob? No, we are kinder than that. We tell him, "Brother, you liked to have stayed too long." We put his dessert in a poke and send him on his way.

4 When I was a child, I took these words for granted. They were part of the language I heard around me, and I breathed them in like air. Only when I began to venture away from the universe that revolved around my grandmother's table did I come to realize that the language of my family was not the language of the greater world. I was embarrassed and ashamed when my town-bred classmates at Rutherfordton Elementary School corrected my speech, but by the time I entered college and signed up for an Appalachian-studies class I wasn't surprised to learn that my family spoke a dialect. I had begun to suspect as much, and was, by that time, bilingual: I spoke in the Appalachian vernacular when I was with my family and spoke standard English when I wasn't. This tailoring of speech to audience, which still feels a shade ignoble to me, is not uncommon among young people from my part of the world. In less generous regions of the greater American culture, the sound of Appalachian dialect has come to signify ignorance, backwardness, intransigence, and, in the most extreme examples, toothlessness, rank stupidity, and an alarming propensity for planting flowers in painted tractor tires.

5 This is not some sort of misguided, Caucasian appeal for ethnicity, nor is it a battle cry from the radical left against the patriarchal oppression of grammar, but the fact is that for me standard English has always been something of a second language. I have intuitively written it correctly from the time I started school, but speaking it still feels slightly unnatural, demands just enough conscious thought on my part to make me question my fluency. When I am introduced to a stranger, when I meet a more showily educated colleague in the English department at Vanderbilt, when I go to parties at which I feel unsure of my place in the evening's social pecking order, I catch myself proofreading sentences before I speak them—adding "g"s to the ends of participles, scanning clauses to make sure they ain't got no double negatives, clipping long vowels to affectless, Midwestern dimensions, and making sure I use "lay" and "lie" in a manner that would not embarrass my father-in-law, who is a schoolteacher from California. Occasionally, even my wife, whose Southern accent is significantly more patrician than my own, will smile and ask, "What did you just say?" And I'll realize that I have unwittingly slipped into the language of my people, that I have inadvertently become "colorful." I'll rewind my sentence in my head so that I can save it as an example of how not to speak to strangers. Only in the sanctity of Granny's house can I speak my mother tongue with anything resembling peace of mind.

6 In 1904, a librarian and writer named Horace Kephart, having recently left his wife and children and suffered a nervous breakdown, moved to the mountains around Bryson City, North Carolina. Although he travelled there initially to distance himself from human contact, he soon recovered enough to take an active interest in the world in which he found himself. An avid gatherer of information and a compulsive list-maker, Kephart spent the rest of his life compiling exhaustive journals and records detailing the geography, history, culture, and language of the southern Appalachians—a pursuit that resulted in countless magazine articles, a celebrated handbook, "Camping and Woodcraft," and two editions of a book entitled "Our Southern Highlanders."

7 Although Kephart had chosen the Appalachians over the deserts of the Southwest somewhat randomly, he arrived in western North Carolina at a particularly fortuitous time for a man of his particular talents. In the roadless hollows of the Blue Ridge and the Smokies, Kephart found a people isolated by their hostile, vertical geography and living largely as their ancestors had, in the later half of the eighteenth century, when the great Scots-Irish migration out of Pennsylvania first filled the region with people of European descent.

8 "No one can understand the attitude of our highlanders toward the rest of the earth," Kephart wrote,

> until he realizes their amazing isolation from all that lies beyond the blue, hazy skyline of their mountains. Conceive a shipload of emigrants cast away on some unknown island, far from the regular track of vessels, and left there for five or six generations, unaided and untroubled by the growth of civilization. Among the descendants of such a company we would expect to find customs and ideas unaltered from the time of their forefathers. . . . The mountain folk still live in the eighteenth century. The progress of mankind from that age to this is no heritage of theirs.

9 Because the Scots-Irish settlers had spoken to and been influenced by so few outsiders, the language they brought with them from Scotland and Ireland, by way of Pennsylvania, had been preserved remarkably intact. And the English dialect that Kephart encountered in North Carolina was in many ways closer to the Elizabethan English of Shakespeare or the Middle English of Chaucer* than to anything that had been spoken in England for centuries. Coincidentally, had Kephart come to these mountains a generation later, his research would have been less definitive. Within a few years after his death, in 1931, road-building initiatives, radio, and the Sears, Roebuck catalogue had begun to open even the darkest hollows of the Appalachians to twentieth-century America. In a very short time, the resulting cultural homogenization had turned the southern highlands into a vastly different world from the one that Kephart had originally discovered.

10 When I first read "Our Southern Highlanders," late last year, it held for me the power of revelation. It told me who I was—or at least where I came from—in a way that I had never fully understood before. All the words I had thought specific to my family had entries in a dictionary compiled from Kephart's research. And all of them—with the exception of "quare," which is a mere two hundred years old—were words of Middle English origin, which is to say anywhere from five hundred to eight hundred years old. Although most of the people I meet today wouldn't have any idea what it's like to eat a bait, Chaucer would have.

11 Of course, words of Middle English origin are mere babes compared with the words of Latin, Greek, and Hebrew etymology that constitute much of our language. The Latin and Greek roots of the words "agriculture" and "barbarian" were old long before the primitive tribes of the British Isles painted their faces blue and grunted in a dialect resembling English. So I am less taken by the age of the words of the Appalachian vernacular which found their way into my grandmother's house than I am by the specific history they hold.

***Geoffrey Chaucer (1340?–1400):** English poet and author of *The Canterbury Tales.*

The word "quare," for me, contains sea voyages and migrations. It speaks of families stopping after long journeys and saying, for any one of a thousand reasons, "This is far enough." It speaks to me of generations of farmers watching red dirt turn below plow blades, of young men stepping into furrows when old men step out. It speaks to me of girls fresh from their mothers' houses crawling into marriage beds and becoming mothers themselves. It bears witness to the line of history, most of it now unmappable, that led to my human waking beneath these particular mountains. If language is the mechanism through which we inherit history and culture, then each individual word functions as a type of gene, bearing with it a small piece of the specific information that makes us who we are, and tells us where we have been. My first cousin Greg and I came down with the same obscure bone disease in the same knee at the same age. For us, the word "quare" is no less a genetic signifier of the past than the odd, bone-eating chromosome carried down through history by one wonders how many limping Scots-Irish. 12

The last time I remember talking to my great-grandfather Womack, he was well into his nineties, and our whole family had gathered on the porch of the house he built as a young man, along Walnut Creek, in the Sunny View community of Polk County. When I tell this story, I choose to remember it as a spring day—although it may not have been—simply because I like to think that the daffodils in his yard were blooming. (My grandmother, who is eighty-three now, helped him plant them when she was a little girl.) At some point, everyone else got up and went inside, leaving Paw Womack and me alone on the porch. I was in high school, a freshman or sophomore, and was made self-conscious by his legendary age. He had been born in another century. His father had been wounded at Gettysburg. A preacher's son, he never uttered a swear word or tasted alcohol. He had farmed with a mule until he was well into his eighties, and he had never got another car after the one he bought in 1926 wore out. He voted for Woodrow Wilson. He was *historical.* I felt that the family had somehow chosen me to sit with him; I felt that I needed to say something. I got out of my chair and approached him as one would a sacred relic. I sat down on the porch rail facing him. I remember his immense, knotted farmer's hands spread out on the arms of his rocker. We stared at each other for what seemed like a long time. Eventually, I blushed. I smiled at him and nodded. He smiled back and said, "Who *are* you?" 13

I said, "I'm Reba's boy. Clara Mae's grandson." 14

"Oh," he said. "Reba's boy." 15

If we ever spoke again, I don't remember it. 16

It seems significant to me now that when I told Paw Womack who I was I didn't give him my name. My position as an individual was secondary to my place in the lineage that had led to my sitting on his porch. I identified myself as a small part of a greater whole. *Who are you?* I'm Reba's boy, Clara Mae's grandson, Tom Womack's great-grandson. *Where are you from?* Over yonder. *Why don't you like watermelon?* I don't know. I guess I'm just quare. 17

Ironically, just as I have learned to appreciate the history contained in the word "quare," I have also had to accept the fact that it is passing out of my family with my generation. Neither I nor my cousins use it outside Granny's house unless we temper it first with irony—a sure sign of a word's practical death within a changing 18 language. Of course, no language is a static property: the life cycles of words mirror the life cycles of the individuals who speak them. Every language, given enough time, will replace each of its words, just as the human body replaces each of its cells every seven years. The self-appointed guardians of English who protest that the word "celibate" means "unmarried," and not "abstaining from sexual intercourse," are wasting their time. "Sounds are too volatile and subtle for legal restraints," Samuel Johnson wrote in the 1755 Preface to his "Dictionary of the English Language"; "to enchain syllables, and to lash the wind, are equally the undertakings of pride."

19 I tell myself that the passing of Appalachian vernacular from my family's vocabulary is not a tragedy, or a sign of our being assimilated into a dominant culture, but simply the arrival of an inevitable end. "Tongues, like governments," Dr. Johnson wrote, "have a natural tendency to degeneration." I tell myself that it is a natural progression for my children to speak a language significantly different from that of my ancestors, but the fact that it has happened so suddenly, within the span of a single generation—my generation—makes me wonder if I have done something wrong, if I have failed the people who passed those words down. Sometimes the truest answer to the question "Who are you?" is "I don't know."

20 Words and blood are the double helix that connect us to our past. As a member of a transitional generation, I am losing those words and the connection they make. I am losing the small comfort of shared history. I compensate, in the stories I write, by sending people up mountains to look, as Horace Kephart did, for the answers to their questions, to look down from a high place and see what they can see. My characters, at least, can still say the words that bind them to the past without sounding queer, strange, eccentric, odd, unusual, unconventional, or suspicious. "Stories," says the writer Tim O'Brien, "can save us." I have put my faith in the idea that words, even new ones, possess that kind of redemptive power. Writers write about a place not because they belong there, but because they want to belong. It's a quare feeling.

Vocabulary

The following terms are identified by paragraph number. Make sure that you understand each term's meaning in its context. If you're not sure that you understand a term, look it up in a college-level dictionary.

renunciation (1)	currency (3)	patriarchal (5)
Victorian (1)	vernacular (4)	intuitively (5)
steadfastly (1)	tailoring (4)	fluency (5)
dialectical (2)	ignoble (4)	showily (5)
archaic (2)	intransigence (4)	pecking order (5)
anachronism (2)	propensity (4)	affectless (5)
clamoring (2)	patrician (5)	exhaustive (6)
lexicon (2)	unwittingly (5)	pursuit (6)
specificity (2)	avid (6)	fortuitous (7)

homogenization (9)	signifier (12)	assimilated (19)
revelation (10)	lineage (17)	double helix (20)
etymology (11)	static (18)	redemptive (20)

Style and Strategy

1. Earley's subject is academic, and his vocabulary is substantial (see above). What is the *tone* of this essay? What does the language contribute to this tone?
2. How much does Earley's audience probably already know about Appalachian culture and language? How does he help them to understand the subject or understand it better?
3. Is Earley defining more than one term or concept? If so, what terms or concepts does he define?
4. Find the specific examples that Earley uses to illustrate his points. What common theme connects these examples?

STYLE AND STRATEGY
1. Although the subject is academic, the tone is somewhat relaxed and familiar. It is established earley, in the introduction. More important, Early conveys examples of Appalachian colloquialisms in believable anecdotes that keep the reader's interest.
2. Paragraph 4 provides clues that the audience knows little about the author's dialect.
3. Paragraph 5 defines a kind of linguistic insecurity. Paragraph 11 suggests a definition of "etymology." Paragraphs 12–17 define "genetic signifier." Via contrast, Earley even distinguishes dialect from "standard" language (paragraphs 18 and 19).

4. Examples of Appalachian dialect appear throughout. Earley discusses them as linguistic phenomena, but also as "the double helix that connect us to our past" (paragraph 20).

Questions for Critical Thinking and Discussion

1. Earley refers to the "homogenization" of U.S. culture: the disappearance of cultural and regional differences so that the people in one part of the country look and act much like the people in other parts. In your opinion, what factors have caused this shift toward uniformity?
2. In the United States alone, languages are lost daily. One reason is that small Native American tribes are losing their elderly members, who in many cases are the last surviving speakers of the tribe's traditional tongue. Earley defines *language* as a living entity, certainly worth our time and attention. Should the government spend federal funds to preserve—or at least to record—dying Native American languages?

QUESTIONS FOR CRITICAL THINKING AND DISCUSSION Item 1 is easier to discuss than item 2, which can be turned into an argument paper based on research. Reserve this one for your more ambitious students.

Suggestions for Writing

Write a 500- to 750-word essay defining one of the following terms:

1. Private language
2. Public face
3. Comfort zone
4. Buzzwords

SUGGESTIONS FOR WRITING Remind students that they will need to fill their papers with effective examples.

WRITING THE DEFINITION ESSAY WITH A READER'S EYE

As you write a definition essay, you will need to be constantly aware of your reader's knowledge of, and interest in, your topic as well as your purpose for writing. The term or concept that you choose to define will largely determine whether you take an objective or subjective (personal) approach to your material. (For more on objective and subjective definition, see pages 335–338.) If

MORE OPTIONS ONLINE
If you would like to read additional definition essays, go to **www.mhhe.com/writingtoday**.

you will be writing a subjective definition, you need to be especially sure that you think like a member of your audience from the prewriting stage through your final draft. The advice that follows will help you think like a reader as you consider your assignment and then prewrite, draft, revise, and edit your extended definition essay.

Issues to Keep in Mind

If you consider the following four issues as you plan and write your extended definition essay, you will have a better chance of making your definition clear for your readers:

1. Using brief definitions
2. Using negative definitions
3. The differences between objective definition and subjective definition
4. Strategies for developing a definition essay

Using Brief Definitions

Providing a brief definition is a good internal strategy that you can use when developing extended definition essays as well as essays that employ other rhetorical options. Often you will need to indicate to your reader the meaning of a term or concept that you are using. Sometimes a more common synonym for the term in question is sufficient, such as in the following example:

> Environmental changes can sometimes be detected by examining a tortoise's carapace (shell).

In other instances, you will need to provide a longer, more detailed definition of a term. Note how this process works:

> name — category — distinguishing features
>
> A "backpack" is a computer hard drive that is portable and is used to copy the contents of one regular hard drive, such as that found in a PC, to another hard drive.

The definition first names or labels the term or item, then shows what type or category it is found within, and then shows how the term or item differs from other terms or items within that category. Thus, a "backpack" is not used as part of a standard computer but is used to copy one computer's contents to another computer.

Writers sometimes make careless errors when writing simple definitions:

CLASSROOM HINT
Discuss these problems in class.

1. **Defining too broadly.** "A car is a four-wheeled, internal-combustion vehicle used to carry people and objects from place to place" does not distinguish a car from a truck.
2. **Defining too narrowly.** "The tomato is a common vegetable that is rendered to produce ketchup" ignores the fact that tomatoes are used in many other areas of food production.

3. **Using a circular definition.** "A word processor is a machine used to process words" tries to define *word processor* by using *process;* for a reader unfamiliar with such a machine, *processor* is probably the term that needs to be defined.
4. **Omitting the category or type.** "In substance-abuse counseling, an intervention is when family members or friends confront the person at risk and try to persuade him or her to enter treatment" neglects to define the category. *Is when* does not give the reader a clear sense of what an intervention actually is: a face-to-face, surprise confrontation. Using *is when* is also faulty grammar.

Using Negative Definitions

Sometimes, defining something by what it *is not* is more effective than merely defining what it *is,* as in the following paragraph:

> The city's new police chief has announced that her emphasis will be on crime prevention—in other words, "proactive" policing, stopping crime before it happens rather than tracking down criminals after the fact. Crime prevention would seem to indicate a more healthy relationship between citizens and law enforcement: community policing, better access to the police to report concerns, and so on. But what has actually transpired is a vast network of speed traps. Although an intended crime is sometimes thwarted by the results of a traffic stop, putting every available officer behind a radar gun (1) ignores neighborhood concerns and (2) raises the old suspicions that the police are just there to raise revenues through the traffic court system. What we are seeing is not crime prevention but a policy that makes local driving an immense pain for residents and makes outsiders glad to leave our city limits behind them.

The writer provides an "ideal" definition of what crime prevention should entail, but the paragraph concentrates on a faulty approach to crime prevention—in the writer's view, what "proactive" police work should *not* be.

Objective Definition and Subjective Definition

The goal of an objective definition is usually to inform the reader about a term or concept. Objective definitions usually avoid personal opinions or biases. However, a subjective definition tries to show the reader a new way of considering a term or concept or even to make a radical change in the reader's opinion of that term or concept. Which approach is the better one for you to take? That depends upon your purpose for writing.

CLASSROOM HINT Consider contrasting objective and subjective definitions in class via discussion and/or short in-class writing exercises.

Objective Definition Suppose that for your next assignment your instructor handed you a topic sheet with the following photograph of a typical dog:

© PhotoDisc.

You are asked to define this creature. In this assignment, your instructor is asking for an **objective definition**, one in which the observation "I like dogs" is probably irrelevant. What your instructor wants, instead, is an essay in which you demonstrate your ability to plan, organize, write, and revise a definition of this familiar type of domesticated animal. Such an assignment might seem like a dry exercise, but it's actually quite useful and a lot harder than it looks.

The main problem with objective definition is to decide what to leave in and what is too specific or irrelevant. Do you need to point out that a dog is a carbon-based life form? Probably not. Do you need to point out that a dog is a mammal? Maybe, if you need to separate dogs from lizards and ticks. Should you say that dogs are descended from wolves and still resemble them in many ways? Yes. The following is a paragraph from an essay responding to this assignment:

> Dogs are descendants of wolves, those rapidly disappearing predators that once prowled most of the world. Early peoples domesticated wolves, probably by the simple device of offering them food and warm shelter. However, the modern dog is still closely related to the wolf: both are fur-bearing mammals with prominent ears, eyes, and nose. Selective breeding over the centuries has produced dog breeds that range from barely 10 pounds to almost 200

> pounds; however, look closely at any dog and you'll see signs of its wild ancestor: the face, the general body shape, the teeth. And although dogs are millennia removed from wolves, they can still revert to feral, predatory behavior.

This paragraph covers a lot of factual ground without lapsing into tedium, proving that seemingly mundane topics can be turned into interesting reading.

Subjective Definition When you write a **subjective definition**, your purpose is different from that of the objective approach. You are trying to influence readers so that they understand a concept from your point of view. When you define *your* ideal (or least-favorite) vacation, evening, car, or article of clothing, the purpose of this essay is different from that of the objective definition.

In the preceding section, we illustrated how one student used a paragraph to define what a dog is. The result was objective and was clearly intended to inform the reader. A different slant on the topic—what is your *ideal* dog?—produces a different result. Now the reader is trying both to inform the reader and to convince him or her that the writer's choice is worthy of consideration. Here is a paragraph from a student's essay on the second topic:

> I first discovered hounds when I was a child spending summer vacations on my uncle's farm. Uncle Ed raised hounds for bird hunting, but by that point in his life he was more interested in the dogs than in chasing quail. I liked his German shorthairs very well. These are mid-sized dogs, usually with a steady temperament and very little viciousness. They like people and join in various activities but are not "needy," a trait I dislike. Dynamo, who is now six years old and whom I raised from puppyhood, is the great-grandson of one of Uncle Ed's hunters. He likes riding in the car but doesn't get cranky if he has to stay home. He likes attention but doesn't demand it. I can leave him at home for a weekend without his going crazy and trashing the place. For me, the German shorthair is the ideal dog to own.

Using subjective definition, the writer is clearly "lobbying" for his favorite breed of dog, trying to convince the reader of the rightness of his preference.

However, note that because your personal view of the topic controls the structure and content of the essay, there is a danger that you will end up writing a "private" essay, one that loses its connection to the reader as you burrow deeper and deeper into your own world. A related danger is that the "private" essay doesn't *define;* it usually just *describes*. For example, when asked to define the ideal living quarters, one student writer decided to use her own apartment as an example and proceeded to describe her (admittedly) well-furnished and desirable abode. Here is one of the body paragraphs:

> The living room is all modular glass and steel, with black leather furniture chosen to match the modular effect. I avoided bright colors here: the wall decorations are all black-and-white prints or photographs. The appliances are also minimized, with the clock wafer-thin against the wall and the television recessed. The carpet is equally muted: a very dark gray.

Why is this décor scheme important to the writer? What does it have to do with the ideal living quarters? The writer has not really defined anything but has instead described her unstated preference with objective, surface details. Note how the following revision makes the description serve the definition:

> Many people over-decorate their living rooms and use too much color, as if they were putting together an outfit for a party instead of providing a suitable environment. The best furniture and decorations are unobtrusive and uncluttered. My living room is all modular glass and steel, with black leather furniture chosen to match the modular effect. The wall decorations are all black-and-white prints or photographs. The appliances are also minimized, with the clock wafer-thin against the wall and the television recessed. The carpet is equally muted: a very dark gray. My living room doesn't occupy me; I occupy it.

Strategies for Developing a Definition

CLASSROOM HINT Reviewing these strategies in class is helpful.

Note how you can use the other rhetorical options to help you develop an extended definition:

1. **Description** (Chapter 6). Defining a physical object virtually requires you to describe it.
2. **Narration** (Chapter 7). Use an anecdote to give your reader a better sense of the term or concept being defined.
3. **Exemplification** (Chapter 8). If you are defining a type of machine, for example, you could list and analyze different name-brand examples of that machine.
4. **Process analysis** (Chapter 9). You could show how the thing you are defining happens or works.
5. **Causal analysis** (Chapter 10). You could show some of the effects of the term or concept when it is used in practice; alternatively, you could explain why a term or concept has come to mean something quite different from its earlier meaning.
6. **Classification** (Chapter 12). A key step in defining a term or concept is showing what type of thing it is, so you could discuss the term or concept in relation to other terms or concepts in the same category.
7. **Comparison/contrast** (Chapter 13). A negative definition explains what a term or concept is *not;* the contrast strategy is obviously useful here.

8. **Argument** (Chapter 14). A subjective definition frequently tries to convince the reader that the writer's point of view is valid and worthy of consideration.

MORE OPTIONS ONLINE
For more help with problem areas in the definition essay, go to **www.mhhe.com/writingtoday.**

Choosing a Topic

Your first step in writing an effective extended definition is to choose a term or concept that you are interested in and can successfully define for your audience. The following guidelines will help you choose a promising topic for your essay:

1. Think about your purpose for writing about this topic. Do you want to write an objective definition that informs your readers about a topic, or do you want to write a subjective definition that amuses readers or convinces them to share your viewpoint? What is the point that you are trying to make?
2. Whether you will be writing an objective definition or a subjective definition, concentrate on finding a topic that you can make interesting for your reader. If you are writing a subjective definition, beware of topics that might lead you to write a "private" essay that your readers will be unable to relate to. Remember, it's not a question of what your preferences are on a given topic; it's a matter of *why.*
3. Avoid a topic that is too large or too vague. Trying to define "love" or "honor" in 500 to 750 words is a recipe for disaster.
4. Consider what your reader is already likely to know about a subject. For example, an objective definition of a supermarket would probably bore most readers; however, a subjective definition of the same term might be quite effective.

Prewriting

To write an extended definition, you need to try to capture the defining features of the term or concept as you plan and prewrite. One student writer tackled the topic "What is the perfect job supervisor?" As he began to think about his topic, he realized that this mythical person had to possess certain general attributes: the ability to be fair, the ability to punish, and the ability to praise. Using clustering, the writer started with this group of three general attributes, then added specific attributes for each of the three general ones. Note that freewriting or brainstorming would also have been a good choice at this stage (see Chapter 2 for more on prewriting strategies).

At this point, see if you can develop a working or preliminary thesis. Does your thesis match your purpose? If so, and if you begin to visualize the direction that your essay will take, you are now ready to organize your prewriting.

Organizing

The writer of the essay on the perfect supervisor produced a sentence outline before beginning his essay. This step helped him see that his essay's structure was logical and balanced. (For more information on outlines, see Chapter 2.)

Drafting

To illustrate some approaches to writing an extended definition, we have included the essay "The Brave and the Humane."

The Introduction

In an extended definition, the introduction needs to present the term or concept to be defined and capture the reader's interest, often by relating the topic to his or her own experience. Introductions often move from general to specific, which is the approach that the student writer has chosen for his essay defining the ideal boss:

The Brave and the Humane

Most people have a number of problems with their job. Even those who like what they do find that most mornings they would rather sleep in or go the beach. However, if work were all fun and games, the company wouldn't need to pay employees for their efforts.

The main demon most people dread at work is the boss. This person probably occupies more space in the average adult American's psyche than Mom, Dad, spouse, or children, largely because of his or her ability to wound us, harm our self-esteem, and even make us feel like moral failures. But what kind of supervisor would be ideal? Many people might long for a weak or absent boss, but most businesses wouldn't keep such a supervisor for long. **Instead, the mythical "perfect boss" needs to have three qualities: the ability to be fair, the ability to punish, and the ability to reward.**

Note the position of the thesis, at the end of the second paragraph, where it follows two paragraphs that have a writing pattern of general to specific.

Consider Your Options

An extended definition can be written to fulfill a variety of purposes. Make sure that you understand your purpose and express it in your introduction. Your choice of introductory strategy can help you do this (see Chapter 3).

The Body

The writer has set up a clear pattern of organization for his essay in his thesis. However, clearly spelling out the essay structure in this way can set up either a mechanical, perfunctory essay or a lively, interesting one. Read on to discover how the student writer carried out his plan:

Everyone wants a piece of the boss. The strategies that employees use to manipulate their supervisors are endless. If Charley has discovered that the boss likes golf, he'll make sure to drop in and schmooze about his iron shot to the eleventh green at Invisible Lakes last Sunday and, maybe, drop off a few half-price greens fee coupons. If Karen knows that the boss has a soft spot for family issues—specifically, kids—she'll keep the boss updated on little Amy's ongoing, time-consuming, and expensive battle with ear infections. Yet when it comes time to decide on rewards for performance (raises, days off, promotions, overtime pay, and so on), the good boss is going to put all personal considerations aside.

The punishment of wrongdoers is another sticky subject. Some supervisors turn into sadistic prison guards at that point, clearly enjoying this part of their job, drawing the process out, twisting the knife. Others have the opposite problem: they can't even look the offender in the eye or form complete sentences. However, the ideal manager gets to the point, clearly stating the problem and the consequences in as short a time as possible. There is no reason for the employee to come away with fears or bad feelings. It's a matter of stating the facts, explaining the situation, and coming to an agreement. Life goes on.

Finally, why can't some bosses ever find a way to praise their subordinates? Some supervisors are like pinch-faced Puritan judges from the seventeenth century. They act as if they're giving up part of their soul if they say "Job well done." Although a good boss can't hand out financial rewards like Halloween candy, he or she must know how a well-judged compliment can motivate employees.

Note how the writer uses comparison/contrast and exemplification as internal strategies to develop the body paragraphs.

The Conclusion

The conclusion of an extended definition needs to reinforce the main point about the term or concept or move beyond it. For example, the student writer could have summarized his extended definition in his conclusion, but a summary would not have added anything to his essay. Instead, notice how he is able to show the logical point to be drawn from his essay:

Even when they have an ideal boss, people will still have problems at work. Most workplaces do not offer much emotional gratification. But the good supervisor will know what people need and what they can tolerate. And most people, if they believe they are being treated fairly, in all senses of the word, will be willing to come back tomorrow and put in an honest day's effort.

Consider Your Options

The conclusion of a definition essay gives you the opportunity to comment on what you have written. Don't summarize here. Use this section to reinforce the significance of what you have written in the body of your essay. (To read more about strategies for concluding an essay, see Chapter 3.)

MORE OPTIONS ONLINE
For more help with the step-by-step development of the definition essay, go to **www.mhhe.com/writingtoday**.

EXERCISE 11.1

Write an outline of "The Brave and the Humane." (For help with outlines, see Chapter 2, pages 41–42.) What does the outline reveal about the essay's organization? Would a different organization work better? Explain.

MORE OPTIONS ONLINE
For more help with revision, go to **www.mhhe.com/writingtoday**.

EXERCISE 11.1 Answers will vary. The following sentence outline is suggested.
I. Background: The ideal boss may not be what most people would expect. Thesis: The mythical "perfect boss" needs to have three qualities: the ability to be fair, the ability to punish, and the ability to reward.
II. The strategies that employees use to manipulate their supervisors are endless.
  A. "Charley" will talk about golf if he discovers that his boss is a golfer.
  B. "Karen" will keep her child-loving boss up to date on her daughter Amy.
  C. Good bosses will put all personal considerations aside when rating employees.
III. The punishment of wrongdoers is another sticky subject.
  A. Some supervisors enjoy being sadistic.
  B. Other supervisors have trouble disciplining employees.
  C. The ideal manager clearly states the problem and the consequences in as short a time as possible.
IV. Some supervisors have trouble praising subordinates.

Revising Your Draft

After you have completed a draft of your extended definition, your next step is to revise it, using your own analysis and comments from classmates or friends. During peer review, answer the questions on page 343 about the draft you are reviewing, whether it is yours or another student's.

After your review for content, you need to go over your and your peer reviewers' responses to your essay and then revise for unity, coherence, language level, and tone (see Chapter 4). When you have revised your draft and are satisfied with it, read your draft for mechanical and grammatical errors. Find and correct major sentence errors (fragments, comma splices, fused sentences), errors in pronoun agreement and subject-verb agreement, and spelling.

Now that you have made your corrections, *read your essay one more time* to catch any errors you may have made during revision and find errors missed during your earlier reviews.

Student Essay

The following essay is Curtis Ray Mosley's response to a definition assignment. The final draft is presented first. Then Curtis's first draft is presented, with his comments about this draft and what he needed to do in the revision stage.

Even the final version of this essay, which won first place in a student writing contest, is strong stuff. Curtis Mosley is working with potentially controversial subject matter here. As you read, ask yourself how you might respond to Mosley's essay if you were to give him comments as a peer reviewer. What are its strengths and weaknesses as a definition of the concept of a "moment of truth"?

Curtis's Final Draft

My "Moment of Truth"

1 A moment of truth is, more accurately, a moment of decision. Faced with an adequate amount of information, the person in a given situation still faces a difficult choice. If good judgment and common sense prevail, then he or she chooses the correct alternative. If not, then he or she walks away feeling like a dope, as I did recently.

2 One afternoon a week or so ago, I was sitting on the lowered tailgate of my friend Bubba's pickup, feeling out of place. The central artery of The

Questions for Reviewing an Extended Definition

1. Does the essay's opening introduce the topic and capture the reader's interest? How could the introduction be strengthened?
2. What is the thesis statement, and has the writer placed it in the best position within the essay? In what ways, if any, could it be strengthened?
3. Is the term or concept that is being defined clear? What is the writer's purpose for defining this term or concept? Has the writer fulfilled this purpose?
4. If the definition is subjective, does the essay speak to an audience, or does it seem written for the writer only?
5. Does the extended definition seem complete? Point out any important defining feature of the term or concept that the writer has left out.
6. Is the organization effective? Should the defining features be given in a different order? If so, what order would be better?
7. Do the topic sentences introduce each defining feature? Is each feature fully developed? Where could the writer use a different rhetorical option to explain a feature more effectively?
8. Does the writer use transitions to guide the reader? Where are transitional words or sentences needed?
9. Does the essay have an effective conclusion? How could it be improved?

Pines Trailer Park in the small town of Bithlo was clogged with wild, screaming children just released from school. I was worried about the impression we gave them, drinking Budweiser at three in the afternoon. The antlike scurrying of the children was disrupted only by the dustdevil swarms of future athletes that marked the frequent basketball goals placed by the road.

A. Some supervisors are like Puritan judges.
B. A good boss knows how a well-judged compliment can motivate employees.
V. The good supervisor will know what people need and what they can tolerate, and when people believe they are being treated fairly, they will be willing to put in an honest day's effort.

3 As I ceremoniously crushed an empty can in my hand, something down the road caught my eye. Walking toward us, parting the throng of children as Moses parted the Red Sea, was the distinctive shape of an attractive young woman. Although she was still twenty-odd mobile homes away, I could not keep my eyes off her. She paused in the road and was joined by another girl, this one a little overweight. They both were adorned in tube tops and cut-off blue jean shorts. The overweight one was bulging over the top, while the thin one hung out the bottom. Neither wore shoes. They

commanded an audience of young boys as they held hands and whispered in each other's ear. Standing in the middle of the road, they were totally oblivious to a car trying to fight its way through.

4 "Where do you think they're going?" I asked Bubba.

5 "Oh, you don't want to mess with them. Trust me."

6 I wondered what he meant. The two girls were slowly coming into focus, and I came to realize their beauty was best admired from afar. Each face was heavily coated in makeup. The thin one had blue mascara streaking back from her eyes like Endora on *Bewitched;* the fat one had red cheeks like Krusty the Clown. Turning suddenly, the two went up to a trailer window, talked for a minute, and went inside.

7 "Bubba, what's the danger here?"

8 "Well, you see, those two are making their early rounds. They're checking out the scene. They want to find out who has some money, beer, or cigarettes, along with anything else a man will give them. That way, later tonight they know where to party."

9 "How do they make a living? Do they have any children?"

10 "Of course they have children. They just don't have any husbands. They're virtual experts in matters concerning food stamps, WIC (Women and Infant Care), and the legal entitlements of child support. Shoot, that skinny one is so good she collects from two guys for the same kid."

11 It all seemed a little professional to me. Could they be prostitutes? How could they finagle every night without a conflict arising between would-be suitors? Bubba's explanation was enlightening. "Take it from me. Those two are slicker than greased owl poop. The good-looking one teases you out of the goods, while the fat one gives her a reason to go home early. It's the old good cop, bad cop with a Bithlonian twist."

12 This would seem to be enough information to convince a reasonable man that he should seek romance elsewhere, but after all of Bubba's warnings, I was still thinking I would like to meet that thin one. I did not have long to wait. Reaching for another Bud, I caught a whiff of fake designer perfume and looked up to find myself face to face with danger.

"Those Budweisers sure look tasty, and you look pretty tasty yourself, working man," she purred seductively. 13

Bubba instinctively grabbed the now tepid twelve pack, pulling it close as if it were a woman's purse on a crowded subway. The thin one positioned her foot on the tailgate between Bubba and me, presenting an erotic barrier that was hard to ignore. The other one was flirting with the now eunuch-like Bubba, to no avail. 14

At this point, of course, I still could have found a way out of the situation. However, my better judgment and overall common sense were growing weaker by the moment. As Miss Piggy asked to turn up the radio in my car (Bubba had blown his speakers), I crumbled under the pressure. Prying the beer from Bubba's hand, I gave them each one. Only two remained. 15

"Hey, maybe I can give you a call sometime?" I sheepishly asked Skinny. 16

"Sure. Got a red?" she replied, grabbing my pack of Marlboros. Without waiting for an answer, she shook out the last of the Mohicans and quickly lit up. She instantly ripped the five Marlboro miles off the side of the pack and stuffed them into her tube top. "I'm sav'n for that Snake River wet-dry duffel bag. It's only three thousand miles. Got a pen?" She squirmed noticeably while writing her initials and number on my now worthless pack of smokes. "I don't want your old lady coming down here to kick my butt," she quipped in regard to the initials. 17

Feeling like Mr. Macho, I surrendered my last beer, bid everyone farewell, and headed for Orlando. After giving up only three beers, five miles, and one Marlboro red, I had procured a phone number and was ready for romance. I was on the East-West Expressway before I noticed my wallet was not in its regular place in the console. Everything became crystal clear, as I remembered the chunky one's request to turn up my radio because her favorite song was on. Furious, I retrieved my cell phone and called the newly acquired number. 18

Listening to the operator's recorded message, "The number you have dialed has been temporarily disconnected," I recalled Bubba's early warning: "You don't want to mess with them. Trust me." 19

Curtis's First Draft

Trailer Park Girls

My peer review partner mentioned that my essay didn't have much of a plot. She suggested that I needed to introduce some sort of story line that entertains readers. I added more description and narration to the final version, including figurative language ("as Moses parted the Red Sea") and humor.

As I read this draft, I began to worry about using the behavior of two people to define an entire group of women. My peer reviewer echoed my concern. I decided that the real issue was my own careless judgment during the encounter and that an analysis of that "moment of decision" was a better topic for a definition essay.

Adding the paragraph placing the overweight girl in the car was all that I needed to set up the surprise ending, when I have my "moment of truth."

1 Sitting on the lowered tailgate of Bubba's pickup, I felt out of place. The Pines Trailer Park in the small town of Bithlo was clogged with wild, screaming children. I was worried about the impression we gave them, drinking Budweiser at three in the afternoon.

2 Something down the road caught my eye. Walking toward us was an attractive young woman. She was soon joined by another girl, this one a little overweight. They both were wearing cut-off blue jean shorts. They commanded an audience of young boys as they held hands and whispered in each other's ear.

3 The two girls were slowly coming into focus, and I came to realize their beauty was best admired from afar. Each face was heavily coated in makeup. Turning suddenly, the two went up to a trailer window, talked for a minute, and went inside.

4 As we drank, Bubba warned me about trailer park girls. "Trailer park girls all have children. They just don't have any husbands. They are all experts in matters concerning food stamps, WIC (Women and Infant Care), and the legal entitlements of child support."

5 "Take it from me. Those two are slicker than greased owl poop. The good-looking one teases you out of the goods, while the fat one gives her a reason to go home early."

6 Even after Bubba's warning, I was still thinking I would like to meet that thin one. I did not have long to wait. Reaching for another Bud, I caught a whiff of fake designer perfume and looked up to find myself face to face with a genuine Bithlo trailer park girl!

7 Bubba instinctively grabbed the now tepid twelve pack, pulling it close as if it were a woman's purse on a crowded subway. The thin one positioned her foot on the tailgate between Bubba and me, presenting an erotic barrier that was hard to ignore. The other one was flirting with the now eunuch-like Bubba, to no avail. Crumbling under the pressure, I pried the beer from Bubba's hand, and gave them each one. Only two remained.

8 "Hey, maybe I can give you a call sometime?" I sheepishly asked Skinny.

9 "Sure. Got a red?" she replied, grabbing my pack of Marlboros. Without waiting for an answer, she shook out the last of the Mohicans and quickly lit up. "Got a pen?" She asked, squirming noticeably while writing her initials and number on my now worthless pack of smokes. "I don't want your old lady coming down here to kick my butt," she quipped in regard to the initials. Against Bubba's advice, I was about to become acquainted with a trailer park girl.

In my final draft I "poured some gravy on the potatoes" by adding more dialogue in the characters' authentic dialect. Finally, I changed the title to reflect my new focus.

EXERCISE 11.2: REVISING

The following is the first draft of a student's definition essay. Working in pairs or in small groups, review this essay. Using the Questions for Reviewing an Extended Definition on page 343, decide what revisions you would suggest. If you have any questions the student needs to consider, write them in the margin or on a separate sheet of paper. If your instructor directs you to, rewrite one or more paragraphs to make them stronger and to eliminate any grammatical or mechanical errors.

SUGGESTED ACTIVITY Consider asking students to meet in writing groups, each of which is charged with producing a more developed and effective version of this essay. Encourage students to use their imaginations or details from their own experience.

EXERCISE 11.2 Answers will vary. Students should point out that the thesis needs to indicate the concept that is being defined; the topic sentence in paragraph 2 needs to be supported with evidence; the topic sentence in paragraph 3 is supported by another assertion, which needs to be backed up with evidence; the personal anecdote backing up the topic sentence in paragraph 3, while relevant, is insufficient; and the conclusion is inadequate.

"TEEN-AGED DISCRIMINATION"

1 'Discrimination' is a hot topic today. Minority groups are sick of it, women are sick of it, foriegners are sick of it. But another group faces discrimination everyday, these are teen-agers.

2 In highschool teenagers are treated like crap, we were used to it. After school, on the weekends, in the summers, are kids treated any better? No!!!

3 Teen-age discrimination takes many forms. One is stores. When young people go to the mall they'can expect to be followed around by store security. This isnt an opinion its a fact. Teens are seen to be either criminals, or criminals about to happen. We want to spend money but we can take it for granite that stores think were their to steel.

4 An other discrimination is police. Last summer I was going fifty in a 35-zone, and got pulled over. Not only did the cop right me a ticket, he gave me a 'young lady' lecture as well. My self of steam suffered that day, I felt like, you know a second class citizen.

5 Teenagers are a target group; no doubt about it. This type of discrimination hurts everytime it hits; although, noone wants to talk about it.

Additional Writing Topics

1. Write an extended definition of one of the following terms:
   a. Road rage
   b. Passive-aggressive drivers
   c. Cyber loafing
   d. A blown semester
   e. The ideal academic advisor
2. **Writing on the job.** At work, you may have heard someone refer to taking a "mental health" day off. What does this term mean? Write an extended definition as a memo for your company's human resources department in which you incorporate both your sense of this term and the interpretations of your co-workers. (See Chapter 17 for help with writing a memo.)

Responding to a Photograph

CLASSROOM HINT
Before assigning either prompt, discuss it in class.

The first humans to walk on the moon were Neil Armstrong and Buzz Aldrin. On July 20, 1969, Armstrong took the photograph of Aldrin that appears on page 349.

1. Write an informal response to the photograph. What do you notice? How does the image make you feel? How does the photograph use the definition option?
2. At the time of this photograph, the moon landing was applauded as one of the greatest exploratory and technological achievements in human history. (To many observers, it still is.) The completely covered "spaceman" seemed to define a new era. Using a combination of library and online research, explore this era, concentrating on the predictions about the new future that space travel would produce. Remember to narrow your topic so that you can adequately address it. Write a documented essay that examines the nature of the "new future" envisioned over thirty years ago. (For more information on documented essays, see Chapter 21.)

Writing About Film

Heathers (1989, R) offers a subjective definition of "popularity in high school." What are the ramifications of this definition as the film unfolds?

Blade Runner (1982, R) attempts to answer the question "What is human?" What are the ramifications of this question as the film unfolds?

Using the Internet

Search the Internet for insights and information to use when writing extended definitions.

1. Many definition topics ask the writer to define an "ideal" or "perfect" example of some subject or thing, such as a day. What might be a perfect day for an avid golfer, tennis player, gourmet, hiker, camper, bowler, beer drinker, basketball player, video-game enthusiast, shopper, or Internet addict? Find three or four Web sites dedicated to a sport or activity you enjoy. Combine information from these sites with your own ideas in an essay that defines what you imagine to be a "perfect day" spent in this sport or activity.

Neil Armstrong, *Buzz Aldrin Walking on the Moon*, July 20, 1969. Original image courtesy of NASA/Corbis. Digital Image © 1996 Corbis.

2. Tony Earley's "The Quare Gene" uses definition to explain a dialect spoken in Appalachia. Until the twentieth century—before the era of universal education and instant telecommunications—there were many regional and local dialects of American English. In fact, most major languages have numerous dialects. Even today, the Chinese dialects of Mandarin and Cantonese differ markedly, and the French spoken in Quebec is quite different from the French spoken in Paris. Even English continues to have many varieties. Consider the differences between the language as it is spoken in the United States and as it is spoken in England, Scotland, Australia, or South Africa. Search the Internet for information about the various forms or dialects of any spoken language of your choice. Then focus on a specific dialect of that language and do some more online research. Use this material in a definition essay that explains the major characteristics of that dialect to someone who has little knowledge of it.

As an alternative assignment, use the Internet to discover information about a particular sect or branch of a world religion. For example, you might search for materials on Hasidic Jews, Coptic Christians, or Shiite Muslims. Again, use the information you find in a definition essay.

CARDS FOR ALL OCCASIONS
POWER FAILURE
JURY DUTY
FLAT TIRE
RENT INCREASE
CROP FAI
NEW MOON
RUG SHAMPOO
LUBE JOB
HAIRCUT
HIGH TIDE

CLASSIFICATION

CHAPTER 12

Writing in Context

You have been asked to start attending the regular Monday morning meeting at Osprey Online. You are sitting with your colleagues at a conference table headed by Bob. "It's quarterly sales report time," he says, tapping a very large folder packed full of paperwork. Bob grins, then slides the mountainous package down the table toward you. "It's your turn. Welcome to the team."

Back in your office, you start to wonder about Bob. He seems to have a certain sadistic quality. But your more important question is right in front of you. Your classes in business school taught you a lot about sales and profit breakdowns, but not how to write about them.

At first, you try to figure this task out on your own but don't make much progress. Then Bob's assistant, Stephanie, suggests using last quarter's report as a guide. You quickly realize that the solution is right in front of you. Virtually all of your division's revenues come from three sources: new software, software upgrades, and outsourced consulting. You take the folder's contents apart and then separate the paperwork into three stacks. The rest of your work day is substantially free of stress, as you organize last quarter's business by category.

***Classification* is a way of organizing material in order to make better sense of it. In the example above, what first seemed chaotic made sense once classification came into the picture.**

SUGGESTED ACTIVITY
Stores are always good examples of classification. Ask students to think of a store they frequent. Have them take five to ten minutes to write a brief classification of the items in the part of the store they are most familiar with (such as different types of music CDs or DVDs, different types of athletic shoes, etc.). Using one or two examples, discuss as a class the basis of classification that each store is using.

HOW DOES CLASSIFICATION WORK?

Classification is a powerful option that allows a writer to make sense of a large subject by dividing it into smaller categories, each one consisting of similar items. In fact, this strategy is sometimes called **division** because the first step requires the writer to divide the larger subject into smaller units. The writer then classifies specific entities according to which smaller category they fit into.

Regardless of the terminology used to describe this strategy, classification is widely employed. In the sciences, for example, classification is a standard strategy. The Swedish biologist Carolus Linnaeus established the taxonomy that we use to classify plants and animals. When we refer to a creature as belonging to a certain family, genus, or species, we are using Linnaeus's system. Similarly, if you find yourself in a chemistry class, you'll probably see the periodic table of elements hanging on the wall nearby, courtesy of Dmitri Mendeleev and Henry Moseley. On this chart, the elements are arranged from top to bottom and left to right, according to their electron structure. The elements of each category behave similarly in chemical combinations.

Classification is not confined to the sciences, however. This method appears in every discipline and in every type of writing. In his classic account of driving the back roads of America, *Blue Highways,* William Least Heat Moon describes the Hopi method of classifying human development:

> The Hopi believes mankind has evolved through four worlds: the first a shadowy realm of contentment; the second a place so comfortable the people forgot where they had come from and began worshipping material goods. The third world was a pleasant land too, but the people, bewildered by their past and fearful for their future, thought only of their own earthly plans. At last, the Spider Grandmother, who oversees the emergences, told them: "You have forgotten what you should have remembered, and now you have to leave this place. Things will be harder." In the fourth and present world, life is difficult for mankind, and he struggles to remember his source because materialism and selfishness block a greater vision. The newly born infant comes into the fourth world with the door of his mind open (evident in the cranial soft spot), but as he ages, the door closes and he must work at remaining receptive to the great forces. A human being's grandest task is to keep from breaking with things outside himself.

Even topics that we try *not* to think about may lend themselves to classification. In 1992 former Vice President Al Gore, Jr., wrote this paragraph as part of *Earth in the Balance,* his plea to clean up the environment:

> Perhaps the most visible evidence of the waste crisis is the problem of how to dispose of our mountains of municipal solid waste, which is being generated at the rate of more than five pounds a day for every citizen of this country, or approximately one ton per person per year. But two other kinds of waste pose equally difficult challenges. The first is the physically dangerous and politically volatile material known as hazardous waste, which accompanied the chemical revolution of the 1930s and which the United States now pro-

duces in roughly the same quantities as municipal solid waste. (This is a conservative estimate, one that would double if we counted all the hazardous waste that is currently exempted from regulation for a variety of administrative and political reasons.) Second, one ton of industrial solid waste is created each week for every man, woman, and child—and this does not even count the gaseous waste steadily being vented into the atmosphere. (For example, each person in the United States also produces an average of twenty tons of CO_2 each year.) Incredibly, taking into account all three of these conservatively defined categories of waste, every person in the United States produces *more than twice his or her weight in waste every day.*

CLASSROOM HINT Reviewing Hunkovic's paragraph in class is helpful.

You can classify by theme, by type, by appearance, by behavior. The way you choose to classify your subject is your **basis of classification.** In his narrative about his middle-school years, student writer Kevin Hunkovic shows the "pecking order" that existed at the ironically named Liberty Middle School (see Chapter 15 for the entire essay):

In 1988 Liberty Middle School had a student body of about 1,700 students, give or take a few hundred. I was overwhelmed by the multitudes of diverse people around me. My classes were huge. There were 40–65 students per class. These numbers dwarfed me as I became a very small part of a whole. Soon after I started the sixth grade, I began to notice a system underlying the way students and faculty interacted with each other. I later realized that it was a social class system. The highest members were the intellectuals, or nerds as they were called. They enjoyed special privileges that others did not have, such as getting to leave class and study alone in the library or move through the hallways without a pass. Then there was the middle class, those who weren't the best or the worst students. This group usually contained the athletes, cheerleaders, and the somewhat popular students. It constituted the majority of the student body. Next, there were the troublemakers, or the Future Criminals of America, as I called them. Those students tended to receive bad grades and get into trouble when they weren't causing it. Above all of this was the school faculty. Until I entered middle school, I thought the faculty were just the people who distributed the information to the students. At Liberty Middle School, however, the faculty took on all the functions of a small government: executives to run it, legislators to make the rules, and judges to punish wrongdoers with detentions. Finally, I noticed a class of outsiders, who for one reason or another did not fit into any category. They weren't mean enough to be in the lower class, or popular enough to converse with the middle class, or good enough at studying to be in the upper class. These students went unnoticed for the most part and were overlooked by teachers in an overcrowded classroom. The fourth class of people slipped through the cracks of the system, so to speak. In other words, they became victims of the institution.

Hunkovic uses classification as an internal strategy here, one that organizes the people of the school into recognizable groups.

In an informative classification essay about a factual subject, such as a report classifying moths or word-processing software, your purpose is to provide your reader with as clear a picture of the subject as possible. In the personal essay, however, your purpose is often both to enlighten and entertain. Therefore, the basis for your classification will be essential to the success of your essay. For example, if asked to classify your blood relatives, you could organize your essay according to genetic proximity—your siblings are closest to you, your parents are next, your extended relatives are further removed, and so on. But an essay on this topic will probably bore its readers. Why not find a more inventive way to classify your relatives? Consider the following categories:

Consider Your Options

Choose your categories carefully when classifying people. A degree of sensitivity is needed here. Be sure to avoid categories that have been used to stereotype or hurt people. (See the second "Writing About Film" topic on page 383 for an example of how classification can be taken too far.)

1. Relatives whom I'd want in my life even if we weren't related
2. Relatives who are in my life only because of blood ties
3. Relatives who are not in my life because they are dysfunctional

This second approach has a much better chance of captivating an audience than the first one. It has more potential: everyone has both beloved and obnoxious relatives. The essay could be either grim or funny, according to the writer's personal circumstances.

As you read the essays that follow, note that the classification strategy always requires three or more categories. If you have a subject that can be broken into only two categories, then you're probably better off using the comparison/contrast strategy (see Chapter 13), which allows you to concentrate on the similarities and differences between the two groups. When you use classification, you examine each group separately.

READING THE CLASSIFICATION ESSAY WITH A WRITER'S EYE

In the four selections that follow, Fran Lebowitz sorts out the types of music that assault her, unbidden; Tom Kuntz offers a satirical analysis of the packaging of breakfast cereals; Martin Luther King, Jr., evaluates three methods of responding to social oppression; and Paul Fussell takes a systematic look at social class in the United States. In the wrong hands, classification can be a dry and boring option; however, note how skillfully these writers make this rhetorical strategy come alive.

The second half of this chapter features strategies for writing the classification essay with a reader's eye (pages 370–377). If you decide to write on one of the topics that follow the four essays, make sure that you have read the strategies section before you begin. Note that additional writing topics are listed at the end of the chapter (pages 381–383).

The Sound of Music: Enough Already

FRAN LEBOWITZ

Fran Lebowitz is known for her satiric commentary on urban living. Her love-hate relationship with city life is the usual topic of her essays, which have been collected in *Metropolitan Life* (1978), *Social Studies* (1981), and *The Fran Lebowitz Reader* (1994). She is also a writer of fiction, a popular lecturer on the college circuit, and an occasional guest on late-night TV talk shows.

In "The Sound of Music," from *Metropolitan Life,* Lebowitz uses classification to comment upon our noisy, intrusive world. This essay is more than twenty-five years old, but as you read, consider whether Lebowitz's conclusions are still valid today.

1 First off, I want to say that as far as I am concerned, in instances where I have not personally and deliberately sought it out, the only difference between music and Muzak is the spelling. Pablo Casals* practicing across the hall with the door open—being trapped in an elevator, the ceiling of which is broadcasting "Parsley, Sage, Rosemary, and Thyme"—it's all the same to me. Harsh words? Perhaps. But then again these are not gentle times we live in. And they are being made no more gentle by this incessant melody that was once real life.

2 There was a time when music knew its place. No longer. Possibly this is not music's fault. It may be that music fell in with a bad crowd and lost its sense of common decency. I am willing to consider this. I am willing even to try and help. I would like to do my bit to set music straight in order that it might shape up and leave the mainstream of society. The first thing that music must understand is that there are two kinds of music—good music and bad music. Good music is music that I want to hear. Bad music is music that I don't want to hear.

3 So that music might more clearly see the error of its ways I offer the following. If you are music and you recognize yourself on this list, you are bad music.

1. Music in Other People's Clock Radios 4

There are times when I find myself spending the night in the home of another. Frequently the other is in a more reasonable line of work than I and must arise at a specific hour. Ofttimes the other, unbeknownst to me, manipulates an appliance in such a way that I am awakened by Stevie Wonder. On such occasions I announce that if I wished to be awakened by Stevie Wonder I would sleep with Stevie Wonder. I do not, however, wish to be awakened by Stevie Wonder and that is why God invented alarm clocks. Sometimes the other realizes that I am right. Sometimes the other does not. And that is why God invented *many* others.

2. Music Residing in the Hold Buttons of Other People's Business Telephones 5

I do not under any circumstances enjoy hold buttons. But I am a woman of reason. I can accept reality. I can face the facts. What I cannot face is the music. Just as there are two kinds of music—good and bad—so there are two kinds of hold buttons—good and bad. Good hold buttons are hold buttons that hold one silently. Bad hold buttons are hold buttons that hold one musically. When I hold I want to hold silently. That is the way it was meant to be, for that is what God was talking about when he said, "Forever hold your peace." He would have added, "and quiet," but he thought you were smarter.

3. Music in the Streets 6

The past few years have seen a steady increase in the number of people playing music in the streets. The past few years have also seen a steady increase in the number of malignant diseases. Are these two facts related? One wonders. But even if they are not—and, as I have pointed out, one cannot be sure—music in the streets has definitely taken its toll. For it is at the very least disorienting. When one is walking down Fifth Avenue, one does not expect to hear a string quartet playing a Strauss

***Pablo Casals (1876–1973):** famous twentieth-century cellist, composer, and conductor.

waltz. What one expects to hear while walking down Fifth Avenue is traffic. When one does indeed hear a string quartet playing a Strauss waltz while one is walking down Fifth Avenue, one is apt to become confused and imagine that one is not walking down Fifth Avenue at all but rather that one has somehow wound up in Old Vienna. Should one imagine that one is in Old Vienna one is likely to become quite upset when one realizes that in Old Vienna there is no sale at Charles Jourdan.* And that is why when I walk down Fifth Avenue I want to hear traffic.

4. Music in the Movies 7

I'm not talking about musicals. Musicals are movies that warn you by saying, "Lots of music here. Take it or leave it." I'm talking about regular movies that extend no such courtesy but allow unsuspecting people to come to see them and then assault them with a barrage of unasked-for tunes. There are two major offenders in this category: black movies and movies set in the fifties. Both types of movies are afflicted with the same misconception. They don't know that movies are supposed to be movies. They think that movies are supposed to be records with pictures. They have failed to understand that if God had wanted records to have pictures, he would not have invented television.

5. Music in Public Places Such as Restaurants, Supermarkets, Hotel Lobbies, Airports, Etc. 8

When I am in any of the above-mentioned places I am not there to hear music. I am there for whatever reason is appropriate to the respective place. I am no more interested in hearing "Mack the Knife" while waiting for the Shuttle to Boston than someone sitting ringside at the Sands Hotel is interested in being forced to choose between sixteen varieties of cottage cheese. If God had meant for everything to happen at once, he would not have invented desk calendars.

Epilogue 9

Some people talk to themselves. Some people sing to themselves. Is one group better than the other? Did not God create all people equal? Yes, God created all people equal. Only to some he gave the ability to make up their own words.

***Charles Jourdan:** an international chain of stores selling high-end shoes, with two locations in New York City.

STYLE AND STRATEGY

1. Lebowitz's purpose is to entertain through gentle satire. Her thesis appears at the end of paragraph 1.
2. Her tone is humorous. Had her purpose been more serious—had she been intent on criticizing a real evil—she might have been sarcastic.
3. This odd approach creates interest because it turns an abstraction into a real "target."
4. Separating each type of bad music into categories allows the author to focus on convincing anecdotes and examples more easily. The categories also allow readers to digest her argument easily. "Epilogue," more appropriate to a long, serious argument, is used for humorous effect.
5. Student responses vary, but invoking God's name imparts a kind of ironic authority to the argument.

Vocabulary

The following terms are identified by paragraph number. Make sure that you understand each term's meaning in its context. If you're not sure that you understand a term, look it up in a college-level dictionary.

incessant (1)	malignant (6)	barrage (7)
unbeknownst (4)	disorienting (6)	

Style and Strategy

1. What are Lebowitz's purpose and thesis?
2. What is Lebowitz's tone? How might she have changed her tone if she had had a different purpose?

3. In the first three paragraphs, Lebowitz *personifies* music—in other words, she treats it as a living thing, with motives and responsibilities. Why do you think she uses personification in this way?
4. Lebowitz uses six subheads—five to indicate her classification scheme and one for her conclusion. Subheads are features normally found in technical documents, not personal essays. Why do you think Lebowitz uses this device?
5. What purpose do the author's frequent references to God serve?

Questions for Critical Thinking and Discussion

1. We do indeed live in a noisy and obtrusive world. Unwanted music, intrusive advertising, and rude people often combine to assault our peace of mind. What can a person do to insulate himself or herself against this collective intruder? What are the consequences of this self-insulation?
2. Should personal privacy be protected by law? Possible areas to consider are noise pollution; the availability of personal information, including income, debt, and shopping habits; and unsolicited calls, e-mails, or visits to the home.

QUESTIONS FOR CRITICAL THINKING AND DISCUSSION Item 1 makes a good prompt for in-class group writing. Item 2 can be discussed in class, then used as a prompt for sustained writing.

Suggestions for Writing

1. In a 500- to 750-word essay, classify the personal invasions that you typically suffer.
2. Lebowitz classifies "bad" music. Write a 500- to 750-word essay in which you classify "good" music.

SUGGESTIONS FOR WRITING Both items are popular with students and produce essays worth reading. Recommend that students adopt a tone similar to Lebowitz's.

Not Sold by Intellectual Weight

TOM KUNTZ

Tom Kuntz is a writer and editor for the *New York Times*, where this essay first appeared in the Money & Business section in 1995. He is also the editor of *The Titanic Disaster Hearings: The Official Transcripts of the 1912 Investigation* (1998) and co-editor (with Phil Kuntz) of *The Sinatra Files: The Secret FBI Dossier* (2000).

Kuntz, like many breakfast eaters, pays close attention to the boxes in which cereal is sold. See if you agree with his conclusions.

1 Ah, those dewy, yawn-filled childhood morns at the breakfast table, when a glazed perusal of the cereal box during milky-sweet crunches of flakes was just the ritual to clear the brain's cobwebs for a new day of rascality. Such nostalgia powerfully stokes today's $8 billion market for breakfast cereal, which is eaten by an estimated 80 million adults, adolescents and children daily. It's not surprising, given such numbers, that the cereal box has become practically a metaphor for artifice and packaging in modern American life. Yet it's the stuff inside that usually gets all the publicity, especially from nutritional critics who say a lot of it is just vile, sweet, overpriced junk. They overlook cereal boxes' cultural value.

2 Which you may not think much of either. Still, boxes can command hundreds of dollars on the nostalgia market. More important: "Walk into any grocery store, stroll

down the cereal aisle, and you'll realize that cereal is more than food—it's an all-American form of entertainment," writes Chuck McCann, the original voice of Sonny, the Cocoa Puffs cuckoo bird ("Wuuwk . . . I'M CUCKOO FOR COCOA PUFFS!"). He wrote this in the foreword to "Cerealizing America: the Unsweetened Story of American Breakfast Cereal," by Scott Bruce and Bill Crawford, a new book that tracks cereal's Elvis-like trajectory from turn-of-the-century wholesomeness to the corny excesses of modern times.

3 If Mr. McCann is right, what's been playing in the cereal aisle lately? From the scores of varieties on the shelves, it's possible to discern several distinct types of boxes.

4 *First up: kiddie cereals. Gone for the most part are the once-common trade-in box-tops and prizes inside (thanks to new marketing methods and greater product liability). Today's boxes are typically cartoonish and character-driven (Tony the Tiger, Cap'n Crunch), offering a crass mix of forced excitement and promotional tie-ins to perhaps the world's most credulous consumers. On the back of Kellogg's Cocoa Krispies is "Coco the Monkey's Marshmallow Adventure," an unchallenging maze through jungle terrain marked by mini-marshmallows (a "free bonus" pack is included inside):*

5 Hey kids! Follow Coco on his adventure through the jungle to discover how Coco uses his mini-marshmallows.

6 "Which weighs more: a pound of marshmallows or a pound of mud?" asks a spotted feline creature leaning on a mug of cocoa.

7 "They both weigh the same, but marshmallows sure taste better," says Coco.

8 "How many S'mores can an elephant eat?" asks an elephant.

9 "As many as he wants," says Coco.

10 (See S'mores Treats recipe on side panel.)

11 *The trail leads to a giant bowl of Cocoa Krispies, watched over, inexplicably, by two thug-like hippopotamuses in dark shades and business suits:*

12 Thanks for joining Coco on his jungle adventure. Have fun trying out all the new ways you can use your mini-marshmallows. How many jungle animals did you see along the way?

13 *Curiously, Rice Krispies, the less-sweet cousin of Cocoa Krispies, pushes dental hygiene on its box, after a fashion, by offering Timmy the Tooth Character Cards. These include the Cavity Goon—a guy with choppers so bad he looks like he OD'd on Cocoa Krispies. Kiddie boxes also resort to self-promotional fun facts:*

14 Get to the center of great taste with [General Mills'] Hidden Treasures. There's a discovery in every bite. That's because inside *some* crunchy sweet squares is a delicious, fruit-flavored center. . . . Here are a few more cool things with surprise centers to grab your attention!

- 15 Geode rocks appear common on the outside, but when you break into one, you'll find a crystal treasure center. The treasure you'll find inside Hidden Treasures is a tasty center of fruit-flavored filling inside special pieces.
- 16 What's inside of a neon light is actually a colorless gas. The only way to shed some light on neon is to pass electricity through it. Give your mouth a charge when you bite into Hidden Treasures.

For Kids of All Ages

17 *Then there are cereals like Wheaties and Corn Flakes aimed at both kids and adults—in particular adults who still like the cereal they ate as whelps. By including*

sports stars on the boxes, the cereals achieve cross-generational appeal, and attract both sports and non-sports collectors. And hey kids! Hey anti-smoking lobby! Check out the subtle way the brand name Winston repeatedly appears on the recent Kellogg's Raisin Bran box featuring the father–son stock car racers Darrell and Michael Waltrip. No, the cigarettes and the cereal don't have the same corporate owners. Still, because the racers' tunics are plastered with corporate plugs, the box has four displays of the logo for the Winston Cup, sponsored by that famous maker of tobacco products hazardous to young lungs! Plus five other mentions of the Winston Cup!

18 Darrell Waltrip has "finished 9th in Winston Cup series points . . . Has won 3 NASCAR Winston Cup championships ('81, '82, '85) . . . trails only Dale Earnhardt and Bill Elliott in career Winston Cup earnings. . . ."

19 *Some boxes continue the tradition of insisting that cereal is not simply cereal. For example, America's Choice Corn Flakes:*

20 That crispy corn taste is just right in the morning with milk and your favorite fruit.

But Don't Stop There!

- 21 Top off your casseroles with the crunchy goodness of Corn Flakes.
- 22 Use crushed Corn Flakes as a coating for oven-fried chicken or fish.
- 23 Mix with any yogurt to add delicious flavor and texture.
- 24 Great taste and wholesome goodness make Corn Flakes much more than a breakfast cereal!

25 *You want wholesome? How about Rice Krispies Treats? "Easy to make and low fat!" though the recipe cautions, "Do not use diet or low-fat margarine."*

For Health

26 *It's enough to make you take up health food. But while the smaller "organic" cereal brands eschew additives, you're not likely to find the phrase "piety- and self-congratulation free!" on any of the boxes:*

27 Health Valley's "Save the Earth" Policy: the grains and fruit in these flakes were *grown without chemical fertilizers, herbicides or pesticides* by farmers using organic methods. Health Valley uses more *certified organic* ingredients than any other food company in the world because George Mateljan, the founder of Health Valley, wants to provide you with nutritious, good tasting foods without polluting our precious water supplies or diminishing our topsoil. . . .

28 *Some organic cereals can be downright depressing:*

29 Remember the Irish potato famine? Billions of rows of genetically identical cereal grains are now planted each year, making entire crops vulnerable to a single rapidly evolving pest or disease. This sameness of fields sown horizon to horizon without interruption demands costly and often dangerous reliance on chemicals to protect crops. And every year what we find in our stores tastes less and less like real food.

30 *Your salvation supposedly can begin with the cereal inside the box, Nature's Path Heritage O's. Also sounding the alarums are Rainforest cereals, launched in 1991 by members of the Grateful Dead:*

31 **Action Alert:** The rubber tappers of the Xapuri Co-op (birthplace of the movement once headed by Chico Mendes, assassinated in 1988, and home of the first Brazil nut-collecting and processing co-op) are under increasing attacks by ranchers & some local government officials. . . .

What You Can Do: Send a letter to Dra. Maria Tapajos Santana Areal & Dr. Erick Cavalcante Linhares, (address) Rua Floriano Peixoto S/N, 69.930-000 Xapuri-Acre, Brasil. . . . Let them know the world is watching. . . . 32

Who are these people? The box doesn't say. 33

For Grown-Ups

Much gauzier, Madison Avenue-style verbiage can be found on the boxes of adult-oriented cereals developed by the big cereal manufacturers in response to the health-food upstarts: 34

Imagine sitting in the kitchen, enjoying a delicious slice of home-baked banana nut bread. Now imagine that wonderful taste—in a cereal. . . . Real banana oven-baked into crunchy oat clusters, mixed with crispy whole wheat flakes and chopped walnuts . . . [Post] Banana Nut Crunch cereal. The delicious taste of home-baked banana nut bread—in a cereal. 35

But for those who don't need their breakfast prose dripping with syrup, you can't get much blunter than the discreet warning on Kellog's All-Bran: 36

Increase your fiber intake gradually. Intestinal gas may occur until your body adjusts. If digestive pain occurs consult your doctor and avoid laxatives. 37

Vocabulary

STYLE AND STRATEGY
1. The categories include cereals that are marketed to children by promising the thrill of treasure hunting; those marketed to the intergenerational crowd, including sports nuts; those marketed to the environmentally sensitive; and those marketed to compete with cereals in the previous group. Of course, students may have a different take on these categories.
2. The thesis is stated in the quotation by McCann in paragraph 2.
3. One conclusion we can draw is that manufacturers should spend less effort on marketing and more on developing healthy foods.
4. The italics represent his commentary. Indeed, these comments comprise the heart of the essay.

The following terms are identified by paragraph number. Make sure that you understand each term's meaning in its context. If you're not sure that you understand a term, look it up in a college-level dictionary.

perusal (1)	credulous (4)	piety (26)
rascality (1)	inexplicably (11)	sown (29)
nostalgia (1)	geode (15)	alarums (30)
metaphor (1)	whelps (17)	gauzier (34)
artifice (1)	tunic (17)	verbiage (34)
trajectory (2)	eschew (26)	discreet (36)

Style and Strategy

1. Name, in your own words, the marketing categories that Kuntz uses to divide his essay. Taken together, do they cover the full range of breakfast cereals? Could any cereal fit in more than one category?
2. What is Kuntz's thesis? Rephrase it in one sentence.
3. This essay has no conclusion. Does it really need one? What conclusion do you draw from Kuntz's essay?
4. Kuntz uses italic type extensively in his essay. What type of information appears in italics? Why does Kuntz highlight this material?

Questions for Critical Thinking and Discussion

1. Many commentators believe that product marketers have gotten out of hand, especially in their attempts to sell to an increasingly younger

target group. Do you believe that small children are harmed by marketing directed at them? If so, what could be done to counter this trend?

2. For a three-hour period, count the number of advertisements that you see or hear. Is the U.S. culture close to "advertising saturation"?

QUESTIONS FOR CRITICAL THINKING AND DISCUSSION Item 1 can be discussed in class quite easily if you ask students to focus on television commercials aimed at children. Suggestions about how to respond to this trend will differ, but students may be able to write an argumentative essay using what is discussed in class.

Suggestions for Writing

1. In a 500-word essay, classify the types of sales pitches found in the junk mail that you receive in a three-day period.
2. In a 500- to 750-word essay, classify the types of television commercials that you regularly experience.

SUGGESTIONS FOR WRITING Both prompts usually produce interesting writing. Remind students that they need to develop each category using specific detail.

Three Types of Resistance to Oppression

MARTIN LUTHER KING, JR.

The American civil rights movement has had many leaders from the 1950s through today, but Martin Luther King, Jr. (1929–1968), was its leader at the most crucial times, from the Alabama sit-ins and boycotts of the 1950s through the national movement of the 1960s. In 1968, King was murdered by white assassin James Earl Ray in Memphis.

King believed in civil disobedience—nonviolent protest against legal inequities. However, many people in the civil rights movement believed that a more forceful response was needed to "shake things up." In the following essay, first published as part of his book *Stride Toward Freedom* (1958), note the delicate balancing act that King is able to achieve in renouncing violence but also decrying acquiescence.

Oppressed people deal with their oppression in three characteristic ways. One way is acquiescence: the oppressed resign themselves to their doom. They tacitly adjust themselves to oppression, and thereby become conditioned to it. In every movement toward freedom some of the oppressed prefer to remain oppressed. Almost 2,800 years ago Moses set out to lead the children of Israel from the slavery of Egypt to the freedom of the promised land. He soon discovered that slaves do not always welcome their deliverers. They become accustomed to being slaves. They would rather bear those ills they have, as Shakespeare pointed out, than flee to others that they know not of. They prefer the "fleshpots of Egypt" to the ordeals of emancipation. 1

There is such a thing as the freedom of exhaustion. Some people are so worn down by the yoke of oppression that they give up. A few years ago in the slum areas of Atlanta, a Negro guitarist used to sing almost daily: "Been down so long that down don't bother me." This is the type of negative freedom and resignation that often engulfs the life of the oppressed. 2

But this is not the way out. To accept passively an unjust system is to cooperate with that system; thereby the oppressed become as evil as the oppressor. Noncooperation with evil is as much a moral obligation as is cooperation with good. The oppressed must never allow the conscience of the oppressor to slumber. Religion reminds every man that he is his brother's keeper. To accept injustice or segregation passively is to say to the oppressor that his actions are morally right. It is a way of allowing his conscience to fall asleep. At this moment the oppressed fails to be his brother's keeper. So acquiescence—while often the easier way—is not the 3 moral way. It is the way of the coward. The Negro cannot win the respect of his oppressor by acquiescing; he merely increases the oppressor's arrogance and contempt. Acquiescence is interpreted as proof of the Negro's inferiority. The Negro cannot win the respect of the white people of the South or the peoples of the world if he is willing to sell the future of his children for his personal and immediate comfort and safety.

A second way that oppressed people sometimes deal with oppression is to resort to physical violence and corroding hatred. Violence often brings about momentary results. Nations have frequently won their independence in battle. But in spite of temporary victories, violence never brings permanent peace. It solves no social problem; it merely creates new and more complicated ones. 4

Violence as a way of achieving racial justice is both impractical and immoral. It is impractical because it is a descending spiral ending in destruction for all. The old law of an eye for an eye leaves everybody blind. It is immoral because it seeks to humiliate the opponent rather than win his understanding; it seeks to annihilate rather than to convert. Violence is immoral because it thrives on hatred rather than love. It destroys community and makes brotherhood impossible. It leaves society in monologue rather than dialogue. Violence ends by defeating itself. It creates bitterness in the survivors and brutality in the destroyers. A voice echoes through time saying to every potential Peter, "Put up your sword." History is cluttered with the wreckage of nations that failed to follow this command. 5

If the American Negro and other victims of oppression succumb to the temptation of using violence in the struggle for freedom, future generations will be the recipients of a desolate night of bitterness, and our chief legacy to them will be an endless reign of meaningless chaos. Violence is not the way. 6

The third way open to oppressed people in their quest for freedom is the way of nonviolent resistance. Like the synthesis in Hegelian philosophy, the principle of nonviolent resistance seeks to reconcile the truths of two opposites—acquiescence and violence—while avoiding the extremes and immoralities of both. The nonviolent resister agrees with the person who acquiesces that one should not be physically aggressive toward his opponent; but he balances the equation by agreeing with the person of violence that evil must be resisted. He avoids the nonresistance of the former and the violent resistance of the latter. With nonviolent resistance, no individual or group need submit to any wrong, nor need anyone resort to violence in order to right a wrong. 7

It seems to me that this is the method that must guide the actions of the Negro in the present crisis in race relations. Through nonviolent resistance the Negro will be able to rise to the noble height of opposing the unjust system while loving the perpetrators of the system. The Negro must work passionately and unrelentingly for full stature as a citizen, but he must not use inferior methods to gain it. He must never come to terms with falsehood, malice, hate, or destruction. 8

Nonviolent resistance makes it possible for the Negro to remain in the South and struggle for his rights. The Negro's problem will not be solved by running away. He cannot listen to the glib suggestion of those who would urge him to migrate en masse to other sections of the country. By grasping his great opportunity in the South he can make a lasting contribution to the moral strength of the nation and set a sublime example of courage for generations yet unborn. 9

By nonviolent resistance, the Negro can also enlist all men of good will in his struggle for equality. The problem is not a purely racial one, with Negroes set against whites. In the end, it is not a struggle between people at all, but a tension between justice and injustice. Nonviolent resistance is not aimed against oppressors but against oppression. Under its banner, consciences, not racial groups, are enlisted. 10

Vocabulary

The following terms are identified by paragraph number. Make sure that you understand each term's meaning in its context. If you're not sure that you understand a term, look it up in a college-level dictionary.

acquiescence (1)	yoke (2)	synthesis (7)
tacitly (1)	corroding (4)	glib (9)
fleshpot (1)	momentary (4)	sublime (9)
emancipation (1)	annihilate (5)	

Style and Strategy

1. King was a Baptist minister and a great public speaker. Note that he uses one of the elements of a spoken sermon: repetition. What is the effect of this rhetorical device?
2. Each type of resistance is discussed in a group of three paragraphs. What does each paragraph in each group accomplish? See paragraphs 1–3, 4–6, and 7–9.
3. Read King's conclusion once more (paragraph 10). Is his contrasting device ("it's not this; it's that") effective? Is King summarizing here, or is he evaluating the points made in his essay?

Questions for Critical Thinking and Discussion

1. King preached patience; Malcolm X (see his essay on pages 255–258) preached direct action. Is violence ever acceptable as a device to effect social change?
2. In your daily life, do racial issues play a large role? Is the way that you see the world affected in any way by discrimination because of race, color, religion, or ethnic origin? If so, how have you responded?
3. Comment on the following statement: "The greatest social development in the United States in the last forty years has been the rise of the black middle class." Do you agree? Why or why not?

Suggestions for Writing

1. In a 500- to 750-word essay, classify the ways that you could respond to a police officer if you were pulled over in a traffic stop.
2. In a 500- to 750-word essay, classify the ways that students at your college or university could respond to unfair policies of the campus administration.

STYLE AND STRATEGY
1. Repetition in this essay imparts an energy and emphasis reminiscent of what we have read or heard in Dr. King's speeches.
2. The first paragraph in each set defines a particular response. The second discusses the philosophical foundations of the response and evaluates their validity. The third explains the outcome or result of each response.
3. He is doing some of both. The conclusion both clarifies and emphasizes what has come before.

QUESTIONS FOR CRITICAL THINKING AND DISCUSSION Item 1 will

produce energetic class discussion, but it can also be used as a prompt for in-class writing. Try using item 2 as a prompt for sustained writing. Item 3 is the most difficult of the group, but students willing to do research might take this one on as an essay project.

SUGGESTIONS FOR WRITING The first item is perfect for students who are not afraid to engage in whimsy. The second can be handled through satire or serious criticism.

Notes on Class

PAUL FUSSELL

Paul Fussell, the Donald T. Regan Professor Emeritus of English at the University of Pennsylvania and noted scholar of eighteenth-century British literature, is well known for his accomplishments in a variety of areas. As an officer in World War II, he was twice wounded and won the Bronze Star and the Purple Heart. He has published thirteen books: on literature, especially poetry; on his wartime experiences; on travel; and on social class. His study of World War I and its surrounding literature, *The Great War and Modern Memory* (1976), won the National Book Award.

Fussell has also studied modern behavior and social expectations. His essays and books on class structure, vulgarity, and modern expressions of personal taste are pungent, biting examinations of the way we live. "Notes on Class," adapted from *The Boy Scout Handbook and Other Observations* (1982), examines a "dirty little secret": our obsession with social class status.

1 If the dirty little secret used to be sex, now it is the facts about social class. No subject today is more likely to offend. Over thirty years ago Dr. Kinsey generated considerable alarm by disclosing that despite appearances one-quarter of the male population had enjoyed at least one homosexual orgasm. A similar alarm can be occasioned today by asserting that despite the much-discussed mechanism of "social mobility" and the constant redistribution of income in this country, it is virtually impossible to break out of the social class in which one has been nurtured. Bad news for the ambitious as well as the bogus, but there it is.

2 Defining class is difficult, as sociologists and anthropologists have learned. The more data we feed into the machines, the less likely it is that significant formulations will emerge. What follows here is based not on interviews, questionnaires, or any kind of quantitative technique but on perhaps a more trustworthy method—perception. Theory may inform us that there are three classes in America, high, middle, and low. Perception will tell us that there are at least nine, which I would designate and arrange like this:

Top Out-of-Sight
Upper
Upper Middle

Middle
High-Proletarian
Mid-Proletarian
Low-Proletarian

Destitute
Bottom Out-of-Sight

In addition, there is a floating class with no permanent location in this hierarchy. We can call it Class X. It consists of well-to-do hippies, "artists," "writers" (who write nothing), floating bohemians, politicians out of office, disgraced athletic coaches, residers abroad, rock stars, "celebrities," and the shrewder sort of spies.

The quasi-official division of the population into three economic classes called high-, middle-, and low-income groups rather misses the point, because as a class indicator the amount of money is not as important as the source. Important distinctions at both the top and bottom of the class scale arise less from degree of affluence than from the people or institutions to whom one is beholden for support. For example, the main thing distinguishing the top three classes from each other is the amount of money inherited in relation to the amount currently earned. The Top Out-of-Sight Class (Rockefellers, du Ponts, Mellons, Fords, Whitneys) lives on inherited capital entirely. Its money is like the hats of the Boston ladies who, asked where they got them, answer, "Oh, we *have* our hats." No one whose money, no matter how ample, comes from his own work, like film stars, can be a member of the Top Out-of-Sights, even if the size of his income and the extravagance of his expenditure permit him temporary social access to it. 3

Since we expect extremes to meet, we are not surprised to find the very lowest class, Bottom Out-of-Sight, similar to the highest in one crucial respect: it is given its money and kept sort of afloat not by its own efforts but by the welfare machinery or the prison system. Members of the Top Out-of-Sight Class sometimes earn some money, as directors or board members of philanthropic or even profitable enterprises, but the amount earned is laughable in relation to the amount already possessed. Membership in the Top Out-of-Sight Class depends on the ability to flourish without working at all, and it is this that suggests a curious brotherhood between those at the top and the bottom of the scale. 4

It is this also that distinguishes the Upper Class from its betters. It lives on both inherited money and a salary from attractive, if usually slight, work, without which, even if it could survive and even flourish, it would feel bored and a little ashamed. The next class down, the Upper Middle, may possess virtually as much as the two above it. The difference is that it has earned most of it, in law, medicine, oil, real-estate, or even the more honorific forms of trade. The Upper Middles are afflicted with a bourgeois sense of shame, a conviction that to live on the earnings of others, even forebears, is not entirely nice. 5

The Out-of-Sight Classes at top and bottom have something else in common: they are literally all but invisible (hence their name). The façades of Top Out-of-Sight houses are never seen from the street, and such residences (like Rockefeller's upstate New York premises) are often hidden away deep in the hills, safe from envy and its ultimate attendants, confiscatory taxation and finally expropriation. The Bottom Out-of-Sight Class is equally invisible. When not hidden away in institutions or claustrated in monasteries, lamaseries, or communes, it is hiding from creditors, deceived bail-bondsmen, and merchants intent on repossessing cars and furniture. (This class is visible briefly in one place, in the spring on the streets of New York City, but after this ritual yearly show of itself it disappears again.) When you pass a house with a would-be impressive façade addressing the street, you know it is occupied by a mere member of the Upper or Upper Middle Class. The White House is an example. Its residents, even on those occasions when they are Kennedys, can never be classified as Top Out-of-Sight but only Upper Class. The house is simply too conspicuous, and temporary residence there usually constitutes a come-down for most of its occupants. It is a hopelessly Upper- or Upper-Middle-Class place. 6

Another feature of both Top and Bottom Out-of-Sight Classes is their anxiety to keep their names out of the papers, and this too suggests that socially the President is always rather vulgar. All the classes in between Top and Bottom Out-of-Sight slaver for personal publicity (monograms on shirts, inscribing one's name on lawn-mowers and power tools, etc.), and it is this lust to be known almost as much as income that distinguishes them from their Top and Bottom neighbors. The High- and Mid-Prole Classes can be recognized immediately by their pride in advertising their physical presence, a way of saying, "Look! We pay our bills and have a known place in the community, and you can find us there any time." Thus hypertrophied house-numbers on the front, or house numbers written "Two Hundred Five" ("Two Hundred and Five" is worse) instead of 205, or flamboyant house or family names blazoned on façades, like "The Willows" or "The Polnickis." 7

(If you go behind the façade into the house itself, you will find a fairly trustworthy class indicator in the kind of wood visible there. The top three classes invariably go in for hardwoods for doors and panelling; the Middle and High-Prole Classes, pine, either plain or "knotty." The knotty-pine "den" is an absolute stigma of the Middle Class, one never to be overcome or disguised by temporarily affected higher usages. Below knotty pine there is plywood.) 8

Façade study is a badly neglected anthropological field. As we work down from the (largely white-painted) bank-like façades of the Upper and Upper Middle Classes, we encounter such Middle and Prole conventions as these, which I rank in order of social status: 9

Middle
1. A potted tree on either side of the front door, and the more pointy and symmetrical the better.
2. A large rectangular picture-window in a split-level "ranch" house, displaying a table-lamp between two side curtains. The cellophane on the lampshade must be visibly inviolate.
3. Two chairs, usually metal with pipe arms, disposed on the front porch as a "conversation group," in stubborn defiance of the traffic thundering past.

High-Prole
4. Religious shrines in the garden, which if small and understated, are slightly higher class than

Mid-Prole
5. Plaster gnomes and flamingos, and blue or lavender shiny spheres supported by fluted cast-concrete pedestals.

Low-Prole
6. Defunct truck tires painted white and enclosing flower beds. (Auto tires are a grade higher.)
7. Flower-bed designs worked in dead light bulbs or the butts of disused beer bottles.

The Destitute have no façades to decorate, and of course the Bottom Out-of-Sights, being invisible, have none either, although both these classes can occasionally help others decorate theirs—painting tires white on an hourly basis, for example, or even watering and fertilizing the potted trees of the Middle Class. Class X also does not decorate its façades, hoping to stay loose and unidentifiable, ready to re-locate and shape-change the moment it sees that its cover has been penetrated.

In this list of façade conventions an important principle emerges. Organic materials have higher status than metal or plastic. We should take warning from Sophie Portnoy's aluminum venetian blinds, which are also lower than wood because 10 the slats are curved, as if "improved," instead of classically flat. The same principle applies, as *The Preppy Handbook** has shown so effectively, to clothing fabrics, which must be cotton or wool, never Dacron or anything of that prole kind. In the same way, yachts with wood hulls, because they must be repaired or replaced (at high cost) more often, are classier than yachts with fiberglass hulls, no matter how shrewdly merchandised. Plastic hulls are cheaper and more practical, which is precisely why they lack class.

11 As we move down the scale, income of course decreases, but income is less important to class than other seldom-invoked measurements: for example, the degree to which one's work is supervised by an omnipresent immediate superior. The more free from supervision, the higher the class, which is why a dentist ranks higher than a mechanic working under a foreman in a large auto shop, even if he makes considerably more money than the dentist. The two trades may be thought equally dirty: it is the dentist's freedom from supervision that helps confer class upon him. Likewise, a high-school teacher obliged to file weekly "lesson plans" with a principal or "curriculum co-ordinator" thereby occupies a class position lower than a tenured professor, who reports to no one, even though the high-school teacher may be richer, smarter, and nicer. (Supervisors and Inspectors are titles that go with public schools, post offices, and police departments: the student of class will need to know no more.) It is largely because they must report that even the highest members of the naval and military services lack social status: they all have designated supervisors—even the Chairman of the Joint Chiefs of Staff has to report to the President.

12 Class is thus defined less by bare income than by constraints and insecurities. It is defined also by habits and attitudes. Take television watching. The Top Out-of-Sight Class doesn't watch at all. It owns the companies and pays others to monitor the thing. It is also entirely devoid of intellectual or even emotional curiosity: it *has* its ideas the way it has its money. The Upper Class does look at television but it prefers Camp offerings, like the films of Jean Harlow or Jon Hall. The Upper Middle Class regards TV as vulgar except for the highminded emissions of National Educational Television, which it watches avidly, especially when, like the Shakespeare series, they are the most incompetently directed and boring. Upper Middles make a point of forbidding children to watch more than an hour a day and worry a lot about violence in society and sugar in cereal. The Middle Class watches, preferring the more "beautiful" kinds of non-body-contact sports like tennis or gymnastics or figure-skating (the music is a redeeming feature here). With High-, Mid-, and Low-Proles we find heavy viewing of the soaps in the daytime and rugged body-contact sports (football, hockey, boxing) in the evening. The lower one is located in the Prole classes the more likely one is to watch "Bowling for Dollars" and "Wonder Woman" and "The Hulk" and when choosing a game show to prefer "Joker's Wild" to "The Family Feud," whose jokes are sometimes incomprehensible. Destitutes and Bottom Out-of-Sights have in common a problem involving choice. Destitutes usually "own" about three color sets, and the problem is which three programs to run at once. Bottom Out-of-Sights exercise no choice at all, the decisions being made for them by correctional or institutional personnel.

The Official Preppy Handbook: a book by Lisa Birnbach, published in 1980, that satirically explains the typical "preppy," or upper-class, lifestyle.

The time when the evening meal is consumed defines class better than, say, the presence or absence on the table of ketchup bottles and ashtrays shaped like little toilets enjoining the diners to "Put Your Butts Here." Destitutes and Bottom Out-of-Sights eat dinner at 5:30, for the Prole staff on which they depend must clean up and be out roller-skating or bowling early in the evening. Thus Proles eat at 6:00 or 6:30. The Middles eat at 7:00, the Upper Middles at 7:30 or, if very ambitious, at 8:00. The Uppers and Top Out-of-Sights dine at 8:30 or 9:00 or even later, after nightly protracted "cocktail" sessions lasting usually around two hours. Sometimes they forget to eat at all. 13

Similarly, the physical appearance of the various classes defines them fairly accurately. Among the top four classes thin is good, and the bottom two classes appear to ape this usage, although down there thin is seldom a matter of choice. It is the three Prole classes that tend to fat, partly as a result of their use of convenience foods and plenty of beer. These are the classes too where anxiety about slipping down a rung causes nervous overeating, resulting in fat that can be rationalized as advertising the security of steady wages and the ability to "eat out" often. Even "Going Out for Breakfast" is not unthinkable for Proles, if we are to believe that they respond to the McDonald's TV ads as they're supposed to. A recent magazine ad for a diet book aimed at Proles stigmatizes a number of erroneous assumptions about body weight, proclaiming with some inelegance that "They're all a crock." Among such vulgar errors is the proposition that "All Social Classes Are Equally Overweight." This the ad rejects by noting quite accurately: 14

> Your weight is an advertisement of your social standing. A century ago, corpulence was a sign of success. But no more. Today it is the badge of the lower-middle-class, where obesity is *four times* more prevalent than it is among the upper-middle and middle classes.

It is not just four times more prevalent. It is at least four times more visible, as any observer can testify who has witnessed Prole women perambulating shopping malls in their bright, very tight jersey trousers. Not just obesity but the flaunting of obesity is the Prole sign, as if the object were to give maximum aesthetic offense to the higher classes and thus achieve a form of revenge.

Another physical feature with powerful class meaning is the wearing of plaster casts on legs and ankles by members of the top three classes. These casts, a sort of white badge of honor, betoken stylish mishaps with frivolous but costly toys like horses, skis, snowmobiles, and mopeds. They signify a high level of conspicuous waste in a social world where questions of unpayable medical bills or missed working days do not apply. But in the matter of clothes, the Top Out-of-Sight is different from both Upper and Upper Middle Classes. It prefers to appear in new clothes, whereas the class just below it prefers old clothes. Likewise, all three Prole classes make much of new garments, with the highest possible polyester content. The question does not arise in the same form with Destitutes and Bottom Out-of-Sights. They wear used clothes, the thrift shop and prison supply room serving as their Bonwit's and Korvette's. 15

This American class system is very hard for foreigners to master, partly because most foreigners imagine that since America was founded by the British it must retain something of British institutions. But our class system is more subtle than the British, 16 more a matter of gradations than of blunt divisions, like the binary distinction between a gentleman and a cad. This seems to lack plausibility here. One seldom encounters in the United States the sort of absolute prohibitions which (half-comically, to be sure) one is asked to believe define the gentleman in England. Like these:

> A gentleman never wears brown shoes in the city, or
> A gentleman never wears a green suit, or
> A gentleman never has soup at lunch, or
> A gentleman never uses a comb, or
> A gentleman never smells of anything but tar, or
> "No gentleman can fail to admire Bellini" —W. H. Auden.

In America it seems to matter much less the way you present yourself—green, brown, neat, sloppy, scented—than what your backing is—that is, where your money comes from. What the upper orders display here is no special uniform but the kind of psychological security they derive from knowing that others recognize their freedom from petty anxieties and trivial prohibitions.

Vocabulary

The following terms are identified by paragraph number. Make sure that you understand each term's meaning in its context. If you're not sure that you understand a term, look it up in a college-level dictionary.

formulations (2)	confiscatory (6)	protracted (13)
proletarian (2)	expropriation (6)	inelegance (14)
hierarchy (2)	lamaseries (6)	corpulence (14)
quasi-official (3)	façade (6)	prevalent (14)
affluence (3)	slaver (7)	perambulating (14)
beholden (3)	hypertrophied (7)	aesthetic (14)
philanthropic (4)	blazoned (7)	gradations (16)
honorific (5)	stigma (8)	cad (16)
bourgeois (5)	inviolate (9)	plausibility (16)
forebears (5)	highminded (12)	prohibitions (16)

Style and Strategy

1. What is Fussell's purpose in writing this essay? Would you guess that Fussell likes his fellow humans, or not?
2. What is the tone of this essay, and how does Fussell's word choice contribute to it?
3. Fussell points out that the traditional three-way categorization of American social class is flawed; he then proceeds to identify nine social classes along with a "floating" class. Which two groups does he compare? How does this comparison add to the essay?
4. Fussell analyzes his nine (plus one) groups in terms of a number of defining attributes. What are these attributes?

SUGGESTIONS FOR WRITING

1. Responses vary, but students have no trouble recognizing Fussell's criticism of classism. They often point out the irony in many of his definitions and characterizations.
2. The tone is somewhat cynical. For instance, note paragraph 7.
3. The author points out similarities between members of the Out-of-Sight groups, both top and bottom. There is an irony in doing so, which contributes to tone and adds interest.
4. Source of money—earned or given—in paragraphs 4–5; visibility or lack thereof in paragraphs 6–10; degree to which one's work is directly supervised in paragraph 11; habits and attitudes as illustrated by television watching in paragraph 12; evening meal times in paragraph 13; physical appearance in paragraphs 14–15.
5. Ask students to outline the essay to discover its organizational principle. Note that Fussell could have simply discussed each of the nine categories under a separate heading.

5. How has Fussell organized his presentation of the categories? What other organization might he have used?

QUESTIONS FOR CRITICAL THINKING AND DISCUSSION The third item is a better test of the students' ability to classify than the other two. However, all three can be used as prompts for in-class group writing and as preparation for class discussion.

Questions for Critical Thinking and Discussion

1. *Snobbery* can be defined as the disparagement of those who are perceived to have a lower status in society. When and where have you experienced snobbery? How did you deal with it?
2. Comment on this statement: "In the past, American society was striated by race. Today, race is less of an issue, and class has become the deciding factor. The average middle-class white family, given the choice of living next door to a poor white family or a middle-class black family, will choose the black family. They share more values." Do you agree? Why or why not?
3. How would you define *poor people*? In your experience, are the poor generally seen as unfortunate victims of circumstance or as unworthy? How do society's assumptions affect the lives and prospects of the poor?

SUGGESTIONS FOR WRITING Both items produce good papers. Remind students choosing item 1 that they need to be faithful to Fussell's definitions. Those completing item 2 might want to create their own categories to discuss social class.

Suggestions for Writing

1. Many people live lives that could place them into more than one of Fussell's categories. In other words, one could be a self-employed dentist (high status) who eats supper every evening at 5:00 (low status), watches almost no television (high status) but is forty pounds overweight (low status). Write a 500- to 750-word essay in which you explain how your life—or that of someone you know—compares to Fussell's classification.
2. Consider your extended family. Write a 500- to 750-word essay in which you categorize the members of your family according to social class.

MORE OPTIONS ONLINE
If you would like to read additional classification essays, go to **www.mhhe.com/writingtoday**.

WRITING THE CLASSIFICATION ESSAY WITH A READER'S EYE

At first glance, classification may seem like a dry, almost boring rhetorical option. However, we have found over the years that some of our favorite essays are classifications. The choices that you make in planning and drafting your essay will largely determine your reader's response, so exploit your opportunity.

Issues to Keep in Mind

In this section, we explore three important topics that you need to think about as you write and revise a classification essay:

1. The method you use to identify a category within a paragraph or section
2. Your purpose for writing a classification essay
3. Your language level

Methods of Explaining Categories

Let's assume that you are classifying teaching styles and are drawing on your own experience to develop the categories. In effect, you are classifying the instructors and teachers whom you've experienced over the years. You find that they fall into three basic groups: the lecturer, the mixer, and the time server. Note that you need to define each type as you introduce it, as in the following paragraph:

> The lecturer does just what the label indicates: lectures, usually from notes. The best of this type is a highly efficient purveyor of information. Teaching a class that won't quite fit into a semester, he or she will cover ground swiftly and effectively. However, this person is a rarity. Most instructors who use the lecture method will cause the class members to be torn between the need to take notes and a desperate desire to fall asleep. An example is my current history instructor (who shall remain nameless). I've always found history to be an exciting, lively subject, full of surprises, but Dr. Lecture seems intent on squeezing the life out of it for me and whoever else in my class seems interested in the subject.

This paragraph first defines the type—*lecturer* can have multiple meanings, and the speaker clearly wants to differentiate between effective and ineffective lecturers—then develops the classification by including an example, his history professor. Would more than one example have worked? Of course it would have, within the boundaries of what a paragraph can hold. Note how the writer uses a different internal strategy, narration, to develop the next paragraph:

> The opposite of the lecturer is the mixer, the sort of person who can work a room at a party. This person probably also has a side job selling Tupperware or Mary Kay. Involvement means everything to this dynamo. The class members are virtually forced to participate because of the barrage of questions and mandatory discussion groups. My psychology professor is an example of this type. Although, on the whole, she is a very effective instructor, she finds psychology to be the most important field of study conceived in human history, and she is amazed when she encounters a student who doesn't share that belief. (She must live in a perpetual state of amazement.) This attitude *does* help involve the student and make class time fly by; however, some days it's just a bit much. Last Monday, for example, one of my "colleagues" fell asleep during class. From the looks of him, he had been out a bit late the night before. Dr. Dynamo tried speaking to him to rouse him from his slumbers; when that failed, she walked over and prodded him,

as if he were a drunk who had fallen asleep on her front porch. He woke up (briefly), stared at her, and said, "Give it a rest, will ya?" Dr. Dynamo was crushed. I sympathized with her on one level, but some days most students in the class find her a bit hard to take.

First, note the skillful transition used to open the paragraph: "The opposite of. . . ." Then the writer uses a definition strategy similar to the one that he employed in his previous body paragraph: he provides a few key details that describe the type of teacher. But after the middle of the paragraph, he switches to a narrative strategy, using an anecdote to illustrate what can annoy students about "Dr. Dynamo's" teaching style. In his final body paragraph, the writer uses yet another development strategy:

Time must pass by slowly for those who have grown sick of teaching. You can spot these people a mile away. They have a slightly glazed look to them, a little distracted, as if they were mildly drugged, which is a distinct possibility. I'm not talking about professors a few years away from retirement; I'm talking about those who are clearly sick of what they're doing. If you get close enough to them to look at their lecture notes, these pages will be yellow around the edges. My feeling is that these individuals are to be pitied, not scorned. They are not like Ms. Krebabble of *The Simpsons,* a contemptible and contemptuous functionary who couldn't care less about her profession. No, these folks have burned out on their career and are careening toward something else. I feel sorry for them.

In the second half of this paragraph, the writer uses contrast to explain what these people are *not.* This isn't a strategy that works in all situations, but it is effective in certain contexts.

As you can see from these examples, you can use definition, description, narration, exemplification, and/or comparison/contrast to explain your categories. You could also use causal or process analysis, depending on your topic and your purpose for writing.

Informative Classification Versus Personal Classification

The example paragraphs we have been discussing are based on one writer's personal experience. Another student who chooses the same topic will likely come up with different categories in which to group his or her instructors. These paragraphs also show that the writer knows how to "externalize" his experiences by explaining his categories so that his audience can understand—and be entertained by—his point of view about instructors. However, some assignments will ask you to take a more objective approach to your subjects. In these situations, your purpose will be to inform.

Note that these two types of classification essays aren't complete opposites. The personal essay also informs, and the informative essay gains nothing by being dry and boring. But the audience for an informative classification essay has different expectations—the readers assume that the writer knows more about the subject than they do. During the prewriting stage, then, the writer needs to spend more time thinking about the needs of his or her readers:

1. How much can the reader be expected to know about this subject?
2. Will I need to define certain terms? If so, what is the best way to do so?

CLASSROOM HINT Consider discussing these two types in class.

For example, in the excerpts from an essay that appear on pages 375–376, the writer is discussing a subject—types of turtles—that most readers will know very little about. Note how each paragraph includes information that the reader needs in order to understand the essay.

Language Level

Self-conscious, artificially formal language is never appropriate; however, many students are tempted to use such language when they write a classification essay, as in the following example:

> To classify breakfast foods is a matter of finding adequate categories. Logical division indicates that nutrition value, time of preparation, and tastiness must be considered. Therefore, in this paper I will classify breakfast foods in the following three categories: foods that are nutritious, foods that take little time to prepare, and foods that taste good.

We don't want to read the rest of this essay. The language alone is enough to repel us. Also, note that the categories are hazy and that they overlap (a breakfast food could be nutritious, easy to prepare, and tasty at the same time). Use concrete language and active verbs to describe your categories. Also, make sure that your categories are clearly distinct from one another.

MORE OPTIONS ONLINE For more help with problem areas in the classification essay, go to **www.mhhe.com/writingtoday**.

Choosing a Topic

When writing a classification essay, you first need to decide whether you will be writing an essay that is primarily informative or primarily personal:

1. If you choose to write an *informative classification,* you are probably thinking of a topic with which you are already familiar. Your purpose will be to explain this topic to your reader so that he or she will gain a better understanding of the subject. However, consider the following two issues:
   - Although you know the subject matter quite well, you should still consider doing some online and library research to look for new ideas and information. For more information on research and on writing documented essays, see chapters 20 and 21.
   - Consider your audience and your purpose as you think about a topic for an informational classification. We have read many classification essays that were technically proficient but on subjects that didn't need

to be explored by using classification—such as "types of socks." The students who wrote these papers obviously thought that they had fulfilled the assignment, but the writer never established a reason for the reader to be interested in these very tedious essays.

2. If you choose to write a primarily *personal classification,* remember that in this context, *personal* doesn't mean "private." Think of your audience. Is the subject that you are choosing going to be one that you can develop to the point that your reader will be thoroughly engaged, or is this an essay that will best be appreciated by the person who has written it?

Prewriting

Once you have chosen your topic, use one of the informal prewriting strategies to generate ideas: listing, freewriting, brainstorming, or clustering. (See Chapter 2 for more on these strategies.) Consider using two steps. First, you could brainstorm the categories that you will use. Then you could use a prewriting strategy for each category to develop definitions, differences between categories, and examples.

At this point, see if you can develop a working or preliminary thesis. If you can do so, you are now ready to organize your prewriting.

Organizing

After you have generated your categories and a sufficient number of examples and developed your working thesis, the best way for you to organize this raw material is to arrange it into an outline. (Chapter 2 covers informal, sentence, and formal outline structures.) As you work on your outline, think about how a body paragraph in a classification essay typically works:

1. General (names the category)
   to
2. More specific (defines and/or explains the category)
   to
3. Even more specific (gives examples of items within the category along with specific information about some of the items)

As well, make sure that you consider the most effective order for your body paragraphs. The normal order is **emphatic**, with the most interesting or complexly developed body paragraph coming last, just before the conclusion.

Drafting

To illustrate one approach to writing a classification essay, we have included the essay "The Last Dinosaurs."

The Introduction

When writing a classification essay, some students write an introduction that is little more than an expanded thesis statement. Remember that an essay's introduction must first establish the essay's *context;* this way, the reader understands the general subject matter and the reasons that the writer has decided to explore it—in this case, by dividing it into separate yet approachable categories. You also need to spark your reader's interest.

Remember also that you don't have to write your introduction first. The writer of our essay in progress wrote this introduction after producing the body of his essay:

The Last Dinosaurs

When people think of turtles, they probably visualize a generic version of this large family of reptiles. Turtles are part of our collective consciousness: children are fascinated by them, and most adults seem to retain a fondness for these creatures. However, there are three very different types of turtles, and the distinctions among them are both illuminating and interesting. **Turtles, terrapins, and tortoises are the three main groups that make up the order Testudinata.**

The writer has used a straightforward thesis statement that indicates the three categories and the order in which he will explain them in the body of the essay.

Consider Your Options

Choose an approach that allows you to convey the context and background in a lively way. (See Chapter 3 for ways to introduce an essay.) You need to introduce your topic sufficiently; otherwise, your reader will not understand why you are using classification.

The Body

The writer has mentioned three types—or categories—of turtles in the introduction. Now he proceeds to develop a paragraph on each category. Notice the development pattern. The first part of each paragraph names the type. Then the writer explains how the type is distinctive from other turtles. Finally, the writer gives specific details to help develop the idea of the paragraph. The pattern used is general, to less general, to specific:

The word turtle is used generically, but the term really applies only to the so-called soft-shell turtles. Most people have never seen one and would be surprised at their appearance. These aquatic reptiles have, as their name suggests, a soft carapace (shell) without the bony plates that form the "armor" common to the other two types. The neck is elongated, and the head is noticeably pointed at the snout. They look quite fierce—because they are. Soft-shells are territorial creatures that will not hesitate to bite an intruder. Swimmers should beware of these aggressive reptiles.

The second group, terrapins, is also found in water. Once again, many people have never seen these or have perhaps seen them only in zoos. These turtles have the bony plates that most of us visualize, and the carapace is very hard. The head is broad, with a rather pugnacious-looking snout. Some terrapins, such as the group made up of snapping turtles, are very aggressive and dangerous. By the time it is fully grown, an alligator snapper may have a head the size of a football; biting off a swimmer's or an angler's finger is no problem for this beast.

The third group, tortoises, is found on dry land, normally in wooded areas. These are what most people think of when the word turtle is mentioned. Tortoises range from a few inches in length to several feet, in the case of the mammoth Galapagos tortoise. Usually, tortoises are not aggressive, and they make fairly good pets. However, a wild tortoise will bite if threatened, inflicting a painful wound on the unwary.

Consider Your Options

Don't summarize here; comment instead. The conclusion allows you to reinforce the importance of what you have just written. (For more on strategies for concluding an essay, see Chapter 3.)

The Conclusion

Having shown the differences among the three groups, the writer now returns to the features that all turtles have in common:

Turtles are said to be the oldest living dinosaurs, and it is clear that they are winners when it comes to natural selection and evolution. The hard shell protects some turtles, and aggressive fighting abilities protect others. All three types continue to occupy a valuable niche in the world's ecosystem.

MORE OPTIONS ONLINE
For more help with the step-by-step development of the classification essay, go to **www.mhhe.com/writingtoday**.

EXERCISE 12.1

Write an outline of "The Last Dinosaurs." (For help with outlines, see Chapter 2, pages 41–42.) What method has the writer used for organizing the categories? What other method could he have used?

EXERCISE 12.1 Answers will vary. The following sentence outline is suggested.
I. Background: When people think of turtles, they are probably thinking of a generic version. Thesis: Turtles, terrapins, and tortoises are the three main groups that make up the order *Testudinata*.
II. The word *turtle* applies only to the so-called soft-shell turtles, which are aquatic.

Revising Your Draft

After you have completed a draft of your classification essay, your next step is to revise it, using your own analysis and comments from classmates or friends. During peer review, answer the questions on page 377 about the draft you are reviewing, whether it is yours or another student's.

After reviewing for content, you need to go over your peer reviewers' responses to your essay and then revise for unity, coherence, language level, and tone (see Chapter 4). When you have revised your draft and are basically satisfied with it, read your draft for mechanical and grammatical errors. Concentrate on finding and correcting major sentence errors (fragments, comma splices, fused sentences), errors in pronoun agreement and subject-verb agreement, and spelling.

Now that you have made your corrections, *read your essay one more time* to catch any errors made during revision and find errors missed during your earlier reviews.

Questions for Reviewing a Classification Essay

1. Does the introduction explain the basis for classifying the topic as well as interest the reader? How could it be improved?
2. What is the thesis statement? Has the writer placed it in the best position within the essay? In what ways, if any, could it be improved?
3. Has the writer fulfilled his or her purpose for writing the essay? Is the writer's tone appropriate for this purpose?
4. Does the way that the writer has classified the topic make sense? Point out any obvious categories that have been omitted. Are the categories differentiated, or could two of them be combined?
5. Is the organization effective? Should the categories be presented in a different order?
6. How do the topic sentences introduce each new category, or how do they introduce a new aspect of a previous category? In other words, point out any topic sentences that do not have a clear role in introducing or further defining a category.
7. Is each category fully developed? Where does the writer need to add more detail to make the distinctions between categories clearer?
8. Does the writer use transitions to guide the reader from one category to the next? Where are transitional words or sentences needed?
9. Does the essay have an effective conclusion? How could it be improved?

MORE OPTIONS ONLINE
For more help with revision, go to **www.mhhe.com/writingtoday**.

Student Essay

The following essay is Sam Leininger's response to a classification assignment. The final draft is presented first. Then Sam's first draft is presented, with his comments about this draft and what he needed to do in the revision stage.

Sam's Final Draft

Fraud Alert

A new brand of retail store has developed over the past several years. The superstore overwhelms smaller, independent competitors with its larger inventory, lower prices, and multiple locations. The chain bookstore is a unique kind of superstore: part store, part library, part café, it's a place where the emphasis has shifted from selling books to getting people to visit, apparently. The staff is extremely nonconfrontational. Most of the time, they won't even acknowledge a customer's existence. It is the policy of these stores not to pressure customers, and they usually provide ample tables and sofas. This laid-back atmosphere has created a new breed of bookstore patron. In fact, there are specific types of customers at these bookstores, and they can be easily distinguished by their purpose for being there.

2 The status-challenged group likes to maintain a high degree of visibility by simply spending an enormous amount of time in these stores. These folks are under the impression that merely setting foot inside a bookstore raises their cultural status. So they grab a few magazines, or perhaps the *History of* Playboy *Magazine Covers,* find a comfortable, visible seat, and begin to pore over their selection with a mock intensity that rivals any politician's. The easiest way to spot these people is to note the frequency with which they look up from their books: almost every time someone walks by, they will stop reading and look up, just in case it's someone they know. One time, I made eye contact with one of them, and I could swear he was silently begging me not to expose him for the fake that he is.

3 The hipsters are also easily recognizable. The patrons of all those coffee houses that have sprung up in the last few years have migrated to the bookstores. You can usually find them in the café section, double latte in hand, or staring lovingly at the shelves in the poetry section. Some of them may even work at the store. Most of the hipsters have some sort of backpack or bag, and most wear Birkenstocks, yet every single one of them has a notepad in which they manically scribble poetry, but only when people are watching. If the café tables are in plain view, this is usually where they set up camp. Some of the wealthier hipsters substitute a notebook computer for actual paper, but there's a greater chance that they are playing solitaire than writing poetry.

4 The worst phenomenon of these stores is the "in-and-outers." These are the people who rush into the store, grab whatever book has been chosen for the best-seller display at the store's entrance, and rush out. Rarely ever seen as more than a blur, these patrons can be observed closely only when the cashier line is backed up. They may blend into the line, but if you notice someone tapping his or her feet and rattling car keys, you may just have spotted the elusive "in-and-outer."

5

These new kinds of shoppers are almost enough to keep me out of the bookstore. I am embarrassed to be seen at the same store as a hipster, although I must admit that it's fun to watch them scamper when you mention that you just saw an employee stocking some new editions of Jack Kerouac's* books. However, the worst group is the "in-and-outers." Not only do they promote the monopoly that these few big bookstores are developing by grabbing the latest romance, spy, or horror novel that has absolutely no literary value, but they also diminish the country's intellectual level faster than professional wrestling. Soon, even these big bookstores with all their excess capital will start to narrow down their selections, because 100 extra copies of the new Tom Clancy book will sell while that collection of essays on Marxism will probably stay on the shelf for months. So the next time you see one of these bookstore types, take action. Hand a hipster a Thomas Pynchon* novel, offer one of the magazine readers a book by Bertrand Russell,* and see if you can steer an in-and-outer to *Jane Eyre* instead of the latest offering from Danielle Steele. You'd be doing your duty for your country.

Sam's First Draft

Fraud Alert

1

A new brand of retail store has developed over the past five years. The superstore uses its massive volume to overwhelm any smaller, independent competitors with a larger inventory, lower prices, and multiple locations. The bookstore has become a unique entity; part store, part library, part cafe, the emphasis has shifted from selling books to getting people to visit, apparently. The atmosphere creates a new breed of bookstore patrons. In fact, there are many different types of customers at these bookstores.

I made my thesis stronger by adding the basis of my classification.

2

The Hipsters are easily recognizable. Remember all those coffee houses? Their patrons have transplanted to the bookstores. You can usually find them

***Jack Kerouac (1922–1969):** an icon of the 1950's counter-culture, also known as the "Beat Generation," a phrase he coined. His novel *On the Road,* published in 1957, has been highly influential.
***Thomas Pynchon (b. 1937):** a respected contemporary novelist. His greatest work, *Gravity's Rainbow* (1973), won the National Book Award in 1974.
***Bertrand Russell (1872–1970):** an Influential twentieth-century philosopher, who is also remembered for his social and political activism. He was a leader of both the anti-war and the ban-the-bomb movements in Europe. He won the Nobel Prize in Literature in 1950.

When I read my draft, I noticed first off that the order of the body paragraphs seemed wrong. I realized that the best approach was to put my categories into the "order of increasing annoyance value," so I switched the first two body paragraphs.

in the cafe section, double latte in hand, or staring lovingly at the poetry section. Every single one of them has a notepad that they scribble manic poetry into, but only when people are watching. Some of the richer Hipsters substitute a notebook computer for actual paper, but there's a greater chance that the solitaire program is being run than the word processor.

I wanted to add more detail, to fill in the picture. For example, I added a fuller description of the status-challenged group.

3 Another group often spends an enormous amount of time in these stores. These folks are under the impression that merely stepping foot inside a bookstore raises their cultural status. So they grab something from the shelf, find a comfortable seat, and begin to pour over their selection with mock intensity. The easiest way to spot these people is the frequency with which they look up from their books: almost every time someone walks by, they will stop reading and look up, just in case it's someone they know.

I needed to tighten the language in the body paragraphs: my first drafts are always more wordy than they need to be.

4 Although the lingering groups are annoying, the worst phenomenon of these stores is the "in-and-outers." These are the people who rush into the store, grab whatever book has been chosen for the best seller display at the store's entrance, and rush out. The best chance to see these patrons is when the cashier line is backed up. They may blend in, but check for people rattling their car keys, and you may just have spotted the elusive "in-and-outer."

5 These new classes of shoppers are almost enough to keep me out of the bookstore; I am embarrassed to be seen at the same store as a Hipster, although I must admit that it's fun to watch them scamper when you mention that you just saw an employee stocking some new Jack Kerouac books. However, the worst are the "in-and-outers." Not only do they promote the monopoly that these few big bookstores are developing, by grabbing the latest romance, spy, or horror novel that has absolutely no literary value, they are sending the country's intellectual level down faster than professional wrestling. So the next time you see a hipster, hand him or her a Thomas Pynchion novel; smack one of the magazine readers in the face with a Bertrand Russell book, and set up a snare for the "in-and-outer," take them in the back, and just beat them senseless until they've agreed that Danielle Steele is not literature.

I changed the ending to make it less shocking and add a final comment.

EXERCISE 12.2: REVISING

The following is the first draft of a student's classification essay. Working in pairs or in small groups, review this essay. Using the Questions for Reviewing a Classification Essay on page 377, decide what revisions you would suggest. If you have any questions the student needs to consider, write them in the margin or on a separate sheet of paper. If your instructor directs you to, rewrite one or more paragraphs to make them stronger and to eliminate any grammatical or mechanical errors.

"Bars"

1 Bars and taverns are popular spots to relax. Although, there are several different types of bars. In this essay I will classify bars and show that they fall in to 3 main categories, and the reader will have a better understanding of this subject.

2 The first classification are neighborhood bars, these are also known as taverns. They specialize in providing constant service to working men and retired men. It takes awhile to become welcome here.

3 Second type are grilles. These are usually franchises, part of the place is a restaurent, the rest is a central bar. These places are sometimes trendy.

4 The third type are my favorite. These are clubs, they are designed for younger costomers. Their is usually a dj, drinks specials an loud music for dancing. Theyre great places to meet women. Some local favorites are: Magma, Club 2004 and the Snake Pit. These places guaranty a classy enviroment by: (1) having a covercharge (2) haveing a strict dresscode (3) security guards. They are hot places to spend an evenning.

5 I hope the reader now understands better the subject of bars. Know what you want, then find the right place for your needs.

EXERCISE 12.2
Answers will vary. Students should point out that the reader needs more background, the second and third paragraphs need to include more details about neighborhood bars and grilles, as paragraph 4 does about clubs, and the conclusion needs to be strengthtened.

SUGGESTED ACTIVITY
Consider asking students to meet in writing groups, each of which is charged with producing a more developed and effective version of this essay. Encourage students to use details from their own experience. You might also ask students to write a similar classification essay about the types of people one might encounter in pizza parlors, fast-food restaurants, or even the college snack bar or cafeteria.

Additional Writing Topics

1. Write an essay in which you divide one of the following subjects into its categories:
   a. Infomercials
   b. First dates
   c. Newscasters
   d. Auto repair companies
   e. College support personnel

2. **Writing on the job.** Think about where you work now or a place where you worked in the past, and write a memo to your manager classifying your customers or clients. Your purpose is to increase sales. (For help with writing a memo, see Chapter 17.)

Responding to a Photograph

RESPONDING TO A PHOTOGRAPH Remind students that both projects rely heavily on classification as a primary method of organization.

By the end of the nineteenth century, the violent conflicts between Native Americans and settlers in the United States were effectively over. Many Native Americans became the legal equivalent of wards of the U.S. government, forced to live on reservations and submit to the new culture and its demands. An unknown photographer took this picture around 1900.

Unknown photographer, Before entering school, Sioux, *Seven Little Indian Children in Four Stages of Civilization*, ca. 1900. The Photography Collection, Carpenter Center for the Visual Arts at Harvard University.

1. Write an informal response to the photograph. What do you notice? How does the image make you feel? How does the photograph make use of the classification option?
2. At the time of the photograph, Native Americans were not classified as full citizens. Using a combination of library and online research, explore the status of Native Americans at the start of the twentieth century. (A good way to narrow your topic is to concentrate on one Native American tribe or on one tribe in a single geographical area.) Write a documented essay showing how Native Americans were classified, viewed, and treated. (For more information on documented essays, see Chapter 21.)

Writing About Film

Antz (1998, PG) shows the hierarchical society of ants. What are the various types of ants shown in the film? How do their categories form the basis for the conflict in the film?

Schindler's List (1993, R) tells the story of Oskar Schindler, who tried to save the lives of Polish Jews during the Holocaust. Because the film takes place during a time when Nazis practiced "human categorization," the viewer is forced to identify people by group. What groups of people are shown in the film? How does Schindler try to subvert the Nazis' classification system in order to save innocent lives?

Using the Internet

Search the Internet for insights and information to use when writing classification essays.

1. Find Web sites devoted to a subject relating to your college major or to an academic discipline that interests you. Focus on a limited subject. For example, instead of researching "biology," try "microbiology," "human physiology," "entomology," or "parasitology"—the more specific the better. Try to limit your search to sites devoted exclusively to your subject, and visit as many sites as you can. Then classify these sites into at least three logical categories. Finally, write an essay explaining the principle you used to classify each Web site. For example, one category might consist of sites maintained by professional organizations. Another might include sites established by colleges or universities. A third might consist of Web sites dedicated to professional, online journals.

   Describe each site thoroughly, and explain the similarities that the within each category share. You will need to use the techniques of description and comparison/contrast as well as those associated with classification. (See chapters 6 and 13 for help with these patterns.)
2. Search the Internet to find the Web sites of online news providers—news services, newspapers, and/or magazines. In a classification essay, discuss at least ten to twelve different sites by organizing them into three or four categories. To classify the sites, consider layout, extent and nature of news coverage, quality of news coverage, editorial leanings, prominence of advertising, or any other relevant governing principles.

DILBERT reprinted by permission of United Feature Syndicate, Inc.

CHAPTER 13

COMPARISON AND CONTRAST

Writing in Context

Bob appears at your cubicle yet again.

"What do you know about optical scanners?" he asks.

"I know what they do. And I know that some of them are geared more toward text processing and some of them are graphics oriented."

"Good," Bob replied. "Here, take this." He hands you two folders. "We need to decide which one of these to buy. Talk to Stephanie if you want the background. I'll need an analysis by Friday."

You start looking through the folders Bob has left with you. They contain mainly sales brochures and listings of technical specifications. You know you'll need to grill Stephanie, and probably other people, before you feel confident about starting the report.

Then it will be a matter of writing an evaluation, a side-by-side examination of the distinctions between the two scanners. Even at this point you can see the "shape" of your report.

You can see its shape because this task so clearly calls for an option known as comparison and contrast, in which two things are compared, often with the aim of producing an evaluation, perhaps an evaluation that will enable readers to arrive at some decision.

SUGGESTED ACTIVITY Dilbert's colleague is comparing engineers to marketers; Dilbert's sarcastic comment suggests that he disagrees. Ask students to think about two groups of people (e.g., students and employees, sports fans and movie fans, etc.) and decide whether members of the two groups are similar or different in some important ways. Have them spend five to ten minutes writing a brief comparison or contrast, and discuss one or two responses as a class.

CLASSROOM HINT Discuss the two patterns presented here in class.

HOW DOES COMPARISON/ CONTRAST WORK?

We frequently engage in the act of comparing. When shopping for food, clothing, cars, or almost any other product, we tend to face multiple choices, not to mention a barrage of marketing intended to sway our decision. Usually, we are able to narrow the field down to a few likely suspects, and then the serious comparison begins.

The same process tends to occur when we choose a service:

- The college or university we'll attend
- The tax preparer who will mediate our relationship with the Internal Revenue Service
- The dentist to whom we'll pay substantial sums of money to inflict pain upon us and disrupt our daily lives

In the case of the dentist, for instance, we might make our choice based on a comparison like this one:

> Dr. Burns is a great dentist, but he's got the patient-relation skills of a repo man. And you have to schedule months in advance. On the other hand, Dr. Chen is young and has not yet shown that she is a "great" dentist, but she's funny, I like her, and she keeps evening hours.

As with comparison and contrast in daily life, writers—whether working on the job, in school, or in other contexts—often use comparison and contrast in order to evaluate. That is, they use it to try to reach a judgment based on a serious and objective look at relevant features of the entities that they are comparing.

However, writers may also use the comparison/contrast strategy in order to inform readers—that is, to illustrate, to describe, or simply to reveal the similarities and differences that exist between two subjects. For example, a writer might describe her two uncles, who are twins. Her purpose might be to show how different the two men are—an approach that would be particularly effective because it would tend to work against the reader's expectations (when most of us think of twins, we automatically think in terms of similarity, not difference). Clearly, the writer's goal is not to "evaluate" her uncles—it's not as if she's trying to convince the reader to buy her uncles or marry them. Rather, she is painting a picture—explaining, perhaps entertaining, showing the reader how twins can be very different. In a similar vein, if your political science professor asks you to compare the U.S. electoral system to the Australian electoral system on an essay exam, he or she hasn't asked for an evaluation of the two systems, but rather for a discussion of the points on which they are similar and different. In short, comparison and contrast can be used for two general purposes: an evaluative purpose and a more general descriptive and informative purpose.

Just as there are two general purposes for using the strategy, there are also two organizational approaches. The **subject-by-subject** method fully examines the first of two subjects being compared and then fully examines the second. A broad outline for such an essay might look like this:

Piano A
- Tone
- Design
- Keyboard

Piano B
- Tone
- Design
- Keyboard

The **point-by-point** method examines both subjects in terms of the first point of the comparison, then examines both in terms of the second point, and so on. A very broad outline for such an essay might look like this:

Tone
- Piano A
- Piano B

Design
- Piano A
- Piano B

Keyboard
- Piano A
- Piano B

In the vignette that opens this chapter, Bob wants information. Specifically, he wants an analysis of key performance and technical issues that will determine which of two scanners will best serve the company's needs. This analysis will probably be easiest for him to read if the writer compares and contrasts the two scanners on one point at a time. Therefore, the writer will probably use the point-by-point method, perhaps selecting these three areas:

- Purpose—to what extent is each scanner designed for text scanning (with less emphasis on graphics scanning) or graphics scanning (with less emphasis on text scanning)?
- Software compatibility—which scanner is better suited for painless hookup to the company's network?
- Processing speed—which scanner gets more work done in a given period of time?

Bob probably doesn't want to be told whether the scanner is beige or gray or to be given interesting information about the development of each product. That information is likely irrelevant to him. He wants to know which product to buy. The areas included in the comparison and contrast are the ones that will help him make this decision. As in this example, in many cases when your purpose is evaluative, you will find a point-by-point organization particularly useful.

However, if your purpose is to inform and describe—to provide readers with a picture of the two subjects—the subject-by-subject method may well be the better choice. This is especially true for comparison/contrast essays that use narration as an internal strategy—for example, comparing and contrasting a wonderful vacation and a horrible one. By analyzing first one event and then the next, you give your readers clear accounts of both events. On the other hand, if you were to use a point-by-point approach here, you'd wind up fragmenting those accounts, in a sense reducing the dynamics of the experiences to mere categories of information (hotels stayed at, meals eaten, places seen, and so on). Your reader deserves better treatment. After all, you are trying to fulfill your purpose of providing a clear picture of the two subjects.

In most comparison/contrast essays, the emphasis will be on contrast. Obviously, if your purpose is evaluative, you want to find and focus on differences. Even if your purpose isn't evaluative, it is usually more instructive and interesting to readers to show how two entities are different than to show how they are similar (however, see page 408 for examples of situations in which comparison is the best option). For example, consider this idea: for decades, American automakers tended to produce a car model and then package it under different "nameplates." A midsize Chevy was virtually identical to a midsize Pontiac, and the same was true of Ford and Mercury and Plymouth and Dodge. Presumably, a buyer might buy a Mercury that was virtually the same as the (normally) lower-priced Ford because the Mercury line had more prestige. Would you want to write an essay comparing these two very similar cars? It's hard to see how you could write a fully developed, interesting paper when trying to compare two items that are so similar. However, keep in mind that comparison/contrast essays that emphasize contrast may also use comparison, just as those that emphasize comparison will surely include some contrasts.

Technically, the comparison/contrast option is not limited to two subjects. A writer could compare three subjects (or four, or ten, or twenty, for that matter). But a three-way comparison asks a great deal of your reader, and any number beyond three would probably be too hard for your reader to comprehend in an essay. The three-way approach tends to appear only in technical/business contexts that use a point-by-point approach. In the opening vignette, for example, Bob could have requested an analysis of three scanners rather than of two. However, for general purposes, most essays concentrate on two subjects only. If a situation seems to call for a three-way analysis, you may find that using a classification or definition approach is a better option.

Consider Your Options

- How might you use comparison/contrast strategies at work?
- How could this approach help you evaluate situations as they arise?

Note also that you can use comparison/contrast to help you develop essays that concentrate on other rhetorical options. For a good example, see Umberto Eco's "How Not to Use the Fax Machine and the Cellular Phone" in Chapter 9 ("Process Analysis"). While showing how consumer technology can come to dominate the consumer, Eco makes a firm distinction between people who need cell phones and those who do not.

The comparison/contrast essay can be difficult to write yet a joy to read, as the following essays indicate.

READING THE COMPARISON/CONTRAST ESSAY WITH A WRITER'S EYE

In the works that follow, Ellen Currie contrasts murder in the past with a more contemporary form of murder, namely, serial murder; Bharati Mukherjee examines two very different ways for immigrants to approach life in a new country; David Sedaris contrasts his fun-loving family with his serious, analytical father; and Barbara Mellix contrasts "home English" with "public English." As you read these essays, note the method of organization used by each author. As well, note how the author uses the comparison/contrast option to achieve his or her purpose.

The second half of this chapter features strategies for writing the comparison/contrast essay (pages 404–414). If you decide to write on one of the topics that follow the four essays below, make sure that you have read the strategies section before you begin. Also note that additional writing topics are listed at the end of the chapter (pages 419–420).

Two Varieties of Killers

ELLEN CURRIE

The work of Ellen Currie, a professional writer, appears frequently in American magazines and newspapers. The following essay, which first appeared in the *New York Times* on August 21, 1986, analyzes a phenomenon that developed in the twentieth century—the serial killer—and contrasts this type of killer with the more "sociable" killers of the past.

1 Henry James,* like many decorous and respectable people, entertained a lively interest in murder. He was a fan of the Scottish solicitor William Roughead, who wrote about real life crime for the first 40 years of this century. James once told Mr. Roughead he was interested in crime because through it "manners and morals become clearly disclosed." He urged Mr. Roughead to write about "the dear old human and sociable murders and adulteries and forgeries in which we are so agreeably at home. And don't tell me, for charity's sake, that your supply runs short."

2 Contemporary supplies of murder, adultery, and forgery remain abundant. But crime seems to me less sociable these days, if I am right in taking "sociable" to mean human and comprehensible and even sympathetic. The crimes get bigger and more horrible, and yet we are not sufficiently horrified by them; we pay less and less attention to the manners and the morals they disclose.

3 Look at the difference, for example, between the crimes of Madeleine Smith, who stirred arsenic into her lover's cocoa in 1857, and the convicted killer Theodore R. Bundy, who has been linked with the murders of 36 women he didn't even know.

4 Madeleine Smith, whose case greatly interested Henry James (he called her a "portentous young person"), was the daughter of a Glasgow architect. In 1855, when she was 19, she crossed paths with a young Frenchman. He was handsome, Mr. Roughead wrote, but "socially impossible." They met in secret and wrote to each other constantly. When they became lovers Miss Smith's letters took on what Mr. Roughead described as "a tropical and abandoned tone." They were indelicate letters, naive and outspoken. Another scholar of crime has pointed out that in a day when sex was supposed to be no more than a woman's bounden duty, Madeleine Smith found it a pagan festival.

***Henry James (1843–1916):** a major American-born novelist who lived most of his life in England. Famous for his large, complicated studies of the well-born and/or wealthy, James came to be considered an arbiter of taste and manners.

Her lover kept her letters, 198 of them. When she accepted an older, richer and more settled suitor, she asked for the letters' return. Wild with jealousy, her lover claimed he would return them only to her father. That prospect drove Miss Smith mad with shame and fear. She bought arsenic. Her lover soon died of arsenic poisoning. She was brought to trial and conducted herself with great dignity. The verdict: not proven. 5

These people are not admirable, but they are real. Their awful situation is comprehensible: a blown up, highly colored version of the kind of dilemma ordinary people face. Madeleine Smith's crime was personal. It was a crime of passion. 6

The case of Ted Bundy is different. To me, it is not "sociable," not comprehensible on any human scale. It is peculiarly impersonal. He didn't even know his victims; they represented an abstraction—women. His are crimes not of passion but pathology. Our reaction to them seems to me to partake of pathology too. 7

According to the reports I have read, some law enforcement officials say Mr. Bundy may have killed more than 36 young women in sexual crimes across the country. (Like Madeleine Smith, Ted Bundy says he is innocent of any crime.) He has been convicted of battering to death, early on Super Bowl Sunday 1978 in the Chi Omega sorority house at Florida State University, two young women. He hideously beat two more young women in the same house and, blocks away, savaged another young woman. He didn't know any of them. Captured and charged, Mr. Bundy was also indicted in the kidnapping and murder of a 12-year-old girl. He didn't know her, either. He was convicted of all charges. His execution, scheduled for July 3, was indefinitely postponed to give his lawyers time to frame an appeal.* 8

The young women Ted Bundy has been convicted of killing, and is suspected of killing, resemble, an investigator said, "everyone's daughter." Their photographs show the sweet faces of their youth, the long hair of the period. Except for those who loved them, their identities overlap now, and blur. These women are not vivid and defined because they did nothing to bring about their deaths. They were not Ted Bundy's angry and discarded lovers. They did not refuse to return his disastrous, impassioned letters. They didn't know him. 9

At first all these deaths of pretty young women attracted wide public notice. But once Mr. Bundy was apprehended, the attention was all on his antics and not on the innocent dead. Bundy is a 20th century phenomenon. He is mediagenic. He is handsome, usually described as a former law student and witty, brilliant, charming, and polished. Oddly, these latter qualities do not come through in any of the several books about him. Mr. Bundy was once active in Republican politics; there are those who profess to believe that he might ultimately have been elected to high public office had he stayed the course. He has twice made dramatic escapes from custody. He has acted as his own counsel in sensational televised trials. He has been the subject of a television movie. Ted Bundy T-shirts, for, against, and smart aleck ("Ted Bundy is a one-night stand"), have enjoyed popularity. So have jingles: "Let's salute the mighty Bundy / Here on Friday, gone on Monday / All his roads lead out of town / It's hard to keep a good man down." Bundy Burgers and a Bundy cocktail had some play in a Colorado bar. Groupies have gathered at his trials. He gets a lot of mail. 10

Theodore Bundy is said by psychiatrists to be an antisocial personality, a man without conscience. In a strange, third person meditation on killings, Mr. Bundy described the rapes and murders as "inappropriate acting out." 11

---

*Ted Bundy was executed in 1989.

12 Perhaps Ted Bundy doesn't labor under a conscience. But how about the rest of us? Shouldn't we feel more revulsion, more grief for those young lives? Something vile has happened to our ideas of what is valuable and what is waste. Perhaps we have seen too much evil and on too grand a scale. We are glib and dismissive of the moral issues. We think Mr. Bundy is good for a laugh. We made him a celebrity. (Richard Schickel, in his book *Intimate Strangers,* about the nature of celebrity in modern society, contends that multiple murderers have grasped the essentials of the celebrity system better than normal people.)

13 Crime does disclose on manners and on morals. If people must kill people, I have to put my dollar down on wicked Madeleine Smith. With her sexy letters, poisoned cocoa, and caddish lover, she dealt in death. But she is piercingly familiar. Ted Bundy's unspeakable crimes and our cheap reaction to them reveal us to ourselves in a strange and deathly light.

Vocabulary

The following terms are identified by paragraph number. Make sure that you understand each term's meaning in its context. If you're not sure that you understand a term, look it up in a college-level dictionary.

decorous (1)	suitor (5)	groupies (10)
solicitor (1)	dilemma (6)	antisocial (11)
portentous (4)	pathology (7)	revulsion (12)
indelicate (4)	antics (10)	glib (12)
bounden (4)	mediagenic (10)	piercingly (13)
pagan (4)	counsel (10)	

Style and Strategy

1. Currie's thesis is in paragraph 7. Would it have been more effective if placed at the beginning of her essay? Explain.
2. Currie uses a subject-by-subject organization. Write a sentence outline of this essay to help reveal her organization.
3. On what points does Currie contrast the crime of Madeleine Smith to the crimes of Ted Bundy?
4. What "choice" is Currie making in her concluding paragraph?
5. What do you think is Currie's purpose in writing this essay?

STYLE AND STRATEGY
1. Placing the thesis in paragraph 7 allows the author time to comment on Madeleine Smith, thereby making the contrast created in paragraph 7 more immediate and credible.
2. Few students have trouble outlining this essay once they realize that comments made about Bundy need not contrast paragraph-by-paragraph with those made about Smith.
3. Paragraphs 5–9 are significant in this regard. Paragraphs 12 and 13 are also important.
4. Her choice is between the more "human," more familiar, crime such as the one committed by Smith and the impersonal, unfathomable type committed by Bundy. The reason for her choice is summed up in the essay's last sentence.
5. This essay is not about murderers; it is about our reaction to them, which is becoming increasingly tepid.

Questions for Critical Thinking and Discussion

1. Madeleine Smith was tried for murder in Scotland, and the verdict was "not proven." Scotland is the only country that has allowed this contingency, which basically means "we know you did it, but we can't prove it." In the United States, on the other hand, the only two definitive verdicts in a criminal trial are "guilty" and "not guilty." Would the U.S. legal system be improved by including the possible verdict of "not proven"?

2. Currie treats Ted Bundy as a modern phenomenon. Actually, serial killers are known to have existed in the nineteenth century and before. It is the sheer *number* of these sociopaths in the past few decades that is remarkable. (At the time of this writing, according to FBI estimates, there are several dozen serial killers on the loose in the United States.) In your opinion, what are some of the possible causes of this increase?
3. Why are we so fascinated by serial killers that we name burgers and cocktails after them? What does this say about contemporary society?

Suggestions for Writing

Write a 500- to 750-word essay in which you contrast two motivations for breaking the rules:

1. Shoplifting because of need versus shoplifting for fun
2. Cheating on school assignments out of desperation versus cheating because of laziness
3. Vandalism motivated by anger over political or economic injustice versus vandalism for fun

Two Ways to Belong in America

BHARATI MUKHERJEE

Bharati Mukherjee was born in India, where she received a bachelor's degree and master's degree before immigrating to the United States in 1961. She attended the University of Iowa, where she earned a master's in fine arts and a doctorate in English and comparative literature. A renowned writer of fiction, Mukherjee has published the novels *The Tiger's Daughter* (1972), *Wife* (1975), *Jasmine* (1989), *The Holder of the World* (1993), *Leave It to Me* (1997), and *Desirable Daughters* (2002). Her short-story collection *The Middleman and Other Stories* (1988) won the National Book Critics Circle Award.

Immigration and identity are frequent themes in Mukherjee's works. The following essay was written for the *New York Times* in 1996 to comment upon controversial proposals and legislation regarding the rights of immigrants.

1 This is a tale of two sisters from Calcutta, Mira and Bharati, who have lived in the United States for some 35 years, but who find themselves on different sides in the current debate over the status of immigrants. I am an American citizen and she is not. I am moved that thousands of long-term residents are finally taking the oath of citizenship. She is not.

2 Mira arrived in Detroit in 1960 to study child psychology and pre-school education. I followed her a year later to study creative writing at the University of Iowa. When we left India, we were almost identical in appearance and attitude. We dressed alike, in saris; we expressed identical views on politics, social issues, love, and marriage in the same Calcutta convent-school accent. We would endure our two years in America, secure our degrees, then return to India to marry the grooms of our father's choosing.

3 Instead, Mira married an Indian student in 1962 who was getting his business administration degree at Wayne State University. They soon acquired the labor certifications necessary for the green card of hassle-free residence and employment.

4 Mira still lives in Detroit, works in the Southfield, Mich., school system, and has become nationally recognized for her contributions in the fields of pre-school

education and parent-teacher relationships. After 36 years as a legal immigrant in this country, she clings passionately to her Indian citizenship and hopes to go home to India when she retires.

5 In Iowa City in 1963, I married a fellow student, an American of Canadian parentage. Because of the accident of his North Dakota birth, I bypassed labor-certification requirements and the race-related "quota" system that favored the applicant's country of origin over his or her merit. I was prepared for (and even welcomed) the emotional strain that came with marrying outside my ethnic community. In 33 years of marriage, we have lived in every part of North America. By choosing a husband who was not my father's selection, I was opting for fluidity, self-invention, blue jeans and T-shirts, and renouncing 3,000 years (at least) of case-observant, "pure culture" marriage in the Mukherjee family. My books have often been read as unapologetic (and in some quarters overenthusiastic) texts for cultural and psychological "mongrelization." It's a word I celebrate.

6 Mira and I have stayed sisterly close by phone. In our regular Sunday morning conversations, we are unguardedly affectionate. I am her only blood relative on this continent. We expect to see each other through the looming crises of aging and ill health without being asked. Long before Vice President Gore's "Citizenship U.S.A." drive, we'd had our polite arguments over the ethics of retaining an overseas citizenship while expecting the permanent protection and economic benefits that come with living and working in America.

7 Like well-raised sisters, we never said what was really on our minds, but we probably pitied one another. She, for the lack of structure in my life, the erasure of Indianness, the absence of an unvarying daily core. I, for the narrowness of her perspective, her uninvolvement with the mythic depths or the superficial pop culture of this society. But, now, with the scapegoatings of "aliens" (documented or illegal) on the increase, and the targeting of long-term legal immigrants like Mira for new scrutiny and new self-consciousness, she and I find ourselves unable to maintain the same polite discretion. We were always unacknowledged adversaries, and we are now, more than ever, sisters.

8 "I feel used," Mira raged on the phone the other night. "I feel manipulated and discarded. This is such an unfair way to treat a person who was invited to stay and work here because of her talent. My employer went to the I.N.S. and petitioned for the labor certification. For over 30 years, I've invested my creativity and professional skills into the improvement of *this* country's pre-school system. I've obeyed all the rules, I've paid my taxes, I love my work, I love my students, I love the friends I've made. How dare America now change its rules in midstream? If America wants to make new rules curtailing benefits of legal immigrants, they should apply only to immigrants who arrive after those rules are already in place."

9 To my ears, it sounded like the description of a long-enduring, comfortable yet loveless marriage, without risk or recklessness. Have we the right to demand, and to expect, that we be loved? (That, to me, is the subtext of the arguments by immigration advocates.) My sister is an expatriate, professionally generous and creative, socially courteous and gracious, and that's as far as her Americanization can go. She is here to maintain an identity, not to transform it.

10 I asked her if she would follow the example of others who have decided to become citizens because of the anti-immigration bills in Congress. And here, she surprised me. "If America wants to play the manipulative game, I'll play it, too," she

snapped. "I'll become a U.S. citizen for now, then change back to India when I'm ready to go home. I feel some kind of irrational attachment to India that I don't to America. Until all this hysteria against legal immigrants, I was totally happy. Having my green card meant I could visit any place in the world I wanted to and then come back to a job that's satisfying and that I do very well."

11 In one family, from two sisters alike as peas in a pod, there could not be a wider divergence of immigrant experience. America spoke to me—I married it—I embraced the demotion from expatriate aristocrat to immigrant nobody, surrendering those thousands of years of "pure culture," the saris, the delightfully accented English. She retained them all. Which of us is the freak?

12 Mira's voice, I realize, is the voice not just of the immigrant South Asian community but of an immigrant community of the millions who have stayed rooted in one job, one city, one house, one ancestral culture, one cuisine, for the entirety of their productive years. She speaks for greater numbers than I possibly can. Only the fluency of her English and the anger, rather than fear, born of confidence in her education, differentiate her from the seamstresses, the domestics, the technicians, the shop owners, the millions of hard-working but effectively silenced documented immigrants as well as their less fortunate "illegal" brothers and sisters.

13 Nearly 20 years ago, when I was living in my husband's ancestral homeland of Canada, I was always well-employed but never allowed to feel part of the local Quebec or larger Canadian society. Then, through a Green Paper that invited a national referendum on the unwanted side effects of "nontraditional" immigration, the Government officially turned against its immigrant communities, particularly those from South Asia.

14 I felt then the same sense of betrayal that Mira feels now. I will never forget the pain of that sudden turning, and the casual racist outbursts the Green Paper elicited. That sense of betrayal had its desired effect and drove me, and thousands like me, from the country.

15 Mira and I differ, however, in the ways in which we hope to interact with the country that we have chosen to live in. She is happier to live in America as expatriate Indian than as an immigrant American. I need to feel like a part of the community I have adopted (as I tried to feel in Canada as well). I need to put roots down, to vote and make the difference that I can. The price that the immigrant willingly pays, and that the exile avoids, is the trauma of self-transformation.

Vocabulary

The following terms are identified by paragraph number. Make sure that you understand each term's meaning in its context. If you're not sure that you understand a term, look it up in a college-level dictionary.

oath (1)	scapegoating (7)	aristocrat (11)
sari (2)	adversaries (7)	cuisine (12)
quota (5)	subtext (9)	ancestral (13)
fluidity (5)	expatriate (9)	referendum (13)
renouncing (5)	divergence (11)	betrayal (14)
mythic (7)	demotion (11)	trauma (15)

Style and Strategy

1. Mukherjee's thesis is suggested in her first few paragraphs but isn't explicitly stated until later. Where is it explicitly stated?
2. Mukherjee uses a point-by-point organization. Write a sentence outline of this essay to help reveal her organization.
3. Is the writer objective in this essay, or is she favoring her choice over her sister's? Explain.
4. Why does the author include (in paragraphs 13 and 14) her experiences in Canada?

STYLE AND STRATEGY
1. Her thesis is stated in paragraph 15.
2. Ask students to write this outline as a homework assignment.
3. This question does not require a definitive answer. It simply encourages close analysis.
4. Doing so allows her to lend credibility to her sister's position on a number of issues. It also shows that a contrast essay can also contain comparisons.

Questions for Critical Thinking and Discussion

1. Does someone living in the United States on a temporary permit have responsibilities to the United States? If so, what are those responsibilities?
2. Some people immigrate to the United States solely for financial purposes. Like the author's sister, they have no interest in becoming an "American." At the same time, many U.S. corporations "emigrate" to countries with lower labor costs and less-stringent regulations. Are these two phenomena comparable? Why or why not?

QUESTIONS FOR CRITICAL THINKING AND DISCUSSION Both items can be used as prompts for group writing followed by classroom discussion.

Suggestions for Writing

1. In a 500-word essay, compare and contrast these two approaches to the college experience: (a) the student who explores the life of the campus, joins clubs, and takes widely varied electives; (b) the student who shows up for classes and leaves the campus immediately afterward.
2. In a 500- to 750-word essay, compare and contrast the following types of romantic relationships: intense and monogamous versus casual and "no strings attached."

SUGGESTIONS FOR WRITING Students responding to item 1 should be reminded to include a discussion of the rewards or effects of each type of experience. Those responding to item 2 should remember that this assignment involves both comparison and contrast.

Family Engineering

DAVID SEDARIS

David Sedaris is a humorist who, along with his sister Amy Sedaris, makes up a comedy team known as the Talent Family. David Sedaris's books include *Barrel Fever: Stories and Essays* (1994), *Holidays on Ice* (1997), *Naked* (1997), *Me Talk Pretty One Day* (2001), and *Dress Your Family in Corduroy and Denim* (2004).

In "Family Engineering," first published in the August 24–31, 1999, edition of *The New Yorker*, Sedaris pits his mysteriously serious father against the rest of his normal, fun-loving family.

1 My father always struck me as the sort of man who, under the right circumstances, might have invented the microwave oven or the transistor radio. You wouldn't seek him out for advice on a personal problem, but he'd be the first one you'd call when the dishwasher broke or someone flushed a hairpiece down your toilet. As children, we placed a great deal of faith in his ability, but learned to steer clear while he was working. The experience of watching was ruined, time and time again, by an interminable explanation of how things were put together. Faced with an exciting question, science tended to provide the dullest possible answer. Ions might charge

the air, but they fell flat when it came to charging the imagination—my imagination, anyway. To this day, I prefer to believe that inside every television there lives a community of versatile, thumb-size actors, trained to portray everything from a thoughtful newscaster to the wife of a millionaire stranded on a desert island. Fickle gnomes control the weather, and an air-conditioner is powered by a team of squirrels, their cheeks packed with ice cubes.

2 Once, while rifling through the toolshed, I came across a poster advertising an I.B.M. computer the size of a refrigerator. Sitting at the control board was my dad the engineer, years younger, examining a printout no larger than a grocery receipt. When I asked about it, he explained that he had worked with a team devising a memory chip capable of storing up to fifteen pages' worth of information. Out came the notepad and pencil, and I was trapped for hours as he answered every question except the one I had asked. "Were you allowed to wear makeup and run through a variety of different poses, or did they get the picture on the first take?"

3 To me, the greatest mystery of science continues to be that a man could father six children who shared absolutely none of his interests. We certainly expressed enthusiasm for our mother's hobbies, from smoking and napping to the writings of Sidney Sheldon.* (Ask my mother how the radio worked and her answer was simple: "Turn it on and pull out the goddam antenna.") I once visited my father's office, and walked away comforted to find that at least there he had a few people he could talk to. We'd gone, my sister Amy and I, to settle a bet. She thought that my father's secretary had a sharp, protruding chin and long blond hair, while I imagined that the woman might more closely resemble a tortoise—chinless, with a beaky nose and a loose, sagging neck. The correct answer was somewhere in between. I was right about the nose and the neck, but Amy won on the chin and the hair color. The bet had been the sole reason for our visit, and the resulting insufferable tour of Buildings A through D taught us never again to express an interest in our father's workplace.

4 My own scientific curiosity eventually blossomed, but I knew enough to keep my freakish experiments to myself. When my father discovered my colony of frozen slugs in the basement freezer, I chose not to explain my complex theories of suspended animation. Why was I filling the hamster's water bottle with vodka? "Oh, no reason." If my experiment failed, and the drunken hamster passed out, I'd just put her in the deep freeze, alongside the slugs. She'd rest on ice for a few months and, once thawed and fully revived, would remember nothing of her previous life as an alcoholic. I also took to repairing my own record-player, and was astonished by my ingenuity for up to ten minutes at a time—until the rubber band snapped, or the handful of change came unglued from the arm, and the damned thing broke all over again.

5 During the first week of September, it was my family's habit to rent a beach house on Ocean Isle, a thin strip of land off the coast of North Carolina. As youngsters, we participated in all the usual seaside activities—which were fun, until my father got involved and systematically chipped away at our pleasure. Miniature golf was ruined with a lengthy dissertation on impact, trajectory, and wind veloc-

---

***Sidney Sheldon (b. 1917):** a Hollywood producer, a director, and the author of popular novels such as *Rage of Angels.*

ity, and our sandcastles were critiqued with stifling lectures on the dynamics of the vaulted ceiling. We enjoyed swimming until the mystery of tides was explained in such a way that the ocean seemed nothing more than an enormous saltwater toilet, flushing itself on a sad and predictable basis.

6 By the time we reached our teens, we were exhausted. No longer interested in the water, we joined our mother on the beach blanket and dedicated ourselves to the higher art of tanning. Under her guidance, we learned which lotions to start off with, and what worked best for various weather conditions and times of day. She taught us that the combination of false confidence and Hawaiian Tropic could result in a painful and unsightly burn, certain to subtract valuable points when, on the final night of vacation, contestants gathered for the annual Miss Emollient Pageant. This was a contest judged by our mother, in which the holder of the darkest tan was awarded a crown, a sash, and a sceptre.

7 Technically, the prize could go to either a male or a female, but the sash read "Miss Emollient" because it was always assumed that my sister Gretchen would once again sweep the title. For her, tanning had moved from an intense hobby to something more closely resembling a psychological dysfunction. She was what we called a tanorexic: someone who simply could not get enough. Year after year, she arrived at the beach with a basecoat that the rest of us could only dream of achieving as our final product. With a mixture of awe and envy, we watched her broiling away on her aluminum blanket. The spaces between her toes were tanned, as were her palms, and even the backs of her ears. Her method involved baby oil and a series of poses that tended to draw crowds, the mothers shielding their children's eyes with sand-covered fingers.

8 It is difficult for me to sit still for more than twenty minutes at a stretch, so I used to interrupt my tanning sessions with walks to the pier. On one of those walks, I came across my father standing not far from a group of fishermen, who were untangling knots in a net the size of a circus tent. A lifetime of work beneath the coastal sun had left them with what my sisters and I referred to as the Samsonite Syndrome, meaning that their enviable color was negated by a hard, leathery texture reminiscent of the suitcase my mother stored all our baby pictures in. The men drank from quart bottles of Mountain Dew as they paused from their work to regard my father, who stood at the water's edge, staring at the shoreline with a stick in his hand.

9 I tried to creep by unnoticed, but he stopped me, claiming that I was just the fellow he'd been looking for. "Do you have any idea how many grains of sand there are in the world?" he asked. It was a question that had never occurred to me. Unlike guessing the number of pickled eggs in a jar, or the amount of human brains it might take to equal the weight of a portable television set, this equation was bound to involve the hateful word "googolplex," a term I'd heard him use once or twice before. It was an *idea* of a number and was, therefore, of no use whatsoever.

10 I'd heard once in school that if a single bird were to transport all the sand, grain by grain, from the Eastern Seaboard to the west coast of Africa, it would take . . . I didn't catch the number of years, preferring to concentrate on the single bird chosen to perform this thankless task. It hardly seemed fair, because, unlike a horse or a seeing-eye dog, the whole glory of being a bird is that nobody would ever put you to work. Birds search for grubs and build their nests, but their leisure time is theirs to spend as they see fit. I pictured this bird looking down from the branches

to say "You want me to do what?" before flying off, laughing at the foolish story he now had to tell his friends. How many grains of sand are there in the world? A lot. Case closed.

11 My father took his stick and began writing an equation in the sand. Like all the rest of them, this one was busy with "x"s and "y"s resting on top of one another on dash-shaped bunks. Letters were multiplied by symbols, crowded into parentheses, and set upon by dwarfish numbers drawn at odd angles. The equation grew from six to twelve feet long before assuming a second line, at which point the fishermen took an interest. I watched them turn from their net, and admired the way they could smoke entire cigarettes without ever taking them from their mouths—a skill my mother had mastered, and one that continues to elude me. It involves a symbiotic relationship with the wind: you have to know exactly how and when to turn your head in order to keep the smoke out of your eyes.

12 One of the men asked my father if he was a tax accountant, and he answered, "No, an engineer." These were poor men, who could no longer afford to live by the ocean, who had long ago sold their one-story homes for the valuable sand beneath them. Their houses had been torn down to make room for high-priced hotels and the A-frame cottages that now rented in season for a thousand dollars a week.

13 "Let me ask a little something," one of the men said, spitting his spent cigarette butt into the surf. "If I got paid twelve thousand dollars in 1962 for a half-acre beachfront lot, how much would that be worth per grain of sand by today's standard?"

14 "That, my friend, is a very interesting question," my father said.

15 He moved several yards down the beach and began a new equation, captivating his audience with a lengthy explanation of each new and complex symbol. "When you say 'pie,'" one man asked, "do you mean a real live pie, or one of those pie shapes they put on the news sometimes to show how much of your money goes to taxes?"

16 My father answered their questions in detail, and they listened intently—this group of men with nets, blowing their smoke into the wind. Stooped and toothless, they hung upon his every word while I stood in the lazy surf, thinking of the upcoming pageant and wondering if the light reflecting off the water might tan the underside of my nose and chin.

Vocabulary

The following terms are identified by paragraph number. Make sure that you understand each term's meaning in its context. If you're not sure that you understand a term, look it up in a college-level dictionary.

transistor (1)	suspended animation (4)	emollient (6)
interminable (1)	ingenuity (4)	sceptre (6)
fickle (1)	dissertation (5)	dysfunction (7)
gnomes (1)	trajectory (5)	reminiscent (8)
protruding (3)	dynamics (5)	symbiotic (11)
insufferable (3)	vaulted ceiling (5)	

Style and Strategy

1. What is the tone of this essay?
2. Provide a one-sentence description of the father, then a one-sentence description of the rest of the family.
3. What is the confusion over the word *pie* near the end of this essay?
4. How does the inclusion of the scene with the fishermen watching the father write in the sand add to the reader's sense of the father's value?
5. Does the author, after comparing the way his father is to the way the rest of the family is, come to an evaluative conclusion? In other words, does the author "choose" one side over the other? Explain your answer.
6. List at least five specific contrasts that Sedaris draws between his father and the rest of the family.
7. Does Sedaris tend more toward the point-by-point or the subject-by-subject approach?
8. Besides comparison/contrast, what other rhetorical strategies do you find here?

STYLE AND STRATEGY
1. Most students recognize the humorous, sometimes cutting tone. Yet behind it, Sedaris's love for his father is evident.
2. Responses will vary. The question is intended to emphasize the obvious contrast.
3. The speaker's father is referring to the mathematical concept "pi."
4. This is an interesting man who expresses his passion for knowledge and discovery in a way that is contagious to *some*. Note that the interest shown by these serious, hard-working men reflects the father's serious and hard-working nature as well.
5. No definitive answer is expected. The question encourages careful textual analysis.

6. Paragraphs 1, 5, and 9 are good places to start the discussion. However, it is also important to note that it is only his family that is not fascinated with the father. Others, as seen in paragraphs 11–16, are.
7. There is more of the point-by-point method here.
8. Narration, description, process analysis, and illustration appear here as well.

Questions for Critical Thinking and Discussion

1. It is said that opposites attract. In your opinion, is this a good way to look for a life companion, or is it a recipe for trouble?
2. What are the implications that this essay raises for the future of the family's children? There are specific issues here (smoking, excessive exposure to the sun) as well as more general issues (frivolity versus seriousness, fun versus industry). What might you predict about the future of the Sedaris children?

QUESTIONS FOR CRITICAL THINKING AND DISCUSSION You might begin the discussion of item 1 with what we are told about Sedaris's family. Item 2 encourages students to analyze and then to speculate on the results of that analysis.

Suggestions for Writing

1. Do you know a couple in a long-term relationship who seem to be "opposites"? Write a 500-word essay contrasting these people and trying to explain why their relationship endures.
2. Which is better, living for the present or building for the future? Write a 500- to 750-word essay contrasting these two approaches to life.
3. Write a 500- to 750-word essay in which you explain how different you are from someone else in your family. Try to focus on a specific area of difference, such as your goals and aspirations or your tastes in music, food, clothing, or movies. Note that your essay should make a point, not just show areas of difference.

SUGGESTIONS FOR WRITING Students attempting item 2 should focus on two people or types of people to generate convincing illustrations of each philosophy.

From Outside, In

BARBARA MELLIX

In "From Outside, In," Barbara Mellix, a college instructor, writes about the gulf that separates her "at-home" language from the language she was and is expected to use in the outside world. The following is excerpted from Mellix's original essay, which first appeared in the *Georgia Review* in 1987.

Two years ago, when I started writing this paper, trying to bring order out of chaos, my ten-year-old daughter was suffering from an acute attack of boredom. She drifted in and out of the room complaining that she had nothing to do, no one to "be with" because none of her friends were at home. Patiently I explained that I was working on something special and needed peace and quiet, and I suggested that she paint, read, or work with her computer. None of these interested her. Finally, she pulled up a chair to my desk and watched me, now and then heaving long, loud sighs. After two or three minutes (nine or ten sighs), I lost my patience. "Looka here, Allie," I said, "you too old for this kinda carryin' on. I done told you this is important. You wronger than dirt to be in here haggin' me like this and you know it. Now git on outta here and leave me off before I put my foot all the way down." 1

I was at home, alone with my family, and my daughter understood that this way of speaking was appropriate in that context. She knew, as a matter of fact, that it was almost inevitable; when I get angry at home, I speak some of my finest, most cherished black English. Had I been speaking to my daughter in this manner in certain other environments, she would have been shocked and probably worried that I had taken leave of my sense of propriety. 2

Like my children, I grew up speaking what I considered two distinctly different languages—black English and standard English (or as I thought of them then, the ordinary everyday speech of "country" coloreds and "proper" English)—and in the process of acquiring these languages, I developed an understanding of when, where, and how to use them. But unlike my children, I grew up in a world that was primarily black. My friends, neighbors, minister, teachers—almost everybody I associated with every day—were black. And we spoke to one another in our own special language: *That sho is a pretty dress you got on. If she don' soon leave me off I'm gon tell her head a mess. I was so mad I could'a pissed a blue nail. He all the time trying to low-rate somebody. Ain't that just about the nastiest thing you ever set ears on?* 3

Then there were the "others," the "proper" blacks, transplanted relatives and one-time friends who came home from the city for weddings, funerals, and vacations. And the whites. To these we spoke standard English. "Ain't?" my mother would yell at me when I used the term in the presence of "others." "You *know* better than that." And I would hang my head in shame and say the "proper" word. 4

I remember one summer sitting in my grandmother's house in Greeleyville, South Carolina, when it was full of the chatter of city relatives who were home on vacation. My parents sat quietly, only now and then volunteering a comment or answering a question. My mother's face took on a strained expression when she spoke. I could see that she was being careful to say just the right words in just the right way. Her voice sounded thick, muffled. And when she finished speaking, she would lapse into silence, her proper smile on her face. My father was more articulate, more aggressive. He spoke quickly, his words sharp and clear. But he held his proud head higher, a signal that he, too, was uncomfortable. My sisters and brothers and I stared at our aunts, uncles, and cousins, speaking only when prompted. Even then, we hesitated, formed our sentences in our minds, then spoke softly, shyly. 5

My parents looked small and anxious during those occasions, and I waited impatiently for our leave-taking when we would mock our relatives the moment we were out of their hearing. "Reeely," we would say to one another, flexing our wrists and rolling our eyes, "how dooo you stan' this heat? Chile, it just too hy*ooo*-mid for words." Our relatives had made us feel "country," and this was our way of 6 regaining pride in ourselves while getting a little revenge in the bargain. The words bubbled in our throats and rolled across our tongues, a balming.

7 As a child I felt this same doubleness in uptown Greeleyville where the whites lived. "Ain't that a pretty dress you're wearing!" Toby, the town policeman, said to me one day when I was fifteen. "Thank you very much," I replied, my voice barely audible in my own ears. The words felt wrong in my mouth, rigid, foreign. It was not that I had never spoken that phrase before—it was common in black English, too—but I was extremely conscious that this was an occasion for proper English. I had taken out my English and put it on as I did my church clothes, and I felt as if I were wearing my Sunday best in the middle of the week. It did not matter that Toby had not spoken grammatically correct English. He was white and could speak as he wished. I had something to prove. Toby did not.

8 Speaking standard English to whites was our way of demonstrating that we knew their language and could use it. Speaking it to standard-English-speaking blacks was our way of showing them that we, as well as they, could "put on airs." But when we spoke standard English, we acknowledged (to ourselves and to others—but primarily to ourselves) that our customary way of speaking was inferior. We felt foolish, embarrassed, somehow diminished because we were ashamed to be our real selves. We were reserved, shy in the presence of those who owned and/or spoke *the* language.

9 My parents never set aside time to drill us in standard English. Their forms of instruction were less formal. When my father was feeling particularly expansive, he would regale us with tales of his exploits in the outside world. In almost flawless English, complete with dialogue and flavored with gestures and embellishment, he told us about his attempt to get a haircut at a white barbershop; his refusal to acknowledge one of the town merchants until the man addressed him as "Mister"; the time he refused to step off the sidewalk uptown to let some whites pass; his airplane trip to New York City (to visit a sick relative) during which the stewardesses and porters—recognizing that he was a "gentleman"—addressed him as "Sir." I did not realize it then—nor, I think, did my father—that he was teaching us, among other things, standard English and the relationship between language and power.

10 My mother's approach was different. Often, when one of us said, "I'm gon wash off my feet," she would say, "And what will you walk on if you wash them off?" Everyone would laugh at the victim of my mother's "proper" mood. But it was different when one of us children was in a proper mood. "You think you are so superior," I said to my oldest sister one day when we were arguing and she was winning. "Superior!" my sister mocked. "You mean I'm acting 'biggidy'?" My sisters and brothers sniggered, then joined in teasing me. Finally, my mother said, "Leave your sister alone. There's nothing wrong with using proper English." There was a half-smile on her face. I had gotten "uppity," had "put on airs" for no good reason. I was at home, alone with the family, and I hadn't been prompted by one of my mother's proper moods. But there was also a proud light in my mother's eyes; her children were learning English very well.

11 Not until years later, as a college student, did I begin to understand our ambivalence toward English, our scorn of it, our need to master it, to own and be owned by it—an ambivalence that extended to the public-school classroom. In our school, where there were no whites, my teachers taught standard English but used black English to do it. When my grammar-school teachers wanted us to write, for

example, they usually said something like, "I want y'all to write five sentences that make a statement. Anybody git done before the rest can color." It was probably almost those exact words that led me to write these sentences in 1953 when I was in the second grade:

> The white clouds are pretty.
> There are only 15 people in our room.
> We will go to gym.
> We have a new poster.
> We may go out doors.

Second grade came after "Little First" and "Big First," so by then I knew the implied rules that accompanied all writing assignments. Writing was an occasion for proper English. I was not to write in the way we spoke to one another: The white clouds pretty; There ain't but 15 people in our room; We going to gym; We got a new poster; We can go out in the yard. Rather I was to use the language of "other": clouds *are,* there *are,* we *will,* we *have,* we *may.*

12 My sentences were short, rigid, perfunctory, like the letters my mother wrote to relatives:

> Dear Papa,
>
> How are you? How is Mattie? Fine I hope. We are fine. We will come to see you Sunday. Cousin Ned will give us a ride.
>
> Love,
> Daughter

The language was not ours. It was something from outside us, something we used for special occasions.

13 But my coloring on the other side of that second-grade paper is different. I drew three hearts and a sun. The sun has a smiling face that radiates and envelops everything it touches. And although the sun and its world are enclosed in a circle, the colors I used—red, blue, green, purple, orange, yellow, black—indicate that I was less restricted with drawing and coloring than I was with writing standard English. My valentines were not just red. My sun was not just a yellow ball in the sky.

14 By the time I reached the twelfth grade, speaking and writing standard English had taken on new importance. Each year, about half of the newly graduated seniors of our school moved to large cities—particularly in the North—to live with relatives and find work. Our English teacher constantly corrected our grammar: "Not 'ain't,' but 'isn't.'" We seldom wrote papers, and even those few were usually plot summaries of short stories. When our teacher returned the papers, she usually lectured on the importance of using standard English: "I *am;* you *are;* he, she or it *is,*" she would say, writing on the chalkboard as she spoke. "How you gon git a job talking about 'I is,' or 'I isn't' or 'I ain't'?"

15 In Pittsburgh, where I moved after graduation, I watched my aunt and uncle—who had always spoken standard English when in Greeleyville—switch from black English to standard English to a mixture of the two, according to where they were or who they were with. At home and with certain close relatives, friends, and neighbors, they spoke black English. With those less close, they spoke a mixture. In public and with strangers, they generally spoke standard English.

16 In time, I learned to speak standard English with ease and to switch smoothly from black to standard or a mixture, and back again. But no matter where I was, no matter what the situation or occasion, I continued to write as I had in school:

Dear Mommie,

How are you? How is everybody else? Fine I hope. I am fine. So are Aunt and Uncle. Tell everyone I said hello. I will write again soon.

Love,
Barbara

Vocabulary

The following terms are identified by paragraph number. Make sure that you understand each term's meaning in its context. If you're not sure that you understand a term, look it up in a college-level dictionary.

acute (1)	balming (6)	embellishment (9)
context (2)	reserved (8)	ambivalence (11)
cherished (2)	expansive (9)	implied (11)
propriety (2)	regale (9)	perfunctory (12)
articulate (5)	exploits (9)	envelops (13)

Style and Strategy

1. Mellix's thesis does not appear until paragraph 9. What is it?
2. Mellix uses a wealth of examples to develop her essay. In your opinion, what similarities and differences do these examples help develop?
3. Comment on Mellix's introduction. Why does it work so well, and what does it help her accomplish so early in the essay?
4. Besides comparison/contrast, what rhetorical options does Mellix use to develop her essay?

STYLE AND STRATEGY
1. The thesis appears at the end of this paragraph.
2. These examples point out differences in language, but they also point out similarities and differences in the people the author mentions. Moreover, they help the reader see the author's "ambivalence toward English." In this connection, discuss the example involving the white policeman, Toby.
3. The anecdote in the introduction illustrates a phenomenon explained in the rest of the essay—that we need to be linguistically versatile to address various audiences and purposes.
4. Narration is present throughout. Analogy appears in paragraphs 7 and 19. Note also the use of dialogue.

Questions for Critical Thinking and Discussion

1. On one level, Mellix is contrasting black English and standard English. What else is she contrasting?
2. Mellix is writing about "the relationship between language and power" in the context of members of a minority group struggling for success in a society where the majority group makes the rules. In your experience, in what other contexts does the relationship between language and power become evident? For example, how might the relationship come into play in areas like school, the legal system, popular entertainment, and computer and other technology?
3. Consider this statement: "Fifty years from now, all this talk about a white establishment and 'official English' will be a historical artifact. America is becoming a nation of color, not just one dominant color." If this statement is true, what are some of its implications?

QUESTIONS FOR CRITICAL THINKING AND DISCUSSION All three items require students to make reference to the text as a jumping-off point for discussion.

SUGGESTIONS FOR WRITING Both prompts encourage interesting writing, but students should be reminded to use concrete illustrations similar to those in Mellix's essay.

MORE OPTIONS ONLINE
If you would like to read additional comparison/contrast essays, go to **www.mhhe.com/writingtoday**.

Suggestions for Writing

1. Are there any advantages to having a "private self" that is very different from the "public self"? Write a 500- to 750-word essay contrasting the private you and the public you.
2. Write a 500- to 750-word essay that recounts a situation in which your cultural upbringing left you uncertain of how to handle the demands of a different culture or context. Possible areas include city versus country, native country versus foreign country, pool hall versus country club.

WRITING THE COMPARISON/CONTRAST ESSAY WITH A READER'S EYE

Students sometimes approach the comparison/contrast assignment as if it were merely an exercise instead of a great opportunity to communicate. All too often, this approach yields mechanical, boring essays that fulfill the assignment's requirements but do little else. Some of these essays seem to have been generated by an artificial intelligence program, not by a real, live human being with a history, with interests, and with ambitions. Your reader deserves more.

Issues to Keep in Mind

As you work on your comparison/contrast essay, keep the following two issues in mind:

1. The need for balance between subjects in a comparison/contrast essay
2. The use of transitions to guide the reader through a comparison/contrast essay

Balanced Subjects

Students sometimes write comparison/contrast essays that technically fulfill the requirements of this rather demanding option, but the essays are weak and ineffective because the two entities that they are contrasting are not "balanced"—in other words, not really suitable for comparison. Contrasting a cockroach with an elephant will almost certainly produce a pointless essay. Contrasting a roadside stand that sells carry-out smoked mullet with a gourmet restaurant is similarly pointless. However, contrasting an African elephant with an Indian elephant has promise, as does contrasting a gourmet French restaurant with a gourmet Chinese restaurant. Be aware of this need for balance; your reader is certainly aware of it.

Using Transitions

Transitions provide the **coherence** that your reader needs to follow your comparisons and contrasts of the subjects. Very often, the difference between a weak essay and a strong one is the absence of transitions in the former case and their skillful use in the latter. Relevant transitions include the following (see also Chapter 3, page 71, for a chart that lists various transitions):

CONTRAST **but, yet, however, on the other hand, nevertheless, nonetheless, conversely, in contrast, still, at the same time, whereas**

COMPARISON **similarly, likewise, in the same way**

CLASSROOM HINT Consider discussing transitions in class especially in connection with the two organizational patterns associated with comparison/contrast.

In the subject-by-subject approach to comparison/contrast, one subject is discussed, then the next subject. Writers using this approach tend to use transitions during the discussion of the second subject in order to establish connections to the first subject. For example, in the following passage the writer discusses one subject and then the other—the viewer's experience when watching a made-for-television movie and when watching a theatrical production—in order to show differences. Notice that although the writer looks at each subject separately, he does not analyze the subjects as if they were completely separate. Instead, as shown by the highlighted words, while discussing the second subject he reminds the reader of the first subject. The writer connects the two pictures he paints.

Made-for-TV movies have a secret attribute that becomes painfully obvious the more you watch them: they are slaves to time. The commercial breaks will arrive at severely structured intervals, and the drama or comedy that you are watching will disappear, replaced by whatever shilling needs to be done. The movie will be structured to accommodate those necessary interruptions. Transitions, moments of high drama, and cliff-hanging scenes are natural places to suspend narrative, so the entire production is designed around the commercial breaks, with logical stopping points built into the story. The effect is of paint-by-numbers drama—the movie has been packaged and trimmed to fit the needs of commercial television.

An entirely different experience awaits the theater-goer. Plays are live, representing an element of risk, and the audience is well aware of this possibility. However, if an actor makes a mistake, there's no going back. Literally, the show must go on. And **unlike dramatic productions made for TV,** plays are characterized by a certain natural, wonderful lack of balance. The play's acts won't be exactly the same length; the show won't start at the precise moment it was scheduled to. Even the audience can be a factor. I once attended a musical put on by a national touring company. The second act, after the intermission, begins with the main character's monologue. He was standing on stage about to speak when the exit door to his right opened and two society types rushed in front of him, oblivious to the fact that they were interrupting the performance. The performer was gracious

> yet funny: "Come on, ladies, take your drinks and have a seat." Then he continued. And, although the perpetrators of this type of "interaction" should be escorted to the back row of the balcony, it represents some of the theater's charm. **In contrast,** in a made-for-TV film, a mass murder/suicide could be in progress, and the idiot box would still break in to push products in the midst of the anguish and suspense.

In the point-by-point approach to organizing comparison/contrast, the two subjects are contrasted in terms of a particular quality or idea. Thus, the essay's body paragraphs must move from one subject to the next, back again, and so on. Appropriate transitions are essential here. The paragraph below is an excerpt from a comparison/contrast of library sources and Internet sources. The other paragraphs of this essay similarly develop other points. Notice the use of appropriate transitions, which are highlighted.

> The main issue that distinguishes library research from online research is trust. Scholarly journals found in a university library tend to be produced in much the same way: Academics submit papers, and the journal's editors send these manuscripts to a panel of experts, who then determine whether they should be published. Much of the scholarship online is similarly "vetted" by experts. **However,** a great many Internet postings are the electronic equivalent of vanity publishing. **In contrast to the process that occurs with traditional print publications,** an online "scholarly journal" could be assembled and posted by a crackpot. This seemingly authentic scholarly journal in fact represents no more authority than what is in the brain of said crackpot and perhaps the brains of his loony friends. **As opposed to the controls in the world of traditional publishing,** the world of the Internet has no mechanism to stop him or her. The unsuspecting researcher, then, may be accessing garbage and not realize it.

MORE OPTIONS ONLINE
For more help with issues in writing the comparison/contrast essay, go to **www.mhhe.com/writingtoday**.

If you reread this paragraph without the boldfaced sections, you will see how much is lost.

Choosing a Topic

What kinds of topics should you consider? If your topics aren't already chosen for you, as in the vignette that opens this chapter, the list of possible topics for a comparison/contrast essay is virtually endless because there are so many different types of subjects to compare and contrast: individual people, groups of people, animals, college courses, and narrative experiences, to name only a few. When choosing a topic, then, your main concern won't be coming up with possibilities but with making sure that the possibilities you uncover are appropriate. The two most important considerations are the size of the topic and the likelihood that it will interest your readers:

1. Limit the size of your topic. For example, "Democrats and Republicans" is much too broad a topic for an essay; it's the subject for a very large book, especially if it includes the historical dimension. What about "neoconservatives versus establishment Republicans"? This is perhaps still a bit broad. But consider a more directed topic involving two politicians: Eileen X, who is a neoconservative, and Thomas Y, an establishment Republican. This topic should allow you to write a manageable analysis, one in which you will have a valuable opportunity to introduce definitions of "neoconservative" and "establishment Republican." The key is to avoid too large a topic, one that requires a very long essay or forces you to write only in generalities.

   At the other end of the spectrum you'll find and need to avoid the severely limited, often strictly personal topic that (a) lacks broader implications and (b) tends to produce a mechanical, by-the-numbers essay. For example, a writer who contrasts a new skateboard with his or her previous one will almost certainly run this risk.

2. Consider your audience. When choosing a topic, always stop and think about your readers: Will your topic interest your audience? One important fact to keep in mind as you think about your audience is that readers love to be surprised, to have their expectations countered by a new idea. With a comparison/contrast essay, there are two very general types of topics that can enable you to surprise your readers.

   The first type of topic is an exploration of differences between two subjects that the reader might expect to be similar. Consider this situation: two companies are leaders in the same industry, constantly battling each other for market share. One company is the type of place that most employees dream of, with flexible schedules, on-site day care, and a history of not laying people off to solve short-term corporate financial worries—in other words, a company run by people who have some sense of the needs of their employees. In contrast, the other company is a hellhole, where maniacal, profit-driven supervisors treat employees like slaves. Flexible schedules are nonexistent. Employees are expected to show up early and leave late. There are no child-care services; children are viewed as a "personal matter" and a "distraction." Management compensates for its blunders by periodically laying off huge numbers of workers and then driving the remaining few into the ground. In short, these equally successful companies have management philosophies that are radically different. Is there a good topic for a comparison/contrast essay here? We think so.

   Or consider topics closer to home. In the introductory pages of this chapter, we discussed the case of the twin uncles who were quite dissimilar. Other topics of this type work equally well:

- Two of your siblings—one must have come home from the hospital in the wrong car
- Two of your best friends, possibly reflecting the fact that our friends meet different needs or correspond to different sides of our personality
- Two college courses that might seem to be "parallel," or at least related, but have furnished you with two very different experiences

With this type of topic, however, make sure that you have your reader in mind as you develop your essay in order to avoid the mechanical, "private" essay discussed above.

The second type of topic is an exploration of similarities between two subjects normally thought to be different. As mentioned in the introduction, focusing on similarities is the less common approach, largely because similarities tend sometimes to be less interesting. But interest isn't likely to be a problem if you're talking about similarities between subjects usually thought to be different. Consider, for example, these potential topics:

- American "southern food" can be found all over the country, whereas Cuban food is much more geographically limited; and, in general, most people don't think of these two cuisines as being very similar. But they are—amazingly so.
- The last fifteen years have seen a growing interest in spiritualism—the so-called New Age movement. Whatever the name may imply and whatever people may think of this movement, a very similar phenomenon occurred at the end of the nineteenth century. Similarities between these two movements are well worth exploring.

Prewriting

Comparison and contrast is a difficult rhetorical option. With that fact in mind, use several prewriting techniques to generate lots of ideas about your subjects. (For more on prewriting strategies, see Chapter 2.)

Freewriting may be the best method for you to choose when developing ideas for your comparison/contrast essay. If you are planning to use the subject-by-subject approach, freewrite on the first subject, then the second; this way, you will be able to review your response to the two subjects and see the points of comparison and/or contrast that link them.

If you are planning to use the point-by-point approach, you could start with an obvious area of comparison and then list or freewrite how each entity relates to that area. If, for example, you are contrasting two people, an obvious area of comparison is personality. You could freewrite on the personality of the first person, then the second. Reviewing your output would show you the major similarities or differences between the personalities of the two people.

If you're not yet sure whether to use a subject-by-subject or point-by-point organization, your prewriting can help you decide. If the results of your prewriting fall easily into categories of differences/similarities, then you should usually use point-by-point. If these areas or categories are not as obvious, use subject-by-subject.

Choosing the wrong strategy can be a dead end. Normally, when students make an inappropriate choice, they have elected the subject-by-subject method when point-by-point development would have worked better. Some writers perceive subject-by-subject to be "easier"—they think it's simpler to cover one subject at a time. In actuality, choosing an inappropriate method will lead to a first draft that is clearly unsuitable and thus to either a painful revision or an entirely new start. *Use the method that is best suited to your topic and the results of your prewriting.*

After you have generated ideas about your subjects, ask yourself these two questions:

1. **Do I have enough material to support my topic?** If not, consider going to the library or on the Internet to look for additional support. (If you plan to research your topic, however, check with your instructor first.)
2. **Can I generate a preliminary or working thesis from my material?** If not, think about your topic some more, and then try prewriting again. You need a working thesis before you begin organizing.

Organizing

Once you have generated a sufficient number of points of comparison and contrast and developed your working thesis, the best way for you to organize this raw material is to arrange it into an outline. (Chapter 2 covers informal, sentence, and formal outline structures.) Sentence outlines work very well for developing the comparison/contrast essay; they establish sufficient structure but can be done quickly.

Whether you employ the point-by-point method or the subject-by-subject method, you should try to use an **emphatic** organization. To illustrate, in the point-by-point method, if you are comparing your two subjects in terms of three areas, your strongest area—the most significant (or startling) comparison or contrast—should be the third one in the body of your essay. In other words, build up to your most important point. If the three areas seem to be of equal importance, use the most logical order when organizing the body paragraphs of your essay. The writer of "Neighborhoods and Memories" (see pages 411–414 in the Drafting section) uses the logic of a **causal chain**, where one event causes another and that event causes a third, and so on (see also Chapter 10) to organize her essay: the friendly atmosphere of the neighborhood had changed, so people felt more distrustful and isolated, and, not surprisingly, property values declined.

If you are using the subject-by-subject method, consider which order of the two subjects will produce the stronger effect on your reader. A typical approach is to write about the more familiar subject first, then show how the second subject is surprisingly different. For example, the essay "Let the Unimportant Things Change" (see pages 410–413 in the Drafting section) explores two visits to a restaurant. The first visit took place when the writer proposed to his future wife, during a very nice evening. Six years later, the couple went back to the restaurant and found that everything about it had changed for the worse. The writer's purpose is to show that love and relationship stability are more important to him than the fate of someone else's restaurant.

Writers using the subject-by-subject method sometimes take the reverse approach. For example, a journalist might explore a degraded, polluted place, describing what a foul setting it has become. Then the writer will contrast this picture to the "old days," drawing upon the memories of current or former residents to develop a picture of a much more desirable past.

When deciding how to order a subject-by-subject essay, consider your purpose: What are you trying to accomplish? Answering this question will help you decide which order to follow.

Drafting

In this section, we present two essays, both dealing with change. "Let the Unimportant Things Change" uses the subject-by-subject method to contrast two experiences and draw a full picture of how change has affected one element of the writer's world. "Neighborhoods and Memories" uses the point-by-point method to look at a before-and-after situation in terms of a set of issues and ultimately to evaluate the changes.

The Introduction

The introductory paragraph or paragraphs of a comparison/contrast essay must establish sufficient context for your audience to appreciate what follows. All too often, students produce very brief introductions when writing this type of essay—sometimes only a pair of sentences. These students are putting all their efforts into the body of their essay and ignoring the importance of the background material that the reader needs. If it helps you, write your introduction after you have drafted the body of your essay.

Notice that the introductions to both of the following essays (1) give readers the necessary context for the essay and (2) state the thesis. In the case of the subject-by-subject essay, the thesis is general, pointing out that the essay will explore change—and the effects of change. In the case of the point-by-point essay, the thesis includes the three areas that will be covered (ambiance, security, and property values) and the nature of the evaluation (the changes are negative).

Consider Your Options

Consider beginning a contrast essay by pointing out how similar your subjects appear on the surface. Consider beginning a comparison essay by pointing out how dissimilar your subjects appear on the surface.

Essay A: Subject-by-Subject Approach

Let the Unimportant Things Change

My wife and I have been married for more than five years now. I proposed to her almost six years ago. At that point I was just out of the Air Force, and Lois was a year past high school. I proposed to her at a suburban family restaurant, and recently, for fun, we went back to have dinner there. **Our experience showed us that time can be counted on to change almost everything.**

ESSAY B: Point-by-Point Approach

Neighborhoods and Memories

I grew up in the Bristol Park neighborhood, near the old armory. My childhood is still the source of some of my happiest memories, and Bristol Park's environment played a large role in creating these happy memories. However, I've been gone for ten years, and my picture of the old neighborhood has been based mainly on memories. Last summer I went back. My aunt Rita was undergoing cancer treatment, and I took care of her during the worst of it. While I cared for her, I got to experience Bristol Park again, and I found that its "quality of life" had changed dramatically. **To be specific, Bristol Park had undergone major, negative changes in three areas: ambiance, security, and property values.**

The Body

The body paragraphs of the two essays offer fairly representative examples of the different kinds of development required by the subject-by-subject and point-by-point approaches. In Essay A, the first two paragraphs describe the experience that the writer and Lois had the evening he proposed, and then the following two paragraphs describe the "parallel" experience they had almost six years later. In Essay B, the writer analyzes her old neighborhood as it is now and as it once was, but this comparison/contrast is controlled by evaluative categories: ambiance, security, and property values. As you read each passage, note how the writer uses transitions to develop and link key ideas. Too often, students writing comparison/contrast essays—especially when using the subject-by-subject method—seem to be working in a vacuum: they are comparing two subjects, but *implicitly,* forcing the reader to make the connections that the writer should have provided. The writers of the two model essays establish these connections skillfully.

The comparison and contrast option allows for a wide range of internal strategies. In the two passages that follow, the writers use narration, description, exemplification, causal analysis, and process analysis to develop their respective thesis statements.

ESSAY A: Subject-by-Subject Approach

Michael's Restaurant was—and is—located in a strip near the Railroad Mall. Six years ago, the strip had just been built, and Michael's was in its heyday. Our fateful night was a Thursday, normally a slow time for restaurants, but Michael's was hopping that night, an attractive, well-decorated place packed with couples and families.

Our server was attentive. I had filled her in on my nefarious plot—to propose to Lois after our dessert order—and the server was doing her part to make our night special. Lois must have wondered why we were treated like royalty, and perhaps she figured everything out after the server left with our dessert order and I produced a ring. I had a little money in those days, and the ring was impressive, if I do say so myself. When Lois gasped her acceptance, our server and her manager came over to congratulate us, and then led the room in applause. It was a perfect night.

What changes six years can bring. The Railroad Mall is now on the verge of being closed, and the surrounding area reflects decay, not hope. The strip where Michael's is located is mostly empty, and, at least on the night we returned, the parking lot was filled with trash.

SUGGESTED ACTIVITY
Consider asking students to outline these two essays in class—see the exercise on p. 414.

When Lois and I visited recently, I noticed that the interior of the restaurant had not been redecorated in the years since our magic evening. The walls needed paint and the carpet was worn in spots. There weren't many people there, a stark contrast to the packed house of six years ago, and most of them were in the bar shouting at a football game. The server was from the group one sees so frequently these days: servers who have apparently never eaten in a restaurant and don't know that glasses need to be refilled and that all elements of a meal shouldn't be served at the same time. The food was mediocre: dry meat and microwaved vegetables. I would have complained to the manager had there been one around.

Essay B: Point-by-Point Approach

The neighborhood I remember was characterized by its friendly atmosphere. Neighbors sat on each other's porches, exchanged recipes, borrowed a cup of flour, ended the day with a martini. We children played in the yards, in the empty fields behind the houses, up and down the sidewalk. The ambiance was friendly and communal. However, the Bristol Park of today is a neighborhood of closed doors and warning signs. My aunt says that she doesn't know most of her neighbors, only third-hand bits of information and rumors about who so-and-so is and what he or she does. Children don't seem to live outdoors the way they used to, either. There are fewer children around, and they must spend their free time in front of a computer or the tube.

A related issue is security. When I was young, people didn't leave their doors unlocked or their car keys in the ignition (I'm not *that* old). However, crime perpetrated by people from outside the neighborhood was rare; we felt safe, and to a large degree we *were* safe. Today, on the other hand, Bristol Park suffers from burglaries and, scariest of all, home invasions. Nonresident cars cruise the streets, and I have to believe that at least some of the drivers are looking for an easy chance. Most of the houses feature burglar bars or yard dogs, in what is clearly becoming a war zone.

Not surprisingly, property values have declined. During the time my parents lived in Bristol Park, their house doubled in assessed value. Today, my old stomping ground is available for about 60 percent of that high-water mark. A similar trajectory is evident all over the neighborhood. This is an area going down, not up, and anyone with money is going to look for something a bit more appealing.

The Conclusion

In the comparison/contrast option, summary is usually a weak way to end an essay. Instead, use the conclusion as an opportunity to draw your analysis together, to comment on the significance of what you have written. Note how the two writers of our example essays have taken advantage of this opportunity.

Consider Your Options

When writing a conclusion for a comparison/contrast essay, consider explaining how the reader might use the similarities or differences you have discussed. Another way to conclude—but *only* in a longer essay—is to summarize your main points, then rephrase your thesis for clarity and emphasis.

Essay A: Subject-by-Subject Approach

I'm glad that Lois and I went back to Michael's on a whim, and not to "relive" our experience, for we would have been sorely disappointed by a trip into a rosy memory. Lois and I haven't changed very much. Our marriage is solid, and we are very much in love. Michael's, however, is a different story. But if one or the other needed to fail, I am glad it was Michael's. There will be other restaurants.

MORE OPTIONS ONLINE
For more help with the step-by-step development of the comparison/contrast essay, go to **www.mhhe.com/writingtoday**.

Essay B: Point-by-Point Approach

It's obviously true that you can't go home again, and I'm glad I spent another summer in Bristol Park to confirm this idea. At least now I won't be tempted to go back and buy my parents' old house in this now unfriendly, dangerous, and declining neighborhood.

EXERCISE 13.1

Write an outline of either "Let the Unimportant Things Change" or "Neighborhoods and Memories." (For help with outlines, see Chapter 2, pages 41–42.) How effective is the approach the writer has chosen (subject-by-subject or point-by-point)? Would the other approach have been a better choice? If so, why?

Revising Your Draft

After you have completed a draft of your comparison/contrast essay, your next step is to revise it, using your own analysis and comments from classmates and friends. Use the peer review stage to make sure that your essay's structure and

Questions for Reviewing a Comparison/Contrast Essay

1. Does the introduction give the reader enough context? Does it capture the reader's interest? How could the introduction be strengthened?
2. What is the thesis statement? Has the writer placed it in the best position within the essay? How could it be improved?
3. Does the essay have a clear and interesting general point? Is the writer doing more than mechanically comparing and contrasting two subjects?
4. Is the approach that the writer chose—point-by-point or subject-by-subject—appropriate for the topic and for the intended purpose?
5. If the essay uses the point-by-point approach, has the writer established coherence by using the appropriate transitions? Where are transitions needed?
6. If the essay uses the subject-by-subject approach, has the writer referred the reader to the contrasts and/or similarities between the two subjects? In other words, has the writer connected the second subject to the first, or do the two subjects seem separate and unrelated?
7. Regardless of the method used, is the analysis thorough and complete? Has the writer left out any obvious points or areas of discussion? If the essay is intended to paint two pictures, are the pictures vivid? If the essay has an evaluative purpose, is the coverage of the two subjects balanced?
8. Does the essay have an effective conclusion? How could it be improved?

content are sound. During peer review, answer the questions on page 414 about the draft you are reviewing, whether it is yours or another student's.

After reviewing for content, you need to go over your peer reviewers' responses to your essay and then revise for unity, coherence, language level, and tone (see Chapter 4). When you have revised your draft and are basically satisfied with it, read your draft for mechanical and grammatical errors. Concentrate on finding and correcting major sentence errors (fragments, comma splices, fused sentences), errors in pronoun agreement and subject-verb agreement, and spelling mistakes.

Now that you have made your corrections, *read your essay one more time* to catch any errors made during revision and find errors missed during your earlier reviews.

MORE OPTIONS ONLINE
For more help with revision, go to **www.mhhe.com/writingtoday**.

Student Essay

The following essay is Sam Leininger's response to a comparison/contrast assignment. The final draft is presented first. Then Sam's first draft is presented, with his comments about this draft and what he needed to do in the revision stage.

In this essay, Sam uses the point-by-point approach to contrast two very distinct kinds of moviegoers.

Sam's Final Draft

The Two Sides of the Aisle

Movie studios are concerned with target markets and audiences: they tailor certain movies for certain types of people. The advertising for the latest Vin Diesel adventure will appeal to different folks than the advertising for the new John Sayles drama. This process works well. When I go to the movies, I get myself ready in different ways, depending on the type of movie I am going to see. Most towns have an art-house theater that plays the independent and foreign releases and a few dozen multiplex theaters (often in malls) that play the big blockbusters, but with independent films gaining a margin of profitability, some of them are leaking on to one of the 37 screens at the local monsterplex. The local cinemas are becoming slightly homogenized, but the audiences are less so: The movie itself defines the crowd it draws. Crowds attending independent films have a few distinct characteristics that separate them from the average viewers of blockbusters.

Independent filmgoers tend to arrive early. The movie is more important to them, whereas it doesn't really matter if a viewer misses the first five

EXERCISE 13.1
(page 414)
Answers will vary. The following sentence outlines are suggested.
Essay A
I. Background: The writer proposed to his wife six years ago at a family restaurant; recently they returned to the restaurant. Thesis: Our experience showed us that time can be counted on to change almost everything.
II. Six years ago, Michael's restaurant was fairly new and in its heyday.
   A. Michael's was an attractive, well-decorated place packed with couples and families.
   B. The server was attentive and came over to congratulate the couple.
III. Michael's Restaurant has gone downhill along with the strip mall where it is located.
   A. The interior has not been redecorated in six years and is looking shabby.
   B. Hardly any customers were there.
   C. The service and the food were bad.
IV. The husband and wife haven't changed much, even though the restaurant has, and that's the important thing.
Essay B
I. Background: I recently returned to Bristol Park, the neighborhood I grew up in. Thesis: Bristol Park had undergone major, negative changes in three areas: ambiance, security, and property values.

II. The atmosphere of the neighborhood has changed.
   A. The neighborhood used to be friendly, with neighborly visits and children playing.
   B. Now neighbors don't know each other and children no longer play outside.
IV. A related issue is security.
   A. When I was young, crime was rare.
   B. Now the neighborhood suffers from burglaries and home invasions, and most of the houses feature burglar bars or guard dogs.
V. Property values have changed.
   A. My parent's house doubled in value during the time they lived there.
   B. Today the house would command 60 percent of the value it once had.
VI. It's obviously true that you can't go home again, and I won't be buying my parent's old house in this now unfriendly, dangerous, and declining neighborhood.

minutes of a natural disaster movie—he or she can still identify the protagonist (that's the good guy, the one with the ruggedly handsome good looks and flimsy backstory) and the antagonist (the latest special effects creation that, although a natural phenomenon like lava or a tornado, somehow manages to chase the hero).

The trip to the concession stand is also a giveaway. The blockbuster crowd loads up on hot dogs, nachos, Twizzlers, and anything else they can carry, drag, or stuff in their or their girlfriends' purses (and, of course, I know men are stuffing things into their girlfriends' purses because the lone moviegoer doesn't happen at blockbusters: just as the movie is an event and not a piece of art, so is the experience an event and not a celebration of art). The independent film fan, however, is rarely there to eat.

Once in the theater, the two audiences have an equal propensity to be rude. The talking is directed differently, though. The independent audience members talk to each other, but loudly enough so that surrounding members can hear; the blockbuster audience tends to talk to the screen. Independent filmgoers are smart enough to realize that these fictional characters cannot hear them.

The major difference during the movie is in the laughter. The blockbuster audience tends to laugh as a single entity, and at obvious moments in the movie there are cues that let them know when to laugh. Independent films are a little more subtle, and not everyone understands the humor. To make up for their insecurities, audience members will sometimes laugh for no reason, at completely inappropriate times, to let others know that they are hip and get all the jokes.

As the movie ends, the differences between the audiences are similar to those at its beginning. The blockbuster crowd races out to the parking lot as quickly as possible. In contrast, the independent moviegoer will often sit courteously through the credits and leave at a leisurely pace, talking with other moviegoers about the film.

Lately, moviegoers have been treated to an increasing number of cross-pollinations: some of the blockbuster crowd are taking a chance on the independent film that makes it to the Gigaplex 9000, and some independent fans are frequenting the latest Hollywood release during the slow time of the year. With any luck, this crossover will be a positive movement: the blockbuster audience may learn to respond to a film in more nuanced ways, and a few of them will even be exposed to higher-quality films. But, more likely, the independent fans may just give in to the ruder ways of the typical moviegoer, and the only place to watch any type of movie in relative peace will be at home—now if I could just get that big screen and film projector installed in the living room.

Sam's First Draft

The Two Sides of the Aisle

Movie studios are concerned with target markets and audiences: they tailer certain movies for certain types of people. The advertising for the latest adventure flick will appeal to different folks than the advertising for the new British art film. And it works. When I go to the movies, I get myself ready in different ways. Most towns have an art-house theater and a few dozen multi-plex theaters that play the big blockbusters, but with independant films gaining a margin of profitability, some of them are showing up at the local multi-plex. Crowds attending independent films have a few distinct characteristics that separate them from the average viewer.

This essay needed more detail—more of a sense of "reality" instead of just commentary.

Independant filmgoers tend to arrive early. The movie is more important to them, whereas it doesn't really matter if you miss the first five minutes of a natural disaster movie. The trip to the concession stand is also a giveaway. The blockbuster crowd loads up on anything they can carry, drag, or stuff in their or their girlfriends' purses. The independant film fan realizes that the concession money supports the movie theater and, not wanting to encourage them, will pass the counter frequently.

I worked on the second and third paragraphs of the rough draft, turning them into three paragraphs.

Once in the theater, audiences are relatively similar—both have the propensity to be just as rude. The talking is directed differently in the two

When I reread the second time, I focused on sentences, many of which were unclear and/or somewhat rough.

theaters, though. The independant audience members must talk to each other, but loud enough so that surrounding members can hear; in the blockbuster theater, they tend to talk to the screen. The major difference, though, is laughter. The blockbuster audience tends to laugh as a single entity, and is given obvious moments in the movie that let them know when to laugh. Independant films are a little more subtle, and not everyone understands the humor. To make up for their insecurities, audience members will often laugh for no reason, at completely inappropriate times, to let others know that they are hip and get all the jokes. As the movie ends, the blockbuster crowd races out to the parking lot as quick as possible, while the independant moviegoer will often sit courteously through the credits and then talk with other moviegoers about the film.

Here is where I broke up the long third paragraph. I also added transitions and a bit more detail.

Lately, some of the blockbuster crowd have been taking a chance on the independant film that makes it to the giga-plex 9000, and independant fans are frequenting the latest Hollywood output. Hopefully, this will be a positive movement; the blockbuster crowds will be given an example of how to watch a film, and a few of them will even be exposed to higher quality films. But, more likely, the independant fans may just give in to the rude ways of the typical moviegoer, and the only place to watch any type of movie in relative peace will be at home.

I added a final comment to strengthen the ending.

EXERCISE 13.2: REVISING

EXERCISE 13.2 Answers will vary. Students should point out the lack of a clear and interesting general point about the two subjects, the need for development in paragraphs 2, 3, and 4, the need for more transitions, and the need for a more compelling conclusion.

The following is the first draft of a student's comparison/contrast essay. Working in pairs or in small groups, review this essay. Using the Questions for Reviewing a Comparison/Contrast Essay on page 414, decide what revisions you would suggest. If you have any questions that the student needs to consider, write these in the margin or on a separate sheet of paper. If your instructor directs you to, rewrite one or more paragraphs to make them stronger and to eliminate any grammatical or mechanical errors.

My 2 Apartments

1 I recently moved to a new place, its much more closer to here. I find that my new apartment has many advantages over my old one; such as, environment, location and furnishings.

My old apartment was five miles from here on a busy highway; so it took me a halfhour to get to school each morning. My new apartment is located about only a mile from campus I could walk if I needed to. 2

My old apartment had a bad environment. The neighborhood was decaying and my neighbor's seemed to be mostly drug dealers and near do wells. My new apartment neighbors are mostly students. There're some great looking girls here. 3

My old apartment looked like a flop house inside. The carpet was awful, the couche was stained and wierd. The stove didnt work. The plumming was strange. My new apartment however everything is new. All the appliances work and every thing smells fresh and new. 4

I'm glad I moved. I feel safer and enjoy life more. 5

Additional Writing Topics

SUGGESTED ACTIVITY
Consider asking students to meet in writing groups, each of which is charged with producing a more developed and effective version of this essay. Encourage students to use their imagination to provide additional details.

1. As we get older, our cars tend to improve. Contrast your current vehicle to your first one. (As an alternative, you might contrast the kinds of clothes you wear now to those you once wore, or the kinds of music or movies you enjoy now to the kinds you used to prefer.)
2. How does the computer that you are now using differ from a computer that you used at some point in the past?
3. Have you ever looked forward to a first date, forming increasingly positive expectations of the person, and then found the reality of the date disastrous?
4. First impressions can be deceiving. They can cause us to misjudge a person and to form opinions about him or her that—positive or negative—are not true. Think about someone you have gotten to know well over a long time. Is your appraisal of that individual's character different from what it was at the beginning of your relationship? Write a contrast essay in which you show how much your opinion has changed.
5. Write an essay in which you explain that your lifestyle is easier than, harder than, or just different from that of your parents or grandparents when they were your age. Focus on three or four major areas of discussion, such as educational or career opportunities, standards of living, family relationships, health—both physical and emotional—the influence of technology, and opportunities for travel, leisure, and entertainment.
6. Contrast the ways in which men and women of your generation complete a common task or ritual. For example, discuss differences in the ways they shop for groceries, clothes, and/or cars. Explain the ways in which men and women prepare for job interviews, get ready for big dates, or drive in

heavy traffic. Then again, you might contrast the qualities that men and women look for in the ideal spouse.

7. **Writing on the job.** Contrast good customer service with poor service in a memo to your co-workers. (For help with writing a memo, see Chapter 17.)

Responding to a Photograph

In 1937 the Ohio River flooded near Louisville, Kentucky. Margaret Bourke-White took the photograph on page below for *Life* magazine.

Margaret Bourke-White, *At the Time of the Louisville Flood, Louisville, Kentucky*, 1937. Photo by Margaret Bourke-White/Time Life Pictures/Getty Images.

1. Write an informal response to the photograph. What do you notice? How does the image make you feel? How does the photograph make use of the comparison/contrast option?
2. The photograph was taken at a time when racial segregation was legal in the United States. The persons shown waiting for emergency assistance are all African Americans; white Americans would use a separate line. Using a combination of library and online research, explore an area of twentieth-century U.S. life that was subject to racial segregation—for example, education, sports, hotels, or restaurants. Remember to narrow your topic so that you can adequately address it. Write a documented essay contrasting the experiences of white citizens and the experiences of African American citizens in this area. (For more information on documented essays, see Chapter 21.)

CLASSROOM HINT Before assigning these items, spend a few minutes discussing the photograph in class.

Writing About Film

In *The Nutty Professor* (1996, PG-13), Sherman Klump is a shy, obese college professor. An experiment goes wrong, and an alter ego appears: Buddy Love. Write an essay exploring the differences between Sherman Klump and Buddy Love.

Rain Man (1988, R) tells the story of two brothers: the younger one is "normal," and the older one is autistic. Write an essay that shows the differences between the two in the first half of the film and then shows the similarities that develop in the second half.

Using the Internet

Search the Internet for insights and information to use when comparing and contrasting.

1. Pick a topic or issue that is related to your academic major or that has been discussed recently in a course you are taking. Find two Web sites that discuss this issue at length. Then write an essay that contrasts these two Web sites. Begin by describing their layouts and organizations and the ease with which they can be used. You can then evaluate the accuracy, completeness, and usefulness of the information presented. You might also evaluate the source or author of the information found in each Web site by researching these people on the Web. Finally, if you have chosen a current political, social, or moral issue—such as handgun control, affirmative action, school choice, or police-community relations—you might compare or contrast the positions your Web sites take. The best way to organize this essay is point-by-point.
2. Go online to learn more about two technological advances or processes that were developed in the last twenty years and that were designed to accomplish the same thing. For example, you might focus on a traditional telephone modem and a digital subscriber line (DSL) as ways to access the Internet, you might research the differences between the analog and digital versions of the cellular telephone, or you might find out about the differences between laser surgery and traditional surgery to correct someone's vision. The best way to organize this essay is subject-by-subject.

"But I see you're having difficulty following my argument."

CHAPTER 14

ARGUMENT

Writing in Context

Just before lunch on Friday, Bob calls you into his office. "Have a seat," he says. "Thanks for putting together the preliminary billing for the Overton Presbyterian package. Just one problem: I've gone over our costs, and we'll need about seven hundred more to break even."

You are immediately angry but try not to show it: "With all due respect, we agreed to put together their project at a reduced rate—and at a firm price. We can't change the rules of the game on these people."

Bob grimaces—not a pretty sight. "I like the idea of us taking on the occasional charity case, but I refuse to lose money on that sort of deal. Get in touch with them and explain why we have to have the extra money."

You eat lunch with Todd, who lives three cubicles down. His take on the situation is not inspiring: "You could change Bob's mind—difficulty rating of 9.9. You could bite the bullet and tell those poor souls at Overton that we need seven hundred more clams. Or you could quit your job to make a point."

At least you'll have the weekend to think it over.

This situation is an example of the contexts in which argument occurs. Bob is not asking for a flat demand to the nonprofit Overton group; he knows that a reasoned, sincere appeal will have the best chance for success.

CLASSROOM HINT Of course, any essay with a thesis is, technically, an argument—even a simple narrative that proves a point. However, you might point out the differences between a classic argument—in terms of the logic it uses, the points it makes, and the need to prove a point—and a simple narrative or exemplification essay. Also discuss the uses of formal argument in law, science, and philosophy; then briefly distinguish between argument and persuasion.

SUGGESTED ACTIVITY Have students spend five to ten minutes writing about a discussion they have had recently in which they and the person they were talking with disagreed about some issue (the issue can be of national, local, or personal significance). Ask them to recall the reasons they gave for their point of view and any objections their partner raised. Discuss one or two responses as a class.

CLASSROOM HINT It is a good idea to review the introduction to this chapter in class.

HOW DOES ARGUMENT WORK?

An **argument** is a communication in which the writer takes a stand on an issue but indicates that he or she is aware that the "other side" has value as well. However, before we go on to elaborate about what constitutes an argument, let's first look at what argument is *not.*

If you and a friend have a screaming set-to, calling each other names and shouting imprecations, this is not an argument. It is a **quarrel.**

If you and a friend have decided to go to the movies this Saturday, perhaps the only issue left to decide is which film to see. You like the idea of *My Life as a Frog.* Your friend wants to see *Total Annihilation: The Day After.* You know little about this second film except that the title sounds certifiably moronic. However, your spiel goes something like this: "I heard that *The Day After* is really cheesy. Let's watch something made for adults for a change. It won't hurt you. I bet you'll like *My Life as a Frog,* and I know I'll hate another stupid disaster film." Here, you are not attempting to argue; instead, you're trying to **persuade** the other person in order to get your way.

However, persuasion is linked to argument in the sense that it is one of the *purposes* of argument. A writer who fairly argues an issue, acknowledging the valid points of the opposing side, may well have as his or her purpose the persuasion of the reader. But consider this situation: American newspapers, newsmagazines, and talk radio include some regular commentators who offer their opinions on the issues of the day. A great many of these pundits consistently favor either a right-wing or left-wing ideology. It is somewhat amazing, to be frank, that these people can look at any public event and turn it into a moral victory for their side and an alarming moral collapse for the other side. However, if you examine the "arguments" of these pundits, you'll find that they are not really arguments at all. They are statements of opinion meant to be persuasive. Typically, these commentators "bend" reality by simply ignoring inconvenient facts and hoping that the audience doesn't notice. These pundits are out to win, just as one person trying to change another person's movie preference is trying to win. After all, winning is pleasurable. But a writer's desire to "win" can override other concerns.

In this chapter, we address persuasion as a purpose of argument, not as a form of writing. Other purposes include arguing for causes of problems, overturning long-standing assumptions, and proposing solutions to problems. Argument is a complex rhetorical option, whereas persuasion is merely a goal.

A skillful arguer can advocate any position on an issue. Consider how debate teams (sometimes called forensics teams) work. These teams are frequently told to research an issue, but they do not know which stance ("pro" or "con") they will be arguing until the moment of the debate. This forces the teams to research the issue thoroughly; a well-prepared team is as conscious of the potential weaknesses of its own argument as it is of the other side's potential weaknesses.

Consider a scenario from the world of law. Susan J. Barrister, a criminal-defense attorney, has just met a potential client, John A. Dubious. Mr. Dubious has been charged with a drug-trafficking offense. He has the money to pay for Ms. Barrister's services, which will cost a great deal if the case goes to trial. And

Mr. Dubious is smart. He tells his potential attorney the charges against him, then tells her a narrative about what happened. The narrative is close enough to the case that the police have prepared, but its implication is that Mr. Dubious is innocent.

Ms. Barrister has dealt with the likes of Mr. Dubious before. She suspects that he is (1) guilty but (2) smart enough not to let her know that. Although she hates representing people from the drug trade, Ms. Barrister has no valid reason to turn Mr. Dubious down. And once she accepts him as a client, her sworn duty as an attorney—as an officer of the court—is to gain the most favorable outcome for his case that she can, without breaking the law or bending the code of ethics that lawyers must follow. After all, she reminds herself, the prosecutor will be doing the same thing, just with a different goal.

Some students dislike the idea of arguing for something in which they do not believe. They worry that such arguments are dishonest and morally suspect. But consider this scenario: you are taking a senior-level history class from a professor who is not known for brooking dissent to his well-established opinions. Your research paper will be on a topic wherein you disagree with your professor—intensely, in fact. You have two choices: (1) try to work against his opinion or (2) toe the line. We aren't suggesting that you choose one or the other, just that similar scenarios are common in the working world. You will have to choose your approach, but in case you are more worried about your grade than about your true opinion, we believe that learning how to argue either side of an issue is a useful skill.

However, for most writing assignments, you will be encouraged to argue the side that you believe. You must be able to consider the evidence, weigh the opposing issues, and favor one side or the other. Obviously, this process is easier if you believe in the side for which you are arguing.

Not all issues are worthy of argument. Consider the following proposition:

> If a pedestrian sees that someone has planted a new flower garden, the pedestrian should attack the garden and dig up all the seeds and plants.

The response to this proposition is cut and dried: no. It's a ridiculous idea and will result in an open-and-shut argument. Instead, argument springs from issues about which intelligent people differ. This very fact bothers some students, who respond to an issue by showing the positive elements of each side, then leave the decision up to the reader. You should reject such an approach. Any issue that is worth arguing and that you care about should allow you to take a partisan stance—once again, with a thorough sense of the strengths and weaknesses of each side before you begin.

As the examples above suggest, you will be writing arguments throughout your college career as well as in your professional life. Assignments in almost any discipline can call for an argument. You might be asked to argue for your interpretation of a poem, play, or novel for a literature class; for or against a public policy for a government class; or for the implications of the results of an experiment in a biology or chemistry class. As part of your job, you may need to propose a solution to a company problem or argue for your evaluation of a product or service.

In the section that follows the professional essays, we talk about the elements—some of them conceptual and some mechanical—that go into an argument. A thorough treatment of argumentation is beyond the scope of this chapter and, in fact, this book. However, we will concentrate on some approaches to the argumentative essay that should help you.

READING THE ARGUMENT ESSAY WITH A WRITER'S EYE

In the works that follow, Walter S. Minot argues that the recent upward trend in part-time employment by full-time college students is detrimental to these students' education; Deborah Tannen contends that Americans are becoming less likely to discuss issues on which they disagree but are more likely just to shout invective at each other; Caryl Rivers, while not asking for governmental censorship, argues that the anti-female bias in modern popular music is influencing young people in negative ways; and Michael Levin points out that torture, a cruel and unusual punishment, may be necessary in some extreme situations. The subject matter of these essays is diverse; argument, as a rhetorical option, can embrace almost any topic on which two reasonable people might disagree.

Following the essays, the second half of this chapter features strategies for writing the argumentative essay with a reader's eye (pages 439–450). If you decide to write on one of the topics that follow the four essays below, make sure that you have read the strategies section before you begin. Also note that additional writing topics are listed at the end of the chapter (pages 455–457).

Students Who Push Burgers

WALTER S. MINOT

Walter S. Minot is a professor of English at Gannon University. He is the author of *Rhetoric: Theory and Practice for Communication* (1981).

Minot published this essay in the *Christian Science Monitor* on November 22, 1988. Does any of his argument touch on an issue in your life as a student?

1 A college freshman squirms anxiously on a chair in my office, his eyes avoiding mine, those of his English professor, as he explains that he hasn't finished his paper, which was due two days ago. "I just haven't had the time," he says.

2 "Are you carrying a heavy course load?"

3 "Fifteen hours," he says—a normal load.

4 "Are you working a lot?"

5 "No, sir, not much. About 30 hours a week."

6 "That's a lot. Do you have to work that much?"

7 "Yeah, I have to pay for my car."

8 "Do you really need a car?"

9 "Yeah, I need it to get to work."

10 This student isn't unusual. Indeed, he probably typifies today's college and high school students. Yet in all the lengthy analyses of what's wrong with American education, I have not heard employment by students being blamed.

11 I have heard drugs blamed and television—that universal scapegoat. I have heard elaborate theories about the decline of the family, of religion, and of authority, as well as other sociological theories. But nobody blames student employment. The world seems to have accepted the part-time job as a normal feature of adolescence. A parochial school in my town even had a day to honor students who held regular jobs, and parents often endorse this employment by claiming that it teaches kids the value of the dollar.

12 But such employment is a major cause of educational decline. To argue my case, I will rely on memories of my own high school days and contrast them with what I see today. Though I do have some statistical evidence, my argument depends on what anyone over 40 can test through memory and direct observation.

13 When I was in high school in the 1950s, students seldom held jobs. Some of us baby-sat, shoveled snow, mowed lawns, and delivered papers, and some of us got jobs in department stores around Christmas. But most of us had no regular source of income other than the generosity of our parents.

14 The only kids who worked regularly were poor. They worked to help their families. If I remember correctly, only about five people in my class of 170 held jobs. That was in a working-class town in New England. As for the rest of us, our parents believed that going to school and helping around the house were our work.

15 In contrast, in 1986 my daughter was one of the few students among juniors and seniors who didn't work. According to the Bureau of Labor Statistics, more than 40 percent of high school students were working in 1980, but sociologist Ellen Greenberger and Laurence Steinberg in "When Teenagers Work" came up with estimates of more than 70 percent working in 1986, though I suspect that the figure may be even higher now.

16 My daughter, however, did not work; her parents wouldn't let her. Interestingly, some of the students in her class implied that she had an unfair advantage over them in the classroom. They were probably right, for while she was home studying they were pushing burgers, waiting on tables, or selling dresses 20 hours a week. Working students have little time for homework.

17 I attended a public high school, while she attended a Roman Catholic preparatory school whose students were mainly middle class. By the standards of my day, her classmates did not "have to" work. Yet many of them were working 20 to 30 hours a week. Why?

18 They worked so that they could spend $60 to $100 a week on designer jeans, rock concerts, stereo and video systems, and, of course, cars. They were living lives of luxury, buying items on which their parents refused to throw hard-earned money away. Though the parent would not buy such tripe for their kids, the parents somehow convinced themselves that the kids were learning the value of money. Yet, according to Ms. Greenberger and Mr. Steinberg, only about a quarter of those students saved money for college or other long-term goals.

19 How students spend their money is their business, not mine. But as a teacher, I have witnessed the effects of employment. I know that students who work all evening aren't ready for studying when they get home from work. Moreover, because they work so hard and have ready cash, they feel that they deserve to have fun—instead of spending all their free time studying.

20 Thus, by the time they get to college, most students look upon studies as a spare-time activity. A survey at Pennsylvania State University showed that most freshmen

believed they could maintain a B average by studying about 20 hours a week. (I can remember when college guidebooks advised two to three hours of studying for every hour in class—30 to 45 hours a week.)

21 Clearly individual students will pay the price for lack of adequate time studying, but the problem goes beyond the individual. It extends to schools and colleges that are finding it difficult to demand quantity or quality of work from students.

22 Perhaps the reason American education has declined so markedly is because America has raised a generation of part-time students. And perhaps our economy will continue to decline as full-time students from Japan and Europe continue to out-perform our part-time students.

STYLE AND STRATEGY
1. The assumption is that we should question the value and extent of work that full-time students undertake. In other words, education should always be the priority. At the heart of the matter is the fact that many students work simply to afford luxuries like those mentioned in paragraph 18.
2. In paragraph 14, he mentions that poor students may have to work. In paragraph 18, he concedes that 25 percent of students who work do save "money for college or other long-term goals."
3. Minot relies heavily on contrast, but he also uses exemplification.
4. No, the essay is fairly short, and his examples are convincing.

Vocabulary

The following terms are identified by paragraph number. Make sure that you understand each term's meaning in its context. If you're not sure that you understand a term, look it up in a college-level dictionary.

typifies (10)	parochial (11)	tripe (18)
scapegoat (11)	preparatory school (17)	markedly (22)

Style and Strategy

1. Minot clearly believes that he and the reader share an assumption. What is this assumption?
2. How does the author show that the issue has two sides?
3. What is Minot's internal rhetorical strategy—for example, narration, comparison/contrast, or process analysis?
4. Minot uses two specific examples of students who work or don't work—the anonymous unfortunate whose case opens the essay and Minot's daughter. Are more examples needed in an essay of this length?

QUESTIONS FOR CRITICAL THINKING AND DISCUSSION Item 1 is a good prompt for in-class writing. Students should be advised to support their answers with concrete illustrations. For item 2, consider listing contrasting arguments on the board. You might then turn this into an assignment for sustained writing in which the student anticipates and responds to opposing arguments.

Questions for Critical Thinking and Discussion

1. As a student, what is your first priority? School? Social life? Work? Family?
2. Some commentators now see higher education as a place where "consumers" (part- or full-time students) "purchase" education on much the same basis as shoppers use to purchase anything—price, convenience, amenities. Others argue that students who take this approach may end up with degrees but will miss out on what the college experience has to offer and enter the workforce at a disadvantage compared to their more-studious colleagues. What do you think?

Suggestions for Writing

1. Write a 500-word essay arguing that a specific group, office, or department fails to accomplish its stated goals because its members spend their time on other pursuits.
2. "American colleges should tighten up requirements for students. (a) More than one absence in a class—except in the case of provable emergency—

should result in the administrative withdrawal of the student. (b) Tests and papers should never be accepted after their assigned date. (c) Students who arrive late to class should be openly reprimanded." Write a 500- to 750-word essay in which you agree or disagree with one or more of the statements above.

3. In 500 to 750 words, argue for a change in school policy that will help students become more successful at their studies.

SUGGESTIONS FOR WRITING The second and third items make for the most well-developed essays. However, you might brainstorm these topics in class ahead of time.

The Triumph of the Yell

DEBORAH TANNEN

Deborah Tannen is a sociolinguist—a scholar who studies language in a sociological context. Her best-known works—*That's Not What I Meant: How Conversational Style Makes or Breaks Your Relationships* (1987), *You Just Don't Understand: Women and Men in Conversation* (1990), and *Talking from 9 to 5* (1994)—explore the differences between female and male communication styles and, especially, how men and women interpret the other sex's communication strategies.

In the following essay, Tannen focuses on a more apparent problem: the current tendency of people on opposite sides of an argument to shout, not to discuss.

I put the question to a journalist who had written a vitriolic attack on a leading feminist researcher: "Why do you need to make others wrong for you to be right?" Her response: "It's an argument!" 1

That's the problem. More and more these days, journalists, politicians and academics treat public discourse as an argument—not in the sense of *making* an argument, but in the sense of *having* one, of having a fight. 2

When people have arguments in private life, they're not trying to understand what the other person is saying. They're listening for weaknesses in logic to leap on, points they can distort to make the other look bad. We all do this when we're angry, but is it the best model for public intellectual interchange? This breakdown of the boundary between public and private is contributing to what I have come to think of as a culture of critique. 3

Fights have winners and losers. If you're fighting to win, the temptation is great to deny facts that support your opponent's views and present only those facts that support your own. 4

At worst, there's a temptation to lie. We accept this style of arguing because we believe we can tell when someone is lying. But we can't. Paul Ekman, a psychologist at the University of California at San Francisco, has found that even when people are very sure they can tell whether or not someone is dissembling, their judgments are as likely as not to be wrong. 5

If public discourse is a fight, every issue must have two sides—no more, no less. And it's crucial to show "the other side," even if one has to scour the margins of science or the fringes of lunacy to find it. 6

The culture of critique is based on the belief that opposition leads to truth: when both sides argue, the truth will emerge. And because people are presumed to enjoy watching a fight, the most extreme views are presented, since they make the best show. But it is a myth that opposition leads to truth when truth does not reside on one side or the other but is rather a crystal of many sides. Truth is more 7 likely to be found in the complex middle than in the simplified extremes, but the spectacles that result when extremes clash are thought to get higher ratings or larger leadership.

8 Because the culture of critique encourages people to attack and often misrepresent others, those others must waste their creativity and time correcting the misrepresentations and defending themselves. Serious scholars have had to spend years of their lives writing books proving that the Holocaust happened, because a few fanatics who claim it didn't have been given a public forum. Those who provide the platform know that what these people say is, simply put, not true, but rationalize the dissemination of lies as showing "the other side." The determination to find another side can spread disinformation rather than lead to truth.

9 The culture of critique has given rise to the journalistic practice of confronting prominent people with criticism couched as others' views. Meanwhile, the interviewer has planted an accusation in readers' or viewers' minds. The theory seems to be that when provoked, people are spurred to eloquence and self-revelation. Perhaps some are. But others are unable to say what they know because they are hurt, and begin to sputter when their sense of fairness is outraged. In those cases, opposition is not the path to truth.

10 When people in power know that what they say will be scrutinized for weaknesses and probably distorted, they become more guarded. As an acquaintance recently explained about himself, public figures who once gave long, free-wheeling press conferences now limit themselves to reading brief statements. When less information gets communicated, opposition does not lead to truth.

11 Opposition also limits information when only those who are adept at verbal sparring take part in public discourse, and those who cannot handle it, or do not like it, decline to participate. This winnowing process is evident in graduate schools, where many talented students drop out because what they expected to be a community of intellectual inquiry turned out to be a ritual game of attack and counterattack.

12 One such casualty graduated from a small liberal arts college, where she "luxuriated in the endless discussions." At the urging of her professors, she decided to make academia her profession. But she changed her mind after a year in an art history program at a major university. She felt she had fallen into a "den of wolves." "I wasn't cut out for academia," she concluded. But does academia have to be so combative that it cuts people like her out?

13 In many university classrooms, "critical thinking" means reading someone's life work, then ripping it to shreds. Though critique is surely one form of critical thinking, so are integrating ideas from disparate fields and examining the context out of which they grew. Opposition does not lead to truth when we ask only "What's wrong with this argument?" and never "What can we use from this in building a new theory, and a new understanding?"

14 Several years ago I was on a television talk show with a representative of the men's movement. I didn't foresee any problem, since there is nothing in my work that is anti-male. But in the room where guests gather before the show I found a man wearing a shirt and tie and a floor-length skirt, with waist-length red hair. He politely introduced himself and told me he liked my book. Then he added: "When I get out there, I'm going to attack you. But don't take it personally. That's why they invite me on, so that's what I'm going to do."

15 When the show began, I spoke only a sentence or two before this man nearly jumped out of his chair, threw his arms before him in gestures of anger and began shrieking—first attacking me, but soon moving on to rail against women. The most disturbing thing about his hysterical ranting was what it sparked in the studio audience: they too became vicious, attacking not me (I hadn't had a chance to say anything) and not him (who wants to tangle with someone who will scream at you?) but the other guests: unsuspecting women who had agreed to come on the show to talk about their problems communicating with their spouses.

16 This is the most dangerous aspect of modeling intellectual interchange as a fight: it contributes to an atmosphere of animosity that spreads like a fever. In a society where people express their anger by shooting, the result of demonizing those with whom we disagree can be truly demonic.

17 I am not suggesting that journalists stop asking tough questions necessary to get at the facts, even if those questions may appear challenging. And of course it is the responsibility of the media to represent serious opposition when it exists, and of intellectuals everywhere to explore potential weaknesses in others' arguments. But when opposition becomes the overwhelming avenue of inquiry, when the lust for opposition exalts extreme views and obscures complexity, when our eagerness to find weaknesses blinds us to strengths, when the atmosphere of animosity precludes respect and poisons our relations with one another, then the culture of critique is stifling us. If we could move beyond it, we would move closer to the truth.

Vocabulary

The following terms are identified by paragraph number. Make sure that you understand each term's meaning in its context. If you're not sure that you understand a term, look it up in a college-level dictionary.

vitriolic (1)	rationalize (8)	winnowing (11)
discourse (2)	dissemination (8)	disparate (13)
critique (3)	eloquence (9)	animosity (16)
dissembling (5)	adept (11)	inquiry (17)
lunacy (6)	sparring (11)	exalts (17)
forum (8)		

Style and Strategy

1. Tannen argues that when argument is reduced to fighting, a variety of effects can occur. List these effects in your own words.
2. Tannen clearly believes that she and the reader share an assumption. What is this assumption?
3. Where does Tannen acknowledge the other side's argument?
4. What does the author mean by "the culture of critique"?
5. Does Tannen ever suggest a way to go beyond the culture of critique and move toward the truth? Explain.

STYLE AND STRATEGY

1. The effects appear in paragraphs 4, 7, 8, 9, 11, and 16.
2. The assumption is that arguments should be seen as tools for critical thinking and for convincing readers or listeners, not as weapons to defeat an opponent.
3. Tannen acknowledges the opposition in paragraphs 16 and 17.
4. The "culture of critique" uses argument as a weapon by which to rip apart the oppositions' arguments, if not their integrity and reputations.
5. Paragraphs 7 and 13 contain hints about ways in which we might get beyond the "culture of critique."

Questions for Critical Thinking and Discussion

QUESTIONS FOR CRITICAL THINKING AND DISCUSSION Students will be able to respond to all three of these items by drawing upon their own experiences.

1. In your opinion, is our culture becoming quieter and more civil or noisier and ruder?
2. Comment on this statement: "These days, people are more likely to resort to shouting at each other because they have lost a certain facility with words. It's hard to listen carefully to what another person has to say and then to respond carefully, especially if there is a disagreement going on. It's easier just to shout."
3. Overt public rudeness seems to be on the rise. All of us have observed bizarre behavior, probably while shaking our heads in disbelief. (The recent account of someone talking on a cell phone during a funeral is *not* an urban legend.) In the past, however, people were less likely to be rude in public, for there was a strong likelihood that they would be chastised for their inappropriate behavior. Why have people become reluctant to speak up during these outbursts?

Suggestions for Writing

SUGGESTIONS FOR WRITING Item 1 demands that students draw specific details from their own experiences. You can prepare students for item 2 through sustained classroom discussion of the Questions for Critical Thinking and Discussion.

1. In 500 to 750 words, argue that an organization or project with which you are familiar has been ruined because of the participants' failure to follow the necessary guidelines or procedures. Stress the negative effects of this breakdown.
2. Is public civility an endangered species? In a 500- to 750-word essay, argue for or against this idea by recalling one or two specific experiences as support for your assertions.

What Should Be Done About Rock Lyrics?

CARYL RIVERS

Caryl Rivers is a journalism professor at Boston University who has written a number of books on modern culture, including *More Joy Than Rage: Crossing Generations with the New Feminism* (1991) and *Slick Spins and Fractured Facts: How Cultural Myths Distort the News* (1996), along with three novels: *Virgins* (1984), *Intimate Enemies* (1987), and *Indecent Behavior* (1990).

The following essay was first published in 1985 in the *Boston Globe*. The questions that it asks are still fresh today.

1 After a grisly series of murders in California, possibly inspired by the lyrics of a rock song, we are hearing a familiar chorus: don't blame rock and roll. Kids will be kids. They love to rebel, and the more shocking the stuff, the better they like it.

2 There's some truth in this, of course. I loved to watch Elvis shake his torso when I was a teenager, and it was even more fun when Ed Sullivan wouldn't let the cameras show him below the waist. I snickered at the forbidden "Rock With Me, Annie" lyrics by a black rhythm and blues group, which were deliciously naughty. But I am sorry, rock fans, that is not the same thing as hearing lyrics about how a man is going

to force a woman to perform oral sex on him at gunpoint in a little number called "Eat Me Alive." It is not in the same league with a song about the delights of slipping into a woman's room while she is sleeping and murdering her, the theme of an AC/DC ballad that allegedly inspired the California slayer.

3 Make no mistake, it is not sex we are talking about here, but violence. Violence against women. Most rock songs are not violent—they are funky, sexy, rebellious, and sometimes witty. Please do not mistake me for a Mrs. Grundy. If Prince wants to leap about wearing only a purple jock strap, fine. Let Mick Jagger unzip his fly as he gyrates, if he wants to. But when either one of them starts garroting, beating, or sodomizing a woman in their number, that is another story.

4 I always find myself annoyed when "intellectual" men dismiss violence against women with a yawn, as if it were beneath their dignity to notice. I wonder if the reaction would be the same if the violence were directed against someone other than women. How many people would yawn and say, "Oh, kids will be kids" if a rock group did a nifty little number called "Lynchin," in which stringing up and stomping on black people were set to music? Who would chuckle and say, "Oh, just a little adolescent rebellion" if a group of rockers went on MTV dressed as Nazis, desecrating synagogues and beating up Jews to the beat of twanging guitars?

5 I'll tell you what would happen. Prestigious dailies would thunder on editorial pages; senators would fall over each other to get denunciations into the *Congressional Record.* The president would appoint a commission to clean up the music business.

6 But violence against women is greeted by silence. It shouldn't be.

7 This does not mean censorship, or book (or record) burning. In a society that protects free expression, we understand a lot of stuff will float up out of the sewer. Usually, we recognize the ugly stuff that advocates violence against any group as the garbage it is, and we consider its purveyors as moral lepers. We hold our nose and tolerate it, but we speak out against the values it proffers.

8 But images of violence against women are not staying on the fringes of society. No longer are they found only in tattered, paper-covered books or in movie houses where winos snooze and the scent of urine fills the air. They are entering the mainstream at a rapid rate. This is happening at a time when the media, more and more, set the agenda for the public debate. It is a powerful legitimizing force—especially television. Many people regard what they see on TV as the truth; Walter Cronkite* once topped a poll as the most trusted man in America.

9 Now, with the advent of rock videos and all-music channels, rock music has grabbed a big chunk of legitimacy. American teenagers have instant access, in their living rooms, to the messages of rock, on the same vehicle that brought them *Sesame Street.* Who can blame them if they believe that the images they see are accurate reflections of adult reality, approved by adults? After all, Big Bird used to give them lessons on the same little box. Adults, by their silence, sanction the images. Do we really want our kids to think that rape and violence are what sexuality is all about?

10 This is not a trivial issue. Violence against women is a major social problem, one that's more than a cerebral issue to me. I teach at Boston University, and one of

---

***Walter Cronkite (b. 1916):** the anchor of the *CBS Evening News* from 1962 to 1981.

my most promising young journalism students was raped and murdered. Two others told me of being raped. Recently, one female student was assaulted and beaten so badly she had $5,000 worth of medical bills and permanent damage to her back and eyes.

11 It's nearly impossible, of course, to make a cause-and-effect link between lyrics and images and acts of violence. But images have a tremendous power to create an atmosphere in which violence against certain people is sanctioned. Nazi propagandists knew that full well when they portrayed Jews as ugly, greedy, and powerful.

12 The outcry over violence against women, particularly in a sexual context, is being legitimized in two ways: by the increasing movement of these images into the mainstream of the media in TV, films, magazines, albums, videos, and by the silence about it.

13 Violence, of course, is rampant in the media. But it is usually set in some kind of moral context. It's usually only the bad guys who commit violent acts against the innocent. When the good guys get violent, it's against those who deserve it. Dirty Harry blows away the scum; he doesn't walk up to a toddler and say, "Make my day." The A Team does not shoot up suburban shopping malls.

14 But in some rock songs, it's the "heroes" who commit the acts. The people we are programmed to identify with are the ones being violent, with women on the receiving end. In a society where rape and assaults on women are endemic, this is no small problem, with millions of young boys watching on their TV screens and listening on their Walkmans.

15 I think something needs to be done. I'd like to see people in the industry respond to the problem. I'd love to see some women rock stars speak out against violence against women. I would like to see disc jockeys refuse air play to records and videos that contain such violence. At the very least, I want to see the end of the silence. I want journalists and parents and critics and performing artists to keep this issue alive in the public forum. I don't want people who are concerned about this issue labeled as bluenoses and bookburners and ignored.

16 And I wish it wasn't always just women who were speaking out. Men have as large a stake in the quality of our civilization as women do in the long run. Violence is a contagion that infects at random. Let's hear something, please, from the men.

Vocabulary

The following terms are identified by paragraph number. Make sure that you understand each term's meaning in its context. If you're not sure that you understand a term, look it up in a college-level dictionary.

grisly (1)	denunciations (5)	cerebral (10)
torso (2)	purveyors (7)	propagandists (11)
gyrates (3)	moral lepers (7)	rampant (13)
garroting (3)	proffers (7)	endemic (14)
desecrating (4)	legitimizing (8)	bluenoses (15)
prestigious (5)	sanction (9)	

STYLE AND STRATEGY

1. In paragraphs 1 and 2 Rivers contrasts the rock lyrics of today, which depict violence, coercion, and perversion, with the rock music of her youth. In paragraph 3, the contrast is clearly between sex and violence, specifically violence against women.
2. Causal analysis is used in paragraphs 4 and 5.
3. The process is the "legitimization" of violence against women through

Style and Strategy

1. What contrast does Rivers draw in paragraphs 1–2 and then again in paragraph 3?
2. What rhetorical strategy does Rivers use in the "what-if" section (paragraphs 4–5)?
3. What is the process that Rivers describes in paragraphs 8–10?
4. In paragraphs 12–14, how does Rivers redefine violence in the media?
5. What solutions does Rivers suggest to deal with this problem?

the media to an audience that, since childhood, has come to accept what the media presents as "accurate reflections of adult reality" (paragraph 9).
4. In these paragraphs, the author distinguishes the violence of some rock songs from violence in other media.
5. Paragraphs 15 and 16 state her advice clearly.

Questions for Critical Thinking and Discussion

1. Our era exhibits a great awareness of the need for sensitivity toward those who are different from us—due to race, sex, sexual orientation, religion, disability, or country of origin. Yet some "differences" seem fair game. Which stereotypes still exist? Why?
2. The 1934 Frank Capra film *It Happened One Night* was the first movie to sweep the major Academy Awards. It was wildly popular, and it retains its appeal today. However, there is a significant problem in the film: the female lead, played by Claudette Colbert, is treated as a helpless idiot by the male lead, played by Clark Gable. Audiences in the 1930s found no problem here; after all, women had a subordinate status in that world. Today, however, audiences approach this film from a different frame of reference, and the treatment of Colbert's character seems, at times, abusive. How legitimate is it for people of today to impose their standards of political sensitivity on works of art and literature produced in accordance with the standards of another era?
3. "One hundred years from now, commentators will look back at us and disapprove of some of our most widely accepted attitudes and actions. At this point, we have no idea what they'll be criticizing us for." Comment on this statement.

QUESTIONS FOR CRITICAL THINKING AND DISCUSSION Items 1 and 3 can be discussed in class, but expect opinions to vary widely. For an informed discussion of the Capra film, you might want to show 5 or 10 minutes of the videotape or DVD in class to illustrate the abusive behavior mentioned in the essay. As an alternative, you can discuss abusive behavior by referencing contemporary television or cinema.

Suggestions for Writing

1. Popular music, like other forms of popular culture, such as films and television programs, is somewhat controlled by its audience. In other words, if the anti-woman message becomes too horrifying, consumers stop buying. But what about Internet sites, which are not subject to the same market controls? In a 500- to 750-word essay, argue for or against this statement: "The Internet contains a vast and dangerous collection of anti-female content that should be regulated."
2. Suppose, as some people argue, that censorship of popular media content should once again become the American norm. In other words, what people could read, watch, and view would be controlled by the standards of 1957. What do you think would happen? Argue your position in a 500- to 750-word essay.

SUGGESTIONS FOR WRITING Encourage students to support their arguments with factual detail and to address opposing arguments.

The Case for Torture

MICHAEL LEVIN

Physical torture is both illegal and unconstitutional in the United States. But could there be times when Americans might regret that fact? Michael Levin thinks so. Levin, a philosophy professor at the City College of New York, originally published this essay as a *Newsweek* "My Turn" column on June 7, 1982.

It is generally assumed that torture is impermissible, a throwback to a more brutal age. Enlightened societies reject it outright, and regimes suspected of using it risk the wrath of the United States. 1

I believe this attitude is unwise. There are situations in which torture is not merely permissible but morally mandatory. Moreover, these situations are moving from the realm of imagination to fact. 2

Death:

Suppose a terrorist has hidden an atomic bomb on Manhattan Island which will detonate at noon on July 4 unless . . . (here follow the usual demands for money and release of his friends from jail). Suppose, further, that he is caught at 10 A.M. of the fateful day, but—preferring death to failure—won't disclose where the bomb is. What do we do? If we follow due process—wait for his lawyer, arraign him—millions of people will die. If the only way to save those lives is to subject the terrorist to the most excruciating possible pain, what grounds can there be for not doing so? I suggest there are none. In any case, I ask you to face the question with an open mind. 3

Torturing the terrorist is unconstitutional? Probably. But millions of lives surely outweigh constitutionality. Torture is barbaric? Mass murder is far more barbaric. Indeed, letting millions of innocents die in deference to one who flaunts his guilt is moral cowardice, an unwillingness to dirty one's hands. If *you* caught the terrorist, could you sleep nights knowing that millions died because you couldn't bring yourself to apply the electrodes? 4

Once you concede that torture is justified in extreme cases, you have admitted that the decision to use torture is a matter of balancing innocent lives against the means needed to save them. You must now face more realistic cases involving more modest numbers. Someone plants a bomb on a jumbo jet. He alone can disarm it, and his demands cannot be met (or if they can, we refuse to set a precedent by yielding to his threats). Surely we can, we must, do anything to the extortionist to save the passengers. How can we tell 300, or 100, or 10 people who never asked to be put in danger, "I'm sorry, you'll have to die in agony, we just couldn't bring ourselves to . . ." 5

Here are the results of an informal poll about a third, hypothetical, case. Suppose a terrorist group kidnapped a newborn baby from a hospital. I asked four mothers if they would approve of torturing kidnappers if that were necessary to get their own newborns back. All said yes, the most "liberal" adding that she would like to administer it herself. 6

I am not advocating torture as punishment. Punishment is addressed to deeds irrevocably past. Rather, I am advocating torture as an acceptable measure for pre- 7 venting future evils. So understood, it is far less objectionable than many extant punishments. Opponents of the death penalty, for example, are forever insisting that executing a murderer will not bring back his victim (as if the purpose of capital punishment were supposed to be resurrection, not deterrence or retribution). But torture, in the cases described, is intended not to bring anyone back but to keep innocents from being dispatched. The most powerful argument against using torture as a punishment or to secure confessions is that such practices disregard the rights of the individual. Well, if the individual is all that important—and he is—it is correspondingly important to protect the rights of individuals threatened by terrorists. If life is so valuable that it must never be taken, the lives of the innocents must be saved even at the price of hurting the one who endangers them.

8 Better precedents for torture are assassination and pre-emptive attack. No Allied leader would have flinched at assassinating Hitler, had that been possible. (The Allies did assassinate Heydrich.) Americans would be angered to learn that Roosevelt could have had Hitler killed in 1943—thereby shortening the war and saving millions of lives—but refused on moral grounds. Similarly, if nation A learns that nation B is about to launch an unprovoked attack, A has a right to save itself by destroying B's military capability first. In the same way, if the police can by torture save those who would otherwise die at the hands of kidnappers or terrorists, they must.

Idealism:

9 There is an important difference between terrorists and their victims that should mute talk of the terrorists' "rights." The terrorist's victims are at risk unintentionally, not having asked to be endangered. But the terrorist knowingly initiated his actions. Unlike his victims, he volunteered for the risks of his deed. By threatening to kill for profit or idealism, he renounces civilized standards, and he can have no complaint if civilization tries to thwart him by whatever means necessary.

10 Just as torture is justified only to save lives (not extort confessions or recantations), it is justifiably administered only to those *known* to hold innocent lives in their hands. Ah, but how can the authorities ever be sure they have the right malefactor? Isn't there a danger of error and abuse? Won't We turn into Them?

11 Questions like these are disingenuous in a world in which terrorists proclaim themselves and perform for television. The name of their game is public recognition. After all, you can't very well intimidate a government into releasing your freedom fighters unless you announce that it is your group that has seized its embassy. "Clear guilt" is difficult to define, but when 40 million people see a group of masked gunmen seize an airplane on the evening news, there is not much question about who the perpetrators are. There will be hard cases where the situation is murkier. Nonetheless, a line demarcating the legitimate use of torture can be drawn. Torture only the obviously guilty, and only for the sake of saving innocents, and the line between Us and Them will remain clear.

12 There is little danger that the Western democracies will lose their way if they choose to inflict pain as one way of preserving order. Paralysis in the face of evil is the greater danger. Some day soon a terrorist will threaten tens of thousands of lives, and torture will be the only way to save them. We had better start thinking about this.

Vocabulary

The following terms are identified by paragraph number. Make sure that you understand each term's meaning in its context. If you're not sure that you understand a term, look it up in a college-level dictionary.

impermissible (1)	hypothetical (6)	thwart (9)
throwback (1)	irrevocable (7)	recantation (10)
realm (2)	extant (7)	malefactor (10)
excruciating (3)	retribution (7)	disingenuous (11)
barbaric (4)	dispatched (7)	perpetrator (11)
deference (4)	pre-emptive (8)	murkier (11)
flaunt (4)	flinched (8)	demarcating (11)
precedent (5)	mute (9)	paralysis (12)
extortionist (5)	renounce (9)	

Style and Strategy

STYLE AND STRATEGY
1. This question sparks interesting discussion, but it is wise to conduct your own poll in class.
2. The difference is documented in historical fact. By beginning paragraph 8 with "Better precedents . . . ," Levin clearly acknowledges this.
3. He does so in paragraphs 7, 10, and 11.

1. In this essay Levin displays a *utilitarian* philosophy. Utilitarians believe that the greater good must be favored over the rights of a few—if the two sides happen to be in conflict. In the fourth paragraph, while admitting that torture is unconstitutional, Levin adds this: "But millions of lives surely outweigh constitutionality." Levin believes that his audience shares this assumption. Is he correct? To what degree would the audience of 1982 differ from today's audience?
2. In paragraphs 3, 5, 6, and 8, Levin paints four scenarios that would justify the use of torture. How does the fourth scenario differ from the first three? Does Levin acknowledge this difference?
3. One of the great strengths of "The Case for Torture" is the way its thesis controls the essay. Throughout, Levin makes sure that the reader knows exactly what he is arguing for—and, just as importantly, what he is *not* arguing for. List the instances when Levin pauses to make his focus clear.

Questions for Critical Thinking and Discussion

QUESTIONS FOR CRITICAL THINKING AND DISCUSSION All of these questions make for very interesting and, at times, heated discussion. The class discussion can provide insight and information students can use in the Suggestions for Writing, which follow.

Utilitarian philosophy raises many interesting and troubling questions. Consider and discuss the following statements and questions:

1. "Telling a lie is morally wrong unless doing so would cause less harm than would telling the truth."
2. "Allowing police to torture a terrorist in order to prevent a tragedy sounds like a good idea, but how would we ever know that torture wouldn't extend to other areas of police work?"
3. "The police used torture off and on in some parts of the United States until the 1950s, when the practice largely disappeared. But wouldn't we all be better off if torture allowed the courts to convict more obviously guilty criminals and get them off the streets?"

Suggestions for Writing

SUGGESTIONS FOR WRITING To get students to exercise their intellectual muscles in response to item 1, urge them to consider laws to which no exceptions apply. Item 2 is the more challenging of these questions, but students who are able to engage in self-reflection write effective papers on this one.

1. Many people believe that every law has its exception. Write a 500- to 750-word essay arguing that a specific law or rule does or does not have an exception.
2. You work for a company that is part of a large, powerful chain. Your manager routinely ensures that each week, you and your co-workers get paid for two fewer hours than you actually put in. One of your colleagues regularly tries to "even the score" by embezzling products and supplies roughly equal to the two-hour discrepancy. Is such behavior justifiable? Write a 500- to 750-word essay arguing your position.

MORE OPTIONS ONLINE If you would like to read additional argument essays, go to **www.mhhe.com/writingtoday**.

WRITING THE ARGUMENT ESSAY WITH A READER'S EYE

Argument is a complex rhetorical option that requires your understanding of issues that are not always present in the other options. The advice that follows will help you think like your reader as you consider your assignment and then prewrite, draft, revise, and edit your argument essay.

Issues to Keep in Mind

You need to consider the following four issues as you work on your argument essay:

CLASSROOM HINT Consider spending substantial time reviewing each of these four sections in class.

1. The language of argument
2. Supporting the essay's claims
3. Logical fallacies
4. Audience and purpose

The Language of Argument

Argument has its own language, a set of terms deriving from historical philosophy and from formal logic. Understanding what these terms mean is more important than knowing the terms themselves; you don't actually use these terms in the course of an argument, but understanding these concepts is crucial to writing an effective argument.

An argument is made up of a series of **claims** (also known as **assertions**); these statements express the writer's belief that an issue should be decided one way and not another. A claim also represents a type of **appeal**, or means of convincing your audience. A writer can, categorically, appeal to **logic**, to **values** or **fairness**, and to **emotion.** However, many—perhaps most—arguments don't use all of these, concentrating instead on one or two types of appeals. The following scenario, the background for an essay that appears on pages 448–450, represents the rare instance in which all three types of appeals can be used:

> Currently, your university charges a good deal for parking. Students pay $100 per year; faculty and staff pay $150. Suddenly, seemingly out

of nowhere, the university president announces that the two amounts will be switched, with students paying the lion's share.

The arguer's response to this situation is complex. There are three claims to make:

1. The shifting of responsibility is not fair. Students are frequently poor; however, faculty and staff have, by definition, ongoing income. This is an appeal to values or fairness.
2. The policy change is bad business. This university competes with other local providers of higher education, and area students are known to "shop" for the best value. The university is running the risk of driving students away. This is a **logical** appeal because it depends on analysis, common sense, and mathematics.
3. Student morale is already low. Because of a series of negative incidents over the past school year, students don't feel very good about the university and their relationship with it. Raising student parking fees while lowering faculty/staff fees just seems like a bit much. Students need good news right now, not more trouble. This is an **emotional** appeal.

Most argumentative essays depend on logical appeals and appeals to values or fairness. Be wary of the overuse of emotional appeals, which can produce an essay that seems manipulative.

Once you have made a claim, you must develop and substantiate it. One method is through **reasoning:** using logical processes to prove an assertion. Another method (which is usually combined with the first) employs **evidence** to back up an assertion (see the next section, "Supporting the Essay's Claims").

Supporting the Essay's Claims

Two ways to substantiate an argumentative claim are by using **reason** and by using **evidence.**

Reasoning

People use two major forms of logic when they think and when they write: **deductive reasoning** and **inductive reasoning.** Deductive reasoning starts from a general principle and applies that principle to specific situations. Inductive reasoning requires you to look at specific examples and then move to a general conclusion. We'll look at deduction first.

The ancient philosopher Aristotle wrote that deductive reasoning takes the form of a **syllogism**, a combination that includes a major premise (a general principle), a minor premise (a specific situation), and the logical conclusion. For example,

- **Major Premise:** All tortoiseshell cats are female.
- **Minor Premise:** My cat is a tortoiseshell.
- **Conclusion:** Therefore, my cat is female.

If both premises are true, then the conclusion must be valid. However, if either premise is faulty, then the conclusion won't necessarily be sound. Notice the problem that occurs when the major premise is faulty:

- **Major Premise:** All computer programmers are solitary people.
- **Minor Premise:** Ed is a computer programmer.
- **Conclusion:** Ed is a solitary person.

The problem comes from the fact that the major premise is based on a stereotype, that of programmers being loners. There are many thousands of computer programmers; expecting all of them to have the same personality type is ludicrous.

Sometimes the problem is in the minor premise, as in the following example:

- **Major Premise:** All baseball players are athletes.
- **Minor Premise:** All jockeys are athletes.
- **Conclusion:** All jockeys are baseball players.

The subject of the minor premise must be the same type of thing as the subject of the major premise. Otherwise, the syllogism is faulty and, in this case, nonsensical.

Many students find deductive reasoning appealing, but it clearly has some drawbacks if improperly applied because the writer can easily end up with an essay built upon faulty conclusions. Many argumentative essays are built, instead, on inductive reasoning.

The inductive process reaches a conclusion by building upon specific information. For example, perhaps you are thinking about buying a car. You notice during your travels that one of the models you had been considering seems to be stranded beside the road alarmingly often. Also, recently the car company recalled that model for safety reasons. You would probably draw the inductive conclusion that this is a car to avoid. Such an approach—building upon facts to reach a conclusion—is an argumentative process that writers—and readers—tend to trust.

Using Evidence

For the most part, good argumentative essays depend on both abstract concepts and realistic evidence. Avoid writing an essay that depends upon abstractions without concrete evidence to back them up. Where can you find evidence to support your claims? The three basic types of evidence are the following:

1. Personal experience
2. Primary research sources
3. Secondary research sources

In a way, **personal experience** is self-explanatory. However, keep in mind that personal experience isn't limited to your own experience but can be drawn from those you know well and trust. Personal experience can be a very rich source of evidence for writers who pay attention to the world around them.

Primary research sources include sources that you develop through your own initiative. If you were planning to argue against a policy, you could gather information on the effects of that policy by conducting interviews, performing surveys, or distributing questionnaires. If your information gathering produces the results you have predicted, you would know that other people have experienced ill effects as a result of the policy, which would be evidence for your thesis. (Note that primary sources must be documented—see chapters 20 and 21.)

Secondary research sources include data, opinions, and other published commentary on a subject. By referring to facts, or data, you establish solid support for your claims. Referring to the published opinions or commentary by recognized authorities on a subject will also support your claims. (Note that secondary sources must also be documented—see chapters 20 and 21.)

Logical Fallacies

Fallacies are errors in reasoning—whether deliberate or inadvertent—that weaken an argument and, of course, the quality of the essay that contains the argument. Fallacious arguments seem dishonest whether or not the writer intended them to be. The following list of common fallacies, with examples, is indicative of the types of errors to avoid:

1. *Appeal to strong emotion, belief, or prejudice.*

   Senator Craven has led the fight to preserve the integrity of the American flag. He is a true patriot. Reelect Senator Craven this November.

   The flag causes strong emotional responses in many American citizens, but besides his devotion to this long-time symbol of American values, what else has Senator Craven done? Is his love of the flag the best way to measure his worth?

2. *Appeal to the unknowable.*

   Yes, the film *Topocat* has careless, haphazard editing, but the director and the editor clearly did this on purpose.

   Unless evidence exists, how can a viewer know the intentions of the director and/or editor? How can the writer know?

3. *Appeal to tradition.*

   Our city's practice of encouraging teenagers to steal cellular phones on the second week of each June is a tradition that shouldn't be questioned. We've always done this, and the tradition has popular support.

   Does the fact that this "tradition has popular support" make it right?

4. *Appeal to the certain rather than the uncertain.*

   The VCR is the best way to watch movies at home. Videocassettes throw a good image, and they last a long time. The entertainment industry is wasting its money if it tries to improve upon the VCR.

   The writer argues that whatever is is preferable to whatever might be. Excuse us while we go hitch up the horses.

5. *Use of a red herring.*

   Yes, Senator Craven is being questioned about his campaign finances. But his fight to preserve American morality will go on. There are forces in this country that would destroy the very basis of all we hold sacred.

   Changing the subject is a very old strategy.

6. *Appeal to false authority.*

The Multitrust Investment Company group of mutual funds looks like a sure bet. Have you seen their commercials with Alice McDear, who plays the grandmother on *The Quiet Neighborhood*? She's probably the most trustworthy figure on TV.

Alice McDear, actress and investment wizard, couldn't be wrong, could she?

7. *Attack the person* (also known as *ad hominem attack*).

Senator Craven's new tax bill has some good points, but I must oppose it. Craven has led a life of depravity and dissolution. His struggles with alcohol are legendary. He has been divorced five times. He may be charged with fraud in the near future.

We weren't really thinking about having Senator Craven move in with us, but we were curious about what is in his new tax legislation. Sometimes, imperfect human beings have innovative ideas that are worth considering.

8. *Oversimplify the opponent's stand.*

Senator Gravely: It seems to me that our criminal justice priorities are wrong. We're letting murderers and armed robbers out of jail in order to make room for people convicted of simple drug possession. Illegal drug possession must be punished, but let's find a way to do it that keeps violent criminals—and drug dealers—in prison for their full sentences.
Senator Craven: Just like always, you're soft on crime, sir.

We're glad that Senator Gravely's argument wasn't any more complicated; clearly, Senator Craven does not want to deal with the reality of what Senator Gravely has to say; he simply chooses to make an easy political point.

9. *Beg the question.*

Sexual perversion is wrong because it's illegal. That's enough for me.

Or is it illegal because it's wrong? Perhaps the writer needs to reconsider the whole situation.

10. *Ask a loaded question.*

Reporter: Senator Craven, Senator Craven, are you still abusing alcohol?

If the answer is yes, the senator looks bad; if the answer is no, the senator still looks bad, if only a little less so.

11. *Use an either/or simplification.*

We should either build the new highway extension using the original plan, or we shouldn't build it at all.

Such a pair of choices leaves no room for other options. The dilemma presented is a false one because there almost always *are* more than two options in any given situation.

12. *Mistake correlation for causation* (also known as *post hoc, ergo propter hoc*).

Every time I wear my black sneakers, my basketball team wins. I'll wear them from now on.

Two events can happen simultaneously and coincidentally; this is **correlation,** not to be confused with **causation** (see also Chapter 10).

13. *Put forth a slippery-slope claim.*

If we let students wear T-shirts with obscene messages on them, the next thing we know they'll be smoking pot behind the gymnasium.

Someone who puts forward a slippery-slope claim sees one change as inexorably leading to a more drastic, horrible change when, in fact, the two events may be unrelated, or one event (stricter gun control) may not necessarily have a catastrophic result (total loss of Second Amendment rights).

14. *Make a hasty generalization.*

Jenkins failed in his first attempt to fix our computer network. Computer programmers usually don't know what they're doing.

Give Jenkins another chance or two before condemning him and his profession. One piece of evidence is not enough to support a generalization.

15. *Create a false analogy.*

Nature shows us through evolution that it continually improves plants and animals through natural selection. We don't have anything to do with this process. Therefore I think we should tell the Department of Family Services to leave the eastern part of our county alone. It's a new, fairly unsettled area, and those people will sort things out on their own.

Human society is not like natural evolution; the analogy is patently false.

16. *Use a non sequitur.* In this type of fallacy, a claim "doesn't follow" the evidence or the previous claim.

Eduardo's Embers is the best restaurant in the city, for the apple pie there is wonderful.

This argument is valid only for those on a strict apple-pie diet. Another example:

I should get a raise at the end of this evaluation period. After all, I got a raise at my last three evaluations.

This writer assumes that what has happened in the past will always happen in the future. If this writer were a machine working in a closed, uniform system, the claim might be valid. However, the writer may have not done enough quality work to justify a raise, slacking off from previous evaluation periods; newly hired colleagues may have raised the level of competition; the company may be experiencing short-term financial problems; the company may have been recently acquired by people who believe that the workers are paid too much already. These are the possible factors that could determine if the writer receives a raise, but he or she ignores them in this simple, flawed argument based on a non sequitur.

17. *Omit vital information.* This is a fallacy sometimes deliberately employed by writers who seek to persuade without offering enough reasons and evidence. "Winning" is key for these writers, not fairness.

    Scenario: Townsend High and Parker High are about to have their traditional end-of-season football game. Two weeks ago, Townsend High ran all over Peabody Memorial, 63–7. However, last week Parker High, without the services of its star quarterback, Lance Archer, who was out with the flu, lost a squeaker against Peabody, 17–16. In the upcoming game against Townsend, Archer is expected to return at full strength. However, a local sports columnist has conveniently ignored this fact while arguing for Townsend's supremacy.
    Columnist: "It seems clear we'll be seeing another blowout by Townsend. Two weeks ago they demolished Peabody Memorial, and I think we'll see the same result when they take on hated rival Parker, who couldn't even surmount lowly Peabody. Fans, this one should be a Townsend whitewash."

    This practice of deliberately omitting critical information is highly annoying and unethical; it depends on the reader's lack of knowledge. Skilled, fair-minded arguers learn to avoid this fallacy.

Consider Your Audience and Purpose

When you make an argumentative claim, consider the effect that it will have on your audience. Through the course of this book we have discussed various aspects of the writer-reader relationship, but in argument, this connection is especially important. In no other type of writing is purpose so inextricably connected to audience as in argumentation. As audiences become increasingly global, audience analysis becomes even more critical As you plan and draft your argument, consider the following questions:

1. **Do the reader and I have a common understanding of the central issues?** Successful arguments depend upon assumptions that the writer and the reader share. Most people share certain assumptions about the importance of fairness, equality, and responsibility. However, assumptions about politics, religion, morality, and other contentious areas can vary widely. For example, a writer who holds a very specialized or radical view of international relations—who believes, for instance, that the United States is a global bully that uses its economic and military powers to get its way with weaker countries—should not assume that such a view will be shared by a general audience. In this case, it is very likely that the writer and the reader will be at odds; the reader will not accept the argument because he or she does not accept the assumptions behind it. If the writer had carefully considered both audience and purpose, however, a different essay could have emerged, one that first tried to establish a common area of understanding with the reader, or at least tried to get the reader to understand his or her view. A writer and a reader can have widely varying political views, but it is still possible for them to find common ground.

2. **Have I presented a fair, well-considered argument?** Your reader does *not* want to read a wishy-washy paper that argues both sides but refuses to back either one. However, your reader wants a sense that you have carefully considered the ramifications of your argument and have taken into account opposing views. An argument that stridently opposes a policy but fails to note the positive results of the policy is easy to criticize. A writer who argues that a social change should occur should not be fearful of acknowledging a valid opposing view. For example, we have read many student essays arguing that marijuana should be legal and for sale. These essays almost always have the following two flaws. First, they are written from a position of narrow self-interest. The writer likes marijuana. Pot is illegal, which makes its use inconvenient and dangerous, so the writer seeks to remove this obstacle. Second, the essays fail to address the enormous effect that legalizing marijuana would have on U.S. society, government, and commerce. The reader of such an essay frequently senses that it is just a plea, not a reasoned argument. A paper that acknowledged and/or recognized the validity of opposing views about legalizing marijuana would be a stronger argument. For example, the paper might acknowledge the fact that smoking marijuana impairs motor responses and judgment and that people driving cars or operating heavy machinery while under the influence of marijuana should be arrested and prosecuted, just as drunk drivers are. It might also discuss the long-term health effects of using marijuana and suggest that warning labels like those for tobacco be used with marijuana. Doing so helps show that the writer has thought about this issue carefully, and it adds to the writer's credibility.
3. **Is my audience likely to agree with me already, be neutral, or oppose my claims?** When writing an argument, be careful to assess your audience carefully. Some readers might be quite receptive to your point of view. Others might not have an opinion at all, or they might be of a different mind and hold an opinion diametrically opposed to yours. In case of the latter, you might have to establish some common ground before stating your opinion explicitly.

MORE OPTIONS ONLINE
For more help with problem areas in the argument essay, go to **www.mhhe.com/writingtoday**.

Choosing a Topic

If your instructor lets you choose your own argumentation topic, consider these guidelines:

1. Avoid open-and-shut issues. If the point of your argument is a foregone conclusion—Why can't we all just get along?—then there's no use pursuing it. Choose an issue that has two or more viable positions; then concentrate on one of these.
2. Avoid narrow, personal topics. If your roommate is a slob and you want to argue that his slobbishness (slobdom?) threatens your ongoing living arrangement, then the only two people who are likely to be interested in this argument are you and your roommate. However, a more *general* topic—the threat that slobs pose to shared living quarters—could work quite well. In this approach, your roommate becomes an example: evidence that you can use.

3. Avoid topics that can't be proved. Students who argue on religious or spiritual topics sometimes find themselves backing up their claims by referring to their faith's authoritative text—the Bible or the Koran, for example. Or they may use their fervent personal beliefs as evidence. If you are writing for a general audience, though, neither approach is valid. Faith is faith, and logic is logic; the two have their own uses, but faith doesn't work as evidence to back up the claims of an argumentative essay. However, we're not stating that religion and religious issues are off-limits in argument. There are a vast number of potential topics in this intriguing category that don't have to be settled by referring to one's faith or to a denomination's doctrines.

Prewriting

Writing an argumentative essay requires the generation of a great many ideas and pieces of evidence. Try this approach: use freewriting, brainstorming, or another prewriting method to generate your claims—the major assertions that you plan to make. Then work to generate reasons and evidence for these claims. How will you back up your claims? Will you need to do some research at the library or on the Internet? (See Chapter 20.) Focus on the types of evidence you will use (see also "Using Evidence," pages 441–442).

After this step, review your prewriting. (If you have produced more information than you can use, don't worry. This situation is always preferable to the opposite situation.) Can you turn your output into a coherent argument? Do you need to do more work before you start the organizing phase? Can you develop a preliminary or working thesis at this point?

Organizing

At this point, organize your prewriting into an outline. (Chapter 2 covers informal, sentence, and formal outlines.) If you use a sentence outline, for example, be willing to revise it or construct a new one if, upon review, you decide that it won't work because it doesn't present your reasons in an effective order or it branches off in an irrelevant direction. Plan on organizing until you come up with a paragraph sequence that suits both your thesis and your purpose.

Consider this strategy: build a sentence outline with annotations. In other words, after you complete your outline, add notes (such as "transition here" and "relevance?") where needed. This way, you'll give yourself an extensive framework to use as you begin drafting.

Drafting

To illustrate one approach to writing the argument essay, we have included the essay "Stuck Again."

The Introduction

The introductory section of an argumentative essay explains the situation—the issue that your argument will address. Depending on the nature of your topic and the extent of your assignment, you may need more than one paragraph to introduce your argument. Be aware of the need for balance: although one paragraph may suffice to introduce a twelve-paragraph essay, a three-paragraph introduction is clearly too extensive for a seven-paragraph paper.

The following introduction sets up the essay on student parking fees versus faculty/staff parking fees that we mentioned earlier:

> Stuck Again
>
> Parking is a sore subject on this campus. There is not enough to go around for both students and employees, and when talking to people who've been here a while, I learned that it's been many years since parking was *not* an issue. There seems to be no solution, either. Located as it is in a congested downtown area, the campus cannot acquire any more land. And the administration has been refused twice in its attempts to gain funds to build a parking garage. **However, the administration's latest decision—to lower the yearly rates for faculty/staff by $50 and to increase student rates by the same amount—is unfair, misguided, and cruel.**

The first paragraph describes the situation, then concludes with the thesis: the writer's stance on the issue. From this introduction, the writer could either have gone on to present a one-sided rant against the university administration or develop a carefully balanced argument. Note how the essay continues.

Consider Your Options

Be thorough in the introduction to an argument. Make sure that your reader understands exactly what you plan to argue. Good strategies include opening with an engaging anecdote or a provocative question. (For more on introductions, see Chapter 3.)

The Body

The first body paragraph reveals that the writer has a comprehensive grasp of the situation—he is not going to write a simple rant stemming from his wounded wallet. But after showing his understanding of "the other side," he needs to bring the focus of his writing back to his thesis, which he accomplishes with the first word of his second body paragraph. Read the following passage carefully:

> I understand that parking is a contentious issue for the administration. I also understand that the administration must deal with a lot of issues related to this situation that students don't hear about. And, on a cynical level, I suspect that the administration may be more worried about pleasing a "permanent" group (faculty and staff) than about displeasing a "temporary" group (students) while still increasing revenues, there being many more students at this campus than employees.

Nevertheless, the administration's decision is patently unfair. Faculty and staff have incomes, whereas students may not. If I were employed here, I wouldn't like the fact that I would have to pay to park my vehicle next to my office, but I would at least have a biweekly paycheck, and I would know that I needed to budget for this expense. Students, on the other hand, tend to run short of funds. Many students are on near-starvation diets. Fifty dollars is a lot of money in that type of situation.

The writer's negative transition (*Nevertheless*) refocuses his argument in the direction indicated by his thesis. In this paragraph he offers a claim based on values and fairness—that the administration's decision is unfair—by using inductive reasoning to back up a logical appeal. The next body paragraph uses a different kind of claim:

This administrative step is also misguided. This city is blessed with a number of institutions of higher learning; our university does not have a local or regional monopoly on college courses. On a practical level, the administration may literally be driving students away. (Excuse the pun.) Many students at this school also take classes elsewhere; more students can take this step.

In this paragraph the student uses a **logical appeal:** that the administrative decision is bad for business and therefore misguided. In the final body paragraph the student introduces an **emotional** appeal:

Finally, the parking decision is just one more piece of bad news for students this year. Some people may have forgotten that the campus was haunted by a series of muggings during the fall term, two fraternity pledges were seriously injured in separate hazing incidents, asbestos was discovered in the women's dormitories, and our football and basketball teams both had atrocious seasons. Student morale is not at its highest level. For the administration to announce this decision at this time is just plain cruel.

The Conclusion

The writer could summarize his argument at this point, but the essay is not long enough to require this step. Besides, summaries tend to sound perfunctory and boring. Instead, he takes a different approach, referring first to his second paragraph, then revisiting his thesis, and finally offering a possible solution to the overall problem:

Although the administration has concerns other than the needs of the campus's students, the recent decision on parking fees seems horribly

Consider Your Options

For the conclusion to an argument, summarizing doesn't work as well as reinforcing your thesis. "Seal your case" at this point. (For more on strategies for concluding paragraphs, see Chapter 3.)

misguided. Rather than adding to students' financial burdens, surely the administration could choose a kinder, gentler course of action. At this point, most students would gladly accept a compromise: Why not make everyone pay the same price? This way, at least students wouldn't feel like they were subsidizing the parking costs of faculty and staff.

MORE OPTIONS ONLINE
For more help with the step-by-step development of the argument essay, go to **www.mhhe.com/writingtoday**.

EXERCISE 14.1

Write an outline of "Stuck Again." (For help with outlines, see Chapter 2, pages 41–42.) How has the writer organized his argument? Would a different organization have been more effective? Why?

Revising Your Draft

After you have completed a draft of your argument essay, your next step is to revise it, using your own analysis and comments from classmates or friends. During peer review, answer the following questions about the draft you are reviewing, whether it is yours or another student's.

Questions for Reviewing an Argument Essay

MORE OPTIONS ONLINE
For more help with revision, go to **www.mhhe.com/writingtoday**.

1. Does the introduction provide enough context to set up the rest of the essay?
2. Is there a clear thesis statement, and is the thesis adequately supported by the body paragraphs? How could the thesis or its support be improved?
3. Does the essay show a sufficient sense of its audience? In what ways has the writer demonstrated common ground with the audience? How could the writer strengthen the connection to his or her audience?
4. Has the writer organized the essay effectively? Does it seem coherent and complete?
5. Has the writer avoided using emotional appeals only? If any emotional appeals have been used, are they appropriate and effective?
6. Has the writer used logical reasoning? Are the essay's claims clear, and are they supported by appropriate evidence? Where is clarification or more support needed?
7. Has the writer avoided logical fallacies? Point out any fallacies that you find.
8. Has the writer indicated an awareness of other positions on the issue, and not just his or her stance? How has the writer dealt with these other positions?
9. Does the conclusion adequately reflect the body of the essay? Is it an effective and satisfying conclusion for the argument? What other strategy for concluding the essay might the writer consider?

After reviewing for content, you need to go over your peer reviewers' responses to your essay and then revise for unity, coherence, language level, and tone (see Chapter 4). When you have revised your draft and are basically satisfied with it, read your draft for mechanical and grammatical errors. Concentrate on finding and correcting major sentence errors (fragments, comma splices, fused sentences), errors in pronoun agreement and subject-verb agreement, and spelling.

Now that you have made your corrections, *read your essay one more time* to catch any errors made during revision and find errors missed during your earlier reviews.

EXERCISE 14.1 (page 450)
Answers will vary. The following sentence outline is suggested.

I. Background: Parking on campus is indequate. Thesis: The administration's latest decision to address this issue—to lower the yearly rates for faculty/staff by $50 and to increase student rates by the same amount—is unfair, misguided, and cruel.
II. Parking is a cumbersome issue.
   A. The administration has to deal with issues students don't hear about.
   B. The administration may be more worried about pleased faculty and staff than students.
III. The administration's decision is unfair. Faculty and staff have incomes, whereas students may not.
IV. The administration's step is also misguided: students can go to other schools, as many already do.
V. The parking decision is just one more piece of bad news for students.
   A. Students have had to cope with crime on campus, hazing incidents, asbestos in dorms, and poor performance by sports teams.
   B. It's cruel to announce this decision at this time.
VI. Rather than adding to student's financial burdens, the administration could choose to compromise and make everyone pay the same price.

Student Essay

The following essay is Sam Leininger's response to an argument assignment. Sam's final draft is presented first. Then his first draft is presented, with Sam's comments about this draft and what he needed to do in the revision stage. Note that Sam's tone is somewhat ironic. While appropriate to his audience and purpose, it is not be the kind of tone you should use in most academic arguments.

Sam's Final Draft

My Simple and Modest Plan

1 People make bad decisions on a daily basis: regular unleaded instead of high octane, fat-free ice cream instead of Ben & Jerry's, the American rip-off City of Angels instead of the classic German film Wings of Desire. Most of these decisions come from a lack of taste, and nowhere is lack of taste more apparent than at the local video store. People are not educated, and don't want to be educated, on the quality of movies. They want to be told what to watch, but in a way that makes them feel like they have a choice. If thirty copies of a particular historical boat movie are prominently displayed on the most visible shelves, chances are likely that this movie will be chosen over the British movie from 1958 that deals with this very same historical boat (that is, if A Night to Remember* is even in the store). If people want some direction, it should be provided in a less subtle and more responsible manner; I propose that a series of tests and levels of rental freedom be established to promote a true understanding of cinema as an art form.

****A Night to Remember:*** a film about the sinking of the *Titanic* in 1912.

2 I understand that taste is a subjective entity and that different people watch movies for different reasons. Some like to see car chases and explosions (and feel that elements like dialogue and character development get in the way); others want to see the guy get the girl, no matter what. I've even been known to watch The Trouble with Mary on occasion. I also abhor censorship and the thought of controlling what people can and can't watch. Freedom with limitations is not freedom.

3 However, someone needs to raise the cultural level of society, and we don't seem to be doing this on our own. Under my proposed system, all new video-club members would take a test to determine their existing cinema knowledge. The test would cover technical aspects, film theory, history, and general aesthetics. The member would then be assigned a level of membership based upon the test results. The higher the score on the test, the more freedom the member has. Someone who performs poorly on the test, for instance, would need every movie to be verified by an employee as suitable before rental. This person could never watch any Charlie Sheen movies. Each member's rental history would be followed closely, with rewards given to those with exemplary rental choices. Watching The General (1927) and Battleship Potemkin (1925) would earn even the lowest scoring members any Farley brothers movie they desire. Also, members can retake the test any time they feel able to move up to a higher level of membership.

4 A few rules would also be established that would apply to all members. First, every tenth movie must be foreign. People are often scared away by subtitles, but some of the greatest films have come from other countries. Repeat viewings would not be allowed on all movies. Multiple viewings would be allowed only for films that have a subtle, layered text with motifs and ideas that may not be understood on the first viewing. A member can rent Kids or House of a Thousand Corpses only once, unless a valid, academic reason is supplied. Every member will get a set number of "guilty pleasure" passes that allow him or her to rent any film without reproach, because sometimes people need to see bad films to appreciate the good ones. And, of course, anyone arguing with the decision of the employee will have his or

her membership revoked until a tribunal can be set up to hear the member's argument.

5

This system would never work, however. If there is one thing that people like more than mind-numbing movies, it is screaming about their right to watch mind-numbing movies. I just want to try to pass on a little bit of the knowledge, admiration, and respect I have for filmmakers who take their art seriously enough not to give Ben Affleck a lead role in their films. You can't walk into an art gallery and buy a velvet painting of dogs playing poker or a sculpture of the fat Elvis, but you can walk into a video store and find more bad films on the shelves than good ones. Until something is done to change the way we view movies, both individually and as an art form, cinema will never be recognized for the art that it is.

Sam's First Draft

My Simple and Modest Plan

1

This first draft is an example of me thinking on paper—it's a very fast, rough draft.

People make bad decisions on a daily basis: regular unleaded instead of high octane, fat-free ice cream instead of Ben & Jerry's, City of Angels instead of Wings of Desire. Most of these decisions come from a lack of taste, and nowhere is lack of taste more apparent than at the local video store. People are not educated on the quality of movies. They want to be told what to watch, but in a way that makes them feel good. If 30 copies of a particular historical boat movie are available chances are likely that this movie will be chosen over A Night to Remember. If people want this direction, I think it should be done in a less subtle and more responsible manner; I propose that a series of tests and levels of rental freedom be established.

2

When I write quickly, I tend to lean on abstractions, and this kind of argument better have specific support if it is going to work. In my second draft I filled in the gaps.

I understand that taste is a subjective entity, and that different people watch movies for different reasons. Some like to see car chases and explosions; others want to see the guy get the girl, no matter what. I also abhor censorship and the thought of controlling what people can and can't watch.

3

However, someone needs to raise the cultural level of society. Under my proposed system, every new member will take a test to determine their existing cinema knowledge. The member will then be assigned a level of member-

I added more details here about my proposed system.

ship based upon the test results. The higher the score on the test, the more freedom the member has. Someone who does bad on the test, for instance, will need every movie to be verified by an employee as valid before rental. Each member's rental history will be followed closely, and rewards given to those with exemplary rental choices. Also, members can re-take the test any time they feel able to move up.

4 A few rules would also be set that would apply to all members. First, every tenth movie must be foreign. Repeat viewings will not be allowed on all movies. Multiple viewings should be saved for films that have a subtle, layered text. And, of course, anyone arguing with the decision of the employee will have their membership revoked until a tribunal can be set up to hear the member's argument.

I proofread my second draft carefully to tighten the language and look for grammatical errors, such as this pronoun agreement problem in the fourth sentence.

5 This system would never work, however. If there's one thing that people like more than mind-numbing movies, it's screaming about their Constitutional rights to watch mind-numbing movies. I just want to try and pass on a little bit of the knowledge, admiration, and respect I have for filmmakers who take their art seriously. Until something is done to change the way we view movies, cinema will never be recognized for the art that it is.

A classmate pointed out that watching movies isn't mentioned in the U.S. Constitution.

EXERCISE 14.2: REVISING

The following is the first draft of a student's argument essay. Working in pairs or in small groups, review this essay. Using the Questions for Reviewing an Argument Essay on page 450, decide what revisions you would suggest. If you have any questions the student needs to consider, write them in the margin or on a separate sheet of paper. If your instructor directs you to, rewrite one or more paragraphs to make them stronger and to eliminate any grammatical or mechanical errors.

SUGGESTED ACTIVITY
Consider asking students to meet in writing groups, each of which is charged with producing a more developed and effective version of this essay. Encourage students to provide additional details from their own experience or from their imaginations (such details should be plausible, however).

"Clear Censor Ship"

1 Last Tuesday Morning I was asked to leave my Economics Class. Its not that I was causing a disturbance, its the shirt I was wearing. The Tshirt was a repro of a popular 1970's shirt with the words "Makin' Bacon," it shows two pigs, well getting it own. My professor, dr. Silva found this offensive and told me to leave and to not return wearing this shirt.

First this is censor ship. I'm expressing myself by wearing this, who is dr. Silva to take offensce? Should we ware uniforms to school, so that dear dr. Silva wont feel threaten?

Second I pay my tuition and abide by the rules and nowhere in the rules is their a picture of my shirt with a notice telling me I cant wear it, if their was, I wouldnt be writing this and dr. Silva and I would not be at war as it is I might have to go over her head.

Im being treated like a child, censored against cause of what I wear and I think alot of students would agree with my gripe. Dr. Silva hasnt herd the end of this issue.

2 EXERCISE 14.2 (page 454)
Answers will vary. Students should point out the personal nature of the topic and the need to make it more general, as
3 well as the absence of evidence to back up the reasons the writer offers ("this is censorship" and the lack of a rule about wearing T-shirts), the either/or simplification ("Should we ware uniforms to school"), the hasty generalization ("I
4 think a lot of students would agree with my gripe"), and the writer's failure to consider—and deal with—opposing views about classroom attire.

Additional Writing Topics

1. In a few countries, such as Australia, adults are required by law to vote in national elections. Should the United States adopt such a law?
2. Nonpayment of child support is a massive problem for single mothers and their children. Should court-ordered child support become a payroll deduction for fathers who have been ordered to make such payments?
3. Should a person be allowed to marry someone of the same sex?
4. In most states, the minimum age at which a person can drive a motor vehicle without supervision is sixteen. However, teenagers are involved in far more than their share of serious car accidents. Should the minimum age be raised to nineteen?
5. Should public school students whose first language is not English and who have limited English proficiency be taught subjects like history, science, and mathematics in their own languages until they become proficient in English? Or should they be mainstreamed into classes where only English is spoken?
6. Should taxpayer moneys be used to fund the education of students enrolled in parochial (church-run) schools? If so, why? And what form should this funding take? If not, why not?
7. **Writing on the job.** At the company where you work or where you used to work, what is one part of the company's procedure for dealing with customers or clients that is ineffective and needs to be changed? Write a memo to your manager arguing for this change. (See Chapter 17 for help with writing memos.)

Ernest C. Withers, *I Am a Man.* © Ernest C. Withers. Courtesy, Panopticon Gallery, Waltham, MA.

Responding to a Photograph

CLASSROOM HINT
Item 2 produces interesting essays. However, you will have to help students narrow their topics. Perhaps you might ask them to address two or three premises behind the arguments for civil rights.

In the 1960s, the civil rights movement took to the streets. Protest marches gave the movement media exposure, with images appearing in national magazines and beamed through the airwaves of network television. Ernest C. Withers took the photograph that appears above in 1968.

1. Write an informal response to the photograph. What do you notice? How does the image make you feel? How does the photograph use the argumentation option?

2. The photograph was taken at a time when African Americans were fighting for equal rights and treatment. Using a combination of library and online research, explore the public arguments that the civil rights movement prompted. Remember to narrow your topic so that you can adequately address it. Write a documented essay examining one of these arguments. (For more information on documented essays, see Chapter 21.)

Writing About Film

Philadelphia (1993, PG-13) depicts a young attorney in a high-powered Philadelphia law firm. Secretly gay, the lawyer has contracted HIV, and his firm fires him under false pretexts. What is the argument that the protagonist (Tom Hanks) and his lawyer (Denzel Washington) develop?

Roger and Me (1989, R) is a documentary by Michael Moore in which Moore depicts the economic and social devastation that occurred in Flint, Michigan, when General Motors decided to close its Flint factory, which had been the area's main employer. In the film, Moore also tries repeatedly to interview Roger Smith, the CEO of GM. What is the argument that Moore develops?

Using the Internet

Search the Internet for insights and information to use when developing arguments.

1. Practice spotting logical fallacies by searching for Web sites that present arguments on both sides of an important social, political, moral, or legal issue of your choice. Spend some time on this assignment by reading the perspectives and opinions that are presented on several different Web sites. Then review the material you have researched, and identify examples of at least five of the seventeen logical fallacies discussed on pages 442–445 in this chapter. In a short essay, explain how each of the examples you have chosen illustrates that particular fallacy.
2. Using information taken from the Web sites you visited in response to item 1, write an argument defending a position on the particular social, political, moral, or legal issue addressed in those Web sites. In the process, present and address arguments that oppose your own so that your reader will know that you have considered both sides of the issue.

   As always, combine the information and insights you have researched with your own ideas, but cite any material you quote, summarize, or paraphrase from another source. Use the Modern Language Association (MLA) format or the American Psychological Association (APA) format, explained in Chapter 21 of this textbook.

PEANUTS
by SCHULZ
"WHEN SHE SAW THE LITTLE HOUSE IN THE WOODS, SHE WONDERED WHO LIVED THERE SO SHE KNOCKED AT THE DOOR. NO ONE ANSWERED SO SHE KNOCKED AGAIN."
WHAT DO YOU THINK WILL HAPPEN?
I CAN'T IMAGINE
"...STILL NO ONE ANSWERED, SO GOLDILOCKS OPENED THE DOOR AND WALKED IN. THERE BEFORE HER, IN THE LITTLE ROOM, SHE SAW A TABLE SET FOR THREE..."
"THERE WAS A GREAT BIG BOWL OF PORRIDGE, A MIDDLE-SIZED BOWL OF PORRIDGE, AND A LITTLE, WEE BOWL OF PORRIDGE. SHE TASTED THE GREAT BIG BOWL OF PORRIDGE..."
"'OH, THIS IS TOO HOT,' SHE SAID. THEN SHE TASTED THE MIDDLE-SIZED BOWL OF PORRIDGE. 'OH, THIS IS TOO COLD.' THEN SHE TASTED THE LITTLE, WEE BOWL. 'OH, THIS IS JUST RIGHT,' SHE SAID, AND SHE ATE IT ALL UP."
I HAVE A QUESTION!
ABOUT WHAT?
WELL, IT'S IN REGARD TO COOLING...IT WOULD SEEM TO ME THAT IF THE MIDDLE-SIZED BOWL WAS COLD, THE LITTLE, WEE BOWL WOULD BE COLD, TOO, RATHER THAN 'JUST RIGHT,' AND..
POW!
I NEVER EVEN BROUGHT UP THE FAR MORE OBVIOUS POINT OF UNLAWFUL ENTRY!
SCHULZ

THE BLENDED ESSAY

CHAPTER 15

Writing in Context

Bob has sent you a memo:

> It's review time. I'll be assessing your first ninety days with the company a week from Friday. Before then, I'd like you to send me an account of your experiences. What did you expect of your new position? What problems did you face? How did you deal with them? How do you think you performed during your probationary period?

Your first thought after absorbing this memo is that the biggest problem you faced was Bob, but you doubt that this fact will appear in your self-review. Past that, you find a jumble of impressions and memories. Certainly, there were expectations that weren't met, and a lot of surprises. There were long-running events that you'll want to briefly narrate, and there were situations whose causes you'll want to analyze and explain. You believe that your first ninety-day period was a success, and you think that Bob shares this belief. However, quite apart from the fact that you don't really trust Bob, in this self-review you should be making a case for yourself, so you'll need to have more than a hint of argument in your account.

In any case, you're going to have to integrate a number of strategies to put together an effective document.

The document Bob is asking for demands that you use multiple rhetorical options in order to explain various aspects of a complex situation: your performance at work. Many complex situations call for such an approach.

SUGGESTED ACTIVITY
Have students consider which rhetorical options Lucy and Linus are using in this cartoon. What other options might Lucy have used in her story? What other options might Linus have used to critique the story Lucy tells?

CLASSROOM HINT
Spend class time reviewing the materials on the next few pages.

HOW DOES THE BLENDED ESSAY WORK?

In the preceding nine chapters, we have discussed individual rhetorical options. Yet in each chapter we have also shown how writers use other strategies inside their essays to strengthen the essays' overall effectiveness. In reality, a writer would find it very difficult to write an essay of any length by using only one strategy. One *could* write a pure description or narration, but the reader might wonder about the essay's purpose. A good essay is one that "seizes" the reader, and it is able to do this precisely because it is generated through a more complicated process, involving multiple strategies. Every week and every month, you can read excellent essays in major newspapers and journals of opinion, and in many or most cases you would be hard-pressed to point out a dominant strategy. The writers organize their work according to the needs of their often complicated subjects.

Let's take what seems to be a simple topic and see what happens. If you were sent to visit a greenhouse as part of a field trip and asked to give an account of your visit, two obvious strategies come to mind: description and narration. But a more thorough approach would also use some or all of the following methods:

- **Definition:** explaining the specialized terms used in the greenhouse business
- **Classification:** discussing how the greenhouse's products are grouped
- **Process analysis:** recounting the steps or procedures used by the greenhouse manager
- **Causal analysis:** discussing why problems occur and what steps are taken to avoid them
- **Comparison/contrast:** examining successful plant species versus unsuccessful plant species, last year's business versus this year's, your expectations of the greenhouse versus its reality
- **Exemplification:** using specific examples to support the general points that you are trying to make

With these ideas in mind, you could write a very thorough account of your visit. There is no need to concentrate on one strategy when you can use several and thereby enhance your account. Notice also that by thinking in terms of these strategies, you might be better able to generate ideas.

You may well find such a combined approach useful when responding to writing assignments in your college classes. We have mentioned that your instructors' assignments sometimes point you toward an obvious strategy: by the wording of the assignment, your instructor is signaling what strategy he or she expects. However, in many instances the assignment is more open, as in the following example: "Describe the political environment in the years leading up to the passage of the Volstead Act."

Prohibition came into being after the passage of the Eighteenth Amendment to the U.S. Constitution. The Volstead Act, which was passed in 1919 to establish the guidelines for Prohibition, was an enormously controversial law. On one side was the temperance movement, whose supporters were concerned about drinking and its consequences—and this was before most people drove cars. On the other side of the debate were the business interests involved in the manufacture, distribution, and sale of alcoholic beverages, along with a large number of citizens who did not want their drinking privileges to disappear. The anti-alcohol forces won, and Prohibition lasted until President Franklin D. Roosevelt engineered its repeal in 1933.

The assignment asks the writer to "describe," but the word is not used in a literal sense here. What the instructor actually wants is for the writer to "tell me what you know, and show me how well you understand the big picture."

What approaches might the writer take? A successful response probably would include some or all of the following strategies:

- **Narration.** The assignment, after all, asks for a discussion of "the years leading up to . . .," so a chronological ordering would be hard to fault.
- **Exemplification.** Specific examples can back up any general statements that the writer makes.
- **Causal analysis.** What spurred the temperance movement? How did the liquor interests first react to the attempts to create a constitutional amendment restricting alcoholic beverages?
- **Process analysis.** How did the temperance movement convince the necessary number of state legislatures to ratify the amendment?
- **Comparison/contrast.** On the surface, the two opposing groups seem radically different, so this approach is an obvious one.
- **Classification.** Did everyone in the temperance movement believe in the same "party line," or were there factions?
- **Definition.** The word *temperance* means "moderation," not "abstinence." This historical irony could be explored.
- **Argument.** Could it be argued that Prohibition was inevitable, given the social, cultural, and political climate of the era? Or could it be argued that Prohibition was a poorly thought out solution to a complex social problem?

Being able to combine rhetorical options as needed is a valuable skill. However, keep in mind that this approach to the essay demands careful forethought, not a haphazard mixing of approaches. A typical blended essay depends on three or four rhetorical options—used as needed when the writer's purpose demands them. They serve the point that the writer is trying to make, not the other way around.

You have studied the dominant rhetorical options, have seen how published writers use them, and have written your own essays that concentrate on one of the rhetorical options. After reading the following essays and the rest of the chapter, you should be ready to write your own blended essay.

Consider Your Options

Reread the anecdote that opens this chapter. Have you faced circumstances on the job or in college that required you to produce a complex, multi-option document or oral response? How did you decide which options to use?

READING THE BLENDED ESSAY WITH A WRITER'S EYE

In the following selections, Scott Russell Sanders explores different perspectives on male privilege, Anthony Bourdain gives the inside scoop on the restaurant business, Elisabeth Kübler-Ross explores the inability of many Americans to deal with the inevitability of death, and Robert B. Reich explains why the gap between rich and poor in the United States is growing ever wider. As you read each essay, look for the strategies that the writer uses.

After each of these essays, we will ask questions about the various strategies used in the essay. Writing topics are located at the end of the chapter (pages 490–492).

The Men We Carry in Our Minds

SCOTT RUSSELL SANDERS

With a bachelor's degree from Brown University, a doctorate from Cambridge University in England, a professorship at Indiana University, and several published books, Scott Russell Sanders would seem to be high up in the American social class system. Yet Sanders comes from a working-class background, and in the following essay, originally published in *Milkweed Chronicle* and collected in his *Paradise of Bombs* (1987), he describes how his background gives him a different outlook on the issue of male privilege.

1 When I was a boy, the men I knew labored with their bodies. They were marginal farmers, just scraping by, or welders, steelworkers, carpenters; they swept floors, dug ditches, mined coal, or drove trucks, their forearms ropy with muscle; they trained horses, stoked furnaces, built tires, stood on assembly lines wrestling parts onto cars and refrigerators. They got up before light, worked all day long whatever the weather, and when they came home at night they looked as though somebody had been whipping them. In the evenings and on weekends they worked on their own places, tilling gardens that were lumpy with clay, fixing broken-down cars, hammering on houses that were always too drafty, too leaky, too small.

2 The bodies of the men I knew were twisted and maimed in ways visible and invisible. The nails of their hands were black and split, the hands tattooed with scars. Some had lost fingers. Heavy lifting had given many of them finicky backs and guts weak from hernias. Racing against conveyor belts had given them ulcers. Their ankles and knees ached from years of standing on concrete. Anyone who had worked for long around machines was hard of hearing. They squinted, and the skin of their faces was creased like the leather of old work gloves. There were times, studying them, when I dreaded growing up. Most of them coughed, from dust or cigarettes, and most of them drank cheap wine or whiskey, so their eyes looked bloodshot and bruised. The fathers of my friends always seemed older than the mothers. Men wore out sooner. Only women lived into old age.

3 As a boy I also knew another sort of men, who did not sweat and break down like mules. They were soldiers, and so far as I could tell they scarcely worked at all. During my early school years we lived on a military base, an arsenal in Ohio, and every day I saw GIs in the guardshacks, on the stoops of barracks, at the wheels of olive drab Chevrolets. The chief fact of their lives was boredom. Long after I left the Arsenal I came to recognize the sour smell the soldiers gave off as that of souls in limbo. They were all waiting—for wars, for transfers, for leaves, for promotions, for the end of their hitch—like so many braves waiting for the hunt to begin. Unlike the warriors of older tribes, however, they would have no say about when the battle would start or how it would be waged. Their waiting was broken only when

they practiced for war. They fired guns at targets, drove tanks across the churned-up fields of the military reservation, set off bombs in the wrecks of old fighter planes. I knew this was all play. But I also felt certain that when the hour for killing arrived, they would kill. When the real shooting started, many of them would die. This was what soldiers were *for,* just as a hammer was for driving nails.

4 Warriors and toilers: those seemed, in my boyhood vision, to be the chief destinies for men. They weren't the only destinies, as I learned from having a few male teachers, from reading books, and from watching television. But the men on television—the politicians, the astronauts, the generals, the savvy lawyers, the philosophical doctors, the bosses who gave orders to both soldiers and laborers—seemed as removed and unreal to me as the figures in tapestries. I could no more imagine growing up to become one of these cool, potent creatures than I could imagine becoming a prince.

5 A nearer and more hopeful example was that of my father, who had escaped from a red-dirt farm to a tire factory, and from the assembly line to the front office. Eventually he dressed in a white shirt and tie. He carried himself as if he had been born to work with his mind. But his body, remembering the earlier years of slogging work, began to give out on him in his fifties, and it quit on him entirely before he turned sixty-five. Even such a partial escape from man's fate as he had accomplished did not seem possible for most of the boys I knew. They joined the Army, stood in line for jobs in the smoky plants, helped build highways. They were bound to work as their fathers had worked, killing themselves or preparing to kill others.

6 A scholarship enabled me not only to attend college, a rare enough feat in my circle, but even to study in a university meant for the children of the rich. Here I met for the first time young men who had assumed from birth that they would lead lives of comfort and power. And for the first time I met women who told me that men were guilty of having kept all the joys and privileges of the earth for themselves. I was baffled. What privileges? What joys? I thought about the maimed, dismal lives of most of the men back home. What had they stolen from their wives and daughters? The right to go five days a week, twelve months a year, for thirty or forty years to a steel mill or a coal mine? The right to drop bombs and die in war? The right to feel every leak in the roof, every gap in the fence, every cough in the engine, as a wound they must mend? The right to feel, when the lay-off comes or the plant shuts down, not only afraid but ashamed?

7 I was slow to understand the deep grievances of women. This was because, as a boy, I had envied them. Before college, the only people I had ever known who were interested in art or music or literature, the only ones who read books, the only ones who ever seemed to enjoy a sense of ease and grace were the mothers and daughters. Like the menfolk, they fretted about money, they scrimped and made-do. But, when the pay stopped coming in, they were not the ones who had failed. Nor did they have to go to war, and that seemed to me a blessed fact. By comparison with the narrow, ironclad days of fathers, there was an expansiveness, I thought, in the days of mothers. They went to see neighbors, to shop in town, to run errands at school, at the library, at church. No doubt, had I looked harder at their lives, I would have envied them less. It was not my fate to become a woman, so it was easier for me to see the graces. Few of them held jobs outside the home, and those who did filled thankless roles as clerks and waitresses. I didn't see, then, what a prison a house could be, since houses seemed to me brighter, handsomer

places than any factory. I did not realize—because such things were never spoken of—how often women suffered from men's bullying. I did learn about the wretchedness of abandoned wives, single mothers, widows; but I also learned about the wretchedness of lone men. Even then I could see how exhausting it was for a mother to cater all day to the needs of young children. But if I had been asked, as a boy, to choose between tending a baby and tending a machine, I think I would have chosen the baby. (Having now tended both, I know I would choose the baby.)

So I was baffled when the women at college accused me and my sex of having cornered the world's pleasures. I think something like my bafflement has been felt by other boys (and by girls as well) who grew up in dirt-poor farm country, in mining country, in black ghettos, in Hispanic barrios, in the shadows of factories, in Third World nations—any place where the fate of men is as grim and bleak as the fate of women. Toilers and warriors. I realize now how ancient these identities are, how deep the tug they exert on men, the undertow of a thousand generations. The miseries I saw, as a boy, in the lives of nearly all men I continue to see in the lives of many—the body-breaking toil, the tedium, the call to be tough, the humiliating powerlessness, the battle for a living and for territory. 8

When the women I met at college thought about the joys and privileges of men, they did not carry in their minds the sort of men I had known in my childhood. They thought of their fathers, who were bankers, physicians, architects, stockbrokers, the big wheels of the big cities. These fathers rode the train to work or drove cars that cost more than any of my childhood houses. They were attended from morning to night by female helpers, wives and nurses and secretaries. They were never laid off, never short of cash at month's end, never lined up for welfare. These fathers made decisions that mattered. They ran the world. 9

The daughters of such men wanted to share in this power, this glory. So did I. They yearned for a say over their future, for jobs worthy of their abilities, for the right to live at peace, unmolested, whole. Yes, I thought, yes yes. The difference between me and these daughters was that they saw me, because of my sex, as destined from birth to become like their fathers, and therefore as an enemy to their desires. But I knew better. I wasn't an enemy, in fact or in feeling. I was an ally. If I had known, then, how to tell them so, would they have believed me? Would they now? 10

STYLE AND STRATEGY

1. Paragraphs 1, 2, and 3 compare soldiers and laborers; paragraph 4 contrasts soldiers and laborers with those "men on television"; paragraph 6 contrasts the author's vision of men with the vision of men held by women he meets at the university; paragraph 7 contrasts the author's two visions of women; paragraph 10 compares and contrasts the author with the daughters of the rich.

Vocabulary

The following terms are identified by paragraph number. Make sure that you understand each term's meaning in its context. If you're not sure that you understand a term, look it up in a college-level dictionary.

marginal (1)	limbo (3)	grievances (7)
stoked (1)	hitch (3)	scrimped (7)
tilling (1)	churned (3)	ironclad (7)
maimed (2)	toilers (4)	expansiveness (7)
arsenal (3)	savvy (4)	barrios (8)
stoops (3)	tapestries (4)	ally (10)

Style and Strategy

1. How and where does Sanders use comparison/contrast? Give specific examples.
2. Where does Sanders use (a) description, (b) narration, (c) definition, and (d) process analysis?
3. What does the author's conclusion reveal about his purpose?
4. How did Sanders's reaction to the "deep grievances of women" (paragraph 7) change over time? What understanding did he gain that made this change possible?

2. Description appears in paragraphs 3 and 5; narration in paragraphs 1 and 3; definition in paragraphs 1, 2 , 3, and 4; process analysis in paragraphs 6 and 8.
3. Students offer various interpretations, but Sanders seems to be attempting definition of self. He is also arguing that the dreams of women are the same as those of men who have

grown up in poor or blue-collar families.
4. In paragraph 9, Sanders makes it clear that he understands why university women hold the views they hold.

Questions for Critical Thinking and Discussion

1. What is your dominant perception of the role of men? Is it different from the one that Sanders describes himself as having had when he was young?
2. What do you think marriage will be like in the future? Will there ever be true equality between men and women?
3. Colleges and universities are frequently accused of being "ivory towers," places set apart from the realities of daily life to such an extent that the opinions of academics are seen to be somewhat dubious outside their areas of expertise. Regarding your college's faculty, what have been your experiences so far?

QUESTIONS FOR CRITICAL THINKING AND DISCUSSION When item 1 is discussed in class, opinions often divide along gender lines. Item 2 makes an interesting prompt for sustained writing, but students should focus on marriage in the future. Item 3 elicits a variety of responses, but if handled correctly, it encourages critical thinking.

Don't Eat Before Reading This

ANTHONY BOURDAIN

Anthony Bourdain is a long-time chef and the author of two novels, *Bone in the Throat* (1995) and *Gone Bamboo* (1997). He published the following article in *The New Yorker* on April 19, 1999. The article's success prompted a publisher to ask Bourdain to use it as the basis of a book, which appeared as the highly regarded *Kitchen Confidential: Adventures in the Culinary Underbelly* (2000). In 2001 Bourdain also published *A Cook's Tour: In Search of the Perfect Meal.* He currently appears on the Food Network as host of *A Cook's Tour.*

"Don't Eat Before Reading This" is an essay in which an industry insider lets the secrets out. As you read Bourdain's essay, notice how he structures his various and fascinating confessions.

1 Good food, good eating, is all about blood and organs, cruelty and decay. It's about sodium-loaded pork fat, stinky triple-cream cheeses, the tender thymus glands and distended livers of young animals. It's about danger—risking the dark, bacterial forces of beef, chicken, cheese, and shellfish. Your first two hundred and seven Wellfleet oysters may transport you to a state of rapture, but your two hundred and eighth may send you to bed with the sweats, chills, and vomits.

2 Gastronomy is the science of pain. Professional cooks belong to a secret society whose ancient rituals derive from the principles of stoicism in the face of humiliation, injury, fatigue, and the threat of illness. The members of a tight, well-greased kitchen staff are a lot like a submarine crew. Confined for most of their waking hours in hot, airless spaces, and ruled by despotic leaders, they often acquire the

characteristics of the poor saps who were press-ganged into the royal navies of Napoleonic times—superstition, a contempt for outsiders, and a loyalty to no flag but their own.

3 A good meal has changed since Orwell's memoir of the months he spent as a dishwasher in "Down and Out in Paris and London." Gas ranges and exhaust fans have gone a long way toward increasing the life span of the working culinarian. Nowadays, most aspiring cooks come into the business because they want to: they have chosen this life, studied for it. Today's top chefs are like star athletes. They bounce from kitchen to kitchen—free agents in search of more money, more acclaim.

4 I've been a chef in New York for more than ten years, and, for the decade before that, a dishwasher, a prep drone, a line cook, and a sous-chef. I came into the business when cooks still smoked on the line and wore headbands. A few years ago, I wasn't surprised to hear rumors of a study of the nation's prison population which reportedly found that the leading civilian occupation among inmates before they were put behind bars was "cook." As most of us in the restaurant business know, there is a powerful strain of criminality in the industry, ranging from the dope-dealing busboy with beeper and cell phone to the restaurant owner who has two sets of accounting books. In fact, it was the unsavory side of professional cooking that attracted me to it in the first place. In the early seventies, I dropped out of college and transferred to the Culinary Institute of America. I wanted it all: the cuts and burns on hands and wrists, the ghoulish kitchen humor, the free food, the pilfered booze, the camaraderie that flourished within rigid order and nerve-shattering chaos. I would climb the chain of command from *mal carne* (meaning "bad meat," or "new guy") to chefdom—doing whatever it took until I ran my own kitchen and had my own crew of cutthroats, the culinary equivalent of "The Wild Bunch."

5 A year ago, my latest, doomed mission—a high-profile restaurant in the Times Square area—went out of business. The meat, fish, and produce purveyors got the news that they were going to take it in the neck for yet another ill-conceived enterprise. When customers called for reservations, they were informed by a prerecorded announcement that our doors had closed. Fresh from that experience, I began thinking about becoming a traitor to my profession.

6 Say it's a quiet Monday night, and you've just checked your coat in that swanky Art Deco update in the Flatiron district, and you're looking to tuck into a thick slab of pepper-crusted yellowfin tuna or a twenty-ounce cut of certified Black Angus beef, well-done—what are you in for?

7 The fish specialty is reasonably priced, and the place got two stars in the *Times.* Why not go for it? If you like four-day-old fish, be my guest. Here's how things usually work. The chef orders his seafood for the weekend on Thursday night. It arrives on Friday morning. He's hoping to sell the bulk of it on Friday and Saturday nights, when he knows that the restaurant will be busy, and he'd like to run out of the last few orders by Sunday evening. Many fish purveyors don't deliver on Saturday, so the chances are that the Monday-night tuna you want has been kicking around in the kitchen since Friday morning, under God knows what conditions. When a kitchen is in full swing, proper refrigeration is almost nonexistent, what with the many openings of the refrigerator door as the cooks rummage frantically during the rush, mingling your tuna with the chicken, the lamb, or the beef. Even if the chef has ordered just the right amount of tuna for the weekend, and has had to reorder it for a Monday delivery, the only safeguard against the seafood supplier's

off-loading junk is the presence of a vigilant chef who can make sure that the delivery is fresh from *Sunday* night's market.

8 Generally speaking, the good stuff comes in on Tuesday: the seafood is fresh, the supply of prepared food is new, and the chef, presumably, is relaxed after his day off. (Most chefs don't work on Monday.) Chefs prefer to cook for weekday customers rather than for weekenders, and they like to start the new week with their most creative dishes. In New York, locals dine during the week. Weekends are considered amateur nights—for tourists, rubes, and the well-done-ordering pretheatre hordes. The fish may be just as fresh on Friday, but it's on Tuesday that you've got the good will of the kitchen on your side.

9 People who order their meat well-done perform a valuable service for those of us in the business who are cost-conscious: they pay for the privilege of eating our garbage. In many kitchens, there's a time-honored practice called "save for well-done." When one of the cooks finds a particularly unlovely piece of steak—tough, riddled with nerve and connective tissue, off the hip end of the loin, and maybe a little stinky from age—he'll dangle it in the air and say, "Hey, Chef, whaddya want me to do with *this*?" Now, the chef has three options. He can tell the cook to throw the offending item into the trash, but that means a total loss, and in the restaurant business every item of cut, fabricated, or prepared food should earn at least three times the amount it originally cost if the chef is to make his correct food-cost percentage. Or he can decide to serve that steak to "the family"—that is, the floor staff—though that, economically, is the same as throwing it out. But no. What he's going to do is repeat the mantra of cost-conscious chefs everywhere: "Save for well-done." The way he figures it, the philistine who orders his food well-done is not likely to notice the difference between food and flotsam.

10 Then there are the People Who Brunch. The "B" word is dreaded by all dedicated cooks. We hate the smell and spatter of omelettes. We despise hollandaise, home fries, those pathetic fruit garnishes, and all the other cliché accompaniments designed to induce a credulous public into paying $12.95 for two eggs. Nothing demoralizes an aspiring Escoffier faster than requiring him to cook egg-white omelettes or eggs over easy with bacon. You can dress brunch up with all the focaccia, smoked salmon, and caviar in the world, but it's still breakfast.

11 Even more despised than the Brunch People are the vegetarians. Serious cooks regard these members of the dining public—and their Hezbollah-like splinter faction, the vegans—as enemies of everything that's good and decent in the human spirit. To live life without veal or chicken stock, fish cheeks, sausages, cheese, or organ meats is treasonous.

12 Like most other chefs I know, I'm amused when I hear people object to pork on nonreligious grounds. "Swine are filthy animals," they say. These people have obviously never visited a poultry farm. Chicken—America's favorite food—goes bad quickly; handled carelessly, it infects other foods with salmonella; and it bores the hell out of chefs. It occupies its ubiquitous place on menus as an option for customers who can't decide what they want to eat. Most chefs believe that supermarket chickens in this country are slimy and tasteless compared with European varieties. Pork, on the other hand, is cool. Farmers stopped feeding garbage to pigs decades ago, and even if you eat pork rare you're more likely to win the Lotto than to contract trichinosis. Pork tastes different, depending on what you do with it, but chicken always tastes like chicken.

Another much maligned food these days is butter. In the world of chefs, however, butter is in *everything.* Even non-French restaurants—the Northern Italian; the new American, the ones where the chef brags about how he's "getting away from butter and cream"—throw butter around like crazy. In almost every restaurant worth patronizing, sauces are enriched with mellowing, emulsifying butter. Pastas are tightened with it. Meat and fish are seared with a mixture of butter and oil. Shallots and chicken are caramelized with butter. It's the first and last thing in almost every pan: the final hit is called "*monter au beurre.*" In a good restaurant, what this all adds up to is that you could be putting away almost a stick of butter with every meal. 13

If you are one of those people who cringe at the thought of strangers fondling your food, you shouldn't go out to eat. As the author and former chef Nicholas Freeling notes in his definitive book "The Kitchen," the better the restaurant, the more your food has been prodded, poked, handled, and tasted. By the time a three-star crew has finished carving and arranging your saddle of monkfish with dried cherries and wild-herb-infused *nage* into a Parthenon or a Space Needle, it's had dozens of sweaty fingers all over it. Gloves? You'll find a box of surgical gloves—in my kitchen we call them "anal-research gloves"—over every station on the line, for the benefit of the health inspectors, but does anyone actually use them? Yes, a cook will slip on a pair every now and then, especially when he's handling something with a lingering odor, like salmon. But during the hours of service gloves are clumsy and dangerous. When you're using your hands constantly, latex will make you drop things, which is the last thing you want to do. 14

Finding a hair in your food will make anyone gag. But just about the only place you'll see anyone in the kitchen wearing a hat or a hairnet is Blimpie. For most chefs, wearing anything on their head, especially one of those picturesque paper toques—they're often referred to as "coffee filters"—is a nuisance: they dissolve when you sweat, bump into range hoods, burst into flame. 15

The fact is that most good kitchens are far less septic than your kitchen at home. I run a scrupulously clean, orderly restaurant kitchen, where food is rotated and handled and stored very conscientiously. But if the city's Department of Health or the E.P.A. decided to enforce every aspect of its codes, most of us would be out on the street. Recently, there was a news report about the practice of recycling bread. By means of a hidden camera in a restaurant, the reporter was horrified to see returned bread being sent right back out to the floor. This, to me, wasn't news: the reuse of bread has been an open secret—and a fairly standard practice—in the industry for years. It makes more sense to worry about what happens to the leftover table butter—many restaurants recycle it for hollandaise. 16

What do I like to eat after hours? Strange things. Oysters are my favorite, especially at three in the morning, in the company of my crew. Focaccia pizza with robiola cheese and white truffle oil is good, especially at Le Madri on a summer afternoon in the outdoor patio. Frozen vodka at Siberia Bar is also good, particularly if a cook from one of the big hotels shows up with beluga. At Indigo, on Tenth Street, I love the mushroom strudel and the daube of beef. At my own place, I love a spicy boudin noir that squirts blood in your mouth; the braised fennel the way my sous-chef makes it; scraps from duck confit; and fresh cockles steamed with greasy Portuguese sausage. 17

I love the sheer weirdness of the kitchen life: the dreamers, the crackpots, the refugees, and the sociopaths with whom I continue to work; the ever-present smells 18 of roasting bones, searing fish, and simmering liquids; the noise and clatter, the hiss and spray, the flames, the smoke, and the steam. Admittedly, it's a life that grinds you down. Most of us who live and operate in the culinary underworld are in some fundamental way dysfunctional. We've all chosen to turn our backs on the nine-to-five, on ever having a Friday or Saturday night off, on ever having a normal relationship with a non-cook.

19 Being a chef is a lot like being an air-traffic controller: you are constantly dealing with the threat of disaster. You've got to be Mom and Dad, drill sergeant, detective, psychiatrist, and priest to a crew of opportunistic, mercenary hooligans, whom you must protect from the nefarious and often foolish strategies of owners. Year after year, cooks contend with bouncing paychecks, irate purveyors, desperate owners looking for the masterstroke that will cure their restaurant's ills: Live Cabaret! Free Shrimp! New Orleans Brunch!

20 In America, the professional kitchen is the last refuge of the misfit. It's a place for people with bad pasts to find a new family. It's a haven for foreigners—Ecuadorians, Mexicans, Chinese, Senegalese, Egyptians, Poles. In New York, the main linguistic spice is Spanish. "*Hey, maricón! Chupa mis huevos*" means, roughly, "How are you, valued comrade? I hope all is well." And you hear "*Hey, baboso!* Put some more brown jiz on the fire and check your meez before the sous comes back there and fucks you in the *culo!,*" which means "Please reduce some additional *demi-glace,* brother, and reëxamine your *mise en place,* because the sous-chef is concerned about your state of readiness."

21 Since we work in close quarters, and so many blunt and sharp objects are at hand, you'd think that cooks would kill one another with regularity. I've seen guys duking it out in the waiter station over who gets a table for six. I've seen a chef clamp his teeth on a waiter's nose. And I've seen plates thrown—I've even thrown a few myself—but I've never heard of one cook jamming a boning knife into another cook's rib cage or braining him with a meat mallet. Line cooking, done well, is a dance—a high-speed, Balanchine collaboration.

22 I used to be a terror toward my floor staff, particularly in the final months of my last restaurant. But not anymore. Recently, my career has taken an eerily appropriate turn: these days, I'm the chef de cuisine of a much loved, old-school French brasserie/bistro where the customers eat their meat rare, vegetarians are scarce, and every part of the animal—hooves, snout, cheeks, skin, and organs—is avidly and appreciatively prepared and consumed. Cassoulet, pigs' feet, tripe, and charcuterie sell like crazy. We thicken many sauces with foie gras and pork blood, and proudly hurl around spoonfuls of duck fat and butter, and thick hunks of country bacon. I made a traditional French pot-au-feu a few weeks ago, and some of my French colleagues—hardened veterans of the business all—came into my kitchen to watch the first order go out. As they gazed upon the intimidating heap of short ribs, oxtail, beef shoulder, cabbage, turnips, carrots, and potatoes, the expressions on their faces were those of religious supplicants. I have come home.

Vocabulary

The following terms are identified by paragraph number. Make sure that you understand each term's meaning in its context. If you're not sure that you understand a term, look it up in a college-level dictionary.

distended (1)
rapture (1)
gastronomy (2)
stoicism (2)
despotic (2)
memoir (3)
culinarian (3)
acclaim (3)
drone (4)
sous-chef (4)
pilfered (4)
camaraderie (4)
purveyor (5)
vigilant (7)
hordes (8)
fabricated (9)
mantra (9)
philistine (9)
flotsam (9)
credulous (10)
demoralize (10)
faction (11)
ubiquitous (12)
trichinosis (12)
patronizing (13)
emulsifying (13)
definitive (14)
toque (15)
septic (16)
sociopath (18)
opportunistic (19)
mercenary (19)
hooligans (19)
nefarious (19)
misfit (20)
supplicants (22)

STYLE AND STRATEGY
1. The thesis appears at the end of paragraph 5.
2. Definition appears in paragraphs 2, 9, 10, 11, and 18. Besides adding interest and clarity, definition helps make Bourdain's "confessions" more credible and convincing.
3. Narration appears in paragraphs 4, 5, and 22. Narration both advances the explanation and establishes Bourdain's authority.
4. It adds to the oddity of the atmosphere the author describes.
5. In paragraph 8, the author mentions the discerning patron who is interested in "dining" on well-prepared food and who knows what's good. In paragraphs 9, 10, 11, 12, 13, and 14, he describes several customer types who really don't know a lot about good food or the restaurant business.
6. Contrast appears in paragraphs 3, 4, 8, 12, 13, 16, and 21.

Style and Strategy

1. What is Bourdain's thesis, and where does it appear?
2. In which paragraphs does Bourdain use definition? What does this option contribute to his essay?
3. Where does the author use narration? What does this option contribute to his essay?
4. In paragraph 17, why does Bourdain include the passage about his after-hours eating habits? Does this inclusion add to or detract from his behind-the-scenes analysis? Explain.
5. The author contrasts two types of very different customers, one of which has various subtypes. What are the two types?
6. What other examples of contrast do you find in this essay?

Questions for Critical Thinking and Discussion

1. Have you ever been involved in a process—during a job, say—that occurs largely away from the public eye? Describe the process, indicating what aspects would be likely to surprise people.
2. How safe are we when we entrust ourselves to strangers? For example, think of car repair, medical care, retail credit-card processing, and the keeping of personal records.

QUESTIONS FOR CRITICAL THINKING AND DISCUSSION
Students can use a variety of techniques to answer these questions if you choose to turn them into writing prompts. However, encourage them to include specific examples, whatever other approaches they use.

On the Fear of Death

ELISABETH KÜBLER-ROSS

A native of Switzerland, Dr. Elisabeth Kübler-Ross (1926–2004) was a pioneer in the study of aging and dying. Her books include the path-breaking *On Death and Dying* (1969); *Death: The Final State* (1974); *On Childhood and Death* (1985); *AIDS: The Ultimate Challenge* (1987); *On Life and Death* (1991);

The Wheel of Life: A Memoir of Living and Dying (1997), her autobiography; and *Life Lessons: Two Experts on Death and Dying Teach Us About the Mysteries of Life and Living* (2000, with David Kessler).

In "On the Fear of Death," which is excerpted from *On Death and Dying*, Kübler-Ross contrasts "natural" approaches to death with "modern" approaches, pointing out that the latter approaches stem from a fear of death that pervades Western culture.

> Let me not pray to be sheltered from dangers but to be fearless in facing them.
> Let me not beg for the stilling of my pain but for the heart to conquer it.
> Let me not look for allies in life's battlefield but to my own strength.
> Let me not crave in anxious fear to be saved but hope for the patience to win my freedom.
> Grant me that I may not be a coward, feeling your mercy in my success alone; but let me find the grasp of your hand in my failure.
>
> —Rabindranath Tagore, *Fruit-Gathering*

1 Epidemics have taken a great toll of lives in past generations. Death in infancy and early childhood was frequent and there were few families who didn't lose a member of the family at an early age. Medicine has changed greatly in the last decades. Widespread vaccinations have practically eradicated many illnesses, at least in western Europe and the United States. The use of chemotherapy, especially the antibiotics, has contributed to an ever decreasing number of fatalities in infectious diseases. Better child care and education have effected a low morbidity and mortality among children. The many diseases that have taken an impressive toll among the young and middle-aged have been conquered. The number of old people is on the rise, and with this fact come the number of people with malignancies and chronic diseases associated more with old age.

2 Pediatricians have less work with acute and life-threatening situations as they have an ever increasing number of patients with psychosomatic disturbances and adjustment and behavior problems. Physicians have more people in their waiting rooms with emotional problems than they have ever had before, but they also have more elderly patients who not only try to live with their decreased physical abilities and limitations but who also face loneliness and isolation with all its pains and anguish. The majority of these people are not seen by a psychiatrist. Their needs have to be elicited and gratified by other professional people, for instance, chaplains and social workers. It is for them that I am trying to outline the changes that have taken place in the last few decades, changes that are ultimately responsible for the increased fear of death, the rising number of emotional problems, and the greater need for understanding of and coping with the problems of death and dying.

3 When we look back in time and study old cultures and people, we are impressed that death has always been distasteful to man and will probably always be. From a psychiatrist's point of view this is very understandable and can perhaps best be explained by our basic knowledge that, in our unconscious, death is never possible in regard to ourselves. It is inconceivable for our unconscious to imagine an actual ending of our own life here on earth, and if this life of ours had to end, the ending is always attributed to a malicious intervention from the outside by someone else. In simple terms, in our unconscious mind we can only be killed; it is inconceivable to die of a natural cause or of old age. Therefore death in itself is associated with a bad act, a frightening happening, something that in itself calls for retribution and punishment.

One is wise to remember these fundamental facts as they are essential in understanding some of the most important, otherwise unintelligible communications of our patients. 4

The second fact that we have to comprehend is that in our unconscious mind we cannot distinguish between a wish and a deed. We are all aware of some of our illogical dreams in which two completely opposite statements can exist side by side—very acceptable in our dreams but unthinkable and illogical in our wakening state. Just as our unconscious mind cannot differentiate between the wish to kill somebody in anger and the act of having done so, the young child is unable to make this distinction. The child who angrily wishes his mother to drop dead for not having gratified his needs will be traumatized greatly by the actual death of his mother—even if this event is not linked closely in time with his destructive wishes. He will always take part or the whole blame for the loss of his mother. He will always say to himself—rarely to others—"I did it, I am responsible, I was bad, therefore Mommy left me." It is well to remember that the child will react in the same manner if he loses a parent by divorce, separation, or desertion. Death is often seen by a child as an impermanent thing and has therefore little distinction from a divorce in which he may have an opportunity to see a parent again. 5

Many a parent will remember remarks of their children such as, "I will bury my doggy now and next spring when the flowers come up again, he will get up." Maybe it was the same wish that motivated the ancient Egyptians to supply their dead with food and goods to keep them happy and the old American Indians to bury their relatives with their belongings. 6

When we grow older and begin to realize that our omnipotence is really not so omnipotent, that our strongest wishes are not powerful enough to make the impossible possible, the fear that we have contributed to the death of a loved one diminishes—and with it the guilt. The fear remains diminished, however, only so long as it is not challenged too strongly. Its vestiges can be seen daily in hospital corridors and in people associated with the bereaved. 7

A husband and wife may have been fighting for years, but when the partner dies, the survivor will pull his hair, whine and cry louder and beat his chest in regret, fear and anguish, and will hence fear his own death more than before, still believing in the law of talion—an eye for an eye, a tooth for a tooth—"I am responsible for her death, I will have to die a pitiful death in retribution." 8

Maybe this knowledge will help us understand many of the old customs and rituals which have lasted over the centuries and whose purpose is to diminish the anger of the gods or the people as the case may be, thus decreasing the anticipated punishment. I am thinking of the ashes, the torn clothes, the veil, the *Klage Weiber** of the old days—they are all means to ask you to take pity on them, the mourners, and are expressions of sorrow, grief, and shame. If someone grieves, beats his chest, tears his hair, or refuses to eat, it is an attempt at self-punishment to avoid or reduce the anticipated punishment for the blame that he takes on the death of a loved one. 9

This grief, shame, and guilt are not very far removed from feelings of anger and rage. The process of grief always includes some qualities of anger. Since none 10

****Klage Weiber:*** German for "wailing wives."

of us likes to admit anger at a deceased person, these emotions are often disguised or repressed and prolong the period of grief or show up in other ways. It is well to remember that it is not up to us to judge such feelings as bad or shameful but to understand their true meaning and origin as something very human. In order to illustrate this I will again use the example of the child—and the child in us. The five-year-old who loses his mother is both blaming himself for her disappearance and being angry at her for having deserted him and for no longer gratifying his needs. The dead person then turns into something the child loves and wants very much but also hates with equal intensity for this severe deprivation.

11 The ancient Hebrews regarded the body of a dead person as something unclean and not to be touched. The early American Indians talked about the evil spirits and shot arrows in the air to drive the spirits away. Many other cultures have rituals to take care of the "bad" dead person, and they all originate in this feeling of anger which still exists in all of us, though we dislike admitting it. The tradition of the tombstone may originate in this wish to keep the bad spirits deep down in the ground, and the pebbles that many mourners put on the grave are left-over symbols of the same wish. Though we call the firing of guns at military funerals a last salute, it is the same symbolic ritual as the Indian used when he shot his spears and arrows into the skies.

12 I give these examples to emphasize that man has not basically changed. Death is still a fearful, frightening happening, and the fear of death is a universal fear even if we think we have mastered it on many levels.

13 What has changed is our way of coping and dealing with death and dying and our dying patients.

14 Having been raised in a country in Europe where science is not so advanced, where modern techniques have just started to find their way into medicine, and where people still live as they did in this country half a century ago, I may have had an opportunity to study a part of the evolution of mankind in a shorter period.

15 I remember as a child the death of a farmer. He fell from a tree and was not expected to live. He asked simply to die at home, a wish that was granted without questioning. He called his daughters into the bedroom and spoke with each one of them alone for a few moments. He arranged his affairs quietly, though he was in great pain, and distributed his belongings and his land, none of which was to be split until his wife should follow him in death. He also asked each of his children to share in the work, duties, and tasks that he had carried on until the time of the accident. He asked his friends to visit him once more, to bid good-bye to them. Although I was a small child at the time, he did not exclude me or my siblings. We were allowed to share in the preparations of the family just as we were permitted to grieve with them until he died. When he did die, he was left at home, in his own beloved home which he had built, and among his friends and neighbors who went to take a last look at him where he lay in the midst of flowers in the place he had lived in and loved so much. In that country today there is still no make-believe slumber room, no embalming, no false makeup to pretend sleep. Only the signs of very disfiguring illnesses are covered up with bandages and only infectious cases are removed from the home prior to the burial.

16 Why do I describe such "old-fashioned" customs? I think they are an indication of our acceptance of a fatal outcome, and they help the dying patient as well as his family to accept the loss of a loved one. If a patient is allowed to terminate

his life in the familiar and beloved environment, it requires less adjustment for him. His own family knows him well enough to replace a sedative with a glass of his favorite wine; or the smell of a home-cooked soup may give him the appetite to sip a few spoons of fluid which, I think, is still more enjoyable than an infusion. I will not minimize the need for sedatives and infusions and realize full well from my own experience as a country doctor that they are sometimes life-saving and often unavoidable. But I also know that patience and familiar people and foods could replace many a bottle of intravenous fluids given for the simple reason that it fulfills the physiological need without involving too many people and/or individual nursing care.

17 The fact that children are allowed to stay at home where a fatality has stricken and are included in the talk, discussions, and fears gives them the feeling that they are not alone in the grief and gives them the comfort of shared responsibility and shared mourning. It prepares them gradually and helps them view death as part of life, an experience which may help them grow and mature.

18 This is in great contrast to a society in which death is viewed as taboo, discussion of it is regarded as morbid, and children are excluded with the presumption and pretext that it would be "too much" for them. They are then sent off to relatives, often accompanied with some unconvincing lies of "Mother has gone on a long trip" or other unbelievable stories. The child senses that something is wrong, and his distrust in adults will only multiply if other relatives add new variations of the story, avoid his questions or suspicions, shower him with gifts as a meager substitute for a loss he is not permitted to deal with. Sooner or later the child will become aware of the changed family situation and, depending on the age and personality of the child, will have an unresolved grief and regard this incident as a frightening, mysterious, in any case very traumatic experience with untrustworthy grownups, which he has no way to cope with.

19 It is equally unwise to tell a little child who lost her brother that God loved little boys so much that he took little Johnny to heaven. When this little girl grew up to be a woman she never solved her anger at God, which resulted in a psychotic depression when she lost her own little son three decades later.

20 We would think that our great emancipation, our knowledge of science and of man, has given us better ways and means to prepare ourselves and our families for this inevitable happening. Instead the days are gone when a man was allowed to die in peace and dignity in his own home.

21 The more we are making advancements in science, the more we seem to fear and deny the reality of death. How is this possible?

22 We use euphemisms, we make the dead look as if they were asleep, we ship the children off to protect them from the anxiety and turmoil around the house if the patient is fortunate enough to die at home, we don't allow children to visit their dying parents in the hospitals, we have long and controversial discussions about whether patients should be told the truth—a question that rarely arises when the dying person is tended by the family physician who has known him from delivery to death and who knows the weaknesses and strengths of each member of the family.

23 I think there are many reasons for this flight away from facing death calmly. One of the most important facts is that dying nowadays is more gruesome in many ways, namely, more lonely, mechanical, and dehumanized; at times it is even difficult to determine technically when the time of death has occurred.

Dying becomes lonely and impersonal because the patient is often taken out of his familiar environment and rushed to an emergency room. Whoever has been very sick and has required rest and comfort especially may recall his experience of being put on a stretcher and enduring the noise of the ambulance siren and hectic rush until the hospital gates open. Only those who have lived through this may appreciate the discomfort and cold necessity of such transportation which is only the beginning of a long ordeal—hard to endure when you are well, difficult to express in words when noise, light, pumps, and voices are all too much to put up with. It may well be that we might consider more the patient under the sheets and blankets and perhaps stop our well-meant efficiency and rush in order to hold the patient's hand, to smile, or to listen to a question. I include the trip to the hospital as the first episode in dying, as it is for many. I am putting it exaggeratedly in contrast to the sick man who is left at home—not to say that lives should not be saved if they can be saved by a hospitalization but to keep the focus on the patient's experience, his needs and his reactions. 24

When a patient is severely ill, he is often treated like a person with no right to an opinion. It is often someone else who makes the decision if and when and where a patient should be hospitalized. It would take so little to remember that the sick person too has feelings, has wishes and opinions, and has—most important of all—the right to be heard. 25

Well, our presumed patient has now reached the emergency room. He will be surrounded by busy nurses, orderlies, interns, residents, a lab technician perhaps who will take some blood, an electrocardiogram technician who takes the cardiogram. He may be moved to X ray and he will overhear opinions of his condition and discussions and questions to members of the family. He slowly but surely is beginning to be treated like a thing. He is no longer a person. Decisions are made often without his opinion. If he tries to rebel he will be sedated and after hours of waiting and wondering whether he has the strength, he will be wheeled into the operating room or intensive treatment unit and become an object of great concern and great financial investment. 26

He may cry for rest, peace, and dignity, but he will get infusions, transfusions, a heart machine, or tracheotomy* if necessary. He may want one single person to stop for one single minute so that he can ask one single question—but he will get a dozen people around the clock, all busily preoccupied with his heart rate, pulse, electrocardiogram or pulmonary functions, his secretions or excretions but not with him as a human being. He may wish to fight it all but it is going to be a useless fight since all this is done in the fight for his life, and if they can save his life they can consider the person afterwards. Those who consider the person first may lose precious time to save his life! At least this seems to be the rationale or justification behind all this—or is it? Is the reason for this increasingly mechanical, depersonalized approach our own defensiveness? Is this approach our own way to cope with and repress the anxieties that a terminally or critically ill patient evokes in us? Is our concentration on equipment, on blood pressure, our desperate attempt to deny the impending death which is so frightening and discomforting to us that we 27

***tracheotomy:** a medical procedure in which a tube is inserted into a patient's neck, thus enabling him or her to breathe.

STYLE AND STRATEGY
1. Paragraphs 1–2 define the author's purpose and audience as well as introduce an important contrast in medical history.
2. The thesis appears at the end of paragraph 2.
3. Paragraph 3 explains why death has always been "distasteful to man and will probably always be." Paragraphs 5, 6, and 7, explain the results of the ability of the unconscious to distinguish between wish and deed. Among these are a kind of guilt that contributes to the nature of our bereavement over the loss of a loved one.
4. In paragraph 8, the author uses an anecdote. Specific objects and practices are mentioned in paragraph 9. The example of the child who has lost a mother is brought up again in paragraph 10. Cultural practices and ceremonies are included in paragraph 11.
5. The thesis is restated in paragraph 12. Note that paragraph 13 signals a turning point in the essay.
6. Description can be found in paragraphs 11, 16, 24, and 26; narration can be found in paragraphs 6, 8, 15, 26, and 27. Paragraph 14 uses causal analysis to explain why the author had "the opportunity to study a part of evolution of mankind in a shorter period." Causal analysis also appears in paragraphs 16, 17, and 18.
7. Responses vary, but the contrast with modern American funeral practices makes the manner in which the farmer died quite preferable.
8. Paragraphs 20–27 use contrast; paragraph 24 uses description; paragraphs 26 and 27 use narration; paragraphs 24, 26, and 27 use exemplification.
9. Responses vary, but some students will suggest that the author might have advocated nonmedical intervention for hopeless cases.

displace all our knowledge onto machines, since they are less close to us than the suffering face of another human being which would remind us once more of our lack of omnipotence, our own limits and failures, and last but not least perhaps our own mortality?

Maybe the question has to be raised: Are we becoming less human or more human? . . . It is clear that whatever the answer may be, the patient is suffering more—not physically, perhaps, but emotionally. And his needs have not changed over the centuries, only our ability to gratify them. 28

Vocabulary

The following terms are identified by paragraph number. Make sure that you understand each term's meaning in its context. If you're not sure that you understand a term, look it up in a college-level dictionary.

eradicate (1)	deprivation (10)	euphemism (22)
morbidity (1)	sibling (15)	hectic (24)
malignancies (1)	embalming (15)	intern (26)
psychosomatic (2)	disfiguring (15)	electrocardiogram (26)
elicit (2)	sedative (16)	tracheotomy (27)
retribution (3)	infusion (16)	pulmonary (27)
unintelligible (4)	intravenous (16)	secretion (27)
omnipotence (7)	taboo (18)	excretion (27)
vestige (7)	pretext (18)	rationale (27)
bereaved (7)	emancipation (20)	impending (27)

Style and Strategy

Paragraphs 1–2

1. What function do paragraphs 1–2 serve?

2. Where is Kübler-Ross's thesis? Restate it in your own words.

Paragraphs 3–7

3. How does Kübler-Ross use causal analysis in this section? Compare her use of causal analysis in paragraph 5 and in paragraph 6.

Paragraphs 8–13

4. How does Kübler-Ross use exemplification in this passage?

5. Where does Kübler-Ross restate her thesis? In your opinion, why does she do so?

Paragraphs 14–19

6. Explain how Kübler-Ross uses description, narration, and causal analysis in this passage.

7. What is your opinion of the anecdote in paragraph 15? In other words, does this "way to die" appeal to you, or does it affect you in some other way?

Paragraphs 20–27

8. Explain how Kübler-Ross uses description, narration, exemplification, and comparison/contrast in this passage.

Paragraph 28

9. Is Kübler-Ross's conclusion effective? In your opinion, what other issues might the author have covered here?

Questions for Critical Thinking and Discussion

QUESTIONS FOR CRITICAL THINKING AND DISCUSSION The first item can be used as a prompt for short writing. The next three can be used as prompts for sustained writing.

1. How would you want the end of your life to occur?
2. In the United States, many people have more medical resources expended for them in the last several days of their life than during the rest of their life altogether. In your opinion, is it a wise idea to expend so much for people who are clearly dying?
3. What is your opinion on the issue of assisted suicide?
4. Have you ever been to a funeral? If so, what were your impressions of what you observed and experienced?

Why the Rich Are Getting Richer and the Poor Poorer

ROBERT B. REICH

Robert Reich was secretary of labor during President Clinton's first term. He is an economist, political scientist, and social commentator whose work has appeared in many prestigious journals. His books include *The Next American Frontier* (1983), *Tales of a New American* (1987), *The Power of Public Ideas* (1988), *The Work of Nations* (1991), *Locked in the Cabinet* (1997), *The Future of Success* (2001), and *I'll Be Short: Essentials for a Decent Working Society* (2002). Reich frequently appears as a commentator on television programs devoted to economic and political issues.

The following essay was originally published in *The New Republic* and is reprinted here in abridged form. The essay is more than fifteen years old, and it reflects data largely from the 1980s. Do you think the trends that he notes have continued?

1 Between 1978 and 1987, the poorest fifth of American families became 8 percent poorer, and the richest fifth became 13 percent richer. That means the poorest fifth now have less than 5 percent of the nation's income, while the richest fifth have more than 40 percent.

2 This widening gap can't be blamed on the growth in single-parent lower-income families, which in fact slowed markedly after the late 1970s. Nor is it due mainly to the stingy social policies of the Reagan years. Granted, food stamp benefits have dropped 13 percent since 1981 (in real terms), and many states have failed to raise benefits for the poor and unemployed to keep up with inflation. But this doesn't come close to accounting for the growing persistence of economic inequality in the United States. Rather, this disturbing trend is connected to a profound change in the American economy as it merges with the global economy. And because the merging is far from complete, this trend will not stop all by itself anytime soon. It is significant that the growth of inequality can be seen most strikingly among Americans who

have jobs. Through most of the postwar era, the wages of Americans at different income levels rose at about the same pace. Although different workers occupied different steps on the escalator, everyone moved up together. In those days poverty was the condition of *jobless* Americans, and the major economic challenge was to create enough jobs for everyone. Once people were safely in the work force, their problems were assumed to be over. Thus "full employment" became a liberal rallying cry.

3 But in recent years Americans with jobs have been traveling on two escalators—one going up, the other going down. In 1987 the average hourly earnings of nonsupervisory workers (adjusted for inflation) were lower than in any year since 1966. Middle-level managers fared much better, although their median real earnings were only slightly above the levels of the 1970s. Executives, however, did spectacularly well. In 1988 alone, CEOs of the 100 largest publicly held industrial corporations received raises averaging almost 12 percent.

4 Between 1978 and 1987, as the real earnings of unskilled workers were declining, the real incomes of investment bankers and other securities industry workers rose 21 percent. It is not unusual for a run-of-the-mill investment banker to bring home comfortably over a million dollars. Meanwhile, the number of impoverished *working* Americans climbed by nearly two million, or 23 percent, during those same years. Nearly 60 percent of the 20 million people who now fall below the Census Bureau's poverty line are from families with at least one member in full-time or part-time work.

5 The American economy now exhibits a wider gap between rich and poor than it has at any other time since World War II. The most basic reason, put simply, is that America itself is ceasing to exist as an economic system separate from the rest of the world. One can no more meaningfully speak of an "American economy" than of a "Delaware economy." We are becoming but a region—albeit still a relatively wealthy region—of a global economy. This is a new kind of economy whose technologies, savings, and investments move effortlessly across borders, making it harder for individual nations to control their economic destinies.

6 We have yet to come to terms with the rise of the global corporation, whose managers, shareholders, and employees span the world. Our debates over the future of American jobs still focus on topics such as the competitiveness of the American automobile industry or the future of American manufacturing. But these issues are increasingly irrelevant.

7 New technologies of worldwide communication and transportation have redrawn the economic playing field. American industries no longer compete against Japanese or European industries. Rather, a company with headquarters in the United States, production facilities in Taiwan, and a marketing force spread across many nations competes with another, similarly wide-ranging company. So when General Motors, say, is doing well, that probably is good news for a lot of executives in Detroit, and for GM shareholders across the globe, but it isn't necessarily good news for a lot of assembly-line workers in Detroit, because there may, in fact, be very few GM assembly-line workers in Detroit, or anywhere else in America. The welfare of assembly-line workers in Detroit may depend, instead, on the health of corporations based in Japan or Canada.

8 More to the point, even if those Canadian and Japanese corporations are doing well, those Detroit workers may be in trouble. For they are increasingly part of an international labor market, encompassing Asia, Africa, Western Europe, and, per-

haps before long, Eastern Europe. With relative ease corporations can relocate their production centers to take advantage of low wages. So American workers find themselves settling for low wages in order to hold on to their jobs. More and more, your "competitiveness" as a worker depends not on the fortunes of any American corporation, or of any American industry, but on what function you serve within the global economy.

9 In order to see in greater detail what is happening to American jobs, it helps to view the work that most Americans do in terms of new categories that reflect how U.S. workers fit into the global economy. Essentially, three broad categories are emerging. I call them: (1) symbolic-analytic services; (2) routine production services; and (3) routine personal services.

10 **1. Symbolic-analytic services** are based on the manipulation of information: data, words, and oral and visual symbols. Symbolic analysis comprises some (but by no means all) of the work undertaken by people who call themselves lawyers, investment bankers, commercial bankers, management consultants, research scientists, academics, public-relations executives, real estate developers, and even a few creative accountants. Also, many advertising and marketing specialists, art directors, design engineers, architects, writers and editors, musicians, and television and film producers.

11 Some of the manipulations of information performed by these symbolic analysts offer ways of more efficiently deploying resources or shifting financial assets, or of otherwise saving time and energy. Other manipulations grab money from people who are too slow or naïve to protect themselves. Still others serve to entertain the public.

12 Most symbolic analysts work alone or in small teams. If they work with others, they often have partners rather than bosses or supervisors. Their work environments tend to be quiet and tastefully decorated, often within tall steel-and-glass buildings. When they are not analyzing, designing, or strategizing, they are in meetings or on the telephone—giving advice or making deals. Many of them spend an inordinate amount of time in jet planes and hotels. They are generally articulate and well groomed. The vast majority are white males.

13 Symbolic analysis now accounts for more than 40 percent of America's gross national product, and almost 20 percent of our jobs.

14 The services performed by America's symbolic analysts are in high demand around the world. The Japanese are buying up the insights and inventions of America's scientists and engineers (who are only too happy to sell them at a fat profit). The Europeans, meanwhile, are hiring our management consultants, business strategists, and investment bankers. Developing nations are hiring our civil and design engineers; and almost everyone is buying the output of our pop musicians, television stars, and film producers.

15 The same thing is happening with the global corporation. The central offices of these sprawling entities, headquartered in America, are filled with symbolic analysts who manipulate information and then export their insights around the world via the corporation's far-flung operations. IBM, for instance, doesn't export machines from the United States; it manufactures its machines in factories all over the globe. IBM world headquarters, in Armonk, New York, exports just strategic planning and related management services.

Thus has the standard of living of America's symbolic analysts risen. They increasingly find themselves part of a global labor market, not a national one. And because the United States has a highly developed economy, and an excellent university system, they find that the services they have to offer are in high demand around the whole world. This ensures that their salaries are quite high. 16

Those salaries are likely to go even higher in the years ahead, as the world market for symbolic analysis continues to grow. Foreigners are trying to learn these skills and techniques, to be sure, but they still have a long way to go. No other country does a better job of preparing its most fortunate citizens for symbolic analysis than does the United States. None has surpassed America in providing experience and training, often with entire regions specializing in one or another kind of symbolic analysis (New York and Chicago for finance, Los Angeles for music and film, the San Francisco Bay area and greater Boston for science and engineering). In this we can take pride. But for the second major category of American workers—the providers of routine production services—the future doesn't bode well. 17

2. Routine production services involve tasks that are repeated over and over, as one step in a sequence of steps for producing a finished product. Although we tend to associate these jobs with manufacturing, they are becoming common in banking, insurance, wholesaling, retailing, health care—all industries employing millions of people who spend their days processing data, often putting information into computers or taking it out. 18

Most people involved in routine production services work with many other people who do similar work, within large, centralized facilities. They are overseen by supervisors, who in turn are monitored by more senior supervisors. They are usually paid an hourly wage. Their jobs are often monotonous. Most of the workers do not have a college education. Those who deal with metal are mostly white males; those who deal with fabrics or information tend to be female and/or minorities. 19

Decades ago, those kinds of workers were relatively well paid. But in recent years America's providers of routine production services have found themselves in direct competition with millions of foreign workers, most of whom work for a fraction of the pay American workers get. Through the miracle of satellite transmission, even routine data processing can now be undertaken in relatively poor nations, thousands of miles away from the skyscrapers where the data are finally used. This fact has given management ever greater power in bargaining talks. If routine production workers living in America don't agree to reduce their wages, then the work often goes abroad. 20

And it has. In 1950, routine production services constituted about 30 percent of our gross national product and well over half of American jobs. Today such services represent about 20 percent of the GNP and one fourth of jobs. And the scattering of foreign-owned factories placed here to circumvent American protectionism isn't going to reverse the trend. So the standard of living of America's routine production workers will likely keep declining. The dynamics behind the wage concessions, plant closings, and union-busting that have become commonplace won't be stopped without a major turnaround in labor organizing or political action. 21

3. Routine personal services also entail simple, repetitive work, but, unlike routine production services, they are provided in person. Included in this employment category are restaurant and hotel workers, barbers and beauticians, retail sales personnel, cab drivers, household cleaners, day-care workers, hospital attendants and orderlies, truck drivers, and—among the fastest-growing of all careers—custodians and security guards. 22

Like production workers, providers of personal services are usually paid by the hour. They are also carefully supervised and rarely have more than a high school education. But unlike people in the other two categories of work, they are in direct contact with the ultimate beneficiaries of what they do. And the companies they work for are often small. In fact, some routine personal-service workers become entrepreneurs. (Most new businesses and new jobs in America come from this sector—which now constitutes about 20 percent of GNP and 30 percent of jobs). Women and minorities make up the bulk of routine personal-service workers. 23

Apart from the small number who strike out on their own, these workers are paid poorly. They are sheltered from the direct effects of global competition, but not the indirect effects. They often compete with undocumented workers willing to work for low wages, or with former or would-be production workers who can't find well-paying production jobs, or with labor-saving machinery (automated tellers, self-service gas pumps) dreamed up by symbolic analysts in America and manufactured in Asia. And because they tend to be unskilled and dispersed among small businesses, personal-service workers rarely have a union or a powerful lobby group to stand up for their interests. When the economy turns sour, they are among the first to feel the effects. 24

These workers will continue to have jobs in the years ahead and may experience some small increase in real wages. They will have demographics on their side, as the American work force shrinks. But for all the foregoing reasons, the gap between their earnings and those of the symbolic analysts will continue to grow if present economic trends and labor conditions continue. 25

These three functional categories—symbolic analysis, routine production services, and routine personal services—cover at least three out of four American jobs. The rest of the nation's work force consists mainly of government employees (including public school teachers), employees in regulated industries (like utility workers), and government-financed workers (engineers working on defense weapons systems), many of whom are sheltered from global competition. One further clarification: Some traditional job categories overlap several of these categories. People called "secretaries," for example, include those who actually spend their time doing symbolic analysis work closely allied to what their bosses do; those who do routine data entry or retrieval of a sort that will eventually be automated or done overseas; and those who provide routine personal services. 26

The important point is that workers in these three functional categories are coming to have different competitive positions in the world economy. Symbolic analysts hold a commanding position in an increasingly global labor market. Routine production workers hold a relatively weak position in an increasingly global labor market. Routine personal service workers still find themselves in a national labor market, but for various reasons they suffer the indirect effects of competition from workers abroad. 27

How should we respond to these trends? One response is to accept them as inevitable consequences of change, but to try to offset their polarizing effects through a truly progressive income tax, coupled with more generous income assistance—including health insurance—for poor working Americans. (For a start, we might reverse the extraordinarily regressive Social Security amendments of 1983, through which poor working Americans are now financing the federal budget deficit, often paying more in payroll taxes than in income taxes.) 28

A more ambitious response would be to guard against class rigidities by ensuring that any talented American kid can become a symbolic analyst—regardless of family income or race. But America's gifted but poor children can't aspire to such jobs until the government spends substantially more than it does now to ensure excellent public schools in every city and region and ample financial help when they are ready to attend college. 29

Of course, it isn't clear that even under those circumstances there would be radical growth in the number of Americans who become research scientists, design engineers, musicians, management consultants, or (even if the world needed them) investment bankers and lawyers. So other responses are also needed. Perhaps the most ambitious would be to increase the numbers of Americans who could apply symbolic analysis to production and to personal services. 30

There is ample evidence, for example, that access to computerized information can enrich production jobs by enabling workers to alter the flow of materials and components in ways that increase efficiency. Production workers who have broader responsibilities and more control over how production is organized cease to be "routine" workers—becoming, in effect, symbolic analysts at a level very close to the production process. The same transformation can occur in personal-service jobs. Consider, for example, the checkout clerk whose computer enables her to control inventory and decide when to reorder items from the factory. 31

The number of such technologically empowered jobs, of course, is limited by the ability of workers to learn on the job. That means a far greater number of Americans will need a good grounding in mathematics, basic science, reading, and communication skills. So once again, comfortably integrating the American work force into the new world economy turns out to rest heavily on education. (Better health care, especially prenatal and pediatric care, would also figure in here.) 32

Education and health care for poor children are apt to be costly. Since poorer working Americans, already under a heavy tax load, can't afford it, the cost would have to be borne by wealthier Americans—who also would have to bear the cost of any income redistribution plans designed to neutralize the polarizing domestic effects of a globalized economy. Thus a central question is the willingness of the more fortunate American citizens—especially symbolic analysts, who constitute much of the most fortunate fifth, with 40 percent of the nation's income—to bear the burden. But here lies a catch-22. For as our economic fates diverge, the top fifth may be losing its sense of connectedness with the bottom fifth (or even the bottom half) that would elicit such generosity. 33

The conservative tide that has swept the land during the past decade surely has many causes, but the fundamental changes in our economy should not be discounted as a major factor. It is now possible for the most fortunate fifth to sell their expertise directly in the global market, and thus maintain and enhance their standard of living, even as that of other Americans declines. There is less and less basis 34 for a strong sense of interclass interdependence in America. Meanwhile, the fortunate fifth have also been able to insulate themselves from the less fortunate, by living in suburban enclaves far removed from the effects of poverty. Neither patriotism nor altruism may be sufficient to overcome these realities. Yet without the active support of at least some of the fortunate fifth, it will be more difficult to muster the political will necessary for change. . . .

On withdrawing from the presidential race of 1988, Paul Simon of Illinois said, "Americans instinctively know that we are one nation, one family, and when anyone in that family hurts, all of us hurt." Sadly, that is coming to be less and less the case. 35

Vocabulary

The following terms are identified by paragraph number. Make sure that you understand each term's meaning in its context. If you're not sure that you understand a term, look it up in a college-level dictionary.

median (3)	dynamics (21)	regressive (28)
publicly held (3)	concessions (21)	rigidities (29)
albeit (5)	beneficiaries (23)	integrating (32)
encompassing (8)	entrepreneurs (23)	prenatal (32)
inordinate (12)	undocumented workers (24)	catch-22 (33)
gross national product (13)	dispersed (24)	diverge (33)
monotonous (19)	demographics (25)	elicit (33)
circumvent (21)	polarizing (28)	enclaves (34)
protectionism (21)	progressive (28)	altruism (34)

Style and Strategy

Paragraph 1

1. What is the function of this paragraph? Why might Reich have used such a sudden and abrupt opening?

Paragraphs 2–4

2. Where is Reich's thesis statement? Restate it in your own words.
3. Locate the use of the following rhetorical options: causal analysis and comparison/contrast.

Paragraphs 5-8

4. In what sense can this section of Reich's essay be seen as an extended definition?

Paragraph 9

5. What is the function of paragraph 9?

Paragraphs 10–17

6. This section analyzes the first group in Reich's three-way classification scheme. How does Reich use definition, process analysis, and exemplification to develop this section?

STYLE AND STRATEGY

1. Paragraph 1 grabs our attention with startling statistics.
2. The thesis appears in paragraph 2: the continuing gap between rich and poor is happening because the American economy is merging with the world economy.
3. Paragraphs 2 and 3 contain causal analysis. Contrast can be seen in paragraphs 3 and 4.
4. These paragraphs define the international corporation and explain how increasing internationalization can cause American workers harm.
5. Paragraph 9 introduces a discussion of the effects of globalization on the nature of jobs held by Americans.
6. Paragraph 10 uses definition and examples; paragraph 11 uses examples; paragraph 12 uses process analysis and definition; paragraphs 14–17 use process analysis and examples.

Paragraphs 18–21

7. Identify the areas where Reich uses the following strategies: description, definition, comparison/contrast, process analysis, and causal analysis.

Paragraphs 22–25

8. Identify the places where Reich uses the following strategies: definition, comparison/contrast, process analysis, and causal analysis.

Paragraphs 26–32

9. What is the conclusion that Reich draws from his study?

10. How does Reich use argument in this section? What possible solutions does he explore?

Paragraphs 33–35

11. What is the function of this section?

12. According to Reich, what needs to happen in order to correct the imbalances that he explores?

7. Paragraph 18 uses definition and comparison; paragraph 19 uses description; paragraph 20 uses contrast and process analysis; paragraph 21 uses causal analysis.
8. Paragraph 22 uses definition and comparison/contrast; paragraph 23 uses comparison/contrast; paragraph 24 uses definition and causal analysis; paragraph 25 uses process analysis and contrast.
9. Paragraph 27 contains the conclusion.
10. In paragraphs 28–32, Reich suggests a change in the income tax; increased income assistance for the working poor; increased funding of public education; an increase in the number of Americans able to use symbolic analysis through increased technical training.
11. This section makes a request and sounds a warning.
12. According to Reich, the "most fortunate fifth need to bear a greater portion of the tax burden."

Questions for Critical Thinking and Discussion

1. Most observers would agree that the United States has a pro-business climate. In your opinion, do businesses have enough, not enough, or too much freedom to operate as they see fit? Refer to your own experiences as a worker and as a consumer.

2. Consider your future. Into what category—following Reich's classification—does the career to which you aspire fall? What might happen to this type of career in the future?

3. One of the trends that Reich mentions is the great mobility of corporations and their willingness to lay off workers suddenly in response to market issues. Do you know of any people who have been affected by corporate cutbacks? If so, how did their lives change?

4. What "advice" does Reich implicitly offer to anyone eighteen years old and unsure about his or her future?

QUESTIONS FOR CRITICAL THINKING AND DISCUSSION Items 2, 3, and 4 produce the best essays. Item 2 invites research. Item 4 requires a close rereading of the text.

MORE OPTIONS ONLINE If you would like to read additional blended essays, go to **www.mhhe.com/writingtoday**.

WRITING THE BLENDED ESSAY WITH A READER'S EYE

Our discussion here is necessarily more general than in the preceding nine chapters. The decisions that you make when writing the blended essay require you to choose the best internal strategies to support your purpose and then to integrate those strategies to produce a unified essay.

Prewriting

The prewriting stage is the point at which many writers realize that they *need* to use multiple options to write their essay. As you use any of the prewriting methods discussed in Chapter 2 to explore your topic and generate ideas, concentrate on finding the logical patterns that result. Look for the possibilities, keeping in mind the rhetorical options that you have learned in the preceding chapters. Keep your purpose in mind as you do so: you are not trying to use multiple strategies in some artificial exercise; your instructor will not grade you on successful and thorough inclusion of several internal options. Instead, you are planning an essay that will support its thesis throughout. Your instructor will be looking for thorough and effective development of each point that you make, no matter which strategy that you have used to develop it.

At this point, you should be able to develop a preliminary thesis. Before proceeding, however, reconsider your thesis in terms of your purpose. Are they compatible? Keep in mind that you may need to revise or replace your thesis after your first draft.

Organizing

When you are satisfied with the results of your prewriting and have developed your working thesis, the best way for you to organize this raw material is to arrange it into an outline. (Chapter 2 covers informal, sentence, and formal outlines.) If you use a sentence outline, for example, be willing to revise it or construct a new one if, upon review, you decide that the first one won't work. Plan on organizing until you come up with a paragraph sequence that suits both your thesis and your purpose.

A very useful strategy for organizing the blended essay is building a sentence outline with annotations. In other words, after you complete your outline, add notes (such as "transition here") where needed. This way, you'll give yourself an extensive framework to use as you begin drafting.

Drafting

As you write your first draft, keep your thesis and purpose in the forefront of your thoughts. A blended essay presents complications, and all too often writers find themselves going astray—spending two paragraphs carefully developing a minor point that deserves only a few sentences, for example. Don't worry too much about this as you write your first draft, but be aware of the potential problem as you revise your draft.

As well, remember the crucial role of transitions in any essay. In a blended essay, transitions help link sections in which you are using different internal strategies; without transitions, the essay might read like three or four individual passages loosely connected to the thesis.

MORE OPTIONS ONLINE
For more help with problem areas in the blended essay, go to **www.mhhe.com/writingtoday**.

Revising Your Draft

After you have completed a draft of your blended essay, your next step is to revise it, using your own analysis and comments from classmates or friends. Use the peer review stage to make sure that your essay's structure and content are sound. During peer review, answer the following questions about the draft you are reviewing, whether it is yours or another student's.

Questions for Reviewing a Blended Essay

1. Does the introduction give the reader enough context? Does it capture the reader's interest? How could the introduction be strengthened?
2. What is the thesis statement? Does it adequately reflect the essay's purpose and development? If necessary to do so, how could it be improved?
3. Is the essay organized in a logical and effective way? How could the organization be improved?
4. Do the internal strategies that the writer has chosen support the essay's main points and help the writer achieve his or her purpose?
5. Where are transitional words or sentences needed?
6. Are the body paragraphs fully developed? Where are additional details, or more-specific details, needed?
7. Does the essay have an effective conclusion? How could it be improved?

MORE OPTIONS ONLINE For more help with revision, go to **www.mhhe.com/writingtoday**.

After reviewing for content, you need to go over your peer reviewers' responses to your essay and then revise for unity, coherence, language level, and tone (see Chapter 4). When you have revised your draft and are basically satisfied with it, read your draft for mechanical and grammatical errors (fragments, comma splices, fused sentences), errors in pronoun agreement and subject-verb agreement, and spelling.

Now that you have made your corrections, *read your essay one more time* to catch any errors made during the revision and find errors missed during your earlier reviews.

Student Essay

Today, Kevin Hunkovic, an accomplished young man, has a healthy level of self-esteem. As he points out in the following essay, which describes a situation that occurred ten years earlier, such was not always the case.

Three Years Without Liberty

1 At age eleven I was just your average American child. I lived primarily between my hat and my heels. Because everything else was taken care of by my parents, I gave little thought to anything except for video games and television. In this fashion I was sheltered from the harsh realities of the world. **Little did I know that I was about to have an experience that**

would alter my outlook toward life forever: I experienced the microcosm of modern society called Liberty Middle School.

2 In 1988 Liberty Middle School had a student body of about 1,700 students, give or take a few hundred. I was overwhelmed by the multitudes of diverse people around me. My classes were huge. There were 40–65 students per class. These numbers dwarfed me as I became a very small part of a whole. Soon after I started the sixth grade I began to notice a system underlying the way students and faculty interacted with each other. I later realized that it was a social class system. The highest members were the intellectuals, or nerds as they were called. They enjoyed special privileges that others did not have, such as getting to leave class and study alone in the library or move through the hallways without a pass. Then there was the middle class, those who weren't the best or the worst students. This group usually contained the athletes, cheerleaders, and the somewhat popular students. It constituted the majority of the student body. Next, there were the troublemakers, or the Future Criminals of America, as I called them. Those students tended to receive bad grades and get into trouble when they weren't causing it. Above all of this was the school faculty. Until I entered middle school, I thought the faculty were just the people who distributed the information to the students. At Liberty Middle School, however, the faculty took on all the functions of a small government: executives to run it, legislators to make the rules, and judges to punish wrongdoers with detentions. Finally, I noticed a class of outsiders, who for one reason or another did not fit into any category. They weren't mean enough to be in the lower class, or popular enough to converse with the middle class, or good enough at studying to be in the upper class. These students went unnoticed for the most part and were overlooked by teachers in an overcrowded classroom. The fourth class of people slipped through the cracks of the system, so to speak. In other words, they became victims of the institution.

3 In this milieu I'm afraid I ended up in the last group of people, mainly because of my shyness and my height. At age eleven I stood at 4 feet 5 inches.

Most people my age were 5 inches to a foot taller than I. The older the student, the smaller I was by comparison. This happened to make me quite vulnerable to the lower class, or the Future Criminals of America. At least twice a day I was attacked by one bully or another. These attacks were never very brutal, although they usually left me holding my stomach and gasping for air. When I recovered from the pain, I'd stand up and attempt to locate where my books had been hidden. It was actually these frequent attacks that prompted me to realize the existence of the underlying system that divided people. Since the unfortunate encounters with a certain mean group of people made absolutely no sense, I tried to find some reason for them. This inspired me to observe closely my environment and the people in it. I eventually came to the conclusion that there were many factors involved. The category to which a student belonged, from bully to intellectual, seemed to be based on the institution's ability or inability to deal with that student. The people that the system could help were benefited by it. The intellectuals and the middle class were among those who did benefit. The others who did not benefit from the school became angry and lashed out at it, which caused the faculty to lash back. This cycle perpetuated itself into oblivion. Unfortunately, I was caught in the crossfire more than once.

4 Because I was very young at the time, every event that transpired seemed momentous and terrifying. Getting beat up almost every day might not have been enough to make me realize the situation and what it implied. I could have easily written the attacks off as the products of bad personalities. It wasn't until the authority figures themselves began to harass me as well that the entire system solidified in my mind. Once while I was waiting for the bus driver to drive me away from school, someone in the back of the bus threw an object that struck the bus driver at the base of her skull. She immediately left the bus, then promptly returned with an administrator. She then made inquiries as to who threw the object. Fearing punishment, a group of several miscreants all pointed at me in unison, while blaming me for the crime. Regardless of my spotless conduct record, I was called in to the office the following day. Because I was so young, I broke down into tears and protested

that I was innocent. I proceeded to give a list of possible suspects, which would have had to be one of the kids who blamed me wrongly. After I left, the administrator had the idiocy to tell everyone that I accused everything I had said in my defense, including the fact that I had blamed him or her for the crime. Each suspect must have given a convincing defense as well, because I was right back in the office the following day facing the same charges, but not before a group of ten students beat me up for telling the truth, with a promise to do it again at the end of the day. Now the criminals and the authority figures were after me simultaneously, all because I was minding my own business and waiting to go home.

5 Just as a doctor slaps a newborn baby, which causes it to cry and to breathe independently, this experience caused just enough mental stress to make me realize how contemporary society functions—and malfunctions. Everything I experienced in that school was a miniature version of the world at large. In essence, my three-year experience at Liberty Middle School woke me from my thoughtless childhood slumber. This realization remains with me to this day.

Let's look at the way Hunkovic constructed his essay and at the strategies he used.

The Introduction

Hunkovic's first paragraph is devoted to description and definition. In providing the background for his essay, he **defines** himself at age eleven, **describing** what kind of boy he was at that age. His thesis, appearing in the final sentence of his first paragraph, indicates that his essay will be a **narration** but also something more than that.

Consider Your Options

What other methods of development might Hunkovic have used to introduce this essay?

The Body

Hunkovic's first body paragraph is a complex **classification** of the people who inhabited Liberty Middle School: four classes of students and a faculty class. Hunkovic first discusses three of the categories of students: intellectuals, the middle class, and the troublemakers. He then classifies the functions of the faculty: executives, legislators, and judges. Finally, Hunkovic tells us about the fourth class of students: the "outsiders," destined to be "victims of the institution," at the mercy of all the other groups.

In his second body paragraph, Hunkovic characterizes himself as an unwilling member of the outsider class. This sets up a **contrast** between him and the "Future Criminals of America" and leads to **examples** of their ongoing persecution of him. He **describes** the characteristics that landed him in this group and the ongoing attacks he endured as a result. The second half of this paragraph is

Consider Your Options

Hunkovic's conclusion makes use of an analogy—"Just as a doctor. . . ." What other analogies might you suggest that could be used to conclude this essay?

devoted to **causal analysis** as Hunkovic tries to ascertain what would lead the troublemakers to behave as they do.

The main part of the third paragraph **narrates** the incident that led to an escalation of Hunkovic's problems and to his understanding more fully the system at Liberty Middle School. The anecdote is followed by an **analysis** of the **process** the school administrators used to get to the bottom of the situation.

The Conclusion

Hunkovic's concluding paragraph confirms what the reader has sensed all along: that his essay has been a subtle **argument** against the unfairness of the school he attended as well as a claim that the school represents, in microcosm, the unfair world that faces us all.

EXERCISE

Write an outline of "Three Years Without Liberty." (For help with outlines, see Chapter 2, pages 41–42.) How has the writer organized his essay? In what ways, if any, would you change the organization?

Additional Writing Topics

1. Analyze and evaluate your life at this moment. Are you doing as well as you had hoped and planned?
2. What single mistake have you made in your life that you would correct if you could go back in time?
3. If you were granted the ability to write one piece of legislation to establish a new law or modify or nullify a current law, what would you propose?
4. What was your high school like? Discuss the building, the people, the curriculum, and the problems and challenges that you faced.
5. **Writing on the job.** For a self-evaluation, predict what your career will be like in ten years. Use your imagination, and be as specific as you can. Your audience is your immediate supervisor and the human resources manager at your company.

MORE OPTIONS ONLINE For more help with the step-by-step development of the blended essay, go to **www.mhhe.com/writingtoday**.

Responding to a Photograph

As World War II drew to a close, Allied soldiers took over areas formerly controlled by the Axis powers. In 1945 Toni Frissell took the photograph of an American soldier examining a bombed church in Italy that appears on page 491.

CLASSROOM HINT Item 1 can be used as a prompt for in-class writing. Item 2 requires careful instructor supervision as students go through the research/writing processes.

1. Write an informal response to the photograph. What do you notice? How does the image make you feel? How does the photograph allow for multiple interpretations?
2. World War II cost the lives of millions of soldiers and noncombatants. It also caused the destruction of vast amounts of property, including many instances of fine architecture and artwork. Using a combination of library and online research, explore the destruction of a major building important for its architecture or the destruction or disappearance of a major

Toni Frissell, *American Soldier in Bombed Church in World War II, Italy, March 1945.* The Library of Congress [LC-F9 02-4504-376-02].

EXERCISE (page 490)
Answers will vary. The following sentence outline is suggested.

I. Thesis: Experiencing the microcosm of modern society called Liberty Middle School altered Kevin's outlook on life.
II. Soon after he started sixth grade, he noticed a social class system underlying the way students and faculty interacted with each other.
   A. The highest members were the intellectuals, or nerds.
   B. The middle class, the majority, contained the athletes, cheerleaders, and the somewhat popular students.
   C. Next there were the Future Criminals of America.
   D. Above all was the faculty, who took on all the functions of a small government.
   E. Finally, he noticed a class of outsiders, who for one reason or another didn't fit into any category.
III. Kevin ended up in the outsider group because of his shyness and height.
   A. His status made him vulnerable to the Future Criminals, who attacked him at least twice.
   B. He tried to find a reason for the attacks, and came to the conclusion that many factors were involved.
   C. The category to which a student belonged seemed to be based on the institution's ability or inability to deal with the student.
      1. The people the system could help benefited from it.
      2. Those who did not benefit became angry and lashed out at it, causing the faculty to lash back.
      3. Unfortunately, Kevin was caught in the crossfire.
IV. Because he was young, every event seemed momentous and terrifying.

collection of art. Write a documented essay that analyzes the importance of the architecture or artwork and then looks into what happened to it during the war and just after. (For more information on documented essays, see Chapter 21.)

Writing About Film

In *Fargo* (1996, R), Jerry Lundegaard, executive sales manager at a car dealership, gets into financial trouble and decides to stage the kidnapping of his wife, Jean, so that he can turn some of the ransom money to his own uses. His plan goes seriously haywire. Write an essay exploring how *Fargo* uses these developmental options: process analysis, causal analysis, comparison/contrast, and argument. (Warning: *Fargo* earns every bit of its "R" rating.)

A. When authority figures began to harass him, the entire system solidified in his mind.
B. On the bus, he was blamed by the bus driver for something he didn't do.
  1. He was called to the office and named some possible suspects.
  2. The administrator told the people he had accused, and he was attacked by the suspects and also blamed by the administration anyway.
V. This experience caused enough mental stress to make Kevin realize how society really functions.

In *Frankenstein* (1931, NR), Henry Frankenstein is obsessed with creating human life. He eventually succeeds, but then everything goes tragically wrong. Write an essay exploring how *Frankenstein* uses these developmental options: process analysis, causal analysis, comparison/contrast, and argument.

Using the Internet

Search the Internet for insights and information to use when developing essays that employ several options.

1. In paragraph 2 of "The Men We Carry in Our Minds," Scott Russell Sanders mentions the effects of the risks and dangers that working men he knew experienced on the job. Research and write an essay that explores the health hazards that people working in a particular industry, occupation, or profession face. For example, you might focus on the black lung that coal miners are at risk of developing, the carpal-tunnel syndrome experienced by office workers, or the long-term psychological or physiological risks of being a police officer.

Learn more about your subject by reading about it online. In your essay you should use multiple strategies—for example, defining the health hazards, analyzing their causes, describing their physical and/or psychological effects, analyzing processes through which they may be avoided and treated, and providing pertinent examples of people or groups of people who have faced them.

2. Robert Reich tells us that between 1978 and 1987, "the poorest fifth of American families became 8 percent poorer and the richest fifth became 13 percent richer." To what extent has this trend continued? Research this question on the Internet, and present your findings in a well-developed essay that cites your sources using the Modern Language Association (MLA) format or the American Psychological Association (APA) format. MLA style and APA style are discussed in Chapter 21 of this textbook.

Part 2 of this book examines the rhetorical options, the basic structures at the heart of the essay. As we point out, these options almost never occur as "pure" forms. Most essays, even if they rely primarily on a particular option, contain strategies derived from other options as well. The nine rhetorical structures covered in Part 2 are starting points that let writers develop essays suited to a specific purpose and audience.

PART 3 APPLICATIONS

Being able to write an essay in any one of the nine options is also a starting point. After the first course in first-year composition, writers find that the world of purposes and audiences expands dramatically. College courses, graduate and professional schools, and the business world dictate that writers build upon what they have learned. Good writers, in other words, think on their feet, improvising to meet the needs of the situation. Very often, whoever requests written work—a history professor, a production manager, a venture capitalist—doesn't care as much about format as about effective results.

Part 3 helps you take the next logical step—applying what you have learned to specific contexts: essay examinations, business documents, essays about literature, and the research paper.

Chapter 16 discusses the essay examination. Too often, when faced with the time limits of an essay exam, students who ordinarily have a good grasp of the writing process will panic, writing as fast as they can whatever they remember in whatever order they remember it. Frequently, the result is a mess. Other, less-worried students justify a casual approach to essay exams with: "Dr. Tompkins teaches history, not English." Actually, if Dr. Tompkins is like most professors, she hates sloppy writing. Faculty from other disciplines frequently ask English teachers "What in the world are you teaching these students? Why can't they write a decent exam?" Of course students can write a decent essay exam—if only they take a few minutes to plan their work before putting pen to paper. Chapter 16 explains how to do so.

Chapter 17 is devoted to the formats used in modern business: e-mail, memos, letters, and résumés. Often, students believe that writing is a peculiar requirement that their college, out of touch with the "real" world, persists in inflicting on them. They are frequently shocked when they get the job they've long dreamed of, only to find that it requires a great amount—and variety—of writing. In addition, supervisors have been known to express anger toward college-trained, entry-level workers who cannot produce coherent business letters. Finally, even getting a good job requires an effective résumé and a strong letter of application.

Chapter 18 discusses a mechanical process that many students find quite problematic: quoting text. Whether you are writing about literature, analyzing a psychological study, or writing a research paper, your ability to quote text accurately and appropriately will be a substantial factor in the ultimate quality of your document.

Chapter 19 looks at writing that for many students is the next logical step after learning the rhetorical options. Writing about literature is an **analytical** process. "Book reports" and "appreciations" completed in high school are passé. Instead, instructors will ask you to read a short story, poem, or play and then explain some aspect of it, such as character development or theme. The successful student displays an understanding of the terminology of literary analysis, the ability to quote from the text and cite quotations correctly, and a strong understanding of the work's meaning. Actually, many students find that literary analysis is not as difficult as they feared.

The research paper is a complicated task that most students dislike and/or fear. We offer a modified description: the research paper is a complicated *yet straightforward* task. As discussed in chapters 20 and 21, it is a rigorous project but not a mysterious one.

Today's student researchers must use both print sources and Internet sources. Chapter 20 discusses both, and it considers the value of the Internet as well as its potential pitfalls. Chapter 21 builds on Chapter 20; it shows you how to use your research findings in a documented essay. We concentrate on the two formats most often required of undergraduates, the Modern Language Association (MLA) format and the American Psychological Association (APA) format. The former is normally used in English and other humanities courses; the latter is used in the social sciences. In addition to describing the steps and requirements of writing a research paper, we present a full-length documented essay written by a student using the MLA format. ●

CHAPTER 16

ESSAY EXAMINATIONS

In the semesters to come, you will find that some instructors rely on objective tests whereas others prefer essay exams. Essay exams have the advantage of indicating more about what the student knows and how the student thinks. They measure not only knowledge but also analytical and organizational skills.

Many students are concerned with only one feature of the essay exam: the time limit. This focus is understandable but potentially dangerous. Writing essays for English classes can be a relatively leisurely task for students, who can take their time drafting, revising, and proofreading. In contrast, having only fifty or seventy-five minutes to complete an exam can be daunting. Some test takers rush through the exam without using what they learned in composition classes; others plan, prewrite, draft, and revise. The latter course is obviously preferable.

STUDY FOR THE EXAM

Before the day of the essay exam, you can improve your chances of success by the amount of time you devote to studying for it. Studying for an essay exam is no different than studying for a short-answer test. Both processes are hard work. However, essay exams often require you to state an idea or opinion or take a position and then to support that statement with information that demonstrates your knowledge of the subject. The facts, opinions, and other information you include will be of your own choosing, yet they will have to relate directly to the question. As such, essay exams require a firmer grasp of the material than do short-answer exams. They also require different approaches, as discussed below.

Consider Your Options

We live in a busy world in which everyone seems to have a very hectic life. Too often, students react to their busy schedules by following a "just-in-time" model that leaves little room for error. However, this approach is not conducive to successful test taking. Try arriving five to ten minutes before an exam, with easy-to-digest food on your stomach. You'll be in much better shape to attack the exam.

READ THE DIRECTIONS

Students often get themselves in trouble on essay exams because they misinterpret or fail to read directions. Directions indicate the instructor's expectations.

- **Answer only what you are asked:** If the directions ask you to "write a fully developed paragraph in response to *seven* of the following twelve questions," writing on all twelve probably won't help your grade. Most instructors will grade only your first seven responses.
- **Meet or exceed minimum expectations:** If the test asks you to write "fully developed paragraphs" and your responses are two sentences long, don't expect a good grade. It's almost impossible to develop an informative paragraph by using only two sentences, and your instructor may view such an effort as slacking. A professor of film studies showed us a student's exam in which each of five questions was to be answered by a minimum of eighty-five words. All five of the responses were between eighty-six and ninety-one words. Obviously, the student cared less about displaying his command of the subject than about crossing the minimal threshold.

The test's directions may ask for "short answers," "paragraphs," or "essays." Therefore, an important part of reading the directions is to distinguish among these three types of responses.

Short Answers

Students frequently equate "short answer" with "single sentence." Most instructors want a bit more. Compare the following two responses to this exam question used in a sports history class:

CLASSROOM HINT Consider bringing in samples of short-answer questions written by colleagues who teach content courses (with their permission, of course). At the very least, you might make such questions available to your college's writing or instructional-support center as tutoring tools for test taking.

What is the significance of the year 1912 to American golf?

Student X: That was the year Snead, Nelson, and Hogan were born.

Student A: Ben Hogan, Byron Nelson, and Sam Snead were all born in 1912. This trio dominated American golf for thirty years, spanning the era from the retirement of Bob Jones to the arrival of Arnold Palmer and Jack Nicklaus.

Note that student A has added information, not simply words. She displays a far wider grasp of and appreciation for the question than student X does.

Paragraphs

A paragraph written in response to an exam question is no different from a paragraph written for an English composition. It needs a topic sentence, internal supports, and evidence. The following response to a political science exam question could have appeared in the text of an out-of-class paper as well:

The electoral college was put in place by the Founding Fathers to ensure stability in presidential elections. Since then, the electoral college—not the popular vote—has determined the results of five presidential elections, the most recent being the Bush-Gore struggle in 2000. For its detractors, the electoral college system, whereby each state sends a predetermined number of electors to reflect the state's vote total, denies the overall will of the nation's voters. For example, Al Gore's national vote total was greater than George W. Bush's. However, the supporters of the electoral college point out that without this system, candidates would concentrate their campaigns in the heavily populated states—New York, Illinois, California, Texas, and Florida, along with a few others—and ignore the rest. Indeed, a map showing who won what in the 2000 race indicates that "most of the country" (in a geographic sense) voted for Bush. The only heavily populated states not won by Gore were Texas (Bush's home state) and, controversially, Florida.

This response is thoughtful and fully developed. The paragraph begins with a topic sentence that is supported by the example of the 2000 presidential election and by a discussion of the Gore-Bush results. More important, it presents specific facts, clearly revealing the student's strong grasp of the material.

Essays

How much longer is an essay than a paragraph? The answer depends on a number of variables, some of which are physical. If the instructor gives you a page and a half of writing space, you should be able to estimate how much text you can fit into it. If the instructor has indicated how long you should spend on each section of the exam and you are given thirty minutes for the essay part, you should plan accordingly. The main requirement, no matter what length is expected, is that you produce an essay with all of its components: introduction, including thesis; body paragraphs with as much development as you can muster; and a conclusion, even if it is a brief one. (See the sample essay at the end of this chapter, pages 501–502, for a sense of how this type of response can be developed.)

ALLOCATE YOUR TIME

Begin by reading all of the directions and all of the questions. As you read them, think about how you will allocate your time:

- **Decide what to do first and what to leave for last.** If the exam asks you to respond to five questions and you are comfortable with four, do these four first. Save the remaining time for the fifth. Otherwise, you might waste time on a question on which you're probably not going to do well anyway.
- **Don't get too comfortable with just one part of the exam.** Many students who are thoroughly prepared for an exam start on the first section—paragraph-length responses—and do so well that they forget that the essay-length section follows. The high marks they make on the paragraphs are brought down by low marks on the essay section. Poor planning, not a lack of study and skills, is the culprit here.
- **Avoid trying to finish early.** When you take an objective test, you answer all questions, you check your work, and then you're done. However, an essay exam is more dynamic—many things can go wrong. Careful students use all the time allotted to them.

INTERPRET KEY WORDS

CLASSROOM HINT Each of these items also makes a good prompt for a short research paper.

The rhetorical options you learned about in the preceding chapters can be used in the essay exam as well. However, the instructor probably won't ask for a specific approach; you will need to interpret key words in test directions to decide on the correct option or options. To see how this works, read through these sample test questions and the analysis that follows each one:

1. *Outline Jean Piaget's theory of psychological development. Use examples to illustrate each stage.*

Here, the student is asked to discuss stages of development—that is, development over time. Thus, *stage* is a key word that clearly suggests **narrative.** Also, because stages together make up a process, with each stage building on the previous one, both **process analysis** and **causal analysis** will work here as well. Finally, the question calls for examples, so **exemplification** is another obvious strategy.

2. *Describe Picasso's* Guernica *and its effect on the viewer.*

There are two key words here—*describe* and *effect*—that direct the student's response.

3. *In the early 1950s, congressional Democrats were split into three factions. Name these groups, and explain how they came to exist.*

Classification is the overriding strategy here, but either **process analysis** or **causal analysis** will be needed to fulfill the second part of the question.

4. *No one has been drafted into the U.S. military for thirty years. Is the decision to have an all-volunteer army a good one?*

This question asks for the student's opinion, so **argument** is the obvious choice. As with all argumentative essays, however, specific **examples** will strengthen this response.

5. *Explain the role of mitochondria in cell division.*

Mitochondria have a role (part) in cell division, which is a process. **Process analysis** (informative, not instructional) is required here.

6. *In 1919 the Volstead Act instituted Prohibition, which lasted until 1933. What was a major unanticipated consequence of Prohibition?*

Consequence means "effect"; hence, the best approach is **causal analysis,** focusing on effects.

7. *In 1980, U.S. voters were asked to choose as their president either Jimmy Carter or Ronald Reagan. What political traditions and outlooks did the two candidates represent?*

Clearly, the student is being asked to concentrate on the differences between Carter and Reagan. **Comparison/contrast** is the likely option, developed point-by-point.

8. *In the 1950s, how did the Polaroid Company market its revolutionary camera?*

The key word is *how;* the emphasis is on **process analysis.**

9. *Historians rank Franklin D. Roosevelt as one of our greatest presidents. Why did fifty years go by before an appropriate national monument was established?*

The key word is *why;* the best approach is **causal analysis,** focusing on causes.

10. *Describe the "ideal Victorian woman" and compare her to the "ideal woman of today."*

Here, *describe* is used loosely. An analytically minded student will realize that *define* is more apt. In addition to **defining** the ideal Victorian woman and the ideal contemporary woman, the student must shift gears and use **contrast.** This approach naturally calls for a subject-by-subject organization: after the first part of the essay defines the Victorian ideal and the contemporary ideal, the second part portrays—in detail—the differences between the modern ideal and its earlier counterpart.

CLASSROOM HINT Here is another example of fast prewriting in response to item 7 on page 499.

Option—Point-by-point contrast

Intro—Carter's policies reflect liberal, Reagan's conservative traditions

2nd—foreign policy

3rd —support for military

4th—tax policy

5th—economic policy

6th—Reagan's policies influence American agenda through 1993 and beyond.

Consider Your Options

This prewriting provides clues on how to develop each paragraph. Notice the variety of options you would use to develop the intended essay:

- Develop the introduction using definition and cause/effect.
- Develop paragraph 2 using narration.
- Develop paragraph 3 using process analysis.
- Develop paragraphs 4–5 using description, exemplification, and contrast.
- Develop the conclusion using exemplification.

PREWRITING ESSAY RESPONSES

We often hear students claiming "I don't have time to prewrite; I barely have enough time to *write*." However, time pressure makes prewriting even more important. We're not referring to formal outlines or lengthy freewriting, just quick, down-and-dirty prewriting that gives focus to your essay and helps ensure that you won't get stuck at one point or another with nothing left to say.

Consider example 6 in the previous section, which asks the student to explain "a major unanticipated consequence of Prohibition." The following is an example of the fast prewriting that will help the student write an essay response:

Option—cause/effect, use effect

Intro—What was Prohib?

2nd ¶—what act. happened: people kept drinking

3rd ¶—problem-how to get booze

4th ¶—unorganized crime

5th ¶—organized crime

Conc.—org. crime still with us today

Running out of time often induces nervousness, if not panic. Having a guide to follow can help control this reaction and keep you working in a systematic way rather than scribbling down random ideas as they come to mind. In addition, such prewriting is an aid to memory, invaluable when you are under stress.

DRAFTING ESSAY RESPONSES

In some ways, a good response on an essay exam resembles an essay written out of class; in others, it does not. For example, both the introduction and the conclusion of a response to an exam question tend to be shorter than those found in formal essays. The body of the exam essay gets the major emphasis because the grader wants to see (1) how much the student knows and (2) how well the student can organize this information. Moreover, because of time constraints, an exam essay will likely not have as much structure as one written out of class.

In most ways, however, the two are essentially similar. One feature that should not be altered or omitted is a clear statement of intent. In other words, both exam essays and essays written out of class must be controlled by a clearly stated thesis, and both must contain clear topic sentences in each body paragraph. You don't need to impose a great deal of structure when writing an exam essay, just enough to help your reader process your response. Of course, you also need to include enough supporting detail to make your response credible and to reveal the full extent of your knowledge.

Sample Essay Exam Response

The essay below was written in response to the following question on a midterm exam in an introductory sociology class:

What are two theories about the individual self and social interaction?

1 How a person defines the self and presents the self in social interactions are two separate but related issues.

Introduction and thesis

2 In one theory, the individual defines the self in terms of the world in which she lives. Charles Horton Cooley put forth the theory of the "looking-glass self" to explain the process of self-definition. This is an imperfect process, but essentially the individual uses others as a mirror (looking-glass) from which to begin to perceive the self. Three steps take place. First, the individual tries to imagine how her appearance, personality, and overall persona are perceived by others. (Am I fat? Am I sullen? Am I likable?) Next, the individual tries to determine how others *judge* this impression. Third, the individual develops a self-concept based on the first two factors.

First theory discussed.

Process analysis used to explain first theory.

CLASSROOM HINT Reviewing this student response in class is helpful. Note that while the overall structure of the response is based on contrast, the second paragraph uses both definition and process analysis; paragraph 3 uses causal analysis and illustration; paragraph 4, which introduces the second theory, uses definition; and paragraph 5 uses causal analysis.

3 As mentioned, the process is imperfect. If in step one the individual is mistaken about others' perceptions, then step two is corrupted because the individual thinks she is being "judged" according to a set of perceptions that do not in fact exist. Also, it seems that Cooley's theory can be extended in the sense that we can develop different self-concepts in different contexts. For example, Jane works in a highly competitive, large office. She is not the brightest of her peers or the most pretty. She has a "low" self-concept at work. However, one night a week Jane volunteers at a soup kitchen for homeless women. Here she realizes that she is perceived as pretty and smart. Her self-concept is "high" in this context.

Cause and effect used to explain a problem with the process.

Example used to illustrate a complication of the first theory.

4 A second, more dynamic theory is put forth by Erving Goffman. He believed that in public, people are actors, rarely revealing their "true selves." Public is the "front stage," according to Goffman, where people "act" according to the needs of the situation. Home is the "back stage," where we can be ourselves.

Second theory discussed.

Analogy used to explain second theory.

5 What complicates the "front stage" is that everyone is aware of the fact that everyone is "acting," so people are alert to the possibility of a poor performance,

Effects of social interaction as acting discussed.

in which someone falls out of his or her role. People are graded on the quality and consistency of their "impression management," their ability to control how they are perceived. Goffman called the ongoing dynamic and its study "dramaturgical analysis."

Conclusion.

Both theories have been attacked for being too simplistic or reductive. However, they are definitely a starting point for understanding the self in society. 6

EXERCISE

EXERCISE Again, you might ask colleagues teaching content courses to allow you to discuss some of their essay questions in class as practice.

Do you have an upcoming essay exam? If so, try to predict from your studying what questions might be asked. Take one of these projected questions, establish a time limit for yourself, and use this chapter's guidelines to write a practice exam essay.

CHAPTER 17

BUSINESS FORMATS

Carla works as an automobile designer. On a typical morning she arrives at work just before her design group's meeting. She checks her e-mail, but because there are so many messages, she prints them out to read during some dead time at the meeting. Her mailbox (the physical one) contains three letters and four memos, which she takes to the meeting as well.

After the meeting, she answers e-mails, writes letters, and writes a memo. She also attends to the "design" elements of her job.

Carla is astonished at how much writing her job requires. "I went to college to learn engineering," she says. However, the world of work requires strong communications skills, both oral and written, along with a sure sense of **audience**, crucial in dealing with colleagues, superiors, clients, and others.

This chapter covers four basic business documents: e-mail, the memo, the business letter, and the résumé, emphasizing standard formats and audience needs.

E-MAIL, MEMOS, AND BUSINESS LETTERS

Electronic mail (e-mail) is a relative newcomer to business. For centuries, the two standard forms of written business communication were memos and letters. Memos are internal documents, sent within a business; letters go outside the business, to clients and vendors. Today, e-mail is used for both functions. However, e-mail has not replaced the memo or the letter. Each format still has a niche in business writing.

E-mail

E-mail is a written message sent from one computer to another. It can be forwarded, saved, or deleted. E-mail saves businesses money when compared to the cost of long-distance telephone calls, and it also preserves a record of the communication automatically, which is normally not the case with a telephone call.

A true convenience, e-mail enables you to send a message to a colleague down the hall and or on the other side of the world. E-mail has other advantages as well. Let's say you make the following phone call: "Ed, the classroom change you requested has gone through. You're in Main Hall 214." Most people would thank you and hang up. Not Ed. He reiterates the reasons he needs the room change (of course, this is the third time you have heard them). He also rambles on about how much the scheduling office must hate him, for this is the third time in two years that he has made such a request. E-mail avoids this problem. Your two sentences are quickly sent to Ed, who probably feels isolated these days, for he receives no phone calls from anyone who can avoid him.

The main issues in writing and sending e-mails are the practical context and the rhetorical context, which includes audience analysis.

The Practical Context

Note that it is very important to include in the subject line a phrase that will provide your reader with an immediate, specific, and accurate idea of the e-mail's contents.

The computer automatically inserts a date and time, so the writer doesn't need to add them. Moreover, like a memo, an e-mail has **To** and **From** lines at the top. Hence, there is no need for a salutation ("Dear Mark"). However, the **From** line might identify the sender as **Jennifer189,073@genericemail.com,** so it's always a good idea to add a "signature line," which usually includes your name and the name of your organization, at the bottom of any e-mail. Note how the practical context affects the following two e-mails, which otherwise contain the same message:

> From: Jennifer189,073@genericemail.com
> To: Mark47,751@genericemail.com
> Subject: Conference rescheduling
>
> Mark: Thank you for your note regarding the conference rescheduling. I was just about to make plane reservations, and you saved me a lot of trouble.
> Jennifer Lewis

> From: Jennifer_Lewis@Bindleburgbarns.com
> To: Mark_Pluta@Bindleburgbarns.com
> Subject: Conference rescheduling
>
> Thank you for your note regarding the conference rescheduling. I was just about to make plane reservations, and you saved me a lot of trouble.

In the second example, a salutation and "signature" are not necessary. However, are there times when they would be helpful? Read on.

Consider Your Options

Proofread your e-mail. At school, sending a hastily keyed and otherwise unexamined message to an instructor will not help your standing in the class. At work, your e-mail messages may well be the only concrete record of your communication skills, an area that your manager will be considering when it is time to evaluate your performance.

The Rhetorical Context

As you will see throughout this chapter, awareness of **purpose** and **audience** is crucial in business communication. The content of your memo, as well as your tone, will depend on whether you are writing to your supervisor (up), your subordinates (down), or your colleagues (sideways). Often, in fact, a message is directed to more than one reader and going in more than one direction. Your content and tone will also be affected by your reason for writing.

If a copy of the e-mail from Jennifer to Mark was being sent to Jennifer's supervisor, for example, the rhetorical context would change. The boss might not know what Jennifer and Mark know, so Jennifer would need to include more information and perhaps make the tone more formal:

> From: Jennifer_Lewis@Bindleburgbarns.com
> To: Mark_Pluta@Bindleburgbarns.com
> CC: Ed_Rowe@Bindleburgbarns.com
> Subject: Conference rescheduling
>
> Thank you for your note regarding the conference rescheduling, from June 17–19 to June 24–26. I was about to make plane reservations when your message came through. I'll now make them for 4:00 p.m. on June 24.

Memos

The **memo (memorandum)** is a staple of corporate and institutional life. Memos are *objective* and *quantitative;* they deal with day-to-day realities such as the following:

- Documenting the progress of projects
- Announcing changes in procedure and policy
- Accounting for time and money spent
- Giving orders
- Making requests

Most companies have policies regarding memo content, format, and distribution. However, the basic format and style of memos do not vary much. Figure 17.1 (page 507) is a memo written from a supervisor to her staff. The four lines at the top are standard. Some companies alter the wording or its order, but **DATE, TO, FROM,** and **SUBJECT** are generic. The handwritten initials of Angela de Jesus indicate her "ownership" of the memo. Memos are never signed, so the initials prevent a subversive employee from floating a document under someone else's name. The subject line ("Complaint messages") is specific and gets the reader's attention.

CLASSROOM HINT If you are discussing this chapter in class, make sure to refer to specific sections of the de Jesus memo (page 507) at this point in the presentation.

Traditionally, the text of a memo is divided into three parts—introduction, body, and conclusion:

1. A memo's **introduction** is usually brief. Functioning like an essay's **thesis statement**, it announces what the memo will cover. Be explicit: "This memo covers . . ." or "This memo explains . . ." saves readers time because it allows them to decide whether the memo is relevant to them before they even read it.
2. The memo's **body** is the reason the memo was written. The body of the memo in Figure 17.1 starts with "Identifying a Complaint Call" and continues through "Routing Complaint Calls." The supervisor outlines steps that customer support representatives should take with belligerent callers.
3. The memo's **conclusion** often restates important content from the body, in this case the supervisor's reasoning. It also fulfills an essential function: asking for a response, especially if clarification is needed. Had de Jesus neglected to ask for questions, an employee could have ignored her message and then tried to justify this act by claiming a lack of understanding.

Formatting

A business writer must make documents easy to read because the audience is probably as busy as the writer. The following features of modern memos expedite the reader's task:

CLASSROOM HINT Note the short paragraphs in the McGillis memo in Figure 17.2 (page 509).

1. **Short paragraphs.** In an essay, paragraphs should be fully developed. Memos use shorter blocks of text. Some paragraphs may contain only one sentence.
2. **Paragraph format.** The preferred format is block style, single spaced, with no first-line indentation but a full line space between paragraphs. (See Figure 17.2.)
3. **Headings.** If a writer divides a message into two or more sections, the body of the memo should include headings, normally styled in bold type. In Figure 17.1, the writer has two issues to address, so she separates them, enabling the reader to process the text more easily.

Figure 17.1: Memo Written to Subordinates

DATE: 18 November 2005
TO: Customer Support Staff
FROM: Angela de Jesus, Customer Support Manager AJ
SUBJECT: Complaint messages

In our last meeting, we spoke about the difference between phone calls from customers needing technical support and phone calls that are really complaints. The following procedure, effective immediately, should be used to handle the latter.

IDENTIFYING A COMPLAINT CALL
Experience tells us that most complaint callers do not have a true complaint; they just need more technical assistance. Some are new users of networked systems and become frustrated when a problem occurs. Therefore, please follow these guidelines when in a situation that may require your supervisor's assistance:

- As indicated above, most complaint callers are more frustrated than angry. If you lead them through their problem step by step—even if you duplicate their first attempt to solve the problem—you may discover where the confusion lies.
- However, be alert to an angry tone, an abrupt or aggressive manner, or dismissive and judgmental comments. Pay special attention to threats of litigation.
- In any case, use your judgment. If you cannot help the client and the conversation worsens, call upon your supervisor.

ROUTING COMPLAINT CALLS
Route any phone message that indicates customer dissatisfaction to your supervisor or to me. If both of us are busy—which happens frequently during normal business hours—put the caller on hold, **but do not go to another call.** Angry people can become even more volatile when trapped on hold. Monitor the time the caller is "parked," and break in every 90 seconds to assure the caller that he or she will be connected to a supervisor soon.

We want satisfied customers. We also want you to find your work fulfilling and nonthreatening. The procedures above should make your job easier and our clients happier. If you have questions, please drop by my office or call me at 1104.

4. **Lists.** A newspaper's business section contains tables listing the values of hundreds of stocks and mutual funds. Each row in the table contains the same information for the different equities listed. Because the paper is presenting parallel information, a table is the most efficient way to display these data. Similarly, a writer can use a list format to quickly and efficiently provide parallel information in business correspondence. (See Figure 17.2 on page 509.) Lists can be either **numbered,** as in Figure 17.2, or **bulleted,** with a round (•), square, (▪), or diamond-shaped (♦) symbol before each item. Numbered lists show a sequence—a chronological list of steps to be followed or a list of items in order of their importance. Bullets are used when listed elements are equal in importance.
5. **Highlighting for emphasis.** In any memo, certain words, phrases, and sentences represent the reason that the memo exists. These can be highlighted—underscored, *italicized,* or **boldfaced**—to indicate their importance. The memo in Figure 17.1 contains a clause in bold type under "Routing Complaint Calls." "**Do not go to another call**" is the most important instruction in the procedure the supervisor is explaining.

   Note that highlighting works best when used sparingly. Memos filled with boldfaced and/or italicized terms are annoying.

Examples of Business Memoranda

Figures 17.1, 17.2, and 17.3 are examples of memos that might be used in the workplace. As noted in Figure 17.1, a customer support manager outlines a new procedure to deal with complaint calls to her staff. The purpose is twofold: to make disgruntled customers happier and to help her subordinates do their jobs. After you reread this memo, answer the questions that follow.

Questions

1. What is the focus (the "thesis") of this memo?
2. Are there issues or details that need clarification? If so, what are they, and how would you clarify them?
3. How would you describe the author's tone? Does she come across as authoritarian, relaxed, or somewhere in the middle? Point to specific words, phrases, or sentences to support your answer.

QUESTIONS

1. De Jesus states her purpose clearly in the last line of the first paragraph.
2. The writer might have included specific examples under "Identifying a Complaint Call." Under "Routing Complaint Calls," she might have provided an alternative to her suggestion for dealing with callers who must be put on hold for long periods. Breaking in every 90 seconds "to assure the caller that he or she will be connected" would not satisfy some people.
3. In general, the tone is reasoned and controlled. Paragraphs 3, 4, and 5 are worth discussing in this regard.

The context for Figure 17.2, the first in a pair of memos, is a church landscaping project on which two employees are working together largely free of supervision. It is essentially a private communication in which Frank McGillis is writing to Victor Espinoza to outline tasks needed to get a job back on schedule. In this case, the writer knows that his reader shares the same information, so he need not explain the context to his colleague. Moreover, both men know that the "Mr. Thompson" referred to in the memo is their supervisor and that

Sara Bannion is a member of the church finance committee. Therefore, McGillis doesn't need to identify them.

After you read both memos (figures 17.2 and 17.3), answer the questions that follow on page 510.

Figure 17.2: Memo Written to Coworker

DATE: April 19, 2005
TO: Victor Espinoza
FROM: Frank McGillis FM
SUBJECT: Completion of Second Presbyterian Project

As discussed in our phone conversation this morning, we know that Sara Bannion is steamed about the landscaping project's running late, but she also knows that we don't control the weather. Here is what we'll need to do:

1. We need to have Melton Environmental Services get back to work on Monday. Randy Melton tells me he has lost the subcontractor he was using because of scheduling overlaps caused by the storm, but he will reassign some of his own employees.
2. Randy says they'll be done by Wednesday. Let's go over there on Thursday. We both trust Randy, but time is tight.
3. The county inspector has agreed to view the site on Friday; all we have to do is call by noon on Thursday.
4. If anything goes wrong, Mr. Thompson has asked for a report and a meeting late in the week, but let's just take care of the situation ourselves.

Further Thoughts

I've asked Randy to call me on my cell phone if he needs to. I'll let you know if he calls.

Before sending the memo to Espinoza, McGillis remembers that he needs to send a copy to supervisor Bob Thompson. This change in audience changes the context as well. McGillis decides to revise the memo, for he realizes that Thompson knows only a little about the project and that he must provide more information, clarify details, and make his tone more formal in order to accommodate the boss.

Figure 17.3: Memo Written to Coworker with Copy to Supervisor

DATE: April 19, 2005
TO: Victor Espinoza
FROM: Frank McGillis FM
SUBJECT: Completion of Second Presbyterian Project

Regarding our phone conversation this morning, we both know that Sara Bannion of the church's finance committee is not happy that the landscaping project will conclude a week after its agreed-upon date, but she also recognizes that we didn't plan for a tornado and a resulting week of chaos. Here is what we'll need to do to finish up quickly:

1. We need to have Melton Environmental Services get back to work on Monday. This was to be our last step before county inspection. Randy Melton tells me he has lost the subcontractor he was using because of scheduling overlaps caused by the storm, but he will reassign some of his own employees to get the job done and honor his contract.
2. Melton says they will be done by Wednesday. If so, you and I should inspect the project on Thursday. We both trust Melton, but time is tight.
3. The county inspector has agreed to view the site on Friday; all we have to do is call by noon on Thursday.
4. If anything goes wrong, Mr. Thompson has asked for a report and a meeting late in the week, but if we can take care of the situation this week a meeting probably won't be necessary.

Further Thoughts
I've asked Randy Melton to call me on my cell phone if problems arise. You have promised Sara Bannion daily updates. Call me if you learn anything new, as I will do for you.

c: Robert Thompson

QUESTIONS
1. Note that the first paragraph of the second memo says that Sara Bannion is on the church's financial committee and that the landscaping is a week behind schedule. It also contains details about the weather, and it reminds the reader that "this was to be our last step. . . ." Item 1 tells us that Randy Melton will "honor his contract." Under Further Thoughts, the writer reminds Espinoza that he has promised SB "daily updates."
2/3. The tone is far more formal in the second memo. McGillis replaces "steamed" with "is not happy." Also "running late" is replaced with "conclude a week after. . . ."

Questions

1. In which section(s) of the second memo in Figure 17.3 does McGillis add more information that Thompson might need to know?
2. In what ways has McGillis altered the tone of the memo?
3. Identify specific lines in which more formal diction has been inserted.

Writing Assignments

1. For a team project, you and three classmates have been assigned to research the city's laws regarding the homeless. You are the group's coordinator. Write a memo to your colleagues to (a) assign responsibilities to each group member and (b) arrange a meeting time/place. Invent facts and details as needed.
2. You are trying to be a full-time student, but your "part-time" job requires more and more of your attention. Write a memo to your supervisor requesting a meeting in which you will discuss ways to deal with the following problems:
   - Being required to work an increasing number of hours
   - Being asked to work the late shift, particularly on evenings preceding early-morning classes
   - Being excluded from decisions about scheduling
   - Being called in to work with little notice, especially at times when you need to be in class
3. What have you learned so far this semester? Write a progress report, in memo format, to your writing instructor. Use a list to discuss important concepts, practices, and techniques you have mastered. Develop each statement fully, but separate it from the next with a bullet or number.

Business Letters

Although business letters serve a variety of needs, they fall into two broad categories: letters that **inquire** and letters that **respond.** For example, sales letters, letters requesting information, and letters of complaint can be categorized as inquiry letters. Letters of explanation or letters conveying information can be considered response letters. Unlike memos, letters are sent outside an organization or business to clients, vendors, and the public. They are normally more formal than memos.

Formatting

The most common—and easiest to produce—style of business letter is full block. The lines are single-spaced, and none of the lines are indented; every paragraph starts at the left margin. Elements—including paragraphs—are separated by extra line spaces. Figure 17.4 on page 513 is an example of full-block style. The company's name, address, phone number, and e-mail address are centered because they are a part of the letterhead stationery.

Type a business letter in a standard font such as Times Roman, Courier, Palatino, Goudy, or Garamond, which are easy to read. Avoid gimmicky display fonts more suited for posters. Also avoid using all-capital letters or a script font. Finally, use a type size no smaller than 12 point (or 10 characters per inch—CPI—if that is how your computer measures type). A letter in 10-point single-spaced type is difficult to read.

CLASSROOM HINT
Other serif typefaces include Schoolbook and Bodoni. Display fonts include Bodoni Bold, Bankscript, and Lydian.

Elements of the Letter

Include the following standard elements in a business letter (see Figure 17.4 on page 513 and Figure 17.5 on page 514 for examples):

1. **Your address or your company's address, telephone number, and e-mail address.** In Figure 17.4, this information appears in the letterhead. If you are using stationery without a letterhead, type this information at the left margin as the first item on the page:

   Altacoma Integrated Digital Services, Inc.
   4197 Crestview Drive
   Altacoma, FL 39999
   904/555-4789
   altacomaids@genericemail.com

   Another option is to type the return address directly below your name, as in Figure 17.5.

2. **The date.** Separate the date from other elements by two line spaces. The date should reflect the day the letter is mailed, not the day it is written.

3. **The inside address.** This is an essential element that is especially useful with "windowpane" envelopes. In Figure 17.4, the letter is addressed to a business, not an individual. In Figure 17.5, the letter is addressed to an individual, whose title is included after his name. If the title and name are too long, put the title on the second line by itself. If the addressee has a title signifying an academic degree, place those initials, such as *M.D.* or *Ph.D.,* preceded by a comma, after his or her name. Alternately, use abbreviations such as *Dr.* or *Prof.* before the name as appropriate. Do not use both abbreviations before a name and initials after a name:

   NOT **Dr. Margaret Bander, Ph.D.**

   BUT **Dr. Margaret Bander**

   OR **Margaret Bander, Ph.D.**

CLASSROOM HINT Stress the fact that writers must use a colon in the salutation of a business letter, even if the reader is addressed by his or her first name.

4. **The salutation.** The first word of the salutation is always *Dear,* followed by the appropriate designation before the addressee's surname. (Always try to find out the name of the person to whom you are writing. If you can't, use *Dear Sir* or *Dear Madam.*) Men are *Mr.* (or *Dr.* or *Rev.,* as the case may be); women who do not have professional titles should be addressed as *Ms.* unless you have discovered that the woman you are writing to prefers *Mrs.* or *Miss.* End the salutation with a colon, not a comma or a semicolon.

5. **The introductory paragraph.** Customarily, the first paragraph of a business letter is short—a few sentences indicating the letter's focus without going into details.

CLASSROOM HINT Remind students that short paragraphs are preferable.

6. **The body.** Organize the body according to your purpose. If your letter deals with a single issue, one paragraph might suffice. If it deals with more than one issue or a series of steps in a process, use multiple paragraphs (see Figure 17.5).

7. **The conclusion.** Like the introduction, a business letter's conclusion tends to be brief. You should normally thank the reader for his or her attention and request a response, if appropriate.

Figure 17.4: Letter Requesting Information

Altacoma Integrated Digital Services, Inc.
4197 Crestview Drive
Altacoma, FL 39999
904/555-4789
altacomaids@genericemail.com

April 15, 2005

Traveler's Plaza Hotel
201 Peachtree Terminus
Atlanta, GA 30202

Dear Sir or Madam:

Our company is sending two managers, Ms. Sara Alvarez and Ms. Maria O'Connor, to Atlanta for three weeks (May 1 to May 21). We are interested in finding out about your hotel's arrangements.

Our representatives will be sharing a room—preferably a suite—and have requested the following:

1. Two double beds
2. A work area
3. Two phone lines and two data ports
4. A kitchen
5. Dry-cleaning service

Please also send us information about entertainment and restaurant options in the hotel's immediate area.

Since we are guaranteeing a three-week stay, we request a corporate package discount. We will be happy to pay in advance by credit card if details can be worked out. Thank you for your attention.

Sincerely yours,

Michael Holgrove

Michael Holgrove, Administrative Assistant
904/555-4789, ext. 2724
mholgrove_altacomaids@genericemail.com

c: Laura Bowen

Consider Your Options

When a financial transaction goes wrong—for example, a problem with a credit card statement or a telephone bill—it's tempting to pick up the phone and abuse a customer service representative. However, such an action will have no legal standing. You must write a letter (be sure to keep a copy) in order to make a legal objection to the disputed billing. Note how in Figure 17.5, Patricia Ogilvie is able to control her anger while stating her case.

8. **The complimentary close and signature line.** The complimentary close has two appropriate forms: *Sincerely yours* or *Sincerely*. This line is followed by the writer's signature, followed by the writer's typed name. If a copy has been sent to another person, the last element in the letter will be a *c:* followed by the secondary recipient's name, as in Figure 17.4.

Letters That Request Information or Adjustment

Figure 17.4 on page 513 is a letter requesting information to which the Traveler's Plaza Hotel should gleefully respond. Notice the level of specificity. The more specific your requests, the better the addressee will be able to respond. Note also the use of a list to enumerate the writer's needs. Had the writer used a narrative style, the result would have been wordy and confusing.

Figure 17.5 is a letter of complaint. It explains what went wrong and requests an adjustment: a refund or discount. In view of the Ogilvies' lost weekend at the Ocean View Mirage Motel, the request for a 50-percent refund seems reasonable. Notice that, despite Patricia Ogilvie's experience at the Mirage, the tone of her letter remains businesslike.

Figure 17.5: Letter of Complaint

June 17, 2005

Mr. Miles Gonagle, Manager
Ocean View Mirage Motel
311 N. Ocean View Drive
Altacoma, FL 39999

Dear Mr. Gonagle:

On the weekend of June 7–9, my husband, Steve, and I celebrated our tenth anniversary at your establishment. Although we had been assured by your brochures that the Mirage is a resort, our stay there was quite disappointing.

First, although we had guaranteed reservations, when we arrived on Friday, June 7 at 6:00 p.m., we were told that our room would not be ready for another hour. Hungry, we decided to eat supper at the Mirage's "gourmet" restaurant, the Gilded Oasis. Several problems occurred with the food and the service:

1. We had to wait seventy minutes between the arrival of our appetizers and the arrival of our entrées.
2. However, the arrival of our "entrées" was really the arrival of only one entrée: my husband's. I was informed by Mike, the waiter, that the kitchen had run out of ingredients for my dinner and that I would need to order another. No matter—my husband had been brought the wrong entrée anyway, so we both had to reorder.

3. When our suppers finally arrived, they were almost cold and tasted like cafeteria food.

Later that night, after we had turned out the lights and were attempting to sleep, two problems arose. One was the palmetto bugs that began dropping from the ceiling onto our bed. We notified the front desk, but the clerk responded that an exterminator would be sent in the morning; there was nothing else that he could do.

We killed the insects ourselves with a rolled-up newspaper, and once again we attempted to sleep. This proved impossible. That weekend, your other guests included the Southeast Convention of the Loyal Order of Field Mice, and their noisy, drunken antics went on into the night. When we called the front desk, the clerk said, "They'll wear out soon enough." Moreover, Mr. Gonagle, we were not told when we made reservations that a convention would be held during the weekend of our stay.

The next morning, Saturday, we checked out, two days early. Our total bill for this horrible night's stay and supper was $271.36, charged to my VISA card. In all fairness, I ask that you credit one-half of this amount to my account. Otherwise, I shall put the entire charge into dispute with VISA.

Please respond to my request by July 1.

Sincerely,

Patricia Ogilvie

Patricia Ogilvie
2801 Vine Street
Framingham, FL 39989
(305) 555-7843
paogilvie@genericemail.com

SUGGESTED ACTIVITY
At this point, you might bring in some sample information or complaint letters you have written or received and ask students to critique them.

Letters That Respond

Figures 17.6 and 17.7 exemplify the second type of letter: a response. They are alternative responses by Michael Delmonica of Altacoma Imaging to a complaint from a corporate customer, Helvetica Reprographics, Inc. The different contexts of these two letters call for different responses.

The letter in Figure 17.6, on page 516, was clearly the easier of the two to write. In it, Delmonica provides Ruth Vanmeter with what is bound to be good news: the problem was caused by a defective belt, which Altacoma will replace. Nonetheless, Delmonica takes care to use an extremely courteous tone, for even if a response letter is favorable, the addressee might be offended by a tone that seems insufficiently concerned and apologetic.

The letter in Figure 17.7 on page 517 is written in a different context. The malfunction is the result of an action by a Helvetica employee, so Altacoma is not responsible. However, Michael Delmonica has to break the bad news to Ruth Vanmeter without angering her; further, he wants to continue the two companies' business relationship. So he sweetens the deal by offering free installation of the replacement power supply and a reinstatement of the warranty. His letter should generate a positive response from Ruth Vanmeter.

Figure 17.6: Letter Granting Favorable Response to Complaint

Altacoma Imaging, Inc.
4107 N. Industrial Road
Altacoma, FL 39999
(904) 555-8575

November 14, 2005

Ruth Vanmeter
Vice President
Helvetica Reprographics, Inc.
11141 Hermes Street
Anniston, AL 33223

Dear Ms. Vanmeter:

Thank you for your phone call and e-mail regarding your MD 3080A photocopier's failure. We have determined that the problem was caused by a defective belt. Please accept our apologies; we will make the situation right.

Because your machine is under warranty, we will send a technician with a replacement belt on Friday, November 19. Your photocopier will be operable by noon on Friday.

Once again, we are sorry for any production delays that our machine's failure has caused. Please accept a one year's extension of your warranty in consideration of your inconvenience. Also, please call or write if you have additional questions or concerns.

Sincerely yours,

Michael Delmonica

Michael Delmonica
Technical Supply Manager

Figure 17.7: Letter Issuing Negative Response to Complaint

Altacoma Imaging, Inc.
4107 N. Industrial Road
Altacoma, FL 39999
(904) 555-8575

November 14, 2005

Ruth Vanmeter
Vice President
Helvetica Reprographics, Inc.
11141 Hermes Street
Anniston, AL 33223

Dear Ms. Vanmeter:

As you know, we sent a technician to Helvetica after we learned from you about the breakdown of your MD 3080A photocopier. During her visit, the technician discovered that while attempting to dislodge a paper jam, someone ignored the safety directives attached to the copier and inadvertently ruined the power supply.

Unfortunately, this action voids the warranty supplied with the MD 3080A. However, we know the inconvenience that you are suffering, and we value our long-term business relationship. Thus, we would like to propose a compromise adjustment: if you will pay for the new power supply, we will be happy to install it for free and to reinstate the warranty on the entire system.

We hope this arrangement is acceptable. Please give me a call, and I'll send up a technician the next day.

Sincerely yours,

Michael Delmonica

Michael Delmonica
Technical Supply Manager

WRITING ASSIGNMENTS
1. Encourage students to use a nonaccusatory but firm tone. Remind them to be as detailed as possible about the effects of their roommates' habits on their attempts to study and on their performance in class and on tests.
2. The tone of such a letter should be professional and appreciative. Advise students to delay the bad news until they have indicated their desire to take the position in the future.

Writing Assignments

1. You share a dorm room with another person. You are studious; your roommate likes loud music, loud conversation, and loud parties. You have not made any progress dealing with the situation. Write a letter to Student Housing outlining your problem and asking for help. Be specific in your request.
2. The Financial Aid office offers you a work-study position next semester in the biology lab. You have complications next semester and don't want the position, but you may want a similar position in the future. Write a letter responding to the offer.

RÉSUMÉS AND LETTERS OF APPLICATION

Students go to college to prepare for a career; before they know it, they graduate and must launch that career. Writing an effective résumé and letter of application is an important skill. The résumé is a summary of the applicant's education and work history; the letter of application is a more personal, persuasive document tailored to the particular position the applicant desires.

Elements of a Résumé

CLASSROOM HINT Explain that the résumé seen here is useful for people who are entering the job market. A "functional résumé," in which experience is organized by type of work, useful for those who are changing jobs.

1. **Address, phone number, and e-mail address.** Note in Figure 17.8 on page 520 that Ronald Hauser lists two addresses and phone numbers—at school and at home—along with his e-mail address.
2. **Career objective.** This is a relatively new feature, for in the past people tended to have only one résumé. Today, most people produce their own résumés on computers, so the career objective can be changed to fit specific job advertisements.
3. **Education.** For young job-seekers, education normally precedes work experience, for they have had little of the latter; education is their main selling point. Too often, however, students mention only their major, their pending degree, and the date the degree is expected. Potential employers will read your résumé to determine how you are different from the next applicant. That's why Hauser mentions his experience as a research assistant and an intern. He points out that he has a high GPA in his major: 3.75. Presumably, his overall GPA isn't as impressive, so he accentuates the positive, always a good idea in a résumé.
4. **Experience.** You may have held part-time or seasonal jobs only. However, listing these will let the potential employer know you have worked successfully. Any job in which you held a position of responsibility—a lifeguard, for example, or a closer for a fast-food restaurant—is a plus. If you have completed a successful term in the military, by all means list this fact. Employers love hiring veterans. Describe your responsibilities using concrete "action" verbs: not *did*, but *arranged, closed, opened, monitored,* and so on.
5. **Computer skills.** List these if you have them.
6. **Languages.** If you are conversant to fluent in a foreign language, mention this important skill.

7. **References.** To guard the privacy of people who have agreed to vouch for you, use *Available upon request.* However, don't send out a résumé until at least three individuals have agreed to recommend you. The opinions of friends, relatives, and members of the clergy carry little weight with employers. Instead, ask for recommendations from professors and job supervisors.

Submit Your Résumé Online

You can post your résumé online by using an Internet job-search service, such as Monster.com or Hotjobs.com. To do this you will have to save your résumé as a plain-text file, which allows prospective employers to scan your résumé for key words and information without having to peruse the entire document, thereby saving them time and effort. Such a document is also known as a *scannable résumé.*

Plain-text files exclude most style elements such as bullets, symbols, underlining, bold type, and italics. Many Internet job-search services allow you to construct a plain-text résumé simply by typing information into fields provided for this purpose. However, you can also save an existing résumé as plain text. To do this, click on your file menu and choose the "Save As" option. Then select one of the "plain-text" choices. For example, Word 97 offers a "Text Only" option.

Once your résumé is saved as a "plain-text" document, you will be able to select and paste it into the job-search service's template or text field. Many of these templates also allow you to provide key words or terms that prospective employers look for as they scan electronic résumés. This important information includes job titles, career objectives, degrees earned, and professional experience.

As is clear from Figure 17.8, the résumé is a dry, somewhat impersonal document, written in sentence fragments and avoiding the word *I.* But the résumé always travels with a letter of application, a much more personal communication.

Elements of an Application Letter

1. **The salutation.** If you are writing to a named individual whose sex is unclear (is "Lee Meyers" male or female?), call the company and ask the receptionist or the personnel department so that you can avoid potential embarrassment.
2. **The introductory paragraph.** This brief paragraph serves only three functions: to announce your application, to tell the employer where you learned of the position, and to indicate your main qualification for the position.
3. **The body.** Normally, this entails two paragraphs, the first on your education and the second on your work experience. Stress how your education and experience have qualified you. However, don't list specific courses you have taken or other, similar information that might bore the reader and weaken the focus of your message.

Figure 17.8: Sample Résumé

Ronald S. Hauser

Bolton Hall, Room 648	48 Sorghum Lane,
Franklin Southeastern University	Apt. 347
Coolmore, AL 35656	Coolmore, AL 35659
(703) 555-2493	(607) 555-8182

ronhauser3@genericemail.com

Career Objective

A position in either business or research involving practical development of alternative agricultural products.

Education

1999–present	Franklin Southeastern University, Coolmore, AL B.S. in food science to be awarded in May 2005. Concentrated on aquaculture and food irradiation. Served three semesters as research assistant for director of aquaculture research center. Interned spring semester 2003 at Logan Biograde, a food irradiation company. GPA in major: 3.75.

Experience

2002–2003	Lorenzo Catfish, Inc., Lorenzo, MS Pond developer/harvester. Coordinated the work of 17 part-time/seasonal employees. Was responsible for maintaining health of crop and maximizing acreage yield. Won Employee of the Month award on three occasions.
1998–2000 (summers)	Wal-Mart, Inc., Coolmore, AL Stocker. Worked both part time and full time between the warehouse and the store. In 1999, coordinated store's fund drive to aid two children of employees who were killed in an auto accident.

Computer Skills

MS Office, MS Word, Quattro Pro, Quark

References

Available upon request.

CLASSROOM HINT You might compare the writing of an application letter to the writing of an essay exam. Just as the essay responds to specifics in a prompt, so should a letter of application respond to specifics in an employment ad.

Figure 17.9: Letter of Application

March 17, 2005

Mr. Wade Michaels, Director
Agrisearch Analytical Association
1442 Gidney Avenue
Bloomington, IN 47999

Dear Mr. Michaels:

I am writing to apply for the position of Innovative Farm Products Coordinator, Southeast Region, advertised on March 12 in the *Atlanta Constitution.* I will graduate this spring with a B.S. in food science from Franklin Southeastern University. My blend of education and experience uniquely qualifies me for this position.

At Franklin, I concentrated in aquaculture and food irradiation. As my résumé indicates, I worked for three semesters as a research assistant for Dr. Herman Lovelace, the director of the aquaculture research center. I also completed a semester internship at Logan Biograde, a company specializing in the development of food irradiation techniques. My GPA in my major is 3.75.

My degree at Franklin has taken me six years to complete, for I took a year and a half off to earn future tuition. I spent that time working directly in aquaculture at Lorenzo Catfish, a massive operation in Lorenzo, Mississippi. Thus, I believe I have learned a great deal about the aquaculture business.

I welcome the opportunity to discuss further my qualifications for this position. If you are amenable, I will travel to Bloomington for an interview at your convenience.

Cordially,

Ronald Hauser

Ronald Hauser
Bolton Hall, Room 648
Franklin Southeastern University
Coolmore, AL 35656
ronhauser3@genericemail.com

Encl.: résumé

Note that a proliferation of the word *I* is inevitable. In Figure 17.9, Ronald Hauser avoids the problem of starting every sentence with *I* by putting transitions at the beginning of his sentences. Note also that in this section you should refer to your enclosed résumé.

4. **The concluding paragraph.** Here, restate your main qualifications for the position, and request an interview. The correct wording is some variation of "I am available for an interview at your convenience." In other words, don't set limitations on your availability.

WRITING ASSIGNMENTS
1. To expedite work on this item, ask students to share their résumés in small groups either in class or via e-mail.
2. Students might apply for actual jobs advertised in newspapers. Ask those who take this option to attach the ads to their letters.

Writing Assignments

1. Write your résumé. After you're done, ask yourself what makes your résumé better than that of one of your peers. What can you do during the rest of your college program to make yourself stand out?
2. What would be your ideal part-time job while in college? Write a letter applying for this position. Invent specific details as needed.

CHAPTER 18

QUOTING TEXT

Chapter 19 discusses writing about literature, and chapters 20 and 21 cover the process of researching and writing an essay using sources. If you are writing about literature or writing a research paper (or writing a literary analysis that uses sources), you need to know how to quote text properly and how to incorporate the text into your work.

Why is this issue so important? Being able to choose and include the proper quotation is essential in a number of different contexts. Along with writers of research papers, attorneys preparing written arguments ("briefs") and journalists writing news articles know that including a key quotation—and doing so properly—can dramatically improve the impact of a document.

In Chapter 21, we explain how to *cite* quotations using the Modern Language Association (MLA) format or the American Psychological Association (APA) format. In this chapter, we concentrate on how to *quote* text, along with how to handle basic citations of page numbers. We'll start with the MLA guidelines and then show how the same example text would be treated in the APA system. However, we begin with some general advice about quoting.

CLASSROOM HINT
Review and stress the importance of these general principles in class.

CLASSROOM HINT
Place special emphasis on item 3.

General Principles for Quoting Text

1. **Quote accurately.** Too often, original text such as "Your sensibilities are what are in question, Mr. John" becomes "You're sensabilities are what is in question, Mr. Johnson." Check your transcription to avoid introducing errors.
2. **Preserve the integrity of your sources.** Later in the chapter we indicate how to elide, or remove, unnecessary text from a quotation. However, never omit text in a way that changes the meaning of a quotation; if a quotation doesn't support your point, don't try to "reshape" it so that it does.
3. **Give full credit to your sources.** Chapters 20 and 21 explain how to avoid **plagiarism**, or the use of someone else's work without giving proper credit. Follow the guidelines in those chapters.
4. **Don't try to merge text from different parts of a source into one quotation.** For example, connecting a sentence from page 5 with one from page 16 by using an ellipsis (see page 527 and page 533) is intellectually dishonest. Instead, introduce and quote the first sentence, followed by its citation; then introduce and quote the second one, followed by its citation, as in the following example (which follows MLA guidelines):

   Rodriguez points out that the winters in his boyhood were difficult: "I grew up in some of the worst weather in the twentieth century" (5). Later, he reiterates his point: "My grandmother told me that she had never seen winters so cold" (16).
5. **Use the correct documentation system for your context.** English and the humanities use MLA; the social sciences use APA. If you try to use APA style in a paper analyzing a poem, for example, you will run into an insurmountable problem: the APA *Publication Manual* offers no guidelines for citing poetry.
6. **When you are writing an essay using quotations, don't refer to them as such.** *Quote* is a verb, not a noun. If you need to refer to text that you have quoted, call it a *statement* or a *passage*, not a *quote* or a *quotation*.

7. **Note that a comma does not precede every opening quotation mark.** In the following sentence, the comma is not needed:

INCORRECT	**Olsen's discussion of, "biosocial ethics" (499) is thorough and informative.**
CORRECT	**Olsen's discussion of "biosocial ethics" (499) is thorough and informative.**

The writer probably wouldn't have considered using a comma if *biosocial ethics* had not been enclosed in quotation marks.

INCORPORATING DIRECT QUOTATIONS: MLA GUIDELINES

The examples in this section are quotations from the following paragraph, which comes from George Orwell's "Shooting an Elephant." (This essay is part of a collection titled *Shooting an Elephant and Other Essays;* the passage is found on page 165.)

> The orderly came back in a few minutes with a rifle and five cartridges, and meanwhile some Burmans had arrived and told us that the elephant was in the paddy fields below, only a few hundred yards away. As I started forward practically the whole population of the quarter flocked out of the houses and followed me. They had seen the rifle and were all shouting excitedly that I was going to shoot the elephant. They had not shown much interest in the elephant when he was merely ravaging their homes, but it was different now that he was going to be shot. It was a bit of fun to them, as it would be to an English crowd; besides they wanted the meat. It made me vaguely uneasy. I had no intention of shooting the elephant—I had merely sent for the rifle to defend myself if necessary—and it is always unnerving to have a crowd following you. I marched down the hill, looking and feeling a fool, with the rifle over my shoulder and an ever-growing army of people jostling at my heels. At the bottom, when you got away from the huts, there was a metalled road and beyond that a miry waste of paddy fields a thousand yards across, not yet ploughed but soggy from the first rains and dotted with coarse grass. The elephant was standing eight yards from the road, his left side towards us. He took not the slightest notice of the crowd's approach. He was tearing up bunches of grass, beating them against his knees to clean them and stuffing them into his mouth.

Note this sentence early in the paragraph: "They had seen the rifle and were all shouting excitedly that I was going to shoot the elephant." Here are three ineffective or incorrect ways and three effective, correct ways to quote and cite this sentence:

WEAK: QUOTATION TREATED AS DIALOGUE

Orwell writes, "They had seen the rifle and were all shouting excitedly that I was going to shoot the elephant" (165).

This writer is using the same method that fiction writers and journalists use to report dialogue:

He said, ". . . ."

She writes, ". . . ."

In a research paper, however, using an introductory phrase or clause will give the quotation more emphasis and context:

EFFECTIVE: QUOTATION PRECEDED BY INTRODUCTORY PHRASE OR CLAUSE

According to Orwell, "They had seen the rifle and were all shouting excitedly that I was going to shoot the elephant" (165).

As Orwell notes with annoyance, "They had seen the rifle and were all shouting excitedly that I was going to shoot the elephant" (165).

SUGGESTED ACTIVITY
Contrasting incorrect and correct methods is worth doing in class. You might also want to quiz the students on this material.

INCORRECT: FLOATING QUOTATION

The tension builds as Orwell receives the gun. "They had seen the rifle and were all shouting excitedly that I was going to shoot the elephant" (165).

Quotations must be *connected* to your text, not detached from it. One way to connect a quotation and add variety to your quoting style is to use subordination:

EFFECTIVE: QUOTATION SUBORDINATED

As he starts out, Orwell realizes that "They had seen the rifle and were all shouting excitedly that I was going to shoot the elephant" (165).

The key word is *that,* which *subordinates* Orwell's sentence to the writer's introduction. (For more on subordination, see Chapter 5.) **Note:** You can also change "They" to "[t]hey." (For more on using brackets, see page 528.)

INCORRECT: COMMA SPLICE

The tension builds as Orwell receives the gun, "They had seen the rifle and were all shouting excitedly that I was going to shoot the elephant" (165).

This writer has tried to join the quoted sentence with the preceding, introductory sentence but has created a comma splice. (For more on comma splices, see Chapter 5.)

CORRECT: QUOTATION INTRODUCED BY COLON

The tension builds as Orwell receives the gun: "They had seen the rifle and were all shouting excitedly that I was going to shoot the elephant" (165).

The colon at the end of the first sentence indicates that the sentence is introducing the quotation. Remember that you must have a complete sentence followed by a colon (*not* a semicolon) before the quoted text begins. After the colon, you may quote one or more complete sentences, as in the example above, or a word or phrase, as in this example:

Orwell's phrasing echoes his title: "to shoot the elephant" (165). This task becomes increasingly significant to him as the narrative continues.

These three methods of quoting from sources will help you integrate source material successfully and add variety to your writing. In addition to these methods, the following guidelines will help you use source material accurately and effectively.

1. **Quoting text containing dialogue.** On page 164 of "Shooting an Elephant" this sentence appears:

   There was a loud, scandalized cry of "Go away, child! Go away this instant!" and an old woman with a switch in her hand came round the corner of a hut, violently shooing away a crowd of naked children.

   To indicate the quotation within this sentence, you need to change Orwell's double quotation marks to single quotation marks:

   According to Orwell, "There was a loud, scandalized cry of 'Go away, child! Go away this instant!' and an old woman with a switch in her hand came round the corner of a hut, violently shooing away a crowd of naked children" (164).

   However, if you are quoting only the woman's speech, you can use double quotation marks:

   The woman seemed both angry and scared: "Go away, child! Go away this instant!" (164).

CLASSROOM HINT Students sometimes have trouble working with dialogue within quotations, so walk them through this subsection carefully.

2. **Using quotation marks with exclamation points and question marks.** In the example above, the quoted sentence ends with an exclamation point. Note that the exclamation point precedes the closing quotation marks, the page citation, and the added period:

   instant!" (164).

   A quotation that ends with a question mark is treated similarly:

   instant?" (164).

   If the exclamation point or question mark is not part of the quotation but ends your sentence that contains the quotation, it follows the closing quotation mark and page reference:

   Ironically, Orwell notes that he "had no intention of shooting the elephant" (165)!

   The writer, not Orwell, is exclaiming here.

3. **Eliding (omitting) text.** Well-chosen quotations can add authority and interest to your writing, but you do not need to quote text that is irrelevant to your point. One way to quote economically is to **elide** (remove) superfluous text. Note this sentence:

   They had seen the rifle and were all shouting excitedly that I was going to shoot the elephant.

   You might want to remove the end of the sentence:

   Orwell writes that "They had seen the rifle and were all shouting excitedly . . ." (165).

   The three dots, called an **ellipsis**, indicate that you have removed the end of the sentence.

   If you are eliding text *within* the sentence, the ellipsis takes the place of the missing words:

The villagers' reaction was immediate: "They . . . were all shouting excitedly that I was going to shoot the elephant" (165).

However, *do not* use the ellipsis if you are removing the beginning of a single quoted sentence:

The villagers "were all shouting excitedly that I was going to shoot the elephant" (165).

You may start a quotation at any logical point in a sentence, but don't omit words in a way that will change the meaning of the sentence you are quoting.

In some situations, you may want to quote two adjacent sentences and elide part of one of them. Note how this procedure is done:

ORIGINAL PASSAGE **As I started forward practically the whole population of the quarter flocked out of the houses and followed me. They had seen the rifle and were all shouting excitedly that I was going to shoot the elephant.**

QUOTED WITH AN ELLIPSIS **"As I started forward practically the whole population of the quarter flocked out of the houses and followed me. . . . shouting excitedly that I was going to shoot the elephant" (165).**

4. **Quoting only a few words.** If you want to quote only a few words from a sentence, don't use the ellipsis; instead, embed the quotation within your sentence:

The concept of an elephant "merely ravaging" (165) a home is a terrifying understatement.

Note that the page reference can also appear at the end of the sentence, before the period:

The concept of an elephant "merely ravaging" a home is a terrifying understatement (165).

5. **Using square brackets to interpolate your own text.** The next-to-the-last sentence in Orwell's paragraph is "He took not the slightest notice of the crowd's approach." Sentences that begin with pronouns can be difficult. (He who?) Note the following solution:

According to Orwell, "He [the elephant] took not the slightest notice of the crowd's approach" (165).

The square brackets indicate that you are adding clarifying information. However, you might try an alternate approach:

According to Orwell, the elephant "took not the slightest notice of the crowd's approach" (165).

Again, you may start quoting at any logical point in the sentence.

Square brackets are also used to indicate an error—either a misspelling or an obvious factual problem—in text that you are quoting. Note the following examples:

As Bohannon writes, "When President Kennedy was killed in 1964 [sic], the nation was horrified" (419).

Rodgers uses this ancient chestnut: "It is better to give than recieve [sic]" (37).

Kennedy was killed in 1963; *receive* is spelled with the *e* preceding the *i*. The use of *[sic]*, meaning "thus" ("that's the way I found it"), tells your reader that you know the source is incorrect.

6. **Using block quotations.** According to MLA guidelines, any passage that (a) consists of more than one paragraph or (b) takes up more than four lines in *your* text must be set off as a block quotation, or extract. Here are guidelines for displaying a block quotation:
   - Don't add quotation marks before or after the quotation or alter any quotation marks that appear within the quotation.
   - Start the extract on a new line with a block indent of one inch from the left margin. Most word-processing programs have a default tab indent of half an inch, so use a double-left indent. If you are quoting more than one paragraph, indent the first line of each paragraph an additional three spaces.
   - Don't indent the right side of the quotation or attempt to center the extract.
   - Double-space the extract, and leave only a double space above and below it.
   - Place the page reference at the very end of the extract, after the terminal punctuation. Note the following example:

   Orwell writes of the building excitement:

   > The orderly came back in a few minutes with a rifle and five cartridges, and meanwhile some Burmans had arrived and told us that the elephant was in the paddy fields below, only a few hundred yards away. As I started forward practically the whole population of the quarter flocked out of the houses and followed me. They had seen the rifle and were all shouting excitedly that I was going to shoot the elephant. (165)

   Use block quotations sparingly. Never use them as a way to lengthen your paper.

CLASSROOM HINT This and the next subsection, on citing page numbers, usually require some explanation in class.

7. **Citing page numbers.** In all of the examples above, note that only a number appears in the parentheses to indicate the page in the source on which the quoted text appears. Do *not* add *page, pg., p.,* or *pp.* If a passage begins on one page and continues to another, then you should indicate the page break this way:

   . . . last word" (41-42).

   . . . last word" (161-62).

Note that the second hundreds digit is dropped if it is the same as the first one: 161–162 becomes 161–62.

EXERCISE 18.1

1. The following passage is excerpted from an article written by John Vardamus Doe and published in a regional magazine. The full article appears on pages 22–23 of the magazine. A student wrote an analysis of Doe's article; part of this analysis appears after the excerpt.

First, read the excerpt. Then read the student's response, which contains ten errors in quoting from Doe's article. Don't try to edit or "smooth out" the response, but look for instances in which the student did not follow proper quoting procedures, and correct the student's errors.

EXERCISE 18.1 The following revision eliminates the student's quoting errors.

Excerpt of Student's Analysis of Doe's Article

Doe's writing is on the debate between the free speech crowd and the morality groups. He asks a question: "How will we reconcile these two issues?" (23). Parents want to protect their children, and adults want to protect their own personal rights to access adult material.

It's true that Internet content can pose problems in public places—libraries, for instance. Before a local library changed its policy, Doe says the assistant librarian had described the situation this way: "It was like walking through an adult bookstore" (22–23). However, the rights of adults need to be considered as well. The main downfall of Doe's writing is his refusal to take a stand:

> Do we want to let adults make adult decisions? Certainly.
>
> Do we want to protect children from clearly inappropriate subject matter? Certainly. (23)

Doe seems to back the morality groups, and to discount the needs of "defenders of 'freedom of choice'" (22). However, he needs to state his case more forcefully and not be afraid to take a stand.

[from page 22] The debate over Internet content rages on. The defenders of "freedom of choice" make up one side, and those who would protect young people and traditional standards of morality make up the other.

In the early days of widespread Internet access, several lessons were learned. For example, Wynton's, an upscale grocery chain, offered free Internet access at each of its stores. The practice was stopped when several instances of shoppers' children accessing porn sites brought objections from both the parents and other concerned shoppers. In another instance, the Fresnell County Library system chose to radically restrict the range of Internet access it provided after complaints of hard-core porn images beaming into the face of every patron who walked past the terminals. According to an assistant librarian, "It was like **[page 23 begins here]** walking through an adult bookstore."

Do we want to let adults make adult decisions? Certainly.

Do we want to protect children from clearly inappropriate subject matter? Certainly.

The Internet offers a whole new world of information and communication, but it offers serious problems as well. How will we reconcile these two issues?

Excerpt of Student's Analysis of Doe's Article

Doe's writing is on the debate between the free speech crowd and the morality groups. He states, "How will we reconcile these two issues" (23). Parents want to protect their children, and adults want to protect their own personal rights to access adult material.

It's true that Internet content can pose problems in public places, libraries, for instance. Before a local library changed its policy, Doe quotes the assistant librarian as describing the situation this way, "It was like walking through an adult bookstore" (23). However, the rights of adults need to be considered as well. The main downfall of Doe's writing is he refuses to take a stand. "Do we want to let adults make decisions? Certainly. Do we want to keep children from clearly inappropriate subject matter? Certainly" (23).

Doe seems to back the morality groups, and to discount the needs of, "defenders of "freedom of choice'" (22). However, he needs to state his case more forcefully and not be afraid to take a stand.

2. **After correcting the quoting errors in the student's response, revise it so that it is a more effective, coherent, and unified analysis of the passage.**

INCORPORATING DIRECT QUOTATIONS: APA GUIDELINES

The examples in this section are quotations from the following paragraph, which comes from George Orwell's "Shooting an Elephant." (This essay is part of a collection titled *Shooting an Elephant and Other Essays* [1950]; the passage is found on page 165.)

> The orderly came back in a few minutes with a rifle and five cartridges, and meanwhile some Burmans had arrived and told us that the elephant was in the paddy fields below, only a few hundred yards away. As I started forward practically the whole population of the quarter flocked out of the houses and followed me. They had seen the rifle and were all shouting excitedly that I was going to shoot the elephant. They had not shown much interest in the elephant when he was merely ravaging their homes, but it was different now that he was going to be shot. It was a bit of fun to them, as it would be to an English crowd; besides they wanted the meat. It made me vaguely uneasy. I had no intention of shooting the elephant—I had merely sent for the rifle to defend myself if necessary—and it is always unnerving to have a crowd following you. I marched down the hill, looking and feeling a fool, with the rifle over my shoulder and an ever-growing army of people jostling at my heels. At the bottom, when you got away from the huts, there was a metalled road and beyond that a miry waste of paddy fields a thousand yards across, not yet ploughed but soggy from the first rains and dotted with coarse grass. The elephant was standing eight yards from the road, his left side towards us. He took not the slightest notice of the crowd's approach. He was tearing up bunches of grass, beating them against his knees to clean them and stuffing them into his mouth.

Note this sentence early in the paragraph: "They had seen the rifle and were all shouting excitedly that I was going to shoot the elephant." Here are three ineffective or incorrect ways and three effective, correct ways to quote and cite this sentence:

WEAK: QUOTATION TREATED AS DIALOGUE

Orwell (1950) writes, "They had seen the rifle and were all shouting excitedly that I was going to shoot the elephant" (p. 165).

SUGGESTED ACTIVITY
Again, contrasting incorrect and correct methods is worth doing in class. To make sure students have mastered the distinctions, try quizzing them.

This writer is using the same method that fiction writers and journalists use to report dialogue:

He said, ". . . ."

She writes, ". . . ."

In a research paper, however, using an introductory phrase or clause will give the quotation more emphasis and context.

EFFECTIVE: QUOTATION PRECEDED BY INTRODUCTORY PHRASE OR CLAUSE

According to Orwell (1950), "They had seen the rifle and were all shouting excitedly that I was going to shoot the elephant" (p. 165).

As Orwell notes with annoyance (1950), "They had seen the rifle and were all shouting excitedly that I was going to shoot the elephant" (p. 165).

INCORRECT: FLOATING QUOTATION

The tension builds as Orwell (1950) receives the gun. "They had seen the rifle and were all shouting excitedly that I was going to shoot the elephant" (p. 165).

Quotations must be *connected* to your text, not detached from it. One way to connect a quotation and add variety to your quoting style is to use subordination:

EFFECTIVE: QUOTATION SUBORDINATED

As he starts out, Orwell (1950) realizes that "they had seen the rifle and were all shouting excitedly that I was going to shoot the elephant" (p. 165).

The key word is *that,* which *subordinates* Orwell's sentence to the writer's introduction. (For more on subordination, see Chapter 5.)

INCORRECT: COMMA SPLICE

The tension builds as Orwell (1950) receives the gun, "They had seen the rifle and were all shouting excitedly that I was going to shoot the elephant" (p. 165).

This writer has tried to join the quoted sentence with the preceding, introductory sentence but has created a comma splice. (For more on comma splices, see Chapter 5.)

CORRECT: QUOTATION INTRODUCED BY COLON

The tension builds as Orwell (1950) receives the gun: "They had seen the rifle and were all shouting excitedly that I was going to shoot the elephant" (p. 165).

The colon at the end of the first sentence indicates that the sentence is introducing the quotation. Remember that you must have a complete sentence followed by a colon (*not* a semicolon) before the quoted text begins. After the colon, you may quote one or more complete sentences, as in the example above, or a word or phrase, as in this example:

Orwell's phrasing echoes his title: "to shoot the elephant" (1950, p. 165). This task becomes increasingly significant to him as the narrative continues.

These three methods of quoting from sources will help you integrate source material successfully and add variety to your writing. In addition to these methods, the following guidelines will help you use source material accurately and effectively.

CLASSROOM HINT Review this section carefully in class, for students often have difficulty with quotations containing dialogue.

1. **Quoting text containing dialogue.** On page 164 of "Shooting an Elephant" this sentence appears:

    There was a loud, scandalized cry of "Go away, child! Go away this instant!" and an old woman with a switch in her hand came round the corner of a hut, violently shooing away a crowd of naked children.

    To indicate the quotation within this sentence, you need to change Orwell's double quotation marks to single quotation marks:

    According to Orwell (1950), "There was a loud, scandalized cry of 'Go away, child! Go away this instant!' and an old woman with a switch in her hand came round the corner of a hut, violently shooing away a crowd of naked children" (p. 164).

    However, if you are quoting only the woman's speech, you can use double quotation marks:

    The woman seemed both angry and scared: "Go away, child! Go away this instant!" (Orwell, 1950, p. 164).

2. **Using quotation marks with exclamation points and question marks.** In the example above, the quoted sentence ends with an exclamation point. Note that the exclamation point precedes the closing quotation marks, the page citation, and the added period:

    instant!" (Orwell, 1950, p. 164).

    A quotation that ends with a question mark is treated similarly:

    instant?" (Orwell, 1950, p. 164).

    If the exclamation point or question mark is not part of the quotation but ends your sentence that contains the quotation, it follows the closing quotation mark and page reference:

    Ironically, Orwell (1950) notes that he "had no intention of shooting the elephant" (p. 165)!

    The writer, not Orwell, is exclaiming here.

3. **Eliding (omitting) text.** Well-chosen quotations can add authority and interest to your writing, but you do not need to quote text that is irrelevant to your point. One way to quote economically is to **elide** (remove) superfluous text. Note this sentence:

    They had seen the rifle and were all shouting excitedly that I was going to shoot the elephant.

    You might want to remove the end of the sentence:

    Orwell (1950) writes that "They had seen the rifle and were all shouting excitedly" (p. 165).

You might want to remove the beginning of the sentence:

The villagers "were all shouting excitedly that I was going to shoot the elephant" (Orwell, 1950, p. 165).

You may start a quotation at any logical point in a sentence, but don't omit words in a way that will change the meaning of the sentence you are quoting.

Note that if you are using APA style, you may elide the beginning of a single quoted sentence and/or the end without indicating that you have done so, unless—perhaps to avoid misinterpretation—you need to let readers know that you are not using the whole sentence. To indicate an omission, you will need to use an ellipsis (see below).

If you are eliding text *within* the sentence, an **ellipsis** (three spaced dots) takes the place of the missing words:

The villagers' reaction was immediate: "They . . . were all shouting excitedly that I was going to shoot the elephant" (Orwell, 1950, p. 165).

The ellipsis indicates that you have removed words from the sentence. APA requires that you use an ellipsis if you elide text within a sentence or if you quote two sentences and elide text from the end of the first sentence and/or the beginning of the second one, as in the following example:

ORIGINAL PASSAGE	**As I started forward practically the whole population of the quarter flocked out of the houses and followed me. They had seen the rifle and were all shouting excitedly that I was going to shoot the elephant.**
QUOTED WITH AN ELLIPSIS	**"As I started forward practically the whole population of the quarter flocked out of the houses and followed me. . . . shouting excitedly that I was going to shoot the elephant" (Orwell, 1950, p. 165).**

4. **Quoting only a few words.** If you want to quote only a few words from a sentence, don't use the ellipsis; instead, embed the quotation within your sentence:

   The concept of an elephant "merely ravaging" (Orwell, 1950, p. 165) a home is a terrifying understatement.

5. **Using square brackets to interpolate your own text.** The next-to-the-last sentence in Orwell's paragraph is "He took not the slightest notice of the crowd's approach." Sentences that begin with pronouns can be difficult. (He who?) Note the following solution:

   According to Orwell (1950), "He [the elephant] took not the slightest notice of the crowd's approach" (p. 165).

The square brackets indicate that you are adding clarifying information. However, you might try an alternate approach:

According to Orwell (1950), the elephant "took not the slightest notice of the crowd's approach" (p. 165).

Again, you may start quoting at any logical point in the sentence.

Square brackets are also used to indicate an error—either a misspelling or an obvious factual problem—in text that you are quoting. Note the following examples:

As Bohannon (2001) writes, "When President Kennedy was killed in 1964 [sic], the nation was horrified" (p. 419).

Rodgers (1999) uses this ancient chestnut: "It is better to give than recieve [sic]" (p. 37).

Kennedy was killed in 1963; *receive* is spelled with the *e* preceding the *i*. The use of [*sic*], meaning "thus" ("that's the way I found it"), tells your reader that you know the source is incorrect.

6. **Using block quotations.** According to APA guidelines, any passage that consists of more than one paragraph or contains more than forty words must be set off as a block quotation, or extract. Here are guidelines for displaying a block quotation:
   - Don't add quotation marks before or after the quotation or alter any quotation marks that appear within the quotation.
   - Start the extract on a new line with a block indent of one-half inch from the left margin, which is the default tab indent of most word processing programs. If you are quoting more than one paragraph, indent subsequent paragraphs one-half inch.
   - Don't indent the right side of the quotation or attempt to center the extract.
   - Double-space the extract, and leave only a double space above and below it.
   - Place the page reference at the very end of the extract, after the terminal punctuation. Note the following example:

   Orwell writes of the building excitement:

   > The orderly came back in a few minutes with a rifle and five cartridges, and meanwhile some Burmans had arrived and told us that the elephant was in the paddy fields below, only a few hundred yards away. As I started forward practically the whole population of the quarter flocked out of the houses and followed me. They had seen the rifle and were all shouting excitedly that I was going to shoot the elephant. (165)

CLASSROOM HINT This and the next subsection, on citing multiple pages, need attention in class.

Use block quotations sparingly. Never use them as a way to lengthen your paper.

EXERCISE 18.2 The following revision eliminates the student's quoting errors.

Excerpt of Student's Analysis of Doe's Article

Doe's writing (1998) is on the debate between the free speech crowd and the morality groups. He asks a question: "How will we reconcile these two issues?" (p. 23). Parents want to protect their children, and adults want to protect their own personal rights to access adult material.

It's true that Internet content can pose problems in public places—libraries, for instance. Before a local library changed its policy, Doe says, the assistant librarian described the situation this way: "It was like walking through an adult bookstore" (pp. 22–23). However, the rights of adults need to be considered as well. The main downfall of Doe's writing is his refusal to take a stand:

> Do we want to let adults make adult decisions? Certainly.
>
> Do we want to protect children from clearly inappropriate subject matter? Certainly. (p. 23)

Doe seems to back the morality groups, and to discount the needs of "defenders of 'freedom of choice'" (p. 22). However, he needs to state his case more forcefully, and not be afraid to take a stand.

7. **Citing multiple page numbers.** Note that if a passage begins on one page and continues to another, then you should indicate the page break this way:

   . . . last word" (pp. 161-162).

   . . . last word" (pp. 41-42).

EXERCISE 18.2

1. The following passage is excerpted from an article written by John Vardamus Doe and published in a regional magazine in 1998. The full article appears on pages 22–23 of the magazine. A student wrote an analysis of Doe's article; part of this analysis appears after the excerpt.

   First, read the excerpt. Then read the student's response, which contains ten errors in quoting from Doe's article. Don't try to edit or "smooth out" the response, but look for instances in which the student did not follow proper quoting procedures, and correct the student's errors.

[from page 22] The debate over Internet content rages on. The defenders of "freedom of choice" make up one side, and those who would protect young people and traditional standards of morality make up the other.

In the early days of widespread Internet access, several lessons were learned. For example, Wynton's, an upscale grocery chain, offered free Internet access at each of its stores. The practice was stopped when several instances of shoppers' children accessing porn sites brought objections from both the parents and other concerned shoppers. In another instance, the Fresnell County Library system chose to radically restrict the range of Internet access it provided after complaints of hard-core porn images beaming into the face of every patron who walked past the terminals. According to an assistant librarian, "It was like **[page 23 begins here]** walking through an adult bookstore."

Do we want to let adults make adult decisions? Certainly.

Do we want to protect children from clearly inappropriate subject matter? Certainly.

The Internet offers a whole new world of information and communication, but it offers serious problems as well. How will we reconcile these two issues?

Excerpt of Student's Analysis of Doe's Article

Doe's writing (1998) is on the debate between the free speech crowd and the morality groups. He states, "How will we reconcile these two issues" (p. 23). Parents want to protect their children, and adults want to protect their own personal rights to access adult material.

It's true that Internet content can pose problems in public places, libraries, for instance. Before a local library changed its policy, Doe quotes the assistant librarian as describing the situation this way, "It was like walking through an adult bookstore" (p. 23). However, the rights of adults need to be considered as well. The main downfall of Doe's writing is he refuses to take a stand. "Do we want to let adults make decisions? Certainly. Do we want to keep children from clearly inappropriate subject matter? Certainly" (p. 23).

Doe seems to back the morality groups, and to discount the needs of, "defenders of 'freedom of choice'" (p. 22). However, he needs to state his case more forcefully, and not be afraid to take a stand.

2. After correcting the quoting errors in the student's response, revise it so that it is a more effective, coherent, and unified analysis of the passage.

CHAPTER 19

WRITING ABOUT LITERATURE

At some time in your college career, you will probably be asked to write about literature. Sophomore literature surveys, humanities courses, and some freshman composition classes often include such an assignment. In order to write about literature effectively, you will have to learn how to analyze it; to understand, appreciate, and use varying interpretations of the same work; and to synthesize the work of scholars with your own opinions and insights.

In this chapter, we concentrate on the type of analysis that readers use to understand literature and the organizational strategies that writers use to respond to topics about literature. We also look at some specific mechanical issues that arise in this type of writing. We start with a short story and then move on to a poem. Note that the *Writing Today* Web site (www.mhhe.com/writingtoday) includes a section that discusses how the techniques used to write about stories and poems need to be modified when a writer analyzes a play or a film.

Whatever type of work you are reading, you need to approach it in a systematic and careful manner. Reading a novel or a book of short stories for the sheer pleasure of it is certainly worthwhile. However, reading literature assigned in a college course is often a far more demanding and time-consuming task than reading the latest best-seller. The very purpose of reading literature in college is to prompt analytical, interpretive, and evaluative responses from students, thereby improving their ability to think critically and to discuss sophisticated ideas intelligently.

To approach a work of literature and to write about it require the same attention to the rules of academic reading and writing that you apply in any other discipline. In addition, you should adhere to the following guidelines.

GENERAL GUIDELINES FOR READING AND WRITING ABOUT LITERATURE

Reading Literature

- Reading, like writing, is a process. To understand and appreciate a short story, play, or poem, you may have to read it more than once. The same is true for a novel, but time constraints might permit you to give multiple readings only to selected passages or chapters.
- As with any text, don't be afraid to underline significant lines or passages or to make marginal notes that will help you construct a coherent analysis of the piece later on. The most common types of notes that students make when reading a short story or play are descriptions or analyses of particular characters, descriptions of setting, or ideas that lead to a fuller understanding of the **theme**—the vision or message about human experience that the author is trying to convey. The most common types of notes students make when reading poetry relate to word choice and figurative language (see Chapter 5), to tone, and to meter and rhyme scheme.
- Make your notes and markings in pencil so you will be able to revise, erase, or replace notes when you read the work a second or third time.
- Adopt an active stance. Reading sophisticated literature demands intellectual curiosity and a willingness to engage the text. For example, to discover the deeper meaning of a short story, you need to do more than simply follow the plot. You need to understand the ironic twists in the plot caused by pure coincidence, setting, or the motives of a particular character. You also need to consider how setting informs tone, and how tone, in turn, contributes to

SUGGESTED ACTIVITY
At this juncture, it helps to annotate a poem or an excerpt from a short story in class to demonstrate the process of reading analytically and its importance.

SUGGESTED ACTIVITY
As you review the sample poem or prose excerpt, ask students to offer questions of their own.

CLASSROOM HINT For example, you might explain that in Latin American literature, dreams and visions become as important as physical occurrences, that in many European countries people wear white to funerals, or that in some Asian cultures the scheduling of an important celebration such as a wedding is often dictated by one's horoscope.

the story's theme. All of these tasks require you to draw conclusions and to interpret what is happening, what is being said, where and when the action is taking place, who is involved, and how one event or character affects another.

- When analyzing literature from another culture, try not to make assumptions based upon what you know of your own culture.

After you have decided on an aspect of the short story or poem to write about and have developed a plan, or outline, for your essay, you are ready to draft your paper. The following guidelines apply to all types of literary analyses.

Writing About Literature

- If you quote directly, summarize, or paraphrase from a primary or secondary source, provide citations for those sources. The piece of literature you are reading and analyzing is one type of primary source. A book, journal article, or other scholarly commentary about that piece of literature is a type of secondary source. The system that is normally used to cite such sources is the one recommended by the Modern Language Association and found in Joseph Gibaldi's *MLA Handbook for Writers of Research Papers,* sixth edition (2003). MLA style is also discussed in chapters 18 and 21 of this textbook.
- Double-check to make sure that you are quoting, summarizing, or paraphrasing accurately. You can find out more about using direct quotations, summaries, and paraphrases in chapters 18, 20, and 21.
- Whether you are analyzing a story, novel, poem, play, or film, use the present tense (sometimes called the *literary present*). For example, at the beginning of John Updike's short story "A&P," the main character, Sammy, *is* a clerk at a grocery store. He *had been* a high school student. Note that the past perfect tense is used for narrative events that happened before the time that you are discussing.
- Refer to authors by their last names.

CLASSROOM HINT Stress the fact that students should not refer to authors by their first names. Too many students still write about "Emily's" poems or "Edgar Allan's" short stories.

WRITING ABOUT FICTION

Short stories and novels are called **fiction.** Although they are narratives, they differ from narrative essays, which are based on real events and are considered nonfiction. Short stories and novels are products of the author's imagination or are imaginative re-creations of real events.

Many first-year English classes that cover fiction have students read short stories rather than novels. When instructors assign a critical essay on a short story, they are normally looking for an essay about a feature or an issue associated with that work—for example, the personality and motives of a character, the use of a particular type of symbol, the effect of setting on the characters and theme. These instructors want more than a simple recounting of the narrative, point by point, event by event—a practice that is unnecessary and that fails to address the assignment.

Useful Terms for Writing About Fiction

In order to analyze a short story and then to use this analysis as the basis of a critical essay, you will need to learn a few literary terms and the way they work together. The following terms will improve your understanding of the elements of a short story as you read and analyze it.

CLASSROOM HINT You might review each of the terms in this list in class, providing examples from the short stories your students have or will have read in your class.

antagonist The character, force, or situation that opposes the *protagonist,* the main character.

character A person involved in the action of a story. In a more particular sense, *character* refers to the personality and motivations of a person.

characterization The way that a *character* is developed by the author.

climax The moment at which the events in the narrative reach a crisis, usually near the end of the narrative.

conflict The struggle that shapes a narrative. Three broad areas of conflict are individual versus society, individual versus nature, and individual versus himself or herself.

denouement The period after a narrative's *climax* in which final questions and details are addressed.

dramatic irony A device created when characters in a short story, novel, play, or film discuss an issue at cross-purposes; each character has incomplete information about the issue but not the same incomplete information. Furthermore, the characters do not realize that each is referring to a different set of facts. Only the audience knows all of the truth. The device's power is due to this gap between the audience's knowledge and the characters' knowledge. See also **irony.**

epiphany A profound revelation experienced by a character as the result of a narrative's events.

foreshadowing The writer's use of hints in a narrative to suggest an upcoming event in the plot.

image A description meant to evoke a mental picture for the reader: "A drowned dog floated by, or was it a bad piñata?" The image of the piñata reinforces the image of the disfigurement caused by drowning.

imagery Images working together to create a desired effect.

irony A discrepancy between appearance and reality: "That the people of the 1920s believed the first world war was the final global battle is **ironic** when the events of the late 1930s are considered." (See also **dramatic irony.**)

metaphor A figure of speech in which one thing is represented by or is compared to another without using *like* or *as*. Thus, "The club scene is a black hole for my wallet" uses the metaphor of *black hole* to describe the financial losses suffered by the writer as a result of club crawling.

motif A recurring word, musical phrase, or visual object with thematic significance: "Each major character in *Death of a Salesman* has his or her 'own' music that announces the character's stage entrance; this motif engages an audience in a very interesting way."

narration The telling of a story.

narrative A story.

narrator The storyteller. The narrator and the author are not synonymous. The narrator might even be a character in the story.

parody A literary work that imitates another literary work in order to ridicule it.

point of view The perspective from which the story is narrated. In **first-person narration**, the narrator (storyteller) is a character in the story who uses *I*. Novels using first-person narration are *Great Expectations, Moby-Dick, Huckleberry Finn,* and *Invisible Man*. The *I* narrator does not have to be the main character; *The Great Gatsby* is told by Nick Carraway, a secondary figure.

Third-person narration does not use an *I* narrator. However, the writer can have the reader experience the plot through the eyes of one character, a technique called **third-person limited omniscience.** A good example is Stephen Crane's *The Red Badge of Courage*. The author can also tell the story from multiple points of view, letting the reader see events from the perspectives of several characters, but again without using an *I* narrator. This approach is called the **third-person omniscient** point of view.

plot The events that make up a narrative.

protagonist The main character of a narrative: "Ruby Turpin is the **protagonist** of Flannery O'Connor's 'Revelation.'" The protagonist is not necessarily heroic, just the main character. See also **antagonist.**

satire A work that ridicules either for entertainment or to suggest reform: "Voltaire's *Candide* is a wide-ranging **satire** of the Enlightenment's belief systems."

setting The time and place of a narrative. Given the differences among cultures, countries, regions, and eras, knowing both when and where a narrative is set is crucial to understanding it.

simile A figure of speech in which one thing is represented by or compared to another by using *like* or *as*. The Scottish poet Robert Burns wrote that "My love is like a red, red rose."

symbol An object used to suggest something else, usually an abstract concept. For example, a broken pair of eyeglasses could symbolize a character's loss of moral perception.

theme The "point" of the story—its controlling idea or message.

Keeping these elements in mind and remembering the general guidelines for reading literature presented earlier, read the following short story, and then consider the two student responses that follow it.

The Answer Is No

NAGUIB MAHFOUZ

Translated by Denys Johnson-Davies

Naguib Mahfouz is the author of almost forty novels and fourteen short-story collections. Much of his work set in his homeland, Egypt. He was awarded the Nobel Prize for literature in 1988.

The important piece of news that the new headmaster had arrived spread through the school. She heard of it in the women teachers' common room as she was casting a final glance at the day's lessons. There was no getting away from joining the other teachers in congratulating him, and from shaking him by the hand too. A shudder passed through her body, but it was unavoidable. 1

"They speak highly of his ability," said a colleague of hers. "And they talk too of his strictness." 2

It had always been a possibility that might occur, and now it had. Her pretty face paled, and a staring look came to her wide black eyes. 3

When the time came, the teachers went in single file, decorously attired, to his open room. He stood behind his desk as he received the men and women. He was of medium height, with a tendency to portliness, and had a spherical face, hooked nose, and bulging eyes; the first thing that could be seen of him was a thick, puffed-up mustache, arched like a foam-laden wave. She advanced with her eyes fixed on his chest. Avoiding his gaze, she stretched out her hand. What was she to say? Just what the others had said? However, she kept silent, uttered not a word. What, she wondered, did his eyes express? His rough hand shook hers, and he said in a gruff voice, "Thanks." She turned elegantly and moved off. 4

She forgot her worries through her daily tasks, though she did not look in good shape. Several of the girls remarked, "Miss is in a bad mood." When she returned to her home at the beginning of the Pyramids Road, she changed her clothes and sat down to eat with her mother. "Everything all right?" inquired her mother, looking her in the face. 5

"Badran, Badran Badawi," she said briefly. "Do you remember him? He's been appointed our headmaster." 6

"Really!" 7

Then, after a moment of silence, she said, "It's of no importance at all—it's an old and long-forgotten story." 8

After eating, she took herself off to her study to rest for a while before correcting some exercise books. She had forgotten him completely. No, not completely. How could he be forgotten completely? When he had first come to give her a private lesson in mathematics, she was fourteen years of age. In fact not quite fourteen. He had been twenty-five years older, the same age as her father. She had said to her mother, "His appearance is a mess, but he explains things well." And her mother had said, "We're not concerned with what he looks like; what's important is how he explains things." 9

He was an amusing person, and she got on well with him and benefited from his knowledge. How, then, had it happened? In her innocence she had not noticed any change in his behavior to put her on her guard. Then one day he had been left on his own with her, her father having gone to her aunt's clinic. She had not the slightest doubts about a man she regarded as a second father. How, then, had it 10 happened? Without love or desire on her part the thing had happened. She had asked in terror about what had occurred, and he had told her, "Don't be frightened or sad. Keep it to yourself and I'll come and propose to you the day you come of age."

11 And he had kept his promise and had come to ask for her hand. By then she had attained a degree of maturity that gave her an understanding of the dimensions of their tragic position. She had found that she had no love or respect for him and that he was as far as he could be from her dreams and from the ideas she had formed of what constituted an ideal and moral person. But what was to be done? Her father had passed away two years ago, and her mother had been taken aback by the forwardness of the man. However, she had said to her, "I know your attachment to your personal independence, so I leave the decision to you."

12 She had been conscious of the critical position she was in. She had either to accept or to close the door forever. It was the sort of situation that could force her into something she detested. She was the rich, beautiful girl, a byword in Abbasiyya for her nobility of character, and now here she was struggling helplessly in a well-sprung trap, while he looked down at her with rapacious eyes. Just as she had hated his strength, so too did she hate her own weakness. To have abused her innocence was one thing, but for him to have the upper hand now that she was fully in possession of her faculties was something else. He had said, "So here I am, making good my promise because I love you." He had also said, "I know of your love of teaching, and you will complete your studies at the College of Science."

13 She had felt such anger as she had never felt before. She had rejected coercion in the same way as she rejected ugliness. It had meant little to her to sacrifice marriage. She had welcomed being on her own, for solitude accompanied by self-respect was not loneliness. She had also guessed he was after her money. She had told her mother quite straightforwardly, "No," to which her mother had replied, "I am astonished you did not make this decision from the first moment."

14 The man had blocked her way outside and said, "How can you refuse? Don't you realize the outcome?" And she had replied with an asperity he had not expected, "For me any outcome is preferable to being married to you."

15 After finishing her studies, she had wanted something to do to fill her spare time, so she had worked as a teacher. Chances to marry had come time after time, but she had turned her back on them all.

16 "Does no one please you?" her mother asked her.

17 "I know what I'm doing," she had said gently.

18 "But time is going by."

19 "Let it go as it pleases, I am content."

20 Day by day she becomes older. She avoids love, fears it. With all her strength she hopes that life will pass calmly, peacefully, rather than happily. She goes on persuading herself that happiness is not confined to love and motherhood. Never has she regretted her firm decision. Who knows what the morrow holds? But she was certainly unhappy that he should again make his appearance in her life, that she would be making of the past a living and painful present.

21 Then, the first time he was alone with her in his room, he asked her, "How are you?"

22 She answered coldly, "I'm fine."

He hesitated slightly before inquiring, "Have you not . . . I mean, did you get married?" 23

In the tone of someone intent on cutting short a conversation, she said, "I told you, I'm fine." 24

Analysis

Here is the topic assigned after discussion of the story:

> Write a 400- to 550-word essay in response to the following statement:
>
> "The Answer Is No" takes place in a traditional culture. The protagonist is an oddity, the rare young woman who is allowed to make her own decisions. As a result, she scorns Badawi's offer of marriage —a daring choice. In effect, she takes the prerogative of a man. However, when Badawi becomes the headmaster of the school at which she teaches, she loses her "male prerogative" and suffers as a "traditional" woman.
>
> Do you agree? (Hint: read the end of the story very carefully.)

Two student responses follow. We have broken each essay into its component paragraphs, accompanied by our comments. The first essay illustrates several errors you ought to avoid. The second is an example of a far more effective response to the question.

First Student Response to "The Answer Is No": Needs Improvement

CLASSROOM HINT Review the critique of the student paper on Mahfouz's story in class. Try to make time to do so when you plan your syllabus.

The Answer Is No[1]

In this story[2] the narrator[3] is a young woman who was sexually abused by a math tutor at the age of fourteen.[4] Years later he becomes the headmaster of the school where she teaches. She loses her male prerogative[5] and lives in fear of him.

Comments

1. Instead of using the title of the story as the essay's title, the writer needs a title that reflects the essay's focus. The writer of the second student response (see page 547) provides insight into her essay's contents and point of view by titling it "An Ongoing Equilibrium." Note that this is a far more intriguing title and serves to draw the reader into the text.
2. The essay starts with "In this story. . . ." A better first sentence would begin with "In 'The Answer Is No,' Naguib Mahfouz portrays. . . ." The title of the story needs to be identified within the text.
3. The young woman is *not* the narrator; the narrator tells the story. She is, instead, the *protagonist,* or main character.
4. After the first sentence, the reader might ask "Who was fourteen, the woman or the math tutor?"

5. To write that a woman "loses her male prerogative" is to repeat part of the question without explaining what that phrase means. Also, *does* the woman "live in fear" of Badawi? Finally, is "loses her male prerogative" an effective thesis?

The story begins with the arrival of the new headmaster, Badran.[1] The narrator is shocked at this unexpected turn of events. She discusses the situation with her mother and worries about implications.[2]

Comments

1. The headmaster should be referred to by his last name, Badawi, not by his given name, Badran.
2. This paragraph is plot summary, but the audience—the instructor—already knows the plot.

The narrator thinks back to the events that had caused her such sorrow. She was fourteen, he twenty-five.[1] Their student-tutor relationship was going well. Then one day, he apparently raped her. He tried to make up for this by promising to marry her when she was old enough. However, she refused when he reappeared when she turned eighteen.[2, 3]

Comments

1. This information is inaccurate. When the protagonist is fourteen, Badawi is thirty-nine.
2. The statement that eighteen is the age of majority is an assumption; eighteen might be the magic number in the United States, but Egypt is a different culture.
3. The paragraph contains almost nothing but plot summary.

When the narrator again meets Badran, with him as her boss, she is fearful.[1] The rest of her working life will be spent under a man[2] who has two reasons for revenge. Her "male prerogative" is gone.[3]

Comments

1. Another reader of this short story might question the word *fearful* and see the protagonist's response as *measured.* Of course, people can have two very different interpretations, both of which are valid. The key is to establish that validity. Thus, the writer of this essay might make reference to the text to support his contention that the protagonist is *fearful.*
2. The phrase *under a man* is unfortunate. Perhaps *being supervised by a man* would work better.
3. A conclusion can serve a variety of purposes, but summarizing plot is not one of them. Perhaps a better conclusion might have explained how the protagonist's losing her "prerogative" makes her a victim. Another interpretation might explain that her reactions to her new situation reveal

strength of character. Still another use of the conclusion might be to reveal the protagonist as a splendid oddity, a woman of independent means with a self-directed future, living in a world where men traditionally make decisions. Indeed, there are many conclusions that could be reached about the character of the protagonist and of the nature of her predicament. That's why forgoing these opportunities simply to retell the story seems wasteful.

The student's essay also suffers from more general concerns. It doesn't answer the question in the writing assignment. This essay is simply a personal response to the story, a useful approach in an informal journal, perhaps, but not what the assignment requested.

Moreover, the essay reflects a lack of understanding of the elements of a short story and the terms used to designate them. Like other areas of study, literary analysis has its own technical terminology. Being able to use these terms will improve your literary analyses (see pages 541–542).

Another weakness of this essay is the absence of direct quotations from the text. Quoting is an invaluable way to support your assertions about a short story. Chapter 18 discusses how to incorporate direct quotations in your essay.

Second Student Response to "The Answer Is No": More Effective

Here is a student's response to the topic that offers a valid thesis and supports it with evidence from the story:

An Ongoing Equilibrium

In Naguib Mahfouz's "The Answer Is No," the unnamed protagonist is an Egyptian woman schoolteacher who learns that an old nemesis has returned to her world. When the protagonist had been fourteen years old, her math tutor, Badran Badawi, had raped her. Years later she learns that he has been appointed headmaster of the school where she now teaches. The story analyzes her complex reaction to this news.

This is an appropriate plot summary. It is long enough to demonstrate an overall grasp of the story without boring the reader. What follows in subsequent paragraphs is analysis.

The protagonist cannot be seen as an "average" Egyptian woman. In that traditional, Islamic country, the future of a woman is more likely to involve marriage and children than a professional position. Yet the protagonist has brains, money, a liberal family, and a ruthless streak of independence: "It had meant little to her to sacrifice marriage. She had welcomed being on her own, for solitude accompanied by self-respect was not loneliness" (544). It is a mistake, then, to read "The Answer Is No" as a harbinger of a dismal future for her. Her peace of mind has been disturbed, but unlike so many other women, she is not trapped. She can either deal successfully with Badawi or move on.

In this paragraph, the student makes good use of a direct quotation that relates directly to and supports an important point.

Again, the student makes excellent use of direct quotation. In addition, she draws a valid, if rather harsh, conclusion about Badawi's vision of women.

The depiction of the rape shows an interesting contrast in perception. The protagonist is the daughter of a wealthy couple, who are able to procure a math tutor for her. However, the math tutor ravishes his pupil as if the right were divinely given: "She had asked in terror about what had occurred, and he had told her, 'Don't be frightened or sad. Keep it to yourself and I'll come and propose to you the day you come of age'" (544). Badawi obviously equates "woman" with "peasant," regardless of the woman's social standing. Thus, he is almost casual about his crime.

Although these paragraphs contain some recounting of plot, they concentrate on character analysis and help to explain the dynamics of the relationship between the protagonist and her rapist/suitor.

Badawi keeps his word, however, and returns to "make things right." Unfortunately, he misjudges the character of his potential "bride": "She had felt such anger as she had never felt before. She had rejected coercion in the same way as she rejected ugliness" (544). Her answer, obviously, is no.

In the years that follow, the young woman devotes her life to her career, never marrying but learning to appreciate her solitude. The news of Badawi's appointment as headmaster comes as a nasty surprise. The man to whom she had once said "For me any outcome is preferable to being married to you" (544) is now her boss. The situation is a tricky one for Badawi as well. He tries to make small talk to her, asking about the intervening years, but finds that his former pupil has an icy wall that will not allow him entrance.

The conclusion is appropriate in that it clearly responds to the assignment. The writer disagrees that the protagonist "loses her 'male prerogative' and suffers as a 'traditional' woman."

Ironically, the person the protagonist has become is a reaction to her childhood assault by Badawi. To see him appointed as her supervisor, however, is intolerable. In effect, she has spent her life avoiding gender domination, and now fate has put her on a strange path. But the protagonist is fortunate in one major respect: she can move on, and many women do not enjoy that kind of independence and mobility.

EXERCISE 19.1

Reread "The Answer Is No." Write a 400- to 550-word essay on the following topic:

> Evaluate the character of Badran Badawi. What does the story tell you about him? In your opinion, does his character change over the years covered by the narrative? What is your sense of this man?

Quote from the story to support your assertions, and cite the appropriate page number(s).

WRITING ABOUT POETRY

Although some poems are narratives, most are not. When you read poetry, you need to pay attention to language, interpretation, and imagery more than to plot and characterization.

A further distinction can be made between types of poetry. Traditional poetry follows patterns of rhyme and meter. On the other hand, modern poetry, which dates from about the time of the nineteenth-century American writer Walt Whitman (1819–1892), has slowly moved away from rhyme schemes and fixed rhythms. By the middle of the twentieth century, many serious poets were writing **free verse**, poetry without intentional rhyming and rhythmic patterns. When analyzing traditional poetry, you need to be aware of the techniques the poet uses to accommodate the needs of his or her chosen form. For example, in the sonnet "On First Looking into Chapman's Homer," John Keats ends by mentioning *Darien,* an archaic name for Panama:

Much have I traveled in the realms of gold,
And many goodly states and kingdoms seen;
Round many western islands have I been
Which bards in fealty to Apollo hold.
Oft of one wide expanse had I been told 5
That deep-browed Homer ruled as his demesne;
Yet did I never breathe its pure serene
Till I heard Chapman speak out loud and bold:
Then felt I like some watcher of the skies
When a new planet sweeps into his ken; 10
Or like stout Cortez when with eagle eyes
He stared at the Pacific—and all his men
Looked at each other with a wild surmise—
Silent, upon a peak in Darien.

The reader might believe that Keats was being willfully obscure unless he or she understands that *Darien* fits Keats's rhyme scheme in this sonnet; *Panama* does not. Keats seems to have been trying to find a word that fit.

In analyzing modern poetry, the reader needs to concentrate more on the role of the speaker, on the use of language, figurative or otherwise, and on the creation of tone, mood, and imagery. Whatever "type" of poetry you analyze, it is always helpful to know something about the literary and historical context in which it was written as well as about the life of the poet. Moreover, knowing the appropriate terminology for the elements of poetry is invaluable. Learning these concepts and the terms for them will help you derive more meaning from the poems you analyze.

Useful Terms for Writing About Poetry

alliteration The repetition of initial consonant sounds in nearby words: "The crow's cackling caw." (See also **consonance.**)

allusion An indirect reference to a well-known person, work of art, or event. Describing a current baseball player as "the new Sultan of Swat" is an allusion to Babe Ruth, the original Sultan of Swat.

CLASSROOM HINT
Again, you might review this list in class, making reference to the poems your students have read or will read in your class.

assonance The repetition of vowel sounds: "The trees freeze in the breeze."

caesura A stop, pause, or break, often signaled by a period, within a line of poetry.

character A figure within any creative literary work. (See also **antagonist** and **protagonist** from the list on pages 541–542.)

consonance The repetition of internal consonant sounds or ending consonant sounds in nearby words: "The brick clicked." (See also **alliteration.**)

epiphany A profound revelation experienced by a character as the result of a narrative's events.

figurative language (See **metaphor, personification,** and **simile;** see also Chapter 5.)

free verse Poetry without a rhyme scheme or fixed meter.

image A description meant to evoke a mental picture for the reader: "A drowned dog floated by, or was it a bad piñata?" The image of the piñata reinforces the image of the disfigurement caused by drowning.

imagery Images working together to create a desired effect.

irony A discrepancy between appearance and reality: "That the people of the 1920s believed the first world war was the final global battle is **ironic** when the events of the late 1930s are considered." (See also **dramatic irony** from the list on pages 541–542.)

metaphor A figure of speech in which one thing represents or is compared to another without using *like* or *as*. Thus, "The club scene is a black hole for my wallet" uses the metaphor of *black hole* to describe the financial losses suffered by the writer as a result of club crawling. In one of his sonnets, Shakespeare compares trees in winter to "Bare ruined choirs where late the sweet birds sang." (See also **personification** and **simile;** see also Chapter 5.)

meter A patterned rhythm of stressed and unstressed syllables found in traditional poetry. The meter of a poem is partly determined by the type of *feet* (combinations of syllables) used:

- Iambic: *collapse* (two syllables with stress on the second)
- Trochaic: *apple* (two syllables with stress on the first)
- Dactyl: *tenderly* (three syllables with stress on the first, and the next two syllables unstressed)
- Anapest: *unappeased* (three syllables with the first two unstressed and the third stressed)

The meter of a poem also depends on the number of feet per line. The terms *trimeter, tetrameter, pentameter,* and *hexameter* refer to lines of three, four, five, and six feet, respectively. When the type of foot is connected to the number of feet, the meter is identified. Here is a line in iambic tetrameter: "I put a hat upon my head." The line has eight syllables constituting four feet. The rhythm is iambic—the stressed syllables are two, four, six, and eight.

metonymy A figure of speech in which a noun is used to evoke associated meaning: "Live by the sword, and die by the sword" probably doesn't refer to a person who owns a sword. Rather, the word *sword* is used to suggest "violence."

motif A recurring word, musical phrase, or visual object with thematic significance: "Each major character in *Death of a Salesman* has his or her 'own' music that announces the character's stage entrance; this **motif** engages an audience in a very interesting way."

narrator The teller of the story. Note that *narrator* does not equal *author.* Frequently, the narrator of a story, novel, or poem is a character within the narrative.

onomatopoeia The use of a word that sounds like what it describes: *squeak, screech, hoot,* and so on.

parody A literary work that imitates another literary work in order to ridicule it.

personification A figure of speech in which human characteristics are ascribed to nonhuman entities: "The full moon smiled kindly at us." The moon can't smile. However, the writer uses personification to build a pleasant tone and illustrate the scene. (See also **metaphor** and **simile;** see also Chapter 5.)

prosody The technical study of poetry. See also **meter** and **rhyme scheme.**

rhyme Matching sounds at the end of two or more lines of poetry: "He stands upon his *feet* / before he takes a *seat.*" See also **rhyme scheme.**

rhyme scheme The pattern of rhyming found in a poem. Some rhyming poetry uses *couplets,* pairs of lines that rhyme. Other rhyme schemes include those used in the English sonnet and the Italian sonnet. (See also **sonnet.**) Traditionally, a rhyme scheme is charted by assigning a letter, starting with *a,* to the sound at the end of a line. Note the following four lines:

I put a hat upon my head,	(a)
I walked out in the street.	(b)
There my boss I chanced to meet,	(b)
I wished I'd stayed in bed.	(a)

This doggerel has a rhyme scheme of abba (head, street, meet, bed). If this poem were to continue—thankfully, it does not—the next new line-ending sound would be assigned the letter *c.*

satire A work that ridicules either for entertainment or to suggest reform: "Voltaire's *Candide* is a wide-ranging satire of the Enlightenment's belief systems."

setting The time and place of a narrative or poem. Given the differences among cultures, countries, regions, and eras, knowing both when and where a narrative or poem is set is crucial to understanding it: "Peter Straub's novel *Ghost Story* is **set** in upstate New York in the early 1970s."

simile A figure of speech similar to a **metaphor.** However, similes use *like* or *as* to create comparisons. Note the difference between these two lines:

METAPHOR **My love is a red, red rose.**

SIMILE **My love is like a red, red rose.**

(See also **metaphor** and **personification;** see also Chapter 5.)

sonnet A fourteen-line poem in iambic pentameter (see also **meter**). The **English** (or **Shakespearean**) sonnet's rhyme scheme (see also **rhyme scheme**) is abab cdcd efef gg. Lines 13 and 14 are called the *couplet.* The **Italian** sonnet has two parts. The first eight lines, called the *octave,* always follow this pattern: abba cddc. The final six lines, called the *sestet,* can use a variety of rhyme schemes. In both types of sonnet, the poet typically uses the first part of the poem (lines 1–12 in the English and lines 1–8 in the Italian) to frame an argument, present a situation, or ask a question. The remaining lines "confirm" or "solve" the situation or problem presented. Thus, for example, a poet writing an Italian sonnet might ask a question in the octave and provide the answer in the sestet.

stanza Two or more lines grouped together and sometimes separated from other stanzas by a line space.

symbol An object used to suggest something else, usually something abstract. For example, a broken pair of eyeglasses could symbolize a character's loss of moral perception.

synecdoche A figure of speech in which a part stands for the whole or in which a general term is used to describe a more specific actor or action: "Five sails approach the harbor" refers to five ships." "Run! It's the law!" actually means "Run! It's a police officer!"

The poem on page 553 is William Wordsworth's "Composed upon Westminster Bridge, September 3, 1802." The model student essay that follows it, "Beauty in a Strange Context," was written in response to this assignment: "Pick one Wordsworth poem from the group assigned, and explain why it is different from the rest."

Guidelines for Quoting Poetry

Chapter 18 explains how to use the MLA style of quoting text. Those guidelines also apply to quoting poetry, with three modifications:

1. Cite line numbers, not page numbers. Include *line* or *lines* with your first reference, as the student paper does on page 554.
2. If you are quoting two or three lines of a poem, separate the lines with a slash (/), as in the following example:

    Wordsworth emphasizes his overwhelmingly positive sense of London at daybreak: "Never did sun more beautifully steep / In his first splendour, valley, rock, or hill; / Ne'er saw I, never felt, a calm so deep!" (9–11).

    Note that the slash is preceded and followed by a space.

3. If you are quoting more than three lines, set off the quotation as a block, as in the following example:

> Wordsworth emphasizes his overwhelmingly positive sense of London at daybreak:
>
> > This City now doth, like a garment, wear
> > The beauty of the morning; silent, bare,
> > Ships, towers, domes, theatres, and temples lie
> > Open unto the fields, and to the sky;
> > All bright and glittering in the smokeless air. (4–8)

Note that the block quotation matches the poem line for line and that no quotation marks are added.

Composed upon Westminster Bridge, September 3, 1802

Earth has not any thing to show more fair:
Dull would he be of soul who could pass by
A sight so touching in its majesty:
This City now doth, like a garment, wear
The beauty of the morning; silent, bare, 5
Ships, towers, domes, theatres, and temples lie
Open unto the fields, and to the sky;
All bright and glittering in the smokeless air.
Never did sun more beautifully steep
In his first splendour, valley, rock, or hill; 10
Ne'er saw I, never felt, a calm so deep!
The river glideth at his own sweet will:
Dear God! the very houses seem asleep;
And all that mighty heart is lying still!

Beauty in a Strange Context

CLASSROOM HINT Reviewing this student paper while making specific reference to Wordsworth's poem is a useful exercise.

William Wordsworth's "Composed upon Westminster Bridge, September 3, 1802" takes a traditional Romantic enthusiasm, the love of nature's beauty, but finds a strange source for this beauty in industrial London. Wordsworth confounds our expectations by praising a sight we would expect him to abhor.

Thesis, the point about the poem that the writer will support.

The Industrial Revolution was in full swing in 1802. London was filled with industry, homes, and air pollution spawned by a reliance on soft coal as a fuel. It was an enormous, filthy place, hardly to be mentioned in the same breath with the natural, untouched beauty of Wordsworth's beloved Lake District, in the western part of England. However, the poet catches the city just before it awakes; the resulting picture is surprising and gains value because of that surprise.

The writer shows how Wordsworth modifies the traditional approach to the form he is using.

"Westminster Bridge" is an Italian sonnet. The octave is regular; the sestet follows the CDCDCD pattern. The iambic rhythm is not perfect; especially in the second half of the poem, Wordsworth strives for a conversational rhythm rather than a strict one. The result is an informal effect—the poet has seen something that amazes him, and the poem reflects this growing surprise.

The writer indicates omitted words with an ellipsis.

In the first line, Wordsworth defines the city's visual beauty by using the negative: "Earth has not any thing to show more fair." It is a "sight . . . touching in its majesty" (line 3). He then uses a simile to show the temporary nature of this sight: "This City now doth, like a garment, wear / The beauty of the morning . . ." (4-5). The poet then uses one of his frequent techniques, listing, to show the power of the scene: "Ships, towers, domes, theatres, and temples" (6) are revealed as a majestic vista, "All bright and glittering in the smokeless air" (8). The key word is "smokeless." The factories are not running; the home fires are banked. Briefly, the city is not corrupted by pollution.

The writer uses well-chosen quotations to demonstrate how Wordsworth portrays the beauty of the city.

The writer explains what the sonnet form contributes to Wordsworth's poem.

Thus ends the octave, whose traditional purpose in the Italian sonnet is to pose a problem, present an argument, or ask a question. Here, Wordsworth sets up a proposal and then uses the sestet to give his summation or evaluation. He points out that never in a rural area did he see the sun "steep" a landscape, using "steep" in the same sense as "brew" (9). Nor has he ever before experienced "a calm so deep!" (11). His conclusion is "And all that mighty heart is lying still!" (14). At first light, London presents a scene of beauty that will surely disappear as the workday begins.

William Blake, Wordsworth's fellow Romantic, believed that even a grain of sand could indicate infinity. In "Westminster Bridge," Wordsworth takes a similar approach: Nature can overpower the stinking industrial hell that London had become by 1802. The reader's surprise at this paradox helps to stimulate the imagination when experiencing the sonnet.

The conclusion refers back to the thesis by mentioning the reader's surprise.

EXERCISE 19.2

Reread "On First Looking into Chapman's Homer" (page 549). Write a 400- to 600-word essay on the following topic:

> This poem is about quest and discovery. What, exactly, has Keats discovered, and how does he indicate his astonishment at what he has found?

Quote from the poem to support your assertions, and cite the appropriate line number(s).

MORE OPTIONS ONLINE
To learn how to write about drama and film, go to **www.mhhe.com/writingtoday**.

CHAPTER 20

THE RESEARCH PROCESS

Many students see the research paper as a complicated, daunting assignment. However, it helps to see it instead as a series of steps, for viewing the research paper as a process is much easier than worrying about the whole picture. This chapter concentrates on the process of focusing on a topic and thesis, finding and taking notes from appropriate sources, and including that information as you plan, write, and revise your paper.

Chapter 21 explains how to incorporate researched material using either Modern Language Association (MLA) style or American Psychological Association (APA) style. In addition, Chapter 21 includes a sample student research paper to illustrate MLA guidelines.

Research can take many forms. If you are in the market for a new car, stereo system, or computer, you might find information about competing models in a consumer magazine. If you want to find a restaurant that will impress your friends yet fit your budget, you might look in the newspaper's entertainment section or in a restaurant guide for your city or state. Of course, academic research is a little more complex. It usually involves finding multiple sources of information and opinion in print and electronic publications located in your college library and on the Internet. In addition, you might have to interview experts on your topic or use information from a variety of other sources, including videotapes, musical recordings, and even paintings.

The process of writing a paper that uses research is more complex than that of writing other papers. However, as with all other types of writing, you will need to start by focusing on a working topic. Of course, your instructor might ask you to write upon a predetermined topic. Whether you are given a general topic or are allowed to choose your own, you will need to focus on a question or aspect of the topic that you can manage to discuss thoroughly given the kind and length of paper you have been asked to write.

In addition, you need to fulfill three responsibilities when completing a research paper that are not necessary when completing other essays:

- Research information relevant to your topic in primary and/or secondary sources and take notes from these sources in an efficient and easy-to-retrieve manner. (See page 559 for a discussion of primary and secondary (sources).
- Incorporate this information into your paper in a way that logically supports your own ideas and conclusions, that is easy to comprehend, and that is placed naturally and correctly.
- Document the sources of this information properly, using an accepted style such as the one recommended by the Modern Language Association (MLA), the American Psychological Association (APA), or other professional organization, as assigned by your instructor. You can find out more about these formats in Chapter 21.

CLASSROOM HINT Take time to review these responsibilities in class. Make sure that students remember that MLA and APA formats are explained in Chapter 21.

NARROWING YOUR TOPIC AND FRAMING A RESEARCH QUESTION

SUGGESTED ACTIVITY Have students participate in a discussion aimed at limiting each student's own research topic. You can also use this method to devise research questions.

If you have a pre-assigned, focused topic, you will find it relatively easy to get started. Such topics often come with the instructor's assurance that they can be researched in your college library or on the Internet. However, topics that you choose for yourself may be more interesting to you personally. As a matter of fact, you may already have a storehouse of information about your topic gained from your own experiences or reading. This information may serve as a foundation to which you can add researched information from primary and secondary sources.

If your instructor wants you to narrow a broad topic that he or she has assigned or to choose your own topic, you will have to limit that topic so that it can be discussed in a paper of the assigned length. This is one of the most important steps in the research process. In many ways, a broad topic is far more difficult to research than a limited one simply because a narrow topic makes it easier to identify sources that are relevant to your task. For example, the following topics are far too broad for a 2,500- to 3,000-word paper:

teenage suicide
environmental risks
alternative fuel sources
computer programming
vegan diets

Instead, try one of the following:

peer pressure as a cause of teenage suicide in American females
the environmental risks of oil drilling in the Great Lakes
the use of ethanol as an alternative fuel source for cars
job and salary prospects for computer programmers in the United States, 2010–2020
the benefits and dangers of following a vegan diet

Once you have established a workable topic, turn it into a general question in order to clarify your purpose and better direct your research efforts. Unless your instructor tells you otherwise, you ought to choose questions whose answers might serve as a thesis that you can support and argue for as you draft your research paper. For example, the topics above might be turned into the following questions:

- To what extent does peer pressure contribute to teenage suicide in American females?
- Are the environmental risks of drilling for oil in the Great Lakes too great for the anticipated return?
- Will ethanol replace or partially replace gasoline as an automotive fuel?
- Do U.S. job and salary prospects make computer programming an attractive major for college students in 2010 through 2020?
- Do the benefits of following a vegan diet outweigh the dangers?

However you frame your question, remember that it is only a starting point. You can refine it at any time as you conduct your research. Remember, too, that the research you do is intended to help you arrive at an answer to that question, an answer that will serve as the thesis of your paper. For example, after doing extensive research on job and salary prospects for computer programmers, you might come up with the following thesis statement: *Qualified computer programmers will have little trouble finding high-paying, satisfying jobs in the second decade of the twenty-first century.*

EXERCISE 20.1

Choose a possible topic for a research paper of approximately 1,250 to 2,000 words. Then narrow that topic and frame a question on which you could base your research. Use one of the sample research questions above as your model.

EXERCISE 20.1 Answers will vary.

CLASSROOM HINT Collecting the work assigned in this and other exercises in this chapter will help you impress students with the fact that research is a long and careful process.

BEGINNING WITH TOOLS FROM THE REFERENCE ROOM

The reference section of your library contains general reference works such as dictionaries and encyclopedias as well as more specialized books, guides, and limited encyclopedias intended to provide an overview of a discipline or a subject. Those devoted to specific fields of study, such as the *Encyclopedia of World Art* and *The McGraw-Hill Encyclopedia of Science and Technology,* are good places to start your research. They provide background information, define technical terms, and include valuable bibliographies of even more specific sources that you might want to research. However, such books are sometimes too general to serve as sources for productive note taking. Check with your professor before using information from such sources.

USING PRIMARY AND SECONDARY SOURCES

Primary sources are original works containing firsthand information and insights that you might make the focus of a research paper or that you might use to support or develop ideas about other works or related subjects. A work of literature; a painting or musical composition; a government, historical, or intellectual document such as the Declaration of Independence or Newton's *Mathematical Principles;* the report of a government or corporate agency; the Bible, the Koran, or other religious document; a contemporary newspaper account; or any other original document or work of art is a primary source. However, information you discover yourself can also be used as a primary source. For example, information that you obtain from interviewing an expert on your topic is also considered primary, as are data collected through questionnaires or surveys that you design and distribute.

CLASSROOM HINT Make sure that students see this distinction clearly.

Secondary sources provide data, analyses, opinions, and ideas from experts other than yourself. For example, if you were writing a research paper on Arthur Miller's *Death of a Salesman,* that play would be your primary source. However, you might also include information about the play from scholarly studies and critiques such as Gerald Weales's book *American Drama Since World War II* and Alan Seager's article "The Creative Agony of Arthur Miller." Secondary sources include written materials—books, journal and magazine articles, pamphlets, Internet sites, and the like.

Only some research papers that you will be assigned in college require the use of primary sources, but virtually all require secondary sources. For example, if you write a research paper on the Great Depression, you might or might not use primary sources such as newspaper accounts written at the time, but you would certainly use secondary sources such as historians' assessments of the causes of this economic calamity. Similarly, a paper arguing for an increased reliance on solar energy might not rely on primary sources such as the records of scientific experiments conducted at a solar observatory, but it would surely include information from reports of such experiments published in journals such as *Scientific American,* which are more accessible to the lay reader.

Your college library is the perfect place to start research. In it, you will find both primary and secondary sources on your topic. However, you can also find a wide range of sources on the Internet. If you have trouble locating any source or need to request an interlibrary loan for a work in another library, seek the help of the librarians. It is their job to help students become proficient at using library resources, and the vast majority are more than happy to do so.

CREATING A WORKING BIBILIOGRAPHY

SUGGESTED ACTIVITY
Consider asking one of your college librarians to lead your class through a library orientation based on the information found in the next several pages.

Before you begin taking notes, you should create a working bibliography. This document will differ from your Works Cited section (MLA style) or References page (APA style) in that a working bibliography contains records of *all* of the books, periodical articles, Web sites, and other sources you search to find information. Works-cited and references sections list only works from which you have taken information for incorporation into your paper.

You can begin your working bibliography by listing titles you have obtained from your background reading in reference texts. Then, as you go along, you can add titles of promising books found in your search of the library's book catalogue, as explained below. Additional entries can be made as you begin to find magazine, journal, or newspaper articles and Web sites that seem relevant.

You may not use every source you record, but the record you keep of your sources will be invaluable. In any case, your working bibliography will be an asset as you prepare your essay's works-cited or references section. Make sure that you record the appropriate information for each type of source. (Chapter 21 discusses the format and content of works-cited and reference entries.) Note that the information you will need to record for a book is different from what you will need for a journal article or for a source from the Internet. Indeed, the content and format for two different kinds of books vary significantly, as do the content and format for materials found in journals or taken off the Internet. For now, be sure to include the following information for any sources you list:

Book:

Author(s)

Editor and translator (if appropriate)

Title and subtitle

Publisher

Date and place of publication

Volume number or edition number (if appropriate)

Periodical article or work found in an anthology (collection of articles):

Author(s)

Editor of the anthology

Translator (if appropriate)

Title of article

Title of journal, magazine, newspaper, or anthology

Date of publication, publisher, and place of publication of anthology

Volume number, issue number, date (for example, 7 July 1999 or Fall 2000 or March 2002)

Electronic source:

Author(s)

Editor or translator (if appropriate)

Publication information if source appeared in print before being published in electronic format.

Title of the Web site or CD-ROM

Sponsor of the Web site or service company publishing the CD-ROM

Title of the online journal, newspaper, or magazine publishing the article, along with any standard publication data for a periodical, such as volume and issue number

Date the work was published electronically or was most recently updated

Date you accessed the work

Complete URL

Consider Your Options

You can record bibliographic (publication) information for all sources in a list on a piece of paper. Another way to store bibliographical information for a source is to record it on a bibliography index card (one for each source), then store these cards in a separate file or box.

A third way to preserve important information about your sources is to photocopy articles in their entirety or relevant sections of a book. Include the title page and table of contents of the publication. Sites found on the Internet can be printed out or saved to a disk. Still another way is to record this information in a computer file.

EXERCISE 20.2

In your college library, find at least one general reference book relating to the research question you framed in Exercise 20.1. Consult the bibliography of these general reference works to find at least five focused sources—books and periodical articles—relating to your research. Copy down all information listed for these five sources. You will use it as you begin to compile a working bibliography.

EXERCISE 20.2
Responses will vary.

LOCATING BOOKS AND ARTICLES ON YOUR TOPIC

Most libraries have computerized their book catalogues to save space and to make searching easier for users. In fact, most card catalogues have been removed from the reference-room floor and put in storage.

Computerized Book Catalogues

In addition to indicating call number, author, title, subject, edition, publication information, and the number of copies the library owns, computerized catalogues tell whether a book is "checked out" or "not on shelf." Some libraries have joined with others to form consortia, or groups to share resources. In such cases, the catalogue will indicate from which member library or libraries a book can be obtained.

The book's call number is a crucial piece of information. A **call number**, which is also printed on the book's spine, refers to the place on the library shelves (stacks) where the book is stored. Some libraries use Dewey Decimal System call numbers; others use Library of Congress call numbers. If your library has open stacks, you can use the call number to find the book yourself. If your library has closed stacks, you can use the call number to order the book at the circulation desk.

Computerized catalogues can be used to search for books by author, title, and subject. Most catalogues provide search directions; they usually appear on an online help menu or in written form near the monitor. Let's say you want to find books for a research paper on air pollution. You might conduct a subject search simply by typing the keywords *air pollution* in the search box. This will probably yield a large list of books, depending upon the size of the collection you are searching. To limit your search and make it more manageable, you might add the word *industrial* or *urban* to your search phrase.

The following is an example of the first screen you would see if you were to type *air pollution* in the search box of LMxAC, the electronic book catalogue of the Libraries of Middlesex Automation Consortium, the system for the college libraries in Middlesex County, New Jersey. It lists the first ten entries on that subject, with sixty-seven others to follow.

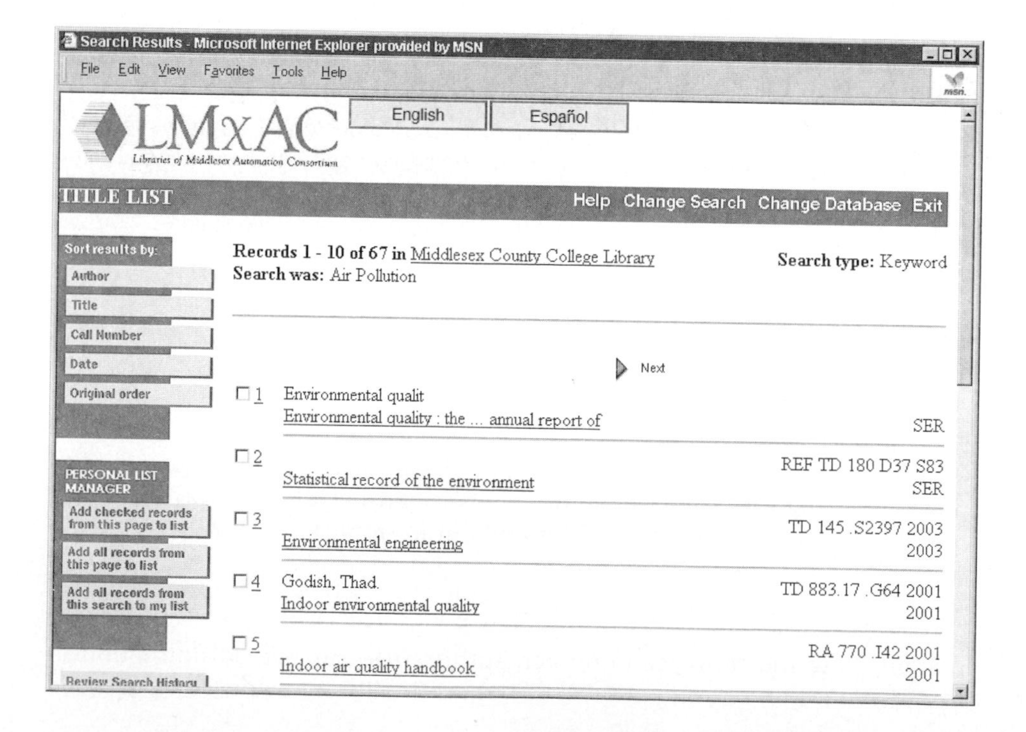

After reading over the entire list of books, you might decide to find more information about several of them. A click of the mouse will usually do the trick (again, you must follow directions appropriate to the system you are using). Here is the entry you would see if you chose one of the books listed—Thad Godish's book *Air Quality.* The entry includes publication information about the book as well as the branch it can be found in, its call number, and its status ("Not Checked Out").

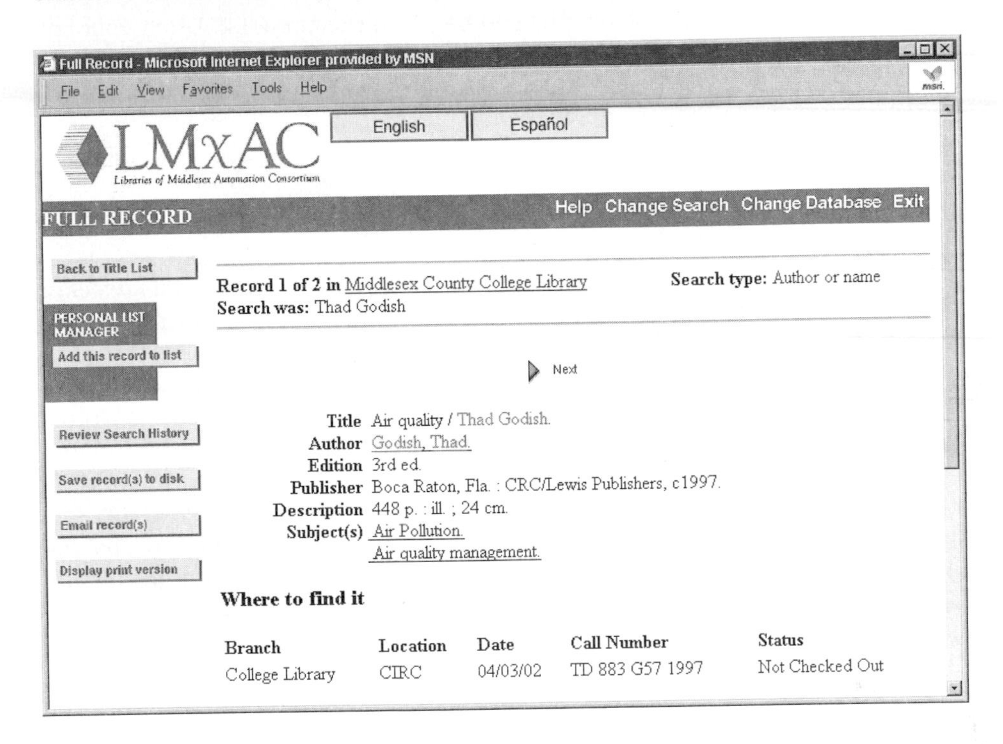

The Traditional Card Catalogue

You may come upon a library that still uses a traditional card catalogue. Such a catalogue usually consists of alphabetically arranged cards indexed by author,

Sample Subject Card from a Traditional Book (Card) Catalogue

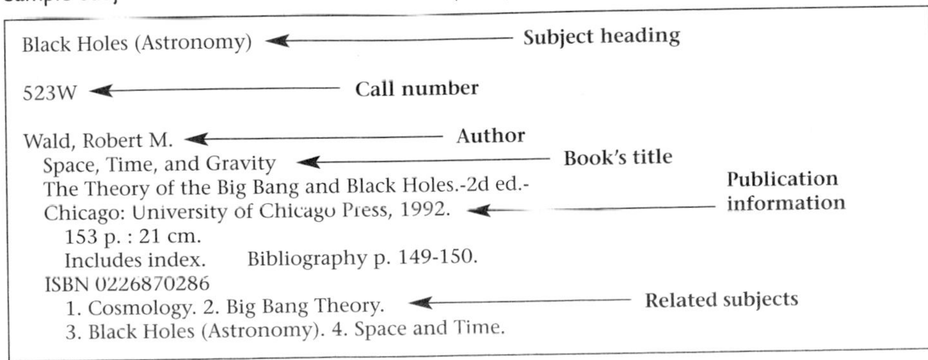

subject, and title. Information for each entry is printed on a card, as in the example on page 563; cards are stored in long, narrow drawers.

EXERCISE 20.3
Responses will vary.

EXERCISE 20.3

Continue the preliminary bibliography you began in Exercise 20.2. Using your college library's book catalogue, locate five books that relate to the research question you chose in Exercise 20.1. Record their pertinent publication information (see the list for books on page 560) in your working bibliography.

Periodical Indexes

Periodicals are publications that come out at regular intervals—daily, weekly, bi-weekly, monthly, quarterly, semi-annually, and so on. The information in periodicals is often more up to date than that found in books, and the publications provide a forum for the research, opinions, and commentary of experts. Periodical indexes are lists of magazine, journal, and newspaper articles—often arranged by author, title, and subject. They can be found in both bound and online versions in the library's reference area. These indexes are limited to information about articles published annually or during another specified period. Some indexes are general, listing articles from a variety of periodicals that appeal to a wide readership. Others focus on articles published in journals and magazines devoted to specific disciplines or fields of interest. You will likely find many indexes in both printed form and as electronic databases. As always, check with your librarian if you are having trouble finding an index.

CLASSROOM HINT You may want to remind students that certain magazines and newspapers are inappropriate for college research. Consider providing your students a list of those publications.

Let's look at three types of periodical sources and at the indexes in which you can find the sources listed.

Magazines, such as *U.S. News & World Report, Time, Atlantic Monthly,* and *Business Week,* contain articles written for general audiences. Magazine articles are researched and written by journalists who might or might not be experts in the fields on which they report. The best-known index for finding magazine articles is the *Readers' Guide to Periodical Literature.*

The *Readers' Guide,* now available in both bound and online versions, contains information from more than 100 magazines of interest to the general public. Arranged by subject and author, each volume of the bound version provides suggestions for using the *Readers' Guide* as well as a legend to abbreviations used. Here is an excerpt from a page in the bound version; the subject is *black holes:*

BLACK HOLES (ASTRONOMY)

Biggest black hole in the universe? J. Horgan. il *Scientific American* 265:32 Jl '91

A black hole found at last? il *Astronomy* 19:22 F '91

Black holes in galactic cores: the research mounts [research by John Kormendy] il *Sky and Telescope* 82: 344-5 O '91

Black holes swarming at the galactic center? [Granat satellite data] M. M. Waldrop il *Science* 251-166 Ja 11 '91

What the first entry contains:

Title of article: Biggest black hole in the universe?

Author: J. Horgan

Note that article is illustrated: il

Magazine in which article appeared: *Scientific American*

Volume number/page number: 265:32

Publication date (July 1991): Jl '91

Here is an entry on black holes found in the online version of the *Readers' Guide,* made available by subscription from the H. W. Wilson Company:

BRGA00065891 (USE FORMAT 7 FOR FULLTEXT)

Black holes in all sizes.

Talcott Richard

Astronomy v. 28 no 12 (Dec 2000) p. 26-8

Document Type: Feature Article

Special Features: il ISSN: 0091-6358

Language: English

Country of Publication: United States

Record Type: Abstract; Fulltext Record Status: Corrected or revised record

Word Count: 538

Abstract: Astronomers have discovered a new variety of black hole. The black hole, which is midway in size between the 2 types of hole identified so far, was discovered lying about 600 light-years from the center M82, in Ursa Major. The breakthrough finding came when astronomers using the Chandra X-ray Observatory compared high-resolution images of M82 with optical, radio, and infrared maps of the same regions. The discovery both opens a whole new field of research and raises the possibility that the Milky Way might contain midsized black holes.

Note that the online version provides an abstract (summary) of the article, which you can use to determine whether the article is relevant to your research project and worth reading in its entirety, as well as a way to access the article in its entirety.

CLASSROOM HINT Remind students that as they progress in their academic majors, they will be asked to rely on professional journals more and more, and on magazines and newspapers less and less.

Journals contain articles devoted to specific disciplines or fields of interest, and they are aimed at limited audiences, usually experts in those fields. Among the most famous are the *New England Journal of Medicine,* the *Harvard Business Review,* and *Publications of the Modern Language Association.* Often, journals are published by colleges and universities and by professional organizations. Articles in such journals are written by experts in the field.

A range of library indexes list information on journal articles. Like the materials they reference, these indexes focus on specific disciplines. Many are published by professional or educational organizations. They are usually bound annually, and some are available online or in electronic format. Many of those published electronically also include abstracts. Among commonly used journal indexes are the *Applied Science and Technology Index,* the *Business Periodicals Index,* the *Arts and Humanities Citation Index,* the *Education Index,* the *Educational Resources Information Center* (ERIC), the *Engineering Index,* the *Guide to Nursing and Allied Health,* the *Index Medicus,* the *Index to U.S. Government Periodicals,* the *Modern Language Association International Bibliography,* the *Music Index, Psychological Abstracts,* and the *Social Sciences Citation Index.*

Here is a sample entry taken from the *Modern Language Association International Bibliography,* an index published by a professional organization made up of teachers of modern language, literature, linguistics, and folklore:

> *Cather, Willa*
> [8429] Saposnik-Noire, Shelley. "The Silent Protagonist: The Unifying Presence of Landscape in Willa Cather's *My Ántonia.*" *MQ.* 1990 Winter; 31(2): 171-179.

What this entry contains:

Subject heading: Cather, Willa

Entry number: [8429]

Author: Saposnik-Noire, Shelley.

Title of article: "The Silent Protagonist:
The Unifying Presence of Landscape
in Willa Cather's *My Ántonia*"

Title of journal (*MQ = Midwest Quarterly*): *MQ*

Year/quarter of publication: 1990 Winter

Volume/issue numbers: 31(2)

Pages on which article appears: 171-179

Newspaper articles can be found by using a variety of indexes. One of the most famous is the *New York Times Index,* which lists articles published in that newspaper. In addition, electronic databases such as the Newspaper Abstracts of ProQuest, a CD-ROM index, offer publication information and abstracts of articles appearing in the *Christian Science Monitor,* the *Los Angeles Times,* the *New York Times,* the *Wall Street Journal,* and the *Washington Post* (see also page 567).

Electronic Databases

In the last decade, computerization has revolutionized library research. Not only have most libraries computerized their catalogues, but they also buy and subscribe to lists of books, articles, and other documents that are delivered via the Internet or stored on computer disks or other portable media. Some of these databases list bibliographical information only—the title, author's name, date of publication, and so on. Others include abstracts (summaries) of articles. Other databases offer copies of whole articles. In some cases, in fact, you can even get copies of entire books—usually classics—on the Internet at no cost.

SUGGESTED ACTIVITY
When students begin using these databases, try to spend time with them in the library to help them become oriented to these electronic search tools. The more coaching you can provide, the better.

Here is a partial list of online databases to which your library might provide you access. As always, check with your librarian to find out exactly what your library offers.

1. **ABI INFORM:** Provides full texts of articles in business and management. It draws articles from more than 1,000 academic and professional journals and trade magazines published worldwide.
2. **Academic Search Premier:** The world's largest multidisciplinary database, which provides the full texts of articles from nearly 3,500 publications.
3. **Anthropological Index Online:** Provides access to articles published in current periodicals found in the Museum of Mankind Library.
4. **Applied Science and Technology Index:** Contains abstracts of articles published in about 400 professional journals in aeronautics, computer science, engineering, and related scientific and technical disciplines.
5. **Cumulative Index to Nursing and Allied Health Literature** (CINAHL): References nearly 900 scholarly journals in the health sciences. It also contains information on books, dissertations, and educational software in the health professions.
6. **ERIC** (Education Resources Information Center): Includes journal articles, reports, and speeches on education.
7. **Humanities:** Offers citations and abstracts of journal articles in art, classics, history, language, literature, music, philosophy, religion, and other humanities. In addition, it provides the full text of some articles.
8. **JSTOR:** A scholarly journal archive, JSTOR stands for Journal Storage. It makes available back issues of important journals in the humanities, social sciences, and sciences.
9. **MOCAT:** The Monthly Catalogue of U.S. Government Documents, which indexes documents published by the federal government.
10. **Newspaper Abstracts:** A service of ProQuest. This index includes citations and abstracts of articles published in the *Christian Science Monitor,* the *Los Angeles Times,* the *New York Times,* the *Wall Street Journal,* and the *Washington Post.*
11. **Project Muse:** Contains citations to articles appearing in more than forty diverse journals published by Johns Hopkins University Press.

MORE OPTIONS ONLINE
For more on library research, go to **www.mhhe.com/writingtoday**.

12. **PsycLIT:** Indexes and abstracts books, journal articles, and dissertations in psychology and related disciplines.

For an example of what you might find if you used one of these online indexes, look at this sample page from the Academic Search Premier. The keywords *air pollution, prevention,* and *automobiles* were used for this search.

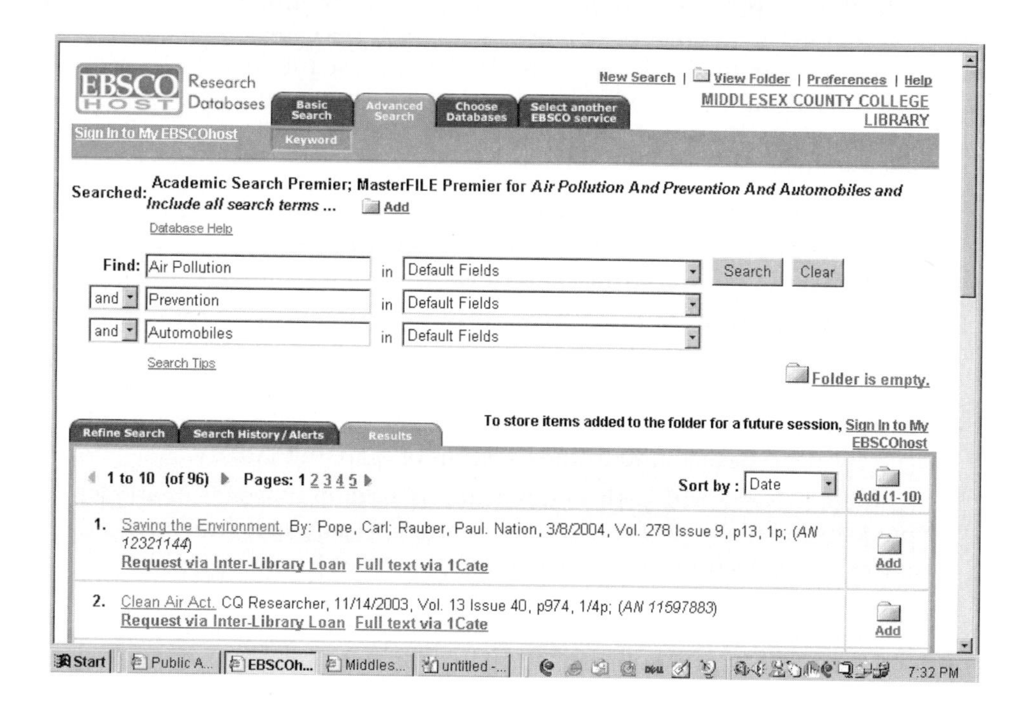

EXERCISE 20.4
Responses will vary.

EXERCISE 20.4

Continue the working bibliography you began in Exercise 20.2. Using resources like those discussed above, locate five periodical articles that relate to the research question you chose in Exercise 20.1. Record their pertinent publication information (see the list for periodical articles on page 561) in your working bibliography.

SEARCHING THE INTERNET

The **Internet**, including the World Wide Web, is a system that connects computers at various research, educational, corporate, personal, and other types of sites around the world. It can provide you with a rich trove of databases, which can yield much valuable information. (In fact, the twelve library databases listed above can be accessed via the Internet.) Students can access whole books, articles from online magazines and scholarly journals, government and organization position papers, government documents, pamphlets, brochures, and a host of other information sources.

However, before you begin to learn to use the Internet as a research tool, you need to realize that the Internet is valuable only if approached with caution and discrimination:

- The contents of the Internet are ever-changing. On one hand, this is an advantage because the Internet can provide access to the most current information on a topic. On the other hand, what you find on the Internet one day might not be there the next, a fact that you should take into account when evaluating your sources. After all, the reliability of such information might be questionable.
- College libraries are run by professionals who can be counted on to order materials prepared by qualified and reputable authors and publishers. Often, specific books, journals, and other materials are requested directly by college faculty. In general, then, you can have confidence that the materials in your college library are reliable, although you still need to read them critically and evaluate their usefulness and relevance to your topic. On the other hand, anyone with access to a server can create a Web site and post information on it. Therefore, when using the Internet you will have to take steps to assure yourself of the credibility, expertise, and reliability of any electronic sources you want to include. For example, if you searched for information about the Greek goddess Aphrodite on the Web, you might find materials by Joseph Campbell, a noted expert on ancient mythology. Then again, you might come up with a research paper on Aphrodite posted on the personal Web site of a college student who wants to show his parents how hard he has been working.
- Unscrupulous people and groups can and do take advantage of the ease of publishing on the Web. For example, hate mongers, racial supremacists, and the like sometimes post false and defamatory information about public figures and about ethnic, religious, or other groups. On occasion, the material is presented in such a devious manner that it seems to be coming from a legitimate news source or a think tank (a professional organization that researches and publishes papers on issues affecting the public). In such cases, it is especially important for you to discover and evaluate the sources of information that you intend to use.

A fuller discussion of how to evaluate Internet sources appears on pages 575–576.

A Brief Glossary of Internet Terms

Browser: Software that allows you to access the Internet. Microsoft Internet Explorer and Netscape Navigator are browsers.

E-zine: Name given to magazines published on the Internet. *Salon.com* is an example of such a magazine. (Many print magazines and newspapers also provide material on the Internet.)

FAQ: An abbreviation for "frequently asked questions." Most Internet browsers, services, and search engines provide a list of such questions so that users experiencing common problems can find solutions quickly.

Home page: The first page you see when accessing a Web site. A home page contains hyperlinks that will take you to other parts of the Web site as well as to related sites. For example, the home page of a professional organization might have hyperlinks to a list of its members, its online publications, and Web sites for other departments as well as to Web sites of other professional organizations in the same or related disciplines.

HTML (Hypertext Markup Language): A computer "language" that allows you to create a Web site.

Hyperlink: A word, phrase, icon, or object found on a Web page that, when clicked, takes you to another page in that site or to another Web site.

Keyword(s): Used in searching the Web and in conducting electronic research, a word or phrase that focuses a search so that you can more efficiently retrieve information on a limited topic.

Mailing list: An electronic discussion group focused on a particular subject or task. Students taking online courses often communicate with their professors and classmates via electronic mailing lists.

Newsgroups: Online forums dedicated to a particular topic on which participants can post comments.

Online: Connected to the Internet.

Search engine: Software that allows you to search for information on a topic by entering keywords. Many search engines provide suggestions that can help make your search more productive.

URL (Uniform Resource Locator): The address of a Web site. Typing a URL into the address box of your browser allows you to connect directly to the site without using a search engine.

Internet Search Tools: URLs, Directories, and Search Engines

If you know the **URL** (Uniform Resource Locator) of a Web site, you can connect to that site directly by typing the URL into the address box of your browser. It is always wise to keep a record of the URLs of Web sites you have accessed; you can do this simply by printing out the site's home page or copying the URL and pasting it into your working bibliography, using your computer's cut-and-paste function.

If you are just beginning your search for information on a topic, however, you will probably want to start by using an Internet browser such as Microsoft Internet Explorer or a **search engine** such as AltaVista, Google, or Lycos. Many Internet browsers and search engines display **directories**, or listings of search categories that will bring you to relevant sites. For example, Yahoo! lists "Arts and Humanities," "Business and Economy," and "Education" among many other categories. Searching for information by using these categories will lead you to sites that people running the search engine have determined are the most useful to their most frequent users. However, such searches might not always produce results that are useful to you. In addition, remember that many Web site creators pay a fee to register their sites with certain search engines. This entitles them to be listed among the sites that come up when you use the search engine's directory. Again, these sites might not be the most appropriate for your search.

Chances are that you will have to conduct your own keyword search via a search engine, which looks through many databases for the keywords you have indicated. Any Web browser can provide you with access to more search engines than you will ever need. However, not all search engines access the same sites. Therefore, searching for the same topic via different search engines might very well produce different results. For future reference, it is a good idea to "bookmark" or include in your list of "favorites" those search engines you find most useful.

Search engines offer users several different ways to limit and refine their searches. With many search engines, for example, if you type in the keywords *AIDS education,* you will find sites relevant both to *AIDS* and to *education.* In some cases, you might be able to refine your search simply by typing your keywords in quotation marks, thereby significantly limiting your yield to sites on topics dealing only with "educational efforts aimed at dealing with AIDS." Fortunately, most search engines provide their users with advice on how to best use their services. For example, using Google's advanced search function can help you refine a search for information on *AIDS education* (see the screens on page 572). To make your search efficient, spend a few minutes reading these suggestions, at least those offered by the search engine you use most often. (See pages 573–574 for tips on using search engines.)

A Brief List of Popular Search Engines

AltaVista (http://www.altavista.com): A useful search engine for academics, it provides access to more than thirty million pages of information.

Excite (http://www.excite.com): This search engine conducts concept as well as word or phrase searches. Thus, if you were to type *AIDS education* in the search box, it might return links to articles on HIV infection and on AIDS prevention as well as links to information on AIDS education.

Google (http://www.google.com): Google provides access to over 3 billion Web pages, and it includes a number of special features to improve searches. It ranks Web sites according to the number and quality of pages that link to them. This is a very powerful and widely used search engine.

Hotbot (http://www.hotbot.com): Developed by a joint venture of the Inktomi Corporation and Hotwired, this search engine allows you to use several configurations of keywords. It searches several different aspects of the Web site, not just its title or metatag (the device created by the Web site designer to enable the search engine to index the site).

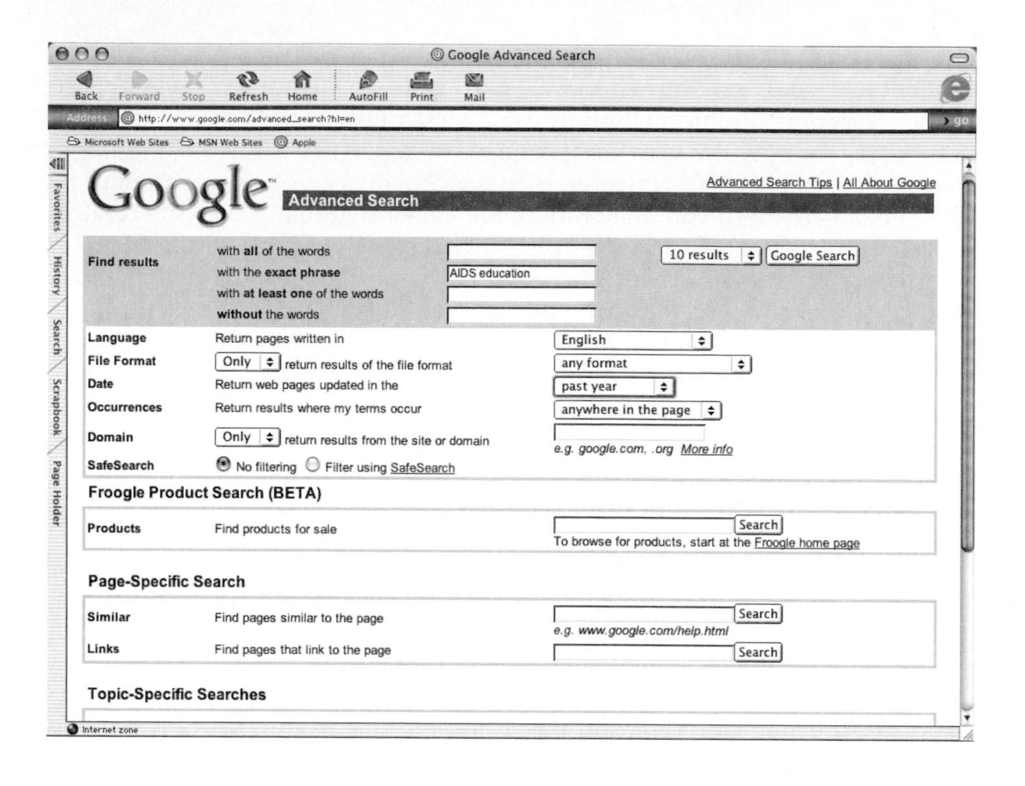
Google Advanced Search
Back Forward Stop Refresh Home AutoFill Print Mail
Address http://www.google.com/advanced_search?hl=en
Microsoft Web Sites MSN Web Sites Apple
Favorites History Search Scrapbook Page Holder
Google Advanced Search
Advanced Search Tips | All About Google
Find results
with all of the words
with the exact phrase AIDS education
with at least one of the words
without the words
10 results Google Search
Language Return pages written in English
File Format Only return results of the file format any format
Date Return web pages updated in the past year
Occurrences Return results where my terms occur anywhere in the page
Domain Only return results from the site or domain
e.g. google.com, .org More info
SafeSearch No filtering Filter using SafeSearch
Froogle Product Search (BETA)
Products Find products for sale Search
To browse for products, start at the Froogle home page
Page-Specific Search
Similar Find pages similar to the page Search
e.g. www.google.com/help.html
Links Find pages that link to the page Search
Topic-Specific Searches
Internet zone

Google Search: "AIDS education"
Back Forward Stop Refresh Home AutoFill Print Mail
Address http://www.google.com/search?as_q=&num=10&hl=en&ie=ISO-8859-1&btnG=Google+Search&as_epq=AIDS+education&as_oq=&as_eq=&lr=lang_en&as_ft=i&as_filetype=&as_q
Microsoft Web Sites MSN Web Sites Apple
Favorites History Search Scrapbook Page Holder
Google
Advanced Search Preferences Language Tools Search Tips
"AIDS education" past year Google Search
Search the Web Search English pages
Web Images Groups Directory News
Searched English pages over the past year for "AIDS education". Results 1 - 10 of about 287,000. Search took 0.28 seconds.
Tip: In most browsers you can just hit the return key instead of clicking on the search button.
HIV / AIDS Information
www.projectinform.org Choose hope over despair. Advocacy, treatment information & more.
Sponsored Link
News: Education Programme for Deaf Learners Launched - AllAfrica.com - Mar 2, 2004
Try Google News: Search news for "AIDS education" or browse the latest headlines
AIDS Education Global Information System (AEGiS) - Enhanced Site
AIDS Education Global Information System (AEGiS) - Site Map. HOME SEARCH KEY TOPICS
Basics Day One Frequently Asked Questions What Do You Know about HIV? ...
Description: AEGIS is one of the largest HIV/AIDS databases in the world, includes the HIV Daily Briefing, updated...
Category: Health > Conditions and Diseases > ... > Immune Deficiency > AIDS
www.aegis.com/ - 13k - Mar 2, 2004 - Cached - Similar pages
AVERT - A UK HIV and AIDS Charity
AVERTing AIDS and HIV. about avert Donate here Contact us. Sections.
AIDS & HIV StatisticsAIDS & HIV Statistics, Becoming infected, Testing ...
Description: AIDS education for young people, including statistics, history, and stories of people living with HIV.
Category: Society > Issues > ... > AIDS > Young People > Organizations
www.avert.org/ - 14k - Mar 2, 2004 - Cached - Similar pages
AIDS Education and Training National Resource Center
Welcome to the AIDS Education and Training Centers (AETC) National
Resource Center (NRC) Web site. Highlights. AETC Network News ...
www.aids-etc.org/ - 9k - Cached - Similar pages
The New England AIDS Education & Training Center
... The New England AIDS Education and Training Center, established in 1988, is one
Sponsored Links
Fight AIDS in Africa
Lend us your voice. Get involved.
Sign up for E-mail Action Alerts.
www.data.org
Aids Education
Aids in the Developing World - Find papers, news, data. Start here.
www.worldbank.org/aids
Outright Speakers/Talent
Gay, Lesbian, Bisexual, Transgender Lectures, Comedy, & Music Agency
www.OutrightSpeakers.com
Date HIV/AIDS Single Now
Dating Center for Singles with HIV/AIDS in Your City. Register Free
www.PositiveSingles.com
See your message here...
Internet zone

Library of Congress World Wide Web Homepage (http://www.lcWeb.loc.gov): This search engine provides information on the contents of the United States Library of Congress, perhaps the largest collection in the world. Its home page offers databases of state and federal government publications. The THOMAS database, named after Thomas Jefferson, provides information on bills under consideration in the U.S. House and Senate.

Teoma (http://www.teoma.com): This is a relatively new search engine that is gaining popularity among academic users. Teoma uses what it calls "subject-specific-popularity" to evaluate a site "based upon the number of same-subject pages that reference it, not just general popularity."

WebCrawler (http://www.webcrawler.com): Now part of the Excite system, WebCrawler searches for keywords in the text of a Web site, not just in its title or metatag.

Multi-Search Engines: Such resources access other search engines and can therefore expand your search significantly. However, because their range is so wide, they work more slowly than other search engines. Examples of multi-search engines are DogPile (http://www.dogpile.com), Metacrawler (http://www.metacrawler.com), and MetaFind (http://www.metafinder.com).

EXERCISE 20.5

Look up a subject such as one of the following using three different search engines:

EXERCISE 20.5 Responses will vary.

1. College literacy standards
2. Ethanol as an alternative fuel
3. Advantages of vegan diets
4. Bilingual education
5. U.S. immigration policy
6. Reducing teenage pregnancy rates

Decide which one finds the greatest number of useful sites and which one is easiest to use.

Three Tips on Using Search Engines

As discussed earlier, all search engines offer specific on-screen help; however, here are three general strategies you might find helpful:

1. **Try a Boolean Search:** Boolean searches use AND, OR, and NOT with keywords and phrases so as to limit searches and make them more efficient. If you typed *victim* AND *crime* AND *compensation,* you would gain access to more sites that contain information about compensating victims of crime, and you would eliminate sites relating to, for example, *compensation for corporate executives* or the *victimization of women in the workplace.* If you searched for *virus* NOT *computer,* you would limit your search to viruses known to medicine.

MORE OPTIONS ONLINE
For more on Internet research, go to **www.mhhe.com/writingtoday.**

2. **Use a Wild Card:** A *wild card* is a character, often an asterisk, that is used with a keyword to search for variations of that word as well as the word itself. For example, typing the keyword *crim** might produce sites containing the words *crime, criminology, criminals,* and *criminality.*
3. **Include Quotation Marks** (" "): Quotation marks tell the search engine to look for the words you have typed in the exact order they appear in the search box. For example, if you wanted to find sites that discuss "standard of living," you would put quotation marks around those words.

EXERCISE 20.6

EXERCISE 20.6
Responses will vary.

Continue the working bibliography you began in Exercise 20.2. Using resources like those discussed above, locate five Internet documents that relate to the research question you chose in Exercise 20.1. Record their pertinent publication information (see the list for electronic sources on page 561) in your working bibliography.

EVALUATING SOURCES

CLASSROOM HINT Try to spend a substantial amount of class time on the evaluation of sources. Bring in examples of sources you consider inappropriate, and contrast them to appropriate alternatives.

As you add more and more sources that you believe are relevant to your research topic and question to your working bibliography, you will realize that some of the sources you have gathered will not be worth using. They may be too general, irrelevant, or even inaccurate. The fact that a book or article has been published does not guarantee the reliability or even the authenticity of its information. The guidelines that follow will help you avoid wasting hours taking notes that will be useless when it comes time to draft your paper.

Tips on Evaluating Sources for Your Research Paper

1. Before you even start taking notes from a work, preview it. Does the work seem to contain enough information relevant to your topic and research question to make it worth your time to read it and take careful notes? Check the index and table of contents of a book, and read its preface or introduction. Skim a periodical article or electronic source. Read subheadings as well as the article's introduction and conclusion. Examine any charts, graphs, or other visual elements that are included.
2. Evaluate the content of the source. Does the author support opinions with facts, reliable statistics, and other trustworthy data, or does he or she rely heavily on unsupported ideas and opinions? Does the author make his or her case logically? Does the work seem balanced, or does the author provide only part of the evidence—the part that supports his or her thesis? Does the work rely on well-documented research, and do the sources of this research seem reputable? For example, contrast these two claims:

People under the age of 30 make high-risk drivers. They cause and are involved in the greatest number of fatal automobile accidents.

According to the authors of "The Insurance Dilemma," an eleven-year study (1990–2000) of automobile accidents published by the Allied Automobile Institutes of North America, "drivers under age of 30 were involved in 45% of all serious collisions (with repair or replacement costs of over $5000) and accounted for 60% of fatalities in such accidents" (44).

3. Does the material presented seem objective, or could it be biased? For example, information on the efficacy of a drug taken from a publication of the National Institutes of Health is likely to be objective, whereas information from a pamphlet published by the manufacturer of that drug will probably be biased in favor of the drug. Most pharmaceutical manufacturers are trustworthy and will provide accurate information, but they are in business to make a profit. Therefore, the perspective from which they provide information is not disinterested.
4. Consider the publication date. For topics in the sciences and technologies as well as in the social sciences, the more current the publication, the better.
5. Consider the author. What are his or her credentials, such as education, years of experience, and professional affiliation? Is he or she a college or university professor or a well-known reporter, commentator, scientist, or other professional in a field related to your topic? Is he or she a member of a respected research institution? Has the author published articles or books on the same or related topics? Are these sources available in college libraries?

   You might want to verify an author's credentials by searching for more information about him or her on the Internet, in your college library, or in *Books in Print,* which would list other book-length works he or she might have written. If you cannot verify his or her credentials, find other sources of information. In addition, you should ask yourself whether the author has a political, artistic, or other bias that makes his or her viewpoint less than objective. If so, is the information still useful if used with caution, or is it so tainted that using it would harm the integrity of your work?
6. Consider the publisher. Is this a respected commercial or academic publisher? Or is this a "vanity" press, which is willing to print a manuscript that other publishers have rejected on the condition that the author agrees to cover all or part of the publication costs? Is the publisher known for putting out inflammatory, biased, or other material that is inappropriate to scholarly research? You can find out about various publishing houses by reading *Literary Marketplace* or *Editor & Publisher,* or by consulting your college librarian or professor.

Tips on Evaluating Electronic Sources for Your Research Paper

CLASSROOM HINT
Make a special effort to discuss the criteria for evaluating electronic sources.

The logic, principles, and good sense that you would apply to a print source are the same as those you apply to all sources, including those found on the

Internet. However, remember that the sources you find in the library have already been screened through a process that involves professionals—college faculty and librarians—ordering materials that they believe will best support the curriculum. Moreover, no publisher with a reputation to maintain can afford to print a text that is poorly prepared, inflammatory, biased, fraudulent, or unfair. You can be fairly confident, then, that most of the print sources available in your college library are appropriate for college research. In the case of articles in scholarly journals, in fact, submissions are often juried—that is, judged for quality by reviewers who are themselves experts in the discipline.

On the other hand, any organization or any person—regardless of education, experience, bias, or intent—can publish on the Internet. No screening process exists for such material. Consider the following *additional* criteria as you decide whether or not an Internet source is appropriate:

1. Who sponsors the Web site or publishes the CD-ROM? Is it a college or university, a research institution, a professional journal, a reputable magazine, or a respected think tank? Is it just a personal Web site that the creator has published by renting space on a commercial server? If the latter, find other sources of information.
2. What is the purpose of the site? Consider the Web address (URL). Addresses for sites sponsored by educational institutions usually end in "edu." Those for city, state, and federal government sites end in "gov." Sites whose addresses end in "org" (organization) need careful scrutiny. As a general rule, groups such as the League of Women Voters, the United Way, or the Girl Scouts provide information that is unbiased; of course, you will have to read the mission or purpose statements of such organizations for yourself to be sure. Other groups, such as the Americans for Democratic Action, the American Civil Liberties Union, and the Young Republicans, also publish a great deal of reliable information, but you must remember that the overall purpose of these organizations may make their views on an issue less than disinterested. Then there are organizations that are so biased that you should never rely on information from their Web sites unless you are trying to expose that bias or analyze its causes and effects. Many Web sites are simply organs of propaganda put on the Web by fringe groups who are trying to advance a political, social, medical, or other type of agenda that would not have been disseminated were it not for the relatively cheap and easy means of publishing on the Web.

   Still another type of address ends in "com," for commercial. Corporations usually use such addresses. If you are considering material posted on a corporate Web site, you need to ask yourself if the material presented is simply informational and objective or if its purpose is to sell you something.
3. What information about the Web site can you find by going to the home page, which may provide more and better information about the author and the sponsor than any single Web page can? You can get to a site's home page by clicking on the home page link.
4. Is the material well written, well presented, and well developed? Is the Web site constructed logically and coherently? Is it updated regularly? Does it include links to other sites? What sites are they? Do they seem

reputable? If the answer to these questions is no, find other sources of information.

5. Was the document published in a print version as well as on the Internet? If not, could it have been? If the document does not meet the criteria for evaluating all sources of information (see the list above), you can't rely on the information that it contains, and you need to find other sources.

MORE OPTIONS ONLINE
For a source evaluation tutor, go to **www.mhhe.com/writingtoday**.

EXERCISE 20.7

Evaluate the sources in the working bibliography you have been developing. Remove sources that are not appropriate according to the criteria for print and nonprint sources discussed above. Do you have enough sources left for you to start taking notes, or should you try to find more sources? If in doubt, consult your instructor.

EXERCISE 20.7
Responses will vary.

TAKING NOTES

When you read, you will want to keep a record of information that is potentially important for your research paper. This is best done by recording notes on index cards (4" × 6" cards are recommended). Use one index card for each fact, idea, opinion, or group of supporting data that you take from a source. This method enables you to organize your notes easily and efficiently once you have finished your research and are ready to begin outlining and drafting.

As an alternative to traditional note cards, you might consider keeping your notes in a computer file or annotating photocopies and printouts of your source material.

- **Taking notes on a computer:** As with note cards, you'll need to take notes in a way that will allow you to organize your information easily. Start each note from a source on a new page, and identify the source of each piece of information. Writing your quotations, summaries, and paraphrases (see pages 578–580) in a computer file can save you time once you begin your paper because you can simply cut and paste information into your draft.
- **Taking notes on photocopies or printouts:** If your paper is brief, and you are not using many sources, this system can work very well. You can highlight key points in your sources on the printout and write notes and ideas in the margins.

Note: Avoid recording information in a notebook or on looseleaf paper. Doing so makes organizing your notes far more difficult later on.

After taking your notes on cards, in a computer file, or on printouts, read over these notes carefully. As you do, general points or major ideas that you might use in your paper will start to emerge. Next, arrange the cards or printouts in a separate pile for each of those ideas. Arranging your notes in this way gives you a preliminary notion of how your paper will be organized—at least in general. Now read over the notes in each pile and arrange the cards or printouts in that pile in the order that will best present the information. If you have taken a lot of notes, you may have to spread your notes on a large table or even

CLASSROOM HINT
You can't stress too strongly the recommendation that it's better to take notes on cards than on 8½" × 11" paper. Try demonstrating the difficulty of using sheets of paper by pretending to draft a paper from notes taken on them. Dramatize the waste of time and possible confusion that is likely to occur. Then illustrate the drafting of a paper using note cards.

on the floor. Doing so allows you to begin to see your paper take form. Once you review your initial "layout," however, you can change the positions of notes, add or delete notes as needed, and make other changes easily and logically. You might even see the need to do more research. In any event, you can then use this arrangement of cards as a model from which to outline your paper.

Note: You can easily keep track of your sources by beginning your note taking with a 3" × 5" "bibliography card" for each source. On it, record all of the publication data you will need to include in that particular source's entry in the works-cited or references section, the list of the sources you used in your paper. You can also transfer this information to your working bibliography. (You will learn more about works-cited and references entries in Chapter 21.)

Bibliography Card

"Are School Vouchers Un-American?"
Gary Rosen, Pages 25-28
Commentary
Vol. 10 Issue 2
Date Feb 2000

Then, at the top of each of your "content" cards, you can simply write the author's last name and the relevant page number(s). If no author is given, use a shortened version of the source's title.

Notes take three forms: direct quotations, summaries, and paraphrases:

Direct quotations use the exact words of the source. Sometimes you will read a passage with insights that are so precise, clear, or moving that you will want to repeat them exactly. A direct quotation is a word-for-word copy of the original, as in the example on page 579. Place quotation marks (" ") around passages you may want to quote as you take notes. The quotation marks will remind you that the information was copied exactly and that you will have to place quotation marks around the passage in your paper. (See Chapter 18 for more guidelines on quoting.)

You can use summaries and paraphrases to present borrowed information, insights, and ideas using your own words and your own sentence patterns. Summaries and paraphrases convey insights and information that you can use as major ideas or as support for those ideas.

Summaries condense information into a shorter form while expressing the main idea. Simply try to focus on the main point or idea the author is mak-

Direct Quotation Note Card

> Rosen 26
>
> "By any measure, public education in America's cities is in deep trouble, and has been for some time. On any given day in Cleveland, almost one of every six students is likely not to show up. In Washington, D.C., a majority of tenth graders never finish high school. And in Los Angeles, school officials recently retreated from a plan to end the practice of 'social promotion,' realizing that it would have required holding back for a year more than half of the district's woefully unprepared students."

ing in a passage or paragraph, and state that idea in one or two sentences that use your own words only. Compare this paragraph from Ernest Albrecht's *The New American Circus* (page 1) with a summary:

> The circus had truly become the best (and often the only) entertainment bargain in town, a display of profligacy that has not been seen outside that wildly prosperous period the United States enjoyed between 1870 and 1915. So abundant were its demonstrations of skill and daring that it required not just three rings to contain them all but four elevated stages as well. Pageants of splendor and inflated grandiosity wound their way around the hippodrome track that encircled the giant tent. In its enormity the American circus had become the glorious embodiment of America's unofficial motto: "All New This Year: Bigger and Better than Ever."

Summary Note Card

> Albrecht 1
>
> In the period of economic growth that spanned the end of the nineteenth and the beginning of the twentieth centuries, the American circus grew into a huge, flamboyant, and extravagant enterprise that met the nation's growing desire for more exciting and lavish spectacles.

A **paraphrase** is like a summary except that it can be about as long as the original. Once again, use your own words while capturing the writer's main idea. Compare a paraphrase of an idea from Vicki Goldberg's essay "Death Takes a Holiday, Sort Of" with the original. Goldberg's essay appeared on page 29 of *Why We Watch,* a collection of essays on violence.

> In the eighteenth century, the popular print, still limited in number, came into its own. The last years of the century saw new and revived graphic techniques, including wood engraving (incising an image on the harder end piece of the wood), which would be vital to the nineteenth-century illustrated press, and lithography. Both permitted much, much larger illustrated press runs. The introduction of photography, in 1839, riveted the eyes of the world on pictures, and by 1851, an easy means of duplicating photographic prints made them cheaper and readily available.

Paraphrase Note Card

> Goldberg 29
>
> At the end of the 1700s, new methods enabled printers to mass-produce illustrations more clearly than before. Thus, illustrations began to appear more frequently in printed materials. One of these methods was lithography. Another was engraving, carving images on wooden blocks, used in the illustrated newspapers and magazines of the next century. In the 1800s, the invention of photography and of inexpensive methods to reproduce photographs further increased the presence of visuals in printed materials.

Note: You might want to include some words from the original in a paraphrase. If so, be sure to put quotation marks around them.

Paraphrase Note Card that Includes Quoted Material

> Goldberg 29
>
> At the end of the 1700s, new methods enabled printers to mass-produce illustrations more clearly than before. Thus, illustrations began to appear more frequently in printed materials. One was these methods was lithography. Another was engraving, carving images on wooden blocks, used in the illustrated newspapers and magazines of the next century. In the 1800s, the invention of photography, which "riveted the eyes of the world on pictures," and of inexpensive methods to reproduce photographs further increased the presence of visuals in printed materials.

EXERCISE 20.8

Find and begin taking notes on one of the sources in your working bibliography. Make sure you have a bibliography card, as well as at least one card that contains a direct quotation, one that contains a paraphrase, and one that contains a summary.

EXERCISE 20.8
Responses will vary.

AVOIDING PLAGIARISM

Schools, colleges, and universities insist on the integrity of their students' work. Plagiarism, which is the use of someone else's words or ideas without giving the source appropriate credit, is a serious offense. It violates the very purpose of education, which is, essentially, the search for truth, and it is usually punished severely. Indeed, penalties for plagiarism can range from failure in the course to dismissal from the college or university.

Most often, intentional plagiarism involves copying something from a source, usually word for word, and using it without quotation marks. However, students who are just learning to write research papers sometimes commit unintentional plagiarism, which can result from any of the following actions:

1. Forgetting to put quotation marks around quoted material when taking notes or forgetting to include quotation marks when placing those notes in the text of the paper.
2. Using material that has been summarized or paraphrased and forgetting to tell readers the source of that material.
3. Paraphrasing or summarizing incorrectly. Inadvertent plagiarism includes accidentally adopting the sentence and/or paragraph structure of the original or including many of the words from the original (except for proper nouns). Note that while this is not done intentionally, it is still a serious problem and may result in a substantially lower grade than the paper could have earned.

CLASSROOM HINT
Plagiarism is an epidemic. Insist on the need for academic integrity. Explain that writing appropriate summaries and paraphrases is hard work and requires some creativity. Follow up with some in-class and out-of-class note-taking assignments. Finally, remind students that instructors can use search engines such as Google to catch intentional plagiarism. All an instructor needs to do is to type in a suspect phrase or sentence into the search box. The key here is to make students aware that the Internet can be used as a tool to catch cheaters. Providing an example will serve as a deterrent.

Contrast a direct quotation from Frank Ancona's book *Myth* with a partially plagiarized paraphrase. Then look at a legitimate paraphrase and summary of the same material.

Original

In *The Interpretation of Dreams,* Freud recognized the difficulty inherent in trying to communicate with the unconscious. He attributed the problem to what he called a "censor." He believed that some elements of consciousness did not want the messages from the unconscious to surface. (23)

Plagiarized Paraphrase

In *The Interpretation of Dreams,* Freud **recognized** how **difficult** it was **to communicate with the unconscious.** He theorized that **the problem** was caused by something **he called a "censor." He believed that some** parts **of consciousness did not want messages from the unconscious to** come out.

Legitimate Paraphrase

To Freud, a "censor" within the conscious mind kept the unconscious mind from communicating with it. In his book *The Interpretation of Dreams,* he theorized that an aspect of the conscious mind prevented troublesome ideas from emerging.

Legitimate Summary

Freud theorized in *The Interpretation of Dreams* that something within the conscious mind attempts to keep out information buried within the unconscious.

The plagiarized paraphrase contains words taken directly from the original. In this case, the student needs to rephrase the note or simply to put the author's original wording in quotation marks.

Keep in mind that you are allowed to "use" the work of another, within reason, as long as you acknowledge and credit this source. On the other hand, a research paper shouldn't be just an unbroken string of direct quotations, paraphrases, and summaries from other sources. Exactly what needs to be cited?

1. A direct quotation of another person's writing or speech, even if only a few words
2. A paraphrase or summary of another person's writing or speech
3. An opinion expressed by another person
4. Statistical data produced by another person
5. Graphic or audiovisual material produced by another person

What kind of information does *not* need to be cited? Only the following categories fall into this group:

1. Common knowledge: U.S. citizens are expected to pay taxes on their income; water freezes at 32 degrees Fahrenheit; most gasoline bought in the United States is imported.
2. "Background" knowledge generated from your research. (Be careful not to interpret this category too broadly.) If you are researching an essay on prison overcrowding in your state, for example, and twelve sources in a row indicate that the problem is serious, you have no need to cite a source for this opinion. However, if one of these sources claims that prison overcrowding is the *most* serious problem afflicting your state, and you express this opinion in any way, you must credit its source. Similarly, if you are researching an article on the salaries paid to major league baseball players in the 1980s and find source after source mentioning the continuing escalation in salaries, you have no need to cite a source. However, if a source points out that salaries increased fivefold during the 1980s, you need to cite this source if you include this information.

MORE OPTIONS ONLINE
For more information on how to avoid plagiarism, go to **www.mhhe.com/writingtoday.**

If you are not sure whether to cite information, be conservative: credit the source. The consequences for being too careful are minimal compared to the damage that plagiarism wreaks.

THE RESEARCH PAPER

The end of the semester is near, and the English composition instructor is grading a stack of research papers. The instructor opens the first one and starts reading. Here is the third paragraph:

> "Students of legal age vote at a surprisingly low rate." (Anderson, pg. 7). According to Anderson, "The franchise given to eighteen-year-olds in 1972 has apparently decreased in value." (Anderson, page 7). "Most people don't become fully engaged in the political process until their late twenties." (pg. 8). And some wait until even later. "Many observers talk of the "senior stranglehold" over the political process." (Anderson, page 8, Fox & Snow, pg. 9).

The instructor might be excused for throwing this "research paper" away and requesting another attempt from the student. The most interesting point is that this paragraph was written *after* the instructor lectured for several class periods about the research paper assignment, showing the class what to do and what not to do—in other words, providing his or her exact expectations. This student clearly didn't get the message or chose to ignore it.

Students' problems with research papers sometimes arise from their tendency to view the research paper with dread. They envision a huge project that is somehow unrelated to what they have already learned. However, you should keep this definition in mind: a research paper is simply a documented essay. The only real distinguishing feature of a documented essay is its use of sources and its need to account for that use in an acceptable manner.

Writing a research paper *is* a complicated process, but this process becomes much more easy to approach when it is looked at as a series of steps. For this reason, the first section of this chapter focuses on the steps that can be taken in approaching any research paper. The next two sections explore the guidelines for producing a documented essay provided by the Modern Language Association (MLA) and the guidelines provided by the American Psychological Association (APA). We also include a sample student research paper that follows MLA guidelines and that illustrates various issues students face during this process. However, keep in mind that your professor might want you to use another style, so always clarify this point before you start drafting the paper.

Chapter 20 covers the process of researching, taking notes, and including researched material as you draft and revise your paper. Here, we show you how to use your research to develop an essay that uses secondary sources.

GENERAL STRATEGIES FOR THE RESEARCH PAPER

Use these strategies for any documented essay that you write:

CLASSROOM HINT Emphasize these strategies in class if you have time. Also, remind students of the need to make a work schedule for their research project before they begin.

1. **Read and follow the assignment.** Each research assignment is different, and each instructor will specify what he or she wants to see. When grading your paper, if the instructor realizes, for example, that instead of using ten sources (five print sources and five Internet sources, as specified), you have

used eight Internet sources and no print sources, your essay is at great risk. The same is true if your instructor asked for a minimum of 1,500 words and you produced 975 words, or if your instructor stated that no more than 25 percent of your essay should be taken up by quotations, summaries, and paraphrases, and half of your essay is material taken from secondary sources.

2. **Don't be afraid to ask for clarification.** During your college career you will be asked to write research papers in a range of courses. Many instructors will spell out the guidelines for these assignments; other instructors might be more vague. Some years ago, one of our students asked a history instructor exactly what he was looking for in his research paper assignment. "You know, a research paper," he responded. "You've taken composition; you know what a research paper is."

   The student pressed for clarification: "I know how to do an MLA-style paper with parenthetical documentation. Will that work?" The instructor answered in the affirmative, and the student was then able to approach the assignment with more confidence.

3. **Use your time wisely.** Most instructors give plenty of time for a research paper to be completed; however, some students don't start the process of researching and writing until insufficient time remains. In other words, instructors see the research paper as a series of steps, but some students begin the process the day before the essay is due.

   Consider this hypothetical situation: if either author of this textbook were given an assignment at 6:00 p.m. on a Monday evening to research and write a 2,000-word essay analyzing Thomas Hardy's "Convergence of the Twain," using no fewer than eight sources, all of them from print publications, with the finished essay due at 10:00 a.m. the next day, the writer would (bleary-eyed, no doubt) turn in a good research paper at or before the assigned time. Keep in mind, though, that we have been studying and/or teaching college English for a very long time. We have learned a few things along the way. Even so, with more time to conduct research, plan, and draft, a "good" effort can become an excellent paper.

   Don't even consider trying to write a research paper the night before it is due. Instead, use your time wisely. If you have three weeks to write a paper, consider scheduling approximately a week for research, a week for drafting, and a week for revision. Better yet, if you have twenty-one calendar days, allot about five days for each of these three steps, leaving a six-day window in case of unexpected problems. For example, sometimes you will need to go back to the library after your first draft. More frequently, the demands of your other classes, your family, your relationships, or your job will find a way to cut into your time. If you become ill during the semester, the illness may well occur toward the end of the term, when, unfortunately, research papers tend to be assigned.

4. **Consider the "shape" of your research paper.** During this semester you have been learning to write essays using various rhetorical options: definition,

Consider Your Options

Your instructor is assigning you a research project, and you will be the project manager. Just as in the working world, you will receive guidelines on how to proceed. When your project is completed, it will be evaluated against those guidelines. The research paper measures not only your ability to write but also your ability to plan a project, coordinate the project's steps, and check the results.

causal analysis, and so on. Can you organize your essay around one of these frameworks? Probably, but check the wording of your assignment. If your instructor asks you to explore the reasons for the entry of the United States into the Spanish-American War, causal analysis is an obvious strategy. If your instructor asks you to explain how the World Bank decides to lend money to developing nations, process analysis will be your choice. Any topic that asks for "the best" or "the ideal" will need both definition and argument. Some research paper topics will require using a blended option in which you combine various approaches (see Chapter 15).

5. **Prepare carefully.** As Chapter 20 indicates, after you have done the bulk of your research, you will have note cards full of information and language that you will want to incorporate into your research paper. However, this information will be of little use if you do not plan how to organize your essay so that you use your researched material to your best advantage. You need to develop a tentative thesis statement at this point. (For more on developing a working thesis, see Chapter 2.) Although your final thesis may vary somewhat from your earliest version, developing this "guiding principle" will help you focus your efforts. Next, you will need to outline your essay. We suggest using a sentence outline. As you saw in Chapter 2, a sentence outline lists, in order, the proposed thesis statement and the proposed topic sentence of each following paragraph. This outline is not carved in marble; you may need to alter it during the writing process. However, a sentence outline gives you a focus and a tentative organization. Such an outline also lets you write the parts of your essay out of order without worrying about a loss of coherence.

6. **Use your sources carefully, and cite them accurately.** The term *research paper* is perhaps misleading. A better term is *essay that uses research for support.* The essay that you turn in should be guided by your point of view and your assertions, backed up by logic, examples, and the support provided by your sources. Your essay should *not* be a hodgepodge of quotations and paraphrases, with your voice occasionally emerging. What you draw from your sources is secondary to what you write in your own voice.

   Some students are troubled by the thought of exploring a subject and then determining what information needs to be cited. Their concern is valid: using someone else's work without giving proper credit can invite a charge of **plagiarism,** which will have decidedly unpleasant consequences for a student's academic standing. Think of the protocol this way: you are allowed to "use" the work of another, within reason, as long as you acknowledge and credit this source. For specific guidelines on what types of information must be cited, see Chapter 20, pages 581–582.

CLASSROOM HINT Although you have undoubtedly talked about plagiarism before, you can reinforce the discussion now. Also, remind students that all information that is not common knowledge—whether quoted directly, paraphrased, or summarized—must be cited. You can't say this too many times.

MORE OPTIONS ONLINE To learn more about how to avoid plagiarism, go to **www.mhhe.com/writingtoday**.

7. **Separate the drafting process from the revision process.** Once you have your essay written, put it aside for a day or two. The essay will look quite different if you give your brain time to concentrate on something else. Revision and writing require two very different sets of skills. Allow yourself time to regroup, psychologically speaking, before you start to review your draft.

THE MLA-STYLE RESEARCH PAPER

The following discussion is based on the sixth edition of Joseph Gibaldi's *MLA Handbook for Writers of Research Papers,* published by the Modern Language Association (2003). It is widely used by writers in the humanities.

MLA uses a **parenthetical** documentation system, also known as an in-text citation system. It involves citing sources in parentheses in the text of the paper. This approach eliminates the need for footnotes and endnotes, except those needed for further explanation of concepts or citations in the text. Thus, an MLA-based research paper ends with a works-cited section, an alphabetical list of all sources actually used—and cited—in the paper. Each entry in this list contains all the bibliographic data that a reader needs in order to find in the original source the information you have cited. Note that any source cited in the essay must also appear in the works-cited list and that any entry in the works-cited list must be cited in the essay.

Parenthetical (In-Text) Citations

A parenthetical (in-text) documentation system such as the one used by MLA identifies quickly and unobtrusively the source of any quotation, paraphrase, or summary used in the research paper. Here is an example of such a citation:

> Johnson writes that "the 1998 influx of tourists strained Central Florida's highways to the breaking point" (22).

CLASSROOM HINT
Going over the correct way to incorporate information from sources and use parenthetical citations will pay big dividends later in the term. If time allows, thoroughly review the next several pages with your students.

The author cited is Johnson; the page from which the quotation has been taken is 22. Alternatively, the author's name can appear with the page number in parentheses following the quotation, paraphrase, or summary. (Note that the period follows the citation.)

> One commentator writes that "the 1998 influx of tourists strained Central Florida's highways to the breaking point" (Johnson 22).

In general, the first method is preferable because the source is named within the text (for more on strategies for quoting text, see Chapter 18). In either case, however, the reader can expect, upon scanning the works-cited entries, to find an entry such as this:

> Johnson, Karen. "Area Infrastructure Not Keeping Up." Central Florida in Review Mar. 1999: 21-24.

The citation and the works-cited entry match, and the entry provides the reader with full information about the source.

Parenthetically citing summaries and paraphrases requires the same approach, with the exception that no quotation marks are used:

> Johnson indicates that the region needs an extra 2,000 miles of roadway (24).

When using a paraphrase or a summary, you should introduce the author's name first and finish with the page reference. Otherwise, the reader will not be able to tell when the paraphrase or summary begins and ends.

Special Cases

CLASSROOM HINT Try to spend a considerable amount of time on these "special" cases. Then test students on their mastery.

Often, you will need to modify these basic citation forms slightly. Here are some examples:

1. Citing two or more sources by the same author. This situation is very common in essays dealing with business or technical topics because writers in those disciplines specialize in an area or have the area assigned as their "beat" by the publication for which they work. In such a case, your in-text citation would include a short title to make clear which article by Johnson is being cited, as in the following examples:

> According to Johnson, "Rapidly shifting demographics in south and east Lake County have upset the formerly tranquil nature of local government" ("Clermont" 28).

> As one observer writes, "Commuters in northwest Orange County are most affected" (Johnson, "Area" 21).

The works-cited entries for such a situation are shown on page 594.

2. Combining direct quotations with your own sentence. To integrate a direct quotation in this way, you need to place quotation marks in the proper places, making certain that the quotation works naturally and correctly with your own language. Include a parenthetical citation that contains the author's name and the page number if the author's name is not mentioned in the text, or just the page number if the author's name *is* mentioned.

> Aletha Huston explains that the government could well end up satisfying "the short-term goal of reduced welfare costs while leading to long-term social problems of school failure and delinquency for children who experience unsafe and inadequate care during their early years" (16).

Chapter 18 has detailed coverage of the process of integrating quotations into your text.

3. Using a direct quotation longer than four lines. MLA format requires that quotations longer than four typed lines be double-spaced and indented 10 spaces or one inch from the left margin. Because the quotation is indented, no quotation marks are used except in cases where quotation marks appear in the original:

> In *India: Myths and Legends,* Donald MacKenzie explains the importance of priests in Indian literature and religion:
>
>> Priests were poets and singers in early Vedic times. A Rishi was a composer of hymns to the gods, and several are named in the collections. Every great family appears to have had its bardic priest and its special poetic anthology which was handed down from generation to generation. Old poems might be rewritten and added to, but the ambition of the sacred poet was to sing a new song to the gods. The oldest Vedic hymns are referred to as "new songs," which suggests that others were in existence. (33)

Note: For a long (block) quotation, the parenthetical citation comes after the period. For a short quotation, which is not set off, the period comes after the citation.

4. Using a source with two or three authors. Name all of the authors in the text of the paper (use last names only):

> Kelemen and Callahan argue that the "financial crises experienced by many American cities have more to do with poor fiscal planning than with demographic factors" (67).

> Spano, Del Vecchio, and Price indicate that "the need for developmental courses in reading is increasing in four-year and two-year colleges alike" (85).

> Research into the spread of Spanish influenza now proves that "the disease killed more people than were killed in all of World War I" (Swanicke, Szilagyi, and De Lisi 14).

5. Using a source with more than three authors. In such cases, you can simply use the name of the first author listed followed by the abbreviation *et al.,* a Latin abbreviation for "and others."

> The history of medicine traces the "derivation of many modern pharmaceuticals to herbs and other natural sources" (Coleman et al. 44).

6. Citing information from a corporate or organizational author. If your source has as its author the Southeastern Maritime Commission, for example, treat it no differently than a source written by a named person. If the corporate author appears with the page number in a parenthetical citation, include its full name:

> (Southeastern Maritime Commission 574)

You can use common abbreviations, such as *Natl.* for *National,* to shorten the name of a corporate author given in parentheses.

7. Citing a source with no author named. If a print source lists neither a person (by name) nor a corporate author, cite the title of the source along with the page number. Never cite "Anonymous," "Staff," or "Wire Reports." Use the full title in the text, but shorten the title to a few words if it appears in the parenthetical citation:

> According to the article "Homeless Focus Shifts to South Patterson," "area authorities want to build a homeless shelter near a subdivision despite residents' objections" (23).

> According to a recent article, "area authorities want to build a homeless shelter near a subdivision despite residents' objections" ("Homeless Focus Shifts" 23).

8. Including a quotation found in another source. If you are using a quotation that your source has taken from yet another source, use "qtd. in" for "quoted in" in the parenthetical citation:

> According to Burke, "The greater the power, the more dangerous the abuse" (qtd. in Frary 18).

9. Including information from a selection in an anthology. An anthology is a collection of works (poems, essays, plays, stories, and the like) put together by an editor. Cite information from such a selection by the name of the author, not the name of the editor. For example, *The Best American Essays 1997,* which is edited by Ian Frazier, contains an essay called "Black Swans" by Lauren Slater. Here's what a citation to this essay might look like:

> Slater celebrates a child's fascination with snow: "There is something satisfying and scary about making an angel, lowering your bulky body into the drowning fluff, stray flakes landing on your face" (144).

The format for a works-cited entry for a work in an anthology is modeled on page 595.

10. Using ideas from an entire work. Indicate the author's name in the text or parenthetical citation. Obviously, no page number can be given. Take this example from *A Drinking Life,* the autobiography of Pete Hamill:

> <u>A Drinking Life</u> chronicles the life of its author, but it also provides insight into the events and people who made history in America from the 1940s through the 1960s (Hamill).

11. Using material from two different authors with the same last name. Simply include both the first names and last names of the authors in the citations or the text:

> Greek sculpture illustrates the "endless struggle between the flesh and the spirit" (Edith Hamilton 65).

12. Including information from two sources in the same sentence. Use a semicolon to separate the authors and page numbers in the parenthetical citation:

> There were important differences in the ways the ancient Greeks and Romans worshipped even though their gods were virtually the same (Romero 52; Christiansen 184).

13. Including material from a work in more than one volume. If you take information from one volume in a multivolume work, indicate the volume number in the parenthetical citation. Separate the volume and page numbers with a colon and a space:

> In the <u>Encyclopedia of Philosophy</u>, Wooldruff explains that the British chemist and physicist Michael Farraday began his career as a bookbinder (3: 18).

14. Including material from printed works that are not paginated or from online sources. In the case of printed sources, you can use paragraph numbers if they appear in the the source; otherwise, you need to cite the entire work (see guideline 10). For online sources, cite the author's name if no page numbers are available. If the source lists no author, cite the title of the online source in quotation marks. As in guideline 7 above, if you place a long title in a parenthetical citation, shorten it to a few words—enough so that your reader can match the title to the appropriate works-cited entry.

15. Using content endnotes. Use such notes only if you need to provide explanations that go beyond what you can place within parentheses. Indicate an endnote by using a superscript number (most word processing programs have an automatic function for this). At the end of your text—before the list of works cited—type the heading *Note* or *Notes,* depending on the number of notes that you have, and use a superscript number again to begin the note, as in the following example:

> There is always the sense, when one reads Percy's novels, of a conscious avoidance of Faulkner, and when Percy does get a bit too close—as in the depiction of Ed Barrett in The Second Coming—the effect is eerie.[1]

This endnote appears at the end of the text:

> Note
>
> [1]Although Faulkner was an occasional guest of Will Percy, Walker Percy never met him there. When Percy and Foote were undergraduates, they once traveled through Oxford, but when Foote stopped to visit Faulkner, Percy claims to have stayed in the car. Although Percy later professed to be somewhat embarrassed by what he saw as callow behavior (see "A Talk with Walker Percy" [85]), his conscious "avoidance" of his predecessor was obviously a lifelong habit.

Chapter 18 includes additional guidelines for quoting, especially quotations that relate to writing about literature. Refer to them as needed.

The Works-Cited List

SUGGESTED ACTIVITY
Again, reviewing this subsection in class will pay dividends down the road. Give open-book tests on this material so that students know they will have to demonstrate mastery even before they complete their research papers. Also, refer to the Works Cited page compiled by Valerie Richfield for the paper that appears at the end of the MLA section of this chapter (page 609).

The last element of your research paper is the works-cited section, a list of entries that tells your reader the sources you have used and cited in the paper. Entries are alphabetized by the last name of the source's author. Sources with more than one author should be alphabetized by the last name of the first author appearing in the work's byline. Sources that don't have named authors, either human or corporate, are alphabetized by the first major word in the title, as shown in the following alphabetized list:

Harper, Leo
Lefou, Ariel
Le Franc, David
Maritime Fisheries Commission
"The Nature of Wax Beetles"
Roth, Michelle
Roth-Lynn, Leo
Rothman, Thomas

1. For alphabetizing purposes, articles (*the, a,* and *an*) are disregarded. "The Nature of Wax Beetles" is alphabetized using the word *Nature*.
2. Le Franc is treated as one word, so it follows Lefou.
3. Roth has fewer letters than Roth-Lynn, and the hyphen is disregarded in Roth-Lynn so that "Rothl" precedes "Rothm."

The Basic Works-Cited Format

Most works-cited entries include author, title, and publishing information. Here is a basic entry for a book by one author:

Peters, Elizabeth. Night Train to Memphis. New York: Warner, 1994.

Note the following:

1. The author's name is inverted, with the last name appearing first.
2. The first line of the entry starts on the left margin. Succeeding ("turnover") lines are indented five spaces or half an inch.
3. The first letter of the first word in the title is always capitalized. The first letters of all other words in the title are capitalized except for articles (*a, an, the*) and prepositions and conjunctions of fewer than five letters (*and, but, to, of, with,* and so on). If the title has a colon, the first letter of the first word after the colon is capitalized. Titles of books and periodicals are underlined.
4. Works-cited entries, like the rest of the essay, are double-spaced.

The rest of this section lists and describes standard MLA works-cited entries. For more information, refer to the *MLA Handbook for Writers of Research Papers,* sixth edition.

MLA Citations—Books

Book with One Author

Percy, Walker. The Moviegoer. New York: Knopf, 1961.

The publisher's full name is Alfred A. Knopf, Inc. As in this entry, use a shortened version of the publisher's name, and never include *Inc.*

Book with Two Authors

Brooks, Tim, and Earle Marsh. The Complete Directory to Prime Time Network and Cable TV Shows: 1946-Present. New York: Ballantine, 1995.

Note that the second author's name is not inverted.

Book with Three Authors

Vander, Arthur, James Sherman, and Dorothy Luciano. Human Physiology: The Mechanics of Body Function. 8th ed. New York: McGraw, 2000.

This is an eighth edition, as noted after the title.

Book with More Than Three Authors

You may type the first author's name, last name first, followed by a comma and *et al.* This is an abbreviation for *et alia,* the Latin for "and others." (If you wish to include all of the names, however, you may do so.)

Malikin, David, et al. Social Disability: Alcoholism, Drug Addiction, Crime, and Social Disadvantage. New York: New York UP, 1973.

This publisher is New York University Press. Any university press should be designated by *UP*.

Two or More Works by the Same Author

Johnson, Karen. "Area Infrastructure Not Keeping Up." Central Florida in Review Mar. 1999: 21-24.

---. "Clermont Council at Impasse." Central Florida in Review June 1999: 28-29.

Note that the two entries are alphabetized by title, with "Area" preceding "Clermont." The three hyphens mean "ditto," Karen Johnson again.

Book with Corporate or Organizational Author

American Psychological Association. Publication Manual of the American Psychological Association. 5th ed. Washington, DC: American Psychological Association, 2001.

Book with an Editor

If you are using information from a book's editor (editors often introduce and comment on work they are presenting), use the abbreviation *ed.* or *eds.*, as in the following:

Garrod, H. W., ed. Keats: Poetical Works. London: Oxford UP, 1970.

This means that you have taken information from Garrod, not from Keats.

If you are using information from the author of a book that has been edited by someone else, place the author's name first, followed by the title, followed by the abbreviation *Ed(s).*, followed by the name of the editor(s).

Twain, Mark. A Connecticut Yankee in King Arthur's Court. Ed. Allison E. Ensor. New York: Norton, 1982.

Book in a Later Edition

Gibaldi, Joseph. MLA Handbook for Writers of Research Papers. 6th ed. New York: Modern Language Association, 2003.

Book in More Than One Volume

Daiches, David. A Critical History of English Literature. 2nd ed. 2 vols. New York: Ronald, 1970.

This is the works-cited format used when you are referring to all volumes of a multivolume work. In the text of the paper, you would cite page numbers by volume: (2: 107), for example. However, if you are citing only one of the volumes of a multivolume work, here is the format for the works-cited entry:

Daiches, David. A Critical History of English Literature. 2nd ed. Vol. 2.
New York: Ronald, 1970.

In the text, you would need to cite page numbers only.

Book in a Series

Knapp, Bettina L. Voltaire Revisited. Twayne's World Authors Ser.: French Lit.
New York: Twayne, 2000.

You can use *Ser.* for *Series* and other common abbreviations such as *Lit.* for *Literature.*

Book of Collected Essays or an Anthology

Montaigne, Michel Eyquem de. The Complete Essays of Montaigne. Trans.
Donald M. Frame. Palo Alto: Stanford UP, 1958.

Frazier, Ian. ed. The Best American Essays 1997. Boston: Houghton, 1997.

Use this format when you want to refer to a whole collection of essays, not an individual essay.

Essay in an Anthology or a Collection

See also page 590.

Montaigne, Michel Eyquem de. "Of Constancy." The Complete Essays of
Montaigne. Trans. Donald M. Frame. Palo Alto: Stanford UP, 1958. 30-31.

Use this format when you want to refer to one essay in a collection, not the whole collection. The translator's or editor's name follows the title.

Translation

Dostoyevsky, Fyodor. Crime and Punishment. Trans. Sidney Monas.
New York: New American Library, 1980.

MLA Citations—Periodical Articles

The three types of articles are journal (academic) articles, magazine articles, and newspaper articles.

Article in a Journal with Consecutive Pagination

Jones, Karen. "Second-Hand Moral Knowledge." Journal of Philosophy 96
(1999): 55-78.

Like most academic journals, this one starts the first issue of each year on page 1 and then numbers consecutively throughout the year. The volume number for 1999 is 96.

Article in a Journal Paginated by Issue

Lützeler, Paul. "Goethe and Europe." South Atlantic Review 65.2 (2000): 95-113.

This journal starts each issue on page 1. This is volume 65, issue number 2 (65.2).

Article in a Magazine Published Monthly

Codman, Ogden, Jr. "The Decoration of Town Houses: Renovating a Manhattan Residence." Architectural Digest Oct. 1997: 164-71.

Entries for magazine articles don't include volume numbers, just dates of publication. Note that all months except May, June, and July are abbreviated.

Article in a Magazine Published Weekly

Branson, Louise. "Children of the Tunnels." Maclean's 8 Nov. 1993: 29-30.

Note the inverted date.

Magazine Article Without Author

"Flour Power." Harper's Bazaar Dec. 1989: 200+.

The page listing (200+) indicates that the article "jumps"; it starts on page 200 but continues after an interval of some pages.

Article in a Daily Newspaper

Tanner, Lindsey. "Study Shows Men Listen with Half a Brain." Lakeland Ledger [Florida] 29 Nov. 2000: A4.

The *Lakeland Ledger* is a local newspaper, so the state (Florida) needs to be added for exact identification. However, newspapers with the city's name in the title or nationally published newspapers such as the *Wall Street Journal* do not need further identification.

Article Unsigned in a Daily Newspaper

"Mexican Drug Cartel May Be Linked to 3 US Dead." Los Angeles Times 12 May 2000: 5.

Simply start with the title of the article.

Editorial in a Daily Newspaper

"The Gun Windmills." Editorial. Wall Street Journal 13 Dec. 1999: A34.

Since editorials are normally unsigned, you can use the same format as you would for an unsigned article except that you must include the word *Editorial* immediately after the title.

Review in a Magazine or Newspaper

Lane, Anthony. "Blown Away." Rev. of Arlington Road, dir. Mark Pellington, and The Lovers on the Bridge, dir. Leos Carax. New Yorker 19 July 1999: 98-99.

Preston, William J. "The Politics of Hysteria." Rev. of Many Are the Crimes: McCarthyism in America, by Ellen Schrecker. Los Angeles Times 31 May 1998: Book Reviews 6.

MLA Citations—Online Sources

Online documentation is evolving. The following is based on the most recent MLA guidelines.

Online Document Retrieved from an Information Database or Online Project

Information databases and online projects are sponsored by a number of organizations, including news and media corporations, professional groups, and educational institutions. Your college or university library may subscribe to several of these resources. They contain abstracts of articles, articles in their entirety, books, chapters of books, poems, and a variety of other materials you might find useful. Cite such sources as follows:

1. Name of author, last name first
2. Title of the work in quotation marks or, if it is a book, underlined
3. Name of the database or project, underlined
4. Electronic publication data, including the date of the electronic publication or of the most recent update; the name of the database or project sponsor; and the version number (if available)
5. The date you accessed the material
6. The uniform resource locator (URL) in angle brackets. If the URL must be divided between lines, divide it after a slash.

O'Hanlon, Larry. "Extreme Measures: The Art of Analyzing Natural Disasters." 25 Feb. 2000. Discovery Channel Online. Discovery Channel. 17 Sept. 2000 <http://www.discovery.com/news/features/disasters/disasters.html>.

The title of the database is *Discovery Channel Online*. The work was published electronically on February 25, 2000. The sponsor of the database is the Discovery Channel. The date the student accessed the material is September 17, 2000. The URL appears in angle brackets.

Online Article from a Scholarly Journal

Loranger, Carol. "'This Book Spill Off the Page in All Directions': What Is the Text of Naked Lunch?" Postmodern Culture 10.1 (1999). 27 Aug. 2000 <http://muse.jhu.edu/journals/pmc/v010/10.1loranger.html>.

Postmodern Culture is an online scholarly journal. Note that the information that is given is similar to information that would appear in an entry for a print journal article (see pages 595–596).

Online Article from a Weekly or Monthly Magazine

Saletan, William. "Electoral Knowledge." Slate 28 Nov. 2000. 30 Nov. 2000 <http://slate.msn.com/framegame/entries/00-11-28_94258.asp>.

Online Article from a Newspaper or News Service

Babinek, Mark. "Railroad Killer Gets Death Penalty." San Francisco Examiner 22 May 2000: 3 pp. 27 May 2000 <http://examiner.com/ap_a/AP_Railroad_Killer.html>.

As in the example above, provide the number of pages if this information is available.

Article Accessed Through an Online Library Service

Hannon, Kerry. "The Joys of a Working Vacation." U.S. News & World Report 10 June 1996: 89-90. OCLC First Search. College of Lake County Lib. 22 Oct. 2001 <http://newfirstsearch.oclc.org/WebZ/FSPag...-64142-ct4j2jzt-cqj0po:entity pagenum=111:0>.

College and university libraries, as well as some public libraries, usually subscribe to at least one online access service. These services allow researchers quick access to periodical articles that are available online. Note that the information from the author through the page range is the same as it would be for a works-cited entry of the print version of the article. This information is followed by the underscored name of the access service, the library, the date accessed, and the URL, which is provided by the access service.

E-Mail Message

Start with the name of the sender, followed by the title of the e-mail (if any) in quotation marks. Next, indicate the kind of document being cited and its recipient. End with the date the e-mail was sent.

Cornell, Pamela J. "Re: Tips on Toddlers." E-mail to the author. 29 Aug. 2002.

Online Book Previously Published in Print Form

Melville, Herman. The Piazza Tales. 1856. ESP: Electronic Scholarly Publishing. 21 Oct. 2000 <http://www.esp.org/books/melville/piazza>.

Melville's book is available in print form and online. The entry for the digital version shows author, title, original publication date, provider, date of access, and URL.

Part of Online Book Previously Published in Print Form

Melville, Herman. "Benito Cereno." The Piazza Tales. 1856. ESP: Electronic Scholarly Publishing. 24 Oct. 2000 <http://www.esp.org/books/melville/piazza/contents/cereno.html>.

"Benito Cereno" is one of the stories that make up *The Piazza Tales*.

Posting to a Forum, Newsgroup, or Discussion Group

Forum message: Start with the author's name, last name first. In quotation marks, provide the title of the posting (if available), followed by the words *Online posting* and the date the message was posted. Provide the name of the "thread" or subject being discussed (if available) and the title of the forum sponsoring the discussion. End with the date you accessed the message, and the URL.

Harrington, J. K. "Publishing." Online posting. 19 May 2000. The Writing Life: Inkspot Writers' Community forums. 25 May 2000 <http://writers-bbs.com/inkspot/threads.cgi?action=almsgs&forum=writinglife>.

Newsgroup posting: Begin with the author's name, followed by the subject of the discussion in quotation marks. Follow this with the words *Online posting,* the date of the posting, the date you accessed the message, and the URL.

Discussion group message: Begin with the author's name, followed by the subject of the discussion in quotation marks. Follow this with the words *Online posting,* the date of the posting, the name of the discussion group if available, the date you accessed the message, and the URL.

Note that such resources may be open to anyone who has access to the Internet, whether or not he or she is an expert on the subject being discussed. Therefore, be extra careful about the validity of the information you take from forums, discussion groups, and the like.

MLA Citations—Miscellaneous Sources

Dictionary Entry

"Carpe Diem." The Random House Dictionary of the English Language. 9th ed. 1966.

Encyclopedia Entry

"Athabascan." Concise Columbia Encyclopedia. 3rd ed. 1994.

Government Publication

United States. Bureau of Labor Statistics. Employment and Earnings. Washington, DC: GPO, 1992.

GPO stands for "Government Printing Office."

Published Interview

Johnson, Paul. "Live with TAE: Interview with Paul Johnson." American Enterprise Sept./Oct. 1998: 20-23.

Begin with the name of the person interviewed. Follow with the title of the interview, if any, in quotation marks. If the interview has no title, simply include the word *Interview* after the subject's name.

Personal, Telephone, or E-Mail Interview

Rodriguez, Dr. Myra S. Personal interview. 6 Sept. 2000.

Personal Letter

Cornell, Matthew Robert. Letter to the author. 9 June 1998.

Begin with the writer's name, followed by *Letter to the author* and the date the letter was written.

Sound Recording

Puccini, Giacomo. La Bohème. Perf. Luciano Pavarotti, Mirella Freni, Elizabeth Hardwood, and Gianni Maffeo. Opera of Berlin Chor. and Berlin Phil. Orch. Cond. Herbert von Karajan. London, 1972.

Begin with the name of the composer, speaker, or singer, followed by the title of the work. Then, if appropriate, include the names of the leading performers, the orchestra, and the conductor. Conclude with the name of the recording company and date of the recording. Note that in this case London is the name of the recording company, not the place in which the recording took place.

Film

Strictly Ballroom. Dir. Baz Luhrmann. Perf. Paul Mercurio and Tara Morice. Miramax, 1992.

MORE OPTIONS ONLINE
For more help with formatting works-cited entries, go to **www.mhhe.com/writingtoday**.

Television or Radio Program

"Mountain Wedding." The Andy Griffith Show. CBS. 29 Apr. 1963.

MLA Research Paper Format

Double-space the essay on white 8½" × 11" paper, using text margins of 1" at the top, bottom, and sides. Use a standard text font, such as Times, Courier, Palatino, Garamond, or Goudy, in 12-point type. Indent five spaces for the beginning of paragraphs, but don't leave extra space between paragraphs.

Unless your instructor asks for a title page, start your essay with this format:

Your Name

Professor _____

Course Name and Section

23 October 20__

Title of Your Research Paper

First line of your research paper.

Notice that all elements are doublespaced, with no extra space between them. For page numbering, use the "header" function on your computer. The header appears at the upper right corner of each page, one-half inch from the top of the page, and consists of your last name and the page number:

Surname 1

The page numbering continues through the end of the document, which will be your works-cited section.

Start the works-cited section on a new page immediately after the end of your text. Center the words *Works Cited.* Then start the first entry on the next line after the head. As with the rest of your essay, this section is double-spaced, with no extra space added.

Once again, follow your instructor's directions if they differ from the above guidelines.

Sample Research Paper in MLA Format

The documented essay that appears on the following pages was written by Valerie Richfield. Her class was researching the condition of the working poor in the United States. Ms. Richfield selected and developed a related topic—subsidies for day care—and then wrote an argumentative research paper that criticizes current U.S. policies.

SUGGESTED ACTIVITY
Review Valerie Richfield's essay paragraph by paragraph if you have time. It illustrates important principles and techniques for the inclusion and citation of research.

Title centered.

Opening paragraphs provide background.

Author of block quotation is introduced in the text. Quotation is indented 10 spaces (1 inch).

Valerie Richfield

Dr. Pharr

ENC 1102.37

25 April 2001

Child Care and the Working Poor

The idea of the "working poor" seems to be a bit contradictory. If people work, then the assumption is that they are making money. In the United States, then, why are so many working people poor? The answer lies in the fact that many people lack the skills necessary for a well-paying job; therefore, these people have limited job opportunities, and the majority of the available jobs provide very low salaries.

The difference between the working poor and the welfare poor is not as distinct as some may believe. A huge overlap actually exists. Both of these groups endure a very uncertain economic life. The welfare poor and the working poor could definitely benefit from a larger job market with higher wages and the availability of affordable health insurance and child care. However, the welfare poor receive money from the government every month, while the working poor depend primarily on themselves.

Of the world's major, industrialized countries, the United States offers a unique situation. As Barbara R. Bergmann points out,

> The countries of Western Europe have programs in place that work to shield children and their families. . . . They have built programs and devoted large sums of taxpayers' money to this effort. On a per capita basis, these countries spend a great deal more money than Americans do for programs benefiting children. They provide income supplements and housing assistance; all of their children have access to medical care under

> national health insurance schemes; some of these countries provide government-sponsored child care that is free or highly subsidized. The availability of such low-cost child care enables many single parents to take jobs and free themselves from total dependence on government cash grants. (5)

The United States takes a more laissez-faire approach that leads to the survival of the fittest. The poor, especially the working poor, are largely expected to fend for themselves.

In this country, one of the many problems the working poor must face is the issue of child care. Since they have such low-paying jobs, the working poor just barely get by, using almost all of their money to pay for the necessities of life such as shelter and food. It is virtually impossible for them to be able to afford the expenses of child care after their vital bills are paid. If the government wants people working in order to escape from welfare, then it is essential that the working poor receive help with the cost of child care, only until they can finance it themselves. Some people argue over how poor parents have to be to receive government assistance. A thoroughly reasonable response is that as long as the parents are working at minimum wage and are unable to completely support their family, it is crucial that government assist with the problem of financing their child care.

Government support for families needing child care is critical for several reasons. The number of women working these days is growing; therefore, the availability of child care is crucial in maintaining their employment. Michele Friedman claims that in the middle decades of the twentieth century, less than 20 percent of mothers were in the work force, but by the end of the twentieth century, the number had

Author's name introduces block quotation, so there is no need to include it in the parenthetical citation.

Widely available information about the working poor does not need to be documented.

Thesis statement.

Paraphrased information from a Web site does not include a page number.

increased to 65 percent of mothers with children six or younger. Subsequently, child care is necessary for the increasing number of women who are trying to sustain their job(s). Moreover, because many of the women belong to the working poor, it is imperative that they receive assistance with financing their children's care. Another reason that child care aid is so important is that people who earn the minimum wage cannot possibly afford child care expenses. Friedman gives an example:

Quotation introduced with a colon. Ellipsis indicates that words have been omitted.

> "Child care expenses can range anywhere from $4,000 to $10,000 a year per child. . . . In 1997, the median annual income of the average female-headed household was $17,256. At such earning levels, child care expenses can easily consume one third or more of the household budget."

In this instance, the expenses of child care would leave very little money for other needs. Therefore, many people are forced to stay home because of their family responsibilities, and they are thus unable to escape from this cycle of economic dependency. The working poor need assistance in order to improve their lives.

The role that the government actually plays in helping the working poor is an important issue. Each state can use the money the federal government grants it in different ways. Harrell R. Rodgers explains how states use this money:

> The states might use some of the funds to subsidize providers of child care services to low-income families. The states would have the option of providing more lucrative incentives to public or private agencies offering child care services to specific low-income parents, such as single parents. (Poor Women, Poor Families 129)

Two works by the same author are listed in the Works Cited, so the title appears in parentheses.

In terms of the issue of financial assistance from the federal government, two questions are crucial: (1) How much help is needed? (2) To whom should it be directed? Many people move back and forth from employment to welfare, making it very difficult at any given time to differentiate between those on welfare and the working poor. Child advocates Theresa Feeley and Deborah Stein maintain that income, not receipt of welfare benefits, should be the deciding factor. If a family's income is below the poverty level, that family should receive benefits. One example of how this process works comes from La Petite Academy, a well-known child care company with centers throughout the United States. The company is affiliated with the government program called Community Coordinated Care for Children (4-C). This program screens families according to their level of income. As Sue Taff, a La Petite director, states,

> If child care is 200 dollars a week, 4-C determines how much government assistance a family will receive depending on their income level. Say the government decides to give that family 75 percent; then it will pay 150 dollars, and the family will have to come up with the difference, which in this case is 50 dollars.

The federal government also offers other support services. The JOBS program is a way for a parent to receive government assistance so that he or she does not have to apply for welfare. Rodgers explains that the "federal government has significantly expanded funding for child care where the parent is enrolled in a JOBS program, where the working parent needs child care help to avoid becoming eligible for AFDC" (Poor Women, Poor Children 159). Such aid is extremely important for the families of the working poor.

Unfortunately, several problems emerge in the administration of government aid for child care. Not enough families receive support from

An idea from a source is paraphrased and credited.

A quotation from an interview with on expert in the topic of the paper.

Since the Works Cited list contains two works by Rodgers, the writer specifies the source she is referencing here.

the government, creating a major problem because of the necessary role that child care plays in keeping parents employed. According to one report, less than a third of working-poor families get help with financing care for their children, while almost 40 percent of "non-working poor and middle-income families" do (Child Care for Low Income Families). If child care for the working poor were more readily available, parents would be able to maintain their jobs without being put on a waiting list for over a year, a situation mainly caused by cutbacks in government funding. As Steve Burghardt and Michael Fabricant of the University of Michigan's School of Social Work explain, "While economic insecurity is driving more and more women into an already discriminatory job market, fiscal cuts in child care programs are marginalizing more and more poor women in their attempts to attain meaningful employment" (97). This lack of funding creates a huge predicament for the working poor as they struggle to become self-sufficient.

Phrase from source is enclosed in quotation marks; source does not have an author, so title appears in parentheses.

Writer includes authors' credentials for added authority.

The situation leads to another major dilemma for the working poor: What about their future? Helping people who are unable to afford child care will benefit them at that particular moment, but their future, along with the future of their children, will still appear to be bleak. The working poor lack the adequate education and job skills that are necessary for them to better themselves by obtaining a well-paying job. For example, the TANF (Temporary Aid for Needy Families) program "creates added hardship for families while not offering the range of long-term supports that would allow welfare clients to become self sufficient" ("Working Families" 4).

The quotation is integrated smoothly into the student's sentence.

These problems are stressful for parents, of course, but the uppermost focus should be on the problems that the children must endure. Their parents serve as role models. Because the parents lack many skills

One commentator writes that "the 1998 influx of tourists strained Central Florida's highways to the breaking point" (Johnson, 1999, p. 22).

In either case, the reader can expect, upon scanning the reference entries, to find a listing such as this one:

Johnson, K. (1999, March). Area infrastructure not keeping up. *Central Florida in Review, 24,* 21-24.

The citation and the entry match, and the entry provides full publication information for the source.

When you are citing summaries and paraphrases in your text, APA requires only the author(s) and date:

Johnson (1999) indicates that the region needs an extra 2,000 miles of roadway.

Special Cases

Often, you will need to modify the basic in-text citation form shown above.

1. Citing two or more sources by the same author. Because APA citations (in contrast to MLA citations) include publication dates, using two or more sources by the same author will usually not cause confusion for readers. The year makes clear to which source in the references page the citation refers.

Johnson, K. (1999, March). Area infrastructure not keeping up. *Central Florida in Review, 24,* 21-24.

Johnson, K. (2000, June). Clermont council at impasse. *Central Florida in Review, 25,* 28-29.

The older of the two entries comes first. If, however, you need to cite two works written in the same year by the same author(s), attach letter suffixes to the year—for example, 1993a and 1993b—which are determined by checking the alphabetical order of the two titles:

Shinzato, L. (1999a). Core beliefs.

Shinzato, L. (1999b). Normal expectations.

2. Citing information from a corporate or organizational author. Treat this source no differently than a source written by a named person; however, if such an author appears in a parenthetical citation, include the entire name with a suggested abbreviation the first time you use it:

(Southeastern Maritime Commission [SMC], 1991, p. 574)

Thereafter, you can refer to *SMC* in your parenthetical citations and avoid repeating the lengthy full title.

3. Citing a source with no author named. If a print source lists neither a person nor a corporate author, cite the title of the source, normally a periodical article. (Never cite "Staff" or "Wire Reports," but note that "Anonymous" should be used if that is how the source is actually credited.) Use the full title if you mention it outside the parenthetical citation. Shorten the title to a few words if it appears within the parenthetical citation:

> According to the article "Homeless Focus Shifts to South Patterson," "area authorities want to build a homeless shelter near a subdivision despite residents' objections" (2000, p. 23).

> According to a recent article, "area authorities want to build a homeless shelter near a subdivision despite residents' objections" ("Homeless Focus Shifts," 2000, p. 23).

4. Citing an online source. If an online source has page or paragraph numbers, cite them to direct your reader more specifically to the source of a quotation. (Use *p.* to refer to a page and ¶ or *para.* to refer to a paragraph; also include the date of electronic publication.) However, since most online sources do not have page or paragraph numbers, you will usually cite the author's name only. If the source lists no author, cite the title of the online source in quotation marks. As in guideline 3 above, if you place the title in a parenthetical citation, shorten long titles to a few words—enough so that your reader can match the title to the appropriate reference entry.

5. Using a source with multiple authors. In the social sciences, many works are written by two or more authors. If a work you are citing was written by a pair of authors, link the two with an ampersand (&) if you are giving the names in parentheses:

> (McPherson & Rico, 1989, pp. 237-238)

However, if you refer to the authors outside the parentheses, don't use an ampersand; use *and.*

If a source has three to five authors, cite all of them the first time you use the source:

> (McPherson, Rico, Maze, & Carter, 1988)

For subsequent citations, either within your text or in parentheses, use the last name of the first author followed by *et al.* ("and others"), as in this example:

> (McPherson et al., 1988)

If a source has six or more authors, use the first author's last name plus *et al.* for any citation, including the first.

6. Using an ellipsis in a quotation. APA uses the ellipsis only in the middle of quoted text, not at the beginning or end, unless it is needed to prevent confusion.

7. Using a quotation longer than forty words. If you are quoting a passage that is forty words or more (not including the citation), set it off as a block. Indent the block five spaces, or one-half inch, from the left margin and double-space the quotation.

8. Using content notes. Although APA emphasizes parenthetical documentation, you may occasionally need to provide explanations about sources or content that go beyond what you can appropriately place within parentheses in the text. In such cases, use a note with a superscript number (most word processing programs have an automatic function for superscript type), and place the note on a separate page with the title *Footnote* or *Footnotes*. The first line of each note should be indented five spaces or one-half inch, and the note or notes should be double spaced.

9. Citing personal communication. APA format includes personal communication (personal/telephone interviews, e-mails, and the like) in parenthetical citations only, not in the references list. To write such a citation, include the initials and last name of the person with whom you communicated and the date.

(M. R. Cornell, personal communication, June 9, 1998)

The Reference List

The last element of your research paper is the reference section. This is a list of entries that tells your reader the sources you have used and cited in your essay. These entries are alphabetized by the last name of the source's author. Sources with more than one author are alphabetized by the name of the first author listed. Sources that don't have named authors, either human or corporate, are alphabetized by title. Some complications may occur, as shown in the following list:

Harper, Leo
Lefou, Ariel
Le Franc, David
Maritime Fisheries Commission
The nature of wax beetles
Roth, Michelle
Roth-Lynn, Leo
Rothman, Thomas

1. For alphabetizing purposes, articles (*the, a,* and *an*) are disregarded. "The Nature of Wax Beetles" is alphabetized using the word *Nature.*
2. Le Franc is treated as one word, so it follows Lefou.
3. Roth has fewer letters than Roth-Lynn, and the hyphen is disregarded in Roth-Lynn so that "RothL" precedes "Rothm."

The Basic References Format

Most entries include author, title, and publishing information. Here is a basic entry for a book by one author:

Peters, E. (1994). *Night train to Memphis.* New York: Warner Books.

Note the following:

1. The author's name is inverted, with the last name appearing first. First and middle names are always shortened to initials. If more than one initial is listed, a space separates the initials: Chesterton, G. K.
2. The first line of the entry starts at the left margin. Succeeding ("turnover") lines are indented five spaces, or one-half inch, as in the example below.
3. The only letters that are capitalized in titles are the first letter of the first word, the first letter of the first word after a colon (if any), the first letter of a proper noun, and acronyms (such as IBM). For example,

   Kendall, D. (1998). *Sociology in our times: The essentials.* Belmont, CA:
   Wadsworth.

4. Note that titles of books, as well as titles of periodicals, are italicized. (Titles of articles in periodicals are not italicized.)
5. Use a shortened version of the publisher's name (for example, Alfred A. Knopf is shortened to Knopf), and never include *Inc.* However, include *Press* or *Books* if it is part of the publisher's name (see the basic entry above).
6. The location of the publisher is indicated by the city and state (represented by the postal service abbreviation):

   Cheyenne, WY

   San Jose, CA

   However, for large, easily identifiable cities (New York, London, Philadelphia, Chicago, Los Angeles), the state is not needed. If the publisher lists more than one city on the title page, use only the first one.
7. References entries, like the rest of the essay, must be double-spaced.

The rest of this section lists and describes standard APA reference entries. For more information, consult the *Publication Manual of the American Psychological Association,* fifth edition.

APA Citations—Books

Book with One Author

Percy, W. (1961). *The moviegoer.* New York: Knopf.

Book with Two Authors

Brooks, T., & Marsh, E. (1995). *The complete directory to prime time network and cable TV shows: 1946-present.* New York: Ballantine.

Book with Three to Six Authors

Vander, A., Sherman, J., & Luciano, D. (2000). *Human physiology: The mechanics of body function* (8th ed.). New York: McGraw-Hill.

Note: If a book has more than six authors, type *et al.* after the sixth name, and follow this with the date.

Book with Corporate or Organizational Author

American Psychological Association. (2001). *Publication manual of the American Psychological Association* (5th ed.). Washington, DC: Author.

Note the use of *Author* in the publisher position.

Book with an Editor

If you are using information from a book's editor (editors often introduce and comment on work they are presenting), use the abbreviations *Ed.* or *Eds.,* as in the following:

Garrod, H. W. (Ed.). (1970). *Keats: Poetical works.* London: Oxford University Press.

This means that you have used information from Garrod, not from Keats.

If you are using information from the author of an edited book, begin with the author's last name:

Twain, M. (1982). *A Connecticut Yankee in King Arthur's court* (A. Ensor, Ed.). New York: Norton. (Original work published 1889)

Book in a Later Edition

Boorstin, D. J. (1985). *The discoverers: A history of man's search to know his world and himself* (2nd ed.). New York: Vintage.

Multivolume Book

Daiches, D. (1960). *A critical history of English literature* (Vols. 1-2). London: Secker and Warburg.

Multivolume Book in a Later Edition

Daiches, D. (1970). *A critical history of English literature* (Vols. 1-2). (2nd ed.). New York: Ronald.

Book in Series

Knapp, B. L. (2000). *Voltaire revisited.* New York: Twayne.

APA does not require the series title and the name of the series editor.

Book of Collected Essays or an Anthology

Frazier, I. (Ed.). (1997). *The best American essays 1997.* Boston: Houghton.

Lynch, R. E., & Swanzey, T. B. (Eds.). (1981). *The example of science: An anthology.* Englewood Cliffs, NJ: Prentice-Hall.

Use this format when you want to refer to a whole collection of essays, not an individual essay.

Essay in an Anthology or Collection

Thomas, L. (1981). Ceti. In R. E. Lynch & T. B. Swanzey (Eds.), *The example of science: An anthology* (pp. 9-13). Englewood Cliffs, NJ: Prentice-Hall.

Use this format when you want to refer to one essay in a collection, not the whole collection.

Translation

Dostoyevsky, F. (1980). *Crime and punishment.* (S. Monas, Trans.). New York: New American Library. (Original work published 1866)

APA Citations—Periodical Articles

Compared to MLA, APA style makes fewer distinctions between journal articles and magazine articles. Volume numbers are required for both types.

Article in a Journal with Consecutive Pagination

Jones, K. (1999). Second-hand moral knowledge. *Journal of Philosophy, 96,* 55-78.

Like most academic journals, this one starts the first issue of each year on page 1, then numbers consecutively throughout the year. The volume number for 1999 is 96.

Article by Two Authors in a Journal with Consecutive Pagination

Benson, J. J., & Loftis, A. (1980). John Steinbeck and farm labor unionization: The background of *In dubious battle. American Literature, 52,* 194-224.

Note that both authors' names are inverted and separated by a comma and an ampersand (&).

Article by Three to Six Authors in a Journal with Consecutive Pagination

Magnusson, W. E., da Silva, E. V., & Lima, A. P. (1987). Diets of Amazonian crocodiles. *Journal of Herpetology, 21,* 85-95.

Note that all three authors' names are inverted and separated by commas, with an ampersand (&) preceding the last author's name. If an article has more than six authors, type *et al.* after the sixth name, and follow this with the date.

Article in a Journal Paged by Issue

Lützeler. P. (2000). Goethe and Europe. *South Atlantic Review 65*(2), 95-113.

This journal starts each issue on page 1. This is volume 65, issue 2. Notice that the issue number is not italicized.

Article in a Magazine Published Monthly

Codman, O., Jr. (1997, October). The decoration of town houses: Renovating a Manhattan residence. *Architectural Digest, 54,* 164-171.

As with an article in a journal paged by issue, the volume number is given, but instead of an issue number following the volume number, the month of publication follows the year: (1997, October). Note that the complete page number is provided for both numbers (164–171) as opposed to the MLA style (164–71).

Article in a Magazine Published Weekly

Branson, L. (1993, November 8). Children of the tunnels. *Maclean's, 106,* 29-30.

This entry differs from that for a monthly magazine only in that the exact date of publication appears: (1993, November 8).

Magazine Article Without Author

Flour power. (1989, December). *Harper's Bazaar, 122,* 200, 213-214.

The entry begins with the article title. Also note the full listing of the pages. (MLA would indicate the pages in this discontinuous article as 200+; APA requires a full listing of the article's pages.)

Article in a Daily Newspaper

Tanner, L. (2000, November 29). Study shows men listen with half a brain. *The Lakeland Ledger,* p. A4.

Note that for newspaper articles, APA requires "p." before the listed page. If the article had "jumped" to a new page for its conclusion, the page listing would look like this: pp. A4, A16.

Essay in an Anthology or Collection

See page 616.

Article or Chapter in an Edited Book

Junod, M. (1987). Visiting Hiroshima: 9 September 1945. In J. Carey (Ed.), *Eyewitness to history* (pp. 638-640). New York: Avon.

Review in a Magazine or Newspaper

Lane, A. (1999, July 19). Blown away [Review of the motion pictures *Arlington Road* and *The lovers on the bridge*]. *The New Yorker, 75,* 98-99.

Preston, W. J. (1998, May 31). The politics of hysteria [Review of the book *Many are the crimes: McCarthyism in America*]. *The Los Angeles Times,* Book Reviews 6.

APA Citations—Online Sources

Online documentation is evolving. Here are some of the most recent APA guidelines.

Online Document Retrieved from an Information Database or Online Project

Information databases and online projects are sponsored by a number of organizations, including news and media corporations, professional groups, and educational institutions. Your college or university library may subscribe to several of these resources. They contain abstracts of articles, articles in their entirety, books, chapters of books, poems, and a variety of other materials you might find useful. Cite such sources as follows:

1. Name of author, last name first, followed by initial(s).
2. Date of electronic publication in parentheses.
3. Title of the work. Capitalize the first major word and proper nouns only.
4. If the work appears in a periodical, indicate the periodical's title and any available publication data appropriate to that type of periodical, including volume, issue, and page numbers. If the work is a section or chapter in a book, indicate the book's title and pertinent publication information. If the work is part of a Web site, indicate the title of the Web site in italics.
5. The date you retrieved the work, followed by a comma and the URL or the name of the database or project from which you retrieved it. Do not add a period after the URL.
6. The item or access number of the work (optional).

O'Hanlon, L. (2000, March 25). Extreme measures: The art of analyzing natural disasters. *The Discovery Channel online.* Retrieved September 17, 2000, from http://www.discovery.com/newsfeatures/disasters/disasters.html

Brown, T. (1998, October). Problems and solutions in the management of child abuse allegations [Electronic version]. *Family & Reconciliation*

Courts Review, 36. Retrieved May 11, 2002, from EBSCOhost database, item 1121380.

O'Hanlon's article was written for the Discovery Channel's Web site. Brown's article first appeared in print and then became part of a database, as indicated by the words *Electronic version.*

Online Article from a Scholarly Journal

Loranger, C. (1999). "This book spill off the page in all directions": What is the text of *Naked lunch*? *Postmodern Culture, 10*(1). Retrieved August 27, 2000, from http://muse.jhu.edu/journals/pmc/v010/10.1loranger.html

Postmodern Culture is an online scholarly journal. Note that the information through the volume and issue number is the same as that which would appear for a print journal article.

Online Article from a Newspaper or News Service

Babinek, M. (2000, May 22). Railroad killer gets death penalty. *San Francisco Examiner.* Retrieved May 27, 2000, from http://examiner.com/apa/AP_Railroad_Killer.html

Online Article in a Weekly or Monthly Magazine

Saletan, W. (2000, November 28). Electoral knowledge. *Slate.* Retrieved November 30, 2000, from http://slate.msn.com/framegame/entries/00-11-28_94258.asp

Note the date of posting: (2000, November 28).

Article Accessed Through an Online Library Service

Hannon, K. (1996, June 10). The joys of a working vacation [Electronic version]. *U.S. News & World Report, 120,* 89-90. Retrieved October 22, 2001, from OCLC First Search database.

College and university libraries usually subscribe to at least one online access service. These services allow researchers quick access to periodical articles that are available online. Note that the information from the author through the page range is the same as it would be for an entry of the print version of the article. The entry ends with the name of the access service. No URL is needed.

Online Book Previously Published in Print Form

Melville, H. (2000). *The piazza tales.* (Original work published 1856). Retrieved October 21, 2000, from http://www.esp.org/books/melville/piazza

Melville's book is available in print form and online. The entry for the digital version shows author, title, original publication date, date of access, and URL.

Part of Online Book Previously Published in Print Form

Melville, H. (2000). Benito Cereno. *The piazza tales.* (Original work published 1856). Retrieved October 24, 2000, from http://www.esp.org/books/melville/piazza/contents/cereno.html

"Benito Cereno" is one of the stories that make up *The Piazza Tales.*

Messages Posted to Newsgroups, Online Forums, Discussion Groups, and Electronic Mailing Lists

1. Begin with the author's name, followed by the exact date of the posting.
2. Type the subject or "thread" name of the posting, followed by any other identifying information in brackets.
3. Close with *Message posted to* and the URL.

Harrington, J. K. (2000, May 19). Publishing [The Writing Life Inkspot Writers' Community Forums, Msg. 3]. Message posted to http://writers-bbs.com/inkspot/threads.cgi?action=*almsgs&forum=writinglife*

Note that such resources may be open to anyone who has access to the Internet, whether or not he or she is an expert on the subject being discussed. Therefore, be extra careful about the validity of the information you take from forums, discussion groups, and the like.

APA Citations—Miscellaneous Sources

Encyclopedia or Dictionary Entry

Earthquake. *Concise Columbia encyclopedia* (3rd ed.). (1994). New York: Columbia University Press.

If the encyclopedia has an editor, then use the format for a book listed by editor.

Government Publication

U.S. Bureau of Labor Statistics. (1992). *Employment and earnings.* Washington, DC: Government Printing Office.

Film or Television Program

Miall, T. (Producer), & Luhrmann, B. (Director). (1992). *Strictly ballroom* [Motion picture]. Australia: Miramax.

Fritzell, J., & Greenbaum, E. (Writers). (1963, April 29). Mountain wedding [Television series episode]. In A. Ruben (Producer), *The Andy Griffith show.* New York: Columbia Broadcasting System.

MORE OPTIONS ONLINE
For more help with formatting APA-style references, go to **www.mhhe.com/writingtoday**.

Personal Communications

In APA style, personal communications appear in parenthetical citations only, not in the references section. Such communications include personal/telephone interviews, e-mails, and other messages that are not archived.

APA Research Paper Format

Double-space the essay on white, 8½″ × 11″ paper, using text margins of 1″ at the top, bottom, and sides. Use a standard text font, such as Times, Courier, Palatino, Garamond, or Goudy, in 12-point type.

The APA format requires a title page. Center the title both horizontally and vertically on the page. The title is followed on the next line by your name (also centered); the last line of the title page is your course and section number (also centered). Your instructor may also require you to include his or her name and the date.

Number all pages of your essay. Use the "header" function of your word processing program to include a shortened version of your essay's title followed by five spaces and then the page number, all flush right at the top margin, such as in this example:

Electromagnetic Variations   1

Note that each page is numbered, including the title page.

Checklist for APA-Style Research Papers

1. Check your quotations for accuracy. Make sure that you have transcribed correctly.
2. Make sure that all of your primary and secondary sources have been properly credited. Check to be sure that you have not created an ambiguous situation for your reader.
3. Credit your paraphrases and summaries, but remember that these do not require a page citation.
4. Make sure that you have used ellipses properly.
5. Format any quoted passage that is forty or more words as a block quotation. Check your essay to make sure you have followed this guideline.
6. Check to make sure that all sources cited in your essay appear in your reference list and that all entries in your references are cited at least once in your essay.
7. Alphabetize and double-space your list of references. Do not number this list.

The last element of your essay will be your reference section. Start this section on a new page. At the top of the page, center the word *References*. Then start the first entry on the next line after the head. Like the rest of your essay, this page is double-spaced, with no extra space added anywhere.

Sample Research Paper in APA Format

You can access a sample paper in APA style written by Joel Darulla, a student in a technical communication course, at the *Writing Today* Web site: www.mhhe.com/writingtoday.

PART 4
GRAMMAR AND MECHANICS

Thinking of grammar as dry and perhaps mundane, students rarely want to study English at the level of sentences. But the truth is that students who can't write effective sentences also can't write effective essays. Essays are, after all, collections of sentences.

The good news is that American English is highly systematic in most areas. In other words, once you learn a particular concept, you will be able to apply it to various writing situations. In addition, once you learn some basic sentence concepts, learning others will become easier.

Chapter 22 focuses on the parts of speech and the way they function. Chapter 23 moves to the working parts of sentences and then explains how you can design whole sentences so that they achieve a specific function.

Chapter 24 analyzes major sentence errors, the ones that cause the greatest grief for most students, and explores several ways to avoid these errors. Chapter 25 discusses the correct use of verbs.

Chapter 26 covers problems with pronouns while Chapter 27 deals with the use of modifiers—various types of adjectives and adverbs, their forms, and their placements. Chapter 28 explains how to punctuate sentences using a comma or commas. As a follow-up, Chapter 29 discusses using other marks of punctuation. Chapter 30 covers mechanics. Chapter 31 explains diction and word choice: the problem of nuance, of "weasel words," and of idiom. This chapter concludes with a look at spelling problems. Chapter 32 is a glossary of usage, discussing often-confused words and distinctions of meaning.

Chapters 22 through 31 are filled with examples and illustrations of the concepts that we discuss. Each of these chapters also contains several exercises so that you can practice "making things right." Our emphasis, as always, is on function. We believe that the logical and most useful response to a student who says, for example, "I think this is a comma splice" is "How are you going to correct it?" ●

Other common nouns are **concrete;** they refer to tangible items:

cats	desks
computers	trees
dust	buildings
sofa	shoes

3. **Count nouns** refer to items that are normally enumerated. They form their plurals by adding *-s* or *-es*. Typically, these are concrete nouns:

horses
boxes
cars
vacuums

However, some count nouns are irregular and retain the same spelling, whether singular or plural:

one moose	seventeen moose
one sheep	forty sheep
one deer	eight deer

4. **Noncount nouns** refer to concepts or to things that are normally not counted but are otherwise identified or measured:

spirituality	oxygen
justice	equipment
rice	poetry
dust	music

Generally, the articles *a* and *an* are not used with noncount nouns:

NOT **a rice**

BUT **the rice *or* rice**

We *weigh* rice; we don't *count* it as we would biscuits: "I made six biscuits and half a pound of rice."

However, note that some nouns are either count or noncount depending on context and meaning:

Jennifer thought that **love** was a fascinating topic.
Francisco has many **loves** in his life.

In the first example, *love* is an emotion (noncount and abstract); in the second, *loves* refers to people or things (count and concrete).

5. **Nouns and their sentence functions.** Nouns function as subjects, objects, and complements.

The **subject** of a sentence controls the verb:

Parker read the novel.
Justice prevails.

The **direct object** of a verb receives its action:

Serena kicked the **door**.

An **indirect object** can—but does not have to—appear in a prepositional phrase, a phrase beginning with a word such as *to, with, of, for, by,* and *in:*

d.o. i.o.
John mailed the **present** to **Joan.**

i.o. d.o.
John mailed **Joan** the **present.**

Joan is the indirect object; *present* is the direct object.

A **complement** appears when the sentence contains a **linking verb,** such as *be, feel, seem,* or *appear* (see page 638) The linking verb connects the subject to its complement.

Alejandro is my **friend.**

A **gerund** is a noun that is formed by adding *-ing* to a verb. Gerunds name activities. For example, adding *-ing* to the verb *play* results in the noun *playing:*

Playing soccer is my young son's favorite activity.

Note that when you add *-ing* to a verb, the result is not always a gerund. In the sentence "My son is playing soccer," *playing* is a participle (see 22k).

EXERCISE 22.1

Underline the nouns in the following paragraph.

Traveling by bus provides a fascinating peek into an aspect of America that many people have not seen. Buses take the back roads, stopping at small towns that time seems to have forgotten. "Good Food" and "Eat" appear in the neon signs of old restaurants. People wave to each other from their cars, and they turn to see who is getting off the bus. Dogs sleep in the streets. Indeed, time seems to stand still. However, the observer has not entered a time warp. Unless the town is very small and isolated, a Wal-Mart store (or a similar competitor) is likely to be nearby. The Internet also provides a link to the larger world. As well, cable and satellite TV services allow small-town residents access to HBO and Bravo, among other options. The world of the small town may look different, but perhaps it is not so different after all.

EXERCISE 22.1
Traveling by bus . . . peek into an aspect of America that many people have not seen. Buses . . . roads, . . . towns that time. . . . "Good Food" . . . neon signs of old restaurants. People . . . their cars, . . . bus. Dogs sleep in streets. Indeed, time. . . . However, the observer has . . . warp. Unless the town . . . , a Wal-Mart store (or a similar competitor). . . . The Internet . . . a link to the larger world. As well, . . . services . . . residents access to HBO and Bravo, . . . options. The world of the small town. . . .

22b PRONOUNS

Pronouns replace nouns or other pronouns. The noun or pronoun that is replaced is called an *antecedent,* "the word that comes before."

antecedent pronoun
The **parents** wished the best for **their** son.

Pronouns are used to create emphasis and avoid repetition. There are eight classes of pronouns: personal, indefinite, reflexive, intensive, relative, interrogative, demonstrative, and reciprocal.

1. **Personal pronouns** refer to specific people, places, and things. They are classified by **case,** the role they play in the sentence:

   I [subjective case] found the letter.
   The letter was found by **me** [objective case].
   The letter is **mine** [possessive case].

   Here are the personal pronouns:

Subjective Case	Objective Case	Possessive Case
I	me	my, mine
you	you	your, yours
he	him	his
she	her	her, hers
it	it	its
we	us	our, ours
they	them	their, theirs

   Remember to use the correct case and to avoid careless sentences like this one:

   INCORRECT **Bill came over to Martha and I, asking if we had heard about the tornado.**

   Take out *Martha and,* and the sentence sounds absurd. You would never write *Bill came over to I.* The correct form is *me,* not *I,* for *me* is the object of the preposition *to.*

   As shown in the chart above, personal pronouns indicate **number**—that is, singular or plural (*she* is singular; *they* is plural). They also indicate gender (*he* is masculine; *she* is feminine; *it* is neuter). Finally, they indicate person (*I* and *we* are first-person; *you* is second-person; *he/she/it* and *they* are third person).

2. **Indefinite pronouns**, as their name suggests, refer to unspecified persons or things. Some are always singular, some are always plural, and some are singular or plural depending upon context.

Always Singular	Always Plural	Singular or Plural Depending upon Context
another	both	all
anybody	few	any
anyone	many	either
anything	several	enough
each		more
every		most
everybody		neither
everyone		none
everything		some
no one		
nobody		

Always Singular
nothing
one
somebody
someone
something

Almost **everyone** in my class **is** here for the game.
Few have stayed behind.
All of the pizza **is** disappearing as we approach the kickoff.
All of our football players **are** ready to do their best.

3. **Reflexive pronouns** refer to the self and always end in *-self* or *selves:*

   The farmer checked **himself** for deer ticks.

   Here are the reflexive pronouns:

myself	yourself
herself	yourselves
himself	ourselves
oneself	themselves
itself	

   Use reflexive pronouns only when they are appropriate. "David and myself made the dessert" should be "David and I. . . ." Also, avoid nonstandard forms, such as *hisself, theirself,* and *theirselves.*

4. **Intensive pronouns** are spelled the same as reflexive pronouns but have a different purpose—to provide emphasis:

   Joan's young daughter baked the cake **herself.**
   We **ourselves** have replaced the plumbing in our home.

5. **Relative pronouns** introduce dependent (subordinate) clauses that act as adjectives. Clauses that begin with relative pronouns refer to an earlier noun or pronoun in the sentence. Remember that *who, whom, whoever,* and *whomever* always refer to people.

who	that
whoever	what
whom	whatever
whomever	which
whose	whichever

   Martha is the only gymnast **who** had a perfect score.

   Here is the car **that** I want to buy.

   The elderly man, **whatever** his relationship to you, is a gentleman.

6. **Interrogative pronouns** are used to form questions:

what	whatever
which	whichever
who	whom
whoever	whomever
whose	

Which is the correct road?
What is the answer?
To **whom** does the future belong?

7. **Demonstrative pronouns** (*this, these, that, those*) are used to show "which one":

This is the hat Carlotta will wear to the wedding.
That is the same problem Judy mentioned.
These are not my shoes.
Those were the paintings we saw in the gallery.

8. **Reciprocal pronouns** (*each other, one another*) refer equally to individual parts of a plural antecedent:

Juan and Maria love **each other.**
The three brothers consulted **one another** regularly.

Use *each other* to refer to a plural antecedent made up of two entities; use *one another* to refer to a plural antecedent made up of three or more entities.

EXERCISE 22.2

In the following paragraph, underline the pronouns. Then identify each pronoun by writing the correct number above it: (1) personal, (2) indefinite, (3) reflexive, (4) intensive, (5) relative, (6) interrogative, (7) demonstrative, or (8) reciprocal.

My friend Gene and I talk to each other frequently. Gene is a successful accountant. However, he has confided to me that he wants to separate himself from his middle-class world and join a carnival. What is wrong with him? Nothing, as far as I can tell. Gene has harbored this fantasy for years, which is why I find myself surprised to learn that I am the only other person who knows about it. Anyone who keeps this type of secret must eventually doubt his or her sanity, and I was quick to assure Gene that everybody has a harmless reverie. I myself sometimes dream about becoming an international hip-hop star, which is a much stranger idea to me than joining a traveling carnival.

EXERCISE 22.2
My (1) friend Gene and I (1) talk to each other (8). . . . However, he (1) has confided to me (1) that (5) he (1) . . . himself (3) from his (1). . . . What (6) is . . . him (1)? Nothing, (2) . . . I (1). . . . Gene . . . this (7) . . . , which (5) is why I (1) find myself (3) . . . that (5) I (1) . . . person who (5) knows about it (1). Anyone (2) who (5) keeps this (7) . . . doubt his (1) or her (1) sanity, and I (1) . . . Gene that (5) everybody (2). . . . I (1) myself (4) sometimes . . . hip-hop star, which (5) . . . to me (1). . . .

22c ADJECTIVES

An **adjective** modifies a noun or pronoun; in other words, it makes the noun or pronoun more specific by describing, limiting, evaluating, clarifying, and so on. In English, most adjectives *precede* nouns:

A **large, brown** dog ran along the **dusty** road into a **small** shack that sat at the foot of a **flower-covered** hill.

The **rusty old** car belongs to Joshua.

Note that nouns can sometimes be used as adjectives:

a **computer** class   a **Ford** dealership   a **rock** concert

In **compound adjectives,** the first adjective describes the second and is connected to it with a hyphen. Collectively, the resulting term modifies the noun:

a **coal-black** fish

Adverbs may be part of such a formation:

an **all-too-common** problem

Adjectives can act as **complements** in sentences with linking verbs (*be, feel, seem,* and so on—see page 638).

SUBJECT COMPLEMENT **I [subject] feel [linking verb] tired [subject complement].**

OBJECT COMPLEMENT **His tone [subject] made us [direct object] nervous [object complement].**

In the preceding sentence, the linking verb is implicit:

His tone made us [feel] nervous.

Do not follow a linking verb with an adverb used as a subject complement, as in the following sentence:

INCORRECT **I feel badly.**

CORRECT **I feel bad.**

Any adjective can be used in its **positive** (base) form as well as in its **comparative** and **superlative** forms. The comparative form is used when comparing two persons or things; the superlative is used with three or more persons or things:

POSITIVE John is **tall.**

COMPARATIVE Betty is **taller** than he.

SUPERLATIVE Calogero is the **tallest** of the three soldiers.

You can find more about creating comparatives and superlatives in Chapter 27.

EXERCISE 22.3

In each of the following sentences, choose the correct word from the choices in the parentheses.

1. This new cologne smells (bad, badly).
2. Of the two paintings, the older one is clearly (better, best).
3. Terry is the (taller, tallest) member of his extended family.
4. Sara is very happy with her new (macintosh, Macintosh) computer.
5. Juan is (tall, taller, tallest).

EXERCISE 22.3
1. bad
2. better
3. tallest
4. Macintosh
5. tall

22d ARTICLES

Articles modify nouns, much as adjectives do (see page 632). Usually, articles are not attached to pronouns, except in sentences such as the following:

Are you **the** one I've been hearing about?

The **indefinite articles** (*a* and *an*) can be used with count nouns that are not specific (see page 627 for a discussion of "count" and "noncount" nouns):

a car   **a** unit   **an** insect   **an** actor

Note that *a* is used before words beginning with consonant sounds; *an* is used before words beginning with vowel sounds. The key term here is *sounds*. Although *unit* begins with a vowel, the *u* is voiced as *y*, so *a* is needed instead of *an*.

When an indefinite article is separated from the noun by one or more adjectives or adverbs, use *a* or *an* according to the initial sound of the modifier nearest to the indefinite article:

an indefinite article

a commonly used article of clothing

Indefinite articles are rarely used with proper nouns. Here is an exception:

There is **a** Robert Kendall here to see you, Dr. Fernandez.

The **definite article** (*the*) indicates a specific noun: ***the** college, **the** elephant, **the** unit:*

The woman [specific person] arguing with **the** store manager [specific manager] is not **a** friend [any particular friend] of mine.

The definite article is sometimes used with proper nouns, but rarely with names:

the Mississippi River	**the** Porsche Boxster
Bennigan's Restaurant	Marisa Tomei

For more on using articles, see 27g.

EXERCISE 22.4

In each of the following sentences, the article is highlighted. Decide if each article is used correctly. If not, revise the sentence so that it is correct.

1. We stopped at **an** highway sign along Route 17.
2. My uncle paid twenty dollars for **a** Uriah Heep album.

EXERCISE 22.4
1. . . . **a** highway sign.
2. Correct

gr 22e

3. . . . **the** restaurant's owner.
4. . . . **an** uncommon situation.
5. . . . at Subway.

3. This soup is horrible; I'm going to complain to **a** restaurant's owner.
4. Her car accident was surely the result of **a** uncommon situation.
5. Let's eat lunch at **the** Subway.

22e PREPOSITIONS

Prepositions connect nouns and pronouns to other words in a sentence. They normally indicate time, place, position, contrast/similarity to, direction, or some other kind of relationship between the noun or pronoun and the words to which the preposition is connecting the noun or pronoun. Many prepositions are single words; others are compound words.

Single-Word Prepositions

about	below	for	through
above	beneath	from	to
across	beside	in	toward
after	between	including	under
against	beyond	inside	underneath
along	by	into	until
amid	despite	like	up
among	down	near	upon
as	during	of	via
at	except	on	with
before	excluding	over	within
behind	following	since	without

Compound-Word Prepositions

according to	except for	in spite of
along with	in addition to	instead of
as to	in front of	on account of
because of	in place of	with regard to
by means of	in reference to	up to

We received a letter **from** our insurance agent.
Mike lives **near** the river.
According to this map, Glenwood is just a few miles farther.
The baseball team won **in spite of** its five errors.

The noun, pronoun, or gerund (a noun ending in *-ing,* which is made from a verb and names an activity) that follows a preposition is called the preposition's **object;** combined, the structure is called a **prepositional phrase.** Occasionally, writers wonder how to structure a difficult prepositional phrase or which preposition goes with a verb to make a verb phrase. Certain objects and verbs "take" specific prepositions; in other words, the correct wording is dictated by custom, not by logic. See Chapter 31, pages 773–776, for a list of many of the troublesome phrases in English. The following are some common phrases:

Angelo and Mark **agreed on** a plan.
Angelo and Mark **agreed to** a meeting.
Angelo and Mark **agreed with** their boss.

The umpire expected the players to **conform to** (not **with**) the rules.

The police have **joined in** the investigation.
The police have **joined with** the FBI in the investigation.

The Murcias **live on** this street.
The Murcias **live in** this house (community, town, county).

Marissa **looked in** the Bible for an appropriate quotation.
Marissa **looked at** the Bible sitting on the altar.
Marissa **looked for** the Bible she had misplaced.
Marissa **looked to** the Bible for guidance.
Marissa **looked on** as the Bible was placed on the podium.

The protestors **marched in** the parade.
The protestors **marched to** the courthouse.
The protestors **marched on** Washington.

Mary **rode on** a bus (train, boat).
Mary **rode in** a car.

The children are **sleeping on** the couch.
The children are **sleeping in** their beds.

Arnold is **working on** a new project.
Arnold is **working in** Tulsa.

Jeff **sat** quietly **at** his desk.
Jeff **sat** quietly **in** his chair.
Jeff **sat** quietly **on** the barstool.

We **parked on** the street.
We **parked in** a municipal lot.

Prepositions are also used with verbs to form multiword (or phrasal) verbs, such as *ran into, call off,* and *pick up*. When prepositions are used in this way, they are called **particles**.

EXERCISE 22.5

In each of the following sentences, fill in the blank with the appropriate preposition. In some cases, more than one answer may be correct.

1. Karen was pleased _____ the quality of her employees' presentation.
2. Franco has lived _____ this condo _____ his elderly father _____ six years.
3. I need to ask you some questions _____ the lunch break.
4. The winner _____ the race was the best _____ many qualified athletes.
5. Go _____ this door to get _____ the security building.

EXERCISE 22.5 Answers may vary.
1. with
2. in; with; for
3. during
4. of; among
5. through; to

22f CONJUNCTIONS

Conjunctions join words, phrases, and clauses. There are four types: coordinating conjunctions, correlative conjunctions, conjunctive adverbs, and subordinating conjunctions.

1. The seven **coordinating conjunctions** are *and, but, for, so, yet, or,* and *nor.* Of these seven, *and, but, yet, or,* and *nor* are used to connect words, phrases, and clauses of equal grammatical weight:

   Carlos **and** Luisa are getting married.

   Finding a house **or** renting an apartment is our next project.

   The rescue worker didn't want to inspect the wreckage again, **nor** did she want to risk missing any survivors.

   As conjunctions, *for* and *so* are used only between independent clauses:

   Brenda's mechanic retired, **so** she had to find a new one.
   Alan will stay home tonight, **for** he needs to study.

   Note: Use the mnemonic FANBOYS (for and nor but or yet so) to remember the seven coordinating conjunctions.

2. **Correlative conjunctions** are pairs of conjunctions that emphasize relationships—*both/and, not only/but also, either/or, neither/nor:*

   Both Larry **and** Gayle are late.
   Lori is **not only** cooking the food **but also** serving the meal.
   Either turn down the radio **or** listen to music elsewhere.

   When you use correlative conjunctions, make sure not to omit part of a pair. For example, don't link *not only* with *but* alone; the expression needs both words: *but also.*

3. **Conjunctive adverbs** (also known as transitional expressions) link independent clauses to show one sentence's relationship to the previous sentence. Like coordinating conjunctions, conjunctive adverbs join items of equal weight:

WITH COORDINATING CONJUNCTION	Sara wanted to go ice skating, **but** the rink was closed.
WITH CONJUNCTIVE ADVERB	Sara wanted to go ice skating; **however,** the rink was closed.
WITH COORDINATING CONJUNCTION	Hungary and Finland are in Europe, **but** their languages are not Indo-European.
WITH CONJUNCTIVE ADVERB	Hungary and Finland are in Europe; **nonetheless,** their languages are not Indo-European.

   Read the two preceding pairs of sentences again. Note that conjunctive adverbs can often provide greater emphasis. In addition, conjunctive adverbs, along with transitional expressions (their grammatical equals), allow writers to show precise relationships, whereas coordinating conjunctions have more general meanings. For a list of conjunctive adverbs and transitional expressions, see Chapter 24, pages 663–664.

Conjunctive adverbs can also be used to introduce a new sentence, as in the following example:

Sara wanted to go ice skating. **However,** the rink was closed.

In this instance, the writer decided to use two sentences instead of one.

Note that conjunctive adverbs can appear *within* a sentence as well:

Sara wanted to go ice skating. The rink, **however,** was closed.

Conjunctive adverbs can also function as simple adverbs:

However isolated a person may be in our world, civilization is never far away.

4. **Subordinating conjunctions** show that one clause of a sentence (the dependent clause) is less important than and is dependent upon the other clause (the independent or main clause). For example, you might write the following:

   We ate dinner; we saw a movie.

   This sentence works fine if you wish to place equal emphasis on each clause or if the relationship between the two ideas in these clauses is not important. But what if you want to create emphasis or indicate a relationship? Here are two ways to do so. As you learned earlier, you can use a **conjunctive adverb:**

   We ate dinner; **then** we saw a movie.

   However, for variety's sake, you might also use a **subordinating conjunction:**

   After we ate dinner, we saw a movie.

   Here are some more examples:

INDEPENDENT CLAUSES	**Ishmael was sent into the desert. His name has come to mean "outcast."**
ONE CLAUSE SUBORDINATED	**Because Ishmael was sent into the desert, his name has come to mean "outcast."**
INDEPENDENT CLAUSES	**James Monroe was James Madison's secretary of state for a brief period. At the same time, he was Madison's secretary of war.**
ONE CLAUSE SUBORDINATED	**James Monroe was James Madison's secretary of state for a brief period while he was also serving as Madison's secretary of war.**

Common Subordinating Conjunctions

after	in order to
although	since
as long as	unless
as soon as	until
as though	when
because	whenever
if	while

For a more complete list of subordinating conjunctions, see Chapter 24, page 663.

EXERCISE 22.6

EXERCISE 22.6 Answers may vary. Here are some possible responses:
1. When John returned home, he learned. . . .
2. Wanda wanted to see a movie; however, George. . . .
3. The bookstore was out of the novel that I wanted, so I. . . .
4. The prices here are ridiculous; moreover, the. . . .
5. Ed won't start college this fall, for he. . . .

Each of the following sentences needs a coordinating conjunction, a correlative conjunction, a subordinating conjunction, or a conjunctive adverb/transitional expression. Supply an appropriate conjunction. More than one answer may be correct.

1. John returned home, he learned that his accountant was running behind on preparing tax returns.
2. Wanda wanted to see a movie; George was tired and wanted to stay home.
3. The bookstore was out of the novel that I wanted, I tried to find it online.
4. The prices here are ridiculous; the service is terrible.
5. Ed won't start college this fall, he didn't mail his application on time.

22g VERBS

Verbs show action (*walk, tell*) or a state of being (*do, seem*).

22g.1 VERB TYPES

There are four types of verbs: transitive, intransitive, linking, and helping (auxiliary) verbs.

1. A **transitive verb** shows action taken by a subject upon an object. A transitive verb always needs a *direct object,* which receives the action and makes the sentence a complete thought.

   t.v. d.o.
   Melissa **hit** the **ball**.

2. An **intransitive verb** does not act upon an object:

   i.v.
   Jason **laughed**.

   Note that some verbs can be both transitive and intransitive depending on the context:

   Joe just **opened** a new ice cream shop.
   The new ice cream shop just **opened**.

3. Unlike most verbs, a **linking verb** does not indicate an action but expresses a relationship or a description. A linking verb connects the subject to its *complement,* a word or words that describe the subject:

   Tapioca **is** an interesting dessert.
   Your CD player **sounds** strange.

   Common linking verbs are *appear, be, become, feel, remain, seem, smell, sound,* and *taste.* (Please note that some of these verbs can also function as action [transitive] verbs: *Maria tasted the peaches.*)

4. A **helping (auxiliary) verb** "qualifies" the main verb by showing its tense and mood (see the discussion of tense, page 641, and mood, page 642):

   Theresa **is** studying tonight.
   Theresa **will** study all of this weekend.
   Theresa **has been** studying all week.

   All forms of *be, do,* and *have* can function as helping verbs.

5. **Modal auxiliaries,** a subclass of auxiliary verbs, further "qualify" a main verb:

   My friends **might** see a movie.
   My friends **could** see a movie.
   My friends **should** see a movie.

6. **Phrasal verbs** consist of a verb plus one or more prepositions. Some phrasal verbs are **separable;** in other words, an object may appear either within the verb phrase or after it:

   Go **pick up** a large pizza for dinner.
   Hoshi **picked** Susana **up** an hour before the concert.

   Other phrasal verbs are **inseparable.** Their parts must remain together:

   The car **broke down** three miles from Ashland.
   We are **looking forward** to your arrival.

22g.2 VERB FORMS

Verbs often change spelling to indicate tense (time). The verb tenses include the present, the past, the future, the present perfect and the past perfect, and the six progressive tenses. You will learn about them in the next section. The change in spelling is minor in regular verbs, more pronounced and harder to predict in irregular verbs.

Regular verbs form their past tenses by adding *-ed* or *-d,* their present participles by adding *-ing,* and their past participles by adding *-d* or *-ed*. They form their future tenses by using *will.* For example, here are the forms for the regular verb *to paint:*

I like **to paint** alone. (base form)

I **paint** alone, but she **paints** with a friend. (present tense)

I **painted** alone. (past tense)

I **am painting** alone. (present progressive tense)

I **have painted** alone. (present perfect tense)

I **had painted** alone. (past perfect tense)

I **will paint** alone. (future tense)

Although most verbs are **regular,** some are **irregular.** The spelling of the principal parts of irregular verbs deviates from the regular pattern, such as with the irregular verb *go: go, goes, went, going, gone*. Check your dictionary. If the principal parts are not listed, the verb is regular. For now, here is a brief list of irregular verbs to use as a reference:

IRREGULAR VERBS

Present	Past	Present Participle	Past Participle
arise	arose	arising	arisen
awake	awoke	awaking	awaked, awoke
beat	beat	beating	beaten, beat
bring	brought	bringing	brought
catch	caught	catching	caught
choose	chose	choosing	chosen
cling	clung	clinging	clung
come	came	coming	come
do	did	doing	done
draw	drew	drawing	drawn
drive	drove	driving	driven
eat	ate	eating	eaten
fall	fell	falling	fallen
fly	flew	flying	flown
forgive	forgave	forgiving	forgiven
get	got	getting	gotten
go	went	going	gone
keep	kept	keeping	kept
know	knew	knowing	known
lay (to place)	laid	laying	laid
lie (to recline)	lay	lying	lain
lie (to speak falsely)	lied	lying	lied
lose	lost	losing	lost
ride	rode	riding	ridden
rise	rose	rising	risen
run	ran	running	run
see	saw	seeing	seen
sit	sat	sitting	sat
speak	spoke	speaking	spoken
teach	taught	teaching	taught
tear	tore	tearing	torn
throw	threw	throwing	thrown
write	wrote	writing	written

EXERCISE 22.7

Each of the following sentences contains an irregular verb in parentheses. Provide the correct form of the verb.

1. The gold dollar (lie) on the ground for three hours before someone spotted it.
2. Mark had (get) fired from three jobs before he finally settled down.
3. The police believe that the suspect is (lie) about her whereabouts on the night of the robbery.
4. The carpenter discovered that he had (tear) his overalls during the morning.
5. Have you (eat) breakfast yet?

EXERCISE 22.7
1. lay
2. gotten
3. lying
4. torn
5. eaten

Three major features of verbs are their tense, mood, and voice.

22h VERB TENSE

Basically, **tense** refers to the time that a verb indicates. There are five basic categories of tense: present, past, future, the perfect tenses, and the progressive tenses.

The **present tense** indicates events occurring at the moment or that happen on a recurring basis:

The race **starts** now.
I **eat** sushi every week.

The **past tense** conveys action that has been completed:

The race **started** on time last year.
I **ate** sushi at Natalia's wedding last Sunday.

The **future tense** conveys future action:

The race **will start** when the referee blows her whistle.
I **will eat** sushi at dinner tonight even if it kills me.

The **perfect tenses** show action spanning different periods of time.

The **present perfect tense** refers to an action in the recent past and/or an action that is occurring in the present and is ongoing:

Eduardo **has spoken** about this issue many times.
The band **has played** for two hours.

The **past perfect tense** is used to refer to a time frame *before* a past time frame:

Luis **had dated** his fiancée before he **entered** the Air Force.

The past perfect in this sentence is indicated by the auxiliary verb *had;* the simple past is indicated by *entered* without *had.*

The **future perfect tense** refers to a future time before a fixed future time:

By the time our vacation has ended, we **will have driven** 2,500 miles.

The **progressive tenses** show ongoing activity. There are six types of progressive tenses:

PRESENT PROGRESSIVE	Reina **is working** as fast as she can.
PAST PROGRESSIVE	Miguel **was visiting** Paris when he died.
FUTURE PROGRESSIVE	Phil **will be jogging** across the state in a charity marathon this week.
PRESENT PERFECT PROGRESSIVE	Angelo **has been collecting** money at our church.
PAST PERFECT PROGRESSIVE	Ingrid **had been trying** to get away when the police arrested her.
FUTURE PERFECT PROGRESSIVE	By next year, the company **will have been conducting** business in Moline for fifty years.

EXERCISE 22.8 Answers may vary.
1. has hosted
2. has been running
3. had qualified
4. will have served
5. will be wearing; is wearing

EXERCISE 22.8

Each of the following sentences contains a verb or verb phrase in parentheses. Given the context of the sentence, provide the correct form of the verb or verb phrase. More than one answer might be possible.

1. The Latino Association (has host) a lecture series for the past five years.

2. Ellen (has be run) every week for three years now.

3. Luis (has qualify) for his current rank two years before he applied for promotion.

4. By the end of the year, Andros (will has serve) over 5,000 pancakes.

5. To pick out Ray at the airport, remember that he (will is wear) a red hat.

22i VERB MOOD

The **mood** of a verb tells the reader how to interpret a particular statement. Verbs occur in three moods: indicative, imperative, and subjunctive.

The **indicative mood,** the most common, is used in declarative and interrogative sentences to convey facts and ask questions:

Mivette **votes** in every election.
My sister **drove** an SUV across the country.
Does Ed **belong** to a labor union?

The **imperative mood** is used for commands, requests, and directions:

Walk carefully on this trail.
Always **back up** the computer's hard drive.
Please **pass** the salt.
Turn right at the next light.

The **subjunctive mood** indicates hypothetical situations, wishes, and conditions contrary to fact. It is also used to make recommendations. Sentences in the subjunctive often contain or begin with *if* and/or *were:*

If I **were** to go to tonight's training seminar, I might impress my boss.
I wish I **were** wealthy, so I could buy my parents a new car.
If cows **were** able to fly, air traffic would be horrendous.

In the first sentence, the writer hasn't decided whether to go or not, so the situation is hypothetical. The second sentence expresses a wish. The third sentence refers to an impossible situation, one contrary to reality.

Note that when the subjunctive appears in the present tense, the base form of the verb is used, as in this sentence, which recommends something:

The auditing committee recommends that the bank **fire** its CFO.

EXERCISE 22.9

In each of the following sentences, examine the highlighted verb. Decide if it is used correctly. If not, revise the sentence.

1. If Kyle **was** more polite, he might have more friends.
2. If cats had thumbs, we **will** never live in safety again.
3. I suggested to my uncle that he **purchase** supplemental health insurance.
4. It is important that you **are** ready to start college this fall.
5. My nephew wishes that he **was** eighteen, not twelve.

EXERCISE 22.9
1. If Kyle were more polite. . . .
2. If cats had thumbs, we would. . . .
3. Correct
4. It is important that you be. . . .
5. My nephew wishes that he were. . . .

22j VERB VOICE

Verbs have two voices: active and passive. The **active voice** is the more common:

s. v. o.
John washed the car.

In the active voice, the subject acts. However, in the **passive voice**, the subject is acted upon:

s. v.
The car was washed by John.

Overusing the passive voice is a common error. The active-voice example above is simple and direct. The passive-voice example is indirect and wordy. Use the passive only when you have a good reason to do so:

The bank **was robbed** last night. [The culprit is unknown.]

Mistakes **were made** in the planning stages. [The writer doesn't wish to embarrass the person responsible.]

The door **was left** open. [By whom? It probably doesn't matter.]

The room **had been** vandalized. [This version is more direct than using the active voice. Writing "Vandals had torn the room apart" does not add any more information, and it contains an additional word.]

Otherwise, avoid the passive voice. The active voice is more forceful and economical.

EXERCISE 22.10

Each of the following sentences uses the passive voice. Decide if the sentence is acceptable. If not, rewrite the sentence so that it uses the active voice.

1. Marisa's car was stolen last week.
2. The cat was chased by the dog for almost a hundred yards.
3. It was felt by Michael that late marriage was better than none at all.
4. After the party, we discovered that the front gate had been unlatched all night.
5. Irregularities were discovered during the IRS auditor's examination of Ellen's tax returns.

EXERCISE 22.10 Answers may vary.
1. Acceptable
2. The dog chased the cat for almost a hundred yards.
3. Michael felt that late marriage was better than none at all.
4. Acceptable
5. The IRS auditor discovered irregularities during the examination of Ellen's tax returns.

22k VERBALS

Verbals are formed from verbs but function as other parts of speech. The three types of verbals are gerunds, participles, and infinitives.

A **gerund** is an *-ing* form of a verb that functions as a noun:

Walking is good exercise.
Sleeping has become a chore for me.

Participles—both present and past—function as adjectives:

The **winning** team will receive a trophy.
The **troubled** young man wandered the streets.

Note that the present participle and past participle can have different meanings:

Lucas is a very **tired** man.
Lucas is a very **tiring** man.

The past participle is normally used to describe how a person or thing has been *affected,* such as in "tired man." The present participle describes the effect the modified noun has on *others.* Lucas is "a very tiring man" because he exhausts others.

Keep in mind that some past or present participles cannot be used as adjectives:

CORRECT **The doomed prisoner was led to the execution chamber.**

INCORRECT **The prisoner was thinking about the day that he heard the dooming news.**

The second sentence is not idiomatic. Although *doom* has a present participle, *dooming,* it should not be used as an adjective.

An **infinitive** is the base form of the verb preceded by *to.* An infinitive can function as an adverb, an adjective, or a noun:

They went to Turkey **to study** Roman ruins. (adverb)
Jason is the person **to fix** your car. (adjective)
To sacrifice is noble. (noun)

gr

22m

EXERCISE 22.11

Each of the following sentences contains a highlighted verbal. First, identify the verbal as a gerund, a present participle, a past participle, or an infinitive. Then indicate the function that the verbal serves—as adjective or as noun, for example.

1. Mr. Walters was a **broken** man after his business failed.
2. This pasta is **disgusting**.
3. **To play** a violin has long been her dream.
4. **Finding** fish is only half the battle on this river.
5. The **tired** racehorse fell back in the stretch.

EXERCISE 22.11
1. past participle—adjective
2. present participle—adjective
3. infinitive—noun
4. gerund—noun
5. past participle—adjective

22l ADVERBS

Adverbs modify verbs, adjectives, or other adverbs by limiting their meaning, describing them, or evaluating them. Adverbs answer questions such as "how," "how often," "when," "where," and "to what extent."

Most adverbs are formed by adding *-ly* to an adjective:

Adjective	Adverb
nice	nicely
cruel	cruelly
terrible	terribly

Notice the spelling change between *terrible* and *terribly.* The final *e* is dropped frequently but not always. For example, *definite* becomes *definitely.* A college-level dictionary will show you which spelling to use. Look up the adjective; then go to the end of the entry to find the adverbial spelling.

However, not all words that end in *-ly* are adverbs—*family, lily,* and *Emily,* for example. And keep in mind that not all adverbs end in *-ly. Well, too, very,* and *almost* are all adverbs.

In addition, some words can act as both adjectives and adverbs:

adj. adv.
Ron owns a **fast** car, but he drives it too **fast**.

adj. adv.
The **early** train will get us there **early**.

22m PLACEMENT OF ADVERBS

Finding the correct position for an adverb can be complicated. Adverbs do not always appear next to the word they modify. The following guidelines will help:

1. When an adverb modifies an adjective or other adverb, it precedes the word it modifies: ***very** rich, **extremely** hungry, **really** too much, **almost** totally destroyed.*

An exception *may* occur when an adverb modifies a present or past participle. In the following sentence, the adverb can either precede or follow the past participle:

The ballet was **beautifully** performed.
The ballet was performed **beautifully.**

However, in most situations, the adverb precedes the adjective or adverb that it modifies.

2. When an adverb modifies a verb, the adverb might appear in several different positions without affecting the meaning of the sentence:

Veronica realized **slowly** that her computer was infected.
Veronica **slowly** realized that her computer was infected.
Slowly, Veronica realized that her computer was infected.

Often, however, changing the position of a verb modifier alters the meaning of a sentence—or makes the meaning unclear. Therefore, always position the adverb so that it clearly refers to *one* verb. Note these alternatives, in which the placement of *frequently* changes the sentence's meaning:

People who **frequently** use discount coupons save money.
People who use discount coupons save money **frequently.**

For more on adverbs and their placement, see Chapter 27.

EXERCISE 22.12

Each of the following sentences is followed by an adverb in parentheses. Place the adverb in the *best* position in the sentence.

1. The food at Mongolian Paradise is delicious. (absolutely)
2. To read is better than not to read at all. (slowly)
3. Dr. Taylor teaches advanced courses. (thoughtfully)
4. Franklin began thinking about studying law. (seriously)
5. Completing this course will require a great deal of work. (successfully)

EXERCISE 22.12
1. The food at Mongolian Paradise is absolutely delicious.
2. To read slowly is better than not to read at all.
3. Dr. Taylor teaches advanced courses thoughtfully.
4. Franklin began thinking seriously about studying law. OR Franklin began seriously thinking . . .
5. Completing this course successfully will require a great deal of work. OR Successfully completing this course . . .

22n INTERJECTIONS

Interjections are short words or phrases that indicate surprise, disappointment, joy, or some other strong emotion:

Oh, no, I've overdrawn my checking account again.
Alleluia! Aunt Martha is finally leaving.

Interjections are connected to the rest of the sentence or sometimes stand alone, as in the second example.

MORE OPTIONS ONLINE
For more exercises, go to **www.mhhe.com/writingtoday.**

CHAPTER 23

SENTENCE PARTS AND SENTENCE TYPES

To be a **sentence,** a group of words must contain a subject and a predicate and must express a complete idea. Of course, most sentences contain additional parts of speech grouped together in clauses and phrases. Sentences can be constructed in several forms: simple, compound, complex, and compound/complex. They can also be classified according to purpose: declarative, interrogative, imperative, and exclamatory.

SENTENCE PARTS

23a SUBJECTS

The **subject** of a sentence is a noun, pronoun, or group of words that (1) completes an action, (2) is acted upon, or (3) is described or explained.

SUBJECT THAT ACTS	**Laura Thompson** battles forest fires.
SUBJECT ACTED UPON	**The orphanage** was destroyed by fire.
SUBJECT DESCRIBED/ EXPLAINED	**The wonderful old cathedral** is more than four hundred years old.

CLASSROOM HINT Students should be encouraged to read this chapter in its entirety at the beginning of the term. Depending upon students' preparation, you might use the exercises in this chapter to test their knowledge and then discuss appropriate sections of the chapter in class.

In the last example sentence above, *cathedral* is the **simple subject**; the **complete subject** is *the wonderful old cathedral*. **Compound subjects** contain more than one subject linked by *and:*

COMPOUND SUBJECT	**Leslie and Jack** arrived an hour after the party began.

Note that **gerunds** (nouns that end in *-ing* and that name an activity) and **gerund phrases** (see 23e) can also be subjects:

MORE OPTIONS ONLINE If you would like to test your knowledge of sentence parts and sentence types before reading this chapter, go to **www.mhhe.com/writingtoday**.

Smoking is prohibited in all campus buildings.

Looking for antiques and shopping for curtains took up their entire day.

Sometimes, subjects are quite long:

The fact that no one ever checked Mark's résumé before we hired him worries me.

23b PREDICATES

A **predicate** is a word or group of words that contains the sentence's verb and any of its modifiers. A predicate makes a statement about the subject. In the following sentences, the complete predicate is in italics; the verb appears in bold.

PREDICATE THAT CONVEYS ACTION	In 1859, Joshua A. Norton *unabashedly **proclaimed** himself emperor of the United States.*
PREDICATE THAT DESCRIBES	Norton ***had** an obviously deranged set of beliefs.*

23c OBJECTS

In addition to acting as subjects, nouns and pronouns can act as direct objects, indirect objects, and objects of prepositions.

A **direct object** receives the action of a predicate:

d.o.
In 1939, Germany attacked **Poland.**

d.o.
Seamus Heaney writes **poetry.**

An **indirect object** is a noun, pronoun, or group of words *for which* an action is completed:

i.o. d.o.
The attacks of September 11, 2001, sent **the United States a horrifying message.**

i.o. d.o.
Bonaparte gave the **French a unique set of laws** known as the Napoleonic Code.

The **object of a preposition** has the same function as an indirect object, except that it is introduced by a preposition such as *by, for, of,* or *to:*

o.p.
To **the French,** Bonaparte gave a unique set of laws known as the Napoleonic Code.

23D COMPLEMENTS

A **subject complement** is a word or group of words that provides information about a subject and follows a linking verb:

s.c.
Shirley Jackson's "The Lottery" is a **masterpiece of short fiction.**

An **object complement** comes after a direct object (see 23c) and describes or explains it:

d.o. o.c.
I call **him** a **genius.**

EXERCISE 23.1

In each of the following sentences, a word or a group of words is highlighted. Identify the word or words as (1) subject, (2) predicate, (3) direct object, (4) indirect object, (5) object of a preposition, (6) subject complement, or (7) object complement.

1. **John's sister** is a nationally known dance critic.
2. In the **end,** you'll see that the training program is worth the trouble.
3. Mark gave **Helen** diamond earrings for their anniversary.
4. Tomoko is **a brilliant painter.**
5. Waiter, the salmon **seems to be a bit off today.**

EXERCISE 23.1
1. 1
2. 5
3. 4
4. 6
5. 2

6. 7
7. 3
8. 1
9. 2
10. 5

6. Charles was angry after his boss called him a **moron.**
7. The police officer closed the **door** and sat in a chair.
8. **The bad news that the early mail supplied** was enough to ruin Dr. Le's day.
9. The family **plans to drive to Nebraska and visit their old neighbor.**
10. When I first visited the physical therapist, I didn't think much of **him.**

23e PHRASES

Phrases do not have both a subject and a predicate. A **phrase** is any related group of words that functions as a unit in a sentence but is not a clause. There are nine types of phrases, and each has a specific function.

1. An **absolute phrase** is a clause without a verb; it modifies an entire sentence (see 23f for more on clauses):

CLAUSE	Her head was aching.
REDUCED TO ABSOLUTE PHRASE	**Her head aching,** Myra tried to steer her car through the snowstorm.
CLAUSE	Its ancient tires were almost flat.
REDUCED TO ABSOLUTE PHRASE	**Its ancient tires almost flat,** the car rested in the shadow of the barn.

2. An **appositive phrase** appears directly after a noun, renaming or otherwise identifying it. Most appositive phrases are set off by commas:

   Softball, **a sport derived from baseball,** is played in many elementary schools.
   My brother, **a stockbroker,** is vacationing in Alberta.
   Our class loved discussing Hemingway's *A Moveable Feast,* **his memoir of Paris in the 1920s.**

   Note that an appositive that specifically identifies a noun is not set off by commas (see also 28c):

   Rita McAlester **the fashion designer** is not the same person as Rita McAlester **the international fugitive.**

3. A **verbal phrase** is a group of words that begins with a past or present participle or an infinitive (see 22k), but that acts as another part of speech:

   Dancing on the piano is prohibited. [noun]
   Having danced on the piano, they were thrown out of the club. [adjective]

4. A **gerund phrase** includes a gerund (an *-ing* form of a verb used as a noun) plus any other words that modify the gerund. Gerund phrases act as nouns and can be subjects or direct objects:

   Driving to work can take me up to two hours. [subject]
   Rita enjoyed **dancing with José.** [direct object]

5. An **infinitive phrase** is made up of an infinitive (*to* plus the base form of a verb) and any other words that modify the infinitive:

   Jason is the best person **to fix your car.** (adjective)
   Lesya stopped at the diner **to eat lunch.** (adverb)
   To live well is the best revenge. (noun)

6. A **noun phrase** includes a noun and its modifying words and phrases:

   Success by accident is a feature of Tom's career. (subject)
   The speaker used **several convincing statistics taken from government sources.** (object)
   The result of the explosion was **an unforgettable shower of sparks and flames.** (complement)

7. A **participial phrase** includes either a present or past participle (see 22k) plus any accompanying words. It frequently describes a noun.

   Mr. Johnson is the man we see **walking beside the lake.**
   Nicholas, a man **shattered by the horrors of war,** is the soldier in the photograph.

8. A **prepositional phrase** consists of a preposition such as *by, in, over,* or *with* and its object as well as any modifying words:

   We decided never to go **to the mall.**
   Beside the couch, Jim had piled copies of the Sunday papers.
   The supervisor rarely showed interest in projects **under her control.**

   English depends heavily on the idiomatic use of prepositional phrases. For a list of "difficult" phrases involving prepositions along with verbs and adjectives, see Chapter 31, page 773.

9. **Verb phrases** contain main verbs preceded by auxiliary verbs:

   I **have been thinking.**
   He **does believe** in you.
   We **will be considering** your proposal.

EXERCISE 23.2

Underline each phrase in the following sentences. Then identify the phrase as (1) absolute, (2) appositive, (3) verbal, (4) gerund, (5) infinitive, (6) noun, (7) participial, (8) prepositional, or (9) verb.

1. Breaking slowly from the gate, the horse was seven lengths behind the rest of the pack.
2. My neighbor, a copywriter for an ad agency, has always believed in extraterrestrial life.
3. "Creativity by design" is our company's latest attempt at a motto.
4. The old man was hurt by the loss of his wife and son in the same year.
5. The fish jumping near the old stump is one that I have hooked and lost three times in the past two months.

EXERCISE 23.2
1. Breaking slowly from the gate (7); behind the rest of the pack (8)
2. a copywriter for an ad agency (2); in extraterrestrial life (8)
3. "Creativity by design" (6); at a motto (8)
4. by the loss (8); of his wife and son (8); in the same year (8)
5. jumping near the old stump (7); in the past two months (8)

6. His foot swollen to twice its normal size (1); up the hill (8); to his car (8)
7. to go (5); to Japan (8); reading about its culture (4)
8. of the best films (8); of the nineties (8)
9. tossing and turning (4)
10. over there (8); talking to Lisa (7)

6. His foot swollen to twice its normal size, Walter struggled up the hill to his car.
7. I've always wanted to go to Japan; reading about its culture fascinates me.
8. The Coen brothers' movie *Fargo* is one of the best films of the 1990s.
9. When people are troubled, tossing and turning can keep them up all night.
10. Michael is the one over there talking to Lisa.

23f CLAUSES

A **clause** is a group of words containing a subject and a verb. Clauses are either independent or dependent. An **independent (main) clause** can function alone as a sentence or be part of a compound, complex, or compound/complex sentence. A **dependent (subordinate) clause** cannot function alone; it must be part of a larger sentence that contains an independent clause.

All clauses, whether independent or dependent, must contain a subject and a predicate. A **subject** is the noun, pronoun, phrase, or clause that functions as the "actor" in the sentence. The subject "acts" through the verb or verb phrase that is the basis of the **predicate**, the verb along with its modifiers.

Having a subject and a predicate distinguishes clauses from phrases, which have a subject but not a predicate, or a predicate but not a subject:

SUBJECT WITHOUT PREDICATE	**the stock market indexes**
PREDICATE WITHOUT SUBJECT	**rose sharply**
CLAUSE	**The stock market indexes rose sharply.**

23f.1 INDEPENDENT CLAUSES

An **independent clause** is so named because it can stand alone as a sentence. An independent clause can be brief or lengthy:

> Go!
> Karen rested.
> Buenos Aires is the capital of Argentina.
> The *Ramayana,* a classic of Sanskrit literature, was written in India in the third century B.C.E.

The third and fourth examples are longer than the first two, but all of the examples include a subject and a predicate. (In the first example, an imperative sentence, the subject—*you*—is implied.)

23f.2 DEPENDENT CLAUSES

A dependent (subordinate) clause differs from an independent clause; it cannot stand alone as a sentence. A dependent clause by itself is a **sentence fragment** (see Chapter 24). Dependent clauses consist of four types: noun clauses, adjective (relative) clauses, adverb clauses, and elliptical clauses.

1. **Noun clauses** begin with *how, that, what, whatever, when, where, whether, which, whichever, who, whoever, whom, whomever, whose,* or *why.* The resulting clause functions as a subject or object:

SUBJECT	**How a two-year-old could program a VCR** is a mystery.
DIRECT OBJECT	I wish Mike would watch **what he is doing.**
OBJECT OF PREPOSITION	We decided to stop at **whichever gas station was closest.**

2. **Adjective (relative)** clauses begin with **relative pronouns** (*that, which, who, whom, whose*) and function as adjectives, modifying nouns and pronouns:

   She is the woman **who was falsely accused of murder.**
   Here is the couple **whose baggage was lost.**
   The Italian and English sonnet forms, **which were developed during the Renaissance,** both contain fourteen lines.

3. **Adverb clauses**, which function as adverbs, begin with a subordinating conjunction, such as *after, although, as soon as, because, in order to, until,* or *when.* (For a more extensive list of subordinating conjunctions, see page 656 in this chapter.)

ADVERB CLAUSE	**After the mechanic fixed the radiator**

   As with other dependent clauses, in an adverb clause, something is missing—the rest of the sentence:

   After the mechanic fixed the radiator, the car was ready to roll.

4. In **elliptical clauses**, a word or words are not present, but the meaning is obvious anyway. Normally, elliptical clauses appear in comparisons:

   Tariq has more money **than I** [have money].
   Bob is as rich **as Geena** [is rich].

gr 23f

EXERCISE 23.3

In the following sentences, underline each dependent clause. Then identify the clause as (1) a noun clause, (2) an adjective clause, (3) an adverb clause, or (4) an elliptical clause.

1. Whoever built this house must have had the plans upside down when he first started.
2. My uncle is a man who was once famous for his yodeling skills.
3. After you finish backing up the hard drive, see if you can find out who was responsible for opening that infected e-mail.
4. Whenever you want to eat lunch is all right with me.
5. When Richard bought his new car, he got a five-year loan because he wanted to keep his payments low.
6. Some financial advisors are known for pushing whichever mutual fund has the highest commission.

EXERCISE 23.3
1. Whoever built this house (1); when he first started (3)
2. who was once famous for his yodeling skills (2)
3. After you finish backing up the hard drive (3); who was responsible for opening that infected e-mail (1)
4. Whenever you want to eat lunch (1)
5. When Richard bought his new car (3); because he wanted to keep his payments low (3)
6. whichever mutual fund has the highest commission (1)

7. as tall as Jared (4)
8. before you come in the house (3)
9. that was stolen in the 1975 burglary (2)
10. so that his overworked father wouldn't have to do the chore on Saturday (3)

7. I know Gene is tall, but is he as tall as Jared?
8. Take off your work boots before you come in the house.
9. This is the painting that was stolen in the 1975 burglary.
10. Robert cleaned the gutters so that his overworked father wouldn't have to do the chore on Saturday.

SENTENCE TYPES

Sentences can be classified according to purpose:

DECLARATIVE	**The officer asked for Jana's driver's license. [states a fact or an opinion]**
INTERROGATIVE	**May I see your driver's license? [asks a question]**
IMPERATIVE	**Give me your driver's license. [gives an order/direction or makes a request]**
EXCLAMATORY	**Oh, my gosh, I have lost my driver's license! [expresses strong emotion or emphasis]**

Within each type, the way that you construct a sentence affects how your reader processes your intended meaning. Your aim is to emphasize the parts of the sentence that are most important and to create sentence variety. Doing so will help communicate your message better and keep your reader's interest.

1. A **simple sentence** contains one main (independent) clause, but it may contain phrases as well. The main clause in the following sentence is highlighted:

   Bordering Honduras and Costa Rica, **Nicaragua is located in Central America.**

2. A **compound sentence** contains two main (independent) clauses connected by a coordinating conjunction (*and, but, for, nor, or, yet, so*) or by a semicolon:

   Some Nicaraguans work in gold and tungsten mines, **but** most are farmers.

3. A **complex sentence** contains a main (independent) clause and at least one subordinate (dependent) clause. In the following sentence, the subordinate clause is highlighted:

   Although Nicaragua had been part of Guatemala and then of the Mexican Empire, it became a republic in 1838.

4. A **compound/complex sentence** contains two main (independent) clauses and at least one subordinate (dependent) clause:

   i.c. i.c.
   Anastasio Somoza took power in 1937, and he continued to rule until 1979,

   d.c.
   when his regime was overthrown by the Sandinista National Liberation Front.

In this sentence, two independent clauses are followed by a dependent clause.

23g CREATING EMPHASIS AND VARIETY: COMPOUND SENTENCES

Simple sentences can be used to convey information effectively, but a steady diet of them will make it difficult for you to emphasize the ideas you want to stress. More important, it will bore your readers. You need to be able to use compound sentences for emphasis and variety. Here are three main ways to join two independent clauses to make a compound sentence: (1) comma plus coordinating conjunction, (2) semicolon alone, and (3) semicolon plus conjunctive adverb or transitional expression:

> The interstate was flooded, **and** the side streets were slick.
> Mark hates yearly reviews; Gail also hates them.
> My relatives are visiting this evening; **consequently,** I need to leave work early.

All three methods work, but which one is best? It depends on context. Using a comma plus a coordinating conjunction is frequently effective. However, some stylists see this technique as a bit too informal to depend on in academic writing. There is a second problem as well: the seven coordinating conjunctions convey a limited range of meaning. Note the problem in the following sentence:

> Andrew was furious about the errors in his credit-card statement, **and** the statement got to him a week late.

Here, the information is adequately conveyed, but only adequately; emphasis is lost. The sentence works much better if a conjunctive adverb is used in place of the coordinating conjunction:

> Andrew was furious about the errors in his credit-card statement; **moreover,** the statement got to him a week late.

Conjunctive adverbs and other transitional expressions have a greater range of meaning than do the coordinating conjunctions; therefore, they allow you to write sentences that are much more focused and precise. (See Chapter 24, page 663, for a list of conjunctive adverbs and transitional expressions.)

For more on using compound sentences in your writing, see Chapter 5.

EXERCISE 23.4

Combine each of the following pairs of sentences by using a comma plus a coordinating conjunction, a semicolon, or a semicolon plus a conjunctive adverb or other transitional expression. Be prepared to defend your choice. You can find examples of coordinating conjunctions, conjunctive adverbs, and transitional expressions in Chapter 24, page 663.

1. Laura was sad. Her friend David was being transferred across the country.
2. The first car we looked at cost $32,000. The next model was only $17,500.
3. This college has a lot of problems. The parking situation is terrible.
4. We won't need you anymore today. Make sure that you check in tomorrow.
5. The software instructions seemed clear enough. The program wouldn't come up on my screen.

EXERCISE 23.4 Responses will vary. The following are suggestions:

1. Laura was sad, for her friend David was being transferred across the country.
2. The first car we looked at cost $32,000; the next model was only $17,500.
3. This college has a lot of problems; for example, the parking situation is terrible.
4. We won't need you anymore today, but make sure that you check in tomorrow.
5. The software instructions seemed clear enough; nonetheless, the program wouldn't come up on my screen.

6. The plane was overbooked, so Mr. Robbins decided to take the airline up on its offer for discounts.
7. Ed opened the door, and he noticed that the office seemed strangely quiet.
8. Andrea is not happy today; she's just gotten some bad news about her tax return.
9. Jane cleaned off her desk; then she started to answer her e-mail.
10. My nephew likes swimming; on the other hand, his sister hates it.

gr 23h

6. The plane was overbooked. Mr. Robbins decided to take the airline up on its offer for discounts.
7. Ed opened the door. He noticed that the office seemed strangely quiet.
8. Andrea is not happy today. She's just gotten some bad news about her tax return.
9. Jane cleaned off her desk. She started to answer her e-mail.
10. My nephew likes swimming. His sister hates it.

23h CREATING EMPHASIS AND VARIETY THROUGH SUBORDINATION

Consider the following sentence:

John opened his mail, and he got a bad shock.

This is a **balanced** sentence, a compound sentence in which two actions (John *opened his mail* and *he got a bad shock*) receive equal weight. But are those two actions equal? Surely, the most important information here is in the second clause. People open their mail six days a week, but they are usually not shocked by its contents. To emphasize the information in the second clause, the writer needs to use **subordination:**

When John opened his mail, he got a bad shock.

An even more effective choice is to place the independent clause first:

John got a bad shock **when** he opened his mail.

Note that all three sentences are grammatically correct; however, the second and third sentences communicate their meaning more accurately and effectively.

You can introduce a subordinate clause with a subordinating conjunction or a relative pronoun.

Subordinating Conjunctions	**Relative Pronouns**
after	that
although	what
as	whatever
because	which
before	whichever
even if	who
even though	whoever
if	whom
in order that	whomever
once	whose
provided that	
rather than	

Subordinating Conjunctions (cont.)

since
so that
so (that)
that
though
unless
until
when
whenever
where
whereas
wherever
whether
while

Because we failed to make reservations, we were not able to get a table.
He will not march in the graduation line **unless he passes chemistry.**
When he was a young man, my father owned a bookstore.
The soldiers **who were honored last night** were part of an airborne division.

In addition to indicating on which idea or part of the sentence you want to place emphasis, subordination can also supply extra information about a subject. In the following sentence, the subordinate clause is highlighted:

Joan was eventually transferred to St. Louis, **which was at least near the town where her sister lived.**

However, note that too much subordination weakens a sentence:

Michael walked to his office, ***which*** **is on Third Street,** ***which*** **is the oldest paved street in the city,** ***which*** **itself is the fourth-oldest municipality in the state.**

Readers of this sentence may feel as though they are being led through doorway after doorway for no purpose. Subordination should not be used to attach stray thoughts or extra facts; rather, it should establish focus and add valuable—albeit secondary—information.

For more on using subordination for variety and emphasis, see Chapter 5.

EXERCISE 23.5 Responses will vary. The following are suggestions:
1. Haiti and the Dominican Republic share Hispaniola, which is a subtropical island in the West Indies.
2. The Delaware Indians, who spoke the Algonquian language, lived in the woodlands of the eastern United States.
3. Because he disagreed with many of the practices of the Roman Catholic church, Martin Luther broke with Rome and founded a sect of Protestantism that bears his name.
4. The Persian Wars of the fifth century B.C.E., which began when the cities of Ionia revolted against Darius I, lasted for over fifty years and resulted in a victory for the Greek city-states.
5. Romulus, who was the legendary founder of Rome, and his twin brother, Remus, were suckled by a she-wolf and were later raised by a shepherd.

EXERCISE 23.5

Combine the sentences in each item by using subordination. You may want to rearrange details as you do so.

1. Hispaniola is a subtropical island in the West Indies. Haiti and the Dominican Republic share the island.

MORE OPTIONS ONLINE
For more exercises, go to **www.mhhe.com/writingtoday**.

gr 23h

2. The Delaware Indians lived in the woodlands of the eastern United States. They spoke the Algonquian language.
3. Martin Luther disagreed with many of the practices of the Roman Catholic church. He broke with Rome and founded a sect of Protestantism that bears his name.
4. The Persian Wars of the fifth century B.C.E. lasted for over fifty years and resulted in a victory for the Greek city-states. They began when the cities of Ionia revolted against Darius I.
5. Romulus was the legendary founder of Rome. He and his twin brother, Remus, were suckled by a she-wolf and were later raised by a shepherd.

CHAPTER 24

MAJOR SENTENCE ERRORS

The first two sections of this chapter concentrate on three of the most damaging sentence-level errors. To receive good grades on college essays, you must avoid sentence fragments, fused sentences, and comma splices. The last section of this chapter discusses three other sentence-level issues: parallelism, appropriate comparisons, and mixed constructions.

CLASSROOM HINT
More and more, college faculty are having to discuss these major sentence errors in class. Schedule some time early in the term to go over this chapter.

frag
24a

MORE OPTIONS ONLINE
If you would like to test your knowledge of major sentence errors before reading this chapter, go to **www.mhhe.com/writingtoday**.

SENTENCE FRAGMENTS

As its name suggests, a **sentence fragment** is an incomplete sentence; it "acts" as a sentence, but it is missing a subject, a verb, or a complete thought.

24a PHRASES AS FRAGMENTS

A phrase, by definition, cannot be a complete sentence. Here are some typical phrasal fragments:

Incomplete Verb Form

FRAGMENT The doctor **thinking** that the patient looked better.

REVISED The doctor **was thinking** that the patient looked better.

Prepositional Phrase Used as Sentence

FRAGMENT You'll find the hammer out back. **Beside the rotary saw.**

REVISED You'll find the hammer out back, beside the rotary saw.

Infinitive Phrase Used as Sentence

FRAGMENT We drove to town. **To buy a new hammer.**

REVISED We drove to town to buy a new hammer.

"Illustration" Phrase Used as Sentence

FRAGMENT Alcoholics can develop many health problems. **For example, cirrhosis of the liver.**

REVISED Alcoholics can develop many health problems—for example, cirrhosis of the liver.

FRAGMENT They were troubled by the motel's location. **Also, the condition of the room they were shown.**

REVISED They were troubled by the motel's location and also by the condition of the room they were shown.

As you can see, many fragments are phrases that clearly belong with an adjacent sentence but that are acting as stand-alone sentences:

FRAGMENT **Wishing that finals week were over.** Jan reluctantly turned back to her studies.

FRAGMENT **To meet our June 1 deadline.** We've got to work hard during the next two weeks.

FRAGMENT **Near the end of its useful life.** The old bridge seemed to sag as heavy trucks strained its rotted timbers.

FRAGMENT Rosa ran to hug her child. **Her eyes filling with tears.**

Of course, you can always correct such fragments by making complete sentences out of them:

CORRECT **Jan wished that finals week were over. She reluctantly turned back to her studies.**

However, a steady diet of such short, choppy thoughts gets boring. Try these other remedies as well:

1. **Treat the fragments as elements of the adjacent sentences:**

    CORRECT **Wishing that finals week were over, Jan reluctantly turned back to her studies.**

    CORRECT **To meet our June 1 deadline, we've got to work overtime during the next two weeks.**

    CORRECT **Near the end of its useful life, the old bridge seemed to sag as heavy trucks strained its rotted timbers.**

    CORRECT **Rosa ran to hug her child, her eyes filling with tears.**

2. **Turn the fragments into subordinate (dependent) clauses and combine them with the sentences they adjoin:**

    CORRECT **Although** she wished finals week were over, Jan reluctantly turned back to her studies.

    CORRECT We've got to work overtime during the next two weeks **if** we are going to meet our June 1 deadline.

    CORRECT **Because** the old bridge was near the end of its useful life, it seemed to sag as heavy trucks strained its rotted timbers.

    CORRECT **As** Rosa's eyes filled with tears, she ran to hug her child.

3. **Turn the fragments into independent (main) clauses and combine them with the sentence they adjoin to make a compound sentence:**

    CORRECT **Jan wished that finals week were over; nonetheless, she reluctantly turned back to her studies.**

    CORRECT **We have to meet our June 1 deadline, so we've got to work overtime during the next two weeks.**

    CORRECT **The old bridge was near the end of its useful life, and it seemed to sag as heavy trucks strained its rotted timbers.**

    CORRECT **Rosa's eyes filled with tears; she ran to hug her child.**

Students frequently write phrasal fragments because they erroneously believe that long sentences are "run-ons" and therefore wrong. But long sentences are just that: long sentences. They may be grammatically correct or incorrect depending on how they're written and punctuated, not depending on their length.

Note that revising some phrasal fragments involves more than merely attaching the phrase to a nearby sentence:

EXERCISE 24.1
Responses will vary. The following are suggestions:
1. Maria decided to wait before buying a new computer because she hoped to find one on sale after Christmas.
2. Believing that tomatoes were poisonous, many people in the nineteenth century refused to eat them.
3. The afternoon rain caused traffic back-ups all over Ft. Lauderdale, a common occurrence there.
4. Will and Jennifer went to the Humane Society shelter, adopted a Siamese kitten, and then went home.
5. Samantha skied carefully down the icy slope to maintain her balance and avoid falling.
6. Many people who are planning a camping trip don't buy sufficient supplies; for instance, they neglect to buy insect repellent and rain gear.
7. Believing that they had extinguished the blaze, the firefighters left the scene.
8. Marisa was considering some important issues, such as whether to quit her job and whether to apply for more school loans.
9. Plymouth is a few miles from here, just past Martinsville.
10. The bank will lend us all we need minus about four thousand dollars, which is a troublesome situation, if I do say so myself.

FRAGMENT	The Secret Service is located in Washington, D.C. **A branch of Alcohol, Tobacco, and Firearms.**
INCORRECT REVISION	The Secret Service is located in Washington, D.C., a branch of Alcohol, Tobacco, and Firearms.

The fragment is now a modifier, but it is in the wrong position, making the reader wonder how Washington, D.C., could be a branch of a federal agency. The writer needs to place the modifier near the word or words it describes.

CORRECT REVISION	The Secret Service, a branch of Alcohol, Tobacco, and Firearms, is located in Washington, D.C.

For more on misplaced modifiers, see 27a.

EXERCISE 24.1

In each of the following pairs of items, one is a complete sentence; the other is a fragment. Combine them to eliminate the fragment. You may need to add, delete, or reorder words.

1. Maria decided to wait before buying a new computer. Hoping to find one on sale after Christmas.
2. Believing that tomatoes were poisonous. Many people in the nineteenth century refused to eat them.
3. The afternoon rain caused traffic back-ups all over Ft. Lauderdale. A common occurrence there.
4. Will and Jennifer went to the Humane Society shelter and then went home. Having adopted a Siamese kitten.
5. Samantha skied carefully down the icy slope. To maintain her balance and avoiding falling.
6. Many people who are planning a camping trip don't buy sufficient supplies. For instance, insect repellent and rain gear.
7. The firefighters left the scene. Believing that they had extinguished the blaze.
8. Marisa was considering some important issues. Such as whether to quit her job and whether to apply for more school loans.
9. Plymouth is a few miles from here. Just past Martinsville.
10. The bank will lend us all we need minus about four thousand dollars. A troublesome situation, if I do say so myself.

24b DEPENDENT CLAUSES AS FRAGMENTS

In the box on pages 663–664, the subordinating conjunctions appear in the middle column. Any single-clause sentence, such as *She had danced all night,* can be changed to a dependent subordinate clause by placing one of these conjunctions before it:

> **after** she had danced all night
> **because** she had danced all night

even though she had danced all night
if she had danced all night

However, the resulting dependent clause is no longer a sentence and must be attached to an independent clause; if not, it is a fragment.

After she had danced all night, Vanessa slept for eight hours.
Vanessa was exhausted **because** she had danced all night.
Even though she had danced all night, Vanessa was able to complete a full day at work the next day.
If Vanessa had danced all night, she would not have gone to work the next day.

Sentence Connectors

Conjunctive Adverbs/ Transitional Expressions	Subordinating Conjunctions	Coordinating Conjunctions
accordingly	after	and
additionally	although	but
also	as	for
as an illustration	because	nor
at the same time	before	or
besides	even if	so
certainly	even though	yet
consequently	if	
conversely	in order that	
finally	once	
for example	provided that	
for instance	rather than	
furthermore	since	
hence	so that	
however	so (that)	
in addition	than	
in brief	that	
in conclusion	though	
in contrast	unless	
in short	until	
in summary	when	
in the same way	whenever	
indeed	where	
instead	whereas	
likewise	wherever	
meanwhile	whether	
moreover	while	
namely		
nevertheless		

Sentence Connectors (continued)

Conjunctive Adverbs/ Transitional Expressions
next
nonetheless
of course
on the other hand
otherwise
similarly
specifically
still
subsequently
then
therefore
thus
to be sure

Subordinate (dependent) clauses that begin with the relative pronouns *which, who, whom,* or *whose* can also be fragments unless they are connected to main clauses:

FRAGMENT **The method of measurement based on the meter is the metric system. Which was first adopted in France in 1899.**

CORRECT **The method of measurement based on the meter is the metric system, which was first adopted in France in 1899.**

FRAGMENT **In Norse mythology, the fates were known as the Norns. Who spun out the destinies of human beings.**

CORRECT **In Norse mythology, the fates were known as the Norns, who spun out the destinies of human beings.**

FRAGMENT **The Norns are probably related to the three witches. Whom we meet in Shakespeare's *MacBeth*.**

CORRECT **The Norns are probably related to the three witches whom we meet in Shakespeare's *MacBeth*.**

For more on relative clauses, see 23f. For help with punctuating sentences with subordinate clauses, see 28b and 28c.

An incorrectly used semicolon can cause what is sometimes called an **internal fragment:**

INCORRECT **Although the stadium is old; it has character.**

INCORRECT **Katie was close to tears; feeling that she had been manipulated.**

In each sentence, a semicolon has been used incorrectly in place of a comma. Keep this idea in mind: in such cases, a semicolon functions as an *internal period;* what comes before or after it must be an independent clause.

EXERCISE 24.2

Read each group of sentences below. Revise as needed to eliminate fragments.

1. The new classroom building was almost a year behind on its construction schedule. Because the contractor had submitted a timetable that was absurd.
2. Once Lucas realized his mistake. He called the branch office again. So that he could catch Ella Hassamin before closing time.
3. The language of the contract was difficult; although the summary at the end made the details clear.
4. I realized that I had been fooled again. After I opened the last envelope in the stack.
5. Whenever a production delay happens. Call the shift manager.
6. After losing his calculus text, missing a biology quiz, and getting a parking ticket, Cameron went home; feeling bitter.
7. The map was old; even though Tina had once lived in the area, the map didn't correspond to her memory of the place.
8. On Friday, the dealership refused to sell Bianca the new van. Even though they had worked out the details on Thursday. To avoid time delays on the busy weekend.
9. Lia married a man from Arkansas. Who owns seven office-supply stores.
10. New students at this university seem to be a bit overwhelmed; while sophomores have the air of those who have seen it all.
11. The front door is standing open. Which bothers me.
12. Eddie is a selfish young man. Whose sole purpose in life is to have fun.
13. Here is my great-grandfather's diary from the early twentieth century. Some of which is fascinating reading.
14. The new candidate for mayor is an interesting person. Who I think will give the incumbent a run for his money.
15. Lora was furious; because she had arrived before the financial aid office was supposed to close and found the door locked.

EXERCISE 24.2
Responses will vary. The following revisions are suggested:
1. The new classroom building was almost a year behind on its construction schedule because the contractor. . . .
2. Once Lucas realized his mistake, he called the branch office again so that he could. . . .
3. The language of the contract was difficult, although the summary. . . .
4. After I opened the last envelope in the stack, I realized. . . .
5. Whenever a production delay happens, call the shift manager.
6. After losing. . ., Cameron went home, feeling bitter.
7. Correct
8. On Friday, the dealership . . . new van even though they had worked out the details on Thursday to avoid time delays. . . .
9. Lia married a man from Arkansas who owns. . . .
10. New students at this university seem to be a bit overwhelmed while sophomores. . . .
11. The front door is standing open, which bothers me.
12. Eddie is a selfish young man, whose sole purpose. . . .
13. Here is . . . twentieth century, some of which. . . .
14. The new candidate for mayor is an interesting person, who I think. . . .
15. Lora was furious because she had arrived. . . .

24c INTENTIONAL FRAGMENTS

Professional writers who use **intentional fragments** know that they are breaking the rules, but they do so for dramatic effect. Advertisements often use this strategy. Nontheless, when you are writing for college courses, using intentional fragments can be risky. What you see as intentional may be considered an error by your instructor. However, you can be secure about using an intentional fragment when answering a rhetorical question (a question to which the answer is obvious). Such questions are usually asked to draw the reader into the text:

CORRECT **Should senior citizens be faced with new taxes? Of course not.**

Writing dialogue for a narrative essay might provide another context in which the use of intentional fragments would be acceptable. Otherwise, avoid fragments altogether in college writing.

EXERCISE 24.3
Responses will vary. The following is a suggested revision:
Martin joined the U.S. Navy to learn a trade and earn some money for college, which he dearly wanted to attend. Although he was short on funds, Martin had applied for scholarships, hoping to pay for college that way. He could get only about half of what he needed for school while his friend David got a free ride to a state university. Consequently, Martin spent four years in the Navy visiting different countries and meeting a variety of people, some of whom became his close friends. Therefore, although joining the Navy had not been Martin's first choice, it turned out to be a worthwhile experience both personally and financially.

EXERCISE 24.3

Rewrite the following paragraph to correct fragments.

Martin joined the U.S. Navy. To learn a trade and earn some money for college. Which he dearly wanted to attend. Although he was short on funds. Martin had applied for scholarships; hoping to pay for college that way. He could get only about half of what he needed for school. While his friend David got a free ride to a state university. Consequently, Martin spent four years in the Navy. Visiting different countries and meeting a variety of people. Some of whom became his close friends. Therefore, although joining the Navy had not been Martin's first choice. It turned out to be a worthwhile experience. Both personally and financially.

AVOIDING "RUN-ONS": FUSED SENTENCES AND COMMA SPLICES

A **fused sentence** occurs when two independent clauses are joined with no punctuation:

FUSED SENTENCE	**I may be wrong I may be right.**
FUSED SENTENCE	**Ed tried to buy a new car however he couldn't get decent financing.**

A **comma splice** occurs when two independent clauses are joined with a comma:

COMMA SPLICE	**I may be wrong, I may be right.**
COMMA SPLICE	**Ed tried to buy a new car, however he couldn't get decent financing.**

As you can see, fused sentences and comma splices are related. Although both are serious errors, they are easy to correct once you find them. The following sections discuss three methods for eliminating fused sentences and comma splices.

24d USE A "FULL STOP" (PERIOD, SEMICOLON, OR COLON) BETWEEN THE INDEPENDENT CLAUSES.

1. If the two independent clauses are not closely related, use a period and form two sentences:

FUSED SENTENCE **Mark drove in from seventy miles away Zoe brought salmon quesadillas.**

REVISED **Mark drove in from seventy miles away. Zoe brought salmon quesadillas.**

COMMA SPLICE **The site-exploration team arrived at the hotel, meanwhile, the company's officers made plans that would change the scope of the project.**

REVISED **The site-exploration team arrived at the hotel. Meanwhile, the company's officers made plans that would change the scope of the project.**

Note that in the last sentence, the presence of the transitional adverb *meanwhile* has nothing to do with the sentence's being a comma splice. Using this transitional word between the two clauses helps the reader process the sentence, but it doesn't cause or prevent the comma splice.

2. If the two independent clauses are closely related, connect them with a semicolon:

FUSED SENTENCE **Zoe brought salmon quesadillas Brian made chicken.**

REVISED **Zoe brought salmon quesadillas; Brian made chicken.**

COMMA SPLICE **Zoe hates chicken, Brian won't eat fish.**

REVISED **Zoe hates chicken; Brian won't eat fish.**

3. If the ideas in the two independent clauses are closely related but a transition is needed, connect the two clauses with a semicolon plus a conjunctive adverb/transitional expression followed by a comma:

FUSED SENTENCE **Zoe is a frequent guest however, we rarely see Mark.**

REVISED **Zoe is a frequent guest;** however, **we rarely see Mark.**

COMMA SPLICE **Mark drove in from far away, Zoe lived next door.**

REVISED **Mark drove in from far away; however, Zoe lived next door.**

You can find a list of conjunctive adverbs/transitions in the box on page 663.

4. If the idea in the second clause is introduced by the first or is caused by the first, consider connecting them with a colon. *Use this method sparingly.*

FUSED SENTENCE **Now came the moment we all feared the building exploded and collapsed.**

REVISED **Now came the moment we all feared: the building exploded and collapsed.**

COMMA SPLICE **Juan knew one thing, he had to find a way out of his deathtrap job.**

REVISED **Juan knew one thing: he had to find a way out of his deathtrap job.**

EXERCISE 24.4
Responses will vary. The following revisions are suggested:
1. (comma splice) The company manufactures . . . home appliances; it also offers. . . .
2. (comma splice) Vacuum the carpet; then mop the floor.
3. (fused) It's not that Jason lacks talent. It's that. . . !
4. (comma splice) The door opened to admit the last person we wanted to see: Sergeant Albertson stood there with a sadistic grin as he watched our discomfort.
5. (fused) We had hoped to take a big vacation this summer; however, our finances didn't really allow us to do so.

fs/cs 24e

EXERCISE 24.4

The following sentences are either comma splices or fused sentences. First, identify the error. Next, revise the sentence by using a period, a semicolon, or a colon. Be prepared to justify your choice of revision method.

1. The company manufactures many interesting home appliances, it also offers factory tours.
2. Vacuum the carpet, then mop the floor.
3. It's not that Jason lacks talent it's that he is late for work three days out of four!
4. The door opened to admit the last person we wanted to see, Sergeant Albertson stood there with a sadistic grin as he watched our discomfort.
5. We had hoped to take a big vacation this summer however, our finances didn't really allow us to do so.

24e USE A COMMA AND COORDINATING CONJUNCTION (*AND, BUT, FOR, NOR, OR, SO, YET*) TO CONNECT THE TWO INDEPENDENT CLAUSES.

FUSED SENTENCE	**Supper wasn't ready my sister practiced her piano lesson.**
REVISED	**Supper wasn't ready, so my sister practiced her piano lesson.**
COMMA SPLICE	**Ed thought the film was wonderful, Maria didn't agree.**
REVISED	**Ed thought the film was wonderful, but Maria didn't agree.**

Note that the proper pattern is always comma plus coordinating conjunction.

Although using a coordinating conjunction is an easy way to fix a comma splice or fused sentence, remember that such connectors describe a limited number of relationships. Overusing this technique can (1) give your writing a monotonous rhythm and (2) fail to express subtle shades of meaning. Frequently, using a semicolon plus a transitional expression produces a more accurate sentence. However, when the context is appropriate, a comma plus a coordinating conjunction works well.

EXERCISE 24.5 Responses will vary. The following revisions are suggested:
1. (comma splice) Tuesday was a gloomy day, and Wednesday was equally bad.
2. (fused) Vito loves bananas, but Eddie hates them.
3. (comma splice) When did you find out, and why didn't you tell me?
4. (comma splice) James committed the crime, or James is lying.
5. (fused) We can't go outside, so let's watch a video.

EXERCISE 24.5

The following sentences are either comma splices or fused sentences. First, identify the error. Next, revise the sentence by adding the appropriate coordinating conjunction preceded by a comma if one is not already present.

1. Tuesday was a gloomy day, Wednesday was equally bad.
2. Vito loves bananas Eddie hates them.
3. When did you find out, why didn't you tell me?
4. James committed the crime, James is lying.
5. We can't go outside let's watch a video.

24f CHANGE ONE OF THE TWO INDEPENDENT CLAUSES TO A DEPENDENT CLAUSE OR TO A PHRASE.

1. **Use subordination.** Subordination reduces one of the main (independent) clauses to a subordinate (dependent) clause. You can subordinate a clause by using one of the subordinating conjunctions from the box that lists sentence connectors on pages 663–664.

FUSED SENTENCE — Enrico left the party early he wasn't in the mood to carouse.

REVISED — Enrico left the party early **because** he wasn't in the mood to carouse.

COMMA SPLICE — Anita studied very hard, she still made a low score on the chemistry exam.

REVISED — **Although** Anita studied very hard, she still made a low score on the chemistry exam.

REVISED — Anita studied very hard **although** she still made a low score on the chemistry exam.

Note in the last revised sentence that when a dependent clause follows an independent clause, a comma is usually not necessary. (For more on commas, see Chapter 28.)

Another way to use subordination is to turn one of the main clauses into a relative clause—a clause introduced by *that, which, who, whom,* or *whose.*

FUSED SENTENCE — The Toltec arrived in Meso-America even before the Aztec they are among the first inhabitants of Mexico.

REVISED — The Toltec, **who** arrived in Mexico even before the Aztec, are among the first inhabitants of Mexico.

2. **Change one of the independent clauses into a phrase:**

COMMA SPLICE — John believes he will do better in economics, he plans to change his major.

REVISED — **Believing** that he will do better in economics, John plans to change his major.

FUSED SENTENCE — On a winter day, we watched the eagles they soared over the Mississippi River.

REVISED — On a winter day, we watched the eagles **soaring** over the Mississippi River.

Note that when the phrase follows the independent clause, a comma is usually not necessary. (See Chapter 28 for more help with commas.)

EXERCISE 24.6

The following sentences are either comma splices or fused sentences. First, identify the error. Next, use one of the strategies covered in this section to revise the sentence.

fs/cs 24f

EXERCISE 24.6 Responses will vary. The following revisions are suggested:
1. (comma splice) Although important, history is not as crucial. . . .
2. (fused) The flood that tore through the valley created. . . .
3. (fused) Danny washed his car and took it for a spin.
4. (comma splice) This is my cat, a very strange creature.
5. (fused) When tax time is over, I'll feel. . . .
6. (comma splice) Walston Industries, which manufactures kites, gliders, and rockets, is. . . .
7. (fused) Reviewing her options once more, Karen made her decision.
8. (comma splice) This useful Web site has an enormous number of links.
9. (comma splice) Leo believed his upcoming work schedule and his course assignment deadlines were hopeless.
10. (comma splice) Interested in Web page design, Yoshi took a class. . . .

EXERCISE 24.7 Responses will vary. The following revisions are suggested:
1. FS Cheating has become a major issue for American colleges; therefore, various security. . . .
2. C
3. CS Load the software; then run the start-up disk.
4. CS Rain can be a blessing; acid rain, however, is. . . .
5. FS Although Ramona . . . recital, she. . . .
6. CS What brand is that, and where. . .?
7. CS The professor is . . . scholar: she has the. . . .
8. FS That's not a squirrel; it's a rat!
9. C
10. CS This is not . . . to see; it's a question of. . . .

fs/cs 24f

1. History is important, history is not as crucial as some would have us believe.
2. The flood tore through the valley it created a new lake near Walston Road.
3. Danny washed his car he took it for a spin.
4. This is my cat, he is a very strange creature.
5. Tax time is over I'll feel more like a human being again.
6. Walston Industries is a very profitable company, it manufactures kites, gliders, and rockets.
7. Karen reviewed her options once more she made her decision.
8. This Web site is quite useful, it has an enormous number of links.
9. Leo believed his upcoming work schedule was hopeless, he felt that his course assignment deadlines weren't much better.
10. Yoshi was interested in Web page design, Yoshi took a class at the local technical college.

Choosing a revision strategy to eliminate comma splices and fused sentences depends upon context. One method will be clearly superior to another in any given situation. Exercise 24.7 asks you to find the best revision method for each defective sentence.

EXERCISE 24.7

Mark each of the following sentences **C** (correct), **CS** (comma splice), or **FS** (fused sentence). Then choose the best strategy to revise each comma splice and fused sentence. Be prepared to defend your decision.

1. Cheating has become a major issue for American colleges therefore various security strategies are being studied.
2. Mammals are warm-blooded whereas reptiles are not.
3. Load the software, then run the start-up disk.
4. Rain can be a blessing, acid rain, however, is something of a mixed blessing.
5. Ramona couldn't attend her son's recital she certainly wanted to.
6. What brand is that, where did you buy it?
7. The professor is a very well-known scholar, she has the respect of her peers throughout the world.
8. That's not a squirrel it's a rat!
9. Sarah shut down her laptop and cleaned out her desk; thus, she said goodbye to seven years at Wentworth Industries.
10. This is not a question of which movie we want to see, it's a question of whether we really want to leave the house in this weather.

COMBINATION EXERCISE

The following passage contains fragments, comma splices, and fused sentences. Rewrite the passage to correct these problems by using the strategies you have learned in this chapter. Reword and combine sentences as needed.

The world has known many calendars. Methods by which to track the passage of time. Today, most of the world uses the Gregorian calendar for business purposes and for conducting international affairs. Indeed, with its twelve months from January to December. This solar calendar is probably the most widely known method of tracking days, weeks, months, and years, it contains 365.25 days per year. One day being added every fourth or leap year. Years in the Gregorian calendar are counted from the birth of Christ, with B.C. (the abbreviation for "Before Christ") being added to years that preceded Christ's birth. A.D. (the Latin abbreviation for "Year of our Lord") being added to years that follow it.

The Gregorian calendar was established in 1583 during the papacy of Gregory III. Scientists and historians realized that the Julian calendar, then in use, was not accurate and needed to be revised, named after the Roman general Julius Caesar, it had been used in Europe since 45 B.C. While the Gregorian calendar was more accurate, it did not receive acceptance throughout Europe for many years, in fact, it was not adopted by the British Empire until 1752. Sweden followed suit in 1753, however, numerous countries in eastern Europe did not adopt the Gregorian calendar until the early twentieth century. In many countries, ordinary people continued to follow the Julian calendar long after the Gregorian calendar had been introduced, this resulted in people using different dates for the same event. In such cases. Events that were recorded according to the Julian method were followed by O.S. ("Old Style") those recorded according to the Gregorian calendar were followed by N.S. ("New Style").

Like the Gregorian calendar, first used in Christian countries and now adopted worldwide. The Islamic calendar has twelve months, it begins in Muhharram and ends with Dhu-al Hijjah. Unlike its European counterpart, however, the Islamic calendar is a lunar instrument, each month begins when the lunar crescent is first seen after the new moon. Years in the Islamic calendar are counted beginning from the Hijra, this is a term referring to the flight of Mohammed to Mecca, whose date corresponds to the year 622 A.D. in the Christian calendar, therefore, dates in the Muslim world are followed by an abbreviation signifying "year of the Hijra." It is interesting to note that because the Christian calendar is based on the movements of the sun and the Islamic calendar is based on the movements of the moon. The latter is about eleven days shorter.

The Jewish calendar has thirteen months, beginning with Nissan and ending with Adar II. With the number of days in each month varying from 29 to 30. Unlike the first month in the Christian calendar, which comes in the winter in northern latitudes. Nissan occurs in the spring. The season of Passover, an important Jewish holiday. The Jewish New Year falls in the seventh month, Tishri, it is at that time that the number of the year advances. The numbering of years in the Jewish calendar is based upon the number of years since the Creation, as recorded in the Scriptures when referring to years in the Gregorian calendar, however, the Jews do not use A.D. or B.C. instead they attach B.C.E. ("before the common era") and C.E. ("the common era") to their dates.

CLASSROOM HINT This is a difficult exercise. You might want to do one or two paragraphs of this exercise in class.

COMBINATION EXERCISE Responses will vary. The following revisions are suggested:

The world has known many calendars, methods by which . . . time. . . . Indeed, with its twelve months from January to December, this solar calendar . . . and years. It contains 365.25 days per year, one day being added every fourth or leap year. Years in the Gregorian calendar are counted from the birth of Christ, . . . birth and A.D. (the Latin abbreviation for "Year of our Lord") having added to years that follow it.

The Gregorian calendar. . . . Scientists and historians realized that the Julian calendar, . . . needed to be revised. . . . Named after the Roman general Julius Caesar, it had been used in Europe since 45 B.C. While the Gregorian calendar . . . for many years. In fact, it was not adopted by the British Empire until 1752. Sweden followed suit in 1753; however, numerous countries in eastern Europe . . . early twentieth century. In many countries, ordinary people . . . introduced. This resulted . . . event. In such cases, events . . . O.S. ("Old Style"); those recorded . . . N.S. ("New Style").

Like the Gregorian calendar, . . . worldwide, the Islamic calendar has twelve months. It begins. . . . Unlike its European counterpart, however, the Islamic calendar is a lunar instrument: each month . . . moon. Years . . . the Hijra. This is a term . . . in the Christian calendar. Therefore, dates . . . "year of the Hijra." It is interesting . . . moon, the latter is . . . shorter.

The Jewish calendar . . . Adar II, with the number . . . 30. Unlike . . . latitudes, Nissan occurs in the spring, the season . . . holiday. The Jewish New Year falls in the seventh month, Tishri. It is . . . advances. The numbering . . . the Scriptures. When referring . . . B.C. Instead they attach B.C.E. ("before the common era") and C.E. ("the common era") to their dates.

fs/cs

24f

OTHER SENTENCE-LEVEL PROBLEMS

24g PROBLEMS WITH PARALLELISM

When you give equal emphasis to two or more things, actions, ideas, or activities, use **parallel** wording: nouns with nouns, verbs with verbs, prepositional phrases with prepositional phrases, and so forth. A sentence that uses parallel structures is both rhythmic and effective. Note the difference between the following examples:

NOT PARALLEL	**Jessica likes several outdoor activities, including swimming, hiking, and to sail.**
PARALLEL	**Jessica likes several outdoor activities, including swimming, hiking, and sailing.**

For a reader, the second sentence is more effective than the first, which is awkward. The first sentence uses two gerunds followed by an infinitive (*to sail*). The second, parallel sentence uses three gerunds (*swimming, hiking, sailing*). Most of the time, you can avoid writing sentences like the first one without a great deal of trouble. The following guidelines will help:

1. Group nouns with nouns:

NOT PARALLEL	**Edwin has arthritis, and he also suffers from a cracked vertebra as well as a nerve that was pinched.**
PARALLEL NOUNS	**Edwin has arthritis, a cracked vertebra, and a pinched nerve.**

2. Group verbs with verbs:

NOT PARALLEL	**At the conference, our project team went to workshops, had a comparison of notes, and then dinner.**
PARALLEL VERBS	**At the conference, our project team went to workshops, compared notes, and then ate dinner.**

3. Group verbals (infinitives, gerunds, and participles) with the same kind of verbals:

NOT PARALLEL	**On the weekends, the district manager likes to walk, golfing, and plays cards.**
PARALLEL INFINITIVES	**On the weekends, the district manager likes to walk, to golf, and to play cards.**
NOT PARALLEL	**Jenn loves dancing, partying, and to go out on the town.**
PARALLEL GERUNDS	**Jenn loves dancing, partying, and going out on the town.**

4. **Group prepositional phrases with prepositional phrases:**

NOT PARALLEL	**You can find these vases in Austin and San Antonio, and you can also find them in Fort Worth.**
PARALLEL PREPOSITIONAL PHRASES	**You can find these vases in Austin, in San Antonio, and in Fort Worth.**

5. **Be careful with correlative conjunctions.** Correlative conjunctions are pairs of conjunctions (*both/and, not only/but also, either/or, neither/nor*) that emphasize relationships. (For more on correlative conjunctions, see 22f.) Note the following sentence:

NOT PARALLEL	**Failing to dress appropriately for the weather can not only ruin a person's day but also leads to health problems.**

The two main verbs—*ruin* and *leads*—are not parallel. Now note the revision:

PARALLEL	**Failing to dress for the weather can not only ruin a person's day but can also lead to health problems.**

When you use a pair of correlative conjunctions, make sure that you use parallel structures within the elements they connect.

For more on parallelism, see Chapter 5.

com
24h

24h AVOIDING FAULTY COMPARISONS

Faulty comparisons are in many ways a kind of faulty parallelism. In an inexact comparison, the writer is sometimes trying to compare two things that cannot be logically compared:

INCORRECT	**The new software company has sold more of its e-mail virus patches than any other software company.**

E-mail virus patches are not comparable to *any other software company.* Note the revision:

CORRECT	**The new software company's e-mail virus patches have sold better than those of any other software company.**

Faulty comparisons can also be the result of an omitted word:

INCORRECT	**Jenkins does more work than any member of her division.**

Isn't Jenkins *in* her division? Adding a word clears the matter up:

CORRECT	**Jenkins does more work than any other member of her division.**

Some faulty comparisons are truly ambiguous:

INCORRECT	**Some people use Internet searches more than librarians.**
CORRECT	**Some people use Internet searches more than librarians do.**
ALSO CORRECT	**Some people use Internet searches more than they consult librarians.**

As Chapter 5 discusses, avoid omitting key words, especially in comparisons.

24i AVOIDING MIXED CONSTRUCTIONS

In a **mixed construction**, the writer starts a sentence with a structure that leads the reader to expect a particular type of sentence. Then, however, the writer goes in a different direction, leaving the reader baffled: the two parts of the sentence are not compatible. Note the following examples:

INCORRECT	**Because he broke his ankle was the reason that Christian gave up basketball.**
REVISED	**Because he broke his ankle, Christian gave up basketball.**
INCORRECT	**The reason for my anger is because of your habitual lack of punctuality.**
CORRECT	**The reason for my anger is your habitual lack of punctuality.**
INCORRECT	**By studying harder improves anyone's chance of success.**
CORRECT	**Studying harder improves anyone's chance of success.**
INCORRECT	**When Einstein relocated to Princeton was a very special honor for that university.**
CORRECT	**Einstein's relocation to Princeton was a very special honor for that university.**

All the incorrect examples above are typical "first-draft" mistakes that often happen because writing and thinking do not occur at the same speed. Writers frequently start a sentence in one direction, then change their minds in midcourse. The revision stage is the point at which careful writers find and correct these errors.

EXERCISE 24.8 Answers will vary. The following revisions are suggested.
1. Mia gives better presentations than anyone else in this company.
2. Dogs like humans; that is the only reason the two species coexist so well.
3. The possibility that humans might live to the age of 150 is being taken seriously by many researchers.
4. Liberals tend to like a powerful federal government more than conservatives do.
5. I want to rest, relax, and plan.
6. Veronica is attractive, funny, and talented.
7. These pickles are more popular than any other brand of pickles.
8. The police chief left town after the mudslide.
9. Ronald likes sardines more than Wanda does.
10. A person who repeatedly fails to wear sunblock can suffer both serious pain and skin cancer.

EXERCISE 24.8

Each of the following sentences suffers from mixed constructions, faulty comparisons, or a lack of parallelism. Revise each sentence to eliminate the error. In some cases, more than one answer is possible.

1. Mia gives better presentations than anyone in this company.
2. Because dogs like humans is the only reason that the two species coexist so well.
3. One idea concentrates on the possibility of humans living until age 150 is being taken seriously by many researchers.

4. Liberals tend to like a powerful federal government more than conservatives.
5. I want rest, relaxation, and to plan.
6. Veronica is attractive, funny, and she has lots of talent.
7. These pickles are more popular than any other brand.
8. After the mudslide is when the police chief left town.
9. Ronald likes sardines more than Wanda.
10. A person who repeatedly fails to wear sunblock can suffer both feeling serious pain and skin cancer.

MORE OPTIONS ONLINE
For more exercises, go to **www.mhhe.com/writingtoday**.

CHAPTER 25

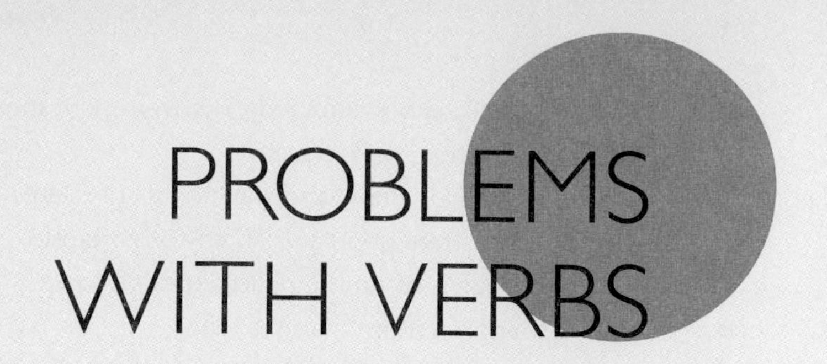

PROBLEMS WITH VERBS

Verbs are among the most important parts of a sentence; therefore, your ability to use them correctly is crucial. Two common problem areas are subject-verb agreement and shifts in tense, voice, and mood.

SUBJECT-VERB AGREEMENT

Properly written sentences have a structural balance: singular subjects are matched with singular verbs, and plural subjects with plural verbs; singular nouns are matched with singular pronouns, plural nouns with plural pronouns. This balance is called **agreement.**

Agreement is in one way different from many other grammatical and mechanical concerns: even professional writers make agreement errors in their first drafts. To make sure that your subjects and verbs agree, you will need to check for agreement problems when revising and editing. Look, for example, at the following sentence:

CLASSROOM HINT
Many students profit from in-class discussion of special agreement problems covered in this chapter, specifically those explained in 25b, 25d–e, and 25j–l.

INCORRECT **There is a number of reasons for my choice.**

CORRECT **There are a number of reasons for my choice.**

Because the verb comes before the subject in this sentence—not the most common order—the writer might easily choose the incorrect verb form. Catching problems such as these in the revision stage will help you keep your final draft free of agreement problems. The sections in this chapter show you where agreement problems are likely to occur and how to correct them. For now, keep the following in mind:

s-v agr 25a

- A subject must agree in *number* with its verb. For example, a singular verb is needed for a singular noun, as in this sentence:

  The **house** that we have owned for many years **sits** on two acres.

- A plural noun requires a plural verb:

  The **houses** that we saw in Tennessee last week **are** well constructed.

MORE OPTIONS ONLINE
If you would like to test your knowledge of verb problems before reading this chapter, go to **www.mhhe.com/writingtoday**.

Most writers have few problems with basic subject-verb agreement. In the sentence "John (work, works) for a large company," the choice is straightforward: *John works*. However, beware of verbs that end in *-ist;* because the verb already has an *-s* sound near the end, it's easy to forget that in a sentence like "The last surviving member of the species (exist, exists) in a zoo," the correct verb is *exists*. Writers must also deal with many situations that are not basic; one of the chief problems in subject-verb agreement is determining whether the subject is singular or plural.

25a SUBJECTS CONNECTED BY *AND*

Two or more nouns or pronouns joined by *and* are called **compound subjects.** These constructions are normally plural:

Walter **and** Luisa **plan** to get married.
Five rabbits, a hamster, **and** a cat **are** the pet shop's remaining inventory.
Going to school **and** working twenty hours per week **have** become difficult for Maureen.

However, if any word or phrase other than *and* joins two parts of a subject, the verb is singular if both parts of the subject are singular:

Walter, **as well as** Luisa, **has** been nominated for chairperson.
Volvo, **along with** Jaguar, **is** owned by Ford Motor Company.
Going to school **plus** working twenty hours a week **is** too much for Maureen.
A case of pneumonia, **in addition to** several double shifts at work, **has** put Louise into the hospital.

25b COMPOUND SUBJECTS TREATED AS SINGULAR CONSTRUCTIONS

Sometimes, two singular subjects joined by *and* are really one entity—person or thing—and they take singular forms:

Track and field **is** Amelia's best sport. (Track and field is one type of athletic activity.)
He believed that *rock and roll* **was** an abomination. (Rock and roll is one kind of music.)
My best *friend and confidant* **is** coming for a visit. (In this sentence, the writer is referring to the same person.)

Two **gerund phrases** linked with *and* can also sometimes be singular:

Going downtown and playing snooker **is** my grandfather's secret vice.

Here, the subject (*going downtown and playing snooker*) is essentially one activity. On the other hand, the following sentence has a compound gerund phrase that clearly indicates two separate activities:

Getting dressed and driving to my date's home **are** the last two steps in the ritual.

EXERCISE 25.1 Responses will vary. The following revisions are suggested:
1. Martha and John **have** signed up for our study group.
2. Tossing and turning all night **is** my response to stress.
3. Correct.
4. Health and safety **was** my least-favorite class in high school.
5. Moss and lichens **grow** on many different varieties of trees.

EXERCISE 25.1

In the following sentences, decide if the highlighted verb is correct in number. If it is not, supply the correct form of the verb, or restructure the sentence so that the existing verb form is correct. Not all sentences contain errors.

1. Martha and John **has** signed up for our study group.
2. Tossing and turning all night **are** my response to stress.
3. Harriet, as well as her sister Jane, **is** expected to attend the public lecture.
4. Health and safety **were** my least-favorite class in high school.
5. Moss and lichens **grows** on many different varieties of trees.

25c SUBJECTS CONNECTED BY *OR, NOR, EITHER . . . OR, NEITHER . . . NOR,* AND *NOT ONLY . . . BUT ALSO*

These connectors join subjects, but the resulting subjects do not act as a compound subject. Therefore, these connectors need a special series of rules for subject-verb agreement:

1. If both subjects joined by one of these connectors are singular, the verb is singular:

   Neither Jane nor he is expected to apply.

2. If both subjects are plural, the verb is plural:

   Neither cats nor dogs are able to fly.

3. If one subject is singular and the other is plural, the verb agrees in number with the closer noun:

   Vitamins or exercise is what Jessica needs right now.
   One CD or two magazines are all Wayne can afford right now.

   This rule also applies if three or more subjects are connected by *or;* the subject *closest* to the verb determines the verb's number:

   Cherries, grapes, or **cake is** all we can offer you for dessert.

   If a sentence is correct but sounds strange, you can eliminate the awkwardness by rearranging the nouns:

   Cake, cherries, or **grapes are** all we can offer you for dessert.

s-v agr 25d

EXERCISE 25.2

In the following sentences, choose the correct word. Rewrite the sentence if the result is awkward.

1. Neither bananas nor grapes (contains, contain) all the vitamins that a human needs.
2. Either Ed or the Johnsons (has, have) bought a new car.
3. Not only floods but also drought (has, have) been a problem in this region.
4. Neither the Walker brothers nor Ellen Hastings (was, were) sent an invitation.
5. Two ducks, a fox, or three turkeys (is, are) what I shall paint today.

EXERCISE 25.2
1. contain
2. have
3. has
4. was
5. are

25d SUBJECTS THAT ARE INDEFINITE PRONOUNS

A **definite pronoun** refers to a specific person: *he, she,* and so on. An **indefinite pronoun**, such as *someone* or *anybody,* refers to a "generalized other." Indefinite pronouns fall into three categories, as shown in the box below.

Indefinite Pronouns

Always Singular		Always Plural	Singular or Plural Depending upon Context
another	no one	both	all
anybody	nobody	few	any
anyone	nothing	many	either
anything	one	several	enough
each	somebody		more
every	someone		most
everybody	something		neither
everyone			none
everything			some

25d.1 INDEFINITE PRONOUNS THAT ARE ALWAYS SINGULAR

Many of the words in the first column *seem* plural, such as *everyone* and *everybody,* but in practice they are always singular. Also, remember that when *each* or *every* precedes a subject, it makes that subject singular:

> **Everyone** in the study group **is** invited to participate.
> **Each** of the four defendants **was** tried separately.
> **Every** detective and lawyer in North America **has** been jolted by the news of McNamara's prison break.

However, when **each** *follows* a plural subject, the verb is plural:

> At the ceremony, the **players each thank** the coach for his dedication.

25d.2 INDEFINITE PRONOUNS THAT CAN BE SINGULAR OR PLURAL

The words in the third column of the box on page 679 are indefinite pronouns, but they do not determine a subject's number; instead, the nouns that they are linked with determine whether the verb should be singular or plural:

> **All** of the **work** on the garage **is** complete.
> **All** of the clerical **tasks,** such as typing, collating, and filing, **are** done by Chris.
>
> **Some** of the **damage is** severe.
> **Some** of the **computers are** still working.
>
> **Either** (**Neither**) the players **or** (**nor**) **the coach is** being fined.
> **Either** (**Neither**) the coach **or** (**nor**) **the players are** being fined.

In the last example, the first sentence uses a singular verb because the subject closer to it, *coach,* is singular. The second sentence uses a plural verb because the subject closer to it, *players,* is plural.

EXERCISE 25.3
1. is
2. awaits
3. believe
4. is
5. have

EXERCISE 25.3

In the following sentences, choose the correct verb. Treat the sentences as a continuous passage.

1. Everyone (is, are) expected to stand in line, Steve.
2. Either success or failure (await, awaits) us.
3. Most (believes, believe) that they will get to the window before the office closes.
4. Some of the procedure (is, are) explained in the company's personnel manual.
5. Neither the deadline nor the three different entry fees (has, have) been announced.

25e SUBJECTS THAT ARE COLLECTIVE NOUNS

Collective nouns, such as *family, team, couple, pair, trio, group, panel,* and *committee,* refer to groups. They often cause subject-verb agreement problems. In American English, these words are usually treated as singular depending on context:

> The **team is** coming out of the locker room.
> The **jury is** still deliberating.
> Her **family is** back together again.

However, they are sometimes treated as plural:

> The **choir raise** their voices in song.
> The **couple are** saying their wedding vows.

What's the distinction? In the first three examples, the collective noun (*team, jury, family*) is acting as a unit. In the last two examples, the elements that make up the collective nouns (*choir, couple*) are acting separately *within* the unit. To test this distinction, you might try to treat the collective nouns in the last two examples as singular:

> The choir raises its voice in song.
> The couple is saying its wedding vows.

The effect is awkward. One solution is to add the word *members* after the collective noun, making the construction automatically plural, as in *choir members*. However, this strategy doesn't work in all contexts. You would never say *the couple members*. In the second example, changing to a compound subject wold produce a more natural-sounding sentence: *The bride and groom are saying their wedding vows.*

s-v agr 25e

EXERCISE 25.4

In each of the following sentences, choose the correct word.

1. The legislature (has, have) passed a resolution praising the governor.
2. After standing to acknowledge the applause of the audience, the orchestra took (its, their) (seat, seats).
3. The hockey team (is, are) arguing among (itself, themselves) about the coach's decision.
4. The family (is, are) planning to go to Manitoba for (its, their) vacation.
5. The awards committee (is, are) still deliberating.

EXERCISE 25.4
1. has
2. their seats
3. are; themselves
4. is; its
5. is

25f OTHER COLLECTIVE NOUNS THAT CAUSE AGREEMENT PROBLEMS

Problems sometimes occur because of a difference between informal English and formal English; other problems represent highly specific developments in English over time.

1. **News:** This word is always treated as a singular noun:

   The news **is** good.

2. **Media:** In informal English, *media* is frequently used as a singular noun. In formal English, however, *media* is always plural. When you refer to the news or entertainment media, you are talking about a collection made up of each specific *medium,* such as print, radio, and television. Hence, *media* should always take a plural verb:

   The news media **are** reporting that the wildfire is being brought under control.

3. **Data:** This word is the plural form of the rarely used *datum.* Although in informal usage a singular verb is often used with *data,* formal English requires a plural verb:

   The data **are** consistent.

4. **Subjects or activities that end in -*s* (physics, statistics, politics, ethics, economics, sports):** These words are singular when they refer to a concept, activity, subject, or academic course but plural when they refer to a specific "set" of individual items:

   Physics **is** my least favorite course.
   The physics of outer space **are** fascinating.

   Statistics **is** my least favorite course.
   The statistics from the two studies **are** consistent.

   Sports **is** her future.
   Team sports **are** dominating the intramural schedule.

5. **Company names:** The name of a single company or institution is always singular, even if it sounds plural:

   Johnson and Johnson **makes** pharmaceutical supplies.
   Ibbotson Research Associates **is** a new company in this area.
   The Organization of American States **is** having an emergency meeting.

6. **Mathematical expressions:** Mathematical expressions are usually treated as singular:

   Notice that 16 plus 24 **is** 40.
   In fact, $(4 \times 2 + 3\underline{x})^3$ **is** the resulting polynomial.

7. **Distances and measurements of time:** When a distance or measurement of time is treated as one unit, it is singular:

   Seven hundred miles **is** a long drive.
   Two hours **seems** like a long time to wait for a doctor.

   However, when a distance or measurement of time is seen as the sum of its individual units, it is plural:

   Five miles of rough road **are** still in front of us.
   Four hours **have** crawled by minute by minute.

s-v agr 25f

In these two examples, five miles will be experienced *mile by mile,* and four hours have been suffered minute by minute.

8. **Word as word/number as number:** When you refer to a word *as* a word or a number *as* a number, the noun is singular:

   Hieroglyphics **is** a very hard word to spell.
   Eight **is** my lucky number.

9. **The number/a number:** *The number (of)* is singular; *a number (of)* is plural:

   The number of guests for our upcoming party **has** been reduced; a number of people **have** called to cancel.

EXERCISE 25.5

In the following sentences, choose the correct verb.

1. The United Nations (has, have) survived decades of political turmoil.
2. The sports media often (fail, fails) to cover events in swimming and water polo.
3. "Eight thousand maniacs" (refers, refer) to the people waiting to buy concert tickets.
4. The number of people who buy umbrellas (is, are) surprisingly small.
5. Statistics (indicates, indicate) that drunken driving is a leading cause of highway fatalities.

EXERCISE 25.5
1. has
2. fail
3. refers
4. is
5. indicate

s-v agr 25g

Special Situations

25g SUBJECTS SEPARATED FROM THEIR VERBS

Don't be misled by intervening words, words that come between the subject and the verb:

Lake Superior, the largest of the Great Lakes, (is, are) a vast body of water.

The subject of the sentence is *Lake Superior,* which is singular, so *is* is the correct verb. However, the word immediately preceding the verb is *Lakes,* and some writers, fooled by the closeness of this word, might want to use *are* instead. Remember to check for the number of the *subject,* not the number of the nearest noun or pronoun. Here are more examples:

A **bouquet** of lilies, mums, and irises **makes** a stunning centerpiece.

Ford, a company that owns many automobile brands, **is** expected to explore various alternative-fuel options.

The **computer,** which has revolutionized both business and personal communications, **was** first used by the military.

EXERCISE 25.6
1. is
2. has
3. are
4. owns
5. seem

EXERCISE 25.6

In the following sentences, choose the correct verb in parentheses.

1. Excitement in all of its sordid varieties (is, are) the principal attraction of the Adelphi Nightclub.
2. The batter for the Montreal Expos (has, have) played for seven different teams.
3. Peanuts, an agricultural mainstay of the South, (is, are) a versatile food source.
4. William, one of five brothers, (owns, own) a car dealership.
5. All voters, regardless of their party affiliation, (seem, seems) interested in debating the bond issue.

s-v agr 25h

25h SUBJECTS AND LINKING VERBS

Linking verbs, especially forms of *be* as well as words like *taste, feel,* and *smell,* connect a subject to a word or words that describe it, called its complement. They cause a unique problem in subject-verb agreement:

	singular	plural	plural
INCORRECT	The main **problem** at the plant **are** production errors.		

	singular	singular	plural
CORRECT	The main **problem** at the plant **is** production errors.		

The subject can sometimes be plural and the complement singular, or vice versa. A common error is to make the verb agree with the complement, but, as always, the *subject* determines whether the verb is singular or plural. If a sentence is correct but sounds strange, remember that you can switch the subject and the complement. Then the verb will change number to match the new subject:

The main problem **is** production errors.
Production errors **are** the main problem.

EXERCISE 25.7
1. are
2. is
3. are
4. are
5. are

EXERCISE 25.7

In the following sentences, choose the correct verb.

1. Penguins (is, are) a tourist attraction in the Antarctic.
2. The problem with this drug (is, are) its side effects.
3. Errors in the programming language (is, are) our focus today.
4. Walking and biking (is, are) good exercise.
5. Driver's licenses (is, are) one item most people carry at all times.

25i SUBJECTS THAT FOLLOW VERBS: INVERTED SENTENCE STRUCTURES

Some English sentences do not use the standard pattern of subject then verb. In a question, for example, the subject comes after the verb. In such instances, make sure that the verb agrees with the number of its subject:

> What **are** the **causes** of the problem?
> **Is this** a good reason for your behavior?

A similar situation occurs in declarative sentences beginning with *here, there,* and *what.* The subject is delayed until after the verb:

> **Here comes** my **aunt,** strolling down the aisle.
> **Here come** my **aunts,** strolling down the aisle.

> What **is** clearly an animal **track** was lifted by the police forensics specialist.
> What **are** clearly animal **tracks** were lifted by the police forensics specialist.

A third type of inverted sentence pattern happens when a writer deliberately switches the normal order for effect:

> Above the mountains **rises** a blinding **sun.**

Here, as always, identifying the subject and its number is crucial.

s-v agr 25i

EXERCISE 25.8

In the following sentences, choose the correct form of the verb.

1. Which (is, are) the correct instructions, this batch or the one over there?
2. Here (is, are) a few interesting questions to contemplate.
3. Through the busy shoppers (moves, move) Bettina, her Christmas buying almost finished.
4. On the barren ridge above the old house (sit, sits) a wolf and her pups.
5. There (is, are) many reasons not to go cave diving.

EXERCISE 25.8
1. are
2. are
3. moves
4. sit
5. are

VERB SHIFTS

As noted earlier, writers frequently need to project themselves into the reader's role and ask "I understand what I mean, but will my reader understand as well?" When writers change verb usage in a sudden or unexpected way (when they make a "shift"), they often cause problems for readers. This section will help you avoid three kinds of shifts—of tense, of voice, and of mood.

25j TENSE SHIFTS

Before we talk about incorrect shifts of verb tense (see also Chapter 22), it is important to note that a writer may correctly change tenses when such a change is called for. For example, a sentence or a paragraph may mention events that happened at different times. Therefore, changing tenses can be logical and necessary. Note the following example:

> In 1946 my father **was** in a quandary. Before World War II he **had been** a college student; however, in 1946 he **wasn't** sure what to do. He felt that the world **was becoming** a much more complicated place. Today, I **feel** the same way.

Four tenses (past, past perfect, past progressive, and present) are used in this paragraph, but this mix is acceptable. However, a sudden tense shift for no apparent reason is not acceptable:

INCORRECT **Bobby rode up on his Harley, and he starts talking a mile a minute. (The action in the sentence either happened in the past or is happening now; the use of both tenses confuses the reader.)**

CORRECT **Bobby rode up on his Harley, and he started talking a mile a minute. (In this version, both verbs are in past tense.)**

A special situation occurs when you are writing about literature, television, or film (you can read about such papers in Chapter 19). In this situation the **literary** present tense is used:

CORRECT **In *Pulp Fiction,* Jules and Vincent are two of the major characters.**

25k VOICE SHIFTS

For most purposes, the **active voice** ("Kevin hit the wall") is preferable to the **passive voice** ("The wall was hit by Kevin"). In any case, mixing voices within a sentence is usually not the best choice:

ORIGINAL **The criminal fled the scene, but he was arrested by the police that afternoon.**

The first independent clause is in the active voice; the second one is in the passive voice. Note how much more direct and forceful the revised sentence is:

REVISED **The criminal fled the scene, but the police arrested him that afternoon.**

As you can see, in the active voice, the subject acts on a direct object. In the passive voice, the subject is acted upon. (To learn more about voice, see Chapter 22.) Here's another example:

ORIGINAL **As Sean ran up the stairs, laughter could be heard.**

REVISED **As Sean ran up the stairs, he could hear laughter.**

25l MOOD SHIFTS

Verbs can have one of three **moods** (see also Chapter 22). The **indicative** mood is the most common; it is used to state facts, make assertions, and ask questions. The **imperative** mood gives commands. The **subjunctive** mood describes hypothetical situations, wishes, or conditions contrary to fact, as in "If I **were** to flap my arms and fly out the window, everyone would be surprised." An inappropriate shift in mood occurs when the writer starts in the subjunctive mood but then switches to the indicative:

INCORRECT **If I were wealthy, I am going to buy a sports car.**

CORRECT **If I were wealthy, I would buy a sports car.**

The original sentence shifts from the subjunctive mood to the indicative; the revised sentence uses the subjunctive in both clauses. In the next example, the writer shifts from the imperative to the indicative:

INCORRECT **Study hard tonight, and then you should rest.**

CORRECT **Study hard tonight, and then rest.**

EXERCISE 25.9

Each of the following sentences contains a shift of tense, voice, or mood. Revise each incorrect sentence.

1. It is believed by scientists that the epidemic will not occur, and parents welcome the good news.
2. American business always concentrated on efficiency, and some of today's firms are models of streamlining.
3. Jeremy is surviving a day in which he had seen his job almost lost, his car almost wrecked, and his house almost torched.
4. If Maria were able to finish college a year early, she will go immediately to graduate school.
5. *Damnation Boulevard* is a good movie, but everyone died in the end.
6. Instruments of the violin family are played with a stringed bow, but guitars, mandolins, and lyres would be played by hand.
7. Part of the German protectorate of Togoland from 1886 to 1914, Togo was administered by the French until 1982, when it becomes a republic.
8. In 1620, the Pilgrims establish Plymouth Colony, which was followed by the Massachusetts Bay Colony. By the 1700s, Massachusetts begins to prosper and had become part of the triangle trade, which involved the selling of molasses, rum, and slaves.
9. President Kennedy establishes the Peace Corps in 1961, and more than forty years later, people with technical skills who are willing to work in underdeveloped countries are still attracted to its mission.
10. White settlements in the mineral-rich hills of South Dakota were opposed by the Sioux Indians under Crazy Horse. With other Indian leaders, Crazy Horse defeats U.S. troops under George Custer at the Little Bighorn in 1876.

EXERCISE 25.9 Responses will vary. The following revisions are suggested:
1. Scientists believe that the epidemic will not occur, and parents welcome the good news.
2. American business has always concentrated on efficiency, and some of today's firms. . . .
3. Jeremy is surviving a day in which he has seen his job. . . .
4. If Maria were able to finish college a year early, she would go. . . .
5. *Damnation Boulevard* is a good movie, but everyone dies in the end.
6. Instruments of the violin family are played . . . lyres are played by hand.
7. Part . . . from 1886 to 1914, Togo was administered . . . it became a republic.
8. In 1620, the Pilgrims established Plymouth Colony, which. . . . By the 1700s, Massachusetts began to prosper and became. . . , which involved. . . .
9. President Kennedy established . . . people . . . who are willing . . . are still attracted to its mission.
10. The Sioux Indians under Crazy Horse opposed white settlements in the mineral-rich hills of South Dakota. With other Indian leaders, Crazy Horse defeated. . . .

COMBINATION EXERCISE

The following passage contains sentences with verb problems. Fix any error that you see.

If someone says that he or she is going to be on time, one hopes that will be the case. If I were to make an appointment with you, you are sure that the appointment will be kept and that I will be prompt. Last Monday I made a tee time for 7:30 a.m. at the Hidden Value Estates Golf Club. My friends Ed and Luis, along with Mike, who is one of Ed's friends, is supposed to meet me at Hidden Value. The course, which is owned by Golf Management Specialists, are located east of the city. I got there first and suspected that traffic problems was the issue, for I waited and waited.

Waiting for latecomers and still remaining patient is not my strong suit. Ed, as well as Luis, are constantly late, and I have no idea about Mike's problems. I sat and listened to the television news, which were bad, as usual. Statistics were indicating that the recent downturn in the North American economies were caused by a number of factors. Either the job market, inflationary trends, or European trade were the main culprit, according to the report. An opposing view countered that the real problem were the billions of dollars in U.S. Treasury bonds owned by the Japanese banks. In my opinion, neither trade issues nor foreign debt are the main issue; I feel that the investor class have just gotten scared of an overheated stock market.

Meanwhile, I was about to lose our tee time—or, should I say, Ed, Luis, and Mike was going to lose it for me. Thirty minutes are not a long time to wait, but the starter and his assistant was beginning to glare in my direction. Golf Management Specialists are not a patient group; it does not hesitate to cancel tee times and then a charge for a missed appointment is levied. Finally, with only a few minutes to spare, my three cohorts arrive in one car. Luis's facial expression and body language was not positive (he had waited for the other two), but we got off at 7:29, as planned.

COMBINATION EXERCISE Responses will vary. The following revisions are suggested:

If someone says that he or she is going to be on time, one hopes. . . . If I make an appointment with you, you can be sure that I will keep the appointment and that I will be prompt. . . . My friends Ed and Luis, along with Mike, who is one of Ed's friends, were supposed. . . . The course, which is owned by Golf Management Specialists, is located. . . . I got there first and suspected that traffic problems were. . . .

Waiting. . . . Ed, as well as Luis, is. . . . I sat and listened to the television news, which was bad. . . . Statistics . . . was caused by a number of factors. Either . . . was the main culprit. . . . An opposing view . . . problem was the billions of dollars. . . . In my opinion, neither . . . is the main issue; I feel that the investor class has just gotten scared. . . .

Meanwhile, . . . were going. . . . Thirty minutes is . . . starter and his assistant were beginning. . . . Golf Management Specialists is. . . ; it does not hesitate to cancel tee times and then levy a charge for a missed appointment. Finally, . . . my three cohorts arrived in one car. Luis's facial expression and body language were not positive. . . .

m shft 251

MORE OPTIONS ONLINE
For more exercises, go to **www.mhhe.com/writingtoday**.

CHAPTER 26

PROBLEMS WITH PRONOUNS

Pronouns take the place of and refer to nouns or other pronouns, called **antecedents.** The word *antecedent* signifies that such nouns and pronouns usually come before the pronouns that refer to them. Keep the advice in this chapter in mind when you revise or edit your papers so that you use pronouns correctly and make them relate clearly and correctly to their antecedents.

CLASSROOM HINT Because many of the problems covered in this chapter find their way into student papers, you might want to discuss it in class in its entirety.

MORE OPTIONS ONLINE
If you would like to test your knowledge of pronoun problems before reading this chapter, go to **www.mhhe.com/writingtoday**.

PRONOUN-ANTECEDENT AGREEMENT

Pronoun-antecedent agreement follows the logic of subject-verb agreement (see Chapter 25). The pronoun agrees in number with its antecedent. Singular antecedents require singular pronouns; plural antecedents require plural pronouns:

> **Karen** asked that I call **her.**
> The Williams **brothers** were annoyed; the hotel had lost **their** reservations.

In addition, pronouns must be in the correct case (subjective, objective, possessive) and must agree with their antecedents in gender (male and female):

> **She** is my Aunt Lil Mcgill; I telephone **her** every week. (The pronoun *she* is in the subjective case; it is the subject of the first clause. The pronoun *her* is in the objective case; it receives the action of telephoning.)
>
> **Lil** is a name **she** took on **her** twenty-first birthday, but **she** is known as Nancy. (The pronouns in this sentence are all female, for they all refer to Lil.)

DETERMINING WHETHER THE ANTECEDENT IS SINGULAR OR PLURAL

p agr
26a

As with the subject in subject-verb agreement, there are many situations in which the writer's main problem is determining the number of the pronoun's antecedent.

26a ANTECEDENTS THAT USE *AND* AND OTHER CONNECTORS

1. **Compound nouns and phrases with *and*:** Antecedents joined by the word *and* usually form a plural compound. Thus, pronouns referring to such antecedents must also be plural:

   Luis and Martina have bought a new home; **they** are delighted to have a home of their own.

   Chile and Argentina are in South America; **they** border each other.

   Sally enjoys **planting** flowers and **reading** mysteries because **they** help relax her.

2. **Compound nouns and phrases with other connectors:** Using other connectors (*as well as, along with, in addition to, plus*) to join two nouns can result in problems:

   INCORRECT **Karen, along with her friend Ed, is coming to the fund drive; they will bring a couch for the auction.**

   In this sentence, *they* has no antecedent because *along with* does not connect *Karen* and *her friend Ed*. The solution here is simple—change *along with* to the coordinating conjunction *and*.

CORRECT **Karen and her friend Ed are coming to the fund drive; they will bring a couch for the auction.**

3. **Compound words treated as singular constructions:** Sometimes, two singular words connected by *and* are actually the same entity. When such words act as an antecedent, refer to them with a singular pronoun:

   My best friend and most exacting critic is my sister; **she** plans to visit next week.

   Whenever I hear **rock and roll,** I have to sing or dance to **it.**

4. **Gerund phrases linked with *and*:** In the following sentence, the subject (*going downtown and playing poker*) is essentially one activity. It should be referred to by using a singular pronoun.

   Going downtown and playing poker is my grandfather's secret vice; he does **it** three days a week.

   On other hand, the following sentence has a compound gerund phrase that clearly indicates two separate activities:

   Getting dressed and driving to my date's home are the last two steps in the ritual, and **they** are the two easiest steps.

p agr 26b

EXERCISE 26.1

In the following sentences, decide if the highlighted pronoun is correct in number. If it is not, supply the correct pronoun or rewrite the sentence. Not all sentences contain errors.

1. Lately, my wife has complained about my tossing and turning all night; **they** are keeping her awake as well.
2. When Bob and Leo went fishing, **he** decided to bring a radio.
3. When a Major League Baseball player leaves the game, **they** can normally expect paid retirement.
4. When Elrod and Lurine got **their** first assignment in the Navy, **they** were shipped to Alaska.
5. When running water and electricity came to our rural cabin, **it** surely made our lives easier.

EXERCISE 26.1
1. Lately . . .; it is. . . .
2. When . . . fishing, they. . . .
3. When Major League Baseball players leave the game, they. . . ; When a Major League Baseball player leaves the game, he. . . .
4. Correct
5. When . . . cabin, they. . . .

26b ANTECEDENTS JOINED BY *OR, NOR, EITHER . . . OR, NEITHER . . . NOR,* AND *NOT ONLY . . . BUT ALSO*

As in subject-verb agreement, using these connectors to join nouns can cause problems in pronoun-antecedent agreement. Note the following basic guidelines:

1. If both antecedents (nouns or pronouns) joined by these words or phrases are singular, the pronoun is also singular.
2. If both antecedents joined by these words or phrases are plural, the pronoun is also plural.

3. If one antecedent is plural and the other is singular, the pronoun agrees in number with the antecedent closer to it.

The first two guidelines are fairly straightforward:

> Either Michael or Edgar left **his** car keys on the counter.
> Either the Parkers or the Robbins left **their** car keys on the counter.

The third guideline is more complex. When a singular noun is connected by *or* to a plural noun, the pronoun's number is determined by *the noun that is closer to the pronoun:*

> Neither my mother nor my sisters found **their** way to my cabin.

But note the problem posed by this sentence:

> Either the Robbins or Edgar left **his** car keys on the counter.

This sentence is technically correct; however, it does not say what its writer intends. To revise, the writer could reverse the order of the two nouns, allowing the pronoun to change number:

> Either Edgar or the Robbins left **their** car keys on the counter.

Remember that *you* control the sequence of your nouns in these situations; make sure that your sentences are logically correct as well as technically correct.

Note also that you can often solve problems by eliminating the pronoun altogether:

> Either the Robbins or Edgar left **a set of** car keys on the counter.

p agr 26c

EXERCISE 26.2

In the following sentences, choose the best term from the parentheses. In some sentences, more than one set of choices may be correct.

1. If you see Jane or Nancy, ask (her, them) to bring some plates.
2. For supper, I think that I'll have either (fishsteaks or pizza, pizza or fishsteaks); (it, they) really (appeal, appeals) to me.
3. (Neither Lance nor Marie) (Both Lance and Marie) (will admit) (refuse to admit) (that she is wrong) (that they are wrong).
4. The specials tonight include not only pork loin but also quesadillas; (it, they) (sounds, sound) wonderful.
5. After a hard night at the casino, (neither the Parkers nor their daughter Ellen) (neither Ellen Parker nor her parents) wanted to risk any more of (her, their) money.

EXERCISE 26.2 Answers may vary.
1. her
2. pizza or fishsteaks, they, appeal; fishsteaks or pizza, it, appeals
3. Both Lance and Marie refuse to admit that they are wrong.
4. they sound
5. neither Ellen Parker nor her parents; their

26c ANTECEDENTS THAT ARE INDEFINITE PRONOUNS

An **indefinite pronoun**, such as *each, everyone, no one,* and *somebody,* refers to a nonspecific person or thing. You can find a chart of indefinite pronouns in Chapter 25, page 679.

26c.1 INDEFINITE PRONOUNS THAT ARE ALWAYS SINGULAR

Such pronouns include *anybody, everyone,* and *something,* as well as many others:

> **Something** must have spoiled in the refrigerator. **It** is probably the fish I left in there last August.
>
> **Everyone** must vote according to **his or her** conscience.

A little more than half the people in the world are female. Unfortunately, English has no single word that can refer to an "indefinite" person of either sex. An informal solution is to write *Everyone must vote their conscience.* However, *their* is plural whereas *everyone* is singular. A better solution is to use the *his or her* construction (as above) or to recast the sentence into the plural:

> All **citizens** must vote according to **their** consciences.

The same approach will work when using words such as *any, each,* and *every:*

> Any **student** who wants to do well in Dr. Oshiro's physics class must make sure that **he or she** is prepared to study.
>
> **Students** who want to do well in Dr. Oshiro's physics class must make sure that **they** are prepared to study.

Another way to fix this problem is to get rid of the pronoun altogether if possible:

> Anybody who forces **his or her** child into show business should be prosecuted.
>
> Anybody who forces **a** child into show business should be prosecuted.

p agr 26c

26c.2 TROUBLESHOOTING

1. Some contexts require singular forms. Consider this situation: your college offers the Landstar Scholarship to a single student. All students are eligible. Hence, the winner will be either male or female. A carefully worded requirement of the scholarship might read like this:

   > **The student** who is awarded the scholarship must present proof of **his or her** completion of thirty semester hours.

   A plural context won't work here: only one winner will be selected. Therefore, using *his or her* is necessary.
2. If you have to use a singular indefinite pronoun, use *he or she* or *she or he.* Avoid *s/he* and *[s]he.* These are not considered acceptable style; furthermore, they can't be spoken.
3. If your context refers to an all-male or an all-female population, use the appropriate singular pronoun to refer to an "indefinite" person. Any player in the National Hockey League can, at this time, be safely referred to as *he.* Any golfer in the LPGA can be referred to as *she.*

EXERCISE 26.3

In the following sentences, choose the correct pronoun. If the result is awkward, rewrite the sentence so that a more natural-sounding sentence results.

EXERCISE 26.3 Answers may vary.
1. his or her; Anyone who wants to participate in the contest better have cooking utensils.
2. his
3. his or her; Everybody who is scheduled for writing conferences must file a proposal with the instructor.
4. his or her
5. their; All the people at this meeting have pledged at least $100 toward the reelection campaign.

1. Anyone who wants to participate in the contest better have (his, her, their, his or her) cooking utensils.

2. A knight in the Middle Ages owed (his, her, his or her, their) allegiance to a fuedal lord.

3. Everybody who is scheduled for writing conferences must file (his, her, their, his or her) proposal with the instructor.

4. Each car mechanic and technician is responsible for (his, her, their, his or her) own certification.

5. All the people at this meeting have pledged at least $100 of (his, her, their, his or her) money toward the reelection campaign.

26d ANTECEDENTS THAT ARE COLLECTIVE NOUNS

Words such as *family, team, couple, pair, trio, group, panel,* and *committee* are called **collective nouns.** They are normally singular, but sometimes they are plural, according to context:

> The **team** emerged; **it** was ready for action.
> The **couple** said **their** vows.

When you use a collective noun, you need to ask the following question: Is the collective noun functioning as one entity, or are the individual members acting separately? In the first example, the team is acting as one entity. In the second example, each of the two people in the wedding ceremony speaks separately; the two people are effectively plural. As noted in the section on subject-verb agreement (see 25e and 25f), you can avoid problems with most collective nouns by adding the word *members*. Consider the following sentence, which is correct and sounds correct:

> The committee has not yet reached its decision.

However, this sentence is correct but *sounds* incorrect:

> The committee are arguing among themselves.

Adding the word *members* helps avoid awkwardness:

> The committee **members** are arguing among themselves.

This strategy works most of the time, except with the collective nouns *couple, pair,* and *duo*. If you use these words alone, you must decide if the context makes them singular or plural when choosing a pronoun.

> The pair walked hand in hand, discussing **their** future.
> This pair [of pants] is worn out; throw **it** away.

26e OTHER COLLECTIVE NOUNS THAT CAUSE AGREEMENT PROBLEMS

In the section on subject-verb agreement, we list a number of collective nouns that cause special problems in agreement (see Chapter 25, page 681). Here is a shortened version of that list—most of these words cause fewer problems in pronoun-antecedent agreement:

1. **News** is singular:

   I heard the news; **it** is good.

2. **Media** is plural:

   A problem with the media is **their** belief that people will never tire of hearing about scandals.

3. **Data** is plural:

   I've checked the data, and **they** seem realistic.

4. **Physics, statistics, politics, ethics, economics,** and **sports** are all singular if they refer to a concept, subject, or academic course:

   Physics is my favorite course; **it** fascinates me.

   My grandfather wants me to go into politics, but **it** is not for me.

   They are plural if they are referring to a "set" of individual items:

   We examined the statistics on car thefts; **they** show a clear pattern.

   Gary has tried various sports, but **they** don't interest him.

5. **Company names** are singular:

   Betty's Wondrous Roses has failed; **it** is bankrupt.

6. **Mathematical expressions** are singular:

   The result we come up with is $(4x + 3)^3/1.5x$; **it** now needs to be tested.

7. **Measurements of distance and time** are singular when treated as one unit:

   Seven hundred miles is a long drive; **it** wears me out.

   They are plural when treated as the sum of units:

   Five years passed slowly. **They** seemed to drift by like a bad dream.

8. **Words treated as words and numbers treated as numbers** are singular:

   When I try to spell *hieroglyphics,* **it** gets twisted around in my memory.

   Eight is my lucky number; **it** always has been.

9. **The number of . . .** is singular:

   The number of attendees was small; **it** was under fifty

10. **A number of . . .** is plural:

    A number of people canceled; **they** didn't want to brave the weather.

p agr 26e

EXERCISE 26.4

In the following sentences, choose the correct word or words.

1. An example of a controversial organization is the United Nations; (it, they) can inspire a number of reactions among people in the United States.

EXERCISE 26.4
1. it
2. they
3. it means
4. it was
5. they keep
6. has; its
7. team members; themselves
8. are; their
9. is; it
10. they; were

2. Golf and swimming are my two sports; (it, they) can keep me occupied in my spare time.
3. When you see the term "teeming millions," (they, it) (mean, means) the bulk of the population.
4. When I drove up to Farber and Associates, (it, they) (was, were) closed.
5. We've rerun the data several times; (it, they) (keeps, keep) coming back the same way.
6. The commission (has, have) announced (its, their) new guidelines.
7. The winning (team, team members) divided the bonus money among (itself, themselves).
8. Tamara and Juan, a newlywed couple, (is, are) planning to spend (its, their) vacation in New Mexico.
9. The Dining and Entertainment Planning Committee (is, are) made up of seven members; (it, they) will make new recommendations next week.
10. When I last saw the baseball team, (it, they) (was, were) taking batting practice.

PRONOUN REFERENCE

p ref 26f

If the pronoun's antecedent (the noun or pronoun it replaces) is vague or ambiguous—or if no antecedent exists—readers may have a difficult time understanding your meaning. Indeed, they may see two or more possible meanings in a particular sentence. The following sections will help you avoid unclear pronoun reference.

26f PRONOUNS WITHOUT APPROPRIATE ANTECEDENTS

A pronoun must have an antecedent, and the antecedent must be an appropriate noun or pronoun, not another word that merely seems like an antecedent.

1. **Don't use an inappropriate noun or an entire clause as an antecedent.**

AMBIGUOUS **Caleb loved the idea of farming, but he had never been on one.**

What does *one* refer to? Obviously, the writer means to link *one* to *farm,* but the word *farm* is not in the sentence—*farming* is.

REVISED **Caleb loved the idea of farming, but he had never been on a farm.**

In the revised version, the noun *farm* replaces the ambiguous pronoun *one.*

AMBIGUOUS **The moving truck collided with an SUV, which left debris all over my front lawn.**

REVISED **The collision of the moving truck with the SUV left debris all over my front lawn.**

In this example, the pronoun *which* has no noun to which it can logically refer. In the revision, the sentence is recast to eliminate the pronoun altogether.

2. **Don't use an adjective or a possessive as an antecedent.**

INCORRECT **Ever since being introduced to Japanese art, Jeff has wanted to visit it.**

REVISED **Ever since being introduced to Japanese art, Jeff has wanted to visit Japan.**

INCORRECT **Decades after Franklin D. Roosevelt's death, the country has finally decided to erect a memorial to him.**

CORRECT **Decades after Franklin D. Roosevelt's death, the country has finally decided to erect a memorial to the thirty-second President.**

In the last example, the writer is trying to link *him* to *Roosevelt.* However, *Roosevelt* is not in the sentence; *Roosevelt's* is, and it is possessive. Technically, then, *him* has no antecedent. This is a fine point, but revision is your best option.

3. **Make sure that the pronoun *it* has an antecedent.** You would be absolutely correct if you wrote this sentence:

Maria wants to buy my old car, but she can't afford **it**.

Here there is an obvious link between *it* and *car.* Also, you would be correct if you used *it* to refer to the weather:

It has been raining all day.

However, when you begin a sentence with *it,* you run the risk of failing to include an antecedent, as in the following sentence, thereby leaving out important information:

AMBIGUOUS **It is generally believed that the Sumerians developed cuneiform writing.**

In reading such a sentence, the reader might ask "Who believes this?"

REVISED **Historians generally believe that the Sumerians developed cuneiform writing.**

Writers can also cause ambiguity by using *it* to mean different things in the same sentence:

AMBIGUOUS **It was raining that afternoon, and it was clear that the party would need to be moved inside or it would have to be rescheduled.**

REVISED **Rain was falling that afternoon, and I realized that the party would need to be moved inside or be rescheduled.**

In the revised sentence, *it* has been eliminated. However, don't get the impression that you should avoid *it* altogether; just avoid conflicting uses of this word. Note the following sentence:

This is my laptop; I bought **it** a year ago, and **it** is worth the high price I paid for **it**.

The word *it* occurs three times in this sentence, but all three instances clearly refer to the laptop computer, so the sentence is not ambiguous.

4. **Don't skip the antecedent altogether.**

INCORRECT	**During the musical *A Chorus Line*, they tell their own stories.**
REVISED	**During the musical *A Chorus Line*, the dancers tell their own stories.**
INCORRECT	**In the latest issue of *Newsweek*, it said the election would be close.**
REVISED	**In the latest issue of *Newsweek*, a reporter said the election would be close.**
REVISED	**The latest issue of *Newsweek* said the election would be close.**

5. **Avoid using the pronoun *you* when you mean a more general word, such as *one*, *anyone*, or *someone*.** Using the pronoun *you* is appropriate if you are addressing the reader directly:

We ask that **you** remit your payment of $150 by December 20.

However, when you really mean the more impersonal *one* or an equivalent pronoun, *you* is inappropriate:

INCORRECT	**As you enter the execution chamber, you notice that everything is white and sterile.**

In the sentence above, the writer presupposes that the reader will actually visit an execution chamber.

REVISED	**As an observer enters the execution chamber, he or she notices that everything is white and sterile.**

p ref 26g

EXERCISE 26.5

EXERCISE 26.5 Responses will vary. The following revisions are suggested:
1. Jeremy hadn't heard from home lately; he wondered if he should call his family.
2. People who have babies soon realize that their lives are no longer their own.
3. His dream of studying at Oxford University was about to come true.
4. Miguel knew rain was possible for that afternoon.
5. The radio station announced that school was canceled.

In each of the following sentences, decide if the highlighted pronouns have appropriate antecedents. If not, revise the sentence to eliminate the problem.

1. Jeremy hadn't heard from home lately; he wondered if he should call **them**.
2. When **you** have a baby, **you** soon realize that **your** life is no longer **your** own.
3. He dreamed of studying at Oxford University, **which** was about to come true.
4. **It** occurred to Miguel that **it** was possible for **it** to rain that afternoon.
5. **They** said on the radio that school was canceled.

26g PRONOUNS WITH UNCLEAR ANTECEDENTS

Follow these suggestions to make sure that pronouns refer clearly to their antecedents.

1. **Make sure that the pronoun has only one possible antecedent.** Sometimes, a writer asks the reader to connect a pronoun to its antecedent when there is more than one possible antecedent. The writer's meaning then becomes unclear:

AMBIGUOUS **When Larry and Gus went fishing, he took a lantern.**

Who? Larry or Gus? Consider this revision:

CLEAR **Gus took a lantern when he went fishing with Larry.**

Most writers who have trouble with pronouns tend to use them too often. When in doubt, repeat the noun or revise the sentence so that the pronoun clearly links to its antecedent.

Connectors such as *as well as, along with, in addition to,* and *plus* can cause problems:

AMBIGUOUS **Peter, as well as Michael, believes in high ethical standards; he says that his business ethics class taught him a great deal.**

After the semicolon, *he* seems to indicate Peter, but the reader can't be sure. Here are two possible revisions:

CORRECT **Peter and Michael believe in high ethical standards; Peter says that his business ethics class taught him a great deal.**

CORRECT **Peter and Michael believe in high ethical standards; they say that their business ethics class taught them a great deal.**

A related problem involves careless use of *which, this,* and *that.* Note the following ambiguous sentence:

AMBIGUOUS **I spent the afternoon waxing the car and buffing it, which is difficult.**

Is buffing difficult? Or waxing? Or, as seems more likely, is the combined task difficult? Here is a possible revision:

REVISED **I spent the afternoon waxing and buffing the car, which is a difficult process.**

As is so often the case with ambiguous pronouns, the writer is simply not using *enough* words to get his or her meaning across.

A similar problem occurs when the writer asks *which, this,* or *that* to carry too much weight. Note the following:

The guest speaker could not keep still. She walked back and forth constantly, and her hands flew around like deformed birds. She also laughed suddenly and inappropriately at several points. **This** drove me crazy.

"This" what? The laughter or the entire experience? The writer probably means the latter, so the final sentence of the passage should be clarified:

This bizarre performance drove me crazy.

p ref 26g

2. **Don't start a paragraph with a pronoun.** The beginning of a paragraph is an ideal place to establish or reestablish an antecedent. If you use a pronoun to start a paragraph, you are asking your reader to think back to the previous paragraph and "retrieve" the antecedent.
3. **Remember that pronouns aren't your only choice.** Use articles—*a, an,* and especially *the*—instead. Rather than using the indefinite *someone,* use (if possible) *people.* This way, you can avoid ambiguity while also avoiding the use of *he or she,* or *his or her.*

WITH PRONOUN	**No one** wants to be frustrated when **his or her** car overheats in traffic.
WITH ARTICLE	**No one** wants to be frustrated when **the** car overheats in traffic.
WITH INDEFINITE PRONOUN	**Everyone** should be concerned about this threat to **his or her** health.
WITH *PEOPLE*	**People** should be concerned about this threat to **their** health.

EXERCISE 26.6
Responses will vary. The following revisions are suggested:
1. Eddie told John that John was fifth in the batting order.
2. The open door and the broken light worried me.
3. The aquarium in the bedroom has a small filter, which I plan to replace.
4. Our manager, Ms. Shinzato, seems to think we're running late, although she hasn't actually said that we are.
5. Correct

p ref 26g

EXERCISE 26.7
Responses will vary. The following revisions are suggested:
Some teams . . . couples on the teams. Couples are untrustworthy. A problem they are having . . . practice. This absence makes . . . ; they . . . slack. It is hard . . . when the team has difficulty holding together.
For example, . . . Laura. . . . Jim's boss frequently makes Jim stay . . . , or Jim gets exhausted, a problem that causes him to miss practices and games. . . . problem. His anger is not a pretty sight to behold.
Jim does his best, and fortunately Laura helps him. Otherwise, . . . solution, for Jim and Laura are our best two players. One night when it was raining, we knew we . . . Jim got there in time. Thank goodness he did. He hit two home runs . . . these hits made the difference.

EXERCISE 26.6

In the following sentences, determine whether the highlighted pronoun is ambiguous. If so, revise the sentence to eliminate the ambiguity. You may be able to use more than one revision method.

1. Eddie told John that **he** was fifth in the batting order.
2. The door was open, and the light was broken; **this** worried me.
3. The bedroom has an aquarium and a small filter, **which** I plan to replace.
4. Our manager, Ms. Shinzato, seems to think we're running late, although she hasn't actually said **that.**
5. Elrod and Lurine were very pleased when **they** finally bought a house.

EXERCISE 26.7

The following passage is filled with ambiguous pronouns. Revise each sentence as needed.

Some teams in the local softball league have started to have problems with couples on the teams. They are untrustworthy. A problem that couples are having can cause one or both of them to miss an important game or practice. This makes it hard on the rest of the team; they have to pick up the slack. It is hard to play a schedule when it depends on each team holding together.

For example, take the case of Jim and Laura. She is normally reliable, but he is not. His boss frequently makes him stay late at work, finishing some project, or he gets exhausted, which causes him to miss practices and games. He also has an anger-management problem. This is not a pretty sight to behold.

He does his best, and she helps him. That's good. Otherwise, our team members would have more frustrations than triumphs, and they would be without a solution. For they're our best two players. One night when it was raining, it was clear that we would lose a weather-shortened game unless Jim got on it and made it to the game. This he did. He hit two home runs in the fourth and fifth innings, and they made the difference.

26h AVOIDING SHIFTS OF PERSON

Personal pronouns can be first person, second person, or third person, as the following list indicates:

First Person	Second Person	Third Person
I	you	she
me	your	her
my	yours	hers
mine		he
we		him
us		his
our		it
ours		its
		they
		them
		their
		theirs

p shft 26h

To use pronouns appropriately and consistently, follow these guidelines:

1. Use *I* to refer to yourself within an essay. In the past, writers were told to avoid the use of *I*, but this restriction is fading.
2. Use *we* to refer to you and your audience when you share values or experiences:

   CORRECT **As Americans, we share a long history.**

   CORRECT **At the end of *The Sound and the Fury,* we realize the mixture of desolation and faint hope that Faulkner has developed.**

3. Use *you* sparingly, only when referring to the reader directly (as in an instructional process analysis, discussed in Chapter 9):

   CORRECT After **you** have tightened the lugs, check the edges of the seal.

   Do not use *you* to mean "a person" or "someone":

   INCORRECT When **you** shoot heroin, **you** are taking a great risk.

   CORRECT When **a person** shoots heroin, **he or she** is taking a great risk.

   CORRECT When **people** shoot heroin, **they** are taking a great risk.

4. Use the third-person pronouns to refer to people, places, things, and ideas:

CORRECT **People who follow a strict exercise regimen may become bored; it can seem like a prison to them.**

To avoid inappropriate shifts when you are using personal pronouns, follow the above guidelines. You also need to understand how to use indefinite pronouns (see 26c, page 692). The following sentence incorrectly shifts from second to third person. It also has problems with pronoun-antecedent agreement:

INCORRECT **When a person sees a student standing outside a locked faculty office at 5:15 p.m. with a blank look on their face, you know that they are seriously adrift.**

REVISED **A student standing outside a locked faculty office at 5:15 p.m. with a blank look on his or her face is seriously adrift.**

REVISED **Students standing outside a locked faculty office at 5:15 p.m. with blank looks on their faces are seriously adrift.**

To avoid shifts in person, use the word *you* carefully, and remember the advice from 26c: whenever possible, don't refer to *a person, a student, a swimmer,* and so on when you can use *persons, students,* or *swimmers* instead. You will then automatically avoid this common—and serious—pronoun problem in your writing.

EXERCISE 26.8

Revise the following paragraph so that it uses pronouns appropriately and avoids shifts in person.

When a student first attends college, no matter how much advice you have received and preparation you have endured, you will be surprised. The student may find that their roommate is new, as the expected roommate has found another place for their domicile. Your classroom may have changed, or you might locate the right classroom but notice that the instructor is not who they're supposed to be. My current roommate is on the men's golf team, and he told me that at the start of this year's practice season, each golfer learned that their coach had suddenly resigned. If you ask me, all this seems to be part of a vast plan to prepare you for the uncertainties of your adult life.

EXERCISE 26.8 Responses will vary. The following revisions are suggested: When students first attend college, no matter how much advice they have received and preparation they have endured, they will be surprised. The student may find that his or her roommate is new, as the expected roommate has found another domicile. The location of a class may have changed, or the student might locate the right classroom but notice that the instructor is not who he or she is supposed to be. My current roommate is on the men's golf team, and he told me that at the start of this year's practice season, each golfer learned that the coach had suddenly resigned. If you ask me, all this turmoil seems to be part of a vast plan to prepare students for the uncertainties of adult life.

PRONOUN CASE

Consider this sentence: "He gave she a present for they anniversary." Something is obviously wrong. *He* is correct, but *she* should be *her,* and *they* should be *their:* "He gave her a present for their anniversary." This example illustrates pronoun **case**, which means that pronouns have different spellings according to their function in a sentence. In the correct version, *He* is in the **subjective case**, functioning as a subject; *her* is in the **objective case**, functioning as an object; and *their* is in the **possessive case**, indicating ownership. (Note that objective-case pronouns can be direct objects, indirect objects, and objects of prepositions.)

26i THE SUBJECTIVE CASE, THE OBJECTIVE CASE, AND THE POSSESSIVE CASE

Here are the subjective, objective, and possessive forms of the personal pronouns:

Subjective	Objective	Possessive
I	me	my, mine
you	you	your, yours
she	her	her, hers
he	him	his
we	us	our, ours
they	them	their, theirs
it	it	its

The pronouns *who* and *whoever* also have different forms according to their function:

Subjective	Objective	Possessive
who	whom	whose
whoever	whomever	

Remember to use the correct pronoun case when you write. Avoid careless sentences such as this one:

INCORRECT **Jamal came over to Nancy and I, asking if we had a copy of the assignment.**

REVISED **Jamal came over to Nancy and me, asking if we had a copy of the assignment.**

The correct form is *Nancy and me* because *me* is the object of the preposition *to.* If you take out *Nancy and,* the sentence sounds absurd. You would never write *Jamal came over to I.* Here are a few more examples:

o.c. s.c. o.c.
Kavan asked **me** if **I** would e-mail **him** the meeting's agenda.

s.c. o.c.
Theresa and Ron are my closest friends; **I** have the utmost respect for **her**
o.c. s.c. o.c.
and **him** OR: **I** have the utmost respect for **them.**

s.c. o.c.
We had a bad scare last night; a police officer almost arrested **us** in a case of mistaken identity.

o.c. s.c.
To **whom** is the letter addressed? **Who** is involved here?

s.c. o.c.
We Americans are a diverse group, but to **us** Americans, certain issues cause little disagreement.

In the last example, the pronoun is the same case as the noun that follows it.

The sections that follow will help you avoid pronoun case errors.

26j PRONOUNS THAT ARE SUBJECT COMPLEMENTS

A personal pronoun connected to the subject by a linking verb—normally a form of *be*—is a subject complement and is in the subjective case:

s.c.
John called; **it** was **he** who left the message yesterday afternoon.

s.c.
The speaker has arrived; that is **she** over by the podium.

As you can see, following this rule can cause some stilted and strange constructions. Note how the second example sentence can be recast for a more natural sound:

The speaker has arrived; **she** is the one over by the podium.

26k PRONOUNS IN COMPARISONS

When writers use *as* or *than* to compare people or things, they frequently omit the verb in the second part of the comparison.

Harley is taller than Mike [is].
Melissa is at least as talented as Gayle [is].

When the second part of the comparison uses a personal pronoun instead of a noun, the pronoun should be in the subjective case:

Harley is taller than **I** [not **me**].
Melissa is at least as talented as **I** [not **me**].

Do these sentences sound awkward? Then "fill out" the comparison:

Harley is taller than I **am.**
Melissa is at least as talented as I **am.**

26l PRONOUNS THAT ARE SUBJECTS OF CLAUSES

When an entire clause is the object of a sentence, the subject of the clause is still in the subjective case:

I hope that **Ron will do well as an intern at Mercy Hospital.**

Note that *Ron* is the subject of the objective clause. If a personal pronoun is used to replace *Ron,* that pronoun must be in the subjective case:

I hope that **he** will do well as an intern at Mercy Hospital.

The pronoun is the subject of the subordinated clause even though the clause is an object; therefore, the pronoun (*he*) should be in the subjective case.

Who and *whom* are troublesome pronouns. Note the difference between the following two sentences:

CORRECT **I must say that the person who is responsible for this mess won't have a job tomorrow morning.**

CORRECT **Please find out to whom I should send this letter.**

In the first sentence, *who* is the subject of the dependent clause (*who is responsible* . . .). In the second sentence, *whom* is the object of the preposition *to;* it is not the subject of the dependent clause.

EXERCISE 26.9

Choose the best form of each pronoun in the following sentences.

1. We realize that (we, us) members of the Widget Club must take our responsibilities seriously.
2. Marina and Miguel are here; see if (he and she, him or her, they, them) want something to eat.
3. Lisa can run faster than (I, me).
4. With (who, whom) has the FBI communicated about the recent kidnapping?
5. Disha is talented; I hope that (she, her) is given a promotion.
6. Rob and (me, I) will be ready soon.
7. It is (I, me) who will be your guide.
8. To (who, whom) is the letter addressed?
9. (Whoever, Whomever) is responsible better start apologizing.
10. Roger has progressed more quickly than Amanda; he is at least as qualified as (she, her).

EXERCISE 26.9
1. we
2. they
3. I
4. whom
5. she
6. I
7. I
8. whom
9. Whoever
10. she

case 26m

26m REFLEXIVE PRONOUNS AND INTENSIVE PRONOUNS

Reflexive pronouns show that a subject is taking action toward itself:

The beetle righted **itself.**
On the hike, Karen made a practice of checking **herself** for ticks.
The ballplayers viewed **themselves** as the country's finest.

The correct forms of these pronouns are *herself, himself, itself, myself, oneself, ourselves, themselves, yourself,* and *yourselves.* Avoid *hisself, theirself, theirselves,* and *ourself.* Also, don't use a reflexive pronoun when it is not needed:

INCORRECT **Jason and myself went to the psychic fair.**

CORRECT **Jason and I went to the psychic fair.**

INCORRECT **The gift is for Bob and yourself.**

CORRECT **The gift is for Bob and you.**

When reflexive pronouns are needed, they're essential; when they're not needed, their inclusion is incorrect.

Intensive pronouns are spelled the same way as reflexive pronouns but have a different purpose—they are used to emphasize a point:

> I checked that report **myself**.
> Jay **himself** admits that the process has flaws.

EXERCISE 26.10

In the following sentences, correct any misuse of reflexive or intensive pronouns. Some sentences may be correct.

1. The four-course Italian dinner was prepared by Carl and myself.
2. Alton Brown hisself couldn't have done any better.
3. You should check out the gourmet cooking yourself.
4. Carl and I couldn't always agree between ourself about certain parts of the recipe.
5. Carl prides himself on his cold antipasto, eggplant Siciliano, and baked ziti.

EXERCISE 26.10
1. . . . Carl and me.
2. Alton Brown himself. . . .
3. Correct
4. . . . between ourselves. . . .
5. Correct

MORE OPTIONS ONLINE
For more exercises, go to **www.mhhe.com/writingtoday**.

case 26m

COMBINATION EXERCISE

Rewrite the following paragraph to correct pronoun problems.

It is certain that hepatitis is an inflammation of the liver. Anyone who gets this disease will know it, for they will become jaundiced, lose their a ppetites, and suffer a loss of energy and a fever. The disease comes in many types, but the most common forms are hepatitis A and hepatitis B. Either form is very dangerous; in fact, they can be fatal. You get hepatitis A from contaminated food and water, but they seem to be able to treat this type with some success. Hepatitis B, on the other hand, can be transmitted when surgical instruments are not adequately sterilized. This is why practicing asepsis is crucial in a hospital and why they work so hard to maintain a sterile environment in operating rooms. Many people have also contracted hepatitis B when receiving transfusions of tainted blood, which is how my cousin Rudy got it. It was him who nearly died in the automobile accident that made the front page of the local paper three years ago. When they brought him into the hospital emergency room, you could see that he had lost a lot of blood. Unfortunately, it was not known that the two pints they gave him were tainted. The donor had not been properly screened for hepatitis; they may have contracted the disease through drug or alcohol abuse.

COMBINATION EXERCISE
Responses will vary. The following revisions are suggested:
Hepatitis is . . . liver. People who get this disease will know. . . . The disease comes . . . hepatitis A and hepatitis B. Either form is very dangerous; in fact, it can be fatal. One gets . . . water, but doctors. . . . This possibility is why practicing asepsis is crucial in a hospital as is maintaining a sterile environment in operating rooms. Many people, such as my cousin Rudy, have also contracted hepatitis B when receiving transfusions of tainted blood. It was he who nearly died. . . . When the paramedics brought him into the hospital emergency room, the doctors. . . . Unfortunately, they did not know . . . hepatitis, and he or she

CHAPTER 27

PROBLEMS WITH MODIFIERS

A modifier is a word or group of words that describes, evaluates, limits the meaning of, or provides more information about another word or group of words in a sentence. Generally speaking, modifiers can be classified as adjectives and adverbs, parts of speech discussed in 22c and 22l.

CLASSROOM HINT This is another chapter you might discuss in class in its entirety.

This chapter discusses problems that you may have with the logical use and placement of modifiers in sentences, the incorrect substitution of adjectives for adverbs, the use of comparative and superlative forms, the sequencing of adjectives, the question of split infinitives, and the proper use of articles.

MORE OPTIONS ONLINE If you would like to test your knowledge of modifiers before reading this chapter, go to **www.mhhe.com/writingtoday**.

27a MISPLACED AND AMBIGUOUS (SQUINTING) MODIFIERS

You will confuse your reader if you place modifiers in the wrong position or if you place modifiers in an ambiguous position. The first situation creates a **misplaced modifier**; the modifier does not refer to what the writer intended:

MISPLACED **Brice solved the problem, a proven leader.**

What did the writer mean for *a proven leader* to do, modify *Brice* or *the problem*? Obviously, the answer is *Brice*. Note the revision:

CORRECT **Brice, a proven leader, solved the problem.**

MISPLACED **A zoologist said that polar bears are the most effective predators on television.**

CORRECT **A zoologist said on television that polar bears are the most effective predators.**

A common problem occurs with the modifiers *only* and *just*. Read the following two sentences:

MISPLACED **I just have five dollars.**

CORRECT **I have just five dollars.**

The first version suggest that the only thing going on in the writer's life is his or her possession of five dollars, an absurd statement. The second version is correct; *just* modifies *five dollars*.

MISPLACED **Frank only worked in Philadelphia for five months.**

CORRECT **Frank worked in Philadelphia for only five months.**

In the first version, *only* modifies *worked*, a structure that suggests that Frank did absolutely nothing else in Philadelphia, such as eat, breathe, and walk, during those five months. In the second version, *only* relates clearly and directly to *five months*.

If a sentence contains the second type of error, an **ambiguous** or **squinting modifier**, the reader must "squint" (look carefully) to determine what the writer intended, as the following example shows:

AMBIGUOUS **Friends who ride in car pools together frequently become angry with one another.**

Here, *frequently* can refer to either *ride* or *become angry*, but which one? The sentence must be rewritten to make the meaning clear:

CORRECT **Friends who ride in car pools together become angry with one another frequently.**

CORRECT Friends who **frequently** ride in car pools together become angry with one another.

Misplaced and squinting modifiers sometimes occur at the beginning of a sentence:

INCORRECT **Staggering on the sidewalk, the police officer approached the drunkard outside the bar.**

To fix the sentence, you can (1) place the word that the modifier refers to immediately before or after the modifier or (2) add a subject and verb to the modifier, turning it into a dependent clause:

CORRECT **The police officer approached the drunkard staggering on the sidewalk outside the bar.**

CORRECT **As the drunkard staggered on the sidewalk outside the bar, the police officer approached him.**

In the example above, the reader can assume that it is the drunkard who is staggering and not the police officer, even if the incorrect sentence seems to say otherwise. In some cases, though, placing a modifier incorrectly may make it impossible for the reader to make such a distinction. In other words, misplaced or ambiguous modifiers cloud meaning:

INCORRECT AND UNCLEAR **Alex found useful books and other resources in the town library that had been donated by a local corporation.**

Did the corporation donate the books and resources, or did it donate the entire library? To make the message clear, the sentence needs to be restructured:

CORRECT **In the town library, Alex found useful books and other resources that had been donated by a local corporation.**

CORRECT **In the town library, which had been donated by a local corporation, Alex found useful books and other resources.**

EXERCISE 27.1

The following sentences contain misplaced and squinting modifiers. Correct them.

1. I only have a week to write this paper.
2. Thrashing the water furiously, the angler hooked the trout.
3. Jim just bought a special gift for his wife, a coffee grinder.
4. The coach only said that she would consider our request.
5. Ella claimed that she was very happy in the restroom.
6. Last Saturday, we went to a French restaurant and then walked home, a rare treat.
7. Spinning out of control, Ed watched in horror as the car slammed into the bridge.
8. They sat through a four-hour meeting and then went out for dinner with their boss, a true horror.

EXERCISE 27.1 Answers may vary.

1. I have only a week to write this paper.
2. The angler hooked the trout that was thrashing the water furiously.
3. Jim just bought a special gift, a coffee grinder, for his wife.
4. The coach said that she would only consider our request.
5. In the restroom, Ella claimed that she was very happy.
6. Last Saturday, we went to a French restaurant, a rare treat, and then walked home.
7. Ed watched in horror as the car spun out of control and slammed into the bridge.
8. They sat through a four-hour meeting, a true horror, and then went out for dinner with their boss.

9. We watched the young pigeons perched on the stone gargoyle.
10. The old man, weary and ailing, opened the letter.

9. Perched on the stone gargoyle, we watched the young pigeons.

10. The old man opened the letter, weary and ailing.

27b DANGLING MODIFIERS

A sentence has a **dangling modifier** when there is nothing in the sentence to which the modifier can actually refer:

INCORRECT **After studying the problem, it became clear that a lot of money would be needed.**

The subject of the sentence is implied, but the reader needs more. Who studied the problem? To whom did it become clear that . . . ?

CORRECT **After we studied the problem, we realized that a lot of money would be needed.**

When writers use the passive voice, as in the example above, a dangling modifier is sometimes the unintended result. Using the passive voice reverses the normal English sentence structure and removes an active subject: "The midfielder kicked the ball" becomes "The ball was kicked by the midfielder" or, more simply, "The ball was kicked." (For more on passive voice, see chapters 5, 22, and 25.)

DANGLING **Arresting the suspect, handcuffs were placed on his wrists.**

DANGLING **Looking over the river, the city's skyline could be seen.**

Here's how to fix these dangling modifiers: first, change the passive to the active voice; second, make sure that the modifier refers to a *stated* subject, not an *implied* one:

CORRECT **Arresting the suspect, the police placed handcuffs on his wrists.**

CORRECT **Looking over the river, we could see the city's skyline.**

dm 27b

Dangling modifiers can also occur even if the sentence is in the active voice:

DANGLING **Before any strenuous physical exercise, a few warm-up activities are necessary.**

CORRECT **People must do a few warm-up activities before any strenuous physical exercise.**

DANGLING **After years of abusing alcohol and drugs, liver disease can develop.**

CORRECT **After years of abusing alcohol and drugs, one can develop liver disease.**

CORRECT **Abusing alcohol and drugs for years can result in liver disease.**

EXERCISE 27.2
Responses may vary. The following revisions are suggested:
1. Feeling bad about the interview, Fred knew that he needed to do more work before the next job application.
2. After a long night, Kama greatly appreciated the rosy daybreak.
3. As I drank hot coffee, the cup slipped from my hand.
4. Running a small business and investing wisely, Mr. Richter amassed great wealth.
5. When growing older, people need to reexamine their priorities.

EXERCISE 27.2

Each of the following sentences contains a dangling modifier. Rewrite each sentence, supplying a subject as needed.

1. Feeling bad about the interview, it became clear that more work was needed before the next job application.
2. After a long night, the rosy daybreak was greatly appreciated.
3. Drinking hot coffee, the cup slipped from my hand.
4. Running a small business and investing wisely, great wealth was amassed.
5. When growing older, priorities need to be reexamined.

27c INCORRECT SUBSTITUTION OF ADJECTIVES AND ADVERBS

Remember that adjectives describe or modify nouns and pronouns. Adverbs describe or modify verbs, adjectives, and other adverbs. Don't use one when the other is called for.

INCORRECT ADJECTIVE **Sam was real sorry for the trouble he caused last week.**

CORRECT ADVERB **Sam was really sorry for the trouble he caused last week.**

In the example above, the adjective *sorry* should be modified by the adverb *really,* not the adjective *real.*

INCORRECT ADVERB **Angela was quickly to praise her boss.**

CORRECT ADJECTIVE **Angela was quick to praise her boss.**

Here, *quick,* an adjective, is needed to modify *Angela,* a noun.

Note that some adjective/adverb pairs have radically different spellings:

Adjective	Adverb
few	less
good	well
many	much

adj/adv 27c

When *good* and *well* are used to describe one's personal health, well-being, and/or appearance they have an idiomatic pattern:

He looks **good.** (appearance)
I feel **well.** (health)
She is finally **well** after her long recuperation. (health)

Otherwise do not substitute *good* for well:

INCORRECT **I played really good today.**

CORRECT **I played really well today.**

Finally, there are no such words as *firstly* and *secondly;* the adjective forms, *first* and *second,* are correct.

EXERCISE 27.3

Revise the following sentences to correct problems with adverbs and adjectives.

1. Iron conducts heat and electricity extremely good.

EXERCISE 27.3
1. . . . extremely well.
2. First, Miguel. . . .
3. Andrea feels good. . . .
4. On an extremely cold . . . the Delaware nearly silently . . . contented and comfortable. . . .
5. . . . treated kindly or humanely . . . . The United States suffered many casualties. . . .

2. Firstly, Miguel wanted to thank his supporters for their contributions and hard work.
3. Andrea feels well about her chances of finding a better job.
4. On an extreme cold Christmas Eve, Washington's army crossed the Delaware nearly silent as they prepared to attack the Hessian troops, who were contentedly and comfortably in their Trenton barracks.
5. The American prisoners of war were not treated kind or humane by our World War II enemies. The United States suffered much casualties as a result.

27d PROBLEMS WITH COMPARATIVES AND SUPERLATIVES

Adjectives and adverbs come in positive (base), comparative, and superlative forms. **Comparatives** are used to compare two people, places, or things. **Superlatives** are used to compare three or more people, places, or things. Here are the three ways that the comparative and superlative forms occur:

1. **The suffixes *-er* and *-est* are added to adjectives and some adverbs of one or two syllables:**

Positive	Comparative	Superlative
dark	dark**er**	dark**est**
happy	happi**er**	happi**est**
fast	fast**er**	fast**est**

However, note what happens with the three-syllable adjective *terrific:*

INCORRECT **terrific** **terrificer** **terrificest**

2. ***More* and *most* are used with adjectives of three or more syllables and most adverbs:**

CORRECT **terrific** **more terrific** **most terrific**

Unfortunately, some adjectives of one or two syllables won't work with *-er* or *-est* suffixes either. The word *common* follows the *more/most* pattern of larger adjectives: *more common, most common.* However, note that if you can attach a suffix to an adjective (such as *dark + er*), don't also use *more* or *most:*

INCORRECT **The cave seemed to be getting more darker.**

CORRECT **The cave seemed to be getting darker.**

3. **Irregular adjectives** change their spellings or form in the comparative and superlative:

Positive	Comparative	Superlative
bad	worse	worst
good	better	best
little	less	least
many	more	most
much	more	most
some	more	most

adj/adv 27d

If you are not sure which form to use in a comparison, say the word with an *-er* or *-est* ending. If it sounds strange, it's probably wrong. However, your best approach is to look up the word in a college-level dictionary. If *-er* or *-est* suffixes are appropriate, they may be indicated somewhere in the entry.

EXERCISE 27.4

In the following sentences, the highlighted words are used incorrectly. Revise to eliminate errors.

1. Robert is obviously **badder** at nine-ball than George is.
2. The lecture on Egyptian art was the **more valuabler** of the two we attended.
3. Among this season's five snowfalls, the **later** was the **worse.**
4. Laura looked **more sadder** after she heard the news.
5. Of the two families, the Agrigentos are the **richest.**

EXERCISE 27.4
1. worse
2. more valuable
3. latest; worst
4. sadder
5. richer

27e PROBLEMS WITH ADJECTIVE ORDER

Cumulative adjectives are a group of adjectives that come before a noun; each successive adjective modifies the adjective(s) and noun that follow (*an old black shoe*). **Coordinate adjectives** modify the noun separately and are separated by commas (*expensive, beautiful shoes*). See 28e for more on punctuating groups of adjectives. Adjectives that precede a noun follow a traditional pattern:

Determiner: a, an, the, this, those, my, their, many, four

Evaluation: great, boring, beautiful, sad

Size: big, small, huge

Shape: circular, square, triangular

Age: old, new, ancient

Color: red, yellow, amber

National or geographic origin: British, German, African

Religion: Catholic, Jewish, Taoist

Material: steel, paper, silk

Noun acting as adjective: garden wall, car phone, school bus, bird house

EXAMPLE In **the large square glass** case, the visitors saw **a wonderful old Japanese silk** kimono.

adj 27e

EXERCISE 27.5

Rewrite the following sentences to correct problems with adjective order.

1. The rectangular large truck delivered a load of antique Italian beautiful furniture to Miriam's red-brick new home.
2. Henry II of England (1133–1189) gained vast French rich lands when he married Eleanor of Aquitaine in 1152.
3. Are radio high-frequency waves harmful to one's health?

EXERCISE 27.5
1. The large rectangular truck delivered a load of beautiful antique Italian furniture to Miriam's new red-brick home.
2. Henry II of England (1133–1189) gained vast, rich French lands when he married Eleanor of Aquitaine in 1152.
3. Are high-frequency radio waves harmful to one's health?

4. Katmandu, the capital of Nepal, sits 4,500 feet above sea level in a stunningly beautiful, fertile valley, which has a great deal of historical significance.
5. An unbroken, centuries-old honor code binds the members of our organization together.

4. Katmandu, the capital of Nepal, sits 4,500 feet above sea level in a fertile stunningly beautiful valley, which has a great deal of historical significance.

5. An honor centuries-old code binds the members of our organization together.

27f PROBLEMS WITH SPLIT INFINITIVES

In most cases, avoid splitting an infinitive. An **infinitive** is a verbal made up of *to* plus the base form of the verb. An infinitive is "split" when an adverb is placed between the two parts of the infinitive:

to **boldly** go

to **wildly** dream

to **slowly** realize

to **carefully** consider

Splitting an infinitive used to be considered unacceptable. Today, however, most style experts recognize that certain sentences are less awkward with a split infinitive. Consider these two sentences:

The thing Jan wants most is **to quickly conclude** this deal.
The thing Jan wants most is **to conclude quickly** this deal.

The first sentence contains a split infinitive; however, this sentence works a lot better than the second one. Then again, you could write this sentence:

The thing Jan wants most is **to conclude** this deal **quickly**.

By moving the adverb, *quickly,* away from the verb and after the object, *deal,* you can avoid both a split infinitive and awkwardness; moreover, the sentence is not ambiguous.

art 27g

EXERCISE 27.6

EXERCISE 27.6 Responses may vary. The following revisions are suggested:
1. . . . caterpillar is slowly going to change. . . .
2. . . . the parents finally decided to go home.
3. . . . to place the glass inside the wire holder carefully.
4. . . . to decide instantly that. . . .
5. . . . it's actually possible . . . to fall in love. . . .

Each of the following sentences contains a split infinitive. Revise each sentence to eliminate it. Reword as needed.

1. In this time-enhanced sequence, the caterpillar is going to slowly change into a butterfly.

2. After waiting for several hours, the parents decided to finally go home.

3. The directions tell us to carefully place the glass inside the wire holder.

4. The evidence led the detective to instantly decide that the perpetrator was known by the victim.

5. I don't think it's possible for a person to actually fall in love at first sight.

27g PROBLEMS WITH ARTICLES

Articles modify nouns in much the same way that adjectives do. However, articles can pose very specific and serious modification problems, as the following guidelines indicate:

1. When you are using an indefinite article (*a* or *an*), choose *a* when the next word starts with a consonant sound; choose *an* when the next word starts with a vowel sound:

   a tire

   a unit

   a precise analogy

   an uncle

   an awful surprise

   Note that the *sound* at the beginning of the next word is key here—thus, *a unit* but *an uncle.*

2. When you use a singular count noun, precede it with an article. A count noun, as its name suggests, denotes something that is normally counted instead of measured:

   a dog **the** monster **an** aviator **the** mayor

   Note that either an indefinite article (*a, an*) or the definite article (*the*) can be used, depending on the context. But also note that if you are using a plural count noun, only the definite article (or no article at all) can be used:

   INCORRECT **A dogs ran down the street.**

   CORRECT **Dogs ran down the street.**

   ALSO CORRECT **The dogs ran down the street.**

3. When you use a noncount noun, do not precede it with an indefinite article. A noncount noun denotes something that is normally not counted but is otherwise identified or measured:

   machinery (not **a** machinery)

   sugar (not **a** sugar)

   However, note that the definite article can be used with noncount nouns in some contexts:

   Linda became interested in the design of **machinery** after she read a book about **the machinery** used to build dams.

4. You can use *the* before any common noun, but in some contexts it is inappropriate. Trouble occurs with nouns that represent general qualities or concepts. When a word such as *wisdom* or *age* is used in a general context—with no specific connection to another noun or concept—don't precede it with *the.*

   CORRECT **This library contains the wisdom of the ages. (*Wisdom* is identified by the phrase *of the ages.*)**

   INCORRECT **The wisdom is a good quality to achieve. (*Wisdom* is a general concept.)**

   CORRECT **Wisdom is a good quality to achieve.**

art 27g

EXERCISE 27.7
Last __X__ Saturday, __X__ Jeremy had __X__ dinner with __the__ head of his __X__ department at __X__ work. After __the (X)__ appetizers and __the (X)__ soup, they enjoyed __a__ main course of __X__ Peking duck and __X__ wild rice. The conversation was not about __X__ work; instead, the occasion was meant to be __a__ get-acquainted evening following __the__ company's new policy. Indeed, __the__ evening went well. When __X__ Jeremy returned to __the__ office on __X__ Monday, he felt __an__ inkling of __X__ hope for his future with __the__ company.

COMBINATION EXERCISE
Responses will vary. The following revisions are suggested:
Ever since the breakup of the former communist state of Yugoslavia in the 1990s, most people have had a hard time distinguishing among the various small countries that emerged in the Balkan peninsula. One of these, of course, is Serbia, which had been the largest of the many regions of the old Yugoslavia. It occupies the west and south, and it contains beautiful mountains and is rich in timber and agriculture. The capital city is Belgrade. Serbia's official language is Serbo-Croatian, which the Serbs write in Cyrillic, the same alphabet used in Russia and some other parts of eastern Europe. Being members of the Eastern Orthodox Church, most Serbs are Christian.
Neighbors to the Serbs, the people of Croatia also speak the Serbo-Croatian language, but they use the Latin alphabet. Being Roman Catholics, the Croats maintain connections with the West. In Serbia, on the other hand, there is a natural tendency to look toward Russia and the East. The second largest of the many former Yugoslavian regions, Croatia lies in the northwest. A region rich in coal, oil, and timber, it is also well-known for its beautiful

art 27g

CORRECT **Julia is at the age at which the world looks rosy. (*Age* is identified by the phrase *at which the world looks rosy.*)**

INCORRECT **Martin is fifty years old but looks as if he were thirty-five; he doesn't have to worry about the age. (*Age* is a general concept.)**

CORRECT **Martin is fifty years old but looks as if he were thirty-five; he doesn't have to worry about age.**

5. When you use a proper noun, remember that it may sometimes need a definite article, but usually not if the noun is a person's name, a place name, or a day of the week or month of the year:

Reese Witherspoon
Nebraska
October
Friday
the Ohio River
the Toyota Corolla

Exception: the United States

The cases in which definite articles are used with names are infrequent and usually involve a sentence like this one:

Is he **the** Wayne Smith who held so many appointed positions in the eighties and nineties?

Indefinite articles can precede singular proper nouns in special contexts:

Ms. Walker, **a** Lisa Androz is on the phone.
We need to go to Wal-Mart; I believe there is **a** Wal-Mart on University Avenue.
Someone has double-parked **a** Ford Ranger outside the front door.

EXERCISE 27.7

A blank line precedes each noun or noun phrase in the following paragraph. Write *a, an, the,* or *X* (no article) for each situation. In some cases, more than one answer is possible.

Last ______ Saturday, ______ Jeremy had ______ dinner with ______ head of his ______ department at ______ work. After ______ appetizers and ______ soup, they enjoyed ______ main course of ______ Peking duck and ______ wild rice. ______ conversation was not about ______ work; instead, the occasion was meant to be ______ get-acquainted evening following ______ company's new policy. Indeed, ______ evening went well. When ______ Jeremy returned to ______ office on ______ Monday, he felt ______ inkling of ______ hope for his future with ______ company.

COMBINATION EXERCISE

Rewrite the following paragraphs to correct modifier problems.

Ever since the breakup of the communist former state of Yugoslavia in the 1990s, most people have had hard time distinguishing the small various countries that emerged in the Balkan peninsula. One of these, of course, is Serbia, which had been the larger of the many regions of the old Yugoslavia. It occupies the west and south. Containing beautiful mountains and rich in timber and agriculture, the capital city is a Belgrade. Serbia's official language is Serbo-Croatian. Writing in this language, it appears in Cyrillic, for the Serbs use the same alphabet used in Russia and in some other parts of the eastern Europe. Being members of the Eastern Orthodox Church, the majority of a Serbian population is Christian.

Neighbors to the Serbs, the language of Croatia is also Serbo-Croatian, but the Croats use the Latin alphabet. Being Roman Catholics, connections with the West seem stronger in Croatia than with the Serbs, where there is natural tendency to look toward Russia and the East. The second larger of the former many Yugoslavian regions, Croats make their home in the northwest. A region rich in coal, oil, and timber, it is also well-known for its Adriatic beautiful beach resorts because of which a tourist lucrative trade was once enjoyed. Tourism has significant decreased since the wars that near destroyed Croatia in the early 1990s.

Bosnia/Herzegovina is found in the central part of the old Yugoslavia, a joint province. Despite having rich mineral deposits, a poverty continues to plague it. With Sarajevo as its capital, Bosnians have been witnesses to great events in history. A most famous is the assassination of Austrian Archduke Francis Ferdinand in 1914 by a Serbian revolutionary who wanted to free the region from Austro-Hungarian control, a event that sparked the World War I. More recently, civil war that engulfed the country killed tens of thousands. Bosnian Serbs, supported by their neighbors in Serbia and Montenegro, fought a bloody conflicts with the Bosnian Muslim population minority, which ended after only international intervention that resulted in a multi-ethnic government.

Adriatic beach resorts. Because of these resorts, the Croats once enjoyed a lucrative tourist trade. Tourism has significantly decreased since the wars that nearly destroyed Croatia in the early 1990s.

Bosnia/Herzegovina, a joint province, is found in the central part of the old Yugoslavia. Despite having rich mineral deposits, the region continues to be plagued by poverty. With Sarajevo as its capital, Bosnia has witnessed great events in history. The most famous is the assassination of Austrian Archduke Francis Ferdinand in 1914—an event that sparked the First World War—by a Serbian revolutionary who wanted to free the region from Austro-Hungarian control. More recently, the civil war that engulfed the country killed tens of thousands. Bosnian Serbs, supported by their neighbors in Serbia and Montenegro, fought a bloody conflict with the Bosnian Muslim minority. The violence ended only after international intervention that resulted in a multi-ethnic government.

MORE OPTIONS ONLINE
For more exercises, go to **www.mhhe.com/writingtoday**.

CHAPTER 28

PUNCTUATING SENTENCES WITH COMMAS

Much misinformation surrounds the use of the comma (,). Many students dread dealing with commas; however, in most cases, comma usage is logical and systematic. The comma appears in six main contexts: in certain compound sentences, after introductory elements, to distinguish nonessential elements, in series, between coordinate adjectives, and by convention—in dates and addresses, for example.

28a COMMAS WITH INDEPENDENT CLAUSES

CLASSROOM HINT In most cases, refering to specific sections of this chapter when responding to papers is enough to help students learn proper comma use.

An easy way to connect two independent clauses and make a compound sentence is by using a comma plus one of the seven coordinating conjunctions (*for, and, nor, but, or, yet, so*—many students use the mnemonic FANBOYS to remember the coordinating conjunctions).

When you combine two independent (main) clauses with a coordinating conjunction and a comma, remember that the comma comes *before* the conjunction:

MORE OPTIONS ONLINE If you would like to test your knowledge of comma usage before reading this chapter, go to **www.mhhe.com/writingtoday.**

The sun slid behind the mountain, **and** night was upon us.
Laura refused to study any longer, **for** she had already put in more than twelve hours.
We tried to start the car, **but** the battery was dead.
Ben didn't like the restaurant, **nor** did he like my cousin.
You can try my computer, **or** you can call customer support about yours.
I worked hard last week, **yet** I didn't get enough done.
The dog couldn't get anyone's attention, **so** he gave up and fell asleep.

Compound sentences can be questions or commands:

What did Melissa say, **and** when did she say it?
Boot the computer, **but** don't turn the printer on yet.

Here are some problem areas that you should keep in mind:

1. Coordinating conjunctions are frequently used to connect two nouns or adjectives:

   John **and** Mary
   poor **but** honest
   young **or** old

   Don't put a comma between these words automatically; make sure that the conjunction links two independent clauses before using a comma.

2. Watch out for sentences with **compound predicates**, two or more verbs and their related words, joined by *and:*

   We **raked the leaves and cut the grass.**

   This sentence is not compound; it has only one subject, so no comma is needed before *and*. However, note what happens if we add the second subject:

   We raked the leaves, **and** we cut the grass.

   Look for two independent clauses, not just the suggestion of them.

3. Remember that using the comma to join compound sentences works *only* with coordinating conjunctions. In the following sentence, the writer has incorrectly assumed that *next*, a conjunctive adverb, can be used in place of a coordinating conjunction:

   COMMA SPLICE **We talked for a while about the new assignment, next we made arrangements to meet again.**

28a

REVISED **We talked for a while about the new assignment; next, we made arrangements to meet again.**

The revised sentence uses the correct punctuation pattern for a compound sentence joined by a conjunctive adverb/transitional expression: semicolon plus conjunctive adverb plus comma. (For more help in correcting comma splices, see Chapter 24.)

The following sentence is also incorrectly punctuated. Can you tell why?

INCORRECT **Maria opened the door, so Bob could bring in the packages.**

The sentence certainly *looks* correct (two apparently independent clauses connected by a comma and *so*). However, in the sentence above, the comma plus *so* can be replaced by the subordinating conjunction *so that.* (See the sentence connectors chart on page 663.) Often, when writers need to use *so that,* they drop the *that* and use *so* alone. The resulting sentence is *not* a compound sentence but a complex sentence, so no comma is needed:

REVISED **Maria opened the door so Bob could bring in the packages.**

EXERCISE 28.1
1. The mayor has not announced her bid for reelection, yet. . . .
2. The new dessert is tasty and low in fat.
3. Martin and his brother John are. . . .
4. Correct
5. I'm going to have to find a new Internet service provider, for. . . .
6. Neither Alice nor Edna knows how to drive.
7. Jarrod wasn't able to study last night, so. . . .
8. You need to drive to town and get. . . .
9. Correct
10. Did the defendant stay at home that night, or was . . . ?

EXERCISE 28.1

Insert commas or delete commas as needed in the following sentences. Some sentences may be correct.

1. The mayor has not announced her bid for reelection yet many people believe that it's only a matter of time.
2. The new dessert is tasty, and low in fat.
3. Martin, and his brother John are going to college on basketball scholarships.
4. Roll up your sleeve, and get ready for a little discomfort.
5. I'm going to have to find a new Internet service provider for the one I use now is as slow as mud.
6. Neither Alice, nor Edna knows how to drive.
7. Jarrod wasn't able to study last night so he's nervous about today's chemistry exam.
8. You need to drive to town, and get some bread and milk.
9. Ed worked two jobs so his daughter could go off to college.
10. Did the defendant stay at home that night or was he instead at the scene of the crime?

28b COMMAS WITH INTRODUCTORY CLAUSES, PHRASES, AND WORDS

A variety of clauses, phrases, and words can precede an independent clause. In almost all cases, put a comma after these introductory elements.

28b.1 COMMAS AND INTRODUCTORY DEPENDENT CLAUSES

A **dependent clause** is an independent clause with a subordinating conjunction at its beginning. Thus, *John learned to swim* is an independent clause, but *After John learned to swim* is a dependent clause. When a dependent clause precedes an independent clause, use a comma to separate the two clauses:

> **Because the puppy had grown so quickly,** we had to buy a new carrier.
> **Even though Martina was ill,** she attended her classes.
> **When we swim,** we get excellent exercise.

When the dependent clause *follows* the main clause, a comma is normally not used:

> We had to buy a new carrier **because the puppy had grown so quickly.**
> Martha attended her classes **even though she was ill.**

A dependent clause can also be *embedded* within a sentence, as in the following example:

> The lecture lasted much longer than scheduled, but **because Michael had nothing else planned that day,** he stayed until the end.

This sentence begins with an independent clause (*The lecture lasted much longer than scheduled*) and then uses a comma plus *but* to connect it to the second independent clause. However, a dependent clause (highlighted) is embedded after the coordinating conjunction *but,* so a comma separates the embedded dependent clause from the second independent clause (*he stayed until the end*).

EXERCISE 28.2

In the following sentences, insert commas or delete commas as needed. Some sentences may be correct.

1. After Gerald Ford became president upon the resignation of Richard Nixon he named Nelson Rockefeller his vice president.
2. My cat doesn't like going to the vet, because she is afraid of dogs.
3. Because the two sides couldn't agree the trial was postponed.
4. Michael naps, whenever he can.
5. The race lasted three hours and although they needed to be in Pensacola by 5:00 they stayed to the end.
6. Andrea took this class so she could get a pay raise at work.
7. While John is a reader his brother Mike is obsessed with computers.
8. The neighbors argued among themselves, while our problems grew.
9. After you leave for town I'll start dinner.
10. Mayra emigrated from Hungary to the United States; after she found a job here she felt good about her choice.

EXERCISE 28.2
1. After Gerald Ford became president upon the resignation of Richard Nixon, he. . . .
2. My cat doesn't like going to the vet because. . . .
3. Because the two sides couldn't agree, the. . . .
4. Michael naps whenever he can.
5. The race lasted three hours, and although they needed to be in Pensacola by 5:00, they. . . .
6. Correct
7. While John is a reader, his. . . .
8. The neighbors argued among themselves while. . . .
9. After you leave for town, I'll start dinner.
10. Mayra emigrated from Hungary to the United States; after she found a job here, she. . . .

28B.2 COMMAS AND INTRODUCTORY PHRASES

When a phrase precedes an independent clause, a comma is *usually* needed:

> **A lifelong nonsmoker,** Jean led the fight to make her company tobacco-free.
> **Feeling good about the progress of his group project,** Curtis took the night off.
> **Loved by all,** the comedian was box office magic.
> **In the last years of his long reign,** the king wondered who would succeed him.

You may choose to omit a comma after a very short prepositional phrase if the absence of a comma does not interfere with communication:

> **During the afternoon** we went to a number of stores.
> **In 1999** people worried about computers crashing because of Y2K.
> **For years** Internet retailers have struggled with security issues.

However, notice the need for commas in the following sentences:

> **In 1994,** 438 cases were filed at the county courthouse.
> **For dinner,** four choices are available.
> **During class,** work options were discussed.

The best advice is to use a comma in borderline situations, especially if you see any chance that a comma's absence might impede the reader's understanding.

EXERCISE 28.3
1. That year, our company. . . .
2. After a long day at the office, Linda. . . .
3. Looked at realistically, Gerald's. . . .
4. Next week or the week after, I. . . .
5. For much too long, Felicia. . . .

EXERCISE 28.3

In the following sentences, insert commas as needed.

1. That year our company earned more money than it had in the previous four years put together.
2. After a long day at the office Linda turned off the computer.
3. Looked at realistically Gerald's conduct at the last meeting was abominable.
4. Next week or the week after I will have to prepare my tax returns.
5. For much too long Felicia has gotten away with bad behavior.

28B.3 COMMAS AND INTRODUCTORY WORDS

Simple adverbs, participles, conjunctive adverbs, and other transitional expressions frequently precede the independent clause. These terms are almost always followed by a comma, with one exception: *then*.

> **Cautiously,** the burglar crept along the ledge and approached the open window.
> **Delighted,** Sally thanked the crowd for the warm reception they gave her singing.
> **For example,** consider the role of the Federal Reserve.
> **However,** your appeal has been denied.
> **Therefore,** the contract was signed.
> **Then** the lawyers went home.

When transitional expressions appear inside a sentence rather than at the beginning, they still require commas (except for *then*):

> Your appeal**, however,** has been denied.
> Consider**, for example,** the role of the Federal Reserve.
> The contract**, therefore,** was signed.
> The lawyers **then** went home.

Finally, use a comma after words or phrases used to address the reader directly:

> Your honor, my client is innocent!
> Peter, we have had enough of your nonsense.

EXERCISE 28.4

In the following sentences, insert or delete commas as needed. Some sentences may be correct.

1. Thus the day ended.
2. Mr. Brooks your client is, nevertheless, implicated.
3. Lisa talked to the class for ten minutes; then it was Juan's turn.
4. On the other hand the new tax proposal does have some merit.
5. Occasionally an estate will auction off some beautiful antique jewelry.

EXERCISE 28.4
1. Thus, the day ended.
2. Mr. Brooks, your. . . .
3. Correct
4. On the other hand, the. . . .
5. Occasionally, an estate. . . .

28c COMMAS AND NONESSENTIAL ELEMENTS

Sentences can contain two types of modifiers. **Essential modifiers** (sometimes called **restrictive modifiers**) are, as their name suggests, necessary for understanding a sentence's meaning. Commas are not used with these modifiers:

> My sister **Lucie** and my sister **Andrea** are both coming to visit.

In this context, each essential modifier answers a question: which sister? Obviously, the writer has more than one.

> Quentin Tarantino's film ***Jackie Brown*** represents a new maturity in the director's work.

Tarantino has directed more than one film; the title *Jackie Brown* answers this question: Which film are you writing about?

On the other hand, **nonessential (nonrestrictive) modifiers** are *not* necessary for understanding a sentence's meaning; instead, they offer extra, explanatory information:

> Ken's only brother**, Chadwick,** will soon become a father.
> Jeremy found his driver's license**, which he thought he had lost,** under the couch.

In both examples, the modifier is *not* essential—there is no "which one" question to answer. In the first sentence, the writer refers to Ken's *only* brother; in the second, it is natural to assume that, like most of us, Jeremy has only one driver's license.

In these and similar contexts, the presence or absence of commas can make a difference in the sentence's meaning. Consider the following pair of sentences:

> My grandmother **who lives in Phoenix** is coming for a visit.
> My grandmother, **who lives in Phoenix,** is coming for a visit.

In the first sentence, both of the writer's grandmothers are alive. The modifier *who lives in Phoenix* serves to answer the question "Which grandmother?" No commas are used. In the second sentence, the writer has only one surviving grandmother, so commas are placed around the useful—but not essential—information that she lives in Phoenix.

In all of the nonessential modifier examples examined so far, *pairs* of commas set off the modifier because the sentence continues after the modifier is finished. If the modifier is the final element in the sentence, however, only one comma is needed:

> I'd like you to meet my grandmother, **who has come all the way from Phoenix.**
> Lois, have you met my only brother, **Chadwick?**

Here is an easy way to decide whether an element is essential or nonessential: if you can remove the word or words from the sentence without changing the sentence's meaning, you can be sure that those words are nonessential and need to be set off with commas:

> Eric's wife, **Catherine,** is the executive of a tire company.
> Our current governor, **James Fallon,** is considering a run for the Senate.
> Chicago, **the largest city in Illinois,** was once destroyed by fire.

The highlighted elements in each of these sentences add information, but they do not identify the nouns that come before them. Eric has only one wife, we have only one current governor, and there is only one major city named Chicago.

In modifiers that describe people, as the previous examples show, *who* is the relative pronoun of choice, whether or not the modifier is essential. But note the difference within each of the following pairs:

> There is the car **that I'm going to buy.**
> There is my car, **which is a Ford.**

> The fish **that the turtle caught** was eaten quickly.
> The fish, **which I caught this afternoon,** is cooking on the stove.

When not referring to people or named animals (pets, celebrity beasts, famous racehorses), writers use *that* (without a comma) to indicate essential modifiers:

> There is the car **that I'm going to buy.**

The modifier *that I'm going to buy* answers the question "Which car?"

Writers use *which* (preceded by a comma) to indicate nonessential information:

> There is my car, **which is a Ford.**

The car has already been identified (*my* car), so the modifier offers only extra information.

EXERCISE 28.5

In the following sentences, insert or delete commas as needed. Some sentences may be correct.

1. We traveled to Albany which is the capital of New York.
2. Ernest Hemingway who is credited with popularizing the term *lost generation* lived much of his life outside the United States.
3. I want you to meet my sister Louise, who coordinated this event.
4. Parker Enterprises is the company, that wanted to buy my uncle's firm.
5. Find me the armadillo that has the virus.
6. No, I mean Joe Morgan the local architect, not Joe Morgan the baseball analyst.
7. Practice and repetition, hallmarks of the serious athlete require dedication and grit.
8. Is he the one, who was recently arrested?
9. Jason told me that the answer was 44 which is incorrect.
10. Over there is my wife Edwina.

EXERCISE 28.5
1. We traveled to Albany, which. . . .
2. Ernest Hemingway, who is credited with popularizing the term *lost generation,* lived. . . .
3. Correct if the writer has more than one sister.
4. Parker Enterprises is the company that. . . .
5. Correct
6. Correct
7. Practice and repetition, hallmarks of the serious athlete, require. . . .
8. Is he the one who . . . ?
9. Jason told me that the answer was 44, which is incorrect.
10. Over there is my wife, Edwina.

28d COMMAS AND ITEMS IN A SERIES

Words, phrases, and even clauses can appear in **series**—three or more words or word groups serving a similar purpose:

> The barn was **old, crooked, and weathered.**
> The energetic pup **raced around the mailbox, ran through the door, and jumped into his owner's lap.**
> **The cold weather lasted until May, the flowers bloomed later than usual,** and **the spring rains caused the creek to flood its banks.**

The commas you see between the items above are necessary to separate one item from the next. But what about the last comma, the one that appears before *and* or *or* in the examples? Some writers—especially journalists—omit it, but in formal writing *using this final comma can help your reader*. Consider the following scenario: you are giving a dinner party and are preparing a list of names of couples and individuals to invite. After the list is completed, you give it to a friend, who will write invitations. The last part of your list reads as follows:

> . . . Anne, Mark and Bob and Wanda

Your friend is confused: "Wait a minute. Who's who?"

You explain that Anne and Mark aren't a couple and will arrive separately. Bob and Wanda are a couple, however. They need just one invitation. Adding a comma before *and* would prevent this confusion:

> . . . Anne, Mark, and Bob and Wanda

Remember, when your choice in punctuation is between giving your reader less "guidance" or more, give more—in this case, remember to use that last comma.

When series items themselves contain commas, use **semicolons** instead of commas to separate those items (see also Chapter 29, page 735). Note the following example, which uses commas only:

> We had a wonderful dinner at the new restaurant: appetizers, including salad and bread, two entrées, veal and salmon, shared between us, and a fascinating dessert.

Readers have trouble with a sentence such as this one because they have to determine the role of each comma. Note the aid provided by semicolons used in place of the series commas:

> We had a wonderful dinner at the new restaurant: appetizers, including salad and bread; two entrées, veal and salmon, shared between us; and a fascinating dessert.

28e COMMAS WITH COORDINATE ADJECTIVES

Writers frequently use more than one adjective to modify a noun or pronoun. When each adjective is working alone to modify its noun or pronoun, the result is a set of **coordinate adjectives**, separated by commas:

> The children brought home an **old, brown, weary** cat.
> Yesterday's hero has become a **bruised, battered, discouraged** man.

How can you decide if the adjectives are coordinate—that is, each modifying the noun separately? Try inserting *and* before the last one. If the result is logical, the adjectives are indeed coordinate and should be separated by commas:

> an old, brown, weary cat
>
> an old, brown, and weary cat

Noncoordinate (or **cumulative**) adjectives serve a different function:

> the **new antique** store
>
> my **former insurance** agent
>
> her **ragged, old softball** glove

Try the test we used for coordinate adjectives:

> the new and antique store

The result is nonsensical. Clearly, *new* modifies *antique store*, not just *store*. The same applies to the second example. However, the third example has both coordinate adjectives and a noncoordinate adjective:

> her ragged and old softball glove

Old and *ragged* are coordinate adjectives, but *softball* is not.

EXERCISE 28.6

In the following sentences, insert or delete commas as needed. Some sentences may be correct.

1. The steep winding road rose through the mountains fell through the valleys and leveled off in the plains.
2. Working hard playing hard and sleeping light are the three methods I use to deal with modern life.
3. A modern, high school should be well administered.
4. When I'm hungry, I dream about a warm, flavorful hot dog.
5. The results were poor, disappointing and infuriating, leading Mr. Perkins to reevaluate the contractor's efforts.

EXERCISE 28.6
1. The steep, winding road rose through the mountains, fell through the valleys, and. . . .
2. Working hard, playing hard, and sleeping light are. . . .
3. A modern high school. . . .
4. Correct
5. The results were poor, disappointing, and infuriating, leading. . . .

28f COMMAS WITH OTHER EXPRESSIONS

Sentences may contain other words or expressions that need to be set off by commas. Some expressions, such as *by the way*, briefly interrupt a sentence's main idea: *Shannon, by the way, has decided not to go to the movie tonight.* Other expressions name a person directly or add information. Transitions, such as *for example* and *on the other hand*, help connect one idea to another (see also 28b). With the exception of a few transitions, such as the word *then*, the following kinds of expressions should be separated from the rest of the sentence by commas:

1. "Not" phrases

   Sheila asked the waiter for ham**, not hamburger.**
   A need for less stress**, not more money,** led Walter to seek a new career.

2. "Echo" questions

   Clare won't be able to attend the graduation, will she?

3. Interjections

   Oh, what a wonderful idea!

28g COMMAS AND CONVENTIONAL USES

28g.1 DATES

If a full date is given, two commas are needed, one after the numerical day of the month and one after the year. However, if the numerical day is not present, no commas are used:

> January 15, 2005, is today's date.
> January 2005 is the current month.

Note that no comma is used when the day comes first: 15 January 2005.

28g.2 ADDRESSES

When city and state appear together, each is followed by a comma:

> Orlando, Florida, is where I live right now.
> Spokane, Washington, is her place of birth.

Placing the comma after the name of the state is seen by many to be old-fashioned; however, this comma is still necessary in today's usage.

28g.3 NUMERALS

Starting with the numeral 1,000, use commas to denote thousands, millions, billions, and so on:

1,435 2,000,000 25,289,074,745

An exception is calendar years: 2004, 1995.

28g.4 DIALOGUE

Reported speech is preceded or followed by a comma, according to context:

> Jeffrey exclaimed, "Marcia, you look heavenly this evening."
> "Thanks, Jeffie. It's just an old outfit," Marcia countered.

However, apart from dialogue, other quoted material may not need to be set off with a comma or commas:

> The words "Bye, bye, Miss American Pie" have a nostalgic ring for people who grew up in the early 1970s.

In situations such as this one, the need for commas depends on whether the words in quotation marks are essential or nonessential to the meaning of the sentence (see section 28c).

28g.5 SALUTATIONS AND COMPLIMENTARY CLOSES

In personal letters, the salutation is traditionally followed by a comma, as is the complimentary close:

> Dear Aunt Lisa,
>
> Sincerely yours,

In business letters, the complimentary close is followed by a comma, but the salutation is followed by a colon:

> Dear Professor Walker:
>
> Sincerely,

no ^ 28h

EXERCISE 28.7

In the following sentences, insert commas or delete commas as needed. Some sentences may be correct.

1. June 15, 2005, will be his fiftieth birthday.
2. Wanda moved from Saint Louis Missouri to Providence Rhode Island.
3. It was a dislike of people not a fear of crowds that kept her indoors most of the time.
4. Oh I guess this will be acceptable Leo.
5. October 2003 is the target date.

EXERCISE 28.7
1. Correct
2. Wanda moved from Saint Louis, Missouri, to Providence, Rhode Island.
3. It was a dislike of people, not a fear of crowds, that. . . .
4. Oh, I guess this will be acceptable, Leo.
5. Correct

28h UNNECESSARY COMMAS

Read the following pair of sentences, both of which are correct:

> As I recall, Marcy, although tiny, devoured the plate of nachos, which was immense.

The dog stretched its rangy legs and ran down the hill just as I realized that she was coming to attack me and my family while we sat contentedly beside a quiet brook that ran through a stand of ancient pine.

The first sentence has fourteen words and four commas; the second sentence has forty-one words and no commas. The need for commas is not determined by sentence length, the "need for a pause," or a desire to provide a dramatic effect. The following examples explain when *not* to use commas:

1. Never use a comma to separate the subject from the verb unless another rule causes you to do so:

   INCORRECT **Walking through the woods, is my favorite type of exercise.**

   Although sentence subjects are usually nouns or pronouns, they can be phrases as well:

   REVISED **Walking through the woods is my favorite type of exercise.**

   This problem frequently occurs when the subject is a noun or pronoun followed by several modifiers. In such cases, writers often think that a "grammatical pause" is appropriate, but it isn't:

   INCORRECT **The boy who grew up in a rustic cabin in the middle of the wilderness, eventually became President.**

   REVISED **The boy who grew up in a rustic cabin in the middle of the wilderness eventually became President.**

   As mentioned, however, a comma may be required by another rule. For example, a nonessential modifier may follow the sentence's subject.

   REVISED **Walking through the woods, an activity I recently started, is my favorite type of exercise.**

   The intervening nonessential modifier should be set off with a pair of commas. (See section 28c.)

2. Connect two items with a comma and a coordinating conjunction *only* when you are joining two independent clauses to form a compound sentence:

   INCORRECT **Leanne showed Rafael the proposal, and asked for his opinion.**

   REVISED **Leanne showed Rafael the proposal and asked for his opinion.**

   REVISED **Leanne showed Rafael the proposal, and she asked for his opinion.**

3. When joining two independent clauses to form a compound sentence, place a comma before, not after, the coordinating conjunction:

   INCORRECT **Larry ate lunch that day in the cafeteria and, Heather decided to join him.**

   REVISED **Larry ate lunch that day in the cafeteria, and Heather decided to join him.**

no ^ 28h

An exception occurs when a nonessential modifier follows the coordinating conjunction:

CORRECT **Larry ate lunch that day in the cafeteria, and, proving that miracles still occur, Heather decided to join him.**

4. In most cases, do not place a comma before a subordinate conjunction that comes after an independent clause:

INCORRECT **Jeremy was excited about going to the play, because his best friend had the lead role.**

REVISED **Jeremy was excited about going to the play because his best friend had the lead role.**

If the subordinate clause is not essential to the meaning of the sentence, though, set it off with a comma. (See section 28c.)

CORRECT **Jeremy enjoyed the play, even though he had seen it before.**

5. Do not use commas to set off essential elements (see also section 28c):

INCORRECT **He is the man, who received last year's Outstanding Community Servant award.**

REVISED **He is the man who received last year's Outstanding Community Servant award.**

6. Do not place a comma between a series containing only two items joined by a coordinating conjunction:

INCORRECT **John, and Mary have moved to Tulsa.**

REVISED **John and Mary have moved to Tulsa.**

INCORRECT **Ed wasn't sure if he'd rather be eating, or sleeping.**

REVISED **Ed wasn't sure if he'd rather be eating or sleeping.**

7. In a series of three or more items, make sure that you place the series comma *before* the coordinating conjunction, not *after* it:

INCORRECT **Your choices are coffee, espresso or, cappucino.**

REVISED **Your choices are coffee, espresso, or cappucino.**

An exception occurs when another rule comes into play:

CORRECT **To get there, you may fly, drive, or, if you'd like, walk.**

In this example, the nonessential element *if you'd like* needs to be set off by a pair of commas. As well, do not put a comma after a series unless another rule requires you to do so:

INCORRECT **Many architects admire the Empire State Building, the Chrysler Building, and the Hoover Dam, as examples of Art Deco design.**

CORRECT **Many architects admire the Empire State Building, the Chrysler Building, and the Hoover Dam as examples of Art Deco design.**

8. Do not place a comma after *like*, *as*, or *such as*:

INCORRECT **Jason prefers old-style heavy metal bands like, Metallica.**

REVISED **Jason prefers old-style heavy metal bands, like Metallica.**

INCORRECT **Small children are likely to engage in such activities as, public displays of emotion.**

REVISED **Small children are likely to engage in such activities as public displays of emotion.**

INCORRECT **Vera enjoys visiting Latin American countries such as, Brazil and Argentina.**

CORRECT **Vera enjoys visiting Latin American countries, such as Brazil and Argentina.**

9. Do not place a comma next to a dash or a question mark.

Sometimes, rules of punctuation can come into conflict with each other, as in the following sentence:

INCORRECT **Mark, who has trouble getting up in the morning, took a second-shift job,—a very bad move,—and then he compounded the error by registering for early-morning classes.**

Dashes always *replace* other marks of punctuation (see also Chapter 29, pages 739–740):

REVISED **Mark, who has trouble getting up in the morning, took a second-shift job—a very bad move—and then he compounded the error by registering for early-morning classes.**

Question marks sometimes need to appear within a sentence, but they should never be followed by commas:

INCORRECT **Guillen's latest novel, *Where to Next?*, is a humorous account of two slackers on the run.**

IMPROVED ***Where to Next?* is Guillen's latest novel, a humorous account of two slackers on the run.**

Note that in the improved sentence, the words have been reordered.

10. In a set of coordinate adjectives, do not place a comma after the last adjective:

INCORRECT **The only item left in the abandoned playground was an old, damaged, swing set.**

REVISED **The only item left in the abandoned playground was an old, damaged swing set.**

EXERCISE 28.8

Some of the commas in the following sentences are unnecessary. Delete these commas, but retain those that are used correctly.

EXERCISE 28.8

1. Cooking a huge supper for her mammoth family was a. . . .
2. Voting or not voting is a choice that we, as citizens, have to face.
3. She walked all the way downtown and stopped at Cloisonné, her favorite shop.
4. The legislature should pass this measure because the people's long-term well-being will be improved if it is passed.
5. Tall, dark, and handsome, the hero of the movie we saw last night was a virtual cliché.
6. All I had to eat today was an old, bruised apple.
7. The new breakfast spot has coffees from many countries, such as Kenya. . . .
8. Knowing the consequences of failure can put. . . .
9. The singer's first number—absolutely guaranteed to please the audience—was his first hit, from way back in 1965.
10. This was the moment that Constance had been waiting for.

1. Cooking a huge supper for her mammoth family, was a chore that Ms. Van Meter had come to dread.
2. Voting, or not voting is a choice that we, as citizens, have to face.
3. She walked all the way downtown, and stopped at Cloisonné, her favorite shop.
4. The legislature should pass this measure, because the people's long-term well-being will be improved, if it is passed.
5. Tall, dark, and handsome, the hero of the movie we saw last night, was a virtual cliché.
6. All I had to eat today was an old, bruised, apple.
7. The new breakfast spot has coffees from many countries, such as, Kenya, Colombia, and Ecuador.
8. Knowing the consequences of failure, can put a student under tremendous stress.
9. The singer's first number,—absolutely guaranteed to please the audience,—was his first hit, from way back in 1965.
10. This was the moment, that Constance had been waiting for.

CLASSROOM HINT Both of these paragraphs are somewhat difficult. You might want to go over one or both of them in class.

COMBINATION EXERCISE
1. Although . . . country, it . . . Ming Dynasty, which. . . . Of course, the most . . . China. Originally . . . the Mongols and the Manchus, the Wall . . . 1,500 miles, from . . . . Because it is so large, no one. . . . It is, instead, a . . . walls, some. . . . In its present state, the Wall. . . . Unfortunately, it never lived up to its purpose, for in the fourteenth century, the . . . China, making it the center of their empire, which. . . . In the seventeenth century, the Manchus also invaded China, and they. . . .
2. The United Nations and the League. . . . Among the most prominent similarities that . . . League is. . . . The League . . . World War I, which. . . . Because "the Great War," as it was then called, was . . . history, many . . . organization that would make World War I "the war to end all wars." At the outset, the . . . the United States, Great Britain, Italy, and France, whose. . . .

COMBINATION EXERCISE

Add or delete commas as necessary in the following two paragraphs.

1. Although China is an ancient country it has few great buildings that date to a time before the Ming Dynasty which ruled the country from the fourteenth to the seventeenth centuries. Of course the most obvious exception is the Great Wall of China. Originally built to keep out northern invaders like the Mongols, and the Manchus the Wall stretches for 1500 miles from the Yellow River to the Province of Gansu. Because it is so large no one person or royal dynasty can claim to have built it. It is instead a stringing together of many walls some of which date back to the third century B.C.E. In its present state the Wall has existed about 700 years. Unfortunately it never lived up to its purpose for in the fourteenth century the Mongols did successfully invade China making it the center of their empire which stretched as far as eastern Europe. In the seventeenth century the Manchus also invaded China and they established a dynasty that lasted until 1912.
2. The United Nations, and the League of Nations have much in common. Among the most prominent similarities, that the UN shares with the now defunct League, is a mission to maintain world peace. The League was founded shortly after World War I which lasted from 1914 to 1918. Because "the Great War" as it was then called was the most destructive war in history many world leaders decided to create an organization, that would make World War I, "the war to end all wars." At the outset the League was conceived by leaders of the United States Great Britain Italy and France whose countries had been victorious.

no ^; 28h

MORE OPTIONS ONLINE For more exercises, go to **www.mhhe.com/writingtoday**.

CHAPTER 29

PUNCTUATING SENTENCES WITH OTHER PUNCTUATION MARKS

You learned in Chapter 28 that correct use of the comma will help you arrange words in a sentence so that your readers will process your message quickly, efficiently, and accurately. The same applies to other marks of punctuation. Learning how to use all of them is essential to controlling sentence structure and communicating clearly.

CLASSROOM HINT Depending on how effectively your students demonstrate mastery over sentence punctuation in their writing, you might want to discuss parts of this chapter in class.

MORE OPTIONS ONLINE
If you would like to test your knowledge of punctuation before reading this chapter, go to **www.mhhe.com/writingtoday**.

29a PERIODS (.)

Periods are used to end sentences and to indicate abbreviations, initials, and decimals.

1. **To end sentences.** The major function of the period is to end a complete declarative or imperative sentence:

   DECLARATIVE **Illinois is the birthplace of Carl Sandburg.**

   IMPERATIVE **Look for the gas station on the left side of the road.**

2. **To indicate abbreviations.** Only a few terms are always shown in abbreviated format:

A.M. or a.m. (ante meridian)	C.E. (common era)
P.M. or p.m. (post meridian)	B.C.E. (before common era)
A.D. (anno Domini)	i.e. (id est—"that is")
B.C. (before Christ)	e.g. (exempli gratia—"for example")

   Most other commonly abbreviated terms should first be spelled out, with the abbreviation in parentheses following the full name—for example, *National Football League (NFL)*—and subsequently referred to by the abbreviation. Some abbreviations take periods; others do not. Usually, titles and college degrees are abbreviated with a period:

Dr. Martin	M.A.
Mr. Sanchez	M.B.A.
Ms. Ishigotu	M.S.
Mrs. Janowitz	Ed.D.
B.A.	B.S.
Ph.D.	J.D.D.

   Abbreviations for addresses and geographical areas tend to use periods as well:

21 Parker Rd.	Boston, Mass.
1497 Summerlin Ave.	Atlanta, Ga.

   However, *USA* is the accepted abbreviation for *United States of America* while *U.S.* is the shorter form. Most writers use the abbreviations recommended by the U.S. Postal Service when referring to states—for example, *CO* for *Colorado* and *GA* for *Georgia.*

   You need to decide whether to add periods to abbreviations in the names of companies and organizations on a case-by-case basis. If you are unsure whether to use the period when abbreviating common terms, however, consult a college-level dictionary.

3. **In initials.** When you refer to people by their initials, put a period after each initial, and insert a space after each period:

E. L. Williamson	G. V. W. Vance IV

   Exception: If a company's name is based on the initials of its founder, follow the company's chosen style—for example, JC Penney or E. F. Hutton.

4. **In decimals.** The period is also used to indicate decimals in mixed numbers:

   The inflation rate of 3.2 percent was very close to the previous year's rate.

29b SEMICOLONS (;)

Semicolons are used to separate independent (main) clauses in a sentence and to separate items in a series when those items contain commas.

1. **To separate independent (main) clauses.** The following sentences both contain two independent clauses connected with a semicolon:

   Poland was once controlled by the Soviet Union; it is now an independent member of the world community.

   Juan's dentist was ill; consequently, Juan needed to change his appointment.

When a semicolon is used in this way, *it acts as an internal period.* The semicolon has the same "weight" as a period, but it allows you to keep both clauses in the same sentence, a choice that is often very effective. For instance, in the second example, the second clause tells readers of something that happened because of the situation explained in the first clause. The two clauses are related; one states a cause, the other an effect.

Because it can separate two independent clauses, a semicolon is one way to correct a comma splice or fused sentence:

COMMA SPLICE	**My sister became seriously ill, therefore, I had to postpone my vacation.**
FUSED SENTENCE	**My sister became seriously ill therefore, I had to postpone my vacation.**
CORRECT	**My sister became seriously ill; therefore, I had to postpone my vacation.**

A semicolon should never be used to separate a dependent clause from an independent clause, however.

INCORRECT	**When I did get to take my vacation; I couldn't decide where to go.**
CORRECT	**When I did get to take my vacation, I couldn't decide where to go.**

2. **To separate items in a series when those items contain commas.** The following example contains items separated only by commas:

CONFUSING	**Our trip to Italy included visits to several historic sites: the Colosseum, the Vatican, and the Spanish Steps in Rome, the ancient streets, taverns, and private homes of Pompeii, and the many temples, amphitheaters, and catacombs in Segesta, Agrigento, and Siracusa, Sicily.**

Readers have trouble processing a sentence such as this one because they have to determine the role of each comma. To make it easier to read the sentence, add a semicolon between each major entry or item:

CLEARER **Our trip to Italy included visits to several historic sites: the Colosseum, the Vatican, and the Spanish Steps in Rome; the ancient streets, taverns, and private homes of Pompeii; and the many temples, amphitheaters, and catacombs in Segesta, Agrigento, and Siracusa, Sicily.**

EXERCISE 29.1

EXERCISE 29.1 Responses may vary. The following revisions are suggested:
1. Florida is an important state; for example, the. . . .
2. Amy isn't an M.D.; she's a Ph.D.
3. V. J. Harris planned on attending medical school; therefore, he. . . .
4. Martha . . . Stockholm Street; however, it was closed.
5. We should work hard and save; we. . . .
6. The college has changed its policy on drop/add; now. . . .
7. Mr. and Mrs. Rogers didn't go to Ontario this summer; instead, they. . . .
8. Don't hold the shift key down. Just. . . .
9. It's been very hot this summer; in fact, we. . . .
10. Starting preschool is stressful for children. For some, it. . . .

Insert periods or semicolons as appropriate in the following sentences. You may have to remove other marks of punctuation.

1. Florida is an important state for example, the vote in Florida decided the 2000 presidential election.
2. Amy isn't an MD, she's a Ph.D.
3. V J Harris planned on attending medical school, therefore, he took many biology and chemistry classes.
4. Martha wanted to explore the new lamp store that just opened on Stockholm Street however, it was closed.
5. We should work hard and save, we should also be kind to those who are less fortunate.
6. The college has changed its policy on drop/add, now the period has been extended to four days.
7. Mr and Mrs Rogers didn't go to Ontario this summer, instead they went to New Brunswick.
8. Don't hold the shift key down just hit enter twice.
9. It's been very hot this summer, in fact, we had four days that set new temperature records.
10. Starting preschool is stressful for children for some, it is a very painful separation.

29c QUESTION MARKS (?) AND EXCLAMATION MARKS (!)

Question marks are normally used to end direct questions:

> How is it that Congress can waste so much money?
> Can you put down two bucks on the four-horse, Lefty?

However, question marks can also sometimes appear within sentences:

> The salmon had returned to their river of birth (who knows how?) and proceeded upstream.

An error to watch for is the question mark used incorrectly to end an implied question:

INCORRECT **She asked if we'd be done by noon?**

CORRECT **She asked if we'd be done by noon.**

Another error is the question treated as a declarative sentence:

INCORRECT **What might have happened if Laura had stayed home that day.**

CORRECT **What might have happened if Laura had stayed home that day?**

Exclamation marks are used to express strong emotion or to emphasize a point:

Put that gun down!
Then he had the nerve to ask for a raise!

In some instances, an exclamation mark can appear *within* the sentence, usually at the end of a sentence in parentheses or set off by dashes:

We saw *In the Bedroom* that night (what a film!) and saw *Lord of the Rings* the next afternoon.

Use the exclamation mark judiciously. It is a very forceful mark of punctuation, and readers can become annoyed if they see it too often ("And the battle was over! General Lee had finally lost!").

Exclamation marks and question marks can appear inside or outside of quotation marks, depending upon the sense of the sentence:

Did Jennifer say that "the committee has already met"?
Jennifer asked, "Has the committee already met?"

The first sentence is a question about a statement. Therefore, the question mark relates to the entire sentence, not just to the quotation. The second sentence is a statement about a question. The question mark relates only to the question, which appears in quotation marks.

The same logic applies when dealing with exclamation marks and quotation marks:

I can't believe that Roxanne has voted to "abstain"!
"Give me liberty," declared Henry Patrick, "or give me a salami on rye with lots of mustard!"

You can find more about using quotation marks in 29h–29j.

EXERCISE 29.2

In the following sentences, add or delete periods, question marks, and exclamation marks where appropriate.

1. Walter asked if we needed any lunch?
2. Is the meeting in the morning or in the evening.
3. "Roger," she shouted, "you are an absolute idiot"
4. The boss has scheduled another meeting (will this madness never end) for Thursday.
5. A restaurant in New York charges over $40 for a hamburger. People who eat there have rocks in their heads.

EXERCISE 29.2
Responses may vary. The following revisions are suggested:
1. . . . lunch.
2. . . . evening?
3. . . . idiot!"
4. . . . meeting (will this madness never end?). . . .
5. . . . heads!

29d COLONS (:)

Colons are used to introduce a list or an example and to show cause-and-effect relationships, as in these sentences:

> Bring the following supplies to the first class: watercolors, bonded paper, and notebooks.
>
> Shaun is what our organization needs most: an excellent programmer.
>
> Ms. Thompson's constant carping has had one very bad effect on our office: no one feels like doing any more than is strictly necessary.

Notice that in each case, the colon means the same as *namely.* If you can substitute a comma plus *namely* for the colon, the colon is logical.

Capitalizing the first word of a complete sentence following a colon is optional. Whether or not you choose to capitalize, be consistent throughout your document.

Colons also appear in the salutations of business letters:

> Dear Dr. Gonzalez:
>
> Dear Personnel Director:

The colon is sometimes useful in sentences that have too many commas:

CHOPPY **Albeit talented, Roderigo, one of my former classmates, is lacking in one area, persistence.**

SMOOTHER **Albeit talented, Roderigo, one of my former classmates, is lacking in one area: persistence.**

Colons are useful, but remember to employ them only when they are needed. They are not needed after introductory phrases like *such as, for instance,* and *for example:*

INCORRECT **Woody Allen has directed many fine films, such as: *Annie Hall* and *The Purple Rose of Cairo.***

CORRECT **Woody Allen has directed many fine films, such as *Annie Hall* and *The Purple Rose of Cairo.***

Note that this rule applies even when introducing block quotations (see chapters 18 and 21).

Never insert a colon after a linking verb (*be, seem, feel, appear,* and so on):

INCORRECT **The only make of car he buys is: Toyota.**

CORRECT **The only make of car he buys is Toyota.**

CORRECT **He buys only one make of car: Toyota.**

Never use more than one colon per sentence:

INCORRECT **Our History of Eastern Europe class began our trip by visiting Poland's two major cities: Warsaw and Krakow, and then we went on to the capitals of Hungary and the Czech Republic: Budapest and Prague.**

CORRECT **Our History of Eastern Europe class began our trip by visiting Poland's two major cities: Warsaw and Krakow. Then we went on to the capitals of Hungary and the Czech Republic: Budapest and Prague.**

29e DASHES (—)

Consider this sentence, which is swimming in commas:

> Browsing through the store, I stopped to listen to the cologne seller's pitch, a stupid choice on my part, and then, somewhat chastened, I headed through the accessories, women's, and home decorating departments.

Although this sentence is correctly punctuated, the reader can't tell which part of it should be emphasized. Adding a pair of dashes helps organize the ideas in the sentence:

> Browsing through the store, I stopped to listen to the cologne seller's pitch—a stupid choice on my part—and then, somewhat chastened, I headed through the accessories, women's, and home decorating departments.

The strongest statement here is *a stupid choice on my part.* Therefore, setting it off with dashes instead of commas makes its significance clear.

Dashes call attention to part of the sentence. They set off nonessential parts of a sentence, as commas do (see Chapter 28, pages 723–724), but they provide much more emphasis than commas. Moreover, as in the example above, they can tighten a sentence's focus.

Here are some guidelines for using dashes:

1. When you are producing a handwritten essay, draw the dash as a continuous line approximately twice as long as a hyphen (see Chapter 30, pages 758–760). The dash should touch both words that surround it; don't add a space in front of or after it. When writing on a computer, use the solid dash if your software supplies it; if not, use two hyphens. In either case, do not insert spaces before and after the dash.
2. Dashes take the place of other punctuation, so a dash should never appear next to a comma, for example:

   INCORRECT **The Marine on the left,—the one wearing all the medals,—is Phil's brother.**

   CORRECT **The Marine on the left—the one wearing all the medals—is Phil's brother.**
3. Commas are used in pairs to set off nonessential modifiers unless the modifier comes at the end of the sentence. Dashes are used in exactly the same way:

   John's funny speech—an abrupt departure from his previous tirade—caught the audience by surprise.

Our group made only seventeen dollars from Saturday's car wash—a major disappointment.

4. Don't overuse dashes. Too many dashes produce choppiness:

CHOPPY **Valerie's research paper on *anorexia nervosa*—the one that received an A+—was used as a model for writing in *Becoming Writers*—a booklet of exemplary student prose that has been published by the English Department every semester since 1979.**

SMOOTHER **Valerie's research paper on *anorexia nervosa*—the one that received an A+—was used as a model for writing in *Becoming Writers,* a booklet of exemplary student prose that has been published by the English Department every semester since 1979.**

29f PARENTHESES ( )

Dashes emphasize information, but **parentheses** are much more subtle, or "quiet." They are used to remind the reader of a fact or a name or to add an interesting comment. Parentheses are always used in pairs:

Luis works for ML Silicone (formerly known as ML Southeast).

A health maintenance organization (HMO) has made us an attractive offer for our group health insurance needs.

We ate at the Salmonella Diner (as always, a bitter disappointment), and then we went to the movies.

Parentheses can replace commas that enclose nonessential elements, but other commas may still be needed, as in the third example sentence above. Without parentheses, this sentence would have been punctuated as follows:

We ate at the Salmonella Diner, as always, a bitter disappointment, and then we went to the movies.

When the commas before and after *as always, a bitter disappointment* are replaced with parentheses, the sentence still consists of two independent clauses joined by *and,* a coordinating conjunction. Therefore, a comma is still needed before *and,* as shown in the example above.

Whole sentences can appear in parentheses, as can independent clauses that the writer wants to embed within a sentence:

Susan's testimony seemed to clear Mark of any wrongdoing. (However, as we learned later in the day, Susan hadn't told all that she knew.)

Jason heroically offered to pay for the education of his two new stepchildren (but he worried about how he would manage to come up with the money).

If a complete sentence in parentheses appears within another sentence, you do not capitalize the first letter of its first word or end it with a period.

Finally, you can use parentheses to enclose a short definition within a sentence:

We installed an anemometer (a device to measure wind speed) on the roof.

29g BRACKETS ([ ])

Brackets have two uses. The most common use is to insert an explanation, comment, or additional material in a quotation:

According to one report, "It [the Porsche Boxster] is the most interesting new European design in years."

Two years ago, a news story claimed that "[Anna] Sadowski and [Samuel] Entremonte [were] the county's highest paid employees."

In the second example above, the writer has added the first names of the employees and changed the tense of the verb in the quotation from present to past in order to fit the context of the sentence. You can also use brackets to indicate a problem within a quotation:

According to Marshall, "When President Kennedy was assassinated in 1964 [sic], the country was in turmoil."

The sentence above has a factual error: Kennedy was killed in 1963. Using *sic* (meaning "thus" or "so"—in other words, "don't blame me") shows that the writer recognizes the error. You can also use this device when quoting text that contains a misspelled word. (See, as well, Chapter 18.)

Another, less common use of brackets is to take the place of parentheses that are needed *inside* other parentheses:

Magra South Ventures (a privately held health maintenance organization [HMO]) is establishing a branch office near our area.

EXERCISE 29.3

The following sentences are punctuated with commas only. Reading the sentences as a continuous passage, insert colons, dashes, and parentheses as appropriate. Be prepared to defend your choices.

1. Our city's downtown section, a perennial topic of conversation, is not improving as hoped.
2. The mayor, a Republican, had promised in her election campaign to try to attract new business to the area.
3. She believed that she knew just what area businesses wanted, tax breaks.
4. However, her plan was voted down by the city council, made up of five Democrats and a Republican.
5. Therefore, the downtown area, formerly just shabby, has gotten worse, a real eyesore.
6. In fact, the building on the corner of Third and Vine, formerly the site of Mammoth Family Shoes, has started to crumble.

EXERCISE 29.3

Responses may vary. The following revisions are suggested:

1. Our city's downtown section—a perennial topic of conversation—is. . . .
2. The mayor (a Republican) had promised. . . .
3. . . . wanted: tax breaks.
4. . . . city council (made up of five Democrats and a Republican).
5. . . . area (formerly just shabby) has gotten worse—a real eyesore.
6. . . . Vine—formerly the site of Mammoth Family Shoes—has started to crumble.

7. The result is inevitable: the building. . . .
8. Its owner—a hideous man—has. . . .
9. . . . Parker (about three blocks down).
10. . . . office: a true architectural eyesore.

7. The result is inevitable, and the building will have to be demolished.

8. Its owner, a hideous man, has threatened the city with a lawsuit if his building is condemned.

9. Go to the stoplight at Monroe and Parker, about three blocks down.

10. From there, you can see the building owner's office, a true architectural eyesore.

29h DOUBLE QUOTATION MARKS (" ")

Double quotation marks have four main uses:

1. To give special emphasis or ironic emphasis to a word or phrase, as in these examples:

The governor's "Look Forward" program is a model of innovation.

Jeremy's "car" is an alarming collection of rusty parts.

2. To show that text from a source is being used verbatim:

According to McPherson, "The decomposition coefficient remains constant at low temperatures."

The lawyer's claim that "the behavior of the police was more criminal than the offense for which my client is charged" will open some eyes in the district attorney's office.

For an in-depth discussion of quoting from secondary sources, see chapters 18 and 21.

3. To report dialogue:

Alice said, "I don't want to disrupt my life right now, John."
John replied, "I hope that you don't see me as a disruption."

Note that when you report dialogue *indirectly,* you should not use quotation marks:

INCORRECT **Did Miguel say that "he was going home"?**

CORRECT **Did Miguel say that he was going home?**

4. To enclose the titles of short stories, poems, articles or essays, chapters, songs, and television episodes or parts of television anthologies. Longer works, such as books, plays, magazine or journal titles, CD titles, film titles, and names of television programs, along with the names of ships and aircraft, are italicized or underlined (see also Chapter 30, pages 756–757).

Here is an easy test to determine whether a title should be in quotation marks or italicized (underlined): you can buy a copy of *Newsweek* magazine, but you can't buy a single article from it. You can buy a book, but not Chapter 7 of that book. You can buy a newspaper, but not an opinion column within that paper. Thus, large, "whole" titles are italicized or underlined; *parts* of a "whole" title are enclosed in quotation marks.

Italicized Title	"Part" Title
Sixty Degrees of the Blues (CD title)	"Fourth Street Hammer" (song title)
Newsweek (magazine title)	"Washington Adrift" (article title)
My Life (book-length collection of essays)	"The War Years" (title of essay)

29i SINGLE QUOTATION MARKS (' ')

Single quotation marks have only one purpose: to replace double quotation marks when the word or words that need to be enclosed in quotation marks are part of a larger quotation:

INCORRECT **According to Walker, "Melville's "After the Pleasure Party" is a dense, almost opaque poem."**

CORRECT **According to Walker, "Melville's 'After the Pleasure Party' is a dense, almost opaque poem."**

Note that magazine and newspaper designers frequently use single quotation marks in unconventional ways, as do the creators of advertisements. Keep in mind that such decisions are made for *visual* impact, not editorial correctness.

29j QUOTATION MARKS WITH OTHER PUNCTUATION

Many writers are uncertain about what to do when it is time to add a closing quotation mark. Where does the period go? What about a semicolon? The following guidelines should help:

1. Periods and commas always *precede* the closing quotation mark, as in the following examples:

   The title of her essay is "Facing Home."
   You've read "Pied Beauty," haven't you?

2. Colons and semicolons always *follow* the closing quotation mark:

   There is a powerful underlying message in Hemingway's "Soldier's Home": the need to bury personal horror.

   Yesterday on the radio, I heard "Maxwell's Silver Hammer"; I had almost forgotten that strange Beatles song.

3. Question marks and exclamation marks should be placed inside the closing quotation mark if they are a part of the quotation or title; they should be placed outside the closing quotation mark if they are punctuating the sentence as a whole:

The title of her article is "They Stole My Children!"
Have you read "Shiloh"?

4. If a closing single quotation mark and a closing double quotation mark appear together, they should not be separated by a punctuation mark:

Baines writes that "Maria's career is encapsulated in 'Jamaica Town.'"

5. If a question mark or an exclamation mark appears within a closing quotation mark at the end of a sentence, a period is not needed:

INCORRECT **The title of her article is "They Stole My Children!".**

CORRECT **The title of her article is "They Stole My Children!"**

When a question mark or an exclamation mark appears within a sentence, an additional comma is unnecessary:

INCORRECT **When asked "Did you know that the contribution was illegal?," the mayor declined comment.**

CORRECT **When asked "Did you know that the contribution was illegal?" the mayor declined comment.**

As an alternative, you can rephrase the original sentence or recast the quoted question as an indirect question:

The mayor declined comment when asked "Did you know that the contribution was illegal?"

When asked if he knew that the contribution was illegal, the mayor declined comment.

EXERCISE 29.4
1. "Are you coming to the game, Eliot?" Maria asked.
2. According to Schellen, "Faulkner's mastery in 'That Evening Sun' is illustrated by . . . conclusion."
3. . . . some coffee, a copy of Vogue, and a copy of the New York Times.
4. . . . the real Titanic.
5. "Jane, your 'little fling,' as . . . consequences," commented Lawrence.

EXERCISE 29.4

In the following sentences, add double quotation marks, single quotation marks, and underlining as needed.

1. Are you coming to the game, Eliot? Maria asked.
2. According to Schellen, Faulkner's mastery in That Evening Sun is illustrated by the almost tossed-away quality of the short story's conclusion.
3. If you're going to the grocery store, bring back some coffee, a copy of Vogue, and a copy of the New York Times.
4. After I saw the film, I actually had a chance to acquire some salvage from the real Titanic.
5. Jane, your little fling, as you call it, may turn out to have serious consequences, commented Lawrence.

29k APOSTROPHES (')

Apostrophes have several functions. Their main function is to signal possession. They are also used with some plurals and in contractions.

29k.1 POSSESSIVES

A possessive is an *of* structure in reduced form. Consider the following passage:

Wanting to see my friend Ed, I went to the house of Ed. Ed did not answer the door, but the wife of Ed said that Ed was in the garage of Ed, working on the 1965 Ford Mustang of Ed.

Fortunately, people don't talk or write this way. Instead, they reduce the *of* structures into more efficient possessive forms. Personal pronouns simply change form to reflect possession: *I/my* or *mine; you/your* or *yours; he/his; she/her* or *hers; it/its; we/our* or *ours; they/their* or *theirs*. However, nouns do not change form. Instead, writers show the possessive forms of nouns by adding an apostrophe (') and *-s* or just an apostrophe (') at the end of the noun.

1. To make any singular noun possessive, add *'s* to the end of the word, even if it ends in *-s, -ss, -x,* or *-z*.

the car's hood

the dictionary's cover

Bob's friend

Morris's friend

Harriss's friend

Moskowitz's report

2. To make a plural noun that ends in *-s* possessive, add an apostrophe after the *-s*.

the cats' dish

the boys' secret

the clouds' darkness

the Harrisses' friend

3. To make a plural noun that does not end in *-s* possessive, treat the noun as if it were singular and add *-'s* to its end.

the men's department

the women's golf team

the children's hour

the people's choice

the geese's nesting area

These three rules have no exceptions, so why do many writers struggle with the spelling of possessive nouns? One reason may be the errors that people see every day. For example, if you go to your nearest department store, odds are that you will see these signs: *Mens, Womens*. You know what these signs mean, but in fact *Mens* and *Womens* are misspelled versions of *Men's* and *Women's*. Constant exposure to such errors does not help the student of English keep apostrophe rules straight.

Another reason that forming possessive nouns can be difficult has to do with the often complex spelling patterns of English. Consider the word *company,* meaning business or firm:

singular: company
singular possessive: company's
plural: companies
plural possessive: companies'

To form the plural possessive of *company,* a writer needs to use the "drop the *-y,* add *-ies*" rule, then place the apostrophe correctly. (For more on spelling, see Chapter 31, pages 776–778.) For many writers, these rules can seem tricky or confusing.

Note that writers often forget to include possessives in constructions such as the following:

John spent a **week's** salary on dinner.
To some people, a good **night's** sleep is an absolute gift.
Years ago, a **quarter's** worth of candy would get you through an entire movie.

In addition, note that nouns and pronouns preceding gerunds are possessive:

Andrea's diving was the only thing we really wanted to see.

The committee seemed unwilling to listen to **his complaining** about the meeting's agenda.

EXERCISE 29.5

EXERCISE 29.5 Responses may vary. The following revisions are suggested:
1. Jean's truck. . . .
2. The four kittens' mother. . . .
3. . . . children's room.
4. Correct
5. The Barretts' house. . . .
6. Correct
7. The men's choir. . . .
8. . . . somebody else's problem.
9. . . . my parents' patience.
10. A security guard's hat. . . .

In the following sentences, make any changes necessary to produce correct possessive forms. Not all sentences contain errors.

1. Jeans truck won't start.
2. The four kittens mother has vanished.
3. Please look in the childrens room.
4. The Subaru's reputation for dependability is well-founded.
5. The Barretts house needs a coat of paint.
6. Give me five dollars' worth of gasoline, please.
7. The mens choir is practicing tonight.
8. For Ryan, it's always somebody elses problem.
9. When I look back, I am astonished by my parents patience.
10. A security guards' hat was found near the bridge.

29k.2 PLURALS OF NUMERALS, LETTERS, AND ACRONYMS

Traditionally, the plurals of numerals are formed by adding *'s,* as in the following example:

The judges gave the first diver two **8's** and a 9.

Similarly, individual letters form the plural by adding *-'s:*

Janine earned four **A's** and one B during fall semester.

An apostrophe may be used to form the plural of an **acronym**, an abbreviation formed from the first letters of a name.

The Pentagon expressed concern over the maintenance of the nation's **ICBM's.**

Recently, however, the trend has been to drop the apostrophe in the plural form of acronyms. In the previous example, *ICBMs* would also be acceptable. Whatever you choose to do, be consistent.

Another recent trend has been to form the plural of a decade without an apostrophe: *1990s*. However, *1990's* is still acceptable. Note that when you drop the century number, you should avoid using numerals at all. Don't refer to the *'80s;* use the *eighties* instead.

As you have seen, the apostrophe is used to form plurals in a few special situations. However, *do not* use the apostrophe to form the plurals of nouns, no matter how great the temptation and no matter how strange the plural noun looks without an apostrophe. Remember that regular nouns become plural with the addition of *-s* or, in a few instances, the addition of *-es*. Notice the correct forms of the following nouns:

Singular	**Plural**
ski	skis
Subaru	Subarus
camera	cameras
potato	potatoes
tomato	tomatoes

29k.3 CONTRACTIONS

Some contractions consist of shortened forms of verbs and the word *not*. The apostrophe takes the place of the deleted *-o* in *not*.

is not = isn't

are not = aren't

cannot = can't

could not = couldn't

A few negative contractions are irregular:

will not = won't

shall not = shan't (now uncommon)

Some verb contractions do not involve negatives, but, as in negative contractions, the apostrophe replaces the deleted letter:

I am = I'm

he is = he's

she has = she's

we are = we're

we have = we've

they are = they're
they have = they've
let us = let's

A few contracted forms are idiomatic noun constructions:

o'clock = of the clock
jack-o'lantern = jack of the lantern

Always remember the important difference between *it's* and *its*. *It's* is a contraction of *it is:*

It's cold outside.

Its is a possessive pronoun:

The horse had lost *its* way in the blizzard.

Also note the difference between *they're* and *their:*

They're about to put *their* house up for sale.

EXERCISE 29.6

Add, move, or delete apostrophes in the following sentences. Not all sentences contain errors.

1. Lets ask the security guard if we can stay late tonight; she frequently let's us do so if her supervisor is'nt on the grounds.

2. This parking lot is full of Volvo's.

3. The 1970s were kind to my aunt; she made her fortune then.

4. Robbie vowed to make all As next semester.

5. As we began to eat, we realized that the spaghetti hadnt been cooked long enough.

EXERCISE 29.6
1. Let's ask . . .; she frequently lets . . . isn't. . . .
2. . . . Volvos.
3. Correct
4. . . . all A's. . . .
5. . . . the spaghetti hadn't. . . .

29l SLASHES (/)

The **slash** has two primary functions: to separate lines of poetry that appear within text and to connect nouns that have a dual role or nature:

1. To separate lines of poetry:

Shakespeare's Sonnet 116 begins with "Let me not to the marriage of true minds / Admit impediments; love is not love / Which alters when it alteration finds. . . ."

2. To connect nouns:

agent/manager
owner/driver

Hyphens are also used to connect nouns; for more information, see Chapter 30, pages 758–760.

/ 29l

COMBINATION EXERCISE

The following passage has problems with the kinds of punctuation marks discussed in this chapter. Revise the passage to correct those errors.

Last Sunday at about 11 am, I was given the companies car and told to take a pair of client's to a baseball game. There are worse assignment's. Theres nothing like going a ball game on a Sunday afternoon, even though you know the home team's players hitting and fielding could be stronger. The Montgomery Eagle's are'nt the strongest team in the league, but their local. Besides, my boss—the person I rely on for my livelihood,—told me to make sure that our client's got they're fill of baseball.

It is rare that I would pay eight dollars to park, however, it was'nt my money, so I forked it over. The ticket's were waiting for us, so in we went to what one local sports writer has labeled "one of the strangest ballparks in the major leagues"! Why is it that the inside of Mountaintop Stadium looks like a malls food court. As I walked around, I wondered where I had seen more places to eat at a stadium? The game started after five minutes worth of delay, for something was wrong with the second basemens glove, and the prima donna refused to use another one!

The Mountaintops manager's must have a strange idea about baseball fans—that we get easily bored—that we need more stimulation than a baseball game can provide—and that we need constant entertainment. Almost every inning had it's attraction: such as trivia contest's, activity's meant for children, and music; music; music.

My clients' seemed to enjoy the game, but they're attention was mostly on the food courts offerings. Im a little worried about the expense report I will have to file because my spending over one hundred and fifty dollar's on beer, hot dogs, and other assorted goodies is sure to raise my boss eyebrows. I hope my companies budget for entertainment it is only a few thousand dollars can take this hit. Perhaps we should have budgeted for antacid's as well. Im sure my client's stomachs could have used them.

COMBINATION EXERCISE
Responses may vary. The following revisions are suggested:
. . . 11 a.m., . . . company's car . . . clients . . . . assignments. There's . . . the home team's players' hitting . . . . Eagles aren't . . . , but they're local. Besides, my boss—the person I rely on for my livelihood—told . . . clients got their. . . .
. . . to park; however, it wasn't my. . . . The tickets . . . labeled "one . . . leagues!" Why . . . mall's food court? As . . . stadium. The game . . . minutes' worth . . . the second baseman's glove—and . . . one!
The Mountaintop's managers must . . . fans—that we get easily bored, that we need . . . provide, and that we need. . . . Almost . . . its attraction, such as trivia contests, activities meant for children, and music, music, music.
My clients seemed . . . their attention . . . food court's offerings. I'm a little worried . . . my spending over one hundred and fifty dollars . . . my boss's eyebrows. I hope my company's budget for entertainment (it is only a few thousand dollars) can. . . . Perhaps . . . antacids as well. I'm sure my clients' stomachs. . . .

MORE OPTIONS ONLINE
For more exercises, go to **www.mhhe.com/writingtoday**.

CHAPTER 30

MECHANICS

This chapter discusses some important practical issues: when to capitalize letters, how to use italics, when to use a written number and when to use a numeral, and how to use hyphens.

30a CAPITALIZATION

CLASSROOM HINT
Depending on how effectively students demonstrate mastery over mechanics in their writing, you might want to discuss parts of this chapter in class.

In the eighteenth century, when the Declaration of Independence was written, capitalization was haphazard. Writers sometimes capitalized words for emphasis, and sometimes they capitalized words for no apparent reason. Today, however, the conventions governing capitalization are well established, and a relatively small number of guidelines cover most situations.

MORE OPTIONS ONLINE
If you would like to test your knowledge of mechanics before reading this chapter, go to **www.mhhe.com/writingtoday**.

1. **Geographical features.** Capitalize the first letter of each word in the names of cities, counties, states, countries, and geographical landmarks:

   Nashville — Painted Desert
   Robertson County — Ohio Valley
   Tennessee — Stone Mountain
   United States

   Besides mountains, deserts, and valleys, geographical landmarks include lakes, rivers, and other bodies of water:

   Lake Tahoe — the Missouri River — Walden Pond

   Also capitalize the first letter of a section of a country:

   Darla grew up in the Midwest.
   The South varies greatly from state to state.

   But don't capitalize directions, such as *east, west, southeast,* and *north,* or adjectival forms—*midwestern, southern*—unless the form is part of the term for an era, study, event, or cultural entity: *Western civilization* or *Eastern customs,* for example.

   Exceptions:
   - **Geographical terms treated as plurals:** the Missouri and Mississippi rivers.
   - **Place names with conventionally accepted lowercase words:** Rio de Janeiro.

2. **Months, days of the week, and holidays.** Capitalize the first letters of names of months, days, and the official names of holidays:

   June — Independence Day
   Tuesday — Thanksgiving

   Do not capitalize first letters of the seasons. For example,

   Memorial Day is the unofficial opening of **summer,** but **Halloween** ushers in the **fall** holiday season.

3. **Countries, nationalities, languages, and religions.** Capitalize the first letters of the names of nationalities, religions, and languages and of adjectives made from those nouns:

   Italy — Italian — Italian painting
   Russia — Russian — Russian wolfhound

Japan	Japanese	Japanese automobiles
Catholicism	Catholic	Catholic nuns
Buddhism	Buddhist	Buddhist priests

An exception is *french fries*. Also, note that when *catholic* is used to mean *universal,* the first letter is not capitalized.

4. **Sacred books.** Capitalize the first letters of sacred texts and of many adjectives made from such nouns. The titles of these books are not italicized (underlined):

the Bible	Biblical authority
the Gospels	Gospel writers
the Talmud	Talmudic scholars
the Vedas	Vedic studies
the Koran (Qur'an)	Koranic references

5. **Historic events, cultural/intellectual movements, and philosophies.** Capitalize the first letters of the names of historic events, of cultural/intellectual movements, and of some philosophies, as well as the first letter of many adjectives made from those nouns:

The Middle Ages	medieval
The Renaissance	Renaissance
Impressionism	Impressionistic
existentialism	existentialist
Romanticism	Romantic

A college-level dictionary will indicate correct capitalization of such terms.

In general, do not capitalize nouns that name political and economic movements unless they are used to name official organizations:

democracy	the Democratic Party
republicanism	the Republican Party of the State of New York
socialism	the Socialist Workers' Alliance

However, in terms such as *Jeffersonian democracy,* the *J* is capitalized because *Jeffersonian* is derived from a person's name.

6. **Course titles.** Capitalize the first letters of major words in the title of academic courses, but do not capitalize words that simply describe a course or that name an academic discipline:

At Wassamatta University, Statistics 101 is a prerequisite for Calculus 240.

But

At Wassamatta University, science classes require students to use their knowledge of statistics and calculus.

In the first sentence, *Statistics 101* and *Calculus 240* are the official names of courses as listed in a college catalogue. In the second sentence, *statistics* and *calculus* refer to the disciplines or fields of study.

Iago got an A in English Literature.

But

Iago has always been fascinated by English literature.

The first sentence in the example above refers to a college course titled *English Literature;* the second example refers to a discipline. Note that *English* is capitalized in both cases because it is an adjective derived from the name of a language.

7. **Names of buildings, ships, air/spacecraft, and animals:**

   the Wrigley Building
   the Alamo
   the *Andrea Doria*
   HMS *Hood*
   the *Challenger*
   Lassie
   Dumbo

8. **Names of companies, organizations, and trademarks.** Capitalize the first letter of names of companies, organizations, and trademarked products. However, do not capitalize names of generic products:

   Union Carbide Corporation was headquartered in Danbury, Connecticut.

   Alcoholics Anonymous has chapters virtually throughout the world.

   Johnson and Johnson controls the "Band-Aid" trademark; competitors call their own products "bandages."

   Only Coca-Cola Bottlers can tempt you to drink "Coke"; other soft-drink makers sell "colas."

9. **Names of people and supernatural entities.** Capitalize the first letter of the names of people, religious figures, and supernatural entities, except when convention requires the use of lowercase letters or when the person in question prefers lowercase letters:

Sinead O'Connor	God	Eve
Eamon De Valera	Yahweh	Gabriel
Alexis de Tocqueville	Jesus	Ariel
bell hooks	Vishnu	Lucifer
e. e. cummings	Muhammad	

Note that the *De* in Eamon De Valera (the first president of the Irish Republic) is capitalized and that the *de* in Alexis de Tocqueville (nineteenth-century French historian) is not. Such distinctions reflect family tradition or conventions developed in different countries. However, bell hooks (contemporary social scientist) and e. e. cummings (twentieth-century poet) chose to represent their names without capital letters, and these choices must be honored. If you are not sure how to spell the name of a prominent figure, look it up in a good encyclopedia or dictionary.

10. **Job and affiliation titles.** When a job or affiliation title immediately precedes a name, capitalize the first word of the title:

    Officer Preston   Uncle Rey
    President Carter   Senator Louis

    However, when a job title is used alone, don't capitalize it:

    The corporation I work for just chose a new president.

    Walker is a long-time senator; she is a close friend of Representative Suzuki.

    Be aware that you can capitalize *President* when used alone if you are referring to the President of the United States:

    The President was greeted by members of the House and Senate with thunderous applause.

    Also note that acronyms formed from job titles appear in all-capital letters:

    Michael is now the chief financial officer (CFO) of Tri-State Data Transport.

    Titles representing family affiliation are capitalized only if they appear with the family member's name or are used in direct address:

    Andrea's **Uncle Ray** served in Vietnam.

    "**Hey, Mother,**" announced Jackie, "I just got engaged!"

    But

    Andrea's **uncle** served in Vietnam.

    "I just got engaged!" Jackie announced to her **mother**.

    Also, family affiliations are not capitalized if accompanied by another adjective: *My uncle Ray* served in Vietnam.

11. **Titles of essays, articles, poems, plays, films, books, and periodicals.** For media titles, follow these guidelines:
    - Capitalize the first letter of all nouns, verbs, pronouns, adjectives, and adverbs.
    - Begin all articles and conjunctions with lowercase letters, unless those words begin or end a title. The same is true for prepositions of fewer than five letters:

    Gone with the Wind   *The Old Man and the Sea*

Exception: Some publishers use lowercase letters for all prepositions, regardless of length. Whichever method you adopt, be consistent.

Suppose that you need to cite in a research paper the following title of a magazine article:

OSPREY IS PRESSING ON WITH EXPANSION WITHOUT FEAR OF SAGGING ECONOMY

The title appears in capital letters because the magazine's designer prefers it that way. However, here is how the title should appear if you are referring to it in your writing.

Osprey Is Pressing on with Expansion Without Fear of Sagging Economy

Note that *Is* begins with a capital letter because it is a verb, even though it is a short word. *With* is a preposition of fewer than five letters, so it is not capitalized. *Without* is a preposition of seven letters, so it is capitalized.

- The first word of a title and the first word of a subtitle (following the colon separating the title from the subtitle) are always capitalized. Note that this rule overrides rules 1 and 2:

  A Worst-Case Scenario: To Succeed in Business Requires Virtual Isolation

Capitalizing Within Sentences

The following guidelines reflect current American standards for capitalizing words within a sentence:

1. Capitalize the first letter of the first word of each sentence.
2. When a sentence appears in parentheses, capitalize the first word only if the parentheses are not embedded in another sentence:

   INCORRECT **After using the transponder, store it in a cool, dark place. (this step keeps humidity from affecting the lithium diodes.)**

   CORRECT **After using the transponder, store it in a cool, dark place. (This step keeps humidity from affecting the lithium diodes.)**

3. If a sentence contains a colon but the text that follows the colon is not an independent clause, do not capitalize the first word following the colon unless the word is a proper noun:

   INCORRECT **The injured man knew what he faced: A long period of rehabilitation.**

   CORRECT **The injured man knew what he faced: a long period of rehabilitation.**

4. If a sentence contains a colon and the text that follows the colon is an independent clause, either capitalize the first word following the colon or leave it in lowercase, but be consistent throughout your paper:

CORRECT **Our softball game was quickly terminated by an unexpected event: Rain came down hard and steadily.**

CORRECT **Our softball game was quickly terminated by an unexpected event: rain came down hard and steadily.**

EXERCISE 30.1

In the following sentences, change lowercase letters to uppercase letters as needed, and vice versa. Some sentences may be correct.

1. the caloosa river splits harbin county in half.
2. my cousin roy works for Eddlestone industries.
3. his brother mike is the chief operating officer (coo).
4. i once had the honor of meeting president carter.
5. the headline in the *rockport times* was interesting: "State To Ban Cow Tipping In Rural Areas."
6. juan orosio drives a volkswagen passat.
7. orosio lives on bennington street in rockport.
8. Orosio used to live in the Southern part of our State.
9. The poetry of e. e. cummings can be difficult to understand.
10. We drove until we almost reached our destination (The Crafton city limits were now only a few miles away).

EXERCISE 30.1
1. The Caloosa River splits Harbin County in half.
2. My cousin Roy works for Eddlestone Industries.
3. His brother Mike is the chief operating officer (COO).
4. I once had the honor of meeting President Carter.
5. The headline in the *Rockport Times* was interesting: "State to Ban Cow Tipping in Rural Areas."
6. Juan Orosio drives a Volkswagen Passat.
7. Orosio lives on Bennington Street in Rockport.
8. Orosio used to live in the southern part of our state.
9. Correct.
10. We drove until we almost reached our destination (the Crafton city limits were now only a few miles away).

30b ITALICS AND UNDERLINING

Most word-processing software allows you to use *italic style,* a style of type in which the letters slant upward and to the right. As an alternative, if italics are not available or you are following a style that requires it, you can use underlining. Italics or underlining can be used in the following situations:

1. To indicate titles of long works or the names of ships or aircraft:

   The Scarlet Letter (novel)
   The Day Lincoln Was Shot (nonfiction book)
   Chicago Tribune (newspaper)
   U.S. News & World Report (magazine)
   Academic Questions (professional journal)
   Romeo and Juliet (play)
   The Pianist (film)
   Law and Order (television show)
   The Barber of Seville (opera)
   Leaves of Grass (long poem)
   Andrea Doria (ship)

Note: By convention the word "the" is capitalized or italicized when the title of a newspaper or magazine such as the *New York Times* or the *New Republic* appears within text.

Remember that parts or chapters of longer works such as those mentioned above are not underlined or placed in italics. Instead, they are put in quotation marks:

"The Prison Door" (title of chapter in the novel *The Scarlet Letter*)
"Allies Land in Normandy" (headline of a newspaper article)
"Great Books in the Undergraduate Curriculum" (title of article published in the professional journal *Academic Questions*)
"When Lilacs Last in the Dooryard Bloom'd" (short poem published in a collection titled *Drum-Taps*)

2. To indicate the fact that a word or letter is being used as a word or letter:

Accommodate contains two *c*'s and two *m*'s.

3. To show emphasis:

The ship sank in only *twelve minutes.*

EXERCISE 30.2

Rewrite the following sentences, using italics and quotation marks as appropriate.

1. Karl Zinmeister, editor of The American Enterprise magazine, wrote an article titled How America's SWAT Team Helped Swat Saddam.
2. Jonathan's reading for the week included A History of the Middle Ages by Joseph Dahmus as well as two plays by Shakespeare: Hamlet and Love's Labors Lost.
3. My high school English teacher recommended that I read the Los Angeles Times each day.
4. Phil and Marna couldn't agree on which Al Pacino movie to rent: The Godfather or City Hall.
5. One of the essays in David Quammen's book The Flight of the Iguana is The Face of a Spider.

EXERCISE 30.2
1. Karl Zinmeister, editor of the *American Enterprise* magazine, wrote an article "How America's SWAT Team Helped Swat Saddam."
2. Jonathan,s reading for the week included *A History of the Middle Ages* by Joseph Dahmus as well as two plays by Shakespeare: *Hamlet* and *Love's Labors Lost.*
3. My high school English teacher recommended that I read the *Los Angeles Times* each day.
4. Phil and Marna couldn't agree on which Al Pacino movie to rent: *The Godfather* or *City Hall.*
5. One of the essays in David Quammen's book *The Flight of the Iguana* is "The Face of a Spider."

30c NUMBERS AND NUMERALS

Rules on the use of numbers and numerals vary from discipline to discipline; however, the rules below work well in the humanities and social sciences.

Spell out the following:

1. Numbers one through ninety-nine (see exceptions on page 758).
2. The first word of a sentence. This rule overrides all others.
3. Large, whole numbers, such as *one thousand* and *three million.*

Use numerals for the following:

1. **Numbers higher than 99**, except for large, whole numbers, as noted above.

2. **Fractions and decimals,** such as 1/7 and 3.14.
3. **Numbers appearing with percentage signs or the word *percent*,** such as 8%.
4. **Street addresses:** 6 Maple Avenue.
5. **Dates:** September 17, 2004.
6. **Sums of money:** He earns $1,574.38 per week.
7. **Volume, chapter, and page numbers:** The information you want appears in Volume 3, Chapter 44, page 567.
8. **Exact times and dates:** 7:43 p.m., 1492 C.E.
9. **Speeds:** Do not exceed the speed limit: 55 mph.
10. **Sports scores:** The Mets won by a score of 3 to 2.
11. **Statistics:** Students in my high school miss an average of only 8 days per year for illness. Faculty average only 4 sick days per year.
12. **Numbers used as numbers:** In the snow, someone had written a large 3.

Exceptions:

1. If one number in a sentence must be expressed as a numeral, use numerals for all other numbers in that sentence:

   Of Dr. Moore's 114 students, 7 withdrew for medical reasons, and 28 withdrew for academic reasons.

2. When two numbers appear together, one number should appear as a numeral:

   The judges gave the diver **three 8's** and **two 9's**.

Use hyphens between compound numbers that you write out from twenty-one to ninety-nine:

Harriet was twenty-nine when she began teaching and sixty-five when she retired.

EXERCISE 30.3
1. Eighty percent. . . .
2. Of his twelve . . . four are nonsense, and eight are plagiarized.
3. My score on the exam was 88.6.
4. She lives at 96 Columbus Street.
5. Of the 368 entries, only 7. . . .

EXERCISE 30.3

Revise the following sentences to correct problems with numbers.

1. 80 percent of the first-year class this year say they are confident about their academic success.
2. Of his 12 "guidelines for success," four are nonsense, and 8 are plagiarized.
3. My score on the exam was eighty-eight point six.
4. She lives at Ninety-Six Columbus Street.
5. Of the 368 entries, only seven got past the first review.

30d HYPHENS

Dashes (see Chapter 29, pages 739–740) are used to *separate* words; **hyphens** are used to *connect* words. Hyphens are used in several different contexts:

1. Hyphens appear in the dictionary entries for spellings of common compound words such as *well-known, cave-in,* and *up-to-date.* If you think that a compound word should be hyphenated, don't guess; look it up in a college-level dictionary.
2. Common prefixes such as *non, pre, post, anti,* and *pro* are sometimes followed by hyphens and sometimes not. Generally, the trend in modern American English is to avoid the hyphen and to use solid word forms: *predetermined,* for example. College-level dictionaries almost always contain many such words, sometimes in list format, to show you whether a prefix needs a hyphen when attached to a given common noun. However, if your dictionary offers no guidance about a specific word, follow this rule of thumb: use the hyphen only if its absence would cause an awkward spelling or make a word difficult to identify. For example,

Without Hyphen	**With Hyphen**
nonessential	non-European
antiwar	anti-establishment
pregame	pre-engineered

In the right-hand column, the hyphens make the term easier to comprehend.

3. Hyphens are used when numbers larger than twenty but not a multiple of ten are written out:

twenty-one   thirty-seven   eighty-four

4. Hyphens are used when simple fractions are written as words:

one-half   two-thirds   three-sixteenths

5. Hyphens are used in typography to even out or "justify" the right margin of a page. Note that you will almost never be asked to produce right-justified pages when writing an essay or a research paper; the major style guides, such as MLA and APA, invariably specify that a manuscript paper should not be justified. But, if you do need to right-justify and hyphenate, your word-processing program will do this task for you. The computer may hyphenate some words incorrectly, however. In American English, words are hyphenated by *sound;* thus, words such as *present, record,* and *attribute* cause problems. Each of these can be either a noun or a verb and will be pronounced differently according to which part of speech they are.

Hyphenated as Noun	**Hyphenated as Verb**
pres-ent	pre-sent
rec-ord	re-cord
attri-bute	attrib-ute

If you are producing a right-justified document, check to make sure that your software is dividing words such as these properly.

6. Hyphens are also used to form **compound adjectives** *when they precede a noun.* In compound adjectives, the first adjective describes the second and

is connected to it with a hyphen. Collectively, the resulting term modifies the noun:

coal-black fish

three-bedroom apartment

late-night snack

country-music awards

student-rights activist

As you can see from the following examples, however, compound adjectives are not always hyphenated:

She wore a **hot-pink** dress.

The dress was **hot pink.**

In the first sentence, the compound adjective precedes the noun, so a hyphen is used for clarity. In the second, the adjective is a complement and appears after the noun it modifies, so the hyphen is not used. Also, simple adverb/adjective combinations do *not* use hyphens.

INCORRECT **an easily-confused clerk**

CORRECT **an easily confused clerk**

However, various three-word adverb/adjective constructions are hyphenated when they *precede* a noun that they modify:

We witnessed an **all-too-frequent** collapse of our baseball team late in the season.

The late-season collapse of our baseball team is **all too frequent.**

COMBINATION EXERCISE

Note: You may want to suggest that students consult a college-level dictionary when responding to this exercise.

The first . . . New Zealand . . . Maori, Polynesian . . . the two islands . . . fourteenth century . . . a Tahitian-like language. . . . 8%. . . . The first Europeans to come to New Zealand were Dutch, . . . seventeenth century . . . Zeeland, a province in Holland.

Eighteenth-century English explorer Captain James Cook visited New Zealand in his ship *Endeavor.* However, . . . European . . . at Wellington. . . . Australian colony of New South Wales, and the British . . . the Maori . . . the northern and southern islands. As a result, the Maori population dropped to below a hundred thousand. (An Academy Award–winning film, *The Piano,* . . . the Europeans and the Maoris during the early days of colonization.) Today, however, the native . . . the Maori number well over four hundred thousand.

In 1907, New Zealand was granted Commonwealth Nation status; in 1931. . . . In both World War I and World War II, the . . . . Allies. Today, New Zealanders . . . the Far East. They . . . Keri Hulme's winning of the Booker Prize for her novel *The Bone People,* which reveals much about Maori life in the second half of the twentieth century. However, New Zealand remains one of most sparsely populated. . . . Indeed, there are far more sheep in this two-island nation. . . .

COMBINATION EXERCISE

Rewrite the three paragraphs that follow to correct problems with capitalization and mechanics.

the First inhabitants of new zealand are thought to be the maori, polynesian people who came to the two-islands of this country in the 14th century and who spoke a tahitian like language. They now make up about eight % of the country's population. The first europeans to come to new zealand were dutch, who arrived in the 17th century and named the place after zeeland, a province in holland.

Eighteenth century english explorer captain james cook visited new zealand in his ship *endeavor.* However, nearly a century had to pass before the first permanent european settlement was established at wellington. At that time, the country was still part of the australian colony of new south wales, and the british fought several wars with the maori to gain control of both the Northern and Southern islands. As a result, the maori population dropped to below 100,000. (an academy award winning film, the piano, released in 1995, explores relations between the europeans and the maoris during the early days of colonization.) Today, however, the Native population has recovered, and the maori number well over 400,000.

In nineteen hundred and seven, new zealand was granted commonwealth nation status; in nineteen thirty one, it became an independent country. In both world war I and world war II, the country supplied troops and materials to the allies. Today, new zealanders enjoy one of the strongest economies in the far east. They have also made contributions to the arts, as illustrated by keri hulme's winning of the booker prize for her novel the bone people, which reveals much about maori life in the 2nd half of the 20th century. However, new zealand remains one of most sparsely-populated countries in the world. Indeed, there are far more sheep in this two island nation than there are people.

MORE OPTIONS ONLINE
For more exercises, go to **www.mhhe.com/writingtoday**.

CHAPTER 31

DICTION, USAGE, AND SPELLING

Diction can be defined as "the words you choose." Being alert to the potentials and pitfalls of diction can help you avoid dull, inaccurate, or verbose writing and, instead, produce lively, vivid, and accurate language. This chapter examines four issues important to clear writing: using the right word, choosing the appropriate language level, using the correct idiom, and improving your spelling.

31a USING THE RIGHT WORD

Over the past six decades, written communication has lost some of its dominance to more visual forms of communication—photographs, drawings, and moving images—and to oral communication. Written communication is still crucial; after all, contracts are not yet written using cartoon figures. Nevertheless, popular culture has edged away from the written word. One result of this trend is that many people today are less familiar with written communication than earlier generations were.

CLASSROOM HINT Reviewing this chapter (or the material on diction in Chapter 5) in class usually pays large dividends. You might review Chapter 5 in detail and then refer your students to the more concise, problem-oriented coverage in this chapter when responding to papers.

This reduced level of familiarity has two major effects. One is a smaller vocabulary. People who don't read very much tend to learn only the words they hear. Frequent readers encounter a greater variety of words since, on the whole, written English employs many words heard less often in conversation. A second effect of the trend away from reading is an unfamiliarity with the way that words "look." Students sometimes turn in essays filled with word forms reflecting the way they *hear* the words, not the way that the words are correctly spelled.

MORE OPTIONS ONLINE If you would like to check your knowledge of diction before reading this chapter, go to **www.mhhe.com/writingtoday**.

An example of the first problem—reduced vocabulary—is seen in the following sentence:

INCORRECT **The movie was dreadful; Rob was disinterested in seeing the sequel.**

CORRECT **The movie was dreadful; Rob was not interested in seeing the sequel.**

The correct form here is *not interested*. Rob doesn't care to see the sequel; the film has bored him. *Disinterested* means "without bias." A judge in a legal proceeding should be disinterested; the judge should pay attention to but not favor either side. The meaning of *disinterested* does not fit the context, something a person who reads a great deal would be more likely to know.

The second type of error, illustrated by the following sentences, shows a writer's almost complete dependence on spoken English:

INCORRECT **My self of steam suffered that year.**

INCORRECT **He attacked the task with avengince.**

INCORRECT **It is no adsaduration to call him the best guitarist of his error.**

INCORRECT **Love of money is the rude of all evil.**

All four of these sentences appeared in the writing of students in a composition course. Each student understands what he or she is communicating; however, college writing demands a precision that the "phonetically transcribed" approach to spelling will never attain.

Two strategies can help you make sure you are using the right word in the right form:

1. Try to read a wider variety of writing than you encounter in your classes and at work. For example, in addition to reading what is assigned, read a related article or book as well. The more you read, the less you will depend upon "heard" English and the more you will be comfortable with "seen" English.

2. Make a dictionary your constant, much-used companion. Learn how dictionary entries work. Use electronic dictionaries as well; they might be even more helpful than print versions. If you can't find your spelling of the word in a dictionary, you may have to look up other combinations. However, incorrectly spelled words such as *adsaduration* pose special difficulties. For example, a computer spell-checker will offer no alternatives to this spelling. In such cases, try looking up synonyms, such as *overstatement,* which the dictionary defines as "exaggeration," thereby providing you with the correct spelling.

31b DENOTATION AND CONNOTATION

A word's **denotation** is its dictionary definition. However, words also have associations not covered by dictionary definitions. What a word *suggests* is its **connotation.** Note the differences between the following pairs of synonyms:

thrifty	cheap
complain	grumble
activist	radical

The words on the left are neutral; those on the right have negative connotations. Being aware of connotation can help you make your writing vivid and emphatic; ignoring connotation can get you into trouble. For more on denotation and connotation, see Chapter 5.

31c GENERAL VERSUS SPECIFIC NOUNS AND VERBS

When writers use specific nouns, they can create more vivid pictures:

GENERAL **David drove up in his new truck.**

SPECIFIC **David drove up in his red 2006 Dodge Dakota.**

The reader of the first sentence gets basic information; the reader of the second gets a mental picture.

A related problem occurs with "weak" verbs, which create boring statements:

WEAK **Ms. Gutierrez spent several years as an office manager.**

STRONGER **Ms. Gutierrez managed an office for several years.**

WEAK **My cousin is a truck driver.**

STRONGER **My cousin drives an eighteen-wheeler.**

The second item in each pair is more interesting and emphatic than the original. For more on using specific nouns and verbs, see Chapter 5.

31d WRITING LEAN SENTENCES

As writers think through concepts on paper or on a computer screen, they often use more words than they have to. As a result, first drafts frequently express the writer's thoughts but are not in a finished, polished form.

Of course, the shortest version of a sentence might not be the best one. You will often need to clear up ambiguities by adding words as you revise your writing. Nonetheless, you should eliminate useless and wordy structures. Compare these sentences:

There is a car coming down the street.
A car is coming down the street.

The only difference between these two sentences is the number of words; the sentences mean the same thing. Starting the first sentence with the empty expletive *There is* adds nothing but words. A similar problem is caused by overusing *it:*

It is a certainty that the proposal will be adopted.
The proposal will certainly be adopted.

These two sentences have the same meaning and emphasis; the only difference is length.

Should you always avoid starting a sentence with the expletive *there* or *it*? No, but if you use these words, ask yourself if they serve a purpose. If not, use a basic subject/predicate structure instead.

As you revise, also weed out bloated phrasing, in which several words are used when one or two suffice:

BLOATED **Due to the fact that** the stock market is shaky, Sarah is investing in a bond fund instead.

LEAN **Because** the stock market is shaky, Sara is investing in a bond fund instead.

Look as well for unnecessary verb or verbal phrases, and reduce them to simple verbs:

BLOATED Joan, I think we need to hold a meeting.

LEAN Joan, I think we need to meet.

Other problems to look for when you are revising for diction are repetition and redundancy. **Repetition** occurs when a word is repeated in the same sentence or in a nearby sentence. It can make your writing tedious:

REPETITIVE Of the ten apple pies in the bake-off, my grandmother's apple pie was the best.

REVISED Of the ten apple pies in the bake-off, my grandmother's was the best.

Redundancy is the result of using two or more words that mean the same thing. In effect, redundancy means saying the same thing twice:

REDUNDANT The dead corpse lay in the narrow alley.

REVISED The corpse lay in the alley.

All *corpses* are dead; all *alleys* are narrow.

REDUNDANT The wealthy tycoon recalled the past history of the company's rise in a very unique industry.

REVISED The tycoon recalled the history of the company's rise in a unique industry.

By definition, *tycoons* are wealthy, *history* is made up of past events, and anything that is *unique* is one of a kind already, so using *very* is unnecessary. For more on how to write efficient sentences, see Chapter 5.

EXERCISE 31.1

EXERCISE 31.1
1. . . . a dog-eat-dog mentality.
2. . . . a well-beaten egg and two cups of flour.
3. . . . for granted . . . aisle.
4. We need to investigate the cost overruns.
5. The sun will rise tomorrow.
6. Many immigrants have problems with the English language.
7. This is an electronic signal locator.
8. Third-quarter profits will probably be about $30 million.
9. The doctor diagnosed my condition.
10. Manuel's letters complaining about the county commissioners' policies prove he is a political activist.
11. . . . implies that he is not happy. . . .
12. . . . led his party. . . .
13. . . . too excited. . . .
14. . . . there are dessert specials.
15. . . . raise my GPA. . . .

The following sentences suffer from the diction problems that have just been discussed. Revise each one.

1. Some people think the business world has a doggy-dog mentality.
2. The recipe called for a well-beeten egg and two cups of flower.
3. The bride took the groom's love for granite as she walked down the isle.
4. We need to undertake an investigation of the cost overruns.
5. It is clear that the sun will rise tomorrow.
6. There is reason to believe that a large number of persons who have immigrated to this country are having problems with the English language.
7. What this is is an electronic signal locator.
8. In all probability, the profits for the third quarter will be in the neighborhood of $30 million.
9. The doctor provided a diagnosis of my condition.
10. Manuel has proved to be a political activist because of his letters complaining about the county commissioners' policies.
11. The tone of our supervisor's memo infers that he is not very happy about the remodeling costs.
12. Last Wednesday, the geologist lead his party into a newly discovered cave.
13. Harriet was to excited to speak.
14. Ask the waiter if their are any desert specials.
15. I hope to rise my GPA this semester.

31e AVOIDING SEXIST LANGUAGE

Words can sting. The use of overtly malicious language to describe women is rarer and rarer these days; however, **sexist language** still appears in speaking and writing because of insensitivity or ignorance. Consider this sentence:

SEXIST **The consultant entered with his assistant, an attractive blonde of about thirty, who helped him set up the presentation.**

The sentence suggests a hidebound and offensive social dichotomy: men are functional, women decorative. This dichotomy is no longer acceptable. Note the revision of the sentence above:

ACCEPTABLE **The consultant entered with his assistant, who helped him set up the presentation.**

Remember these guidelines when you write:

1. Avoid job titles that imply gender. In the 1920s and 1930s, the famous pilot Amelia Earhart was labeled in the media as an "aviatrix," as opposed to an "aviator." Still with us today are the hard-to-get-rid-of *waiter/waitress* distinction and a distinction that plagues film and theater: *actor/actress*. Note this list of old-fashioned job titles and their modern equivalents:

Gender-Linked Title	Gender-Free Title
repairman	technician
mailman	letter carrier
fireman	firefighter
policeman	police officer
chairman	chair
congressman	representative

Keep in mind that you do not need to use such bizarre terms as *waitperson* and *ombudsperson; server* and *mediator* will suffice.

2. When you write about both men and women, treat each sex equally. What's wrong with the following passage?

SEXIST **The two candidates, William Rogers and Sara Gonzalez, were introduced to the audience. In his preliminary remarks, Rogers said that he would focus on lower taxes. Ms. Gonzalez, however, spoke on improving local roads.**

The writer is being inappropriately polite, identifying the male candidate as "Rogers" but the female candidate as "Ms. Gonzalez."

REVISED **The two candidates, William Rogers and Sara Gonzalez, were introduced to the audience. In his preliminary remarks, Rogers said that he would focus on lower taxes. Gonzalez, however, spoke on improving local roads.**

In the revised version, the writer refers to both candidates by their last names.

A similar problem occurs when a writer identifies groups containing both males and females as if they included males alone:

SEXIST **At the convention, the doctors and their wives enjoyed the best the Sunset Resort had to offer.**

We doubt that the female doctors brought their "wives":

REVISED **At the convention, the doctors and their spouses enjoyed the best the Sunset Resort had to offer.**

3. Use pronouns fairly and accurately. English lacks a single pronoun to refer to an indefinite person of either sex. This shortcoming causes problems with accuracy and *agreement* (see also chapters 25 and 26). Writers need to avoid using *he* or *she* alone or plural pronouns such as *they, them,* and *their*

to refer to singular indefinite pronouns, such as *anyone, everybody,* or *someone,* or to nouns used in a general sense, such as *any doctor* or *the average teacher:*

SEXIST **Everyone** must vote according to **his** conscience.

SEXIST **Any student** who wants to do well in Dr. McDonald's economics class must be sure **he** is prepared to study.

INCORRECT **Everyone** must vote according to **their** conscience.

INCORRECT **Any student** who wants to do well in Dr. McDonald's economics class must be sure **they** are prepared to study.

The preferred pronoun forms are, instead, *he or she, him or her,* or these forms in reverse order:

CORRECT **Everyone** must vote according to **his or her** conscience.

CORRECT **Any student** who wants to do well in Dr. McDonald's economics class must be sure **she or he** is prepared to study.

The pronouns and antecedents in the two sentences above agree in number, and the revisions avoid sexism. However, an essay that is filled with *he or she, him or her,* and *his or her* becomes tiresome. On the other hand, almost all sentences with indefinite pronouns can be revised with plural nouns, as in the following example:

CORRECT **All citizens** must vote according to **their** conscience.

The same approach will work with nouns used in a general sense:

CORRECT **Students** who want to do well in Dr. McDonald's economics class must be sure **they** are prepared to study.

You should use *he, him,* or *his* alone or *she* or *her* alone only when the context is male only or female only, as in the following:

A British cavalry officer of the 1850s could be sure that **his** future depended not only on **his** abilities but also on the politics of the chain of command.

Any member of this sorority who violates the finals-week quiet hours will have **her** room assignment voided.

The possibility that a nineteenth-century British cavalry officer *could* have been a woman disguised as a man or that a male college student *might* be passing as a sorority member is negligible and not worth considering.

For more on pronoun-antecedent agreement, see Chapter 26.

EXERCISE 31.2 Responses will vary. The following revisions are suggested:
1. Joan . . . is better at fishing than anyone I've ever known.

EXERCISE 31.2

In each of the following sentences, determine whether the highlighted term is acceptable. If it is not, replace it with a more appropriate word or rewrite the sentence.

1. Joan has broken another line-class record for sea trout; she is the best **fisherperson** I've ever had the pleasure to know.

2. Each officer to be honored must wear **his** dress uniform.
3. A grandmother must be careful not to compete with **her** grandson's parents for **his** affection.
4. An employee of a defense plant must show **his** ID upon entering.
5. The American coal miner of the 1830s saw the potential end of **his or her** life about twice weekly.

2. . . . his or her dress uniform.
3. Acceptable
4. . . . an ID upon entering.
5. . . . his life about twice weekly.

31f USING FIGURATIVE LANGUAGE AND AVOIDING CLICHÉS

Figurative language is a way to amplify the description of a subject by comparing the subject to something else that is not *literally* like the subject but is like it in a compelling way. As Chapter 5 points out, using figurative language effectively is a matter of degree. Make sure your language is fresh, and try to avoid clichés, overused and worn-out figures of speech. (You will read more about clichés later in this section.)

As discussed in Chapter 5, there are three main categories of figurative language:

1. A **metaphor** compares two things directly by claiming that the subject and its description are one:

   The Internet startup company proved to be a huge vacuum cleaner that sucked up its investors' money.

2. A **simile** compares two things by using *like* or *as:*

   Jason says that after his back surgery, he looked **like a defective banana.**

   Robbins turned as green **as turtle soup** when he heard about the burglary.

3. **Personification** attributes human characteristics to nonhuman entities:

   The forest **whispered** of a simpler, more peaceful existence.

   The darkening sky **wore the garments of doom.**

A well-turned figure of speech is highly effective and can be the difference between good writing and memorable writing. However, a straightforward sentence without figurative language is better than a sentence that is labored or strained:

STRAINED	**The dog pulled at its leash like a hound of hell.**
STRAIGHTFORWARD	**The dog pulled urgently at its leash.**

The first example might be appropriate in some contexts, but the second would work in all contexts.

Two other problems can occur when you are using figurative language: a **mixed metaphor** and a **cliché.** A **mixed metaphor** results when a writer uses two unrelated figures of speech in the same sentence:

MIXED METAPHOR	**On a motorcycle, Andrew becomes an angry bulldog who rockets through town like a missile.**
REVISED	**On a motorcycle, Andrew becomes an angry bulldog, snarling and growling as he races through town.**
MIXED METAPHOR	**The arena of love can be a snarl of confusing roads.**
REVISED	**Love can be a snarl of confusing roads, with signs that lead in different directions.**

In each of the revised versions, two figures of speech are used, but they are clearly related.

A **cliché** is a worn-out phrase that readers have heard many times. Including such figures of speech can make your writing flat and boring:

CLICHÉ	**My salary increase was the icing on the cake; being assigned to a new department was all I had requested.**
FRESHER	**My salary increase was a real bonus; being assigned to a new department was all I had requested.**

Most people have read *icing on the cake* numerous times. In the revised version, a more straightforward construction and avoids sounding hackneyed and stale.

EXERCISE 31.3 Responses will vary. The following revisions are suggested:
1. Using . . . dullness. Always avoid clichés.
2. . . . committee disbanded . . . were rejected.
3. . . . like bees that had been invited to a country bake-off.
4. Simply, we . . . the company's balance sheet before investing.
5. Hawaii will see a blizzard before. . . .

EXERCISE 31.3

In each of the following sentences, replace the highlighted expression with a more effective word or phrase. Different answers are possible.

1. Using too many clichés is an illness whose symptoms include dullness; avoid them **like the plague.**
2. The exploratory committee **kicked the bucket** after its first suggestions **went south.**
3. During the shoe sale, customers **swarmed** into the store **like bees** in a **barroom brawl.**
4. **In a nutshell,** we should have reviewed **the bottom line** before **jumping in feet first.**
5. **It will be a cold day in Hell** before Wanda Jane becomes a church member.

31g AVOIDING FILLERS, EUPHEMISMS, AND JARGON

Empty language and language offered without a sense of audience are a waste of effort both for the writer and the reader. Three varieties of misguided language are fillers, euphemisms, and jargon.

1. **Fillers** are well-known but essentially empty expressions used when a more basic expression—or none at all—would suffice:

   all in all

   needless to say

   first and foremost

golden opportunity
safe and sound

2. **Euphemisms** are sensitive or "safe" terms used to refer to unpleasant realities that reflect bodily functions, sexual activities, and death, to name a few. The deceased are sometimes said to have "passed on" or to have "met their Maker." People who have lost their jobs are said to have been "downsized." These are weasel words, language designed to avoid reality:

UNNECESSARY EUPHEMISM	**Jane is in a family way.**
REVISED	**Jane is pregnant.**

In addition, euphemisms can be misleading by masking the seriousness of a condition or situation:

UNNECESSARY EUPHEMISM	**Subjects in the psychological study were high-strung.**
REVISED	**Subjects in the psychological study suffered from anxiety disorders.**

With the subjects of bodily functions and sexual relations, however, a polite level of euphemism is expected. "I need to go to the restroom" is always preferable to an explicit account of what one plans to do there. "The young couple made love for the first time" raises no eyebrows. The key is to avoid language that fears its subject or that seeks to lie about the true nature of its subject.

3. **Jargon** is the specialized language used in a particular field or discipline. It is language used among engineers, chemists, accountants, and other specialists. Jargon is perfectly acceptable—in fact, useful—as long as it is not used outside the field or discipline to which it belongs. Only when a specialist speaks to nonspecialists does jargon become an issue.

JARGON	**The publisher warned the author that the book's front-matter was too long.**
REVISED	**The publisher warned the author that the book's introductory section was too long.**

If you need to use a word or phrase that you know will be jargon, define the term the first time it appears. Then use it as needed. However, this approach has its limits. If you define several such terms, you risk overwhelming your reader.

EXERCISE 31.4

Look for fillers, clichés, euphemisms, and jargon in the following sentences. Replace each inappropriate word or phrase.

1. The company's accountants input new data into the computer in order to complete the product's projected-cost assessment.
2. The guests flocked to the buffet table, swooping down and tackling anyone in their way.

EXERCISE 31.4 Responses will vary. The following revisions are suggested:
1. The company's accountants entered new data into the computer in order to assess the product's projected cost.
2. The guests crowded around the buffet table and eagerly filled their plates.

3. Please kill that stupid fly.
4. The new testing center stopped the cheating problem before it began.
5. The commission found that the company's new regulations were appropriate.

3. Please eliminate that stupid fly.
4. The new testing center has nipped the cheating problem in the bud.
5. All in all, the commission found that the rules and regulations that the company had put into place over the specified period of time were appropriate.

31h USING THE APPROPRIATE LANGUAGE LEVEL

Writers vary their level of language according to the nature of their audiences. When you write a letter or an e-mail to a lifelong friend, you probably use informal language and a friendly tone. However, if you were to write a proposal seeking funding for a research project, you would avoid such informality.

Language level is determined in part by the level of formality of the words used. Dictionaries commonly identify three levels of formality:

1. **Formal** words are used in scholarly or legal contexts. Typically, these words have Latin or Greek roots. A resident of North America might seldom hear these words spoken; they are far more common in print. Here are two examples:

   propinquity (existing close together)

   censorious (highly critical)

2. **Standard** words make up the text of popular magazines and daily newspapers, as well as most college writing. These words are of a level most likely to be understood by the average reader. For example, the standard alternative to the more formal *propinquity* would be *nearness*. The alternative to *censorious* might be *negative*.
3. **Informal** words are found in conversation and in conversational writing, such as e-mail messages. They are not appropriate in college writing. Here's an example:

   When I started college a year ago, I bought a new computer. (Actually, my parental unit bought it for me.) It had all the bells and whistles, top of the line. Now—just one year later!—it's like it has suffered some weird aging disease. It's slow against the Net, and the word processing gizmos are, like, ancient. I need a new box!

   Informal language often includes colloquial language and slang.

   Colloquial language is informal language that is peculiar to a geographical region. For example, in parts of New England, long sandwiches are known as *grinders,* while in other parts of the country they are known as *submarines* or *heros*. In the South, you might hear someone tell you to beware of a "pig in a poke." In other words, never buy a product without seeing it first.

   Slang consists of temporary, stylish language forms that reflect popular culture and are traditionally used more by young people than by older people. (The example above is filled with slang.) Like colloquial language, slang is usually inappropriate in college-level writing because (1) your audience might not understand it and (2) slang has no fixed, permanent meaning.

Note the difference among language levels for the following terms:

Formal	Standard	Informal	Slang
altercation	quarrel	fight	rumble
unsophisticated	rough	rube	scrub
comely	attractive	cute	hot

When you write for your college classes, use standard English. (For more on levels of language, see Chapter 4.)

31i USING A CONSISTENT LANGUAGE LEVEL

Sometimes, college students stray from general English in a paper. They might suddenly slip into informal English; later, their vocabulary might suddenly become quite elevated, as if they had just discovered a thesaurus. Remember the importance of using standard English consistently. Sometimes, you'll need a more formal word, and sometimes—when quoting dialogue, for instance—you might have to use slang, but these should be exceptions, not common occurrences.

EXERCISE 31.5

The following sentences are written in general English but stray from that category. Revise as needed.

1. Jan had not expected to receive so much calumny because of turning in her research notes beyond the deadline.
2. The small town was populated largely by rubes.
3. Worrying about a math exam won't get you anywhere; you need to chill a bit, then form a study plan.
4. Mr. Banks is a good supervisor but a real hard-nose about punctuality.
5. The smell coming from the restaurant was truly odoriferous.

EXERCISE 31.5
Responses will vary. The following revisions are suggested:
1. Jan had not expected to receive so much criticism. . . .
2. . . . by rural people.
3. . . . you need to relax, then. . . .
4. . . ., but he is firm about punctuality.
5. . . . was truly disgusting.

31j USING THE CORRECT IDIOM

Many English phrases are **idiomatic**; that is, certain combinations of words are acceptable, but similar phrases are not. *On the contrary* is standard, but *in the contrary* is meaningless. Unfortunately, when you are trying to decide which construction is correct, logic won't help.

Most troublesome idioms in English involve prepositions. The following list includes combinations that commonly cause problems:

accuse of: She was **accused of** embezzlement.

accustom to: I'm not **accustomed to** luxury.

adhere to: We **adhere to** a code of ethics.

adjacent to: The restaurant is **adjacent to** a dry cleaner.

advice on: I need some **advice on** this mutual fund.

advise of: The detective **advised** us **of** the new developments.

advise to: Dr. Sanchez **advised** me **to** take microeconomics.

agree on: Let's **agree on** a plan.

agree to: I'll **agree to** her demands on one condition.

angry with: Cathy is **angry with** Rob.

apologize for: We need to **apologize for** our loud party.

apply for: He **applied for** the management position.

assent to: The administration **assented to** the students' demands.

benefit from: We have **benefited from** her advice.

blame for: I took the **blame for** my brother's antics; I **blame** him **for** getting me into trouble.

bored by: James was **bored by** Karen's constant talking.

bored with: I'm **bored with** staying home and watching television.

capable of: Cats are **capable of** great mischief if left unattended.

compliment on: The judge **complimented** the jury **on** their promptness.

comply with: Please **comply with** our guidelines, Mr. Roberts.

concerned about: Janet was **concerned about** her children.

concur with: I **concur with** Jane; we must change our level of customer service.

confide in: Laura **confides** only **in** her mother.

confide to: Laura **confided** the secret **to** me.

confident of: The incumbent is **confident of** success in the upcoming election.

conform to: This design **conforms to** the county building code.

consent to: I **consented to** the new regulations.

decide on: Have you **decided on** which film to see tonight?

derive from: The recipe was **derived from** an eighteenth-century cookbook.

despair of: Wayne **despaired of** ever finishing his degree.

deviate from: This type of orchid **deviates from** the norm.

devoid of: The musical's cast was **devoid of** talent.

different from: Baseball is **different from** cricket.

discourage from: The new legislative guidelines **discourage** students **from** changing majors.

disdain for: Julie has a great **disdain for** unmotivated students.

embark on: Today, we **embark on** a new chapter in our company's story.

foreign to: This kind of fish is **foreign to** my taste.

hinder from: Working part time can **hinder** a student **from** studying properly.

hindrance to: Too much background noise can be a **hindrance to** careful thought.

implicit in: His motives are **implicit in** his actions.

in accordance with: We have drawn up the contract **in accordance with** our notes from the meeting.

independent of: The French researcher reached her findings **independent of** the Russian scientist.

in search of: We are **in search of** the truth.

insight into: The lab report should give us some **insight into** the patient's condition.

interfere in: Veronica loves to **interfere in** her friends' lives.

interfere with: My love of partying **interfered with** my studies.

involve in: How did you get **involved in** this mess?

involve with: Are you **involved with** that organization?

mistrustful of: Sometimes it's too easy to be **mistrustful of** a friend.

neglectful of: The new security guard was **neglectful of** the compound's perimeter.

oblivious of (*or* to): Middle-class people are frequently **oblivious of (to)** the plight of the homeless.

opposition to: My **opposition to** rezoning is well-known.

partial to: I am **partial to** chicken cooked in any manner.

peculiar to: This orchid is **peculiar to** only one very small part of Brazil.

preferable to: Success is **preferable to** failure.

prevent from: The police **prevented** me **from** parking near my house.

protest against: I must **protest against** this madness, sir!

receptive to: Oddly, Mr. Younger was **receptive to** my plan.

renege on: The bank **reneged on** our original agreement.

responsible for: The captain is **responsible for** the people on the ship.

responsible to: She is **responsible to** her supervisors.

rich in: The dessert was **rich in** carbohydrates.

sensitive to (about): Jason is **sensitive to** (or **about**) questions regarding his past.

similar to: This car is **similar to** my old one.

superior to: This wine is **superior to** others of its type.

suspect (*verb*) of: He has long been **suspected of** embezzlement but has never been caught.

unaware of: Dr. Vershinsky was **unaware of** his class's boredom.

variance with: These specs show a large **variance with** our original blueprints.

void of: This movie is **void of** any redeeming qualities.

wary of: Be **wary of** telephone sales pitches.

yield to: Don't **yield to** temptations too early; think before acting.

EXERCISE 31.6

EXERCISE 31.6
1. . . . consented to the request . . . and will not interfere with. . . .
2. . . . benefit from in his new job.
3. Michael embarks on . . . be involved in. . . .
4. . . . concerned about. . . .
5. . . . different from. . . .

The following sentences contain unidiomatic expressions. Reword as necessary.

1. The factory management has consented with the request for the installation of more safety equipment and will not interfere on meetings called by union officials.
2. Juan has an education that he will benefit with in his new job.
3. Michael embarks in a new career; he will be involved with matters related to national security.
4. The new coach was not concerned for the future of the team.
5. Rita always wants to be different than everyone else in her dorm.

31k IMPROVING YOUR SPELLING

Modern English is derived from a hodgepodge of languages. As a result, English spelling is not always predictable. Some lucky writers process language *visually;* they "see" words as they think them. However, most people process language orally, and to spell correctly, they must depend on phonetics and their memory.

For any writer who is uncertain about how to spell a word—and this includes a lot of us—a dictionary provides invaluable help. If you make a point of looking up words when you are unsure of their spelling, eventually you will remember them. Keep a list of "corrected spellings" for your reference. Also, remember that most good spellers are habitual readers.

The following guidelines will help, but they almost always include exceptions. Use your dictionary whenever you are not sure about how to spell a word.

1. *ie* or *ei:* Use *i* before *e* except after *c* and except in words pronounced without the long *e* sound (as in *see* or *beat*).

field	ceiling	neighbor	foreign
grief	conceit	sleigh	height
niece	conceive	vein	heir
relief	deceive	weigh	stein

   Exceptions are *fiery, neither, seize, species,* and *weird.*

2. Final *e:* Drop a silent final *e* before suffixes beginning with a vowel; keep a silent final *e* before suffixes beginning with a consonant:

guidance	virtuous	nineteen
wasting	lovely	sincerely

Exceptions are *dyeing* (fabric), *ninth, truly,* and *courageous.*

3. Changing *y* to *i:* When adding a suffix, change a final *y* to *i* except before a suffix beginning with *i:*

cry, crying, crier
forty, fortieth
rely, reliance

4. Forming plurals: Most plurals are formed by adding *-s* to the singular form; plurals of nouns ending in *s, ch, sh,* or *x* add *-es.*

bassists	cars	foxes	lunches
cables	handfuls	dishes	mosses

An exception is *stomachs.*

Singular nouns ending in *y* preceded by a consonant form the plural by changing the *y* to *i* and adding *-es.*

berries, caddies, lobbies

Singular nouns ending in *o* preceded by a consonant usually add *-es,* but note the exceptions:

heroes, potatoes, tomatoes, zeroes
ghettos or ghettoes, mosquitos or mosquitoes
Exceptions: hippos, jumbos, pros

Here is a list of eighty commonly misspelled words:

accommodate	continuous	hypocrisy	predominant
acquaintance	criticize	imitation	prejudice
aggravate	definitely	independent	prevalent
all right	desperate	intelligence	privilege
a lot	develop	irrelevant	proceed
altogether	disappoint	irresistible	prominent
amateur	disastrous	knowledge	psychology
analysis	dissatisfied	license	questionnaire
argument	embarrass	loneliness	receive
athletic	environment	maintenance	recommend
bureaucracy	existence	maneuver	repetition
calendar	exaggerate	mischievous	rhythm
category	feasible	necessary	schedule
cemetery	February	noticeable	separate
competition	gauge	occasionally	succeed
condemn	government	occurred	susceptible
conscience	grammar	parallel	temperament
conscientious	guard	personnel	unanimous
conscious	harass	possess	undoubtedly
consistent	hurriedly	preceding	villain

sp 31k

MORE OPTIONS ONLINE
For more exercises, go to **www.mhhe.com/writingtoday**.

EXERCISE 31.7

Sixteen of the following words are misspelled. Provide the correct spellings.

1. definatly
2. paralel
3. wholly
4. personell
5. accomodation
6. independent
7. resistence
8. seperate
9. occurrance
10. mispell
11. catagory
12. cematery
13. aggrivate
14. bureaucracy
15. disasterous
16. goverment
17. develope
18. hypocrisy
19. predominent
20. mischievious

EXERCISE 31.7
1. definitely
2. parallel
3. Correct
4. personnel
5. accommodation
6. Correct
7. resistance
8. separate
9. occurrence
10. misspell
11. category
12. cemetery
13. aggravate
14. Correct
15. disastrous
16. government
17. develop
18. Correct
19. predominant
20. mischievous

CHAPTER 32

A GLOSSARY OF USAGE

The following glossary contains words that are commonly misused or misspelled, along with pairs or groups of words that are commonly confused.

CLASSROOM HINT In most cases, you will need to refer to entries in this chapter only when responding to student writing. However, you might want to discuss some of the more chronic problems in class.

a, an These are the two indefinite articles. Use a before a word beginning with a consonant sound; use an before a word beginning with a vowel sound. For example, one starts with a consonant sound: a one-term president. Hour starts with a vowel sound: an hour.

absolutely Avoid using this word to produce redundant expressions such as *absolutely perfect* and *absolutely unique.*

accept, except *Accept* is a verb: "Will they **accept** our proposal?" *Except* is normally a preposition: "Everything is finished **except** the letter."

access, excess *Access* means "entry," "entrance," or "availability to": "Susan was denied **access** to sensitive files." *Excess* means "too much of," "surplus," or "redundancy": "When buying meat, have the butcher trim off the **excess** fat."

adapt, adopt *Adapt* means "to alter to fit": "The armadillo has **adapted** to life in Florida." *Adopt* means "to take in" or "accept": "We **adopted** our new dog at the humane shelter."

adverse, averse *Adverse* means "unfavorable" or "hostile." *Averse* indicates "unwillingness," "reluctance," and even "repugnance." "She is not **averse** to going sailing as long as we don't encounter **adverse** weather."

advice, advise *Advice* is a noun; *advise* is a verb: "I did not like my boss's **advice**, for she **advised** me to find other employment."

affect, effect *Affect* is almost always a verb: "The weather forecast **affected** our plans." In the social sciences, *affect* is sometimes used as a noun to mean "normal human responses": "The psychopath showed a chilling lack of **affect.**" *Effect* is almost always a noun: "The **effect** of the storm was profound." However, *effect* can also be used as a verb, as in "to **effect** change," meaning to cause change to happen.

again, back Avoid using these words to create redundant phrases such as *reiterate again* and *return back.*

aggravate This word is often confused with *irritate* and *annoy.* However, *aggravate* means "to worsen": "The symptoms of my cold were **aggravated** because I was able to get only three hours' sleep." "Children can **irritate** [*not* **aggravate**] their parents by making unreasonable requests."

a half a Avoid; use either *half a* or *a half,* according to context: "I had **half a** [*not* **a half a**] cantaloupe; then I drank **a half** [*not* **a half a**] quart of water."

ahold Not a word—use *hold* instead: "The diver tried to get **hold** of the side of the rescue boat."

ain't This is a nonstandard contraction of *am not, are not,* or *is not.* Avoid it unless reporting dialogue.

all ready, already *All ready* indicates that everyone or everything is prepared: "They were **all ready** to go." *Already* is an adverb meaning "at this time" or "before this time": "Laura had **already** finished eating when her son called."

allude, elude *Allude* is a verb meaning "to mention indirectly": "The senator **alluded** frequently to the *Iliad.*" Note that *allude* does not have the same meaning as *refer,* which means "to mention directly." *Elude* means "to avoid capture or censure": "The escaped convict **eluded** the police for three days."

allusion, illusion An *allusion* is an indirect "reference": "In *Paradise Lost,* Milton makes **allusions** to the classics and to the Bible." An *illusion* is a "mirage," a "fantasy," or a "misperception": "Anna is under the **illusion** that everyone is capable of doing good and avoiding evil."

alot Avoid—use *a lot,* meaning "much" or "many," or *allot,* a verb meaning "to divide among."

alright Avoid—the correct spelling is *all right.*

alternately, alternatively The first word means "in turn," "in sequence," or "in rotation": "Meetings of the committee are held once per month **alternately** in Hightstown and Princeton." *Alternatively* refers to a "choice": "You can pay full tuition; **alternatively,** you can join the work-study program and have your payments reduced by 20 percent."

altogether, all together *Altogether,* an adverb, means "completely": "We were **altogether** disgusted with the new film." *All together* is a phrase meaning "in a group" or "in a collection: "My family was **all together** this Christmas."

alumnus, alumna, alumni, alumnae Use *alumnus* to refer to a college graduate of either sex; use *alumni* for more than one graduate. Avoid *alumna* and *alumnae,* which are outdated and sexist.

among, between Use *among* to connect more than two; use *between* to connect two: "**Between** you and me, Dr. Justino is **among** the best three surgeons in the state."

amoral, immoral *Amoral* means "without moral principles." "Jerry believes there is no right and wrong in this world; he has a thoroughly **amoral** philosophy." *Immoral* has an even stronger negative connotation and means "sinful," "evil," or "depraved": "The Holocaust was the manifestation of an utterly **immoral** philosophy."

amount, number Use *amount* to refer to entities that are normally weighed or measured, not counted, such as rice, sugar, and sunshine. Use *number* for entities that are normally counted, such as peaches and people: "The **amount** of fog made driving on the highway unsafe; the **number** of people trapped in their cars was astounding." See also **few, less.**

ampersand (&) Do not use this symbol to mean "and" in college writing unless it is part of a company's name or is required by a particular documentation style.

an, a See **a, an.**

and etc. Avoid this redundancy; in fact, *etc.* alone should be used with caution. See also **etc.**

and/or Avoid this clumsy construction except in legal and scientific writing.

and so, and therefore Redundant phrases—use *so* or *therefore* instead.

angry at This is a nonstandard form. Use *angry with* instead.

angry, mad *Angry* refers to an emotional state. In college writing, use *mad* to mean "insane" or "deranged": "How can you be **angry** with someone who has obviously gone **mad**?"

any, any other Using *any* instead of *any other* can sometimes create illogical comparisons: "Anna is better at mathematics than **any** student in her class." This sentence claims that Anna is even better than herself, an absurdity! The correct version is "Anna is better at mathematics than **any other** student in her class."

anyone, any one *Anyone* is an indefinite pronoun meaning "a person." *Any one* is a phrase referring to an individual singled out from a group: "**Anyone** is eligible; **any one** of us could win."

anyways Not a word—use *anyway* instead.

appraise, apprise *Appraise* means "to set a value on"; *apprise* means "to inform": "The jeweler **apprised** her clients that their ring had been **appraised** at $100,000."

apt, likely These words are synonymous. However, don't confuse *likely* with *liable* (see also **liable**).

around *Around* refers to position. Avoid using it to mean "near" or "about" in formal writing: "**Around** the fort, the remains of which are **near** Santa Clara, were amassed **about** one thousand enemy soldiers."

as, like When comparing, use *like:* "Joan is **like** her sister." When subordinating an independent clause, use *as* (or *as if, as though*): "Ed was late, **as** we knew he would be." Avoid using *as* in place of *because* or *while:* "He was late **because** [*not* **as**] he had to wait **while** [*not* **as**] the mechanic fixed his car."

as regards Avoid—use *concerning* instead.

assure, ensure, insure *Assure* means to "affirm" or "pledge." *Ensure* means "make sure" or "make certain." *Insure* means "to guarantee against destruction, loss, or harm": "We **assure** you that enough monies have been put aside to **ensure** his release." "Reggie is an executive with a company that **insures** businesses against loss by theft, fire, or natural catastrophes."

awful, awfully *Awful* means "awe-inspiring." However, it has taken on the popular meaning of "horrible" or "dreadful." In speech, *awfully* sometimes replaces *very.* Avoid both of these popular uses in college writing: "News of the **appalling** [*not* **awful**] conditions in the city's hospitals spread through the media **very** [*not* **awfully**] fast."

awhile, a while *Awhile* is an adverb: "We ran **awhile.**" *A while* functions as a noun and is often used as the object of a preposition: "I thought for **a while** about Bianca's proposal."

bad, badly *Bad* is an adjective: "Edwin is not a **bad** man, and I'm sure he feels **bad** about losing his temper." Note that the second *bad* is used as an adjective complement, a word that describes the subject *he. Badly* is an adverb: "We played **badly** all day at the new golf course."

basically Do not use this word as a filler, as in "**Basically,** we feel sorry for Mike because of his wife's illness."

being as (being that) Do not use to mean "because": "I believe that my sixteen-year-old daughter is ready for college **because** [*not* **being as** or **being that**] she has compiled an outstanding academic record in high school."

beside, besides *Beside* is a preposition that means "adjacent to": "The parking lot is **beside** the store." *Besides* is an adverb that means "in addition to" or "except for": "**Besides** her regular job, Karen does freelance work; Andre, on the other hand, has no other sources of income **besides** his printing business."

between See **among, between.**

both Avoid redundant expressions such as "they both agree" or "both together."

breath, breathe *Breath* is a noun: "Slow down and take a **breath.**" *Breathe* is a verb: "'**Breathe** deeply,' said the doctor."

broke This word is informal for "insolvent," "without money." Avoid this use of *broke* in college writing.

but Do not join this word with other negative conjunctions, as in *but yet* and *but however.*

can, may *Can* refers to ability or possibility: "**Can** the helicopter make it to the accident scene in time?" *May* refers to permission: "No, you **may** not put your feet on my sofa!" *May* is also used as a synonym for *might:* "We **may** get this project finished on time; it's too soon to tell."

cannot The verb *can* plus *not* is usually spelled as one word. However, if you need to stress the *not,* separate the two words and underline (italicize) *not:* "You **can *not*** drive from Los Angeles to San Francisco in two hours."

can't hardly Avoid this double negative; use *can hardly* instead.

can't help but This is an informal construction. Instead, use *can't help:* "I **can't help** loving you!"

capital, capitol *Capital* is the noun for a city that is the governmental center of a county, state, province, or country. However, it can also refer to money or financial resources. *Capitol* refers to the building in which lawmakers and other government officials meet: "Arriving in the **capital** by train, the senators proceeded directly to the **capitol,** where they presented a bill to cut **capital** spending."

censor, censure To *censor* is to remove from a document materials that are considered offensive. To *censure* means to "condemn," "admonish," or "strongly criticize":

"Let's hope that the courts will **censure** the government if it attempts to **censor** the press."

center around Inaccurate—use *center on* instead.

childish, childlike The first of these words carries a negative connotation: "Though he is fifty years old, his behavior at meetings is often childish." The second word has a more positive meaning: "There is a childlike innocence in Mary's eyes."

cite, site, sight When writing a research paper, students *cite* by identifying the source of a quotation or of other information. *Site* refers to a place in real or virtual space: "The proposed **site** of our college's off-campus center can be examined on our Web **site.**" When used as a verb, *sight* means "to see" or "to spot." When used as a noun, *sight* means "vision."

climactic, climatic *Climactic* is the adjective form of *climax:* "The car chase was the movie's **climactic** scene." *Climatic* is the adjective form of *climate:* "Her job is to monitor **climatic** changes at the South Pole."

complement, compliment, complementary, complimentary *Complement* means "to complete" or "to fit with": "Uma's green handbag **complemented** her outfit." As a verb, *compliment* means "to praise," and as a noun, *compliment* means "a word of praise." Rarely used, *complementary* is the adjective form of *complement:* "The dress had a **complementary** belt." *Complimentary* means either "praising language" ("The boss was **complimentary** about our report") or "free of charge" ("The hotel room came with **complimentary** theater passes").

conscience, conscious The first word is a noun; it refers to a moral faculty: "Hitler lacked any semblance of a **conscience.**" *Conscious* is an adjective, meaning "awake": "Was Ray **conscious** when he wrote his history paper?"

contemptible, contemptuous A person or an act that is *contemptible* is worthy of our contempt. A person who is *contemptuous* has contempt for someone or something: "Luisa was **contemptuous** of her boss, for his treatment of female employees was **contemptible.**"

continual, continuous *Continual* means "habitual" or "normally repeated": "Rob's **continual** drinking was the reason Miranda left him." *Continuous* means "ongoing without interruption": "The pistons' pumping was **continuous.**"

could of Avoid; use *could have* instead. See **of.**

council, counsel, consul A *council* is an administrative body: "The city **council** voted today on the zoning request." *Counsel* is advice: "I sought my grandfather's **coun-sel** on handling my debt." A *consul* is a civil servant stationed in another country: "As **consul,** she has worked at the embassy for nine years."

couple Be accurate. Do not use this term to refer to more than two.

criteria, criterion These terms derive from Latin. *Criterion* is the singular; *criteria* is the plural: "We focus on one **criterion** for promotion: productivity. To a lesser extent, however, we also consider other **criteria**, such as loyalty, punctuality, and effort."

cute Avoid this informal term for "attractive."

data A plural noun—use plural verbs and pronouns with *data:* "The data **were** [*not* **was**] insufficient.

definite, very definite The second of these terms is redundant. *Definite* suffices.

desert, deserts, dessert One travels on a camel through the *desert.* However, as a verb, *desert* means "to abandon": "They **deserted** their disabled aircraft and began walk-ing across the **desert** in search of water and food." *Deserts* is a noun meaning "appropriate reward or punishment": "The killers got their just **deserts.**" *Dessert* is a fruit or sweet eaten at the end of a meal.

deviant, deviate The first is a noun, the second a verb: "A **deviant** is one who **devi-ates** from social norms."

usage 32

device, devise *Device,* a noun, refers to an instrument, machine, or tool. *Devise* is a verb meaning "to create or make": "Archimedes **devised** a **device** that used solar power to burn the sails of Roman ships."

differ from, differ with Use *differ from* to indicate dissimilarity: "Lemurs **differ from** meerkats." Use *differ with* to indicate disagreement: "Our local film critic **differed with** the New York critics' opinion of *The Matrix.*"

different from, different than Use *different from:* "Pasta is **different from** risotto."

discreet, discrete *Discreet* means "judicious about revealing sensitive or private matters": "Senator Bing wishes his aide had been **discreet.**" *Discrete* means "separate" or "distinct": "The park contains three **discrete** areas of interest: the zoological area, the botanical gardens, and the water park."

disinterested, uninterested These words are often used interchangeably, but their meanings are quite different. *Disinterested* means "unbiased" or "impartial": "The mediator was renowned for her professional **disinterest** when settling labor disputes." *Uninterested* means "not interested": "I am **uninterested** in modern sculpture; it does not move me."

due to Do not substitute *due to* for *because of.* "She lost her job **because of** [*not* **due to**] the recession." However, *due to* is permissible when used to describe the subject of a sentence. In such cases, it is used directly after a form of *to be:* "In the 1930s, the run on the banks was **due to** a massive loss in depositors' confidence."

due to the fact that Avoid this needless filler. Use *because* instead.

each and every Avoid this redundancy by using either *each* or *every,* not both.

eachother, each other Always spell as two words.

economic, economical *Economic* refers to the study of economics: "The president's **economic** advisors resigned after the new unemployment statistics were released." *Economical* means "frugal" or "thrifty": "Shopping at discount clubs is an **economical** way to provide for a large family."

effect See **affect, effect.**

e.g. Short for the Latin *exempli gratia,* which means "for example." Avoid using this abbreviation in most college writing, except in parentheses or in footnotes. In any case, always follow *e.g.* with a comma.

elicit, illicit *Elicit,* a verb, means "to draw forth": "The new rules for fraternities **elicited** the approval of the student newspaper." *Illicit,* an adjective, means "illegal": "The athlete was accused of using **illicit** drugs."

emigrate, immigrate A person *emigrates from* a country; a person *immigrates to* another country.

eminent, imminent Both are adjectives. *Eminent* means "important" or "prominent": "The **eminent** historian gave a fascinating public lecture." *Imminent* means "immediately going to happen": "The thunderstorm is **imminent.**"

enthused, enthusiastic *Enthusiastic* is preferred in college writing.

equally as Avoid this redundancy. Use *as* by itself: "This pizza is **as good as** [*not* **equally as good as**] the one I had in New York."

especially, specially Use the first of these words in college writing; the second is colloquial.

etc. Short for the Latin *et cetera* ("and other things"). Avoid this abbreviation in most college writing, except in parentheses or in footnotes. Do not use it with *and,* for *and* is already part of the Latin term.

eventhough, even though Always spell as two words.

everyone, every one *Everyone* is an indefinite pronoun meaning "a person." *Every one* is a phrase meaning "all members of a group": "**Everyone** is eligible; **every one** of us should enter."

except, accept See **accept, except.**

explicit, implicit *Explicit* means "stated clearly or directly": "The directions were **explicit**, but Raymond managed to get in trouble anyway." *Implicit* is the opposite, meaning "suggested but not stated directly": "**Implicit** in my ninety-day review was a sense that the company is doing better as a whole."

extant, extent *Extant* is an adjective meaning "in existence" or "not extinct": "Scientists believe that only twenty **extant** reptile species are left in the area." *Extent* means "degree" or "amount": "Doctors removed the scar tissue to the **extent** possible."

facilitate Avoid this bureaucratic jargon; use *help* or *aid* instead.

farther, further Use *farther* to refer to actual distance: "It is **farther** to Detroit than it is to Chicago." Use *further* to mean "a greater degree" or "more": "After **further** debate, we decided to adopt Plan A."

fewer, less Use *fewer* to refer to countable things: "There are **fewer** cars on the lot now than there were this morning." Use *less* to refer to things that are normally measured, not counted: "There's **less** rice than usual in the dish."

finalize Avoid; use *finish* or *complete* instead.

flaunt, flout To *flaunt* is "to boast" or "to display ostentatiously." To *flout* is to "treat with contempt, sneer at, or disdain": "Avery does not hesitate to **flaunt** his wealth. Knowing he can pay any traffic fine, he **flouts** posted speed limits and parks wherever he likes."

formally, formerly *Formally* is the adverb form of *formal,* which indicates an adherence to particular rules, ceremonies, and conventions. Synonyms for *formerly* include *previously* and *in the past.*

former, first; latter, last Use *former* and *latter* to refer to one of two items; use *first* and *last* to refer to more than two items.

get Avoid using this word to mean "bother" or "affect": That music really **bothers** [not **gets**] me.

goes Avoid using this verb to mean "says."

good and This expression is informal. Instead, use "very" or "well": "She returned from her vacation **well** [*not* **good and**] rested."

good, well *Good* is always an adjective: "This pasta is quite **good.**" *Well* is normally an adverb: "We played **well** together." Use *well* as an adjective only to refer to personal health: "Three months after his bout with pneumonia, Mr. Oshiro finally feels **well** again."

got, gotten *Got* is the past tense of the verb "to get"; *gotten* is its past participle. Don't confuse them. "Shortly after Maurizio **had gotten** [*not* **got**] promoted for the third time, he **got** an even better job offer and left the company."

hanged, hung *Hanged* is the past tense and past participle of the verb *to hang. Hanged* refers to killing by suspending from a height: "The prisoner **hanged** himself in his cell." *Hung* is also the past tense and past participle of *to hang,* but it means "to suspend" a thing or "to fasten" it on a wall or hook: "The portrait was **hung** in the living room."

hardly See **can't hardly.**

highschool, high school Always spell as two words unless you are quoting.

hisself Not a word—use *himself* instead.

hopefully Some writers avoid this form because its use can result in the omission of important information: "**Hopefully**, you will take the job." Who is doing the hoping in this sentence? A better alternative is "**I hope** you will take the job."

how Don't use *how* when you mean that: I learned that [*not* **how**] he had been arrested.

i.e. Short for the Latin *id est* ("that is"). Avoid using this abbreviation in most college writing. However, if you must use *i.e.,* follow it with a comma.

if and when Avoid this filler, which means "if."

if, whether *If* is used in sentences that express a condition. *Whether* is used to indicate an alternative: "**If** you lend me $10, I will accompany you to the movies tonight **whether** we go to the Bijou Theater or to the Star Cinemas."

illicit, elicit See **elicit, illicit.**

immigrate, emigrate See **emigrate, immigrate.**

imminent, eminent See **eminent, imminent.**

impact Use *impact* as a noun rather than a verb in college writing. When you need a verb, try *affect:* "Will the dip in the stock market **affect** our income? If so, what will be the **impact**?"

implicit, explicit See **explicit, implicit.**

imply, infer Use *imply* to mean "suggest"; use *infer* to mean "interpret" or "conclude": "Speakers **imply,** but listeners **infer.**"

incidence, incidents The first term refers to frequency or rate of occurrence. The second is the plural of a word that means "event," "occurrence," or "specific case": "The **incidence** of polio decreased dramatically after the Salk vaccine was introduced. There have been no **incidents** of the disease in this country for decades."

incredible, incredulous The first term means "unbelievable"; it relates to statements and phenomena. *Incredulous* describes people who are skeptical or unwilling to believe that a statement or phenomenon is true: "Naturally, I remained **incredulous** about his excuse for being late; considering the fact that he is an inveterate liar, his story about having two flat tires remains **incredible.**" Note that *incredible* is sometimes informally used to mean "unusual," "unique," or "spectacular." Avoid this usage in college writing: "Jason's 55-yard field-goal kick was **spectacular** [*not* **incredible**]."

infact, in fact Always spell as two words unless you are quoting.

ingenious, ingenuous Synonyms for *ingenious* include *intelligent, innovative,* and *inventive. Ingenuous,* on the other hand, means "innocent," "naïve," and "without guile": "Although Michael is **ingenious** at fixing cars, he is remarkably **ingenuous** when it comes to matters of the heart."

in regards to Avoid; use *in regard to* or *regarding* instead.

inside of Avoid this redundancy; use *inside* or *within.*

inter-, intra- *Inter* means "between" while *intra* means "within": "Susan has just competed in an **interstate** college field hockey tournament. She learned to play the game only last year, when she joined her college's **intramural** league."

irregardless Not a word—use *regardless* instead.

is when, is where Students sometimes use these constructions when defining a term, as in this case: "Communism **is where** (or **is when**) the government owns the means of production." But *communism* is neither a time nor a place; it is an economic system. A better alternative is "Communism is an economic system in which the government owns the means of production." Note that in the second example, *communism,* a noun, is being defined by the noun *system,* not by the adverb *when* or *where.*

its, it's *Its* is a possessive pronoun that means "belonging to it": "The new SUV has **its** virtues." *It's* is a contraction of *it is* or *it has:* "**It's** been three years since Sara took a vacation." Note that *its'* does not exist.

kind of/sort of Avoid these informal terms.

latter See **former, first; latter, last.**

lay, lie *Lie* means "to recline": "I think that I will **lie** down for a while." *Lay* means "to put (something) in a lower position": "Jack **lays** the manual down on the desk."

The past-tense form of *lie* is *lay:* "Alice **lay** down for a few minutes after supper." The past-tense form of *lay* is *laid:* "Rosa **laid** the packages down and searched for her car keys."

leave, let *Leave* means "to depart"; don't use *leave* in place of "let," which means "permit": "**Let** us go now," not "**Leave** us go now."

lend, loan Never ask: "Can you **loan** me a dollar?" *Lend* is a verb; *loan* is a noun: "Bankers **lend** money, but they make **loans.**" The correct wording of the question above is "Can you **lend** me a dollar?"

less, few See **few, less.**

let's us Avoid this redundancy; use *let's* instead.

liable *Liable* means "obligated for" or "legally responsible for." Do not use it to mean "likely": "Susan is **likely** [*not* **liable**] to be promoted."

lie, lay See **lay, lie.**

like, as See **as, like.**

lite Always spell as *light* unless you are quoting.

loose, lose *Loose* means "not tight": "The nut holding the boiler plate was **loose.**" *Lose* means "to misplace" or "to be defeated": "We need to make sure not to **lose** the backup disk."

lots, lots of Avoid these informal constructions in formal writing. Instead, use *much, many,* and *a lot.*

many, much *Many* is used with count nouns such as pounds, inches, people, and cars. *Much* is used with noncount nouns such as rice, string, and equipment: "**Much** water has passed under **many** bridges."

may, can See **can, may.**

may be, maybe Both terms mean "perhaps" or "possibly," but the first is a verb phrase while the second is an adverb. Keep this distinction in mind: "**Maybe** the sun will shine; if not, the picnic **may be** postponed."

media This noun is the plural of *medium.* It agrees with plural verbs and pronouns: "The **media are** [*not* **is**] divided on this issue; in fact, **they have** [*not* **it has**] many different approaches to the problem."

might of Avoid; use *might have* instead. See **of.**

most Don't use to mean *almost.*

myself Correct when used as either a reflexive pronoun ("I pinched **myself**") or as an intensive pronoun ("I rebuilt this carburetor **myself**"). However, avoid using *myself* as part of a sentence's subject: "Rita and **I** [*not* **myself**] met with the college president yesterday."

nice This is an almost meaningless word because so many unrelated meanings have been attached to it: "likable," "kind," "good," "attractive," "polite," "friendly," "considerate," "suitable." In college writing, always choose a more specific alternative.

nite Always spell as *night* unless you are quoting.

nohow, nowheres Avoid—these are not words.

nowhere near Avoid—use *not nearly* instead: "Ten is **not nearly** [*not* **nowhere near**] enough."

number, amount See **amount, number.**

of Avoid using *of* to replace *have:* "I could **have** [*not* **of**] been a contender."

off of Avoid this redundancy; use *off* by itself: "Jason fell **off** the roof."

oftentimes *Often* works just as well and is less trouble to write.

on account of Avoid this wordy construction. Instead, use *because* or another synonym.

orientate British English uses *orientate;* American English uses *orient,* which means "to familiarize with" or "to place in a particular position": "Faculty advisors will **orient** students to the new regulations." "The church's large rose window was **oriented** south."

outside of Avoid this redundancy; use *outside.*

passed, past *Passed* is the past tense of the verb *pass:* "I **passed** the test" or "The former club president was glad she had **passed** her responsibilities on to her successor." *Past* means "former" or "previous" (when referring to time) or "beyond" (when referring to place or time): "We turned off the road just **past** the first bend; there a **past** president of our club had built a cabin."

patience, patients *Patience* is a virtue; *patients* are people under the care of doctors or dentists.

percent, percentage Use numbers with *percent* (9 **percent**), but use *percentage* when referring to a general concept: "A large **percentage** of voters skipped Tuesday's runoff election."

persecute, prosecute The first item means to "oppress" or "tyrannize": "In Russia, Jews have been **persecuted** since the time of the czars." The second term means to litigate or to bring charges against in a court of law: "Abigail was **prosecuted** for tax evasion."

personal, personnel *Personal* is an adjective that means "individual," "intimate," or "relating to 'person'": "Residents of Sunnyvale Nursing Home can make **personal** choices regarding room décor." *Personnel* is both a noun and an adjective. It refers to the employees or members of a business or organization: "**Personnel** at Acme Electrical Suppliers, including those who work in the **personnel** office, have voted to accept pay cuts."

plenty Do not use to mean "very": "This stew is **very** [*not* **plenty**] good, Mom."

plus Do not attempt to substitute *plus* for a coordinating conjunction: "It was late when we got home, **and** [*not* **plus**] the dishes still needed to be washed." *Plus* is a preposition: "Our tax owed **plus** the late penalty amounted to over eight hundred dollars."

precede, proceed *Precede* is a verb that means "to come before": "The bridesmaids **preceded** the bride by three steps." *Proceed* is a verb that means "to continue": "**Proceed** with your task, Wentworth."

predominant, predominate These words are not interchangeable. *Predominant,* the adjective form, is used to describe the leading or most important member of a group: "The **predominant** feeling is that the company president will be replaced very soon." *Predominate,* the verb form, indicates that one thing has more importance than others: "In the arts, modernist philosophy **predominated** during much of the twentieth century."

presently *Presently* means "very soon." Do not confuse it with *currently:* "Howard will be here **presently; currently,** he is in the restroom."

principal, principle As an adjective, **principal** means "dominant" or "most important": "The **principal** cause of the fire was an electrical short." As a noun, it refers to a school administrator ("the **principal** of Oakwood Elementary") or the base value of a loan or an investment ("drawing the interest but leaving the **principal** alone"). *Principle,* a noun, means "an axiom or theory" ("the **principle** of unintended consequences") or a moral belief ("Karen is a person of **principle**").

proceed, precede See **precede, proceed.**

quiet, quite The first is an adjective meaning the absence of sound; the second is an adverb meaning "very." Be careful not to confuse the spellings of these words.

quite, rather Overused as modifiers: "The airport was **quite** huge." "The hotel room was **rather** tiny." Neither *quite* nor *rather* helps here. In each case, the adjective is stronger when not afflicted by *quite* and *rather.*

quotation, quote Do not use *quote* as a noun: "My **quotation** [*not* **quote**] comes from a story by Flannery O'Connor." Remember also that text is not a quotation until you have borrowed it: O'Connor's **sentence** becomes your **quotation.**

raise, rise *Raise* is *transitive,* meaning that it must be used with a direct object: "The elderly farmer **raised** sunflowers." *Rise* is *intransitive,* meaning that it does not take an object: "The sun **rises** each day."

rather, quite See **quite, rather.**

real, really *Real* is an adjective that is frequently misused as an adverb. Use **really** instead: "You are **really** [*not* **real**] quiet today." However, **really** is often overused in a different way. How does "It is a **really** great film" improve upon "It is a great film"?

reason is because Avoid—use *reason that . . . is* instead. Instead of "The **reason** they postponed the game **is because** of bad weather," use "The **reason that** they postponed the game **is** bad weather."

refer back See **again, back.**

respectfully, respectively Use *respectfully* to mean "showing respect": "I **respectfully** ask that my interview be moved to next Friday." Use *respectively* to mean "in the order indicated": "On the exam, Robert, Tomoko, and Sarah made A, A–, and B+, **respectively.**"

rise, raise See **raise, rise.**

sensual, sensuous *Sensuous* relates to things that are pleasing to the senses: "A **sensuous** wind blew warm and fragrant breezes across the bay." *Sensual* relates to gratification of the physical senses, especially as they relate to sexuality: "In the Renaissance, painters felt free to depict the **sensual** qualities of the human form."

set, sit *Set* is a transitive verb (it takes an object) meaning "to place" or "to put"; *sit* is an intransitive verb (it doesn't take an object): "**Set** your luggage on the rack, and **sit** on the couch."

shall, will *Shall* was once used to indicate the future tense with the pronouns *I* and *we.* Today, *will* is almost universally used.

should of Avoid—use *should have* instead. See **of.**

so Don't use to mean "very": "It was **very** [*not* **so**] hot today." But note: "It was **so** hot today **that I stayed inside all afternoon.**"

some Don't use *some* as an intensifier: "Hurricane Hugo was a **terrible** [*not* **some**] storm."

sometime, some time, sometimes *Sometime* is an adverb that means "at some indefinite point in time": "Matthew will be taking his college entrance exam **sometime** in the near future." *Some time* is a phrase made up of the noun *time* and the adjective *some:* "We hiked for **some time** before we reached the river." *Sometimes* is an adverb meaning "on some occasions": "**Sometimes** I stop at the Hungry Lion for a hamburger."

somewheres Not a word—use *somewhere* instead.

sort of, kind of See **kind of, sort of.**

stationary, stationery Use *stationary* to mean "unmoving" or "fixed": "The sailboat has a **stationary** mast." Use *stationery* to mean writing paper and envelopes: "We bought this expensive paper at the **stationery** store."

suppose to, supposed to The correct form is *supposed to.*

sure, surely *Sure* is an adjective: "This investment is a **sure** thing." Do not use *sure* as an adverb; use *surely* instead: "The introduction to this proposal is **surely** stupid."

than, then These words are frequently confused. Use *then* as an adverb signaling a time transition: "**Then** the concert ended." Use *than* as a comparative conjunction: "These pretzels are harder **than** the last batch we bought."

their, there, they're These words are easily confused. *Their* is the possessive form of *they:* "They checked **their** bags at the curb." *There* can be either an adverb of location—"The exercise room is over **there** by the pool"—or an expletive, a word that delays the appearance of the subject—"**There** are many reasons for the boss's anger." *They're* is the contraction of *they are:* "**They're** going to Cancun for a vacation."

theirselves Not a word—use *themselves* instead.

through, thorough As an adverb, *through* means "by way of." As an adjective, it means "completed." *Thorough,* meaning "completely," is an adjective. Don't confuse the two by misspelling them.

thru Always spell as *through* unless you are quoting.

thusly Avoid—use *thus,* which is an adverb already and does not need the extra *ly.*

till, until Both words mean the same thing. However, *till* is less formal.

to, too, two These words are frequently confused. Use *to* either as a preposition—"Bill is going **to** Omaha"—or as part of an infinitive—"**To** look at museum paintings is one of Bill's great pleasures." Use *too* as an adverb meaning either "also" or "excessively": Sarah is **too** tired to go to the party; Andrea is **too.**" Use *two* to mean the number, either as a noun or an adjective: "Martin earned **two** degrees at the university."

toward, towards In American English, *toward* is preferred.

try and Avoid—use *try to* instead.

uninterested, disinterested See **disinterested, uninterested.**

unique Do not try to qualify *unique.* "Fairly unique" or "somewhat unique" are contradictions in terms. Something is either unique, or it is not.

usage Avoid unless referring to language choice: "His **usage** of old-fashioned words seems strained and affected." Otherwise, stick with *use:* "His **use** [*not* **usage**] of the car is limited to weekends."

use to, used to *Used to* is correct.

utilize, utilization Avoid this bureaucratic jargon; stick with *use* for both the verb and the noun: "We will **use** [*not* **utilize**] every means at our disposal."

very definite This term is redundant; write *definite.*

wander, wonder Don't confuse these. They mean very different things: *Wander* means to "roam." *Wonder* means to "think" or "consider."

ways Avoid using this term to refer to distance: "Colorado is a long **way** [*not* **ways**] from here."

were, where Don't forget the letter *h* in *where.*

where Do not use to mean "that": "I heard on the radio **that** [*not* **where**] the big garden-supply store is going out of business."

where . . . at Avoid colloquial expressions such as "Where is my car at?" Instead, write "Where is my car?"

who, whom *Who* is a subject; *whom* is an object: "**Who** is the college loan officer?" "**Whom** did you speak with about your loan?"

whose, who's These words are frequently confused. *Whose* is the possessive form of *who:* "**Whose** fishing rod is this?" *Who's* is the contraction of *who is:* "**Who's** out in the garden?"

-wise This is a nonstandard noun ending. Don't write "**Math-wise,** I need a tutor." Instead, write "I need a tutor for math."

would have, would of The correct form is *would have.*

your, you're These words are frequently confused. *Your* is the possessive form of *you:* "Here are **your** tickets and itinerary, Karen." *You're* is the contraction of *you are:* "**You're** going to be late if you don't get started."

CREDITS

Text Credits

p. 15 From Suzanne Britt, "Neat People vs. Sloppy People," *Show and Tell*, Morning Owl Press, 1982. Reprinted with permission from the author. **p. 65** From Cecil Adams, *The Straight Dope Tells All*. Copyright © 1998 by Chicago Reader, Incorporated. Used by permission of Ballantine Books, a division of Random House, Inc. **p. 66** From Gabriel García Márquez, *Love in the Time of Cholera*, translated by Edith Grossman. Copyright © 1988 by Gabriel García Márquez. Used by permission of Alfred A. Knopf, a division of Random House, Inc. **p. 139** From Thomas McGuane, "Roanie," in *Some Horses* by Thomas McGuane. Used by permission of the author. **p. 144** From Maxine Hong Kingston, "Photographs of My Parents" from *The Woman Warrior* by Maxine Hong Kingston. Copyright © 1975, 1976 by Maxine Hong Kingston. Used by permission of Alfred A. Knopf, a division of Random House, Inc. **p. 147** From Hildegard Knef, *The Gift Horse*, McGraw-Hill, 1971. **p. 151** From Sherman Alexie, "Family Portrait" from *The Lone Ranger and Tonto Fistfight in Heaven* by Sherman Alexie. Copyright © 1993 by Sherman Alexie. Used by permission of Grove/Atlantic, Inc. **p. 176** From Lynda Barry, "The Sanctuary of School," *The New York Times,* January 5, 1992. Copyright © 1992 by The New York Times Co. Reprinted with permission. **p. 179** From Sandra Cisneros, "Only Daughter." Copyright © 1990 by Sandra Cisneros. First published in *Glamour,* November, 1990. Reprinted by permission of Susan Bergholtz Literary Services, New York. All rights reserved. **p. 182** From Annie Dillard, "The Chase," in *An American Childhood* by Annie Dillard, pages 45–49. Copyright © 1987 by Annie Dillard. Reprinted by permission of HarperCollins Publishers, Inc. **p. 186** From George Orwell, "A Hanging" in *Shooting an Elephant and Other Essays* by George Orwell. Copyright © 1931 by George Orwell. Copyright © 1950 by Harcourt, Inc., and renewed 1979 by Sonia Brownell Orwell. Reprinted by permission of Harcourt, Inc. and Bill Hamilton as the Literary Executor of the Estate of the Late Sonia Brownell Orwell and Secker & Warburg, Ltd. **p. 212** From Phyllis Rose, "Shopping and Other Spiritual Adventures in America Today" in *Never Say Goodbye* by Phyllis Rose. Copyright © 1990 by Phyllis Rose. Printed with the permission of the Wylie Agency, Inc. **p. 215** From Brent Staples, "Just Walk on By," *Ms.,* September, 1986. Used by permission of the author. **p. 219** From Lars Eighner, "On Dumpster Diving" in *Travels with Lizbeth* by Lars Eighner. Copyright © 1993 by Lars Eighner. Reprinted by permission of St. Martin's Press, LLC. **p. 224** From Harry F. Waters, "Life According to TV," *Newsweek,* December 6, 1982. Copyright © 1982 Newsweek, Inc. All rights reserved. Reprinted by permission. **p. 246** From Jerry Jesness, "Why Johnny Can't Fail." Reprinted, with permission, from July 1999 issue of *Reason* magazine. Copyright © 1999 by Reason Foundation, 3415 S. Sepulveda Blvd., Ste. 400, Los Angeles, CA 90034, www.reason.com. **p. 252** From Joan Gould, "Binding Decisions." Reprinted by permission of Harold Ober Associates, Incorporated. Copyright © 1989 by Joan Gould. First published in *Memories,* February/March, 1989. **p. 256** From Malcolm X, "A Homemade Education" in *The Autobiography of Malcolm X* by Malcolm X and Alex Haley. Copyright © 1964 by Alex Haley and Malcolm X. Copyright © 1965 by Alex Haley and Betty Shabazz. Used by permission of Random House, Inc. **p. 259** From Umberto Eco, "How Not to Use the Fax Machine" and "How Not to Use the Cell Phone" in *How to Travel with a Salmon and Other Essays* by Umberto Eco. Copyright © Gruppo Editoriale Fabbri, Bompiani, Sonzogno, Etas S.p.A., English translation by William Weaver. Copyright © 1994 by Harcourt, Inc. Reprinted by permission of Harcourt, Inc. **p. 284** From Barbara Ehrenreich, "The Cult of Busyness." Reprinted by permission of International Creative Management, Inc. Copyright © 1990 by Barbara Ehrenreich. **p. 287** From Natalie Angier, "Is War Our Biological Destiny?" *The New York Times,* November 11, 2003. Copyright © 2003 by The New York Times Co. Reprinted with permission. **p. 291** From Gore Vidal, "Drugs" in *Homage to Daniel Shays: Collected Essays* by Gore Vidal. Copyright © 1970 by Gore Vidal. Used by permission of Random House, Inc. **p. 293** From Richard Rhodes, "Hollow Claims About Fantasy Violence," *The New York Times,* September 17, 2000. Copyright © 2000 The New York Times. Reprinted by permission. **p. 318** From Nancy Gibbs, "When Is It Rape?" *Time,* June 3, 1991. Copyright © 1991 Time, Inc. Reprinted by permission. **p. 320** From Judy Brady, "Why I Want a Wife," *Ms.,* Spring, 1972. Copyright © 1970 by Judy Brady. **p. 322** From William Raspberry, "The Handicap of Definition." Copyright © 1982 The Washington Post Writers Group. Reprinted with permission. **p. 325** From Annie Dillard, "So This Was Adolescence" in *An American Childhood* by Annie Dillard, pages 222–225. Copyright © 1987 by Annie Dillard. Reprinted by permission of HarperCollins Publishers, Inc. **p. 328** From Tony Earley, "The Quare Gene," *The New Yorker,* September 21, 1998. Copyright © 1998 by Tony Earley. Story originally appeared in *The New Yorker,* September 21, 1998. Reprinted by the permission of Regal Literary, Inc. as agent for the author. **p. 355** From Fran Lebowitz, "The Sound of Music: Enough Already." Copyright © 1978 Fran

Lebowitz. Reprinted by permission of International Creative Management, Inc. **p. 357** From Tom Kuntz, "Cereal Boxes: Not Sold by Intellectual Weight," *The New York Times,* October 22, 1995. Copyright © 1995 by The New York Times Co. Reprinted with permission. **p. 361** From Martin Luther King, Jr., "Three Types of Resistance to Oppression" by Martin Luther King, Jr. Reprinted by arrangement with the Estate of Martin Luther King, Jr., c/o Writers House as agent for the proprietor, New York, NY. Copyright © 1958 Dr. Martin Luther King Jr., copyright renewed 1986, Coretta Scott King. **p. 364** From Paul Fussell, "Notes on Class" in *The Boy Scout Handbook and Other Observations* by Paul Fussell. Copyright © 1982 by Paul Fussell. Used by permission of Oxford University Press, Inc. **p. 389** From Ellen Currie, "Two Varieties of Killers," *The New York Times,* August 21, 1986. Copyright © 1986 by The New York Times Co. Reprinted with permission. **p. 392** From Bharati Mukherjee, "Two Ways to Belong to America," *The New York Times,* September 22, 1996. Copyright © 1996 The New York Times. Reprinted by permission. **p. 395** From David Sedaris, "Family Engineering," *The New Yorker,* August 24–31, 1999. Copyright © 1999 by David Sedaris. Reprinted by permission of Don Congdon Associates, Inc. **p. 400** From Barbara Mellix, "From Outside, In." Originally appeared in *The Georgia Review,* Volume XLI, No. 2 (Summer 1987). Copyright © 1987 by The University of Georgia./© 1987 by Barbara Mellix. Reprinted by permission of Barbara Mellix and *The Georgia Review.* **p. 426** From Walter S. Minot, "Students Who Push Burgers," *Christian Science Monitor,* November 22, 1988. Copyright © 1988 by Christian Science Publishing Society. Reproduced with permission of Christian Science Publishing Society via Copyright Clearance Center. **p. 429** From Deborah Tannen, "The Triumph of the Yell," *The New York Times,* January 14, 1994. Copyright © 1994 The New York Times. Reprinted by permission. **p. 432** From Caryl Rivers, "What Should Be Done About Rock Lyrics?" Used with permission of the author. **p. 436** From Michael Levin, "The Case for Torture," *Newsweek,* June 7, 1982. Used by permission of the author, Michael Levin, Professor of Philosophy, City University of New York. **p. 462** From Scott Russell Sanders, "The Men We Carry in Our Minds" from *The Paradise of Bombs.* Copyright © 1984 by Scott Russell Sanders. First appeared in *Milkweed Chronicle.* Reprinted by permission of the author and the author's agents, Virginia Kidd Agency, Inc. **p. 465** From Anthony Bourdain, "Don't Eat Before Reading This," *The New Yorker,* April 19, 1999, pp. 58–61. Used by permission of the author. **p. 471** From Elisabeth Kübler-Ross, "On the Fear of Death" from *On Death and Dying* by Dr. Elisabeth Kübler-Ross. Reprinted with the permission of Scribner, an imprint of Simon & Schuster Adult Publishing Group. Copyright © 1969 by Elisabeth Kübler-Ross; copyright renewed © 1997 by Elisabeth Kübler-Ross. **p. 477** From Robert B. Reich, "Why the Rich Are Getting Richer and the Poor Poorer," *The New Republic,* May 1, 1989. Copyright © 1989 by Robert B. Reich. Reprinted with permission from the author. **pp. 525, 531** From George Orwell, "Shooting an Elephant" from *Shooting an Elephant and Other Essays* by George Orwell. Copyright © 1931 George Orwell. Copyright © 1950 by Harcourt, Inc., and renewed 1979 by Sonia Brownell Orwell. Reprinted by permission of Harcourt, Inc. and Bill Hamilton as the Literary Executor of the Estate of the Late Sonia Brownell Orwell and Secker & Warburg, Ltd. **p. 543** From Naguib Mahfouz, "The Answer is No" in *The Time and the Place and Other Stories* by Naguib Mahfouz. Copyright © 1991 by the American University in Cairo Press. Used by permission of Doubleday, a division of Random House, Inc. **pp. 562, 563** Reproduced with permission from Libraries of Middlesex Automation Consortium, Middlesex County College, New Jersey. **pp. 564, 565** Book page and on-line entry: From *Reader's Guide to Periodical Literature, Black Holes.* Copyright © 1991 by H.W. Wilson Company. Reprinted by permission of the H. W. Wilson Company. **p. 566** Reprinted by permission of the Modern Language Association of America from *Modern Language Association International Bibliography.* Copyright © 1990 Modern Language Association. **p. 568** Used with permission of EBSCO Publishing. **p. 572** Used by permission of Google Marketing Department. Screen shots reprinted by permission from Microsoft Corporation.

INDEX

A

M

N

Y

Abbreviations and Symbols for Revising and Editing Your Work

Abbreviation	Meaning
adj	Problem with an adjective (27c–27e, pp. 711–714)
adv	Problem with an adverb (27c–27d, pp. 711–713)
art	Problem with article use (27g, pp. 714–716)
cap	Capitalization error (30a, pp. 751–756)
case	Problem with pronoun case (26i–26m, pp. 702–706)
cl	Edit for clarity (pp. 763–764)
cliché	Eliminate cliché (p. 123; 31f, pp. 769–770)
com	Faulty comparison (24h, pp. 673–674)
coord	Faulty coordination (pp. 104–111)
cs	Comma splice (pp. 106–107; 24d–24f, pp. 666–670)
dict	Word choice problem (pp. 114–129; 31a–31c, pp. 763–764)
dm	Dangling modifier (27b, p. 710)
fig	Problem with figurative language (pp. 121–123; 31f, pp. 769–770)
frag	Fragment (p. 110; 24a–24c, pp. 660–666)
fs	Fused sentence (pp. 106–107; 24d–24f, pp. 666–670)
gr	Problem with sentence grammar (22, 23, pp. 625–658)
hyph	Hyphen needed/not needed (30d, pp. 758–760)
idiom	Problem with idiom (p. 126; 31j, pp. 773–776)
inf	Language too informal (pp. 88–89; 31h–31i, pp. 772–773)
ital	Problem with italics or underlining (30b, pp. 756–757)
jarg	Eliminate jargon (31g, p. 771)
log	Faulty logic (pp. 442–445)
m shft	Mood shift (25l, p. 687)
mix	Mixed construction (24i, p. 674)
mm	Misplaced modifier (27a, pp. 708–709)
num	Numbers and numerals (30c, pp. 757–758)
p agr	Pronoun–antecedent agreement (26a–26e, pp. 690–696)
p ref	Pronoun reference problem (26f–26g, pp. 696–701)
p shft	Shift in person (26h, pp. 701–702)
pred	Predication (verb) problem (22g–22j, pp. 638–644)
pl	Error in the plural form of a noun (31k, p. 777)
red	Redundant (pp. 119–120; 31d, pp. 764–766)
ref	Pronoun reference problem (26f–26g, pp. 696–701)
rep	Repetitious (p. 116; 31d, pp. 764–766)
sexist	Sexist language (31e, pp. 766–768)
sl	Avoid slang (pp. 88–89; 31h, pp. 772–773)
sm	Squinting modifier (27a, pp. 708–709)
sp	Spelling error (31k, pp. 776–777)
split inf	Split infinitive (27f, p. 714)
sub	Faulty subordination (pp. 104–111)
s–v agr	Subject–verb agreement (25a–25i, pp. 677–685)
t shft	Tense shift (25j, p. 686)
trans	Transition needed (pp. 71–72)
usage	Usage problem (32, pp. 779–790)
v shft	Voice shift (25k, p. 686)
vb	Problem with verb form (22g–22j, pp. 638–644)
wordy	Wordy sentence (pp. 117–118, 127–128; 31d, pp. 764–766)
^,	Comma needed (28a–28g, pp. 719–728)
no ^,	Unnecessary comma (28h, pp. 728–731)
.	Period (29a, pp. 734–735)
;	Semicolon (29b, pp. 735–736)
?	Question mark (29c, pp. 736–737)
!	Exclamation mark (29c, pp. 736–737)
:	Colon (29d, pp. 738–739)
—	Dash (29e, pp. 739–740)
( )	Parentheses (29f, pp. 740–741)
[ ]	Brackets (29g, p. 741)
" "	Double quotation marks (29h, pp. 742–743)
' '	Single quotation marks (29i, p. 743)
' (over a caret)	Apostrophe (29k, pp. 744–748)
//	Parallelism needed (pp. 114–115)
^	Add a word or words
X	Obvious error
∼	Transpose words
#	Add a space
⁀	Close up space
??	Unclear

Powered by *CATALYST* (www.mhhe.com/writingtoday), *Writing Today* helps students throughout the writing process:

If you need help with . . .	see these pages in the text	follow this click path in *CATALYST*—section > title
Abbreviations	734	Editing > Abbreviations
Active vs. passive verbs	643	Editing > Verbs
Adjectives and adverbs	711–714	Editing > Adjectives and Adverbs
Apostrophes (’)	744–748	Editing > Apostrophes
APA documentation style	610–622	Research > Bibliomaker Research > Sample Paper in APA Style
Argument essay	422–457	Writing > Writing Tutor: Arguments
Articles	714–716	Editing > Parts of Speech
Blended essay	458–492	Writing > Writing Tutor: Blended Essay
Body paragraphs	55–60	Writing > Paragraph Patterns
Business writing	503–522	Writing > Résumés and Business Documents
Capitalization	751–756	Editing > Capitalization
Causal analysis essay	278–315	Writing > Writing Tutor: Causal Analysis
Classification essay	350–383	Writing > Writing Tutor: Classification
Clichés	123, 769–770	Editing > Clichés, Slang, Jargon, Colloquialisms
Coherence	70–72	Writing > Coherence
Colons (:)	738–739	Editing > Colons
Comma splices	106–109, 666–669	Editing > Comma Splices
Commas (,)	718–732	Editing > Commas
Comparison and contrast essay	384–421	Writing > Writing Tutor: Comparison/Contrast
Concluding paragraphs	60–63	Writing > Conclusions
Coordination	104–111	Editing > Coordination and Subordination
Dangling modifier	710–711	Editing > Dangling Modifiers
Dashes (—)	739–740	Editing > Dashes
Definition essay	316–349	Writing > Writing Tutor: Definition
Descriptive essay	134–171	Writing > Writing Tutor: Description
Drafting	43–50	Writing > Drafting and Revising
End punctuation (. ? !)	734, 736–737	Editing > End Punctuation
Evaluating sources	574–577	Research > Source Evaluation Tutor (CARS)
Exemplification essay	208–243	Writing > Writing Tutor: Exemplification
Faulty comparisons	673–674	Editing > Faulty Comparisons
Fused sentence	106–109, 666–669	Editing > Run-on Sentences
Hyphens (-)	758–760	Editing > Hyphens
Idioms	126, 773–776	Editing > Word Choice
Introductory paragraphs	52–55	Writing > Introductions
Internet, searching for sources	568–574	Research > Using the Internet
Italics (underlining)	756–757	Editing > Italics
Jargon, euphemisms	770–771	Editing > Clichés, Slang, Jargon, Colloquialisms
Library, searching for sources	559–568	Research > Using the Library
Misplaced modifier	708–709	Editing > Misplaced Modifiers
Mixed constructions	674	Editing > Mixed Constructions